Robert Mannyng of Brunne

The Chronicle

Medieval & Renaissance Texts & Studies

Volume 153

Robert Mannyng of Brunne
The Chronicle

Edited

With Introduction, Notes, and Glossary

by

IDELLE SULLENS

Medieval & Renaissance texts & studies
Binghamton University
1996

Library of Congress Cataloging-in-Publication Data

Mannyng, Robert, fl. 1288–1338.
[Chronicle]
Robert Mannyng of Brunne : the chronice / edited with introduction, notes, and glossary by Idelle Sullens
p. cm. — (Medieval & Renaissance texts & studies ; v. 153)
ISBN 0-86698-137-3
1. Great Britain—History—To 1485—Poetry. I. Sullens, Idelle. II. Title. III. Series.
PR2056.A63 1996
821'.1—dc20 95-25413
CIP

This book is made to last.
It is set in Garamond,
smythe-sewn and printed on acid-free paper
to library specifications

Printed in the United States of America

Dedicated to
Robert William Ackerman
Teacher and Defender

CONTENTS

PREFACE

This edition of *The Chronicle* completes the publication of the works of Robert Mannyng of Brunne, 1303–1338, which was begun by the edition of *Handlyng Synne* in 1983. During the many years of work on the manuscripts surviving, I have incurred numerous debts to other scholars, mainly to those who have responded promptly and generously with information and copies of essential documents. Others have read parts of the work in progress and made valuable suggestions or asked penetrating questions which helped greatly to clarify the results. I am grateful to all of them.

The dedication of this volume to Robert William Ackerman, my advisor and champion at Stanford, is a tribute to one of the most eminent Middle English scholars in this century. When I solicited his sponsorship, it was a much more difficult time for women who aspired to become editors in this rather narrow specialty. Professor Ackerman defended me, encouraged me, and made my scholarly career possible in the most direct way.

Among the scholars in England and elsewhere in Europe who have been of most direct assistance are Rosamund Allen, Lesley Johnson, Angus McIntosh, M. L. Samuels, Thomas M. Smallwood, Matthew Sullivan, Stephen Sullivan, Thea Summerfield, and the late Sarah M. Horrall in Canada. Among American scholars I owe special thanks to Gretchen P. Ackerman, Joseph Bingaman, Juris G. Lidaka, James Pratley, and Robert P. Stepsis. For direct encouragement and lasting friendship, I am greatly indebted to Clifford Josephson and his wife Kathleen, my colleague DeForest Sweeney, and especially to Anne Conway Scott who has provided constant support and many essential bits of information.

The librarians who have facilitated my work and permitted me to examine the manuscripts and locate documents include the Keeper of Western Manuscripts at the Bodleian, Oxford; W. W. S. Breem at the Library of the Inner Temple, London; E. G. W. Bill of the Lambeth Palace Library; and Miss P. M. Baker of the University of London Library. Permission to publish Petyt MS 511, Vol. 7, was graciously given by the Masters of the Bench of the Inner Temple; permission for use of Lambeth MS 131 was granted by the trustees of Lambeth Palace Library. Use of the fragment of MS Rawl. D.913, fol. 5 was granted by the Keeper of Western Manuscripts, Bodleian Library. On many occasions, Mary Anne Teed and her staff at the Monterey Peninsula College Library have rescued me by promptly locating materials that were unavailable except through their loan network.

Publication of this work would never have been possible without the patient encouragement of Professor Mario A. Di Cesare and his wife, Lee, and the staff of Medieval & Renaissance Texts & Studies. For their direct contribution at all stages in the preparation of these editions, I can never adequately express my thanks. The errors, of course, are mine; the value of the editions to future scholars is assured, in good part, by the publisher who has never failed me.

Robert Mannyng of Brunne
The Chronicle

Introduction

Prologue

Robert Mannyng of Brunne's *Chronicle* was first edited by Thomas Hearne in 1725, but he presented only the second part. He stated that the first part would be of little historical interest to his readers; it was merely another version of the long-famous Historia Regum Brittaniae by Geoffrey of Monmouth (1136).[1] Mannyng's *Chronicle,* Part I, was subsequently edited by Frederick J. Furnivall for the Rolls Series in 1887.[2] These editions by Hearne and Furnivall have been the only printed texts of the *Chronicle* except for a transcript of the first 5383 lines of Part I by Aemilius W. Zetsche in Anglia IX (1886). Both Furnivall and Zetsche chose the version of the *Chronicle* preserved in Lambeth MS 131 [L] for their editions, while Hearne edited the Petyt MS 511 Vol. 7 [P] from the Inner Temple Library, London. (L has only 4973 lines of Part II.) An edition of the single leaf in Bodleian MS Rawlinson Miscellany D. 913 [R] which has lines corresponding to 12550–699 of P (Part I) was printed in 1892 by Eugen Kölbing.[3]

It is time for a reexamination of Mannyng's work, for these early editions do not provide an optimum text for further study of his *Chronicle.* The major considerations justifying a new edition are: (1) errors and peculiarities in all the older editions, (2) their inaccessibility except in major university libraries, and (3) the necessity for an accurate text to support studies of Mannyng's language. A reappraisal of his stature in the early fourteenth century as an important translator of Anglo-French literature for an audience using the English language is long overdue.

Though Mannyng's works—the earlier *Handlyng Synne,* begun in 1303,

---

[1] Hearne's edition was reprinted in his *Works,* vols. III and IV: *Peter Langtoft's Chronicle (as Illustrated and Improv'd by Robert of Brunne) from the Death of Cadwalader to the End of K. Edward the First's Reign* (1810). See his preface, p. LII: "The first Part, therefore, of Robert of Brunne is nothing but Geffry of Monmouth, and that too translated into English from a French Author." Part II, based on Petyt with footnotes for Lambeth has also been edited by Robert P. Stepsis, "An Edition of Part II of Robert Mannyng of Brunne's *Chronicle of England*" (unpublished Ph.D. diss., Harvard University, 1967).

[2] F. J. Furnivall, ed., *The Story of England by Robert Manning of Brunne, A.D. 1338.*

[3] In *Englische Studien* 17. See the description of the MSS and the discussion of dialect below.

and the *Chronicle*, completed in 1338—have been cited thousands of times in scholarly studies as well as in the language references (OED and MED and many glossaries), we have been hampered by the limitations of the older editions. The major difficulty arises from Furnivall's choice of the late copy in a version of the *Chronicle* which does not represent the author's Lincolnshire dialect: the Lambeth manuscript is a copy of the work translated by a South West Midland reviser, while the Petyt manuscript closely preserves the language we would expect from Mannyng, even though it is doubtless a later copy.

One of the earliest scholars to recognize the value of Mannyng's work was Hearne's friend John Bridges, who commented, "It is very strange, that this Author has never been taken notice of or quoted. In my Opinion, it far exceeds *R. of Gloucester*, both for the matter and manner of his story."[4] This early eighteenth-century judgment was seconded by Sir Frederic Madden, commenting in the 1840 edition of Thomas Warton's *History of English Poetry:* "Warton does not treat Mannyng with sufficient justice. As a smooth and easy versifier, with an extraordinary power of imitating the meter of his original, there is no poet previous to Chaucer his equal, and when compared with Hampole and Nassyngton, his followers, he rises immeasurably superior."[5]

Mannyng's *Chronicle* survives in only these manuscripts. P is the most complete, while L ends midway in Part II. The single leaf preserved in R has just enough of the text to be tantalizing, but not enough to justify any firm conclusions about what might have been in the text before and after this fragment. I have used the Petyt manuscript [P] as base text for this edition because it is the oldest and the North East Midland dialect of South Lincolnshire is representative of the area where Mannyng says he was

[4] Bridges's comment (quoted by Hearne) is preceded by: "This Translation was taken at first for *Robert of Gloucester* by the total Ignorance of the Owners." See n. 34 below for details of the confusion that has resulted from the ascription which appears on a flyleaf in the Petyt MS.

[5] I am indebted to Gretchen Ackerman for this quotation from her unpublished article, "Sir Frederic Madden and Warton's *History of English Poetry*," citing the edition by Richard Taylor (London, 1840): "See Madden's spirited defence of Mannyng's poetic style in a note to *HEP*, I, 72 (n. 20)." See also her article, "Sir Frederic Madden and Arthurian Scholarship," in V. M. Lagorio and M. L. Day, eds., *King Arthur Through the Ages* II, especially pp. 35–36. Many modern scholars (for inexplicable reasons) ignore Mannyng and sometimes slight his achievement. His obscurity today is reflected in a comment by J. A. Burrow in a popular reference, *The Oxford Illustrated History of English Literature*: "Chaucer was perhaps the first Englishman deliberately to write for posterity in his native tongue" (p. 1). Whether Mannyng had "posterity" in mind is debatable, but he was certainly explicit about the deliberate use of English in his work.

born. Variant notes from the later Lambeth manuscript [L] have been added (in parallel, so far as possible, in the right hand column) and variants from the Rawlinson manuscript [R] are also given for the parallel passage in Part I.

I have adopted an unorthodox editorial method because neither P nor L preserve complete texts. It is clear that the scribes of P attempted to shorten the text in several passages, and that the L scribes were copying an exemplar that had been translated to a different dialect, augmented, and generally edited, but rarely improved over what Mannyng originally wrote. The differences in the texts are demonstrated by showing the variant readings from L (and R) beside the corresponding lines in P. The variants are selective, using a period [.] to replace each word in P's line that is virtually the same in L. To make better sense of the variant line, sometimes more of the words have been included to clarify differences in L. The usual method of adding footnotes to the text would not adequately illuminate these differences (especially in syntax) nor would footnotes demonstrate the nature of the editing and rearrangement which was done by the reviser or the scribes in the text of L. Showing the variants adjacent to the lines of the P text also avoids a great deal of unnecessary repetition of words from P in footnotes. The scribes in P, moreover, left many careless errors which are quite easily seen by comparing the parallel variant lines in L.

Rather than attempt to second-guess the scribes and add conjectures about Mannyng's original version by emendation, I have presented the most accurate readings I could, based on my perception of what the manuscripts provide. The result is not going to please all scholars: those who believe that it is possible to reconstruct a Middle English text from the evidence of several manuscripts will not find a reconstruction in this edition. They will find the bare unemended lines with all their obvious faults. There are some suggestions, however, for possible reconstruction in the appended text notes applicable to passages where I have found other evidence to illuminate Mannyng's text, mainly based on comparison with his sources. Many of these suggestions could be accepted as emendations if we could ascertain accurate texts of the manuscript sources which Mannyng might have used, chiefly in Wace's *Brut* and Langtoft's *Chronicle.* But the available editions of these sources must be consulted with caution: the manuscripts that Mannyng used for his translation are not likely to be the same manuscripts that have survived, though the general plan and sometimes the precise language of the sources may appear in his translation. For example, when English words for translation were not available, Mannyng frequently used a French word from the source. Most of the diction so appropriated is indicated in the text notes, and the glossary provides other examples. Where Mannyng was translating faithfully, the passages are also identified in the notes.

Both P and L ultimately derive from an exemplar made one or more generations after Mannyng finished his work in 1338; they are divided into two parts and have the same general plan. This two-part arrangement has been necessarily retained in this edition because all subsequent scholarship depends upon it. The total number of lines in the complete text in P is 24,304: Part I has 15,946 and Part II has 8358. A leaf at the beginning of L has been torn out, and several others are missing in Part II; the manuscript ends imperfectly at line 4973 (corresponding to the Petyt text). A substantial number of lines survive in L, however, which were either deliberately or erroneously omitted in P, and several passages of varying length have been added in the version of the work that survives in L. All these differences are included in the variant notes.

The L manuscript was written long after P, and presents a copy based on a much revised version, substantially translated to a different dialect. The reviser of L's exemplar, nevertheless, used a text that was similar to the one that was the source of the text in P. The scribes of L were only copyists; neither of them could have been the reviser who translated the L text, for there are many instances of miscopying the exemplar. In contrast, the main hand that copied P was very likely the one who abbreviated the text and made some other changes that were not in his exemplar. The omissions in P and the additions in L are shown in the side notes and explained where appropriate in the notes appended to the text.

The evidence of a basically close relationship in the texts of PL in an earlier recension is partly supported by the very similar Latin captions included in both manuscripts (see n. 61); conjecturally, the ultimate common source may have been a professional copy made in a scriptorium. Though written some years later than Mannyng's time, P might have been a copy made in one of the Gilbertine houses and kept there. Since Mannyng credits the priors of the Gilbertines (or masters of individual houses) for his choices of material to translate, it is likely that copies of his books were retained for the use of members of the order. All the houses he mentions were in Lincolnshire and this dialect is very consistent in P. We might assume that the P manuscript itself did not travel far, and that Mannyng's *Chronicle* was not in demand elsewhere. But more than one copy of the authorial version must have been made and exported since at least one was available to the reviser who wrote the exemplar of L. It is likely that this reviser, from the South West Midlands, was working directly from a first generation or possibly later copy. The dialect of L indicates that its two scribes also used the language of the reviser, though many of Mannyng's North East Midland forms survive throughout the text, especially in rime words. The differences between P and L, however, are sufficient to prove that neither L nor its exemplar was translated directly from P itself.[6]

Though Hearne knew of the incomplete Lambeth manuscript, he did not include any variant readings from it in his edition of Part II. His chief concern was to publish older manuscripts as contributions to history. Furnivall's objective, on the other hand, was to preserve the language of older literature. He was a philologist, not an historian. His choice of L as the basis for his edition of Part I is explained in the introduction to his edition.[7] He had edited Mannyng's earlier work, *Handlyng Synne,* for the Roxburghe Club in 1862, employing a South East Midland manuscript, Harley 1701, as base text, which he believed was more representative of Mannyng's language than any of the other manuscripts containing Mannyng's work.[8] In choosing between P and L, his decision was further influenced by his belief that L was the earlier manuscript, and that its dialect was closer to the dialect of Harley MS 1701.

Furnivall's choice of the Lambeth MS 131 was justified for his immediate philological purpose, and he was rather apologetic about the fact that the *Chronicle* was actually history. Yet the *Chronicle* was commissioned as a contribution to the corpus of historical documents in the "Rolls Series." Furnivall had transcripts of both manuscripts for Part I, and completeness was no doubt another consideration: L has approximately a thousand more lines than P and has fewer obvious scribal errors. If one accepts Furnivall's (unfortunately misguided) convictions about the dialect and the date of the L manuscript, one must acknowledge that L was a logical choice for his base text.[9] Mannyng's

---

[6] The discussion of dialect follows the description of the MSS below. The basic dialect in L resembles that of several other documents from South Wiltshire.

[7] See *The Story of England* I (1887), p. xx. Furnivall's authority on dialect was Dr. Richard Morris, who was then editing the nearly contemporary *Cursor Mundi,* published by EETS between 1874 and 1892. See Sarah M. Horrall (1989) for an account of the MSS Morris edited. The study of dialectology was in its infancy in these years. Furnivall's efforts to gather evidence for the language of Middle English MSS underlie the modern dictionaries, but many errors lay in the path.

[8] Furnivall re-edited *Handlyng Synne* for the Early English Text Society without an introduction in 1901, 1903 (EETS OS 119, 123). See my edition, *Robert Mannyng of Brunne: Handlyng Synne,* Medieval & Renaissance Texts & Studies, vol. 14 (Binghamton: MRTS, 1983), pp. XXVII–XXVIII.

[9] Furnivall's curious classification of *Handlyng Synne* as history and the later *Chronicle* as fiction appears in his introduction, p. xiv. The reason appears to be that Mannyng "englishes the romances of Geoffrey of Monmouth and Wace," thus justifying classification of the subject matter of all three as "romance." Furnivall's other scholarly pursuits delayed him in completing the edition; he apologizes for the annoyance he had caused by what appeared to be dalliance: "Now, under great pressure of other work, the present Introduction has been written, on the urgent remonstrance of the Deputy Keeper

authentic dialect, however, is preserved consistently only in P.

The earlier editions were accurate and carefully printed, on the whole, though lack of line numbers in Hearne's edition has caused difficulties in citation. Moreover, Furnivall's annotation for P as a variant manuscript is often erratic: he regularly included lines from P in his text (which were omitted in L), leaving the contents of both manuscripts confused. Also, the line numbers in his edition were garbled near the end, but the errors were merely noted and the printers were not required to correct them. Using the early edition of Wace published by Le Roux de Lincy (1836, 1838), Furnivall noted the lines in Mannyng's translation which were different from those of Wace. The later standard edition of Wace by Ivor Arnold (1938, 1940) is based on different manuscripts, leaving Furnivall's analysis of limited value today.

For other shortcomings, the editors must be excused. Diligent scholars have corrected some of the errors in the earlier transcriptions, and our methods of dating manuscripts have improved, though neither P nor L is as yet firmly dated. Many misreadings in these editions have been corrected in citations in the *Middle English Dictionary;* where the L text is significantly different in Part I, MED regularly provides alternate readings from P. (Some of these corrections appear to have been based on consultation of the manuscripts.) Lack of variants from L in Hearne's edition of Part II, however, has limited the MED editors to citations occurring only in P. Since P is frequently faulty, or altered by omission, we are forced to depend on L for the contents of many passages as well as for correction of P's errors. The reviser of the exemplar of L was probably responsible for many of the differences, but the meticulous L scribes deserve credit for preserving a less faulty text than the one that survives in P. Individual words in the text of the *Chronicle* in both manuscripts show much variation in spelling, but they must belong to Mannyng's vocabulary, however orthographically erratic, when examples are found elsewhere in his works. The fact that the reviser who created the L exemplar introduced language that was not in the original version should also be taken into account. The evidence of editing and change in idiom from the usage of Lincolnshire to that of the South West Midlands is abundant throughout L.[10]

---

of the Records. I can only ask mercy for its shortcomings, and for the long delay which has taken place in the production of the book; pleading also that this delay has not been due to mere laziness, though I acknowledge that it was wrong in me to do other work and leave this volume undone." *The Story of England I,* p. xxiii.

[10] The language of the whole *Chronicle* includes many terms unrecorded elsewhere in Middle English. Words that are cited in OED or MED with references *only* to Mannyng's works are so marked in the Glossary.

During the years when Mannyng was actively translating (1303–1338 as he said), very few major literary texts in English appeared, and almost all of those surviving are found in later manuscript copies. Thus his works, *Handlyng Synne* and the *Chronicle*, are essential for the study of the language in use during the first years of the fourteenth century. Though *Handlyng Synne* does not survive in any manuscript that has Mannyng's own dialect, the lexis retains much of the diction he used in the *Chronicle*. He left a substantial body of verse: 12,678 lines in the longest complete manuscript of *Handlyng Synne* and 24,304 lines in the *Chronicle*, a total of 36,982 lines. Without Mannyng's work, our knowledge of early fourteenth century English would be very much more limited.

Among the other poetic texts contemporary with Mannyng's works, for example, are the historical compilation attributed to "Robert of Gloucester,"[11] the northern *Cursor Mundi*,[12] (both ca. 1300) and the col-

[11] There is no evidence that Mannyng knew the work attributed to "Robert of Gloucester," though he certainly knew most of the sources of this very dull poetic history. The first edition was published by Hearne (1724), reprinted in vols. I and II of *The Works of Thomas Hearne* (1810), and reedited by William Aldis Wright for the Rolls Series (1887). Anne Hudson's article, "Robert of Gloucester and the Antiquaries, 1550–1800" (1969), adds useful information on both of these editions. The work survives in two recensions in fourteen MSS (including fragments) widely scattered in date and provenance. The oldest (MS C, Cotton Caligula A. XI) is dated in the first quarter of the fourteenth century while the others date from a century or more later. The different recensions of the work were done by different authors. The confusion of Mannyng's *Chronicle* with the work of "Robert of Gloucester" is doubtless attributable to erroneous notations in MS P (see the description of the MS below). The putative author and Mannyng were discussed by Thomas Baker (1656–1740), a friend of Hearne, in Baker MS 41 (Cambridge University Library MS Mm.1.52), f. 262v, with speculations concerning the identity of "Robert of Gloucester." See Hudson, p. 326, n. 33. "Robert of Gloucester" was once alleged to be the author of the "Lives of the Saints" also. Skeat's edition of Laud Misc. MS 108 (the "Havelok" MS) makes this attribution (EETS 4, p. xxxv). "Lives of the Saints" is actually the earliest version of the *South English Legendary*, ed. by Charlotte D'Evelyn in EETS 235, 236 (1956) and 244 (1959). See vol. III, especially pp. 15ff. The tendency to give credit to a "known" author, in spite of evidence to the contrary, including the fact that "Robert of Gloucester" is only named in a revised version of the work and was probably not the original author, seems to apply here. Similarly, Mannyng was once credited with the translation of Bonaventure's "Medytacyuns" solely because of its appearance in the MSS with *Handlyng Synne* by the first editor of this late fourteenth century work, J. Meadows Cowper (EETS 60, 1875, p. xiii).

[12] The early northern version of *Cursor Mundi* was edited by Richard Morris (see above, n. 7). The southern version is published in several parts in a series begun under the general editorship of Sarah M. Horrall (d. July 27, 1988), at the University of Ottawa, 1978–. See Horrall's posthumous article, "'For the Commun at Understand': *Cursor Mundi* and its Background" (1989). The work is (generically) a vernacular biblical paraphrase, but is best described as "a chronologically arranged narrative of world history," according to Horrall. She says that the classification of *Cursor Mundi* with Mannyng's *Handlyng Synne* is misleading (p. 97).

lection in the "Auchinleck manuscript"[13] (ca. 1330), along with the North East Midland "Havelok" and some English romances in various other manuscripts that are presumed to have been written in the first part of the century. Mannyng depended on some version of "the romance of Richard" in Part II, for example, frequently referring to it as if he assumed it would be familiar to his readers. Mannyng's own references to other contemporary works have provided clues to their dating and attest to his wide knowledge of the literature available in English in his time.[14]

Mannyng was not an anthologizer. He made use of the literature he knew in frequent casual references, but his main purpose was to translate his specific sources in a coherent historical account. Like his models, Wace and Langtoft, he was composing (or in his own term, compiling) a unified work rather than a collection of short pieces that had some chronological or thematic plan without any poetic continuity. Some of his references to added details are intended to reinforce the authenticity of the texts he was translating; others provide gratuitous information. The fact that he chose to add supplemental matter before and within the translation of the named major sources does not detract from his plan. All the allusions and snippets are carefully integrated and suitable transitions are provided where necessary. No doubt the arrangement of the preliminary matter in the first part, the 726 lines that form a kind of prelude to the whole work, followed

---

[13] The contents of the "Auchinleck MS" (National Library of Scotland MS Advocates 19.2.1) have been published in separate editions; a facsimile edition of the MS was edited by D. A. Pearsall and I. C. Cunningham (London, 1977). See n. 14 below for the lists of separate editions. See the analysis in Julia Boffey and John J. Thompson, "Anthologies and Miscellanies: Production and Choice of Texts," in *Book Production and Publishing in Britain, 1375–1475* (1989), pp. 279–315. A facsimile of two folios is on p. 296. Boffey and Thompson say that the MS can be associated with the North East Midlands area (p. 295). See Edwards and Pearsall, "The Manuscripts of the Major English Poetic Texts," in the same volume, pp. 257–58 and notes, pp. 272–73.

[14] See J. Burke Severs, ed., *A Manual of the Writings in Middle English, 1050–1500* vol. I (1967), 13. For "Works of Religious and Philosophical Instruction," see vol. VII (1986), 2255ff. Dating of the MSS is in the list provided in MED, "Introduction," and in *A Linguistic Atlas of Late Mediaeval English* (LALME). A useful list is in Robert W. Ackerman, "English Rimed and Prose Romances," in *Arthurian Literature in the Middle Ages* (ALMA), 480–519. He provides dates and brief discussions of twenty-three separate Arthurian Tales, including a few from Mannyng's time: i.e., "Arthour and Merlin" (1250–1300), "Sir Tristrem" (ca. 1300), "Libeaus Desconus," "Sir Perceval of Galles," and "Sir Launfal." The earliest surviving version of "Richard" is in the Auchinleck MS. Another romance dated in the first quarter of the fourteenth century is the North West Midland "Seege or Batayle of Troy" (ed. by Mary E. Barnicle, EETS OS 172, 1927). Derek Pearsall, "The Development of Middle English Romance" (1965), lists fifty romances which have been edited (pp. 93–95, n. 7). Dieter Mehl, *The Middle English Romances of the Thirteenth and Fourteenth Centuries* (1969) has extended analyses of the works contemporary to Mannyng's. See Mehl's Appendix, p. 285, n. 3, for a list of the seventeen romances in the Auchinleck MS.

similar plans in other historical manuscripts. He does not identify all his diverse sources in this part, perhaps because so many models were available that he assumed his readers would recognize what he included.

Mannyng's earlier work, *Handlyng Synne* (1303), was also conceived as a unified work, and though it was designed to follow the basic structure of his major source, the *Manuel des Pechiez,* he made many substitutions and additions to the tales in the Anglo-French poem. From one perspective, *Handlyng Synne* is a kind of anthology of short stories, but the whole poem is systematically arranged to cover a body of narrative matter prescribed by the doctrinal imperatives of contemporary confessional manuals.

Handlyng Synne survives in ten manuscripts: three complete manuscripts, two that were probably complete originally, and five manuscripts with excerpts incorporated in later anthologies.[15] None of these manuscripts of *Handlyng Synne* preserves an authoritative text for the study of Mannyng's dialect. A major source for the language of Lincolnshire in Mannyng's time, therefore, is in his *Chronicle*, though several manuscripts from that area have been identified as the work of scribes with similar or analogous dialects. Only "Havelok," which is (in its most complete contemporary copy) basically similar dialectally, though very mixed from scribal alteration, approximates the language in Mannyng's work. As indicated above, several pieces can be identified as works originating in the North East Midlands, but a most significant body of the surviving literature from the earlier fourteenth century is in Mannyng's work.[16]

---

[15] Appendix I, p. 377 of my edition has a list of the MSS. BFH are the complete MSS and DO were probably once complete. The excerpts are: MSS C ("The Ten Commandments"); A has a single story; SV has a selection entitled the "Sacrament of the Altar" in the published version, Horstmann (1892). The recently identified Westminster MS (W) also has a single tale.

[16] See the discussion below of the "Havelok" interpolation in L, with references to the various editions; see n. 45, and the text notes for ll. 538ff. in Part II. The language is that of South Wiltshire, of course, for this passage is a substitution for a shorter passage in P. For an analysis of the language see Angus McIntosh, "The Language of the Extant Versions of *Havelok the Dane*" (1976). On Laud Misc. MS 108, McIntosh says: "I shall not dispute the solid evidence for the original version having been composed in Lincolnshire, but ... [Laud MS 108] is written in a kind of Middle English ... characteristic of Norfolk rather than Lincolnshire" (p. 36). In n. 5, p. 48, McIntosh provides information on the other South Lincolnshire documents he discusses to establish provenance. G. V. Smithers, ed., *Havelok* (1987) analyzes the language (pp. lxxv–lxxxix) with frequent references to Mannyng's work: "Useful confirmation of a general kind is provided by Robert Mannyng, and by links with his vocabulary as well as his phonology and accidence" (p. lxxxix). See also Smithers' mention of possible links to *Handlyng Synne* in "Havelok." The two passages he cites (pp. lxxi–lxxii) that are "commonly regarded as direct imitations by Mannyng" are based on lexical coincidences. Smithers himself concedes that the evidence is thin. The LALME list of Lincolnshire MSS

Although we do not have a surviving manuscript of *Handlyng Synne* that represents Mannyng's language at the time he wrote, we must take this early work into account in evaluating his achievement. The glossary shows that many distinctive words and phrases as well as the probably authorial rime words have survived several recensions and translations to other dialects. The scope of the whole poem survives in the complete (BFH) manuscripts and in some of the passages of the Osborn manuscript (O), particularly the tale of the "Drunken Priest" (at line 6546). This tale is almost certainly authorial as it is derived from a tale in the source, *Manuel des Pechiez.* Perhaps most important, *Handlyng Synne* continued to be of interest to other scribes or anthologists for almost a century and a half after Mannyng wrote, though the later manuscripts (CDO) containing substantial surviving parts of the text are not precisely dated. The single short tales appearing in diverse anthologies (ASVW) argue for a wide distribution of copies.

Mannyng's sources and his translation of them are discussed in detail below and in the notes to the text of both parts of the *Chronicle.* For the structure of the whole work, however, a preliminary comment is necessary to put the *Chronicle* into perspective, since the text has regularly been described erroneously. The relationship of Part II to Langtoft's text, for example, is mislabelled in all the references that follow Hearne's title for his edition. The text of the *Chronicle* is a whole work and should not be described as two separate works.[17] Mannyng's clearly stated purpose was to compile a history in English verse of the British and English people from the "beginnings"; he was following the example of many other

(County Lists) is in vol. I, pp. 210–15; there are very few literary MSS among them. The editors state that "From before about 1350 there are very few sources for northern or north Midland English . . ." (I:3).

[17] J. Conway Davies, *Catalog of Manuscripts in the Library of the Honorable Society of the Inner Temple,* I (1972), relies on the statement in Hearne's edition quoting Mr. Anstis, a trustee of William Petyt, who said the P MS was "written about the same time that the author liv'd, *viz* at the beginning of Edw. 3rd's Reign." (Hearne's Appendix, p. CII). Davies' description of P identifies the contents as "two entirely separate translated works which have been combined together, the second part, written slightly later than the first, being coalesced into it" (p. 219). There is no reference to the source for this information, nor for the following: "The date 1338, which is the year of Robert Mannyng's death, may be accepted as correct for the second part" (ibid.). Davies' catalog is very useful for a succinct history of the circumstances of the acquisition of Petyt's MSS by the Inner Temple Library; see p. 36: Petyt's bequest included funds for publication and obligated the trustees to make the arrangements. I have not found any corroboration of Davies' statements concerning the "separate works" and a date for Mannyng's death. Davies' date for P is almost certainly too early. I have relied (in part) on Davies' description of some of the scribbles and other data written in the MS, particularly for the names of persons, which are extremely difficult to decipher.

historical compilers who preceded him, most of them named in his text. Part I is a translation of the French *Roman de Brut* of Wace (1155), with additions from various other sources in French, Latin, and possibly English. Nearly all of Part II was translated from the Anglo-French verse chronicle by Peter of Langtoft, a Bridlington canon (as Mannyng tells us in lines 187–88 of Part I), whose work was also the basis for a few passages near the end of Part I. These sources and Mannyng's reasons for choosing them are explained in his preface (Part I, lines 55–70), where he states his objectives in undertaking the translation, adds comments on the intended audience and style of poetry to be employed, and provides attributions to his sources for the main body of the work.[18]

In the course of preparing this edition, I found that it was necessary to transcribe the microfilm and verify the transcripts in the manuscripts at the libraries where they are held. I also consulted the older editions of the *Chronicle* and editions of the sources to correct doubtful readings because those editions were printed before the invention of microfilm.[19] But misreadings in the editions are ubiquitous: MED notes hundreds of them for their citations of Mannyng's language from the printed editions, as well as citations from Thomas Wright's edition of Langtoft's chronicle. Though these editions have been indispensable, there are many readings in the manuscripts that were misinterpreted by the editors or conjecturally emended. Where a major misreading involves the meaning of a line or

[18] The text of Mannyng's prologue in P (ll. 1–198), which evidently also occupied the first folio in L but was torn out, may have been disarranged in an earlier copy (or in P itself). It is not as logically organized as Mannyng's work usually is. If a scribe rearranged it, he also cleverly rewrote some of the lines to accommodate what he had done. For example, the text in ll. 125–62 could go just as well after l. 200 (i.e., after f.2r c.1). The first column on f.1v (ll. 83–124) could have originally been the second column (after l. 40), but some adjustment of the text would also have been necessary. If Mannyng began with the explanation of his translation, proceeded to outline the matter, then discussed his sources, the line order as it survives in P appears to be somewhat disarranged.

[19] Among other indispensable references is the English translation of the "Vulgate" version by Lewis Thorpe, *Geoffrey of Monmouth: The History of the Kings of Britain* (Penguin reprint, 1980), based on the oldest Latin MS, Cambridge University Library MS 1706, which was the base text for Acton Griscom's edition of 1929. Thorpe employs the traditional divisions of the work, which facilitates the citations. Some of the Latin MSS are now becoming available in a new series published by D. S. Brewer; see the review of this series by L. M. Matheson (1988), who also describes the series of proposed publications of the *Historia Brittonum* by Nennius, a major source for Geoffrey. References to several volumes in these two series are given in the notes below. The standard edition of Wace is by Ivor Arnold, *Le Roman de Brut de Wace* (*SATF* 1938, 1940). The only edition of all of Langtoft's work is by Thomas Wright, *The Chronicle of Pierre de Langtoft* (RS, 1866). The resemblances between Langtoft's MS B and Mannyng's translation are detailed in Wright's variant notes throughout. See the short list of references to works containing Mannyng's sources at the beginning of the text notes for both parts of Mannyng's *Chronicle*.

passage, it is noted in the text notes. Many words in Furnivall's edition, both in the text and in his footnotes, required correction. Hearne was particularly prone to confuse u/n or c/t, including his curious reading of "Hanelok." The manuscript scribes themselves must have perpetuated some of these confusions by misreading their exemplars, and confusion of letters has been noted by almost every modern editor of Middle English manuscripts. Whether my perception of these differences in individual words is better than that of earlier editors is a question that will no doubt be resolved eventually by other scholars. For a conspicuous example of the perpetuation of misreadings, see the text notes in Part II for lines 538ff., the "Havelok" episode in L that has so exercised scholars concerned with that work in its various versions.

From as long ago as the publication of Hearne's edition of Mannyng's *Chronicle,* Part II, editions of Middle English works frequently present a reinterpretation or modernization of the manuscripts the editors have chosen. Too often, these editions obscure the original meaning of some of the lines simply through unfortunate misreadings or other misperceptions. And editors following them regularly insist that they have improved and corrected the text. Yet even the most skilled editor (with a magnifier of the highest power) can err. The result may be an edition that does not reflect the original of the author's work nor even a faithful transcript of any one manuscript in which that work happens to survive.

Those of us who have been permitted to verify transcripts from microfilm copy of manuscripts that are not otherwise easily accessible discover that what seemed to be a reliable reading in black and white often appears quite different in the actual manuscript. Shadings of ink, the marginal scribbles lost in the photographic process, the nuances of color in initials or captions are not easily discerned in microfilm copies. We must rely in part on earlier editions done by those pioneer editors (or their assistants) who transcribed the manuscripts before microfilm was invented. But the risk of accepting misreadings in these older editions is always present. Optimally, all important manuscripts would be available in facsimile, which would theoretically make accurate editions possible for everyone.

No scholar will disagree that reliable transcripts of manuscripts are essential, and if an editor can do more than provide accurate readings, so much the better. But the attempt to reconstruct an authorial text by emending a manuscript which is not a holograph seems to me to be arrogant. To choose the method I have found most useful in this edition, however, is to risk offending those scholars whose major concern is recovery of an author's original composition by comparison of many different documents and then choosing what seems to the editor to be the best reading to provide an emended text. Making the effort to recover what these surviving manuscripts provide (regardless of their faults) as evidence of the original work is the necessary first step. In the present edition, I chose the P text, mainly because of its dialect and earlier date, and added variant notes in parallel from the revised version in the L manuscript; this seemed the least confusing way to deal with the manuscript evidence. The glossary for Mannyng's works from all the manuscripts, including fragments and selections in anthologies that have survived has, of course, made the perception of accurate readings somewhat less difficult: even diction that is garbled or misread by a scribe from his exemplar can often be identified in other manuscripts and the misreading noted. The discovery of the same diction, however orthographically distorted, in *Handlyng Synne* as well as in the *Chronicle* has made interpretation of his language more precise. The fact that all but two of the manuscripts (PR) containing parts of Mannyng's works are translated from dialects other than his own, however, is still a major editorial hazard. Thus, the survival of Mannyng's *Chronicle* in P is extremely fortunate: without it, scholars would lack a substantial amount of information about the language of southern Lincolnshire in the early fourteenth century.

Mannyng's Biography

Robert Mannyng was a native of Bourne (Brunne) in Lincolnshire, and was probably a canon in the English Gilbertine order. Though he makes no claim to membership in the order, he mentions his familiarity with several of the Gilbertine priors and masters as if they were intimate colleagues. These names occur in the passages in both works where he gives us a few facts about his life.[20] There is no evidence for his birthdate, but it could have been as early as ca. 1265 or as late as 1280. He was evidently a student at Cambridge some time before 1306, for he mentions attending a feast there in honor of a brother of Robert Bruce, who was king of Scotland,

[20] The biography references are given in my edition of *Handlyng Synne,* applicable to pp. XII–XIII, nn. 2–4 on p. XXXIX. Some additional data is included in the discussion here. Furnivall notes: "The name of the present wapentake in which Bourne is, is Aveland, in Kesteven." (*The Story of England* I, p. iii). Mannyng nowhere actually says that he was a canon, but his knowledge of matters pertaining to liturgy and the duties of parish priests suggests first-hand experience. See Sally Thompson, *Women Religious: The Founding of English Nunneries After the Norman Conquest* (1991), 73–79 on the Gilbertine houses and 133 on the role of the canons in the order. She refers to *The Book of St. Gilbert,* R. Foreville and G. Keir, eds. (Oxford, 1987) and to the continuing study of the Gilbertines by Brian Goulding (p. 73, n. 123).

1306–1329. In Part II of the *Chronicle,* he writes:

> Now of Kyng Robyn salle I ȝit speke more
> & his broþer Tomlyn, Thomas als it wore,
> & of Sir Alisandere, þat me rewes sore,
> þat boþe com in skandere for dedes þei did þore.
> Of arte he had þe maistrie, he mad a coruen kyng
> in Cantebrige, to þe clergie, or his broþer were kyng.
> Siþen was neuer non of arte so þat sped,
> ne bifore, bot on, þat in Cantebrigge red.
> Robert mad his fest for he was þore þat tyme,
> & he sauh alle þe gest þat wrote & mad þis ryme.
> [8225–34]

The interpretation of this passage requires some conjecture: did Robert the Bruce, later king of Scotland, make the feast in honor of his brother Thomas, or was it Alexander who made the feast, with the other brother in attendance? There is evidently some distortion of the facts, and of the text itself, in these lines. A. B. Emden has suggested that "coruen kyng" may be a scribal error for "commencyng," thus the sense of the passage is much improved.[21] In the subsequent lines Mannyng writes of the "skandere" involving the Bruce brothers:

> Sir Alisander was hie Dene of Glascow,
> & his broþer Thomas ȝed spiand ay by throw
> where our Inglis men were, not in clerke habite,

[21] See A. B. Emden, *A Biographical Register of the University of Cambridge to 1500* (1963), 100. He suggests that "coruen kyng" is "a scrivener's mistaken rendering of the unfamiliar term 'commencyng,' meaning 'a commencement feast.' " Stephen Sullivan, "*Handlyng Synne* in its Tradition" (Ph.D. diss., 1978), discusses this passage and its implications (pp. 83–84), and cites Langtoft's version of the first three lines: "Du fols rey Robyn qe voet plus parler / De sir Thomas de Breus se poet amentiner / Et de sir Alexander de qi me dout le quoer" (Wright ed., II:374). Sullivan concludes that the feast was in honor of Alexander and remarks: "It is important to assert that the English writer is concerned with the career of the Bruces, and only incidentally, if at all, with his own biography" (p. 83). The passage is quoted by Ruth Crosby, "Robert Mannyng of Brunne: A New Biography," (1942), p. 28, also assuming that Alexander was the scholar. Crosby, however, considers lines 8228–34 an interpolation; Mannyng was perhaps using these lines as an excuse to reveal his intimate acquaintance with the Bruce brothers; the "Robert" named in line 8233 evidently refers to the future king of Scotland rather than to Mannyng himself. Was a line omitted between 8233 and 8234 that could have resolved this ambiguity? Both Crosby and Stephen Sullivan cite other references which have been made to these lines as evidence for Mannyng's and the Bruces' being at Cambridge; it is a passage regularly quoted for support in matters concerning the history of the Bruce brothers. Emden's conjecture, in fact, about the possibly mistaken word "commencyng" appears in his biographical information for Alexander Bruce.

& non wild he spare, bot destroied also tite;
þorgh þe Kyng Robyn þei ȝede þe Inglis to spie.
[8235–39]

In the lines following, Mannyng describes how the Bruces were apprehended as they came from church on Ash Wednesday, then were taken to King Edward who condemned them to be hanged and drawn. With slight differences in the nature of the sentence, Mannyng follows Langtoft's account in this passage. Lines 8233–34, however, are not in Langtoft's version. Mannyng's purpose was to insert a sly comment indicating that the Bruce brothers were contemporaries, evidently his fellow scholars, and he has changed Langtoft's condemnation of them sufficiently to reveal that he held them in high regard in spite of the unfortunate spying episode that gave King Edward an excuse to execute them. Most scholars have accepted the interpretation that Mannyng was present when one of the Bruce brothers was admitted Master of Arts; this is a significant detail in Mannyng's biography, providing an approximate date and a clue to his activities.

It is notable that Mannyng moderates Langtoft's account of this period in many ways. Instead of precisely translating the lines in which Langtoft expresses his virulent hatred of all Scots, Mannyng attempts to treat the Scots more evenhandedly. He omits much of the vituperation that we find in Langtoft's version. This difference in attitude does not fully explain the changes in the text, however, particularly in the short biographical passage above. Earlier in Part II, Mannyng used different (or altered) versions of the political songs that deal scurrilously with the Scots, a device that had been introduced by Langtoft for his own propagandistic purposes.[22] Even in a period of extreme hostility between the Scots and the English on the northern borders, Mannyng was humane in his judgment while Langtoft never neglected an opportunity to denounce the enemy. Possibly some of the hatred had diminished in the period between the times when Mannyng and Langtoft wrote, but it is more likely that Mannyng tempered his remarks because he remembered his fellow scholars at Cambridge with kindness.

---

[22] For the political songs, see the discussion of Mannyng's use of sources below. M. Dominica Legge proposed that Langtoft revised and altered his work several times, the final version reflecting his bitterness when Edward II came to the throne. See her *Anglo-Norman Literature and Its Background* (1963), p. 179. The details of MS history which would explain Langtoft's revisions have not yet been satisfactorily recorded, though J. C. Thiolier in a book (1989) and several articles has made an attempt to do so. The best account of the various recensions is that of Thomas M. Smallwood, "The Text of Langtoft's Chronicle" (1977).

In the prologue to *Handlyng Synne,* Mannyng tells us that he was in residence at the Gilbertine mother house at Sempringham where he began the translation of the Anglo-French *Manuel des Pechiez* in 1303 (ll. 60–76). Whatever his status among the Gilbertines was, he was evidently employed as a poet and translator, living at the priory for fifteen years; the first ten years were during the tenure of "dan Ione of Cameltoun," then five years with "dan Ione of Clyntone," while "Dan felyp" was "mayster" of the [Gilbertine] order. Though this account probably was added when the translation was finished, it is very circumstantial. Some of the records of the Gilbertine houses support the dates for the priors and masters, though there are some divergences in spelling of the names. Prior John de Hamilton of Sempringham is recorded in 1301 and 1312; John de Homerton (?Hamerton) was elected Master in 1276, Philip de Burton in 1298. John de Glinton appears in the list of priors in 1325 and 1332; he was elected Master of the order in 1332, and resigned in 1341. It is possible that "dan Ione of Cameltoun" (ll. 67–68) was John de Hamilton, and "Ione of Clyntone" (l. 71) was probably Glinton.[23]

In his prologue to the *Chronicle,* Mannyng adds a detail about his further employment:

> In þe thrid Edwardes tyme was I
> when I wrote alle þis story.
> In þe hous of Sixille I was a throwe;
> Danȝ Robert of Malton þat ȝe know
> did it wryte for felawes sake
> when þai wild solace make. [139–44]

If Mannyng began the *Chronicle* at the beginning of Edward III's reign in 1327 and completed it in 1338 (so dated at the end of Part II), he must have devoted most of his time to the work. One may surmise that he began somewhat earlier, for eleven years would be scarcely enough. The Gilbertine house at Malton was a retreat house for the canons, and Sixhills was a major house as well. They doubtless appreciated Mannyng's long historical narrative.

Ethel Seaton discovered what she considered external evidence for Mannyng's biography in the will of a widow, a parishioner of St. Cuthbert's in Lincoln: Avice de Crosseby calls him "Sir Robert de Brunne . . .

23 "Victoria County History for Lincolnshire," vol. 2, ed. by William Page (London, 1906) lists these Gilbertines on pp. 184–87. Matching the names is, of course, conjectural. Mannyng's poem as it appears in the Bodley MS 415 was translated to the South East Midland dialect and doubtless copied many times, increasing the probability that the names were altered.

chaplain," and names him as one of her executors in 1327.[24] When she died on "3 Ides Sept.," probate was entered and "administration granted to Robert de Brume [*sic*]." The name occurs three times in Avice's will. She left him ten shillings and a *ciphum* or goblet ("without a foot, which is called 'Nutte' "). If this document correctly identifies our author, Mannyng was employed as a chaplain in Lincoln several years before he completed his *Chronicle* in 1338, and his clerical duties may have been assigned even earlier, probably during the years when he was also translating. More precise connections would be desirable, yet an assumption that he served as a chaplain is consistent with other aspects of his life as revealed in his writings. The Gilbertines, like several other contemporary orders, appropriated churches in this period and provided chaplains when necessary. Mannyng's tone in *Handlyng Synne* clearly implies that he was writing for preachers, precisely the audience we would expect to be employed as chaplains.

The name "Robert of Brunne" has recently been discovered in several other documents. Possibly more than one person with this name was employed as a clerk at the time that Mannyng lived. The name as recorded in contemporary documents does not necessarily prove identification as our author. Juris G. Lidaka, challenging Seaton's assumption, explored this question and found the names of other Roberts of Brunne in Lincoln: citing Lincolnshire bishops' registers, the following ordinations occurred during the period May 19, 1290 to September 19, 1299:

> "Among unbeneficed subdeacons, Robert son of Thomas of Bourne (Brunne), from Lincoln" 18 December 1294
> "Among unbeneficed deacons, Robert of Bourn (Brunne), t. Revesby Abbey for all holy orders" 26 February 1295
> "Among unbeneficed priests, Robert son of Thomas of Bourn (Brunne), from Lincoln, t. Revesby Abbey."[25]

---

[24] See Ethel Seaton, "Robert Mannyng of Brunne in Lincoln," *Medium Ævum* 12 (1943): 77. Seaton refers to a will printed in translation in C. W. Foster, ed., *Lincoln Wills Registered in the District Probate Registry at Lincoln. Vol. I: A.D. 1271 to A.D. 1526* (Lincoln Record Society Publications, 1914), 6–8. See Vincent Gillespie, "Cura Pastoralis in Deserto" (1989); he illuminates the pastoral activities in the thirteenth and fourteenth centuries and mentions some of the books owned by members of these orders. See pp. 180–81 on the Carthusians working in the dioceses of York and Lincolnshire. The authorship and use of manuals and handbooks of religious instruction do not seem to be exclusive to any one order. This observation is confirmed, in a general way, by the evidence of copies of parts of *Handlyng Synne* made by scribes in diverse MSS not connected with the Gilbertines. The standard reference on churches and other dependencies of the various orders is David Knowles and R. Neville Hadcock, *Medieval Religious Houses: England and Wales* (2d ed., 1971). See pp. 194–99 on the Gilbertines.

[25] This information appeared in a 6 January 1994 posting on Internet [Bitnet: Lida-

Matthew Sullivan has reported another dozen references to Robert of Brunne, one of them with the Mannyng surname (in 1314) and another referring to Robert "the son of Nicholas [of Bourne] the forester" who was involved in a Lincolnshire land transaction. These references (from 1287 to 1345), as well as other documents naming "Robert of Brunne" that have not previously been published, portray him, in Sullivan's words, as "a substantial landholder in Bedfordshire and Cambridgeshire who experienced a fair amount of legal trouble (much of his own making), had some experience in the legal profession ... and maintained some contact with his birthplace."[26]

These references to a Robert of Brunne whom Sullivan assumes to be our author are quite diverse. The activities associated with the name are not very consistent with the presumptive employment of a clerical poet and translator: they involve legal documents concerning ownership and transfer of land, accusations of theft and assault, perversion of justice, and attacks on clerics and scholars at the University of Cambridge. Moreover, we have the odd circumstance that "Robert son of Thomas of Bourne" was ordained in 1294 in Lincolnshire, and at the turn of the century, Robert, "son of Nicholas [of Bourne] the forester" appears. There is always the possibility of error in a record of this kind, of course, though it would be very strange, as Professor Lidaka has pointed out, to find two different fathers for the same person. Along with Ethel Seaton's conjecture that Mannyng was a chaplain in Lincoln in 1327, positive identification of all these Roberts as our author admits of some doubt.

Though Mannyng's reference to himself in *Handlyng Synne* (at line 61)

---

ka@WVNWVSC]. In subsequent correspondence, Professor Lidaka has helpfully given permission to quote him; he is persuaded that more than one Robert of Brunne must have flourished at this time. The list of ordinations is from Rosalind M. T. Hill, ed. *The Rolls and Registers of Bishop Oliver Sutton,* vol. 7, pp. 60, 63, 71. A subsequent posting from Peter Binkley adds: "The 't.' must stand for titulus, meaning that Revesby [Cistercians] theoretically promised him a living. This doesn't necessarily mean he was a monk himself, just that the abbey was his patron. Religious houses needed secular priests to serve as vicars in appropriated parishes. Bishops were responsible for the upkeep of any excess clergy they ordained, ... so they were careful to record titles for all ordinands; but a good number of these titles were fictitious, and religious houses were often used for this purpose." Posted 6 January 1994 [binkley @let.rug.nl].

[26] Matthew Sullivan, "Biographical Notes on Robert Mannyng of Brunne and Peter Idley, the Adaptor of Robert Mannyng's *Handlyng Synne,*" *Notes and Queries,* n.s. 41 (September 1994): 302–4. In response to my inquiry, Dr. Sullivan writes that "the sources upon which the article is based are largely printed and are all noted in the article itself. Most of the source material derives from local history series (some quite obscure) ..." (letter of 15 January 1995). An earlier article is "The Author of the *Manuel des Péchés*" in *N&Q* (June 1991): 155–57. Both pieces refer to Sullivan's D. Phil. thesis, "The Original and Subsequent Audiences of the *Manuel des Péchés* and its Middle English Descendants" (University of Oxford, 1990).

does not include his surname, the manuscripts in which "Robert of Brunne" appears could have lost the name Mannyng in earlier copies. In the *Chronicle*, however, he emphatically states "Robert Mannyng is my name" (l. 136). No doubt he had a father, whether it was Thomas or Nicholas, but one or both of these must be inapplicable. The only identification that applies with reasonable certainty must be based on the text of Mannyng's works, leaving us much room for conjecture.[27]

At the beginning of Part I of the *Chronicle* (ll. 139–44), Mannyng says that Robert of Malton, possibly the prior at Sixhills or the Gilbertine retreat house for canons at Malton, asked him to undertake the translation of the *Chronicle*, which he completed in 1338, according to the last lines of Part II:

> Now most I nede leue here of Inglis forto write,
> I had no more matere of kynges lif in scrite;
> if I had haued more, blithly I wild haf writen.
> What tyme I left þis lore, þe day is for to witen:
> Idus þat is of Maii left I to write þis ryme,
> B letter & Friday bi ix þat ȝere ȝede prime.
> [8353–58][28]

Thus we have firm dates Mannyng himself provided for the beginning (in 1303) and end (1338) of his works, a probable date (before 1306) for his studies at Cambridge, and a possible clue to his employment as a chaplain in Lincoln ca. 1327. These dates are not inconsistent with the possibility that he could have been sponsored by Revesby Abbey for ordination

---

[27] In his 1994 article, Sullivan's reference for 1314 has: "Robert (here with the Mannyng surname), living in or near Bedford, was accused of disturbing the peace." The source is J. Godber, "Two Cranfield Manors," *Bedfordshire Historical Society* 25 (1947): 4–6. For the reference to "Robert Son of Nicholas the forester" the source (in n. 2, p. 302) is J. W. Clark, ed., *Liber Memorandum Ecclesiae de Bernewelle* (Cambridge, 1907), 298. All of the instances giving evidence of Robert's activities are carefully documented in Sullivan's notes, op. cit. For the 1307–11 citation, "Robert was alleged to have perverted the course of justice during the trial of Walter of Langeton, Bishop of Coventry and Lichfield." The reference is A. Beardwood, ed. *Records of the Trial of Walter Langeton, Camden Society* 4th series, 6 (1969): 44. Mannyng's *Chronicle* ends with the death of Edward I in 1307, of course, but he has a couple of references to Walter at lines 6792–93 and 6911–12, both following Langtoft's account on pp. 260 and 274 (Wright, II). There is no suggestion of partisanship nor of any close acquaintance with Langton, though it is possible that Langtoft knew the bishop during the years when he was Edward I's treasurer or chancellor. Langton's quarrel with Edward II more or less corresponds to the years 1307–11. If Mannyng had any direct dealings with Langton or was involved in some way at the bishop's trial, one would expect some allusion, since the *Chronicle* was still being written during the next quarter century, ending in 1338.

[28] The Latin caption following these lines in P corrects "B" letter to "D": "littera dominicali D prima ix tempore Regis Edwardi tercii a conquestus xi."

during 1294 and 1295 as subdeacon, deacon, and priest though he was not necessarily either a Cistercian or Gilbertine at that time. That the name appears in the records of the Bishop in Lincolnshire suggests that he did not have a specific commitment to one of the established orders. The bishop's registers would include secular priests but not necessarily those ordained in the orders.[29]

The choice of the chronicle as Mannyng's subject was a curious departure, representing a very different genre from the religious instruction in *Handlyng Synne.* Though Mannyng asserts that he undertook the compilation of a long historical work merely for the entertainment of his fellows, he does imply that he had a didactic purpose at the beginning. He is a humble translator of Wace and Langtoft: "And I, Robert, fulle fayn wald bringe / in Ynglis tonge þer faire saiynge" (I, 197–98). Throughout, he reminds his readers that the life of a king is instructive, if not always exemplary, and that the narrative of good kings' lives should provide a model for moral behavior. Still, there is no doubt that Mannyng simply loved a good story, long or short. He comments early on that he chose to translate Wace over Langtoft because Wace included all the contents of the British history (as Geoffrey of Monmouth had compiled it in Latin) but "Pers ouerhippis many tymes" (I, line 64). This justification is characteristic of an author who had made a much more interesting work of the material he found in the *Manuel des Pechiez,* his rather plodding French source for *Handlyng Synne.* D. A. Light's comment concerning the *Brut* of Wace would also apply to Mannyng: "The defining characteristic of a poet is not his skill in handling detail, it is his controlling and unifying vision which at least to some degree must be seen as giving shape and significance to his work as a whole."[30]

Thorlac Turville-Petre has recently argued that Mannyng's *Chronicle* was perhaps undertaken as a Gilbertine venture into contemporary politics. Since the work was an "assignment," so to speak, by a superior of the

[29] R. P. Stepsis's dissertation conjectures that a manuscript of Mannyng's *Chronicle* might have been preserved at Sixhills which was the exemplar for P (n. 2, p. xxxi). Sixhills is about fifteen miles northeast of Lincoln and fifteen miles southwest of Grimsby. In *Handlyng Synne,* Mannyng locates his home town, "Syxe myle besyde sympryngham euene." (l. 64). Revesby Abbey is northeast of Sempringham and about the same distance southeast of Sixhills. Bourne is directly south of Sempringham, about six miles even on modern maps.

[30] Light, "The Arthurian Portion of the Roman de Brut of Wace" (1970), contests critics of Wace's work who thought he was merely a "talented versifier" (n. 20, p. 14). J. S. P. Tatlock, *The Legendary History of Britain* (1950), discusses Wace's stance as a "professional literary man," and points out his naming himself and "the dates of beginning or ending or his conditions of life at the time" (p. 464). All of these aspects are equally characteristic of Mannyng.

order, this argument has merit. Turville-Petre explores the political situation of the Gilbertine houses in Mannyng's time, the relationship of the order to the barons and the monarchy, and assesses Mannyng's audience. His discussion includes conjectures about the reasons the Gilbertines might want to have the *Chronicle* translated and whether there was a political purpose behind the choice.[31]

Mannyng was undoubtedly aware of the political events of his time, though his opinions are not always categorically stated. He seems to be mainly concerned about recording the events, rarely passing judgment on them. Where his judgments do appear, however, he is usually translating his source in Langtoft's chronicle. In the account of Edward I's dealings with his barons, for example, the king's failure to share his wealth is a fault that caused much of the friction. In an extended criticism of Edward, Langtoft condemned him in a passage which Mannyng translated in these words: "ffeyntise, liþt duellyng, on mornes long to lie" (II, 7587) and later, "wille without reson, conseile of wise men fle, / wynnyng forto hold, & gyue not largely" (7590–91). Langtoft's last line is: "Conqueste retenir sanz fere largetez" (Wright, II, p. 326). One cannot directly attribute these political judgments to Mannyng, but he evidently agreed with them in part. Where he moderated or altered his source, as in the references to the Bruce brothers, he obviously disagreed with Langtoft.

Among the original amendments to his source in Part II, Mannyng adds a few particulars concerning Edward I's parliament at Lincoln in 1300:

> At þe Pask afterward his parlement set he,
> þe gode Kyng Edward at Lyncoln his cite;

[31] Thorlac Turville-Petre, "Politics and Poetry in the Early Fourteenth Century: The Case of Robert Manning's 'Chronicle,' " (1988), 1–23. One interesting facet discussed is the Wake family connection. In *Handlyng Synne*, there is a garbled line (in Mannyng's statement about his home territory) which was evidently miscopied at some early stage of the MS history: "Of brymwake yn kesteuene" (l. 63) which is identical in MSS B and H, and is "bringwake" in MS F. MS D, however, has "Brunnewake," which is doubtless correct. MSS H and F are copies of B, but none of these scribes corrected the error, and F changes the word to try to make sense of what he found in B. Howard Naish's note for this line further clarifies the matter: "D's Brunne Wake is undoubtedly the correct reading. . . . It seems likely that *Brunne* received its cognomen from the ancient family of Wake. Hugh Wac came from Normandy in 1166 and married the heiress of the Norman FitzGilbert, lord of Brunne. In 1279, Baldwin, lord Wake, obtained a licence for a market weekly on Saturdays, and one annual fair." *Handlyng Synne and Medytacyuns* (1936). The matter is important to Mannyng's biography in a peripheral way because of Lord Wake's dealings with the Gilbertines, as Turville-Petre outlines them, pp. 10, 20–21. See Lesley Johnson's comments on Turville-Petre's argument in "Robert Mannyng's History of Arthurian Literature," (1991). Johnson's reservations pertain to his assertion that Mannyng's *Chronicle* was an expression of English antagonism toward the Normans (pp. 145–46 and especially her n. 32).

> at Sant Katrine hous þe erle marschalle lay,
> in þe brode gate lay þe Brus, erle was he þat day;
> þe kyng lay at Netilham, it is þe Bisshopes toun,
> & oþer lordes þer cam in þe cuntre vp & doun.
> [7611–16]

These details are not in Langtoft; it is possible that Mannyng was in Lincoln in 1300, or perhaps he was acquainted with persons who knew the lodgings of the king, the "erle Marschalle," and "þe Brus." This passage is one of several that reveal Mannyng's awareness of the political situation in his own time. He did not follow Langtoft when other incidents were of more interest to him or were matters of personal observation. The reference to the lodging of the Marshall was probably to the Gilbertine priory of St. Catherine outside Lincoln, originally founded as a house for canons.

A lifetime of service, perhaps including some years as a chaplain, and at least thirty-five years devoted to translating two major works from French, suggests that Mannyng lived at least sixty years. We have no evidence of the date of his death, though some scholars have assumed it to be in 1338, perhaps from a misreading of his epilogue to the *Chronicle.* He might have lived another ten years, up to the time of the Black Death.[32]

The Manuscripts of Mannyng's Chronicle

The manuscripts of Mannyng's *Chronicle* are:

- P: Petyt MS 511, Vol. 7 (Inner Temple Library, London) [Part I: 15946 lines; Part II: 8358 lines]
- L: Lambeth MS 131 (Lambeth Palace Library, London) [Part I: from line 199, parallel to P with several additions; Part II: lines 1–4973]
- R: Rawlinson Miscellany MS D. 913 (Bodleian Library, Oxford) [one folio, Part I: lines 12550–699 of P].

P. Petyt MS 511, Vol. 7 (Inner Temple Library, London)

The Petyt manuscript is on vellum, approximately 285 x 210 mm., with

[32] See n. 17 above on the information in Davies' catalog of the Petyt MSS. Matthew Sullivan concurs on the possible end of Mannyng's life: "In 1345 Robert and others were accused of theft of horses and goods, and serious assault, at Pulham, Norfolk. Mannyng more than likely died of plague during the late 1340s. . . ." Though I have reservations about accepting the accusation that Mannyng was guilty of theft in 1345, especially since he would have been very old then, his death in the plague of 1349 "that killed nearly half of the civilian population of Lincoln, and almost two-thirds of the clerical population" is certainly likely. Sullivan (1994), n. 4, p. 303.

Latin captions and rubrics mostly added by the scribe, and other embellishments done by an illuminator in blue and occasionally in red. The date of the manuscript has been variously, arbitrarily conjectured but not confirmed. Part of an older library catalog page bound in at the front has "XIV Cent." On leaves at the beginning and the end are the names of Robert Haxe, and of an early owner: "Iste liber pertinet Edmundo Pymond, vic. de Laghton"; Sir Jhon Chume and John Turner appear elsewhere. In addition, the manuscript has a notation concerning an early disposition: "this buke be delyverd at the syngn of the Bell in Doncastre for to be send to John Wyre dwelling at the parsonage of Laghton, a° 1522, x° die Marcii." With the signature of John Turner is the instruction: "Sell this book for v^{s} if you can." John Wyre and Edmund Pymond may both have been vicars in "Laghton"; John Turner is likely a later owner.

The date of the manuscript as given in the index to *The Middle English Dictionary* is "?a1400, (1338)"; that is, the work was composed in 1338 (as Mannyng states at the end of Part II) and the manuscript is probably dated within the twenty-five years before 1400. Though a date in the last quarter of the fourteenth century is still conjectural, I believe it is probably correct. The paleography also supports this dating: the hand is a modified anglicana that resembles the hands in several contemporary manuscripts.[33] The approximate period when the manuscript was written is also suggested by numerous citations of words in OED and MED which were current in contemporary manuscripts.

Cataloguers and other scholars who have examined P at various times

---

[33] The MSS of Mannyng's works are listed in "A Bibliography of Middle English Texts," published as a preliminary index for the MED (1954), 58. See M. B. Parkes, *English Cursive Book Hands, 1250–1500* (1969), especially pp. xvii–xix. The main hand in P has the characteristics of anglicana formata rather modified by the letter forms of the more cursive script which began to appear in the third quarter of the fourteenth century. I have consulted several sources containing facsimiles: Andrew G. Watson, *Catalog of Dated and Datable MSS in the British Library, ca. 700–1600* (1979); Cyril E. Wright, *English Vernacular Hands: From the Twelfth to the Fifteenth Centuries* (1960); older authorities with facsimiles include Charles Johnson and Hilary Jenkinson, *English Court Hand, A.D. 1066 to 1500* (2 vols., repr. 1967). For the fifteenth century and later, see Jean F. Preston and Laetitia Yeandle, *English Handwriting, 1400–1650* (1992). The main hand in P is quite typical of the anglicana formata script. "There is ample evidence that from the second half of the fourteenth century onwards scribes were seeking to adapt the regular anglicana formata, to evolve a version of this variety of script for use in vernacular books" say A. I. Doyle and M. B. Parkes, "The Production of copies of the *Canterbury Tales* and the *Confessio Amantis* in the early Fifteenth Century" (1978), 207. The quotation concerns "scribe D" of Trinity College, Cambridge MS R.3.2, whose hand is illustrated (especially in plate 49) and discussed at length. "Scribe D" also appears in ten other MSS of this period (p. 177); most of his letter forms are very similar to those in the P MS of the *Chronicle,* but the dialect, of course, differs. See the discussion of the P scribes' work below and n. 58.

have made other notes perpetuating confusion about the contents. A fragment of an earlier binding on the verso of the third prefatory page attributes the work to "Robert de Gloucester" and "Petrus de Langtoft," with a pencilled note beneath: "See Petyts own Catalogue, vol. 2, p. 155." On the next sheet, evidently kept from an earlier binding, are three pencilled notes: "Robert of Gloucester. Not Peter Langtoft as in the catalogue. J. C." The next note has: "+ this is not so. The volume contains both Robert of Gloucester and Peter Langtoft. W. fs." The third note, the only one which is correct, has: "Not true. The volume only contains Robert of Brunne's *Chronicle*; the first part of which is translated from the French of Wace and the latter portion from the French of Peter of Langtoft. From fol. 96 to the end was published by Hearne. F. M." This last note was almost certainly written by Sir Frederic Madden, who probably examined the manuscript at the Inner Temple Library before it was rebound in 1850. Madden discussed both the P and L manuscripts in his edition of *Havelok* for the Roxburghe Club in 1828 and was the first to notice that P and L differ.[34] A cryptic note in a later hand at the right margin of the first folio, about mid-page, is: "to my lovinge friend."

None of these notations help to identify the provenance or date of the manuscript.[35] The location in "Laghton" (the Doncaster area) in 1522 might be a useful clue if a further search for provenance is required. The dialect of the manuscript has been authoritatively established in South Lincolnshire, however, within the area Mannyng claimed as his place of birth at Bourne.[36] Explaining the erroneous attribution to "Robert of

---

[34] *The Ancient English Romance of Havelok the Dane* (Roxburghe Club, 1828). See Robert W. Ackerman and Gretchen P. Ackerman, *Sir Frederic Madden* (1979). Madden's "Havelok" is item 7 in Bibliography A, p. 46. The first note and possibly the second (signed "J. C." and "W. fs.") were in MS P before it was submitted to Hearne by his friend John Bridges. See n. 4 on the notations and n. 11 above on "Robert of Gloucester." The reference to "Petyt's own Catalog" is Petyt MS 523 in the same collection at the Inner Temple Library.

[35] Professor Angus McIntosh of the University of Edinburgh writes: "Thirty years ago, Dr. A. I. Doyle of Durham told me that the MS (Petyt) was (at least temporarily) in the Doncaster area in the early 16th century" (in a personal letter, August 15, 1985). Dr. Doyle may have gotten this information from the note cited above in the MS itself.

[36] The analysis of the language of P is in Angus McIntosh, M. L. Samuels, Michael Benskin and others (LALME is the usual abbreviation), III, LP (Linguistic Profile) 38, pp. 253–54, for Lincolnshire; the LP appears on the Lincolnshire map (3) in vol. IV: 336. See Angus McIntosh, "The Language of the Extant Versions of 'Havelok the Dane,' " (1976): "There are in particular two early texts which may be assigned with some confidence to South Lincolnshire [i.e., BM Addit. 23983 and Merton College 248]. . . . Another text of rather later date that may be ascribed with some assurance to the same region is that of Robert Mannyng's *Chronicle* in . . . MS. Petyt 511" (p. 39). His criteria are discussed at length thereafter, distinguishing the language of Lincolnshire from that of W. Norfolk. His mention of the Petyt MS is incidental: the purpose of the article is to establish that

Gloucester" is not difficult. A cataloguer who did not take the trouble to actually read the manuscript, or who was unfamiliar with Middle English dialects, was to blame. An "old English Chronicle" by Mannyng, who was not as well-known as "Robert of Gloucester," was simply misidentified. It is a grievous error: Mannyng introduced himself in line 4 of the first folio.

A most interesting peculiarity of P is a preliminary page bound in the volume, containing a passage that has the same lines given in the text of f. 110v (Part II of the *Chronicle*, lines 1223–1264). The page is worn and partly defaced as a result of being the first sheet in a manuscript that has been rebound, perhaps more than once. In its present condition, the leaf appears to have been pasted to the earlier binding but removed to be kept with the rest of the manuscript. Thomas M. Smallwood suggests that the leaf "must have been intended to be part of the manuscript, but was discarded to become a fly-leaf, while the text was rewritten on what is now f. 110v. It was probably rejected because it was written on the recto of a leaf when a verso was needed; a sheet cannot be refolded to make a recto page, once written, take a verso position."[37] The leaf has nothing at all on the reverse, but it is in the hand of the scribe who was responsible for most of the manuscript. Comparison of the words in the preliminary folio with the text of f. 110v and with the same passage in the Lambeth manuscript (f. 84v) supplies more evidence of the ways in which the P scribe habitually altered his text. Smallwood concludes: "In over half the lines he has altered the choice or arrangement of one or more words in one version or the other (or conceivably both)" (p. 553). (The Lambeth version of the lines in this short passage shows additional changes, probably revisions of the text.)

L. Lambeth MS 131 (Lambeth Palace Library, London)

Lambeth MS 131 is written on paper, approximately 305 x 212 mm., with the text ending at f. 131, followed by two blank leaves with marginal markings drawn as if the scribe intended to continue. The first leaf has been torn out, but a bit of the stub remains with the first letters of a few lines, indicating that L originally began with the same text we have in P, that is, with the prologue to Part I (ll. 1–198). There are several other folios missing in Part II of L: single leaves between ff. 92–93 and 104–105,

---

the language of "Havelok" in Bodleian Laud Misc. MS 108 is characteristic ("in all main essentials") of Norfolk, while the original version of the poem was composed in Lincolnshire (p. 36).

[37] "Another Example of the Double-Copying of a Passage of Middle English" (1986), 551. A transcript of the leaf with the parallel text from f. 110v is on pp. 551–52. Smallwood dates P ca. 1360–90.

three leaves are missing before two blank leaves at 107–108, and a lacuna of 115 lines on f. 110v. (This gap in the text is a scribal error, probably the result of turning an extra page of the exemplar while the scribe was making a copy.) The numbering of the leaves is not accurate, for the manuscript pages were numbered before and again after the leaves were lost. The older catalog of the Lambeth library dates the manuscript "Sec. XIV" while the later catalog (1930) has "Cent xv."[38] Dating in MED is "a1450," or the second quarter of the fifteenth century, which is supported by the characteristic letter forms of the two hands represented in the manuscript.[39]

L was part of the original Lambeth collection acquired by Archbishops Bancroft (d. 1610) and Abbot (d. 1633), and was among the manuscripts rebound after 1664 by Archbishop Sancroft (1617–1693), who catalogued the first 576 manuscripts in the collection and added many volumes to the library.[40] E. G. W. Bill's catalog of the manuscripts includes a supplement

---

[38] See H. J. Todd, *A Catalogue of the Archepiscopal Manuscripts of the Library at Lambeth Palace* (1812), p. 15, and M. R. James, *A Descriptive Catalog of the Manuscripts in the Library of Lambeth Palace* (1930), pp. 210–11. Several plates in Watson (1979) have examples of hands closely resembling those in L: e.g., plates 451 (dated 1442), 519, 520 (dated 1451).

[39] The discussion of secretary hands is in Parkes (1969), p. xxi and plate 12(ii). Compare plates 23 and 24 in C. E. Wright (1960): plate 23 (Cotton MS Vespasian D. viii) is dated by Wright 1450–1475, and has similarities to the second scribe in L and the hand in CUL MS Ii.4.9 (MS C of *Handlyng Synne*), as well as the piece added to Harley MS 1701, "Robert of Sicily," which is not the same hand as in the rest of the MS. Another set of plates for copies of this last item is in Lillian Herlands Hornstein, "King Robert of Sicily: A New Manuscript," (1963), p. 456. Coincidentally, four of her illustrations are from *Handlyng Synne* MSS: V (ca. 1390), S (ca. 1400), H (Harley 1701, probably ca. 1450 for this piece), C (ca. 1450). The fifth is from BM Harley 525 (ca. 1475). (These dates are from MED.) VS are in hands somewhat similar to the anglicana represented in P of the *Chronicle,* while C is more typical of the fifteenth century. C. E. Wright's dating of Harley 1701 (plate 13, f. 12v, *Handlyng Synne* ll. 1751–1826) is clearly too early: "written about AD 1380"; his judgment is a cautionary example, however, for the variety of anglicana represented in this MS can be found in MSS from before 1380 to well into the fifteenth century. He suggests comparison to plate 14, one of the C-text MSS of "Piers Plowman" (BL Cotton Vespasian B. xvi), which he says was "written not later than AD 1400." Wright's introduction has the following caveat: "As regards the dating of vernacular MSS. it must be stated frankly and by way of warning (where no internal evidence is available) this is to be regarded for the most part as tentative only . . ." (p. xvi).

[40] E. G. W. Bill, *A Catalogue of Manuscripts in Lambeth Palace Library* (1972), has a detailed history of the collections, with an analysis of the shelfmarks in the volumes that were in the library before and after the rebinding done by Sancroft. The shelfmark "M.22" is written on the bottom right hand corner of the first leaf in L, which is pre-1647; the later shelfmark (after 1664) is "E. z. 3," indicating that the first leaf in the MS (which probably had Mannyng's prologue) was missing at a very early date, before the MS was acquired for the Archbishops' collection. Ker's supplement includes a comment on L: "The hand changes at f. 80 . . . to one of distinctly xvth cent. type in my judgment" (p. 211). Both hands are clearly fifteenth-century secretary in style, but the second hand seems to be rather later than the first.

to M. R. James' catalog (1930) by N. R. Ker. The rebinding of the manuscripts, their removal to Cambridge and their return in 1664 are also discussed in the study by Sears Jayne and Francis R. Johnson, *The Lumley Library: The Catalog of 1609,* which adds an interesting dimension to the history of Lambeth MS 131. John, Lord Lumley (?1534–1609), a famous bibliophile in the reign of James I, acquired the nucleus of his library from Archbishop Thomas Cranmer (who gathered manuscripts when he was presiding over the dissolution of the monasteries). Lambeth MS 131 was among the manuscripts that came to the Archbishops' collection from Lumley's library at some point during the years just before and after 1600. The Lumley signature that appears on the first page in L is identical to signatures in other Lumley volumes that have been identified. As an interesting coincidence, the manuscript of Langtoft's chronicle which most closely suggests the text followed by Mannyng in his translation (MS B, Royal 20. A. XI) was also in Lumley's collection.

The L manuscript has a number of names and other indications of prior ownership throughout. At the top of f. 1: "A chronicle of England in olde Englische meeter from Brute to K. Richarde y^e .i. made by Piers of Langtofte Chanone of Bridlington and putte into Englishe ryme by Robert de Brunne iuxta Depinge .v. infr. f. lxxiii." This identification is evidently in the same hand as the signature at the bottom of f. 1, "Lumley." The librarian or keeper of Lumley's manuscripts was probably responsible for these notations. At the end (f. 132) following the page caption, "Richard," entered by the scribe before he stopped, are clumsily written names of "Richard" and "John" and the comment: "Note this Book imperfect the French copies of Peter Langtoft in the Cotton Library and allso in the Heraldes office end with the Reigne of King Edward the first." The manuscript in the "Heraldes office" is possibly the Langtoft B manuscript (Royal 20. A. XI), identified with the Arundel collection which became part of the Royal archives when Lumley's manuscripts were dispersed.

The names at the end of L seem to be pen-trials, but they are much later than the last scribe's hand on f. 131. On f. 133v are some scribbled accounts with the name of an early owner, now nearly indecipherable, "Jhon [? Wackman] his boke." On f. 134r are more notes by "Jhon" in the right margin, followed by two lines, "At Wenchestere ouere a parlement the / helde there the beshop of [?ba]," unfinished, perhaps a comment about some lines from the text. The last page, f. 134v, is blank except that it has been ruled by the scribe, and a page has been torn from the binding thereafter.[41]

---

[41] R. P. Stepsis (1967), pp. vii–ix, has a more detailed list of the marks in the MS for

The missing pages at the beginning and end of the L manuscript might indicate one or more intermediate bindings of the volume before Sancroft rebound it in the 1660s. The loss of the first page, however, suggests that the manuscript may have been armigerous or that it had other marks of ownership which an early manuscript collector did not wish to reveal. Considering the sources of the original collection acquired by Archbishop Cranmer, one is tempted to think that the monastery or other institution holding the manuscript at the time of the dissolution might have been responsible for this mutilation, or the collector himself was attempting to conceal its source.

The first leaf of L (beginning with line 199 of the text of P) has a graphic genealogy interspersed between the columns and in the right margin; the personages named in the text, Noe and his sons Sem, Cam, and Iaphet are in separate circles in the middle of the page, while the descendants named in lines 260ff. are identified in separate connected circles in the margin. The genealogy is continued on f. 1v in the same fashion, and this is the last "illumination" in the whole manuscript. These embellishments take the place of captions to identify the relationship of the persons appearing in the text on these pages.

Many of the scribbles and notes by later hands throughout the manuscript suggest that it was often read and probably used for reference over a long period of time. There are marginal notes in English, for example, on ff. 72r, 72v, and 76r. On f. 79r: "Kynge Edgar endowed (?) the abbey of Crowland ..." and on f. 79v under the side captions: "her it raynyd blode" and "the gret cite Kerlion ..." with other words evidently meaning that the city was destroyed. These notes occur near the text at lines 797

---

ff. 72 to the end. He notes the line at the top of f. 93: "This ys antone wakman ys boke," and reads the line on f. 133v as "Jhon wakman his boke." Stepsis uses the caption from L (f. 73) at the head of his transcript of Part II: "Incipiunt Gesta Angliae per M. Petrus de Langtoft transporta in lingua materna per Robertus de Brune iuxta Depyng." According to Jayne and Johnson, the cataloguer of Lumley's library in 1596 was Anthony Alcock; the 1609 catalog which they edited is a copy of Alcock's work (p. 32). The note at the top of f. 73 relative to "iuxta Depinge" is probably also by Alcock. Wright's ed. of Langtoft has this comment: there were two parishes named Langtoft, "one near Market Deeping in Lincolnshire, the other in the East Riding of Yorkshire. . . . [The latter, say Hearne and Wright] . . . is only a few miles west of Bridlington" (Wright, I: vii). See Jean Claude Thiolier, (1989), p. 45 and nn. 4, 5. Thiolier's description of MS B of Langtoft's chronicle is the occasion: "Sur le f° 1, noms de [Henry Fitzalan, earl of] Arundel et [John, lord] Lumley." See the discussion of Mannyng's use of sources below on the B MS of Langtoft and its relationship to his translation. I am indebted to Thiolier for the reference to the volume by Sears Jayne and Francis R. Johnson. See also Stepsis' article, "The Manuscripts of Robert Mannyng of Brunne's 'Chronicle of England' " (1969), pp. 132–33, on the missing folios in L. All these missing parts are noted in the variant L notes in the text of this edition wherever they occur.

(Crouland) and 860 (Kerlion) of Part II; they are evidently commentaries by a later reader. Many folios have additional rubrics not done by the scribes, some of them in abbreviated Latin scribbles which may have been a later user's own method of indexing the contents. Some of these additions are scarcely readable now and have proved to be of no help in elucidating the text. Some of the captions supplied when the manuscript copy was first made are in the margins, but after f. 80r when the second hand begins, most are within the text itself, executed in a textura style to distinguish them from the secretary style of the text.

The first scribe of L (ff. 1 to 79v) was evidently copying an exemplar which had been translated (and revised) from a manuscript in Mannyng's own dialect. Although his work is not faultless, there are few omissions of words or lines that survive in P. (Some of these differences, of course, may be accounted for as additions in P.) The second scribe, who begins on f. 80r (at line 879 of Part II), employed the same exemplar and simply stopped copying at line 4973. His work is very likely datable to a somewhat later period; perhaps the manuscript was left incomplete by the first scribe and the second undertook to do more of it but did not finish. This second scribe introduces some changes in the handwriting style and spelling as compared to the first. It is possible that the second scribe also made further changes in the text, recasting some lines to suit himself. There is one dislocation: lines 1321–40 (of P) appear in L after line 1625. These lines have the account of the death of Godwin and may properly belong where they occur in L; the passage is an interpolation in both manuscripts, but Mannyng probably added it himself.[42]

Since Mannyng changed from couplets in the manner of Wace for his translation of Part I to a longer line in Part II, evidently to suggest the different style of Langtoft, the differences between the two scribes in L are more marked.[43] The first scribe's lines do not differ so much from the poetic design of the text in P; in contrast, the practice of the second scribe (from f. 80r on, line 879) is quite inconsiderate of Mannyng's poetry. A few random examples (from Part II) will illustrate:

2471 P: At Corue his kastelle sperd depe in a dongeon
L: At Corff in þe castel hous ful fast in a dongeon

[42] See the text note for ll. 1321–40, Part II. Compare Wright's ed. of Langtoft, pp. 378 and 398. Though Godwin is cursorily mentioned, his death is not described in either place by Langtoft. Stepsis (1967, p. xxxix) points to a passage in the French *Estoire De Seint Edward le Rei* (RS 3, 1858), ll. 3277–337; compare Part II, ll. 1590–622 in the present edition on King Edward. This passage has been considerably revised in L.

[43] See Stepsis' discussion (1967) of Mannyng's versification in Part II, pp. xciv–xcix, and my comments on his use of sources below.

2475 P: togider prisoned iii ȝeres & dayes þam fed
L: to gederes in to prison ȝeres & dayes yfed
3270 P: our Inglis duelled þer vnto þe pes were pleyn
3271 P: þo þat þer were beforn wild no more com ageyn
3270 L: Þe Englissh host dwelled þere vntil þe pes was pleyn
3271 L: So þat þe Freynsche þat þere were wold no more com agayn
3486 P: At Westmynstre tok þe coroun of ȝork Bisshop Geffray
L: At Wynchestre was þat bar þe Croys of Ȝork Buschupe Geffrey
3543 P: to whom Acres salle be ȝolden also tite
L: To wham with worschupe Acres schal ben ȝulden als tid

Though many of the lines in L improve the sense of the text, the addition of words, for whatever purpose, reveals a tendency to be more prosaic and less aware of the shape of Mannyng's verse. We have no way of substantiating whether the text in P is correct, of course (and the manuscript is full of obvious errors throughout), but the alterations in L, especially in the last fifty folios, have no more authority and frequently seem to be gratuitous amplifications. Styles in poetic narrative were changing in the fifteenth century, and there are clear indications that history in prose was also supplanting poetic works of the type represented in Mannyng's *Chronicle*. By the mid-fifteenth century when the L manuscript was written, the English prose *Brut* manuscripts had proliferated from a translation (ca. 1400) of a French prose version of English history. The fashion to prefer recording mere facts in prose rather than to make a precise copy of a long narrative poem is already evident in the work of the second hand in L.[44] The extent of the revision of Mannyng's original work in this late manuscript amounts to much more than "modernization" or translation from the original dialect.

The differences between P and L in Part I are the result of two different factors: the work of the reviser that survives in the L copy and the P scribe's habit of shortening his work. The disturbance of the rime pattern in the revised lines in L may not seem particularly important, but it certainly shows that the reviser (or the L scribes) was indifferent to the

[44] See Lister M. Matheson, "Historical Prose," in *Middle English Prose* (1984), pp. 209–48, for a survey of the various forms of the prose *Brut* and its evolution. Matheson says: "The English *Brut* is a legendary and, in its later section and continuations, a historical chronicle of England. . . . It was translated into English about 1400, and the English text received in its turn a number of continuations by a process of accretion over the next sixty years" (p. 210). The work was edited by Friedrich W. D. Brie, *The Brut or the Chronicles of England* (2 vols. EETS o.s. 131, 136; 1906, 1908). Brie used Rawlinson MS B.171 (Bodleian) for most of his edition: "the oldest English copy of the *Brut* known to me." He dates this MS ca. 1400 on the basis of paleography.

style of Mannyng's verse. Whether the P scribe was merely careless or also making changes from his exemplar cannot be determined precisely, but comparison with Mannyng's sources occasionally suggests that authorial diction might have been lost. Wright's frequent complaints that Mannyng "imperfectly understood" Langtoft's French (in Part II) are only partly justified: I suspect scribal error in successive copies of Mannyng's sources rather than his own failure to translate correctly. Most of these passages are identified in the text notes.

The many copies of manuscripts of Wace's text which were made in the fourteenth century attest to the continuing popularity of French poetic history; Mannyng's translation was ahead of its time, but he perceived that making the British history accessible to an English-reading audience ("þat þe Latyn no Frankys con") in his own age was a worthy endeavor (lines 3–10, Part I). A century later, the reviser who was responsible for the exemplar of L might have been attempting to "correct" Mannyng's text to conform to details in a later Wace manuscript as well as to translate it to his own dialect. The alterations in diction between the P and L manuscripts also reflect changes in the language during the several decades between copyings of the manuscripts as well as differences in the customary usage of Lincolnshire as compared to that of the locale where the revised exemplar of L was written. The hundreds of words in P that were changed in L are evident in the glossary as well as in the variant notes to the text.

The major difference in content between P and L in Part II is the insertion of the "Lambeth Interpolation," a version of the "Havelok" story (at line 538) that may have been derived from Gaimar's *L'Estoire des Engleis,* or as some scholars have suggested, from a version of the Havelok tale written even earlier than Gaimar's history. This passage has been the subject of a great deal of scrutiny by editors of "Havelok," and all agree that it was an addition to Mannyng's *Chronicle*. It is very likely the work of the reviser of the whole text in L. The lines in P (519–38) for which L substitutes the different version of the story are certainly Mannyng's own contribution and not a translation of Langtoft's very sketchy account (Wright, I: 318).[45]

---

[45] See text note for ll. 538ff., Part II. Alexander Bell edited Gaimar's history and dates it ca. 1150 (making Gaimar a contemporary of Wace). In all four of the MSS containing Gaimar's English history, Wace's *Roman de Brut* precedes Gaimar, and there is evidence that Gaimar had written a "British history" which was replaced by the Wace version. See Bell's introduction to *L'Estoire des Engleis* (1960). See also M. Dominica Legge, *Anglo-Norman in the Cloisters* (1950), 104–5, and her *Anglo-Norman Literature and its Background* (1963), 27–32. Bell contends that Gaimar was the source for the Anglo-Norman version of the Havelok story ("Le Lai d'Haveloc") as well as the short (82 ll.)

R. Rawlinson Miscellany MS D.913 (Bodleian Library, Oxford)

A collection of miscellaneous documents is bound together in R without regard to any logical relationship among them. The leaves are of different sizes, some separately mounted (inlaid), apparently arranged according to the whim of the binder. A single leaf with lines corresponding to 12550–699 in the text of Part I is the fourth item. The manuscript also includes parts of other identified works which were among the Rawlinson documents. According to J. A. Burrow, the manuscript is "a collection of separate fragments bound together by the Bodleian Library at least a century after it received his collection in 1756."[46]

Among other documents in R is a set of "Ordinances" (ff. 44r–51v) of the Gild of St. George, Norwich, from ca. 1442, and a single leaf from the "Prick of Conscience" (f. 9r–v).[47] None of these disparate works can be identified as related in any way to the fragment of Mannyng's *Chronicle* and they are not related to each other in date or provenance.

The R manuscript also contains fragments of a Wace text, listed as manuscript *X* in Arnold's edition, but not collated to establish his text of Wace. Arnold identifies the following folios which have short passages from Wace, with the line numbers of his edition:[48]

f. 83r–v:	lines 7029–148
f. 84r–v:	lines 7391–510

interpolation in L. See the recent edition of *Havelok* by G. V. Smithers (1987), especially pp. xix–xxiv. It is certain that Mannyng was unaware of Gaimar's long tale (ll. 45–814 in Bell's edition), as MS P merely laments that no story was to be found about Havelok: "Bot I haf grete ferly þat I fynd no man / þat has writen in story how Hauelok þis lond wan" (519–20). In L, these lines and the following eighteen are omitted and the interpolation is given instead. See Edward Kirby Putnam, "The Lambeth Version of *Havelok*" (1900). Putnam contends that "the Lambeth Interpolation is derived from a form of the story earlier than Gaimar" (p. 14).

46 "Poems Without Contexts," from a paper delivered at the Conference of University Teachers of English, Southampton, 1978. Burrow discusses a set of poems on a leaf of parchment which have all been published elsewhere (pp. 8–9). For this leaf, "The paleographers agree ... the handwriting belongs to the first half of the Fourteenth Century, perhaps somewhere near 1325" (p. 7). The R MS has been shelved with the numbers 1262 and 1370 (Bodley SC 13679, 14099) at various times, but when I examined it, the MS was located with its original mark, Rawlinson D.913.

47 The "Ordinances" are among the Norfolk items listed in LALME, I: 151 and 222, referring to the MED dating (list of MSS, p. 42). The "Prick of Conscience" is identified in LALME with the language of Soke (Peterborough), p. 151. R also has a fragment of the "Prose Merlin"; a related fifteenth-century English translation is in Cambridge University Library MS Ff.3.11. See Norris J. Lacy, ed., *The Arthurian Encyclopedia* (1986), 438.

48 MS *X* is listed on p. XIII of Arnold's introduction with no other information except this list of ff. In his analysis of the classes of MSS which would have parallels for ll. 4000–8000, the fragments in MS *X* are omitted. See pp. XLI–XLVII.

f. 92r:	lines 4346–64
f. 92v:	lines 4453–71

The whole manuscript includes pages that may have been held in various libraries or scriptoria or possibly by private owners; Rawlinson probably acquired them long after the institutions owning them were dissolved. A comparison of the folios from Wace and the text of the single leaf in R with the lines corresponding to Mannyng's text (in P) would not illuminate the text of the *Chronicle* since these passages are thousands of lines apart. Unless some connection could be discovered concerning the provenance of the folio from R, or other parts of the manuscript from which it was detached, we have only the evidence for a comparison with the corresponding lines in PL. It is, indeed, a fragment "without context."[49]

There is a close resemblance between R and P: R begins with a column corresponding to f. 75v c.2 of P. In a majority of the lines in R, the diction and syntax also match P; the dialect and orthography are very similar in RP. The R text could be somewhat earlier or later than P, though the paleographic characteristics (of ca. 1400) are not very different from the forms in P. The leaf is inlaid on paper and is bound in reverse (bound in on the right side).

Another kind of relationship is evident between R and L. They include twenty-six lines in this passage (which comprises 150 lines in P) that are not in P. To establish the Wace text which Mannyng might have translated in this section would require a search of the other Wace manuscripts, a task that would yield nothing useful beyond the text surviving in R. The evidence seems to indicate that P was deliberately shortening the text in this passage, while L and R copied all of whatever exemplars they were using. Comparing the LR texts firmly supports the fact that R is a copy of a manuscript in Mannyng's own dialect (or at least in the same dialect

---

[49] The passage in Arnold's text of Wace which corresponds to the parallel text in PLR is at lines 12000–12169 and includes most of the lines in LR that are omitted in P. Rawlinson's acquisitions also included the miscellaneous parts of various MSS now bound in Rawlinson Poet. MS 145. According to Ewald Zettl, "After Hearne's death, in 1735, the volume was acquired together with the rest of his collection by Rawlinson, from whom it passed into the possession of the Bodleian Library." It might be possible to discover that MS R was also part of Hearne's collection. Zettl's comment concerns seven leaves of the *Anonymous Short Metrical Chronicle* (EETS o.s. 196) which he edited in 1935, p. xxiv. The list of misbound leaves in MS 145 is on p. xxiii. He says that Hearne received them from his friend John Murray. Zettl refers to Philip Bliss, *The Remains of Thomas Hearne, M. A.* (London, 1869) on the contents of Hearne's library. I regret that Bliss's book is not available to me. Though Hearne included some passages from Part I as notes in his edition of Part II, he could easily have missed discovering that the single leaf in R was a copy of a few lines in Part I, even if he did actually possess it.

represented in P) while the dialect of L is quite different. The possibility that a complete R manuscript was the exemplar for P needs much more proof than the fragment provides, but this is an interesting conjecture. Another bit of evidence appears in the similarity of the page captions and side-notes in all three manuscripts: obviously, the same exemplar, a manuscript copy at least one generation beyond Mannyng's original, underlies all of them.[50]

Summary: The Manuscripts

The survival of Mannyng's *Chronicle* is important to Middle English scholars for several reasons. Though the precise date of P has not been established, it was certainly written later than Mannyng's date of completion of his work in 1338. P doubtless preserves much of the authorial text, since the language represents the dialect area of Lincolnshire. We may assume that at least one recension intervened and that P was probably written after the mid-century and likely twenty to thirty or more years later. The main hand in P uses the anglicana letter forms similar to those in many other manuscripts dated in the last quarter of the fourteenth century, but there are no other clues for the dating, so far as I have been able to discover. The diction in P has been regarded as representative of Mannyng's own language by those scholars who have disagreed with Furnivall's choice of south-east and south-west Midland manuscripts for his editions of both of Mannyng's works.[51]

The language of P is not a translation from one dialect to another, nor is there much evidence that the scribe changed the exemplar he used to impose his own dialect. There is some evidence, however, that the main hand in P sometimes employed habitual spellings differing from those in his immediate copy text.[52]

---

[50] A more explicit analysis of the resemblances and differences in PRL follows; see n. 61 below on the Latin captions in these MSS. I have revised my opinion of the relationships in PLR from that expressed in the very brief description of R in my edition of *Handlyng Synne* (p. XXXV and n. 41). As the side notes in the text indicate (Part I, lines 12000–12169), I have relied in part on the transcript of R published by Eugen Kölbing (1892), pp. 166–71. I have deleted his added punctuation and capitalization that are not in the MS. Since the last column in the MS is now virtually unreadable, I have consulted his transcript (with gratitude) to decipher some of the doubtful words.

[51] See n. 36 above and the discussion of dialect below. The early study of dialect by Moore, et al., published in 1935 is seconded, but with qualifications, in Angus McIntosh's statement concerning Mannyng's language in P (1976, p. 39) in his discussion of South Lincolnshire texts. See the LALME analysis of P (LP 38) for detailed evidence (III: 253–54).

[52] The matter of translation from one dialect to another is discussed in LALME I,

In Part II, another factor applies: Mannyng changed his style from couplets in imitation of Wace to a longer line with varying stresses, adding mid-line rimes as well as end-rime. The rimes within the lines are the chief source for some of the strange spelling and outright inventions of words not recorded elsewhere in Middle English. After approximately the first thousand lines in Part II, the mid-line rimes are persistent in P but are frequently lacking in L. Either the reviser who wrote the exemplar or the scribes of L chose to ignore Mannyng's poetic design, perhaps because they thought such embellishment did not enhance the "facts" of the text, or the scribe of an intermediate manuscript may have altered Mannyng's work. The evidence of editing, especially expansion for clarification, is abundant in L.

The consistent end-rime in P is evidence of close attention to eye-rime throughout the manuscript, as if the scribe willingly sacrificed customary spelling in favor of consistent rime words. In a few passages in Part II, however, the influence of Langtoft's verse pattern occasionally appears, with a long stretch of identical rimes rather resembling the French *laisses.* Mannyng's copyists were devoted to English couplets with rime words appearing to be very similar, in spite of the frequent necessity to invent strange spellings for complete conformity.

The Lambeth manuscript, preserving a revision of Mannyng's *Chronicle* that was translated from a North East Midland exemplar, has many changes in diction, not only because of the differences in dialect but also because the revision was done several decades after Mannyng's time. L also has many errors that can be attributed to scribal misreading of the exemplar. The reviser apparently tampered with the individual lines and sometimes added explanatory matter, though he kept closely to the overall design of whatever manuscript he was using. There are some minor orthographic differences between the two hands in L, but the dialect is generally consistent in both: it is a confused language that has the appearance of the South West Midlands dialect of the scribes, but much of the original Lincolnshire language also remains, especially in rime words. Some differences between P and L appear in changes to the diction that the reviser (or the L scribes) evidently thought was archaic. In many places, moreover, it is clear that the language of the authorial text was simply misunderstood. The reviser's usual remedy was to recast the whole line, but he also substituted or invented diction. It is possible that the P scribe made similar changes, but they are hard to detect.

Appendix I, pp. 29–32. The consistency of the dialect from the beginning to the end of P argues that the scribes (and especially the main hand) were using a dialect quite similar to Mannyng's own.

Evidence for an early common source underlying both P and L is suggested in the Latin captions and marginal annotations which are very similar in both manuscripts. I have not included these tags in this edition because they are clearly not authorial. They are included in Furnivall's edition of Part I, in side notes in Hearne's edition and again in Stepsis's edition of Part II. (The interpretation of the expansions of the Latin varies among these earlier editions.) Some of the captions appear within the text, and many pages have headings identifying the personages with which the text is concerned. The captions in P appear to have been added by the scribe as he was writing his text, though large capitals may be the work of an illuminator, as several of the initials at the beginning of paragraphs are omitted. The caption style in L, however, is clearly scribal and is set off from the text by a change from the secretary hand to a bold textura, frequently underlined. By comparison, the main hand in P did the captions in a slightly larger anglicana script with the same letter forms he used in the text. He also added the captions applicable to the work of the alternate scribe who did eight short passages (675 lines) in Part I.

Mannyng's professed objective, to write for an audience reading English, argues against assuming that this Latin apparatus appeared in his original manuscript. As he states in his introduction, he was translating Wace and Pers "for the luf of symple men / þat strange Inglis can not ken" (Part I, 77–78). He did not expect his readers to be literate in Latin or French. In comparison, there are no Latin captions in manuscripts BFH of *Handlyng Synne*, though Mannyng probably wrote the work for a clerical audience originally, men who might be expected to understand Latin. (A few Latin inscriptions appear in some of the shorter excerpts in later manuscripts, probably as an indexing device.) Latin captions are the characteristic marks of later ecclesiastic or commercial manuscripts, perhaps added to conform to the style of a scriptorium and not necessary to the text itself. They have some value beyond embellishment: most are identifications, and they might be useful to a reader searching for one passage or another. Rubrication of historical manuscripts was often added by scribes in earlier manuscripts and the practice became standard later. Julia Crick says: "Rubrics are not strictly speaking part of the text but particularly open to interpretation by scribes." She notes that "the overwhelming majority of *Historia [Regum Britannie]* manuscripts are rubricated. Of the 214 manuscripts surveyed, only thirty-nine lack rubrics; twelve of these are fragmentary and so may originally have had them. Rubrics were added before the fourteenth century in three of the remaining twenty-seven."[53] Rubrics are usually in red ink, but the term can apply

[53] Julia C. Crick, IV (1990), 121. The convention of rubricating MSS or adding Latin

generically to any caption or Latin tag in the margins, not necessarily in another color.

In assessing the comparative value of the surviving texts of Mannyng's *Chronicle*, however, it must be acknowledged that P is faulty, careless, and scribally sloppy throughout. In fact, much of the difficulty with unusual diction is the result of an unusual number of errors which might well have been corrected if the main hand, as well as the second hand whose work is identified below, had been more careful in copying. However, the text of L (as shown in the parallel notes to the text) corrects the obvious scribal errors in many instances, restoring words that P carelessly dropped and suggesting the original syntax of lines that are garbled in P. The question of which manuscript best presents the whole *Chronicle* text (so far as PL are parallel) cannot be resolved, though the dialect and earlier date of P justify its choice as the base text for this edition. Most of the omissions made by the main hand in P, especially of couplets and short passages, were probably done to shorten the text, though some of these omissions may have been in the exemplar. The scribe regularly omits words and letters without any indication of correction, which suggests that in many passages he was copying mechanically and inattentively. The evidence of mechanical copying is notable throughout L also. In spite of the evidence of extensive revision in L, many of its lines that were omitted in P must have been authorial.[54]

To determine how much of the surviving text in P might be considered Mannyng's work, some other evidence can be considered. In the eight short passages executed by the second scribe in Part I (from f. 23r to f. 52v), only four lines have been added in the comparable passages in L: at 7432, L has a gratuitous comment on the Saxons, "Hengistes compaynie," and the reason that Britain was then "cald Engelond," which is probably an addition by the reviser. However, the 675 lines written by the second scribe in P were very likely faithfully copied from the exemplar, and the text seems to be more complete rather than abbreviated as it often is in the rest of the manuscript. But the lines done by the second scribe have an unusually large number of variants in spelling as compared to the work of the main hand or the parallel lines in L. Thus, the deduction that the main

identifications is older than the MSS of the *Historia* and becomes obligatory in the period after Mannyng wrote. By the time the oldest MS of the English prose *Brut* was written (ca. 1400), each chapter had a caption describing the contents. Stephen G. Nichols, "Philology in a Manuscript Culture" (1990), puts the matter of rubrication and illumination of MSS in perspective from the point of view of philology in general.

[54] M. L. Samuels identifies the "mixed" dialect aspect in L as an "overlay." The detection of layers in single texts is described in LALME, I, 4.2.1, p. 24. (See n. 73 on dialect below.)

hand in P was responsible for the omissions in his text is compelling. This conclusion is also supported by the omissions from P in the parallel passage in manuscript R.[55]

By comparison, L has few major dislocations of lines or passages. There is only one substantial passage dislocated (Part I, at 4871), obviously an exceptional change in L. The P manuscript alone, however, would not suffice to establish the complete text of Mannyng's original version: the revised L manuscript preserves many lines and passages omitted from P that may or may not be Mannyng's work, but the appearance of many of them in his sources suggests that they were probably in the authorial text. In hundreds of lines, the differences in P are plainly scribal errors which can be understood only by reference to the parallel text of L.

The sources of the longer additions and revisions in L are obscure, but these passages suggest that the reviser was a conscientious scholar who had a wide knowledge of the romance literature in French and acquaintance with other historians, some of them unfamiliar to Mannyng and possibly later than the early fourteenth century. Since there is no way of determining how much of the P text is authentic, it is difficult to isolate the passages which the reviser of L contributed. The text in L is not necessarily a more precise version of the *Chronicle,* however; many of the added lines supporting the "authentic history" are gratuitous amplifications or explanations. They confirm the impression that the reviser intended to verify and add details from other sources which may not have been available to Mannyng. The damage to Mannyng's verse is notable: the revisions often ruin the scansion of his verse, reducing his lines to something closer to prose. Many passages in L, however, are attempts to clarify what the reviser thought might be misunderstood.[56]

The mixed language of the text in L, a copy from a revision in the dialect of South Wiltshire, may have been created in part by the L scribes.

---

[55] Furnivall noted some of the scribal changes in P in his edition of Part I on pp. 259 (nn. 9, 10), 262 (n. 14), 275 (n. 9), 289 (n. 8), and 292 (n. 5). He was intrigued by the *qw-* spellings in the passage on f. 23r and the shorter passage beginning on f. 44v. His annotations remark the odd verb and noun endings (–in, -is, -id) elsewhere. He missed some of the passages done by the second hand and was not certain that only one alternate scribe's work was represented. The different word endings in this scribe's lines also appear consistently in the fragment in MS R.

[56] The passages which were probably additions in L are identified in the text notes for both parts. Some of the changes in L which are likely to be attributable to a reviser were noted in Sir Frederic Madden's 1828 edition of *Havelok.* He discusses these revisions and adds: "The Lambeth MS . . . has evidently been revised by a later hand, which has abridged the Prologues, omitted some passages, and inserted others." Quoted from Walter W. Skeat's re-edition of *The Lay of Havelok the Dane* (EETS e.s. 4, 1868), p. xi. Skeat includes direct quotations from Madden's Roxburghe Club edition.

They certainly could have introduced further alterations if the copy was made much later than the exemplar. The "modernization" of the diction probably also deleted some of Mannyng's authentic language. The notes to the text record these variants as well as the passages demonstrating the considerable rewriting of individual lines and couplets.[57]

Scribes in the Petyt Manuscript with some Questions on Orthography

Two scribes prepared manuscript P, both writing in the North East Midland dialect, but the hands differ in obvious ways. The main hand, who writes most of the manuscript, is always legible and seems to treat his exemplar with respect, except for his omission of couplets or longer passages that he thought were dispensable. In spite of careless errors and failure to mark corrections, his work is generally competent and clear. This scribe (hand A) employs virtually the same style throughout the manuscript, a fluent anglicana typical of the later fourteenth century, somewhat modified toward the end of Part II to a more cursive style. The changes in letter forms from the beginning to the end of the manuscript are not significant; some of these may be explained by the fact that completion of the whole manuscript must have taken a long time. Comparison of the early folios with those later in the manuscript shows a minor increase in fluency, but no change in the hand.

The second hand (B) executed eight passages from f. 23r to f. 52v in Part I, including complete folios and parts of others:

	Number of lines
(1) f. 23r: mid-column 1 to end of f. 24r (ll. 3705–934)	230
(2) f. 39v: near end of column 1 to end of f. 39v (6489–539)	51
(3) f. 44v: the entire folio (7293–376)	84
(4) f. 45r: column 2 to end of f. 45v (7419–544)	126
(5) f. 47r: both columns (7713–96)	84
(6) f. 49r: mid-column 2 to end of f. 49r (8115–33)	19
(7) f. 49v: mid-column 1 to end of f. 49v (8159–217)	59
(8) f. 52v: half of column 1 only (8638–59)	22

57 A curious recurrent alteration in L is the frequent substitution of Wynchestre for Westmynstre (e.g., at line 3486 in Part II). Since the dialect of L reflects forms of the region in the South West Midlands closer to Winchester, this alteration is probably deliberate rather than erroneous. Wright's edition of Langtoft notes a similar confusion: "It is rather singular that nearly all of the MSS. of Pierre de Langtoft fall into the error of confounding Worcester with Winchester" (p. 378, n. 7).

Altogether, the second scribe was responsible for only 675 lines. Though his work is certainly not error-free, he is usually more meticulous than the main hand in such matters as capitalization and correction of his own errors. B's hand is coarse, the pen untrimmed, and he sometimes appears to be rather uncertain of his text. The letters are crowded and the lines straggle, though he evidently tries to copy the same letter forms used by A. The style of handwriting, on the other hand, permits considerable variation. B uses two or three different forms of the same letter, often all in the same line of text. When the hand changes, B's conscious effort to copy the letter forms of hand A is notable.[58]

The major differences between the hands are in the letters *d, r, s, u* or *w*, capital *I* (a modified long *i*), *y*, and *thorn*. The final stroke of *k* tends to slant down close to the line in B, whereas A uses a short horizontal stroke that often ligates with the following letter. B has very short descenders, especially for *r, s, f*, and *y* or *thorn*. These minor stylistic differences are quite clear except in some of the transitions when the hands change within a column. The letter forms represented do not provide absolutely conclusive evidence for only one alternate hand, however: comparing the different passages might suggest the possibility that more than one scribe did some of them if one considers only the overall impression of roughness in hand B. However, an exhaustive comparison of the work of the two hands, even taking B's considerable variety of letter forms into account, does not support the hypothesis suggested in Furnivall's tentative notes that more than one hand did the passages I have identified as B's work.[59]

---

[58] See the discussion of anglicana letter forms in Parkes (1969). The style in P represents the "second stage" developments (p. xviii) illustrated in plate 12. See also A. I. Doyle and M. B. Parkes (1978). Illustrations of the plates for "Scribe D" of the *Confessio Amantis* (e.g., p. 176) have letter forms resembling those in the Petyt MS. Though P is likely earlier than the MSS discussed in Doyle and Parkes, the main hand is representative of the anglicana formata style that persisted for many years. Following the list of the ten MSS where "Scribe D" is represented, they comment: "A number of scribes seem to have used this version of anglicana formata, and at first sight they are difficult to tell apart, particularly since the salient characteristics of this version lie in the refinement, the careful proportions and disciplined qualities of the handwriting" (pp. 177–78).

[59] See n. 55 on Furnivall's comments. I would cheerfully defer to the judgment of expert paleographers on this matter. The variety of letter forms and the arrangement within the eight short passages (especially the change of hands in illogical places) is the justification of my conclusions. Others may agree with Furnivall that more than one scribe wrote the passages not done by the main hand (A). If there were more than two scribes in the MS, however, some other differences would probably show up in the diction and spelling to distinguish the work of a third hand. The glossary records the usage of hand B in the lines he wrote and examples of hand A's usage appear in the same entry for the same words. I do not find any distinct evidence of any other hands, though the spelling is notably aberrant in many of B's lines. See Margaret Laing, "Dialectal

Perhaps inexperience could account for the different appearance of B's hand as compared to the assured style of A. The alternate hand may be that of an apprentice. There is certainly no apparent logic in the change from one hand to the other in the middle of a column. That the two scribes were simply alternating periods of copying, both using the same exemplar, is very clear.

There is no major difference in dialect between A and B, yet B uses characteristic diction and spelling that evidently comes from a different part of England than that shown in the customary usage of hand A. We may be confronted with an extreme case of scribal individuality, however, rather than an indication of regional custom. These differences, which are demonstrated in all the eight passages executed by B, are not dialectal but orthographic, for example:

(1) qw- for wh-: qwen (3851), qwere (7332), qwat (7336, 7376), qware (7469)

(2) doubling of final letters: mett-grett (rimes at 3817, 3818), grett (3856), grett-sett (rimes at 7455, 7456, 7749, 7750), wee (3933, 7375, 7749), ȝee (7296, 7533, 7757), iff (7361), off (for *of*, 8657), ȝitt (8133)

(3) preference for *u* or *w*, *v* or *u* where hand A would use the alternate letter: hou (for *how*, 3733, 6538, 7358, 7438, 7439), hov (7743, 7751, 8217), nov (for *now* 8188, 8215), slou (for *slouh* 6539 in rime, 7789, 8126), sloh (7768), sleu (3731, 3734), heu (3769); ȝow (7295); owt, owte, owtyn (3742, 3807, 3837, 3838, 3892, 3918, 7737, 8656; cp. *with outin* 7716); miscellaneous instances in which A would use the alternate letters: Suimmes (3753), swilkone (3751), swaloud (3756), (cp. sualhid 3771, swalud 3773), swerd (3769), swere (3844, 3849), swiþe (7310), sau (for *saw*, 7769, 7773, 7793), swete (7490)

(4) inconsistent spelling for *þorgh*: þroru (7350), þoru (7741), þorh (7727), þrou (7756, 8126)

(5) plural nouns end in -is instead of -es (as in hand A): bodis (3738, 6491), bestis (3775), freendis (3924), frendis (7502), landis (6524), Peihtis (7323, cp. Peightes 7304), stedis (7326), nedis (7330), enmis (7367, 7376, 7541), schippis (7420), handis (7754), stonis (7782), dintis (7786), wordis (8162), wodis, hillis (8174), armis (8211) [These -is endings are not always consistent; whether B is copying his source or using his own spelling is not clear.]

(6) verb endings: B regularly prefers -is to -es for the present forms, -id to -ed for past forms, often omitting the preceding vowel: robbid (3727,

---

Analysis and Linguistically Composite Texts in Middle English" (1988), p. 85, for a discussion of methods of distinguishing scribal hands.

7306), distroid (3743), opind (3771), leuid (3855), amendid (3865), gadird (3881, 8168, 8193), sualhid (3771), deid (for *died,* 3772), discordid (3796), hopid (3832), louid (3866, 3878, 3919; cp. *loued* 3871, 7366, 7522); hatid (3871, 3926), endid (3875), departid (3886), coround (3898), passid (6507), mustird (6524), kepis (7293), lastid (7327), askid (7458, 7506, 8207), lerid (7460, 7462), callis, letis (7466), louis (for *loves,* 7469), louedis (8213), bidis (7371), drinkis (7473), semid (7491), consentid (7501), dispisid (7518), takis (7753, 7765), sittis (7755), puruaid (7760), scapid (7781), didis (8131), duellid (8161), mons (for *mones,* 8133, 8655), wons (for *wones,* 8654), forgetis (8209), praid (8644), kennis (8189; cp. rime *rennes,* 8190)

(7) B regularly uses -ir in words customarily spelled -er in hand A, though A sometimes uses -yr instead of -er. In these examples from B, the change may sometimes have been for purposes of rime: wondirful (3747), aftir (3833, 3906), vndirfong (3893), suffir (3840), oþir (6499; cp. rime *tothir,* 6498), þidir (7320, 7442, 7795), togidir (7311, 7336), bettir (7342), chambir (7451), childir (8123, 8165), fadir (8210, 8216), sikir (7530, 7533)

(8) miscellaneous differences: B prefers -ou- medially where A uses -o-; B prefers -gh- to A's -h-; B frequently uses *alls* or *alls so* for *as;* B often spells out *wyt* where A usually abbreviates. B prefers *es* for *is* and *be* for *by*. The last letter in a word spelled with *y* is often *i* in B's hand: dai (3835, 7317, 7335, 7728), enmi (7370), mi (7360).

Listing these differences between the P scribes only proves that two scribes were involved. If B is an apprentice, he does not improve very much from f. 23 to f. 52. There are a number of instances, however, in which hand A also departs from his usual practice, especially in the noun and verb endings, but these examples are scattered from beginning to end of the manuscript.[60]

The possibility that hand B is copying the text they both used more faithfully than does A cannot be proved, but a similarity in some of the above examples from hand B can also be demonstrated in the fragment of manuscript R (ll. 12550–699). (None of the passages done by hand B are parallel to the R fragment.) The following examples are selective. If an exemplar very like R was used by the P scribes, the forms we find in hand B may be more representative of that exemplar than the habitual usage in hand A. (I have included the comparable examples from L to make the spelling comparisons more complete since many of the lines in this passage

[60] See Angus McIntosh, "Towards an Inventory of Middle English Scribes," (1974), 602–24. His discussion of the problems arising in the analysis of scribal habits is especially useful. In P, for example, the main hand regularly uses a slash through *ll* and often spells the word out, as in *-lle.* I have interpreted the slash as a normal abbreviation for this scribe.

were omitted in P.) These examples are not sufficient to justify any firm conclusions, but they are suggestive:

Line number in P:	**P**	**R**	**L**
12551	sawe	sauh	saw
12554	fors	foris	fores
12561	bi	be	by
at 12566	———	drouh	drow
12567	touh	touh	tow
at 12570 (P om. 17 lines)		to fruschid	to frusched
		heu	hew
		þreu	þrew
		thurgh	þorow
		stedis	stedes
		stomblid	stumbled
		fil	feld
		mani	manye
		kneu	knew
12571	bated	abatid	abated
12572	hated	hatid	hated
12575	knaw	knowe	knowe
12578	ony	ani	any
	———	ouht	ought
12579	wald	wild	wolde
12582	wild	wild	wold
12585	bolded	boldid	bolded
12594	þorgh	thurgh	þorow
12613	said	seid	seide
12658	bussed	buschid	enbusched
12672	defended	defendid	defended
12681	spors	sporis	haste
12687	tendid	tent	tente

In addition, there are several examples of P's preference for *suld,* while R has *schuld* and L uses either *scholde* or *schuld,* and there are a few other insignificant spelling differences.

In two places in the PRL parallel passage it is clear that P simply erred, as in the dropped lines after 12566 of P where the scribe manipulates the rime word of the following line, and in 12569–570 where P has combined three lines into two. Here, the logic of the passage suggests that the RL version is correct. The passage of seventeen lines omitted after line 12570 in P is probably an example of shortening; the differences in 12571–575 support the impression that RL have an authentic text while P has been altered.

The close resemblance of PR, especially in spelling (except for the word endings and differences noted above), is reinforced by an identical caption at line 12659, where L differs, and the illuminated capitals of PR are in the same place in several lines.[61] But most important, P and R usually have the same diction and syntax where L differs. It is possible that R and P are copies of the same source manuscript. If any other pages should be recovered from the fragmentary R manuscript, however, it might be possible to make a case for R as the exemplar of P, but the single folio that survives does not provide enough evidence.

As most scholars agree, there is little to be gained by studying the comparative orthography of manuscripts written in the later fourteenth and early fifteenth centuries. The idiosyncracies of the scribes can outweigh valid evidence of authorial usage. As Angus McIntosh has said: "It is noteworthy that a very considerable ... orthographic revolution affected the written English of most areas over the course of the fourteenth century: it is not merely that the spoken language changed during that period, but that the conventions for setting down even what had not changed underwent marked modification."[62] The examples above cannot identify Mannyng's own customary usage with any certainty, of course, but the language as a whole can be assessed with reasonable accuracy from the recurrence of words in both of his major works as listed in the glossary. What the exemplar of P actually demonstrated in its spelling, and what the text of the R fragment might suggest about that exemplar, are questions still unanswered.

---

[61] The suggestive Latin captions in the PRL passage are:

	P	R	L
12560	——	Ecce mirandum est de fortuna per totum	[¶ at 12561]
12600	——	De vassalacione Britonum	Vassalacio Brytonum
12618	[¶ at 12619]	De incarceratis	De Romanis incarceratis
12634	Nunciatum est parties Imperatori	Totum nunciatum inperatori	Nunciatum est hic Inperatory hoc Infortunium
12659	Ecce de Romanis qui nocte precesserunt britones in abscondito et ecce pugna inter partes	Ecce de Romanis qui nocte precesserunt Britones in abscondita & ecce pugna inter partes	Exe pungna inter Brytones & Romanos qui de nocte eos precesserunt

I have consulted Furnivall's edition for the expansions in L and Kölbing's edition for R. The first *n* in pungna (L, 12659) is Furnivall's expansion.

[62] McIntosh, "The Language of ... *Havelok*" (1976), 37.

Dialect of the Manuscripts: Earlier Studies

The dialect of Lincolnshire in the fourteenth century is faithfully represented in the P manuscript; in spite of spelling variations, the dialect of the two hands is substantially the same. Manuscript R is also in the same dialect, and is very close to P orthographically as well. In L, the forms usually analyzed to determine the dialect of a manuscript, however, are South West Midland, while the language retained in rime words is more consistently North East Midland. Consequently, identifying the dialect of L has been difficult. Early scholars have relied on Furnivall's choices of a South East Midland manuscript for *Handlyng Synne* (BL Harley MS 1701) and the Lambeth manuscript of the *Chronicle,* and citations in OED and MED have depended mainly on Furnivall's editions. The edition of Part II by Hearne based on P has corrected the perception of what might have been in Mannyng's own text to some extent, at least in matters of diction, but the persistence of the impression that Mannyng's dialect was represented in Furnivall's editions has sent many scholars off in the wrong direction.

In the year before Furnivall's edition of the *Chronicle,* Part I, was published, the first of several studies of Mannyng's language appeared: A. W. Zetsche presented his transcription of the first 5383 lines from L.[63] His dissertation (Leipzig, 1887) justifies the manuscript choice as follows: "Der Schreiber des Lambeth Ms. gehöt sonach dem östlichen Mittellande an, vielleicht derselben Grafschaft, Lincolnshire, die auch unsern Dichter hervorbrachte" (p. 53). Zetsche's dissertation included a phonological analysis of both manuscripts (PL); variant notes from P were in his edition for *Anglia* published the year before.[64]

In 1891 Oskar Preussner's dissertation (Breslau) was published, a study of Mannyng's translation of Langtoft based on Hearne's edition of Part II and Wright's edition of Langtoft, and it was followed the next year by an

[63] "Chronik des Robert von Brunne," in *Anglia* 9 (1886): 43–194. Most scholars of Mannyng's works will necessarily go through the same process that I have in preparing these editions. It would be a disservice to them to avoid an evaluation of the earlier scholarship and merely offer my conclusions. Accordingly, it seems to me to be a useful exercise to outline the major work that has been done since Hearne's (1725) edition. Future scholars need not waste a great deal of time on some of the early studies. Let us get on with the business of critical studies with an optimally accurate text. Edward D. Kennedy's list of references in vol. VIII of the *Manual* (1989), 2811–18, includes all of those in this discussion and many others concerning related matters.

[64] Furnivall's edition of Part I appeared with the date 1887, but he was certainly working independently. Zetsche's dissertation has an acknowledgement of "J. G. [*sic*] Furnivall's edition" of *Handlyng Synne* (Roxburghe Club: London, 1862) on p. 1, n. 4. He evidently did not consult the Furnivall edition of the "Story of England" because it was not yet available.

article with the title, "Zur Textkritik von Robert Mannyng's Chronik."[65] The article depends entirely on his dissertation and seems to be mainly an extended list of text notes, ostensibly adding to his own work, but he unintentionally perpetuates some other misjudgments.[66]

The dialect study done by Oskar Boerner, *Die Sprache Roberd Mannyngs of Brunne und ihr Verhältnis zur Neuenglischen Mundart* (Halle, 1904), is representative of the misdirection thus far attained: according to Stepsis, Boerner "gives a detailed description of Mannyng's language based on a comparison of *Handlyng Synne,* the *Meditations,* and the first part of the *Chronicle;* but he uncritically accepts the Harleian manuscript of *Handlyng Synne* and the Lambeth manuscript of the *Chronicle* as his working texts and pays absolutely no attention to the Petyt manuscript" (p. xlviii, n. 53). Boerner's study is still frequently cited for the description of Mannyng's language, but one wonders whether scholars who cite this reference have read it attentively.

The reverence for earlier authority persisted in the massive study of Mannyng's vocabulary by Hubert Gburek, "Der Wortschatz des Robert Mannyng of Brunne in *Handlyng Synne*" (diss., Erlangen, 1977). Gburek chose to analyze the version in Harley MS 1701 chiefly on the basis of a presumptive earlier date for this manuscript; he cites the dating of 1380 in C. E. Wright's *English Vernacular Hands* (1960) in the comments accompanying a plate (13, f. 12v) from the Harley manuscript. Wright would not have approved this use of his tentative dating, for he specifically qualified his conjectural dating of the plates for manuscripts that had no other supporting information.[67]

---

[65] In *Englische Studien* 17 (1892): 300–314. Another study appeared the same year, M. Thümmig, "Über die altenglische Übersetzung der Reimchronik Peter Langtoft's durch Robert Manning von Brunne" in *Anglia* 14 (1892): 1–76. This is an extensive analysis of the rimes and other aspects of Langtoft's language compared to Mannyng's translation. He cites Zetsche (in *Anglia* 9) and uses the editions of Furnivall (1887) as well as Hearne (1725) for the *Chronicle,* and Wright's edition of Langtoft (1866). This study appears in most bibliographies. Thümmig's analysis was based on his 1889 dissertation, published in 1891.

[66] For example, Stepsis comments on Preussner's claim that the source of the "romance" of Richard was *Estoire de la Guerre Sainte:* "Anyone . . . can see that it has no relation to the Middle English *Richard* or to Mannyng" (1967, p. xliii, n. 48).

[67] See n. 39 above on Wright's caveat. Gburek cites my dissertation (Stanford University, 1959) but evidently he only read the abstract in *DA* 20 (1959), 664. He rejects the fact that BL Harley MS 1701 is a copy of Bodley MS 415. Gburek's discussion of his choice of MS H (p. 22) is part of his review of some of the other MSS of *Handlyng Synne* (pp. 19–32). He also rejects the judgment of E. J. Arnould, *Le Manuel des Péchés* (Paris, 1940), that H "doit être une copie, directe ou indirecte, de celui d'Oxford [B]." (Quoted from Arnould, p. 315, n. 2). Here, Gburek insists that H could not be a copy of B since H is older (p. 31, n. 2).

Robert P. Stepsis undertook an exhaustive analysis (1967) of the dialect in PL using only the rime words. In his analysis for P, the results were as expected, but the analysis of L went awry: the confusion of dialect characteristics in this late manuscript, translated to a South Wiltshire dialect in the fifteenth century, and probably further altered by the scribes, left Stepsis' analysis inconclusive. Stepsis lists samples of the internal rime from Part II, demonstrating differences between P and L; but his use of only the rime words for his analysis precluded a precise localization.[68]

In the analysis of dialect characteristics by Samuel Moore, Sanford B. Meech, and Harold Whitehall (1935), the dialect problem is stated as follows:

> The language of the Petyt manuscript is highly consistent and homogeneous. The forms that occur in rime are the same as those that occur within the line. The Lambeth manuscript of the *Chronicle,* edited by Furnivall, has the forms of the Petyt manuscript, but with a considerable mixture of south East-Midland forms. In MS Harley 1701 of *Handlyng Synne,* edited by Furnivall, the south East-Midland forms greatly predominate and the forms of the Petyt manuscript occur only occasionally or not at all. But both the Lambeth manuscript and Harleian 1701 have regularly in *rime* the *-(e)s* third singular, *-nd* present participle, and *are,* which the Petyt manuscript has both in rime and within the line. We believe, therefore, that the Petyt manuscript, though not localized, may be relied on as reflecting approximately Manning's [*sic*] own language.[69]

One might assume from the above statement that the Lambeth manuscript and Harley MS 1701 [H] are in the same dialect, but the case is otherwise. H is clearly South East Midland, while L has a mixed southwestern dialect. In addition to the forms mentioned above, L regularly uses *-eþ* in third singular verbs, the preverb *y-* or *i-*, adverbs with *-like* endings, and in nearly all words within the line, L has *-yng(e)* in the present participle. The second hand in L (in Part II) has a predominance of *-u-* spellings, as in *fulely* for *fouly* (as in P), *huld* for *helde, suster* for *sistere, hurde* for *herd,* as

[68] Stepsis' conclusions for P (pp. xlix–xciii) corroborate the Moore, et al., study, *Middle English Dialect Characteristics and Dialect Boundaries* (1935), p. 55. See his discussion of the differences in PL on pp. xiii–xiv, and his summaries of dialect characteristics on pp. lxvii–lxix and xcii–xciii.

[69] Ibid., p. 55. This pioneer work was partly revised by Albert H. Marckwardt in *Historical Outlines of English Sounds and Inflections* (1951). For an appraisal of these earlier dialect studies, see Angus McIntosh, "A New Approach to Middle English Dialectology" (1963), 1–11.

well as the other consistently southern forms noted by Moore, et al., in Part I. None of these dialect characteristics by themselves would be conclusive in a late manuscript, but comparison with other nearly contemporary manuscripts that show the same evidence permits somewhat more precise conclusions.[70]

Furnivall, as noted above, was misled by his conviction that the South East Midland Harley MS 1701 of *Handlyng Synne* really represented Mannyng's dialect. Though the authorities who advised him should probably bear some responsibility, his choice of manuscripts as base texts for both of Mannyng's works was unfortunate, at least for the purpose of presenting texts in an authentic Lincolnshire dialect. After he had transcribed both P and L, his choice of L as the better text of the *Chronicle*, however, is not at all unreasonable, for L is certainly more complete in Part I, and the careless scribal omissions would persuade an editor that P's text is often defective. But Furnivall's justifying the choice of L for his base manuscript on the basis of the dialect was an error. Unfortunately for some of the scholars who followed him, their whole work was based on studies of dialect. Their conclusions apply to the dialect of manuscripts containing late copies, but the evidence for Mannyng's own dialect is not in them.

The studies of dialect based mainly on phonology by Moore, Meech, and Whitehall, and the revision by Albert H. Marckwardt (1951), have been largely superseded by the recently published data in *A Linguistic Atlas of Late Mediaeval English* based on analyses of hundreds of manuscripts.[71]

---

[70] See Marckwardt (1951) pp. 75ff., section 65, for a list of the phonological elements related to French spelling. Among the alterations in his list that may be significant are these: *æ* is nearly always *e* in P, sometimes *u* in L; in P, *u* is regularly *o*, especially with *n* or *m;* the *u* as in *hus* has become *hous; u* is sometimes *ui* in L; the MSS differ on *c* or *k:* P customarily has *k* while L is often ambivalent. I am not convinced that these differences have anything to do with French spelling; they are all matters of customary usage within the locale represented in the dialect of the MSS. For an example of the language of the South West Midlands, see W. Nelson Francis, *The Book of Vices and Virtues* (EETS 217, 1942). He discusses the Simeon MS (BL Additional 22283) [S] on pp. li–lii, and prints the text of a tract on "The Ten Commandments" from S in Appendix I, pp. 316–33. This MS also contains the version of a selection from *Handlyng Synne* with the title, "Septem miracula de corpore cristi," which appears in almost identical form in the Bodleian Vernon MS (Eng. Poet A.1) [V]. This excerpt is printed by Carl Horstmann, ed. (with side-notes by Furnivall) in *The Minor Poems of the Vernon MS* (EETS 98, 1892), pp. 198–221. See my edition of *Handlyng Synne,* pp. XXXI–XXXIII.

[71] Angus McIntosh, M. L. Samuels, Michael Benskin and others; LALME is the usual abbreviation. This work approaches the whole question from a non-phonological perspective which is defined in the introductory essays. The dialect of P is in "Linguistic Profile" (LP) 38, analyzed in vol. 3, pp. 253–55. LR are not individually analyzed, but see vol. 3, pp. 543–47 for analyses of other Wiltshire MSS linguistically similar to L. Among these, LP 5411 is especially interesting: London, College of Arms MS 58, with *Robert of Gloucester's Chronicle* (ed. by Hearne in 1724) and *Richard Coeur de Lion* (ed.

LALME outlines a new direction for studies of Middle English, especially for manuscripts dating from ca. 1350 on, by providing a new method for the analysis of dialect. In the light of LALME's criteria, it is clear that any conclusions about Mannyng's language must be based on P: the survival of his own diction in the other manuscripts containing parts of his work, in spite of translation to different dialects by later scribes, is demonstrated in the glossary to this edition, which includes the language from the *Chronicle* and *Handlyng Synne* and the significant variants in the later copies.[72]

The data analyzed for P (LP 38 in LALME, III) confirms that the dialect of southern Lincolnshire consistently appears, representative of the area where Mannyng was born and made his translations. Although we are faced with confusing dialect evidence in L, some other conclusions can be drawn from the dialectally translated language of this version. The main consideration is that the L copy was made a century or more after Mannyng wrote, when many changes in the language had occurred. Many of the revisions in L are words substituted for what must have been in Mannyng's lexis but were considered to be obsolete when the translation (or the L manuscript) was made. Some of these terms, of course, were substituted because the Lincolnshire usage was unfamiliar to South Wiltshire scribes. Much of the language in the revised L text departs entirely from what must have been in Mannyng's original version, and in some passages the meaning is considerably altered as compared to the lines in P.

Professor M. L. Samuels, writing before LALME was published, advised that the dialect in L resembles several other South Wiltshire manuscripts, and identified the mixed language as follows:

> The overlay in these hands is likely to be S. Wilts.... The MSS closest to these upper layers in language [are]: (1) Public Record Office, Exchequer TR Council and Privy Seal, No. 29 (The Fry Letters, Wilton and Salisbury); (2) College of Arms MS HDN 58 (Robert of Gloucester and Richard Coeur de Lion); (3) Canterbury Cathedral MS D.13 (Prick of Conscience); (4) Salisbury Cathedral MS 39.[73]

---

by K. Brunner in 1913, variants), p. 547. LP 5411 reveals the close similarity in the dialect of this MS with our L MS from the same area. The MED index (p. 42) dates this MS in 1448, which is not far from a possible date for L.

[72] See Angus McIntosh, "Some Words in the Northern Homily Collection," (1972), 196–206. He lists "some one hundred and fifty words and phrases found in seven or eight of the more important manuscripts" of NHC which attest to "the extraordinary interest of the vocabulary" (p. 196). A comparison of his list with the glossary for Mannyng's language is instructive on the typically "northern" diction. The connection of the NHC to *Handlyng Synne* is also indicated in correspondences of the tales in both. See Appendix II, the analysis of the tales, in my edition, pp. 381ff.

[73] From a personal letter dated 29 September 1985. The LP numbers in LALME III

To describe the peculiarities of dialect exhibited in L as an "overlay" is very useful. Where the scribes were adding to their exemplar or recasting lines for whatever purpose, the southern forms are abundant. Where we find the texts of L and P are very close, the mixed forms in L still reflect the North East Midland original source; the meticulousness in retaining the rime words, however incongruous, is marked, especially in the work of the first scribe of L (through f. 79v).

As this review of the dialect studies indicates, the phonological analyses for all of Mannyng's surviving work have been done repeatedly. Unfortunately, these analyses could not directly address the obvious questions about Mannyng's authentic language because the earlier editions were based on manuscripts translated to other dialects. Once a manuscript is accepted as attributable to a specific author, the language of that manuscript should provide some basis for discovering what that author wrote. Until now, none of Mannyng's manuscripts have been edited in a way that permits legitimate conclusions about the dialect of his time and place. Even though the validity of the P manuscript as a major source for his Lincolnshire dialect has been recognized since 1935, no scholar has had an accurate text of the whole *Chronicle* in hand. Except for Hearne's 1725 edition of Part II (or the 1810 reprint in Hearne's *Works*), the necessary resources for further study have not been readily available.

The changes in methodology for studying the dialect of late Middle English manuscripts which are presented in LALME and in the separate studies by the authors of that work render further phonological analyses of Mannyng's language in the surviving manuscripts moot. Thus, it would be redundant to repeat Stepsis' phonological analyses of the language in Part II of the *Chronicle,* and his conclusions on the dialect of L are now superseded. The glossary to this edition, however, provides citations for word forms that should be useful to scholars concerned about the details of dialect.[74] The line numbers for these citations in the texts are included.

---

for these MSS are: (1) 5361 (p. 546); (2) 5411 (p. 547; see n. 71 above); (3) 5420 (p. 548); (4) 5371 (p. 546). A complete list of the Wiltshire documents analyzed is in LALME I: 248–49. Professor McIntosh, commenting on Samuels' conclusions, wrote: "my impression of L . . . is that it must, linguistically at any rate, lie fairly close to some underlying NE Midland text. Otherwise not so many forms characteristic of that area, even *not* in rhymes, would have got through" (Letter of 15 August 1985). See LALME, I, 4.2.1, p. 24, on the detection of "layers" in single texts.

[74] Stepsis includes line numbers only for the text of his edition, Part II, in the dialect analyses. Line numbers are not given in his glossary; it is simply a list which the reader can consult for a definition when an unfamiliar word is encountered in the text. To use his glossary, reference to specific lines in the text is impossible and there are no comparisons with Mannyng's language in Part I or *Handlyng Synne.* Some of the definitions, though imaginative, derive from the context and are not always precise. In 1967, only a

Where there are differences, such as dialectal variation and substitute diction in L, both the P and L words are cited. The diction in *Handlyng Synne* is added at the end of each entry (because all the manuscripts are later than manuscript P of the *Chronicle*) where applicable, to demonstrate how Mannyng's language was retained or altered in the manuscripts preserving various translations into other dialects.

Mannyng's Use of Sources

Discussion of Mannyng's sources for his *Chronicle* and the use he made of them requires consideration of several factors: (1) We have only inaccurate (and sometimes inappropriate) editions of the sources, and until better texts become available, all information from older editions must be regarded as provisional, in part.[75] The exception is the excellent edition of Wace's *Roman de Brut* by Ivor Arnold. (2) Contemporaneity of texts does not mean that one author knew the work of any other. Many of the

---

few of the first fascicles of MED were available to him, and for many of the strange words, he relied on Hearne's readings, which were often inaccurate; some of these, however, have been corrected in later MED entries. The editors frequently cite a reading based directly on the P MS.

[75] The reliability of editions of Mannyng's sources has been discussed by many later scholars. Since only one edition has appeared for Langtoft's whole chronicle, the choice is limited. See notes below on the edition by Thiolier of a part of the work (1989). Thomas Wright's reputation among other scholars was not always favorable. William Benzie, in *Dr. F. J. Furnivall: Victorian Scholar Adventurer* (1983), quotes a letter from Edwin Guest to Furnivall (April 27, 1861) with an ironic slur about Wright, adding a note: "Thomas Wright, philologist and editor, was a member of the Roxburghe Club and the Camden Society. He was a pioneer in Anglo-Saxon and medieval antiquarian studies, but much of his work is very careless and full of errors" (p. 92, n. 72). By comparison, although Thomas Hearne was sometimes ridiculed for his antiquarian eccentricities, his editions have retained their usefulness and his reputation has not suffered in our own century. See Stuart Piggott, *Ancient Britons and the Antiquarian Imagination* (1989); he says that "Thomas Hearne [was] lampooned as *the* antiquary in Pope's *Dunciad*" (p. 22). See Anne Hudson's vindication of Hearne with reference to his edition of "Robert of Gloucester": "The achievement of Hearne is difficult to overestimate" (1969), 331. D. C. Douglas, *English Scholars, 1660–1730* (2d ed., 1951), devotes an entire chapter to Hearne and quotes him regularly in the discussion of other scholars in the period. In Hearne's lifetime, there was no other scholar with such wide-ranging interests, and the number and quality of his editions is amazing. In the next century when interest in Middle English studies was at its height, Furnivall was involved in so many different scholarly activities that he was regularly blamed for perpetuating errors, and he sometimes invited invidious criticism. See Benzie for a generally sympathetic biography; Sir Frederic Madden's opinion of Furnivall was very low: "As to that jackanapes Mr. Furnivall, I think it is a matter of great regret he should be allowed to edit any works of the [Early English Text] Society. His style of writing is thoroughly disgusting, and his ignorance is on a par with his bad taste." Quoted by Benzie from Madden's diary of March 25, 1868, pp. 130–31.

sources now considered to have been in existence at the beginning of the fourteenth century were not necessarily available to Mannyng. (3) The problematic dating of manuscripts forces us to resort to conjecture about which manuscripts Mannyng might have actually used for his translation; assessing the influence of a source is unreliable when we have only hypothetical information about the dates of those works.

Inattention to these aspects has affected the scholarship on Mannyng's works for more than two centuries. The best one can do is attempt to evaluate what we can substantially prove and to trust Mannyng's own statements about what his objectives were in translating his sources. He includes many lines in the text of the *Chronicle* attesting his determination to give credit to his sources and to verify the accuracy of his information. At the beginning of his *Chronicle*, Mannyng explains that he will translate the "Breton" history and then will tell the history of the English according to Peter of Langtoft's chronicle. For the "Brute" from Aeneas to Cadwallader, however, he chose to use the French version of "mayster Wace" because Wace tells the whole story: "þe Latyn alle rymes / þat Pers ouerhippis many tymes" (Part I, 63–64). Indeed, Wace translates the British history by Geoffrey of Monmouth at length, while Langtoft condenses and abridges the matter summarily, sometimes with little regard for the "facts" in the original *Historia Regum Britannie.* Geoffrey's history was regarded as authentic by Mannyng and most of his contemporaries, though some early scholars had expressed doubts about his veracity. The evaluation of history as fact or fiction, which is the habit of our own contemporaries, was simply not a consideration.

Langtoft's plan was that the story of his hero, Edward I, should be the culminating episode in the whole historical poem. His choice of the style of the *chansons de geste,* though outmoded in his time, and the many passages extolling Edward's deeds, suggest that he considered the older history to be of secondary importance to his main objective. As a consequence, he wrote a sketchy version of the earlier chronicles. Wace had undertaken a meticulous translation of Geoffrey's *Historia* for quite different reasons: his concern was to write historical narrative poetry, stylistically distinctive.

Mannyng's comment that "Pers ouerhippis" some of the details is actually from four lines in one of the Langtoft manuscripts, BL Royal MS 20. A. XI [B], which appear at the end of the first part of Langtoft's chronicle. These lines confirm Mannyng's judgment of his source:

Le livere mestre Wace counte plus parfit
E dit tut la lettre qe Peres trop salit.
Peres par tut lessa meint bone respit

Qe bon fust a lire e aver la delit.[76]

The scribe who wrote the Langtoft manuscript [B] was taking some liberties with the text, for the comment quoted above certainly was not written by Langtoft himself. But this manuscript has a version of Langtoft's text that was very similar to the one Mannyng used for his translation as the notes to Wright's edition attest throughout. Wright cites nearly as many passages from Mannyng's work as he does for all four of the other variant manuscripts of Langtoft.[77]

Mannyng's choice of sources, not only of Wace and Langtoft, but also of the other historians and various authors he used to augment his narrative, is indicated in many places throughout the *Chronicle*. Some French and English romances of his own age are mentioned, as well as Ovid and Juvenal. Some of his citations of sources in Part I are translated from Wace, but many of them acknowledge sources written after Wace's *Roman de Brut* was completed in 1155. Mannyng also comments frequently on matters concerning translation, giving alternate meanings in French and English. His direct use of Geoffrey's *Historia* is also evident: he often adds "as the Latin says" when he wants to support a particular detail. He is especially concerned about fidelity to the works of other poets, deploring

---

[76] Wright's edition, I: 264. Wright included annotation for four of the Langtoft MSS in addition to his base MS, BL Cotton Julius A. V [A]. See the list in Smallwood, "The Text of Langtoft's Chronicle," (1977), 219–230. The variants Wright collated were from MS [B] above, and BL Royal MS 20. A. II [C], College of Arms MS Arundel LXI [D], and parts of College of Arms MS Arundel XIV [E] which has the history only from 1272, the reign of Edward I. See Wright's description of the MSS he edited, I: xxii–xxvii, and further remarks in II: vii–xvi. Smallwood lists sixteen MSS and classifies them according to their contents, pp. 219ff. See n. 41 above on J. C. Thiolier's work; his list of MSS includes some extraneous documents that could not be considered authentic sources for Langtoft.

[77] Thiolier describes another MS that does not appear in Smallwood's list: Sidney Sussex College MS 43 [U] (noted in R. S. Loomis' article, "Edward I, Arthurian Enthusiast," 1953, p. 126, n. 53). Thiolier's description of MS U concludes with a statement suggesting that this MS, or one with a closely similar text, might have been used by Mannyng because of localization and resemblance to MS B (p. 132). The localization, however, depends on a note on f. 20 of U suggesting a connection with the Cistercian monastery at "Swyneshead" in Lincolnshire in the reign of Henry VIII (1529). Some of the other contents of MS U do suggest a relationship with MS B: the political letters and Boniface VIII's "Bull" and the Prophecies of Merlin which are also in MS B (f. 183v). See Wright, II, App. I (pp. 386–424) for "Supplementary Matter Which Follows the Text of Pierre de Langtoft in MS. B." (The comment quoted above from MS B on Pers' omission of details does not appear in MS U, according to Thiolier.) Since Thiolier edited only MS E and the very few lines surviving in MS F (Bodleian Fairfax MS 24), the value of his study lies almost entirely in the description of the MSS. For a corrective view of the value of MSS EF, see Smallwood, "An unpublished early account of Bruce's murder of Comyn" (1975), and "The Prophecy of the Six Kings" (1985), as well as his classification of the Langtoft MSS (1977).

the debasement of original texts by careless later speakers or writers (e.g., ll. 83–112).

In Part I, Mannyng adopts the poetic form of his source, Wace's four-stress couplets. It is the form of his earlier work, *Handlyng Synne,* adopted from the *Manuel des Pechiez,* and thoroughly familiar to him. The superiority of Wace's poetic style was acknowledged and much imitated in the twelfth and thirteenth centuries. The octosyllabic couplet was innovative: according to Rosalind Field, "the classic form of the Old French epic is that of the ten- or twelve-syllable line gathered into *laisses* of varying length, linked by monorhyme or assonance. From the mid-twelfth century it gave way before the new fashion for the octosyllabic couplet." Not only was the popularity of Wace's *Brut* attested in the survival of a substantial number of manuscripts and fragments, but the work was also chosen for the early English translation by Laȝamon (ca. 1200), in the borrowings by continuators of "Robert of Gloucester" (ca. 1300 originally and additions thereafter), and Langtoft himself had abridged Wace's work in the earlier parts of his chronicle. The dependence on Wace by the authors of both the French and English versions of the later prose *Brut* also supports Mannyng's judgment of Wace's poetic narrative.[78]

Before Mannyng begins his translation of Wace's *Roman de Brut*, he provides a prologue with a version of ancient history (from lines 201 to 726) that could have been based on similar accounts in many earlier manuscripts. He credits the Trojan story to "Dares þe Freson" (l. 145), the traditional source for these episodes, but Mannyng actually used a quite different version, which varies in many details from Dares Phrygius' *Historia de Excidio Troie.*[79] Though lines 429–454 have a text that is essentially the same as in many other medieval manuscripts citing Dares as their authority, Mannyng departs from the usual version thereafter. According to E. B. Atwood, Mannyng's source was a Latin version of the Troy story from which he drew details concerning Paris and the battle of

[78] See Field, "The Anglo-Norman Background to Alliterative Romance" (1982), 60. See also M. Pelan, *L'Influence du "Brut" de Wace sur les romanciers de son temps* (1931). Analysis of Wace's style and influence is in Arnold's edition, especially pp. XCIIff. and references. See Matheson, "King Arthur and the Medieval English Chronicles" (1990), 253ff. See n. 84 below on Laȝamon.

[79] Julia C. Crick, IV, (1990) identifies twenty-seven MSS that contain versions of Dares, "the single work most frequently associated with Geoffrey's *History*" (p. 38). For the Trojan genealogy, Crick identifies four MSS (pp. 43–4), including one that has "Ciprus is the son of Cetinus, but in the others, his father is Ieuan or Yawan." Compare Mannyng's ll. 262–66, Part I. In one MS, Arundel XXII, the Middle English poem entitled "The Seege or Batayle of Troy" constitutes a prologue to the *Historia.* Dieter Mehl writes: "The fall of Troy was widely considered to be a kind of prelude to the history of England" (1969), p. 20.

the bulls, the encounter with the "thre wicches," and the voyage to seize Helen (the prize promised by Venus), all of which (ll. 455–711) differ substantially from Dares' account. As Atwood says, "[these] episodes are distinctly not part of the Dares narrative. The most plausible conclusion, it seems to me, is that Mannyng did not use Dares at all.... The closest Latin source seems to be the *Compendium Historiae Trojanae-Romanae,* and there is no reason why he may not have drawn directly from that source."[80]

Mannyng's use of other historical sources, however, is not always so clear. The genealogy of Brutus, for example, along with the forebears of the Trojans back to Noah and his antecedents, is embellished with various Greek and biblical characters (ll. 202–427). This genealogy could have been modeled on or directly translated from a Latin (or possibly French) source, but it was certainly not from Dares. Genealogies were ubiquitous introductions in medieval historical works; Mannyng may have used a source ultimately derived from the British history attributed to Nennius (fl. early ninth century) whose genealogies comprise a major part of his work. Geoffrey himself had made limited use of them in his brief account of the ancestry of the Trojans. In Nennius, the ancestors appear in descending order from the earliest names and again in reverse, just as Mannyng recites his account. At line 387, the repetition is pure embellishment: Mannyng announces that he will give the "kynde" now "ageynward vnto Noe."[81]

---

[80] See Elmer Bagby Atwood, "Robert Mannyng's Version of the Troy Story" (1938), 13. See also Atwood and Virgil K. Whitaker, *Excidium Troiae* (1944). Copies of Dares preceded the *Excidium* in two of the MSS they edited. The two works were "probably regarded as alternate versions of the Troy story" (p. lii). Atwood cites the *Compendium* ed. by H. Simonsfeld in *Neues Archiv der Gesellschaft für ältere deutsche Geschichtskunde,* XI (1886): 241–51. It might be possible that the source MS Mannyng used, with a version of the *Compendium,* also had a version of Dares preceding it, justifying his attribution in l. 145. See Margaret J. Ehrhart, *The Judgment of the Trojan Prince Paris in Medieval Literature* (1987), especially pp. 65–69.

[81] Stuart Piggott, "The Sources of Geoffrey of Monmouth" (1941), 269–86, demonstrates the "wholesale plundering" of Nennius in the *Historia.* Geoffrey used the "Pre-Roman King List" for names and then attached tales (many fictional) to the characters named. See John Morris, ed., *Nennius: British History and The Welsh Annals* (1980), 19, for Brutus, and p. 22 for the genealogy in reverse back to Noah. Mannyng's immediate source is not the same, but the method of naming ancestors is demonstrated in Nennius. The Trojan genealogy used by Geoffrey is generally attributed to Nennius as the ultimate source, but not by Geoffrey himself: he says his authority was Gildas. According to Piggott, "Geoffrey seems to have regarded [Gildas] as the author not only of the *De Excidio [Britanniae]* ... but also of the Nennian compilation" (p. 272). See Lewis Thorpe's translation of *The History of the Kings of Britain* (1966): "It is now accepted that [Geoffrey] had at his disposal something closely related to M. S. Harley 3859 ... the contents of which are Nennius' *Historia Brittonum* [with other works]" (p. 15). Morris' edition also uses Harley MS 3859, which he notes "is certainly not the first edition, but is very probably the second," and dates the MS AD 828 or 829 on internal evidence (p.

Although Mannyng failed to identify his source for the genealogies other than the attribution to Dares (l. 145) and the Bible (l. 204), he regularly alludes to other historical sources, most of them standard references available in his time, and often adds comparisons where there is disagreement among them. He specifically mentions Gildas (confused with Nennius), Bede, Henry of Huntingdon, and William of Malmesbury, as well as literary sources, songs and earlier romances, lives of saints, and other biographies.[82] The obligatory prologue (ll. 201–428) is the dullest passage in Mannyng's *Chronicle,* but when he begins the tale of Troy (at line 429), his translation takes on narrative verve and becomes quite colorful. Here we first find the poet's enthusiasm for circumstantial story which was evident throughout *Handlyng Synne.*

Where Mannyng mentions Gildas, he usually follows his immediate sources. ("Nennius" appears in the *Chronicle* as the name of a character who fights a duel with Ceasar, as in Geoffrey and Wace.) But Mannyng knew the sources, evidently at first hand, from the Gildas-Nennius history, for he cites Gildas (ll. 10407 and 10412) in referring to Geoffrey's account of Arthur and the failure of both Gildas and Bede to mention the illustrious British king. But since the genealogy in his prologue appears before the *Brut* of Wace and Geoffrey's *Historia* begin (at line 727), he was obviously relying on some other sources.[83]

Mannyng's text in Part I, mainly translated from Wace's *Roman de Brut,* begins with the departure of Aeneas from Troy (l. 727) and ends with the reign of the last British king, Cadwallader, who lost his land to the Saxons. This is the plan of both Geoffrey and his translator, Wace, who

1). Geoffrey's version of the Nennian genealogy is substantially rewritten, however, and was not Mannyng's immediate model. The matter of confusion between Nennius and Gildas (fl. early sixth century) is discussed below, n. 82. See David N. Dumville, ed., *The Historia Brittonum 3: The Vatican Rescension* (1985) for a discussion of the MSS of Nennius that survive.

[82] Specific references are in the text notes. The contents of the work by Gildas were often attributed to Nennius as a result of confusion in late MSS. Geoffrey cites Gildas as well as Bede, who credited Gildas for parts of his own early history. (Geoffrey's citations may have been included merely to give his narrative the appearance of authenticity.) Bede, however, did use Gildas for the period covered in Gildas. See the *Ecclesiastical History,* Chapter XXII, for ca. 383 to ca. 545. The "Gildasian Recension" is number 5 in a series of new editions. See David N. Dumville, ed., vol. 3 (1985); see also Dumville and Michael Lapidge, *Gildas: New Approaches* (1984; a chronology for Gildas' work is on p. 83).

[83] See Antonia Gransden, *Historical Writing in England, c. 550 to c. 1307* (1974), pp. 1–28, on Nennius, Gildas, and Bede (AD 672/3–735). She says that Bede's "grasp of historical method was unique in the middle ages" (p. 24). R. W. Hanning, *The Vision of History in Early Britain* (1966), surveys the historians from the sixth to the twelfth centuries, from Gildas to Geoffrey of Monmouth.

made many additions and alterations to the Latin prose work. Mannyng is faithful to Wace's version except in a few passages where he cites information based on Geoffrey. From about line 13400 on, Mannyng departs from the Wace text more frequently, adding details from Langtoft and Bede, and generally rewrites the story without entirely abandoning the outline of events as given by Wace.[84]

Part II of the *Chronicle* begins with a short reprise on Cadwallader's death and continues through the end of the reign of Edward I (d. 1307), generally following Langtoft's text. Since the events of Edward's reign were contemporary, Mannyng adds details from personal knowledge, such as those in his account of the parliament at Lincoln in 1300 (at lines 7609ff.). He credits Langtoft with the authentic history of his time, however, and frequently adds "þis is Pers sawe" to insure that his source is understood truly. (He may have also added some of these credits to distinguish Langtoft's version from his own additions.) Modern historians have remarked that Langtoft was a major authority for the events of Edward's reign. Gransden comments that Langtoft's Book III, "as a contemporary account of events by an intelligent and observant writer, is an important authority especially for Anglo-Scottish relations."[85]

---

[84] Ivor Arnold used these base MSS for his edition of Wace: the first 12,000 lines from a MS in the library of M. Boies Penrose [his MS P] and the rest from Durham Cathedral MS C. IV.27.1 [D]. See pp. LVII–LIX. Arnold found it necessary to change MSS at about the same place in Wace as the place where Mannyng begins to rely on other sources. The Wace MS D has many variants close to the text in Mannyng's translation. The question of Wace's sources is discussed in Neil Wright's edition of *The First Variant Version* (1988) of the *Historia*. Wright concurs with Robert A. Caldwell, "Wace's *Roman de Brut* and the Variant Version" (1956), that Geoffrey was not the author, but the Variant was a redaction of the Vulgate text done by an anonymous contemporary writing in Geoffrey's lifetime. That the Variant was Wace's main source has been long established (see Wright, p. lxx); Wright also says that Wace "draws only supplementary material (almost exclusively in the second half of the poem) from the Vulgate *Historia*" (p. lxxvii). The analysis of the contents of both versions of the *Historia* is given in detail in Wright's introduction, including an account of several episodes that differ from the version in Arnold's edition of Wace as compared to the Vulgate. Some of the episodes which Mannyng seems to have drawn directly from Bede (Wright, pp. xlii–xlix), for example, are of particular interest in appraising the sources Mannyng used. If a Wace MS containing these passages could be identified, Mannyng's dependence directly on Bede would accordingly be reduced, even though he included attribution to Bede in his text. Arnold's edition of Wace notes many of Mannyng's changes (2:791ff). See also D. A. Light (1970) for explanation of some of the nautical terms, p. 164. Arnold used different MSS from those edited by Le Roux de Lincy (1836, 1838), and omits many lines appearing in the earlier edition. See J. S. P. Tatlock (1950) for an appraisal of these differences (p. 466, especially n. 12) and the translation of Wace by Laȝamon (p. 487).

[85] Gransden (1974), p. 477, n. 83. She relies on the comments in Legge's two studies of Anglo-Norman literature (1950, 1963) for many of her judgments on Langtoft's work. Other contemporary sources for this period have some of the same information, however. Gransden's discussion of Walter of Guisborough (pp. 470–476), for example,

It is possible to see Langtoft's chronicle, in the first two "books," as Legge calls them, as a lengthy epitome of the then-recognized British and English history. The first book is drawn generally from Geoffrey or Wace; the second is from various sources, especially the works of monastic chroniclers in the eleventh to the thirteenth centuries. The third book is an account of Langtoft's own times, which he based on other chronicles and to which he then added his own personal knowledge of events. Many passages in this part suggest that Langtoft's purpose from the beginning was to provide a rationale for Edward's continuing wars against the Scots and struggles to maintain English rights in Gascony and other parts of the French territories which his grandfather, King John, had lost. Langtoft's theme was the restoration of English overlordship, regaining the empire of the fabulous Arthur.

Mannyng does not depart from Langtoft's text in very many places, but his emphasis is often different. Some of his additions seem to be a kind of modernization, as if a later perspective was necessary; he tries to avoid including Langtoft's rhetorical passages expressing outrage, particularly against the Scots. (He may have been following a different manuscript text for some of these parts, however.) But the translation is essentially a faithful English version of Langtoft's work.

Near the end of the *Chronicle,* Mannyng made some substantial revisions: for some of the "political songs" in Langtoft's text there are additions, alterations, and substitutions. These songs begin at line 6423 and end at line 8068 (Part II), as follows:

---

includes the comment: "In places [Walter's account] seems to derive from the same source as Peter of Langtoft" (p. 471). Harry Rothwell, editor of *The Chronicle of Walter of Guisborough* (1957), points to a very few passages where Langtoft's account is "related to" Walter's. There are only nine notes on this concurrence. His introduction (p. xxvi) makes the matter of sources as clear as possible in consideration of the state of the MSS of Walter's chronicle. Langtoft did not use Walter as a source, though the passages cited by Rothwell were evidently drawn from the same or similar sources: "It is inconceivable that Langtoft took them from Walter" (p. xxvi, n. 3). On the other hand, Michael Prestwich, biographer of *Edward I* (1988), refers repeatedly to both Langtoft and Walter for evidence, often in the same notes, on the history of Edward's reign. Since Walter's compilation was probably done between ca. 1300 and 1305, he was Langtoft's contemporary. Both included personal knowledge or hearsay in their accounts of these events. Legge (1950) notes (p. 72) that the Anglo-Norman historian Jordan Fantosme (in Henry II's reign) may have influenced Langtoft, particularly in matters of poetic style. Part of Legge's discussion of Langtoft's sources is unreliable; she intended to study the matter further, but did not complete her plans (p. 74, n. 1). The three "Books" in Langtoft's chronicle are I: Brutus to 1066; II: 1066 to death of Henry III; and III: Edward I (Legge, p. 73).

Lines:	Incipit:	In Langtoft ed., pp.
(1) 6423–6428	"For Edward gode dede . . ."	222
(2) 6599–6604	"Þikit him & dikit him . . ."	234–36
(3) 6683–6688	"Whan ȝe haf þe pris . . ."	244
(4) 6711–6716	"Þe Scottis had no grace . . ."	248
(5) 6735–6736	"Þe Scottis . I telle for sottis . . ."	252
(6) 6765–6778	"Þe Walsh & þe Irish . . ."	254
(7) 6813–6826	"Þise Duȝepers . com to þe freres . . ."	260
(8) 8063–8068	"At London is his heued . . ."	364

(The text of this edition of Mannyng's *Chronicle* presents the line arrangement as closely as feasible to the version in the P manuscript. Wright's edition of Langtoft arranges the short lines to conform to the tail-rime scheme in passages written in both French and English. The actual arrangement in Langtoft's manuscripts is not indicated in Wright's edition.) Except for the first of these songs, all have "Couwe" marked in the margin near the incipit. At line 6779, the margin notes "Exemplum," presumably to identify a short homily: "Priue pride in pes es nettille in herbere / þe rose is myghtles þer nettille spredis ouer fer" (6779–80). The tail-rime pattern of these passages is inexplicably continued in lines 6827–52, mostly translated from Langtoft, who writes in his usual *laisses* for about seventeen lines (Wright's edition, pp. 264–66), with the last part in a florid outburst of tail-rime (p. 268). At 6827, Mannyng seems to despair of a literal English rendering: "Now tels Pers . on his maners . a grete selcouth." But the lines following are partly an interpolation and partly a commentary on Langtoft's allusion to Merlin's "tales."

Considering Mannyng's condemnation of tail-rime in his introduction (at lines 85–92 of Part I), the marginal addition of "Couwe" identifying the songs in P is almost certainly not authorial. The traditional tail-rime pattern usually has a twelve-line stanza with varying and frequently complicated rimes. The scribe copying P, however, had a much simpler idea of this verse arrangement. The passages so marked are clearly not stanzaic: there are three short lines, all written as one line, which preserves the rimes only for the third line. The effect is the same as if these passages were still written in couplets, with internal rime for the first two parts of each line. Mannyng invented his own rime pattern as a way of producing the effect of Langtoft's verse without obscuring the meaning of the lines.

The differences between Langtoft's versions of the songs and Mannyng's rendering are complicated by the fact that Langtoft erratically resorted to English in several songs: in (2), (4), and (5) the whole song is in English; (3), (6), and (8) begin in French but the last stanza (six lines in the edition) is in English; (7) also begins in French, but the last twelve lines are in English. Wright's notes on these passages include several variations from other manuscripts as well.

Mannyng's changes indicate that he was familiar with the popular songs current during the Scottish conflict and was not reluctant to improve on his source or change the emphasis.[86] Scholars generally concur that Mannyng substituted different versions, at least for the parts that are quite different from the lines in Langtoft, but whether he was quoting oral versions or using songs already written down by others is in dispute.

Mannyng's favorite historian was certainly Bede, the unassailable authority for the authentic history of England up to the middle of the eighth century. He mentions Bede twenty times (though some of these references were in his sources). Toward the end of Part I of the *Chronicle,* sometimes following hints in Langtoft, he attributes several passages directly to Bede. In these passages, however, we must also consider that there were different versions represented in the Wace manuscripts, depending on Wace's use of both the Variant and Vulgate versions of the *Historia.* Whether Mannyng's source manuscript differed substantially from the text in Arnold's edition is a matter for further study. (See n. 84 above.) Throughout the last two thousand lines of Part I, Mannyng regularly cites Geoffrey and Bede for details. It is possible that his manuscript of Wace had some or all of these differences, but Mannyng's meticulousness in citation and his frequent comments on other specific sources imply that he

[86] See Pearsall, "The Development of Middle English Romance" (1965), 107–8 for a general discussion. The differences in Mannyng's text may, in many cases, be attributed to some other immediate MS source rather than to the MSS Wright edited, though MS B is closer to Mannyng's text than to the other variant Langtoft MSS. Smallwood (1977) comments on the different versions of the songs in MSS EF, which "represent a separate independent revision" of Langtoft (p. 224). See R. M. Wilson, *The Lost Literature of Medieval England* (2d ed., rev. 1970). Wilson refers to Mannyng's *Chronicle* frequently in his chapter on "Historical Narrative" for clues to works that have not been preserved. He comments: "Several of these songs on the Scottish wars are found elsewhere. Some of those in Langtoft and Mannyng appear in slightly different forms in the *Brut* and Fabyan" (p. 206). He also notes: "The differences in Mannyng suggest that he also had access to the English originals; . . . most of his additions appear to give the authentic flavour of the original poems" (loc. cit.). R. H. Robbins, ed., *Historical Poems of the Fourteenth and Fifteenth Centuries* (1959), has an excellent discussion of the genre and an edition of a large number of poems. The separate publication of *The Political Songs of England,* edited by Thomas Wright (1839), is cited by the MED as the source for the language of "Songs Langtoft" ("Plan and Bibliography," 1956, p. 75). For the English snippets in Langtoft, LALME I analyzes the language from Wright (1839) for Arundel MS XIV [E] (p. 214) and concludes it is from the Crowland area of Lincolnshire; see also Arundel MS 61 [D] (p. 117) from Adlingfleet, near Goole, West Riding of Yorkshire. The English verses in the Paris MS Bib. Nat. 12154 do not have enough lines "to assess adequately, but language possibly of S Westmorland or SE Northumberland" (LALME I: 248). Two different versions of Langtoft's chronicle are in this MS, BN in Smallwood's list, the "Anstis" MS known to Hearne.

was rearranging his material as he wished. Much of the passage concerning St. Augustine (ll. 14475f.) and the English history thereafter, particularly during the time of Penda, his adversaries and successors, seems to be drawn directly from Bede with a few details from Langtoft. The dates are given exactly as in Bede, and Mannyng's account demonstrates that he knew the *Ecclesiastical History* very well. His last lines in Part I (15934–46) are a graceful tribute to Bede, an invocation.

Mannyng's Poetic Style

Mannyng consistently follows Wace's octosyllabic couplets in Part I. In Part II, however, he changed his style to translate Langtoft, whose verse pattern was difficult to translate into English. Even though Mannyng admired and praised his model, the epic style of a *chanson de geste* that Langtoft used was archaic. His attempts to imitate Langtoft's monorimed *laisses* appear in a few short passages, but the rime pattern must have become tedious and evidently interfered with the sense of the narrative. Langtoft was not the most accomplished master of French verse either. Unfortunately, being an Englishman, he was capable of execrable French. As his editor says, Langtoft's language

> is singularly corrupt. Grammatical inflections are set at nought at every step, and accusatives are used for nominatives, and plurals for singulars, and the converse, with so little care, that not unfrequently a sentence will bear two contrary interpretations, between which a knowledge of the historical events to which it relates will alone enable us to make our choice. . . . Even Pierre de Langtoft's notions of metre appear to have been not always correct, for his lines have sometimes too few feet, and sometimes (though less frequently) too many; but we may perhaps allow this to be in some degree the fault of the copyist.[87]

[87] Wright I: xxix–xxx. M. Dominica Legge (1950) comes to Langtoft's defense, more or less: "He wrote in a very old-fashioned style, employing the monorhymed *laisse* in alexandrines, for all the world as if he was writing a *chanson de geste* in the twelfth century. He uses the same strong caesura as other Anglo-Norman writers. . . . As for Langtoft's literary merits, they are few, but exist nevertheless. He writes with the verve and swing which so offend French ears, but which are characteristic of Anglo-Norman writers such as himself, Matthew Paris and Jordan Fantosme" (pp. 71–72, 73). Wright's expectations of Langtoft may have been exaggerated. His last sentence, blaming the copyist(s), is important. Evidence of carelessness by later scribes is all too common and a proper edition of Langtoft might reveal that his French was not as bad as Wright asserts.

If Mannyng's verse is less than inspired in Part II, we might be justified in blaming his source, at least for making the task of translation difficult. His compromise was to produce a longer line of varying stresses (usually five or six) rimed in couplets, and after the first thousand or so lines, he added a rime at mid-line as well as at the end. Langtoft's long stretches of monorimes would tax any translator who was concerned about his verse making sense and conveying explicit information. The octosyllabic couplets Mannyng used in Part I must have been very much easier to manage.

The appearance of the verse in Part II of P may also owe a great deal to the scribe: each line has a dividing mark [.], but this does not always (nor even regularly) indicate half-lines with varying stresses. (L does not have this device.) This punctuation is arbitrary and does nothing for either sense or scansion. Most lines have three or more stresses in each half line except where the diction suggests that a scribal error or alteration has occurred. The internal rime and end rime, however, are consistently observed. Evidently Mannyng was not overly fussy about faulty scansion, but even so, many of his lines are wrenched by the obviously erratic punctuation of the scribe. These observations apply particularly in the last part of the *Chronicle* beyond the point where the L scribe stopped (i.e., at line 4973, where there is no alternate text for comparison with P). Mannyng was attempting to create a verse pattern that would clearly convey the meaning and still have some recognizable poetic form. There are, however, a few stretches of monorime here and there. One example is in lines 4097 to 4114, where both P and L keep the same rime for eighteen lines. Other examples are in 5047–52 (six lines rime with the preceding couplet in 5043–44), and 5053–62 (ten lines rime in -oun). Mannyng was not necessarily using Langtoft's actual rimes: he was trying to translate the French into English with rime equivalents that had the same meaning.

The internal rime, though consistently maintained in P after a rather tentative beginning, has no logical relationship to the mark that divides the line: the effect is simply to produce eye-rime, even when the spelling is quite obviously distorted; the sense of the rime word is also sometimes irrelevant to the meaning of the rest of the line. In the last example above, *Geffroun* (5061) has been invented to rime with the preceding nine lines. (Compare *Geffrey* in 5043.) Examples of altered spelling occur throughout, with no possible explanation other than the necessities of internal rime: e.g., *wem-Durhem* (1884–85), *buke-tuke* (1886–87), *feste-meste* (2182–83), *Roberd-sperd* (2224–25, where L has *stret* for *sperd* and alters the whole line), *laid-purtraid* (2298–99, the usual spelling is *purtreit*), *Durham-gleam* (2328–29, where the meaning of *gleam* is very obscure). These examples could be multiplied throughout Part II of the manuscript. My impression is that Mannyng's original text did not include all of these instances of altered diction and that a subsequent copyist is probably to blame for some of them. The fact that the internal rime words begin after the first thousand lines of Part II strongly suggests some kind of scribal alteration: the rimes might have been present in the earlier lines and ignored by a scribe until he decided to copy accurately. On the other hand, since many lines in L do not have internal rime where revision or scribal editing appears, it is difficult to decide which lines with rimes in P might have been in Mannyng's original.

Mannyng was not alone; many other authors faced the same difficulties in translating French into English. The author of "Sir Ferumbras," for example, translated a version of the Old French *Fierabras* which survives in a holograph manuscript, Bodleian Ashmole 33. His method permitted him to retain a close relationship with the French source, but he also imposed internal rime.[88] It is notable that the scribe of P, in spite of his carelessness throughout the manuscript, makes a conscientious effort to preserve the rimes. The coinages, especially to create internal rimes, raise many questions about Mannyng's language, but there are altogether too many neologisms to justify giving entire credit to the scribe of P. Mannyng, of course, wrote his translation before the language had assimilated enough new English words to suffice; where diction failed him, an invented word, or an older term used with a new meaning, was employed.

Judging Mannyng's verse on its own merits is only just: he followed an acknowledged master in Wace, and attempted to translate Langtoft's verse in spite of difficulties. If he had been writing an original poem instead of a translation, his work would perhaps have been even less exemplary, as we can see in the preliminary passages where he was probably translating from Latin prose (e.g., in Part I, lines 201–438 where many lines have only three stresses). On the other hand, many of the passages translated from Bede's Latin prose, especially in the last part of Part I, are as carefully composed as one might wish, though Mannyng may have used a Wace manuscript which included some of these passages. He was writing history in verse, he took the history itself seriously, and though he was concerned about poetic style, accuracy was even more important. His verse shows considerable narrative skill: it is smooth and graceful, rarely end-stopped

[88] See Stephen H. A. Shepherd, "The Ashmole *Sir Ferumbras:* Translation in Holograph" (1989), pp. 103–21. The MS has evidence of dating in two places, 1357 and 1377. See also E. G. Stanley, "Rhymes in English Medieval Verse: from Old English to Middle English" (1988), pp. 19–54. Stanley remarks: "The texts have come down to us transmitted by scribes most of whom show little respect for the integrity of their exemplars, little respect even for their author's wording and usually none at all for his orthography" (p. 20).

or harsh. He follows Wace's typical embellishments occasionally, including repetition, rhetorical parallelism, and antithesis. The best features in Wace are the vivid descriptions and the imaginative reconstruction of scenes, and Mannyng keeps most of them in his translation. One may weary of the endless bloody battles, the mindless valor of knights, or beheadings and mutilations, but they are all part of the tradition of historical narrative poetry and Mannyng did not flinch when portraying them.

Mannyng's Influence

The manuscripts in which excerpts from *Handlyng Synne* are included may indicate a wider circulation of this early work than the number of surviving manuscripts have revealed. Evidently there was an audience for Mannyng's poem in the latter part of the fourteenth century that was not localized in Lincolnshire nor confined to the Gilbertine establishments that he said he was writing for. More anthologies may yet be discovered with parts of his work that have thus far escaped identification. Since *Handlyng Synne* was composed very early in the fourteenth century, it was available to later compilers of religious poetry who used Mannyng's tales, either in their original form or altered to fit the kind of anthology in which they were copied. On the other hand, if one judges popularity by the number of manuscripts remaining, we have, in fact, many more surviving manuscripts of the French works from which Mannyng translated, a majority of them written after the mid-fourteenth century. The *Manuel des Pechiez* and Langtoft's chronicle, Mannyng's major contemporary sources, as well as Wace's *Roman de Brut,* were all copied many times after Mannyng did his translations.

Whether Mannyng had a direct influence on later poets needs further study. There is one confirmed example: Peter Idley used *Handlyng Synne* in the fifteenth century as a major source for his *Instructions to His Son.* Idley's choice indicates the durability and pertinence of Mannyng's work, at least to one poet who acknowledged his debt.[89]

[89] The *Manuel des Pechiez* survives in twenty-five MSS and fragments. See my edition of *Handlyng Synne,* App. I, p. 378 for a list. Identification of a short selection from *Handlyng Synne* in the Westminster Cathedral Diocesan Archives MS H.38 [W] appears in Horrall (1990), 214–27. Charlotte D'Evelyn edited *Peter Idley's Instructions to His Son* (MLA, 1935). Her discussion of Idley's use of Mannyng (p. 45f.) has been modified by the discovery of another MS: "It is clear from a version of the *Instructions* in an early sixteenth-century MS recently acquired by the British Library, Addit. MS 57335, a version unknown to its modern editor, Charlotte D'Evelyn, that Idley realized his intention (as expressed in the Prologue to Book 2) of reworking *Handlyng Synne* in its entirety and covering the Ten Commandments, the Seven Deadly Sins, Sacrilege, the

The surviving manuscripts that contain all or parts of *Handlyng Synne* allow some conclusions about the existence of other copies at some time in the fourteenth century (or later), in addition to Mannyng's original text:

(1) An exemplar for Bodley MS 415 [B] (from which FH are copies) was likely a translation into a South East Midland dialect before ca. 1400. LALME's analysis (LP 6620 for B, LP 7780 and 7650 for F, and LP 6630 for H) establishes the dialect; F was apparently the work of a "literal" copyist. Other parts of the composite manuscript analyzed, all in the hand of the same scribe, are in the University of London Library Sterling MS V.17, "Piers Plowman" (C text) and "Estorie del Euangelie," assigned by LALME to South Worcestershire. The copy [F] of *Handlyng Synne* with the *Medytacyuns* was the first item in this manuscript, once intact before the first part was sold to the Folger Library. The second item is the English prose version of "Mandeville's Travels," the Boies Penrose manuscript, now in Princeton University Library.

(2) Two exemplars must have existed for the Norfolk manuscripts, C and D. C was shortened and revised to some extent, probably by the scribe of the manuscript (Cambridge University Library Ii.4.9, LP 621); D is the first part of what was probably once a complete version, judging by the abrupt ending followed by catchwords on f. 21v. Only the "Ten Commandments," lacking ninety-five lines, remains in this manuscript (LP 4646).

(3) An exemplar, probably in the dialect of the South West Midlands, was copied in SV; the versions in these two manuscripts are almost identical and it is very unlikely that there were two different exemplars. Whether either one is a copy of the other is doubtful, though the manuscripts are closely related in other ways. The LP for Vernon (Bodley Eng. Poet. A.1) [V] is 7630, but Simeon (BL Addit. 22283) [S] was not analyzed in

---

Seven Sacraments, the Twelve Points of Shrift, and the Twelve Graces of Shrift. He was not an accomplished poet, and his work, although it enjoyed contemporary popularity . . . makes tedious reading today." Robert R. Raymo, "Works of Religious and Philosophical Instruction," in *A Manual of the Writings in Middle English, 1050–1500*, vol. 7 (1986), 2258. Gburek (1977) asserts a relationship of the Dulwich MS 24 [D] to Idley's work. His judgment is based on a comparison of passages from D and Idley and attribution to the dialect of Kent: "Das Dialektgebiet ist Kent" (p. 21). However, LALME III, 354–55, analyzes the D MS (LP 4646) and identifies it as one of two MSS by a scribe named "Rose" (the other is Cambridge, St. John's College MS 28, B6) and places the dialect in Norfolk. The Kentish dialect in Idley MSS ought to appear, but as D'Evelyn notes, there is no significant trace of this dialect in his language (p. 58), even though the author said that he was a native of Kent. Matthew Sullivan has provided biographical information in "The Author of the Manuel des Péchés" (1991), William of Waddington, a secular canon of York. Sullivan discusses the biography of Peter Idley (1994), and says he is preparing an edition of BL Addit. MS 57335 (p. 303, n. 5). See n. 26 above.

LALME. (See n. 70 above.)

(4) The snippet in manuscript A (Bodley Ashmole MS 61) is probably a copy of a copy that had a text close to that of manuscript B (or possibly F or H). The manuscript is analyzed in LALME (LP 71) with the dialect of Leicestershire.

(5) The excerpt in manuscript W (see n. 89) is perhaps a copy of a copy, though the text is very close to that of manuscript B. It might have been a copy of H as there is a gloss on one line (3672) that also appears in BH and nowhere else; however, the exact diction in BW strongly recommends B as a more immediate source for W. (Not analyzed in LALME, but the language does not differ from that of the other South East Midlands manuscripts.)

(6) The exemplar of manuscript O (Osborn MS a.2) was probably a mid-to-late fifteenth century translation to a northern dialect, perhaps done in the area of Durham where the manuscript was kept until ca. 1957. The dialect is analyzed in LALME (LP 521, 484, and 471 for three of the hands) as "Northern" but not placed on the maps locating the Northern manuscripts. (This manuscript was known to James Orchard Halliwell who cited it in his dictionary of archaic words as the "Bowes manuscript.")

The probable existence of at least five exemplars (leaving the excerpts from A and W in doubt) attests to a wider audience for *Handlyng Synne* in several areas during the later fourteenth century. The fact that the work was translated in the South East and South West Midlands and in the North might suggest that Mannyng was rediscovered and his work copied for different purposes than he originally intended. Only the complete manuscripts (BFH) and D have the prologue in which Mannyng names himself. Manuscript O is mutilated, beginning at line 2501. All the rest (ACSVW) are anthologies and Mannyng's work is copied without identification of the author. Most medieval literature, of course, was deliberately anonymous. What we would call plagiarism was the customary method of compiling anthologies. Mannyng was one of the rare authors who not only identified himself but also specifically acknowledged his sources and gave his reasons for and methods of employing the works of others.

Mannyng's *Chronicle,* on the other hand, was not copied by many scribes, perhaps because the taste for history (or fiction that passed for history) was shifting to works in prose in the later fourteenth century. The proliferation of manuscripts of the prose *Brut,* for example, in both French and English (and even Latin), a few contemporary with but most postdating Mannyng's work, is an indication of a growing preference for unembellished historical facts. The convention of poetic history (or more precisely, historical narrative in verse) had been partly supplanted by prose in Mannyng's own lifetime. By the end of the century, the English *Brut,* translated from a French prose *Brut* that was composed at about the same time as Mannyng wrote his *Chronicle,* began to achieve extraordinary popularity. At least 170 manuscripts of the English *Brut* survive, as well as fifty in Anglo-French and fifteen in Latin; the English version was published by Caxton in 1480 and its popularity continued during the century thereafter. There were thirteen printed editions between 1480 and 1538.[90]

---

[90] See Matheson (1984, and "Printer and Scribe," 1985). The question of whether the English prose *Brut* was indebted to Mannyng's *Chronicle* is not entirely resolved, and many eminent scholars have made this assumption, each depending on his or her predecessors. The pertinent references are in M. D. Legge (1950, p. 73 and 1963, p. 280), Brie (in *Geschiete und Quellen,* 1905, pp. 17ff., 33), and Gransden (1974). Gransden's discussion depends chiefly on Legge, ending with this statement: "Robert Mannyng was himself a Yorkshireman, and his English rendering of Book III of Langtoft's chronicle became the source for the English prose *Brut*" (p. 480). Why Legge (and Gransden) inconsistently moved Mannyng to Yorkshire after identifying his place of birth at Bourne in Lincolnshire remains a very curious error, wholly unsupported. See John Taylor, *English Historical Literature in the Fourteenth Century* (1987), 110–14, 150–51. Taylor also cites Legge, as above. The original compilation of the French prose *Brut* ended with the death of Henry III (1272) and was composed near the end of the thirteenth century. A later, longer version was the basis for the English translation. Parts of this work cover the same era as in Mannyng's *Chronicle,* Part II, ending with the death of Edward I (1307). But the treatment in the English *Brut* is terse and perfunctory, not in the least poetic, and for the historical events after 1333, the accounts are all in continuations of the French version, translated to English ca. 1400, long after Mannyng's time. Madden's discussion of the English *Brut* ("Prose Chronicles of England," 1856) includes the comment: "The English version, in general, agrees tolerably well with that of the *revised* French text . . . which is certainly the original followed by the translator" (p. 3). The revised French *Brut* appears in MSS nearly contemporary with Mannyng's time (oldest: Dom. A. X, ca. 1332; Royal 20. A.iii, ca. 1345; another in BL Addit. MS. 18462; see Brie (1905) for other citations). Thus a French work that was the basis for the English translation more than half a century later would scarcely need to borrow from Mannyng's *Chronicle.* If older MSS of the English *Brut* should eventually be identified, the problem would need to be restudied. It is possible that Langtoft's chronicle could have provided some of the details for periods down to 1307, of course. See Matheson (1984), p. 218, on Woburn Abbey MS 181. It is a prose chronicle including a *Brut* continuation that was described by Madden (in BL Egerton MS 2257) which, according to Matheson, "appears to be a paraphrase of Robert Mannyng of Brunne's *Chronicle,* Part 2. . . . The basis of the paraphrase may have been a text of Mannyng similar to that found in Lambeth 131, which contains the interpolated Havelok story . . . and Brie (1905) deduced that this meant that the story differed from that found in Langtoft's *Chronicle.*" The version that appears in this MS "begins with Alfred and ends with Edward I . . ." (loc. cit.). This matter needs further study, and Woburn Abbey MS 181 is not published. Matheson does not note that the L MS ends (l. 4973, reign of Richard I) long before the reign of Edward I: MS L could not have been the direct source, for the extent of the text would obviously be impossible. However, an antecedent MS, perhaps rather like the exemplar of L (for which the scribe left an incomplete copy), might have been the source of part of the Woburn text. Brie quotes Madden (from Egerton MS 2257) throughout his description and discusses the Woburn MS as one of the English versions of the *Brut* (pp. 100–102). Madden also included a comment on this MS in his short article (1856, quoted above): "In the library of the Duke of Bedford, at Woburn, is preserved a manuscript English Chronicle, compiled and written in 1448 by Rycharde

The French prose version is ultimately based on Wace's *Brut;* as a result, the English translation of ca. 1400 sometimes employs language suggesting that of Mannyng's *Chronicle,* but the resemblance is mainly in occasional phrases which surely were translated from Wace. I cannot endorse the theory that Mannyng was a direct source for the English *Brut* as there are major differences in arrangement and treatment of the text. I do not find any passages that appear to have been directly derived from Mannyng, though the continuity of episodes and narrative details often suggests a similar underlying source, probably ultimately from Wace. As observed above, the comparison of sources is necessarily dependent on the editions of those sources; for the *Brut,* we have only the edition by F. W. D. Brie, (1906, 1908) based on only three manuscripts. The oldest is Rawlinson B. 171 of ca. 1400, while the others are later.

The direct influence of Mannyng on another poet is asserted by Mary Hamel in her edition (1984) of *Morte Arthure.* The dialect of this remarkable poem is ultimately that of Kesteven in Lincolnshire and the diction includes many of the words in Mannyng's vocabulary. Hamel's use of the similarity in language to establish a direct influence from Mannyng, however, is not convincing, mainly because the *Morte Arthure* poet completely transformed his source material into alliterative verse. Since Hamel necessarily used the *Chronicle* text in Furnivall's edition based on L, the correspondences to Mannyng's language are diluted by the South West Midland translation, except for a few examples where she quotes P. These are chiefly verbal echoes, not direct borrowings. If the *Morte Arthure* poet used a source that represented Mannyng's authentic *Chronicle,* it would necessarily have been in some manuscript intermediate between P and L. But Wace's *Brut* was the poet's major source: his indebtedness to Wace accounts for the structure and arrangement of the poem, as other scholars have confirmed. The language of *Morte Arthure* preserves some of the usual idiom found in Mannyng's *Chronicle* in P, though at least two generations must have elapsed between the probable earliest date for P and the composition of the alliterative poem ca. 1400–1402. But the text of the *Chronicle* in L, another half century or so later, reveals that much of Mannyng's language has been altered or obscured. By relying on Furnivall's edition, Hamel is handicapped: the content of the passages she cites which she

---

Fox of St. Alban's, which commences with the reign of Alfred (AD 872), and as far down as the end of the reign of Edward I. is borrowed from the older historians; but from this date onwards to the siege of Rouen (6 Hen. V.), where it ends, it is identical with the English *Brute*" (p. 4). See the edition of *Des Grantz Geanz* by Georgine Brereton (1937). This Anglo-French poem served as a prologue to the longer French prose *Brut.* Brereton has some cogent observations on the earlier (1905) work of Brie.

believes were dependent on Mannyng could have been derived ultimately from a translation of Langtoft but would not necessarily indicate that Mannyng was the direct source of the language. For passages which were evidently derived from Wace (or possibly Laȝamon's translation of Wace), Hamel is able to support her discussion more adequately. In her text note for *Morte Arthure* 4226, for example, Hamel quotes Mannyng's lines 13693–98 (in the present edition, Part I) and notes that Mannyng was here "following Langtoft": the passage describing the duel of Arthur and Modred is not in Arnold's edition of Wace. But the fact that a confrontation occurred in the decisive battle between the two is the only applicable point. There is no resemblance between the details in the *Morte Arthure* version and the passage rather loosely translated by Mannyng from Langtoft.

A somewhat better case could be made for the account of the arming of Arthur in the *Chronicle* (ll. 9880ff.) compared with the *Morte Arthure* lines at 900–919. Some of the specific terms for armament are reflected in the L (revised) account. The next fifty lines in L, however, demonstrate considerable rewriting. The "arming of the hero" was a romance convention, of course, and Hamel notes that "Gawain and the Green Knight" and "Seige of Jerusalem" also have such passages (p. 287, n. 900–913). After checking the references in Hamel's edition, I am forced to conclude that the evidence for a direct influence from Mannyng is very doubtful, in spite of the undeniable resemblances between the Kesteven idiom in the *Chronicle* and the later alliterative poem. I do not find any significant parallels in diction in the passages Hamel cites, nor any distinctive phrases or syntax in Mannyng's lines that apply to the same subject matter in *Morte Arthure*.[91]

---

[91] Mary Hamel, ed., *Morte Arthure: A Critical Edition* (1984). The only surviving copy of the poem is in the "Thornton MS," Lincoln Cathedral Library MS 91 (an anthology of ca. 1420–30). A facsimile edition is in *The Thornton Manuscript,* ed. by D. S. Brewer and A. E. B. Owen (1975). Hamel cites Angus McIntosh on the language, "The Textual Transmission of the Alliterative *Morte Arthure*" (1962), 232–34. Hamel says that the poet used Geoffrey, Wace, Laȝamon, and Mannyng, all four together, and that her conclusions are based on a "line-by-line collation"; her analysis is based on the proper names (pp. 6, 25). On the matter of romance literature conventions, see Charles Foulon, "Wace" (in ALMA, 1959): "But set two medieval French poets to describe independently the arming of a knight, a sumptuous feast, or a combat with a giant, and it will be a miracle if there are no precise correspondences, even of phrase" (p. 102). John Finlayson, himself an editor of *Morte Arthure* and one of the discoverers of Malory's Winchester MS which borrowed parts of the alliterative poem, comments on the premises of Hamel's edition: "This multi-chronicle view [of the poem's sources] strikes me as a little thin, though it is one way of accounting for the variety of posited resemblances. An examination of some of the footnoted resemblances, however, did not seem to me to provide conclusive evidence" (Finlayson's review, 1988, pp. 936–39). See

We owe an enormous debt to the historians who persist in extracting information about medieval events from any possible sources. Though they uniformly reject the fictional origins of the genre that includes Mannyng's *Chronicle,* nevertheless the fiction that Geoffrey created to fill a gap in the "true history" underlies a major part of the subsequent literature. It was the stuff of the whole tradition for several centuries. To try to find some direct influence on later poets in Mannyng's work, to differentiate his specific formulation in English poetry as distinct from the work of the anonymous authors who followed him, is not easy. In the English prose *Brut* and also in the *Morte Arthure,* the verbal echoes from Wace, it seems to me, are stronger than the intimations which might have come from Mannyng's translation.

The reign of Edward III saw an increased awareness of English history and the wars with France contributed to a new pride in English as a literary medium which is adumbrated in Mannyng's unapologetic statements about his use of English in the first lines of his *Chronicle.* Nevertheless, since French was still the literary language of most upper-class English readers during the fourteenth century, Mannyng's English *Chronicle* was evidently not well-known in his own time. And since he wrote in a dialect unfamiliar to southern Englishmen, other copies would have to be translations. Mannyng's version of the poetic history was evidently not popular enough in the late fourteenth or early fifteenth centuries to justify the labor of making many additional copies. Though the original dialect may have been an impediment to wider circulation, the *Chronicle* was at least

---

William Matthews, *The Tragedy of Arthur* (1960), who contends that the chief chronicle sources were Geoffrey, Wace, and Laȝamon (p. 20). I was dismayed to find that Hamel gives Wace the name "Robert," which does not appear in Arnold's edition of Wace, nor in Houck's study (1941), nor in Light's dissertation (1970). The only other scholar (so far as I have discovered) who calls him "Robert Wace" is W. R. J. Barron (1982), p. 72. Tatlock (1950) makes a point of this matter: noting that Wace names himself fifteen times in his five known works, "the ambitious Wace gives himself but this one name" (pp. 463–64). See Lesley Johnson, "Robert Mannyng's History of Arthurian Literature," (1991) for a cogent discussion of the matters included here. She comments that "material from the Chronicle was used in the composition of the alliterative *Morte Arthure* " (p. 146, n. 32) and refers to Mathesen's discussion of the "paraphrase of Mannyng's version" identified in the compilation of Richard Fox's chronicle (see n. 90 above). Johnson's note, carefully supported by recent authority, shows how easily conjectural scholarly positions can become embedded in subsequent studies. Even the most alert of us have difficulty appraising the validity of extrapolations from earlier studies. The critical scholarship on Mannyng is still a rather small part of what has been done on the whole body of Middle English works, but even what has been published is often marred by the unavailability of adequate editions. The present edition of Mannyng's *Chronicle* should provide some answers to Johnson's comments at the beginning and end of her article (p. 129, n. 1 and p. 146.)

well-enough regarded to be translated in an exemplar that was copied by the later scribes of L who converted his then-archaic language to fit their own locale. The triumph of prose as the preferred medium for history certainly contributed to the popularity of the English prose *Brut* and was perhaps a factor in the eclipse of Mannyng's work.

I regret that I have not found more convincing evidence of Mannyng's direct influence (except for Peter Idley) on later fourteenth- or fifteenth-century literature. Just because I have not found it, of course, does not mean that it does not exist. His language, as preserved in P and in the reflections of his language as translated in L and the diverse variant manuscripts of *Handlyng Synne,* however, is a very substantial legacy. Without it, our knowledge of the lexis of fourteenth-century literature would be much impoverished.

Presentation of the Text

The text of Mannyng's *Chronicle* survives, as described above, in two versions: the earlier, and I believe, the version nearest to his original intentions, is in P. The later L manuscript is based on a revision of the work, and though it preserves many lines lost from P, it also has lines added by the reviser and shows many changes to conform to a dialect different from Mannyng's own. For these reasons, the text of P (with line numbers for that manuscript only) is the base text for this edition, with side notes giving the alternate readings in L, through all of Part I and through line 4973 of Part II (where the L manuscript ends), and for the fragment in R (Part I, 12550–699).

In order to present the whole text economically, some necessary annotation is included in the side notes, such as differences in the order of lines and the rearrangement of longer passages; for other textual matters, especially for the sources other than Wace or Langtoft from which Mannyng derived material, a list of text notes is added at the end of each part.

In the side notes, there are some accommodations: where a line in L differs entirely from the line in P, the whole line is given; where some of the words are the same in P and L, the side note for L has a period [.] replacing each of the words that is the same in P. This method is not customary, as I am aware, but I believe that it provides precise information without distracting the reader.[92] In some lines, however, more of the

[92] I am indebted to my publisher, Mario A. Di Cesare, for this plan. In the earlier volume of Mannyng's work, *Handlyng Synne,* most of the variant MS readings were added at the end of the text; however, the *Chronicle* presents a different kind of textual

information from L is included where it would be difficult to see the variant syntax or logic. For example, at f. 42r c.2 through f. 44v c.1 (Part I, lines 6918 to 7292), there are corrections, additions, and editorial changes in abundance in the L version. Most of the variant lines, however, end with the period [.] because the L scribe was using the same rime word as in P. Another example is in the thirty-six lines of 8388 to 8423 where thirteen lines have variant readings but the rime words are the same in PL. The reviser adds much detail but keeps the basic pattern of the line as he found it in his source.

The usual editorial license appears in some of the text notes, for they include suggestions for interpretation which may be useful to a reader concerned with passages that can be compared with texts of other works. The references to sources cited there are for further information, not necessarily to support one interpretation or another.

Though we have only the one alternate manuscript [L] for practically all of the *Chronicle* text, it illuminates many passages in which the base manuscript [P] is probably or certainly defective. Some of these differences are discussed in the text notes as well as in the side notes, especially for the passages representing significant revisions in L. For some lines, I have ventured conclusions as to whether the text in one manuscript is preferable to the other; all these instances are cited in the text notes but not cross-referenced in the side notes. The objective of making this very long historical narrative accessible to the reader without requiring constant flipping to the end of the book for essential information has governed the arrangement and content of the side notes to the text.

In the text notes, I have avoided conjecture about inaccurate or possibly spurious lines except in those instances where another source or analogous work provides help in interpretation. For example, the account of Richard I in Part II (beginning at line 3485, the coronation in 1189) derives ultimately from one or more narratives written by Richard's contemporaries who may have accompanied the Crusaders, but the "romance of Richard" to which Mannyng frequently refers has not yet been identified and may never be. Though Langtoft's chronicle is the immediate text being translated, many of Mannyng's allusions to the "romance" are not in Langtoft's manuscripts; it is clear that Mannyng had a copy of the "romance" to supplement Langtoft's account. For some of these lines the text notes refer to other (later) versions of the Richard story where the details are striking-

---

arrangement which is better managed by showing the text of P and the L variants side by side on the page. This method does not actually provide a parallel text edition, but the differences between the MSS are clearly shown and problems of syntax and errors in one MS or the other are minimized.

ly similar. Probably Langtoft used the same sources, which were so familiar in his time that he neglected to include the frequent attributions we find in Mannyng's translation. On the other hand, because Mannyng also assumed the currency of the Richard "romance," his allusions to it excused him from repeating some of the details in his own version. Generally, Langtoft included acknowledgement of sources rather sporadically, while Mannyng was meticulous in identifying almost all the authors whose work contributed to his narrative.

The differences in scribal practice have been discussed above. Some specific orthographic peculiarities of the scribes, however, require a further note. Both manuscripts P and L are clear and readable; R has, because of mutilation and detachment of the leaf from its original manuscript, several difficult passages, particularly in the last of the four columns. My verification of this manuscript left many words in doubt, with the result that I found the transcript published by Eugen Kölbing in 1892 to be very helpful.[93] Though the R fragment is not essential to establish the text except in the brief passage where it is parallel to PL, it is important for some insights on the possible history of the manuscripts.

The main hand in P has some individual peculiarities:

(1) A stroke is often added over *n* in meaningless positions; the mark does not mean a doubling of the letter, but it may indicate that the scribe was distinguishing *n* from *u*, for example: *man̄, smyten̄, when̄, wyn̄.* A more remote possibility is that it was an indication of a short vowel preceding. I have omitted this mark in the text since it is impossible to interpret it, and the meaning of the words is clear without cluttering the lines unnecessarily.

(2) The double *l* in all positions has a stroke through the two letters which evidently indicates a following *e.* This abbreviation is not usual in the other manuscripts I have transcribed, but the invariable practice of indicating the spelling *-lle* in P is frequently reinforced when the word is spelled out, as in *alle.* Accordingly, this mark is treated as a customary expansion in this manuscript. There are many instances when *h* has a slash through the loop, an apparently meaningless stroke, which is ignored because there is no orthographical justification for it and it does not

---

[93] See n. 50 above. The R fragment has suffered more than usual mishandling in its unknown past. Kölbing also edited *Arthour and Merlin* (Leipzig, 1890). In his introduction, he advanced the theory that this poem and *Kyng Alisaunder* and also *Richard Coeur de Lion* were all by the same author. Several scholars have referenced this matter, including Brunner (1913, pp. 34–35), Ackerman (in ALMA, p. 486), and Pearsall (1965, pp. 100f). G. V. Smithers, ed., *Kyng Alisaunder* (EETS OS 227, 237; 1952, 1957), follows Kölbing's theory and attributes *The Seven Sages of Rome* to the same author (see introduction, p. 41). See Pearsall's discussion on pp. 101–2.

indicate a contraction or expansion, just a flourish.

(3) The main hand is very erratic in capitalization. Though the second scribe in this manuscript conscientiously capitalizes the first word in almost every line, the main hand rarely bothers. He does not capitalize proper names consistently, but these are easily distinguished. To make the text more intelligible, I have capitalized the proper names of people and places, regardless of the scribe's indications. The first words of lines are capitalized when they begin a new sentence, though these capitals may not represent what actually appears in the manuscript except when there are other indications that a new paragraph begins. In attempting to punctuate the text, I found that alterations in capitalization were inevitable. My original intention was to indicate punctuation and capitalization as closely as possible to the practice of the scribes, but I have deferred to the judgment of readers who found the text unnecessarily difficult without modern conventions.

(4) The main hand occasionally shows subtle changes in style, employing different letter forms, sometimes smaller or larger, perhaps because the manuscript was copied over a very long period of time and the scribe may have been engaged in other work. One example is the later use of a loop at the top of the lower-case letter *i*, which becomes customary at about line 12000 of Part I and consistent in Part II of the manuscript. The letter has a slightly longer descender than the single stroke used earlier in the manuscript; the scribe perhaps wished to make his script more legible by this device. The differentiation between *i* and *j* is complicated: I have transcribed all instances as *i* because *j* is not distinguished as a separate letter form.

(5) In many passages, the scribe has added a period [.] to indicate internal punctuation, as in the list of names of places (1243–46). I have omitted this mark in the text in favor of consistent punctuation. Throughout Part II, the period in mid-line is employed without any logic whatsoever. It sometimes indicates a caesura, sometimes points to internal rime, but mostly it means nothing at all. I have added customary punctuation simply to help improve the sense of the text. In the political songs in Part II, however, lines which could be broken up into shorter lines are also punctuated with a period [.] in the manuscript; in these instances, the scribe was punctuating to indicate tail-rime lines. I have left these marks as they appear in the manuscript (where the marginal annotation "Couwe" is added) as there is no other satisfactory way to show the scribe's intentions.

The usual abbreviations in both P and L have been silently expanded: *re, er,* the stroke for *per* or *pro,* the stroke to indicate a vowel preceding *m* or *n.* Both manuscripts also abbreviate for *þ*^{t}, *þ*^{u} and *þus.* A curl at the end of a word to indicate an *e* differs from the abbreviation for *-us* which has a longer stroke. These expansions are all clearly indicated by the scribes and present no difficulties. Only the expansion of *re* or *er* is sometimes arbitrary, but I have tried to expand consistently, especially in rime words.

The scribes in L are more particular in capitalizing the first letter of each line and the names of persons and places. Often, the capital is only an enlarged character similar to the lower-case form, but the intention is clear. Many lines in L begin with the ampersand for *and* or the customary letter form for *þ* (thorn) or *ȝ* (yogh); these characters are not much enlarged, but the intention to capitalize the first letter of each line is generally consistent otherwise. In both manuscripts, many new "chapters" or divisions of the text are distinguished with larger initials done by illuminators, and the same artists have evidently supplied some of the major Latin captions, also occasionally the marginal notes and paragraph marks. I have omitted these captions and other miscellaneous notes in the text, for it is very doubtful that they were included in Mannyng's original manuscript. The close concurrence of these Latin additions in PRL suggests that they were originally added by a copyist of one of the earlier manuscripts, perhaps in the first copy made after Mannyng's own text.[94] The captions in L are usually written by the scribe when they occur within the lines of text; they are obviously copied, and not always accurately, from an exemplar that included them. The other captions in P (usually identifications) throughout the manuscript, including passages done by the second scribe, are all the work of the main hand, except as noted above.

The carelessness of scribes in P, especially the main hand, is notable: there are dropped words and omitted lines throughout the manuscript, and they are rarely marked for correction. In fact, the P text in many passages would be nonsense without the alternative reading we find in L. There are also many transpositions of lines in P that make much better sense in the order they appear in L. (All these are indicated in the side notes.) The first scribe of L (who wrote from the beginning of Part I through f. 79v of Part II) is not faultless, but he is much more conscientious about corrections,

---

[94] See n. 61 above for one example. Vincent Gillespie, "Vernacular Books of Religion" (1989), has a discussion of the ways in which scribes imitate the exemplar in format and apparatus: "Accurate scribal work might well have consisted not only in careful attention to the copying of the text but also in the perpetuation of the structures and layout of the text in the scribal exemplar" (p. 332). The complexity and content of the apparatus in the examples he provides indicate varying uses in these works. My conclusion that Mannyng's own original MS did not contain the Latin apparatus in PLR is explained above.

If poetic narrative MSS followed some known convention in these copies, the contents would simply have been made to fit into some frame: names of the kings as they appeared in the text, for example, comprise most of the captions at the heads of folios.

usually underdotting his error within the line, occasionally adding a word in the margin and marking it as a correction. I have transcribed all these peculiarities *as the scribes intended them to be read* and have added comments only for disarrangements and transpositions that were necessary for intelligibility.

A reader who is not concerned about Mannyng's sources will not need to refer to the text notes at the end of each part. For the reader who only wants to enjoy Mannyng's *Chronicle* without interruption, the text and its side notes alone should suffice. The only emendations in the text appear in passages where the manuscript has blemishes; the text notes explain the reasons for emendation where it was required. The information needed to emend the text, of course, is given in detail in the notes, but I have avoided imposing a hypothetical interpretation on the evidence, such as supplying words in the lines of the text for which there is no clue in the manuscript at all. The scribes who had access to Mannyng's own version (or intermediate copies) were far better qualified to record what they found in their exemplars, and even when they made mistakes or deliberate changes, they were preserving the only surviving evidence of the original work.

BIBLIOGRAPHY

The following abbreviations are used in this bibliography:

ALMA — *Arthurian Literature in the Middle Ages.* Roger Sherman Loomis, ed.

ANTS — Anglo-Norman Text Society. Oxford.

BBIAS — *Bibliographical Bulletin of the International Arthurian Society.*

EETS — Early English Text Society.

LALME — *A Linguistic Atlas of Late Mediaeval English.* Angus McIntosh, M. L. Samuels, and Michael Benskin, eds. 4 vols. 1986.

MRTS — Medieval & Renaissance Texts & Studies. Binghamton, New York.

N&Q — *Notes and Queries.*

NM — *Neuphilologische Mitteilungen.*

PMLA — *Publications of the Modern Language Association.*

RES — *Review of English Studies: A Quarterly Journal of English Literature and the English Language.*

RS — Rolls Series.

SATF — Société des Anciens Textes Français. Paris.

TPS — Transactions of the Philological Society. Oxford.

Ackerman, Gretchen P. "Sir Frederic Madden and Arthurian Scholarship." In *King Arthur Through the Ages*, ed. Valerie M. Lagorio and Mildred Leake Day, 2:27–38. New York: Garland Publishing, 1990.

Ackerman, Robert W. "The English Rimed and Prose Romances." In *ALMA*, 480–519.

——. "Sir Frederic Madden and Medieval Scholarship." *NM* 73 (1972): 1–14.

—— and Gretchen P. Ackerman. *Sir Frederic Madden.* New York: Garland Publishing, 1979.

Ambroise. *The Crusade of Richard Lionhart.* Ed. and trans. M. J. Hubert and J. L. La Monte. Columbia University Records of Civilization, vol. 34. New York, 1941.

The Anglo-Saxon Chronicle. Ed. and trans. G. N. Garmonsway. New York: E. P. Dutton, 1953.

Arnould, E. J. *Le Manuel des Péchés: Étude de littérature religieuse anglo-normande (xiiime siecle).* Paris: Libraire E. Droz, 1940.

The Arthurian Encyclopedia. Ed. Norris J. Lacy. New York: Peter Bedrick Books, 1986.

Arthurian Literature in the Middle Ages. Ed. Roger Sherman Loomis. Oxford: Clarendon Press, 1959.

Ashe, Geoffrey. " 'A Certain Very Ancient Book': Traces of an Arthurian Source in Geoffrey of Monmouth's *History.*" *Speculum* 56 (1981): 301–23.

Aspin, Isabel S. T., ed. *Anglo-Norman Political Songs.* ANTS, vol. 11. Oxford: Basil Blackwell, 1953.

Atwood, Elmer Bagby. "Robert Mannyng's Version of the Troy Story." *Texas Studies in English* 18 (1938): 5–14.

—— and Virgil K. Whitaker. *Excidium Troiae.* Cambridge, Mass.: Medieval Academy of America, 1944. Repr. Kraus, 1971.

Barnicle, Mary Elizabeth. *The Seege or Batayle of Troye: A Middle English Metrical Romance.* EETS o.s., vol. 172 (1927).

Barron, W. R. J. "Alliterative Romance and the French Tradition." In *Middle English Alliterative Poetry and Its Literary Background,* ed. David Lawton, 70–87. Cambridge: D. S. Brewer, 1982.

Bede. *The Ecclesiastical History of the English Nation.* Intro. by Dom David Knowles. New York: E. P. Dutton, 1954.

——. *Historia Ecclesiastica Gentis Anglorum.* Trans. Leo Sherley-Price. Baltimore: Penguin Classics, 1955.

——. *Bede's Ecclesiastical History of the English People.* Ed. and trans. Bertram Colgrave and R. A. B. Mynors. Oxford: Clarendon Press, 1969.

Bell, Alexander. "The Epilogue to Gaimar's 'Estoire des Engleis.' " *Modern Language Review* 25 (1930): 52–59.

——. "Maistre Geffrei Gaimar." *Medium Ævum* 7 (1938): 184–98.

——, ed. *L'Estoire des Engleis by Geffrei Gaimar.* ANTS, vols. 14–16. Oxford: Basil Blackwell, 1960.

Bennett, J. A. W. *Middle English Literature. The Oxford History of English Literature I, Part 2.* Oxford: Clarendon Press, 1986.

Benskin, Michael and Margaret Laing. "Translations and *Mischsprachen* in Middle English Manuascripts." In *So Meny People, Longages and Tonges: Philological Essays in Scots and Medieval English Presented to Angus*

McIntosh, ed. Michael Benskin and M. L. Samuels, 55–106. Edinburgh: Authors, 1981.

Benzie, William. *Dr. F. J. Furnivall: Victorian Scholar Adventurer.* Norman, Okla.: Pilgrim Books, Inc., 1983.

Bill, E. G. W. *A Catalogue of Manuscripts in Lambeth Palace Library. MSS. 1222–2860.* Oxford: Clarendon Press, 1972.

Boerner, Oskar. *Die Sprache Roberd Mannyngs of Brunne und ihr Verhältnis zur Neuenglischen Mundart.* Halle, 1904.

Boffey, Julia and John J. Thompson. "Anthologies and Miscellanies: Production and Choice of Texts." In *Book Production and Publishing in Britain, 1375–1475,* ed. Jeremy Griffiths and Derek Pearsall, 279–315. Cambridge: Cambridge Univ. Press, 1989.

Brereton, Georgine E., ed. *Des Grantz Geanz: An Anglo-Norman Poem.* Oxford: Basil Blackwell, 1937.

Brewer, D. S. and A. E. B. Owen, Introduction. *The Thornton Manuscript: Lincoln Cathedral Library MS 91.* London: Scolar Press, 1975; 2nd ed. rev., 1978.

Brie, Friedrich W. D. *Geschichte und Quellen der mittelenglischen Prosachronik: "The Brute of England" oder "The Chronicles of England."* Marburg: N. G. Elwert, 1905.

——, ed. *The Brut or The Chronicles of England.* Part 1. EETS o.s., vol. 131 (1906); Part 2, EETS o.s., vol. 136 (1908). Reprint, Kraus, 1960, 1971.

Brook, G. L. and R. F. Leslie. *Laȝamon: Brut.* Vol. 1, EETS o.s., vol. 250 (1963) [Text lines 1-8020]; vol. 2, EETS o.s., vol. 277 (1978) [Text lines 8021–16079].

Brunner, Karl. *Der Mittelenglische Versroman über Richard Löwenherz.* Wiener Beiträge, vol. 42. Vienna: Wilhelm Braümuller, 1913.

Burrow, J. A. "Poems Without Contexts." *Essays in Criticism* 29 (1978): 6–32.

——. "Old and Middle English." In *The Oxford Illustrated History of English Literature,* ed. Pat Rogers, 1–58. Oxford: Oxford University Press, 1987.

Caldwell, Robert A. "The 'History of the Kings of Britain' in College of Arms MS. Arundel XXII." *PMLA* 69 (1954): 643–54.

——. "Wace's *Roman de Brut* and the Variant Version of Geoffrey of Monmouth's *Historia Regum Britanniae.*" *Speculum* 31 (1956): 675–82.

Chadwick, Nora K. *Studies in the Early British Church.* Cambridge, 1958. Repr. Hamden, Conn.: Archon Books, 1973.

Cowper, J. Meadows, ed. *Meditations on the Supper of our Lord, and the Hours of the Passion, by Cardinal John Bonaventura the Seraphic Doctor. Drawn into English Verse by Robert Manning of Brunne.* EETS o.s., vol. 60 (1875).

Crick, Julia C. *The "Historia Regum Britannie" of Geoffrey of Monmouth 3: A Summary Catalog of the Manuscripts.* Woodbridge: D. S. Brewer, 1988.

——. *The "Historia Regum Britannie" of Geoffrey of Monmouth 4: Dissemination and Reception in the Later Middle Ages.* Woodbridge: D. S. Brewer, 1990.

Crosby, Ruth. "Robert Mannyng of Brunne: A New Biography." *PMLA* 57 (1942): 15–28.

Davies, J. Conway. *Catalogue of Manuscripts in the Library of the Honourable Society of the Inner Temple.* Vol. I. (The Petyt Collection: MSS 502–533.) Oxford: Oxford University Press, 1972.

D'Evelyn, Charlotte, ed. *Peter Idley's Instructions to His Son.* Modern Language Association of America, Monograph Series 6, 1935.

—— and Anna J. Mill. *The South English Legendary.* Vol. 3 (Introduction by D'Evelyn). EETS o.s., vol. 244 (1959). Repr. Kraus, 1969.

Douglas, David C. *English Scholars, 1660–1730.* 2nd ed., rev. London: Eyre and Spottiswoode, 1951.

Doyle, A. I. and M. B. Parkes. "The Production of Copies of the *Canterbury Tales* and the *Confessio Amantis* in the Early Fifteenth Century." In *Medieval Scribes, Manuscripts and Libraries: Essays Presented to N. R. Ker*, ed. M. B. Parkes and Andrew G. Watson, 163–210. London: Scolar Press, 1978.

Dumville, David N., ed. *The "Historia Brittonum" 3: The "Vatican Recension."* Cambridge: D. S. Brewer, 1985.

—— and Michael Lapidge, eds. *Gildas: New Approaches. Studies in Celtic History 5.* Woodbridge: The Boydell Press, 1984.

Edwards, A. S. G., ed. *Middle English Prose: A Critical Guide to Major Authors and Genres.* New Brunswick: Rutgers Univ. Press, 1984.

—— and Derek Pearsall. "The Manuscripts of the Major English Poetic Texts." In *Book Production and Publishing in Britain, 1375–1475,* ed. Jeremy Griffiths and Derek Pearsall, 257–78. Cambridge: Cambridge Univ. Press, 1989.

Ehrhart, Margaret J. *The Judgment of the Trojan Prince Paris in Medieval Literature.* Philadelphia: Univ. of Pennsylvania Press, 1987.

Ellis, Roger, ed. *The Medieval Translator: The Theory and Practice of Translation in the Middle Ages.* Cambridge: D. S. Brewer, 1989.

Emden, Alfred B. *A Biographical Register of the University of Cambridge to 1500,* 99–100, 388. Cambridge: Cambridge Univ. Press, 1963.

Field, Rosalind. "The Anglo-Norman Background to Alliterative Romance." In *Middle English Alliterative Poetry and its Literary Background.* ed. David Lawton, 54–69, 136–40. Woodbridge: D. S. Brewer, 1982.

Finlayson, John. Review of *Morte Arthure: A Critical Edition,* ed. Mary Hamel. *Speculum* 63 (1988): 936–39.

Fletcher, Robert H. *The Arthurian Material in the Chronicles.* Harvard Studies and Notes in Philology and Literature, vol. 10. Cambridge, Mass.: Harvard Univ. Press, 1906; Reprint, New York: Burt Franklin, 1958.

Foulon, Charles. "Wace," In *ALMA,* 94–103.

Francis, W. Nelson, ed. *The Book of Vices and Virtues.* EETS o.s., vol. 217 (1942).

Frappier, Jean. "The Vulgate Cycle," In *ALMA,* 295–318.

Frazer, R. M. Jr., trans. *The Trojan War: The Chronicles of Dictys of Crete and Dares the Phrygian.* Bloomington: Indiana Univ. Press, 1966.

Furnivall, Frederick J. *The Story of England by Robert Manning of Brunne, AD 1338. Edited from MSS. at Lambeth Palace and the Inner Temple.* 2 vols. RS, vol. 87. London: Longman, 1887.

——. *Robert of Brunne's "Handlyng Synne," AD 1303.* 2 vols. EETS o.s., vols. 119, 123. London: Kegan Paul, 1901, 1903. [Orig. pub. Roxburghe Club, London, 1862.]

Gburek, Hubert. *Der Wortschatz des Robert Mannyng of Brunne in "Handlyng Synne."* [Diss. Friedrich-Alexander-Universität, 1977.] Bamberg: M. Schadel, 1977.

Gildas: De Excidio Britanniae. Ed. and trans. Michael Winterbottom. In *The Ruin of Britain.* History from the Sources, 7. Chichester: Phillimore, 1978.

Gillespie, Vincent. "Vernacular Books of Religion." In *Book Production and Publishing in Britain, 1375–1475,* ed. Jeremy Griffiths and Derek Pearsall, 317–44. Cambridge: Cambridge Univ. Press, 1989.

——. "Cura Pastoralis in Deserto." In *De Cella in Seculum,* ed. Michael G. Sargent, 161–81. Woodbridge: D. S. Brewer, 1989.

Gillingham, John. "The Unromantic Death of Richard I." *Speculum* 54 (1979): 18–41.

Gransden, Antonia. *Historical Writing in England, c.550 to c.1307.* Vol. 1. Ithaca: Cornell Univ. Press, 1974.

Griffin, Nathaniel E. *Dares and Dictys: An Introduction to the Study of the Medieval Versions of the Story of Troy.* Baltimore, 1907.

Halliwell-Phillips, James Orchard. *A Dictionary of Archaic and Provincial Words, Obsolete Phrases, Proverbs and Ancient Customs from the Fourteenth Century.* London, 1889. [Orig. pub. John Russell Smith, 1847, 1850.] Repr. London: Bracken Books, 1989.

Hamel, Mary, ed. *Morte Arthure: A Critical Edition.* Garland Medieval Texts No. 9. New York: Garland Publishing, 1984.

Hanna, Ralph III. Review of *King Horn: An Edition Based on Cambridge*

University Library MS Gg.4.27 (2) with an Analysis of the Textual Transmission, ed. Rosamund Allen. Garland Medieval Texts No. 7 (1984). *Speculum* 60 (1985): 936–39.

Hanning, Robert W. *The Vision of History in Early Britain: From Gildas to Geoffrey of Monmouth.* New York: Columbia Univ. Press, 1966.

Hearne, Thomas, ed. *Peter Langtoft's Chronicle (as Illustrated and Improv'd by Robert of Brunne) from the Death of Cadwalader to the End of K. Edward the First's Reign.* 2 vols. Oxford: Printed at the Theater, 1725. Reprint in Hearne's *Works,* vols. 3 and 4. London: Samuel Bagster, 1810.

Hector, L. C. *The Handwriting of English Documents.* London: Edward Arnold Publishers, 1958.

Hornstein, Lillian H. "King Robert of Sicily: A New Manuscript." *PMLA* 78 (1963): 453–58.

——. "Romances on Historical Themes." In *A Manual of the Writings in Middle English, 1050–1500,* vol. 1, ed. J. Burke Severs, 158-61. New Haven: Archon Books, 1967.

Horrall, Sarah M., ed. *The Southern Version of "Cursor Mundi," Vol. I.* Ottawa: Univ. of Ottawa Press, 1978.

——. "'For the commun at understand': 'Cursor Mundi' and its Background." In *De Cella in Seculum: Religious and Secular Life and Devotion in Late Medieval England,* ed. Michael G. Sargent, 97–107. Cambridge: D. S. Brewer, 1989.

——. "Middle English Texts in a Carthusian Commonplace Book: Westminster Cathedral Diocesan Archives MS. H.38." *Medium Ævum* 59 (1990): 214–27.

Horstmann, Carl, ed. *Altenglische Legenden.* Neue Folge. Heilbronn, 1881. 339–40. [Ashmole MS 61].

——. "Septem miracula de corpore cristi." In *The Minor Poems of the Vernon Manuscript.* EETS o.s., vol. 98 (1892). 198–221.

Houck, Margaret. *Sources of the "Roman de Brut" of Wace.* 161–356. University of California Publications in English V, no. 2. Berkeley: Univ. of California Press, 1941.

Hudson, Anne. "Robert of Gloucester and the Antiquaries, 1550–1800." *N&Q* n.s. 16, 214 (1969): 322–33.

——. "Middle English." In *Editing Medieval Texts: English, French, and Latin Written in England,* ed. A. G. Rigg, 34–57. New York: Garland, 1977.

Jayne, Sears and Francis R. Johnson, eds. *The Lumley Library: The Catalog of 1609.* London: The Trustees of the British Museum, 1956.

James, M. R. *A Descriptive Catalog of the Manuscripts in the Library of Lambeth Palace.* Cambridge: Cambridge Univ. Press, 1930.

Johnson, Charles and Hilary Jenkinson. *English Court Hand, AD 1066 to 1500.* 2 vols. Oxford, 1915. Repr. Frederick Ungar, 1967.

Johnson, Lesley. "Robert Mannyng's History of Arthurian Literature." In *Church and Chronicle in the Middle Ages: Essays Presented to John Taylor,* ed. Ian Wood and G. A. Loud, 129–47. London: The Hambledon Press, 1991.

Kane, George, ed. *Piers Plowman: The A Version.* London: Athlone Press, 1960.

Kennedy, Edward D. "Chronicles and Other Historical Writing." In *A Manual of the Writings in Middle English, 1050–1500,* vol. 8, Albert E. Hartung, gen. ed., 2625–28, 2811–18. New Haven: Archon Books, 1989.

Ker, N. R. *Medieval Manuscripts in British Libraries.* Vol. 1. Oxford: Clarendon Press, 1969.

Knowles, Dom David and R. Neville Hadcock. *Medieval Religious Houses: England and Wales.* London: Longmans Green, 1953; 2nd ed. 1971. 149, 194–99, 203.

Kölbing, Eugen, ed. "Ein Fragment von Robert Manning's Chronik." *Englische Studien* 17 (1892): 166–171. [Rawl. Misc. MS D. 913, olim. 1262, 1370. MS R, Chronicle, Part I, lines 12550–12699.]

Laing, Margaret. "Dialectal Analysis and Linguistically Composite Texts in Middle English." *Speculum* 63 (1988): 83–103.

Leckie, R. William, Jr. *The Passage of Dominion: Geoffrey of Monmouth and the Periodization of Insular History in the Twelfth Century.* Toronto: Univ. of Toronto Press, 1981.

Legge, M. Dominica. "A List of Langtoft Manuscripts With Notes on MS. Laud Misc. 637." *Medium Ævum* 4 (1935): 20–24.

——. *Anglo-Norman in the Cloisters.* Edinburgh Publications in Language and Literature, vol. 2. Edinburgh, 1950.

——. *Anglo-Norman Literature and Its Background.* Oxford, 1963.

Light, David Anthony. "The Arthurian Portion of The Roman de Brut of Wace." Ph.D. diss., New York University, 1970.

Loomis, Roger Sherman. "Edward I, Arthurian Enthusiast." *Speculum* 28 (1953): 114–27.

——, ed. *Arthurian Literature in the Middle Ages.* Oxford: Clarendon Press, 1959.

——. "Layamon's Brut," In *ALMA*, 104–11.

Loyn, H. R., ed. *The Middle Ages: A Concise Encyclopaedia.* London: Thames & Hudson, 1989.

Machan, Tim William, ed. *Medieval Literature: Texts and Interpretation.* Medieval & Renaissance Texts & Studies, vol. 79. Binghamton: MRTS, 1991.

McIntosh, Angus. "The Analysis of Written Middle English." *TPS* (1956): 26–55.

——. "The Textual Transmission of the Alliterative *Morte Arthure.*" In *English and Medieval Studies Presented to J. R. R. Tolkien*, ed. Norman Davis and C. L. Wrenn, 231–40. London: George Allen & Unwin, 1962.

——. "A New Approach to Middle English Dialectology." *English Studies* 44 (1963): 1–11.

——. "Some Words in the 'Northern Homily Collection.' " *NM* 73 (1972): 196–206.

——. "Towards an Inventory of Middle English Scribes." *NM* 75 (1974): 602–24.

——. "The Language of the Extant Versions of 'Havelok the Dane.' " *Medium Ævum* 45 (1976): 36–49.

McIntosh, Angus, M. L. Samuels, and Michael Benskin. *A Linguistic Atlas of Late Mediaeval English.* 4 vols. Aberdeen: Aberdeen University Press, 1986.

Madden, Frederic. *The Ancient English Romance of Havelok the Dane, Accompanied by the French Text.* Roxburghe Club. London: W. Nichol, Shakespeare Press, 1828.

——. *Syr Gawayne.* London: Bannatyne Club, 1839.

——. *Laȝamons Brut, or Chronicle of Britain: A Poetical Semi-Saxon Paraphrase of the Brut of Wace.* 3 vols. Society of Antiquaries of London, 1847.

——. "Prose Chronicles of England Called the Brute." *N&Q* 1 (2nd series, January 5, 1856): 1–4.

——. "Notes on Early English MSS." British Library, Egerton MS 2257. [Unpublished.]

Matheson, Lister M. "Historical Prose." In *Middle English Prose: A Critical Guide to Major Authors and Genres*, ed. A. S. G. Edwards, 209–49. New Brunswick: Rutgers Univ. Press, 1984.

——. "Printer and Scribe: Caxton, the 'Polychronicon,' and the 'Brut.' " *Speculum* 60 (1985): 593–614.

——. Review of *The "Historia Brittonum," 3: The Vatican Recension*, ed. David N. Dumville (1985); and *Geoffrey of Monmouth, 1: Bern, Burgerbibliothek, MS. 568*, ed. Neil Wright (1984). *Speculum* 63 (1988): 147–49.

——. "King Arthur and the Medieval English Chronicles." In *King Arthur Through the Ages*, 2 vols., ed. Valerie M. Lagorio and Mildred Leake Day, 1:248–74. New York: Garland Publishing, Inc., 1990.

Matthews, William. *The Tragedy of Arthur: A Study of the Alliterative "Morte Arthure."* Berkeley: Univ. of California Press, 1960.

Mehl, Dieter. *The Middle English Romances of the Thirteenth and Fourteenth Centuries.* New York: Barnes and Noble, 1969.

Merrilees, Brian. "Anglo-Norman." In *Editing Medieval Texts: English,*

French, and Latin Written in England, ed. A. G. Rigg, 88–106. New York: Garland, 1977.

Middle English Dictionary: Plan and Bibliography. Ed. Hans Kurath and Sherman M. Kuhn. Ann Arbor: Univ. of Michigan Press, 1956.

Middleton, Anne. "The Audience and Public of 'Piers Plowman.' " In *Middle English Alliterative Poetry and its Literary Background*, ed. David Lawton, 101–23, 147–54. Cambridge: Boydell and Brewer, 1982.

Mills, M[aldwyn], ed. *Lybeaus Desconus.* EETS o.s., vol. 261. London: Oxford Univ. Press, 1969.

Moore, Samuel, Sanford B. Meech, Harold Whitehall. *Middle English Dialect Characteristics and Dialect Boundaries. Essays and Studies in English and Comparative Literature.* University of Michigan Publications in Language and Literature, vol. 13. Ann Arbor, 1935. 1–60.

Moore, Samuel. [Revised by Albert H. Marckwardt] *Historical Outlines of English Sounds and Inflections.* Ann Arbor: George Wahr Publishing Co., 1951.

Morris, John, ed. and trans. *Nennius: British History and the Welsh Annals.* History from the Sources, vol. 8. London: Rowan & Littlefield, 1980.

Morris, Richard, ed. *Cursor Mundi.* EETS o.s., vols. 57, 59, 62, 66, 68, 99, and 101 [by H. Hupe] (1874–1893). Repr. 1961–66.

Murray, James A. H. *The Romance and Prophecies of Thomas of Erceldoune.* EETS o.s. 61 (1875); Repr. Kraus 1987.

Naish, George Howard. "*Handlyng Synne* and Medytacyuns." Ph.D. diss., University of London, 1936.

Newstead, Helene. "The Romances Listed According to Probable Chronology and Dialect of Original Composition." In *A Manual of the Writings in Middle English, 1050–1500*, vol. 1, ed. J. Burke Severs, 13–16. New Haven: Archon Books, 1967.

Nichols, Stephen G. "Introduction: The New Philology." *Speculum* 65 (1990): 7–8.

O'Loughlin, J. L. N. "The English Alliterative Romances." In *ALMA*, 520–27.

The Oxford English Dictionary: Compact Edition. 2 vols. Oxford: Oxford Univ. Press, 1971.

Parkes, M. B. *English Cursive Book Hands, 1250–1500.* Oxford: Clarendon Press, 1969. Repr. Berkeley: University of California Press, 1980.

——. *Pause and Effect: An Introduction to the History of Punctuation in the West.* Berkeley: Univ. of California Press, 1993.

—— and Andrew G. Watson, eds. *Medieval Scribes, Manuscripts, and Libraries: Essays Presented to N. R. Ker.* London: Scolar Press, 1978.

Parry, John Jay and Robert A. Caldwell. "Geoffrey of Monmouth." In *ALMA*, 72–93.

Partner, Nancy F. *Serious Entertainments: The Writing of History in Twelfth-Century England.* Chicago: Univ. of Chicago Press, 1977.

——. "Making Up Lost Time: Writing on the Writing of History." *Speculum* 61 (1986): 90–117.

Paton, Lucy Allen. "Les Prophécies de Merlin." New York: Modern Language Association, 1926. 1: 3–50.

Pearsall, Derek. "The Development of Middle English Romance." *Mediaeval Studies* 27 (1965): 91–116.

——. "Texts, Textual Criticism, and Fifteenth Century Manuscript Production." In *Fifteenth Century Studies: Recent Essays*, ed. Robert F. Yeager, 121–36. Hamden, Conn.: Archon Books, 1984.

—— and I. C. Cunningham, Intro. *The Auchinleck Manuscript: National Library of Scotland Advocates MS. 19.2.1.* London: Scolar Press, 1977.

Pelan, Margaret. *L'Influence du "Brut" de Wace sur les romanciers de son temps.* Paris, 1931.

Pickford, Cedric E. "Miscellaneous French Prose Romances." In *ALMA*, 348–57.

Piggott, Stuart. "The Sources of Geoffrey of Monmouth." *Antiquity* 15 (1941): 269–86.

——. *Ancient Britons and the Antiquarian Imagination: Ideas From The Renaissance to the Regency.* New York: Thames & Hudson, 1989.

Preston, Jean F. and Laetitia Yeandle. *English Handwriting, 1400–1650.* Pegasus Paperbooks. Binghamton: MRTS, 1992.

Prestwich, Michael. *Edward I.* Berkeley: Univ. of California Press, 1988.

Preussner, Oskar. *Robert Mannyng of Brunne's übersetzung von Pierre de Langtoft's Chronicle und ihr verhältniss zum originale.* Diss., Breslau, 1891.

——. "Zur Textkritik von Robert Mannyng's Chronik." *Englische Studien* 17 (1892): 300–314.

Putnam, Edward K. "The Lambeth Version of 'Havelok.'" *PMLA* 15 (1900): 1–19.

Raymo, Robert R. "Works of Religious and Philosophical Instruction." In *A Manual of the Writings in Middle English, 1050–1500*, vol. 7, Albert E. Hartung, gen. ed. 2255–78; 2467–582. New Haven: Archon Books, 1986.

Robbins, Rossell Hope, ed. *Historical Poems of the Fourteenth and Fifteenth Centuries.* New York: Columbia Univ. Press, 1959.

——. "Political Prophecies"; "The Merlin Prophecies"; "The John of Bridlington Prophecies"; "The Thomas of Erceldoune Prophecies"; "Tags in Langtoft and Mannyng." In *A Manual of the Writings in Middle English, 1050–1500*, vol. 5, Albert E. Hartung, gen. ed. 1516–27; 1400–1403. New Haven: Archon Books, 1975.

Roberts, Brynley F. and Daniel Huws. "Another Manuscript of the Variant Version of the 'Historia Regum Britanniae,'" *BBIAS* 25 (1973): 147–52.

Rothwell, Harry, ed. *The Chronicle of Walter of Guisborough, previously edited as the chronicle of Walter of Hemingford or Hemingburgh.* Camden Society, 3d series, vol. 89. London: Offices of the Society, 1957.

——, ed. *English Historical Documents, 1189–1327.* Vol. 3. David C. Douglas, gen. ed. Oxford: Oxford Univ. Press, 1975.

Scott, Ronald McNair. *Robert the Bruce: King of Scots.* New York: Peter Bedrick Books, 1989.

Seaton, Ethel. "Robert Mannyng of Brunne in Lincoln." *Medium Ævum* 12 (1943): 77.

Severs, J. Burke. "Romances." In *A Manual of the Writings in Middle English,* 1050–1500, vol. 1, Albert E. Hartung, gen. ed. New Haven: Archon Books, 1967.

Shepherd, Stephen H. A. "The Ashmole *Sir Ferumbras:* Translation in Holograph." [Ashmole MS 33.] In *The Medieval Translator: The Theory and Practice of Translation in the Middle Ages,* ed. Roger Ellis, 103–21. Cambridge: D. S. Brewer, 1989.

Shonk, Timothy A. "A Study of the Auchinleck Manuscript: Bookmen and Bookmaking in the Early Fourteenth Century." *Speculum* 60 (1985): 71–91.

Skeat, Walter W. *The Lay of Havelok the Dane.* EETS e.s. 4 (1868). Repr. Kraus, 1981. [Rev. Kenneth Sisam, 1915.]

Smallwood, Thomas M. "An unpublished early account of Bruce's murder of Comyn." *The Scottish Historical Review* 54 (April 1975): 1–10.

——. "The Text of Langtoft's Chronicle." *Medium Ævum* 46 (1977): 219–30.

——. "The Prophecy of the Six Kings." *Speculum* 60 (1985): 571–92.

——. "Another Example of the Double-Copying of a Passage of Middle English." *NM* 87 (1986): 550–54.

Smithers, G. V. *Havelok.* Oxford: Clarendon Press, 1987.

Stanley, E. G. "Rhymes in English Medieval Verse: From Old English to Middle English." In *Medieval English Studies Presented to George Kane,* ed. Edward D. Kennedy, et al., 19–54. Woodbridge: D. S. Brewer, 1988.

Stepsis, Robert P. "An Edition of Part II of Robert Mannyng of Brunne's Chronicle of England." 2 vols. Ph.D. diss., Harvard University, 1967.

——. "The Manuscripts of Robert Mannyng of Brunne's 'Chronicle of England.'" *Manuscripta* 13 (1969): 131–41.

——. "Pierre de Langtoft's Chronicle: An Essay in Medieval Historiography." *Medievalia et Humanistica* n.s. 3 (1972): 51–73.

Sullens, Idelle, ed. *Robert Mannyng of Brunne: "Handlyng Synne."* Medieval & Renaissance Texts & Studies, vol. 14. Binghamton: MRTS, 1983.

Sullivan, Matthew. "The Author of the *Manuel des Péchés.*" *N&Q* (June 1991): 155–57.

——. "Biographical Notes on Robert Mannyng of Brunne and Peter Idley, the Adaptor of Robert Mannyng's *Handlyng Synne.*" *N&Q* (n.s. 41, September 1994): 302–4.

Sullivan, Stephen A. "*Handlyng Synne* in its Tradition." Ph.D. diss., Gonville and Caius College, Cambridge, 1978.

Summerfield, Thea. "Context and Genesis of Pierre de Langtoft's *Chronicle.*" In *Literary Aspects of Courtly Culture,* ed. Donald Maddox and Sara Sturm-Maddox, 321–32. Cambridge: D. S. Brewer, 1994.

Tatlock, J. S. P. *The Legendary History of Britain.* Berkeley: Univ. of California Press, 1950.

Taylor, John. *English Historical Literature in the Fourteenth Century.* Oxford: Clarendon Press, 1987.

Thiolier, Jean Claude. *Édition Critique et Commentée de Pierre De Langtoft: Le Règne D'Édouard Ier.* CELIMA, Université de Paris XII, Creteil, 1989.

Thompson, Sally. *Women Religious: The Founding of English Nunneries After The Norman Conquest.* Oxford: Clarendon Press, 1991.

Thorpe, Lewis, intro. and trans. *Geoffrey of Monmouth: The History of the Kings of Britain.* Baltimore: Penguin Books, 1966; Repr. 1980.

——. "Orderic Vitalis and the 'Prophetiae Merlini' of Geoffrey of Monmouth." *BBIAS* 29 (1977): 191–208.

Thümmig, M. *Über die altenglische übersetzung der reimchronik Peter Langtoft's durch Robert Mannyng von Brunne.* Halle, 1891. Diss., Leipzig, 1889.

——. "Über die altenglische Übersetzung der Reimchronik Peter Langtoft's durch Robert Manning von Brunne." *Anglia* 14 (1892): 1–76.

Todd, Henry J. *A Catalogue of the Archiepiscopal Manuscripts in the Library at Lambeth Palace.* London, 1812.

Turville-Petre, Thorlac. "Politics and Poetry in the Early Fourteenth Century: The Case of Robert Manning's 'Chronicle.' " *RES,* n.s. 39 (1988): 1–28.

Victoria County History: A History of the County of Lincoln, Vol. 2. Ed. William Page. London, 1906. 179–95.

Wace. *Le Roman de Brut.* Ed. A. J. V. Le Roux de Lincy. 2 vols. Rouen, 1836, 1838.

——. *Le Roman de Brut de Wace.* Ed. Ivor Arnold. 2 vols. Paris: SATF, 1938, 1940.

Watson, Andrew G. *Catalog of Dated and Datable Manuscripts c. 700–1600 in the Department of Manuscripts, the British Library.* London, 1979.

Weber, Henry, ed. "Richard Coer de Lion." In *Metrical Romances of the Thirteenth, Fourteenth, and Fifteenth Centuries,* vol. 2. Edinburgh: Archibald Constable, 1810.

Wilson, Richard M. *More Lost Literature in Old and Middle English.* Leeds Studies in English, vol. 5, 1936.

——. *The Lost Literature of Medieval England.* 2nd ed. rev. London: Methuen, 1970.

Wright, Cyril E. *English Vernacular Hands From the Twelfth to the Fifteenth Centuries.* Oxford: Clarendon Press, 1960.

Wright, Neil, ed. *The "Historia Regum Britannie" of Geoffrey of Monmouth, 1: A Single-manuscript Edition from Bern, Burgerbibliothek MS. 568.* Cambridge: D. S. Brewer, 1984.

——. ed. *The "Historia Regum Britannie" of Geoffrey of Monmouth, 2: The First Variant Version, a Critical Edition.* Woodbridge: D. S. Brewer, 1988.

Wright, Thomas, ed. *The Political Songs of England from the Reign of John to that of Edward II.* London: Camden Society vol. 6, 1839.

——. *The Chronicle of Pierre de Langtoft.* London: Her Majesty's Stationery Office, 1866. 2 vols. RS, vol. 47. Repr. Kraus 1964.

Wright, William Aldis. *The Metrical Chronicle of Robert of Gloucester.* London: Her Majesty's Stationery Office, 1887. RS, vol. 86. 2 vols. Repr. Kraus 1965.

Zetsche, Aemilius W. *Über den ersten Teil der Bearbeitung des 'Roman de Brut' des Wace durch Robert Mannyng of Brunne.* Diss., Leipzig, 1887.

——. "Chronik des Robert von Brunne, von Anfang bis zu Christi Geburt." *Anglia* 9 (1886): 43–195.

Zettl, Ewald, ed. *An Anonymous Short English Metrical Chronicle.* EETS o.s. 196 (1935).

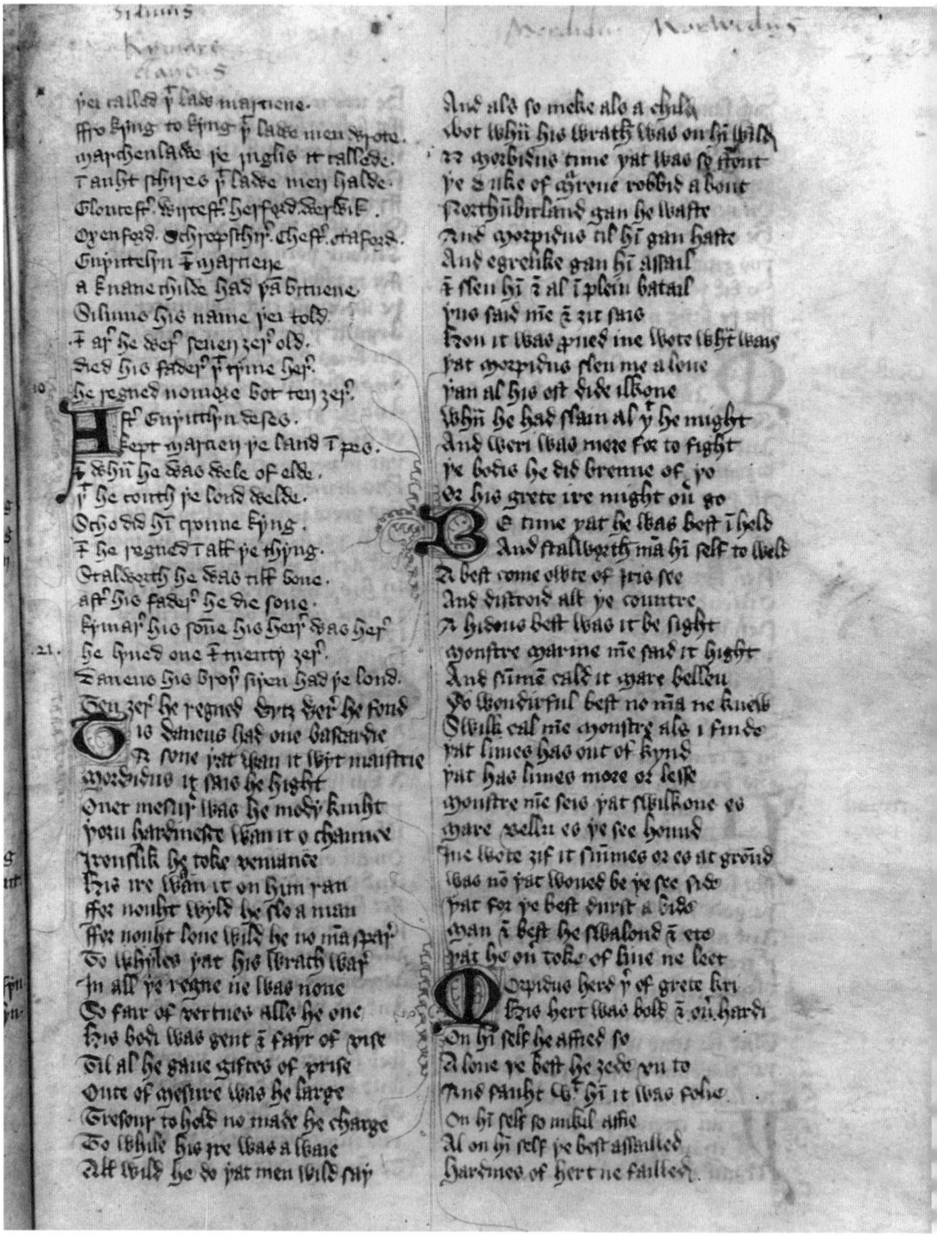
Sidimus

Kymare

claud. 5

Merlin Northedys

þei called þat lade martiene.
ffro king to king þat lawe men wrote.
Marchenlawe þe inglis it callede.
In aught shires þat lawe men halde.
Gloucestre. Wircestre. herford. Werwik.
Oxenford. Schropschire. Chestre. Stafford.
Guyntelyn and Martiene
A knawe childe had þai bitwene
Sisilius his name þei told.
And ar he were seuen zere old.
Died his fader þat tyme her.
10 He regned noumore bot ten zere.

After Guyntelyn dedes.
Kept Marcien þe land in pes.
And whan he was wele of elde.
þat he couth þe lond welde.
Scho did him crowne king.
And he regned in alle þe thing.
Stalworth he was and wise bone.
After his fader he die sone.
Kimar his sone his heir was her
21. He lyued one and twenty zer.
Danius his broþer siþen had þe lond.
Ten zere he regned with wer he fond

This Danius had one bastardie
A sone þat wan it wiþ maistrie
Morvidus it sais he hight
Ouer mesure was he mody knight
þoru hardinesse wan it o chaunce
Irenslik he toke vengaunce
His ire wan it on him þan
ffor nouht wylde he slo a man
ffor nouht lone wild he no man spare
So whiles þat his wrath ware
In all þe regne ne was none
So fair of vertues alle he one
His bodi was gent and fayr of prise
Til al he gaue giftes of prise
Oute of mesure was he large
Tresour to hold no made he charge
So while his ire was a waie
Alle wild he do þat men wild saie

And als so meke als a child
Bot whan his wrath was on him wild
In Morvidus time þat was so stout
þe duke of Moreyne robbid about
Northumbirland gan he waste
And Morpidus til him gan haste
And egrelike gan him assail
And slen him and al in plein batail
þus said men and zit sais
Bot it was ended ine wote wht wais
þat Morpidus slen me a lone
þan al his ost dide ilkone
Whan he had slain al þat he might
And weri was mere for to fight
þe bodis he did brenne of þo
For his grete ire might nou go

Be time þat he was best in held
And stalworth man him self to weld
A best come oute of þis see
And distroid all þe countre
A hidous best was it be sight
Monstre Marine men said it hight
And summe calde it Mare bellen
So wonderful best ne man ne knew
Swilk cal men monstre als i finde
þat limes has out of kynd
þat has limes more or lesse
Monstre men seis þat swilkone es
Mare bellu es þe see hound
Ine wote zif it summes or es at ground
Was non þat wones be þe see side
þat for þe best durst abide
Man and best he swalond and ete
þat he ou toke of line ne leet

Morpidus herd þat of grete kin
His hert was bold and ou hardi
On him self he affied so
Alone þe best he zede vn to
And faught wiþ him it was folie
On him self so mikil affie
Al on him self þe best assailled
Hardines of hert ne failled.

Petyt MS 511, Vol. 7, f. 23r. By kind permission of
the Masters of the Bench of the Inner Temple.

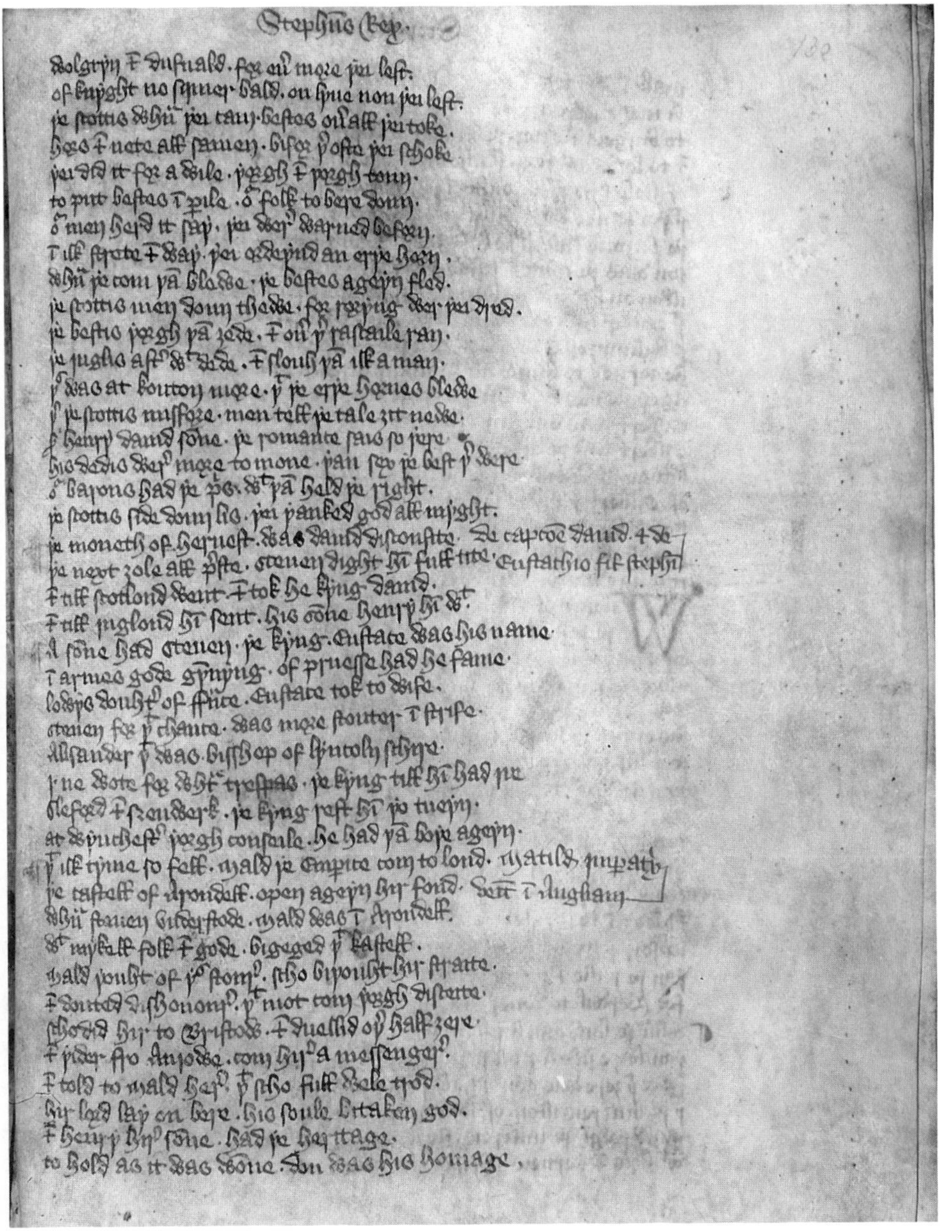
Stephanus Rex.

Wolgrym & Dufnald. for an more þei left.
of knyght no squier bald. on lyue non þei left.
þe Scottis whan þei can bestes on alle þei toke.
hors & nete alle samen. bifor þe oste þei schoke
þei did it for a wile. þorgh & þorgh toun.
to putt bestes in pile. our folk to bere doun.
our men herd it say. þei were warned beforn.
Tille strete & way. þei assemblid an erþe horn.
whan þe com þat blast. þe bestes agayn fled.
þe Scottis men doun thast. for ferdyng wer þei dred.
þe bestis þorgh þam zede. & on þe rascaile ran.
þe Inglis after with drede. & slouh þat ilk a man.
þat was at Coutton more. þat þe erþe hornes blewe
þat þe Scottis misfore. men telle þe tale ȝit newe.
Sir Henry Dauid sone. þe romance sais so here
his dedis were more to mone. þan sho þe best þat were
our barons had þe pris. with þat held þe right.
þe Scottis side doun lis. þei þanked god alle might.
þe moneth of heruest. was Dauid disconfite. De captione Dauid & de
þe next ȝole alle prest. Steuen dight him fulle tite. Eustathio fil Stephi
& tille Scotlond went. & tok he kyng Dauid.
& tille Inglond him sent. his sone Henry him with.
A sone had Steuen þe kyng. Eustace was his name
In armes gode gynnyng. of prouesse had he fame.
lowys douhter of France. Eustace tok to wife.
Steuen for þat chance. was more stouter in strife.
Alisander þat was bisshop of Lincoln schire.
in ne wote for what trespas. þe kyng tille him had ire
Slefford & Newerk. þe kyng reft him þo tueyn.
at Wynchester þorgh counsaile. he had þat bere agayn.
þat ilk tyme so felle. Maud þe Empres com to lond. Matildis imperatrix
þe castelle of Arondelle. open agayn hir fond. venit in Angliam
whan Steuen vnderstode. Maud was in Arondelle.
with mykelle folk & gode. bisegesd þat castelle.
Maud souht of þis stoure. scho bisouht him strayte.
& wited dishonoure. þat not com þorgh disceite.
Schoued hir to Bristowe. & dualled o half zere
& þider fro Aniowe. com hir a messengere.
& told to Maud her. þat scho full wele trod.
hir lord lay on bere. his soule bitaken god.
& Henry hir sone. had þe heritage.
to hold as it was wone. Son was his homage.

Petyt MS 511, Vol. 7, f. 130r. By kind permission of the Masters of the Bench of the Inner Temple.

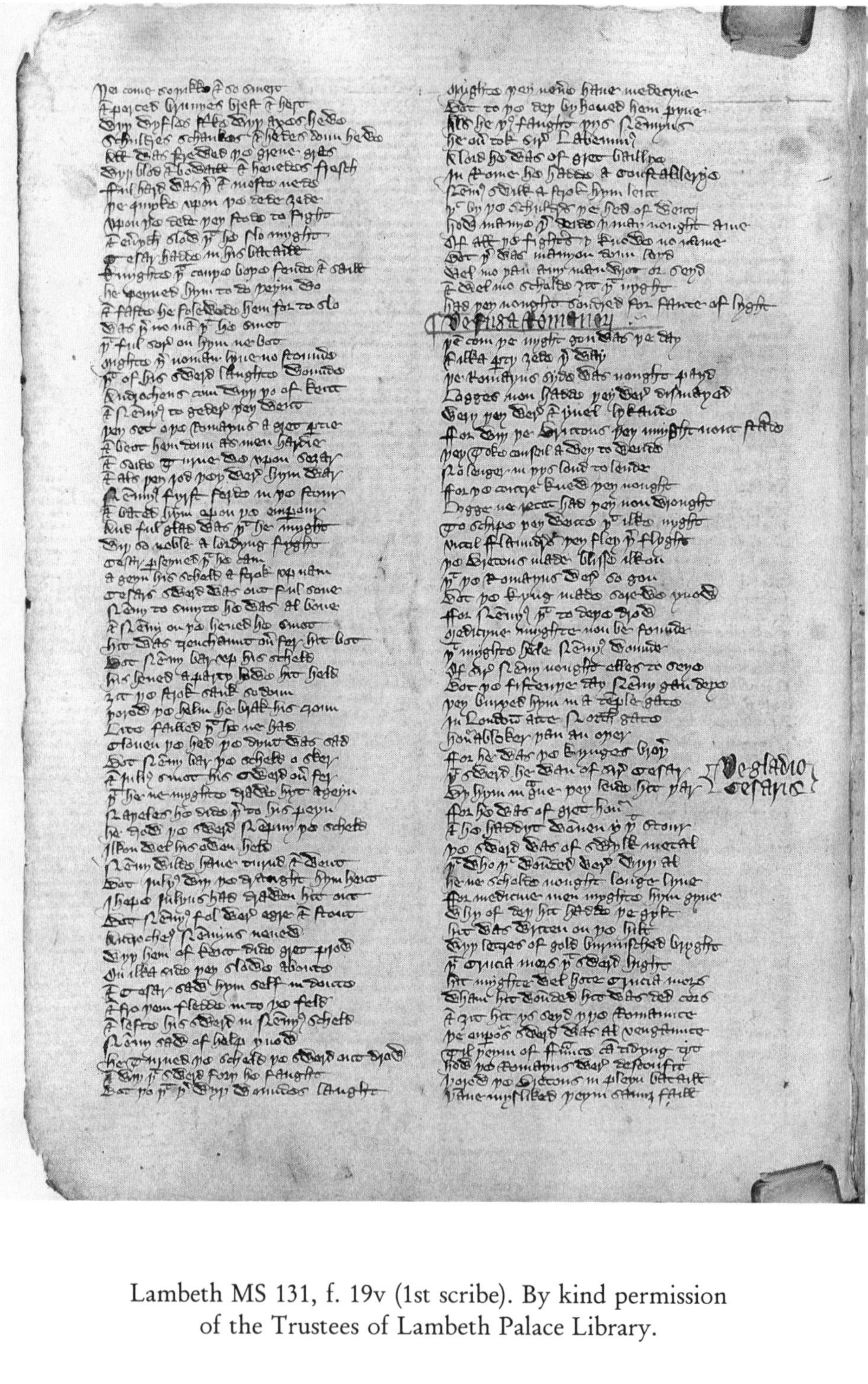

Lambeth MS 131, f. 19v (1st scribe). By kind permission of the Trustees of Lambeth Palace Library.

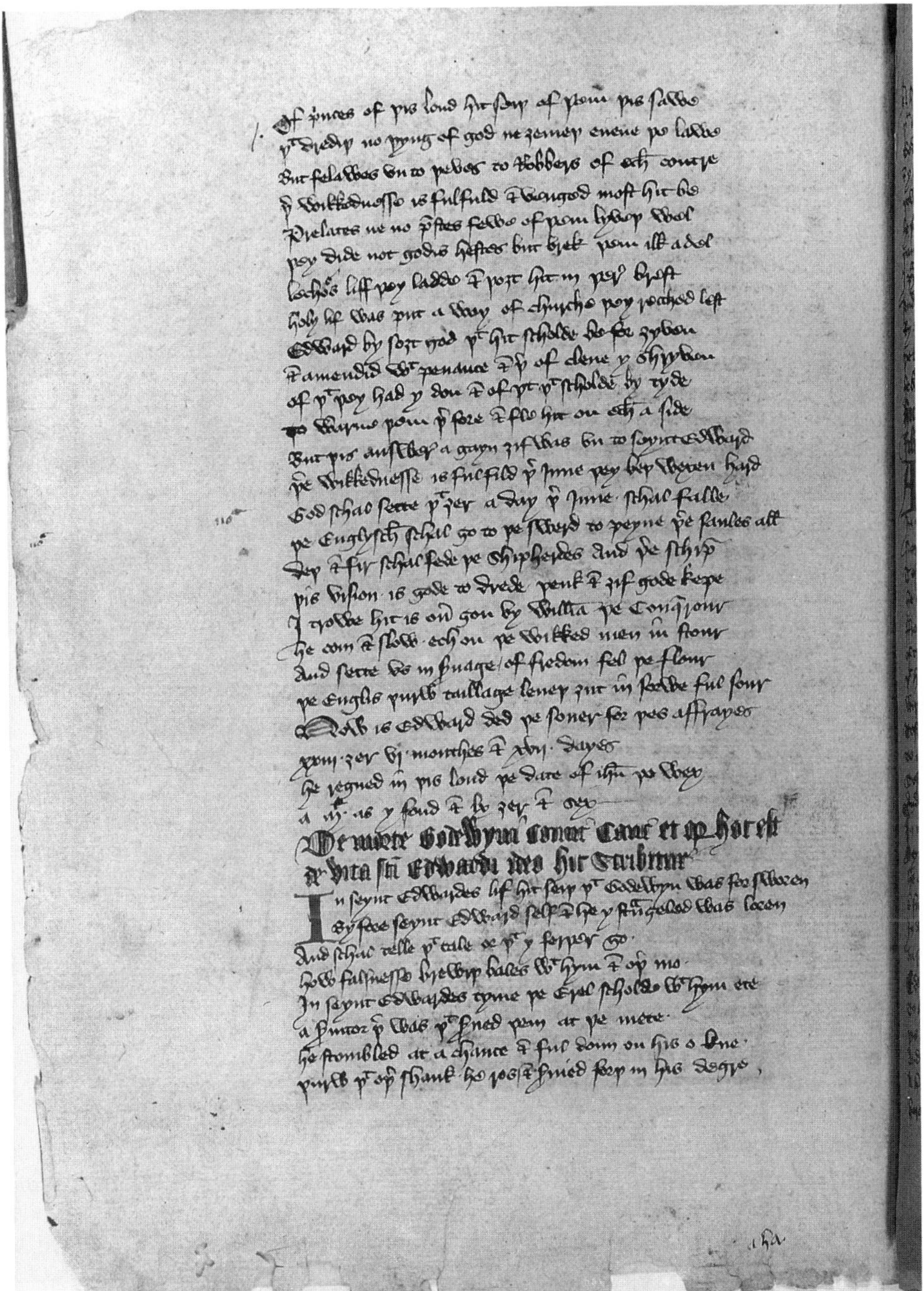

Of princes of þis lond hit sayþ of þem þis sawe
þat dredeþ no þyng of god ne ȝemeþ euene þe lawe
But felawes ben to þeves to robbers of ech contre
þe wikkednesse is fulfild & wrongod most hit be
Prelates ne no prestes kepe of þem lyveþ wel
þey dide not godis hestes but kept þem ill a del
lechours liff þey ladde & þoȝt hit in þer brest
holy lif was put a way of churche þey rechid lest
Edward by forþ ȝed þat hit scholde be for ȝyven
& amendid wt penaunce & þai of clene y shryven
of þat þey had y don & of þat þat scholde by tyde
to wayne þem þe sore & flo hit on ech a side
But þis answer a gayn ȝif was ben to seynt Edward
þe wikkednesse is fulfild þe tyme þey ben woren hard
God schal sette þat ȝer a day þe tyme schal falle
þe Englysch schal go to þe swerd to peyne þe saules all
Der & fir schal fede þe shipherdes and þe schip
þis vision is gode to drede þenk & ȝif gode kepe
I trowe hit is ouer gon by willam þe Conquerour
he com & slow echon þe wikked men in stour
and sette vs in seruage of fredom fel þe flour
þe englis þurgh tallage leveþ ȝit in sorwe ful sour
Now is Edward ded þe soner for þis affrayes
xxiiij ȝer vj monthes & xvij dayes
he regned in þis lond þe date of ihū þo was
a m^t lxvj is y found & lx ȝer & [illegible]

De morte Godwyni comitis Cancie et [illegible]
ex vita sancti Edwardi [illegible]

In seynt Edwardes lif hit seyþ þat Godewyn was for sworen
By fore seynt Edward self & he y strangeled was soon
And schal telle þat tale or þat y ferþer go
how falsnesse bytrayþ hales wt hym & oþer mo
In seynt Edwardes tyme þe erl schold wt hym ete
a seruitor þat was þat serued þem at þe mete
he stombled at a chance & ful doun on his o kne
þurgh þat oþer schank he rose & serued forþ in his degre

Lambeth MS 131, f. 89v (2nd scribe). By kind permission of the Trustees of Lambeth Palace Library.

The Chronicle

PART I

[1ra] *The first 198 lines are lacking in L, as a page has been torn out.*

Lordynges þat be now here,
if ȝe wille listene & lere
alle þe story of Inglande
als Robert Mannyng wryten it fand
& on Inglysch has it schewed,
not for þe lerid bot for þe lewed,
ffor þo þat in þis land won
þat þe Latyn no Frankys con,
ffor to haf solace & gamen
in felawschip when þai sitt samen.
And it is wisdom forto wytten
þe state of þe land & haf it wryten:
what manere of folk first it wan
& of what kynde it first began.
And gude it is for many thynges
for to here þe dedis of kynges,
whilk were foles & whilk were wyse,
& whilk of þam couth mast quantyse,
and whilk did wrong & whilk ryght,
& whilk mayntend pes & fyght.
Of þare dedes salle be my sawe,
& what tyme & of what lawe,
I salle ȝow schewe fro gre to gre
sen þe tyme of sir Noe,
ffro Noe vnto Eneas,
& what betwix þam was.
And fro Eneas tille Brutus tyme,
þat kynde he telles in þis ryme,
ffro Brutus tille Cadwaladres,
þe last Bryton þat þis lande lees.
Alle þat kynde & alle þe frute
þat come of Brutus, þat is þe Brute.
And þe ryght Brute is told nomore

þan þe Brytons tyme wore.
After þe Bretons þe Inglis camen,
þe lordschip of þis lande þai namen.
South & north, west & est,
þat calle men now þe Inglis gest.
When þai first amang þe Bretons
þat now ere Inglis, þan were Saxons.
[1rb] Saxons, Inglis hight alle oliche,
þai aryued vp at Sandwyche
in þe kynges tyme Vortogerne
þat þe lande walde þam not werne,
þat were maysters of alle þe toþire.
Hengist he hight, & Hors his broþire,
þes were hede, als we fynde,
where of is comen oure Inglis kynde.
A hundreth & fifty ȝere þai com
or þai receyued cristendom,
so lang woned þai þis lande in
or þai herde out of Saynt Austyn.
Amang þe Bretons with mykelle wo,
in sclaundire, in threte, & in thro,
þes Inglis dedes ȝe may here
as Pers telles alle þe manere.
One mayster Wace þe ffrankes telles
þe Brute, alle þat þe Latyn spelles
ffro Eneas tille Cadwaladre.
Þis mayster Wace þer leues he,
and ryght as mayster Wace says,
I telle myn Inglis þe same ways,
ffor mayster Wace þe Latyn alle rymes
þat Pers ouerhippis many tymes.
Mayster Wace þe Brute alle redes,
& Pers tellis alle þe Inglis dedes;
þer Mayster Wace of þe Brute left,
ryght begynnes Pers eft
and tellis forth þe Inglis story,
& as he says þan say I.
Als þai haf wryten & sayd
haf I alle in myn Inglis layd
in symple speche as I couth
þat is lightest in mannes mouth.
I mad noght for no disours,
ne for no seggers, no harpours,

bot for þe luf of symple men
þat strange Inglis can not ken.
ffor many it ere þat strange Inglis
in ryme wate neuer what it is.
And bot þai wist what it mente,
ellis me thoght it were alle schente.
[1va] I made it not forto be praysed,
bot at þe lewed men were aysed.
If it were made in ryme couwee,
or in strangere or enterlace,
þat rede Inglis it ere inowe
þat couthe not haf coppled a kowe;
þat outhere in couwee or in baston,
som suld haf ben fordon,
so þat fele men þat it herde
suld not witte howe þat it ferde.
I see in song, in sedgeyng tale
of Erceldoun & of Kendale:
Non þam says as þai þam wroght,
& in þer sayng it semes noght.
Þat may þou here in sir Tristrem,
ouer gestes it has þe steem
ouer alle þat is or was,
if men it sayd as made Thomas.
Bot I here it no man so say
þat of som copple, som is away.
So þare fayre sayng here beforn
is þare trauayle nere forlorn;
þai sayd it for pride & nobleye
þat non were suylk as þei,
and alle þat þai wild ouerwhere,
alle þat ilk wille now forfare.
Þai sayd in so quante Inglis
þat manyone wate not what it is;
þerfore heuyed wele þe more
in strange ryme to trauayle sore,
and my witte was oure thynne,
so strange speche to trauayle in.
And forsoth I couth noght,
so strange Inglis as þai wroght.
And men besoght me many a tyme
to turne it bot in light ryme;
þai sayd if I in strange it turne,

to here it manyon suld skurne,
ffor it ere names fulle selcouth
þat ere not vsed now in mouth.
And þerfore for þe comonalte
þat blythely wild listen to me,
[1vb] on light lange I it began
for luf of þe lewed man,
to telle þam þe chaunces bolde
þat here before was don & tolde.
ffor þis makyng I wille no mede
bot gude prayere when ȝe it rede.
Þerfore ȝe lordes lewed
ffor wham I haf þis Inglis schewed,
prayes to god he gyf me grace:
I trauayled for ȝour solace.
Of Brunne I am if any me blame,
Robert Mannyng is my name.
Blissid be he of god of heuen
þat me, Robert, with gude wille neuen.
In þe thrid Edwardes tyme was I
when I wrote alle þis story.
In þe hous of Sixille I was a throwe;
Danȝ Robert of Malton þat ȝe know
did it wryte for felawes sake
when þai wild solace make.
Dares þe Freson of Troie first wrote
& putt it in buke þat we now wote;
he was a clerk & a gude knyght.
When Troie was lorn, he sawe þat fight.
Alle þe barons wele he knewe:
he tellis þer stature & þer hewe,
long or schorte, whyte or blak,
alle he telles gude or lak.
Alle þer lymmes how þai besemed,
in his buke has Dares demed,
both of Troie & of Grece,
whatkyns schappe was ilka pece.
Of manyon he reknes & sayes,
both of Troiens & of Gregeis,
þat it were oure long to telle;
& many wald not þerin duelle
þare names alle forto here,
bot þe Latyn is fayre to lere.

[2ra] Geffrey Arthure of Minumue
fro Breton speche he did remue
& made it alle in Latyn
þat clerkes haf now knawyng in.
In Gloucestre was fonden a buke
þat þe Inglis couthe not rede no luke.
On þat langage þai knew no herde,
bot an erle þat hyght Roberde,
he prayed þat ilk clerk Geffrey
to turne it fro þat speche away
in to Latyn as it mente
þat þe Inglis mot know þe entente.
ffor Geffrey knew þe langage wele,
in Latyn he broght it ilka dele.
Siþen com a clerk, Mayster Wace,
to make romance had he grace,
& turned it fro Latyne
& rymed it in Frankis fyne
vnto þe Cadwaladres,
no forer: þer makes he ses.
Als Geffrey in Latyn sayd,
so Mayster Wace in Frankis layd.
Þe date of criste was þan þis lyue,
a thousand ȝere fifty & fyue.
Than com out of Brydlyngton,
Pers of Langtoft, a chanon.
Als Mayster Wace þe same he says,
bot he rymed it oþer ways.
He begynnes at Eneas:
of alle þe Brute he tellis þe pas,
& sþen alle þe Inglis dedis;
feyrere langage non ne redis.
After þe Inglis kynges, he says þer pris
þat alle in metir fulle wele lys.
And I, Robert, fulle fayn wald bringe
in Ynglis tonge þer faire saiynge.
God gyf me grace wele to spede, *[L begins with this line.]*
þis ryme on Inglis forto rede.
[2rb] Now of þe story wille we gynne.
When god toke wreke of Caym synne,
þe erth was waryed in his werke,
as in þe bible says þe clerke.
Þerfore god sent a flode

& fordid alle flesch & blode,
man & beste þat beren lyues,
bot foure men & foure wyfes.
So mykelle was þan mans trispas
þat alle þat euer of Adam was
within a thousand ȝere & mo,
in þat flode were lorn alle þo.
Bot Noe & his thre sonnes
& þer wyfes, þe bible it mones,
were non worþi in goddes syght,
ne non bot þes þat lyued ryght.
Þes were þai þat escaped þe deth:
Noe, Sem, Cam, & Iapheth .Seem Cam & Sapheþ
& þer wyfes þai with þam nam, ...þat wiþ þem nam
þo þat now ere of þes aught cam. .....þys folk þey cam
This Noe sonnes, ȝe haf wele herde
how þai departid alle þe werlde: ....þys werd
þei parted it in thre partys
& names gaf at þer deuys.
Asie, Aufrik, & Europe,
þes ere þe partys wele I hope.
Sem was eldest, he ches Asie;
Cam toke Aufrik to his partye;
Iapheth Europe he toke,
& þis departid as says þe boke. .þus þey parted als...
How many landes in ilk of þise,
ilk a partye has þer assise.
In Asie fyften landes are,
bot þer names we seie namare:
India, Assiri, & Partie,
Sire, Pers, Med, Mesopotamie,
Capadoce, Palestyne, Armenie,
Cilice, Cades, & Arabie,
alle Egypte, & Libie,
þise ere þe landes in Asie.
[2va] Tille Aufrik tuelf landes lang
þat Cam tille his parte vnderfang:
Cirennes, Pentapolis, Liddia,
Ethiope, Tripolitan, Biȝancia,
Getulie, Natabrie, Numedie,
Mauritan, Tinguitanie,
Sirtes, þe more & þe lesse,
ffor þe tuelft teld it es.

ffouretene landes ere in Europe	ffiftene....
was Iapheth parte, þer es þe pope:	Saphethes partie þer dwelleþ..
Rome, Calabre, Spaygne,	Romanie Calabre Poille &.
Macedone & Almaygne,	
Tracie, Dalmatik, Pannonie,	
Coloyne, Galle, Aquitanie,	Lange dok ffraunce Acquitonie
Bretayne, Ireland; þes be þe best,	
& alle þe North toward þe west.	
Now salle we telle, as we fynde,	
how Eneas com of Iaphet kynde.	....Saphethes.
fful myrke it is for to here	
bot alle gate a man may lere.	
Noe god saued fro þe deth,	.þat god saued fro deþ
his son was sir Iaphet.	
Iauan, his son þat com of hym,	
he had a son þat hyght Cetim.	
Cetim son, Ciprius hyght,	
a man of fame & of myght.	
So mykelle þat tyme was his fame,	
þe lande of Cipre for hym had name.	
Of þis noble sir Ciprius	
was a son men called Cretus;	...þat hight.
þis Cretus an Ilde he aught,	
þe name of hym, Crete it laught.	
Cretus son hyght Celius,	
& Celius son was Saturnus.	
Saturnus son hyght Iubiter;	
in astronomye he lered fer.	
Þis Iubiter had tua wyues,	
kynges doghters, faire lyues:	
þe ton hyght Maye, þe toþer Electra;	
þer fadere hyght Atlans of þam tua.	...Aclas...
For Atlans, a hille men called	.Aclas alle hise..
Mons Atlantis, if it now hald.	.Aclatis....
[2vb] Þat hille was so hii, men lette,	.....as men hit leet
þat heuen men sayd it vndersette.	...seye hit vnder feet
Þis noble kyng, sir Atlas,	
in his lordschip a tre þer was	..Orchard....
þat gilden apples it bare euermore,	
alle þe tymes þat appilles are.	....apples wore
Alle tymes a dragon þam kepte;	& alwey on dragon..
siþen were þei stollen whils he slepte.	
Þis Iubiter lay Dam Maii bye	

& gatte of hir sir Mercurye.
Of Electra he gatte anoþer,
Dardanum, Mercury broþer.
Iubiter lufed wele more Maye
& Mercury þan þe toþer tuaye.

[*L adds:*] Wel more Maye & Mercurium
Þan Electra or Dardanum

ffor luf of Maye, he did calle
þe monyth of May þat we knaw alle,
ffor in þat Monyth made þai fest,
þat tyme þai helde fairest & Mest. ...helden most honeste
Dardan gaf hym to chyualrye, Þys Dardaum....
Mercury gaf hym alle to clargye.
Þis Dardan was a noble kyng; .Dardanus....
his godes schewed hym mykelle thyng
& bad hym tille Ytalie ...gon til.
toward Samo thorgh Tracie.
Tracie forsoth is a lande,
Samo a cuntre, I vnderstande,
þe whilk Dardan thorgh mastry
made þam both one, Samotracie.
Samotracie at his dyuise, .haþ at..
siþen he went vnto ffryse
& gaf name when he þer cam, ..hit name....
after hym self, Dardaniam.
Þe name of ffrise cald Dardanie
as he cald Tracie Samotracie.
Of þis Dardan com a son,
Erictonius, þat þare gan won. Erictorius....
Þis Erictonius a son he gatte, .Erictorius....
Troys, a noble man was þat,
of rygfulnes & of pite; .rightfulnesse & pitee
ouer alle praysed was he .alle oþer...
for a ryghtfulle man & heende. .....hende
Of hym is mynsyng withouten ende,
[3ra] ffor he mad a cyte of ioye
& after his name cald it Troie.
Of þis Troys, þe story mones,
com of hym tuo noble sonnes.
þe tone hight Ile, þat oþer Assarake;
þise ware þer names þe story spake.
Ile was after his fadere kyng;
he mad a cyte, a faire biggyng,

& after hymself he named it right,
Ilie after Ile it hight.
Of þis Ile a son was on,
& his name was Laomedon.
Þis Laomedon a batayle ches;
he was slayn with Hercules.
Of Troie was made destruction
thurgh Iason, kyng Pelles son.
Of þis is noght to telle here;
it is noght of oure matere.
Of Laomedon com Priamus,
Volcontus, & Ysipulus,
& a doghter of hym cam:
hir name was Esionam.
Of Priamus, eldest & more,
he had a son men called Hector
& oþer sex & doghteres tuo.
Þe names may ȝe here of þo:
Alisander, Paris, Deiphebum,
Helenum, Troil, Amphimacum,
& tuo doghtres þat of hym cam,
Cassiandram & Polixenam.
Of Troys beforn anoþer son,
Asserake, ȝe herde me mon.
Of þis Asserake now geten is
a son men cald Capis,
& of Capis Enchis was,
& of Enchis com Eneas;
þis is þe kynde fro gre to gre
betuen Eneas & Noe.
Now donward it is þus
fro Eneas tille sir Brutus:
Sir Eneas had sonnes tua;
Askaneus was be Dame Creusa.
[3rb] In þe batayle of Troie amang þe pres,
his wyf Creusa þer he hir les.
Whan þis Duke, sir Eneas,
fro þe batayle ascaped was,
he com to þe land of Latyne,
& þer he weddid Dam Lauyne.
Latyn hight þan þo landes
þer men says þat Rome standes.
Be Dam Lauyne, þat lady,

he gatte a son þat hight Siluy;
his eldest son, Askaneus,
he gatte a son, Sisillius;   . . . child Cycillius
þat ilk Sisilli gatte þat man,
Brutus, þat alle þis land wan.   . . . . . first wan
Of Brutus com sir Loqeryne, ... Lokeryn
Camber, & Albanak, euen in lyne;   Kamber Albanak Euen Iulyn
how þa departed þis land in thrinne,   . þey . . . . .
þat may ȝe here alle within.
Now haf I sayd alle þe kynde
vnto Loqeryn as we fynde.
Now agaynward vnto Noe:
schortly to say, wille þou see
þe kynde of alle þat I are spak, ... y er of spak
& of Troys, Ile & Assarak.   . . Troies sones . . .
Lokeryn com of Brutus;
Brutus was geten of Sisillius;
Sisilli, Askaneus son was,
& Askaneus com of sir Eneas;
Eneas com of Enchise;
Enchis, Capis son was he;
Capis com of Assarak;
Assarak of Troys blode brak;
Troys com of Erictonius;
Ericton com of Dardanus;
Dardan com of Iubiter;
Iubiter was Saturnus heyre;
Saturnus com of Celius,
& Celius com of Cretus,
& Cretus com of Ciprim,
& Ciprius com of Cetim;
Cetim com of Iauan,
& Iauan of Iaphet gan,
[3va] & Iaphet com of sir Noe;
of Assarak þis is þe degre.
Now salle we say of Ile partie: . . . . . ylke .
Hector com of Priamy;
Priamus com of Laomedan;
Laomedan of Ile began;
Ile com of Troius,
& Troius of Erictonius;
Ericton com kyng Dardan;   Erector cam of . .
Dardanus of Iubiter ran,

& Iubiter com of Saturnus,
& Saturnus of Celius;
Celius com of Cretus,
& Cretus com of Ciprius;
Ciprius of Cetim gan,
& Cetim com of Iauan;
Iauan, Iaphet son was he,
& Iaphet com of sir Noe;
of Troys sonnes þise are þe kyndes
þat both in to Noe byndes.
Now lordynges, it were to wyten
why þe batayle of Troy was smyten:
þe last myschaunce & þe peyne
was for þe quene of Grece, Heleyne;
þe kynges wyf of Grece scho was
þat Paris rauyst thorgh a cas.
Þat were was in tymes seere
lastand tuo & tuenty ȝeere.
ffor þat were þe barons fledde
þat were in Troie born & fedde.

[*L adds:*] How hit bigan þe laste bale
Listneþ & schal telle þe tale

Of Troie þe first destructon
com thorgh Iason, Pelles son,
þat wan þe rame with þe fleeȝ of golde,
þat neuer man of erth molde
mot it wyn before thorgh fyght;
bot sir Iason, þe gude knyght,
wan þe ram with þe gilden flees
& stroyed Troie alle þe citees. ...wiþ alle..
Bot þe kyng, sir Priamy,
bigged it agayn fulle nobly
& vouted it oft ston alle corn, .vitailled hit of ston & corn
was it neuer so faire beforn;
[3vb] bot siþen þe last sorow & peyne
was it neuer bigged agayne.
How it began þe last bale,
listes a partie of þe tale.
In Troie was a duke of pris,
Priami son, þat hight Paris.
Custom was be þo dawes
in tyme of þe olde lawes,
þat knyghtes suld kepe bestis,

as I haf herde rede in gestis.
Þe bible wittnes wele þis thyng
of Moyses & Dauid þe kyng.
Suld non bot of gentille blude,
Erle or duke or als gude,
bestis kepe bot he were knyght,
& stalworth in armes to fyght,
& hardy & honoure, ...of honur
he kepte bestis in þe pastoure.
Suilk on was þis ilk Paris,
a duke, hardy knyght, & wys. ...& a knyght wys
He kepte bestis in þe felde
as a knyght armed with schelde.
As þis Paris sat at his hole,
out of Grece þan com a bole.
To Paris bestis was his draght,
& with Paris bole he faught.
Ilkon oþer gan fast assayle,
& Paris beheld þer batayle.
Þai faught so long it was a wondere;
at þe last þei ȝede asondere.
A noþer day he com agayn
& faught togydere, þise boles tueyn.
So faught þai many dayes long,
felons batayles & fulle strong. ffelenous....
Paris sayd, "Now salle I see
whilk is worþi to haf þe gree,
& whilk of þam maystri salle haue,
for to coroune hym I vouchsaue." To coroune hym y vouche hit saue
A day þai faught so felonlike,
stalworþely to gydere gan strike.
So long þai faught, at þe last ....þat atte.
[4ra] þe bole of Troie doun was cast.
When Paris saugh his bole doun,
þe bole of Grece he gaf þe croun,
& þat was gret curtasye
to gyf þe bole þe maystrye
& latte hym go crouned quite
þat had don his bole despyte.
Þer beside thre wicches ware,
ladyes were cald, in þe eyr did fare.
Þe þre stod & behelde
þe boles batayle in þe felde

& praysed mykelle sir Paris
þat he gaf þe bole þe pris.
Þai sayd he was a man of skille
þat gaf þe dom þat felle þer tille,
ffor he þat was þe pris worþi,
he crouned & gaf þe maystri. .corouned hym....
Þise þre ladyes were of myght;
þat mast was, Iuno scho hight, Þe principale Iuno..
þat oþer Pallas, þe þrid Venus.
Alle þre ladyes hight þus:
Iuno, scho was gyffere of myght;
Pallas gaf wysdom & right;
Dam Venus, scho gaf luf tille man.
Betuex þise þre a strife began,
whilk of þam were fayrest;
at Paris dome þai wald it kest.
Dame Iuno sayd, "It am I."
Þat oþer sayd, "Nay, certanly! ....truely
To Paris dome we graunte alle,
þe whilk of vs salle fayrest falle."
Dame Iuno said hir auyse:
"We salle do it on Paris
& he salle oure domesman." ..schal ben..
Þat oþer said, "We graunte þan.
Now," scho said, "we graunte alle.
Go we now & mak a balle
& gyf it Paris, alle þre, ..we hit...
& pray we hym for specialte
to gyf it hir þat semes best
of vs þre to be fayrest." ...whilk ys.
Þis ilk counselle þai toke to pay;
[4rb] when it suld be, þai sett a day.
Here now of a quante gyle Hereþ...quynte wyle
how alle þre thoght a wyle: .eche of þo þoghte oþer gyle
are þat day com þat þai sette,
Iuno with sir Paris mette.
"Paris," scho said, "I salle þe seye
a priuete betuex vs tueye. ....beye
We thre ladyes haf ordeynd so
þat alle þre schalle com þe to,
& tak þe a balle & preye þe
to gyf it þe fayrest of vs þre;
& whom þou gyffes, it is our deuys,

scho salle for euer bere þe pris;
& if I myght beseke þe so,
þou wild gyf it me, Iuno.
I salle graunte thorgh my poere, ..þe graunte þorow my power
in Troie ne suld be þi pere." ..schold neuere...
Paris, "Dame, grant mercy; Parys seide...
als þou wilt, þan wille I." Right als..al so..
When scho was gon, com Pallas
for þat same þat Iuno was:
scho prayed Paris as scho had said,
þat þe balle were to hir layd.
"Of wisdom I salle gyf þe grace
ouer alle oþer in ilk place."
Paris said þat was curteyse.
"It may be, lady, as þou seys." Hit...ȝyt...
When scho was gan, com Venus ...gon cam dame.
& to Paris scho said þus:
"Paris," scho said, "we ladyes are
þre in grete thoght & in care,
& þou may abate þat gylte ...bate al..
of vs alle if þat þou wilte.
I am," scho said, "on of þo
þat is in thoght to þe to go.
A day we sette to þe to come
for to stande at þi dome.
A balle," scho said, "we salle þe bryng,
& pray þe oppon alle thyng
þou gyf it hir þat fairest semes;
for þi dome vs alle quemes,
& if þou gyf it me, Paris,
[4va] I salle gyf þe a luf of pris,
þe fairest lady þat now lifes,
for þe balle & þow it me gyfes." ...ȝif þou hit..
Paris thoght & stude þan stille;
to þat luf turned alle his wille.
He said, "Iuno hett me powere;
þerof," he said, "is no mystere.
Kyng son I am & lord salle be.
Powere inogh salle com to me.
& Pallas hight me grete wisdam;
wisere of Troie es ne þan I am. In Troye nis wyser...
Of þise gyftes is no nede;
to luf þat lady is alle my spede."

To þat gyft his herte gaf alle.
“Venus,” he seid, “þou getes þe balle.
If þou me halde þat þou has hette,
þou getes þe balle at ȝour day sette.”
Þai graunted both at þer pay,
& com alle þre at þer day
& betaght Paris þe balle; .bytok...
at his þai stode alle. .his dom þey stoden.
Paris toke þe balle in hande.
“So faire ladyes ere non lyffande,
bot me thynk of ȝow þre
Dame Venus semes fayrest to be.
Haf here þe balle, Dame Venus,
fairest to be me thynk reght þus.”
Þis lady Venus was alle glad;
þe toþer were for wrath mad. ....wrayth al.
Venus was with hym certeyn; .held wiþ hym.
þe toþer boþe were hym ageyn.
Powere & wisdom he forsoke,
& woman luf þertille he toke.
Dame Venus said tille sir Paris,
“Þou salle do at my deuys: .schalt don at myn auys
purueie þe,” scho said, “veire & gris,
faire iuels, purpure & bys.
Do dight a schippe with saile & ore
right as þou a merchand wore.
Of alle quantise þat þou may se,
haf vnto þi schippe with þe;
do mak þerin a fulle fayre bedde
[4vb] with clothes of gold be it alle spredde.
Þi schippe without be fulle faire dight
likand to þat lady sight;
þerin to Grece salle þou wende.
In a hauen salle þou lende
þer þe kyng is & þe quene,
& when scho has þi schippe sene,
scho salle ȝern on alle wyse
forto se þi merchandyse.
Bot luke þou schew non of þo
bot scho wille in to schippe go, ...in to þy..
& when scho heres þat tiþing,
scho salle pray fulle fast þe kyng
to gyf hire leue to se þi ware

to bye þerof þat so ryche are.	
Luke þou schew no man noght of þe	. . . noman nought
bot he wille in to þe schippe go,	Til þat sche first be hider brought
ffor out of witte woman ȝernes	
þat man forbedes hir & wernes.	
Bot when is broght in to þi schippe,	& whan scheo his brought vnto . .
be þe hande redy þou hir kippe	
& curtasly þat scho be ledde	
& sette hir faire on þi bedde.	
Do curtene it alle aboute	. cortine . . .
þat scho se no thyng withoute,	. . . nought wyþynne ne wyþoute
& when scho is on þi bed sette,	
luke wele þat þi schippe be gette	
þat non com vndere þi telde	Lat . . . . .
mo þan þou may lightly welde.	
Luke þi schippe it be vnfest	
& þi folk be alle prest,	
& what thyng þat scho wilt craue,	
do it hir redy to haue	
þat scho tente to no thyng els	
bot tille þat ware þat þou hir sellis.	
When redy is þin apparaile,	
þat þi men haf vp þi saile,	Lat . . . . . .
& at þou be tuo myle or þre	. loke þou be . . . .
or scho within þe se.	Ar scheo wite wyþynne . .
Do þan þat lady witte	& . . . . to wyte
how iuels wile hir sitte."	How þy . . . .
Paris did as Venus kende	
[5ra] & dight his schippe wele I wende	. . þe schip wel he wende
with alle quantise þat were gay	
& aryued þer þe kyng lay.	. . vp þer . . .
Menelaus hight þe kyng;	
he sent to witte what maner thyng	
was in þe schippe forto selle.	
Ryche iuels, þai gon hym telle,	
bot non ne myght for gold no fee	
out of þe schippe gete ought to see.	
Þat herd telle þe quene Heleyne;	
nyght & day scho did hir peyne	
of þe kyng to haf grantise	
to se þat ilk merchandise.	
What with wele or with wo,	
leue scho gate þider to go.	

Vnto þe schippe was scho broght.
Paris þe duke forgate he noght
þat he did als Venus bad;
þe quene com, in his herte was glad.   ffor þe quene comynge he was fol.
ffayre iuels forth þai drogh
& schewed þat lady right inogh.
To whils þei ryches befor hir cast,
þai drowe þer saile vpon þe mast.   Þer sayl þey drow vp by..
Þis lady Heleyne gaf no tente,
ne non of hirs þe schippe out went;   ....how þe schip..
within a throwe, tuo myle or thre,
was þe schippe within þe see.
When þai were fro þe land,
Paris toke þe quene be þe hand.
"Welcom, Heleyne, ert þou to me!   .he saide art...
For þe I com to þis contre.
ffor I haf þe, mykelle is my ioye;   Now y haue þe....
þi fairehede salle amend alle Troye.
Þou was gyfen, þat gyft I haue;   .were me gyuen....
alle my trauaile I vouch it saue."
I kan not say of þat lady
whedire scho were or sary,   Wheþer scheo was glad or sory
bot when hir lord þe kyng it wist,
ioye to make hym ne list.
After his barons alle he sent
& schewed þam how he was schent: ...how þat...
þat a schippe of Troie was comen,
[5rb] þe quene thorgh treson has nomen.
When þai alle wist þe grete dispyte,
with o wille þai said fulle tyte,
þei suld neuer reste no lende
to destroye Troye withouten ende.
Herfore began þe sorow & peyne,
þe slauhtere of Troye for þis Heleyne.
Þe slauhtere was in batayles sere
lastand tuo & tuenty ȝere
betuex þe Troiens & þe Gregeis.
Storyes witnes it & sais   Als þe stories wytnesses..
at a bataile þat þai sette,
at ones Troie & Grece þai mette;   Troye & Grece at ones.
at þat bataile þe Troiens lees   .which....
& fled fro þat mykelle prees.
Þat myght fle, fled aschore   ....ay whore

& Troie destroyed for euermore.
Alle þe world makes ȝitt menyng
how Troie was stroyed for þis thyng.
Clerkes wyse in buke it wrote;
þorgh þer writyng we it wote.   . whiche wrytynge wel alle hit.
Þai wrote þe names of þe kynges
& of alle þat oþer lordynges,
whilk were men of most honoure
þat fled fro þat grete stoure.
A grete lord of Troie þer was,
men called duke Eneas.
ffro þat gret slauhter he fled,
his son Askaneus with hym led.
Son ne douhtere he no mo   . . . had he namo
when he fled þe cite fro.
In þe slauhter amang þe pres
hys wyf Creusa he hir les.
Þis Eneas fled hym self to saue
withouten ouþer ȝoman or knaue.   Hys sones lif & his to haue
With mykelle vitaile & tresore gude,
he charged tuenty schippes on flude.
He duelled long in þe see
& many escaped he.   . . perille ascapede he
With alle þe wo þat he gan drye,
he com to þe land of Italye.
Ytalie was þan þe name   . was kalled þenne
[5va] þat land þer now men Rome ame.   Þe land þat Rome now standes ynne
Of Rome þat ilk tyme was noght,
ne long after was it wroght.
Eneas þat had alle þat trauayle,
what in þe se & in batayle,
at þe last he gan aryue
in Ytalie, a londe plentyue.
Þe water hate Tiber þer þai londe nome;   By þe water of Tyber land þey nome
be þat water standes Rome.   By whilk water now standeþ.
The kyng of þe londe, Latyn hight,
a riche man & mykelle of myght,
rychesse inouh his lond to welde,   & hadde ynow. . . .
bot þat he was smyten in elde.
He worchipped mykelle sir Eneas
& fayn of his comyng was,
& seid if he wald leue stille,
he wille gyf hym lond at wille.

Latyn þe kyng had non heyre
bot a maden suyth feyre; ..maide..
þis damyselle hight Lauine.
Þe kyng said, "Sho salle be þin.
I wille þat þou after myn endyng,
my douhter wed & be þe kyng."
Bot þerto graunted not þe quene:
scho þat anoþer had bene. Scheo wold....
ffor he did not als wald his wyf,
þerfor ros a new stryf.
Þer beside a ryche man,
Turnus he hight, lord of Tuscan.
Þis Turnus had lufed Lauine, ...yloued.
& herde seie þat þe kyng Latyne
had gyffen his douhter sir Eneas,
& had enuye þat it so was.
ffor Turnus had luffed hir long or he
& grantise had his wyf to be,
he bed his body, his ouer myght,
with Eneas alle one to fyght.
Sire Eneas was þerof fayne;
þei smyte togydere, Turnus was slayne. .faught....
Eneas wedded þat mayden ȝing;
sho was quene & he was kyng. Þen was scheo quen....
Siþen fand he non þat hym noyed
[5vb] ne noght of his londe destroyed;
siþen he wedded Lauine his wyfe
had he þe londe withouten strife. He held....
In pes foure ȝere he regned wele;
within þo ȝeris he mad a castele
& gaf it name thorgh ilka toune
after Dame Lauine, Lauioune.
In þe ferth ȝere, last of his lyfe,
of hym conceyued Lauine his wyfe,
& or þe childe felle to be borne,
ore was Eneas dede beforne. Sire Eneas was ded.
When Lauine tyme was fulfilled,
of hir was born, as grace it wild,
a knaue chylde men called Siluius.
His toname was Pollinius.
Askaneus, Eneas son ..oþer sone
þat com with hym, I gan ȝow mone, ...as ȝe wel mone
after his fadere þe londe he toke;

his broþer Silui he did to loke. ..Syluius he dide hit.
Silui his half broþer was,
geten of his fadere, Kyng Eneas.
Askaneus did mak a cite,
þe name Albe gaf it he.
Askaneus lete Dame take .let dame Lauyne.
þe castelle þat Eneas did make, [*Om. L. A later hand adds this line at the folio bottom.*]

& alle þe lond þat felle þer tille,
Dame Lauine held it at hir wille.
Þe Maumet þat Eneas brouht fro Troie,
in Lauion he sett þam with ioye.
Siþen com Askaneus his son,
brouht þam to Albe þer he gan won,
& þerin had þai neuer rest;
þe morn þai were agayn alle prest ffor o þe morn þe were...
at þe castelle of Lauion
& wilde not duelle in Albe, his toun.
He ne wist no was certayn
in what maner þai com agayn.
He regned four & thritty ȝere
in pes withouten wo & were.
When Askaneus did his endyng,
Silui his broþer regned kyng
þat was born of Dame Lauine;
[6ra] þe heritage he had in lyne.
A son þan had Askaneus;
his name was Sisillius. .brother highte Sysillius
Þis ilk child Sisilli
luffed Lauine nece & lay hir by,
& scho als sone wex with childe [*These lines are probably*
as ȝong men do þat be wylde. *transposed in both MSS.*]
Þe kyng did his clerkes calle
& bad þam cast lotes alle, ...loke þer bokes alle
what suld of þat childe com, ...bycome
gude or ille, what maner dome. ..wykke...
Þei said þai fond, as þam was wo,
fadere & modere he suld slo,
& out of lond go for chance ......þat chaunce
& siþen com to gude cheuisance.
Passe he suld mony a stoure
& siþen com tille grete honoure.
Þai fonde siþen as þei seid:

when he was born his moder died, Þat of his burþe...
his modere deied also suythe.
Þe childe lyffed; þai were alle blythe.
Brutus þus his name þei teelde. .....teld
When he was fiften ȝere elde,
his fadere & he to wod þei wente;
to venery he gaff his tente.
A herde of hertes son þei mette;
at triste to schote, Brutus was sette.
He auysed hym apon a herte,
betuex passed his fadere ouerthuerte, Hys ffader passed bytwyxt.
& with þat schote his fadere he slouh,
bot his willand not it drouh. Al vnwylland þat draught he.
When Brutus sawe his fadere dede,
he ne wist what was best rede; .nyste...to red
for dole & drede, away he nam
vntille þe lond of Grece he cam. Tyl Grece fro when his fader.
Þe folk of Troie þer he fonde
þat in seruage lyfed in þat londe. Þat lyuede in seruage y þe.
Helenum, Priami son,
with sex thousand þer gan he won,
& ȝitt mo lordynges inouh
þat þe Gregeys to seruys drouh,
þat Pirrus held in treuwage.
[6rb] Achilles son was þan of age.
Brutus was þer bot a throwe
þat his name manyon gan knowe .manyon his name gon wel.
for his mykelle hardynesse, ..grete.
for curtasie & largesse.
Mykelle lufed hym, his own kynde
& oþer tille hym were fulle mynde
gret gyftes forto gyfe, ..þey gon hym.
& seid, "If we myght frely lyfe,
ouer vs alle wille þe make ...we wolde..
Kyng, if þou wild vndertake.
Oure folk is waxen for þe maystri,
& stalworth ere, & fulle hardy. ....right.
If we had one þat we dred
þat vs vnto bataile led,
& mayntende vs, & lered also
what in bataile we suld do,
I trowe he suld alle our seruage, Syker scholde he haue...
to fredam bringe or asuage.

Seuen thousand now we are
of knyghtes redy to bataile ȝare,
without sergeantes & oþer pedale   ....pytaille
þat ere not forto sette in tale.
If þou wilte vndertake þis thyng,
we wilt þe mak our allere kyng, ...alder.
& at þi biddyng we wille bowe;
doute þe noght we are inowe."
Als þei tille spak oft þus,   ...hym spek often.
a bachelere men Assarakus   ..men calde.
was born in þe lond of Grece.
Of þat blode he had a spece,
ffor his fadere was Gregeis,
his modere of Troie, þe story seis.
His fadere was a lordyng,
þe most of þe lond saue þe kyng,
& gate hym opon bastardye
be one of Troie in rebaudye.
& for he gate hym on his rage,
he gaf hym in heritage
þre castelles þat were gude
tille his clothyng & his fude.
His breþer wild haf reft it hym
[6va] bot he bare hym so stoute & brym.   ....grym
ffor þe Troiens with hym helde,
þe boldelyer bare vp his schelde.
ffor he was on þat wild þam saue
& at his castelle rescet haue
with his counselle & his socoure,
made þei Brutus þer gouernoure,
& with his wille & his lokyng   [*Om. L*]
was sir Brutus chosen Kyng.   [*Om. L*]
Brutus sawe & vnderstode
his folk was alle strong & gode,
& hymself wele of myght
þam forto defende in fyght.
He did force þe castelle wele,   ..enforce þe casteles.
his folk warned ilk a dele,   ..he warned...
& bad þam to þe castelle drawe.
Þo þat were of Troie lawe,
men & women, childere ilkone,   ...& children.
þat to hym had mad þer mone,
þer godes þidere suld þei lede   & þidere scholde þer godes.

vnto þe castelle for doute & drede.
When þai had þer gudes led,
beside þe castelle bussed & spred,
& Brutus sawe his men wele dight,
alle redy vnto þe fight,
Brutus did write a brefe
vnto sire Pandras, kyng & chefe.
Þis is þe brefe þat he sent . . . lettre . . .
þat Latyn vndrestode þus ment: Þe latyn y vnderstonde . .
"For þe schame & þe outrage
þat is done þe noble lynage
of Kyng Dardan, our ancessoure,
at myschefe is in dishonoure.
In caytifte long haf þei layn,
bot now þai hope to com ageyn.
In o wille alle haf þei spoken
& in o counselle þei ere alle loken, In o conseil alle ar þey .
me to haf vnto þer heued, [*Transp. L*]
& with þam alle I am beleued. [*Transp. L*]
I send to þe þer allere sawe . . . . . alder .
þat to þe wod þei wille þam þan drawe.
Þer is þam leuere lif in wo,
[6vb] in wildernes with bestes go,
ffor haf wille þer fre . to haue þer wille fre
þan in thraldom haf plente.
No maugre þou þam con
þat þe wille in fredom won. Þaw þey wolde . . .
It is þer kynde fredom to haue;
þat owe be lord, now is he knaue. ffor þat whylom was lord . . . .
Ne meruelle þe if þei haf grace Merueille þe nought . . . .
franchise & fredom to purchace,
for ilk wild be at þer myght . . man wolde ȝyf he .
in fredom to lif as ryght. . . lyue als hit ys .
Þerfor þei pray þe with gude wille,
& I comande for drede of ille,
þat hiþen forward þou grante þam fre
& no more in þi seruage be.
Sire, we ask þe bot skille: . kyng we . . . .
graunte vs to go where we wille."
When þe kyng herde þis writte, . . . had herd . .
hym merueyled out of his witte
þat þe Troiens were risen on heght;
þei wild be fre or þei wild feght.

He did suyth mak somons
for his erles & barons, — . alle his . . .
& for his broþer, sir Antigon,
Sir Anacletun anoþer on. — . . & oþer on
He teld þam þei of Troie were rysen
& thouht to make þam alle agrysen.
When Brutus wist alle þer boste
þat þe kyng purueyd an oste,
befor in þe kynges weye
Brutus did hym busse & leye
with þre thousand armed & mo.
Þe kyng Pandras wende sauely go,
bot Brutus ros of his bussement
& slouh alle þat he myght hent.
Þe Gregeis schad sone osondere;
þei were vnarmed, it was no wondere.
In a water hate Askalon,
þidere þei fled manyon — . in flowe .
& dronkend þer a fulle gret frape; — . drenkled . . wel gret .
þe toþer he closed, þei myght not scape.
Many were dronkend & mo were slayn; — . . drenkled . . . .
[7ra] þe kyng fled with fulle grete payn.
Þe kynges broþer, Antigonus,
he sawe þe chance felle on þam þus.
His folk he relied þam to hym — . . . relyed hym to
& seid, "Fraist ȝitt what we may do? — ffor to assay eft what þey might .
Schamly ere we discomfite. — . he sais ar we desconfit
Late þam not pas fro vs so quite."
When þei were togydere comen,
ageyn þe Troiens boldly þei nomen.
Þan began a scharpe bataile:
egrily þe parties gon asaile
with bowe, with lance, with suerdes dynt, — . . & spere & . .
so scharpe þei com, þe Gregeis tynt. — Bot atte þe laste . . .
At þat metyng, amang ilkone
taken was sir Antigone,
& a lord, sire Anacletun, — . an oþer . .
& þe most of þam born doun. — . best of hem were born .
Þe to preson Brutus þam led; — Þyse two prisons . . .
of þam of Grece, fo þer fled. — . . . . fewe . .
Pandras þe kyng had sorow & site — . . . . . in sight
þat he was so alle discomfite,
& þat his broþer taken was.

He com ageyn vnto þat pas
& wend haf fonden Brutus þore.
Help he had & purueied more,
bot Brutus was to his castelle gone
with Anacletun & Antigone,
& warnised þam with men of armes
for he dred desceyt & harmes.
Whan þe kyng fond hym þer nouht,
to besege þe castelle he thouht.
Vnto þe sege he hym hasted;
his purueiance he wold were wasted.
Berfreis did make to gyf assaute
þat Brutus myght falle with faute; .....y þe faut
to magnels he did mak stones, .mangeneles....
with þere assaute kast alle at ones.
Þei within stude in kirnels, ...karneles
with alblastes schote ageyn quirels;
þe grete trees fulle vnride,
þei kest ageyn on ilk a side.
Enginours had þei with þam inowe .þey hadde wyþynne.
[7rb] þat þei without agayn þam throwe; At þeym..to þrowe
[*L adds:*] Þat non dyrste comem þe wal ney
Bot for drede hel þeym a drey
þei kast wilde fire with engynes,
brent þer bretasks, ropes, & lynes, ..bretaxkes...
cables, cordes, tymbere þer was.
Who was wo bot þe kyng Pandras. ..þen wo bot..
The kyng saw it myght not vaile, Bot he saw hit...
þer assaut ne þer trauaile.
He drouh hym þien & gaf þam place
& began fast to manace.
He did mak for fens a dyke
about þe castelle a grete stryke,
& closed in alle Brutus oste
þat non myght ascape at coste. ...skape by no cost
Þe kyng did it palace ʒitt eft, ...ʒyt pale hit.
bo þre entries nouht was left. Bot þre entres non..
Þe kyng did so wele loke þo
þat non of þam myght passe hym fro
to do Brutus no suate, ...suwaute
so wele was loked ilk entre.
The sege was harde to þam within,
& þei without myght nouht wyn,

ne nouht ne suld of fulle long, — .....ful fer longe
if it ne were for hunger strong.
Defaut þei dred comand aforn: — Þe faute..comynge byforn
þe oste was mykelle, litelle had corne. — ....& lite..
Þai asked Brutus of counseile,
what þei suld do for more vitaile.
"Counseile vs or it be gon!
It is fulle late whan we haf non. — ..to.....
Whan we haf non vs to fede,
þe castelle most vs ʒelde nede." — ...we ʒelde for nede
Þus þei seid, þo men were wyse,
& Brutus bethouht hym of quantyse:
quantise behoues hym nedly thynk
þat his enmy salle wate a blenke.

[*L adds:*] & mykel peril byhoues hym haue
Þat auntres hym his frend to saue

Brutus had in his prison
Antigon & Anacleton.
Brutus toke hym be þe toppe
& seid, "Hedeles salle þou hoppe;
bot þou do as I þe saye,
of my hand salle þou deie,
both þe kynges broþer & þou,
[7va] & both may þou saue ʒow." — ..myght þou saue now
"Sir," he seid, "do ʒour wille,
bot if I myght saue vs fro ille, — How mygh y vs saue..
say me, sire, on what manere,
& if I may, I wilt ʒow here."
Brutus seid, "Þou salt go — ...schalt go
to nyght at bedtyme without mo — Alone to nyght wyþouten mo
to þam þat loke þe ton entre,
& seie to þam as I seie þe.
Seie þou has stolne þe kynges broþer
out of prisoun & non oþer.
Into þe wod þou has hym led
& farþere myght þou not for dred, — Bot ferrer may....
for þo men þat þe wod loke
þat hym no þe þei ouertoke.
Bot ilkon bid þam com with þe
þat no man behynd be,
& we salle be bussed þer beside,
& if I may, þei salle abyde
þat þei go not vs to wreie

ne desturble me my weie."
Anacletus granted wele
if Brutus were treste as stele. ..wold be tryst..
Þat his lyf he wild hym saue,
Brutus did hym sikernes haue.
Anacletus forth he went
& did as Brutus had hym sent.
At bedtyme whan men were to reste,
Brutus with his folk alle preste,
wele armed went þer weie.
Þer he had purueied in a valeie ..knew by o valeye
in þe wod beside þe entre,
he bussed þam in partys þre.
Whan alle were bussed, man & stede,
Anacletus he gan hym spede
& com to þam þat kepte þe pas,
& seid fro Brutus stollen he was.
Alle þei knew hym þat þer were ..kende....
& asked hym how he com þere.
Sire Antegon, þe kynges broþer,
þei asked where he lyued as oþer. ..ȝif....
He seid, "Þe kynges broþer & I
[7vb] ere scaped out fulle quantly.
In þe wod I haf hym hid
for sight of men, if so betid,
if any had perceyued vs
& led ageyn tille Brutus; ..vs a geyn..
bot alon dar he not go,
þerfor I com after mo.
Þe gyues about his fete þei ryng,
& I alon dar hym not bryng.
Comes with me, I salle ȝow lede
þer he es & has grete drede."
Þei trowed hym þat he soth seied,
& schette forth alle a braid ...al in a breyd
in to þe wod alle on a route,
& thouth of no treson doute. Þey þoughte...ne doute
Anacletus forth þam led
tille Brutus folk þer þei were spred,
& Brutus perceyued alle þer tide, ...pryde
vmbilapped þam on ilk side, & bylapped hem...
so þat non ne myght scape,
bot alle were slone at a frape. ...flayd...

Com neuer non of þo agayn
þat myght þam werne, knyght no suayn.
Brutus parted his oste in þre — Þen parted Brutus....
& sette þam alle in certeynte,
how priuely þei sulde go
withouten noyse, without wo.
"Noþer behynd ne beforn,
ne smyte not no man born
tille I com þer þe kyng lis,
& men with me of gude auys;
& whan I am at his pauilloun,
I salle blawe a grete soun.
My horn þat ȝe wele knowe,
a blaste to ȝow I salle blowe,
& whan I haf blowen a blaste, — [*Transp. L*] Þen spares non bot sles on.
spares non, bot slo alle faste, — [*Transp. L*] When þat y haue blowe þat.
slepand, wakand þat ȝe may fynd
þat es of þe Gregeis kynd."
Whan Brutus his horn blewe,
his men it herd & wele it knewe;
þei spared non bot slouh right doun
[8ra] on & oþer, erle & baron,
þei slouh þam alle at þer wille. — ....right at..
On slepe þei fonde þam alle stille,
had no grace ne pouste — Hadde þey....
to arme þam ne to fle.
Behynd, befor, on þam þei cam,
vnneþis ony a wey þer nam.
If any escaped thorgh chance,
it felle þam a foule vengeance: — ȝit bifel þem as foule a chaunce
on grete roches felle þei doun
& alle to frusshed bak & croun,
or were dronkend in wateres depe, — Oþer þey were drowned...
vnneþis couth any þam kepe.
Brutus toke þe kyng, Pandras,
& alle þat in his pauillon was
withouten any kyns ille;
vnto þe morn he held hym stille.
In þe mornyng at þe son rysyng,
Brutus led Pandras þe kyng
vnto þe castelle, his owen holde,
& did hym with knyghtes bolde. — ...kepe wiþ..
Siþen toke Brutus alle þe tresoure

þat he had won in þat stoure,
& gaf his knyghtes largely,
& oþer þer of had curtasy. .als til oþer fol corteysly
Þe toþer day counseile he toke
thorgh þe comoun, & bad þam loke Amanges þe.....
what were to do of kyng Pandras
þat halden in his prison was,
wheþer þei red hym forto slo
or quitely late hym alle go.
"Counseils wele now alle of þis
þat non ne seie þat I do mys."
Manyon seid þer auys,
on & oþer þat were wys.
Þis counseile was oft on hand
to tak a partie of þe land
& euer haf it in heritage,
frely withouten seruage,
& to haf a quitance
of þe barons for alle chance.
Oþer seid þat þer were
[8rb] þam were bettere elles where.
"Ask we leue at þe kyng,
& go we seke vs oþer wonyng
with our childere & oure wyues,
for þi þat hates alle day striues."
Þis tuo skilles forth þei cast,
whilk to tak were þe best.
A knyght vpstert as þei spak þus,
his name was Membricius.
"Alle þe resons ȝe haf forth brouht,
þe best of alle seie ȝe noght.
Certis, þis were our most profite,
with luf & leue he quede vs quite, ...queþe vs quyt
and gyf vs schippes in to wende,
& of vitaile as he is hende,
& oþer thyng þat we haf nede;
to charge þam with vs to lede .chargen hem wiþ...
& to our lord Brutus, our kyng,
Ignogyn his douhter ȝyng.
Lat vs þan go do our best
& seke vs lond on to rest,
for if we duelle with þam here,
we be þam neuer leue ne dere.

Þat we did now, þan salle þei thenk — What we did ones þey schold wel.
& wate vs with a wikked blenk;
salle we neuer rightly haf pes,
bot wate with som wikked res. — .wait vs....
Grete ferly ne were it nouht
for mykelle wo we haf þam wrouht,
for we haf slayn of þer kynde
þat we myght ouertake or fynde; — ...eyþer take..
þerfor siker mot ȝe be:
whan þei se tyme or haf pouste,
þis bale wille þei eft vs brewe.
Our olde mysdedis þei wille mak newe; — ..skaþes....
& þus men seie & oft is founde,
of olde sore comes greuous wounde.
Non of vs, alle wele I wene,
þat wene haf don þam treie & tene. — .we naue.....
Þer frendes þorgh vs haf þai lorn
or þer gudes away haf born,
& þo þat lyf þat now ere left,
[8va] vengeance on vs þei wille seke eft,
ffor þei salle waxe & we salle wane.
Whan we be fo, þei salle be manie. — ..ben fewe....
If we ouht falle & þei ouht rise,
þei salle tille vs be suylk iustise — ....do swylk.
þat alle our Troiens ilkone salle deie;
þerfor I rede ȝe chese þe weie,
if þat our kyng þerto wille rede,
els gos oure kynde to dede."
Þan cried alle & spak at ons, — ..þey alle....
"Sir Membrice seis wele for þe nons;
at þis counseile consent we alle,
non better for vs may falle."
The kyng þei brouht forth anone
& his broþer Antigone,
and asked hym leue for to go
withouten any more wo.
Þei asked hym what þei wold haue
& if he vouched on þam saue,
& his douhter to be þer quene
þat was ordeynd þam betuene. — Als hit was...
Þe kyng sawe þer myght was more
þen his was, þat dred he sore.
He granted þam ilka dele

to go at þare awen wille. . . . þer wylle wel
"At ȝour wille ȝe may haue . . . ȝe me haue
& my douhter ȝe may craue; . . . . me.
I se I may no noþer do. . . . . non oþer.
Myn enmy bos me gyf hir to. . enemy most y . . .
[*L adds:*] My moste fo & my feloun
Schal haue my doughter to warisoun
Bot of o thyng is my ioye,
he is þe douhtiest man of Troye
& comen of þe noblest blode;
þat me gladdes most in mode. . now gladeþ most my.
I grante ȝow schippes ȝour folk to lede,
& vitaile þat ȝe haf of nede,
more þan is ȝour deuyse, Wel more . . . .
if at þe lond may it suffise." ȝif þat þys . . . .
The kyng sent hys messengeres
vnto þe hauens in costestes seres, . . . & costes sers
þat alle þe schippes on water mot saile
suld be brouht tille o ryuale;
þer þei suld chese þe beste
[8vb] þat were most or strangest. . . . oþer strengeste
Whan þei had chosen at þer pay,
þei charged þam, day be day. . . þey fro day to.
Of þe best in ilk cuntre,
þei led to schippe grete plente.
The kyng did his douhter bringe
& gaf hir Brutus in weddynge,
& did hym better on alle wyse
þan Brutus asked or ony of hyse.
For ilkan, baron & knyght, . alle þat þer were Baroun . .
had gyft of hym after his ryght. Þey geuen hym after þer myght
Whan þe Troiens were alle dyght,
with saile vpon mast on hyght, . . . þe mast vpright
with ankere & ore & oþer ware,
& were alle redy forto fare,
whan þe wynd was wele þam lent,
þei toke þer leue & forth þei went.
Whan were redy to saile, When þey were . . .
þre hundreth schippes þei were be tale, . . . þer was in taille
& foure mo, þe story seies,
whan þei departed fro þe Gregeys.
Tuo days þei sailed & tuo nyght
þat lond no hauen reche þei myght.

Þe þrid day in þe euen tyde,
in Leogice þei gan ryde.
Leogice þan es an Ilde;   . þat ys . .
þat tyme was it wast & wilde.
Man ne woman non þei fonde;
outlandes had wasted þat londe
& þe godes awey had born.
Bot buk & do & herte with horn
in þat ilde þei fond inowe,
þat þei slouh & to schippe drouh,
& stored þam wele of venyson
þat lasted þam long seson.   . . . a long .
Als þei went þorgh þat cuntre,
þei vnto a waste city   . come vntil . . .
& fonde þerin a temple stande,
whilom þe folk misleuande   Þat whilom . . mys lyuande
worschipped þerin maumetrie.
Diane in liknes of a ladie,
woman liknes þe fende did take;   Wyþ man lyknesse . . . .
[9ra] in þat liknes þe folk did make
an ymage & worschipped þat same;
Diane was þat fendes name.
In þis tempille stode a cage, ... yn a gage
suilk a maner like an ymage.   Swich an Erlyk man ymage
Þe folk þat had þer rescet
leued on þat maumet;
þat fende telled þam mykelle thyng
to hald þam in mysleuyng.
On fele maneres sho schewed þam signe,
þerfor whilom þei held hir digne.
To Brutus þan was it tolde
how in a tempille þat was olde,
fonde þei an ymage
þat whilom had grete seruage
of þe folk þat þer was wone
& þe token ȝitt wille mone.   . . . ȝit wil we mone
Brutus toke tuelf of his peres,
eldest & of faire maneres,
& a preste of þer lawe,
sir Gerion, as seis þe sawe.
Brutus gan þe ymage loute;   . alone to þe ymage gan .
he alone, þei left withoute.   & alle þe oþere . .
In his reght hand, whan he com ine,

he brouht a coppe of mylk & wyne;
þe mylk was of a white hynde.
He souht Diane with herte fulle mynde: Bysoughte Diane wyþ hertly .
scho wild hym schewe certeyn thyng ... schewe som ..
in worde or oþer tokenyng, .. oþer elles oþer .
what gode land he mot won in
in pes, he & alle his kyn.
Ouide witnes it & seis
þat it is non oþer weis: *[The following two lines are in red, evidently done by the illuminator; they seem to be midline captions in both MSS.]*

Diua potens nemore terror siluestribus
apris . Cui licet amfractus

Nien tymes he mad þis prayere
with soft wordes in symple chere,
as scho was godes of powere, *[Transp. L]*
with nyen knelynges befor þe autere. *[Transp. L]* As scheo was a god of power
Nien siþes he ȝede aboute
& kiste þe autere & gan it loute.
Þe mylk þat he about bare,
[9rb] in a fyre he cast it þere.
Afterward, þus we fynde,
he toke þe skyn of þe hynde
& spred it þer on þe grounde,
& sleped þeron a welle gude stounde.
Brutus thouht, when he was leid,
Diane com to hym & seid,
"Ouer France toward þe west
is an Ilde, on of þe best.
Wele likand is þer wonyng ffol lykynge...
& plenteuous of ilk a thyng,
ffrute to bere, gode es þer londe;
þe geantȝ haf it now in honde.
Albion is now þe name;
þhorh þe salle it haf oþer fame: Þorow þe.....
þer salle þou gyn a newe Troie,
to alle þi kyn newe ioie, Til al þy kynde..
& þe kynde þat comes of þe,
thorh alle þe werld wirsciped salle be;
& þat ilde þat þou has herde, ... þou hast of herd
with þe see on ilk half is sperde." .... alle halue ys spred
Brutus ros & vp hym sette.
He þouht on his dreme þat he mette

& þanked Diane hir gude wille;
& if scho myght his dreme fulfille
þat he mot þat ilde take,
in hir name he suld do make
a tempille gude & ymage hende,
& wirschip hir tille his lyfes ende,
& tolde his dreme sir Gerion   He telde....
& to þe toþer tuelf ilkon.   .tyl þise oþer..
So glad þei were, forth þei ȝode
to þer schippes þat were on flode.
Þer sailes drowe þei reght hie, ...right on hey
with þe wynd gan þei flie;   Byfore þe wynd faste..
vmwhile est, vmwhile west,   Vmwhile west vmwhile est
ere schippes dryuen in many tempest.   Þer.....
What with wele, what with wo,
in thritty daies, less ne mo,   Þe þrittyþe day...
into þe see of Aufrike
þei com & passed a grete strike;
a lough of water of salyns
[9va] & oþer louhes of Filistyns,
þe grete louh of Rusticiodan
betuex þe hilles of Daȝardan.   ....Daȝaran
Þei mette robbours of outlandes;
þorgh þei passed with dynt of handes,   Þorow þem þey.....
ffor þei gan þam fast assaile.
Þe Troiens partid alle þer bataile,   .Trogens passede...
& had þer vitaile ilk a dele
þat þei were of stored so wele.
Þei passed þe water of Maluan
& aryued in þe land of Mauritan.
Þer þei com vnto þe londe
& toke þe vitaile þat þei fonde;
fro þe to see vnto þe toþer,
þei robbed alle on & oþer;
þei charged alle þat þei mot lede,
set vp þer saile & forth þei ȝede.
With alle þer schippes & alle þer pres,
þei com to markes of Hercules.   .comen to þe Merkes..
Hercules was douhty a man;   .was so doughti.
out of Troie þider he wan   .....cam
bi þe see as he wan bi londe.
A piler of bras þer þei fonde
þat he did sette for honour

þat þider was he conquerour.
Þer fand þei Nikers þat mery song
þat drecched þam ferly long;   [*Om. L*]
in þe west see es þer wonyng.   [*Om. L*]
As women mery þei syng,   [*Om. L*]
& þo þat listen to þer song,   [*Om. L*]
out of þer weie þei turne wrong, ... to turne hem .
or þei forget þer schippe to stere,
for þer song þat þei here.   Þorow . . . . schold here
So ere þo nykeres fast aboute
to bring schipmen þer it es doute,
to som suelhu, to turne or steke,   . . swelw . . . .
or ageyn roches breke;
þerfor it is a grete perile
schipmen to listen þertille.
Þe Troiens knew þer song wele;
þei listend to þam neuer a dele.
Þei had herd telle beforn
[9vb] how scippes were for þam lorn.   . schipes had ben wyþ hem forloren
With peyne þei passed at þat tide;
vpon Spaigne þer flet gan ride.
Þer þei fond at a ryuage
grete folk of Troie lynage,
þat on of þer ancessoure
fled fro Troie out of þat stoure
als þei did, ilk a man,
whan þei of Grece Troie wan.   . . . . to Troye cam
Corineus hight þer ledere;
he mantend þam in pes & were.   & meintened hym . . . .
He was a man as a geant;
tille hym þei drowe as to warant.   . . . . alle to waraunt
Þis Corineus had grete ioie
whan he wist þei were of Troie.
To Brutus men he was fulle meke
& asked if þei ȝede lond to seke.
Þei seid, "We wille wend with ȝow,"   [*Transp. L*]
þat þei mot fynd vnto þer prowe.   [*Transp. L*]
So Corineus & his partie
went in Brutus companye.   Wente forth . . .
Brutus luffed wele Corineus,   [*Om. L*]
a frende of hym for sir Brutus.   [*Om. L*]
When þer flote with alle þer wayne
turned fro þe lond of Spaigne,

on þer reght hand toward Peyto,
þe wynd þat half bare þam so ..to þat half bar hem to
þore þe see receyues Leyre.
Alle þer flote com with grete eyre,
& þer he metis with þe see. [*Transp. L*] Leyre rennes þorow many contre
Leire rennes þorgh many cuntre; [*Transp. L*] And euere he metes wiþ þe se
þer flotes boþe þer gan duelle,
seuen days fully to telle.
Out of schippes þei went grete route ..þe schipes....
& spred þe cuntre alle aboute.
Goffare was kyng of Perters. ....Peyters
He sent knyghtes & squyers
to witt who made on hym pres, .waite.....
& wheþir þei souht were or pes.
Numbert hight þat bare message, .he highte...
for he knewe dyuers langage.
Corineus was gone to chace,
[10ra] venyson to tak o grace;
with hym were tuo hundreth men
to serche about in felde & fen.
With Numbert mette Corineus,
& Numbert spak tille hym þus:
"Be whos leue & whos warant
ere ȝe here alle chasant, ...chasand
& be whos rede ere here ...conseil are ȝe.
for to destroie þe kynges dere?
Here ne suld ȝe mak no chace
bot þorgh me or þe kynges grace,
& þe kyng forbed ilkon
þat no man suld tak here non.
How dar ȝe do suylk a thyng
withouten leue of þe kyng?"
Corineus spak as he þouht,
"Of ȝour kyng ne witte we nouht;
for hym ne wille we leue to do,
ne for his bode com hym to.
We know þe for no messengere,
ne hymself þof he were here."
Numbert sone his bowe bent
& schotte, bot Corineus glent. ....bleynt
Corineus was wroth, I trowe.
He sesid Numbertis bowe
& brak his bowe on his heued.

Hys felawes fled & dede hym leued, ...lefte hym ded
& ʒede & talde þe kyng Goffare .wenten to telle..
how men away his venyson bare.
Ilka dele þei tolde hym howe
þat Corineus Numbert slowe.
Goffare suore he suld him venge;
of mykelle folk he mad a renge
forto com on Brutus oste; .falle...
& Brutus spied be what coste, ..aspied on..
& sent vnto his flete on flode
þat þare rascaile to schippe alle ʒode,
& þer vitaile with þam lede
tille þei wist how he suld spede.
"Ne com not out, I ʒow forbede,
tille I com, for doute & drede."
His men of armes þat with him was,
[10rb] þei went ageyn to kyng Goffare.
Þe ostes sone togider mette,
with dynt of launce togidere sette. .spere & swerd to gedere.
Þe Peteuynes wele on þam souht;
þe Troiens stode & failed nouht.
Þei stode wele a grete partie;
non wist who suld haf maistrie.
Corineus for tene wex wode
þat þe Peteuyns so wele stode.
Out of þe renge he ʒede beside
& ches hym folk þat durst wele bide,
& trauersed þe Peteuyns bataile;
þan began þei for to faile. ...mykel to.
Þorgh þer oste he made þam weie,
on ilka side he did þam deie.
Corrineus þer his suerde les;
an ax he wan in alle þat pres. ...wan sone yn þat.
As auenture was it com to hand: ..fel hit cam til.
ageyn þat mot no man stand
noiþer behynd ne beforn;
þat he ouertok, þe lyf was lorn. ..ouer raught....
Þe Peteuyns stode & behelde
how Corrineus fauht in þe felde.
Þei saw his grete hardynesse
& his strokes were euer fresse; ...þat were ay.
befor hym euerilkon þei fleih,
ageyn hym nouht non ne deih. ffor drede of his hand to deye

When he sawe þat þei gaf bak,
he folowed þam & to þam spak:
"ffals folk, why fle ȝe?
Fle ȝe alle only for me? ... for drede of me
I am alle one, Corrineus,
& for me on ȝe fle alle þus!
Turne ageyn! What haf ȝe souht? .....þought
Fend ȝour land & fle nouht.

[*L adds:*] Turn a gayn & comes blyue
By tuo by þre by foure or fyue

Fend ȝour land, men hardy. & fend..as men.
Ȝow folowes non bot only I."
Suard, a knyght of þe kynges oste, Swerd......
herd his pride & his boste;
with tuo hundreth knyghtes & sueyn
on Corrine turned ageyn. .Coryneus..
On alle half about hym þei ȝede;
[10va] he fled þam nouht for no drede;
with þat ax he hym bewent.
Sir Suhard a stroke he lent; .Swerd....
with þat stroke his body clef,
into þe erth his ax dref.
Þe toþer alle had no foson
þan þe lomb ageyn þe lyon. Þan had þe....
Brutus com in þat stounde,
manyon slouh & leid to grounde; .he slow....
with þe Troiens was no fayntise.
Suhard was slaen & alle hyse. Bot Swerd was slayn...
Vnneþis scaped þe kyng o chance;
he ȝede & souht hym help in France. .ȝed to seke hym...
It hight not France, þe name was Galle;
Galle was it called þat tyme alle. .....tyme of alle
Þe tuelf Duȝperis of pris
departid þe lond in tuelf parties.
Ilkan of þise, Goffard þei hight
with þe Troiens for hym to fight,
& do þam alle to fle þe lond,
or do þam deie with dynt of hond.
Goffard thanked þam alle tuelf,
& ilkan gedred oste hymself.
Brutus & his men of Troie
for þer wynnyng made grete ioye,
& discomfite had þer enmys.

A castelle þei did mak of pris
in þe cuntre as þei nam,
on a faire hille þei restid & cam. ..... rested þam
A castelle þai mad to haf rescette;
beforhand ore was þer non sette,
toun no castelle þat no man witten,
bot as in olde story is writen.
Þorgh þat makyng þat þei did same,
Tours had gynnyng þerof & name. . had þey gyuen hit þe .
Toures called þat wyde is kid . was cald....
þorgh a knyght þat dede bitid.
Whan þe castelle was made & sette
& þer godes þerto fette,
bot tuo days sen it was dight,
com Goffare with alle his myght
on þe Troiens to gyf bataile,
& þer castelle þei gan assaile.
[10vb] Whan þe kyng sawe þat hille,
to his men he said his skille:
"Lo, þai haf mad a toure
fforto abate myn honoure! . abesen our .
Sorow in herte wille me slo
bot I be venged or þei go.
Þerfor, Lordes, pray ȝow alle, . . y preye . .
helpes now þat it may falle.
Arme vs suyth alle redy,
assaile we þam douhtily."
In tuelf batailes redy to fight, [*Transp. L*]
þei armed þam, baron & knyght, [*Transp. L*]
to gyf assaut þei were alle boune. ... al wer þey bone
Þei of þe castelle com out sone;
þei smyte togidere also smert
with fulle egre wille of hert.
Þer was bataile of no lite, Þat bataille was nought a .
so felonly þai gan to smyte.
In þer strokes at þe first tide, At þassemble in ...
þe Troiens had þe better side,
for wele in tuo thousand or mo . wel vnto twey ...
þe Troiens slouh sone of þo.
Þe tuelf batailes þe Troiens brak
& did þe Frankes go o bak. ... ffrensche arere hem bak
Þe Frankes þan kest a crie, . ffrankysche þenne ...
þer foreyn men drouh þam nehi Þerfore men drowe to . .

& stode ageyn & smyten sore,
& þer folk wex ay more.
Þei com ay fresh & stoden wele,
& drofe þe Troiens to þer castele.
Þan had þe Frankes þe fairere ende;
with force agayn did þam wend. Þat ded hem wyþ force ageyn to.
Alle þat day þei held þam fight
tille þam failed day light.
Þei withdrouh, tille loges þei ȝede;
þe nyght com nere þei most nede. ..was come þey..
Þe Troiens þat had bene in tirpelle,
at mydnyght toke þer counselle
þat Corineus out suld go
with his own oste & oþer mo, ...no mo
& busse in a wod beside. .busche hym....
"Þe Frankes oste ȝe salle here bide,
[11ra] & whan þer oste be alle comen,
& ȝe be ageym þam nomen, ..haue a geyn þem.
þen salle þei se þat ȝe ere fo.
Þei salle not drede on ȝow to go;
& tak non auysement,
for ȝe ere þei salle not tent, ..ar fewe þey schol..
& ȝe salle abate ȝow hardily,
for at þer bak I com redy.
Þe maistrie salle ours be,
for couward els hold ȝe me."
Corrineus he dight þam ȝerne
& went out at þe day sterne,
& bussed þam on a rowe
þat þe Frankisse kouth þam not knowe. .. Frensche moughte þem..
Þe Peiteuyns com at þe morn tide;
þe Troiens ageyn þam gon ride.
Turnus, a knyght, Brutus cosyn,
he partid þe oste of þe Peiteuyn
& rode þer oste alle þorhout:
mot non bere his strokes stout.
Meruelly was he hardy; Merueyloslike...
his hardines was foly.
In alle þe oste ne had he pere
of no strength þat men mot here.
Bot þe geant, sir Corrine,
ȝit was he als strong as he;
he trost hym mykelle on his myght; .triste to mykel...

ouer ferre he ȝede on þam to fight.
He had slayn, þe story seis,
sex hundreth Peiteuyns & Franceis;
siþen com alle þe Frankisse route
& closed hym in alle aboute
or euer com Corrineus,   Er þan ouer cam.
ore was he slayn, þis knygh Turnus.   Er.... knyght.
Right to dede as he was cast,
Brutus abatid hym ferly fast   . hasted...
& toke þe body fro þam alle
ore he of his hors gan falle,
& bare it vp vnto his toure.
Þer was he beried for honoure.
For luf of Turnus, þat gude knyght,
Tours hes now þe name right.   Toures in Tureyne now hit hight
[11rb] After Toures, þat ilk Cite,
Turoyne hate alle þat cuntre.
Brutus com ageyn to þe fight   . retorned to þat.
& Corrineus halpe at his myght;   ... wiþ al..
þe Frankisse oste was þam betuene.
Bituex þam tuo þei mad alle clene
of Frankisse & of Peiteuyns;
þei ley in dikes & in kynes.
To what stedes þei mot þem hide,   Þey soughten how þey mought..
to bataile wild þei no lenger bide.
Whan alle was fled & þe felde was playn,
Brutus turned his oste agayn;
ilkon to þer castelle went
& þer þei held a parlement.
Þer parlement, þis was þe ende:
euerilkon to schippe suld wende,
& drawe þer vitaile vnto þe see
& weyue alle þat cuntre.
Whan þei had don as I ȝow saie,
þei sette vp saile & furth þer waie.   ..... went..
Þei sailed day & on þe nyght   .. boþe day & nyght
þat neuer striken, bot ay vpright,
to þei aryued, as our buke says,
in Dertmuthe in Toteneys.
Alle holy com þer flote
in Dertmuthe at a schote.
Þat is þe Ilde þat Dame Diane
hete Brutus & his kynde alane.

Out of þe schippe þei com to land
with mykelle ioye, I vndirstand.
Whan þei wist þat þei were sette
to won þer Diane had þam hette
in þat Ilde of Albion,
& þanked þer godes euerilkon,
þat ilk tyme was not late,
fulle long tyme als says þe date.
Þe tyme Brutus aryued here
a thousand & tuo hundreth ȝere,
so mykelle was it þer beforn
are Ihesu was of Mary born.
In þat tyme were here no hauntes
of no men bot of geauntes.
[11va] Geant es more þan man,
so says þe boke, for I ne kan.
Like men þei ere in flesch & bone;
in my tyme, I saw neuer none.
Of membris haf þe liknes, . . haue þey .
þe lymes alle þat in man es.
Tuenty geantȝ were in þis lond;
of one þe name writen I fond,
Gogmagog þus was told;
for he was strong, grete & bold,
Gogmagog þus men hym calle;
it says he was most of alle.
Þe Troiens whan þei þe geantȝ sawe,
with þer bowes at þam gan drawe,
& also with darte & spere;
þe geantȝ couth þam not were.
Vp to þe hilles fro þam þei wonde
& left þe Troiens þe playn londe.
A day þe Troiens mad þer feste
after þe maner of þer geste,
with carols & with oþer glewe, Wyþ caroles trompes & pypyng
for ioie of þer wonyng newe. . . . . newe wonyng
As þei had carolde alder best
& ilkon suld haf gon to rest,
so com þe geantȝ þat ilk nyght
& on þe Troiens smyte dounrght. . . . . . doun ryght
fformast was sir Gogmagog,
he was mast, þat fule frog.
Þei fauht with trees þat þei vpdrouh;

I kan not say whilk þei slouh,
oþer wapen had þei non,
bot smite with trees or kast with stone.
When þei had fouhten & wend to fle,
in to þe hilled agayn to be, ...hilles...
are were þe Troiens þam before
& gaf þam wondes depe & sore,
& slouh þam þe mast parte
with bowe, with spere, & with darte. .spere & bowe swerd & dart
Gogmagog þe Troiens toke;
Brutus sayd þat þei suld loke
wheþir he were stranger or Corrineus. ...strenger..
A place to play ordaynd Brutus.
[11vb] Corrineus was wele ogrante
for to wristille with þe geante.
On o felde fast bi þe see, .a Clyf....
þe wristelyng was set to be. .wrastlyng was ordeyned..
Alle þei ȝede, ȝenge & olde,
þat wristelyng forto beholde.
Corrineus vpstirt first
& with a cloth his body girt,
streit in þe flank did hym lace;
he com & stode forth in þe place,
& Gogmagog ros vp sone.
He had hym dight & was alle bone.
Þe first pulle so hard was sette
þat þer brestes togidere mette;
ouer bakkes, handes þe cast, Þeir handes ouer bakkes þey.
syde to syde was set fulle fast.
Þer was turne set to turne, ...ageynes turn
þat waikest was behoued scurn; ...byhoued spurn
forset befor, forset behynd, ..& eke.
with krokes ilkon oþer bynd. ....gan bynde
Oft about ilk oþer threwe;
þe stem stode whan þei blewe; ...vp so..
þei handeled boþe sore þer nekkes,
chynnes, chokes, gaf hard chekkes; .chekes...
þer teth gnaisted with nese snore, ...nose.
hurteld hedes set fulle sore;
ilk oþer pulled, ilk oþer schoke,
with fete in fouche ilk oþer toke; ...fourche...
with trip forset ilk oþer to gyle.
In lifte & writhyng þei fraist vmwhile; ..in..sayed.

ilk oþer fro þe erth did vp rise
with strength more þan with quantise.
Gogmagog proued his strength;
tuelf elbous he was o length.   Twelue Cubyte....
In armes Corrineus he lauht
& on hym drow so strong a drauht
þat þre ribbes brak in his side
& had nere cast hym þat tide.
Þan was Corrineus oschamede
þat he was for geant lamede.   ...for þe Geaunt.
He recouerde his strength for tene;
of scathe he wild hym nomore mene.
[12ra] Alle with ire þe geant he hent;   Wyþ þat þe Geaunt..
in his armes so hym went
þat Gogmagog began to suoune
& bare with þe bank doun,   .bar hym....
doun of þe roche he lete hym falle.
Þe name ȝit, Faleise men calle.   Þerfore ffaleys men gon hit.
Are he com doun was flesh & bone
alle to ryuen fro stone to stone.
A grete þer he lay dede;   .gret þrowe....
þe water of his blode was rede.
Whan þe geantȝ were o dawe,
þe Troiens had more no awe.   ..hadden na more.
Tounes, houses did þei make,
& mesured lond & did it stake
þat his owen ilk did knowe;
þei tilled lond & did it sowe.
Þat tyme þis lond hight Albion.
Whan Brutus com, þat name was gon;
ffor Albion was Brutus wayne,
þerfor he did it calle Bretayne.   ......Brutayne
Whan he & his of Troie nam,
Troiens were called to þei þer cam.   ...til...
After þe Troiens, þe name was set:
for þe name of Brutus, first was Bret.
Afterward it turned eftsons,
for Brutus his folk was called Bretons.
Þat name held of Bretoun   ..held hit..
long sen þe Incarnacioun
tille Gurmunde com & here gan aryue;
þe Bretons away did he dryue.
Neuer siþen vnneþis non ros   Vneþe siþen any on.

þat long bare any los.
Þerof is spoken mykelle in dede;
nere at þe ende, ȝe may it rede.
Corrineus sesed a gude partie
of þe lond, for he was worthy.
Þer Corrineus did bataile,
þat cuntre he toke to Waile. ....þat hyghte Waille
Of corn & kataile þat is winnyng, .Corni & Waille þat was.
had Cornwale þe name gynnyng.
Cornwaile com of Corrineus,
& Bretayn com of sir Brutus.
[12rb] Ilkon þer frendes drouh .to þeym þer frendes.
& bigged lond for þer prouh;
fro stede to stede gan þei wende;
þer best was, þer wild þei lende.
Þei multiplied & wele throfe
& wex ryche, cante & kofe. ...kant & cof
In a fo ȝers, alle þe kynde
of folk wex þei mykelle mynde.
Brutus biheld þe mountayns
& auysed hym on þe playnes,
biheld þe wodes, water, & fen
where was eyse wonnyng for men.
Als waters rynnen, wele he behelde,
& þe medew with ardawfelde, .mede wiþ þe eryed feld
what frute he hopid it wild bere.
His folk wex fast þe lond to were,
þouht in his hert he wald make He þoughte in herte he wolde do.
a new biggyng for Troie sake.
A stede he chese, he ȝede to see ..to seche he...
where him thouht best & most eyse.
A water he fond & called it Tamise
after his langage on his wyse.
"I wille here, our kynde to ioye, Y schal sette her....
a cite for þe luf of Troie;
for Troie was so noble cite, ...a Cite
Newe Troie þe name salle be."
Newe Troie long it hight
tille quant men com of langage light, .som..wiþ..
schorte speche had þei in haunte
& called Newe Troie, Trinouaunte.
Alle is one, who so it knewe,
Trinouant & Troie Newe.

Troie Newe is Trinouant,
tuo wordes in one & nouht is want.
Þen com a kyng, Lud was his name,
& made a ȝate in þe same;
Kaer Lud þe name lauht,
for luf of Lud þe toune auht.   ....þat hit laught
ffor to haf hym renoune,   ...of hym.
Kaer Lud þei called þe toune.
Whan Sessons com, þat name ne couth: .Saxons.....
þer owen spech was best in mouth.
[12va] Þei called Luden & London;   ..hit Ludden..
þer þe name com eft son,   Þus....don
London on Sesson langage.
Anglis hold þat heritage,   Now Englysche holden..
als oþer of nacions,   .men of oþer.
þat haf bene here siþen þe Bretons,
has þe names of cuntres
bien charged, lawes & fees,   Ben chaunged &...
fro þe first þat þei were named
als outen folk haf hidere samed.   .straunge folk han hider y samed
Whan Brutus had set his cite
& burgeis set & gaf þam fee,
in lawe wisly to welde
& pes to haf in ȝouth & elde,
he regned foure & tuenti ȝed   .....ȝer
in alle Bretayn, fer & nere.
Alle Bretayn be olde tales,   Al was Brutaigne...
England, Scotland, & Wales:
þise þre were þan alle one
þat are was called Albion.
Albion hight þise londes þre,
for þei ere closed alle with þe see.
Brutus had with Ignogin
þre childire: þe eldest hight Lokerin,
þe toþer Camber, & Albanak.
Þise lyued behynd Brutus bak
& biried hym, þise sons thre,
whan he was dede in his cite.
Þise þre breþer, in luf & pes,
parted þe lond & ilkon ches
& were paied of þer partis   .held þem payed on þer.
als þe þre remes lis.
Lokerin ches first, he was eldest,

þis lond of Logres, it felle hym best.
[*L adds:*] Logeres hit ys after his name
ffor Lokeryn Logers had hit þe name

Camber tille his parte gan ȝerne
northwest þe water of Seuerne,
in length, in brede, as it gan lie,
& for his name called it Cambrie.
Cambrie it hight, be þo tales,
alle þe lond þat is now Wales; Þat lond þat now ys cleped.
& for þe quene, dame Galaes,
for luf of hire þat name þei ches.
[12vb] Som say, for oþer reson,
Gales was called for Duke Galon;
whilom þis duke was of powere
& grete renoun had fer & nere.
Albanak was ȝongest of alle;
þe mast wodelond gan hym falle.
Albanak called his partie
after his name, Albanie.
Albanie hight þat is Scotland, ..þat now ys.
as I salle telle ȝow who it fand. ...ȝow telle how y fand
Þe name of Scote, þe first rote,
it was gyfen a mayden, Scote.
Scote was Pharaon douhter, þe kyng;
to Scotland was scho weddid ȝing
& was to hire giffen & scho it auht;
of hire þe name Scotland lauht.
Humbert, a kyng of Huneis, Numbert....
a robbour he was, it sais.
He robbed þe ildes alle about;
of felon men he had grete route. .lyþer.....
Of Albanie men to hym spake,
bot a childe was Albanake. Þat was a childes Albanak
With Albanak fayn wald he fight;
Albanak herd, agayn hym dight, & Albanak faste...
bot Albanak son he slouh. ..sone þer..
His folk fled & southward drouh
& plenyd vnto Lokerin, ..þem to sire Lokeryn
how þei ascaped with mykelle pyne.
Lokerin vnto Camber sent;
þei gadred oste & þider went.
Ageyn þam com sire Humbert;
of þam both was he not ferd.

In an arme of þe see	
mette þei togidir alle þre;	
þe breþer had more powere þen he.	. Bretons were wel mo . .
In þat water, fast gan he fle;	. to þat water þey dide hem .
he ascaped nouht for no thyng;	Þey ne ascaped . . .
he dronkend þer, Humbert þe kyng.	& so þer drenkled Humbert . .
ffor Humbert gan þer misfalle,	
Sir Lokerin did þat water calle	
Humber after sir Humbert,	
for he dronkend þer in a pert.	. . dreynte þerin in apert
[13ra] ffro Almayn sir Humbert cam,	
þe ildes he robbed als he nam.	
Sir Lokerin toke þat he had reft;	
þre maydens in his schyppe were left.	Þre faire maydenes . . . . .
Þe kynges douhter of Germine	
was þe fairest of þase þre.	. . . . alle þre
Sir Lokerin ȝened mykille þat may,	. Lokery byheld faste . .
scho was fairest vnto his pay.	
Tendirly he did hir ȝeme;	
of alle women scho mot hym queme.	. . scheo was most til hys .
Estrild þat mayden hight;	
was non fairere in Lokerin sight.	. . so fair . . .
Corineus ȝitt lyued he þo;	
a douhter had & childere no mo.	He hadde a doughter & . .
He had spoken with Lokerin	
to wed his douhter Guendoline.	
Lokerin & he were in conount	. . . . . couenaunt
& þei both had made þe graunt,	
bot for þe luf of faire Estrilde,	
Lokerin haf broken it wilde.	. . . hit fayn he wylde
Corrineus herde it sone say;	
þer Lokerin was he toke þe way.	
An axe in his hand he toke;	
on Lokerin lothely gan he loke	. . loþliche . . .
& wrothfully to hym he spak;	. angrily til . . .
ne bot wreth of his mouth brak.	
He sayd, "Lokerin, þou ert a foole!	
Þi self dightes þe to doole!	
Þi dede of me þan salt þou haue,	
þer fro no man salle þe saue.	
Why has þou my douhter forsaken	
þat in treuth þou had taken?	
Þat is þe þank þou me kons.	. . . . þat þou me cones

	I halpe to wyn þat þou in wons;	. hope . . . . inne wones
	I serued þi fadere in many nede,	
	& ille ʒeldes þou me my mede.	
	I auntred me in many chance	
	þi fadere, Brutus, for to auance.	
	Many stroke gaf in many stoure	
	to bring þi fadere tille honour,	
	& ʒit þi self auance I wilde,	
	bot for on þei calle Estrilde	
[13rb]	forsakes my douthter Guendolene	. . doughter .
	& dos me dispite & tene.	
	Tille þou wote I am olyue,	Whil þou wost . . .
	salle þou haf non oþer wyue.	
	Þou bringe þe in foule fame,	
	& dos me dispite & schame	. . . gret onoy . .
	& my douhter Guendoline,"	
	& layd hand on sir Lokerin	
	& wild haf venged his tene,	. wolde han venged þer . .
	& lordynges schet þam bituene	Nadde lordes schoten hem .
	& departed þam o tuynne,	
	& prayd Corrineus to blynne.	
	Þei conseiled sir Lokerin;	
	he ʒede & wedded Guendolin,	
	bot he forgat on no manere	
	faire Estrild þat was hym dere.	
	In London he did hire kepe	
	vndere þe erth in a celere depe.	
	Estrild was lang þare,	
	seuen ʒere & somwhat mare.	
	Whan Lokerin suld vnto hir go	
	& duelle with hir a day or tuo,	
	vntille his wyfe þan tald he	
	þat he suld go in priuete	
	& stilly mak his sacrifise	
	vnto his godes with his seruyse,	
	for openly ne felle in nouht	. . . . hit nought
	to do þat seruise þat he wroht.	. . . . . he had wrought
	So long he played with Estrilde	
	þat scho had a mayden childe,	
	Sabren it hight, white so glas,	. . . as whit as .
	& fairere þan þe modere was.	
	Guendolin a son had þan,	. . child . .
	a childe þat hight Maddan.	. sone . . .

Corrineus had it to loke;
whan tyme was, set it to boke.
Whan Corrineus was dede,
dame Guendolin he misbede.
For hir fader did hym tene,
he drofe a way dame Guendolene
& toke Estrilde tille his quene
als dame Guendolene had bene.
[13va] Scho sawe no bettire myght auaile,
scho gadred an oste in Cornwile; .....Cornewaylle
tille hir frendes scho pleyned hire.
Agayn Lokerin þei gan þam atire
with grete oste out of mesure.
Opon a water men calle Esture,
in Dorcester schire, þei mette
& to batale smertly sette. ...swyþe þey.
Þe kyng was slayn with a schote,
þe oste discomfet ilk a crote. ..destruyed...
Þe quene had þe heiere hand:
scho did seise alle þe land.
Scho did take faire Estrilde
& Sabren þat was hir childe,
& did þam in a water cast.
Þe name for þam is rotefast: ffor þeym þe name ys roted fast
Seuerne it hate for þe child Sabren,
for þat childe þe name we ken.
Þat tyme þat þis chance felle
lyued þe prophete Samuel.
Guendolene was þan stoute;
scho did þe folk vnto hire loute.
Ten ȝere with Lokerin had scho bene
& siþen fiften wynter quene.
Whan Madan couth kepe his thyng,
in hir lyue was he kyng. ....he mad.
To Cornwaile scho turned eft
to kepe þat hir fadere left.
Madan gate opon his wyfe
tuo sones þat lyued in strife; ...ay lyued..
Malyn hight þe eldest broþer,
Membrice men called þe toþer.
Madan regned fourty ȝere
& left his sonnes þe lond in wehere. ....þat lond in wer
Þise breþer were euer wroþe;

for þe lond þei stryuen boþe.
Membrice for treus to Malyn sent
in pes to hold a parlement;
Membrice to treson drouh,
his broþer Malyn priuely slouh.
Þorgh slauhtere & treson
had Membrice þe region.
[13vb] Þis Membrice he wex vnkynde,
fordid þe gude men we fynde, .god men þat he myght.
reft þam ouþer land or lyfe,
& forsoke his wedded wyfe
& haunted þe syn of Sodom,
& vnkyndly to bestis com.
Tuenty ȝere had he space
& as he went to wod to chace,
with wolues alon he mette. Many....
As deueles þai about hym sette, Also þeues abouten hym þey.
lym fro lym hym alto rente;
Membrice so to dede wente.
Saul regned in Iudea
& Eresteus in Lacedemonia.
Ebrauk, his son, was of age,
had þis lond in heritage.
He was a fulle noble knyght;
a grete nauye he gert dyght. ...he dide hym.
He was þe first man of þis lond
þat robbed bi see & sond. ....oþer by sond
With þe Cornwailes he stode to chance;
þei & he robbed alle France;
þei robbed tresore & vitaile;
home to Bretayn gan þei saile
whan he had tresore & feeȝ; ...y now tresour & fe
in þe north he mad a Cite.
Kaer Ebrauk he called þat toun,
anoþer, Aklud, opon Breton,
Kaer Ebrauk first men spak;
siþen men calde it Eborak.
ffrankys spech is not so like:
for Eborak þei calde it Euerwyk.
Aklud he called Maydens Toun;
Kaer Lauerok is now þe renoun.
Maydens castelle, bi þat day,
with maydens had he þer his play.

Sexty wyntere he regned in lyue;	.....lyues
he had tuenty sons with tuenty wyues,	
& þritty douhtres bi þo same.	
Of þe sons listen þe mame:	.þyse children lystneþ þer name
Brutus Greneschelde, Margadu,	
Sisillius, Regin, Bladu,	
[14ra] Moruid, Lagon, Ebollan,	Moryod..
Kinkar, Spadan, Gaul, Pardan,	Kynbar...
Eldade, Chagus, Cherm, Luor,	...Luwor
Lud, Assarak, Buel, Hector;	
þise ere þe sonnes names right.	
Listens how þe madens hight:	Now lystneþ how...
þe first hight Gloyglin,	
Otidas, Aurar, Ninogin,	Otyda..
Garadid, Rodan, Guedan,	..Gwedian
Maylure, Echab, Tangustel,	[*Transp. L*] Angart Gwenlode Medlan
Engard, Guenlode, Medlan,	[*Transp. L*] Mayleure Echab Tangustel
Stadut, Kambreda, Methael,	.Lambrada.
Gaat, Eheyn, Neest, Egorgon,	.Echeyn..
Gladus, Abren, Langon, Egron,	
Edra, Abalac, & Angues,	...Agues
Anor, Staliad, & Galaes.	.Stahad Angalaes
Galaes was ientilere lady	Galaes was þe gentilest.
þan þe toþer nyen & tuenty.	.any of al þe oþere...
Anor scho was fulle curteise	
& wele couth demene rycheise.	...demeyne Richeyse
Gloglyn, scho was eldest,	
& scho was of maneres best.	
Alle were þei dight, maydens gent,	....þyse madenes.
& into Lumberdy were sent	
tille þe kyng Silui, Latyn son,	
at bring þam to warison.	To brynge þem..
Alle were þei gyuen as þei ȝode	
to þe Troiens, men of gode.	
Þe tuenty breþer, als it says,	
to purchace þam went þer ways;	..hem þey wente..
þei did þam vnto Almayne	
& alle þe lond was þer wayne.	
Brutus Grenschelde, þe eldest son,	
in þis lond he left to won.	
Tuelue wynter regned here	
in pes & in gode manere.	
He had a son hight Leyle;	

he mad a toun with his conseyle,
Karlel it hatte, men say,
bot Leil, agayn þat he suld dey,
pered fast in his elde   Preyed....
& his lond couth not welde.   ffor his lond he mought..
[14rb] Ilk on oþer were souht;
for doute of him left þei nouht,
ne he couth no bettir Iustiser.   ...be no iustyser
He regned fyue & tuenty ȝere.
In his tyme was þe prophete Amos,
& Hien & Aggeos,
& þe prophete Ʒacharie
in his preched þei prophecie.   .þat tyme preched.
Leyl lygges at Karlele, þer þe story spak;
Brutus lygges at Ʒork beside Ebrak.
After Leile regned Rudhudibras;   ...Rehudybras
to iustise þe folk noble he was.   ....fol wys..
He acorded alle his barons,
pes to hold he made þam somons.
He mad Wynchester & Cantirbyre
& þe castelle of Chestirschire.   ....Chestebury
One spak þer & prophecied,   A while on spak þanne..
Aquile, men sais he lied.   Bot som men seide þat he.
Rudhudibras in his powere
regned nyen & fourty ȝere.
After þe kyng Rudhudibras,
Bladud his son crouned was.
Bladud did many maistri:
he gaf him tille Nigromanci;
þe hate bathe he did mak   Hote bathe he dide.
for mykille gode to mans sak.
He did ley þer it springes   ...þerin.
tunnes of bras, quante þinges   ...wiþ queynte.
þat makes þe water euer hote;
what is þerin no man wote.
Bathe for bathyng þe name hight;
beside þe bath, a temple he dight.
Þe temple name was Minerue,
þe folk to resceyue & serue.
A fire he did mak þerin,   After he...
euer to birne & neuer blyn.
Bladud wrouht many meruaile,
many a gude þat ȝit auaile,   .god þyng þat ȝit wyl vaylle

At þe last he wild flie:
fedirhames he mad slie. ...hym sleye
[At Lond]on he toke his flight, *[P has a hole in the MS; the repair*
[& fley] fer as he myght. *has failed. Emendations are from L.]*
[14va] Apon þe temple of Apolyn, Vpon a temple sire.
þeron he felle & mad his fyn.
Sir Apolyn so doun hym cast
þat body & bon alle to brast.
Tuenty wynter was he kyng;
at London he mad his endyng.
After hym regned Leire
þat was his son & his heire.
Fourty wynter regned he;
opon Sore mad he a cite.
Kaerleir he did it calle,
Leicestre þe name is now withalle.
Þre douhters had sir Leire,
myght he haf non oþer eire;
þe eldest hight Gonorille
þe toþer Ragau, þe þrid Gordille. ..Ragaw...
Gordille scho was ȝongest
& hire lufed þe fadere best.
Leyre, whan he was in elde,
his lond myght he not welde.
His douhters he thouht gyf husbondes,
bituex þam departe his londes. & twyxten hem parten..
Of þam first wald he here Bot of hem first he þoughte.
whilk of þam had him most dere:
he asked of ilk bi þam self alon, .assaied ilk...one
þe eldest first of ilkon.
He com & spak to Gonorille:
"Douhter, say me now þi wille,
how mykille wild þou me loue
if þou were lady me aboue?"
Whan þat word scho herde neuen,
scho suore bi þe godhed of heuen
wheþire scho were mayden or wyfe,
scho wild luf hym als hir lyfe.
"Douhter," he saied, "grant mercy;
of me þou getes grete curtasie."
He com & spak to Ragawe.
"Douhter, sey me soth sawe. ...þe soþe sawe
How mykille lufes þou me with wille?"

& Ragawe thouht of Gonorille.
Scho said, "Fadere, I luf þe mor[e]   [*P has a hole in the MS.*]
þan alle þat in þis world euer wore."
[14vb] "Douhter, þat is luf inouh.
Þi lufyng salle falle for þi prouh."   . . schal be . . prow
He com to Gordille þe ȝongest;
of boþe þe toþer he lufed hir best.
Scho wist how hir sistres said;
of a gyle it was a braid.
"Douhter, how mykille lufes þou me?"
"Fadere," scho said, "I salle say þe.
Als my fadere I haf þe loued
& euer salle to be reproued."   . . more schal to be proued
"Loues þou me no more, my dere?"
"Ȝis, fadere, þou listen & here.
Right as þou has, so ert þou worþi;
so mykelle luf to þe ouh I."
Þat word toke he ille to hert.
He vnderstode it alle ouerthuert.
Scho said not glosand to his wille
als Ragawe did & Gonorille.
Þerfor he ansuerd þus agayn:
"Of me þe þink grete desdeyn
& has myn elde in despite;
of myn for euer þou ert quyte.
Þou sais not als þi sistres sais   . . . . . sistren .
of þin ansuere so curtais;   Þyn answere his nought . .
þerfor I salle myn heritage
gyf þi sistres in mariage.
Þei salle departe þam bituene,   . . depart hit þeym .
& þou þerfro quyte & clene.
Of þam alle I chirest þe maste, ... loued . .
& now I se þou lufes me leste."
Gordille no more wild say
ne stryue agayn bot ȝed hire way.
Ne he said no more to hire;
he went a way fulle of ire.   Bot wente fro hure al in ire
In þis tyme þat þei were wroþe,
he maried þe toþer douhtres boþe.
Þe kyng of Scotland þe ton wedde,
Hennis of Cornwaile Ragawe hom ledde.
Þei acorded alle at þer paie
to parte þe lond bi his daie.   . . . . al by . .

Dame Gordille with wrath scho went;
of many men, mykille was ment
[15ra] þat scho had no warisoun,
noþere rent of lond ne toun,
& he forbed hir lord to take
in his lond, for warison sake.
Þerfor aschamed hir so sore . he schamede hure .
& hir forþouht mykelle more . . ouer þoughte . .
þe wraþe of hir fadere þe kyng
þan þe tynselle of oþer thyng. Wel more þan any . .
Aganippus, þe kyng of France,
herde speke of Gordille chance,
how men said of hir grete pris, Alle men leyde on hure . .
þat scho was faire, curtays, & wis.
He þouht if he myght hir haue,
alle his honor suld scho saue. . . . . sche haue
He sent messengers to Leyre;
to wedde his douhter he was in speyre,
bot Leyre had ȝit forgeten, . . . nought ȝit .
how lightly scho of him had leten.
Leyre sent him agayn to say
he had gyfen his lond to douhtres tuey. His land was gyuen to his . .
Hir body on him he vouched saue;
with hir nouht els myght he haue.
To Leyre he sent eft agayn . . . . ȝut eft .
& teld hym for certayn . seyde Leyr . .
þat he asked non oþer thyng
bot only his douhter ȝyng;
& Leyre granted þam alsone, Leyr þen . . also sone
with hir to wend þai mad þam bone.
To schippe þei went & vp þe saile,
asked þei non aparaile.
Now is hir fallen fairest chance: . . . . þe fairest .
Gordille is mad quene of France.
Lo, þo men þat kyng Leyre Þenne þe men . . .
had ordeynd to be his heyre,
þei suffred hym no thyng to take,
his awen propir for to make.
Hewyn, þe duke of Cornwaile, When þe Duk . .
þe south to hym gan he taile. Al þe souþ tyl hym gan .
Meglan, kyng of Scotland, Manglanus þe kyng . .
þe north toke to his hand. . . he tok hit til . .
Leyre was at þer baundon

& þei set him to liuerison;
[15rb] þe set honorable to be   Þey sette hym...
with fourty knyghtes of meigne.
Leyr was payed of þat conant;   .held hym...coueinaunt
to hold him þat, þei suore þe grant.
With Maglanus was Leyr þe kyng   .Manglanus....
fulle wele serued at þe gynnyng.   .....comyng
Sone afterward, þei filled Leyr   ...fillede of.
& did his lyuere to apeyr.
After apayrment of his lyuere,
were abatid of his meygne;
þe quene, his douhter Gonorille,
hir thouht most scorne & ille
of þe meygne hir fadere held;
grete outerage scho it teld.
Scho said vnto Maglanus,
"Fouly hold we þis meygne þus   ffolyly.....
þat mykelle thyng alle day notes,
& my fader in elde dotes
to hold suylk a squyery
& grete costage in riotry;
þerfor I rede þou do as I say,
lat som of þise go forth þer way."   ...hem go þer.
Þan was ordayned to lesse þer men,
of fourty knyghtes abatid ten.   ...abyde þe ten
Þan was Leyre rente abatid;
he auanced hir þat first him hatid.   ..first hure þat hym.
Scho was first maried of alle,
& first did scho his honour falle.
Allas, fo childere men fynde   .to fewe...
þat to fadere & modere be kynde.
Now gynnes Leyr to mislyke.
"Sone," he said, "þei gynne me suyke.
Of myn aboue, I am put lowe,   ffro myn alone....
& ȝit more within a throwe.   ..scha more...
Mine oþer douhter wille I proue
what scho is worth to my behoue."   Þey scheo be wroþ...
He dight him with his apparaile
& went him in to Cornwaile.   To wende in to.
He had not bene þer fully a ȝere   .dwelt nought þer fullyk..
þat þei ne mad hym grete dangere
& lessed his knyghtes, his oþer men,
of thritty þei abatid ten,

[15va] & ȝit of tuenty abated fyue;	
þan wald Leyr haf ben of lyue.	
"Allas," he said, "I hider cam,	
fro wik vnto wers I nam."	
To Gonorille ageyn he ȝede;	
he wend scho wald amend his nede,	.... heue mended ..
haf gyffen him as he had beforn.	... als scheo hadde .
Scho suore þat god lete hir be born,	.. by god þat hure leet ..
þat scho ne wild, day ne nyght,	
holde bot him & a knyght.	
Þan began Leyr to sorowe	
& ment his mone euen & morowe.	
þe grete rychesse he had beforn,	
alle it was away lorn.	
"Now ouer long o lyue haf I bene	To longe a lyue haue y be
þat þis euer I suld haf sene.	Þat euere scholdy þys day se
fforbisen bi me men may take	Ensample of me ...
& warned be for my sake.	. warnyng of sibbe ...
I had richesse, now haf I non;	
my witte & my happe is gon.	... al myn help ..
[*L adds:*]	Lady ffortune þou art chaungable
	O day art þou neuere stable
	No man may of þe affye
	Þou turnes hym doun þat er was heye
	Þat now ys doun vpward þou turnes
	Wyþ þe nys non þat he ne mournes
	Bot þere þou gyuest þy loue lokyng
	He ys worschiped als a kyng
	& whom þou turnest þy lokyng fro
	Sone ys he doune yn sorewe & wo
	Þe vnkynde þou wilt vp reyse
	Þe kynde þou puttest to meseysey
	Wyþ Kyng & Erl when þe myslikes
	Þer welþe a wey to wo þou strykes
Whan I had gold & welth inouh,	
my frendes vnto me fast drouh;	Þen fondy frende þat to me.
now pouert put me beforn	.. ys put ..
þat alle þer sight of me is lorn.	
Þer luf suld longe to þorgh right,	... lange to me ..
þei mak of luf semlant ne sight.	Þat schewe me of loue ...
Dame Fortune, þi lufly loke	
& þi gode wille fro me þou toke.	
Whan I blamed my douhter ȝyng	

& gaf no kepe to hire kennyng,
þat said me soth apertly:
als I had, so was I worthy;
& als so mykille scho lufed me,
scho said better þan I couth se.
Hir word no þing I vnderstode,
bot made me wroþe, I couth no gode.
I perceyued not what was hir tente,
bot now I fele what scho mente. — ..fele y wel...
I fele it wele þe soth it endes;
Whidere may I to seke me frendes? — ..y now to...
If I seke hir for any frame
& scho me weyue, scho nes to blame, — Þey sche me.....
[15vb] for I defendid hir my londe,
ne nouht I gaf hir ne fonde. — ..hure gaf ne hure..
Neuerþeles, hir wille I seke;
I fond hir euer gode & meke.
Wisdom sho has me tauht;
wisdom salle mak hir with me sauht.
If I may nouht bring hir þer to,
wers þan þe toþer may scho not do.
He said a thyng I salle now proue: — Scheo seyde......
als hir fader sho wald me loue,
& als sho said, proue salle I
hir kyndnes & hir curtasy."
Whan Leyre had long sore sighed, — .....syked
his mone ment & mislyked,
he dight him als o chance
& ouer þe se he ferde to France. — Right ouer..forþ into.
At Kaleis vp heuen he hente;
to þe quene priuely he sente.
At a cite he abode
tille a man þe massage rode — Whyle a man his message.
& telled þe quene alle his cas,
& how he vp aryued was,
how his douhtres with him wrouht; — ...had wyþ..
alle his mischefe forgate he nouht.
Gordille, whan scho wist þe pleynt,
hir faire colour gan alle to feynt.
Alle þat scho had in hir powere
scho bitauht it þe messengere,
& bad him go for to atire him — ....hym forte atyre
with honour, forto com speke with hire.

"Biforhand send my lord þe kyng Bot byforn sendes....
& warne him of his comyng."
Þe messenger sped him suythe
& brouht Leyre tiþing blythe;
vnto a noþer Cite he ȝede
& dight him þat him was nede. ...al þat hym..
Whan he was dight at his wille,
he sent to þe kyng & to Gordille
þat he was aryued in þat cuntre
to speke with þe kyng, his douhter to se.
Whan he wist þat Leyre suld com,
ageyn fulle faire þei nom Agaynes hym ful...
[16ra] & faire resceyued him for þe quene ..receyues hym aforn..
as a man he had not sene.
He comanded in his kyngdam
to wirschip him where he cam.
Whan he had duelled longe space,
he teld how his douhtres did him chace.
Sire Aganippus was curtais;
he samned an oste of Franceis .samned...his ffraunceys
& com with Leyre ouer þe see
to help to wyn ageyn his fee.
Gordille with hir fader went,
with leue of hir lord his hoste sent.
Þe dukes bifor þam þei fond; ..sone byforn hem..
þei slouh þam boþe & wan þe lond.
Þre ȝere after was he kyng;
in plenere seisen did his endyng. .ful seysyne made..
Dame Gordille he mad his heyre.
In Laycestre laid scho hir fadere Leyre
in a temple solempnely;
þe name was temple Iani. .temple highte temple Iany
Sone after þat chance felle þus,
died hir lord Aganippus.
In hir widouhed scho had þe honour
fyue ȝere as conquerour.
Hir tuo sistres had tuo sons;
how þei did þe story mones.
Gonorille son hight Morgan,
þe toþer Condage, a noble man.
Whan þis Morgan & þis Condage
waxen were & of age,
to Gordille þei gaf bataile,

& scho agayn did þam trauaile.
First were þei boþe ouercomen;
at þe last, Gordille þei nomen
& held hir long in þer prison;
for hir myght go no raunson.
Whan no raunson myght for hir go,
hir self for sorow did scho slo.
Whan Condage & Margan
of Gordille þe lond þus wan,
Condage toke, als him thouht best,
ouer Humber þe Northwest,
[16rb] & Margan þe south he ches.
Bot tuo ȝere held þei þe lond in pes;
bot couetise þat neuer restis,
venom amang men it kestis.
Margan had enyous felawes ..enuiouse.
þat wikkedly said to him sawes:
þam were leuere were þen pes;
he listend þam & þat he ches.
Þus þei said vnto Margan:
"Þou ert eldest & baldest man
& has bot half & ȝit þe lest,
& he ȝongere & has þe mest;
& þat is alle þin owen gilte;
þou may haf alle if þou wilte. ..haue hit al ȝyf þat..
To ride, if þou wille bigyn,
alle þe lond may þou wyn.
Þou getis folk out of noumbire ...wyþoute.
to seise þe lond beȝond Humbire.
If þou bigyn forto ride,
Condage salle not abide." .schal nought þe.
Margan did after conseile ..atte her.
& wrouht himself to wroþerheile.
He passed Humbir, destroied þe lond,
& brent & robbed alle þat he fond.
Condage herd it sone seie;
he dight his oste to stop his weie.
Margan herd telle þat Condage
com with grete oste & outrage;
he turned bak, bigan to fle
south fro cuntre to cuntre;
fer in to Wales fled Morgan,
& Condage folowed & hym ouerran,

& þer in Wales Morgan slouh.
Þorgh þat has it name nowe: Þorow hit haþ þat þe . .
Clou Morgan is now þe name
for Morgan died in þat same.
Þan had alle sir Condage
þe lond holy in heritage.
Þritty wynter was he kyng;
in pes he made his endyng.
In his tyme was Ysaie
& preched þan þe prophecie,
[16va] & þe prophete Osee
þat tyme lyued he, Y þat tyme þan . .
& þe emperoure Romulus
& his broþer Remus.
Þise tuo breþer mad Rome
þer holy kirk gifes his dome. . . chirche gyueþ þe .
Þre hundreth ȝere & foure score
& seuenten þus felle before, . . . fer .
regned kynges in þis landes
ar Rome were set þer it standes. . . . . þer hit now .
After þis kyng Condage,
Ryual, his son, held þe heritage;
þre days in his rayned blode
(I ne wote why ne vnderstode),
& wex so mykille mynde of flies,
men died bi stretes & bi sties.
Alle men had þerof grete drede
tille it sesed & ouer ȝede.
After þis kyng Ryual, . þe kynges tyme .
Gurgustius, his son, had alle.
After þis Gurgustius, . his sone .
regned his son Sisillius.
After þe kyng Sisilli
was Lago kyng, cosyn Gurgusti. . . . his cosyn ney
After Lago was Kynmare kyng,
Sisilli son, & had þe þing.
After Kynmare regned þan
his son þat hight Gorbodian.
Gorbodian had tuo sones,
fulle enuyous þat ȝit of mones; . enemys . . men .
þe eldest hight sir Ferreus,
þe toþer men called Porreus.
Might neuer pes be þam bituen,

ne non acorde bot euer tene.
To whils þer fadere was o lyue,
for þe reume gan þei stryue. ..Royalme gon þey to.
[*L adds:*] Al þus þey ferde wiþ gret enuye
Whilk scholde haue þe seignurie
Porrex was eldest & most felon; Porrex was ȝongest...
his þouht was ay on treson
þer þorgh he thouht his broþer slo. Where þorow he moughte...
Þe toþer herd þat did hym to go
into France for doute of gyle.
Þe kyng Siwarde he serued a while
[16vb] & gadred þer a partie, ...god party
with schippes com ouer baldely,
& to his broþer gaf bataile.
He died sone, it myght no vaile;
bot at þe first was he slayn
& alle his folk, knyght & suayn.
Iudon, his moder, herde wele how
þat þe ton þe toþer slouh.
Scho lufed mykille þe slayn broþer
& dedely hated sho þe toþer;
for als vnkyndly as þei wrouht,
an vnkynes sho þouht. Þerfore vnkyndenesse..
A nyght hir son to bed was gon,
on hym com his moder Iudon.
Ilk of hir maydens a knyfe bare;
Porrex throte a tuo sho schare
& on peces alle to hewe; ...hym al to.
suylk a vengeance no man knewe.
Long men spak of þat chance
of Iudon & hir vengeance.
Whan þise breþer þus were gon, ...werre bygon
here of blude was þer non Eyr.....
þat myght haf þe heritage.
Was nouht left of þe right lynage,
tille fyue kynges left þe lond Bot to..þey lefte..
þat fourty wynter þe were fond.
Ilk of þam þat mast myght ....most was of.
benam þe powere of his myght. .þat oþer of his right
Mesure no lawe held no man
bot who so myght of oþer nam; ......wan
þat richest were most bare þam stoute,
in lawe ne luf wald non loute.

Þat tyme in Scotland regned Statere;
in Logres was þe kyng Pincere;
Rudak was kyng of þe Walsch men,
& Cornwaile had þe duke Cloten.
Cloten of kynde was next of alle
to whom þe heritage suld falle,
bot for þe toþer were most of myght,
þei gaf nouht of alle his right.
Þis duke Cloten had a childe,
[17ra] a douhty bachelere & wylde;
þat tyme he was most worþi ..was he man most.
& faire waxen & wele on hii.
Donwal Douhty was his name,
of curtasie had he þe fame;
ouer þam alle passed his powere,
for first he slouh kyng Pincere
& seised þe lond tille his bihoue;
opon Statere wild he ȝit proue.
With force of armes he gan to ride;
Statere & Rudak he þouht to bide.
Rudak & Stater herde son say,
þei suore togidere on him to dey.
Ageyn Donwalle þei brouht þer oste
in tuo parties bi diuers coste. In to halues...
Rudak of Wales had þe to side;
toward þe north Statere gan ride.
Þei brent & slouh, nouht wild þai spare;
of castelle & toun alle made þei bare.
Donwalle herd þis lond þei wasted;
he dight his oste & to þam hasted.
He mette with þam & did þam stande;
þe were in felde þritty þousande.

[*L adds:*] Gret noise at her samnyg was
Wiþ trompe & taber & horn of bras

Grete strokes & sore sette
were gyfen when þei togider mette.

[*L adds:*] Helm þorow smyten & many a scheld
Many a knyght was feld in feld
Of many hauberks was hewen þe maille
Longe þey stode & gaf bataille

Non wist who suld haf þe maistri,
þe parties boþe were so douhti.
Donwalle was werreour gode;

him forþouht þe so wele stode.   . ouerþoughte þey . . .
Sex hundreth of his weled he out   . . . . he colede out
þat proued were herdy & stout;
he did þer armes alle doun ley
priuely beside þe wey
& armed þam on alle manere,
als þer enmys armes were.
Þer scheldes toke, helme & gleyue,
þer enmys for to disceyue;
þei did alle at his auys
& toke þe armes of armes of his   . . . . of þere enemis
þat dede ley & alle þer quantise,   . leyen dede wyþ here queyntise
& dight þam on þer enmys wyse.
Donwalle said, "Comes alle with me
& als I go, so salle ȝe."   . þider as y go . . .
[17rb] Þei ȝede spiand here & þere
in wate bataile þe kynges were.   . what . . . .
Whan þei wist, alle at ons
trauersed þam for þe nons,
als þei had ben on þer partie
& side bi side riden þam bie.
Þe kynges to þam gaf no tent
bot forþe in þer bataile went.
"Haf at," said Donwalle, "now is leisere,"
& seised Rudak & Statere
& boþe at ons lightly slouh,   . . . ones þeym . .
& of þe pres þam smertly drouh,
& cast þer armes of þe vnknawen,
& armed þam eft with þer awen.
Whan þei had þer armes nomen
& to þere oste ageyn comen,
fast þei folowed on þam alle.   . . fullen opo þem .
Sone þer force doun gan falle;
þe toþer side stode stoute in stoure,   . . . stod nought . .
for þei had tynt þer gouernoure.   . . . lost . .
Þei fled to wodes & mountanes,
for slayn were þer cheftanes.
Whan Donwalle had þe maistrie,
his pes he did set & crie,
þat so gode pes was neuer ore
ne þer after salle neuer more.
A croun of golde he did make,
suylkon neuer for kynges sake

was in Bretayn wrouht beforn
on kynges hede set ne born.
He stabled suylk pes & grith,
& with his seal confermed it with,
þat ilk a temple & ilk cite
suld haf & hald þis dignyte:
þat if a man had don trispas,
robbed or slayn or oþer cas,
if he to a temple cam
ore men him with handes nam,
or tille a Cite go his way,
of ille suld no man to him say;   Non yuel schold men til hym eft.
& also to þat at plouhes ȝede,   ..to hem þat at..
if any man did ille dede   ...dede hem yuel.
[17va] or to merket if on suld go,
if any man did þam wo,   ȝyf men dide hem any.
it was told for felonye
& worþi were þerfor to dye.
ffourti wynter was he kyng;
at London he mad his endyng.
A temple þer he did make
for þe pes & concorde sake.
In þat temple mad for pes
was he laid & þer he ches.
Of him were tuo noble sones
as þe story of þam mones:
Belyn þe eldest, þe toþer Brenne;
Donwalle þer fadere god I bikenne.
Belyn & Brenne parted þe lond
on þis maner als I fond:
Belyn lete Brenne of him holde   Brenne schold of Belyn holde
fro Humber north his lond he tolde.   His lond fro Humber Northward..
Ilk a dele vnto Cathenesse
held Brenne of Belyn, more & lesse.
Seruyse suld he do þer fore,
he & his for euermore.
Belyn held to his partie
Logres, Wales, & Cornubie.
So þei held it fyue ȝere
in pes & in faire manere.
Bot contek & couetise
out of the north wille algate rise, ...alwey.
for þus men said be olde dawe

& ʒit it is a comon sawe:
sothron dere gos northward
& northren were to þe south is hard; ..werre.....
bot northren dere & southron were
non dredes oþer þei com not nere;
bot northren were þat is to doute,
& souhren dere þe north dos loute. .southern der....
In Brennes tyme, as ʒe may here,
it ferd on þat ilk manere.
About Brenne were losengeres,
bakbiteres & werreoures.
One þer was þat wikly spake, ...ful euele.
bituex þe breþer raised contake; To whette Brenne to reyse.
[17vb] þus he spak alle with treson
(I gyf suylk cristes malison),
"We haf meruaile in our thouht
bot non to þe dare say nouht,
þat of so mykelle an heritage
þat long & brode is in passage,
þat þi fadere had in his balie
þou has þerof so litille partie; & hast....
for als lytelle as þou ʒit has, And ʒit als litel as þow has
þou salle him serue at alle cas.
Wille þou hald long þat wyse
to serue þi broþer in alle seruyse?
Ert þou thralle or bastard,
or more vile, or more cuhard, ...coward
þat þou salle do him þerfor homage
& ert of þe same parage?
Þe fadere him gate, he gate þe,
& of a modere born er ʒe;
siþen ʒe boþe breþer are
of o fadere & o modere ware,
wherfor has Belyn & whi,
of þe & þin suylk sengnori? ....swych seygnury
Brist it þat þou with þe bond, Brest a two þat ilke bond
do him no seruyse for þi lond.
ffor Lord ne holdes þe Belyn, .no lord holdeþ..
no more salle þou hald him for þin.
Trowe tille vs & our consaile;
to þi wirschip it wille auaile;
tille non of þi vassallage
sawe we neuer do suylk outrage.

Þorgh whos quantise & whos arte
ches Belyn him þe best parte?
Þer falles non oþer chesyng to:
mast salle haf þat mast may do.
Þou ert more worth & more hardi:
þat haf we sene certaynli.
Whan þou slouh þe Duke Cenflo
þat alle Moreiue longed to,
þat alle Scoteland wild haf wastid,
þi douhtynes to dede him hasted.
I trowe of þis þou þouht beforn
bot priuely þou has it born,
[18ra] þat we ne suld nempe it for drede. ....mynge for.
Now rede we þe do it in dede
& fond to wyn it ilka dele;
doute þe nouht þou may fulle wele,
for we ne salle þe neuer faile,
vntille we lyf & may trauaile. Þe while we lyue...
If þou ne trowe þat we þe say,
do þe ouer in to Norway;
þe kynges douhter þou take,
þi partie may þou better make;
haf þou Norwey & Scotland
& vs alle vnto þi hand.
Ageyn no land suld þou wend
þat þou gete þe fairere end;
ne Belyn durst þe neuer abide
if þou ageyn him wille ride.
If þou haf þouht mak þe bone,
go bityme & com right sone,
alle bi þe side of Moreiue,
þat Belyn þe not perceiue. ..no þyng aparseyue
Per auentour he wild him greue
if þou toke wife withouten leue,
or oþer ways men wald him saye
þat þou had of him non aye."
On þis maner þei conseiled him so
& Brenne triste þer conseile to.
He passed ouer, in Norway gan ryue
& asked þe kynges douhter to wyue.
Þe kynges name was Alfynges;
he graunted Brenne his askynges,
holy Bretayn for to wyn

when he wild his were begyn.
Oft tiþing to Belyn was brouht
whider Brenne ȝede & what he þouht. ......sought
Belyn had þan suspecion
þat for felony was it don,
& þouht he suld within a while
his owen desceite himself begile.
He said, "On stelth he sekis praie; .....sekes hym.
if salle not help ȝit þat I maie, Hit...ȝyf þat..
ne salle not Brenne bede me treget ......trypet
þat I ne salle turne with a forset." ....turne hym...
[18rb] Belyn seised Northhumberland,
kastelle & toun into his hand. Boþe Castel & toun tok...
Alle þat were Brennes beforen,
for werre he stroyed þam with corn, ...storede...
& folk inouh to þam he send .....dide sende
ageyn Brenne forto defend.
Himself ȝede with an oste
& rengid bi þe seis coste;
hauen & lond þei him withset, .to aryue þey..
bot þorgh bataile or baret.
To Brenne men brouht broth tiþing ....brod.
þat Belyn had seised his þing.
He had his wyf & was alle ȝare
with faire folk on flode to fare.
Liþerly liked þat Lady gent;
scho wepe weddyng & mykelle ment, .wepede...hit ment
for scho had luffed long before
þe kyng of Danmark, or Brenne com þore,
& þe kyng had luffed hire.
Long scho was of his desire;
þe kyng of Danmark hight Gutlake. .....Goodlak
Scho sent him letter þat þus spake: ..hym a....
"Long I lufed þe kyng of Danmark; Longe haue......
þat luf is lokyn & leyd in ark.
An vnkoth one of fer salle fong
þat luf þat þou has lufed long,
& bot þou com, rescous to make, ...rescours..
neuer in armes salle me take." ...schalt þou..
Whan Gutlak wist, his herte was drede
þat Brenne a way his wyf suld lede.
He did samen alle his flete
& Brenne & he in see gan mete. ......þey met

Whan boþe þe flotes com at frusse, ...come at a frosche
þe first hurtyng gaf a grete crusse. ..hortlyng....
End to end & side to side,
þe heiest of burde best felle his tide; ...bord....
fast þei fauht, boþe flotes
perced schippes with alblast schotes, ...arblast.
with axe & suerd ilk oþer on hewe,
in to þe water ouer borde threwe. .....bord þey.
On boþe parties were þe gode,
bot þe Danes best þei stode:
[18va] speres & dartes þik þei schote,
& perced þorgh Brennes flote.
Brenne fled & was discomfite,
& Gutlak seised a schippe fulle tite.
Als auenture felle, þat schip he wan
þat scho was, Brenne leman. ..was inne Brennes.
Whan he had won þat he souht,
of alle þe toþer gaf he nouht,
& Brenne fled with saile & ore;
his wyfe he les, he pleyned sore. ....þat playned he sore
Whan Gutlak had þat may in hand,
he ȝerned fast vnto þe land;
als he sailed his lond toward,
here of a chance þat him felle hard:
in þe see a storme it grewe,
þe water rored, þe wynde blewe,
þondred, reyned, leuende lyght, ..lemed.
þe skye wex blak as it were nyght;
þe see gan fight, þe wawes ros,
þe stremes wex & þam at gros. ....þem agros
Þer schippes alle in perille were:
ropes, burdes, brosten aywhere.
Maste & saile doun it lussed,
cordes, kables, kastels frussed; ...tofruschēd
to know þer names, I am alle wille.
Alle þat þer was were in perille.
Þer flote sone was alto spred
& into diuerse londes fled.
Fyue days at þe leste
lasted þan þat grete tempest.
Gutlak þre schippes had & no mo;
with þam he scaped in peyn & wo
& aryued vp in þis lond,

& fayn he was þat hap he fond,	
for luf of his leman	Bot for þe loue...
þat in þe tempest wex alle wan.	
He ne wist what land ne porte	
he was aryued for miscomforte;	
bot þei þat keped þe see side	
& sauh þe schippes to hauen ride,	....til haue glyde
þei toke Gutlak, þat may so gent;	Godlak þey toke wyþ þat may.
[18vb] to Belyn of þam mad present,	...hem þey made.
& alle his men with him þei toke;	
& Belyn did þam alle to loke,	
for waited what tyme or whenne	ȝyf he wayted....
þat he myght here tiþing of Brenne.	
Þo þat were take with þe mayden	
vnto Belyn þe soth sayden,	
how Brenne ilkadele had wrouht	
& þe kyng of Norwey souht,	
& how Gutlak had him mette	
opon þe se with strong barette.	
Brenne wild not long abide;	
his flote gadred on ilk a side	
ariued vp in Albanie	
with grete force & gode nauie.	
He sent to Belyn messengeres,	
men of gode, knyghtes & squyeres,	Of worthy knyghtes..
praied him to delyuer his wyfe,	Preynge forto deliuere..
& his castels, & bate alle stryfe;	
& bot he wild ȝelde þam on haste,	
more of his suld he waste.	
Belyn gaf nouht of his manace.	
He þouht he suld ȝit him chace	
& sent him bode be his men bolde,	
þat he had taken, þat wild he holde;	
for his prayng, no thyng wild do,	..praieres noþyng..
ne for his luf no more þan so.	
His folk redied & alle dight	..were al redy &.
ageyns Brenne forto fight.	
Biside a wod hate Kalenteres	...at Kalenters
mette þe breþer with þer baneres.	
Þe tone þe toþer mykelle hated;	Eyþer oþer mykel þey.
fersliere þei þam abated;	Þe felonloker...
dartes tille oþer þei schote fast,	
grete stones with slenges cast,	

scharp lances þorgh scheldes smote,	
bright suerdes þorgh helmes bote;	
som bi nekkes seised sore,	Sone . . þey sesede .
with kyues smyte togidere aiwhore,	. knyues smyten to deþ .
þorgh hede & throte, breste & bak,	
frussed togider þe nekkes brak.	
Þe Bretons bolded stifly to stande;	
[19ra] þe norþeren nouhted ay fleand.	& nought þe norþerne bot were .
To flote þei fled ilk bataile sere,	. flyght . . . . .
& Belyn folowed & nehed nere;	. . . . neyghed hem .
thousandȝ, hundrethes fleand he slouh	Two þousand fleyng he þer slow
als þei vnto þer schippes drouh.	
Brenne, þat mad mast þat wo,	
with peyn escapid þat slauhter fro.	. . he skaped þe . .
Vneþis a schip in hauen he hent,	. he skaped þe hauene . .
his tuelf & he to se þei went;	
alle he les bot þo tuelue;	
to France he went with þam himselue.	
ffiften thousand were þor told	. . slayn were told
of men slayn without in hold.	Wyþoute prisoners þat were . .
Whan alle þis wo was brouht to ende	
& Brenne in to France gan lende,	. . . . . . wende
Belyn vnto Ȝork he went	
& þer he held his parlement.	
He asked his barons & spake	
what suld be don of Sir Gutlake.	
Gutlak beforn sent Belyn	. . sent to .
out of prison þer he was in,	. . . . . lay .
þat of Belyn wild he holde	
alle honour if he wolde,	Al his honour ȝif þat . .
Danmark his lond, quyte & clere,	
& gif him trewage ilk a ȝere.	
Sikere þerof he wild him make	
with treuh & gode ostage take,	. bond . . . to take
withþi he myght lede sauely	
his lemman withouten vilany.	
Belyn had fulle grete desire	
to haf trewage of his empire.	
Þorh leue of þer parlement,	
Gutlak & his lemman went.	
Whan had don his homage,	. he had sworn & don omage
othe suorn & gyfen ostage	& bondes mad . . .
to Belyn forto hold conant,	. . to halde þer couenaunt

forto wend he had þe grant.
Gutlak to go sone was ȝare
with schippe vnto his lond to fare.
Belyn wele held his honour — .held wel þenne..
& wisely was gode gouernour.
He lufed pes at his myght, — ...wyþ al..
[19rb] pesabille men he held to right;
his lond Bretayn he ȝode þorghout — ....went.
& ilk cuntre beheld about,
beheld þe wodes water & fen;
no passage was maked for men, — & no passage fond he mad..
no hegh strete þorgh cuntre, — Ne...no contre
ne to burgh ne Cite.
Þorgh myres, hilles, & valeiȝ — ....vales
he mad brigges & cauceiȝ,
hie strete for comon passage,
brigges ouer wateres did he stage.
Þe first he mad he cald it Fosse;
þorghout þe lond it gos to Scosse.
It begynnes at Toteneis
& endes vnto Catheneis. — .endeþ þenne at Cateneys
Anoþer strete ordand he
at Southampton vpon þe se — ffro....
& gos to Wales to seynt Dauy, — To Mene yn Walys Seint Dauies now hight
þe toun hight Menne þat tyme redy; — Ikenyldestrete reches ful ryght
tuo kauceȝ ouer þe lond o brede — .causes...in lengþe & brede
þat men ouerthuert in passage ȝede.
Whan þei were mad als he ches, — ...maked...
he comanded tille alle haf pes;
alle suld haf pes & fredam
þat in his stretes ȝede or cam,
& if it were any of his
þat fordid his franchise,
forfetid suld be alle his þing,
his body taken to þe kyng. — & hym self....
Brenne þat was gon to France,
him schamed sore of his chance
þat it was so wyde spred,
& þat his lemman away was led.
Himself & his tuelue felawes
serued þe kyng ȝeris & dawes.
Knyght he was, curtais & wys,
ouer alle he had los & pris.

Whan any knyght toke his lyuere,	What ony knyght hadde to þer.
his was largest for he was fre.	
Mikelle was he praised of pruesse	
& fulle wele lufed for his largesse.	
He couth inouh of curtasi	..mykel..
[19va] & faire bare him as man worþi.	
Whan his los was þorgh runnen	
& in þe lond his pris had wunnen,	
with whom he mad any soioure,	
he praied for help & socoure	
forto conquere his heritage	
þat Belyn held with outrage.	..reftym..
He ȝede to Burgoyn to Duke Segwyn,	
besouht of help ageyn Belyn;	Bysought hym....
þe duke lufed his company	
& gaf him of his tresory.	
Brenne was in spech curtais,	
a konand knyght on many wais.	& konnynge. by..
He couth of wod & of ryuere,	...chas...
inouh of gamen on oþer manere,	..game of here.
gentille of body with faire visage,	
he semed a man of hie parage.	
He was meke to serue & briche,	& was plesaunt & seruisable
& þe duke was noble riche,	Þe Duk was Riche wyþoute fable
bot of his body had he non heire	
bot a mayden ferly faire.	
Inouh scho had þat tyme of elde	
þat scho mot tak lord to welde.	...take a...
He spak lufly, wisely & stille,	
& serued þe duke at alle his wille,	
& wele him paied alle his dedes,	
& oueralle wele sped his nedes.	..wel he...
Þe duke his douhter gaf him to wyue	
to haf þe duche after his lyue,	
saue þis he had þe speire	Þen þoughte þe Duk þat hym fel feir
þat god gaf him a son tille heire.	..had sent hym suche on..
Brenne obessed him curtasly	
& said, "Sir Duke, grant mercy."	
Þei him lufed & held him dere,	Al men hym.....
& he þam paied on alle manere.	Ech man hym payed wel his.
Not was it siþen a tuelmoth ende,	ffel þanne wyþynne þe tuelf monþ.
suylk a grace god gan sende	....gan hym.
þat he died, þe duke Segwyn,	

& of þe duche Brenne toke seisyn.	Of al þe....
His barons þat lufed him wele before,	
after lufed him mykille more;	
wele lufed him ilk a Burgoilun	
[19vb] & knyghtes of oþer nacion.	...þeyr.
He had lond inouh & rente,	..þe lond wyþ al þe.
& ȝeng lemman faire & gente.	And a ȝong lady...
In alle þis weth forgat he nouht	..his welþe...
how Belyn had with him wrouht,	
& held þo londes þat his suld be.	
Bot whan he sawe his tyme eise,	
sent for knyghtes & squyers,	He sent....
souht his frendes, hired souders,	ffrendes he soughte & waged.
with grete oste com to Normundy	
& purueied him þer a nauy.	..þer a gret nauye
Whan he sawe tyme, had wynd at wille,	.hit was.....
he passed þe se withouten ille.	
Belyn herd wele þat he cam;	
with folk inouh ageyn him nam.	
Sone were þei armed within a lyte	Þer bataylles assembled...
& were in poynt forto smyte.	.redy were almost to fyghte
So com þer modere, dame Tonuenne,	
þat bare boþe Belyn & Brenne;	
bituex þe ostes, trembland for drede,	
alde scho was, haltand scho ȝede,	ffol old scheo was haltyng..
oueralle scho asked where was Brenne.	
At þe last men gan hire kenne,	
& Brenne herd say þat it was sche	
& said, "Modere, welcom be ȝe."	
Hir armes about his hals scho cast.	....nekke..
Boþe þe ostes biheld þam fast;	.ostes wondred þer ate.
vnto hir girdille hir cloþes scho rent	
& naked befor þe ostes went.	
Vnto Brenne gretand scho spak,	
hire fingers wraste, þe blode out brak;	
scho trimbled & sighed inerly,	...sykede inderly
handes, face, breste alle blody.	.& face...
"Dere son, where has þou bene?	.child scheo seid....
Now þank I god I haf þe sene!	
Son," scho said, "listen to me	...list now..
& do as I salle conseile þe.	
Lo, here þe pappes þat þou soke,	.....þou on.
þise armes ere þat þe biloke.	..hit arn...

Here es þe wombe ȝe boþe in ware,	
þis is þe body þat ȝow bare.	. body ȝow bar wiþ wo & kare
I am scho þat for ȝow knelid;	
[20ra] þink on þat sorowe þat I þan felid.	Now þenk ....
Schew no sorowe more me beforn;	Ley now .....
for him þat lete ȝow of me be born,	
lay doun þin armes, me forto saue;	
wille nouht þat I for þe dede haue.	...... deþ .
Þou mysdos þat þou now fondes	
to bring aliens of vnkouth londes	.. straungers of outlandes
vs forto robbe, vs forto slo,	.. robben & to slo
þin owen demeyns to wirke wo.	Rest þe let þy mod ouer go
Þou has no mo breþer in wolde.	
Dede is þi fadere, þi modere is olde.	Þy fader ys ded ....
Suffire for no þing olyue	
þi pure frende away to dryue;	. pore frendes ...
þou suld present vs & gyue	
& help vs alle forto lyue,	.... in pes to .
bot þou comes to reue our socoure	
þat suld be our mayntenoure.	
Do þis foly now to slake.	Lef folye & y vndertake
If þou on him wille pleynt make,	
& if I fynd he has þe gylte,	
he salle amend as þou wilte.	... right als ..
If þou say he did þe fle,	Bot ȝyf þou seist ....
I say nay, þe wrong is in þe:	... witnesse on þe
þou began first alle þe wrong;	ffyrst þou bygonne al yn .
þe foly es alle on þe long.	So al þe folye ys on ..
Þe first foly in alle dedis	... & yuele dedes
whan þou vnto Norweie ȝedis,	
wife to take without his leue.	... wyþouten leue
Þan schewed þou þou wild him greue	Þat schewede þou mentest hym to .
& brouht þe north him to assaile;	. broughtest Norn men ...
þou sped nouht at þat bataile.	Þerfore þou lostest þy .
Þi blame is now ȝit fulle grym	
þat suylk an oste bringes on hym,	
þat is tille our disheriteson	& schapest oure desherytysoun
& to þis lond destruccion.	. þys londes .
So mykelle ille wild he not þe	.. yuel ....
if his powere so wele myght be.	Al þey his power so mykel ..
Brenne, son, what þinkes þou?	
Come tille acorde for þi prow;	.. acord now ...
lay doun þi suerd, do way þi schelde,	

widraw þi folk out of þe felde   Wyþdraw......
& seke þe pour charite;   ..þe pes for.
[20rb] þe same salle he do to þe."
Brenne hir praiere vnderstode;
for luf of hir changed his mode.
His helme & hauberk he did vnlace,
alle bare hede with open face,
come he with his modere Tonwenne;
þe same did Belyn to Brenne.   & also dide...
Þer modere did þam togidere kisse;
for þat sauhtlyng was mykelle blisse.
More of wreth was þer nouht spoken;
with luf in armes ilk oþer loken.
Þusgate endid þe breþer wreth,   Al þus þen ended...
þer tene turned gamen & gleth.   ...to game & glathe
Fro þien to London þei went   .þeþen....
& þer þei held a parlement.
Of þer parlement was þe end:
to wyn France wild þei wend.
Belyn ded somon his Bretons
& Brenne alle his Burgoylons.   ..haþ alle..
Bi tyme & terme þat þei had set,
boþe ostes at þe hauen met
& schipped ouer in to France,
þe lond to wyn awnterd þer chance.   To wynne hit þey hoped was..
Bituex þam was a bataile done;   .hem was þen...
þe force of France felle fulle sone;
þei dured nouht to fight in felde.
Þe breþer did þam to þam ȝelde,   ...hem to þeym.
Castels þei seised fer & nere
& wan þam alle within a ȝere.   ..alle ffraunce wyþynne..
Whan alle þe folk was at þer dome,
þei said þai wald wend to Rome,
& leue non þat þei fond
bot if þei held of þam þer lond.
Þei sent about to diuers costes,
of douhty folk gadred ostes
forto wyn pris & prow.
Þai passed þe mountayns of Mongou,
Taurinus þei toke, & Iuorie,
& alle Citeȝ of Lumbardie:
Vrcels, Pauie, & Tremoyne,
Melan, Plesance, & grete Boloyne.

Þei passed þe water of Tauron
[20va] & þe hille of Mount Bardon;
þei robbed þorgh Tuscan
& alle ouer rode & þorgh ran.
As þei robbed londes aywhore, ..Ryfled...
Rome þei neghed ay þe more.
Romanes dred for to die .dredden hem...
for þe tiþng þat þei herd seie. .þo tydynges....
Alle day of passand men þe herd
þat tuo breþer wan alle þe werld. ......werd
Þei of Rome had chose þat ȝere
tuo noble men of grete powere
þat þei suld, when þei had nede,
þer folk vnto bataile lede
& saue þer londes, hald þam to right,
for douhtiest þei were in fight.
Sir Prosenna þe ton hight so,
þe toþer men called sir Gabao.
Þise tuo were þer conseiloures
& spak vnto þer senatoures:
what þei wild, how had þei tight,
þe Cite ȝelde or stand to fight.
Þe sene said þei were affraid;
non þam withstode bot þorgh alle straid.
"With suylk to fight we haf non oste,
for þei haf folk with þe moste;
& if we myght our pes haue
þorgh mekenes & our godes saue,
& our self at þer pes lyue,
golde & siluer we wille þam gyue.
Ouer þat þei salle haf trewage
to passe & do vs non outrage,
for stronge it were for our Cite
to be destroyed & alle þe cuntre."
In alle þer drede & alle þere dome,
þe breþer com & seged Rome. ....byseget.
Þorgh comon assent of þe senatours,
þei present þe breþer grete tresours;
for to be in þer auowri,
trewage þei granted þam forþi.
Þe breþer toke of þam ostage,
tuenty childere of þer best lynage,
& of þe richest of þe toun,

[20vb]	þei present þam as for raunson.	.presented....
	Þus was þe pes bituex þam granted,	
	bot litelle while þei it haunted.	..þrowe...
	Belyn & Brenne remoued þer oste;	
	bi Lumbardie þei went þat coste	
	for to were on þe Almayns	To werren opon þe Alemaunt3
	& heue trewage at remanans.	.take.of þe remenaunt3
	Þei were destorbled þorgh Romayns	..letted by þe Romayns
	þat conaunt brak, ros þam agayns;	
	& proue þei wild þer hardynes	
	& said þei wild do more prowes.	
	Þei sent for knyghtes alle aboute	
	& gadred oste grete & stoute,	
	wele armed were in alle conrey.	..in ilke a conreye
	After þe breþer toke þer wey,	
	on þam þei þouht to smyte alle fresse,	
	in þe mountayns hald þam at stresse	...to holdem at destresse
	þat non of þam suld more come	
	of þe breþer oste to Rome.	...eft..
	Þei sent massages on þer partie	
	vnto þe Almayns, þe breþer to spie,	
	þat ilk a pace þei suld so waite;	...pas....
	in þe mountayns hold þam so straite,	
	if þei suld passe on oiþer side,	
	with force þei suld þam ouer ride.	
	Þer on ilk a side þei ros	Al þus on.....
	to haf þe breþer oste in clos,	
	& at þer passyng in to þe mounte,	
	þe Almayns suld be in þer frounte.	
	Þorgh for of gode ordenance,	Þorow force of þer god.
	þei suld not passe be no chance.	
	Whan Belyn perceyued þer felony,	
	þei conseild þam on þer party,	
	þat Brenne suld turne ageyn	
	to withstand þe oste Romeyn,	
	& Belyn suld on his side	
	ageyn þe oste of þe Almayns ride;	
	& whilk of þam best mot spede	
	suld turne & help þe toþer at nede.	
	Whan Romeyns wist þat Brenne suld com	
	& toke þe gate ageyn to Rome,	Þey toke þe wey...
	þat Brenne suld negh Rome nere	...neighe Rome no ner
[21ra]	& þe breþer osondere fere.	

Þorgh a spie, Belyn herd say
& tauht Brenne a gaynere way
to trauers þam alle ouer þer score,
& passe þe Romeyns wele before.
Þe ches giours þe cuntre knew
to lede þam way treste & trew
& bring þam wele to þat strete
þer þam behoued þe Romeyns mete.
Þei ioneyd boþe day & nyght   . iourneyed . . . .
als so stilly as þei myght,
withouten noyse or any crie,   Wyþoute noise cry or how
vnto þe entre of Mongu;   . . . . Moungow
& whan þei were in þe valeie,
þer leders said, "Þis is þer weie.
Bi þis þei com it is certayne:
non oþer may þei gayne."   Oþer wey haue þey non ageyn
To þat passage þei com at nyght;
þe mone schane faire & bright.   . . schon ful . . .
Brenne þam bad bere þam priue
withouten noyse to tyme be.   . . til tyme schold be
Sone after come þe Romeyns route;
of non þei had drede ne doute.
Be þe mone þat bright schone, ... so lyght schon
þe sped þam fast furth to gone.   . . . faste swythe . .
At þe passage þei glift ine;   . . . glyfte þey þer eyene
ageyn þe mone sawe þei schyne
helmes, hauberkes, scheldes vplift.
Þan were þe Romeyns alle oglift;
þe Bretons had þe Romeyns biden,
also suyth to þam þei riden.
Brenne þam boldid, bad þam wele smyte,
"Felle ȝour fos, þei wild ȝow byte!"   . . . þat wolde . .
Þe Bretons on alle halfe þam assailed;   Oueral þe Bretons þeym .
þe Romeyns route felle & failed;
þei had no tome fer to fle   . nadde no tome for . .
ne to tapise in stede priue.   Ne place to huyden hem priue
Þe Bretons bouweld þam & hewe,
in buskis, bankis, doun þam trewe;   . . . . . þrew
þe slauhter lasted alle þe nyght
tille it sprong þe dayes lyght,
& alle þat day afterward
[21rb] vnto þe nyght was bataile hard.
Þe nyght departed þam osundere;

þo þat escaped it was wondere.	Þat any . . . a wonder
Þe toþer day in þe morn tide,	
toward Brenne Belyn gan ride;	
fer fro his broþer ne wild he go,	
what chance so betid of mo,	
& Brenne þat befor nam,	
a bode vnto Belyn cam.	
Whan þei were togidere comen,	
boþe vnto Rome nomen	
& biseged it aboute,	
& þei of Rome were fulle stoute.	
On alle sides þei set engynes	
at Brenne ordenance & Belynes.	
Minours had þei inouh & slie,	
þe walle to hole & vndermye;	. . to perce . .
þei within defendid þam wele,	
at þat tyme les not a dele.	
With alblastis schote querels vnride;	
inouh men brouht & laid beside,	
with grete stones þei þam affreide.	
Þe Romeyns were not dismeide;	
þei lanced dartes, bowes drowe,	
fele þei fellid, many slowe.	. . . & manye .
Þe breþer left þer assaute alle	
& perced no thyng of þe walle.	
Long lasted þat ilk chance,	
to þe breþer grete noyance.	
Galwes did þe breþer renge;	
of þer blode þei wild þam venge.	
Þe galwes þei reised right hie	. . . . vp ful heye
(þe Romeyns myght it wele se),	. . wel myght hem se wyþ eye
& hanged ilkon þer ostagers,	. hongeden alle . .
burgeis sones, lordes, pers;	
þer kynde, I trow, had sororew & wo;	Þat . . . . sorewe . .
to schames dede þei sawe þam go.	. . deþ þat . . .
Alle only þerfor were wroth,	. olyke . . .
& alle said & suore þer oth,	
in pes ne suld þei passe quite	
bot þei were venged on þat despite;	. . . wroken . . .
& þise men tristed þe Romeyns to,	On . . . . . þo
[21va] Prosenna & sir Gabao,	On Prosenna & on sire Gabao
for þise were to Lumbardie	. . . gon to Lumbardye
to procure Rome more partie.	

After þam abode þe Romeyns,
a day to com þei set certeyns;
þat day was nere of þer comyng.
Þe Romayns þat day mad þer samenyng
& were right fulle egre & stoute,   . ber hem ful egrely . .
armed þam, & issued oute;   Þey armede hem & isseden .
& on þe breþer fast þei souht,
& þei ageyn spared þam nouht.
Als þei fauht best in stoure,
com þe tuo men with alle þer socoure   . her chefteyns wyþ more .
vpon þe breþer & ilkon fresse;   Oþe breþere þey fullen alle on a res
þan were þe breþer in hard stresse.   . . þey boþe . . destres
Þe Romeyns opon þe toþer parte,
þe toþer side, Poiles & Lumbard,
& fellid fele of þe Burgoilons,
& called cowerde & huresons.   . . þem coward3 hore sons
"We salle do 3ow drink 3our blode   . . 3ow do drynke 3our owen .
& spare our water in the flode.   . . . . of Tyber flod
On þis haf Mongou, what do 3e
to chalange vs of our fe,
& þat 3e henge our childir hie,
þat vilany 3e salle abie.
To 3ow it was a wikke conseile;   . . was hit an yuel .
þat 3e salle se fulle wroþerheile."   . schul 3e fele to wroþer hayl
With suylk vpbraid þei þam missaid   . . vmbreides . . .
& grete strokes on þam laid.
Obak ageyn þei did þam go
& did þam bray & crie for wo.
Belyn & Brenne were dismaid
þat þe Romeyns so þam affraid;
þe Bretons sauh þer side þede lowe,
þe rimethed þam to rest a throwe.   Þey rempede þem . . . .
In þer restyng þei gan þam mene,
a parlement mad þam bituene,
& gadred þer folk agayn to fight,
armed newe & renged right;
in sere batailes set þam osundere, ... a sondres
both bi thousand3 & bi hunderes
of hardiest & defensables,   Of þe . . .
[21vb] & þer maistres & constables,   Made þey Mayster Conestables
& bad þam in þer batailes holde
þat non fro oþer flit ne folde.
Þo þat were strong, hardi & wight,

formast were þei set to fight;
beside were set to þer socoure   [*Om. L*]
archers to maynten þam in stoure.   [*Om. L*]
Þe alblasters on þe toþer side,   [*Om. L*]
ilkon for oþer better to bide,   [*Om. L*]
doun on fote þe moste gan light;   [*Om. L*]
on fote þei renged þam to fight.   [*Om. L*]
Þei bare þe lances vp & doun
on maner of a cheltroun,   On þe . . . scheltroun
& non for wele ne for wo,
ne suld forþer þan oþer go,   . . byforen oþer go
ne go suythere þan a pas, ... softe paas
at ons to smyte whan com a kas;   . . . . as comeþ þe cas
& non baldere þan oþer be,   . . schold baldere . . .
ne no man fro oþer fle.
Whan þei had set ilk bataile
on what manere þei suld assaile,
trompes blewe & greilles rong;
of boþe parties to batale sprong.
On ilk a side were strokes inouh;
lances did þei brest & bouh.   Speres dide þem . . .
After lances þat þei sette,   . þe speres . . .
siþen with knyf & suerd þei mette;
ilk oþer on ran, ilk oþer to stike, ... to styke
opon þe dede ȝede þe quike.
Alle to telle I ne kan,
bot lorn þer were many a man.
Þe Breton sawe non oþer weie:
þer behoued þam lyue or deie,   Þey most wel fyghte oþer elles .
or alle to wyn or alle to lese;
one of þo behoued þam chese.
Þe best fighters bare forth þe breste,
archers & alblasters þam neste, ... next
þe Milleners & centeners   . Mylers & þe Centaynes
folowed fast on þe Romeyns.
Sir Gabao, þer gouernoure,
he batid him on þe Bretons stoure;
bot slayn was þis Gabao
[22ra] þat alle þer trist was vnto,
& Prosenna was born doun;   . . . brought right doun
on him þe Bretons wan þe toun.   . hem . . . . .
Prosenna þei toke alle quike
& perced þe Romeyns batile þike,

& alle þer force doun þei slouh,	
& to þe Cite fast þei drouh.	
Þe toun mot þei defend nomore;	
þei were slayn, cheiftayns þat wore.	Þe cheftayns were slayn þat þer.
Þe breþer com vnto þe Cite	
& fond þerin riches plente.	
Belyn gaf Brenne alle þe empire	
& he was emperour & sire;	
þe folk of him had grete doute;	
His fomen þorgh force did he loute.	. . . . . þem aloute
Long he regned Emperoure	*[Om. L; at folio bottom*
	by a later hand.]
þat neuer Romeyn durst stir him stoure.	. . dirst Romayn stire in his.
Belyn to Bretayn gan turne;	
he wild no langere þer soiorne,	
& whan he com vnto þis lond,	
þe old Citeȝ þat he fond,	
he closed þam & mad þam newe;	
þe walles he raised triste & trewe.	
In Wales he did mak a toun,	
Kaerusk, he called it opon Breton,	
for it standes opon Vsk,	
a water þat rynnes bi bank & busk,	
siþen men called Kaerlegion.	. . caldit.
Liste now why þe encheson:	. . what was . .
whilom Romeyns had þis land	
in þer demeyns, in þer hand,	
whan Romeyns com for þer trewage,	
at Kaerusk þei held ostage,	
& þer þei mad þer maste duellyng,	
for þer was ese of mykille þing	
at Kaerusk in Clamorgan.	
Þe wynter þei duellid þer ilk man	
& for þei had so long þer hold,	
Kaerlegion þe name was told.	
Com diuers men of þer langage	. after . . diuerse language
þat schorte to speke haf vsage,	
& schortid it with name & soun,	
[22rb] & brak þe word to Kaerlioun.	. afterward kaldyt Carlyon
Legion is noumbre of folk þat wex	
sex þousand, sex hundreth sexti & sex.	
Þus many euer fro Rome cam	. . alwey . . .
þat ay vnto Kaerlion nam.	. . for truwage to Carlyon nom

Whan Belyn Kaerlion had set,	
þe walles raised & folk to fet,	
vnto London he toke his way	
& þer he duellid many a day.	
þer he did a ȝate bigyn	.... gate.
ouer þe water þat schippes com in,	
& ouer þe ȝate he mad a toure;	.. þat gate....
þerin he held long soioure.	
He raised alle his fadere lawes	
& did þam hold bi his dawes.	
Dome he gaf wysly & right,	
trewth he held wele at his myght.	Trowþ held he wel wiþ al..
Mikelle plente was in his tyme;	
of no man more may we ryme.	On no mannes more may men.
Long he lyued þe lond to welde,	... longe to welde
& faire he endid in his elde;	
for of þat ȝate þat Belyn auht,	
of Belyn þe name it lauht.	
Long men called tille now late,	
after Belyn, Belyns gate.	
Þorgh schort langage I told ar how,	
Billinges gate men calle it now.	
Whan he was dede, sir Belyn,	
þe popille for him had sorow & pyn;	. people......
for many a man fulle sore grete	
þat day þat he his lyf lete.	.... ys lyf for let
Þei did mak for his honoure	
a barelle of gold of his tresoure,	
& brent his body, flesch & bone;	
in þat barelle þei laid ilkone.	Iþe barel of gold...
More wirschip þam þouht it so	
þan his body in erth to do.	
Whan þe barelle was alle dight,	
barred alle & burnessid bright,	& wel y burnuscht fair &.
vp in þe tour þei mad a stage	
& hang it befor þe passage,	. heye it henge...
þat alle þat passed, more & lesse,	
[22va] praised Belyn for his pruesse.	Schold preyse....
After Belyn, Gurguynt, his sone	
had þe heritage be resone.	
Gurguynt Bertruk was his name,	
a man of gode þer of had fame.	Of gret godnesse he bar þe.
Pes to loke & right to hold,	

He likynd his fadere, Belyn þe bold.
Þat Belyn left he held it wele,
noyance had neuer a dele;   . had he . . .
bot þe Danes þei forsoke
to gif treuage þat Belyn toke.
Gurguynt þouht he had right þerin;
his treuage he wild alle gate win.
He gadred schippes did com,   His host he gadered & . . .
set vp saile & forth þei nom,   Þey set . . . . . .
bot Gurguynt wan son þe pris.   [*Transp. L*]
To bataile samned boþe partis;   [*Transp. L*]
himself in bataile slouh þe kyng
& toke homage of ilk lordyng,
& his treuage did restore
as his fadere had it before.
Whan he had taken of þam ostage,
Gurguynt went on his viage.
He passed forth be Orkeneie;
þritty schippes he mette on þe weie,
charged fulle & with vitaile,   . wyþ folk . . .
bot þei ne wist whidire to saile.
Pantaleus þer maister hight,
þat mayntend þam & held to right.
Gurguynt asked what men þei were,
what þei souht & whi com þere.
Pantaleus spak curtasly:
"We ere men of pes, seke auowery, ... sekyng .
wayfarand men þat wald haf grith.
We ask þe leue to speke þe with."
Pes wild nouht þe kyng breke;   Þe kyng ne wolde no pes .
with luf he gaf hym leue to speke.
He said, "We ere men of diuers lynage,
exilde of Spayn, com bi þis ryuage;
if we any stede fond
on to reste a certeyn lond,
a ȝere & half þer haf we went.   ffor oþer half ȝer þus . . .
[22vb] Hunger & þriste, colde has vs schent.
Many a coste þorgh haf we souht,   . . . haue we þorow sought
lond on to lend fond we nouht;
& we ere alle noyed þerfore,
for our trauaile & grete lore.
Bot, Lord, if it were þi wille,
suffre vs reste on þi lond stille;

seruyse þerfor wille we do,
þi men bicom if þou wille so."
Bot Gurguynt wild þam not grante
of his to haf a remenante;
nouht forþi he gaf þam conseile
toward Ireland to set þer saile,
& of his schippes lent þam tuaie
to tech þam þe right waie.
Ireland þat tyme was bigged no þing
with londes, ne toun, ne man wonyng. .hous.....
So long þei sailed þe se þorgh ronen,
alle gate to Ireland ere þei wonen;
þei striken saile & ankere cast,
vp to land þei 3ede right fast.
Alle fond þei wildernes & wilde; .þey fond wast..
þei spred about in ilk an ilde.
Sone þei mad ardawe felde, ..maden eryed.
þei loged þam & timbred telde; ....tymber.
þe folk wex & fostred more, ..wax faste...
& tilled þe lond about aywhore.
Pantaleus þei mad him kyng;
in Ireland mad he first wonyng.
Whan Gurguynt had þam þider sent,
home vnto his lond he went;
þritty 3ere in þis lyfe gan lende;
at Kaerlion he did his ende.
When Gurguynt had don his fyn,
after him com his sone Guytelyn, Regned his sone Gwyntelyn
a gude man for þe maistrie.
His wyfe hight Dame Marcie.
Dame Marcie was mykelle in pris,
of landes lawe was scho wis. ...scheo was ful wys
Scho studied fast to mak þe lawe;
for hire þei called it be þat dawe,
in þe Bretons tyme, as I wene,
[23ra] þei called þat law Marciene.
ffro kyng to kyng þat lawe men wrote;
[*L adds:*] & Englysche kynges 3it hit wot
Marchenlawe þe Inglis it callede; Marchenlage....
in auht schires þat lawe men halde,
Gloucester, Wircester, Herford, Werwik,
Gloucestre Chestre Warewyk Oxenford
Oxenford, Schropschire, Chester, Staford.

Hereforde Wynchestre Schropschire Stafford

Guyntelyn & Marciene
a knaue childe had þam bituene;
Siluius his name þei told,
& are he were seuen ȝere old,
died his fadere þat tyme here.
He regned nomore bot ten ȝere.
After Guyntlyn deses,
kept Marcien þe land in pes,
& whan he was wele of elde
þat he couth þe lond welde,
scho did him croune kyng
& he regned in alle þe thyng. — Y telde ȝow his Regne in alle.
Stalworth he was tille bone; — ...yn armes.
after his fadere he die sone. — Bot...he deyde.
Kymare, his sonne, his heire was here; — Þenne com his heir Kynmar.
he lyued one & tuenty ȝere. — & Regned on &..
Daneus, his broþer, siþen had þe lond;

[*The second scribe begins in P.*]

ten ȝere he regned wytȝ were he fond. — ....wyþ werre..
Tis Daneus had one bascardie, — Þys..on bastardie
a sone þat wan it wyt maistrie.
Morwidus it sais he hight,
ouer mesure was he mody kniht. — He was a merueillous mody.
Þoru hardinesse wan it o chaunce,
irouslik he toke veniance. — Egreliche...
His ire, whan it on him ran,
ffor nouht wyld he slo a man; — .....no man
ffor nouht loue wild he no man spare — ffor loue wold he noman.
to whyles þat his wrath ware.
In alle þe regne, ne was none
so fair of vertues alls he one;
his bodi was gent & fayr of vise.
Til al he gaue giftes of prise;
oute of mesure was he large:
tresour to hold no made he charge.
To while his ire was awaie,
alle wild he do þat men wild say,
[23rb] and als so meke als a child — .also meke was as..
bot whan his wrath was on him wild. — Tyl þat..wax...
[I]n Morbidus time þat was so stout, — [*Capital I om. in P.*]
þe Duke of Moreue robbid about;
Northumbirland gan he waste,

and Morpidus til him gan haste	
and egrelike gan him assail,	. Angerly . . .
& sleu him & al in plein batail.	& þer hym slow . . .
Þus said men & ȝit sais	
hou it was proued I ne wote what wais	Þat . . . y not what weys
þat Morpidus sleu me alone	. . . mo men alone
þan al his ost dide ilkone.	
Whan he had slain al þat he might	
and weri was more for to fight,	. was al wery more to .
þe bodis he did brenne of þo	
or his grete ire might ouer go.	
Be time þat he was best in held	Þe tyme . . . . . elde
and stalworth man himself to weld,	& stalwordest hym self . .
a best come owte of Iris see	. . . . of þe . .
and distroid alle þe countre.	
A hidous best was it be sight,	
Monstre Marine men said it hight;	
and sum men cald it Mare Belleu,	
so wondirful best no man ne knew.	
Swilk cal men Monstre, als I finde,	
þat limes has out of kynd;	
þat has limes more or lesse,	
monstre men seis þat swilkone es.	
Mare Bellu es þe see hound;	
I ne wote ȝif it suimmes or es at ground.	
Was non þat woned be þe see side	
þat for þe best durst a bide.	. durste for þat best .
Man & best he swaloud & ete;	
þat he ouer toke, of liue ne leet.	
Morpidus herd þer of grete kri;	
his hert was bold & ouer hardi.	
On him self he affied so,	
alone þe best he ȝede vnto	
and fauht with him; it was folie	
on himself so mikil affie.	. . . mykel forto .
Al on himself þe best assailled,	Hym self alone þe . .
hardines of hert ne failled;	Gret hardynesse hym non ne .
[23va] with launce first he to him scet	. spere . . . . schet
and woundyd him, he was so grete.	
When he had schoten & to him kast,	
þan with swerd heu on him fast.	
Ouer nere he com in þat fightyng,	
he opind his mouth & sualhid þe king.	He gaped wyde & swelwed . .

Þus gate deid sir Morpidus, [*Om. L*]
so did þe best þat swalud him þus. [*Om. L*]
ffor þe king men make grete mone; . . . . made . .
þe bestis ded comford ilkone. . . deþ conforted .
Morpidus had sons v, . . . fyue
and all left behind him on liue: . . þey leftym byhinde alyue
Gorbodian, fairest & flour,
and Argail, and sir Elidour,
Iugenes, & sir Peredour.
Alle fiue were kynges of honour;
Gorbodian was flour & prise,
he was trew, rihtfulle, & wise. . . . feyghtful . .
Neuer Kyng with so mikille loue
ouer lond ne folk ne was aboue; . no lond regned aboue
neuer witand he ne leih, . louede he no lye
ne dide wrong to man þat deih. No dide men wrong lowe ne heye
He was kyng ful mesurable; [*L adds:*] To don alle right he was ful stable
loue and pes his time was rife.
Ten ȝere he liued þere in his life.
In Treniouant þer he lise; . Trenouante . . .
his broþer him leid at his deuise.
Argail þat next him was born,
was kyng as he had ben beforn.
Wykkidli þan gan him falle,
ffor he discordid with þam alle;
þe gode men he abeised mikille,
and aueanced þo þat were fikille. . auaunsed . . . swykel
Þat tresour had, he it þem reft; Þe tresor þey hadden he . . .
bleþely wild lie, þe sothe he left; He loued wel lyes þe soþes . .
trewe men ne louid he noght,
glad he was whan wo was wroght.
Þe Barouns conseild þem betwene;
þe lond him reft quite & clene. . . þey refte hym . . .
Þan coroned þei sir Elidour,
man of pite and of socour.
Argail þat was driuen owt,
[23vb] he ȝede to princes oueral about
ffor help to haue his regne ageyn,
bot his trauaille was in vain;
none wild help restore his pert, ... perd
ffyue ȝere he was in poueret. Þen lyued he ffyue ȝer . .
Sone aftir þe fiue ȝere ende,
Elidour þoru a wode suld wend

ffor to play be a riuere;
þe wode men calle Kalamiter.   Þat wode men caldit Calduter
Argaille þer sir Elidour mett;
on knes sir Elidour he grett
and asked him grace & mercy,
and he graunt him alle redy.
Of him he had grete pite
þat in pouert suld him see,
his armes about his nek he cast;
his grete pouert he pleined fast.
Whan þei had long ment his mone,
tille Aclud þei went ilkone;
in his chambre he dide him be
þat none ne wist bot in priuete.
Here now of sir Elidour
how he did his broþer honour.
Elidour feined him seke to lie
and said he hopid for to die.
Aftir his Barouns he sent
and þei alle to him went;
a dai was ordaind for to be
þat þei suld viset him & see;
withowtin nois to him suld go
on alle one withowtin mo   . alone . .
and speke soft & priuely,
ffor he might suffir no kri.
Ilke one did þe kyngs wille;
alls þei come in, held þem stille.   . . . . þey held hem .
As þei come in, þe kyng þem toke
and did þem swere on þe boke
ffor to do Argail homage.
Were he neuer of so hi parage,
wild he ne wild, þat suld he do,
or þe dede he suld go to.   Oþer þe deþ schold he . .
Þus sunderleps he did þem swere   . sonderlypes . . . .
to Argaille suld þei feche þe bere.   . . . . faiþ bere
[24ra] Qwen þei had alle sworn on othe
tille Argaille leue or lothe,   . . wer hem lef or loþ
Elidour & þei alle went
to Ʒork & held a Parlement.
Elidour þer þe cround leuid   . . . Coroune leued
& sett it opon Argaille heued,
and said, "Here gyf I Argaille, ... y þe Argayl

þe croune of Bretain holike alle."
Þan said men of sire Elidoure
þat he of pite was frute & floure
þat forsoke þe regaunte ...regalte
and gaue it his broþer for pite.
Þerfor in ilk a lordyng hous
was he called Elidoure þe pitous.
Argaille amendid his maners,
louid his barouns, made þam his pes; &....þem pers
was non of alle so mesurable
ne of his worde so wise no stable.
Alle his wikked tecchis left
whan he toke þe croune eft.
Alle him loued þat ore him hatid,
ffor alle his vices were abatyd.
Ten ȝere he regned in honour
and syn fel in a langour
and endid his life fair & wele;
þei berid him at Karlele.
Syr Elidour eft þei chese
þat louid so mikille pite & pese;
bot Iugens & Perodours
again him were ẇereours. ..gonne be.
Pryuely gadird þei partie
and toke him alle with trichery;
at London þei did him in hold
in a prison hard & cold.
Peredour and Iugenes
þei departid þe lond and ches.
Iugenes toke alls him þought best,
be Northen Humbyr est and west;
Peredour had þe toþer partye
and a throw alle þe seygnorie. & in a þrowe...
ffor Iugenes lyued bot seuen ȝere
wyt owtyn ayr quite & clere,
[24rb] Peridour gan it vndirfong;
bot he ne ioyed it neuer long, ..reioysed hit nought.
ffor þe ferynges dede him toke. ..ffeuerynges deþ..
With sin it whan, with schame forsoke. ...wan wiþ sorewe hit.
Þan broght þei forth sir Elidour
and coround him with grete honour;
þris had he takyn þe coroun. When he had take..
He did þat time þe folk somoune

to see þe schathes his broþer had done	...skaþes....
and amend þam als so sone.	
Of folis was he gode iustise,	.folyes....
he reft neuer man his franchise;	
he gaue ensample of alle wisdam	
þat þe lond or aftir him cam.	Þat helden þe.....
Large of hert, of wille free,	
he hight Elidour of pite.	
In alle his time was alle ende,	....hit was hende
	[*L adds:*] In alle godnesse his lyf gan ende
in Aldburgh Castel was he laid;	
Glud þat time þe name was said.	Klud......
Aftir Elidour of pite,	
his cosin had þe regaute,	
þe eldest sone of Gorbodian,	
sythen Argail sone þat hight Margan.	
Þis Margan was gode & meke,	
his gode wille was nouht to seke;	
lord tille alle withowtyn ille,	He was god lord..
and alle him louid with gode wille.	
After Margan, Algaylle sone	
Emmanius had þe region;	
Emmanius was Margan broþer,	
bot his maners was alle other.	
He cowthe him neuer freendis gete,	
tille alle he had niht and hete,	....ire & hate
and alle hatid him reght sore;	
and he did ille tille alle þat wore.	ffor he......
Ilkone þei fond him veniaunce fulle;	
with yuel men did him manie a pulle.	.schrewes he dide hem many yl.
Sex wynter he regned in þis liue	.....his lyf
in felonie & in ille striue;	
alle þe comune said reht þus,	
"Wee hate him, so dose he vs."	
Opon þat, þam counseild þei	Þer opon conseillede.
[24va] & drof him out of lond away.	The first scribe resumes in P.
Þus þei reft him þe kyngdam	
& no man wist where he cam.	
Þan mad þei a Parlement	
& chese a kyng þorgh alle assent,	
þe comon of þe region,	[*Om. L*]
Iugenes sone, Yualon.	
Iuallo gaf him to trauaile	

alle to gode þat mot auaile.
He did mak many estres,
he likned his gode ancestres; And lykned muche...
bot lif was no stounde, Bot his lyf lasted..
þe dede him cast to þe grounde. Ouer sone had deþ cast hym to.
Whan Yuallo mad his endyng,
Peredour sone þei chese to kyng.
After Peredour sone deces,
was Eledour sone, Gerunces.
After Gerunces was Catillus,
after Catillus, Coylus, ..was Coyllus
& þan Porrex, & þan Cheryn.
He was a drynkere of wyn;
ouer mykelle drynk he ches;
his ȝouth alle þerin he les
in drynk & in drunkenes;
he did neuer oþer pruesse.
Bi his wyf he had þre sones
& alle were kynges, þe story mones,
ilkon after oþer were. Ilkon were after oþer
ffulgenius was eldest broþer,
Eldadus, Andragius, .& Androcheus
þe toþer breþer called men þus;
lytille while was ilkon kyng,
alle did þei sone þer endyng.
Andragius sone hight Vrian;
he regned a ȝere & died þan.
After Vrian, Eliud men ches;
he had his tyme þe land in pes.
After Eliud, Endacius,
& þan Doten, siþen Gurguttius;
siþen Marian, faire in chere, .was Merian...
he couth of wod & ryuere;
in alle maner of venrie,
[24vb] him liked best suylk maistrie.
Ladies bed him luf inouh,
bot his luf to non wild bowe
bot only vnto his wyf; .onlyke til his owen.
so endid Marian his lyf.
After Marian was Bleludo,
his sone, & couth of wod also;
large he was & gaf bleþely,
he spared of non þat was worþi;

alle him lufed, he was fre,	.men hym loued for...
erle, baron, & oþer meingne.	..& Knyght &..
After þis nobille Bleludo,	
Capis was his name so;	Cam Capes hys name was.
after Capis, Oeneus,	
after Oeneus was Sisillius;	
after Sissili was Blegabret	..com Glegabret
þat was a syngere of þe get.	A syngere of þe beste get
Of song & of mynstralcie	
of alle men gaf him maistrie;	
þe note he couth of alle laies	
& mynstralcie alle þe saies;	Of mynstrecye al þer assayes
he couth so mykelle musik & chyme	......chume
þat þe pupille said, in his tyme,	..people in..
he was god of fithelers,	..þe best of.
of iugelours & sangesters,	
for he was euer glad & gamen;	
fele in seruise held he samen.	
Of ioie & song was his spelle,	
was he not irous no felle,	..neyþer irous ne.
bot led his lyf in Melodie	
vnto þe tyme þat he suld die.	
After him Archinaul was,	..was Archynaul
pesabille (god haf his soule) he was.	.he was God haue ys saul
After him com his sone, Eldol;	
it sais he had a foltid pol	
for he was euer licheros,	
of women euer couetos.	..ouer.
A ientille woman if he mot fynd,	
were scho neuer so noble of kynd,	
whedire scho were weddid or nouht,	
	[*L adds:*] His lecherie he wolde haue y wrought
& for encheson of his foly,	
men hatid him; he was worþi.	
[25ra] After Eldol, þis foltid fon,	
was his sone hight Redion.	
Redion had þe kyngdam	
& after him Redrik cam;	
siþen was Famur & Missel	
& after hym, kyng Pirchel.	
Pirchel had fare hede with heire,	
þorgh gifte of kynd þat was heire;	.....was er
somwhat was faire out of kynd	.was hit....

þat of his heire writen we fynd.
After him com Caporus,
siþen his sone, Eliguellus;
þis Eliguellus fulle wys was he,
man of mesure wele auyse.
After him regned his sone Hely,
holy togidere ȝeres fourty; ffully . . .
a noble man & a wys, . . . was he & . .
he died & at Castre lys. ffaire he deyd & at . .
Hely had þre sones wyght;
þe heldest son Lud hight; . eldest . . he highte
þe toþer was Cassebelan;
þe þrid, Nenny, a douhty man.
Lud was eldest, most of age;
him felle to haf þe heritage.
Knyght was he, gode in stoure,
& metegift man, viandoure. & lyberal man & vyaundour
Citeȝ & kastels new did sette,
of þe olde he mad gude rescette.
He lufed London best of alle;
he closed it about with walle. Þerfore vmb closedit wyþ a .
Many ere þe close men se ȝit stande
þat Lud did mak whils he was lyfande.
For baroun & for burgeis sake
grete stedes to þam did make; . . til hem dide he make
þerfore men said, & ȝit men may,
þat neuer befor vnto þat day
made kyng befor so fele citeȝ,
ne castelle ne clos þat ȝit men ses.
Tille Luddes tyme, men held þat haunt
to calle London Trinouaunt;
for þe luf of Lud ilk dele
þat wonned þer long & closed it wele,
[25rb] & was of him so grete renoun,
Karelud men called þat toun.
Þan com oþer men were strange,
for þe Lud, London did chance; . . . . . hit chaunge
þan com Sessons, men of Angle, . . Saxoyns . . .
as þei couth on þer langage iangle,
fro Kaerlud called it Ludden,
þat couth þei best com on & ken;
þan com Normandȝ & Frankis
couth not com on to calle it þis.

For Ludden, Lundres þei calde; . London Londres þey hit.
on Frankis ȝit þat name men halde. ȝit Frensche men þat name.
Be remouyng of kyndes strange ffor Regnynge of Kynges.
for diuers spech, langage men change;
þat has þis lond often wonnen,
þorgh riden & þorgh ronnen,
ere þe names changed þerfore;
som names ere lesse & som more.
I hope fo tounes þat now ere . . þe . . . .
holde þe names þat first were.
Whan sir Lud, þe gude kyng,
was dede & mad his endyng,
beside his ȝate þei him laid;
for his name Ludgate is said.
He it mad & he it auht;
Ludgate for him þe name lauht.
Of Lud were left tuo childre ȝing,
lond to kepe couth þei no thyng;
þe eldest hight Androcheus,
þat oþer Tenuacius. . . men calde.
Cassebelan was þer eam,
þe next sibbe of þer team.
He kept þe childre & þe lond;
men held him, faire he þam fond. . . hym Kyng . . . .
He mayntend þe lond to þe right;
he was curtais & douhti knyght;
þe folk he couth wele iustise,
of þam he had faire seruise.
Whan þe childre were of elde
þat þei couth Lordschip welde,
in tuo erldams he did þam seise,
wirschiply alle at þer eise. Worschipfoly . . . .
[25va] Androcheus had þorgh assent
London & þe erldam of Kent;
þe toþer broþer had þe baile
of þe erldam of Cornwaile.
Whan ilk was seised in his erldam,
were called erles where þei cam. Þey were . . . . .
To whille þe kyng & his cosyns
in luf loked alle þer lynes; . . loken ar þer.
richesse had þei inouh to wille
ne of þe lond dred þei non ille, & of no lond . . . .
ne neuer thorte haf dred no tide. . . þurt hem haue . . .

Bot ouerwenyng of herte pride
ros a discorde þam bituen
þat long in þis lond was sene;
foure hundreth ȝere it lasted & nyen
in þis lond, þat first pyne.
It bigan, as ȝe may se,
of Cassebelan & Androche.
Þorgh sorow þe Romeyns wan   . whilk sorewe . . .
treuage of Cassebelan
þat mot neuer wyn it beforn,   . . nere be wonne byforn
tille þer luf þorgh pride was lorn.

[*L adds:*]Whyle þer loue to gedere held
Might neuere no Romayn bide þem in feld
Þat þey ne chased þorow force of fight
Cesar of Rome & al his myght

How it began bituex þam bale,
listes & I salle rede þe tale.
[I]n þe tyme of Cassebelan,   [*Capital I om. in P.*]
Iulius Cesar, a mighty man,
þat tyme was Emperour of Rome;
of knyghthede he bare þe blome   Of alle knyghtes . . . .
of alle þo þat tyme were herd, ... men of herd
for he conquerd alle þe werld.
Als he was douhty knyght & gode,
in clargie wele him vnderstode;   . . . he hym .
of conseile was he man fulle wys
& of manhede he bare þe pris.
His giftes he gaf largely,
he wist to whom & was worþi;   . . . . hit was worthi
fals & felon he couth knowe,
þe ouer proude he held þam lowe.
Þe Romeyns were þan of pride,
for þei had won on ilk a side,
londes oueralle þam aboute
& gaf þam treuage for doute.
[25vb] Whan Iulius had wonen þo þere,
forþer he þouht to conquere.
Long ne wald he soioure ne reste
tille he had won toward þe weste.
Hardy Iulius, knyght war & wys,
praised of pruesse, powere, & pris,
he gadred oste of knyghtes ȝong
of alle nacouns þat spak with tong,   . . nacions . . . .

& toke his leue at þe Romeyns
to wyne londes lungeteyns. — . wende fro þem for longe teymes
Weste he said he wild wend
to wynne to þe werldis end.
Whan Iulius was wele dight inouh,
he passed Lumbardie & Mongouh. — . . Burgoygne & Moungow
ffirst he wan alle Burgoyne,
ffrance, Nauerne, & Gascoyne,
Pettew, Normandie, Lesse Bretayne;
siþen he went tille Almayne, — . went agayn til .
alle he wan ar he þien nam;
sþen to Boloyn & Flandres cam — Siþen to . . . he cam
& alle conquered vnto þe see;
alle gaf treuage to Rome in fee.
Whan alle was won, wele held him paied;
bi þe se he ȝede a day & plaied.
Toward þe see, he egh gan kest, — . . . his eye gan .
fast biheld vnto þe west.
"What is ȝone lond I ȝondere se,
& what folk euer þerin be?"
Men him told it was a lond
þat þe folk of Troie first fond.
Brutus hight þer first cheftayne,
& after him it hate Bretayne;
þo heires þat of him ere comen,
in heritage þai haf it nomen.
Iulius ansuerd & said right þus:
"Wele haf I herd of sir Brutus."
He said, "He com of Eneas kynde,
bot rightly born, nouht we fynde.
We com of Eneas þat hald þo landes — He com . . . . . .
þer Rome our cite now it standes.
If he were born of Eneas kyn,
þorgh I set chalange þerin. — Þorow kynde y . . .
[26ra] Chalange I wille þat lond þorgh right
þat Eneas kynde had of myght. — . . . gete þorow .
Es ȝon þat ilde þat ȝe me kenne
þat Belyn was of & Brenne,
þat our cite of Rome wan,
our seene destroied ilk a man? — Oure see & destruyed . . .
Wele salle þei witte tille I am here
þat Rome es now of more powere,
& right it were & reson it wilde

þat þei tille vs treuage suld ȝelde.
Ȝon ilde was Belyns & Rome was his;
grete skille haf þan þorgh þis   . . haue y þenne . .
forto sette chalange þerin
þat his lond was þorgh right to wyn.
Bi lettre wille þam first somoune   . lettres woly hem . .
to here þer wille & þer respone;   . . . . what þey respoune
nouht ne wille passe þe see   . . woly passe . .
tille I witte how þei ansuere me.
If þat þai my pes chese
& ȝelde it me, þei salle nouht lese.
If þei ne wille bot with stoure,
I salle dereyn þe lond for oure."
Þan did Iulius write a brefe
& schewed þam how he was chefe,
& how his kynde first it wan,
of Eneas com Brutus, þat man,
& siþen was Belyns heritage.
He wild it wyn or take treuage.
Þe letter com to Cassebelan
þat he suld com Iulius þat man.   . . . bycome sire Iulyus man
Cassebelan brak þe seel osundire;
of treuage askyng he had wondire.
Anoþer he did write þare   . lettere dede he wryte .
& sent ageyn vnto Cesar,   . sent hit . . .
alle in ire & in tene,
& þe writte þus mykelle wild mene:
"Cesar," he said, "we haf meruaile
& gre disdeyn withouten faile,   . gret . . .
þat of ȝow Romeyns rennes suilk los,
& long it lastes & fer it gos,   . to longe hit lastes after . .
þat ere of so grete couetise
þat non bot ȝe may haf franchise;
[26rb] & alle þe siluer & alle þe golde,
& alle linage þat lien on molde, ... lyuen . .
tille ȝour dome wille þam drawe,   . . . wil ȝe þem .
withouten reson, withouten lawe.
Alle þe tresore ȝe drawe ȝow to,
what wille ȝe þer with do?   . . . þer wyþ al do
& we þat ere at þe wordes ende, ... wordes ende
in an ilde lif & lende,
ȝit wille ȝe nouht passe vs forbi
bot ȝorgh treuage greuosli;   Wyþoute truage askyng .

& we þat suld be ȝour peres,	
ȝit wille ȝe mak vs treuageres.	
If þou, Iulius, wild mak assay	Þerfore Iulius ȝyf þou wilt.
to com tille vs & sette vs day,	& of þy comynge sette vs a day
I trowe þou suld litelle spede,	...schalt fol euele.
if þou wild proue it with dede.	Come on & proue hit in dede
Euer ȝit haf we lyued fre	
in þis lond, bot now for þe,	
& we suld life also freli	...lyue als.
as ȝe Romens & reson whi,	
for ȝe & we ere alle a kynde,	Syn we ar comen alle of o.
comen of a rute & a rynde;	& of o rote & of o.
for we ere comen of Eneas,	Þat ys to seyn..
frely born als euer þou was.	
Þerfor if þou þe biþouhtis	
& after skille & reson wrouhtis,	In skil & reson as þou oughtest
þou suld not sette vs in seruage	...put vs to.
þat ere of þin awen lynage.	Syn we ben of...
We salle be peris to ȝow of Rome,	
in alle fredom haf euenly dome.	
Als þou ert ientille & of grete pris	Vs wondreþ at ȝowre nurture of pris
þat suilk vilany in þe now lis,	
in seruage to putte vs to;	
& we wote nouht how we salle do,	
ne neuer lerid ne nouht wille lere,	
if þat we may, in no manere.	
Of alle our kynde, I wist no man	
þat couth of seruise ne ȝit kan;	
ne we ne knawe on what wyse	
we suld serue seruage seruyse.	
Fre we ere, so salle we be,	
if god wille, Cesar, for þe.	& ȝyf God wyl we schul..
[26va] Witte þou wele be our ansuere,	
tille we may ourseluen were	While....
& fend our lond & our franchise,	
of vs getis þou neuer seruise	
ne treuage, I gyf þe a gyue.	.neuere truage schol we þe gyue
Þat is to say, to whils we lyue,	
we wille be fre & hold honoures	
als did beforn our ancessoures."	
To Iulius suilk a lettre þei sent,	
& whan he wist þe entent	
þat if he wild haf treuage,	

nedeli borde him mak passage; — Nede byhoued hym..
þan did he mak schippes & bargis
foure score with grete charges.
So grete were non þat tyme for were, — ..byfore were neuere for.
ne non so heuy charge myght bere, — ..þat so gret charge..
withouten oþer schippes smale
þat were not telde of in þat tale. — .we nought telde byforn in.
Whan Iulius was alle redy
to go to schippe, þei mad a cry.
His folk com into schippe right fast
& did drawe þe saile on þe mast; — .drowe þer saylles vp heye on.
þe wynde blewe & gan þam dryue. — Þen blew þe wynd....
At a hauen þei gan vp ryue
þer Temse & þe se togidire comen;
bot ar Cesar þe land had nomen,
þer was spred bi þe se side
faire folk to fight, Cesar to bide.
Cassibelan was redy at Douere
& rengid him bi þe ses ouere. — ..his men by þe ouere
His stiward hight sir Belyn,
conseilere was he gode & fyn. — Of conseil was....
He had don com þorgh somons — ..do comen..
on ilk half erles & barons;
þe kynges neuoȝ þe to partie, — ...com wyþ gret partie
on þo tuo he might affie: — To hem he myghte hym wel.
[*L adds:*] Þe eldest highte Androcheus
Þat oþer broþer Tenuacius
Androcheus & his lordynges Londreis, — ..his Loundreneys
Tenuacius with his Cornwaleis;
Sire Nennius, lord of Caunterbire,
þe noblest of alle þe empire.
Þe kyngis broþer was sir Nenny;
Androche was in his company,
[26vb] & oþer folk grete plente.
With ostes were þer kynges þre:
Erudionus, þe Scottis kyng,
Britalles with þe Walsh gaderyng,
of south Wales com Ignertet; — ....kyng Ignarcet
þise þre were in a batale set.
With þer fre wille þise þre cam
for to defend þar fredam.
Ilkon gaf conseile to go
or þe Romeyns were loged mo,

or þei had any rescet taken,
or þei wild hald þam waken.   Þey þoughte þey wolde hem a wake
Whan alle were set in ilk bataile
& whilk of þam suld formast saile,   & schept ho scholde formest assaille
toward þe Romeyns fast þei nom.
Whan Cesar saw þat þei suld com,
he cried on his, "Armes ȝow!   . . to hys men . .
Þe Bretons ere redy & com now."   . . . . . come right now
Son were þer ostes to gidere mett
& to bataile rengid & sett,
þe parties smert smyten togidre;   [*Om. L*]
with scharp suerdes on helmes gan glidre,   [*Om. L*]
þer schaftes þorgh schoten body & schelde.   [*Om. L*]
Many on felle & many vphelde;   [*Om. L*]
many tome sadille & hors ostray,   [*Om. L*]
many douhti knyght doun þer lay,   [*Om. L*]
& many one wonded & lay to blede,   Many on wonded lay þer . .
& many stode & fled for drede;
knyghtes iusted, archers drowe,
of boþe parties were feld inowe.   . . . fol manie þey slowe
Þei com so þikke & so smerte,
perced hauberk, breste, & herte;   & perced brunyes . . .
with staues striken, with axe hewe,   . wyfles . . . .
þe schuldres, þe schankes doun threwe.   Schuldres schankes & hedes . .
Alle was strewed þe grene gresse
with blode & bowes & herneis fresse;   . . . bowaille & heuedes .
no ferly was it behoued nede   fful hard was þer & moste .
þe quyk opon þe dede ȝede;
opon þe dede þei stode to fight
& alle slouh þat slo myht.   . eueryche . . he slo myght
Cesar had in his bataile
knyhtes þat couth defend & saile;   . . . boþe fende & .
[27ra] he peyned him to do þam wo,
& fast folowed þam to slo.
Was it non þat he smote   . þer no man . . .
þat ne þe dede sone him bote;   . ful sore on hym ne bot
myght no man lyf no stounde
þat of his suerde toke any wounde.
Androche com with þam of Kent,
& Nennius, togidere þei went;
þei gadred þam a gode partie   . set o þe Romayns a gret .
& batailed þam as men hardie,   . beot hem doun . . .
& "Turne we opon Cesar!"   . seide turne . . .

& als þei rode þei were of him war.
Nennius first ferde in to þe stoure
& abatid him on þe Emperoure,
& glad was þat he myght
with so grete a lordyng fight. ..noble...
Cesar perceyued þat he cam;
ageyn his stroke his scheld vp nam. ..scheld a strok..
Cesar suerde was out fulle sone;
Nenny to smyte he was alle bone,
& Nenny in þe hede he smote;
it was trenchand, ouer fer it bote; ..trenchaunt....
bot Nenny bare vp his schelde,
his hede lowe a parti helde,
ȝit his stroke sank so doun
þorgh þe schelde & brak his croun; ..helm he brak..
litille failed þat he ne had, Lite.....
clouen þe borde, dynt was sad; ..hed þe dynt..
bot Nenny bare þe scheld o skere
& Iulius smot his suerde ouer fere
þat he ne myght drawe it ageyn.
Neuerþeles he did his peyn; Naþeles he dide þerto..
he drouh his suerde, Nenny þe schelde,
ilkon wele his owen helde.
Nenny wild haf turned & went;
Iulius ageyn with þe drauht him hent.
I hope Iulius had drawen it out,
bot Nennius folk were egre & stout.
Androche, Nenny neuow,
with þam of Kent did grete prow;
on ilk a side þei slouh aboute,
& Cesar sawe himself in doute
& fro þam fled into þe felde,
[27rb] & left his suerde in Nenny schelde;
& Nenny sawe of help inouh.
He turned þe schelde, þe suerde out drouh
& with þe suerde forth he fauht;
& þo þat þer with wondes lauht
myght þei neuer haf medicyne,
bot to þe dede bod þam pyne. ...deþ by houed hem.
As he fauht, þis Nennius,
he ouertoke sir Labennius;
lord he was of grete bailie,
in Rome had a constablie. ..he hadde a constablerye

Nennius suilk a stroke him lent	
þat be þe schuldres þe hede of went.	
How many died, I may not ame;	
of alle fighters I knew no name.	
Bot manyon doun was laied,	
mo þan any wrote or said,	Wel mo þan any man...
& mo suld if þat þe nyght	& wel mo scholde ȝit þat.
had ne sondred þam & left þer fight.	.þey nought sondred for faute of lyght
The nyght com, gon was þe day,	Þen com þe nyght....
& ilk a partie ȝede þer way.	
Þe Romeyns side was not paied;	
loges non had, þei were dismaied.	
Wery þei were & ille likand	....yuel.
with þe Bretons þei myght not stand.	
Þe toke conseile away to wende,	
no langere in þis land to lende,	
for þe cuntre knowe þei nouht.	
Loge ne rescet had þei non wrouht;	
to schippes þe went þat ilk nyght,	
vnto fflandres flegh þer flight.	
Þe Bretons mad blis ilkone	
þat þe Romeyns were so gone,	
& þe kyng mad sorow inouh,	
for Nennius to dede drouh.	..þat to deþe.
Medicyne non myght he founde	.myghte non be.
þat myght hele Nenny wounde.	
Of sire Nenny nouht els to say:	
he died on þe fiftend day;	Bot þe fiftenþe day Nenny gan deye
þei biried him in a temple gate	
in London at þe north ȝate,	
honorablie more þan anoþer,	honurabloker.þan.
for he was þe kynges broþer.	
[27va] Þat suerde he wan of sir Cesar,	
bi him in graue þei laid it þar,	
for he was of grete honoure,	
& he had won it in þat stoure.	..haddyt wonnen y þat.
Þat suerd was of suilk matal	
þat if any were wonded with al,	.who þat wounded were..
he myght not long liue,	
for medecine men mot him gyue.	
Whi of dede it had þe gilt,	
it was writen on þe hilt,	
lettres of gold burnissed bright,	Wyþ lettres....

þat "Crucia mors" þe suerd hight;
[*L adds:*] Hit myghte wel hote Crucia mors
Wham hit wounded hit was ded cors
& ȝit men say, as sais þe romance, ..hit ys seyd y..
þe empourer suerd was alle vengeance.
Tille þam of France com tiþeng tite
how þe Romeyns were discomfite
þorgh þe Bretons in pleyn bataile;
þan mysliked þam sanȝ faile
& for cowardes þamseluen ches
þat þei were at þe Romeyns pes.
Þei conseild þam a day certayn
vpon Cesar to turne agayn.
In þer conseile þei said þus:
"As þe Bretons chaced Iulius,
ȝit salle we fonde so to spede
to do sir Iulius fle for drede.
Þe Bretons be not ȝit so bolde
als we ere, ne men of tolde, ..haue ben men..
& so lightli did þam loute,
ȝit salle we fond to chace þam oute.
It ere inouh þat first haf grace
forto wynne & robbe & chace,
& siþen turnes þer pray to pyne.
Lightly þei wyn, lightly þai tyne;
þer lordschip salle we abate,
for alle þe world þe wyn with hate."
Þus þei said þat þei wild do,
& ȝit alle day men teld þam to, ...so
þat þe Bretons wild fond a flight,
France to help, þe Romeyns to fight. fforto fele þe Romayns myght
Þat sawe mad þam wilde & wode
& raised þam more vp in mode;
[27vb] bot son þer boste was in grith
whan Iulius had spoken þam with.
Sir Iulius was fulle quaynte;
wisdom he couth & wordes faynte.
A felon couth he fulle wele daunte, .folet couþe he wel adaunte
to proude men þer wille graunte.
Wele couth he pay þe couettouse;
he wan þe wille of þe enuyouse.
Wele couth he bere him meke & ful wel couþe bere..
whan his force was to seke. ..strengthe was for..

He wist þe Frankis men were fikelle,
þei forced þem agayn him mykelle; — & how þey forcedem...
& his men were ille dight — ....yuel.
& weri for fouhten in fight. — Wery & wounded al..
Leuere him were in luf to loute
þan com to bataile & be in doute. — .in bataille to ben..
Þe Bretons had þam hasted so
þat tyme in dede myght þei nouht do.
With faire wordes þam to him drouh
& gaf þam giftes riche inouh, — ...giftes & Richesse.

[*L adds:*] ffor of his giftes he was ful large
ffor schame þey moughte hym namore charge

& more hette þam if þat he myght — ..he byhet þan gyue..
þe Bretons wyn with force of fight.
Pouere men he gaf franchise,
claymed þam quite of alle seruise;
þo men þat he had fled þe cuntre, — ..he hadde flemed..
to com agayn he gaf þam fre,
& to haf þer heritage
& restored þam þer damage. — ..þeym of here.
Whan þis grete lordynges
sawe Cesar offer þam suilk thynges,
golde & siluere at þer wille,
in pes alle þei held þam stille.
Mikelle es richesse of powere;
sone had he bated wo & wheere. — ....wo & wer

[*L adds:*] Sone had he turned wrong to right
Sone had he blent þe Coueytous sight

Of Cesar & þe frankis boþe, — [*Transp. L*]
sone made he frende þat were wrothe, — [*Transp. L*]
for þo þat him beforn hatid,
for his giftes were alle abatid.
Þat compassid foly & outrage, — .schopen hym yuel &.
þei mad him feaute & homage,
at his conseile forto lende
agayn þe Bretons if he wild wende.
[28ra] Whan sir Iulius, lord & sire, — .sire Cesar...
had pesed & suaged alle þer ire,
he conseild with an engynoure
& did mak a meruailous toure
in Boloyne; Odre is þe name;
so wrouht is non bot þat same.

Bineþen, it is in strange compas,
brode & þik þe gynnyng was,
& euer it nerewes, risand on heght,
semegrelere & more streght; & semeþ griller & . .
selcouth stages ere þerin,
wyndous cast, coruen with gyn.
His tresore he laid þer in to loke,
only þer alle þat he toke,
& himself lay in þe toure
whan he dred him for his tresoure.
Tuo ȝere he duelled þer in France
& dighted it for were o chance, ... werre in alle chaunce
& sent bailifs to gadre his feeȝ
& raised his treuage of Citeȝ.
Whan alle was gadred in ilk partie,
in Odre þei laid it in tresorie.
In þo tuo ȝere he did him dight
vppon þe Bretons eftsons to fight. & made hym to Brutayne right
He did dight a flete on flode,
sex hundreth schipes grete & gode,
& said, "Ȝit wille mak assay . . . wyly . .
vppon þe Bretons, spede if I may;
bot I myght conquere Cassibalan, . ȝif y may . .
I praise nouht els alle þat I wan.
Alle my conqueste praise I nouht,
bot þe Bretons to trew be brouht."
Whan it was dight alle, alle his flete . . . . al his flet
with gode folk & vitaile sete,
þei sette vp saile þe schippes kemse, Þe schipes seyled day & nyght
þe wynde þam drofe in to Temse. Til þey come in to Temese right
Þus þei wende at þe first tide,
þer nauye to London holy suld ride.
Alle at ons þei suld vp saile
& to þe Bretons gyf bataile.
Þe Bretons wist it wele inouh,
bot what þei did, listen how. . of þer sleigþe lystneþ now
[28rb] Long peeles & grete did þei make, . pyles . . . . .
fast in Temse did þam stake,
euerilkon with iren schod;
agayn þe schippes stod ilk an od,
fulle wele set & sikerly,
myght non wele scape forby. Þer myght . . ascape .
Right at a folle flowe of flode, . atte fulle se of .

alle sex hundreth schippes gode. Com alle. . . .
Sikerli þei wend haf nomen
& to London at ons comen.
Þei were within bot a lite
are on þe peles þai gan smyte.
Þer myght men se þat stode on brinke
schippes in to water sinke; . in to þe . .
þe tone vnto þe toþer hurte,
mastes falle, togidere burte; Þe mastes faste . .
som ouerturned & lay on side,
burdes riuen out holes wide,
ropes reueld, snarled in line. [*Possibly*] suarled
Ropes Ryuereled & swerued . .
Ilk oþer dered & did pine,
lond ne hauen myght þei non take
so fast on pelis gon þei stake.
In ille tyme out þei nome, . yuel . . . .
ille þei sailed & þidire come. Yuel þey ryued þat þider .
Cesar sawe þat grete vnhap
þat in þe water was suilk a trap,
iren schod was ilk a pele.
He þouht þat so was ilk a dele.
Many of þam turned agayn
& said þat wendyng was in vayn;
he did þam alle go vp to lond,
man & hors þer þei best fond,
bi bankes vp abouten went,
& piked þam pauillons & tent. . pyght . . . .
Right as þai piked þer pauilons, . . . picched . .
com Cassibalan with þe Bretons.
Erles, barons, knyghte, suaynes . . . squiers
asperly fellid on þe Romayns.
His neuoȝ & his oþer kynde, . neuew & oþere of his .
with alle þe help þat he mot fynde,
þe kyng ascried þam on his wise; . . asemblede in noble wyse
with þe Bretons was no fayntise.
[28va] At þer loges as þei þam sette,
þe Bretons with þam þer þei mette;
[*L adds:*] Þeyr egre comyng þe Romayns aboden
ferweis at þer first comyng, [*Om. L*]
þer armour herd þe crusse & ryng. [*Om. L*]
At þer loges þe Romeyns biden, [*Om. L*]
agayn þe Bretons stifly riden; Ageyn þe Brutons stifly þey stoden

as a walle þer hardynes helde	. . . þe scheltrom held
& did þe Bretons go bak in felde.	& Ruysed þe Brutons abak . .
ffirst þe Romeyns fulle wele stod	
agayn þe Bretons in felde ȝod,	. . . . bataille ȝoden
& fer bakward did þam go;	
manyon slouh & wrouht wo.	
Þan was wroth Cassibalan;	
for tene befor þam alle he wan	
& bare þe breste on þam before,	
& after him þe Bretons gan bore,	
& euer was fresch folk comand	
& did þe Romeyns agayn stand.	
So within a litelle þrowe	
men amed þam, & wele it sowe	
tuo so many Bretons þare	
als he had þer, Iulius Cesare,	
& did þe Romeyns agayn fle	. . . . . to fle
& slouh þam, þo schame was to se.	. . . schame was hit . .
Hardi Cesar, noble kyng,	
þat neuer abaist for no thyng,	. . so bayscht was . . .
he sawe þe force of þe Bretons,	
& his to þam had no fosons;	. . . . . . fuysons
þe Bretons als wode rengid route,	
of dede ne dynt had þai no doute.	
Þei slouh & feld & mad þam way;	
þei mad no force to lyf or deie.	
Cesar perceyued þat fulle wele;	
he did turne his folk ilk dele	
ageyn to þer schippes wende,	
& himself was in þe last ende	Bot hym self lefte til . . .
ageyn to þe Bretons to fight,	
to whils his folk to schip þam dight.	
Bi þe lond his schippes did ride	
to kepe his folk at ilk a tide;	
whan alle were in & saile on maste,	
Cesar com in alderlaste,	
& alle þat were of his conrey	
[28vb] vp with saile & forth þer way.	Hyed þem faste & wente þer.
Euen als lyn þe wynd gan dryue;	. as lyne . . . .
at Odre, his toure, did vp ryue.	. . . . gon þey aryue
Cesar soiornde þer wel long	
to hele þat were wonded strong,	. hele þem . . . .
& man & hors forto reste,	

& ordeynd what was for him beste.
Þe kyng, douhti kyng Cassibalan,   ..of þys lond.
& þe Bretons, ilk a man
had ioy for þe mykelle pris
þat þei had won of Cesar tuys.
Þe Romeyns mykelle sorow made
& þe Bretons were alle glade.   Þat þe Bretons were so glade
[*L adds:*] Cesar & hyse were dismayed
Bot þe Bretons were wel payed
ffor ioie þey hadden þo batalle wonnen
& Cesar twyes had ouer ronnen
To god þei hight to mak a feste
with alle þe comune of þer geste.   ...commes lest & meste
Þat day he sette of sacrifise,
his vowe to hold with fair seruise,
Cassibalan sent messengers
for barons, knyghtes, & squyers
of his demeyns, alle þe pedaile   .....pytaille
þat him serued at þe bataile,   .hadde hym serued in.
þat þei suld alle to London come
on peyn of forfetore & dome.
Wyf & childe with þam suld lede;
þo þat halpe him in his nede,
& alle þei come with hert glad
in riche atire, als he bad.
Man & wife, childre ȝonge
þat couth go & speke with tonge,
alle þei com vnto þe cite,
feirere folk myght no man se;
& ilk a man at his auenaunt
mad offryng als was þer haunt.
Þis fest day was so hii   ...þat was..
was of fourti þousand kii   Were offred fifty þousand ky
& þer þritti þousand hyndes,   ..to þre þousand.
wilde walkand bi wod lyndes,
& a hundreth þousand schepe;
þe tale af foules gaf no man kepe,   Þe noumbre of foules....
so fele þer were myght no man ame,
what of wilde & what of tame.
Whan done was þe sacrifise,
[*L adds:*] & feste holde in þer beste wyse
[29ra] mynstrals bigan to glewe & ryme   ...blowe..
as þer custom was þat tyme.

Knyghtes & squyers mad burdis   ....bourdys
in þer quantise of purpure & bis   & hem desgysede in...
& oþer bachelers skirmed fast,
wristled, skipped, stones kast.   Wrastlede lepen..
In felde in toun at ilk a way
ilkon plaied þat he couth play.
Whan alle had plaied at þer wille
& suld haf ben alle stille,   ...ended & ben al.
tuo wald skirme þat com of cas,   ..skyrmen as fel þe.
Heulyn & Hereglas.   Sire Huwelyn & Irelgas
Ireglas was þe kynges cosyn,
Androche nouowe was Heulyn;   .neuew..
þis tuo togidere skirme algate,   ...wolde skyrme.
þorgh pride of hert þan com hate;
þorgh þan gan wordes rise   Þorow hate þen gan þer..
of boþe parties of ille asise.
Whan ilk had said oþer wouh;   ...seyd til..
with wreth to smyte, þe edge drouh.
Þorgh a mischance, I wote it was,
Heulyn sleuh þer Ireglas.
Whan þe kyng þat chance herd say,
þe feste was turbled & mirth away,   ...sturbled & aweye
for þe kyng was fulle feloun
& hastif vnto vengeance boun.
Þe kyng said vnto Androche,
bad him on peyn of alle his fe,
Heulyn him forto send   .his cosyn hym..
þat felony forto amend,
& in his courte haf iugement
þorgh comon or þei went.   Þorow þe Comunes er þat..
Androcheus þouh with herte fulle wo,   .þoughte....
"If I him send, he salle him slo."
Androche sent agayn fulle tyte
& of his courte asked respite.
"A lord I am, a courte I haue
þorgh whilk I may dampne him or saue.   .þat wyl y hym dampne..
If it be ouþer baron or knyght,
pleyne him þer & haf his right.   ...he schal haue right
Þe courte þat þou bides me to,   & þe souereynte þou takest þe.
it suld be myn & salle be so.
[29rb] Þou wote it is myn heritage;
þou bedis me mys & outerage."
Whan þe kyng herd his ansuere,

he suore he suld on him were,	
& þat he had he suld him reue	
heritage ne nouht him leue;	. . . . byleue
& Heulyn suld he slo,	
for Ireglas suld he go.	ffor þat outrage þat had do
On þis manere departed þer feste;	
with luf bigan, endid with cheste.	
Cassibalan was Androche eame,	
Luddes broþer of þat teame;	
Androche & Tenuace,	Androcheus was Luddesone & .
Lud sons boþe, I told or space.	As y forn telde in oþer place
Whan Lud died, þei ne couth	
kepe þe lond for ouer ȝouth.	
Cassibalan þerfor vndertoke	
þe lond & þam to kepe & loke,	
& þorgh þe wreth now of þis thyng,	
makis Androche a chalangyng.	
Now ilk a day þe kyng fondes	
to robbe & brenne Androche londes.	. brenne & struye . .
Androche sawe his felon wille	
þat þe kyng wild him spille.	. . . þoughte hym to .
He sent to him his messengere	
& praied þe kyng faire manere,	. . . . in fair .
no more destroie his londes so,	
bot mak acorde bituex þam tuo;	
& praied him if he wild it mone,	. . . þat he wolde mone
þat ha was his broþer sone	. he . . . .
& heire of alle þat heritage,	
"Þat þou me reues als outerage."	. . . reuest wyþ outrage
Þe kyng was so felon res,	. . . of so . .
he not here his praiere no pes,	. ne wolde here of preyere ne .
bot vengeance take for any thyng	
bo fallis vmwhile ille for a kyng.	Þat falles ful yuel . . .
Androche sawe no bettir bote.	
"To suffre," he said, "I nede mote."	Suffren he saide nede y mot
His pleyn londes lete him haue,	. . . he let . .
& his forceletes did saue.	Bot his forteletes he . .
With him to hold he fond no man,	
so cruelle was Cassibalan.	
[29va] Fle ne wald he neueradele,	
ne lese þat he mot holde wele.	
Androche said, "What is to spede?	. asked . . . rede
No man dar me help for drede,	

& help me bos haf alle gate;	. . . byhoues haue . .
nede me chaces vnto þe ȝate.	. . dryueþ vntil . .
[*L adds:*]	ffor þe kyng assent wil nought
	Þat y haue pes als y haue sought
	Siþen y ne may haue no rest
	On oþer halue y schal do my best
Fulle mykelle anguys wilde I bide	
forto felle þe kynges pride.	
A foly to do & slek a more;	. . . . . fle a wel more
men hold it wisdom & lore	
to do a foly, ȝit were it skille	
to delyuer a man fro more perille;	
& wele it were to suffire a wo	
forto venge him on his fo.	
Wele I wote & haf in herte	
þat it salle vs boþe smerte,	
bot ȝit me likes þat greuance,	
if I may take of him vengence.	
What so salle betide, alle gate	. . schal me . . .
þe kynges pride I wille abate;	
I may not els with him dele."	
A lettre he wrote & did it sele	
& sent it priueli to Cesar,	
tille Odre, his toure, for he was þar.	
What he wrote & þider sent,	
þus I vnderstond þe entent:	
"To Cesar, hardy, war & wys,	
whos pruesse men praises in pris,	
of Bretan, Androche þe Breton,	
Sire of Kent, Lord of London,	
to send þe gretyng is my rede,	Sendeþ þe gretynge wyþ his god .
whilom to whom I desired dede.	Þat whilom wylned to þe ded
Cesar, oft haf men sene	
þer tuo haf hated & fomen bene,	
þat siþen haf lufed togidere wele,	
tristeliere þen any stele.	Tristiloker . . .
After hate, luf wille be,	
& after wirschip men se	& after schame . . .
þus betides many gate	Þus hit . . .
of som þat long haf bene in hate.	. . þer longe has ben hate
We souht our dede alle þat we myght,	Ilk soughte oþer deþ . . . .
whan we fondid in felde to fight.	. . met vs . . . .
[29vb] Bot so it felle to boþe our prowe	

þat nouþer am I slayn ne þou.
Ageyn vs bataile has þou nomen,
& tuys haf we þe ouercomen;
bot witte þou now for certayn,   .lef þou wel þis..
if þou wille com eft agayn,
of Kent ne thurte þe fle þat coste   ...þertestow fle..
þof I were þer with alle myn oste;
& þof þe kyng þat tyme com þere,
ne thurte þe fle for alle his here,   Ne þart þe....fare
for þorgh my help & me   ....& þorow me
has þe kyng don þe fle,   ...do þe twyes.
& þorgh þe dyntes of my honde,   [*Om. L*]
defended þe kyng his londe;   [*Om. L*]
& for me þe lond þou les,   ffor by me....
& for me fled þi mykelle pres.
Þerof now I repent sore   ...repente me.
þat I did ageyn þe þore.
Þerfor þorgh me þou salle be brouht
to wyn þat lond als þou had þouht.
Now me forþenkes þat I noied þe, ...þe noyed
& þat þe kyng of þe destroied, ...þe so.
for he has born proude þerfore   .syn he haþ boren hym in to proud wyse
to his barons out of score;   Til his barons & to alle hyse
siþen with me ne had he wille   And syþen hadde he neuere.
in pes me suffre a day be stille.
My lond to waste he wendes aboute, ...goþ.
my frendes to slo & druye þam oute.
Miself he wald exile, & chace,
& slo, also is his manace.   ..als hit ys..
My god I tak witnes vnto,
I serued nouht he suld do so.
My neuow to dede he wild haf demed;
for þat encheson am I now flemed,   .y wyþstodit he haþ me.
for I wald not do his wille,
suffir him my neuow to spille.
I salle þe telle how it bigan
bituex me & Cassibalan.
For þe honoure & þe pris
þat we had ouercomen þe tuys,
þe kyng did þe folk somon
þorghout þe lond of ilk a toun
[30ra] þat alle of valow, moste & leste,   [*L om. 4862–4871*]
suld com to London to his feste,

grace tille our god ȝelde
with sacrifise, as lawe wilde,
graces ȝolden with sacrifise.
Whan we had don our seruise,
diuerse folk in stedes did samen
& diuersly plaied þei gamen.
With skirmyng þei bigan to play
& ilk oþer with word myssay.

[*The following passage in L repeats 4706–4737 in P.*]

Irelgas was þe kynges cosyn
Huwelyn he was neuew myn
Þyse togydere wolde skirme algate
Þorow proude hertes þer wax hate
Þorow hate þer gon wordes ryse
On boþe partys on yuel assise
Whan ilk had seid oþer wow
Wiþ wraþe to smyte þe egge drow
Þorow a meschaunce y wot hit was
Huwelyn slow þer Irelgas
When þe kyng herde þys seye
Þe feste was trobled & myrþe aweye
ffor þe kyng was ful felon
& hastif vntil vengaunce boun
Þen seid þe kyng vntil me
Comaundynge vp peyne of al my fe
Huwelyn hym for to sende
Þat ffelonye for to amende
And in his court haue iugement
Þorow þe comunes ar þat þey went
Þan þought y wyþ herte ful wo
Ȝif y hym sende he scholde hym slo
Y sende hym ageyn ful tyt
& of his court asked respit
A lord y am a court y haue
Þorow þat wold y hym dampne or saue
Ȝif hit be eyþer baron or knyght
Þat pleyneþ hym þere he shal haue right
Þe court þat þou bedes me to
Hit schold be myn & schal be so
Þou wost hit is myn heritage
Þou beodes me mys & outrage

[*For this passage, P has the following, lines 4872–4893.*]

My neuow was þer Heulyn,
& þe kyng had þer a cosyn;
þe kynges cosyn manaced fast
& drouh his suerde at him in hast.
My neuow saw þat & on him stirte,
held his suerde for doute of hirte.
Of trewe men þus I it herd:
bituex þam tuo þus it misferd
þat þorgh a wond þat he lauht þore,
vp ne ras he neuer more;
oþer wais no man ne wote
whedire he felle or he him smote
Þe kyng of þis apechid me
& comandid on alle my fe,
þat I his body to him sent
& at his courte take iugement.
I hoped wele he wild him slo,
þe ton suld for þat oþer go,
þerfore I douted him to sende.
I said I had a courte, I wende,
& lordeschip as a man of myght;
com pleyne him þer & tak his right;

[P and L are parallel again at 4894.]

& for I þus agaynsaid him,
es he to me þus brothe & brym — He ys . . . wroþ & brym
& manaces me, day bi day,
to brenne or slo if þat he may.
Wharfor, Cesar, I shewe it þe
þat þou my socoure agayn him be
& help in my wo so hard, — . help me . . . . .
& com hider in gode forward,
& þorh me salle þou haf Bretayne,
& I for þe be brouht of payne. — . . þorow þe brought out of .
[30rb] Ne haf þou no suspicion
þat I say it for any treson;
I wild no suilk a thyng begyn
for þis reme forto wyn, — Al . . . .
bot com & mak no duellyng
& rescowe me agayn þe kyng.
If þou spede not in þe first ende, — ffor þou myshappedest y . . .
now salle þou spede are þat þou wende.''
Cesar herd what he besouht

& straitly turned it in his thouht,
& schewed it his barons about,
whedire þei held it certayn or dout.
Þeron þei conseild þat þer ware;
þan at þe last, said Cesar
þat he ne wild for his sond no sawe
putt him in perille ne in awe,
ne for a biheste of boste
wild he so sone eft samen his oste.
"For I haf herd say fele sithe
þat faire hotes makes foles blythe."   ..byhestes makeþ..
Cesar sent him bode agayn,
if he wild holde his worde certayn,
send he suld him ostagers,
men of gude, barons, pers,
or els wild he not com þer
vnto his tyme better were.
Androcheus dred him of treson
þat þe kyng wild bisege þe toun.
His sone, Senna, to Cesar sent
& þritty oþer þidere went   ...wyþ hym þey went
of þe best þat he mot fynde,
next born of his awen kynde.
Cesar receyued þam with honoure
& did þam Odre, his toure.   ...alle in Ordre..
Siþen als son as he mot hie,
he dight his oste & gode nauie,
& priuely aryued vp at Douere
& loged þam bi bank & ouere.   ...by þe cost al ouer
Androcheus com to Cesar þidere
& conseild þam boþe togidere,
how þei suld wirk & on what wise
agayn þe kyng in bataile rise.   .....to rise
[30va] Renoun ran þat ouer reches   Tydynges ronne þat ouer al.
to ilk a man mad þei spechis;   Ilk man til oþer made þer.
speche men told þe kyng tiþand   Til men tolde þe Kyng tydant
þat þe Romeyns were aryued on land.
Þe kyng þeron conseild him sone
on þam to renne, mad him bone,
& had in herte grete meruaile
þei rose so sone eft in bataile.
He wend of þam haf had no warde
bot him felle þer a chek hasarde, ...ful harde

& als sone as he myght,	
toward Douere his oste he dyght.	
To Cesar was told in haste	. . was hit . . .
þat þe kyng was comand faste.	
Cesar conseild with Androche	
þat he wald out of þe cite	. . wolde come . . . .
& turne sidenen in a valeie,	. . a sidenhand o valeye
alle armed, bide þam in þe weie,	
& renge þam redy in ordire right,	. arraied þem in renges .
whilk aschelle suld formast fight.	& assigned whiche bataille first schold fight
Whan Cesar had set alle his oste,	. . . arrayed al . .
a thyng he comandid moste	
þat non suld for wele ne wo	
on fro oþer out of renge go,	
ne non prese ne stirte before,	
ne hold behynd in coward score,	
bot renge þam sadly side bi side;	. passe forþ sadlyk . . .
vntille þei com, þei suld abide,	Til þey com þer þey . .
& þan baldely auentour his chance,	. stoutly hem þanne o þe bretons auaunce
resceyue him with suerde & lance.	& felle þem doun wiþ . . .
Androche bussed him priuely	. enbusched . .
with fyue hundreth armed redy	. fif hundred men . .
on þe kyng assaute to make,	
bituex þam if þei mot him take.	. hem ȝyf he myghte . .
Cassibalan on his way gan spede,	
of non bussement had he drede;	. . enbuschement tok he hede
þer ostes boþe he neihed ȝerne.	
Whan he was not fro þam ferne,	
ouer a hille þan lay his waye	
& as he com into þe valaye,	
he sawe þe Romeyns spred in þe felde,	. . . . fresche y . .
redy renged with helme & schelde.	. enbatailled wiþ spere . .
[30vb] Als he mad him redye	. sone mad he hym.
& discried þam with a crye,	. loude ascried þem on har .
& to schot arowes & dartes,	. sone þey schoten . . .
fulle felonli boþe partes.	. . on boþe .
Androche at þe first comyng,	
of his enbussement gan he springe;	
alle fresly on him he com fulle hote	. . he com on hem . .
& bakward on þe Bretons smote.	
"Ay," said þe kyng, "here disceite!	Ey . . . here ys deseit
Betuex þam tuo I am holden streite."	. . . þey holde vs .
He ne mot not perce þe oste Romeyn,	

ne he ne myght turne ageyn;
behynd, befor, he sawe perille;
on side he trauersed to a hille;
nede behoued him or be in clos,
on boþe sides he sawe his fos.
He said himself he was betraist. ...þo he..
Þan were þe Bretons alle obaist; .....abaischt
ilkon þat mot fle, þei fled;
þat best mot renne, best þam sped.
Better es fle þan foly bide .was..worse abide
whan socour comes on no side. ffor socour þer cam on none.
Vnto a hii hille þei fleih; Vntil....drowe hem to
he wist no bettere þat þam deih, Bettere wistey nought what for to do
& are þei mot þat hille take,
many a croune men myht se crake.
Whan þei had alle þat hille nomen, ...þe hil al.
þam þouht þei were to castelle comen;
no more Romeyns durst com þam nehi, Non of þe.....
bot held þam fro þe hille o drehi.
Þe hille was round busked about; ...strong..
þe Bretons had of no man doute, Þat..of Cesar hadde no doute
for ilk man toke a tre to stalle,
trostere þan a castelle walle. As tristi as...
Cesar biheld of þe hille þe heght ..to þe hilles heyght
þat with non assaut, ne with sleght,
myght he wyn þer forcelete.
Sege about þe hille he sette Þerfore a sege abute hit set
þat þei myght noure aboute, ..ne myghte no wer.
bot þorh þam alle passe oute. ..hym haue issue.
He did sette in stedes seres ....wardes.
knyghtes to waite & squyers, ..wachem..
[31ra] & he þam hewe trees, .also he dide..
þe sties to stop & þe entres;
& he forgat not fulle lihtly .....lyghtly
how þei chaced him with maistri, .þey had....
bot often teld in þer vys & ofte þey...auys
how þei chaced þam tuys. ..bifore had...
"Now salle I ȝelde if I may, ...hit ȝif þat..
or ȝe departe fro me way." .....away
Allas, it suld so gate betide, ...euer so.
so bolde as Bretons mot non abide,
for þei had chaced tuys þat man
þat alle þe world þorgh bataile wan;

& ʒit þei stode stifly ilkon
whan þei wist of socour non,
ʒit suffred þe not to be nomen
of him þat þei had ouercomen. ....had er.
Bot Dame Fortune had turned hire whele,
doun to wo þat are was wele;
for þo þat vp were wont to be, ...abouen were wond..
donward þam now turnes she.
Þise Bretons þat were in clos
& biseged with þer fos
had þei noþer drink no mete,
ne nouht myght purchace ne gete.
Þei dred no sauht of bataile,
bot what may þat help or vaile;
whan of mete is defaute,
hungere wynes at þe first saute.
It is no castelle so stalworth dight, Þer ys...strong idight
hungere it wynnes withouten fight;
withouten wapyn or armoure,
hunger ʒeldes castelle & toure.
Gude castelle dredis no powere,
emperour, kyng, no kaisere,
ne oþer help men haf at nede,
bot of hungere is alle þe drede.
Þer force has mad of assais, ...manye.
hungere it wynnes in fo days.
Þre days þei were in þat tourment
þat hungere had þam nere schent.
Cassibalan had sorow in wolde
how he mot escape þat holde.
[31rb] On alle halue he sawe Romeyns
redy forto do þam peynes;
he had no force with þam to fight
& hungere had nere reft þer myght.
Mikelle he dred Iulius Cesar,
more þe hungere þat þei had þar;
of þe tuo þan had he weie, He moste chese on of tweye
ʒelde him to Cesar or for hungere deie.
Tuo days & tuo nyghtes tille ende,
no man wald he biseke no sende.
Þe þrid, he þouht how best mot be
& sent his sonde to Androche.
I ne who did þe message, .ne wot ho...

wheþer knyght, squiere, or page.	
"Androcheus, I send him to saye	. . . þe . .
he suffire me not schamly die.	Suffre me . . to deye
I haf not serued it greuosly,	Þaw y mystok me .
bot I pray him of mercy;	I prey þe of me haue þou .
þof I did him a hastifesse,	Þaw I dide an hastynesse
I wille amend if his wille is.	Y schal hit amende as . . .
A man salle not his owen kynde	
dampne for a defaute we fynde,	
for men has oft wist & sene	. hit haþ ofte be . . .
þat wrath bituex kynde has bene,	
& whan þe wrath was brouht to ende,	
siþen ilk oþer has bene fulle hende;	Syn han þey ben ful feyþful frende
& say him, if his wille be,	I preie þe now ȝif þy . .
þat he be now curtais to me.	. þou . . . . .
Bid him þenk on no misdede	I biseke þe þenk . . .
bot schew now kyndenes in þis nede,	. . me þy . . . .
& saue me now befor Cesar	
& euermore I wille be ware;	
to þe may neuer falle honour	
if me betide misauentour."	
Androche herd þe kynges pleynte	
þat nere was recreant & teynte,	
& ansuerd him alle at robours.	. . . . . reburs
"Has now þe kyng nede of my socours?	
What has my lord ouht herd or sene?	
Seuen nyght ȝit ne has it bene	
þat he wild me exille, & reue	
alle my londis & no þing leue,	
[31va] & þerto þrette me to slo;	
wher he haf laten þat mode ouergo,	. . haue now laten . . .
my lord þat bare him are so stoute,	
for no praiere to luf wild loute.	
I said it suld not falle him wele	. wiste hit wolde . . . .
þat he bare him ouer cruele.	. was so fers & . .
Withouten skille were we wrothe	
& þat salle now repent vs bothe,	
& aldermost skath wille falle	
on him self for vs alle.	
It fals no kyng do felon rees	Hit falleþ . . to . .
as lion in þe tyme of pes,	
ne in tyme of were to dare	
to fle for drede as dos þe hare.	

Þat he fled, I say not so,
bot his cruelte wille him fordo.
He auanced him tille his ilkon, ...til vs.
he venquised þe emperour alon.
He alon neuer him wan
more þan did anoþer man,
bot þorgh me & my knyghtes
þat wounded were in many fightes,
& oþer þat were als douhty
& wele better þan he or I;
þorgh þer dede & our trauaile,
wan Cassibalan þe bataile,
ffor whilk he mad his nobille feste
& sais it was his awen conqueste.
His barons þat were his peres,
of his conquest were partineres. ....parceners
ffor he þat wele standes in stoure
he awe haf partie of þe honoure. .aughte haue part...
Þe kyng may himself wite,
bi him alon salle it nouht wite. ......byte
Þo þat halp it for to wynne, ...hym hit...
þei owe be partinere þer ine. Wel oughte þey be parceners..
Bot wele am I venged on him,
þat now es meke, þat are was grim.
Now seþen þat he sekes me ....bisekeþ.
to haf mercy & pite, On hym to haue...
& I salle, certes, if I may spede,
[31vb] help him now in þis nede. ....his gret.
I may not els for no þing;
he es myn eam, my lord, my kyng.
I may not faile, no I ne wille. .ne may nought faille hym ne...
He mekes him, I wille do skille. Syn he hym mekeþ....
I am venged on him inouh;
now wille I fond to do his prow."
Androcheus, wys knyght & war,
on one he ȝede vnto Cesar; Anon he...
on knes befor him sette.
Iulius Cesar fulle faire he grette:
"Sir Iulius, þou ert myghty man. ...art a..
Conquered þou has Cassibalan;
vnto þi mercy wille he come ....he now.
& ȝelde þe treuwage vnto Rome.
Take of him now þat treuwage,

of þe to holde his heritage.
With luf þou lat him com to þe;   ..let hym now...
þou askes nouht els of alle his fe,
bot only of þe to holde.
He it grantes & I it wolde.
Iulius, haf of him mercy.
Þi wille to do we ere redy."
Iulius Cesar wild him not here;
defly he herde his praiere.   fful deflike herde he..
He passed forth as he not herde,
tille Androche no thyng ansuerde.
Androche had þer of disdeyn
þat Cesar toke his praiere in veyn.
He stirte vp with euelle wille.
"Abide, Cesar, & stand right stille!   & bad Cesar stonde a whyle.
Þis londe is ȝolden to þi bailie;
þorgh me has þou þe seignorie.
Þat I þe hight holde couenant   ...hight y..
& no more wille be o graunt   .more getes þou nought of.
þe seignorie of þe empire;
þat may þou haf as lord & sire.
Þou has þat, what wille þou more?
God wille not, þat oþer weis wore,
þat þou myn eam prison or slo.   ....schost prisone..
Nay, Cesar, so salle not go.   ...schal hit..
He salle not be so lightly slayn,   Þat he schol be...
[32ra] tille I haf þat myght & mayne   While þat y haue....
þat him fro dede I may rescue.
He es myn eme, I his neueue.
He norissed me, he es me dere.
If þou ne wille my praiere here, ...my biddyng.
I parte fro þe; haf gode day.
Do þan to him alle þat þou may."   Do now til.....
Cesar passed forth & stode,   Þen cam Cesar forþ..
þouht he was of kynde blode,
& þat he said it was skille,
& he did his witte þertille.
Whan he had alle cast in þouht,
he graunted þat he had bisouht;   ..al þat he had sought
ostages asked þe parties
& granted were at þer auys,   .þey wer graunted...
& treuwage þei granted so.
Als þe lond was taxed to

þre þousand punde ilk a ȝere,
at termes sette to pay plenere,
of alle þe lond gadred & tan.
Þen brouht þei forth Cassibalan
& did Cesar & him kisse;
for þat acorde was mykelle blisse.
Before or þis, neuer I fonde . þis tyme . . .
þat any man conquerd þis londe,
tille Cesar com & mad conqueste

[L omits 5222–5261 but sustitutes a passage of 74 lines, providing a different version. P bases its version generally on Wace. See below at 5261.]

as ȝe haf herd in þis geste.
Euen sexty ȝere þis was beforn
þat Ihesu criste was born.
Here withalle acordes saynt Bede,
þe gestes of Ingland first ȝe rede.
Whan alle þis was brouht tille ende
& fele went to se þer frende,
þus say þei þat know þe estre
þat Iulius funded first Excestre.
Excestre it hate, þis skille is whi:
þe water hate Ex þat rennes þerbi.
Tille wynter were gon, Cesar gan bide
& went home in þe somers tide.
For grete luf & specialte,
he toke with him sir Androche,
& led with þam men of ostages
[32rb] of þis lond, þe best lynages.
Seuen ȝere lyued Cassibalan
siþen Cesar þis lond wan;
to ȝelde þe treuage he was fulle mylde,
ne he had noþer wife no childe.
In Ȝorke, forsoth, he did his endyng
& biried þer as a kyng.
Tenuacius was erle of Cornwaile,
had þe regne alle in his waile;
he was Androcheus broþer.
Androche was went, þer was non oþer;
bot he regned fulle litelle space;
he died sone, Kyng Tenuace.
After sir Tenuace fyne,
þei crouned his sone Kymbelyn.

He was norissed at þe courte of Rome;
he was gode knyght, wiseman in dome.
At Rome, tille Kymbelyn was þare,
he mad him knygh, Augustus Cesar.
Ten ȝere he regned kyng
& in þat ȝere he mad endyng.
Ihesu criste þat ȝere was born,
so had a prophete tald beforn.

[*L substitutes the following passage for lines 5222–5261 in P.*]

Þenne returned Cesar wiþ hye
To Romeward after his victorie
Bot ȝe schul here a wonder þyng
Þat fel in Rome after his wendyng
He had þer mad chef of þe Cite
Sire Crassus & sire Pompee
When þey had so al þe maistry þer
& he nought returned þe fyfte ȝer
Þey racoillede þe Romayns til her wylle
Ageyn Cesar þat fel hem ylle
ffor Iulius destruyde Rome þan
& slow þer Lord & Gentilman
& Crassus he slow in a tour hey
Bot Pompeus skaped & faste fley
fforþ in to Poylle he chased hym wel
Þer he byseged hym in a castel
Braundys hit highte as men tolde
Bot þat myghte he nought longe holde
Bot in to Egipte þen schiped he
ffor wel wend he þer siker haue be
Bot Cesar hym suwed yn to þat contre
& spak to þe kyng sire Tholome
Wiþ him was sire Pompe ytake
Bot for drede of Iulius sake
He nolde meyntene hym namore
Bot his hed dide smyte of þore
& sentyt Iulius til present
& þerwyþ he to Romward went
In al his moste nobleye in Rome
Right yuele þey schope for hym ful sone
His barons wiþ treson dide hym deye
Bot Greffes hym mordred for enuye
Tweye neuews he hadde bot sone non
Þe eldest was cald Octouyon

Þe Romayns corouned hym saunȝ faille
Þen sesed he Braundys & Itaille
Of Poylle & Grece he tok þauow
& of alle þe Reomes byȝonde Moungow
And al þe Oryent þat oþer sesed
& tok tys part þat þe oþer leued
Of þritty Reomes euery Kyng
Were enclinaunt til his coronyng
Such wraþe bytwixte þe neuews ros sone
Þat wiþ batailles to feld þey come
Octouion þat oþer slow anon
& his men desconfyted echon
Þen hadde Rome such renoun
Þat al þyng was in here baundon
Þen gaf þey til þe emperour
A newe name for gret honour
Augustus Cesar þe calde hym þere
ffor þei ouer alle oþere were
& after þat he þat name had
Þe Romayns were þe more ydrad
ffor þemperour had þen vnder hand
Al þe werld boþe se & land
Bot Cassibolan was ful ioyous
Þat þis werre was ended þus
ffyftene after he regned in pes
Bot no child ne lefte at his deses
Þerfore þe corounede sir Tenmace
To gouerne þe Reome he hadde grace
Cassibolan was ded as was pite
& buryed at ȝork þe gode Cite
Wiþ Iulyus went forþ sire Androche
& his broþer reioisede þe regalte
After cam Kymbely Tenmace sone
Þat had ful gret grace of Rome
Of alle his truage þey relesed hym þer
While he scholde regne & lyuen her
So þat he neuere ne payed non
To Rome ne to Octouyon
He meyntend euere his lond in pes
& leftyt his sones after his deces

[P and L are parallel again at line 5262.]

In þis lond þan was a Deuyn;
his name was called Teselyn.

. his tyme was here . .
. . . . Telesyn

He told þe Bretons many selcouth,
alle fond þei trewe he said with mouth.
He bad þam leue withouten erroure:
"Now is born our saueoure;   ffor now....
now is toward ioy & blis.   .ys vs....
Of a maiden, a child born is.
Alle mankynd salle he saue.
Ihesu, þat name salle he haue."
Þis worde þat þer prophete said,
þe Bretons in hert wele it leid.
Many day þat worde þei held;
þei fond it soth þat he þam teld.
Was no folk in alle þe werld
trowed so sone whan þei ouht herd
preche ouht of Ihesu lawe,
ne to þe faith so sone wild drawe.
Þan was a þousand ȝere gone
þat Brutus aryued in Albion,
[32va] & tuo hundreth, sais it mo,   .þerto two hundred ȝer.
þat Kymbelyn to dede gan go.
Als long as he regned here,
with þe Romeyns was he dere;
þei asked him neuer þer treuage,
neuerþeles at terme & stage,   Neyþer in his ȝougþe ne in age
he ȝalde it curtasly & hende   [*Om. L*]
in pes tille his lyues ende.   [*Om. L*]
Of Kymbelyn tuo childere left
þat þe Romeyns þer treuage reft.
Witherus hight þe eldest broþer,   Wyder....
Arwigar men cald þe toþer.
Sir Widere had þe heritage;
a douhty knyght in vassalage.   A man he was of gret corage
Proude he was & ouer stoute;
Romeyns ne wild he luf ne loute,
bot where so euer he þam fond,
he did þam alle void þe lond.
Claudius was þan Emperour
of Rome, maister gouernour.
Skorne him þouht & suore his heued
þat treuage suld not so be leued.
He suld haf it ageyn fulle wele,
disherite Widere of ilk a dele.
Of Romeyns he gadred oste

	& hied suyth vnto þis coste.	..fast til Bretaigne.
	Hauen he toke at Porchestre;	
	Karepers hight þan þat estre.	Kaer Perys....
	He wend haf taken þe toun in hast,	
	bot he failed of his tast.	Possibly cast
	Þan tende Claudius with alle;	.tened...
	befor þe ȝate did mak a walle,	
	to famen þam was þe encheson;	[*Transp. L*]
	no vitaile suld com to þe toun.	[*Transp. L*]
	Bot Widere, Arwigarus &	.Wyder & Arwygarus
	with ten þousand mad þam rescus.	.twenty þousand...
	Sir Claudius & his partie	
	fled fast to þer nauie.	
	Þe best Romeyns in batailes sere	
	stode som ageyn Widere,	
	& fauht with him long stounde;	
	of boþe sides lay dede on þe grounde.	
[32vb]	A Romeyn þer was, a noble baroun,	
	his name was sir Hamoun.	
	He was þe emperour conseiloure;	
	a gode knyght he was in stoure.	.noble.....
	He houed & biheld Widers,	
	how he bare him stoute & fers,	
	Romeyns to felle, Romeyns to slo,	
	vnneþis mot any ascape him fro;	
	how wisely his folk he led,	
	how to bataile he þam spred,	
	withouten tinselle slouh Romeyns	.los slow þe.
	& eft alied þam wele ageyns.	.syn relied his men.
	He sawe wele tille he mot lyue;	...weel he mought hit leue
	treuage wild he neuer gyue.	Þat oþer truage wold he no.
	[*L adds:*]	Ne þe Romayns schuldit neuere wynne Whyle Wyder rengned kyng þerynne
	He þouh what maner thyng	.þoughte þorow...
	he mot best slo Widere þe kyng.	
	Þat ilk noble Hamon Romeyn	
	spoiled a Breton þat was slayn,	Dispoilled...he fond.
	& with þe armes of þat Bretoun,	
	he armed him, sir Hamon,	..hym seluen Hamoun
	& went on þe Bretons side;	
	& als þei rode, gan he ride,	
	& þer langage to þam he spak.	[*Om. L*]
	Toward þe kyng þe bataile brak;	[*Om. L*]

þe armes desceyued þam ilk dele,	
& on þer langage he spak wele.	
He lerid it at þer ostagers	. had lered at our .
þat were at Rome treuagers.	
He called þe Bretons bi þer name	
& þei ansuerd ageyn þe same,	
& euer he neghed ner & ner	[*Transp. L*]
tille he com to þe kyng Widere;	[*Transp. L*]
& þidere he sawe þe kyng ride,	Þys Hamon rod ay side by side
þis Hamon rode ay side by side;	To sle þe kyng his tyme tabide
þe kyng to him gaf no tente.	
Hamon saw þat, a knyfe out hente,	Þat saw Hamoun . . . .
vndire þe arme, þe kyng he stiked.	. þarmoure . . . .
Priuely fro þam alle he priked.	
Arwigarus, his awen broþer,	
perceyued þat or any oþer	
& þouht it were grete foly	
þer forto grete or krie.	Þere to grede or forto crie
[33ra] He toke þe kynges conisance	
þat non suld perceyue þat chance,	
& had his priuies euerilkon	An bad his priues .
nouht so hardy to mak mone,	
"For wist our folk we were þus traist,	
it suld mak þam alle obaist.	
Wist þe Romeyns þat þis chance wore,	
it suld aforce þam wele more.	
If ȝe were bolde, bes now boldere;	. we were bold now be we .
I salle maynten forþe þis were."	& y schal vndertake . .
He was was wele armed on his stede;	. . wel armed & . . .
to gyf bataile he gan him spede.	Toward þe . . . . .
Was þer non þat wild him feyne	
whan þei sawe þe kynge seyne;	. . . . kynges seigne
so wele he bare him & austere,	
þei wend it were þe kyng Widere.	
Þan myght men se knyghtes stoute	
þat perced þorgh þe Romeyns route;	
þe Romeyns ne myght togider holde	
so were þe Bretons egre & bolde.	
Sire Claudius with his partie,	
to water fled to þer nauie;	. þe water fledde wyþ his meynye
þat myght not to þe water fle,	
vnto a wod fledden he.	
Hamon þat alle þe oste led,	

to þer schippes fast he fled.
He spirred after þe emperour
whider he mad his retoure. — Whider ward....
Men inouh to him gan say
þat to þe water he toke his way.
Þe kynges broþer, Arwigare,
how Hamon fled he was wele ware.
At þe water Hamon doun light,
into a bote Hamon him tight. — ...Hamon had tyght
Com Arwigare befor at þe bote, — Byforn cam Arwygar atte bot
Sir Hamon hede of he smote;
for Hamon left þer his heued,
þe name of him þer is leued; — ......bileued
& for encheson of þat Hamon,
for him þei cald þe toun Hampton;
for chances þat haf ben tid — .swylke chaunces..bytid
er names of tounes cald & kid.
[33rb] Whan he was fled, þe Emperour,
& Hamon slayn at þe retoure,
& alle were driuen to þat coste,
to Wyncestre he led his oste. — Þe kyng to Wynchestre lad..
Tille Arwigarus þiderward nam, — When...
Claudius eft to lond cam
& com ageyn to Porchestre,
brak þe walles & brent þat estre.
Alle he brent vp & doun
& exilde þe men out of þe toun. — .chaced men....
Befor it was a noble cite, — ....god.
siþen com it neuer þat bounte. — Syn...to þat.
Whan had destroyed Porchestre, — .he had destruyed þus.
þan he went to Wynchestre;
þerin he seged Arwigare
& alle þer euer with him ware;
gode engynes did he make,
þe walles to breke, houses to schake.
Arwigare held it a vilte
so seged in a toun to be;
he said he wild not þer in lie.
Who so felle to wyn þe maistrie, — To wham euere happede..
ouþer wild he wyn or lese los,
or he suld more be holden clos. — Er....halde inclos
He went out into þe felde
& alle his knyghtes with helm & schelde.

He batailed þam vnto þe fight
with archers gude, wele dight,
& mene folk alle in fere
were wele sette on gode manere.   . wysly . . . .
Betuex þe parties was bot lite,
þat þei ne suld togidere smyte.
Þe wisest men of þat cite
conseild þam if better myght be.   . . how best . .
Mykelle þai dred þer gode to tyne
& slauhter of þe folk & pyne.
Þei said, "Þe pes were better haue, ... to haue
our toun & our godes to saue,
þan forto life in were & strife,   . . lyue in werre . .
lese our godes & tyne our life."
Þei toke a man of honoure
& sent vnto þe Emperoure   . . hym to . .
[33va] to witte at him whedire he ches
forto haf were or pes.   To haue þe werre oþer þe .
Þe Emperour said als he þouht,
"Were to haf wild I nouht;
I ne ȝerne nouht of ȝoure
bot þat Rome haf his honour."

[*L adds:*] Ne y ne wilne wyþ no man fight
So þat Rome mot haue his right

Þei graunted alle at his auys;
þei suore þe pes boþe partys.   And sworen . . in boþe .
The Emperour honoured mykille þe kyng
& bed him a fulle faire thyng: . profred . . . . .
"Sir Kyng," he said, "a douhter I haue
& on þe I vouch hir saue,
if þou wille myn ow bicom   . . . . owen bycome
& ȝelde treuage vnto Rome."
Arwigare graunted þerto
& to treuage ȝeldyng also.
In Wynchester were ostiled boþe,   . . . þey hosteld .
& frendes were þat are were wroþe.
Þe Emperour to Rome sent
for Genuys, þat maiden gent.
In duellyng of þis messengers,
þei samned knyghtes & squiers;
with grete oste went þer way
& wan to Rome alle Orkenay   . . þe ilde of .
& oþer ildes þat þer are;   . . . . . ware

with him was sir Arwigare.   .help of..
Claudius regned þat ilk tyme,
as saynt Bede sais in his ryme,
siþen Ihesu was born of our lady,
þer fele ȝers sex & fourty.
Þe messengers þat went to Rome,
in þe somores tide þei come
& brouht þat maiden Genuys,
gentille of body & faire of vys.
Þat tyme com þe Emperour home,   Þan cam hom þemperour
mirth þei mad at þer tocome   Þan mad þey myrthe in halle & bour
to wedde þat may in stede auenant,
couenant to hold & sikere grant.   Þe...siker þey graunt
Vpon Seuerne in a vale
þat rych was & ese,
bituen Ingland & Wales
forto mene of þo tales,   To telle ȝow þe soþe tales
[33vb] & for wirschip of þat may,   Þat for þe....
a toun þei set þer þat day.
Gloucestre first hight it þus   [*Om. L*]
for þe Emperour, sir Claudius.   [*Om. L*]
Þe Emperour þer a sone;   ..gat þer..
of þat childe þe name we mone,
Gloy, he hight, born in þat estre,
& for þat Gloy hat it Gloucestre.
Arwigar wedded þer Genuys
in Gloucestre with mykelle pris;
þer was he crouned & sche,
nobilly, with solempnite;
& whan þe feste was brouht tille end,
Claudius to Rome gan wend.   ...ageyn gan.
I fynd writen, ȝow to teche,
þat tyme ȝede saynt Petir to preche;   .in Nero tyme seint Peter gan.
fro Antioche þat tyme he cam,
þorgh prechyng brouht it to cristendam
& was comen late to Rome,   ...right in to.
& preched þer of cristes dome.
Whan gon was sir Claudius,
in Bretan regned Arwigarus.
Of himself he lete right mykille,
boþe proude was & a partie fikille;   But proud he was....
þe treuage to Rome gif ne wolde,
he deyned not of þam to holde.   ffor he dedeyned of...

Þe Romeyns þouht an outrage
so to lese þer treuage.
Þei sent after Vespasian, ..hyder.
maister of Rome was he þan;
at Douere vp wild he aryue,
þe kyng it herd, þider gan dryue. ....& þyder..
Þe Latyn sais, I wene, Ebru, As hit ys founden in Ebru
Douer hight þan Ritipu.
Defended Vespasian þe lond; Þer fended he...
þer sailes ageyn on mast þei wond
& sailed bi þe londes side
tille Toteneys, þer gan þei ride;
fond þei non þat did þam qued, ffor þy now hit dide hem qued
ne non þat þam þe land forbed. Þat þey hem so þat lond.
Tille Oxenford þei gan alle ride
to take þe toun in þe euen tide,
[34ra] Karpenhuelgoit, opon Bretoun, Karphuelgoit..
on Inglisse, Oxenford þe toun;
þe toun of þam had no doute.
Seuen nyght þe seged it withoute;
þe kyng als son as he myght,
oste gadred, þidere him dight; ..& þider..
sonere ne mot he þider wend. Raþer ne myghte..
Bot at þe seuen daies end,
he com in a morn tide
& smyte togidere on ilk side. Sone þey assembled on boþe.
Fro morn tille euen bataile þei nomen,
& nouþer side was ouercomen.
At euen þei ȝede alle osundere,
alle wery, it was no wundere. Al were þey wery....
On þe morn, þo þat were left
armed þam to bataile eft; Þey armed....
bot þe quene, Dame Genuys,
scho acorded boþe þe partys.
Scho peyned hire acorde to make
for luf of þe Romeyns sake.
Algate scho peyned hir so
þat acorde scho brouht þam to;
alle þe wyntere scho did þam bide
tille it was þe somers tide.
Þe pes þe granted, þe parties suore, Þe pes was take...
& Vespasian to Rome fore. Bot Vaspasian swor first byfore
Þe kyng fro þat ilk day,

alle his lyue ȝalde Rome þer pay.

[*L adds:*] Hys oþ ne let ne neuere falle
Bot ay worschiped Romayns alle
And wyþ help of Vaspasian
Al Irlonde he wan

Þe folk, þe lond, he couth wele loke;
gode kyng he was, we find in boke. — At Colchestre he lis we...
A boke, men calle it Iuuenal,
of stories it spekes alle;
at Gloucestre it sais he lies, — ..þer hit lys
& þe quene, Dame Genuys.
Marius, his sone of Genuys born,
was kyng als his fadere beforn.
A wilfulle man was Marius, — .myghtful...
of faire speche meruaillus.
His fadere tyme he was at Rome
with þe kynde his moder of come.
Wele he contend him in his land;
þe folk serued him at hand. — Þer blessed hym boþ fre & bonde
[34rb] In Marius tyme felle þis ferlik:
in Scotland vpryued a Peiht, Rodrik.
Kyng Peiht com fre Cice; — Kyng Peyt cam out of þe se
a man he was fulle of malice. — Þat neuere had mercy ne pite
Mykille he lufed to robbe & reue;
Scotland to waste wald he not leue.
Als he ȝed & robbed fast, — ..wente...
Marius met him at þe last.
Marius had folk inouh; — ..god folk.
þe Peiht, Rodrik, smertly he slouh.
For þat Marius slouh þat Peiht,
he did set a ston þourh sleht — ..þer set a ston þorow sleight
forto schew his pruesse,
& for mak þe menyng fresse; — .forto....
for in þe ston he did write,
& for þat writyng men may wite — Whar þorow euery man..
& testemons þat auenture, — Hit wytnesseþ þe.
& tellis þe discomfeture
how Marius slouh þe Peiht Rodrik,
þe ston was set for þat ferlik.
Þe men þat þer woned & are, — Þo men þat weren & ȝit are
þei calle þat ston Westmare.
Þe men of þat cuntre say ilkon — Þat Contre folk seyen.
þat it is cald after þat ston, — Þatte countre is cald...

for þe ston Westmare, Westmerland;	
þus in Latyn writen I fand.	
Whan Rodrik þe Peiht was dede,	
men gaf Kyng Marius to rede	
to take þe Peihtes, more & lesse,	
deliuer a partie of Catenesse	Deliuere hem....
to tile & haf in heritage,	
for it was wast & sauuage.	...bot wast..
Þe herberd þam eueraywhere,	
in stedes ese þat best were.	
Women of Bretan wald þei haue,	
bot þe Bretons vouched non saue;	
þei did þam into Ireland	
& toke wyues at þer hand.	
Of þo tu kyndes, Ires & Peight,	.two kyndes Iris..
ire & tene es wele on heght.	Sorewe & tene hit broughte..
Marius, kyng in his lyf here,	.þe kyng....
lyued nyen & fourty ȝere	
[34va] & biried is at Salesbiri	
þat standes on a playn fulle miri.	
After Marius þat lyued long,	
Coyl, his sone, þis lond gan fong;	
he was norist at þe courte of Rome.	...y þe toun..
Of alle lawes he gaf right dome;	
þei of Rome lufed him wele	
for þei fond him trewe als stele.	
Coyl couth of many quantise	
& many artes on sere wyse;	
was he neuer nygon ne nyce,	
ne he had neuer non ille vyce.	.neuere vsed yuel.
Ten ȝere he regned wele & riche;	....her al fully
he ligges biried at Norwiche.	At Norwiche byried ful worþyly
After þis gode kyng Coylus,	
regned his son, sir Lucius.	
He was large & curtays,	
þe first cristen kyng, men says.	
Re Lucius Bretannie	Al þis land so fair and fre
	[Line 5636 in P must be a caption from a previous copy.]
Þorh him was brouht to cristiante.	þorow.....
Whan he herd þe lawe of criste,	
how in his men were baptiste,	..his name..
of his miracles men spek rife	
& of þa apostels holy life,	..þapostles..

& how god for þam wrouht
þat to þe cristendom were brouht,
he sent to þe Pape Eleuthere,
besouht als his fadere dere,   . hym as . . .
to send him men myght him baptise,   . . . a man . . .
of cristes lawe lere him þe wise.
Whan þe herd þat tiþing,   . þe Pope herde . .
he þanked Ihesu, heuen kyng,
þat in his tyme he wild so wirk,
Bretayn to bring to holy kirk.
Tuo clerkis he sent hider to preche,
bisshopes þei were, þe lawe to teche;
þe to clerk hiht sir Danuan, ... Dunian
þe toþer, men cald Bisshop ffagan.
Þise tuo bisshops baptiȝed þe kyng
& alle his meigne at þer comyng.
Þorgh þe kyng had grauntise   . . . & his .
as þe lawe is & right assise,   Þey ordeyned þe lawe in . .
[34vb] ordeyned þei Archbisshop see   Þey ordeigned ilka bischop þer.
& bisshopes vndere þam to be.   . Erchebischopes abouen hem . .
In þis lond were temples olde,   . hys tyme . . .
auht & tuenty grete men tolde;   Eyght . . flamins . .
þe Latyn sais þe temple flamyns,   . . calleþ temple flamins
som of Mahoun & of Appolyns,
som of Diane, som of Berit;
tuo Archeflamyns were þer ȝit.
At London was þe Archeflame   . . . þer chef flamee
& at ȝork þe toþer se;
þe toþer flamyns in þe lond ware
als þe bisshop sees now are.
Þise temples of maumetrie
þei turned fro þat heresie   . . alle fro þer eresyes
& halowed þam to cristes werk,
& ordeynd kirkes with preste & clerk.
Lond, light, rent, & catelle
þat to þo temples longed & felle,
& alle oþer aportenance,
he gaf it to þer sustenance.
To a diocise longed a cite
& ordeynd parisches for to be;
to parsons & to vicaries
was graunted grete seignories.
Whan Bretayn was cristen alle

	& þe newe lawe brouht to stalle,	
	ioyfulle was sir Lucius	
	þat sawe þe folk turned þus.	
	In cristen lawe, als he ches,	
	þerin he endid in godes pes;	
	at London he died & þer he lies,	At Gloucestre . . . þer lys
	& his soule in Paradis;	. . . wente to .
	þe date of criste men told so here,	
	a hundreth & sex & fyfti ȝere.	Was an hundred & fyue . . .
	Withouten heire Lucius es dede;	
	þe Bretons couth þer of no rede.	
	Wo was þam he had non heire;	
	to be þer lord had þei no speire;	. haue a lord þey were in .
	þe were bigan omang þam alle	[*Om. L*]
	to whom þe seignorie suld falle.	[*Om. L*]
	Fro lond to lond, fro man to man,	
	of þis to Rome tiþng ran	. þat . . tydynge .
[35ra]	þat dede was sir Lucius,	
	& þat we wered amang vs.	. . he werreyed ageyns vs
	Þei chese Seuere, a senatour,	. . Sauer a senatour emperour
	& mad him maister gouernour.	. . . maister & .
	He brouht hider tuo Legions;	
	þe Bretons to þam were felons.	
	Seuere werid on þam fast,	. werreyed . . .
	many he conquerde & cast,	
	& fele oþer had disdeyn	
	forto hold of any Romeyn.	
	Vmwhile þei fauht, vmwhile fleand,	
	Seuere þam chaced to Scotland.	. þey . . .
	Þe Bretons chese þam þer a kyng,	Þen chose þe Bretons þeym . .
	ffulgence he hight, a lordyng,	
	& folowed þam with þe Peihtes	He felawed hym . . .
	þat euer were lefe to fehtes.	. . . ful of deseites
	Outlandes þat were fled,	
	alle suilk with þam þei led.	
	In a cuntre men did grete schame,	
	Deire was þan þe name	Dene . . þer of . .
	fro Scotland vnt Thrilwalle,	. . in to Þurlewal
	Peihtlond þei told it alle.	
	ffulgence south him hasted,	
	þe lond about his folk wasted.	. . al aboute was .
	Seuere fled southward ageyn,	
	þe Peihtes robbed & mad alle pleyn.	

Whan Seuere had folk on þam eft ran, ffulgence wyþ Peytes on hem þey.
þe Peihtes fled þan ilk a man.
Som tyme þei bataile bide, ..wolde þey..
sum tyme fled on ilk a side;
often did þei Seuere tene.
ffulgence with þe Peihtes kene
long dured þat robberie, ...reuery
þat Seuere mot þam neuer com bi,
tille he did mak an ouerthuert dike
bituex þe tuo sees a fulle grete strike,
& set þeron a palis with poynt, .þeron a Pale wel y poynt
þik & hii, fulle wele ioynt,
& closed þat side of þe lond;
ouerthuert est & west it bond.
Siþen þat tyme it was in clos;
neuer non, of alle his fos,
[35rb] durst non of þam forþer fele
bi þat side robbe ne stele.
Fulgence toke consele at wyse,
at þe Peihtes & oþer of hyse,
to were ȝit more opon Seuere
& robbe & reue hym fulle nere. .hym to chace fer & ner
To Peihtes he gaf gifte grete
& praied þam þei wild not lete,
bot gadred a god company
on þe se in his nauy.
Whan þei had gadred þer oste
in his schippes bi þe sees coste
in stedes þer þei sawe ese, Þe host was schiped & went to se
þei aruyed vp in best contre
& beseged Ȝork aboute;
alle þe cuntre to þam gan loute.
He sent to grete lordynges
& het & gaf þam riche þinges;
for faire hote & gyfte þei toke, ...giftes þat..
þe Emperour Seuere þei forsoke.
Seuere toke his oþer Bretons
& gadred togidere his legions; .asembled his.
toward Ȝork fast þam dight,
to remoue þam had he tight;

[*L adds:*] When þey were comen wyþynne a lyte
Þe batailles gonne to gedere smyte

felly þei fauht, for þer was slayn

on ilk side þer chieftayn.
ffulgence was first felled to grounde,
& Seuere was slayn in a stounde.
Þe Romeyns for Seuere besouht
þat his body to ȝork was brouht
& biried þerin solempnely,
& his oþer frendes him by.
Þis ilk Emperour Seuere
regned seuenten ȝere;   Regned her..
siþen criste was born of þe Virgyne,
nien score ȝere euen & nyen.
Of þis Seuere þat died þere,
tuo knaue childre were;
þe ton men kalled Bassian
& þe toþer Getan.   Þat oþer had to name Cetan
Getan modere was Romayne,
of men of gode, knyght & suayne.   Comen of gode...
[35va]   [*P repeats 5784–5785 in error.*]
Bassian was born of a Brette;
þe Bretons of him þe better lette.
Romeyns toke þis ilk Cettan
& crouned him & com his man;   ....bycome..
þe Bretons with Bassian helde
& of þe reme him þe schelde.   ....highte hym..
Ilkon on þer partie
held with his kynde douhtily.
Þus gate with mengyng & with mong,   Al þus wyþ megge...
bituex þam wex were strong.   ..wax þer werre.
Algate ilk oþer so long ouer ran
þat slayn was sir Getan.
Þe Betons eftsons þei ches   .Bretons...
Bassian kyng, & had þer pes.
A ladde was in þis lond, of fame,
Karausius þus was his name.
Hardy he was & conand, ...ful connynge
stalworth of body, wele fightand;   ...& wel fightynge
in many nedes assaid he was.
Of prowesse men men praised þis Karas;   ..men preised..
born he was of pure linage   ....pouere.
& litille had of heritage.
Fairer & better state he helde   Gretter & fairer stat..
þan he rent had or lond in felde.   .wolde his rentes or...
A grete empris durst vndertake;   Grete emprises he..

more lufed he were þan pes to make.	
Þat tyme on þe se to wend was doute,	
mariners robbed ildes aboute;	
myght non at hauens duelle no be	. atte hauenes reste ne be
for outlandes þat com bi þe se.	. outlandesmen . . by se
Karausius þan him bithouht;	
þe senators of Rome he souht	
& talde þat outlandes flete,	. tolde hem . . .
Bretayn alle about bisete.	
He said, "Wille ȝe gyf me leue	. . ȝif ȝe wil . . .
þe robbours on þe se to greue,	
& gif me chartire & auourie,	. . chartre of a vowerye
þe se to loke with my nauie,	
I salle þam warant þorgh treuage	. scholde ȝow warante ȝoure .
þat non outland salle mak passage."	
[35vb] Þei graunted him þer leue to haue	
þat he suld þer treuage saue.	
Chartre þei gaf him with þer seale	
þat he suld to þam be leale.	
Karais his leue at Romeyns nam	
& schewed þe chartre þer he cam.	
Quicly he gat him mariners,	Sone gat he hym .
schippes gode, busses, coggers;	Wiþ schipes Barges & Balyngers
disherited men þat were fled,	He desired . . . .
& robbours, alle suilk he led.	Þeues & Robbours swylk . .
Ille dedy men þat were wyght,	Yuel dedy . . . .
of outlandes, þo þat he myght,	
of suilk he gadred companyes	
born & norissed in felonyes.	
Whan þis Karais had geten him oste,	
of many he serched þe coste;	. manye a land he . . .
fro an ild to anoþer he ȝede;	
was it non þat þei ne had drede.	Of no þynge ne hadde þey .
Men he robbed, londes wasted,	
fro a stede tille anoþer he hasted.	
Neihburs nere & fer fro,	To ney neygheburs & ferþer fro
to alle he did scaþe & wo;	
alle he toke þat he mot take,	
mesure wild he no man make	He nolde mesure to no . .
þat outlandes befor had lefte.	
He spared non, bot alle he refte;	
to saue þe folk Karais was suorn.	
He wers þan oþer beforn;	Bot he was worse . . .

mikelle he wan, ȝit ȝerned he more.
His folk wex & spred aywhore;
castels, tounes, doun he threwe;
for lord he wild þat alle him knewe.
So fer he farde to wyn him wayne,   ...sayled....
at þe last, he aryued in þis Bretayne.
Priuely with þe Bretons he spak
& said, "Ȝe se not ȝour lak;
ȝour kyng can not himself were,
& if ȝe wild me gode faith bere,
I suld delyuere ȝow of þe Romeyns, ...out of peynes
alle þis lond of þar dimeyns."   And al ȝour land of ȝour Romaynes
He ȝede to þe Peihtes & said þe same.
If ȝe wild alle with a name
[36ra] mak him kyng of þer empires,
alle wild he mak þam lordes & sires.   He wolde þem make...
Þis Peihtes ware with þe kyng priue,   Þo were þe Peytes....
& in þis lond grete plente,
bot Karais wist þat þei were fikelle.
He glosed þam & gaf þam mykelle   Þerfore he......
& þei hette him withouten faile:
if he with þe kyng toke bataile,
to Karais partie suld þei go
& þe discomfet & slo.   And þe kyng...
Whan þei had alle Karais hight,
Bretons, Peihtes help at þer myght,   Bretons &.....
Bassian he gan deffie
& with foule wordes ascrie.   ....hym descrie
So long lasted þer manace,
to batale were þei brouht in place.   ..þey comen in to.
Karais partie dred not þe kyng,   [*Om. L*]
ne Bassian Karais no þing.   [*Om. L*]
Bassian affied him on þe Peihtes;
inouh of bataile þei couth sleihtes,   In bataille þey knewe many.
þerfor his triste was on þam more
þan on alle þe oþer þer wore,
for he gode triste to þam had.
Richely often þam he clad,
& als þe partis gaf bataile,
iusted, chaced, & gan assaile.   .& chased...
Þis ilk Peihtes were traitoures;
ageyn þe kyng turned in þe stoures
& with Karais partie helde,

& traised þe kyng in þe felde,	. traysched . . right in . .
& slouh þer sir Bassian	
& alle his folk ilk a man.	
Þus þei traised him in nede,	
sir Bassian þat did þam fede,	
& Karais leihtly wan þe lond;	
ageyn him partie non he fond.	
Karais gaf þam for þer seruise,	
among þe Scottes grete franchise,	
so þat Peihtes & Scottes kynde	
ere alle now one, so men fynde.	
When þei of Rome tiþing herd	
þat Karais with þis lond misferd,	. . . Bretaygne þus ferde
[36rb] þei sent hidere tuo legions	. . . þre.
with tuo of þer baldest Barons;	
Allet & Gallus, þer names hight,	Allectus & Walwes . . .
wise men of were, hardy & wight.	. . . . . in fight
Þei com vp ryuand out of þe se	. . pryuely . . . .
& Karais wild haf reft þam entre,	
bot maugre Karais, on him þei nam,	. . . . . . wan
& slouh Karais þat falsnes gan,	. . . þe fals man
& alle þat were of his kynde,	
stroyed þam bi rote & rinde,	Destruyed hem . . . .
& þo þat þe Romeyns forsoke	
& to Karais partie toke.	
The Bretons sawe þe Romeyns aboue	
& Romeyns mot þen neuer loue.	
Treuage to Rome wild þei non send,	[*Transp. L*]
for fayn þei wild þer fredam fend.	[*Transp. L*]
After þer Barons þei sent	. . . þo þey .
t chese at þer parlement	To chesen at þat .
a kyng þat mot ageyn þam vale,	
Asclepedoth, erle of Cornwaile.	
Whan he was chosen, he did somoune	
alle Bretons fro toun to toune.	
Alle suld com þat were of elde	[*Transp. L*] To bataille schold com . . . .
to bataile go or wapen welde,	[*Transp. L*] Þat alle þat myghte . .
to London ageyn Alletus	
& his felaw, sir Gallus.	
A day þe Romeyns mad sacrifise	
in þer temple, als was þer wise.	I þe temple as was gyse
Right in þer solempnite,	
biseged þe Bretons þer Cite;	

þe Romeyns herd noys & cri,
& cried, "Has armes!" alle on hii, ..as armes on hy on hy
& did þam out into þe felde,
boldly on þamself gan belde
& fauht with þe Bretons fast;
bot þe Romeyns route tobrast,
for Allet side & his meigne
ȝede alle doun & mot not fle;
alle þat were on þat partie
ascaped bi strete no stie. Ascaped þer non by stret ne.
Gallus sawe þer side ȝede doun;
bi tyme he fled vnto þe toun
[36va] & þe ȝates after þam sperd,
to kirnels & to walles ferd,
& to þe toure vp on hie,
& did þe Bretons hald þam o drie.
Asclepedoth, þat was with oute,
sawe þe Romeyns had no doute.
His brefis he did write & send .lettres.....
after Bretons fer & hend, .mo bretons...
þat þei suld com & sege make
about London, Romeyns to take.
For þe sonde of Asclepedoth,
com þe of Wales & com þe Scoth; Come Walschemen & many a Scot
on ilk a side alle þei cam
þat longed to þe kyngdam.
Barfreis did þe Bretons raise, Engyns....
& magnels gode for to praise, .mangenels ful gode to.
& frussed þe walle of þe cite;
with strength wan þei þe entre. ..on þeym þey had entre
Þen mygh men þe Romeyns deie, .myghte men se...
on hepes ligge in ilk a weie;
neuer befor suilk slauhter was
of þe Romeyns at no pas.
Þe Romeyns þat were so schent,
to priue forceletes þei went
for þe Bretons þam to hide, ffro þe Bretons for..
þer life to length ay be tide. .....byside
Bot þe Bretons held þam so streite,
þe scaped nouht for no disceite.
Vnglad was Gallus; he mad his mone Sory was Walwes &...
& said vnto þe Bretons ilkon, .preyed....
"Lordynges, wille ȝe lat me go

vnto Rome þer I com fro,	
& my men forto saue?	
A legion no mo we haue,	O legion & namo wold y craue
a legion mo ne lesse,	Þo þat mystaken haue more or.
for þam I ask forgyfnesse,	
with lyfe & lymme away to fare	& let vs senglely a wey.
out of þis lond for euer mare."	
Þe Bretons granted þam þer bone	
& þe Romeyns ȝalde þam sone.	
Of þe toures þei com alle doun	
to þe pes into þe toun.	
[36vb] Als þe Romeyns ȝolden were,	
þe Scote, þe Walsh, with alle þer here,	
com with grete noys & hu,	
toke þe no tent of pes ne tru.	
Of þe Romeyns smyte ilk a heued;	
lord ne ladde was non bileued.	....þer non leued
Gallus þei his vnþank	Walwes þey tok al his vnthank
& led him tille a brokes bank;	.leddym to Atyngal...
his hede gird of he was last,	Þer left he his heued he was þe.
his body into þe broke kast.	... Atyngal cast
For he in þat water lay,	
þe broke men calle to þis day	.Riueres name was turnd þat.
on Inglis, Gualebroke,	..tonge hit hat Walbrok
for Gallus þe dede þer toke.	.þat Walwes his deþ..
Whan regned Asclipedoth,	Þenne..
nouþer he lufed schrew ne sotte;	Neyþer was he...
feste he held at his crounyng	
& ten ȝere he regned Kyng.	
In his tyme was an Emperour,	
Dioclician, a werreour.	
He sent hider Maximian	
& stroied & slouh ilk criste man	.....Cristenman
þat he on þis half Mongou fond;	
tille he come vnto þis lond,	
alle he stroied & brouht to schame	
þat cristened were in Ihesu name;	
to cristen men did felonie	[*Transp. L*]
Dioclician on his partie.	[*Transp. L*]
Vndere him & Maximian,	
her was slayn sayn Alban	Þey slowe at Verolame seint.
& saynt Iue & saynt Aaron;	
þo were in Wales in Kaerlion.	...ware at.

Þe bisshops with alle þer clergie
þat leued in Ihesu or in Marie,
alle þei slouh þat þei fond,
bot if any ascapid þe lond. — fful fewe ascaped fro þer hond
So fele was neuer slayn in stoure
of Corsayntes vndire Emperoure.
Þat tyme þe date of Ihesu wex
tuo hundreth ȝere, foure score & sex.
In Colchestre was a lordyng
of whom þe toun had begynnyng,
[37ra] Sir Coel his name hight,
of noble lynage & man of myght.
He wered on Asclipedoth
for he had born him als a sot,
& suffred mykelle Maximian — ..to mykel.
þat he þorgh his lond so ran
þe cristen blode for to slo.
Þe Bretons were wroþe & wo, — Þer fore were þe Bretons wo
þerfor þei crouned sir Coel; — [*Transp. L*]
Asclipedoth bare him not wel. — [*Transp. L*]
Whan Maximian was at Rome,
on Asclipedoth toke þei dome.
Sir Coel him in batail slouh
for he fro Maximian him drouh. — ....hym yuel wyþdrow
Þis Choel had a douhter feire,
of clergie couth & was his heire;
sone ne douhter had ne no mo
þat þe heritage mot to go.
Scho was hir fader ferly dere; — ..to hure...
he did maistres hir forto lere.
Þat scho couth þe lond ȝeme, — ..moughte bettere...
lord to take þat hir wild queme. — & lord..as hure wolde byseme
Þis ilk mayden hight Heleyn,
a gode woman & a certeyn.
Þe Romeyns herd & were fayn
þat Asclipedoth was slayn.
Þei sent hider a man of pris,
Constancius, both ware & wys. — .þat was noble..
Alle Spayne he had won to Rome
þorgh treuage at þer dome;
was no man þan of his bounte
þat men wist so mykelle as he.
Þat Constant þat wan Spayn

aryued vp in Britayn.	He aryued her in Brutaigne
Choel, þat wist his comyng,	
he dred Constant ouer alle þing.	
Choel sent to him messengers	
& said he wild, on faire maners,	
holde of him if þat he wilde,	
& redely his treuage ȝelde.	
Constant seid he wild skille	
& consentid to his wille.	
[37rb] Þe Romeyns sawe þei were aboue	..seyde...
& fayn þei were of pes & loue.	
Was it not a moneth long	
þat Choel toke an euelle strong;	
aght days he lay & no mo,	
siþen died as we salle do.	& deide & wente þer we schal go
Constant sawe þis ilk Heleyn;	
þis lond was of hir demeyn.	...al of..
He sawe þat scho was ferly wys	
& of beute bare þe pris.	
He þouht himself wele besette	Hym þoughte he myghte wel be byset
to wedde þat maiden & bate barette;	
he was kyng & scho quene.	Þen was he kyng...
A knaue child was þam bituene,	
Constantyn was his name told;	
& whan he was elleuen ȝere old,	
his fadere felle in a sekenesse	
þat to þe ded it mad him stresse.	
Whan Constant had don his fyn,	.Constantyn had y mad..
[*L adds:*]	In Euerwyk toun þey byried him
	fful Ryaliche wiþ gret honur
	ffor he was a worþy Emperour
	Whan þenterement was done
þei crouned his sone Constantyn,	Constantyn his sone þey coronede sone
& whan he was wele of age,	.þe more he wax in.
wele lufed him his baronage.	Þe bettere loued hym..
Gode knyghtes to him drouh	God chiualrie..he drow
for he was large & gaf inouh.	
If his fadere were of bounte,	
ȝit was þe sone more þan he.	
Constantyn was man of quantise;	
	[*Line order differs in L:*]
in his ȝouth he was als wise	Þer wyþ he was a noble iustise
as eldere were in þer mast pris,	In his ȝouthe he was als wys

þerto he was noble Iustis.   As elder were y þer moste pris
For his modere he lufed Bretons;
for his fadere, of Rome alle barons;
of þise tuo kyndes was he born,
& of þe noblest men beforn.
At Rome þan was an Emperour
did þe Romeyns dishonour,   Þat . . . gret desonour
his name was Maxcencius.
Proude, stoute, & malicius,   . & fers & .
he wasted þe honour of þe toun.
Þe noble men, brouht þam doun;   . . . he brought þem .
þe ordre of þer sene abatid he
& reft þam þer dignite.
[37va] Some þat hatid him, of þo
left þer feeȝ, þam to go   . . fes dide hem . .
hider to Bretayn to Constantyn,
for he was born of þer lyn.
Þei praied him wild mak defens   . . . he wolde . .
& bate þe pride of Maxcens,
bisouht als he was knyght, ... worþy knyght
of þer sene hold vp þe right.
Þe Bretons alle praied him so,
with him þei wild consent þerto.
Long þei bisouht & he at ende   . . preied bot at þe ende
granted þam þider to wende.   He granted . . . .
He dight his folk, knyghtes, squiers,   . tok wyþ hym knyghtes & .
men with alblastes & oþer archers.   . . bowes & arblasters
His moder eames, wys men of dome,   & his moder ful wys . .
with him went vnto Rome;   . . . þey alle vntil .
for þei were men of honours,
he did þam in ordre of senatours;
þe ton hight sir Leonyn,   . . . sire Huwelyn
þe toþer Trahern, þe þrid Maryn.   . . Iohern Eroert & Maryn
Wardeyns he left gode certayn,   . . ordeined gode & .
þis lond to kepe tille he com ageyn.
Whan Constantyn to Rome cam,
þe mastrie fro Maxcens he nam
& was himself Emperoure,
& Maxcens doun with dishonoure.
To sir Leonyn he gaf a wife,   . . Huelyn . . . .
of noble kynde was sho rife.
Of þat wife Leonyn wan   . . . sire Huelyn .
a child men cald Maximian.

This wardeyns þat Constantyn toke   I þe wardeyns tyme . . .
alle þis land forto loke,   Þe Bretons . . .
com Octauus, an Erle of Wales,
sesid þis lond, dounes & dales.   & sesed . . boþe dounes . .
Þis Octauus was man of myght;   Þy Erl of Walys . . . .
in Bretayn he cleymed right.
Wardeyns & scherefes he slouh,
bedels, bailifs, did schame inouh.
Constantyn to Rome was went;
to gretter nedis he gaf his tent;
he ne myght þan on no wise,
hider com to make iustise.
[37vb] He sent hider sir Traherne,
þe lond to kepe & gouerne.

[*L adds:*] Two legions wiþ hym he ladde
Toward Bretayne þey hem spedde

At a hauen þat þei fond,
Sir Traherne toke þe lond;
to Porchestre went sir Trahere,   . Wynchestre wente þis .
tuo days he soiorned þere;
to him þe toun he did ȝelde,
be þer wille þei ne wilde.
Maugre þers, þe ȝald þat estre;   . . þey ȝolde þe .
siþen he ȝode to Wynchestre.
Sir Octauus with many schelde
was befor him in þe felde
& gaf to him batale stoute,
þe Romeyns perced þorghoute.   . . ofte perced þe rout
Octauus gretter force had,
þe Romeyns route alto schad;
he did þam to þe hauen fle
vnto þer schippes on þe se;
þei set vp saile hie on mast,
toward þe north sailed fast.
He ryued in Scotland & loged his oste,
robbed & reft at ilk coste.   & Pylede & Robbed . . .
To Octauus son com tiþand
þat Trahern robbed in Scotland.
Octauus gadred ost aywhare
& hied fast þat he were þare;   . hyed hym . . . . .
oft he said with grete pride
þat Trahern suld not dur abide.
Bot his ouerhope gan faile;   . . ouerwenyng . .

Trahern stode vnto bataile ..& bod.
& did Octauus forto fle
into Norwey ouer þe se.
Octauus þat fled for ferde,
spak vnto Kyng Comperde He spak vntil þe Comperd
for help & socour for ȝerne ....he preyde.
to wyn þe lond of Traherne.
Priuely sent he to þis lond ageyn
to þo þat were tille him certeyn,
þat þei suld fond on alle wise
to slo Trahern with som quantise.
Trahern þat tyme sped wele inouh.
Ageyn to þe south Trahern drouh,
[38ra] & did him croune kyng to be
& regned with solempnite.
A day of London he suld out ride, ..to.....
his fomen spied wele what tide
& busched þam bi þat strete
þer þei hoped him to mete. ...þe kyng..
Sir Trahern of non him dred,
þerfor no folk with him he led.
At a passage as he went,
þei put þam of þer bussement; .breken of þeyr enbuschement
þat him hatid for Octauus, Þo þat....
slouh þer sir Trahernus.
For Octauus þei sent þer sond
& seised him eft in þe lond,
& crouned him as he was ere;
& alle þat com with Trahere,
euerilkon þei did þam slo,
ascaped non bot with wo.
Siþen in pes þe lond gan welde
& long lyued to right gode elde.
Whan he had regned in þis lond here
þe tyme of tuo & þritty ȝere,
he sawe of him was non heire .sey þat of hym cam..
bot a mayden child feyre.
He said, who mot his douhter haue,
þe lond forto loke & saue?
Fele of his frendis gaf reson
to send to Rome for a baron,
his douhter forto gif to wyue,
so myght þei haf pes þer lyue. ...pes haue in þer.

Oþer þer were þat lufed Conan,
þe kynges cosyn, a noble man;
þei conseild to mak him his heire,
he myght best, þis was þer speire. ... in þeir espeir
Þan spak þe erle of Cornwaile,
sir Karaduk, & said sanȝ faile
he wild not conseile þerto,
ne it were nouht wele to do,
heir to mak his cosyn Conan, To make his eir sire.
bot send after Maximian,
þe eldest son of Leonyn, ... Huelyn
Heleyn cosyn & Constantyn. Eleynes ...
[38rb] "His fadere is Breton, þis is certeyn,
& on his modere side Romeyn,
gif him þi douhter in mariage.
Wisemen he is & wele of age. Wys man ......
If þou gaf it vnto Conan,
þi douhter maried to a noþer man,
he suld fond whan he mot wele,
þe lond of him to wyn ilk dele.
He suld þenk & wele myght,
þe lond suld be his þorgh right.
Bot ȝe do als I say,
of pes es þer non oþer way."
Þe kyng held him to þat conseile;
þerfor bigan a tirpeile
bituex Conan & Karaduke;
þe to þe toþer gan rebuke. ffor Conan gan þat oþer.
Conan stouted him with wordes þore; & reuiled hym ...
if he had durst, he wald more.
Sir Karaduk had litelle awe
of his manace or of his sawe.
Þe kyng bisouht sir Karaduk
send to Rome his son, Maurik, To sende .....
& praie him opon alle þing
Maximian to Bretayn bring.
Whan Maurik to Rome was comen,
he saw grete partie was nomen
bituex þis Maximian
& Valentyn & Gracian,
þe stryue to haf þe empire,
þe breþer þe better partie. .. hadde þer partie most seure
Sir Maurik Maximian fond .. þer Maximian.

& told him he was of þis lond,
& bad him leue alle þat of Rome — Anon he bad him take leue..
& vnto Bretayn smertly come,
þe kynges douhter forto take.
"Þi parte may þou þe better make." — Þou may þy party...
Whan Maximian þo tiþinges herd,
with ioy to Bretayn with Maurik he ferd;
was non abide ne no duellyng,
Maximian com to þe kyng.
At Southampton Maximian gon ryue
& asked þe kynges douhter to wyue.
[38va] Octauus was þan at ese;
of his douhter he did him sese,
& alle rengne ilk a dele, — Wiþ al þe Reome ilkadel
& bad him regne richely wele. — ...Richely Regne & wel
Conan was wroth & mad grete boste
& alied him to þe Scottis coste.
Octauus his eem he gan manace,
& Maximian to were did chace.
Bot Maximian gaf nouht of him;
he stode ageyn Conan fulle grim.
Conon oft of him wan, — fful often Conan...
so did of him Maximian.
It is þer chance þat were begyn,
som tyme to lose, som tyme to wyn.
Whan þei togidere had wered long,
men of gode ȝede þam among,
did þam acorde in luf & pes,
so þat Maximian nouht les.
He het him þan for his eam sake,
riche man he suld him make;
þre ȝere in pes withouten fight,
he drouh to tresour þat he myght.
He said he wild stande to chance — ....assaye þe.
on þe se to wend & wyn France,
& fro þien vnto Rome — ..þenne wende to.
of his enmys to take dome,
& of alle þat with þam helde
agayn him fightand in þe felde.
Whan he had folk & was redy,
to schip þei went hastily;
þe southwest þei passed þe se, — Toward south west....
aryued vp in a cuntre;

Anmoriche was þe name, Armoriche . . .
bot now it has oþer fame.
Humbald þerin was lord & sire,
of Anmoriche held þe empire.
He did somon alle his barons
to chace away þe Bretons. A wey to chace & felle . .
Þe Bretons were of more myght;
Humbaldes men þei slouh doun riht,
þei had no force to turne agayn.
Alle þei fled, knyght & suayn,
[38vb] fiften þousand was þer slayn.
Maximian turned agayn
& ioyfulle was þat he so sped,
þe lond had wonnen, þe folk was fled. Þat lond held women þe men were.
He toke sir Conan bi þe hande
& on him louh with faire semblande.
"To haf a reume, þou were worþi. [*Transp. L*] To manne Armoriche þou were.
Conan," he said, "þou ert douhty. [*Transp. L*]
Ses þou now þis faire cuntre,
fulle pleytiuous & wele ese, . plentyuous & ful ayse
þe lond to tile, gode is to wyn,
wodes, wateres, inouh þerin,
forestes fulle of faire deere,
fresch riuers ese & nere.
I sawe neuer in my lyue
so faire a lond ne so plentyue.
On þe, Conan, I vouch it saue,
þat þou it weld with ioy & haue.
Bretayn þe grete was þe hete,
& on þe were it fulle wele sete. . . . . byset
Bot for me þou has it lorn;
ille wille to me þerfor has born. Þer fore to me yuel hastow .
Forgif me now ilk a dele,
& haf þis lond & brouk it wele;
þis is þe hete þat I þe hight, . . . heste . . . .
& better salle whan I haf myght. . . y wolde ȝyf þat y .
Þis lond we salle clens of þise,
þe Bretons salle þe lond iustise;
non oþer folk salle duelle here in,
þan mai þou weld þe lond with wyn."
Conan of him resceyued þe gifte
& Maximian to kyng him lifte,
& Conan mad him feaute

of him to hold alle his fe.
Maximian spak to þe kyng.
"Þis lond is þe Bretons winnyng
& for þat encheson,
þat it is conquest þorgh Breton, ...conquered þorow.
it salle hate Lesse Bretayn,
& we Bretons to be chieftayn;
& I command ȝow alle onlyche .....oliche
þat no man calle Anmoriche." ....hit Armoriche
[39ra] Fro þat day vnto þis same,
Anmoriche has lost þe name
& now is called Bretayn with alle;
I trow þat name salle neuer falle.
Maximian to his demeyns
he seised þe cite of Reyns;
þat were þer in þe toun þam left;
durst neuer non of þam rise eft.
Maximian þat þe lond toke,
constables castels did loke; Tounes & Casteles dide he.
faire ouer alle he fond, ffaire countres....
bot þer was non mot tile þe lond.
He þouht he wild to Britayn send
after men, sibbe & frende, .men boþe..fremde
& forto puplise þe lond & tile, Þe lond to multeplie & to.
þat oþer ne suld þerto haf skil.
He did com of pure pedale, ...pore pedaille
a hundreth þousand þat mot trauaile,
& þritty þousand of knyghted gode
to fende þam to tile þer fode.

[*L differs*:] To laboure & to tyle þer fode
Wyþ þritty þousand men of armes gode
Þe londe fro enemis to fende & were
Þat Vtlandeys scholde þem nought dere

Þan was Conan crouned kyng
& had þe regne in kepyng,
þer for to lyue & deie,
& Maximian went forth his weie.
Als he went, Maximian,
France & alle Lorenge he wan;
þat him þouht was not inouh:
to Rome he þouht & þider drouh.
He þouht to venge him of þo
whan he Rome first ȝede fro, Þat greued hym at Rome when he scholde go

þo breþer bring to ille fyne,
Gracian & Valentyne.
He com to Rome fulle austerly, ... hastely
þe tuo breþer toke þar maistry; Þat o broþer tok he..
þe toþer he did with force fle
& held þe empire in dignite.
Þan was þe fourtend emperour ..he þe fourtenþe.
siþen Augustus þat bare þe flour.
Þe date of criste was þan euen
þre hundreth ȝere, seuenty & seuen.
Whan Maximian ferd fro Bretayn,
of Dinotus mad he ceiftayn, ...cheftayne
[39rb] & kept þe lond tille his behoue; To kepe......
for a lele man did him proue. .trewe & feyþful he...
Sir Karaduk broþer, I spak beforn, ..þat y spak of.
was Dinotus & ȝongere born; ..broþer & ȝonge.
bot dede þat tyme was Karaduk.
His sone þat hight Maurik,
þat ȝede to Rome Octauus message, ...Rome in..
with Dianoth had his heritage. ..he kepte..
A douhter had Dinoth & no ma;
þat maiden hight Vrsula. Hure name was cald dame.
Þo þat were driuen fro Anmorike,
þe Frankis & þei fleand olike, .Frensche..felawed.
ros agayn Conan to fight; & rysen....
bot Conan mayntend wele his right;
for þem he les neuer nouht
whan þei on him bataile souht.
To do his folk be more þorgh skille Þen was Conan meued of skyle
& þe lond herberw & tille, Hys lond to edefie & to tyle
& þe sikerer for to lyue, .þat þey moughte þe sikerere.
wyfes he þouht þam forto gyue.
Frankis women wild þei non take
þat þe blode no monge suld make
to haf cleyme þorgh heritage,
ne dowerie þorgh mariage;
vnto no blode þei wild þam binde
bot vnto þer owen kynde. .only to...
Conan þerfor sent his sonde
to Dinoth þat kept þis londe,
to send him his douhter Vrsele,
with non oþer wild he dele,
& ientille douhtres vngyuen .Gentil damysels.

þat were of waxdam & wele þriuen,	.able to mennes companye were.
sergeanȝ douhters & frankeleyns,	Squyers...
to gif to knyghtes & to sueyns;	
oþer maydens comen of thralles,	
to be maried as þam falles.	
Alle þat he myght, he suld him send,	
with warison he suld þam mend.	
Dinoth granted to send him hire;	
richely did hir attire.	& Richely þen...
Alle þo þat he gete myght,	
lordes douhtres wele dight,	
[39va] elleuen þei were bi tale,	Enleuen þousand....
of ientille women grete & smale;	..blod...
oþer þat were of lowere kynde,	
auenant þat þei mot fynde,	Þe auenauntest þey..
sexti þousand so many þei ware	
redy to schip ouer se to fare,	
wele dight ilkon for þe nons;	
at London þei schipped at ons.	
Whan þei had alle þat þam felle nede	[*Om. L*]
& were bitaght þo þam suld lede,	[*Om. L*]
drouh þer saile hie on mast,	
bitauht þam god & sailed fast.	
Whan þei com in deppest flode	
& wende haf sauf passage & gode,	
ros a tempest rorand loude;	
	[*Line order differs in L*:]
myrk was þe skie, grete was þe cloude,	& reyned al doun wyþ a blak.
þe wynd was wode & þam ageyn;	Derk was þe skye gret was þe reyn
mirk was þe skie, grete was þe rayne;	Þe wynd was wod þem ageyn
þe skie ferd it suld doun falle.	...as hit...
Wondere wawes agast þam alle;	
so gret risand one ouer oþer,	.þey arysen..anoþer
auailed nouht mast no roþer;	Þat þeym nauaillede...
þe wynd, þe water, so fast fouht,	
nouht to saue, nouht ne douht.	Þem to saue was non þat þouht
Þritty scippes þei were no mo;	.schipes þer...
þe sexti þousand to dede ȝede þo.	
Þe elleuen fer were dryuen,	Þe oþere enleuene ful fer..
in Babarie þer vp ariuen.	.Barbarie þey..
Tuo Saracens were kyngis of pris,	
þe ton Melga, þe toþer Guanis;	Þat on highte Melga...
Guanis was kyng of Huneis,	

	Melga of Peihtes, it seis.	. . . was kynge hit seis
	Þis Saracens wild haf layn þam bi,	
		[*The second scribe begins in P.*]
	bot þei ne bot þei ne wild of no uilani.	. . nolde of no vileny
	Leuer þem wer die with drede	
	þan to lychery þer bodis bede;	
	with martirdam þei did þem die.	
	At Coloyn men sais þei lie.	. . now men sais . .
	Þise two Sareȝins herd wele say,	Þenne herde þise to Sarsyns.
	þe force of Bretain was away.	
	Grete ost with Maximian went,	
	to Conan xxx thousand sent.	
[39vb]	What with ton, what wit þe tothir,	
	here left no force a geyn oþir.	
	What dide Melga & Guaneis?	
	Gadir ost of outlandis,	Bot gadred . . .
	with a grete flete on flode to ride,	. gret nauye o þe se þey.
	& com in alle b Scotland side.	. . . . by Scotlande syde
	With wo & were þei did grete noie,	
	Westmore land alle gan þei stroie,	
	al þe Northe cuntre þei wasted;	
	þei passid Humbre, southt þem hastid.	. . . & southe hem.
	In no countre þei ne fond	Non encountre . . .
	bot husband men þat tilled lond,	
	& werkmen & oþer pedail	
	þat couthe not werre no of batail.	
	Ȝif ony of swik stode again,	. any swyche stod ought agayn
	with armed men sone were þei slain.	
	Ilk man fro his oun gan fle;	
	þat ne myght, slain was he.	& þo þat ne . . . .
	How suld a lond be dreded	. . þat londe kepe hym fro harmes
	þat of knigthes es al nakyd;	Þat naked ys of men of armes
	a lond heuedles in time of nede,	
	ouer al es sorow & drede.	
	So was þan bot kry & calle care;	& so . . . . & kare
	of help & socour þei were al bare.	
	To while þei had þer bold barouns,	
	sauely held þei castels & touns.	
	Ouer al landis þei mustird myghtes	. . . . schewed þer myghtes
	to whyle þei had þer gode knyghtes;	Þe whyles . . . noble.
	þei ches þat were baldest & fers,	Þen chose þey of most bolde . .
	to Rome þam sent as messagers	& sent hem to Rome . .
	ffor help to syr Maximian,	

and he sent þem sir Gracian.
With him come two legiouns
þat wele socourd þe Bretouns.
Þis Saxins þeues þei dreue away,
Þise Sarsynes þeues...
into Ireland ilkone fled þei.
[I]n þis at Rome ros Valentyn
[*Capital I om. in P.*]
..tyme at...
and all his kynd, eam & cosin;
with him com a kyng of þe est,
...kynges...
Theodosius, so sais þe gest.
Mo þan twenty as seyþ..
Þrou tresoun, I ne wote hou,
Bot þorow treson....
algate Maximian þei slou.
[40ra]
[*The first scribe resumes in P.*]
Þo Bretons þat Maximian led,
som þei fleuh & som fled.
..slowe somme were fledde
Valentyn seised alle eft
Þan sesed Valentyn Rome..
& alle þat Maximian him reft.
This tiþing com to Gracian
þat he was dede, Maximian.
How Valentyn slow Maxymian
He did him croune of alle Bretayn;
[*Transp. L*]
he sawe him self cheftan.
[*Transp. L*] & saw he was here Cheuentayne
Þis was his custon & his haunte:
[*Transp. L*] ffor...custume...
he bare his as a tiraunte.
[*Transp. L*] And bar hym heye as..
Pouere men, to do þam wo,
out of þer right to put þam fro,
& right many of þam he slouh;
þe ryche he lufed wele inouh.
What did þe mene folk & þe poueraile,
.......pedaille
samned þam a grete bataile;
to priue conseile þei gan þam renge,
of Gracian þei wild þam venge.
Þe biseged him priuely
Þey byseded hym sodeynly
& toke him siþen par maistry,
& his body al to hewe;
þe peces vnto þe hondes threwe.
Þe Romeyns þat were with him comen,
smertly ageyn to Rome nomen.
Melga Guanis herd wele how
Melga Guaneys...
þat þe poueraile Gracia slow;
..poraille Gracian.
fro Ireland þei com & were fayn
þat sir Gracian was slayn.
Þei gadred alle þe outlandes
of Norweie men, with Daneis,

of þe Scottis, with men of Ireland,	
& ouer sette alle Northombirland;	
þei passed Humber, robbed & brent.	...Pylede..
Þe Brentons sawe þer land alle schent,	Þen sawe þe Bretons....
& þer folk so schamly deie,	[*Om. L*]
& þei had no myght stop weie,	.....to stoppe þer weye
	[*L adds:*] ffor nought þat þey couþe don or seye
no throwe in pes mot þei rest.	
Þei conseild þam how it were best;	
þei sent vnto þe senatours	
of Rome for help & socours,	
als men þat þei on affied	....most on.
& in seruage to þam alied,	
[40rb] help þam on hast now in þer nede;	To helpe hem......
with robbours lyued alle day in drede,	ffor ay þey lyue wyþ Pylours..
& þei suld neuer, for wele ne wo,	
more out of þer conseile go	.....do
bot þam þat þam auht to haue,	.ȝelde hem þat þeym...
if ȝei wild help þam to saue.	.þey..now...
Bot þe Romeyns forgat nouht	
what to þam befor þei wrouht,	.schame byforn þey had hem.
so often & so fele siþe	
whan þe mot þer felony kiþe.	
Neuerþeles agayn þei sent	Natheles twoo legions..
þat sone com, als hap hent,	...as hap þem lent
deliuerd þam of þer enmys;	
to Scotlond fled Malga Guanys.	
Þis Romeyns tok þer conseile take;	..dide þem..
a walle opon a dike did make	
fro þe est vnto þe west,	..est se...
ageyn þer foos to saue þam best.	
Stone þei did gadre & graue,	
& masons alle þat þei mot haue;	
ouerthuert þe lond þat is þe brede,	
þei mad þat walle ar þei ȝede,	
for bi þe north end com alle þo	
þat to þe lond brouht were & wo.	
Þat contre hight þat tyme Deire;	
of þis half þe walle in Ȝork schire,	
on þe toþer half, I vnderstond,	
men cald it þan Peihtlond.	...þenne þe Peytes lande
Whan þis walle was alle dight	
& wardeyns set bi day & night,	

þe walle forto defend & loke
þat þei no more scathe toke,
toward þe south gan þei wend.
Whan þe walle was brouht tille end,
at London set a parlement; ..þey sette..
þe hie folk alle þidere went,
þorghout þe lond ilk lordyng,
& þus þei said at þer samenyng:
"We wille wend fro ȝow to Rome
& neuer hidere send ne come.
Be ȝe douhty & lere of armes
& quicly defend ȝour harmes, ...ȝow fro harmes
[40va] ffor we ne may suffre þe costage [*Transp. L*] Ne endure þe grete costage
so often com so fer viage." [*Transp. L*] ffor we ne mowe come so fer viage
Þe Bretons alle said þer ageyns. ..seyde alle þer geynes
Þan stirt vp one of þe Romeyns,
a wise man & wele spekand,
& said, "Lordynges of þis land,
listens now tille I haf said,
þe Romeyns reson on me is laid.
Lordes," he seid, "many tyme lore
haf we suffred þis lond fore,
& befor vs our ancessours,
& we for ȝow haue hard stours. ffor ȝow han had ful..
Treuage ȝe gaf & somtyme nouht;
whan we it had, dere we it bouht.
Litille þer of we were amendid;
more for ȝow we haf dispendid. ffor ay for ȝow wel more we spended
If o ȝere wele tille vs ȝe it ȝolde,
tuo ȝere after ȝe ne wolde.
If any kynges ȝe were vs trewe, ȝyf o kynges tyme ȝe...
tuys als mykelle ȝour wrong was newe; To so mykel after....
to while ȝe myght ouht stand ageyn, Til whan ȝe mighte onst..
lofed ȝe neuer man Romeyn.
Whan ȝe com vnto þis lond, Ay when we....
to lese our right cheson ȝe fond, ...som cheson..
& oþer wronges tille vs inouh,
& aldermast our men ȝe slouh. An alderworst....
Now ȝe haf nede, ȝe vs biseke,
& hete vs þan to be vs meke.
Whan we haf holpen ȝow in caas,
þan do ȝe wers & more trispas.
Tille vs ȝe bare ȝow als leons

& waite vs with som tresons,	
& to withhold vs our rightes,	
ouer wikly gif & þat with fightes.	Oþer yuel hit gyuen....
Wele better vs were it alle forsake	
þan suffre þe wo we þerfor take.	
It is grete coste we won fer hiþen,	Our costes ar grete & wone..
& ȝe haf nede & ere beneþen;	
& we may not com alle way,	..ne mowe nought come al day
do now ȝourself as ȝe may.	....ȝe best may
May we ons take to Rome,	
for no man salle we eft here come.	
[40vb] To saue ȝour self bigynnes now,	
for we no more wille maynten ȝow.	
Wittes wele ȝour ancessours	
were strong & hardy conquerours,	.bolde...
Belyn, Constantyn, & Maximian;	
alle londes to Rome þei wan,	
mayntend þamself & did pruesse.	
Bot now of ȝow oþer ways is,	.....weis hit esse
I ne wote where; it is long	
on ȝow comes non oste so strong	
þat ȝe ne myght ȝourself defend.	*[Line order differs in L:]*
Bot ȝe ere alle gon out of kynd,	Ȝyf any grace on ȝow myghte desende
ȝour wikkednes now ȝe fynd.	Bot ȝe al gon out of kynde
If any grace of ȝow descend,	Ȝour wikkednesse now ȝe fynde
turnes ageyn & waxes bold,	
& thynk on ȝour ancessours old	
þat þe riche regions conquered,	
for fight ne fondyng were þei ferd.	
Fulle late salle ȝe now conquere;	
þat route of rascale may ȝow fere.	Syn route....ay fere
Now salle be sene what it may vaile	
whan outlandes wille ȝow assaile.	
We haf closed þer most nede was,	..ȝow closed....
& if ȝe defend wele þat pas	
with archers & with magnels,	....mangeneles
& kepe wele þe kirnels,	....Carneles
þer may ȝe boþe schote & cast.	
Waxes bold & fende ȝow fast;	
[L adds:]	Þer Outlandeys aryues & Rydes
	Makeþ þer hauenes to kepe þo sydes
	& at oþer recettes fele
	Þat non alien on ȝow stele

þinkes ȝour fadres wan franchise,	
be ȝe no more in oþer seruise,	
bot frely lyf to ȝour lyues ende.	
We wille fro ȝow for euer wende."	We taken now leue fro ȝow to.
At þat word was mykille cri,	
manyon wepe fulle doelfulli.	
Was þer nouht els to say,	
þe Romeyns þam kissed & went away	. . . . . wente þer weye
& said þam for certeyn,	
þei wild no more com ageyn.	. ne wolde her neuere come eft.
Guanius Melga had þar spies	Gwanyus Melga . . .
waitand bi stretes & sties,	
how long þe Romeyns suld soiorne	
& whan þei suld to Rome turne;	
[41ra] & als sone as þei nam,	
Melga Guanis to þis lond cam,	Melga Gwaneys . . . .
robbed & brent Northumbirland.	
Ageyns þam no cuntre ne fand;	. hem non encountre þei ne.
mad þei neuer stynte no stalle	
tille þei com to þe Romeyns walle.	
Þe Bretons were redy þeron aboute	
to gyue bataile to þam withoute;	
þer mot men se on boþe parties	
schaftes schoten bituex enmyes,	A scharp schour . .
arwes, querels þikli flie,	
with slenges caste stones hie.	
Þo þat on þe walle fauht,	
so mykelle skaþe non lauht;	fful mykel scaþe sone þey.
þo þat newe were dubbid knyghtes,	
þei ne couth not ȝit of fightes.	. couþe bot litel þo . .
Þei couth not þe querels scurne	[*Om. L*]
ne no quantise in bataile turne.	[*Om. L*]
Þe arwes com als þik as reyn;	
þei couth not couer þam þer ageyn,	. . . coeuere þer eye . .
& als þikli com þe stones	
with þe dartes & alle at ones.	. schot of dartes al . .
Vnneþis myght non kepe his iȝe,	
he was in poynt bakward to fle.	
Was þer non so hardy Bretoun	
þat him þouht long tille he were doun.	
Þei without were myand alle;	. . . mynynge.
þe walle þei holed & did it falle,	
& filled in fele stedes þe dike;	

þe walle & þe way was euen like,   Þat wal & wey was euene y like
& mad þer þorgh pleyn passage
with carte & wayn to hors & page.
Þei robbed & slouh alle aboute;
þei fand non þei had of doute.
Befor or þat no man fond   . þat tyme . . .
so many at ones slayn in þis lond,
with doelfulle dede & so vile
of ȝonge knyghtes & gentile.
Somtyme Bretons bare þe pris;   Whylom Bretons . . .
þat pruesse now doun lis,   Now al þer prowesse doun hit.
þorgh þam salle it neuer rise
bot þorgh grace of þer quantise.   . . . . oþer.
[41rb] To Rome þei sent to þe senatours   Þen sent þey to Rome . . .
& praied þam eft of more socours;
þe Romeyns said þei ne wold
to Bretayn neuer com þei suld;   . . þey neuere come ne.
on oþer half þei had to do,
þei wild no more be trauailed so,
bot gete þam help where þei might haue;
þei wild þam nouþer slo ne saue.
Þat tyme þe Romeyns þis forsoke,   Whan þe Romayns þus vs.
þe birth of criste was writen in boke,
foure hundreth ȝere & nien were gone
siþen Ihesu tok flesch & bone.   . . of Marye . . . .
Alle þe clargie of þe cuntres,
& lordes of londes & feeȝ,
com alle to a comon conseile   At Londone þey toke þer.
how þei mot turne þat tirpeile.   What myght hem helpe in þer.
Þei said, "Aliens alle day vs noies
& þe cristen blode distroies;
bot Ihesu criste visite vs sone,
we cristen men salle be fordone."
At London was þan þe bisshop se
whan cristendom gan first to be;
þe Archbisshop hight Guncelyns,
a holy man, clerk in deuyns.   . ful holy clerk was . .
Þis Archbisshop his conseile toke
at þo þat þe lond suld loke,
þat he wild wend to Lesse Bretayn
þer Conan somtyme was cheftayn.
Adroel hight, þe kyng was þan,   Aldroan . . . . .
þe ferþe kyng after Conan.

Þe bisshop went in to þat lond,
sir Adroel þe kyng he fond; .Aldroel þer...
þe kyng resceuyed him curtaisly.
His fame was gode, his state hie;
he asked what he so fer souht
& what tiþing þat he brouht.
"Lord," he said, "ȝow þar not wene,
why I am comen ȝe may wele mene,
& what encheson me hidere led
þat I to ȝow so hasty sped.
Ȝe ne ere not born so late,
ne bituex vs so fer þe gate,
[41va] þat ȝe haf herd tiþnges say
how aliens dos vs schamly deie.
Siþen Maximian went vs fro,
haf we lyued in sorow & wo,
þat þis lond þorgh conquest wan
& gaf it þin ancestre Conan.
Oure douhty folk alle with him went;
siþen we were neuer bot schent.
Dounward siþen haf we gon,
frendes fond we fo or non ...fewe..
þat euer wild vs socoure or were;
inouh we fynd þat wille vs dere. Bot to fele we.....
Somtyme Bretons londes wonnen,
renoune of þam þorgh remes ronen;
now ere þei not so mykelle of myght
þat þer londes may hold to right.
Þei of Rome halp vs whilom,
now þei forsake vs alle & som,
for þer wonyng & grete costage .fer....
þat oft misferd in þer passage. ..mys spedde...
Of folk we ere inouh ȝit leued,
bot keper ne no kyng to heued
þat can our folk to bataile lede,
ne our enmys to haf of drede.
Bot we haf help at þis tyme now,
of oþer landes or of ȝowe,
we couer not our cursed care .kenne neuere oure..
so fer doun beneth we are.
I ne may not telle for sore herte
alle our sorow, how it is smerte,
þat we haf had & ȝit haue,

bot if god wille, nouh may vs saue.   Bot God wyle nought may..
Þerfor I am to ȝow comen
als tille kyth & our kyn nomen,   .to kyþ of oure kynde.
for ȝe ere Brettis & we Breton.   ...Brutes...
For þat skille & þat reson,
help vs now to venge our fo
als we wild ȝow if ȝe were wo.
Þorgh right lawe writen we fynd
þat men auh to help þer kynd,
[*L adds:*] & hit ys also worldes honur
At nede þer frendes for to socour
& if no sibred of kynde cam,   Þey no sybrede...
help ȝe suld þe cristendam."
[41vb] Whan Adroelle herd þe bisshop speke,   ...so Gwyncelyn.
for sorow him þouht his herte wild breke
þat þe teres ran of his ine,   Þe teres ronnen out...
for þei were in so grete pyne.
Gretand ageyn he him ansuerd.
"For þe doel þat I haf herd,
I salle do alle my trauaile
þat I to ȝow may help or vaile,
bot Frankis men me chace ageyn.   [*Transp. L*]
If I myght, myself wald fayn   [*Transp. L*] ....y wolde.
þei were on me alle þat þei may.
Miself am þer at ilk assay.   ...a ylka fray
I wille not leue my litille þing,
myn heritage, for more wynning.
I haue a broþer, sir Constant,
a werreour gode, man valiant;   God werrour &..
with tuo þousand, I salle him send
of knyghtes gode ȝour lond to fend.
Him to Bretayn salle þou lede,
þorgh godes grace, wele to spede."
He sent þan for Constantyn
& betauht him sir Guncelyn.
Whan Guncelyn beheld þe knyght,
þe hand he lift þat was þe right,
& gaf Constant þe benyson.
Þe knyght befor him kneled doun;
þe bisshop foure wordes said,
þe wordes ere of Latyn laid:
"Christus vincit, Christus regnat;
Christus vincit, Christus imperat."

Bitauht him knyghtes tuo þousand, — Þe kyng þen bitaughtym four.
tuo þousand squiers þam seruand, — Of men of armes wel seruand
& þre þousand of men of fote.
Þe kyng said, "Þise may do bote
to saue ȝour lond ilk a dele.
My kynde þerin grete þam wele."
Sir Guncelyn ryued at Toteneys
& sir Constant with his herneys;
þat herd þe Bretons alle aboute
þat are sculked for drede & doute, — Þo þat er.....
out of woddes & mountayns
þat durst not are com to þe playnes.
[42ra] To Constant com men inouh
þat þer enmys ouer alle slouh.
He did him into Westmerland;
þe cuntre alle wast he fand.
Alle þe lond leie it lay,
þe folk for pouerte fled away, — ...fere wer..
had þei nouht vnto þer fode
bot bestis wilde & fisch in flode.
Þer enmys þei brouht of lyue,
þe remanant out of land gan dryue.
To Cirecester sir Constant went
& held þer a parlement.
Sir Guncelyn gaf him þe croune;
fayn was þan ilk a Bretoun.
Wife he toke, auenant & gode,
sibbe þe bisshop, of Romeyns blode.
Þre childre of hir he gate auenant,
þe eldest hight his name Constant.
He did him norish at Wynchestre
& mad him monke in þat estre; — .ȝald hym...same estre
þe toþer sone hight Aurelius,
his toname was Ambrosius;
þe þird child, Vter hight,
he lyfed lengest & best was knyght.
Þe bisshop þorgh leue of þe kyng,
had þo tuo in his kepyng;
if Constant had lyued any seele,
he suld haf mendid þis lond wele.
Ten ȝere he regned & no mo; — Two ȝer.....
listen how a traitour did him slo.
One Vortiger, of Wales blode,

þat neuer in treuth no while stode,
he ȝerned mykelle þe kyngdam.
Listes how þis treson for him cam.
In þe kynges courte serued a Peiht
þat was þorgh Vortigers sleiht;   ....deseit
þis Peiht long with þe kyng had bien,
of treson he þouht ay bituen.
He ȝede with þe kyng a day   Þys Peyt......
into an herber alone to play;
it was perceyued of non
whidere þe kyng & þe Peiht was gon.
[42rb] Þe kyng of treson wend nouht,
bot þe Peiht þeron þouht.
Als þei boþe togidir sat
& speken of many what,
þe kyng tille him gaf no tent;
þe Peiht saw þat, his knyfe out hent   Þat saw þe Peyt & his...
& smote þe kyng to þe herte,
& fled away als so smerte.
Priuely þe fame ȝede
þat Vortiger gart do þat dede.   .fforteger had don..
Vortiger was of þe Walsherie,
an erle þat lufed tricherie;   Þat euere louede.
quante he was & fer couth þenk
to compasse a wikked blenk.
Faire he spak þer he wild gile,
& þer he hated, wald he smyle.
Wele couth he praise & lak som dele,
& treson couth he teche wele.
Som þer ere þis tyme here
þat of him þar no thyng lere.   .craft of hym nought nedeþ.
The clergie for þis mad a semble, ...dide make asemble
whilk of þe childre kyng mot be,   ...children best kyng..
bot þei were so litelle & ȝong,
reson couth þei nouht with tong.
Constance was eldest & more;   Constant....
he was a monke, a man of lore.
Þei seid it myght not be don   ..atones alle & som
to take him fro religion.   Þem noughte nout reue hym..
"Of no right we se no way   Ne lawe nolde hit by..
a monk to take fro his abbay."
To take on þe tuo þer conseile ches.   ..an oþer þe Conseil.
Vortiger stirt vp in þe pres   Þen stirte vp Forteger in al..

& said, "It is to drede no þing
of þe monke to mak a kyng.
He is eldest, of þe abite no tale, ...habite..
þe toþer ere ȝong & ouer smale.
I grant non oþer kyng to be.
Alle þe synne I tak on me."
Non oþer consented to þat dome, ..assented...
þe monk suld a kyng bicome;
þei dred suilk a þing begyn.
Bot Vortiger dred not þat syn;
[42va] what he wald do non durst him warne.
To Wyncester he hied him ȝerne;
he asked leue at þe Prioure
to speke with Constant in þe parloure.
"Constant," he said, "þi lord is dede,
þi breþer ȝenge, what is þi rede? ..ar ȝonge....
I wild þou had þe heritage,
for þou ert man most of age.
Wille auance my rent, my fe, Wiltow.....
& luf me wele & triste on me?
Þis blake cloþes salle þou loth
& in riche I salle þe cloth; .y þe richest y...
þi monkhed salle alle weyue, ..þow schalt..
þe heritage of þe reaume resceyue."
Þis monke ȝerned seignorie, ..was blent wyþ veyn glorye
abite, ordre lete ouer flie. Abyte & ordre he let al.
He ȝerned pride þan prue, ffor..more pryde..
& more vice þan vertue; .wel more...
þat Vortiger askid, he him hight
& þerto his trouth him plight. ....he dide hym.
Out of his abite he him schoke
& siþen out of þe abbay toke;
in faire cloþes he him cled,
with him to London he him led. ....Constant he.
Was no man þat said him nay; ...wyþ seyde hym o nay
þei sawe it was þe mokes pay. .....monkes.
To somoun þe folk, non ne beed, ...anon þey bed
& þe archbisshop þat tyme was ded.
With him to London Constant he led. *[P repeats 6983 in error. L om. here.]*
Þat felle to mak þe corounment,
þerto non oþer durst consent,
bot Vortiger þe croun forþe fet
& on Constant hede it set.

Was þer non oþer beñyson, [*Om. L*]
bot Vortiger set on þe croun [*Om. L*]
& Constant þe croun toke,
habite & ordre alle forsoke;
þus to wirschip gan he lende,
with schame departid at his ende. ..he parted...
Vortiger had alle þe maistrie,
þe kyng at wille, þe marchaucie. ....& þe marchalsye
Alle togider þe kyng he led,
[42vb] & alle he did þat he him red,
þe kyng, as Vortiger wild, ..dide al as fforteger.
& alle his conseile he fulfild.
He sawe þe kyng couth no gode
ne kynde skille nouht vnderstode;
on clostire skille couth he maste, [*Om. L*]
& his breþere with þe leste; [*Om. L*]
he sawe þe force of þe barons falle
& his state hiest of alle; & saw.....
þe folk discord nouht in a wille, [*Om. L*]
þan he þouht in hert fulle stille [*Om. L*]
to haf þe regne on his side. & þoughte þe Regne haue in..
Here a desceite he spak þat tide: Her whuche a.....
"Of o þing, sir, I wote right wele,
þer of ȝe auh to witte som dele,
þat þe Danes with þe Norweie ..Daneys wyþ men of Northweye
on ȝow wille lyue & deie, ..wyl þey...
for þou ert no kyng of armes; & for þou art no Knyght..
þe more þei waite þi lond with harmes,
on vs þei wille þe soner haste, ...þis somer.
þi castels tak, þi lond to waste.
Here of I rede þou take ȝeme .....nyme.
þe lond to fende, þi folk to queme.
In castels set þi warnisours ..he sette garnysons
for drede of oþer traitours; .þe drede of oþer traysons
to þo þat þe castels couth loke,
to suilk I wild þat þou þam toke."
Þan said þe kyng to Vortigere,
"Take þe kepyng in þi powere; Tak þou þe lokyng...
as þou wille, it salle be so,
ouer þe wille I no man do. ..wol y þat...
Þe castels alle I þe biken, ...bykenne
& loke þat no man slo ne bren.
In þi conseile þan am I; ...onlyk..

loke to me þou do treuly
of cite3 & of tresore alle,
as þou wilt, right so it salle." Right as . . so be hit schal
Þan was Vortiger at ese;
þe forcelettes he did him seise. ffor alle þe strengþes he gan to .
Now has Vortiger þe forcelesse, When he had alle þys forceresses
cite3, tounes & alle þe richesse, Wyþ Cites . . . richesses
[43ra] 3it he þouht on oþer wise
to contreue a fals quantise.
"Sire," he said, "wille þou do . . . 3yf þou wilt .
þat I salle conseile þe to?
Þi lond salle þou fulle wele saue
& of þin enmys no drede haue. . do þyn enemys of þe stond awe
Sende for knyghtes þat can of sleghtes,
quante men ere alle þe Peihtes. & þat ar bolde men in feyghtes
Late þam be alle þi souders,
of alle kyndes þei know þe maners;
for if þei be þi courte within, . . . be y þy . .
what tyme so any were begyn, On whilk side þat werre .
þou may send þam aboute Þen may þou . . .
to serche of whom is moste doute. . . . wham þer ys . .
Þorgh þe Peihtes & þer frendes, Þaw . . . . kendes
[*The L scribe corrects* frendes *to* kendes .]
may men witte how mykelle wendes."
Þat ofte han schewed þey were oure frendes
Þe kyng to Vortiger þus said,
"My purueiance on þe is laid;
do right as þi self wille,
tak & leue als þou sees skille,
how many þat þou has of nede. Als manye as . . . .
Better þan I, þou wote þe dede."
Vortiger had his wille inouh,
a hundreth Peihtes to þe court he drouh;
of castels, of tounes, of tresorie,
of alle he had þe maistrie.
He gaf þe Peihtes what þei wild,
alle þer askyng he fulfild;
he honoured þam suyth mykille.
Wele he wist þat þei were fikille;
with mete & drynk he made þam glade,
& oft drunken he þam made.
He praised fast in his sawe . preised hem faste . . .
& ouer alle did þam forth drawe;

bifor oþer he þam honoured, — fforby alle oþere...
þat mistere had, he þam socoured.
Þerfor comonly ilk a Peiht
beforn alle þei said on heiht,
þat Vortiger was more curtais
þan þe kyng was any wais,
& semed better to bere þe honoure
þan þe kyng or his ancessoure.
[43rb] In ilk stede als þei ferde, — ...whare..
þus þei said ne rouht who herde; — ...þey ne roughte ho.
& for þe Peihtes of him said þis,
Vortiger þer of had blis; — ....gret blys
& þe more þat þei him praised,
þe more he þam vp araised.
A day it was to þam he dranke
forto haf of þam þanke, — .gete of hem more.
& als þei sat drunken & songe, — .right as þey dronke..
com Vortiger þam alle amonge
& said to þam, "God glade ȝow here,"
bot euel he lete with sory chere.
"Knyghtes," he said, "mykille I ȝow loue.
I haf hulpen to ȝour aboue; — ..ȝow holpen...
more I wild if I had ouht.
Þis lond is þe kynges & myn is nouht.
Here haf I nouht þat ouht amountes;
þat I spende of, I ȝelde acountes,
for in þis lond haf I nouht; — ...contre...
fro fer it comes þat me is brouht.
To serue þe kyng I do my tent;
of him haf I no lond ne rent,
þat I may nouht hold to me
forty sergeanȝ on alle my fe. — .squiers....
If I more had, it were ȝour prowe,
bot nedes I mot departe fro ȝowe, — Þer fore nede y mot parte..
& þat forþenkes me fulle sore. — ..ouer þynkes...
Pore I am & may no more, — ffor pouere......
bot if ȝe se þat I ouht mende,
boldly to me com or sende,
& I salle fonde at alle ȝour nede
both forto clothe & fede."
Vortiger þan turned his bak.
ffals he was & fayntise spak,
& þo þat had drunken wele

trowed his falsnes ilk a dele. ..sawes...
[*L adds:*] His word to truþe al þey hit turned
Þat he to falsnesse had performed
Þei said tille oþer, "What haf ȝe mynt?
Þis curteis man now haf we tynt; ..Knyght....
þis folted kyng serues vs litelle, ...he gyueþ vs.
a monk kan nouht bot his chapitille.
To slo þat folte, wele were it done;
a better myght we haf fulle sone.
[43va] Go we & slo þat vnþrifte
& Vortiger to kyng lifte.
He were worþi to haf empire
& better he semed lord & sire
þan þis monk þat nouht can.
Go we & slo þat foltid man;
he has no kynde þat vs þar drede ......þarf.
þat myght maynten ost ne lede,
ne himself salle neuer be nouht.
Go we do þat we haf þouht." .we & do....
To while þer wille was þus hote,
þei stirte to his chambire, his hede of smote;
with þe hede suyth þai went,
to Vortiger þei mad present.
Þei gan to crie, "Here may þou se
þat we wille auance þe!
Þis monk is dede, do þou þi wille: ....now do..
tak þe croune & hold vs stille."
Vortiger sawe þe kynges hede;
ioyfulle he was þei had him reued, Glad he was þey haddyt..
neuerþeles he couerde him quantly.
Semlant he mad he was sory
& more to did his felonye. .for þat dide þo Peytes deye
Þerfor in London did he crie And at Londone he did.
þat alle þe Peihtes þat men mot wite,
þer hedes of suld men smyte. ..scholde al of be.
Manyon were þat trowed & said
þat non of þam had handes laid
on þe kyng with ille manere
withouten conseile of Vortiger,
& þe Peihtes said þe same,
þat þei did it for his frame.
Þat had þe childire in kepyng, Þo þat þe children had..
Aurelius, Vter, & boþe ȝeng, .& Vter boþe.

dred þat þorgh conseile of þo	
þat slouh þe kyng, þam wild slo.	
Þerfor þis conseile þei toke,	
to Bretayn sent þam to loke,	
to Kyng Budice of þer kynde;	
& noblie he did þam fynde	Þat ful nobly dide..
& honoured þam þorgh alle þe lond;	
[43vb] whan tyme was, armes þam fond.	
Vortiger had alle þe lond,	..al in kepynge..
castels, citeȝ in his hond,	.& cites al in..
& at his wille þe folk he led;	
his powere was no man he dred.	ffor his power noman..
He sauh his chance wele wild falle;	He sey fortune toward hym.
he regned kyng ouer alle.	And regned þen kyng ouer þeym.
Of tuo thynges wakned his wouh:	
on þe Peihtes þat he þam slouh,	
þei called him traitoure with manace,	
& to mischefe þei suld him chace.	..meschaunce....
Anoþer þing men him telde,	
whan þe childere were of elde,	Þat whan.....
þei suld venge Constant þer broþer;	
were him wele & hope no noþer.	War....non oþer
In tyme þat Vortiger regned riche,	Whyle þat fforteger þus..
þre schippes aryued at Sandwiche	
with faire folk & wele dight.	
Hengiste & Hors þe maistres hight,	
of faire stature withouten lak	
& a selcouth spech þei spak.	
Þis Vortiger þat held þe honoure	
at Canterbiri mad soioure;	
to þe kyng men tiþing told	
þat a faire folk with faces bold	
at Sandwiche late gan aryue,	
so gentille of schap is non of lyue.	.faire y schape were non alyue
Þe kyng said, "If suilk be comen	
& in pes haf hauen nomen,	.peysibly þe hauene han.
in pes late þam take þer reste,	
& with my pes to do þer beste;	
& if þei speke with me in pes,	
& in þat wende as þei ches."	.right so wende...
Whan þis breþer, Hengist & Hors,	
had leue of þe kyng & þe ports,	
þei dight þer fers to fare myri	He greyþed his feres to fare al.

to speke with þe kyng at Canterbiri.	
Whan þei com to þe kyng þei grette	
& alle þei were bi him sette;	
þe kyng biheld þis bachelers	
were faire of schap & face clers,	
[44ra] how þei were mad so gentilly,	
fairest of alle þer company.	
Þe kyng said, "Of what lond be 3e?	Þen seyde þe kyng of whenne..
What haf 3e souht to þis cuntre?"	
Hengist was eldest & more;	
for alle his he ansuerd þore.	..his feres onswered he.
"In Sessoyne were we born & fed,	.Saxoyne.....
þien hidere our god vs led.	ffro þennes.....
If þou wille alle þe manere,	.3e wil wite...
whi & on what manere,	..for what we ar com here
to telle þe, sir, gif þou me leue	
þat þou ne þin with me greue."	
Þe kyng gaf him grantise,	
& Hengist tellis on his wise.	..teldym þen in..
"Sir Kyng," he said, "if þou euer herd	
so waxand folk in alle þe werld,	
ne so genderand, ne so plentyue,	
ne so graciouse þrod to þriue	...kynde..
as we ere of our kynde,	
in no lond salle men fynde;	
ne so selcouthly to gendre,	.selcouþloker so..
ne haf so many childre tendre	
& waxen men, women inouh,	..boþe men &..
þat alle þare duelle ne mouh.	....þey ne mowe
For whan þe folk is waxen & largid	
& þe lond is ouer charged,	
oure princes perceyue þer ere so fele,	
þe 3enge, þorgh þei do wele	..dur þey nought out.
þat ere of fiften wynter elde	Bot þulke of twenty..
or more, þat kan þam kepe & welde.	
On stronge men lotes þei kest	
& bid þam go purchace þer best	
to seke oþer lond & lede,	
so mykille pupille may it not fede.	
Mo childre þer ere þan our gendrure	...are of oure.
þan bestis ere in our pasture,	
& for we so multiplie,	
we ere þe kynde of Germanie.	.ar of....

Þis tyme, on vs felle þe lote,
þerfor of lond nede we mote
to seke vs oþer on to lende,
& hidere our godes did vs wende."
[*L adds:*] Mercurius þat vs saues & schildes
Haþ vs brought vnto þys yldes
[44rb] Whan þe kyng herd þam neuen god, ...hym nemne a God
he asked him how þei trod ..þenne...
& what þe goddes names hight
on whilk þei trowed þat had myght. .wham..had most myght
He said, "We haf goddes sere
to whom we mak autere: ffor whos wyrschip...
Mars, Iubiter, & Saturnus,
Diane, & Mercurius;
þise ere goddes of our paen lay
þat we wirschip at þer day,
& mo goddes ȝit we hold
als our ancessours befor vs told.
Bot ouer alle we wirschip mest .on ouer....
Mercurius & hold his fest.
Mercuri is on our langage
Woden, lord is our vsage.
Oure ancessours set it so;
þe ferth day we halow him to.
For we þat day worschip him alle,
Wodenesday þat day we calle.
Withouten anoþer we haue, .hym an oþer..
a godes þat we for help craue;
on our spech we calle hir Fre,
þe sext day hir worschip we.
For Fre we calle it Freaday .....ffryday
& worschip hir on paen lay."
Þe kyng said, "Ȝe leue alle wronge!
With fals goddes ȝe mak monge.
On suilk es nouht forto leue;
it ere fendes & salle ȝow greue. ...þat schol ȝow.
Þat fulle sore forþinkes me.
Neuerþeles," he said, "welcom ere ȝe.
Faire men ȝe ere & stalworth seme,
& if ȝe wille serue to queme, .ȝe wyl serue me..
euerilkon I wille ȝow take
& riche men I salle ȝow make.
Þe Peihtes waite me with wo;

þe Scottes als vs robbe & slo.	..also vs brenne..
If it be so ȝe may me vaile	
to venquis þam in pleyn bataile,	
giftes salle ȝe haf fulle gude	
to ȝour cloþing & ȝour fude.	
[44va]	[*The second scribe begins in P.*]
Þe north kepis ay wele þat cost;	& kepes wel ay þe Northe cost
þine comys euere alle oþer ost.	ffro þennes comen ouer al þeyr ost
Loke I finde in ȝow no faintise;	
ȝee salle me serue of swilk seruise."	
On þis manere come þe Sessouns	
þrou Vortigere among þe Bretouns.	
Hengest toke leue at þe kyng	
to lond for to bring his þing,	.Londone.....
and sone com to þe court again	
with mani fair knight & swain.	
Was it not long sethen þei were comen,	Wel sone after þat...
þe Scottis, þe Peightes bataille nomen	
& come in fast vnto þis lond,	.comen faste in til..
robbid & brent alle þat þei fond;	Pylede......
reght to Humbir water þei come,	
þe kyng with his Sessouns agains þam nom.	
Þe Sessons wer þer of fulle blithe,	
dyght þem wele & þidir swiþe.	Þey arrayed hem wel & þydeward.
Þei smite togidir bataille smert;	
þe Peihtis were euere eger of hert.	
Þei stode first wele & hardlie;	..wel furst & hardyly
ffor þei wer won haue maistrie,	...wond to haue þe.
þei wend haue had þer old custome.	
Lenger again þe Bretouns nome,	Þe lenger...þey nome
þer wening þat dai þei tint.	
Þe Sessons did þem bakward stint	
& were discounfet at þat dai,	[*Om. L*]
þe Sessons bare þe prise a wai.	[*Om. L*]
Þe king was þan a ioiefulle man	Þen was þe kyng a ioly.
þat he þe bataille of þam so wan.	
Þe king lete mikille of þe Sessons	Þen let he mykel...
& did amend þer liueresons;	
þe king gaue Hengist of his maners	....faire.
in Lindesai in stedis sers.	In Kent & fele oþere..
Þis loue lastid betuex þem long,	
ffeithfully wele & strong.	
Hengist saw þe werld wild skape	.sey til hym þe word wold schape

his nedis for to spede in rape.	..to spede þen had he rape
He saw oþer do þer quantise	
qwere of auauntige mote rise.	Wher of...
Alls þoght he to sai some þing	& also þoughte he þan...
ffor to plese wit alle þe king.	
[44vb] On a dai be king he sat,	...by þe...
togidir spekin of mani qwat;	
he saw þe king was wele at ese,	.....mury..
with þis counseille he gan him plese.	
"Sir King, þou has done me honour	Sire he seis ȝe han do..
& mikille I haue had of ȝour.	....y take..
If I haue serued þe to wille,	
bettir I wille forward fulfille;	
& mikille I haue herd & sene	
alls I haue in þi court bien.	Syþen y.....
Þou has nouþer baron no knight	
þat alle þe hate at þer might.	..ne hate þe wyþ her.
Of tuo childer I here þem speke;	
of þe ful herd þei salle þem wreke.	Þat on þe harde schul..
Þer lege louerdes þei suld be	
þroru heritage of fadir fee.	Þorow..þer faderes fe
In scort time suld þei come,	& bynne schort terme schul..
of me & þe take herd dome;	& of vs boþe...
& þis es comune sau of alle,	
an iuelle ending of þe suld falle.	
Þus þei þe with ille manace	..þrete wyþ manace
and to procure & puriace.	.ful yuel þey procure & purchace
Whan I here þem þus ȝelpe,	
þan þink I hou I mote help.	...how y myght ȝow helpe
Into Sesson wild I send	Þer fore to Saxoyne...
ffor mi sib kind & oþer frende.	
Iff I had here childer & wife,	
þen were I holdin on limes & life,	
þe for to socour & saue.	
On alle þe purtenaunce I might haue,	Wyþ al þe strengþe...
þe sikerer mote þou be for me,	
& I suld be loued bettir for þe.	...deserue more loue of þe
Of alle þin enmis þou ne fond,	ffor...þaw þey wild fond
þat durst þe reue a fote of lond.	Ne durste nought reue þe....
ffor I þe loue & serue treuli,	
haue I on me mani enmi	
and I lig euer so nakid side,	
& oure fomen sprede fulle wide.	

ȝif I had ani forcelete
to haue on siker rescet,
..þer inne som syker recet
þen might wee more be siker
..we þe more..
qwat time our enmis gaue us biker.

[45ra]
[The first scribe resumes in P.]

Þerfor it were prowe to þe
þat I had oiþer castelle or cite
sauely in forto slepe
Where inne y mighte sauely.
þat non enmys on vs lepe.
Wele more þan þei wild me doute
[*Om. L*]
þan þei do now I ligge þeroute."
Þan said þe kyng to Hengist,
"Þorgh sond I wild þi folk wist
Þorow sonde.... hit wist
þat þei were whan we had nede,
..were her....
inouh þei salle haf to mede.
To gif þe a toun I ne may,
for þou ert of þe paen lay;
foly it were more þan resoun
to gif a paen a cristen toun.
Of oþer þing þe entirmet,
of toun getes þou no rescet."

[*L differs for four lines:*]
Said Hengist, "If þou wille nouht
ne dar not gif I þe of souht,
on of þi maners þat I haue,
grante it me myself to saue,
Syn þou seide Hengist wyþseyst þat me
A skylful preiere þou graunt me
Of þy maners þat y mot haue
Wher inne þat y may my lif saue
ne no more lond, wide no side,
þan I may sprede a boles hide."
Alle þat grantid Vortigern
Þat graunted anon kyng.
& he sent for his frendes ȝern.
A boles hide he brouht þidere,
on thuonges he karue it alle togidere
& knyt it alle on o thuonge;
& als fer as it was longe
& euenly als mykille on brede,
þe lond he toke it ouer ȝede.
Þat lond about he did it stake,
a forcelet þer on did make.
On his langage he gaf it name
Castelle of Thuonges þe first fame;
siþen as schorter speche felle,
þei called it Thuangcastelle.
Hit was called þong castel
Frankis men couth not so seie;

þei called it Castelle de Correie;
þat vses men biȝond þe see,
& Breton called it Kaer Karre.
Whan Thuangcastelle was al closed, . Þongcastre . . .
þe name giffen ouer alle alosed.
[45rb] [*The second scribe resumes in P.*]
ffor þo þat Hengest sent his sonde,
of þem come xiii schippis to londe Þer comen sexten schipe . .
with mikille folk, knihtes, swaines,
and oþer þat were of his demeins.
In a schip with geentille men
come Hengist doghter, sche hight Ronewen,
a fair woman & a loueli, . ȝong woman & louely
auenaunt gret & fair was hi. . & fair & semly
Þis lewid men seie & singe,
and tellit it was a maydin ȝinge; . telle þat hit was mayden Inge
writin of Ingge no clerk may ken
bot Hengest douhter Bonewenne. . of . . Ronewenne
Alle þe folk Hengest fore sent,
to Thuang Castelle ilkone þei went. . Þoncastre . . .
[*L adds:*] ffro Angle a Contre in Saxonye
Comen alle Hengistes compaynie
So þat for Angle y vnderstond
Bretayne was cald Engelond
A day Hengest him purueid Þen Hengiste faste hym.
& sent vnto þe king & seid,
praid him as he louid his grith,
a night herber him with; Þat he wolde ony night . . .
a day a sop ete & drinke . . to ete a sop . .
& see his werke hou þat him þinke,
& of his folk hou him þoght,
& held þo þat to him dought. . wyþholden . . . . .
Þe king his werk fain wild he see; Hengistes werk fayn . . .
he ȝede þidir alls in priuete.
Whan it saw, wele he it praised When he hit saw . . . .
þat þer myght folk be wele asaied; & . . . be folk wel aysed
& þo knightes þat late cam,
ffor þer sond with him þei nam.
Hengest þat day did his might
þat alle wer glad, king & knight;
and as þei were best in glading
& wele cop schotin, knight & king, . . cuppe schoten . . .
of chambir Bonewen so gent, ffro chaumbre cam Ronewenne . .

before þe king in halle scho went.
A coupe with wyne sche had in hand,
& hir hatir was wele farand.   . hure atyr . . .
Before þe king on kne sett,   Byfore . . o knes sche hir.
& on hir langage scho him grett: In hure langage ful faire . .
"Lauerid king, Wassaille," seid sche.   Wassayl my lord wassail . .
Þe king askid what suld be;   Þen asked þe kyng what þat myght.
on þat langage þe king ne couthe.
A knight þer langage lerid in ȝouthe,
[45va] Breȝ hiht þat knight, born Bretoun,   Breyþ . . . . .
þat lerid þe langage of Sessoun;   Þat wel spak langage . .
þis Breȝ was þe Latinier,   . Breþ . . kynges latynier
what scho said told Vortiger.
"Sir," Breȝ seid, "Ronwen ȝow gretis
& king callis & lord ȝow letis.
Þis es þer custom & þer gest
whan þei are at þe ale or fest.   . . arn at þer fest
Ilk man þat louis qware him þink   . . . . þer hym best þynk
salle say 'Wosseille' & to him drink.
He þat bidis salle say 'Wassaille';   . . haldes . . .
þe toþer salle say again 'Drinkhaille.'
Þat sais 'Wosseille' drinkis of þe cop,
kissand his felaw, he giues it vp.
'Drinheille' he sais, & drinks þer of,
kissand him in bourd & skof."
Þe king said as þe knight gan ken,
"Drinkheille," smiland on Ronewen.
Ronwen drank as hire list
& gaue þe king, sine him kist.   . . . . & syn hym.
Þere was þe first Wassaille in dede
& þat first of fame ȝede.   Þat now & euere þe fame.
Of þat Wassaille men told grete tale
& Wassaille whan þei were at ale,   . vsed wassail . . . . þale
& Drinkheille to þam þat drank,
þus was Wassaille tane to þank.   . . . take . .
ffele sithes þat maidin ȝing   fful often þus þys mayden.
Wassailed & kist þe king.
Of bodi sche was right auenant,
of fair colour with swete semblaunt.
Hir hatire fulle wele it semid;
meruelik þe king sche quemid.
Oute of messure was he glad,
ffor of þat maidin he wex alle mad.

Drunkenes þe feend wroght;	Þe ffend & dronkenesse hit.
of þat paen was al his þoght.	
A meschaunche þat time him led,	As meschaunce . . . spedde
he asked þat paen for to wed.	
Hengist wild noght draw o lite,	& Hengist wernde hym bot.
bot grauntid him alle so tite	. . hure hym . . .
& Hors his broþer consentid sone;	
hir frendis said it were to done.	. . seyd alle hit was . .
[45vb] Þei asked þe king to gife her Kent	
in douary, to take of rent.	
Opon þat maidin his hert so cast,	
þat þei askid, þe king made fast.	What so þey asked . . . .
I wene þe king toke hir þat day	
& weddid hire on paiens lay.	
Of prest was þer no benison,	
no mes songen, no orison.	
In seisine he had hir þat night;	
of Kent he gaue Hengist þe right.	
Þe erelle þat time þat Kent alle held,	
Sir Goragon, þat had þe scheld,	
of þat gift no þing ne wist	
to he was cast oute with Hengist.	Til he was dryuen out . .
Þe paens counseille he vndirstode	. . . þe kyng.
& dispisid þe Cristen blode,	
& alle þe cristen him forsoke	
ffor he to þe paens toke.	. he hym to . . .
His owne kin hotid him most;	. . kynde hated hym mest
his childir loued him alle lost.	. . . . alder lest
Beforn or þat he had a wif,	Byfore tyme he . . .
bot dede had depart þer lif;	. deþ had departed . .
with þat wife he had thre sons	
þat held again him for þe Bretons.	
Þe eldest hight sir Vortimer,	
Þe toþer Passence & Katiger.	. . Pacens & Catyger
Hengist went with þe king about	
to be sikir for drede & dout.	
He said, "I see on mani gate	& seyde y se hit . . .
þat of sum for me has hate,	. þou for me of summe hast.
& I am, sikir mote ȝee be,	
hatid for þe loue of þe.	
Þou art mi sone be þis skille:	
þou has my doghter, law it wille;	. . . . as lawe . .
I am þi fadir alls in honour	

to be þe a gode counselour.
If þou wilt regne, traist on me wele
and help on my party sum delle.
If þou wilt greue þine enmis,
I salle þe counseille a gode vis; ....by god auis
send aftir my sone Octa,
and for his Cosin Ebissa, ...Ebsa
[46ra] [*The first scribe resumes in P.*]
& for a nobille man, Kerdike; ....Knyght Kerdyk
in alle Sessone ere non þam like.
Þise ere feihters, nobille in stours, Þey ar fighters & noble iustours
& quynte men & werreours;
gif þam lond in þe north to lende,
þi werre comes in euer bi þat ende.
Fro þin enmys þei salle þe were
þat nouht of þin salle robbe ne dere, ...schulle þey dere
so may þou haf to þi decese .myght..til þy deses
of þis half Humbere þe lond in pese."
Þan said þe kyng, "Send after þo
& of þe best if þore be mo."
Hengist had his sondes sone,
þam to bring, þei were alle bone.
With þam com a flete on flode,
þritti schippes & alle gode;
knyghtes þat wild wend for wages,
with Octa come to þe ryuages. ..wenten...
After þat flete come ouer þe see,
schippes vmwhile bi tuo bi þre, ...or þre
[*L adds:*] By foure & fyue by six & seuene
By eyghte & nyne by ten & enleuene
in a throwe were mo paen men
or als many as þe cristen.
Þe Bretons sawe þis; þei were noied, Þis seye þe Bretons & were onoyed
& said þe kyng þe lond destroied;
þei praied him he suld not drauh To þe kyng þey pleyned in curteys sawe
paiens agayn cristen lauh,
& said, "Greteli þei gynne vs greue; Bygynneþ gretly vs to greue
to wend away, sir, gif þam leue;
alle, or þe most partie,
to cristendom ȝe do vilanie."
Þe kyng ansuerd & said, "Nay,
I sent for þam, þei serue to pay."
Whan þe Bretons herd þat þe kyng

wild not leue for no þing,
at London þei set a parlement
& Vortimer to kyng þei hent,
þe eldest sone of Vortigere;
he was a douhti bachilere.
Þis Vortimere did krie a kri
þat no Sessone were so hardi
in his demeyns duelle no be,
noiþer in burgh ne in cite,
[46rb] smertli alle did þam out kest;   Anon alle out he dide hem.
among þe Bretons non mot rest.   ... myghter non.
Þe kyng, for luf of his wife,
held þe Sessons, mantende stryfe.   . wyþ þe Saxons & meyntend.
His sone had þerwith enuy,
sawe his fader mantend foly.
He spied þe Sessons where þei were
& chaced þam als hunde dos hare.   ... as hound doþ þe hare
His folk was gode, himself douhty,
& mantend wele his party.
Boldeli bolded on him þe Bretons
agayn his fader & þe Sessons;
foure tymes bataile þei nomen
& euer þe Sessons were ouercomen.
Þe first bataile was opon Derwent,
þer were þe Sessons schent;   ... Saxons alle y schent
þe toþer at Breford at a broke,
þer eftsons bataile þei toke.
Þer was Hors & manyon oþer
agayn Katiger, Vortimere broþer;
gretli ȝerned ilk oþer to assaile   . þey ȝernde....
& boþe were slayn at þat bataile.
Þe þrid tyme, in Kent at a hauen,
to þer schippes as þei were drawen,
þe fled to þe Ilde of Tenet;   [*Transp. L*]
þer were þei so harde biset,   [*Transp. L*]
fro biȝond Humber to þat Ilde
was no Sesson so bolde ne wilde
þat he ne did him þider chace;
for alle þe kyng þei fond no grace.   . in ffortiger....
Þe Bretons folwed þam & slouh;
þo þat scaped to þe Ilde þei drouh.   .....hil..
In þe Ilde þei assailed þam þerin
with botes as þei might to þam wyn;

bi þe se side on þam þei karfe,
on þe toþer side for hunger þei starfe.
Þe Sessons sauh on ilk side wo;
þare best it were to wende þerfro.   & þoughte best were...
Þei sent þer sonde to Vortiger
þat he wild praie sir Vortimere   ...so sende to Vortymer
to gif þam leue away to wende
withouten scaþe, als he was hende.   .slaughter....
[*L adds:*] ffor þey ne leften nyght ne day
Þem tasaille wyþ strong afray
[46v c.1] In þis treus, leue to gete,   His trewes þer fore fond vs..
þe Sessons drouh þam alle to flete
& dight þer schippes & set vp saile,
left wife & childe & oþer apparaile.   ......porayl
On þis maner, away þei scapid;
into þer awen lond þam rapid.   Ouer se til oþer land þeym.
Vortimer did þan restore
þat for þam had any lore.
Kirkes he did raise & make
þo þat Hengist did doun schake,
& godes seruys be songen & said   & dide......
þat for þe paiens long was laid,
& he sent hidire þe bisshop Germayn,   [*Transp. L*]
he sent to Rome to saynt Romayn.   [*Transp. L*]
With him com saynt Loys,   Þen com wyþ hym seint Lowys
a holy bisshop & a wys,
þei were sent þe lond to asoile;
he kept þe see of þe apostole.   ...sege...
Þise tuo turned þe folk agayn
to leue þe cristen lawe certayn.   .Crist & to his lawe ageyn
Many þorgh þam saued was
þat are was gyuen to sathanas;
þorgh þam schewed god many vertue
þat in þis lond did grete prue.
Whan þei had stabled godes lawe
for miracle & þorgh þer sawe,   Þorow.....
a noþer sorow com vp ryfe
þorgh Rowen, Vortiger wife.   .Ronewenne..
Scho mad a drynk þorgh treson
& Vortimere scho did poson;   ....Poyson
scho poisond him þat loued criste
for þe paien, hire fadere Hengiste.
Whan Vortimere wist he suld deie,

leches to lif couth him not seie.
He sent after his barons bolde,
betauht his tresour to holde	. hem alle his . . .
& said, "Takes conseile & rede;
of me is non, I am bot dede.
Knyghtes of sonde I rede ȝe take	Men of armes swyþe . .
bi þe se side quikly to wake,	By alle þe costes . . .
þat no Sesson on ȝow aryue
ne resceyue non for þing olyue.
[46vb] Holdes þis state þat I ȝow wan
& trauaile ȝe as I began;	. trauailleþ forþ . . .
& if ȝe do als I ȝow rede,
on ȝow to com þei salle drede.
Bi þe se side birie me þere
þe sight of me salle þam afere.	. . . . ȝyt schal hem fere
Do mak a toumbe þat long may laste,
þe sight þer of salle þam agaste;
on alle maner ȝe mak it hie
þat I be euer agayn þer ie;
þus way on me þat salle þei skurne	Þat wey of me þan . . .
þat neuer haf grace on me to turne."
Þus he þam tauht, þus he þam said,
& befor þam alle he deid.	. þenne byforn þem . . .
Did þei nouht his comandment;	Bot þei dide . . .
þe dede conseile is sone ouerwent.
His body to London þei bare
& in þe cite biried him þare.
Þan wex Vortiger right stoute
als he are was regned þorghoute.	. . fore dide he regned.
Ronwen þan hir lord bisouht
þat Hengist agayn were brouht.	. . myghte ageyn be.
Tille his wife his wille he went;
after Hengist bi letter sent
to com slily he suld fonde,	. . sleightly . . .
bot bring not mykelle folk to londe.	& litel folk wyþ hym brynge . .
[*L adds:*] So þe barons þem nought mispaye
Ne þe comun folk affraye
"It is no nede grete folk to haue,	Hit nedeþ no þyng . . . .
Vortimere ligges dede in graue."
Whan Hengist herd þo tiþinges,
he þankid his godes & mad offrynges.
He dight him folk, þre hundreth þousand	. . . . an hundred þousand
of armed men, brouht þam to land.

Many Bretons dred þam þan sore	. a Breton þen dredde hym .
& so suld oþer þat þan ne wore.	
Whan þe herd Hengist was comen	
with mykelle, hauen had nomen,	& wiþ mykel folk þe lond . .
he dred him sore & ment his mone.	
Þe Bretons were greued euerilkon;	
þei said þei suld fond þer myght,	& seide þey wolde do . .
& do him flie þorgh force of fight.	To sle þem doun wyþ force & .
Hengist herd say, what loud, what stille,	
þe Bretons to him had wikked wille.	
[47ra]	[*The second scribe resumes in P.*]
Himseluen was euer fulle felon;	
he sent to þe king alle in treson	
þat he wild speke with him pes,	. . . . wyþ alle in pees
& sempely with outin pres.	. simplely . . .
Pes he asked, pes wild he seke;	
to him in pes he wild him meke.	
He wild not þe Bretouns greue	
ne dwelle with force again þer leue,	
bot chese þem self as þei wild seie	
or at þer wille go home þer weie.	Wheþer we schul dwelle or go our .
At þat couenant, at þat deuis,	On . . & þat deuis
þei had treus of boþe partis.	
Whan þe partis to treus were broght,	
who wild haue wend of treson þoght.	Hengist of treson hym byþought
Þorh treist & treus on on assent,	. trist of trues of . .
þei set a dai of þe parlement	
opon þe plain of Salesberi	
beside þe Nunnis of Ammesberi.	. . Merueille of Aumbresbyry
He bad Hengist no grete folk lede,	Þey . . . . . .
bot simpli no man suld drede,	. senglely come & noman .
& what louerding he gan mete	
alls he þem dred, so suld he lete.	
Hengist sent him bode again	
þat he wild come vnto þe plain	
with owtin armour on oni wiht,	
ffor drede of contek & of fiht.	
To þat plein þei come þat day,	
of Salesbery, þe first of May.	
Mani a man þoru somouns	. . . wyþoute .
of þe Sessons & of þe Bretouns,	
heres now hov Hengist wroght	Hereþ . . . þought
þis tresoun who wild haue þoght.	& what treson he schop to be wrought

"ffelaus," he said, "what so be tides,	
puruey ȝou kniues egid boþe sides	Get ȝow knyues egged on . .
& bere þaim priuely þat non ne se,	
in ȝoure bosums be ȝour the.	. . hoses harde by ȝour kne
When wee haue þem & þei vs grett,	
ilkone be sidyn oþer sett;	& ilkon of vs by a Breton.
on alle manere fondis hov	. . . . how
on of þem & on of ȝow.	Ay . . . anoþer of ȝow
Takis oute ȝour sexis whan I seie,	Nymeþ . . . when y so say
handis on ȝour felawe leie,	
[47rb] on þe Breton þat sittis ȝou next,	
& smyte with knife þrou bak or brest;	& stykeþ hem ded þorow . . .
alle gate þat ȝee him slo,	[*Om. L*]
no poer haue ferer to go."	[*Om. L*]
Whan þis treson to þem was said,	. Hengist to þem þus had.
ilk a man a sexe puruaid	. . Saxon . . .
& come to þe playn of Salesbiri,	
ffair felichip & ful meri.	. felawschip . . .
Whan þei were alle sett in fere	
as he had said on þat manere,	
"Takis out ȝour sexis," said Hengist.	Nymeþ . . . . .
What it ment, þe Bretons ne wist,	
bot þe Sessons þer sexis droh,	
his felau next þe Sessons sloh.	
Þe kyng sau þat & vp he stirt,	
bot Hengist toke him be þe scirt	. . laughtym by . .
& held him alls so stille as stone	
þat he mote help to saue none.	
Þe Bretons sau þei were betraist,	
so sodenly þei were obeist	fful deolfuly were þey þenne abayscht
& þer liues so sone reft,	Þat so sodeynly had þer lyues.
ffo of þe lordings were þer left.	& so fewe lordes as þer were.
Þer were slain of barouns bold	ffor . . . . knyghtes.
thre hundirth & sexti told,	. . . . Bretons tolde
alle riche men, euerilk one,	. were þey lordes . .
ffor whilk þe lond made mikil mon;	
& þo þat scapid out of þe place,	
wit stonis fauht wen þei had space,	
ffehtand þei fled as þei had nede.	
Þe Erelle of Gloucestre was in þat drede;	
a tree he laght & þer with smote,	
his dintis on þe Sessons bote.	
Þis erille, sir Eldof he hight,	Sire Eldok þe noble Erl so.

to stond his dint non ne might.	His dint wyþ stonde no Saxon.
He slou þer of þe Hengist men,	ffor he . . . Hengistes men
as it tellis, seuenti & ten.	. . . twenty . .
He bare him so in þat prees,	
of wound he was wemles.	Þat of. . . .
Þei sau he was schapid with þe liue;	. . . scaped so . . .
at him þei kast many a kniue.	& kesten after hym . . .
Þer his hors was, þidir him sped,	
on him to Gloucestre he fled.	& to Gloucestre on þat hors he ȝede
[47va]	[*The first scribe resumes in P.*]
He warnyst so alle þe toun,	
it had no drede of no Sessoun.	Þat þey ne dredde . .
Sessons wald haf slayn þe kyng,	
bot Hengist wild not for no þing.	
He bad þam leue, "Do him bot gode,	
for he has auanced my blode.	. . . auaunced mykel . .
As in lawe he is my sone,	
els suld he oþer waies mone."	
Þe led him vnto London	Þey ledde hym þenne to .
& þer did him in prison.	
London was þers; to Lyncoln þei hastid,	
Wyncester & Ȝork þei tok & wastid.	
Vortiger sauh how þat it fore;	
þat þei asked, he þam suore;	What þey hym . . . .
forto be out of þer prison	
& of alle maner raunson,	& quit of . . .
he graunted þam to haf Southsex,	
& Estsex, & Mydellesex;	Oxenfordschire & .
for þei merched opon Kent	
þat he gaf Ronuen to rent,	
& forto mene of þo tresons	. . . ȝyt of þe .
of þe sexis & þe Sessons,	
haf þo cuntres þerfor toname	Þo countres haue þer of þe name
Sexis, for þe Sessons schame.	
Whan þe kyng, sir Vortiger,	Sire ffortiger þe kyng þankede god þo
was laten go quyte & clere,	Þat so quit & sker had lat hym go
toward Wales fled he ȝerne	
fer away biȝond Seuerne;	
þer he duelled & mad soioure	
& here now how he mad his toure.	Now hereþ how he þer made . .
He did send after þe clergie,	
wise men of astronomie;	Þe wysest men . .
at þam alle conseile he toke	

how he might him sauely loke, ..myghtym safliest lok
ageyn his enmys to defende
if oste biseged him as he wende.
Þus red him his conseilours
to mak a strong castelle & tours,
þat non with force myght it take
ne with non engine perbrake. ..engyns hit Perebrake
Whan it were dight at his auys,
warnissed agayn his enmys, To warnyschit...
[47vb] in fele stedes þan ches he
where was best & most ese.
On a hille, Mount de Tire, ..hil hight...
þer on was his desire. ...his moste.
Masons slie he brouht þertille, .brought he þenne.
began a kastelle opon þat hille; Bygonne þat Castelwerk o..
morter did mak, stone did fet,
& sped þam fast þeron to set.
Alle þat þei mad þe day vp right
was fallen doun opon þe nyght.
Oft þei les alle þer iorneis,
þat þei mad lay doun on knes. Þat what made....
Þe kyng sauh it misfare so;
þe maistres he did com him to ....eft com..
& praied þam telle what þing it deres
þat þe erth his werke ne beres,
& if þei myght, þe suld fonde
to witte what myght do it stonde.
Þis wise maistres lotes caste ...þer bokes kest
for þat werke þat wild not laste. Why þat werk ne wolde..
Þei fond in þer lotes kestyng .fondyt þenne in þer musyng
a grete selcouth & tald þe kyng,
"ȝif any myght a childe fynde .ani man....
þat no fader had of mankynde,
if he were taken & slayn on one, ...slayn sone
& menged his blode with morter & stone,
vpon þat morter þat blode were in,
might men þe werke sauely begyn."
Þe kyng als sone his sondes sent;
fro toun tille toun þorgh Wales went.
In ilk a cuntre, þorgh ilk a schire,
he had his spies forto spire,
& in oþer londes seres
sent þe kyng his messengeres.

Tuo togidere about þei ȝede,
þe better forto spire & spede.
Tuo of þise went þorgh Wales,
of suilk a childe ȝif þei herd tales.
So fer in to þe lond þei cam, ...nam
þat Kaermerdyn þei nam; Atte last to Kermerdyn þey cam
befor þe ȝates in þe way,
sauh þei many childere play.
[48ra] Bituex tuo a strife þei herd, . to þer....
of grete vpbreide ilk oþer ansuerd; .. reprefs...
þei withstode & gan abide
forto here þe childir chide.
Whan wrath comes, þan is vpbreid; .. bygynneþ þen comeþ vmbreyd
alle þat men wote is þan forth seid;
so did þei whan þei were wroþe. ...þat weren.
Danubius, Merlyn, þus hight þei boþe. Dynabus.....
Dinabȝ seid, "Lat be, Merlyn.
Ȝif þou vpbreid, þe schame is þin. . þou me vmbreyde....
I am born of hiere kynde
þan any man of þe may fynde;
it auht þe schame alle þi lyue,
þat þou, Merlyn, with me wild stryue,
for I am of kynges blode .. am come...
& þou, Merlyn, ert not so gode.
Ȝi kynd & myn is no þing euen,
ne þi fader kan þou not neuen,
ne neuer him sauh, ne nouht knewe, ...seye ne hym ne knew
ne of what kynd þat he grewe,
ne no man of þe may kone. Þer wot no man of wham þart come
Þerfore I hold þe no mans sone."
Þe messengers listend & þouht
þat suilk a childe had þei souht;
þe spired at men of þe cite
þat Dinabus seid, if it myght be.
Þei of þe cite seid ilkon, [*Transp. L*]
þat fader wist þei him haf non. [*Transp. L*]
"His moder we knowe þat him bare,
of his fader ne wote we whare.
His moder kynd alle we knowe,
bot his fader neuer we sowe. ...we neuere sawe
Sho was þe kynges douhter, Demetie, ...Dymenice
of Wales had half partie; .. he hadde..
sche is nonne of religioun

at seynt Petir kirke of þis toun."
Þei ȝede to þe Maire of Kaermardyn;
on þe kynges half, asked Merlyn
þat neuer ȝit no fader had.
His moder with þam als þei lad; ..also wyþ hym..
þe Maire wild þam nouht werne,
bot sped þam on þer way fulle ȝerne;
þei com to kyng Vortigere.
[48rb] He welcomed þam on faire manere.
"Dame," said þe kyng, "welcom be þou.
Nedeli at þe I mot witte how, Nedlike.... wyse how
who þan gate þi sone Merlyn,
& on what maner was he þin."
His moder stode a throwe & thouht
are sche to þe kyng ansuerd ouht.
Whan scho had standen a litelle wight,
scho said, "Bi Ihesu in Mari light, ..by Marye bright
þat I ne sauh him, neuer ne knewe
þat þis knaue on me sewe, Hym þat þis child...
ne I ne wist, ne I ne herd Y ne wiste neuere....
what maner schap with me so ferd; ..wyght....
bot þis þing am I wele ograunt,
þat I was of elde auenaunt.
One com to my bed I wist,
with force he me halsed & kist. &..me clipte & kyst
Als a man I him felte
& als a man he me welte.
Als a man he spak to me,
bot what he was myght I not se.
So ofte to my bed he cam,
me ofte kist, in armes nam,
& knewe me als a man suld do.
Bifore no siþen did neuer non so.
Þusgate conceyued I þis knaue,
& als I wist, told I ȝow haue."
Þan did þe kyng a maister calle,
Magaunt he hight, wisest of alle.
He asked if it myght be so,
þat þing als scho teld þam to.
"Ȝa," said þe maister to þe kyng,
"it may betide of suilk a thyng.
We fynd writen in our skrites
of suilk a maner of spirites,

bituex þe moyne & þe erth won, ..mone...þei wone
so saið our bokes þat we con. .telleþ vs.....
Somwhat tak þei of mans kynde
& menge it with angels, we fynde;
for þer wonyng is in þe eyre,
vmwhile to þe erth þei mak repeire.
Mikelle scaþe do þei nouht.
[48va] Drecchyng bi poyntes haf þei wrouht; ..tymes...
manes nature vmwhile þei take,
þat is þer myght, þei may so make
whan it is tyme of þer powere,
to haf liknes of bodies sere. .....here
What tyme þei tak it, wote no man
bot he þat alle may wite & kan.
Þise spirites do women schame;
incubi demones is called þer name.
ffendes in bedde, so þei sayn, ...as our bokes.
þat many women haf forlayn.
On þis maner myght Merlyn
be geten & born, in oure deuyne."
Þan said Merlyn, "Sir kyng, þou has
sent after me, say me what cas:
what þou wilt, say me þi wille,
whedir it is for gode or ille."
Said þe kyng, "Þou salle here.
For þe I sent, at þe to lere.
A kastelle I haf begunnen
& lost þerfor þat I haf wunnen. .lore þer on....
Alle þat þei mak þeron on þe day, ...þer on a day
a nyght holy stand it ne may; O nyght alone....
& eft whan þe begyn þe walles,
oiþer it sinkes or cleues or falles;
& fayn I wald þe werke haf hasted
& mykille of myn þerfor is wasted.
Bot þus say alle my diuinours
þat neuer salle stand walle ne tours,
bot þi blode þeron be schad,
þou þat neuer no fadere had."
Þan said Merlyn, "Þat wild not god
þat suilk fals worde so suld be trod, ..a fals schold be bytrowd
þat þorgh þe mengyng of my blode,
þi toure suld stonde strong & gode.
I salle proue þam fals forsuorne

if þou bring þam me beforn;
þo þat on me lotes kast
& said my blode þi werk mot fast, ... myght makyt fast
I salle þam proue for liers olde,
þo ilk maisters þat þe so tolde."
Þe kyng did þam com ilkone
[48vb] ageyn Merlyn himself alle one.
"Maisters," he said, "What haf ȝe said?
What lotes haf ȝe on me laid,
for þis þyng is þus farand,
þe kynges werk þat may not stand?
Kan ȝe say non oþer cheson
whi þis kastelle falles doun,   . þat þis Castel þus . .
& if ȝe kan non oþer say,
whi it falles a certeyn way?   . þat . . som certeyn .
How couth ȝe with þat þorgh my blode,   . . . wyte . . . .
his toure myght stand stark & gode.
Sais what þing is in þe grounde
þat it may not be hole & sounde,   . . ne may stande hol ne .
& sais what þing þat it help myght
þat it mot stand vp right,   . þys Castel myght . . .
& if ȝe kan not, do him wite
what þe fallyng may with site.
Þat ȝe haf said, it is bot fabille
þat my blode suld mak it stabille.
Say him now alle þe disturbance
& whereof coms alle þat chance."   . . comeþ þat wonder chaunce
Þo maisters þat said þat devyne,   Þise maistres of astronomie & of .
ansuerd nouht vnto Merlyne.   . . o word to .
Whan Merlyn sauh þei ansurd nouht,
vnto þe kyng he said his þouht:
"Sir kyng," he said, "gif now þi tent.
Beneth þe erth at þe fondement
is a water rynnand depe
þat makes þi werk to slide oslepe;   . . . . slyden o slep
& certeyn þerof þou be,
do graue þe erth alle vp & se."
Þe kyng did com grauers inouh   . . . . mynours .
þat þe erth vp cast & drouh.
As Merlyn said, þe water þei fonde.
"Þe wise maisters of þis londe,   Ȝe maistres seid Merlyn . . .
if ȝe can telle vs now here
what meruaile is in þis ryuere,

sais now þe certeynte,	Seyeþ now þe righte.
3e þat deuyned þe dede of me."	
Þe masters alle stille stode;	....þey stod
þei seid noiþer ille ne gode.	
Merlyn to þe kyng gan turne.	Þen toward þe kyng Merlyn..
[49ra] "Do scoupe þis water & turne þe burne;	
sikes 3e do graue & groupe,	
þe water in þam men salle scoupe."	..þer inne...
Þe kyng did folk inouh	..dide come..
þat þe water with scoupes vp drouh.	
Whan þe water was out clene,	
Merlyn schewed what it wald mene.	
He said to þe folk alle at ons	.telde þe folk...
þat in þe grounde lay tuo holle stones;	
bituex þe stones were tuo dragons;	
þat did him mak alle þis somons.	
"Do now þis stones were otuynne,	.þat þo stones..
þe dragons salle 3e fynd þer inne."	
Þei brast þe stones vp als tite	
& fonde a rede dragon & a white;	
þis rede dragon was grym to se,	
felle to fight semed he;	
þe white was so grimly in sight	..was nought so grym of sight
ne so felle semand to fight.	
"Sir kyng," seid Merlyn, "to me þou herk:	
þise dragons fordid þi werk,	.two dragons...
for whan þi werk on heght larged,	
þe grounde satled & þam ouercharged;	Þen schok þe ground &..
þan moued þei, þe water alle quoke,	..þey hem....
& þe werk abouen to schoke.	
Of þat I say, nouht I leih."	...seyde nought y ne ley
Vp into þe aiere þe dragons fleih	
& fauhte so long it was selcouht;	
flammes of fire com of þer mouht.	.as fyr fley fro..
Alle þe folk said comonly,	
þe rede þei hopid suld haf mastri.	Þey hoped þe rede..þe maistri
What þei had long togidir smyten,	When.....
spouted sperkes, bolued & biten,	Spatled spouted belewed..
wipped with wenges, ouerwarpen & went,	Wyppyng..ouer wepen..
kracchid with clawes, rombed & rent,	Cracchyng..rubbed & brent
þe batelle lasted day & nyght	
vnto þe toþer day light.	....was lyght
Þe folk wondred þat þe white dragon	

to þe rede had any foson;
at þe ende, þe white a flaume kast
þat þe rede bolned & brast.   . . . bolnede . .
Whan it was dede, þe rede dragon,
[49rb] þe white ȝede & laid him doun;
þre dais he lyued & no mo,
þe ferth day he diede for wo.   . . . . . y trowe for wo
Vortiger þat sauh þis chance
asked Merlyn þe signifiance,
& praied him telle what it wild mene,
whedir it tokned ioy or tene.
Merlyn said þan many þinges:
what in þis lond suld tide of kynges
þat in Blase boke is writen;   . are in Blase bokes write
þo þat it haf, þei it witen,   Þey þat hauyt mowe hit wyte
& in Tholomer & sir Auntayn;   . . . . . Amytayn
þise had Merlyn bokes playn.
Þise þre wrote his prophecies
& were maistres at sere parties.   . were his . . . .
Som haf þam mykille in hande
þat can not þam vnderstande.
I say for me, I haf no witte
to open þe knottis þat Merlyn knytte;
non may say more þan he has said,
ne nouht þerto may be laid.
Merlyn spak on suilk manere
tille it be gon, non may it lere.
Þe king held Merlin in mikylle prise,   [*The second scribe begins in P*.]
ffor his saing was sothe & wyse.
In Vortiger time, Merlin, men told,   . . . men hit told
he was þat time tuelue ȝere old.   . . . . bot twolf . .
Þe king besought him þat he wild seie
what maner dede he suld dye.   . . deþ þat he schold .
"Sir king, to wite haues þou desire.
War þe wer þe wele fro fire,   Al way war þe wel . .
ffro Constant childir þat are comand,
and sone salle ariue here on land.
Þou signifise þe rede dragoun
þat slou þer broþer þrou tresoun,   . ffader & broþer slowe wyþ .
& it menis þer bataille strong
þat þou haues þer lond with wrong.   . . hast halde . . . .
Þe white dragoun es signefiance
þat þei salle take of þe vengeance.

An euelle þou didis, þou slou þer broþer,   ffful yuel þou slowe þer ffader & .
þou made þe king, þat es a noþer.
Þe þrid combrance þat ȝitt þe mons,
[49va]   [*The first scribe resumes in P.*]
þou resceyued þe paiens Sessons.
On alle half comes þi wo;
þe Sessons wille þe waite to slo.
Þe toþer half þe heires salle com
& aske þer lond of þe þorgh dome;
þei ere now sailand in þe see,
be tyme I rede þat þou fle.   Awey by tyme y rede þow .
Þei salle aryue vp at Toteneis
to morn with hors & herneis;
to ren on þe, þei salle þam renge,
fadere & broþer þei salle venge.
Þer þou wote best refute to haue,   . . wenst best recet . .
fle now suyth þi self to saue.
Ȝit salle I warne þe of þis þing:
Aurelius salle first be kyng
& he salle lyf bot a stounde,   . . . lyue nought . . .
þorgh poyson salle he be brouht to ground.
Vter, his broþer, after salle be   . . . after hym . .
kyng & regne als did he.
Vter sone coms out of Cornwaile   . . schal com fro .
als a feihtand bore in bataile.   . . fyghtyng bor . .
Þe traitours of þe þat he may fynde,
he salle fordo & alle þare kynde.
Of pruesse he salle haf pris   . . . . haue þe pris
& distroye alle his enmys."
Merlin left & spake no more;   [*The second scribe begins in P.*]
at Vortiger he toke leue þore,   Þen fforteger tok his leue .
ne Vortiger duellid nouht;   ffo þes tydynges dwelt he .
of Merlin wordis he had þouht.   On . . was al his þought
Þe toþer day, as Merlin said,
Toteneis was be layd   . . vmbyleyd
with schipes with þe childir ost
& spred aboute be þat cost.
Bretons herd þat & were bliþe;
þei gadird þem & þidir swiþe
to þat were or sundird wide,   Þo . . a sondred ful .
come to Toteneis on ilk a side;
lordis ridin & fote men ran,
Bretons were bliþe ilk a man.

Hengist before had done þam sculk
in wodis, in hillis to krepe & hulk,
& had slayn nere alle þe barouns
[49vb] with þer sexis of þe Sessons.
Þei were þan bold for þer coming.
Þei toke Aurelius & made him king;
with þe Bretons was blis eneugh, ...ynough
& þret Hengist to wakin his wouh.
Þis tiþing come to Vortiger
þat Aurelius & Sir Vter
were comen & had sesid þe lond,
þem to venge ȝif þei him fond.
For þat tiþings & þo tales,
he fled & wanisid him in Wales. ...warnyschet...
Genoyre hight his castel name;
I ne wote ȝif it haue nov þe same.
Þe hille hight Cloart þer men it kennis,
beside Wye, a water þat rennes. & byside þe water of Weye.
Þe contre þat it standis in,
þe name þer of hiht Hergrin. .....Dergryn
Þidir gadird his folk & þer vitaille
& warnisid it ȝif ouht might vail. .warnyschet hem....
Þis ȝong king & his broþer
with mani a Breton, one & oþer,
& folk with him þat he brouht,
in Wales, Vortiger þei souht.
Þei beseged his castelle Genoire .byseced straite his castel
& fondit ȝif þei might it peire. ffele arewes þey schotten & quarel
Þei cast þer to on mani gate;
þei had þer to fulle grete hate.
In þe ost was þe erelle of Gloucestre,
of Wales he knew alle þe estre;
Eldof he hight, man of honour
& herdy kniht, gode wereour.
Þe King Aurelius askid him rede
ffor to venge his broþer dede, ...his fader ded
& said, "Sir Erelle, þou forgetis ilk dele
þat my fadir feffid þe wele
& gaue þe armis & made þe kniht;
siþen my broþer in alle his might,
& if þou louedis him feitfully, ...louedest.feyþfuly
help me to venge his enmy.
Lat nov no gode wille be wane,

	bot help to venge my fadir bane,	
	& þink hov he þe paens drough	Þenk o þe Payens þat sexes drow
[50ra]		[*The first scribe resumes in P.*]
	þat Hengist at þe parlement slouh."	& at þe Parlement þe lordes.
	Whan Eldolf herd he mad suilk mone,	
	þei cried, "Has armes!" euerilkone	
	to mak assaute to þam withinne,	
	bot þe castelle was ille to wynne.	
	Þei comandid þat alle olike	..to al men lyk
	with brusche suld com & fille þe dike.	
	Whan it was fulle, fire þei fet	
	& on a lowe at ons it set;	
	þe low was mykelle & vpward stegh	
	þat it in to þe castelle fleih	
	& vp in to þe toure it went	
	þat alle þe houses about brent.	
	Castelle, hous, & þer atire,	.houses wyþ al..
	man & best alle was on fire.	
	Tille alle was brent wald it not blynne;	
	þe kyng himself was brent þer inne,	
	& alle his folk, euerilkone	
	brent to dede, bodi & bone.	
	Of ilk a traitoure suilk is þe ende;	
	laste of his life with ille salle wende.	
	Of a traitoure is alle of spoken;	
	of Hengist walde þe kyng be wroken.	
	Whan Aurelius & sir Vter	
	were venged wele on Vortiger,	
	alle þe lond ouer alle aboute	
	with luf he did it tille him loute.	
	Whan he wist þat alle þe land	
	was vnto his wille bowand,	
	he said he wild no langer bide;	
	agayn þe Sessons wild he ride,	
	delyuer þe lond of þam clene.	.....al klene
	"Þei haf vs wrouht mykelle tene."	...do ful mykel.
	Hengist herd þo tyþinges say,	
	toward Scotland he toke his way;	
	þe south cuntre he alle forsoke,	
	ouer Humber þe way he toke.	
	At Scottes & þe Peihtes þere,	
	he hoped of help if nede were.	
	Þe kyng him spied, whan he it wist,	...spedde....

toward þe north after Hengist.
Whan Bretons herd þe kyng passed Humbere,
[50rb] so fele com myght non þam nombere. ..to hym come men myghtem nowt.
Toward þe north alle waste he fond,
was þer non left mot tille þe lond.
Castels broken, tounes brent,
Holy kirk robbed & schent, ..was broke &.
paiens Sessons alle had reft, Þyse Payens Saxoyns...
þe kyng sauh nouht was left.
Alle he hight it to restore
if he had life eft to com þore. 3yf he myght lyue & eft..
Whan Hengist herd þe kyng cam, ..wyste þat...
for him he wist þe way he nam; .drede he ne wyste what wey..
fer to fle, it myght not vaile,
nede bord him stand to bataile. Bot nede he mest byde.
He called his folk & bad þam reste.
"ffelawes," he said, "what is þe beste?
Þis Bretons folow fast & nehi; ...vs faste & ney
vs behoues be quaynte & slehi.
In bataile now we wille vs fraiste; ...þey...
loke þat 3e be trewe & triste.
Drede not þer grete company:
if we stand, þei wille son flie. ..wel stande sone schul þey.
Wele 3e wote what Bretons are,
þei faynte son if non þam spare.
Standes stifly a þrow agayn, .styf & truely.
þan gif þei bak & þe felde alle playn.
We schul þen of hem make feldes pleyn
With litille folk many a tyme, .fewe we han seyn...
we haf þam sundred & smyten in suyme.
Mak 3e no force of þer grete oste; Tak 3e non hede of þeyr..
wele 3e wate þei ere bot boste.
A fals folk we febille heued, & fals folk wyþ..
for þam our wed salle not be leued.
He is a childe þat þam ledis
& kan nouht 3it of suilk dedis,
& we ere noble werreours
& has ben proued in many stoures.
Standes now wele agayn 3our fo,
raunsoun for vs non may go.
Defend our lyues, best is to chese,
now alle to wyn or alle to lese."
Whan Hengist had þam comforted þus,

þey armed þam alle at a frusse
& rode fulle soft & semely
[50va] agayn þe Bretons withouten cri.
Þei hoped vnarmed þe Bretons mete
& alle vnarmed on þam schete. ..vnwarned...
Bot þe Bretons, ilk a conrey,
were als wele armed as þei;
þei had of þe Paiens drede,
nyght & day armed þei ʒede.
Þe kyng herd say þei com þat side
& to bataile þei wild abide;
a felde þei chese faire & brode,
he went þidere & þer abode.
Þre þousand knyghtes of his meyne .hundred....
þat com with him ouer þe see,
alle douhti knyhtes fro ferne fette, ...ferne he fet
bi þe to side alle were sette. Boþe batailles þen sone..
Of þe Walsch he toke tuo companyes,
pathe to waite, stretes & styes,
þat þe paiens suld for no nede
þe hilles take, if þam felte drede,
& þe wodes he did so loke
als wele, þat non þam toke,
þat if any þidire drowe,
þe Walsch men sone þam slowe;
þe stalworthest to fight & fende,
his awen bataile suld be hende.
Whan his barons were set & dight, ..batailles....
renged alle redi to fight,
þe men of kith þat he wele knewe, ...kuythe....
þat he wist were treist & trewe,
þam he did bere his banere
& he fro þo was nouht fer.
Sir Eldolf was euer him bi
& oþer Barons also were nehi.
"Lord," said Eldolf, "had I þat grace
Hengist forto mete in place,
wele burd me þe treson mene .oughte....
þat is on þe playn ʒit sene;
þe floure of alle þis empire
was slayn beside Ambirschire,
þe day first of clene May.
With mykille I scaped away; ..wo y..

vnneþis to Gloucestre I cam	. . . . wan
[50vb] þat þei were slayn ilk a man."	Elles had we be slayn . . .
Als sir Eldolf þus ment his mone,	
com Hengist & his men ilkone	
& vmbileid alle þe felde,	
redi armed with helm & schelde.	
Nouht fulle long sen þei were comen	Sone after þat . . .
þat þe bataile was with þam nomen;	
boþe þe parties felonly hated,	. partys ful felly .
þe soner togidere þei þam abated.	. . . . . raped
Þer mot men se strokes sette	
bituex enmys þat smertli mette;	. . . scharply .
sore he smote þat smerte couht smyte,	[*Om. L*]
bitterly bote þat best myght bite.	[*Om. L*]
Ilkone peyned oþer to slo	[*Om. L*]
for euerilkone was oþer fo.	[*Om. L*]
Mercy was on noiþer partie,	. was non . . .
ne no raunson bot alle suld die.	
Þorgh schelde & hauberk lances brast,	. Plate & hauberk þe spere out .
doun to dede ilk oþer kast;	
þat doun was cast, die suld nede,	. . . . þem lye most .
hors & man opon þam ȝede.	
Fulle wele fauht þe paien men	
& mykelle bettere þe cristen.	. . . þan dide Cristen
Þe paien force fast gan falle,	Bot sone after þer force . .
oppon þer goddes þei cried alle.	
Þe cristen cried help to criste	
agayn þe paien force Hengiste;	
þe cristen men þer batale brak	
& sondred þam þat þei gaf bak.	When þey wer sondred þey turd þe .
Many were slayn as þei fled,	
fleand þei sparpled & spred.	
Whan Hengist sauh his folk fleand,	
his force failed & myght not stand.	
Þei fleh to þe castelle of Coningesborgh;	
he wend haf bene saued þer þorgh.	
Þe kyng it herd & after ȝerne	
to entre þe kastelle he wald him werne.	Þe entre of þe Castel him for to werne
He cried & said, "Folow fast & slo,	& cried þen faste folewe we to .
for þise ere þei þat did ȝow wo!"	
Whan Hengist herd þe kyng him sued,	
þorgh castelle wild he not be rescued;	
it was bot pyne, wele had he herd,	

[51ra]	withouten socoure in kastelle be sperd;	
	leuere him were hold him withoute,	
	auenture him he was in doute,	Þat held he betere & lasse.
	þan þe kastelle closed inne,	. yn castel be closed.
	for he ne wist who suld him out wynne.	
	He sauh no þing mygh more auaile	3it þoughtym best myght hym.
	þan forto stand to bataile.	To relye his folk & gyue.
	He gadred his folk þat were ostray	
	& said he suld 3it mak assay.	ffor he wolde 3it eft..
	Þe paiens to bataile turned agayn,	
	fulle egrely, boþe knyght & suayn,	
	ageyn þe cristen hardeli	
	& discried þam with a cri.	. ascryed þem þanne wyþ a gret.
	At þer criyng, þe cristen lees,	. þat comyng...
	so stifly þe paiens on þam gan pres.	
	Greuous & grym was it to se,	Grysly......
	fo noiþer partie wald biþeli fle.	Syn.. wold blyþely.
	In auenture was þe kynges side,	
	bot his men halp wele þat tide,	.. þre hundred knyghtes....
	þat com out of Litelle Bretayn,	
	opon þe paiens þei mad bargayn.	ffor þis Paiens þey feld doun playn
	Vpon þe paiens þei trauersede þe felde	
	& þe kynges side wele vphelde,	
	bot þe paiens so fast fouht,	
	þei hoped of no socour þat douht	
	& wist wele þat þei myght nouht	ffor wel þey wyste þat þe ne myght
	ascaped þorgh force of fight;	Ascape wyþoute strengþe..
	þerfor þei fauht as þei were wode,	
	abated þam bold & stifly stode.	
	Als þei were boldest in þer baret,	
	Eldolf & Hengist togider met.	
	Sir Eldolf Hengist wele knew;	
	his herte agayn him gros & grew;	
	if it so did, fulle wele it auht,	
	grete encheson mad þam vnsauht.	
	He þanked god he hoped fulfille	. preied to God his desir.
	of Hengist forto haf his wille.	
	With scharp spere tille him he ran	.. swerdes to gyder þey.
	& Hengist kept him als a man,	
	Eldolf stroke fulle wele he sat,	
	Hengist agayn anoþer smat;	
	þer myght men se tuo iuste & turne	.... fighteres bolde
[51rb]	for doute of dede non wild scurne.	. dynt of deþ spare þey ne wolde

With scharp suerdes þei dubled dyntes, — .swerdes of werre double.
þe sparkes fleh as fire of flyntes;
if Eldolf help ne had ben nehi,
Hengist had had þe better parti.
Bot þe erle Gorleus of Cornwaile
com in alle þe most trauaile.
Whan Eldolf sauh þe erle cam,
more hardynes in herte he nam,
for belde of him to Hengist went — fful egrely þanne til Hengist he went
& bi þe naselle him he hent, — ...vyser he hym.
& held it tille on seised his nek; — ...til he had sesed..
þe paiens were mate with þat chek.
"Merci, Ihesu, þat þou it wilde, — Þanked be Iesu....
þat I haf ȝerned, now is fulfilled;
now haf I taken our most fo
þat has vs wakned many wo;
þis is þe honde, wo mot him be,
þat neuer of vs had pite.

[*L adds:*] Þis hound y soughte now y hym fond
He was heued to struye þis lond

Sir erle, þis honde, þis comlyng,
on my halue present him þe kyng, — ....hym to þe kyng
& say his enmy is ouercomen.
Now þis honde, Hengist, is nomen."
Þan was Hengist fouly schent,
fettred, to þe kyng him sent.
Þe kyng did him kepe fulle streite,
in chynes bonden fo desceite. — .cheynes.for deseit
Hengist sone þat hight Octa,
& his cosyn, sir Ebissa,
with mykille pyne boþe escaped;
Ȝork to take þei þam raped.
Bot whan þei had þe toun taken,
warly þei waited & held þam waken.
Þe toþer þat left fled here & þere,
be dounes & dales, in wodes aiwhere.
Þe kyng was ioyfulle þat he so sped,
Hengist taken & his folk fled;
to Konyngesburgh þe kyng gan turne,
þerin þre daies he mad soiorne,
þe wounded for to hele & rest,
þe paiens fro þe cristen kest.
In þat tyme þat þei þer lay,

[51va] þe barons alle, þe toþer day, .Bretons....
to conseile þe kyng kalled þam to,
of Hengist what were to do; Þe best to wite....
whedir þei red him forto slo, .Hengist þey reddem hym to.
hold him in prison, or late him go. Or hym enprisone....
A bisshop ansuerd, sir Eldadus,
sire Eldolf boþer, & said þus: .Eldokes broþer & seide right.
"I deme Hengist þe same wayes
als in þe bible of Samuel sais.
Samuel did Agag to dede,
Kyng of Amalech was þat quede,
a fulle proude kyng, riche & kene,
tille godes folk he did ay tene. ....wroughte al tene
At alle his myght wo þam wrouht [*Om. L*]
& euer werre on þam souht. [*Om. L*]
He robbed þer godes & tounes brent
& slouh alle þat he myght hent;
suilk mischefe myght not dure.
He was taken at a discomfeture
& brouht befor Saul þe kyng,
how he had don to here endyng. ffor his mysdedes to haue demyng
Saul asked what iugement
Agag suld haf or he went. Schuld Agag haue er þat..
Þan ros þe prophete Samuel,
kepere of þe folk of Israel,
& opon Agag handes laid,
tille him & alle þis wordes said:
'Agag, þou has manyon trauailed,
manyon slayn, manyon assailed,
many lond mad waste & wilde,
many widow, many faderles childe.
Þorgh þe has bene lorn & slawen,
many saule of body drawen; ..& bodies brought of dawe
þe same waies salle þi soule be refte;
childeles for þe þi mode be lefte.' ...þy moder ys left
Agag siþen he alle to hewe,
þorghout þe cuntre þe peces threwe
& said, 'Ouer alle þou has don wo;
of þe ouer alle salle wondryng go.'
Als þe prophete gaf dome þorgh lawe,
so suld ȝe do Hengist of dawe." .schal...to drawe
Whan Eldolf herd him so say
[51vb] & haly schewed euen way, .þat holy wryt schewed þat..

smertly with þe dome alle hote,
Hengist hede of he smote.
Þe kyng did lay þe body in graue
on þat maner þat paien salle haue.   I þe manere of Payen lawe
Siþen quicly þe kyng him sped,
dight his ost, to ȝork þam led.   He ȝared his host....
[*L adds:*] Þe toun & his enemys for to wynne
Hengist sone þan was þerin
& many lordes of his kynd,   .oþer manye lordynges þer ware
& som in þe cuntre myght men fynd.   .....in mykel kare
Þis Octa studied in his þouht;
to stand to fens auauile nouht.
Socour to send, he wist of non;
þer socour was foreuer gon.
He couth se no better bote
bot forto falle þe kyng to fote.   .auntre & falle....
Felle it to wisdom or foly,
he suld auenture him merci to crie,   ..auntre....
& alle his men red him þertille,
neuerþeles it was his awen wille.
Out of þe toun ilkon þei cam   ...Tour...
als prisons barefote þei nam.
Octa had don, in stede of streeng,
about his nek a chyne heeng,
& on his knees, fulle myldely, ...fel mekely
& said, "Sir kyng, Merci, Merci!
Alle our godes ere vs failed,
þat we on trowe nouht auailed.   ....haue vs nought vailled
Þi god is of more myght;
þat we in leue ere not so right.
He schewes miracle for þi loue;
we ere bineth & þou aboue.
We ere ouercomen, þerfor I com
merci to haf, to þe we nom.
Haf here þis chyne & do þi wille.
Whedir þou wille vs saue or spille,
we ere paid whedir þou wilt.
I am oknowe I haf þe gilt,   We arn aknowe we haue agilt
to haf our lyues if þou it grant,
what so þou sais we hold conant
to serue þe tille our lyues ende
ne neuermore agayn þe wende."
[52ra] Þe kyng was fulle of pite.

He said, "Lordynges, what say ȝe?
What conseile wille ȝe me gyue,"
he said, "rede ȝe þat þei lyue?"
Þan spak þe Bisshop Eldadus
vnto þe kyng Aurelius:
"Wele is worþi mercy to haue
þat mekely mercy wille craue;
ageyn mercy who so is grym,
god has not mercy on him. . wyl haue no mercy of.
To þi mercy þei mad assay,
mercy þei seke haf, if þei may.
Bretayn is large & long,
in many stedes waste among.
Delyuer þam lond þer ȝe se skille,
late þam trauaile þeron & tille;
bot I rede ostage ȝe take,
sikernes þei salle ȝow make,
in alle seruys to be trewe,
& ȝour mercy salle þam be newe.
In þe bible ensample bigan,
þe folk of Gabaoth, þat with wrong wan
of þe Iues & siþen it les,
at þe Iues besouht for pes; . . . þey bysoughte.
of þer wrong asked mercy,
& þei granted alle redy. . . . hem al.
Sen þei had mercy & pite,
wers þan þei suld we not be. . . . schul nought do we
At þe Iues ensample nimmes,
grante þam merci, lyfe & lymmes."
Þe kyng granted þam his pes
as þe bisshop Eldade ches;
biside Scotlond he gaf þam londes;
þei tilled & were gode hosbondes.
Or þei went, he toke ostages,
childere of þer best lynages.
Fiftene dayes his courte gan lie;
he did somon alle þe clergie,
bisshopes, abbotes of þe cuntres, [*Transp. L*]
& gaf þam londes, rentes & fees. [*Transp. L*]
Schireues, bailifes he sett aywhore, . . . sente.
his rentes to gadre & to restore.
[52rb] Masons, wrightes, kirkes did make
þat þe paiens did doun schake,

þat were fordon þorgh Hengist,
were wrouht agayn to serue crist.
ffro þiþen to London he went; .þenne..euene..
þe toun he fond paired & schent,
kirkes, houses beten doun;
to þe kyng þei ment, þam of þe toun,
þat many of þe best burgeis
were fled, & ilk man ȝede his weis.
He bigged it eft þat are was playn,
clerkes, burgeis, did com agayn,
& gaf ilkon agayn þer estre.
Siþen he turned to Wynchestre,
bigged kirkes & houses þere
als he had don elswhere.
Siþen he ȝede to Salebiri
& to þe Abbey of Ambisbiri,
& to þat stede he toke his way
þer Hengist did þe Bretons deie.
Þare biriels he þouht to honoure
with som þing þat ay myght doure,
& frithe þat stede þer þei lay
þat myht last tille Domesday. .hit myght...
He did masons deuyse & cast
what werk mot langest last.
With þe kyng, a clerke was þore,
his name was sir Tremore,
was Archbisshop of Kerlioun.
He did þe king in reson, .seyde..a god reson
if he wild mak a werk of fyne,
"Send ȝour sond to seke Merlyne.
Mak þis werk may no man
gif suilk conseile as he can.
He can ȝow telle what salle betide;
after him, I rede ȝour werk abide."
Þe kyng said, "It salle so be;
mykille I desire Merlyn to se.
Of his wisdom wild I here,
he sais selcouthes many manere." .telleþ wondres on..
At a welle fer in Wales,
Baynes it hight, bi olde tales,

[52va] *[The second scribe begins in P.]*

þe messager þer Merlyn fond.
"Come speke with king, he sent his sond." ...þe kyng....

Whan he come before þe kyng,
ioye he made for his comyng
& honourd him for he was wyse,
& cherisid ouer alle oþer of prise. ..him ouer....
He praid him with fulle louand speche, ..hym wel wyþ louely.
what suld betide he wild him teche.
"Sir kyng," said Merlyn, "certis nay;
to opyn my mouth I dar ne may,
bot if it be a behouely þing at nede
þat were warnyng or tokyn of drede, ...dede
& ȝit with grete lounes of hert ....lownesse..
þat pride turn noght ouertheurt. ...hit nought ouerthwert
ffor if I spake þrow pryde or bost,
or for scorn agayn my gost,
þat ilk gost þat in me wons
þat alle me kennys & alle me mons,
owt of my mouth it wild him draw,
off my conyng reue me my saw,
þat no more myght I speke with mouthe
þan anoþer þat noght ne couthe.
Þerfor of suilk priuete [*The first scribe resumes in P.*]
þink not þer on. Lat it be. ....but let..
Þink on þat whi þou me souhtes;
bring þat ille end whi þou me brouhtes.
If þou wille mak a werk stedfast
þat faire wille euermore to last, ..wyl be & euere to.
send for þe stones þer þei stand
þat þe Geantȝ brouht tille Ireland.
Rounde about ere þei set,
out of Aufrik were þei fet;
ilkon on oþer is set vpright.
No man in erth has now þat myght
forto tak doun o stone,
ne set þam eft, es þer none."
Þan said þe kyng & on him louh,
"It were þan grete ferly how Sertes þat were selcouþ ynow
þat þo stones þat þou of sais
ere so heuy & of suilk pais,
þat non has force ne fosoun
to remoue þam vp ne doun,
[52vb] & ere so fer ouer þe see.
Who myght þam þan bring to me?"
Þan said Merlyn to þe kyng,

"Quayntise ouercomes alle þing.
Strength is gode vnto trauaile.
Þer no strength may, sleght wille vaile;
sleght & conyng dos many a char,
begynnes þing þat strength ne dar;
with sleght may þou þe stones wynne
& in Bretayn set þam in,
þer þou ne salle with strength ...schalt wyþ no strengthe
remoue þam a stone length.
In Aufrik were þei compast & wrouht;
Geantȝ tille Ireland fro þiþen þam brouht
& set þam on a hille fulle hii
with engyns fulle quayntly.
ffirst, whan þei were compast newe,
þei did grete gode to þo þam knewe;
þo þat were seke & lauht scathes, ...or had laught.
wesch þe stones, did it in bathes;
þat felt þam greued of grete þinges,
bathed þam of þe self wasshynges Wasched þem....
& heled wele of þer pyne,
had þei non oþer medicyne."
Whan þe kyng herd of þer vertu
þat þei mot falle þe folk to pru,
he had longyng for þam to go;
& of þat wille were oþer mo
þe stones to Bretayn forto bring
þat Merlyn mad of sermonyng.
Þei ches Vter, þe kynges broþer,
þe kyng offred himself þe toþer;
of folk þei led fiften þousand
agayn þe Iris forto stand.
With þam went Danȝ Merlyn
for þe stones to mak engyn.
Whan Vter with his folk was ȝare,
þei went to schip ouer þe se to fare
& aryued vp bi þat coste;
þe Iris kyng gadred his oste,
agayn þe Bretons þei com ȝerne,
þe lond if þei mighte þam werne.
[53ra] Þis Irisch kyng þat regned þare,
his name was sir Guillomare.
Whan he wist whi þei kam
so fer viage, for þe stones nam

[*L adds:*] He scorned þem on his langage
So fer for stones to make passage

ouer þe see tille anoþer lond,
for þei ne stones hender fond
& said, "Þo stones þei salle haf here,
þei salle bie þam first fulle dere.
If we may, salle not spede ffor ȝyf we may þey . . .
þo stones out of our lond to lede."
He scorned & said, "It salle be nouht;
þei salle faile þat þei haf souht."

[*L adds:*] Þys kyng byhigt hem foul despit
Bot wykke þey were to desconfyt

So long he manaced & þrette,
at þe last, togider þei mette;
at þer metyng was no lite . . . hit was nought lyte
þat þei gon togidere smyte.
Fulle wele fauht boþe parties,
bot þe Bretons wan þe pris;
þe Iris couth not so wele feiht,
ne of armore had þei no sleiht,
ne were þerof so wele bone;
þerfor þe Iris fled fulle sone.
Fro stede to stede þei fled to skulk
on hii hilles to hide & hulk. . heþ & hilles . . in hulk
Whan þe Bretons had don þat chace
& rested þam a long space,
Merlyn had þam alle at ones
to þe hille to se þe stones.
Killomare hight þat hille
þore þe Geantȝ brouht þam tille.
Þis Bretons renged about þe feld,
þe karole of þe stones beheld.
Many tyme ȝede þam about, fful often ȝede þey .
biheld within, biheld without,
alle þei said, so said þe kyng,
þei sauh neuer so selcouth þing.
How þei were raised þei had wondere
& how þei suld be brouht o sondere;
with þat worde þei þam rescued, [*Om. L*]
þei ne wist how þei suld remued. [*Om. L*]
Merlyn said, "Now makes assay
to putte þis stones doun, if ȝe may,
[53rb] & with force fond þam to bere;

þer force is mykille, þe lesse wille dere." ....lesse wyl þem.
Þe oste at ons to þe hille went
& ilk man toke þat he mot hent;
ropes to drawe, trees to put,
þei schoued, þei þrist, þei stode o strut
on ilka side, behynd, beforn,
& alle for nouht, þer trauaile lorn.
Whan alle þe had put & þrist, .þey ofte hadde put..
& ilk man don þat him list
& left þer puttyng manyon,
ȝit stired þei not þe lest ston.
Merlyn wist it suld not vaile,
strength of body ne trauaile. ...ne myght nout vaille
He bad þam alle draw þam odreih,
"Þorgh strength ne com ȝe þam neih."
A litille he stode, siþen him bi went. Al stille he stod....
He spak bot non wïst what he ment;
þei sauh his lippes stir vp & doun,
bot non herd his coniurisoun.
Whan he had gon alle aboute
within þe karole & withoute
& said his coniurisons,
agayn he cald þe Bretons
& said, "Now may ȝe lightly bere
þise stones to schip withouten dere.
Go now alle & spedis ȝow,
for ȝe salle welde þam wele inouh."
Als Merlyn þam tauht & said,
into schippes þam lightly laid;
þan had þei won þei fer had souht,
to þe playn of Salesbiri þam brouht,
of Aumesbiri beside þe abbay,
& was at þe Whitsonenday. .hit was atte Whitemonday
Þe kyng did mak somons
of bisshopes, erles, & barons,
& oþer folk of noble geste, ..lordes of þe nobleste
& did him croune at þat feste.
Þre daies sat þe feste of fode; ..laste þe feste fode
on þe ferth day, gaf he giftes gode:
kroces to clerkes of pris,
to saynt Sampson & saynt Dubris.
[53va] Seynt Dubris he gaf Kerlion,
Ȝork he gaf to saynt Sampson;

þis gaf he at his crounment
& many mo bi comon assent,
bifor þe lordes þat com þider.
Merlyn set þe stones togider;
als þei were ore in þat certayn,
stand þei now vpon þe playn.
Within þe compas of þe stones
er biried alle þe lordes bones
þat Hengist at þe parlement slouh,
here beforn ȝe herd wele how.
Of Vortigere þat þe kyng brent,
was left a sone þat hight Passent.
For drede of Aurelius & Vter,
vnto Almayn he fled fer
& purchesed him folk on þe see .purchaced.....
& aryued vp in þe north contre.
Tounes stroied, contres wasted,
þe kyng herd say & þider hasted. .....sone hym hasted
Whan Passence herd þe kyng cam,
agayn to þe se his way he nam;
þer he com fro, he durst not wend;
vpon Ireland his flete gan lend.
He spak so with þe kyng of þat land
þat he was his wele willand,
vpon Bretayn a route to renge
& on þe Bretons þam to venge.
Passence chalanged his fader wones,
þe kyng for robbery of þe stones;
treuth togider boþe þei plight
to tak vengeance at þer myght
with alle þe force þat þei mot gete,
& in Wales aryued þer flete. In Walsche lond...
Þei spred about ilk cuntre.
Meneue, þei toke þat Cite;
Meneue is langage on Bretoun,
& now it hate saynt Dauid toun.
In þat tyme þat þei com þus,
seke lay our kyng, Aurelius.
At Wynchester, many a day,
long þer bedered he lay
[53vb] þat he mot noiþer couer ne deie
bot euer languest one weie. .ouer more languisched on.
Als he lay seke, bode was him sent

þat Vortiger sone Passent
in Wales was, & þe Iris kyng,
on him to mak chalangyng.
He chalanged him of robberie,
Passent of dede of felony.
Þe kyng said, "Vter for me salle go;
þat I ne may, me is wo."
Vter said, "I am redy."
He did somond alle priuely — His folk somonde . .
with hors & armes redy to ride,
& com to him he suld þam bide;
& long it was in þe somons,
& þe buskyng of þe barons.
Dred þei were þe kyng suld die, — [*Om. L*]
& in to Wales fer was þe weie; — [*Om. L*]
gude stound it was ar he þam wan — God whyle . . . . . .
into Walis ilk a man.
In alle þis drecchyng as þei gon duelle,
of one Appas I salle ȝow telle.
Appas was a Sesson,
wele couth contreue a treson.
He fened him to be a leche,
& couth speke diuers speche.
A day to Passent Appas spak,
treson he þouht & out brak. — . . . . out hit.
"Passent," said Appas, "wele I wote
bituex þe kyng & þe is hatered hote.
What wille þou gif me & I salle go
þe kyng Aurelius forto slo?"
Passent said, "I salle gif þe
a þousand pound of gode mone,
withþi þi word be certeyn
to say me whan þou has him slayn."
Appas said, "Wele I graunt."
Passent said, "I hold couenant."
Appas spak Latyn parfite
& clad him a monkes abite; — . . hym in . . habyt
als a monk, he did him schaue,
contenance couth he fulle wele haue.
[54ra] Venom for salue with him he nam.
Als a monk to courte he cam,
for iuels couth he medicyn make.
Þe kyng, he said, he wild vndertake;

if he wild do at his quayntise,
so he wild do him vp ryse. Sone he scholde....
He tasted his pouce, saw his vryne;
he said he knew his medicyne.
Þe kyng ȝarned his hele mykelle; ..ȝerned...
he wend not a monk were fikelle.
He did him in kepyng of þat feloun
& he gaf him drynk poysoun,
happed him warme & bad him slepe
þat in his lymmes it suld alle lepe.
Whan þis Appas his nedes had sped,
also suythe away he fled.
Sone after in a throwe,
þe kyng it wist & men wele knowe, ...sowe
þat he suld algate deie.
He prayed men suld him leie
at þe stonhenges in graue,
his biriels forto mene & saue.
On þis maner þe kyng was dede
& biried als after his rede.
Vter þat tyme in Wales was
þat þe kyng was poysond with Appas.
Als he was dede, ros a sterne
þat many man beheld ȝerne;
comete is cald in astronomye,
kynges dede wille it signifye;
fro þat com a beam fulle bright
onlik one þat lemed light.
Þe lemyng was both rede & schire
like a dragon þat sparkeld fire.
Was noiþer erle no baron .þer neuere...
þat þei ne likned it tille a dragon:
tuo brondes com out of his mouthe
þat lightend þe est with þe southe; ..Est West & Souþ
opon France lighted þat one,
þe toþer vnto Mongu schone;
þe þrid vnto Ireland ȝede;
in seuen branches gan it sprede,
[54rb] & alle were þei schynand
on þe watere & on þe land.
Þis ilk mervaile þat þus was sene,
men wondred what it mot mene.
Sir Vter, þe kynges broþer,

meruailed more þan any oþer. Hym merueilled . . anoþer
[*L adds:*] Merueillyng he was affrayed
Of þat affray he was nought payed
He praied Merlyn fulle specially
to telle him what it ment & why. Þe toknyng þer of to telle . .
Merlyn sauh it with sir Vter; Þen sey Merlyn þat . .
sore sighyng, he fecched it fer . sykede & feightit fer
& stode als he were in duale,
no worde said bot wex alle pale.
Whan his spirit was comen agayn,
þouht þat may not help es vayn.
"Ihesu he," he said, "sore may þai mone, Seid Merlyn sorewe . . .
alle þat in Bretayn wone;
lorn þei haf þer noble kyng
þat brouht þam of encomberyng . . . . Saxons encombrynge
out of þe paiens Sessons handes . . . false Payens .
þat manyon brouht to bitter bandes."
Whan Vter herd his broþer was dede,
he bicom als heuy as lede.
"Allas," he said, "now has Bretayn
lorn hym þat was a noble cheftayn."
He sighed for sorow, dole was to se.
Merlyn said, "Vter, late be.
Þer not bote es ouer sore ne sorowe;
þe lif may no man bie ne borowe.
Of dede may non no bale bete,
þe sorow bos men nedes lete; . . nedly byhoueþ men .
bot hast þe suythe on þin enmys: . haste . . . . .
of þe bataile þou getes þe pris
of þe Iris kyng & Passent; To morewen schul þey boþe be schent
to morne salle þei boþe be schent. & al þer folk boþ sleyn & hent
Siþen salle þou crowne take, . schaltow þe Coroune .
þe pes to mayntene & to make.
Þe sterne þat þou ses so rede
betoknes euere þe kynges dede;
þe dragon þat semes flaumand so hie,
þiself it menes þat is hardie.
Þe bronde þat schynes of his mouth . . . schyned out of . .
þat spredes boþe este & south,
þat is of þe salle com a sone,
[54va] douhty of dede, manyon salle mone.
Alle France salle to him loute,
vnto Mongu men salle him doute.

Þat oþer þat schone west so euen,
toward þe west it spred in seuen, ..Norþ hit...
a douhter it is, I vnderstand,
þat maried salle be beside Scotland.
Hir heires mene þe seuen brondes
þat salle welde alle þo londes."
Sir Vter listend ilk a dele
how Merlyn comforted him wele.
He bad his oste reste alle nyght,
on morn arely to bataile dyght.
Þe Iris wist whan þei suld com,
þei dight þam & agayn þam nom; & made hem redy alle & some
stalworthly togidir fouht,
þe Iris sone nouh ne douht, Bot þe.. were brought to nought
for þe Iris kyng & Passent
were slayn & þer oste alle schent,
& þo þat with þe life scaped,
to þer schippes fast þam raped;
& þei þam folowed in to þe se, Of þo þat fledden to..
þat was ouertaken, slayn was he.
Whan alle was slayn þey mot ouerhent,
to Wynchester sir Vter went.
In þe way he mette a messenger
þat tald alle tille sir Vtere,
on what maner þe kyng deied
& beried was þer als he seid
at þe stonhenges solemply, .Stonhenges so louely
with þe bisshopes & alle þe clergy.
As Vter com ridand in þe strete,
þe folk on him gon sore grete,
&, "Sir, haf mercy on vs! & seyde.....
Dede is þi broþer Aurelius
þat mayntend vs in alle his myght;
take þou þe croune þat is þi right
& be our hede for we it ȝerne,
& fende vs fro our enmys ferne."
Sir Vter sauh it was to do,
his heritage of blode also. ffor his heritage hit was...
His barons þider he did somoune
[54vb] & made a feste & did him croune.
For Merlyn told þat tokenyng
þat Vter suld be douhty kyng,
& of him suilk heires suld be

named þourh alle cristiente, Alosed þorow out..
& for þe dragon he sauh in sight
bitokend himself kyng þorgh right,
he did mak tuo dragons
þorgh conseile of his barons;
þe ton he did befor him bere
at ilk tyme he ȝede to were;
þe toþer dragon he did wirke,
it hang at saynt Petir kirke. & heng hit at...
For þat skille & þat cheson
was he cald Vter Pendragon.
Pen is hede on Walsche langage,
dragon is said on our vsage.
Pendragon was his toname
in alle his life for þat same.
Octa, Hengist sone, þat was
forgyuen before his trispas, When Aurelius furgaf..
& þe kyng gaf him & his meigne
londes in þe north cuntre,
whan he wist þat he was dede
þat þam þe lond first forbede,
of him he gaf nouht þat was newe;
to him he þouht neuer be trewe.
What did þis schrewe, þis fals Octa,
conseiled with his cosyn Cosa; ....Ebessa
with alle þo of his awen kynde
& oþer Sessons þat þei mot fynde,
& fele of þo with þam went
þat scaped fro þe slauhter of Passent,
þat fro Vter in Weles fled, ..Vter handes fled
þei com to Octa & he þam led.
Biȝond Humber alle þe land
Octa toke vnto his hand,
alle tille Scotland in lengthe & brede.
To ȝork siþen alle þei ȝede,
þe toun forto sege & wyn;
þei fendid it þat was þerin. .defended hem faste wyþyn
Þe kyng þe sege wild remue,
[55ra] þe toun agayns þam rescue;
he þouht not long to abide,
he gadred folk on ilk a side.
Whan he was comen, he abode nouht,
bot on þe paiens bataile souht;

& þe paiens fulle egre & stoute,
þorgh þe Bretons held þam oute.
Paiens, cristen, many were slawen, Payens &....
many saule of body drawen. & many a sowle fro..
Þe Bretons þat tyme myght not spede;
bak þei turned, þei sauh nede;
þe paiens after folowed fast,
& many on to dede kast.

[*L adds:*] Whider to fle þey were al wyl
Þe Payens hem chased vntil an hyl

Damer, þe hille so hight,
þe Bretons toke it, þo þat myght.
Hiie & narow, fulle strayte to prikke,
about busked with hesils þikke. .y busched wyþ þornes.
Whan þe Bretons þe hille had taken,
with sege þe paiens held þam waken;
bot it was at þe nyght,
þam to assaile þei ne myght.
Þei loged þam stille in þe playn,
þe Bretons were in þe montayn;
þe paiens to þer loges gan lepe,
wery þei were & felle on slepe.
Þe kyng had of himself grete drede
& of his folk þat he suld lede,
how he suld escape þam fro;
þer ways were stopped þat þei suld go.
Þe erle of Cornwaile was on þe hille,
Gorleus he hight, a man of skille,
wisest þe held him of ilkon;
to him for conseile þei ment þer mone.

[*L adds:*] ffor he was man of gret queyntyse
& neuere louede no cowardyse

He seid, "For conseile ȝe com me to;
I salle ȝow conseile if ȝe wille so.
Mercy to god first salle we krie
& mende vs alle of our folie,
& pray Ihesu our saueoure
to bring vs fro þis misauntour, .schulde vs fro mysauentour
& gif vs grace & powere
ageyn þis paiens þat sege vs here
þat vs cristen wo has wrouht, ..often wo han vs.
[55rb] & him for Lord knowe þei nouht,
þat he today stande vs bi,

of his enmys to haf maistri.
If he wille help, our Lord Ihesus,
who may þan agayn vs?"
To his conseile granted alle
& opon Ihesu þei gan calle,
& hette to mak amendment,
þat tyme to scape if he þam lent.
"Arme vs," he said, "now priueli, . ȝow . . pryuely
& go we stille withouten kri.
Þei ere on slepe, I am sikere;
þei traueld fast to gif vs bikere.
Þei wene not we dar vs abate,
for þei discomfet vs so late.
Þei hope to morn at þe son risyng,
vs to slo & tak our kyng.
Arme vs suyth & go we doun
withouten any more sermoun."
Þei armed þam sone, knyght & suayn,
priueli com doun in to þe playn,
& fond þam slepand als he said;
vnarmed ilkon were laid.
Whan þe Bretons were spred about,
in þer oste within & without,
þer was slauhter withouten pite;
was non for mercy ȝolden fre.
Þorgh wombes, þorgh brestes, speres bote;
hedes, handes, fete of smote,
to arme þam þei had no space
ne to fle had þei no grace.
[*L adds:*] ȝyf any fledde þat fle myght
Þe merknesse saued þat nyght
Octa & Cosa o lyue þei toke, . . Ebessa . . . .
at London in preson did þam loke.
Whan þis paiens were discomfite,
toward þe north þei went fulle tite,
Northumbirland, Scotland, þorgh rode
als it was fer, long, & brode.
Þo men þat non myght ore iustise,
alle he drouh to his seruyse;
ouer alle he sette suilk pes,
better neuer no man ches.
Whan he was kyng kid fulle couthe, ... kyd & couþ
he toke his gate in to þe southe.

[55va] At London his Pasch he held	
with erle, baron, & knyght of scheld.	
Bisshopes, abbotes he did somoun,	
& riche burgeis & oþer of toun.	
He did comand opon þer life	
þat wedded man suld bryng his wife	
& if he wild, his oþer meigne	*[L differs, four lines:]*
	& oþere honeste of his meyne
þat were auenant in courte to se.	Man or woman wheþer þey be
Man or woman þat were honeste,	Al he bad vntil his feste
alle he bed vnto his feste.	Þat were worþy & honeste
Whan alle were comen þat suld or wild,	
innes taken & fulfillid,	
& at þe kirk seruys said,	
in halles & hales burde laid,	
þe kyng was sette & serued of mes.	
At þe toþer end was a des,	
þer satte þe barons of pris,	
þe erle of Cornwaile agayn his vis;	
bi him sat Igerne his wyfe,	
of hir fairhed was spech ryfe.	
In alle þe regnė so faire was non,	
ne of suilk was þer non.	. . . kynde bot scheo al on
Oft þe kyng had herd hir praise,	
how scho was faire & curtaise;	Þat . . fair god & curteyse
mikelle he desired hir to se.	
Whan he hir sawe, more lufed he;	
þe sight of hir him alle to brast.	. . . . . . to blast
His hert on hir agayn he cast;	
wheder he ete or drank, said ouht or nouht,	
Igerne was euer in his þouht;	
com scho neuer out of his hert,	
to hir was his ie ouerthuert.	. . . his eye euere .
Bi his priueȝ of he hir grette	. . . often hure grette
& his presentȝ befor hir sette;	
oft on hir luke & & on hir louh,	Often hure lout & on . .
& made semlant on hir inouh.	. . . of loue ynow
Hir contenance was & hir semlante,	
scho not withsaid ne, ne nouht grante.	. . ne seyde ne nought wold .
Þe kyng of hir nouht vnderstode	
in contenance bo stable & gode.	. . but . . .
What lauhynges & oþer tihtes,	What for laughynge . . .
what for presentȝ & oþer sightes,	. . . . . delites

[55vb] þe erle perceyued & þouht fulle ȝerne:
þe kyng lufed his wife Igerne.
He þouht þat faith he ne wild him bere
bot he in pes his wife myght were.
Vp he stirte fro þe borde;
to þe kyng he spak no worde.
His wyfe bi þe hand he hent,
& called his knyghtes & þien went.
Hastily þer hors was bone
& to Cornwaile þei com sone.
Ore he was ȝare, redy to wende,
þe kyng comanded, as he was hende,
þat he suld com to courte agayn,
els did he vilte tille his souerayn; Or he dide vylenye...
& if he wild not com blethely,
kepe him wele, he were his enmy. Waite hym wel as for..
Þe kynges sonde he wild not here,
he mad no force of his praiere.
Whan þe kyng wist he wald nouht
com agayn als he besouht,
he manaced him with felle herte,
& said it suld him sore smerte.
For alle þe manace ne wild he bide,
bot he ne wist what suld betide.
Tuo castels he had in Cornwaile,
he warnisced þam with vitaile. Þo he warnisched..
In þe castelle of Tintagelle
he did his wyfe to kepe welle;
of defens it his grete los, ..hit hadde gret.
with see & fen it is in clos. .dyk & se hit...
Whoso kepes þe ȝate in nede,
in oþer stede þar him not drede;
þer he did hir be ȝemed & sperde Þer inne scheo was ȝemed..
& he tille his oþer castelle ferde.
Þider he led his souders
to kepe þe kyng at sautes sers.
In þat castelle þat he to cam I þat Castel was þat...
was alle þe force of his erledam.
The kyng wist he mad purueance
agayn him at stand to chance; ..to stand..
þe kyng als son purueyd oste,
þer þe erle was, biseged þat coste.
[56ra] Þe castelle þat þe erle was in,

he biseged it for to wyn;
alle a seuenyght þe kyng þer lay, ..wyke....
he spilte his tyme, sped of no pray.
Of þe erle nouht he wan,
ne did scathe to no man,
for þe erle kepte euer þe comyng
him to socour, þe Irisch kyng.
Þe kyng sauh þe sege was waste,
Igerne to haf he wild him haste.
He was gretly anoyed
þat his tyme so destroyed.
He cald Vlfyn, his priue baron,
to conseile him of gude reson.
"Vlfyn," he said, "conseile þou me;
my best conseile I tak of þe.
On Igerne I am anamorde strong.
I die if it last long.
I ne may slepe, wo I waken; ....wyþ wo y wake
so am I in hir luf taken,
ete no drynk may I nouht,
hir luf benethen has me so brouht; So lowe hure loue haþ me.
luf has me wonded, dede I drede. .dereþ me so to deye..
I ask conseile how I may spede."
Said Vlfyn, "I here meruailes!
Þou lufes his wife & him assailes.
Wenes þou þerwith to be aboue,
þorgh were to wyn his wife to loue?

[*L adds:*] Hure to loue þou com to late
Hure loue to gete hure lord to take

At whom toke þou þat conseile,
to luf in tene & with tirpeile?
Conseile of þis can I non kest;
of suilk conseile Merlyn can best.
He can inouh of suilk craftes,
of alle figures he turnes þe schaftes." ..vigures....

[*L adds:*] ȝyf he can kenne þe no weye
Igerne to wynne can no man seye

Þorgh þe conseile of Vlfyn,
þe kyng sent after Merlyn;
Merlyn com þe kyng beforn.
He said, "Merlyn I am forlorn; .....ner lorn
conseile me if þat þou can,
& I salle euer be þi man.

I haf nere lorn witte & life
for Igerne, þe erles wife.
[56rb] Help me now, þat I hir haue,
& what þou wilt I vouch it saue."
"Sir kyng," said Merlyn, "god forbede
þat þou for hir suld be in drede,
in drede for to haf þi dede. ffor Igerne to haue þe ded
Are suld I do an oþer rede,
þou salle hir haf withouten pyne,
bot I wille haf no þing of þine. & ȝit wol y haue nought..
Bot, sir Vter, þou wote it wele:
strong es þe holde of Tintagele,
& scho is loken þerin so straite,
bot þorgh quayntise or disceite
no man may hir out take
þorgh engyne þat man may make,
for tuo men þat without be ....oughtes be
may kepe þe issheu & þe entre;
& þof alle be it wik to wyn,
fulle wele I salle do þe þerin. ..schal y þe brynge.
For alle maner forme þat es
kan I turne þe liknes; ...til oþer.
a face forto be like anoþer,
& his agayn vnto þe toþer. .a body vnto þat oþer

[*L adds:*] Stature of body speche & heryng
& countenaunce of ylka þyng
Y schal chaunge what so þey are
Ilkon schal wene þat oþer ware

Þe erle specially with him ledes
tuo knyghtes, douhti of dedes;
sir Bretelle hate þe ton, .Bertel þen...
þe toþer hate sir Iordon;
þise er his priue conselors.
To þer liknes I salle tourne ours:
in þe erls liknes I salle þe dight,
& I salle be Bretelle, his knyght, Y schal be lyke Bertil..
like Iordon salle be Vlfyn.
Þus salle we com þe castelle in:
alle þre at euen salle we go
to þe castelle withouten mo,
& speke þer speche & þer facounde.
We salle com in on a stounde;
drede þe not of no man

for quayntise þat any kan, ffor no....
& þou salle haf hir at þi wille,
þi grete ȝernyng to fulfille."
Alle þat euer Merlyn teld,
als gospelle þe kyng it held.
[56va] Þe kyng comandid tille on certayn,
þe oste to kepe tille he com agayn.
Merlyn þam charmed þorgh vertue,
colore & cloþing did remue,
contenance, spech þe same asise.
He turned þe kyng on þe erles wise
& he & Vlfyn be þo sightes, ...to alle.
als Bretel & Iordon his knyghtes. ....þe Erles knyghtes
At euen þei com to Tintagelle,
& þo þat wend haf knowen þam welle
resceyued þam with glad chere
als þer erle leue & dere. .hit were þe Erl...
What þei wild, non wild þam werne;
þe þat nyght lay bi Igerne, Þe kyng lay þat nyght..
& scho conceyued of him þat nyght
Arthure, þat was so mykille of myght.
In þe oste was it told on one
þat non wist whidire þe kyng was gone.
His ordenance þei alle forsoke
þat to þe kyng kepyng toke;
þei armed þam to mak assaute
for þei had of hede defaute,
& went forth in þe morne tide;
non for honour wild oþer bide, .for oþer...
ne bataile set ne rightly renge, Of bataille set þey no right.
bot ilkone forth þe kyng to venge.
Was þer non held right aray [*Om. L*]
bot ilkone went to þe assay; [*Om. L*]
[*L differs, four lines:*]
on ilk a side þei gaf batayle, Þen gon þey assaille boþ fer & hende
þe erle agayn gan fast assaile. Þe Erl ageyn þem faste ga fende
As he & his stode þem to fende, As he stod er he lest wende
he was slayn or þei wende. He was schot to deþe & made his ende
Whan he was dede, his side gan slaken,
lighly was þan þe castelle taken. Lightly.....
Þo þat ascaped with þe life
brouht tiþing to þe erles wife.
Hir lord was slayn in þe mornyng,

þe castelle taken vnto þe kyng.
Þe kyng himself þo tiþinges herd;
he stirt vp & þam ansuerd,
"Late be þo tales, þei be not trod.   ..ȝour tales to tene my wyf
I am o life, I tanke it god.   Y þank God y am her on lyf
[56vb] To telle suilk tales men to greue,
lesynges ere not forto leue.   ..nought to byleue
I wote wele þei er in doute;
vnwarned fro þam I went oute.
For whan I out of þe castelle ȝede,
I spak to non, þat is þer drede,
ne said whidir þat I suld go
for doute & drede of my fo;   ...treson...
& for I com not suyth agayn,
wene þei now þat I am slayn.
Bot þat my folk doun is born,
slayn, & þe castelle lorn,
it may do tene & greuance;
bot I lyf, þank god þat chance.
I salle me haste, out wille I wende,
pes to seke, þe kyng is hende;
are any more scaþe falle,
I wille acorde with þam alle."   ...me wiþ þem.

[*L adds:*] ȝyf he wyþ sege sperre me her yn
More wo þan ys þen scholde bygyn

To þat conseile Igerne red.
Alle tymes þe kyng scho dred.
In armes boþe ilk oþer hent,
þe kyng hir kist & out he went.
Whan þei were passed alle þre,
ilkon was as felle to be
& com dryuand vnto þe oste,
for þe erle he spired moste.
"Who gaf conseile forto go
þe castelle take, þe erle to slo?"
Þe sothe sone was him told
of on & oþer, simple & bold.
Þe kyng þerfor was wo inouh;
he wrathed with þam þat him slouh.
Bot long ne wild he þerfor morne;
to Tintagelle agayn gan torne,
& to þam of þe castelle spak
& said, "I rede ȝe turne bak, ...ȝour bak

for he þat bataile on me beede,
þe erle, ȝour lord, he is dede.
Of non salle ȝe fynd socoure
agayn me to stand in stoure."
Whan þei herd þe kyng þus said,
þer socour lorn, þer hede doun laid,
[57ra] þe castelle on one to him þei ȝold
& lete him do what he wold.
He ȝede on one to Dame Igerne.
Als he had don told hir ȝerne,
alle how he bi hir lay,
& how he went fro hir away.
"I am," he said, "withouten wyfe
& þou ert singelle woman of lyfe;
I wille þe wed if þou wilt so."
Igerne consented wele þer to: Dame Igerne consented . .
"Of no disceit ne wist I,
bot of þi weddyng grant mercy."
Þe childe scho had conceyued beforn,
whan tyme felle, it was born.
Arthure was þe childes name,
a noble man of grete fame.
A douhter þei had, Anne scho hight,
þat gyuen was tille a douhti knyght,
vnto sir Loth of Lonneis.
His sone was Wawan þe curteis.
Siþen regned Vter long
& þan felle in an euelle strong;
bedrede long he lay . doun ful longe . .
& languysced fro day to day. . . so forþ fro . . .
Þo þat kept Octa, Hengist sone,
& Cosa at London in presone, . Ebessa . . . .
þei were greued of long lokyng,
& Octa gaf þam mykille þing.
For giftes gyuen often & grete,
þei lete þam scape of prison lete . . . . of þe prison sket
& went with þam ouer þe see
in to Sessone, þaire contre.
Octa þer gadred grete oste,
toward our kyng he lewe boste. . . . þey blewen bost
He purueid him a flote on flode
with knyghtes & with archers gode; . men of armes & . .
toward Scotland þei gan vp ryue,

robbed & brent, men brouht of lyue.
Oure kyng þat lay in langoure,
of him was no help, no socoure;
his lond forto fend no were,
he myght not rise armes to bere.
[57rb] Þerfor he bad alle his barons
to do after sir Loth somons,
for he was knyght of gode auys, ...doughti noble & wys
douhty man, large & wys. & sley Cheuentayn of god auys
Sir Octa þat had folk inouh,
þe Bretons ouer robbed & slouh. Oueral þe Bretons þei pyled..
He bolded him with mykille pride
þat þe kyng myght go ne ride. ...ne myghte...
[*L adds:*] To meschef he putte al þat he fond
Man & wyf þorow al þys lond
Bot Loth oft with him mette
& oft chaced him with barette;
many tyme of him he wan
& him oft ouer ran. .eft on hym þat oþer.
[*L adds:*] Hit ys Custume þat werre bygynne
Some to lese & somme to wynne
Loth fulle son did him fle Lot ful often...
& chaced him vnto þe se;
bot grete disdeyn of þe Bretons ....þe Barouns
þat wild not go at Loth somons, ...come for Lotes.
þam þouht þam als gentille of blode
& als mykille in stede stode
at ilk tyme or more þan he,
& als mykelle of rent & fe;
þus þei deleyd, long was þe drede, ..delayed....
to þe kyng sawe how it ȝede.
For Octa, alle þe north he wan,
& of þe south to saynt Alban;
þis wan he for þe barons defaut
þat for Loth wild gif non assaut.
Alle þe lond to þe kyng pleyned
þat þe barons alle þam feyned.
Bot here now of þe kyngis wille.
He ne left for sekenes ne for ille
þat he ros vp fulle austere
& did mak him a littere,
kirneld as a hors bere, Corneled....
& said þus þat alle myght here:

"Now salle I se who salle withstand
& who wille com at my sond."
He somond þo tille his were .. firste þo ...
þat deyned not for Loth com nere;
þei com & were sore of grisen .... ful sore agrysen
whan þei wist þe kyng was risen.
To þe toun of Verolhram .... Wyrolhram
þe kyng & alle þe barons cam.
[57va] At saynt Alban þer ligges he,
Verolhram hate þat cite.
Þe kyng com þat toun to wyn, Þer com þey to þe toun wyþ.
Octa & his were alle þerin.
Þe kyng seged it aboute,
did mak engynes strong & stoute;
þe toun was so strong & fyne,
it had no doute of non engyne.
Octa & his were fulle bold;
þei had gode folk & siker hold,
& seid it was schame to bere fere .... neuere fere
for a half dede man in a bere; Of half a dedman lyggyng on.
for to hold þer ȝates loken Ne for swyche on to kepe þe..
& cowardise of þam be spoken; Cowardyse of vs scholde..
for to haf of suilk on drede
þat in a bere to bataile ȝede.
Allas, he was no cristen man,
þis Octa, þat so fer wan.
His ouerwenyng & his pride
did þam open þe ȝates wide
& com stoutly in to þe biker,
bot þer hap was not siker;
þer fals trouth did þam misfalle, ffor synne of Octa fals & fursworn
þat felle to wyn, he wan þam alle. Dide al his felawes & hym be lorn
Slayn was þer sir Octa
& his cosyn, sir Ebissa;
oþer inowe þat escaped, .. ȝit þey skaped
vnto Scotland þam raped
& chese a prince, sir Colgrym,
þat was Octa cosyn.
Long þei lenged bi þat coste .. lendend ...
& gadred þam an oþer oste.
Bot for þis nobille ouercomyng
þat god gaf Vter our kyng,
ffor ioy he stirt out of his bere

as he had bene hole & fere,
alle armed in irne & stele
& bolded his barons wele,
& said þus, standand & louh,
"More wirschip as men say now ..ys as me þynkeþ now
in a bere forto lie,
in sekenes to wyn þe maistrie,
[57vb] þan be a man hole & sound
& schamfully leid to þe ground. .schamely lygge ded on.
Octa dispised me many day
for I seke in my bed lay;
scornfulle wordes þei me bede
& cald me bot a man half dede.
Þe halfdede man fulle felonlik
has slayn his fo hole & quik. ...fos boþ hol..
Þe hole & quike er dede & fled,
ȝit lifes þe seke man þat lay in bed;
ȝit wille I folow þam þat fle.
Do dyght ȝow alle & wend with me;
for no sekenes salle I leue
þat I salle exille þam & reue,
& ȝelde þam þe hard stoures;
my lond þei destroied & ȝours."
Whan þe kyng had said his wille,
his barons bad him beleue stille
tille he were warisced of his sekenes
or a partie suaged les. .his penaunce y swaged.
Þus departed þe barons
& chaced after þe Sessons.
Whan þer chace was alle left
& þe Sessons gadred eft,
þei conseld þam & toke þer rede,
how mot do þe kyng to dede. .þey might do....
Þei said if þei mot him destroie
he had non heire þat suld þam noie,
& als long as he mot lyfe,
bataile durst þei non him gyfe,
bot it were þorgh poyson ....tresoun
to gyfe him venom or poyson. ...venym & poysoun
Þei chese men þat couth suilk dede;
to go þider, þei gaf þam mede.
To Verolhram þei bad þam go
to fond þe kyng forto slo.

In pure wede þei did þam dight .pouere.....
& com þidir þat day seuenyght.
Alle maner langage þei couthe
þat comes wele in traitours mouthe.
Þei ȝede about þe courte to spie
where þei myght do þer traitorie.
[58ra] So wele þei sped neuer þer pray .yuel þey spedde of..
þat þei myght com þer þe kyng lay; ..ne myght.....
alle gate so long to courte þei ferde
þat þei perceyued & oft herde
þat for certeyn was it tolde,
þe kyng drank nouht bot water colde
þat was best for his peyne,
& euer of a welle certeyne
þat sprong vp beside his halle,
& best water forbi alle;
non oþer þing þouht him so gode
þat best agayn h euelle stode. ...his yuel.
Whan þat his dede so souht .þo þat....
wist þer wiles auailed nouht,
þei ȝede & venomed þis ilk welle
þat he of drank as þei herd telle.
When þei had þer wikked dede, ..had don þat..
out of þe toun son þei ȝede
& were listenand whan þei herd seie .ay lystned what...
þe kyng were ded or suld son deie. How þe kyng schold..
Þe kyng whan þe water drank, ..whan he...
he wex blak & bolned rank
& died son within a throwe,
bifor his men þat þei sowe; ..meyne þat hit.
& so did fele oþer mo
þat drank þerof to dede gan go.
Þis lasted a gode while
tille men perceyued þat gile;
þan ȝede þe comone alle at ones,
stopped þat welle with erth & stones;
so long bare þei erth þer tille,
þer are was welle now is a hille.
Whan sir Vter, our kyng,
was dede & don his endyng,
at stonhengis als he said,
beside his broþer men him laid.
Þe Archbisshop his conseile held,

erles, barons, knyghtes of scheld,
ilkon after oþer sent
to com to þe comon parlement,
& after Vter sone, Arthure,
to com to Cecestre burgh   . . . Circestre þe noble.
[58rb] & bitauht him þe croune
þorgh comon graunt of ilk baroune.
Fulle ȝong he was lond to ȝelde,   . . þen was he lond to welde
fiftene ȝere was his elde.
At Cicestre þat tyme þare,
croune on hede nouht he ne bare.   Was first tyme þat he croune.
Som of his thewes I wille discrie
(I trowe I salle not mykelle lie).
Kraftely he did mans dedis,
douhtiest knyght at alle nedis;
man of myrth most in halle   Þan of myrþe most was . .
& glad to gle his gestis alle.   Glad chered louely & lordlyest of.
Agayn þe proude, proud man was he;
agayn þe meke, suete & ese.   . . . debonere . .
Hardiest himself to fend,
bliþeli gaf, largely wald spend;
þat nedefulle was & him bisouht,
þat he myght, warned he nouht;   . . . he werned hym.
mykille lufed he ioy & worþi þing,
douhty dedes mad of menyng.
Nobilly his courte he led,
richely alle his he fed.
Ilk day com tiþinges newe,
gestis of ioy with knyghtes trewe;
ouer alle princes þe prise he nam
of curtasie & of wisdam.

[*L adds:*] Was no þyng so noble of þewes
As men reden of hym & schewes

When he had taken þe regalte,
an othe he mad, his wille fre,   & mad oþ by his . .
þat þe Sessons suld neuer haf pes
in stede of his þer þei ouht ches.
His fader & his eam þei slouh
& oþer wo þei wrouht inouh.
He did somond þe folk & fette,
largely he gaf & wele þam hette,
bad þam be redy with him to wend;
þei passed Ʒork to þe north end.

Colgrine of Sessons was cheftayn
after þat Octa was slayn; Syn Octa was at Wyrolhram.
þe Scottis men wer at his crie,
þe Peihtes with þam were redie,
ageyn Arthure at alle þer myght
& redy with him forto fight.
[58va] Beside þe water of Duglas
þer þei mette at a pas,
þe parties bold þat wele wild bide. ..were bolde & þoughte wel.
Many was slayn on ilk a side;
discomfite was sir Colgrine,
vnneþis fled he with mykille pyne. .he scaped...
Toward ʒork Colgrine flegh,
Arthur folowed bi bank & begh. .hym pursued faste & ney
ʒork he toke for drede & doute
& Arthure seged him withoute.
Colgrine had a broþer on þe se,
Balduk, þat had grete meyne.
He bode þe kyng of Almayne
þat com with oste toward Bretayne;
son him was told of on & oþer,
þat Arthur had biseged his broþer, ..byseged Colgrim..
how he was in bataile discomfite.
To lond he drouh fulle tite;
in a wod bi þat coste,
fyue myle he bussed fro þe oste; ..Balduk busched...
þus many was in his company:
sex þousand armed alle redy,
þat suld haf stolne þat ilk nyght
opon Arthure redy dight. ..al redy.
A man perceyued þer enbussement
& tille Arthure bodword sent.
Whan Arthure wist þat þei wer þore,
he cald to conseile þe erle Cadore
þat was Lord of Cornwaile;
his life to lese ne wald he faile.
"Cador," he said, "Balduk with gile
es bussed hiþen bot fyue myle. .enbusched fro vs four.
Tak sex hundreth of gode knyghtes,
þre þousand oþer if þou myghtes;
alle vnwarned on þam falle,
lightly may þou wyn þam alle."
Sir Cador dight him alle redy

& went withouten noyse or crie;
alle vnwarned þer þei ware, ..right þore..
wele to smyte wild he not spare.
More þan half was slayn þat frap, Þe most del was slayn of..
vnneþis myght any escape.
[58vb] If any of þam escape myght,
þn mirknes saued þam þat nyght. .derknesse....
[*L adds:*] & wode letted þem to renne
Þe redy wey couþ þey nought kenne
Balduk fled, durst not abide,
fro busk to busk on ilk a side.
Lost he had his men ilk one,
conseile couth he tak at none
how he myght his broþer help;
of tynselle myht he mak his ȝelp, .gret los mighte....
fayn he wald with him speke,
bot of his enmys he ne myght him wreke.
He couth of notes & of laies,
of harpe he knew alle þe saies. &...knew þasayes
He feyned him a ioguloure ...as a iogelour
& com to þe oste of kyng Arthure.
His hede, his berde, he did half schaue, ...al schaue
men wend he were a folted knaue;
als a glewman gan he syng
& couþe a partie of harpyng.
Long he ȝede þus aboute,
non ne wend of gile ne doute.
Bot he was boþe wili & slehi,
þe walle he neghed fulle neghi.
He spak to þam & þei him knewe;
a rope doun þei him threwe
& he knytte him þerin alle,
& þei drouh him ouer þe walle.
Neuerþeles þei wer at mischefe
for to scape þam were lefe;
bot son com þam tiþinges gude
þat sex hundreth schippes gude ....on flode
out of Almayn wer comen,
& in Scotland had hauen nomen.
To Arthur com tiþinges alle quike
þat þidir suld com Kyng Cheldrike
with folk mykille on ilk a side
þat Arthure dar not abide.

Þe best frendes þat wer him couth
conseld him to turne south
& gif no bataile at þat tyme,
bot lat his folk sprede & ryme.
"His folk is felle & fulle austere   ...fresche...
& tuys so felle as we haf here;   ...fele....
[59ra] & if þe folow vs ouer Humber,
þe soner salle we þam cumber.
Þan salle vs com folk ay fresch
& þei salle euer wax þe lesse."
To þat conseile he gaf gode tent;
fro þiþen to London he went.
Þe folk had þan sorow & wo,
þei dred þat alle to dede suld go;
þat had castels, þider þei drouh,
þat non had, þei þam slouh.
To holes, to hilles men crept for nede;
þat sikerest was had grete nede.   ....ful gret drede
Men gaf Arthure in conseile
to send for his cosyn Oheile,
Kyng of Bretayn, his sister sone;
bi letter his nedes gan him mone
& praied him of help a stounde,
[*L adds:*] Or elles he scholde go to grounde
"Bot if I help of þe now haue,
or of som oþer, my lond to saue,
within a thorwe it salle be lorn   ..þrowe....
þat our forfadres had beforn;   ..auncestres han..
& schame it were tille our lynage
so son to lese myn heritage."
Ohel vnderstode his nede.   fful wel he vnderstod..
With alle þe powere þat he myght spede,
he mad no long soiornyng;
hors & armes he did bryng,
fiften þousand helmes cleres
withouten sergans & archeres.
Gode wynd þei had þat gan þam dryue,
at Southhampton he did vpryue.
Mykille ioy mad kyng Arthoru   ...sire Arthurgh
& faire resceyued in toun & borgh;   ..receyued hym in...
wild þei mak no long delay,
þei had no drede of non affray,
bot sent messengers smert;

folk com him tille with gode hert.
To Lincoln com ilk a baron
for Cheldrik had seged þe toun;
withouten noise, spech, or cri,
þei com to Lincoln alle stilli.
No scaþe ȝit þe toun had taken,
[59rb] for þei within held þam waken.
Þe oste was ariued on a throwe,
þat trompe ne horn non did blowe, Bot horn ne trompe dide non.
ne oþer dyn on non manere
tille alle was splaied ilk banere.
Alle þei wrouht at on auys,
priuely felle on þer enmys.
Neuer ȝit befor of no Sesson
was are so grete destruction
in no stede þat men wist whare,
sex þousand slayn was þare;
þei kest þer armes, þer horses lete,
naked þei fled on þer fete;
into þe water fast þei ran,
of þam was dronkeld many man.
Þe Bretons on þam were euer preste,
þei þoled þam to haue no reste. .suffred þem nought....
A wod beside hight Calidoun,
þat now men calle ffiskertoun,
bi þe water side þe wod was set,
þerin had þei grete rescet.
Þe Bretons bihalued þe wod about
þat no Sesson durst com out.
Arthure did it luke so strait
for on þe nyght he dred disceit.
He did hewe trees & pikke,
& palased it alle about þikke.

[*L adds:*] Tre ouer tre stok ouer stok
As þikke as men myghte hem schok

His oste was loged on þe toþer partie
þat non com in ne ȝode forbie;
þo in þe wod had no mete,
ne non þam brouht þat myght ouht gete,
ne nouht had purueid þer beforn
noiþer brede, mele, ne corn.

[*L adds:*] Þey were so hasted faste þey fley
Bot helpless weren fer or ney

Þre daies it was þei nouht ete,
ne nouht drank, þat was wete;
þei sauh wele þat þei suld deie,
þorgh for mot þei mak no weie. .force myghte þey...
Þei conseile oþer weis: .toke conseil..
to leue armes & herneis,
in pes to þer schippes go
withouten any more wo,
& þei suld leue gode ostages,
þe best men of þer lynages, Þer...noblest lynage
[59va] & gif him treuage ilk ȝere
in pes withouten wo & were;
& Arthure gaf þam þe grantise
forto wend in þat wise. .wende forþ on..
Ostages he toke a remanant ...atte remenaunt
þat þei suld hold couenant.
He delyuerd þam schippes withouten harmes
& left robes, herneis, & armes; ..þer robes & harneys of.
sengli to schip þei went,
nouht was þam gyuen ne lent.
Ȝit he did grete curtesi
þat with þe life gaf þam merci.
Þei set vp saile, þe wynd þam blewe;
so fer þei sailed þat non þam knewe.
Whan þei were so fer born
þat we of þam þe sight had lorn,
ȝit þei þouht treson & gile; Ȝut þoughte þey more...
þei turned þer flete in a while.
Bituex Ingland & Normandie,
hiderward dight eft þer nauie
& entred in to Dertmue;
was þer non mad þam rescue. Neyþer fond þey arest ne.
At Toteneis þei toke lond, ..toke þey hauen &.
alle ȝede to dede bifor þam fond. ....þat by forn hem.
In þe cuntres þei spred aboute
to go to dede, alle was in doute.

[*L adds:*] Robes þey refte armure þey tok
Tounes brente houses doun schok

Þe cuntres trauersed þei ouerthuert;
ouer alle was wo & noure quert. .....no whar.
Douerschire & Somerset Deueschire..
& a partie of Dorset,
alle þei wasted & robbed þe gode,

was þer non þat þam withstode.
Knyghte þat felle haf ben at home,   Þe knyghte þat aughten....
with Arthure to Scotland nome;
þe Sessons did so mykelle scaþe,
þe robbed to þe toun of Bathe.
Bot þei of Bathe held þam oute
& þei biseged it aboute.
Arthure wered on þe Scottes,
for þei did as fole sottes,
helped Colgrine & Cheldrik
ageyn þer lord don so wik.
[59vb] Bot whan he wist þe Sessons   ....þat þe Saxons
brak þe couenant & did tresons,
& had biseged þe toun Bathe, ...toun of.
he said, "Þe Sessons falses me rathe!"   ... Saxoyns false me ful raþe
Þer ostages ilk on he heng
hie on galwes with a streng.
Whan þer ostages to dede wer don,
toward þe souht he hied son.   .þe souþ he hyed hym.
Ohel, his cosyn, & his meyne,
he left seke in a cite;
in Aklud þerin he lay,
þat was þe name be þat day.
With alle þe folk Ohelle mot spare
toward Bathe Arthure was ȝare.
Cheldrik sege he wild remue,
his men within he þouht rescue.
In a pleyn vnder a wod side,
Arthure did his folk abide,
to arme þam alle & ordeyne
whilk suld go with whilk seyne.
Himself was armed fynly wele

[*L amplifies this passage*:]

with gode chambres of iren & stele   Wyþ sabatons & spores & iaumbers of stel
Doublet & quysseux wiþ poleyns ful riche
Voydes breche of maille wyþ paunȝ non liche
& a hauberk þat non was suilk;   Hauberk wiþ plates y burnuscht ful wel
Vaumbras & rerbras wyþ coters of stel
abouen an acton mad of silk   Þer opon an Aketon wyþ stof & al sylk
His cote of armes þer on in world was no swyik
& gird with Calaburn, þe gode bronde,
a better com neuer in kynges honde;
ten fote long was þe blade,

in Rameseie þe merk is made;	..& oþer stedes....
fro þe hilte to þe pomelle	
tuelue inche grete þat tyme as felle,	Was twenti vnche large meten ful wel
þe brede of þe blade seuen inche & more.	
I trow þat wild smyte sore.	Wond was hit y þat world smite ful.
Arthure luffed it wele inouh,	[*Om. L*]
mishapped him neuer whan he it drouh.	[*Om. L*]
His helme was gode, non better on molde,	An helme he had on his hed no betere vpom molde
þe naselle befor was alle of golde;	A Riche corounal wiþ perre al of brent golde
þe bendeles of gold burnyst bright,	.nasel & bendeles..ful bryght
a dragon aboun selcouth in sight.	Þer opon a dragon...
About his nek hang his schelde,	
Pridwen it hight, many it bihelde;	
þer on was purtreid next him bi	
þe image our suete Lady,	..of oure swete leuedy
[60ra] in ned to behold hir face,	
ageyn his enmys to haf grace.	
His lance grete, he cald it Ron,	.spere was gret....
with iren befor suilk was non.	.an hed by fore ful noble þer on
[*L adds:*]	Hit was long & swyþe gret Þer was no scheld þat he ne þorow schet
Whan þe kyng was armed wele	
& his folk ilk a dele,	...dight ilka.
alle softly he bad þam go	
þat non suld befor oþer þro,	
tille þei com to þe batale;	
bot þe Sessons durst not assaile,	
bot fled vnto a hie hille	
þat non mot wele wyn þam tille;	
þei held þat hille as castelle strong	
& defendid þam fulle long,	
as þei were closed within a walle;	
bot at þe last it stode no stalle.	
Arthur sauh þe hille was taken	
& long mot þei hald þam waken;	
tene him þouht þei fro him brak,	
& to his men þus he spak:	
"Lordynges," he said, "þis hille is hie	
& we may not com þam nehi	
bot it were long destresse;	..were þorow..
þe length wald I schorten lesse.	..fayn woldy..
Agayn to Scotland wald I be,	

Ohel, my cosyn, fayn wald I se."
He monessed þam with wordes smerte — .bad þem...
& bad þam be gode of herte. — Þat schold alle....
"Lo, here befor vs þan ere þo
þat has vs wrouht mykille wo; — ....ful muche.

[*L adds:*] Þyse are þat han wasted our lond
Þat riche was & farre vs fond
Þise are þat slowe our auncessours
Als wel myne als ȝoures
Þis ar þo þat vs assailled
& often in werre vs trauailled

venge vs now we se þam here,
late þam bie our godes dere.
Þei haf don vs many trauaile, — Lat þeym bye þey toke byforn
quyte þam þat þei scored on taile, — & let hem now lese for we haue lorn
& I salle ȝelde, if þat I may,
þat othe þei suore þe toþer day. — Þe fals oþ.....

[*L adds:*] Þer turnyng y wole rescowe
Þat þey come til Dertemuwe

If I may not with þam mele, — ȝyf I may ought...
hand to hand strokes dele,
þei salle neuer eft haf powere
in bataile to negh me nere."
With þat worde he smote his stede,
befor þam alle, vpward he ȝede.
[60rb] His lance fulle wele he bare þe poynt,
þe schelde befor fulle wele ioynt;
þe first Sesson þat with him met,
his daies were no lenger set;
þan bigan Arthur to crie
agayn þis paiens, "Help me, Marie!"
& bare on þam þe brest before.
After him þe Bretons gan bore,
"Þe first stroke þan is myne,
on I mette & mad his fyne."
Þan mot men se þe Bretons strike
& felled þe Sessons douhtilike.
Ilkon wald haf bien þe breste — [*Om. L*]
& at his power Arthure neste, — [*Om. L*]
& he þam egred so with sawe — Arthur þen egred þem...
for schame þat non mot þam withdrawe; — ..ne myghte þey hem.
þei bihalued þam aboute
& riden þorgh þe Sessons route;

on ilk a side doun þei fleih
& euer Arthure vpward steih.
Caliburne drawen in his hand,
was non his dynt mot withstand
þat ne him behoued nedis deie,
þerfor þei fled & gaf him weie.
So fele he slouh & brouht to schame,
for þus þei counted þat couth þam ame,
fyue hundreth he slouh mo alone ffour.....
þan his oste did ilk one.
Dede was Balduk, slayn Colgrine;
Cheldrik fled with mykelle pyne;
toward þer schippes to Totneis
þei fled & left þer oþer herneis.
Lightli to go, wightli to fle,
þei left alle & fled to þe se.
Arthure perceyued wele inouh
þat to þer schippes þei fled & drouh.
He bad Cador of Cornwaile
tak ten þousand of gode aparaile
& after þam suyth him spede,
& ouertak þam þat fled.
For Arthur to Scotland went,
Ohel a messengere him sent
[60va] & said þe Scottes had seged þe castelle
& had nere taken sir Ohel.
Cheldrik fled to his nauy,
bot Cador was quaynt & wily;
be a bigate to Toteneis lay, ..bywey...
Cador & his tok þer wey,
& to þe hauen wele ore cam .....raþer.
ar any Sesson to schip nam.
Cador þe mene folk toke
þe schippes, gaf þam to loke,
& bad þam houe fer fro þe land ...ryde....
þat Sessons rauht no bote in hand.
Siþen went he with alle his oste
& in þe cuntres kept þe coste,
& kept þam euer as þei come.
Bi ten, bi tuelue, vmwhile þei nome,
armour, robes, had þei cast Armure &....
þat þei were light to fle fast;
þei had bot suerdes on þer hippes,

son to com vnto þer schippes.
As þei passed þe water of Tyne,
were þei war of Cador syne.
Whan þei it sauh, þei held þam schent;
vp & doun away þei glent. Hider & þyder...
Als þei tok þe hille of Tenwik,
was he slayn, Kyng Cheldrik; Þer...þe kyng.
þe toþer þat wend wele haf scaped,
to þe dede were alle to fraped.
Whan þe com þer, þei wer vnfayn, [*Transp. L*]
þo þat scaped to þe hauen vnslayn, [*Transp. L*]
for þei were kept at þe brynk,
into þe water did þam synk.
On alle halue wex þam wo,
to woddes, to hilles, fled som of þo,
þam to hide þat non wist
tille þei died for hunger & thrist. ......þirst
Whan Cador had mad þe cuntre clene
þat no Sesson was more sene,
he hied fast toward Scotland;
in Aklud, Arthure he fand
& Ohel with him, his cosyn,
of his sekenes warissed fyn,
þe Sessons þer sege remued. .Scottes...
Whan Arthur com, Ohel rescued,
[60vb] alle þe cuntre gan þei weyue
& fled away vnto Moreyue;
þer þei hoped best to be
& klosed þam in a strong cite.

[*L adds:*] Þere þey hoped Arthur to byde
A geyns þem what wolde bytyde

Arthure wist it certeynly,
þei gadred ageyn him party.
He hied him þiderward fulle ȝerne,
& þei herd say & fled ȝit ferne,
vnto a louh, Louh Lumine, Right vnto þe Louh Lumyne
a selcouth þing it is to se.
In þat louh er sexty iles;
in þo þei duelled long whiles,
& ilk an ile has a rochere
& a water depe & clere;
in þo roches foules reste
& ernes brede & mak þer neste.

If any sorow or any wo,
or any were or any þro,
salle in þat lond tide or gynne,
alle þo ernes þat brede þerinne
salle crie & ȝelle & mak rere
þat alle þe cuntre about salle here,
& fight togider foure daies or fyue,
& alle to pulle þer fedres & ryue. ....þe feþeres..
Þis Louh Lumine men calle,
sexti watres þerin falle,
& alle duelle þerin ilkon;
non rynnes to þe se bot on.
[*L adds:*] Wyþynne þis lough had þey dwellynge
Þe Scottes for Arthur oure kynge
Arthure biseged alle þo louhes
& gadred oste, chalans & trouhes, ..botes chalans & trowes
þat non myght bring þam ne gyue
mete ne drink withalle to lyue;
so within a litille while
so mykille hunger was in þat ile,
men sauh þam bi hundrethes & þousandȝ
lig dede for hunger on þe sandȝ.
[*L adds:*] Men seye þem go & falle right doun
ffor hunger þat was lord of toun
Guillomar, þe Iris kyng,
com ouer þe se with many lordyng
to help þe Scottis in þer nede. ...Saxons...
Litille, I wene, he mot spede.
He ryued vp be þat coste
þer Arthur lay & alle his oste.
Arthure & his agayn him nomen,
þe Iris was son ouercomen.
[61ra] He did þe Iris with force to fle
agayn tille Ireland ouer þe se.
Arthur nouh ȝit ne left But ȝyt Arthur nought..
þat he þe Scottis biseged eft.
Þan com þe bisshopes of þe land
& religious relikes bringand,
& praied Arthure of mercy;
& with þam com many lady,
alle barefote & alle bare heued,
þe haire rent or litille leued;
ȝong childere with þam brouht,

reuly gretand, mercy bisouht,
mekely felle doun to his fete;
bisshop, abot, & alle grete, Byschops Abbotes & ladis . .
& asked him mercy & pes.
"To saue þo childer helples,
þis ladies þat þis sorow haue,
ȝelde þam þer lordes þer life to saue.
[*L adds:*] 3eld vs þo þat are on lyue
Let hem nought alle to deþe dryue
Late vs not alle so dere bie
þe fals Sessons felonie,
for it was neuer our wille
þat þei com here to do ȝow ille.
Of þer comyng we no frame, . . . had we . .
þer duellyng did vs mykelle schame.
Alle day wer we with þam noied,
our lifelade þei ete & stroied;
catelle þei bare away & spended.
We had no hede þat vs defended;
þat we þam halp es no trispas,
maugre ours for soth it was;
þer force was more þan ours,
we wist of non to haf socours.
ȝe wote þei ere of lawe paien,
& we, als ȝe, ere men cristen;
þerfor þei did vs þe more wo.
At ilka tyme boþe to & fro,
wo did þei vs, wars haf we now; . dude þey vs & worse haue .
& þat is non honour to ȝow,
vs to slo þat crie mercy
& die for hunger dolefully.
Þou has vs won, leue vs þe life,
lord to lady, hosband to wife,
[61rb] & gife vs lond on to lyue;
trewe hostage we wille þe gyue.
Þorgh reson þou suld vs spare, . righte reson . . . .
for we ere cristen as ȝe are,
& if we die in suilk destresse,
kristendom es mykelle þe lesse.
Þan is þe perille mykelle more . . þy peryl mykel þe .
þat þou wrethis criste so sore."
Arthure wist þei said reson,
wele excused þam of þe Sesson;

for þe Bisshopes þat him bisouht . byschope & clerkes...
& þe relikes þat þei brouht,
& of þe ladies him rewed sore,
& ȝong childer þat þer wore,
he granted þam alle þat þei ches,
life & lymmes & his pes.
Ohel beheld þe louh, þat lake,
& tille Arthure þus he spake:
"Arthure," he said, "I haf mervaile
of þis louh & of þe entaile;
& many iles I teld sexti
& ilkon has a roche hi,
& many ernes nestes, . so manye..
& þer crie þat ilkon kestes;
ferly me þink how it may be A wonder me þynkeþ hit..
of ilk a þing þat I se."
Þan said Arthure vnto Ohele,
"Of þis me mervailes neuer a dele,
bot of anoþer is selcouþe more,
& so salle þe whan þou comes þore.
Þat louh is here in þis cuntre,
cornerd as a cheker quarre;
xxti fote of length þe brede es Twenty fot of lengþe as...
& fyue fote it has of depnes;
in þe water at foure corners
ere fisches in foure maners;
þo þat ere in þe to cornere
neuer coms þe toþer nere,
ne þe fisches alle foure,
non with oþer meng noure; Ne wyþ oþer menge ne voure
ne no partyng es þam bituene
of erth ne stone bot water clene;
[61va] ne oþer þing þat man may wite
þat mot þer mengyng with site.
I ne wote if it be þorgh kynde
or crafte of clerk þat he mot fynde. ...clergie as men may.
Of anoþer is more selcouth
& þat louh is in þe south,
to Wales beside Seuerne.
Whan þe flode flewes þerin ȝerne,
þe water waxes no þing on hie,
þan þe flode com neuer þer nehie.
Als long as þe flode þerin flewes,

þe water of þe louh ne grewes
in no stede bi bank ne bre
þat any may perceyue or se.
Bot whan þe flode drawes agayn
& es þe ebbe in certayn, ..atte þe ebbe.
þan begynnes þe louh to flowe
& ouer bankes to renne & rowe.
With risand wawes & with grete,
fer about wille he wete; .aboute hym...
if it be a couth man of þe cuntre
þat gos þider þe water to se,
& fles þo wawes þat so wetes, .feleþ.....
it rennes on him & doun betes. .....doun hym.
Oft of þo þat so haf gon
haf bien drenkled manyon;
if any conand man of þo
stand stille or sidelynges go,
he may stand on þe brinkes.
Als long as him gode þinkes,
salle he neuer latche scaþe,
ne haf wettenes ne waþe."
Ohel said, "It is selcouth þing
& ferly who mad þe gynnyng."
Þan did Arthure bemes blowe,
hornes & bellis þat men mot knowe,
þat he wild þien turne
& remue his oste fro þat burne.
His barons þat com fro ferne,
he bad þam wend home ȝerne ..hem renne hom ryght.
to witte how it fore at home,
to glad þer wifes whan þei come;
[61vb] with mykelle & mykelle play .mykel ioye...
went þe oste hamward þer way.
Of Arthure mad þei mykelle pris,
how he was hardy, large, & wis,
& said neuer ore in Bretayn
was so noble a cheftayn.
Vnto ȝork Arthure gan turne
& alle þe ȝole mad þer soiurne.
On ȝole day mad he feste
with many barons of his geste.
Mikille enpaired was þe toun,
kirkes, houses, beten doun;

þer burgeis wer bigged riche;
wasten & way was alle o liche,   Wast & Eyuere was hit liche
þe bisshop slayn with þe Sessons   ..was slayn wyþ þe Saxons
& oþer many religions.
Alle did he bigge it agayn
as it was in þe right certayn;   ...byfore certeyn
him serued a preste, a fulle gode man,
his name was sir Piran,
he gaf þe Archbisshopes see   .gaf hym...
& bad him kepe þat dignite,
& Holy Kirke agayn restore
þat þe Sessons wasted before.
Pes he did ouer alle crie
þat non did oþer vilanie.

[*L adds:*] But in lawe right & skyle
Husebandemen bad hem tyle

Frankelyns þat had disherison,
he did þam in ilk a toun,
gaf þam agayn þer heritage,
restored þam oþer damage.   ..þer oþer.
Þre þer were, douhti & gode,
noble men of kynges blode:
Loth, Auguisel, & Vrien;
þe north longed to þise þre men.
Þise þre departed þe north lond
þorgh Arture gift, as I fond;   .Arthures gift y vnderstond
to Loth he gaf alle Lounes,
alle þe cuntre right als it es;
Scotland he gaf sir Auguisele,
Vrien had Morey tille his dele,   ..Murreue...
& alle to hold of him þer þing,
for Arthure was þer chefe kyng.
[62ra] Sir Loth þat wedded Anne,
Wawan, þer sone, at Rome was þan
to norise, as þe romance sais.
He hight Wawan þe curtais.
Whan Arthure had his land iustised
& alle don as he auysed,
Genoyre he wedded, mad hir quene;
norised with Cador had scho bene.
Scho was sir Cador cosyn
& born of þe Romans lyne,   .born was....
& hir moder of Roman kynde;   ffor hure moder was...

so fair as scho mot no man fynde.
Inouh scho couth of curtasie,
large giffer, spekand lufely;
of body was scho auenant,
faire contenance with suete semblant.
Alas, þei mot non heire haue,
noiþer maiden childe ne knaue.
Whan wynter colde was alle away
& hete comen of somers day,
a flete on flode Arthure did ȝare, [*Transp. L*]
& faire wedir on se to fare, [*Transp. L*]
& said he wild to Ireland
& wynne it to þe Bretons hand.
Long tyme wild he not waste;
he did somond his folk on haste,
erles, barons, knyghtis, squiers;
alle þe ȝongest bachelers
þat wele myght & best couth
stand in were & were of ȝouth.
On Ireland his flete gan lend,
vp to land gon þei wend,
vitaile to seke, mele or corne,
bestis slayn to schip was borne,
lyuelod þat þei mot gete
to sustenance vnto þer mete.
Ilk a dele to schip þei drouh
& vitailed þam wele inouh;
to Guillomare, þe Iris kyng,
com sone bode of þer comyng,
þat Arthure was aryued þere,
alle his lond forto conquere.
[62rb] Þe folk pleyned þam about,
þer godes was lost & þei in dout;
þe Iris kyng did folk somoun
þorghout þe lond of ilka toun,
to gif bataile agayn Arthurh [*Transp. L*]
of vpland & of burgh. [*Transp. L*]
Whan boþe parties com to fight,
þe naked Iris was not dight;
hauberk ne schelde ne myght þei bere,
ne fro þe arwes couth þam not were,
þei had sene neuere non are;
o side þei fled hider & þare,

ilkon mad oþer agast
& conseld þam to fle fast
to wodes, to hilles, þer lyues to saue;
oþer socoure wist þei non to haue.
Þe kyng fled tille a wod side;
Arthure folowed & did him bide,
& alle with force him þer toke;
& he suore on þe boke
to hold of him his heritage
& ȝelde him ilk a ȝere treuage;
þerto he gaf him gode ostage
to hold of his feaute & homage. .holden his fewte..
Whan þat was pesed & brouh to ende, ...brought..
tille Island he dight him to wende. Til Ingelond dight...
Island son alle he wan, Irland....
for lord knew him ilka man. ..þey knew...
Geneweis, þe kyng of Orkeney,
how Arthure wan herd wele sey,
so did Doldan of Gotland,
& Rumarek, Kyng of Wentland;
tille alle þre was it told
þat Arthure was conquerour bold.
Þise þre kynges him dred ...þey hym.
for þe grete oste he led,
þei durst not stand him agayn,
ne þei had non oste certayn;
ne þei ne wild þer lond destroye,
ne him ne þam togider noye.
Þe best conseile þei toke on hand
& went tille Arthure tille Island, ..to Arthur into Irland
[62va] & for þer landes mad alle pes.
Arthure þam þanked þat þei so ches;
lufly he tok þer feaute
for þei com with þer wille fre.
Whan alle siker & certeyn, .al was...
to Ingland he com ageyn,
& whan þei wist þat he cam,
with ioy alle ageyn him nam.
Tuelue after þat comyng, Twelf ȝer...
in rest, in pes, he regned after kyng, ..& pes he regned kyng
þat neuer no were on him nam ..on hym no werre bygan
ne he wered on no man.
He toke so mykille of curtasie

withouten techyng of any him bie
þat non myght con more,
noiþer þorgh kynde ne crefte of lore. ....craft..
In alle ansuere he was fulle wys;
of alle manhede he bare þe pris.
Of non þat tyme was suilk speche
þat tille his nobleie mot reche,
not of þe emperour of Rome
þat he ouer him bare þe blome,
in alle manere þat kyng suld do,
non oþer had grace þerto.
He herd neuer speke of knyght
þat losed was of dedes wyght,
þat he ne ȝerned him to se
& for to haf of him mercy; ....hym of meyne
if he for mede serue him wold,
he ne left for siluer ne for gold.
ffor his barons þat were so bold
þat alle þe world pris of told,
for no man wist who was best
ne in armes douhtiest,
did he ordeyn þe rounde table
þat men telle of many fable. .ȝit men...a fable
At þer burde in tyme of mete,
alle þo douhty knyghtes suld ete;
non sat within, non sat withoute,
bot alle euen round aboute;
non sat first, non sat last,
bot pere bi pere euen kast;
[62vb] non sat hie, non sat lawe,
bot alle euenly forto knawe; ..euenlyk men myghte þem.
non was set at þe ende,
bot alle o round & alle wer hende;
non wist who of þam most was ..whiche of pris..
for þei sat alle in compas.
Alle at ons doun þei siten,
at ons ros whan þei had eten;
alle wer serued of a seruys,
euenli alle of on assise.
What knyght had bene in alle þe world
þof his los had bene wele herd, Had his los be neuere so wel byherd
were he Frankis, wer he Breton,
Normand, Flemmyng, or Burgolon,

[*L adds:*] Spaynard Gascoyn or Angeuyn
Scot Irische Pykard or Peyteuyn
Daneys Norneys or Selander
Henner ffryson or Katelaner
Arragoneys Lombard or Brabaunt
Prouyncial Nauerner or Alemaunt

of whom he held his fe or how,
fro þe west vnto Mongow, ..West Est vntil.
he was told of non honoure
bot he had bene with Arthoure
& hadde taken of his lyuere,
cloth or þing þat knowen mot be. ..queyntise....

[*L adds:*] Of ferne landes many on namen
& til þat court for worschyp camen
To lere honur & curtesy
& here þe prowesse of knyghtes hardy
& to here þe faire gestes
þat knyghtes broughte & telde at festes
Somme come to se his faire wonyng
& se & here þere selcouþ þynge

Pore men lufed him alle
& riche honoured him in halle;
fele kynges of ferne thede ....stede
sent him gyftes for doute & drede.

[*L adds:*] Þey wyst hit wel ȝyf þey wold ryde
His werre durste no kyng abide
Kynges aforced þer casteles aboute
ffor alle landes of hym hadde doute
Þat ȝyf he come he scholde þam lese
Or gyue hym truwage as he wold chese
Þer fore ilkon at þer myght
Aforced þer Cites & wel þeym dight

[I]n þis tuelue ȝeres tyme [*Capital om. in P.*] But in....
felle auentours þat men rede of ryme;
in þat tyme wer herd & sene
þat som say þat neuer had bene;
of Arthure is said many selcouth
in diuers landes, north & south,
þat man haldes now for fable,
be þei neuer so trew no stable.
Not alle is sothe ne alle lie, Al ys nought soþ ne nought..
ne alle wisdom ne alle folie;
þer is of him no þing said

þat ne it may to gode laid;	.hit ne may be to godnesse.
more þan oþer was his dedis	
þat men of him so mykelle redis.	
[*L adds:*]	Ne were his dedes hadde be writen
	Of hym no þyng men scholde haue wyten
Geffrey Arthur of Menimu	...Monemu
wrote his dedis þat wer of pru	
& blames boþe Gildas & Bede,	
whi of him þei wild not rede,	.þey wolde nought of hym.
[63ra] siþen he was pris of alle kynges,	Syn he bar þe pris of alle Cristen kynges
þei wild not write his praysynges,	& write so litel of..
& more wirschip of him was	.....spoke þer was
þan of any þat spekes Gildas,	Þat of any of þo þat..
or of any þat Bede wrote	
saue holy men þat we wote.	
In alle londes wrote men of Arthoure;	
his noble dedis of honoure,	
in France men wrote & ȝit write;	
here haf we of him bot lite.	Bot herd haue we....
[*L adds:*]	Þere fore of hym more men fynde
	In farre bokes als ys kynde
	Þan we haue in þys lond
	Þat we haue þer men hit fond
Tille Domesday men salle spelle	
of Arthure dedis, talk & telle.	
Now is Arthure of pleyn age;	
he conseils with his baronage	
& his gode knyghtes him redde	
þat he had fostred & forth fedde.	
He said he wald wend to France	...wolde ouer se..
& wyn it with dynt of lance.	
Bot first he wild to Norweie;	...seide he wolde..
þe kyng sent, he hoped to deie,	..had sent hym bode....
"& Loth, my niouh, salle be his heire;	...neuew....
to mak him kyng I am in speire.	
His neuow he is of next degre,	
of blode is non heire bot he.	....nerrer þan he
Sichelyn said & þus þouht,	Right as he seyde also he.
he wend þe barons wold so haf wrouht.	
Bot whan þei saw þat he was dede,	
þei tok þam tille a noþer rede.	
Loth to haf þei him forsoke	
& a noþer kyng þei toke.	

Þus þei said with o mouþe,   ffor alle þey....
þei wold haf no man vncouþe.   ....kyng.

[*L adds:*] Þey hoped nought þey schold hym fynde
Als godliche as þer owen kynde

Aliens, þei said, he wild auance
þat suld be þer apurtenance.
A hede þei wild haf þam aboue
þat þam wild auance & loue.
Þorgh þat conseile & þat reson,
Ricolf þe ches, a baron,
& crouned him & mad him kyng;
þus gate hast Loth lorn þat þing.   & þus haþ Lot...
For help Loth men has souht,   ..seid Arthur Loth haþ bysought
to faile him ne may I nouht.   ffaile hym by no weye wol y.
[63rb] I wild his honour & his right
& help þerto þat I myght.   & þat schal y hepe at my.
Ricolf croune I wild abate
þat þe Norreis gaf him late."
Tille Arthure com folk inouh,
to schippes on flode fast þei drouh;
þe wynd blewe & gan þam dryue,
vp in Norweie gan þei ryue.
Ricolf was gode, he wild not fle
ne remoue him out of cuntre.   ....of þe.
He gadred oste, for wele he wend
agayn Arthure him to defend,
bot his wenyng was alle vayn;
Ricolf & his was alle slayn.   ffor...wer alle þer.
Whan Arthure had Norweie wonnen,
þe barons ouer riden & runnen,
Loth, his niouh, he gaf þe croun   ..neuew....
after Ricolf þat was doun.
Loth mad Arthure feaute
as to his chefe ouer þat fe.
Loth sone, sir Wawan,
had bene at Rome to lere Romayn,
with Supplice þe pape to wonne,   ...Apostoille..
honour to lere, langage to konne;
þer was he dubbid knyght
& holden hardy, strong, & wight.
Sir Supplice had don his ende;   When Supplice....
to Bretayn home Wawan gan wende.
Now is Wawan comen home

& Loth is fayn of his come; ffful blithe ys Loth al...
noble he was & curteis,
honour of him men rede & seis. Mykel honur of hym euere men.
He lufed mesure & faire beryng,
pride ne boste lufed he no þing;
fals & fikelle lesyng he hated, Vnkynde false & fykele..
auauntour alle suilk he bated; Lesynges alle swilk..
more he gaf þan he hette,
more he did þan terme of sette.
Now is Loth in Norweie seised
& Wawan is comen & preised. ..comen þat mykel ys.
Alle þo men þat were of myght,
in þouth þat couth ouht of fight, Þat weren ʒonge & couþe..
[63va] þat lufed more were þan pes,
Arthure alle suilk men ches; .til hym alle swyche.
of suilk gadred he manyon
& schippes on se fulle gode won.
Whan his oste was stiffe & stark,
he went to schip to Danmark; .schiped to wardes.
Achil þat was kyng of Danes
sauh & Noryeis com alle at anes, Saw Bretons & Noreys....
with Arthure to wyn his lond
& to destroie alle þat þei fond.
Bot Achil þouht as kyng wys;
he sauh Arthure ouer alle had pris. Þat Arthur oueral hadde þe.
He wist wele he suld conquere
his lond of him if he com þere,
bot he said if he suld not so, ...he wolde nought so
[*L adds:*] Hym seluen ne his lond fur do
ne suffir his folk to be slayn,
ne his tresour spend in vayn,
ne his castels be casten doun,
ne kirke to robbe ne bren toun.
Bot faire he spak & wele hette,
giftes gaf & wisly sette, & wysly gaf giftes wel bysette
þat of Arthure he had grantise
þe lond in pes for his seruyse,
& Arthure his seruyse toke;
homage he suore on þe boke.
Arthure was glad þat he þus wan,
so son þe kyng bicom his man.
ʒit him þouht he wild wyn more; But ʒut he þoughte to wynne wel.
of þe best knyghtes he ches þore,

& squiers gode, & slie archers, ..bolde & gode.
þat loued were & knew þe maners;
I ne wote þe hundrethes ne þousandȝ ...how manye þousandes
þat he gadred in þo landes;
of folk he mad purueiance .gret folk mad he.
for he said he wild to France.
Flandres he wan, Bolayn he toke,
tounes, kastels, for him quoke;
so wisly his folk gan lede,
stroied he no lond as he ȝede.
He toke no þing fer no hend
bot mete or drynk or hors prouend;
ȝit tok þei non with maistrie,
[63vb] bot bouht it þer it was to bie.
Þat tyme þat þis chance gan falle,
þat now hate France þan hight Galle.
Þe Romayns þat tyme it helde,
was þan no kyng bare croun ne schelde;
ilk ȝere toke þei þer of treuage
sen Iulius Cesar wan it in seruage.
Frolle, a douhty bachilere,
had it in kepyng many ȝere,
to þer behoue gadred þer rent To Romayns byhoue...
& at termes home it sent, ...to Rome..
or bare it himself to þe Emperoure.
ffrolle was hardy man in stoure; ..a ful hardy...
he was comen of Romans blode,
he douted non þat agayn him stode. .dredde.....
Alle day tiþing men him told
þat Arthure with oste bold, ..com wyþ host ful.
& no man myght duelle no be,
bot he held of him his fee. But ȝif he...in fe
ffrolle herd þat & was right wo, Þat herd ffrolle & was ful.
& said it suld not so gate go. .....þat wey.
He did somond alle to come
to him þat held þer fee of Rome,
forto bring hors & armes

[*L adds:*] Þe lond for to fende fro harmes

& douhtily togidir stand
agayn Arthure þat was comand.
Long ne was it bituex þam sette Hit was nought longe...
þat þer ostes togider mette.
ffrolle misfelle at þe first pres,

nere alle his best folk he les;
what slayn & ouer schaken,
nerhand himself was taken;
it was ferly þat he fled, ..no wonder...
so grete an oste Arthure led
no man couth noumbre it no say
þe folk he tok comand in þe way.
It was no lond þat he þorgh souht,
euer þe best with him he brouht
þat douhty was on hors or fote,
wild he, ne wild he, forþe he mote.
Som went for his faire speche
& som for drede of oþer wreche;
[64ra] & som for he gaf largely,
& som for his grete curteisy,
& som for tynselle & doute of dede, ...los....
knowlegyng to him þei bede;
of France many a lordyng
com & held of him þer þing. Comen to holde....
Frolle fled fast vnto Paris,
it was strongest cite of pris; ..þe strengest...
agayn Arthure þat mot him saue, [*Transp. L*]
he knowe no better rescette to haue; [*Transp. L*]
nyght & day did his trauaile
to store þe toun with vitaile. .warnische....
Mykille folk to Paris fled
& Arthure fast þider sped;
& Arthure vnderstode wele
þer purueiance ilk a dele; Þe purueaunce of ffrolle...
þerfor he hasted sege to sette,
þer purueiance forto lette.
Arthure seged him so straite
þat ffrolle myght with no disceite,
of vitaile help him at nede,
bi lond ne be water lede.
Nere a moneth þus men telde .al a monþe as..
þat ffrolle þe cite of Paris helde.
Alle þat tyme Arthure þer lay,
he ne remoued nygh ne day; ...night..
so mykelle folk was þer inne
þe soner gon þer faute begynne. .raþer bigan þer fight to gynne
It was spended þat þei in drouh,
þei had no tyme to drawe inouh;

for hungere gan þei mak mone,
men & women, childir ilkone,
if ffrolle wild als þei wolden,
þe toun were fulle son ȝolden.
Þei praied ffrolle þorhout þe burgh
to make pes with Arthurh.
ffrolle sauh þei pleyned sore
& þer vitaile was no more,
& sauh wele þat þei alle wilde
þe toun vnto Arthure ȝelde,
& þat þouht him schame & vile.
Himself had leuere be in perile,
[64rb] auenture him his dede to take
þan with his wille þe toun forsake,
strength of body are wille I fond.
Vnto Arthure he sent his sond:
if þat he wild bituex þam tuo
togider fight withouten mo,
& whilk of þam were ouercomen,
slayn or with force nomen,
tak him þe lond at his wille
so þat þe folk not spille.
Þat bode com Arthure wele to hert;
his gloue he gaf vp als so smert
& toke ostage on boþe partys
of Arthure & of Paris; . Arthures host . . .
þe bataile suld be in a playne
bituex tuo waters, Marne & Seyne.
Whan þei were armed & redy dight
& comen þer þei suld fight,
men mot se folk tremble & quake,
on boþe parties grete doele make.
Handes wreng, on knees falle,
on godes name to crie & calle
þat he mot wynne þat pes wild haue
& þe lond fro were mot saue.
Arthure stude & bihelde, . folk stode . .

[*A strip has been torn from fol. 47 of L.*]

redy dight with helm & schelde,
& praied god interly
to graunt Arthure þe victory. . . . . maistri
Þise tuo Knyghtes þat forþe were fette,
nobilly dight, on hors wele sette,

to assay þam how þei were wight,
þe lance to raise, þe scheld to ryght;
ho mot wele telle & soth say,
suilk were non þat tyme als þai.
Ilk of þam was horsed wele,
in armes strong als þe stele;
bi sight non mot chese þe best, ..myght non þer...
[*The mutilation of L ends here*.]
whilk semed to be þe douhtiest. Ne whilk þen semed.
[*L adds:*] Ne whilk schold wynne ne haue þe gre
By sighte myghte þer non hit se
Whan þei wer boune, redy to smyte,
& þer horses sundred a lyte,
with speres þei smote þe bridelle braide,
þer scheldes sette, on lance forþe laide.
[64va] Þer horses at þer powere ronnen,
þe parties wend alle lorn or wonnen.
Bot ffrolled failed of his dynt .ffrolle....
(I trow his stede oside stynt)
& Arthure smote him in þe schelde;
þe iren was gode & wele helde, .hed was god & ful..
& ffrolle out of his sadelle caste
als fer as þe lance mot laste.
ffrolle vpstirt & sidelynges glent,
his schelde dight, his lance he hent, ..dressed his launce vp.
tille Arthure stede þe poynt he bare
þorgh þe breste, þe hert it schare.
Arthure felle, he most nede,
he was on fote, dede was his stede.
Þe Bretons sauh he had þat falle,
þam þouht for wo þei alle to sualle;
þe erthe stonyed for þer crie, ..dunede...
to passe þe water þei were redie;
þe treus to breke, þei were fulle wilde
to haf gon ouer into þat ilde.
Bot þei sauh him son vp agayn;
þei withstode þan & wer fayn.
Whan he was vp, he had no reste;
with ffrolle to fight, he was alle preste
& laid his hand to Caleburne
þat neuer for armes wild scurne;
þerwith on ffrolle fulle sore he souht
& ffrolle agayn dred him nouht.

Agayn Arthure he stode & stynt,
nouht abaist for him no dynt.
His suerde drawen, he lifte it hie,
on Arthure he lete it flie.
Þe dynt was grete for he was strong;
þe fire out flegh, þe sparkes sprong;
þe helm he clefe & þe bacyn,
& þe coife þat was so fyn;
þe suerd was scharp & wele bote,
in þe forhede Arthure he smote
þorgh þe flesch vnto þe pan,
after þe stroke þe blode out ran.
Whan Arthure felte þat he was wonded,
noiþer he stynt ne stounded; Noþyng he ne stinte . .
[64vb] fulle of ire, with coloure teynt,
was he noiþer abaist ne feynt.
Kaleburne he had in hand,
he toke him bir, þe stroke teisand;
aboun his helm fulle fast he drefe,
to þe girdille þe body clefe. Hed & nekke & breste he .
Þei of þe cite mad dole inouh
& þe Bretons þerfore louh.
What sorow so þei mad algates,
agayn Arthure þei opened þe ȝates
& lete him in & alle his,
& mad him homage & seruise.
Whan he had homage of lefe & lothe,
ostage he toke to hold þer othe.
At Paris to soiorne he ches;
bailifs he sette to ȝeme þe pes.
He parted his oste & þe halfendele . . . . in haluendel
betauht he vnto sir Ohele . . þem to . .
& bad him go to wyn Burgoyne,
Nauern, Peitow, & Gascoyne,
& Lorenge, if þat he myght
assay þam with luf or fight.
Ohel did his comandment;
he toke þe folk & þidir went
& wan alle þo þat I haf said; And alle þo landes . . . .
to gyfe treuage on þam he laid.
Witard, þe duke of Peiters, Gwichard . . . .
was a felle knyght & a fers.
Forto kepe his heritage,

he wild gyfe no treuage;
often he turned Ohel þe vis,
& oft of him wan þe pris,
& oft ageyn him he les.
Are he wild com vnto þe pes,
Ohel destroied nere alle þe lond
þat he withouten kastelle fond,
alle was destroied & reft,   . . . & al was reft
þe vineis þei ne left.   . selue vynes . . .
Whan Witard sauh nere alle was lorn,   . Gwytard . . . . .
so he myght not be forborn,   . þat he ne mighte be byforn
he sauh it was non oþer bote;
he ȝede & felle Arthure to fote
[65ra] & mad him homage & feaute,
of him to hold alle his fe.
Siþen lufed Arthure Witard wele,   . . . Gwytard ful .
non so mykelle bot only Ohele.
Þe toþer cuntres south fro France,
Arthur wan to his aliance.
Whan Arthur had alle þo landes
wonnen with dynt of handis,   & wonne hem . . . his handes
to þo men þat trauailed sore,
wele of elde þat with him wore,
ȝalde þam þer sonde & þer seruise;
vnto þer cuntres bad he þam wise.
Þo þat were ȝong & wilde
& had noiþer wife ne childe
þat lufed to bere helm & schelde,   & louede . . spere . .
nyen ȝere in France he þam helde.
Many selcouth be tyme seres   . wondres by times sers
betid Arthur þo nyen ȝeres.
Many proude man lowe he brouht,
to many a felon wo he wrouht.
[*L adds:*] Enuyous men he hated alle
Þe mysproude ful lowe dide falle
Þer haf men bokes, alle his life,   . . . bokes of . . .
þer ere his meruailes kid fulle rife;
þat we of him here alle rede,
þer ere þei writen ilk a dede.
Þise grete bokes, so faire langage,
writen & spoken on France vsage,
þat neuer was writen þorgh Inglis man;
suilk stile to speke no kynde can.

Bot France men wrote in prose, . ffrensche men wryten hit . .
als he did, him to alose.

[*L adds:*] In prose al of hym ys writen
Þe bettere til vnderstande & wyten

At þe Pasch at Paris, Arthur at Pasches . .
he held his fest of grete pris;
tille alle þo þorgh him had lorn,
restored he as þei had beforn;
riche or pure, gentille or þralle,
þat he þam auht, he paid þam alle;
after þat he was worþi,
he ȝald þer seruise largeli.
To Kay þat was his steward,
Aungers he gaf tille his part.
He gaf also sir Beduere,
þat was of fe his botelere,
[65rb] he gaf him in fee alle Nomondie; . . . . . . Normandie
þat tyme men say it hight Neustrie. But þenne hit was cald.
Boloyn he gaf to sir Holdin,
þe Mannes to Borel, his cosyn. And Mayne . . . .
He gaf giftes of honours
& londes & rentes tille vauasours.
Whan he had feffed his barons
& mad his priueȝ lordes of touns,
þe next Aprile whan somer gan,
to Inglond went ilk a man.
Whan men wist þat þei were comen,
agayn Arthur fast þei nomen;
þei mad ioy, non myght more, . . suche ioye . . be more
his long duellyng forþouht þam sore.
Ladies kist þer lordes suete,
modres on childir for ioy grete;
sons welcomed þer fadres home
& mad myrth at þer tocome.

[*L adds:*] Lemmans leue ilk oþer kest
Of more þey esed hem when þem lest

Neuous, nyftes, sistir, broþer,
ilk a frende welcomed oþer;
þei stode in ilk strete & stie,
in gashadles men passed bie . grete Routes . . for by
to spir at þam how þei had faren,
& whi þat þei so long waren,
& how þei sped of þer conquest,

& whan þei wan so fer est, . what.....
& how þei ferd in alle þer wo.
"We wille no more ȝe far vs fro,"
& þe teld þam alle þer chance, . þen þey teld....
how Arthure had wonen France
& of mervuailes þat þei had sene,
& in what perile þei had bene.
Þo lordynges of þis lond
þat Arthure befor him fond,
riche presentȝ þei him sent.
His long duellyng mykelle ment,
& he agayn was fulle curteis,
some gaf he hors or oþer herneis;
gladly he gaf & largely
forto schewe his curteisy.

[*L adds:*] ffor to schewe his grete prowesse
& do by knowe his grete Richesse
& for to speken of his dedes
Þat alle kynges doutes & dredes

Þei conseiled him his lond somoune;
at Whitsonday to do him croune,
[65va] at Karlion & Klamorgan . . in Glamorgan
did somond þidir ilk a man.
Karlion was þat tyme riche,
Rome & it likned liche.
It standes on þe water of Vske, . . . a water men calleþ .
to Seuerne renne bi bank & buske.
In Vske men mot þider wend,
outlandes fer þat þider wild lend;
on þe to side ran þat ryuere,
on þe toþer, forest fulle of dere.
Venison þer was inouh,
plente of fisch in water þei drouh;
large medes with gres plente,
lond to tille, non better mot be;
tuo kirkes were in þe toun,
þat tyme had þei grete renoun.
Of saynt Iulie was þe ton,
& þe toþer of saynt Aaron;
saynt Iulie in martirdom gan die,
Nonnes were at his abbeie.
At saynt Aaron was þe bisshop see,
þe hede kirke of þat cite,

þat of Arthure was foundoure,
did set it in saynt Aarons honour.
Þer were chanons of clergie
þat knewe wele of astronomie;
to knowe þe sternes þer wittes leid,
& tille Arthure oft tymes seid
þat what þing þat he was aboute,
he suld spede withouten doute.
Fele was þan a Karlioun, [*Capital F is illuminator's error.*]
Wel was þat tyme at.
bot sen þat tyme has it gon doun,
for þe plente of fisch & flesch,
wod & water, hay & gresse,
of housyng & oþer esement,
bi water & lond, men brouht & sent.
Arthure said he wild þer hold
feste with his barons bold,
& at þat samenyng ..þat selue.
he said he wald be crouned kyng.
Messengers he did sende
for kynges & dukes fer & hende,
[65vb] & for erles & barons,
knyghtes of kastels, lordes of tounes.
A legate fro Rome was sent
forto mak þe corounment.
Archbisshopes was þer þre;
at London was þan þe se,
þe toþer was at Euerwik;
at Karlion was saynt Dubrik.
Of Scotlond, þe kyng Auguiselle
þat tille Arthure was fulle lele;
of Murreue, Kyng Vrian,
with him com his sone Iwan.
Stater of South Wales alle,
of North Wales, Kyng Cadwalle;
Cador, erle of Cornwaile,
for Arthure had many trauaile;
Morioud, erle of Gloucestre, Sire Moryoud þe...
Maurice, erle of Wirecestre, Sire Mauryce þe..Wyncestre
Gurguynt, erle of Herford,
& sir Beus of Oxenford;
sir Vrgence þat was of Bathe, ..þe Erl..
þer þe Sessons did scathe;

sir Cursalle of Chestre was.
Of Dorcester, sir Ionathas,
Amorand, erle of Salebiri,   Emoraund þe . . .
& Kinmare, kyng of Canterbiri;
sir Baruk of Cirecestre
& sir Iugence of Leicestre;
sir Argal, erle of Werwik,   . Ergal þe . . .
his men com to courte fulle þik.
Of þer childir it sais þer names,
to neuen þam here it ne frames.   . nemne hem here litel hit .
Þer was Porsud sone, Donant,   . . Porfodes . .
& sir Regin sone, Elant;
& Cohel sone hight Keneus,   . Coyles . . .
& Katelle sone Katellus,
& oþer names selcouth to telle;
it is not on þam to duelle.
Þise serued at þe rounde table;
to rekne þam alle it is fable, ... but fable
so many were in chambir & halle,
men suld irke to telle þam alle.

[*L adds:*] What of þo þat y fond writen
& of þo þat fewe men wyten
Hit are but fewe þat can þem telle
& þo þat can þer to ne wyl dwelle

[66ra] Outlandes kyngis þat of him helde,
þat bowed vnto Arthure schelde,
Guillomare, kyng of Ireland   [*Transp. L*]
þat he wan with his hand;   [*Transp. L*]
þe kyng of Danmark, sir Askil;
Loth of Norweie com him tille;
Gonweis, kyng of Orkeneye,
of Island he com in his weye;
Doldan, kyng of Gouteland,
Kynmare, kyng of Wentland,   & Reumarek . . .
Ligere, þe erle of Boloyne;   [*Transp. L*]
of Nauere, þe kyng, & of Gascoyne;   [*Transp. L*]
of fflandres, þe erle Holdin,
& of Chartres, þe erle Gerin;
he was a man noble & fers,
with him com alle þe Duȝepers;
& sir Witard, þe erle of Peiters,   Sire Gwytard . . . .
& sir Key, lord of Aungers;   . . Caye . . .
of Nomondy, sir Beduere,   . Normandie . .

of fe, þe kynges Botilere;
of Bretayne, þe kyng Ohel, [*Transp. L*]
of þe Mans, þe erle Borel. [*Transp. L*]

[*L adds:*] Sire Ohel & þo of ffraunce
Þey were of noble contenaunce
Wel clad & arayed y þe richest
& horsed alle for þe best

It was no baron of alle Spayne,
no þien vntille Almayne,
þat he ne tille Arthure feste ferd,
þat douhty was & þerof herd;
som himself forto se
& to be holden of his meyne, ..byholde his meyne
& som to se of what wise
þei ordeynd þat faire seruise;
& som to se þe table rounde
þat neuer ore or þat was founde, ..byforn þat tyme..
& som to se his faire paleis,
som to behold his riche herneis,
som þe folk to behowe,
& som his knyghtes forto knowe;
& som for his gyftes gode,
& som for his noble fode;
som com for haf baily ...to haue bailly
& som to lere curteisy.
Whan Arthure courte was alle plenere
& alle comen fer & nere,
þe erþe about stired & quoke,
[66rb] so fast hors & man þer schoke;
þer was puttyng, þristyng, & þro
with fotefolk þat com to & fro,
innes forto teme & take;
þat non had, pauillons did make.
Þer maistres, marschalles ferd aboute,
delyuerd stedes within, withoute, .innes wyþynne &.
bordes brouht, cordes & kables,
mad maniores to stand in stables. & made mangers....
Þan mot men laddes lede ...se þe ladies lede
many faire palfrey & stede.

[*L adds:*] In mud in mires to soille & dasche
Siþen in wayers to watre & wasche
Syþen to wype & to mangers teye
Hey & prouende byfor þem leye

Þan com chambirleyns & squiers
with robes riche on many maners,
to folde, to presse, & to pike,
& som to hang & to strike,
mantles, forres of grete pris, .forours of riche.
menyuere strinkled with gris. Of meneuer stranlyng veyr &.

[*L adds:*] Oþer pelure yknowe þer were
Þe names of þem y ne wot what are
Lomb or boge conyng or hare
Y ne knowe me nought in swylk chaffare

On þe morn þe fest suld be,
com þe Archbisshop of his degre;
with him of Rome þe legate ....cam þe legat
& oþer bisshopes of mener state;
& right als þe story sais,
Dubrice crouned him in his palais,
& þe legate of Rome & he
did þat sollempnyte.
Whan he was crouned on þat wise,
to þe kirke þei ȝede to þe seruise.
Þe tuo Archbisshopes þat þer ware,
þei led him, his armes vpbare,
& sette him in a riche chaiere
þer he suld his seruise here;
foure suerdes of golde were borne
with foure kynges him beforne,
þat seruise felle ilk a schelde. ..fel to þer.
Whan Arthure his fest helde,
þe kyng of North Wales & of Scotland
& of South Wales, writen I fand,
of Cornwaile, þe Duke Kadore,
þe ferth suerde bare he þore;
þof his state were not so hii,
ȝit was he man most worþi. ....ful wel.
Dubrice þat was noble prelate
[66va] & of Rome þe legate,
þat office did, þei myght best; ..þey dide þey..
of dignite þei wer hiest.
Þe quene Gunuere on hir side
was serued with mykelle pride,
for scho had befor sent
after ladies, maidens gent, .leuedys & maydens.
þat were of hir awen kynde

& oþer of pris þat scho mo fynde.	......myght.
[*L adds:*]	Quenes Cuntesses oþer laydys mo
	Comen to mayntene þe fest þo
In hir chambir apon a palle	
þei crouned hir with a corounalle.	
With scho was crouned, þe ladies	When scheo....
led hir to þe kirke of saynt Iulis;	
þer were nonnes of religioun	
& þer suld hir messe be don.	
Þer to be, so þei ches,	To ben a twynne...
forto departe þer mykelle pres	
þat myght not be in o stede,	
for folk vnrid & mykelle krede,	
foure ladies went þat assise	...þe same.
as þe kynges did Arthurus seruise.	
Foure doufes befor hir bare,	.white douues byforn..
þo ladies þe kynges wyues ware;	
after þam com oþer ladies	
richeli clad in purpure bis;	..in pourpre & bys
[*L adds:*]	In cloþes of golde þat schon so schene
	& oþere in scarlet & in grene
alle were þei richely dight	
& gay to behold in sight.	Þer was neuere seyen swyche a.
	[*L differs, four lines:*]
Grete presse was at þe procession,	I trowe þer were many doude
ilkon proudere þan þe lion.	Þat proudly spak for noble schroude
	Ilkon oþer faste byheld
	And of þe faire mykel was of teld
Whan þe procession was gone,	
þe messe bigan son on one.	
Þer mot men se faire samenyng	
of þo clerkis þat best couth syng;	
with tribille, mene, & burdoun,	
of manyon was suete soun	
of þo þat songe hie & lowe	
& þo þat couþe organes blowe.	
Inouh þer was of mynstralcie	
& of songe faire melodie;	
þer mot men folk com & go	.myght men se folk...
to þe kirkes boþe to & fro,	
of knyghtes & of squiers bolde	
[66vb] to liste songe, ladies to beholde;	

[*L adds:*]	ffro þat o kyrke to þe oþer þey ran
	Where was þe beste wyste no man
	At neyþer þem þoughte þey dwelled longe
	Ne nought were ful to here þe songe
if it had bene at þer pay,	
þat songe had lasted alle þat day.	
Whan þe messes were don	. . . were boþe .
& homward were alle bon,	. . þey were . .
þe kyng did of his tire þare	
þat he to þe kirke bare	
& toke anoþer of lesse pris;	
þe quene did þe same wise.	
[*L adds:*]	Þeir heuy atir þey dide of boþe
	& in lightere dide þem cloþe
Þe kyng into his paleis	. . com vntil . .
& sat at þe mete þat ilk weis;	
þe quene tille a noþer ȝede	
& þe ladies with hir gan lede.	
Somtyme was custom of Troye	But Custume was whilom in .
whan þei mad fest of ioye,	
men togider suld go to mete,	
ladies bi þam self suld ete;	
[*L adds:*]	Þe Bretons had þe selue vsage
	Þey were of þe Troiens lynage
þat ilk vsaga was at þat feste,	. ilk vsage . . . .
þe women com amang þer geste;	No womman cam . . .
þe women withouten men suld be	
bot seruitours of meyne.	. . . here meyne
The kyng was vp at þe des,	. . . set vp . . .
about him þe mykelle pres;	Þer was in ful . .
about him þe lordes sate,	But . . . lordynges sat
ilk a lord after his state.	
Sir Kay was stiward, chosen of alle,	
to serue befor þe kyng in halle.	
His cloþing was riche & fyne	
& þe pelore of hermyne;	
with him serued befor þe kyng	
a þousand in þe same cloþing;	
out of þe kichyne serued sir Kay	
& alle his felawes þat day.	
Sir Beduere on þat oþer partie,	
he serued of þe boterie;	. . . . botelerye

with him was, clad in hermyne,
a þousand þat brouht þe wyne. ...serued of..
[*L adds:*] Was þer non þat serue bad
But he in riche pelure were clad

Þe kynges couþe sir Beduere bare,
he ȝede befor þat þer ware; & ȝede byforn al...
after him com alle þe route
þat serued þe barons alle aboute.
Þe quene was serued richely,
[67ra] hir seruantȝ were signed redy .seriauntȝ were assigned.
in alle office forto serue,
& befor þo ladies kerue;
many vesselle was þer riche,
of sere colours not alle liche,
of metes many maner seruise
& sere drinkes on þat wise.
Alle þe nobley couth I not telle,
ne myght stonde þeron to duelle; Ne y naue no stounde...
þe names to say of þe richesse
ne þe men of pruesse, .of þe...
ne þe curteisie, ne þe honour; [*L differs:*] Was þer no lond in al þe werd
of cristiente þer was þe flour. Of gode knyghtes so mykel of herd
Was þer no knyght so hie of blode,
ne had so mykelle werldes gode,
þat þerfore suld be holden of pris,
bod he in dede were proued þris; But......
þris proued at þe leste,
þan was he alosed at þe feste.
Þan suld his armes þat men knew
& his cloþing alle o hew,
þat same quantise his armes had,
in þat same he suld be clad.
His wife was clad in þe same coloure
for hir lord was of honour. ...was man of.
If ane were douhty & syngle man,
he suld che him a lemman, Þen schuld he chese...
els suld he not be loued
bot he had bene in bataile proued.
Þo ladies þat were holden chaste,
for no þing wold, no do waste;
þo ladies were clad in one
& be þer cloþing men knew ilkone.
Whan þei had eten & suld rise,

ilk man dight him on þat wise
þat he couth in play;   . . best couþe inne.
vnto þe felde he toke his way
& parted þam in stedes sere
to play ilkon on þer manere.
Som iusted þat couth & myght
forto schewe þer stedes lyght;   . . . . . wyght
[67rb] som skipped & keste þe stone
& som wrestild fulle gode wone;   . . skirmed . . .
darte schotte, lances kast,
& þo þat couth skirmed fast.   . . . couþe wrastled.
Ilkon played þe gamen he couth
& maste had vsed in his ȝouth;
þat best did in his playeng,
he was brouht befor þe kyng,
& þe kyng gaf him mede
þat he was paied or he ȝede.
Þe ladies on þe walles stegh
forto behold alle þer pleih;
who so had lemman þore in place,
toward him turned þe face;   . . . boþe eye & face
on boþe sides ilk oþer beheld,
þo on þe walles, þo in þe feld.
Iogelours were þer inouh
þat þer quantise forþe drouh.
Mynstrals many with dyuers glew,   Many mynestrales þorow out þe toun
souns of bemes þat men blew;   Som blewe trompe & Clarioun
harpes, pipes, & taboures,
ffithels, citolles, sautreours,
belles, chymes, & synfan,
oþer inouh neuen I ne kan.   & . . þat nemne y . .
Sangsters þat myry song,   Gestours singers . . .
sounde of glew ouer alle rong;   So gret murþe was þat ouer . .
disours inouh teld fables
& som plaied with deeȝ at tables;
& som at þe hasard fast   . . pleide at hasard.
& lost & wan bi chance of cast;
som þat wild not of þe tablere
drouh forth meyne of þe chekere.
With drauhtes quante of knyght & roke,
with grete sleiht ilk oþer suoke;   & oþer sleyghtes ilk oþer byswok
at ilk matyng þei said "Chek!"
Þat most les, sat in his nek.   . . þer loste sat y þe blek

Þre daies lasted þe feste	..þe feste sat
(I trow was neuer non as þat);	..neuere non was lyke þat
& whan it com Wednesday	
þat þe folk suld parte away,	..people..to wende þer way
þe kyng gaf gyftes riche,	..þem gaf his..
þo to his seruise were briche,	.þat til....
[67va] & for þer seruise held þer fee3,	...seruises held hem at.
he gaf þam burghes & cite3;	& somme he gaf burwes..
abbot & bisshop, auanced his rent	....þer rent
or þei fro þe courte went.	
Þat of oþer londes were	And oþere þat of strange..
þat for luf com þere,	..worschip were..
he gaf stedes & coupes of golde,	
non richere aboun molde.	& oþere iuels þe beste on.
Som gaf he hauberkes, som grehond3,	
som riche robes worth many pond3;	...wyþ..
som mantels with veire & gris,	
& som ma3ers of riche pris;	
som helmes & hauberkes,	& somme..somme.
gode palfreis he gaf to clerkes;	
bowes & arwes he gaf archers,	
runces gode vnto squiers;	Rounsyes...
som he gaf hauberions,	[*Om. L*]
som plates, & som aktons,	[*Om. L*]
som he gaf knyues of plyght,	... Plates & swerdes..
& som suerdes richely dyght.	Somme Gyrdles & knyues ful..
Vnto disours þat teld þam gestes,	[*L differs, six lines:*]
	Somme gaf he ewer & basyn
he gaf cloþes of wyld bestes;	& somme Pelure of fyn Eremin
som gaf he pelore of hermyn,	Vnto disours þat telde þem gestes
som lauour of siluer with bacyn.	Gaf he cloþes or wylde bestes
	Lyouns lepards þat wold þem take
	Beres & apes boþe white & blake
Was þer non ouht worþi	
þat he ne gaf him bliþely.	
After þat his state was lyfte,	
so he rewarded him with gyfte.	
Right as þis giftes were in gyffyng	
& alle serued, knyght & kyng,	
Arthure sat opon þe des,	
aboute him his mykelle pres	
of kynges, erles, & barons,	.. Dukes Erles..
of vnkouth knyghtes & Bretons,	& of straunge lordes..

& suld haf taken leue & went,
tuelue messengers to him were sent
fro þe Emperour of Rome.
Tuo togidir faire þei come
into þe halle Arthure beforn,
with olyue branches in handes born,
with softe pas & fulle seine
grette Arthure & his meyne.
[67vb] Þei said þei were messengers
komen in pes & faire maners,
out of Rome þien fulle fer
fro þe Emperour Lucius Ybere,
"þat is our lord & our dere. ....lef & dere
Bi vs he sendes þis letter here
& þe comandes on alle weies
þou do als þis letter seis."
Þe letter in his hand þei leid.
Liste now what þe charter seid:
"Lucius, þat Rome has in balie
& ouer þe Romeyns þe maistrie,
he sendes tille Arthure þe Breton
als on of his enmys felon.
Me meruails mykille, & ilk Romayn,
& meruailand we haf disdeyn
þat þou dar bere þe so hie,
agayn a Romayn ons open þin ie.
I wonder of þe bost þou makes
& at whom þou conseile takes,
ageyn Rome to reise strife
whils þou wote a Romeyn o lyfe.
Þou gaf þi self a sory chek
agayn Romeyns to reise contek,
þat alle erþe þorh dome demes
& hede of alle þe world it ȝemes.
Þou wote not, ȝit wist salle it be,
ne nouht þou sawe, bot þou salle se
how grete it is to wreth Rome
þat alle þe world iustise with dome. ...werd schal iustice & dome
Ageyn kynd has þou gon;
reson ne mesure has þou non.
Whiþen com þou what þing þe boldes,
our treuage takes, & has, & holdes,
our londes reues vs als þou wildes,

& tille vs no thyng þou ȝeldes?
What right has þou þervnto?
Þi foly it is þat þou did so.
If þei may long so with þe leue
þat we þorgh þe þam not reue, ..þorow force....
þan may þou skorne & say to where ...seye & scorne þe wheþer
þat þe woulf fles for þe wethere,
[68ra] & ȝit þat he so long slepe
þat durst not wake to assaile a schepe,
or a goot þe woulf did dare,
or þe grehunde fled for þe hare;
bot suilk a þing may not betide,
no more salle it on our side.
Oure ancessoure, Iulius Cesar,
wan Bretayn, ert þou not war,
& toke treuage þerof long;
foure hundreth ȝere we gan it fong,
& of oþer ildes aboute
þat þorgh þe ere we now withoute.
Ȝit has þou don vs more vilete
þan alle þe losse we telle to þe,
þat þou ffrolle our seruant slouh, ...baroun.
ffrance & Flandres fro vs drouh.
For þat þou has of Rome no doute
ne to his lordschip wille þou loute,
I mak þe somons vnto Rome
& I comand þe to come
folowand at þis next heruest;
it salle not help cheson to kest,
bot com & mend þin vnright
þat þou slouh ffrolle our knyght,
& amend on oþer way
of þat w kon more to þe say. ..we conne to þe.
If it be so þou mak delay
& wille not com at þi day
ne bewe tille our comandment, .come...
þan telle I þe þat þou ert schent. .telly þe outrely schent
Þorgh force, ffrance I wille þe reue;
of Bretayne nouht a fote leue.
I wene not þou wille abide,
& if þou do þou salle þe hide.
I trowe nouht on þis half þe se & siker on þys...
þou salle dur schewe þe to me, .schalt nought dur....

& if þou on þis halfe bees,
if I kom, forsoþe þou flees; At my comyng...
& þou salle not tapise a nyght to slepe
þat I salle do þe stirte & lepe,
& bring þe to Rome in bandes,
& leue þe in þe Romeyn handes."
[68rb] [A]t þat word was noyse & crie [*Capital A is missing in P.*]
of þe Bretons þat stode nehi;
othes þei suore þat þei suld die
þat brouht þat lettre of vilanie,
"& for his luf þat sent ȝow hidere,
þe salle be hanged alle togidere." ȝe.....
Litelle letted þat men þam hirte, ..þey nadde be slayn or.
bot sir Arthure þan vpstirte.
"Bretons," he said, "hold ȝow stille!
Messengere salle haf non ille; Þe messegers schul...
non ille haf, non ille here, Ne neyþer ille haue ne.
bot com & go in faire manere.
Messengers of Rome þei are,
in pes þei com, so salle þei fare.
Þer message þat þei haf said,
a lord þei haf on þam it laid."
Whan þat dynne was wele pesed
& eft þei had þer setes sesed, ..hadde þeir sittynge.
þe kyng toke tuo or þre ..toke wyþ hym two..
of his wisest barons priue
þat best couth conseile tille honour,
with him þei ȝede in tille a toure;
þe name þer of was in haunt,
als I fond, þe Toure Geaunt. As y fond writen...
Arthure þer sat & þei beside
to conseile how best mot betide.
Sir Cador spak first & louh,
"Sir Kyng," he said, "I salle say ȝow:
often in study haf I bene
& in grete drede ay bituene,
þat þorh idelnes of pes
ere Bretons feble & hertles.
Idelnes norisches bot euel
& mykelle temptacoun of þe deuel; Temptacion of flesche &...
idelnes mas man right slouh .makeþ man ful.
& dos pruesse falle fulle louh;
idelnes norisches licherie

& dos vs tent to suilk folie;
idelnes & long reste,
ȝouth in waste a way wille keste,
& dos men tent to foly fables,
tille haȝardrie, to deeȝ & tables.
[68va] We haf now alle þis fyue ȝere
vsed rioterie mystere — Lyued in lechours mester
þat þorh reste & suilk soioure
haf we lost grete honour.
A long while haf we slept
þat no man wakand on vs kept;
bot I þank god & our Lady,
now ere we wakned a party.
Som grace is ronen in þe Romens þouht — ...ronne in Romayns herte
þat þei chalenge on vs souht — ...vs so smerte
for to haf our londes & feeȝ, — Vs to bynime oure...
alle our conquest in oþer cuntreeȝ.
If Romeyns be so coreious
þat þei wille do as þei send vs,
ȝit salle Bretons wyn þam los
of Romeyns þat in renoun gos. — ....Rome gos
Long pes lufed I neuer,
ne nouht salle, þof I lyf euer."
Þan spak Wawan þe curteise,
"Meruaily, Cador, þou seise!
After were, gode is pes,
& after wo, þe wele god ches.
In pes is don grete vassalage;
for luf men dos many rage." — ...doþ gret outrage
At þat word þei sat doun,
þe kyng & ilk a baroun.
Whan þe kyng sauh þam set,
alle þat were to conseile fet,
a while he þouht, þan lift his heued — Þe kyng þoughte a þrowe....
whan þei had þer carpyng leued. — ....ianglyng.
"Barons," he said, "þat er here,
ȝe ere my felawes & me fulle dere.
Whan I lese, ȝe haf parte þerin;
ȝe ere my felawes whan I wyn.
Whan wo or were has me comen,
ȝour parte with me haf ȝe þer nomen.

[*L adds:*] As felawes in prosperite
& felawes in aduersete

Whedir I haf won or lorn,
3our hap with me haf 3e born;
þorgh 3our help & 3our auys
haf I won mykelle pris.
Bi water, bi lond, I haf 3ow led,
3orgh 3ow in nede I haf sped.   Þorow . . . haue y wel.
[68vb] Alle tymes haf I fon 3ow trewe,   Euere y haue founde 3ow.
3our conseile euer gode & newe;
alle þe londes þat I haf wonnen,
withouten 3ow was nouht bigonnen.
Þe Romeyns, 3e haf wele herd,
þat here is folden & vp sperd,   By þys lettre þat here ys.
me & 3ow þei manace fast,
with grete wordes wene me gast.
If god wille help me & 3ow,
þer manace is no þing þer prow;   Þeir þret schal nought be for . .
of vs get þei neuer nouht
bot it be fulle dere bouht.   . 3if hit be ouer dere abought
Þei haf grete power & fulle riche,
non is þer pere ne to þam liche;   Þer nis no power to þeires.
þerfor bus vs befor purueie   . we moste bifore.
what we wille do, what we wille seie,
auant like & resonabille,   & auenauntly . .
& þat we say hold it stabille.
A þing befor þat men wille rede,   . . for þought . . . .
it is better mayntend in nede.
Ane arowe þat is schot 3e se,
ouþer bos men fend it or fle;   Eyþer bihoues hit men . . . .
þe sam wyse bos vs do,   . same weys byhoues . .
þe Romeyns haf schoten vs to.   . . han yschoten . .
Conseiles now & couere vs rathe   Now conseille we . . . .
þat þer schotyng do vs no scathe.
Trewe þei ask, so haf þei had;
þat is behynd, send þam þei bad,
of þis lond & oþer mo;
& France wille not forgo,   . . wil þey nought.
for Bretayn wille first ansuere,   . . wil y . .
writen in letter, þat þei salle here;   . . . . . . bere
ansuere for 3ow & me
wille I þat þis lettre be.   Þat lettre wil y þat hit so.
Þus wille I say & þus write,
my skille listens me a lite:
Cesar of Rome þis lond first wan

þorgh fight & force of man.
Þe Bretons þat tyme mot not defend;
treuage bord þam to þam send, Trewe byhoued þem to.
& force, ȝe wote wele, is no right,
bot pride out of mesure myght.
[69ra] It is no skille, ne lawe non makes
þing þat þou þorgh force takes,
& suylk gyftes men salle fordo
þat with wrong was taken so.
Þei vpbraide vs of our ancessours
þat þei ouercome with hard schours; ...þem..stours
of þe pouerte þei mak vpbraide
& of þe treuage befor saide.
Of þis þei mak auancement
þat here befor our fadres schent;
so mykelle awe we greue þam þe more ..oughte.....
& þei ere halden vs to restore.
We awe to hate þat þei haf hated Wel oughte we hat hem þat...
& bete doun þo þam abated. & bere hem doun þat..
Þei wille do vs þe same outrage,
& say it is þer heritage,
to haf our godes & vs reuyle.
Þei salle not bide eft þat whyle,
bot with þer reson & þer dome,
I wille set chalange on Rome, Wyþ skile y may chalange.
& with þer skille I may wele So wyþ skile & reson...
þe lond of Rome ask ilk a dele.
Belyn was kyng of Bretons
& Brenne, duke of Burgolons;
þise breþer of Bretayn born,
Rome conquered here biforn
& of þe Romeyns toke treuages,
& hange tuenty of þer ostages
befor þer ine þat þei mot se,
& siþen conquered alle þat cite.
Whan Belyn turned to Bretayn,
he mad Brenne of Rome cheftayn
& bad him gouerne alle þe honoure,
& he regned als emperoure.
Now wille I leue Belyn
& speke I wille of Constantyn,
Constancius sonne & Elyns,
þat held Rome as his demeyns.

Constance of Rome had senyorie faire
& Constantyn was his ayre,
& I am ayre of Constantyn;
þorgh þat descent Rome salle be myn.
[69rb] Maximian, Leonyne sonne,
kyng of Bretayn, at Rome gan wonne.
He wan Neustrie, þe Lesse Bretan,
& alle ffrance, & Almayn,
& Mongou, & Lumbardie,
& of Rome had þe seingurie. ..... seignurye
Þise were myn ancessours of schelde
þat þe honour of Rome helde.
Now þorgh skille haf ȝe knowen
þat Rome ouh to be myn owen, ..by reson schold be..
als wele as Bretayn þers,
þorgh olde ancetrie tille heires. ..auncetrie..
Rome had treuage & it forsoke
& myn ancessours of Rome trew toke.
Þei cleyme Bretayn & I Rome;
þat we boþe cleyme, it is to come.
Late þam wyn it if þei may,
ȝit haf I kept it alle my day.
ffrance I wan of ffrolle, þer knyght,
to kepe it lengere þei no myght; ....he hadde no.
þei wan it þorgh force as I it wan,
with force so myght anoþer man.
[*L adds:*] Wherto chalange þey so bolde
Þat þey ne myghte no lenger holde
Þorgh skille haf þei no seruise .right skil....
bot þorgh force & couetise; But al....
[*L adds:*] Þat ys to anoþer al so fre
Als hit was to þeym or me
þe emperour makis his manace ..makeþ vs gret.
out of þis lond me to chace
& in bondes to Rome lede.
God wille not he so spede!
Litille he me praises & dredes lesse; Y preyse hym litel & drede hym lesse
if he to me seke pruesse, ..on me wil seke.
a countir he getis or he go, Encountre..er þat..
me eft salle not manace to slo, Þat eft ne schal he me manace ne.
ne to non of myn do ille.
So salle we do him change his wille;
bot whan þei com to chalangeyng,

bring Rome & I salle Bretayn bring,
& whilk of vs most may ....þat most.
bere Rome & Bretayn boþe away."
Whan Arthur had said his reson,
wele was alowed with ilk Breton;
with o worde þei said alle at ons,
"Wele haf ȝe said, Sir, for þe nons."
[69va] Whan þei were stille a partie,
Sir Ohel spak þat sat him bie,
& said, "No man ȝong no alde
suld ouht amend þat ȝe haf talde.
Bot sen þou sees þat þou ert thrette
& may not passe withoute barette,
somon þi folk, mak þam ȝare, ...& make..
& sette þam day whan þou wille fare.
Mak no long drecchyng þerto,
for I wille if þou wille so,
& passe Mongow in to þe mouns, ...mountȝ
& hold þe day of þi somouns;
& if we wend with þe togidere
& he se þat we com þidere,
so may tide, þan salle him rewe
þat he began þe bale to brewe;
& it tides often stoundes
þat on bigynnes, himself confoundes. .who so bygynneþ..
I trowe þat god wille vs auance;
grace is toward & gode chance.
Þe emperour sendes after þe,
seke him þan whare so he be,
& bede baldlie on him bares, .baldely bede we on hym þe.
so may we se who vs chares. Sone schul we se þen ho ys.
Sette þe emperour in suilk drede
þat neuer to courte eft dur þe bede. .he tys court nere dur vs.
Loke what sais þe prophecie,
Sibille þe sage þat wille not lie:
þre Bretons of Bretayn salle come,
þorgh fyne force gouerne Rome;
tuo er passed, wele we mene, ffoure ar passed...
þou ert þe thrid salle do þam tene. ..þe fifte schal...
[*L adds:*] Þe fifte þou art y wot hit we
Þat Rome schal haue ilkadel

Sen so is ordaynd to betide,
wharto salle þou long abide; .schold we longe.

[*L adds:*] Auaunce now boþe þy self & ous
Oure wil to helpe ys coraious
Y dar wel seye so hastou founde
ffor we ne doute no dynt ne wounde
Ne deþ ne prison ne langour
So wilne we faste þyn honour

leue nouht, bot fast þe spede,
& I salle help, if þou haf nede,
with ten þousand gode knyghtes   Come wyþ . . of . .
with hors & armes at alle rightes;
& if þou for tresure lette,
alle my lond I salle wed sette
for golde & siluere þe to take
or þou þi wendyng forsake."   Er þou þis viage schuld .
[69vb] Saynt Dubrice, þe holy man,
at Sir Arthure leue toke þan
forto change his habite
& bicome ane heremyte;
& Dauid, Arthure eam, it toke
þe Archbisshop see Dubrice forsoke.   . Erchebischopriche þat . .
After þe speche of Sir Ohel
spak þe Kyng Auguisel

[*L adds:*] Sire Lothes broþer & sire Vrien
Alle þre were doughti men

& said, "If þou wille were bigyn,
speke now to þo þat ere herein,
þe best of alle þi baronage
þat herd & wote þe message,   . wyte & herden . .
& witte þer wille what þei wille do,
& what þei may help þe þerto.

[*L adds:*] Now ys tyme to purueye
Of help & god conseil to seye
Alle þo þat of þe holde
Riche lordes & barouns bolde
Þat oughte to helpe þe þorow skile
& wel y trowe þat so þey wyle

No tiþing neuer I vndirstode
þat gladed me so mykelle in mode
als with þe Romeyns forto werre
þat alle men in þer daungere sperre.
I may þam nouht luf no preise,
for þei ere proud & vncurteise.
Gode men so mykelle þei dispise,

þei may not lif bot in þer seruise;
& þei ere men of non honour,
bot couetouse to gedir tresour.
[*L adds:*] Gode men wyþ al to noye
& þer londes to robbe & struye
I trowe þam salle mysbetide   ..þei schul ȝit.
for þer couetise & pride;
of þis þat þei haf vs sent,
þei salle be wrothe or it be ent.
[*L adds:*] Wonder were elles or art me failles
But þey pleye wyþ repentailles
Bot þof þe neuer had it begunnen,   & þaw þey neuere...
we suld þorgh reght on þam haf runnen
for to venge our ancessoures,
& bate þer pride als þei wild oures.
Þei say þai had of vs trewage   .seide þey had of þeym.
& chalange it for heritage;
I trowe þat þei þam neuer non gaf
bot thorgh force þam ouer haf,
as theues robbed þam & reft;
þat wille we chalange of þam now eft.
[*L adds:*] Wyþ force þey gaf hit to þe Romayns
Wyþ force we wil haue hit agayns
So harde oure force may to þem byte
Þat alle oure scaþes schul þey quyte
We haf wonnen in many stoure,
ouer alle we haf born þe floure;   & ouer al born awey..
so salle we ȝit þer pride abate
for þer couetise & þer hate.
[70ra] Þat we haf, I set at nouht   ..haue wonne....
bot þe Romeyns to rounge be brouht;   .ȝif þe Romayns to ryng..
no þing desire I mare
þan þiderward we redy ware,
& þat we were at þe bataile
to se whilk suld best assaile.
Þer salle we wyn pruesse & prowe,
hors & armes, tresore inowe;
if god vs grante our life to saue,
þat we þam ask, we salle it haue,
Rome & alle þat þer to langes.
Þan salle we right þat þerto langes;   ....þat now vs wranges
if god vs grante vs forto venge,
ȝit salle we fond to wynne Lorenge   Toward hym we schal wynne.

& Almayn, if þat we may;
alle gate we wille mak assay.
Als I say, so wille I rede
& alle þe same wille do in dede. — .þat ilke wil...
If god me grante wele to spede,
tuo þousand salle I with me lede
& fotefolk inouh gode at nede;
if god wille, we salle not drede." — ...noman schul we.
Whan Auguiselle his tale had told, — .þe Scottysche kyng had his tale told
alle þei said, with tong o fold,
þat schent he suld be of þam alle
on whom þat wendyng suld not falle.
Whan ilkon had said his wille,
Arthure listend & sat stille,
did calle a clerk with inke & penne,
bad him write, he suld hym kenne.
Als he had said in alle maners,
he tauht it to þe messengers,
faire folden & we seilde, — ..& wel enseled
& to þer maister was it deilde,
& did þam alle grete honour;
inouh he gaf þam of tresour,
& bad þam say to þe emperour
þat Arthure, of France gouernour,
& of Bretayn chefe & flour,
salle defend boþe toun & tour. — & schal defendit castel..
[*L adds:*] & be þer warant & socour
Ageyns Romayns to stonde in stour
"Say ȝour lord I wille not lette
to com þat day þat he has sette,
[70rb] no treuage ȝelde bot forto fette. — ..to ȝelde but trewage to.
Loke he be redy do þat he hette."
Þe messengers þer leue toke,
toward Rome þei way schoke — ..þer wey þey.
& teld þe emperour whan þei come,
þe grete nobley of Arthure home;
how mykille folk þei with him fonde,
so douhty non is in no londe,
& in what stede his courte he held,
& alle þe state þerof þei teld;
how curtaisly to þam he spak,
nouht bot wisdom of his mouthe brak.
"Non is o lyue, kaiser no kyng,

þat semes so wele his beryng,
no is so curteis þerwith alle.
His giftes ere large & standes in stalle;
it is no kyng to his costages   Þer ys no kyng doþ suche.
of mete & drinke, no to gyue wages,   ..ne drynke ne giftes of.
ne suilk seruise is þer none
in no courte bot his alle one.
To ask him trewe, it is for nouht,
ne non to bring has he þouht   [*Om. L*]
He þenkes to ask ȝe þien brouht   .....þennes.
þat ȝe þam reft, it salle be bouht."   [*Om. L*]
Þe chartere þei schewed þer barons
& said, "Suilk ere Arthure respons."
Whan þe Romeyns had wele herd
how þe messengers ansuerd,
& þer chartre acorded wele
vnto þer saw ilka dele,
þat Arthure wild no seruise do,
bot haf treuage, þe letter wild so.
Þei said to þe emperour alle aboute,
"With force ȝe salle do him loute,
[*L adds:*] Passeþ Moungu wiþ host right stoute
& if he com, we salle him þoute, ...route
reue him his renge, maugre his snoute!"   &..his regne...
[*L adds:*] & wyþ righte force hold hym wyþoute
Whan Lucius wist Arthure respons
& sawe þe wille his barons,   He saw..of his.
he did somone withouten delay
to be redy be þe tuenty day,   ...byn þe twentyþ.
with hors & armes to wend alle preste
agayn Arthure toward þe weste.
[*L adds:*] ffor y schal nere stynte no stounde
Til y come þere þat þey hym founde
[70va] ffirst com Epistrot, þe kyng of Grece,
& sir Ethion, duke of Boece,
Sir Hurtak, þe kyng of Turkeis,
a duhty knyght & curteis;   .doughti..a curteys
Pandras, kyng of Egipte,
& of Cice, kyng Ipolipte.
He was of grete seignorie,
a hundreth cites of his balie.
Out of Sire com Ewandere,
& out of ffrise þe Kyng Teucere;

out of Babiloyn, sir Micipsa,
& out of Spayne, sir Alifatina;
out of Mede, þe Kyng Bokius,
& out of Libie, sir Sertorius;
out of Bitinie, sir Polidetes,
& out of Tire, þe Kyng Serses;
Sir Mucensar out of Aufrik,
a lond ferne a fulle grete strike.

[*L adds:*] But he broughte tresor gret plente
& fair folk & fele to se

Þo þat were of þe senatours,
men of Rome most of honours,
of þam com Marcelle, Lucius Katelle,
Octa, Gaius, & sir Metelle
& oþer inouh of þe same kynde
þat no man may þer names fynde.

[*L adds:*] & þey alle þe names wer founde
Me þynkeþ hit were but tynt þe stounde
To write þe names of so fele hounde
Þat were vncristned in þys mounde

Whan alle were comen, simple & bolde,
foure hundreth þousand were þei tolde,
& a hundreth & foure score,
alle of armes, men telle bifore, . armed men hit telles .
withouten fote men & sargeancie,
þat þe noumbre can non discrie.
Whan alle were þat þider suld come, . . were comen . . . .
at Lammes þei remoued fro Rome . þe Lammesse þey wente . .
& toke þer way towerd Mongu . . . . toward Moungu
with mykelle noyse, crie, & hu.
Whan Arthure parted his meyne
& suld go þer þei wild be,
be name he mad þam alle somons
or þei went, alle þe barons,
& praied þam of help at þer myght.
Bot þat þei saued wele þer right
& how mykille ilkon mot bring,
þat wild he wit ouer alle þing.
[70vb] Ireland, Gotland, & Norweie,
Danmark, Island, & Orkeneie,
sex score þousand þei him mette,
of alle þo londes gadred & fette.
Knyghtes were non of alle þo

þei kouth not ride, þei suld go.   Bot oþere þat on fote most go

[*L adds:*] On fote by houed þem bere þer armes
Dartes Gauelokes & Gysarmes
Þat was þe manere of þer lond
Þey hadde non oþer ne non þem fond

Of Normandie & Angeou,
of Pikardie & of Peitou,
& out of fflandres & Boloyne, ... of Brabant
fourescore þousand withouten essoyne.   . . . want

[*L adds:*] So mykel scholde þey fynde of fe
& namore was þer ryght to be

In France was tuelfe lorde fers   . . were þanne tuelue lordes fers
þat man cald Duȝepers;
þise Duȝepers, lordes of ffrance,
to Geryn of Chartres had aliance.
Ilk of þam fond a hundreth knyghtes
þat felle þer fe at alle rightes;
ten þousand hette sir Ohel,
& tuo þousand sir Auguisel,
& Arthure of þis ilk lond,
sexti þousand knyghtes fond
withouten fote folk & archers,
& sargeanȝ & alblasters.
Of þise fond I þe noumbre writen   . . y ne fond no noumbre ywriten
& of no mo kouth men witen.
Whan Arthure wist þe certeyn
how fele ilk kyng suld bring ageyn   What ilk lord scholde brynge hym .
of men of armes of gode aray,
he praied þam com & set a day;
at Barbflete in Normondie,
þidere suld com alle þer nauie,
& ilkon him certeynly hette
to be þer at þe day sette.
Þan went alle home, kyng & knyght,
& purueied þam þat þei were dyght.
Arthure had a cosyn,
Modrede hight þat traitour fyn;   . he highte a . .
noble knyght he was in stoure,
bot to his eame was he traitoure.
He betauht him his lond to kepe;   Arthur bitaughtym . . . .
him had bien better haf liggen to slepe,
for he lufed þe quene priuely,
Arthure wife, & lay hir by;

[71ra] was nouht perceyued bituex þam tuo,
who wild haf wend it had bien so. .schuld haue trowed....
[*L adds:*] Who wold haue went so synful lyf
Þat þe cosyn had leyn by þe Emes wyf
& namely of swylk a man
Þorow al þe werld his los of ran
Arthure bitauht him Goneuere þe quene;
allas, if myght oþer wais bien, .þat euere hit scholde so ben
& þe lond, alle bot þe crowne, .al þe lond saue..
& dight his oste to Southamptoune. .schop his host..
Þer schippes in þe hauen riden,
þer Arthure & his folk abiden;
þer mot men se maryners,
many wight man in schippes sers,
ropes to right, lynes to lay,
bi bro, bi bankis, to tache & tay; By banke & brymme....
kables to knyt about þer mast,
þe saile on ȝerd fest þei fast; ....þey feste ful fast
ankres, ores, redy to hande,
roþers, helmes, right to stande;
boulyne to set, boulyne to hale, .on bouspret to sette &.
bordes, keuiles, atache to wale. Cordes kyuiles atached þe.
Whan alle was redy in gode poynt,
vnto þe lond þe schippis ioynt;
som stode in schippe & som on land, ...somme on sand
brigges, plankes, kest to þe sand. .& plankes þey caste to land
With men, with horses, forto charge
galeis, cogges, schippes large, Cogges barges & schipes.
brouht in helmes, hauberkes, & scheldes
& alle þat men in bataile weldes.
Hors in to drawe, hors in to dryue,
men hied in after bilyue. ..þer after yn ful blyue
Whan alle were in & mad ȝare
& þei on þer way suld fare,
to þam on þe lond þei spak to eft, ..o land þey preieden.
& praied þam grete þer frendes left; To grete þer frendes þat þey had left
on boþe parties was heuy chere
whan frendes departed, leue & dere. [*Om. L*]
Whan alle were in & was on flote,
maryners dight þam to þer note,
þer takille forto dight & taile,
vnto þe wynd, wele forto saile;
ankers vpwond, saile drouh hie, .o bord sayl drowen.

þe wynd blow, þer schippes gon flie, ..blew wel....
& þo maistres þat were slie, .þe mariners...
ilkone did þer maistrie.
[71rb] Som aforced þe wyndas,
som þe lofe, som þe betas;
þe maister maryners stode bihynd, ..mariner was.
þe schip to stere to þe wynd.

[*L adds:*] Queynte he was & right hardy
& engynous man & sley
Þat first fond schip on se to fare
& turnde wyþ þe wynd þer he nyste whare
Lond to seke þat he saw nought
Ne whiderward he schulde be brought

Arthure had wedir at wille,
sauely sailed withouten ille.
His folk was ioyfulle & glad lete,
þei red þam right to Barbflete. ffor þeire pathe fare to.
At þe midnyght, men gaf gode kepe,
Arthure felle on slomer & slepe; ...slomber..
in his slepe as he gon lie,
him þouht he sauh a bere flie,
a long & an vgly beste, An hugely gret a lothly.
& flouh fast toward þe este;
on þe toþer a dragon vpstegh, O þat oþer syde...
into þe weste him þouht it flegh;
of his mouth a flaume com out,
þe lond, þe water, schone about;
þe bere assailed þe dragon
& he defendid him as a leon.

[*L adds:*] Wonderly ilk oþer gan assaille
& strong was þanne þer bataille

Fulle scharpli ilk oþer smote,
bitterly þei blew & bote;
þe dragon was suyfte & suyftly suypte, ...& sleyly swypte
þe bere in his klawes clipte
& þriste him so þat he to braste,
& doun into þe erthe him caste.
Arthure of his slepe woke,
grete tent on his dreme toke.
He asked clerkes sat him aboute
whedir it ment drede or doute.
"I wild wit what it mot mene,
whedire it tokned ioy or tene,

& whedire it was help or dere
þat þe dragon slouh þe bere."
Som þer were þus it discried,
himself þe dragon signified,
& þe bere som geaunt,
he suld him mak recreaunt;
fro fer suld com & do grete wo
& þorgh he suld him slo. & þorow force....
Som oþer wais gan it rede,
bot alle said he suld wele spede.
[71va] Þan said himself, "I trowe it menes
þis werre & many oþer tenes
bituene me & þe emperour,
late god alle worþe my creatour."
At þat word þe day gan spring,
þe sonne ros in þe mornyng; ..ros faire...
& at þe sonne risyng in gode tyme,
þei com to Barbeflete or prime;
of schippe fulle sone to lond þei ȝede,
in þe cuntre about gon sprede.
He said he wild his folk abide,
þo þat were not comen þat tide.
Long stounde duelled he nouht
þat tiþinges men to him brouht
þat þidere comen was a geaunt,
& long þer had bien his haunt;
out of Spayn was he comen
& had sir Ohel nece nomen.
Mayden Heleyn was hir name,
he hir toke to do hir schame .had hure taken....
& had hir brouht to a hille
þat non may, ne dar com tille.
Michaels mount men calle it now,
þore þe geant Heleyn slouh;
was þer non altere no no chapelle ...auter ne no.
þat tyme þat þis chance felle.
About þat hille þe water flowes,
komes þer non þat he ne rowes;
it was non þat had þe myght
þat with þat geaunt durst fight.
Som þer were wold somtyme fond, ...vmwhile wylde.
assailed him bi water & lond;
bot he gaf nouht of þer assaute,

for þei felle in alle defaute, ..fulle euere in þeir.
for grete roches at þam he caste
& þer schippes to rofe & braste.
Many were dronkled, fele were slayn,
þo þat escaped, it was with payn;
þerfor þe cuntre was nere alle fled,
þer wonyng forsoke, þer godes led,
& left þe lond waste & wilde
for man or beste, wife or childe.
[71vb] Þe geaunt name was Dinabroke,
a grimly man on to loke. .grysly man was...
Whan Arthure had herd þe pleynt
how with þe geaunt þe folk was teynt,
he cald sir Kay & Beduere
& ilk of þam toke a squyere;
armour did with þam lede ..þey wiþ hem.
& ilk of þam toke a stede.
He wild shew it to no mo
þat he suld to þe geaunt go;
if alle had wist he went so one,
þe oste had bien abayst ilkone.
He trasted wele on godes grace
þat he durst schewe him his face,
& on his owen valiantise
þat he durst take þat emprise.
Alle þat ilk nyght þei riden
þat þei neuer stynt ne biden,
tille it was in þe morn tide
þat þei sauh wele þore biside
a bote standand at a stage;
þat hoped þei was þe passage. Þen..þere was..
Tuo hilles within þe water wore,
þe tone lesse, þat oþer more. Þat on was lasse...
On þe more hille was a fire,
fro fer þei sauh it bren schire.

[*L adds:*] Þe lasse hil was nought so drey
ffro þe more but euene ney

Anoþer fire was on þe lesse hille;
þerfor Arthure was alle wille
on whilk hille þe geaunt was,
ne non couth ken him þe right pas.
Þan bad he Beduere go
to serche þe hilles to & fro,

"& whan þou wote þe certeyn,
hie þe þan to me ageyn."
Beduere did him in þe bote
& vp on þe next hille smote;
Beduere smote & him auised .stod...
whiderward þe wais wised.
Þe next way he toke vp hie,
& as he went, he herd a crie;
grete pleynt he herd on make,
a partie gan his herte quake.
[72ra] He wend it had þe geaunt bien
þat his comyng had wist or seen.
He drouh his suerde als smerte
& gadred hardinesse of herte,
& þouht if he with him mette,
with him to fight he wald not lette;
bot alle þat þinkyng was bot veyn,
for on þe hille aboun þe pleyn,
he fond a fire brennand hie
& a towmbe new þer bie.
As he bare his suerd in hand,
bi þe towmbe he sauh on sittand,
a woman & nere alle naked,
about hir hede hir haire schaked.
Biside þe towmbe þis woman lay
& often said, "Weleway!"
& ment þe vilany & þe peyne,
& said, "Allas for þe, Heleyne!"
Beduere sauh þe towmbe newe
& of hir dole his hert gon rewe.
Whan scho perceyued Beduere,
scho said, "Caitife, what dos þou here?
Som synne has þe hidere brouht
þat þi dede here has souht. ..deþ her hastow.
Þis day is þe schaped to die
if þe geaunt þe se with i3e.
Þis ilk hille suythe þou weyue
þat he þe nouht perceyue."
"Wife," he said, "par charite,
lete þi gretyng & speke with me,
& say me what þou ert, & whi
þou wepes here so doelfulli,
& who is laid in þis graue.

Say me soþe, so criste þe saue."
"I am," scho said, "a wo bigone,
a helples þing, a waried one;
I grete for mayden mishap.
At souke I gaf hir of my pap, Þat whilom y norished at . .
I norisshed hir of my breste; & souke y gaf hure . . .
þis is hir towmbe þat þou seste.
Heleyn scho hight, Ohels nece,
of flesch was not so faire a pece.
[72rb] To norisch, to me scho was bitauht. . . sche was me taught
Allas þat while I euer hir auht!
So com þis feende to þis cuntre
& toke boþe hir & me,
& brouht vs vnto þis hille
þat no man dar com vs tille.
Heleyn he wild haf forlayn,
scho ne myght not with þat payn.
He was so grete ouer mesure . . . huge . .
& scho was ȝong & myght not dure;
for grete destrisse hir hert braste,
in his armes scho ȝald þe gaste;
& in þis toumbe I hir laid,
& so it is als I haf said."
He said, "Wharto duellis þou here
sen scho is dede þat was þe dere?"
"Sir," scho said, "I wille þe telle
if þou durste so long duelle,
for I se þe of body auenaunt
& gentille man be þi semblaunt.
Whan I sauh hir so schamly die,
my witte was lorn & aweie.
With force he did me leue stille,
his lichorie in me to fille. . . . . to fulfille
On god himself I take witnesse
þat alle maugre myn it is;
at ilk a tyme þat I him se,
I wild be sonken for I ne may fle;
& I hope he comes sone . . trowe he comeþ right.
his licherie with me to done.
I telle þe dede if þou here bides,
no þing þe saues ne hides.
Suythe to fle, I gyue þe rede,
I wild not se þat þou were dede.

ȝonder is he, I salle þe kenne,
on ȝon hille þer þou sees brenne,
sone to com his tyme salle be;
þerfor, sir, I rede þou fle   . sire Knyght . . . .
& late me haf myself my sorow;
my wille is to die tomorow."
Of hir wo sore him forþouht,
bot he ne wist what hir douht,
[72va] ne he to mak long duellyng.
He turned agayn to þe kyng;
als scho him said, so he told
how Heleyn died & scho in hold,
& he suld fynd þe geaunt,
in þe more hille was his haunt.
"Out of þat stede þe smoke comes fro,
we may him fynd if þat we go."
ffor Heleyn had Arthure sorow inouh
& bod to while þe flode widrouh.
Vnto þe ebbe a stounde þe bode;
with þer hors þei ouer rode
& went bot a schorte pas   . . . . softe .
tille þei perceyued where he was.
Þer stedes & þer palefreis
þer squiers held with oþer herneis,
bot sir Beduer & sir Kay
ȝede vp with Arthure þe way.
Arthure, "I wille proue myself   Arthur seide y . . my might
with þe geaunt alle one to fight.
Hold ȝow here bihynd a lite,
alle one on him I wille first smyte;
tille I may myself saue,
oþer help non wille I haue.
Me þink it were no vassalage,
þre tille one it is outrage.
Neuerþeles, if ȝe se nede,
better is help þan ouerdrede."

[*L adds:*] ffor men seye hit ys folye
In strengthe to mikel for to affye

Þei said for pruesse ne for ȝelp,
if it were nede, þei suld help.   . . . . . wolde hym help
Arthure alle one þe hille toke
vnto þe geaunt, Dinabroke.
Be a mykille fire he sat

& roste suynes flesch fulle fat,   Rostyng a swyn gret & .
som rosted & som was sothen.   & oþer flesche biside was sode
His bryne, his berde, þerwith was broþen   ......al lothen
& alle to solied with þe spikke   ..to soilled...
(I trow þat sight was lothelik).
Arthure þouht to haf þe grace
to come or he toke his mace.   To smyte er....
Whan þe geaunt of him was ware,
ferly he had had how he com þare,   fferly he hadde how...
[72vb] & stirte vp alle oglifte,
& toke his mace vp forto lifte.   His grete mace..
Arthure auised him wele inouh;
as he his mace vpward drouh,
Arthure bare to him his launce   ..on hym wyþ..
to encombire him o chaunce.
Long þei fauht a gode while,
bot Arthure kouth mykelle of gile.

[*L adds:*] Nere sleighte & queyntise hadde ben & gile
Somme had be combred þer in a whyle
ffor kyng Arthur neuere er was
Bystad in so hard a cas

Dinabrok agayn him stode
with his mace as geaunt wode,
for þre men withouten þe ferthe
suld not lifte it fro þe erthe.   ..haue stired his mace from .
He sawe wele how he mad mynt   ......his mynt
& with þe mace teised his dynt.
He wist þe stroke suld be grete;
vnder his schelde alle he schete
& agayn þe stroke it helde,
& þe geaunt smote on his schelde;
so was þe dynt heuy & strong,   & wyþ þat dynt so...
þe hilles alle about rong.

[*L adds:*] & al þat was þer inne hit schok
When Arthur þat dynt so huge tok

Arthure was stonyed, stakerd, & stynt,
bot he felle not with þat dynt.
Anoþer stroke ne wild he bide,
bot etild him to smyte o side;   .peyned.....
with his suerd Caliburne,
scharply he gan him turne;
þe suerd he lift wele on hie,
his schelde he availed a partie,   & valede his scheld..

& o long his forhede he smote;   Endlong his forehed he hym .
þe suerde bote wele & he was hote,
& entamed boþe his bryne
þat alle þe skynne hang ouer his ine;
with þat stroke he had ben slayn.
His mace he held þer agayn
& his hede a partie glente
þat som of þe stroke it hente;
noþeles, wele was it set,
þe blode ouer his ine get   . . al ouer his eyen hit schet
þat he les alle his sight;   Þen lost he þer . . .
þen was he woder forto fight.   Þen wax . . . .

[*L adds:*] Þen was he woder þen he was or
ffightyng als a wylde bor
Þe same weys so dide he
When he sey þat he myghte nought se

He ne lefte for suerd ne for hirte
þat he vnto Arthure stirte.
[73ra] About his mydelle armes laid
& on Arthure so sare he braid,
on heght he lift him foure fete;
& as he him doun lete,
vpon his knees he him kast.
Arthure proued his force fast,
our lady halp, his wille was gode,
with force he ros & vpstode.

[*L adds:*] & Arthur was algate queynte
& his wille was neuere feynte

On þat side he bare his schelde,
þe geaunt nouht he ne helde;
with þat he wroþe & turned his side
& did his armure open wide.   . . . armes . .
Whan he him felte fro him broken,   . . . self was fro . .
þat his body was not stoken,   & . . . . . loken

[*L adds:*] fful lyght hym þoughte þat he was oute
Wiþ Caliborne þen ran he aboute

on þe geaunt with his suerd he smote
& Caliburne sore bote.   . . . vpon hym bot
Þe geaunt glent þider & þidere;   . . . hider & tyder
þe blode him blent, he ne wist whidere.   . . so blent hym . . . .
He grapte about if he mot hent,
& Arthure euer about him went
& smote him sore with wondes fele,

nouht of him ne wild he spele;	
& at a turne þe geant stynt,	
Arthure gaf him so grete a dynt	
þan doun in to þe hede it drafe,	O þe hed þat in to þe nekke..
þe panne in to þe schuldres klafe;	& in to þe schuldres þe panne he clef
ȝit he after Arthur rauht	
& Arthur drouh his suerd a drauht.	Arthur wyþ drow....
[*L adds:*]	Þat he stombled & gaf a cry
	A dredful & a loþly
Whan he felle, he gaf a lasch	
as with a blest had fallen an asch.	...blast had falle..
For þat falle Arthure louh;	
he was venged wele inouh.	...hym þoughte y now
[*L adds:*]	ffro ferre he stod & loked on hym
	& seyde he was a Geaunt grym
He bad Beduer þat he suld go	
to smyte þe hede þe body fro,	
& bitech it a squiere,	.bytake...
to schewe it alle þe oste pleynere.	
He teld Beduer & sir Kay	
þat he had neuer so grete affray	
of no geant bot of one	
& þat geant hight Ritone.	
He did mykelle wonder & wo	[*Om. L*]
& many kynges did he slo,	fful many kynges had he don.
	[*L differs to 12134.*]
[73rb] & alle þer berdes he did of flo.	.flow þe berdes of alle þo
A pane he mad of alle þo	Til a pane as a furour he did hem tewe
& as a forrour he did þam tewe;	
se how Riton was a schrewe.	Loke ȝif Ryton were nought..
Þat geant Riton sent his sond	
to Arthure fro fer lond	Til..ferne.
& said he suld mak him aferde,	
bot he flouh of his awen berde	
& sent it him tille his paene,	
to mensk it þer it was wane;	
& if he sent it blithely	
he suld do it most curteisy,	..set hit most worschipfuly
for he suld vrle his pane withalle	
about with a filette smalle;	
& if Arthure wild nouht	
do as Riton him besouht,	
redy him sone als he myght	Greyþe hym as sone as he.

fo Riton wild with him fight, ffor Ryton wolde...
& whilk of þam mot oþer slo,
his berde suld do of flo ..he scholde don..
& haf þe pane ilk a dele,
þerwith about vrle it wele.
Arthure vnto Riton went,
in bataile slouh Riton & schent, ..he slow hym..
& wan þe pane & his berde;
on þe mounte de Rame he was conquerde. ...Derane...
Siþen fond Arthure non
bot Dinabrok, als was Riton,
þat euere did tille him in dede .neuere.....
þat he had of so mykelle drede.
Þer þei him slouh, þer þei him leuede;
Beduer toke a squiere þe heued
to bere & schewe þe oste aboute,
whare þei were & in what doute.
Sir Ohel fulle sore it ment
þat his nece was so schent.
A faire chapelle for hir did make
of our lady, for Heleyn sake;
sen þat tyme scho was þer laid,
for Heleyn, Heleyn toumbe is it said.
[*L adds:*] & so men han cald hit ay
Eleynes toumbe vnto þys day
Whan þe oste was alle comen & ȝare,
þo þat suld with Arthure fare,
[73va] no while wild he þer lie,
bot passed sone alle Normondie.
His flok wex where so he cam, .folk.....
þe douhtiest with him he nam
out of castelle & cite,
& passed Burgoyne, alle þat cuntre
vnto Ostun, þider he þouht. .Hostun...
Þien tiþinges tille him men brouht
þat þei of Rome com with grete route
& toke þe cuntre alle aboute.
Als Arthure suld a water passe,
Albe, it sais þe name wasse,
alle day tille Arthure men told,
with passand men & spies bold,
þat þe emperour was þer beside;
to conseile him how best mot tide, ..what best myghte bytide

his pauillons, his pencels þikke,	
nouht fer þien had þei doun pikke.	..fro þenne had þey don wyk
"Þer er so many Romeyns,	
& þou has non oste þam agayns,	.þyn host may nought..
foure ere agayn on of þine.	.haþ he agayns...
If bataile go, þou salle tyne."	& 3if 3e assemble þou most.
Arthure said, "Godes help is nehi.	
He wote who salle haf þe maistri."	
He left not for no manace.	
Vppon Albe, a strong place,	..in a..
a kastelle did he raise & sette	
if him were nede to haf resette.	.he had nede to take.
[*L adds:*]	Smertly to make þei were al bon
	Wyþ folk ynow & sone had don
Whan alle was endid, vp in þe toure	
he did his herneis & his tresoure,	He leyde in.....
if chance com þat him bord fle,	...þei moste wyþdrawe
to reste þer in tuo daies or þre.	..hem þere a litel þrawe
Whan þe castelle was alle dight,	
defensable for kyng & knyght,	
he sent messengers to wend;	.ordeynd...
to þe emperour he þouht to send	
tuo erles of noble lynage,	..þat were of..
& wele spoken, of gode langage;	
Gerin of Chartre3, a man of pris,	
Beus of Oxenford, anoþer fulle wis;	Wiþ Beofs of Hamptone...
with þise tuo went sir Waweyn	
for he couth speke þe speche Romeyn.	.he spak wel...
[*L adds:*]	ffor he had longe wiþ hem ben
	& his connynge þey hadde wel sen
	ffor þat skile Arthur hym sent
	Þat he wist best what þeir speche ment
[73vb] Arthure tauht þam þus to say	
whan þei suld wend þer way:	
"Say þe emperour he go to Rome	
& to ffraunce no hender come,	
ne to no lond þat I wan,	
ne be chalenged þorgh no Romayn.	.chalange hit as man.
Þo er myn & myn salle be;	
Romayn of þam salle neuer haf fe.	
If he wille not turne agayn,	
bid him stand to bataile playn	.hem abide þe..
& auenture vs alle to chance	..at alle chaunce

whilk salle derayne þe Reme of France.	To dereyne þe ryght of Rome &.
So long as I may it saue,	
ffrance salle he neuer haue.	Þe Romayns schul hit..
With bataile say him I it wan,	
& so defend it fro ilk man.	& schal.....
With force þerof had þei first fe,	
with force þei lese it ageyns me;	
& now with bataile salle be sene	
who salle haf it quite & clene."	
Þe messengers þat went þo nedis	
horsed þam on gode stedis,	
& armed þam at alle rightes	
as felle vnto gode knyghtes;	
oþer Bretons herd here of say	
& led þam alle þre on way,	.wente to mete hem bifore..
& praied þam forto do	...hertely for to.
som þing, or say þe Romeyns to,	
þat þe werre mote alle gate go	
or þei com þe courte fro.	
"It has bien long manaced & þrette	
& now so nere togider ere sette,	But so ney to gydere were we nere set
schame it were þat ouþer ȝede	
withouten bataile or manly dede.	...vaillaunte.
If so betide þat it begynne,	
ȝit salle Bretons pruesse wynne."	
[*L adds:*]	Þer to algate dos ȝour trauail
	& þat we may we wil ȝow vaille
Wawayn said, "In alle manere	
of vs salle þei som tiþng here,	...ȝe som tyding.
& if ȝe se þat we ouht duelle,	
tiþing þerof salle men telle."	
Þe messengers passed a mountayn	
& þan a wod, & siþen a playn;	
[74ra] of þat playn a partie heldid	
& þeron were þe Romeyns teldid.	
Fulle semely, withouten boste,	
þei com ridand þorgh þe oste;	
þe Romeyns on ilk side aboute,	
of þer tentes þei com oute	
þe messengers to behold,	
þat semed noble men & bold.	...bodies..
Þei asked what tiþng þei brouht	...tydynges..
or þider for þe pes þei souht.	

With non þei stode ne tales helde
tille þei com to þe emperours telde.
Whan þei were at his pauilloun,
þer befor þei light doun,
bitauht þer hors to þer pages, & bitok.....
to stand stille at certeyn stages.
Bifore þe emperour com alle þre
& said þer message as men avise,
Gerin & Beus, boþe fulle wys,
& þe emperour said his auys
& teld agayn boþe fast. .spak ageyn þeym..
Bot Wawayn said at þe last, .þenne spak Wawayn atte.
"We ere comen fro Kyng Arthoure
to þe, sir Lucius, þe emperoure.
His knyghtes ere we to lyue & deie;
his message I salle þe seie.
Þis is þe gretyng þat he þe sendes: ...message....
He comandes þe & defendes
þat nouht of France þou entirmet
ne no fote þiderward þou set.
ffraunce he holdes as his demeyng, ffor.....demeynes
& euer salle for alle Romeyns;
& if þou of him ouht chalange,
& he þorgh bataile wille him venge; Þorow bataille wil he..
þorgh bataile first wan ȝe France
& lese it eft þorgh þat chance.
Agayn Arthure ȝe it les,
þorgh bataile þe parties ches; ..as þe party.
[*L adds:*] & now ys holde as his conqueste
& schal while þe sonne ryseþ est
& if þou sette chalange þerin,
þorgh þe bihoues it wyn, Þorow bataille byhoueþ þe..
þorgh bataile salle it be dereynt,
þi chalange & alle þi pleynt,
[74rb] & sone set withouten delay. ..assigned..
Com to morn & proue þi day
& wyn it if þou wyn salle,
or alle lese, or haf it alle. ..to lese or wynne hit.
If þou wille not turne agayn,
þat þou duelles it is in vayn." Al þy dwellyng is..
[*L adds:*] ffor þou hast lorn & we haue wonnen
So ferre we haue þy lond ouer ronnen
Þan said þe Emperour to þam þre,

"To turne agayn, it salle not be.
ffrance is myn, þider wille I go.
If I it lese, me salle be wo.   ffor ȝif I lese hit me...
If I haf lorn at vnskille,   & ȝif..lore hit..
I salle wyn it whan grace wille."   ..hit wynne eft when god.

[*L adds:*] Þus he seide for wel he wende
Þey hadde no force Fraunce to fende

A knyght þer was hight Quintelyn,
sibbe þe emperour & his cosyn,
contrariosly to Wawayn spak
& vilensly behynd his bak.   .vyleynlike he gan hym lak
"Bretons," he said, "ere bot auantours
& manace mykille at rebours.

[*L differs, 7 lines:*] Þer bostful wordes ar nought to seke
Þer dedes ar nought worþ a leke

Ȝe manace ay, it salle be so,   Ȝe manace ay hit schal ben so
þe dede is nouht þat ȝe do.   Ȝour dedes ar noughte þat ȝe do
Alle bostely ȝe þrete;   Al day bostfuly ȝe þrete
do in dede, þe manace lete."   Doþ hit in dede manace ȝe lete
Wawayn listend him inouh   Wawayn hym listed & gram low
& smertly his suerde out drouh,
& smote his hede of alle quite,
& bad his felawes hors þam tide, ...tyt
& said vnto þe Romeyns alle,
"Bretons salle rise & ȝe salle falle!"

[*L adds:*] Ȝow were wel bettere at Rome burgh
Þan reyse baner a geyn Arthurgh

Sir Wawayn his hors hent
& homward alle þre went.
Þe courte was fraied, no wonder was.   .knyght.....
Þe emperour cried, "Allas, Allas!
Slayn þei haf sir Quintelyne
here now befor myn ine!   Now right here byfore..
If þei escape vs alle fro,
mervaily may men telle of þo."
Romeyns ran out of pauillons
suythe after þe Bretons.   & hasted fast...
Ilkon toke þat þei mot hent
& after riden & went.   ..þem prykede faste..
On þer was þat had a stede
þat befor alle oþer ȝede,
[74va] & cried loude, "Abide, Abide!
If þou dar, turne & to me ride."

Sir Gerin herd what he said,
he turned him & his spere forth laid,
& of his gode hors him caste
als fer as þe lance wild laste.
Sir Gerin said as he lay þore,
"Þi hors þe bare ouer fer before."
.... ouer faste.

[*L adds:*] 3it were þe bettere ha ben at þe ost
Þan fort ha foched þy deþ wyþ bost
& haue holde þe fer o drey
ffor now þe ouer þynkeþ þou come so ney

Beus of Oxenford loked o bak
Beofs . . þen loked.
& listend how þat Gerin spak.

[*L adds:*] Saw þe Romayn ded þer lay
& his hors wente forþ o stray

Sir Beus þouht, "I am to blame
bot I do anoþer þe same."
He turned his hors & abode
& to anoþer Romeyn rode;
with his lance he bare him in
& wyþ his spere....
þorghout þe þrote beneth þe chyn.
Gaspand he felle & lay alle strekid
Gapyng he lay at erþe al.
as he was with þe lance chekid.
Sir Beus said, "For þat þou gapid,
to þe mete fulle sone þou raped.
...fuer sone hym.
Bot lig now stille ore þat þou ete,
& if þi felawes þe ouer gete,
to þam may þou þe soþe say,
Sey þe messegers wente here forþ god spede
þe messengers went bi þis way."
& wiþ suche musseles he can 3ow fede
Anoþer com ridand fast beforn,
a noble knyght of Rome born,
Marcelle it sais þat he hight,
Marcels hit seyþ his name.
& his hors was ferly wyght.
. hadde an hors was ferly lyght

[*L adds:*] Of þem alle last horsed he was
& passed þe formest a gret pas

For fast hieng als of chance,
And for gret haste...
he had forgeten at home his lance.
With sporse he smote, þe hors gan schake,
He sporede his hors forþ faste..
he wend wele Wawayn to take.

[*L adds:*] & seyde hit were ful gret ferlik
But he broughte Wawayn to þem al quyk

Wawayn hed selcouth fer fro
. wondred hym ferne.
þat his hors mot so wele go,
for Marcelle neihed Wawayn right hend,

Wawayn to tak, wele he wend;
bot his hors com so smertly
& passed Wawayn fast by,
& als he bi Wawayn glent,
Wawayn had his suerde out hent
& clefe his hede at a dynt;
þorgh þe helme to þe sadille it stynt. — . helm þat at þe breste . .
[74vb] His gode armure auailed nouht,
with þe drauht, þe erth he souht. — Wyþ þat strok to . . . .
In his fallyng, said Wawayn,
"Marcelle, I rede þou turne agayn
& go to Quintelyn to helle,
& on my half þou him telle,
& say þe Bretons þat ȝe þus chace,
wele more do þan þai manace, — . . con do þan .
& more þai gife þan þei hete. — Sey Quyntalyn we hym by þe grete
Bi þe, Marcelle, Quintelyn I grete." — & more wol gyue þan we wol hete
Now togider þei gon drawe
& oþer þre þei did of dawe.
Langer to iuste ne mot þei stand,
bot þam defendid & were fleand. — . . . al wyþdrawande
Þe Romeyns on ilk half þam went,
with suerdes & lances strokes lent. — . . . spere strokes þey .

[*L adds:*] But neuere for strok þat þey þer tok
Of stirop ne sadel out ne schok
Ne drowen blod ne gaf þem wounde
Ne stopped þem þer wey no stounde

Þat Marcelle had a nevowe,
wele horsed vnto his prowe;
in his way Marcelle he fonde,
slayn he lay on a londe. — Liggyng slayn þer . . .
After þe messengers trauersed þe felde,
Wawayn houed & bihelde
þat he com so grete a spurne,
he had no tome his hors to turne. — . . . leyser . . . .
Vnto he com amang þam alle,
of his hand his lance lete falle. — & of . . . spere . .
He wend Wawayn wele to smyte, — [*Transp. L*]
drouh his suerd scharpe to bite. — [*Transp. L*]
As he lift his suerde hie,
at his hand Wawayn lete flie
& smote of hand & arme
so þat he did no more harme.

Anoþer stroke he suld haf had,
bot with þe Romeyns þei were ouerstad;
so ferly fele after þam schoke
þat alle gate þe wod þei toke — But for al hem....
þat was bituex þam & Arthure holde,
þe new castelle I ore of tolde.
Arthure, our kyng, þat was at home,
wondred þe messengers not come.
Sex þousand he sent for drede
to socoure þam if þei had nede;
[75ra] þei com & passed to þe wod side
& þer stode forto abide. — ..wyþstode..
After þe messengers þei gaf tent
if þei of þam had any glent;
þe sauh grete folk in parties sprede
þat folowed þre þat to þe wod ȝede.
Þan perceyued knyghtes & squiers
þat þo þre were þe messengers
þat þei com for & after souht;
priuely þei stode, auised þer þouht,
siþen gaf þei a crie fulle grete,
at ons opon þe Romeyns schete,
alle vnwarned in þer vis.
Þen spred þe Romeyns in partis;
som þat fled were ouertaken
& som prisonde, holden waken; — ...& halden waken
som slayn & beten doun,
fulle was giffen for raunson. — .fewe were leten to.

[*L adds:*] Wiþ mikel wo any ascaped
Þat he ne was fruscht & al to fraped

A noble man was þer of Rome,
of alle knyghtes he bare þe blome,
Petreus his name hight;
a riche man, mykille of myght, — .worthi man & mykel..
what for richesse & gode knyght, — ..his prowesse...
ten þousand he had þorgh right. — ..men he ladde in fyght
He herd of þe Bretons assaute
& how þer men were at defaute;
smertly with ten þousand scheldes
socoured þer men in þe feldes. — To sokere hem go we to..
With ten þousand þat he brouht,
on þe Bretons hard he souht,

þat maugre þars he did þam go ..þeires....
into þe wod þer þei com fro;

[*L adds:*] O þe playne myghte þey holde no place
Þat to þe wode he gan þem chace

& whan þei were in wod teld,
agayn Petron þer owen held.
Petreus oft on þam gan presse,
bot mykelle of his folk he lesse,
for þe Bretons stirt out & slouh
& eft in to þe wod þam drouh.
Bi þe wod side in a brusse
was many fight & many frusse. ..a stour & many a frusch
[A]rthure marvailed ferly strong [*Capital omitted in P.*]
þat þe messengers duelled so long,
[75rb] & what þam letted or for whome
þat þe sex þousand home ne come.
He cald Nu, sonne Sir Yder, Þen cald he swyþe..
þat was a douhty bacheler.
"Tak fyue þousand & smertly fare;
þe sex þousand sek where þei are." ...sekeþ...
Sir Yder did as he him bad; ....Arthur.
for his wendyng fele were glad.
As Yder & his folk forth ferde,
grete noyse vnder þe wod þei herde;
þan hied þei a fulle gode pas,
þei dred sore þer was som kas. ..þem sore of som mys cas
Yder sauh how þat Wawayn,
Gerin, & Beus fauht oþer agayn;
in þe moste pres Yder sprong
& gaf a crie, þe wod alle rong;
þan were þe Bretons wele abouen,
þe Romeyns route bakward schouen.
Yder perced þe Romeyns route, When Ider had met wyþ...
of dynt no dede had he no doute;

[*L adds:*] Lytel þey þoughte hem self to saue
So fayn þey wolde þe werre haue

þe Romeyns þei ouer riden & runnen
& þer gode stedis wonnen.

[*L adds:*] & þe Romayns atter power
Stryken & stoden ageyns Ider

Many were on boþe partis
slayn forto wyn þe pris.

Petreus þat I of told,
þe riche Romeyn & so bold,   .noble Romayn fers & bolde
he was mayntenure of þat bataile;   .mayntende þer.
his folk he set right to assaile.   & sette his folk wysly..
[*L adds:*] Wel couþe he stande wel couþe he scurne
& faire wyþdrawe hym & eft returne
With him & þam were many chaces,   Bytwyxt þem...
fele turnynges & fele wanlaces;
þat hardy was, he fond hardy;
who so couth iuste fond redy.   ....he fond.
[*L adds:*] Þat wel couþe fighte þer fond his fere
Þat nought ne couþe þer myght he lere
Alle þe Bretons ostrey rode,   ...oft astray þey rod
non held togider ne oþer bode;
so þei ȝerned to haf þe were,   [*L differs to 12509.*]
ffor prowesse þat þey ȝernde al day
& so faire armes to bere,   [*Om. L*]
& to do som dede þat day,   [*Om. L*]
þerfor þe rode on þat aray;   .þey nere of non.
þei ne rouht how þei ȝede,   .nadde warde how þat..
bot þat þei did of armes dede;   ..prowesse wer do...
[75va] to do som þei ȝerned alle day,   [*P repeats 12503–4 in error.*]
þerfor þei rode at non aray.
Petreus was auised more,   .bygan auise hym.
his best men about him wore;
he kouth in werre wele stand in stoure
& at nede seke him socoure.   ..his nede gete..
[*L adds:*] fful wel he halp þere help failled
& wel hym rescowed when he was sailled
Gode tent on alle his men he toke,
where þei straied, whidire þei schoke,
& alle relied þam wele ageyn
þat ilkon wist his certeyn.
Beus of Oxenford perceyued wele
þe comyng of Petron ilkadele;
withouten losse suld þei not go
bot if þei mot Petron slo,
slo or take in þe felde,
for his comyng þe Romeyns vpheld.   ..confort þe Bretons.
[*L adds:*] Hider & þider þe Bretons went
Al out of array & were ney schentÞe best
Bretons of þam alle,   ..Barons...

Beus to conseile gon þam calle.
"Lordes," he said, "spekis with me,
þat tille Arthure wille leaute.
Begunne we haf a contek
& Arthure wote not of þis chek;
[*L adds:*] Wyþoute his welyng is þis tyrpeyl
Þer fore y cald ȝow to conseil
if it falle wele, wele salle vs be;
if it ne do, we gete maugre.
Bot we in þis first stoure
haf þe gre & bere þe floure, — Haue þe pris....
I telle vs schent ilk a man,
& mykelle maugre we it began;
it was ȝour conseile als wele as ours,
ȝe praied vs to begyn þise stours.
Þerfor peyn ȝow to do — Þe bettere þer fore peyne...
þing þat I salle conseile to;
fonde we now euer ilkon
forto slo ȝon ilk Petron; — ffort acombre þylke.
quikke or dede, vs bus him haue
if we to day our folk salle saue,
els salle we neuer gon hiþen
þat we salle mykelle be bineþen.
Þerfor, lordynges alle togidere,
folowes whore I turne or whidere,
& help wele whan ȝe se nede;
if we gete him, wele we spede."
[75vb] Alle þei said, "What so betides,
[*The fragment in R begins.*]
we salle ride þat way þou rides." — We schul þe folewe wher þou rydes
R: We schul ride þat wei þou rides
[*LR add:*]
Go we þanne þat God vs a vaille
R: Gawe þan þat God vs availe
So þat we of hym ne faille
R: Þat we of him nouht ne faile
Beus aspied & sawe fulle sone, — Beofs aspied & saw hym sone
R: Beus aspied & sauh hym sone
"I se Petron, mak ȝow alle bone!"
Beus smote his hors with þe spors — Beofs......
& þei after, ouer felde & fors; — ......fores
R:......foris

wild he neuer stynt no sesse
vntille he com in alle þe presse ..cam in to alle..
R: ...in.in al..
þer Petron was & to him rode. ....til hym rod
R:....til hym rod
Hors tille hors þat þei bestrode,
Beus tille him fast was alied, Til hym ful faste Beofs allied
R: Beus til him fast was alied
on his felawes Beus afied. & on hys felawes wel hym affied
R: On hys felawes Beus affied
Bi þe nek Petron he hent, Beof by þe nekke Petron hent
R: Beus be þe nek Petron hent
doun to þe erþe boþe went; & doun til Erthe boþe þey went
R: & doun to þe Erthe boþe þei went
Beus felle doun be his wille Beof fel doun al by..
R: Beus fell doun be his wille
& held Petron stone stille. ...al ston stille
R: ...right ston stille
Beus did þer a grete wile Beof...ful gret.
R: Beus did þer a gret wil
& did himself in a pile; & putte hym self in gret perile
R: & did him self in peril
[*LR add*:]
Beofs held sore & Petron drow
R: Beus held sore & Petron drouh
Petron wild go bot Beus was touh. Petron had go nad Beofs be tow
R: Petron wild go bot Beus was touh
Romeyns Petron wild rescouh, Þe Romayns Petron wilde rescouse
R: Romeyns Petron þei wild rescouse
þe Bretons ageyn þam fast sette, But Bretons ageyn þem faste gan brouse
R: But Bretons ageyn þem gan brouse
with scharp lances togider mette. ..speres to gidere sett
R: With scharp launces to gider sett
[*LR add 17 lines not in P*:]

R:
& al to fruschid þat scheldes met
Whan þer launces might nouht serue
Þer swerdes drouh ful scharp to kerue
With hardi hert ilk oþer on heu
In armes hent of sadels þreu
Helmes bouwed & thurgh stoken
Scheldes clef & swerdes broken
Hauberkes riuen & al to mailed

L:
& al to frusched þat þey wiþ.
When speres myght namore serue
Þer swerdes drowe ful faste..
......hew
....sadeles þrew
Helmes bowed & þorow were steke
....breke
....fur mailled

Stedis slayn stomblid & failed	Stedes slayn stumbled & failled
Men were slayn & fil to grounde	....feld to grounde
& mani cast þat had no wounde	& manye cast....
So þikke to gidre þei were in þrong	..þey were to gydere..
Ilk oþer wroth ilk oþer swong	..wroþ...
Ilk oþer of sadels wrast	& ilk....
& vnder hors fet were cast	..hose fet wer cast
Non kneu oþer þei were so neih	.knew....ney
Bot bi þer speche or bi þer cri	.....by þer cry
	[P resumes with couplets transposed.]
Þe Bretons fast on þam bated	*[Om. LR; see below.]*
& þe Romeyns sore þam hated;	*[Om. LR; see below.]*
þe Bretons cried þe Kyng Arthoure	Bretons cried kyng Arthour
	R: Þe Bretons cried þe King Arthur
& þe Romeyns Lucius þe Emperoure.	& Romayns Lucius Emperour
	R: Þe Romeyns Lucius Emperour
	[LR add 12571–2 here:]
	Þe Bretons faste on þem abated
	R: Þe Bretons fast on þem abatid
	& þe Romayns ful sore þem hated
	R: & þe Romeyns sore þem hatid
Non kouth knaw for certeyn	Þer couþe non knowe for certeyn
	R: Non couthe knowe for certein
whilk was Breton, whilk Romeyn,	...whilk was Romeyn
	R: ...whilk was Romeyn
bot bi þer spech þat þei spak;	But by.....
	R: Bot be þer speche þattei spak
or ony out of þe pres brak,	.any...pres ought brak
	R: Or ani out of þe pres ouht brak
fayn wald Wawayn Petron haue,	.wolde...
	R: Fain wild Waweyn..
& Beus wild þei alle gate saue.	& Beofs wold....
	R: & Beus wild þei algate saue
He brak in tuo þer mykelle pres,	..in to þe mykel pres
	R: He brak in to þer mikel pres
forto smyte wild he not ses.	To smyte sore wold he nought ses
	R: Wel to smite wild he nouht ses
	[LR add 4 lines not in P.]
R:	L:
On alle sides he smot aboute	On alle sides he smot aboute
& mad him gate among þe route	..þeym rounn þorow out..
Was þer non stod in his weie	......weye
Þat his dint ne did him deie	..dynt ne dide hym deye

[*P resumes here.*]

Sir Yder on þe toþer side,
Sire Ider on þat oþer syde
R: Sire Ider on þat oþer side
& Gerin durst non abide;
ffor Geryn durste no Romayn byde
R: & Gerin durst non abide
ilk for oþer bolded þer herte
Ilk on for oþer bolded here hert
R: ...boldid þer hert
& þer strokes were so smerte
& smyten strokes so grete & smert
R:.....smert
þat no Romeyn durst bide þer dynt,
bot fer o bak did þam stynt.
..on bak dide þem.
R:.....þem stint
Þan was Petron alle oglifte;
Þen...a glyft
R: ...al o glift
þe Bretons vp Beus lifte
...sire Beofs lyft
R: ...sire Beus lift
[76ra] & horsed him wele agayn,
...ful wel a geyn
R: ...ful wel a geyn
& toke Petron þe Romayn.
...þe maister Romayn
R: .tok Petron þe maister Romeyn
With him vnto þe wod þei fled,
[*Transp. LR*]
& wiþ hym vntil wode..
R: ..vntil þe wode..
þorgh alle þe pres þei him led
[*Transp. LR*]
Þorow al þe pres...
R: Thurgh al þe pres þei him led
& did him þer he mot be siker,
& eft alle new bigan þe biker.
....bygonne to byker
R: And eft al newe be gan to biker
Bot þei had no gouernoure
But þen had þey..
R:....gouernour
þat kouth maynten þat stoure,
Þat couþe meyntene þem in stour
R: Þat couth mayntene þe stour
no more þan þe schip can
Namore þan schip or barge can
R: Nomore þan þe schip can
þore it failes steris man.
Þere hym wanteþ a steres man
R: Þer it failes steresman
Bretons broched among þam alle,
Þenne broched þe Bretons...
R: Bretons brochid...
many hors þei did doun falle;
Man & hors þey dide doun falle
R: Man and hors þei dide..
þat were fallen, þei ouer schoke,
& þe fleand þei ouertoke;
& þo þat fledde þey ouer tok

R: & þe fleand þei ouertok

som þei slouh & som þe held,
& som þei spoiled in þe feld.
Alle were slayn þe maste frap,
....moste frape
R:....mest frape
fo þei were þat myght it scap;
ffayn wer þey þat myghte a scape
R: Fo þer were þat might ascape
þan turned agayn alle þe Bretons
& com to þe wod to þer prisons,
& laid þam alle with Sir Petron,
& led þem....
R: And ledde þem....
& present Arthur with ilkon;
.presented...
R: .presentid...
& he þanked þe messengers
Þen þanked he his messegers
R: And he þankid his messagers
& alle þe toþer þat were þer fers,
...oþere...pers
R:.......pers
& said if it be wonnen,
& seide hem ȝyf hit may be wonne
R: And seid ȝif it be wonnen
þe werre þat was begonnen,
Þe game þat we haue by gonne
R: Þe werre þat was begunnen
He suld amend þer rent & fe,
.wolde amende....
R: He schold amend þer rente þer fe
if þat tyme mot tide & be.
Ʒyf þat tyme myghte bitide or be
R: Ʒif þat time miht betide & be
Þe Kyng did his prisons loke,
wardeyns þat þam vndertoke.
Wiþ wardeyns þat hem.
R: Wardeins þat þem.
Þus said men of conseil wis,
Þen seide....
R: & seid....
he suld þam send vnto Paris;
Best was to send hem to Parys
R: He schuld þem send vntil Paris
& men of armes suld þam lede,
Wiþ men of armes þat scholde..
R:....schuld þem.
haf þam in courte it were drede.
To hold hem.....
R: Haue þem.....
Þan was ordeynd with þam to go,
Þen...hem schold go
R: Þan....þem schuld go
for waityng & for takyng fro,
ffor rescours &...
R: For waiting....
Kador, Borelle, & Erle Richere,
& sir Beduere, his botelere.
Noble of blode were alle þise,

& in þe mornyng suld þe rise
R:...morwnyng schuld þei.
& conueie þe passages alle
To conueye hem...
R: And conueie þem...
þer most desceit & drede mot falle;
[76rb] & whan þei were passed ilkone,
þe mene folk suld þan alle one.
Let oþer mener wiþ hem forþ gone
R: Þe mene folk schuld þan allone
Þe emperour had his spies
..had ful gode spies
R: Þe emperour...
þat had knowyng of boþe parties;
..knowynge on..
R: ..knowyng on..
þei com & told him beforn
...teld hym oþe eue byforn
R:.....on euen be forn
þat þe prisons arly at morn
...erlik at morn
R: ...erlik at morn
vnto Paris suld be led
Vntil Paris schuld ben led
R: Vnto Paris schuld be led
to hold þam þer þei ere o dred.
Þe emperour bad tak ten þousand
Þen bad þemperour take ten þousand
R: Þe Emperour bad take þre þousand
to go þat nyght beforhand,
....fer byfore hand
R:....fer bifore hand
rescous of þam if þei mot make
Rescours of þeym ȝyf þey might.
R: Rescous of þem ȝif þei might.
& þe prisons fro þam take.
Þise were þo þe emperour sent
þat on þe nyght before went:
Sertorius, of Libie kyng & sire,
R:..Lubie...
Sir Ewander, þe kyng of Cire,
Sire Ewander...Syrie
R: Sire Ewender...Cirie
Karice, Katelle, & sir Wilteres;
þise were of Rome kynges peres.
Þise were chosen be somons
to mak rescous of þe prisons.
Þei toke þe way at euen late
& þey toke.....
R: Þise tok.....
& passed befor our men þe gate;
& whan þei in þe way cam
....þat weye.
R:....þat weie.
þat right forþe to Paris nam,
in þat way gan þei reste,
priuely bussed þer þei sauh best.
& priuely enbusched þer þey sey.
R: And priueli buschid þer þei sauh.

[12659 is the first line of the fourth and last column of the R fragment which is almost unreadable now. The transcript is based partly on Kölbing's edition (1892).]

Als þei were bussed redy to bikere, ...busched...
R: ...buschid...
com Arthure men, wend haf bien siker;
noþeles ȝit had þei doute,
þerfor þei did sonder þe route.
Sir Borelle & erle Kadore R: Sire Borel & þe erl Cador
with þer folk riden before, ...riden byfore
R: ...redi be fore
Sir Beduere & erle Richere,
þise were þe prisons nere.
With þam com fyue hundred ..come men fif hundred
R: ..come men fiue hundred
þat fro þe prisons not sundred; ....were nought sundred
R:....were nouht sundred
on Borelle & Kador þat formast went, R: Sir Borel & Cador...
þe Romeyns sideslepis on þam glent ..a side on hem glent
R: ..o side on þem glent
& felonly on þam gan strike, R: ..to þem..
& þei defended douhtilike. ..defended hem doughtilyke
R: And þei defendid douhtilike
Sir Richer sauh & Beduere herd
þat wikked men þe way sperd .þer Enemis þer weyes sperde
R: ...þer weies sperde
[76va] & with þer felawes fast gon fight,
armed men with suerdes bright.
He did prisons þer withstand, Þey dide þer prisons..
R: ..þe prisons..
þe mene men tok þam on hand,
in saufe stede with þam to bide .siker.....
R: .sauf stede....
tille more sikernes myght tide. ....bityde
R:....be tide
With spors ilk man toke his stede .haste.....
R: .sporis.....
to help þer felawes in þer nede; R:.....hire nede
þan bigan Britons to bolden
& þer partie wele vpholden. R: ..partis..
Þe Romeyns ran amang Bretons ....þe Bretons
R:....þe Bretons
forto seke þer prisons; To seke after þer prisons

R: Forto seke among þer prisons
Britons to slo tentid þei nouht,
Þe Bretons to slo tente..
R: Þe Bretons to slo tent..
hot here & þare þe prisons souht;
But hider & þyder...
R: Bot hider & tider...
to while þei ȝede about to seke,
& while.....
R: Bot while.....
þe sped not worþe a leke,
Þey ne spedde....
R: Þei spedde....
for mykelle of þer folk þei les
as þei souht about with res,
Als þey soughten in þe pres
R: Als þei souht a boute be þe res
for þe Bretons togidere riden,
Þe Bretons hollyk to gyder riden
R: ...to gidre.
at þer assautes togider biden;

[*LR add:*]
To gyder wente to gydere camen
R: To gidre went to gidre camen
In alle stedes were þey samen
R:....þei.

for þei togidere so wele held,
lay many Romayn in þe feld.
Þey slowe þe Romays doun in.
R: Lay mani Romeyn in..
In foure batailes þe Bretons þam sette,
In foures Routes....
R: In foure batailes....
þe sarer with þe Romayns þai mette.
Þe sykerer wiþ þe...
R: Þe sarrer with þe Romayns mette
Sir Kador with his Cornwales,
Sire Cador wyþ þe Cornewaleys
R: Sire Cador with his Cornwaleys
[*The R fragment ends here.*]
Sir Beduer with his Herupeis,
Sir Borelle & Sir Richere,
ilkon had þer batailes sere.
Þe Romeyns ouer alle about wend,
..al aboute wond
fast þei les & nouht fand.
..lore & nought ne fond
Ewandere, kyng of Libie,
Ewanden þe kyng..
sauh þe Romeyns force doun flie.
He relied his folk a stounde
& sauh þe prisons mot not be founde.
He bad þam tent alle to þe bataile; [*Transp. L*]
to seke þe prisons is tynt trauaile. [*Transp. L*]
He sette þam alle in suilk certeyn
þe better partie þei wan ageyn;

of þe Bretons þei feld inowe	
& foure of our best men slowe.	
Heere Yder sone, þe Bretoun,	Sire Iders sone..
& Heriglas of Periroun,	.Irelgas & Peryron
[76vb] Sir Alidouk of Tintagelle	
þat lord was of þat castelle,	
& Maurik, Kador, Keneis,	
oiþer Bret or Walsch whedir it sais.	Souereyne knyghtes þey were..
Þe erle Borelle, a lordyng,	
him smote Ewander þe kyng;	
in at þe mouthe, Borelle he bare,	
þorghout þe þrote, a tuo it schare.	
Whan þei sauh how Borelle felle,	..seye sire Borel fel
þe Bretons þei alle to suelle	ffor wo þe Bretons al to swel
þat þei so þer lordes les.	
Of þe Romeyns were grete pres,	Wyþ þe Romains grete.
agayn a Breton seuen men told;	.o Breton were ten Romayn
if ne grace had bien, alle had bien sold.	Nere grace had ben al had be slayn
[*L adds:*]	Al had ben ded & doun born
	& þer prisons had ben lorn
Bot Vttred, a lord of Peiters,	
he was keper of foreris,	..Cheftayn of fforreyers
he com driuand þat ilk while,	
for it was told him alle þat gile	.....of gyle
þat Romeyns com, rescowes to make,	
Bretons to slo, þe prisons take.	
With him com þre þousand knyghtes	
& archers gode at alle rightes,	
& on þe Romeyns smote fulle tide	....smyten ful tit
þat had our Bretons discomfite.	
Þer scharp lances on scheld forþe laid,	..speres & scheld..
a hundreth smote doun at þe first braide	..þei felde atte..
þat neuer eft þei no ros	
of þe Bretons to wyn los.	
Þan were þe Romeyns alle abaiste,	
& alle was schent þat ore was traiste;	
þei wend Arthur & alle his oste	
had folowed þam in to þat coste.	
Þe Peiteuins fast þam assailed	
& þe Bretons nouht failed.	
[*L adds:*]	Þe ton quiked þe toþer to lyue
	Þe Romayns to greue fast gon þey stryue
Þe Romeyns gaf bak & fled,	..in haste turnde..

þei had no klos, ouer alle þei spred;   ..no clos but oueral spredde
to þer loges þer þei þam busshed,
þei fled & þei þam alle to lusshed.   ..& þer wer al..
Ewander, þat slouh Borelle,
& fyue hundred with Sir Katelle,
were alle slayn & don in holde;
withouten lordes, more were tolde.
[77ra] Þat þei wold haf, alle þei haden,
prisons inow away laden;   .y nowe alle þey ladden
þer batale was, þei turned ageyn   .þe bataille was...
& souht ilk Breton fro Romeyn;   .tryde þe Bretons fro ilk.
to seke Borelle, his men had haste
& fond him sone ȝeldand þe gaste.   Þey fond..ȝeldyng..
Þe wonded men to saue þei souht
& þe slayn to erþe brouht.   ....erþe þey.
Þe first prisons þat Arthure sent,
þo þat wer charged, to Paris went;
þe toþer prisons þat þei last hent,
of þam to Arthur þei mad present,
& teld him alle þer descent,   ..þem wel of þeyr deseit
how þer hap was nere ouer streit
& how Vttred was þer socoure,
& mayntend þam in þat stoure,   .grately meyntende þem in.
& bad him boldly to bataile wende.
Of þe emperour gat he þe fairere ende;
þe emperour herd how þe Bretons sped
þorgh þe help of Vttred,
& þat Ewandere was slayn,
& þe toþer don to payn.
Grace tille wild non betide   .til hym wold..
bot euer mishapned his side;   ..mys happed on..
þerfor mykille he was dismaied;
þat werre was gunne, he was not paied.

[*L adds:*] Al þe day he studied & þought
Wheþer he wylde werre forþ or nought

Forþe to werre mykille he dred,   To take þe bataille...
for he at no tyme sped.   ..no tyme byfore ne.
Of þis to conseile, he ne wist at whame,
or leue alle tille anoþer cam;
if he left tille a noþer wore,
þan suld him schame þat he com þore.

[*L adds:*] Þus he þoughte to do or lete
ffor drede of Arthur þat was so grete

Bot þis conseile he had of som,
þat he suld remue tille Oscom .....Oston
& passe be Langres, þat contre,
þat nyght to reste in þe cite.
At þe morn he gan to ride
& com to Langres in þe euen tide.
Arthur herd sone say .herde hit..
þat tille Ostum he toke þe way How to Oston....
& wild nouht tille bataile stand
tille him com more help tille hand.
[77rb] Þerto Arthur nouht ne radde
so long abide tille he folk hadde,
bot als priuely as men myght,
he did his oste remue þat nyght
& lete Langres on þe left,
& þe way tille Hoscum him reft. ....Ostun..
Bi a gate þat he wist gayn, By o weye....
he passed hilles, wod, & playn,
tille þei com þer þe strete lay hi
in a valeie hate Suesi;
þorgh þat vale alle camen
þat fro Hoscum to Langres namen.
Whan þei were þer, he bad þam reste,
& siþen ilkon þer armour keste; .....on kest
to be redy whan þei mette, ...what tyme..
smertly togider sette Swyþe on hem..
þer herneise & þer frapaile
þat felle not be in bataile. ...to be..
Vnder a hille sette þam þere ...he set..
as þei armed men were; ....alle were
whan þe Romeyns of þam had sight,
þe mykillehed suld mak þam ofright. ....þem aflight
A legion þe kyng ches & toke,
þe erle of Gloucestre had þo to loke
(a legion is folk þat wex ...of folk..
sex þousand, sex hundreth, sexti & sex),
& tauht on a hille to bide. ..hym on an hil..
"Moue not for ouht þat may betide
tille þat I com & I se nede,
þorgh þe way may stand & spede; .þe we may...
if suilk auentur tide or be ...bytide..
þat þe Romeyns turne & fle, ...turn bak..
folow after þan & slo, .þou after þenne..

in gode tyme þider þou go."
Sir Morinth said, "It salle be don."
3it toke þe kyng a legion
of douhti knyghtes horsed wele
þat bare name of þe best eschele; Þey bere þe name....
in more sight wer þo sette,
himself was chefe & þam gette; ....he þem.
þo were þe rounde tabille praised Þey were þo þat....
þat he had norised & vpraised.
[77va] Among þo was his dragoun
þat Arthur bare for gonfaynoun;
þe toþer wer set at his pay
in auht batailes of gode aray. On eyghte....
Alle wer þei knyghtes gode
& hardy men þat wele stode.
He besouht þam at þer myght
whan þe fotemen suld fyght,
þat þe hors folk com ouerthuert Þat horsmen come.
& trauersed þe Romeyns smert,
in ilk batale was tald euen.
Þus fond I writen as I salle neuen:
fyue þousand, fyue hundred, fifty & fyue
of þe noblest knyghtes o lyue,
wele armed at þer wille
& had no doute of non ille.
Þus wer þei sette, als I fynd,
foure befor & foure bihynd.
Bituex þise foure was folk þe moste,
alle þe comon of þe oste.

[*L adds:*] On hors on fote arrayed ful wel
Þat were nought set in non eschel
Þe fotmen also ful doughti ware
In ilka bataille for to fare

In ilk bataile of lordynges,
tuo cheftayns chosen, erles or kynges:
Auguiselle had þe first bataile
with Sir Kador of Cornwaile;
Beus of Oxenford þe secound, Beofs..hadde..
Gerin of Chartres halp him þat stound;
Achille of Danmark þe þrid correie, A child....Conreye
with Sir Loth, kyng of Norweie.
Þe ferth had Ohel of Bretayn,
with him was Wawayn chefetayn. & wyþ hym was þe gode Wawayne

After þo foure, oþer foure ware	
rengid & set to bataile ȝare.	
Of one was Kay iustisere,	Of þat on...
& with him Sir Beduere;	
Beduer had his Herupeis,	[*Om. L*]
Kay, Angeuins & Chinnoneis.	[*Om. L*]
Þe toþer eschelle had Sir Holdyn	
& Sir Witard, þe Peiteuin.	..Gwitard..
Þe thrid had Iugens of Leicestre	.seuenþe....
with Sir Ionathas of Dorcestre;	
þe erle of Chestre, Sursalem,	....sire Cursalen
& of Bathe, þe erle Vrgen;	Baruk of Circestre of Baþe Vrgen
[77vb] þe auhtend was to þam alied,	.eyghteþe bataille to þem was.
Arthure on þam wele affied.	fful mykel on þem Arthur.
Þe sargeancie & þe archers	
& oþer noble alblastrers,	
þo were set withouten þe pres	
to kepe þe Romeyns at þe trauers;	
bifor Arthure suld þise alle wende	
& Arthure was in þe last ende.	
Whan had set ilk bataile	.Arthur had set..
& tauht þam how þei suld assaile,	
listens þe grete curteisie	
he spak tille his barons on hie,	.....alle on hy
& þe mykelle praisyng he made,	
his men to bold, þer hert to glade:	
"Barons," he said, "ioy me ledis	
whan I think on ȝour gode dedis,	.....doughti.
for ȝour thewes & ȝour conqueste,	
& euer I fynd ȝow hardy & preste.	
Ȝour pruesse it waxes ay,	..& nobleye hit wexeþ ay
maugre þo þat wild say nay.	
Whan I thynk on ȝour gode dedis,	..byþenke on ȝoure godnesse
þat Bretayn our lond in ȝour tyme es	
hede of thritty kyngdames,	
& lady so men hir names,	.lorde ouere þem as men hit.
for þat ioy my hert is tikelle;	
in god & ȝow I affie mykelle	
þat ȝit salle we our lond auance	
þorgh godes grace & ȝour gode chance.	
Of dedes of armes ȝe haf þe pris	
& ouercomen þe Romeyns tuys.	& haue....
Mi hert me giffes þat grace it schapes,	

& tyme neghes & þerto rapes
þat we salle þis day in þe were
fro þe Romeyns maistrie bere.
Norweie, Danmerk, haf we ouer runnen,
& France þorgh bataile wonnen. ffraunce & fflaundres þorow bataille ȝe wonne
Wele salle we wynne þe lesse worþi,
whan of þe best we haf maistrie. Syn ȝe of þe beste hadde.
To seruage þei wene vs to drawe
& giffe þam treuage þorgh awe,
& France to reue vs rote & rynde;
suilk folk wene þei here to fynde
[78ra] als out of þe est bring. Als þey out....
Women kan better of fightyng!
On criste salle we hope & affie
ageyn þe houndes of Payenie;
for houndes salle ȝe neuer fle
ne Romeyns ere not als we. & Romayns ar nought worþ a be
Wele I wote & wele salle wite, .wot y & ȝe schul.
þat I salle se who wele smyte, ...ho wel schal.
for I salle be at ilk dede
& I salle help at alle nede."
Þat he said was wele herd Þys þat he....
& alle at ons him ansuerd: ....þey hym.
maistri no pes wild þei non ȝelde;
bataile was set, bataile þei wilde.
[*L adds:*] Þey wylde deye þer in þe feld
But ȝyf þe maystrie wyþ hem held
Þei suore alle þat mot be suorne;
what chance so was laid him beforne,
þat ilk chance þei wild haf alle,
gode or ille, whedir god lete falle. God or wykke wheþer God..
Lucius Yber was born in Spayn,
of Rome emperour & chefetayn.
Ȝong man inouh was sir Lucie,
þritty ȝere & more, not fulle fourty. More þan þritty but nought.
Don he had in þat age
many douhti vassalage; Many a..
for he was strong to stand in stoure, ...lastynge..
had þei mad him emperoure. Þer fore was he mad.
On þe morn arly, on a thrum ......þrom
þei moued fro Langres tille Hoscum .....Ostum
with mykille folk & grete route,
in length & brede spred aboute.

Be spies þe emperour herd say
þat Arthur had trauersed his way.
He perceyued his boldhede
& sawe þat he had no drede, ...hadde of hym..
& ouþer burd him to bataile stand   Þat eyþer bihoued hym...
or turne ageyn & be fleand.
To turne ageyn were cowardise
& þat were schame to alle hise.   ....til hym &.

[*L adds:*] Kynge Prynces & Dukes alle þo
Þat were wyþ hym two hundred & mo

For conselle he cald his men to,   To conseille alle he calde þem.
to wite of þam how he suld do.
"Lodes, peres, men of honours,   Lordes....
douhti bodies, gode conquerours,   .lordes..
[78rb] 3e er comen of þo ancessours
þat wele stode in alle stours.
Þorgh þam is Rome, 3e haf herd, ...wel haue 3e.
holden hede of alle þe werld,
& so salle I gyf 3ow a gyue
als long as I may lyue.

[*L adds:*] Þey wonne þe londes þat we now heyre
Schame hit were we scholde now peyre
Gentil þey were oure kynde hit mones
Of doughti fadres of doughti sones

Þerfor dos now þat in 3ow es,
liken þour fadres douhtynes,   Likneþ 3our fadres in doughtines
bot it were in bataile pyne   Better.....
þan fader heritage to tyne.

[*L adds:*] & þat schul we on none wyse
Heritage lese for feintyse
Þyse wordes for yuel seide y nought now
ffor y fond neuere feintise in 3ow

3our fadres wer gode, so er 3e,
or better þan þei, it may so be;
3e se & wate als wele as I,   3e wyte & se as...
þat bi þat way we suld go bi,
vntille Hoscum it is withsette   .Ostum...
bot with bataile or barette.

[*L adds:*] I ne wot wheþer þey be robbours
Or þeues þat wolde haue ought of ours
Þat weye þey haue vs wyþsted
Þat y scholde 3ow haue inne y led

I trowe þei wend þat I had skurned,

for I now ageynwerd turned;   ffor þat y...
nay, for soþe þat þouht I nouht,
I wild þei had on vs more souht.
[*L adds:*] Ouer fer byfore vs þey han hopped
& oure right passage haue þey stopped
Þer forgate salle þam not auaile.
Arme we vs, gyue þam bataile,   .vs & gyue we þem.
& do þam bakward to be born   To do þem bak be dryuen &.
þat vs er passed so fer beforn;   Þat passed vs...
if þei stand, we salle þam smyte;
if þei fle, þan salle þei wyte
þat þer pride has þam schent   Þer pryde þat hem so haþ.
þat þei our way bifor vs hent."   ..þe weyes byfore vs wente
Whan Lucius had þus said,   ...þus gat.
alle þei stirt forþe at a braide   fforþ þey ferde alle...
& armed þam ilkon wele,
& sette ilk man tille his eschele.
Kynges & dukes of paien   ..Prynces..
wer medled among cristen
þat þer londes of Rome held,
& in þer werre seruis of scheld.
Be centiners & millers   by milers & by centeners
sette þei þer batailes sers;
hors folk, fotemen, on ilk partie   Horsmen fotfolk...
wer som set louh, & som hie,
after þat þam gode þouht
[78va] þat wer of pruesse in bataile douht.
Whan þei were dight & sette
in tuelf batailes þo þat þam gette,
doun with þe hille þei com þe way
alle sarrely vnto valeie.   ..in to þe valeye
Alle þe to side to þe Romeyns,   & þat o syde toke..
Arthure þe toþer euen ageyns;
[*L adds:*] Þe Romayns comen fro ward þe west
& Arthures folk were al prest
on boþe sides þei gan to blowe
& trumped als a fulle gode þrewe,   Trumpes & pipes a wel god þrowe
blowand neghed nehi & nehi,   Þe batailles neyghed...
sadly passand & softeli.
Whan þei sauh þei nehi mot mete,   ...þat þey might.
with bowes & alblastes gan þei schete.
Dartes launced, stones kast
on boþe parties þikke & fast;

vnneþis mot any open his ie
so þikke at ons gon þei flie,
als þikke as snowe þat snewe
or as haile þat stormes blewe.
After schotyng, þei striken lances, [*Transp. L*] .þat schot þey schote launces
þorgh scheldes smyten & þorgh pances; [*Transp. L*]
fer wais mot men here þe frusse, ...brusche
a þousand braken at þe brusse. ....o frusche
After lances, suerdes smyten, ..wyþ swerdes.
& oþer wapens þat biten, & wyþ axes & daggares þat wel.
þer was bataile merueilous,
neuer ore so perillous. .non byfore..

[*L adds:*] Ne non so asper ne so þyk
ffor ilk was oþer euen quik
Þat wel couþe feighte he fond his mecche
Cowardie halp þer no wrecche
[*The next two couplets are transposed in L.*]

Hard togider gon þei hurte, fful harde....
þe ton ageyn þe toþer burte;
so hard þe parties togider toke
þat alle þe valeie about schoke;
som þat were striken turned [*Om. L*]
& defended, strokes skurned; [*Om. L*]
fele doun felle & many stode, Manye doun fulle & fele þer.
& many ley dronkled in blode; .mani on lay...
many knyght of sadelle was kast, ...wrast
& many stede with him was wrast; ....hem were cast
& many oþer went ostray,
þe bidelle broken, sadelle away. .bridles broken & sadeles.
Wele þei fauht & long stounde, ...a ful long.
inouh of fight ilk oþer founde; Ilk fonded oþer to haue to grounde
so siker to wynne was no Romeyn So vaillauant was neuere..
[78vb] þat myght bring þe Bretons abak agayn, ..þe Bretons ruyse ones.
ne þe Bretons of þam nouht wan,
so wele stode ilk a man.
Noþeles, foure batales of ours
were ay fightand in þo stoures. Had hard encountre & scharpe.
Auguiselle & Sir Kadore, Agusel...
Beus & Gerin, þise ȝede before; Beofs...were þor
Achil, Loth, & Sir Ohele,
& Sir Wawayn þat did so wele,
þise foure were þe comon oste; ..wyþ þe..
alle had fulle hand alle most. .had þey....

Was þer non kouth lightly chese   Noman mighte þer wel.
who suld wynne ne who suld lese.   Whilk of þem schold wynne or.
To þat eschel to bataile spred   Til þat o bataille forþ.
þat Kay & Sir Beduer led;
þei sauh þe Bretons nouht wan,
þe Romeyns held as þei began;
to þam þei said þei suld alle gate,
in alle þe pres þei gan abate.

[*L adds:*] In to al þe þrong þer was þykkest
Kay & Beduer in gonne brest

Wele fauht Beduer, so did Kay;
þo þat þei hitte, dede þei lay.
Þus said þo þat stode nere, ...þem ner
neuer stiward ne botelere
þat serued kyng no kaisere,
so wele halp at þat powere.   ....here.
Mikille þe did & more suld
if þei had liffed & criste it wold.

[*L adds:*] Byfore þey breke þe Romayns route
Þer folk folewode & hadde no doute
Many a strok þey gaue & tok
Out of þer sadeles mani on schok

Sir Beduer among þam presed,
Romeyns to sle he ne sesed;
on þe toþer side, Kay ne blan,
for he feld hors & man;   ..feld doun...
if þei þamseluen kouth haf mythed,   ...couþe haue meþed
& þer strokes kouth haf lithed,   & als þer...leþed
& þer folk wild haf abiden
þat þei had togider riden   And alle to gidere þat þey had.
tille þe toþer batailes had comen,
& þan alle at ons nomen,
of þam grete pruesse had bien told,
& saued þer lyues lightly was sold.   ...bodies þat sone were cold
Allas, if þat god had wilt
þer hardinesse þamself spilt;
þei þouht to perce þe oste þorghout
[79ra] & wist þamself strong & stoute;   ffor þey hadde hertes ful fers &.
on þamself ouer mykelle affied,
þer men to þam wele alied,   ...hem were so allyed
þat þei ne rouh where þei ȝede,   ...roughte...
no tentid not þei were in drede.   Ne nought rewarded how....
A bataile þei met & smote þerin,

not Romeyn, it was Saraȝin; Nought of þe Romayns but of.
of Mede he was, Bockus he hight,
kyng he was & fulle god knyght.
A grete oste Bockus led,
þe erles were hardy & nouht dred.
Vnto þam alle smertly riden, Right on þem alle fulbut þey.
þer was bataile fulle wele smyten.
Bituex þe hondes Saraȝins,
& Herupeis & Angeuyns,
Bockus rode with a gleyue, .rod in wyþ..
fayn he wild Beduere disceyue;
in at at þe breste Beduere he smote, .att þe brest...
þe gleyue was scharp, ouer fer it bote.
Hauberk & scheld þorgh he brak,
þe dynt com out at his bak. Þe spere fley out al...
Beduere felle, non myght him saue,
bot Ihesu criste his saule haue.
Kay fond Beduer þer he lay,
fayn he wald haf þe body away;
of alle men he lufed him most.
He relied his men in þe ost & þenne gan faste relie his.
& gaf bataile to þam of Mede,
with force he did þam flit þat stede;
as he suld his body vpfange, ...þer þe body.
he was duelled a litille to lange; .dwelled þer on a...
com Sir Sertor, kyng of Libie
with mykelle folk of paemie, .gret power of Paynye
& on Sir Kay smot fulle sore ....smot he þore
& wonded him ferly ille þore. ...ferly sore
Bot for no wo, ne wonde, ne dynt,
þe body he ne left ne tynt.
His gode folk was him about
& halp him of þat mykelle dout;
þe body to þe dragon brouht,
maugre þo þat on him souht.
Beduer kosyn, Ireglas, Sire..hight Irelgas
[79rb] whan he wist þat hard cas,
of his frendes & his kynde,
& oþer þe best þat he mot fynde,
þre hundreth with helmes bright, .hundred men...
wele horsed & alle dight;
whan he had samend þam ilkone,
"Lordynges, to ȝow I mak my mone.

At þis nede, helpes now,
of þo þat myn eam slow. ..houndes þat...
Of Bockus þe kyng of Mede,
spies him in alle stede." Aspieþ hym wel in ilka.
Þei serched alle vp & doun
tille þei sauh his gonfaynoun;
þer þei it sauh, þider gon þei drawe,
"A, Kaliburne!" þe cried a thrawe. On Kaliborne þey...
Yreglas no man withstode,
his eam to venge he was wode.
He dred non of alle þe renge
bot þat he mot his eam venge;
fulle wele halp his felauhes alle, ..hym halp þen...
with lances þei did many on falle,
on þam riden þat doun were kast,
& Bockus trauersid at þe last. ..bataille trauailled fast
Whan þei tille his bataile were comen,
so wele þei did þat þorgh þei nomen.
Yreglas was euer before,
his folk after him held þat skore;
side & oþer þei left no þing
vntille þei fond Bockus, þe kyng.
Whan Yreglas was wele auysed,
his hors on him þe bridelle wysed.
He teised his dynt, Bockus to smyte,
þe suerd was gode & wele wild bite;
þe helme clefe, þe hauberk taar,
þorgh þe breste þe suerd in schaar. Þorow out...swerd hym schar
(I trowe þe soule to helle went.)
Bot Yreglas bi þe arme him hent
þat þe body felle not doun,
& laid ouerthuert þe arsoun; He leide hym ouer þwert hys.
þe knyght was gode, þe hors strong,
he turned þerwith out of þe þrong,
þe body to þe dragon bare;
[79va] his men wele halp about him ware. Wel holp his men þat...
Beside his eam his body threwe
& on pecis alle tille hewe; ...hym al to.
alle to hewen þei him lete, ...þer he hym let
hondes & foules his body ete.
Whan Yreglas had don þis pris,
"Felauhes," he said, "grant mercies.
Turne we now on þam agayns

& folow fast on þe Romayns,
& on þam þat nouht ne leue,   ..þise houndes þat mys byleue
þat our cristen mykelle greue."

[*L adds:*] Þey turnde ageyn as men hardy
Þen myghte men here noise & cry
Swerdes helmes men mighte se glyder
& sparklyng as þey smyte to gyder

Holdin, þe erle of fflandres, helde
Briges & Blemes vnder his schelde;   Gaunt & Bruges...
he contred with Alifantyn of Spayn,   [*Transp. L*]
of a bataile he was chefetayn;   [*Transp. L*]
so long þe tone þe toþer assailed
& ilkon oþer so trauailed,
þat slayn was Alifantyn
& also þe Erle Holdyn.
Liger, þe kyng of Boloyne, ...Babilloyne
iusted with þe erle of Boloyne;   Rod to þe Erl of.
slayn was þe erle, so was þe kyng,
& oþer þre did þer endyng,
Baluk, Vrgens, & Sir Cursalle,
& ilkon was grete folk with alle.   Wiþ ilk was....
Sir Vrgens, of Bathe was sire,
Baluk, erle of Wilcheshire,   & Baruk of Circestre & Wilteschire
& Cursalle, erle of Chestre was,
þise wer slayn at þat pas;
þer men gaf bak & turned ageyn
& com tille Ohel & Waweyn.
Suilk tuo knyghtes wele to leue   ...ful wel þou leue
was non siþen Adam & Eue;
þer men & þei were gode ilkon,
in pres, in playn, þei douted non;
þo þat first on þe Bretons brak,
þer chefetayns slouh, did þam gyf bak.
Alle þei slow & did þam fle
& turned þam ouer iambe leue;   ....þat men myght se
so had strokes þe Bretons gaf,   .harde....
þe Romeyns route þei alle ouerhaf,
[79vb] þat Romeyns, wild þei ne wold,
fled vnto þer egle of gold.
(Egle is herne on Inglis roun,
þat was þe Romeyns gomfaynoun.)   ....gunphanoun
Þer þe fond þe emperour,
of alle Rome þer was þe flour.

Whan þei sauh þei com so nere,	
þe Romeyns were fulle austere.	
[*L adds:*]	Nere herd þey seye ne sawe hit writen
	Swilk a stour to Romayns smyten
A douhty erle þat hight Kynmare,	
with Sir Ohel þat tyme was þare;	
don he had grete vassalage,	
þe Romeyns slayn at ilk a stage.	
[*L adds:*]	Mighte no Romayn him a scape
	Þat to þe deþ he dide hym rape
It sais a fote man a disceit drouh,	A fotman þenne his bowe vp.
þis Erle Kymare algate he slouh,	& Erl Kynmar atte lasste he.
& tuo þousand of Bretons	...of þe.
withouten noble men of ronons.	.men of grete renouns
Þre gode men þer were wight,	.noble knyghtes..& wyghte
Iaguȝ it sais þe ton hight;	Iugens..þat on so.
out of Boloyn þiþen was he,	
a toun, I wene, or a cuntre;	.borough y were or a cite
þe toþer hight Ricomarkus,	
þe þrid men cald Bocklonius.	
Þer was not þre in alle þat stoure	
þat wrouht after so grete honour;	
if þei had bien dukes or kynges,	
of þam had bien grete praisynges.	
[*L adds:*]	Þer was no Romayn bitwyxt hem cam
	Þat awey wyþ lyf fro þem nam
	Were he neuere so doughty
	On lyue passed non forby
Right to þe emperours bataile,	....owen bataille
þei ne rest Romeyns to assaile;	..lefte...
Romeyns sauh þei did grete wouh,	
þei closed þam & alle þre slouh.	
Whan Wawayn wist, & Sir Ohel,	
þat þer gode folk doun felle,	
was neuer libard no leon,	
ne wilde woulf, ne dragon,	
was so wode bestis to bite	
as Wawayn was, Romeyns to smyte.	
Sir Ohel als on his partie,	
manyon dede did doun lie;	.dide he ded..
& þe Romeyns wele defendid,	Þe Romayns wel þem.
grete strokes on þe Bretons spendid.	
Wele were þei smyten & wele smote,	[*Om. L*]

Bretons þe biten, Bretons þam bote. [*Om. L*]
[80ra] Wawayn was euer fresch & preste;
whan oþer ne myght, þan was he beste.
Was no helm with stele so rank
þat his suerd ne þorgh it sank. ...þorow out ne sank
[*L adds:*] Ne hauberk non wyþ maille gret
Þat his spere ne þorow schet
Þat tyme manyon did he deie,
þo þat myght, mad him weie;
among þe most, euer he presed,
his hard strokes nouht ne sesed.
Right to þe Emperour Lucius,
of þe Romeyns he mad rescus.
Lucius was ȝong, inouh had elde,
hardy & stalworth armes to welde;
þritty & more, lesse þan fourty, Bytwyxte þrytti & fourty
was þe elde of Sir Lucy.
He knewe wele Sir Wawayn
& he him fulle wele agayn;
ilk on oþer auisement set
& þe emperour wele he let.
He hoped with Wawayn to fight
for he was man praised of myght,
& if he myght eskape of chance,
þerof at Rome wild him auance.
After þe sight ne þrow abiden, Right anon no þrowe.
bot smertly togidir riden;
þer schaftes scheuerd & fleih in felde,
bot þei felle nouht ne donward helde.
[*L adds:*] Gode were þer brunyes & stronge of maille
Þer fore þer dyntes myghte nought vaille
To smyte with suerd, smertly þei hasted,
on many maners ilk oþer tasted;
[*Line order differs in L:*]
on what he mot bring to grounde, Ilk oþer to slo ilk oþer to wounde
þei proued bineth & aboun; How eyþer myght oþer brynge to grounde
ilk oþer slo, ilk oþer wounde, Þei proued byneþen and a bouen
with suerd poyntes sidelynges schouen. ...sadly þei schouen
[*L adds:*] fful wel þei couþe ilk oþer assaye
& þer as was peril ilk oþer affraye
fful sone schuld eyþer to deþ haue gon
ȝyf þey nadde be let of non
þe Romeyns perceyued þe bataile hard;

þei alied þam at þer standard & relyed þem to þe.
& com to socour þer emperoure
þat was in a perillous stoure;
fulle litelle failed, he ne had bien lorn;
þer were þe Bretons bakward born,
fer þei fled, on þam was wonnen, Bretons wyþ drowe & Romayns.
& many on ouer riden & ronnen.
Þer was Wawayn in grete doute,
þe pris of Rome was him aboute.
[80rb] Ohel & he eskaped þam þorgh
& com & teld tille Arthorgh .wente & teld hit..
þat þei had bien at þe standard,
& nere alle slayn & dryuen bakward.
Whan Arthur sauh his men gaf bak,
þe Romeyns boldly on þam brak,
& poined þam ouerpriked with pres,
þei fled bak & þe feld les. & þey wyþ drowen hem & erþe þey.
No lenger þan wild he bide,
ne myght if he wild saue his side.
He com criand with his bataile,
"Bretons, ageyn Romayns assaile! Agayn ȝe Bretons þe Romayns.
I am Arthur þat salle not faile;
at alle ȝour nedes I salle ȝow vaile.

[*L adds:*] Y am Arthur þat hider ȝow ledde
Þat neuere in feld for no man fledde
Ne deþ ne dynt ne bataille dredde
In alle stours wel haue y spedde

I am Arthur salle mak ȝow way,
Romeyns to ryme, Romeyns to fley. & Romayns to Rome for drede do fleye
Loke þat none of ȝow recreie,
ne þat ȝour fight feynt ne feie. Ne at þys iourne...
Þink now on ȝour gode bountes,
so fele haf won londes & fes. How fele we haue....
Today ne salle I of feld fle ...y fro þys feld.
tille alle be won or lorn þorgh me."
He smote his stede & forþe gon go,
Romeyns to felle, Romeyns to slo;
þo þat sauh it mot wele say,
so mykelle folk for him gon die;
so many helmes for him þorgh dryuen,
scheldes clouen, hauberkes ryuen
þat Kaliburne had þorgh biten,
hedes, schankes, armes of smyten. .armes legges..

I may not say alle ne howe,
at ilk a dynt a man he slowe.
As þe leon for hunger snacches
& slos þe beste þat he first kacches, .sleþ.....lacches
so ferd Arthur with ilkone;
man ne hors lyue left none. Many hors men a lyue..
Whom so he myght reche or smyte,
þof he wonded him neuer so lyte,
leche crafte couth him not saue, ...seye
no medicyne þat he mot haue. ffor any medisine nede most he deye
Alle for drede befor him fleih As þe wolf chaseþ þe schep
as schepe agayn þe woulf ne deih; He dide þe Romayns by fore hym lep
[*L has the following line, but crossed out*:]
Byfore hym for gret drede þey fleye

[80va] & as Arthure after þam schoke,
Sertor of Libie he ouer toke.
His hede he smote of at a dynt;
for armour þe suerd ne stynt.
Said Arthur to þo þer ware,
"Schame þe tyme þou armes bare
þat þou come so nehi &...me so ney
Kaliburne to mak blody!"
Arthur ouertoke anoþer pres,
þe kyng of Bitinie, Polidetes,
of a lond of paemie;
a selcouth Arthur lete flie, .wonder strok...
bi þe schuldres þe hede of plat,
þe hede felle doun, þe body vpsat.
Þorgh Arthure wordes & dedes traiste,
þe Bretons bolded, Romayns abaiste;
noþeles, Romeyns wele abode,
ageyn þe Bretons stifly rode
& laid at as þei were wode; .foughten....
with grete strength ageyn þei stode.
Arthure sauh þei wild not skurne,
strokes he gaf with Kaliburne.
Þe emperour soiorned nouht; Þemperour þenne taried.
on Arthur folk sore he souht.
Þe emperour ne Arthur our kyng
myght not mete for no þing.
[*L adds:*] Mikel was þe pres ful þykke þe þro
Þey myghte nought mete Arthur was wo
Wele fauht Breton & wele Romeyn,

a þousand in a þrowe was slayn;
non mot wit who suld ȝit wyn   Myghte noman wyte ho...
ne whas was ouer no whilk was in.   Ne whiche of hem wer oute ne.
Þer was þe flour of boþe parties
& noiþer bare ȝit þe pris.   .neyþer side....
Morinth, of Gloucestre chefetayn,
moued aboun on þe mountayn.
He sauh þe bataile was long
& non fled out of þe throng.
He had a legion of folk þat wex
vi M, vi hundreth, sexti & sex.   Sex þousand sex hundred...

[*Line order differs in L.*]

Him þouht þat Arthur had nede,   And alle knyghtes wyþ helm on stede
he sauh þat non gaf þe feld   & þoughte þat Arthur hadde nede
& tille þe Bretons þer owen held,   He sey non þat hym ne gaf þe feld
& alle knyghtes with helm on stede.   & til þe Bretons þer owen held
[80vb] He þouht þorgh of a lyte,   ..þorow help...
þei suld þe Romeyns discomfite;
& forto maynten Arthure tene,   ..venge Arthures.
of þe Romeyns þei suld mak clene.
He com doun alle priuelie
þat none ne herd noise no crie;
behynd þer bak he com alle hote,   .þe bank....
& on þe emperour side he smote,
& þer bataile perced þorghout;
þan þei bessed þat are was stout.   Þen gon þey baysche....
Þe Romeyns no langer biden,
þe Bretons folow & þam ouer riden,
& fleand, lightly þam slouh,   .al fleynge...
& spoiled þam & alle to drouh;
sþen had þei no grace to stand   Syn......
ne myght recouer bot euer fleand.   ..relye...
Þe emperour was slayn o chance
þorgh þe body with a lance.
I kan not say who did him falle,
bot Sir Wawayn, said þei alle.   ...men seide hit.
In þe last bataile þat in sprong,
he was slayn þam among;

[*L adds:*] Þe certeyn can þer noman ame
But sire Wawayn bar þe name

amang þe dede þei him fonde
& with a lance was his wonde.   ...spere...
Þe Romeyns alle fast fled

& þe paiens for drede spred.
Whilk of þam þat suiþest nam, ...swyþest.
þe Bretons kept þam as þei kam.
Many of þam lete þei go;   [*Transp. L*] ffor wery manion let..
þei were werie alle to slo.   [*Transp. L*]
Þe blode ran doun as water stremes
in kynnes, in creuesse, & in semes;   .chynes.....
gode stede & palfreis
ȝede o strey, ilk þer weis.
Arthur was glad þat þorgh þer dome
he had abatid þe pris of Rome,   Had so abated þe pride..
for so said alle þe Romeyns   ffor byforn seyden...
þat non mot stand þam ageyns;
þerfor Arthure þanked god alle myght,
gaf him þe maistrie of þam þorgh fight.   Þat gaf.......
He did seke alle þe Bretons,
erles, knyghtes, & barons,
[81ra] & did þam bere to þer cuntres   ...carie...
& biried þam at þer cites,
to hermitages & abbeis
þer men holy bedis sais.   ..holy bodies leyes
He to þe body of þe emperour   He tok.....
& did it kepe with grete honour;
to Rome it sent to do in graue,
oþer treuage suld þei non haue.
"If þei oþer lord fond   ..any oþer..
to ask treuage of Arthure lond,
oiþer Bretayn or of ffrance,
him suld falle þe same chance;
& Arthure praies ȝow for þe arrerage
to resceyue þis treuage,   Þat ȝe receyue now..
& if ȝe challange any mare,   ...chalange hym..
he salle ȝow send suilk als þise are."
[K]ay þat was wonded biforn,   [*Illuminator's error*: Þ.]
vnto þe bastelle was he born.   Vntil þe Castel...
He compassed or he ȝede,   ..hit in lengþe & brede
boþe þe length & þe brede   Er he to þe bataille ȝede
& gaf it name Chinnun   ....& cald hit Chymoun
(I ne whi no bi what reson).   ..wot why ne what.
Sir Kay liffed not bot a stound,
he had so many dedely wound.
Þei biried him at an heremitage
bisid Chinnun, at a passage.

At Bayon in Normundie,
þe seid Sir Beduere suld þer lie;
þei beried him at a kirk namcouht ......name couþ
without þe ȝate toward þe souht. .....souþ
To fflandres þei bare þe erle Holdyn,
in Terruane biried him in. .Tyrewane þei...
Sir Liger was born to Boloyne,
& Arthure left in Burgoyne.
Alle þe wynter duellid þer in,
tounes he did many bigyn;
in somer he þouht to Rome haf gone
if he had lettyng of none.
He was passed þe mountayns playn
bot Modrede did him turne agayn.
A day als he to mete went,
out of þis lond lettres were sent;
[81rb] right als his trompes blewe,
a messengere þat he wele knewe
þe lettres in his hand laid,
& tille him with mouth said ..his owen mouþ he.
þat Modrede, his sistir sonne,
had don him grete tresonne,
& had taken of þe lond homage,
& don in kastellis gode hostage. .leyd in casteles gret.
Ȝit wille he not be þor bie
bot waite him with more vilanie. .waiteþ þe more.
His wife tille his hore gon drawe Þy wif til hys hore haþ.
agayn cristen mannes lawe,
"& Cheldrik, kyng of Germinie,
com & brouht grete partie; Ys comen &...
biȝond Humber vnto Scotland,
Cheldrik has þat in his hand,
& alle þat longes vnto Kent,
vnto Cheldrik ȝeldes rent; Vntil Cheldrik gyue þey.
to hold with Modered at his myght,
trouth togider haf þei plight.
Seuen hundreth schippes ligge bi þe stronde;
fourscore þousand er comen to londe
of men of armes withouten pedaile, ...pytaille
ageyn ȝow comes to gyf bataile."
Whan he had tille Arthur teld ..had þus...
how Modrede no faith him held, ..no feyþ ne trouþe..
& synfully had raised stryfe,

his lond him reft, forlayn his wyfe,
he mad his pleynt to Sir Ohel,
praied him to kepe ilk a del,
Burgoyn & France wele; ...boþe wel
tille him he trosted als to be stele. ...tryste as to þe.
"Vnto Bretayn I wille me spede,
þe outlandes with me lede;
on Modrede wille bataile bede ..wil y..
& take vengeance on his misdede.
Litille I praise alle my conqueste
þat I haf wonnen est or weste, ...in þys Est
if I left now Bretayn my fe, ȝyf y now leue...
myn heritage þat felle to be.
I salle me hie agayn to com,
on alle manere I wille to Rome."
[81va] He iorneid fro land to land
tille he com to Whitsand.
He pleyned of Modred ..hym sore..
þat fro his conquest him fled. ....had don hym.
Arthur had purueid him flete, ...a flet
at Whitsand was in water sete.
Modred herd þat tiþng, ..wel þat tydyng
bi Whitsand com Arthur þe kyng;
Modred gadred oste togidere ..his hostes.
of his & oþer þat com þidere.
Arthure he hoped wele to abide, ...he durste.
withset þe hauen on ilk a side;
þe lond wild not Modred lese,
ne repent him, ne to þe pes chese.
He wist himself so coupabille,
to ask pes, it were bot fabille.
Arthur did his flete eft dight,
to Romneie þe red þam right.
Bot or þei wer of schippes nomen,
ore was Modred þidere comen Er was Moddred ageyn hym.
& letted him to haf entre;
þe mot nouht com out of þe se. Þey..come vp fro..
Bot Arthur men myght with trauaile,
fals Modred gon þam assaile, ..þey gonne.
& he agayn fulle bold, ...was ful.
for he had so siker hold.
Arthure folk was wele more schent,
for to þer schippes þei gaf þer tent

to stere boþe þam fer & hend, ..þem boþe...
& tent it nouht þereself defend; Þey tenden nought hem self to fende
ne myght þam not fro arowes couere
to whils þei stode on bankes ouer;
þerfor wer many at mischefe
& þer tinselle more grefe. ..lost was..
Als þei to lond fro botes stirte,
many were slayn & fele hirte;
at suilk a chance & suilk a caas, & mescheuously þen fel such cas
Sir Wawayn þore ded was. Þat sire Wawayn slayn þer.
Sir Auguiselle of Scotland
bi him lay dede on þe sand. .....his hand
Þe sothe I saw neuer writen how, ..ne sawe y write ne how
whedir bowe or suerde þam slow.
[81vb] þer many wer slayn þare
þat Arthur pleyned him sare,
bot non bi þe tendele ....tenþe del
als Wawayn & Auguisele. ... Agusel
[*L adds:*] He had so mikel sorewe for þo
Þat he þoughte in non oþer wo
Þer sorow mot neuer forgete, Þeir sorewe myght he..
siþen ete he neuer bliþely mete; ....gladly.
bot whan his folk land had taken,
a partie his sorow was ouer schaken.
Modred myght haf no dure
ne nouht stand his meyne; Ne no fot helden..
[*L adds:*] Þaw þey were fele þey were nought prest
Þey had be norisched in pes & rest
þei couþe not togidere wonne, ...fighte ne to gydere wone
ne in tyme stand ne schonne,
as Arthur folk in werre couth
þat it vsed in þer ȝouthe. .had hit vsed fro tyme of.
Þat ilk day at Romneie,
Arthur many one deie .dide manion.
of Modred folk here & þare,
& mo suld if þe nyght ne ware.
Arthur sauh þe day faile;
he bode & stynt, his folk to tale.
He gaf tent tille his owen conrey,
to whils fled Modred away.
Alle þat nyght Modred fled
to seke reste, bot ille he sped. ..recet but yuele..
He wend London wild him reseue;

þei wild him not bot lete him weyue.
Temse & London he passed alle,
at Wynchestre toke he stalle;
þer he herberwed alle nyght,
ageyn þer wille, alle þorgh myght.
Of þe burgeis he toke feaute
& homage at þer maugre.
Arthure wild no soiorne make
Modred forto slo or take, — But Moddred wold he sle . .
bot þe sorow did him pyne
of Sir Wawayn his cosyne, — . . Gawayn his dere .
& Auguisel þe Scottis king.
Arthur was at þer birieng — . made here .
at Wibiri þat is in Wales;
þer lig þei boþe, sais Pers tales.
Now turnes Arthur sorow & drede — . comeþ al Arthures . . .
to venge him on fals Modrede.
[82ra] Day ne nyght ne wild he blynne
to sege Wynchestre, Modred þer inne.
He did þe cuntre somon alle out
& vmbileid þe toun about;
Modred sauh he was in clos
& bised with his fos. — . byseged . . .
He þouht if he long lay,
he suld not wele wynne away,
þat nedly taken suld he be,
& maugre his, ȝelde þe cite.
Among his men he mad a crie
& bad þam arme þam alle redie
with him to fight, leuer he wild
þan his vnþankes to þam him ȝeld.
His batails set, how þai suld renge, — . men in bataille gan þem .
& went out him forto venge;
þe parties son togider ran,
lorn was þore many a man.
Modred partie ȝede alle doun,
his folk had no foysoun.

[*L adds:*] Hit was no wonder he hadde no grace
ffor traitour scholde nought spede in place

He sauh his side no tyme sped,
he had misdone, þe kyng he dred. — ffor his misdede . . . .
Himself he þouh forto saue — . . þoughte algate to .
sen he myght no grace haue.

His priue3 alle to him he toke,
þo þat Arthur alle forsoke,
[*L adds:*] Þo þat Moddred hadde forþ brought
Þat neuere louede Arthur nought
priuely with þam fled away   ..hem he..
& left in bataile þat oþer conray;   ..þer al his..
to Southampton he toke þe stie
& hired him schippes alle redie,
& son onward were to saile;   .swyþe anon þey gonne forþ.
for drede he fled to Cornwaile.
Þo þat Modred bihynd left,   ...byhinde hym.
alle wer slayn & lyue reft,
& wan þe doun of þam ilkone;   ...toun...
bot wo was him Modred was gone.
Sir Vrien sonne, Iwein he hight,
gentille of blode, fulle gode knyght,
Auguiselle cosyn was Sir Iwein.
In Scotland he mad a cleyme;   Þe Reme of Scotland he gan to.
for he was next of his kyn,   [*Om. L*]
þerfor mad he cleym þerin.   [*Om. L*]
[82rb] He gaf Iwein in heritage   .left hit til...
& he mad Arthur homage.   .Iweyn...
Iwein had lauht grete honour,
agayn Modred he stode in stoure.
[*L adds:*] & dide & seyde Moddred gret schonde
Þe while Arthur was out of londe
At 3ork to soiourn was þe quene
& herd what was þam bituene.   Scheo herde what wo hem was.
Modred ne myght in bataile dure
bot euer was disconfeture.   ..was at.
Scho þouht scho was mykelle to blame
for þe vilanie & þe schame
þat Modred had brouht hir in,
& with him had layn in synne
& wedded hir agayn þe lawe;
he ne left for kynd ne godis awe.   ....kyng...
Scho hoped ille it suld bind ende,   ..þat hit scholde yuele.
hir noble lord so to schende.   ...so foule to.
[*L adds:*] & hure self for euere y schent
So mykel sorewe in herte scheo hent
Scho fled away out of þe toun
into Wales to Kaerlioun;
scho did hir in þat Nunrie   .3ald hure til þat.

& toke þe vaile for hir folie;
þerin scho was hid & sperd
þat non of hir more herd.
Modred had seised Cornwayle,
alle þe toþer lond gan him faile. — ffor al Ingeland...
He sent about to lond sers
after knyghtes þat wer souders, — .knyghte & souders
paien, cristen, knyght of scheld,
alle þat wild at sonde he held.

[*L adds:*] He sente for Irysche & Noreys
Þe Saxons come wyþ þe Daneys
Þat hadde nought on to lyue
Lond he seyde he wolde hem gyue
He highte & gaf to forthe his sped
As man byhoues þat haþ gret ned

Arthur sone ouer þouht — But Arthur sore..
if he wist what him douht.
He dred mykille þe grete comyng,
paiens among þe cristen bring.
Arthur wild no lenger bide;
he gadred folk vpon his side, — ...on ilka.
alle þe cuntres vntille Humber, — Of...heþen to.
many he had, it sais no nomber. — fful manye þer were as seys þe.
If Arthur had lenger abiden,
þe sikerer myght Modred haf riden.
Whan þe kyng had folk inouh,
vnto Cornwaile he him drouh
& com in bi þat coste
þer Modred lay with his oste. — .þat Moddred logged..
[82va] Modred said he wild not fle,
he wild stand what chance mot be; — But abyde what chaunce so.
he suld ore put himself to deie
or he suld eft fle aweie.
Modred had fourti þousand
in a wod busshed to stand.
Beside a water, Tambre, I wene,
þat was þe parties bituene; — .þe parties ran.
strong was þe ostes, grete was þe hate;
hatered togidir did þam abate. — & wrathe to gydere...

[*L adds:*] Þorow hate & ire to gydere þey ran
& Payens loues no Cristen man
Þerfore þe bataille was merueillous
& þe slaughter more hydous

On boþe parties wer slayn fele,
for non wild oþer forbere no spele. .þer non wolde oþer spele
Whan Arthur sauh Modred felon,
he rode to him with grete raundon;
befor did bere his dragon, .hym dide...
Modred to smyte als a leon.
Modred he smote & he smote him,
on boþe parties wer wondes brim; .....grym
Modred side gan misfalle,
he was slayn & his men alle;
& þer was slayn in þat stoure
of þe rounde table þe floure

[*L adds:*] Þe faire ȝonglynges so mykel y preised
Þat Arthur had norisched & vp reysed

þat Arthur gadred of alle landes, .he had gadered...
þat douhtiest were of þer handes;
& Arthur himself þore,
men sais, he wonded sore; Men seyþ he was..
for his wondes wer to drede,
þerfor þei did him lede .he dide hym self.
into þe ilde of Aualoun;
& þus sais ilk a Bretoun
þat o lyue þer he es,
man in blode & in flesch, Lyuende man wyþ blod &.
& after him ȝit þei loke.
Maister Was þat mad þis boke, .Wace....
he sais no more of his fine
þan dos þe prophete Merlyne. Þat doþ...
Merlyn sais fulle meruailous
þat Arthur dede was doutous;
þerfor þe Bretons drede .ȝyt þe..
& sais he lyues in lede;
bot I say þei trowe wrong,
if he life, his life is long. ffor ȝyf he now lyue....

[*L adds:*] & ȝyf he lyue þys ilke day
He schal lyue for euere & ay

[82vb] Bot þe Bretons loude lie; Nought þan y trowe þe Bretons.
he was so wonded þat him burd die. ....he moste dye
Þise wer lordes of renoun
þat on Modred side ȝede doun:
Bruming, Egbrith, Elais, Cheldrik,
Gillarion, Gillaselle, Gillomar, Gilopatrik. .Syllatel.Gylopayk
Þo þat died on Arthur side

þat wer lorn þat ilk tide:
Egbriht of Norweie, Askille of Danmark,
Kador & Cassibalan, douhti men & stark,
& many oþer lese þer life, ..oþer lordes...
many widow þat ore was wife. .lady wydewe þat..
Arthur was born tille Auiloun
þe ȝere of þe incarnacoun,
four hundreth & tuo & fourti ffyue hundred & two &.
sen Ihesus lighted in Mari. ..lyghte in virgyne.
ffor þe regne men were in speire, But al þe Roialme was..
for of his body was non heire.
Bot Kodor sonne, hight Constantyne,
of Cornwaile, Arthur cosyne,
he bitauht him kepyng, .tok hym þe Roiame in.
vntille he com, bad him be kyng.
Of Modred wer to sonnes left
þat þe lond wild him haf reft;
proude men & riche wer þei,
þei sauh þe force ȝede alle aweie;
þe gode knyghtes þat þer ware
was slayn & þe lond alle bare.
Þei sauh þat Arthur nouht com,
to haf drede, þei ne wist of whom.
Þe newe kyng nouht þei dred;
þei gadred folk & ostes led.
Þo Sessons þat Modred held
þat skaped vnslayn of þe feld,
to þam alle þei wer alied;
þe kynges ouer alle þei aspied. .kynges men....
Of London þei seised þe cite ..þat on...
& þe best of alle þe cuntre;
þe toþer Wynchestre & alle þe schire, Þat oþer.....
& wend haf bien lord & sire.
Costantyn herd of þer estre Constantyn....
& hied him ȝerne to Wynchestre,
[83ra] & in a kirke he him fond,
for alle kirke ne wild he wond; ..þe kirke....
befor þe autere, seynt Amfiballe,
quikely smote his hede of alle. His hed he smot of quitly.
Whan þe ton þus gate was dede,
on þe toþer bataile he bede,
bot he durst not him abide;
in a kirke he gan him hide,

bot þat stode him tille no prow,
for in þe kirke he him slow.
Þre ȝere holy was he kyng;
at þe stonhengis did his endyng,
for Konan, his kosyn, þer him slouh
þorgh treson, I ne wote how,   Treterously but y not.
& in þe stede is he laid   ...same stede ys.
within þe karolle, þe story said.
After him, kyng was þat Konan   ..was kyng his cosyn.
þat was a folte, a misproude man.
Pes kouth he non ȝeme his lyue;
he suffred his folk to fight & stryue.
Þe barons werred þam bituen,   [*Transp. L*]
in cites was euer contek & tene.   [*Transp. L*]
His men & he wer seldom sauht   .....sonder.
& oft tymes togider fauht;   By stoundes often..
it semed wele he couth no gode,
he fordid his owen blode.
His oþer eam he toke with werre & wouh
& boþe his eam sonnes he slouh,
for þei were right heires of þe lond
þat after him felle of blode men fond.   ...self....

[*L adds:*] Þer fore he was þe more to blame
Þat his owen blod so broughte to schame

Foure ȝere he regned & in treson
& died in dampnacion;
he regned & died in feble hap;   ...dide his..
after was kyng, Sir Vortap.   And after hym regned..

[*L adds:*] In þe Latyn ys writen þus
Hys ryghte name ys Vortapus

[I]n Vortapus tyme ros þe Sessouns   [*Capital omitted in P.*]
to haf wonne þe lond eftsouns;
þer chance was gode in þer tisyng, ...þeir rysyge
grete skathe þei did vnto þe kyng.
His seconde ȝere, his grace kam,
hardinesse in herte he nam,
hired soudeours, gaf þam wages,
& distroied Sessons lynages
[83rb] þat non durst in his lond abide,
bot þorgh treuage at terme & tide.
Foure ȝere he had þe lond in pes,
at London he mad his deces.
After him was his cosyn Malgo;   ..cam his sone.

alle manhede he gaf him to.
Alle men had of him doute,
he wan þe ildes alle aboute
& of kynges toke feaute
as whilom was wont to be.

[*L adds:*] Of doughtinesse of body feir
He lyknede his auncestre als heir

Of knyghtschip nobilly he proued,
alle his kynd wele he loued.
Large he was of gyftes gode, ...ȝyftes bolde
tresore wild he neuer holde,

[*L adds:*] He let nought þat day to lyuen
But he had som what of his gyuen

þat alle with him were glad & blythe
& þanked god for him oft siþe. ..hym ful many.
His þrid ȝere was ille to lyke:
he ȝede to synne sodomyke; .vsed þe..

[*L adds:*] Þe synne of Sodome as men fynde
Is a sinne ageynes kynde

at Wynchestre at his bathyng,
sodanly mad he endyng. ..he his.
After Malgo, Karice þei ches,
a nyce man, luffed no pes.
He was ay sorowfulle & wroþe,
þerfor he was alle men loþe;
þe Sessons herd he was gremiand
& þouht he mot not dure ne stand;
ouer alle about him þei ros,
& oþer aliens, Bretons fos
þat com with Gurmund bi þe se side;
þe nauie of Gurmund spred fulle wide.
He destroied þe Bretons alle
& þer name for euer did falle,
& þe name of þe lond lorn
þat hight Bretayn long beforn.
A þousand ȝere or þe incarnacoun,
hight it Bretayn for luf of Breton,
euer vnto Gurmund cam;
þe name of Bretayn away he nam.

[*L adds:*] Listneþ now a litel pas
When Gormound cam & what he was

Gurmund was a noble knyght,
of noble linage, mykelle of myght;

[*L adds:*] Stalworþe of body hardy of wille
He dredde noman for god ne ille

kyng sonne he was of Aufrik,
fer in haiþenes a fulle grete strik; Þat is in heþenesse a ful fer.
[83va] of alle Aufrik was he heire,
bot he was in anoþer speire. .þer of ne tok he ward ne.
Aufrik he gaf tille his broþer
& said he wild purchace him oþer,
& said he wild toward þe West,
bi þe se side to mak conquest,
& croune wild he neuer bere
bot he it wan with force of were.
Merlyn, þe clerk, long biforn
of Gurmund spak or he were born,
& said þe woulf opon þe se
suld do alle þe Bretons fle;
þus said Merlyn with herte sore.
Þe Bretons tyme for euer more,
tille Cadwaldre & Conan,
þer bones wer brouht agayn with man.
Fulle wele he kald him woulf of drede;
he robbed ouer as he ȝede. ..oueral...
He purchaced þorgh robberie .purchased hym..
men inouh & faire nauie.
A hundreth & sexti þousand bolde
of men of armes & bowmen tolde, ...knowe & tolde
withouten gelde & maryners,
sergan ȝ gode & archers, & sergaunt ȝ & gode.
schippes he had, I ne wote how fele,
alle he toke & non wild spele.
Water & lond, long & brode,
alle ouersailed & þorgh rode.

[*L adds:*] Ildes þorow ȝede kynges ouer cam
Þeyr landes sesed þer godes nam

So long he farde on se sailand,
kynges slouh bi se & sand;
alle holy his flete gan dryue,
vpon Irelend wild he ryue. .Irland he gan aryue
Þe lond son tille him gon falle,
Iris kyng he did him calle;
siþen he wild to Bretayn, Þen seide he he wolde..
with þe Bretons to mak bargayn. ....make a newe.
Sessons wer many ȝit in þis lond

þorgh treuage þat men þam in bond,	
& whan þei felt þam out of myght,	...felde hem ought..
in Hengist lond þei cleymed right.	
Tuancastre, Lindesey, & Kent,	
of þise Hengiste had rent,	...furst hadde.
[83vb] & þat Octa his sonne	..he gaf...
bi Scotland þer bigan wonne;	
þei chalanged it of auncestrie,	
alle was Hengist partie.	.þat was..
Oft þei wan it þorgh dynt	
& oft it ageyn tynt;	
[*L adds:*]	Often þer fore þey gaf hostages
	& also ofte made þey homages
	To þe Bretons oþ þey swor
	& often ageyn þer oþ þey for
þei held no lenger feith no ryght	Neuere held þey....
tille þei sauh tyme þat þei myght,	Þan...& terme of.
þat a kyng was dede or doun	
or if a feble on had þe croun.	
Þan þei ros, on Bretons runnen,	
vmwhile lese, vmwhile wonnen.	.þey les vmwhile þei wonne
[*L adds:*]	ȝyf a discord were bitwixt þe Bretons
	Euere medlande were þe Saxons
	On wham so ros contek or wo
	Þe Saxons were redy þeym to slo
	Northumberland was al þeyr home
	Þere þey wonede þennes þey come
	Hit was gyuen þem first to bigge
	Al wast was hit wone to ligge
	But þer dwellynge mended þat contre
	Wel bettere þan hit was wone to be
Of Gurmund ȝede þe word wide	
þat alle londes he wild þorgh ride;	
paien he was, þei herd wele telle,	
þe cristendom forto quelle.	Cristen men to struye &.
Whan þei herd of him speke,	....hym þus.
þei hoped he suld þam wreke;	
with þe Bretons þei mad pes	
to whils messengers þei ches	
& sent to Gurmund ouer þe se,	
& hette to hold of him þer fe,	
withþi he wild com to Bretayn	
& gif it þam & be chefetayn,	

he himself lord & kyng; & be hym....
withþi þe held of him þat thyng
þat leued on his owen lawe,
& bryng þe cristen alle odawe.
"For ȝe er paien & so er we;
o lawe we wild alle on be, ...þat al schuld be
& suilk a kyng wild we haue
þat þe paien lawe mot saue."
Fast him þei souht & þus þei hette,
& Gurmund had redy his flete So þat Gurmound mad redy..
& said he wild auenture his chance,
his paien lay forto auance.
To schippe he went at a tide,
on Norþehumberland gan he ride.
Gurmund acorded with þe Sessons
to voide þe lond of alle Bretons
& gyue þe Sessons in fe ageyn; .gyue hit.....
of þis mad þei forward certeyn,
[84ra] & þat þei suld gyue him treuage,
& þer to suore & gaf hostage.
Ouer alle þan was sorow & drede
whan þe paiens bigan to sprede,
for þei of non had mercy
bot alle died dolefully.

[*L adds:*] Þe Cristen blod er was gentil
Was turned to Payen so vyl

Þe Sessons led þe Aufricanes
& destroied þe cristen wanes;
knyghtes, clerkes, to dede were done
& namly alle religion.
Was non spared of cristens tong,
noure women no childir ȝong. Neyþer....
Bisshopes, abbote, þat relikes had,
whan þei fled, away þam lad,
& many in þe erþe dalf
þat men fynd now on many half.

[*L adds:*] Crosses belles men haue founden
In welles in watres vp haue wounden
Þat tyme were casten so to saue
ffor þey myghte nought alle wyþ hem haue

Corsayntes bones with þam þei bere,
& hid in erþe many ȝit are.
Alle fled þat fle myght,

þat hardiest was alle ofright.	Þe hardiest was ful sore afright
Theon, archbisshop of London,	
to þe wod fled & was not fondon;	
Sir Thadoke, þe archbisshop of ȝork,	
lyued in kerres as dos þe stork;	
þei lyued with herbes of ryuere,	....of þe.
in with bestes at stedes sere.	.wast wyþ....
Non þam toke to kastelle no toure,	
for þei of non wist socoure;	..wyste of no.
halles, chambres, alle þei lete,	
to Wale many fled on fete;	.Walys fele fledde..
& som þat mot hauens hent,	
in schippe to Litille Bretayn went.	
Þe mene folk & þe poraile	
fled to Wales & to Cornwaile.	
Þe kyng fled fro coste to coste,	
he myght not gete togider oste	
þat durst stand Gurmund ageyn.	
Erle, baron, knyght, no sueyn,	
for non wild stand, bot alle fle,	[*Transp. L*]
ne þe kyng durst him not se.	[*Transp. L*]
Seynt Bede telles in his gestis	
how þe Bretons brak godes hestis;	
[84rb] why þat mischefe on þam gon falle,	..meschaunce gan on þem.
in his boke he writes alle.	
Auht he writes, I telle þe þre	Of eighte þat he.....
in stede of auctorite:	..of an.
propir profete & priue hate,	
ȝong men conseile þei toke algate.	
Befor alle, þise þre þei ches,	
mast þorgh þise Britayn þei les.	
Gurmund souht fast & spirde,	
þe kyng to mykelle he desired.	..to haue...
Carice to folow fast him sped,	
& euer Carice bifor him fled;	
to Cirecestre algate he wan,	
& Gurmund & ilk an Aufrikan	..hym folewede þe Aufrican
biseged þe toun a fulle long while,	
& brent it with a quaynte gile.	
He telles first of a mischance	
of Lowis kosyn of ffrance,	.Kyng Lowys...
his was kalled Isambert.	His name...
He did him self foly apert;	

to Gurmund com & with him spak,
his cristendom forsok & brak
to venge him on his eam, Lowis,
þat had him fled out of Paris. ...flemed...
A deuele he was, þe soþe was sene,
þat god forsoke, his eam to tene. Our God to fursake hys...
Gurmund had spied ouer ilk estre .aspied oueral..
how he mot bisege Cirecestre. .best he...
Tentes & pauillons þei sette,
engynes did mak & fette;

[L adds six lines that appear below in P at 14017–23. Variants from L appear after the corresponding lines of P.]

on dayes þei wrouht on þer clos,
on nyghtes woke for þer fos. ..þey woke...
Þof alle þer clos was right gode,
a skille þei sauh & vnderstode
þat at þe last, wild þe ne wild,
þe toun burd þam nedly ȝeld.
Þei wist it wele & noght wend,
þe toun for euer mot þei not fend. ....þey mighte defende
For þat þouht þei wer dismaied, Nought for þan...
for gile alle day þei were affraied;
neuerþeles, þei hald þat þei mot haue, [*Om. L*]
so long þe mot þer lyues saue. [*Om. L*]
[84va] Þe toun he seged alle about ....so straite.
þat þei within myght not out;
þei within ageyn þam kast,
with timbir & stone klosed þam fast; ....þey closed..
engynes on walles þei had inouh,
out of kirnels alblastes þrewe.
Þei withoute of þam assailed, [*Line order coincides here.*]
þe toun was strong for nouht traualed. ....in veyn trauailled
Gurmund sauh it helped nouht,
þe sautes þat he on þam souht,
& long burd him þer lie ..byhoued þem þare to.
or he wan it with maistrie. Er he schold wynne hyt..
A kastelle about þe toun did make,
bretaskes, kirnelles, þer in to wake; Bretaxed & carneled....
Isambert þe ton he toke,
þer estres forto spie & loke;
anoþer he toke his owen barons,
þe þrid he gaf þe Sessons.
Vnto himself he mad a toure,

þerin he lay & held soioure;
þerin he ȝede vp & doun
& spied þe estres of þe toun.
Þei of þe toun wer bold & stoute,
bitymes vmwhile com þei oute
alle armed as men hardy,
& did þe paiens grete vilany.
Bituex þam was many manace ....a chace
& did þer lyues alle in grace; .putte þer lyues ofte..
of þei did þam many chek fful often dide þey many foul.
& of þei were in þe brek; .often were þey...
on boþe sides to wynne pris,
boldly bede ilk oþer þe vis.
[*L adds:*] But þey wyþoute were euere þe mo
Ageyn to toune dide þem go
Boþe half slouh many man, On eyþer half slewe þey manye a.
Bretons, Sessons, & Aufrikan.
Whan þei had driuen þe Bretons in,
þe walles myght þei not wyn; .Walsche men....
þe toun long þer owen held,
þe oste without lay in þe feld
& had destroied alle þe cuntre,
& oþer þer next tuo or þre. ffourty myle about & þre
Bot listens now a selcouth
þat euer felle be norþe or souh. .neuer er fel by norþ ne souþ
[*L adds:*] Ne neuere contreued in elde ne ȝouþe
Ne conseil gyuen of mannes mouþe
[84vb] Þe paiens without laid many lymes, ...leide nettes & lynes
sparowes þei toke alle day bi tymes;
after, nottes þei toke, .þat luytel notes..
holed þam, kirnels out schoke,
did in þe skellis fire & tunder,
bronston, flax, þis was a wunder. Brymston &.....
[*L adds:*] & feste þem by þe sparewes fet
At euen homward fleye þem let
Þe sparowes fleih at euen to rest
tille houses þer þe wont to nest; ...þey were woned..
in eues þei crepte & in þak, ...in þe þakkes
in hay & in korn stak;
þe tundir, bronston, & fire hote,
kindled on lowe & vp smote.
Þe Bretons wist not how it brent,
ne on what maner þe fire was sent;

þei armed þam redy to fight;   ..þeym alle...
our fo þei wer & had no myght.   Ouer fewe......
Þe kyng in to Wales ascaped
& þo þat myght, with him þam raped.
Siþen herd I not telle of whom
widirward Carice bicom.   Whiderward..
Þusgate Cirecestre was taken
þat long held þe paiens waken;
& for it was with sparowes brent,
þo men þat þorgh þe cuntre went
on Inglis kald it sparowes toun,
on Frankis, Cite de Moshon,   & Frensche men Cite de Mischeroun
forto mene þe quantise
how sparowes brent it on what wise.   .hit was wonne &...
Gurmund stroied many cites,   [*L om. eight lines, to 14095.*]
many kastels & cuntres;
many heremytage & abbay
þorgh him wer brent & brouht away,
& many fair toun mad wasten
þat neuer ʒit was bigged ageyn.
In many tokne is sene
þat whilom ware, now is alle grene.
Whan Gurmund þe lond alle wonne,   ..had al ouer riden & ronne
þe Bretons ouere riden & ronne   & Bretayne til his hand al wonne
þat non so hardy durst him abide   .no Breton...
ne ageyn him in bataile ride,
to þe Sessons he gaf þe lond
þat in Norþehumbirland first fond.   .he in...
[85ra] If Gurmund did so, he did right;   And ʒyt dide Gurmound....
he sikerd þam before & hight,
& þo þat ʒerned Hengist þing,
þorgh Gurmund had þer ʒernyng.
Þorgh Gurmund had þei þe lond of Kent   ffor he gaf þeym....
þat fro Hengist blode was went.   .longe wyþ Hengistes...
A lynage out of þe ildes did alie   ..of þe out ildes he..
þat longed vnto Saxonie;
men þei wer of grete honoure
& douhty forto stond in stoure.
Anglis cald þei þat kynde
to know where men mot it fynde.
Gurmund þe lond to þam it gaf,
þe toþer Sessons he þam ouer haf
& mad þam souereyns to be,   ..Anglische soueryns for..

& þei suld hold of him in fe. — ffor to holde hit....
In Northfolk was first þer wonyng,
Estangle it hight for þer comyng.
Anglis þat cuntre first þei aught
& of Anglis Estangle it lauht.
I fond in maistre Wace boke,
of Pers of Langtoft also I toke,
& of Gildas þer to I laid
right as Pers þerof said.

[L adds:] Of alle þre bryng y to place
Gyldas Peres & Maister Wace

Þe Sessons acorded for no þing
þat þe Anglis suld be þer kyng;
þe had wele leuer þei said — Þey.wel leuere þe Saxons.
þe lond were in parties laid,
þan þe Anglis of þe out ildes
suld be chefe of þer gildes. — ....alle þer gyldes
Gurmund sauh þei acorded nouht;
he parted þe lond als him þouht. — ......best þought
In Kent, a kyng ordeynd he,
Canterbirie was þe chefe cite;
Southsex was þe toþer estre
& þe chefe toun Cirecestre; — ....was Chichestre

[L transp. two couplets:]
Midelsex þe thrd fonden, — Westsex þe þrydde of renoun
þe chefe toun þan was London; — & Wyltone was þer chef toun
Westsex þe ferthe of ronoun, — Middelsex þe ferþe founden
Wilton was þe chefe toun; — Þe chef toun þanne was Lounden
Estangle þe fifte kyngriche,
þe chefe cite was Northwiche;
[85rb] Southfolk longed als þertille,
of Estangle it is þorgh skille;
þe sext was Merce, now is Lyndesey,
þe hede toun to Lincoln ley;
þe seuente reame of rent & fe, — ..roialme....
fro Humber alle þe north cuntre
vnto Scotland as it lis,
& ȝork þe chefe toun of pris.
In Gildas boke þus I fond
þat Gurmund departed þe lond; — ..parted Ingelond
siþen vppon France he ran
to wyn it, for Arthur it wan.
Now haf Anglis þe seignorie

þat er kynde of Germenie,
þat Sessons als now ere on, Þe Saxons als þat now..
spred in þis remes ilkon.
Ilk a kyng diuersed his lawe, ...desired..
of alle mot no man say no sawe;
so fele þei wer now & now,
what þei wrouht couth non say how.
Bot þat Saynt Bede of þam sais,
els suld non haf knowen what wais,
no story forto haf writen;
bot þat Saynt Bede dos vs witen
whilk wer gode & whilk els, ...were elles
& of bisshopes als he tels
þat ȝe in his boke rede,
to telle it here, it is no nede;
& it were a diuers þing Hit were a degyse.
bot whan þe lond was tille a kyng.
Long after þis, writen I fond,
how a Breton chalanged þis lond.
Engle, þe story sais he hight,
he brouht a champion to fight.
Skardyng hight þis champion
þat com with Engle þe Breton.
On alle þe lond he set chalange,
his ancessours wild he venge
& tak vengeaunce of þe Englis
þat chaced þe Bretons out of þis.
Alle þe Englis Engle dred .Anglys þys Engle.
for þe gret powere he led.
[85va] Engle sent vnto þe barons,
& alle þe kynges he mad somons,
to hold of him alle þer right
or he suld wyn it of þam þorgh fight,
oiþer þorgh bataile playn in felde,
or with champion staf & schelde.
Þis Scardyng was ferly strong,
als a geant grete & long,
þat non for drede durst auenture on him, ...auntre..
so was he strong, mykille, & grym.
For drede of Engle & Skardyng,
þei mad Engle chefe kyng;
for þis Engle þe lond þus wan,
England cald it ilk a man.

Whan Engle had þe lond þorgh,
he gaf Skardyng Skarburgh
toward þe north bi þe se side,
a hauen it is, schippes in to ride.
fflayn was his broþer, so sais a tale
þat Thomas mad of Kendale.

[*L adds:*] Of Scarthe & fflayn Thomas seys
What þey were how þey dide what weys

Maistre Edmunde sais, as me mones,
þat Engle had nien sonnes; ..hadde Nynetene sones
þis niented sons after þer fader deuys, .Nynetene.....
departed þis lond in nienten partys;
of þo parties, fond I non writen,
bot a partie þat I kan witen.
Þe nientend partie was þat þing .Nynetenþe....
þat longed to Saynt Edmund þe kyng.
Þis is þat oþer skille I fond
whi it is cald Inglond.

[*L adds:*] Als Maister Edmond þer of seys
& as he seys y seye þat weys

Bot of Inge sauh I neuer nouht
in boke writen ne wrouht;
bot lewed men þer of crie .....speke & crye
& maynten þat ilk lie. ..al wey vp þat.
Maystre Wace telles his skille,
þe Englis wer not of o wille
a kyng ouer þam to sette,
ne be to him als sugette, .for to be til on.
bot þorgh conseile of þam alle
deuysed þe reames as best wild falle.
Whan ilkon had his porcion,
held him kyng & bare croune,
[85vb] he acordes with Gildas;
as Gurmund gaf it, so it was.
Many a werre bituex þam ros,
& fele tymes frendes & fos, .often were þey...
þe strangest on þe wakest ran ....febleste.
& ilk on oþer werre bigan.
Long lasted alle þat care
þat o kyng croune ne bare; ...þe chef coroune non.
no kirke halowed, no messe songen,
no childe cristned, no belle rongen,
fyuescore ȝere, & som say more, ...seuene.

þat non leued on cristen lore.
In alle þo fyuescore ȝere
was no story writen of here.

[*L adds:*] ffor hit was al Payenie
Þe certein couþe non descrie
Ilk on oþer werre sought
& ilk in seruage oþer brought
And ilk of oþer tok men in hold
& ilk of oþeres men þey sold

In alle þis werre & þis wo,
merchanȝ com ay to & fro
& bouht þe childre of þis lond,
in stedes to sẹlle, þei þam fond. — ....þer þey hem.
Þo þat were taken in ostage,
þei sold þam schipmen þat mad passage.
So faire a kynd in alle þe werld
ne non so trewe þat men of herd,
als þe Englis þei after spired, — .were þe Englys þat men of.
ne of no kyng men so desired. — ...kynde...

[*L adds:*] And marchaunȝ come mo childre to bye
Rather þan oþer marchaundie
& solde hem in londes dere
ffor þey were so white & clere

We Englis auh more luf god & drede — Wel more oughte Englys loue...
þan any nacoun of any lede,
for a grace god has þam gyuen,
forbi alle kyndes þat lyuen,
als faire ere comon pedale — ..are þe comune.
as þe lordes & of þe entale.
Gif Englis euen kepyng, — .Englische man..
mete & drenk & oþer þing,
es no man fairer of colour — ...of so fair.
ne so clene, of suete sauour. — ..cler ne of so..
To Rome men led þam to selle.
Saynt Bede, so herd I telle,
to Rome, he sais, merchanȝ þam led
& seld þam þer & forth fed;
as þei to selle were oft sette,
on þam to se, þe folk wele lette.
Many burgeis of þat cite
com þe childre forto se; — ..faire childre to se
[86ra] amang alle þo þat þider nam,
a tyme Saynt Gregore with þam cam.

Whan he sawe þat semly sight,
wheþen þei wer he wald wite,
for he said he sawe neuer are
so faire ch[ildr]e of hide no haire. [*Bookworms at work here.*]
..childre of huyde ne her
“Of what lond,” he said, “þis childer be?”
Þei said, “Of Bretayn, a cuntre.” Men....fer contre
He said, “Faire folk is þer in.
Þer faces to se, it is grete wyn.
Whedir be þei cristend or non?” .ar þei Cristen he seide..
“Þei er,” þei said, “paiens ilkon.”
“Allas,” he said, “so faire mankynde
þat þe fende in pyne salle bynde!
[*L adds:*] So fare persones so bright of ble
Þat in merknesse euere schul be
How,” he said, “þis kynd men calle?” Þeyr kynde he asked how men þem.
“Anglis,” þei said, “hate þei alle.”
“Angle,” he said, “a name of grace,
for angels er þei like of face,
& suilk to be heires of heuen. & wel oughte swylk be...
Þer name is Angle, angelle to neuen.
Of Bretayn þei er, ȝe tolde beforn,
what hate þe cuntre þei wer in born?”
Þei said, “In þe North of þe schire,
þe cuntre men calles it Deire.”
“Deyire,” he said, “wele say ȝe.
Fro godes ire þei salle fle .....falle &.
& be called to his mercie,
with angels in blis to wonne him bie.
What hate þe kyng, can ȝe me telle?” ..þer.....
“ȝa, sir,” þei said, “he hate Elle.” ....þeir kyng hight.
Saynt Gregore at þat name louh.
He said, “Þat name is wele inouh!
Fulle wele,” he said, “certes ȝa.
It betoknes Alleluya,
Alleluya, a song of honoure
to wirschip criste our saueoure.”
Saynt Gregore to pape ȝede ...þe Pope.
& bisouht him for our nede .prayede...grete.
þat he mot to Bretayn wende,
þer cristendom bi him sende. & Cristendom by hym þem.
He said his wille were wele þerto
if þat þe pape wild so.

[86rb] Bot þe courte wild not consent
þat Saynt Gregore so fer went,
for he was in lite next forto be ...ablest next Pope to.
after him þat held þan þe se.
Whan he was pape, forgat he nouht;
on our nede fulle wele he þouht.
He sent hider Saynt Austyne,
at þe ilde of Teneth he com ine,
þat is þe est side of Kent.
In Teneth lond Saynt Austyn hent
& in þe tyme of his comyng,
of Kent, Ethelbert was kyng, ..Ethelbright..
& þe kyngdom of Ethelbright
tille Humber was he chefe in right.
Ethelbert as we fynd
was of Hengestis kynd.
Gurmund þam seised in þat kyngdam,
þe kynd þat of Hengist cam.
Þis word of Saynt Bede I toke,
þe fifte capitle of þe boke; .fifte chapitre of þe secounde.
þorgh þat capitle, I wist, ..chapitre al y.
bituex Ethelbright & Hengist:
Hengist sonne, Oysk was his name,
kyng of Kent, noble of fame;
for fame of Oysk, of Kent kynges,
long wer kald Oyssynges.
Þis Oysk was noble & so ferlike,
his sonne men cald Oyrike.
Octa com of Oyrike,
& Octa sonne hight Irminerik,
Irminerik sonne hight Ethelbright;
þus sais Saynt Bede þe kynd ȝede right.
Of Ethelbright haf I told þe kynne,
now turne ageyn to Saynt Austyne.
Þe lengthe of þis ilde, Teneth, ...þe Ilde of Tenet
sex myle is it mette ..þen ys þe met
& þre myle is þe brede;
bi tuo waies þat men it lede,
& of þis ilde, boþe þe endes
alle about þe se wendes.
Into þis ilde Saynt Austyn cam,
fourti felawes with him nam,
[86va] of Frankis & religions, .Cristene & of.

to mak þe kyng somons   ..Ethelbert.
þat he suld to Rome wend,
to know þe life withouten end
þat Ihesu criste, lord of myght,
in þe Virgyn Mary lyght,
& is & euermore salle be
sothfast god in trinite.
Whan he wist suilk men were comen   .þe kyng wiste....
& in þe ilde had hauen nomen,
þat did ne said to no man ille,
he bad þei suld leue stille
& be serued þat þam was nede
of mete & drynk withouten drede,
tille himself com þam to
to wite at þam what þei wild do.
Þe kyng had herd say biforn
þat Ihesu was of Marie born,
& had tauht a new lawe;
oft þerof he herd in sawe,
& his wife was cristen,
in France born of Frankis men.
In suilk forwarde scho him toke
þat scho hir lawe not forsoke.
Þat lady name was Dam Berke,
& with hir com a clerke,   Wyþ hure cam ouer a noble.
a bisshop hight Sir Leothard,
to hold his wife þat forward;
þe kyng suld not fordo hir faith,
noiþer for leue ne for laith.   ..loþ lef ne leythe
Þe kyng a day tille Austyn sette
to com to þe ilde of Tenet;
þe kyng durst com no courte tille, ...couert.
bot stode & bode vnder a hille;
for wychecrafte he had doute,
of courte, þerfor, he held him oute;   Þer fore of Couert....

[*L adds:*] In Toune ne hous ne com he nought
ffor drede of gyle þat mighte be wrought
Þat his poer mighte hym be raft
Þorow word or werk of wychecraft

þus he hoped & wele wend,
after him þerfor he did send.
Whan his bodword tille Austyn cam,   ..message...
his felawes alle with him he nam

& befor þam bare a croyce — .byforn hem dide...
of siluer, & alle with a voyce
[86vb] sang þei þe letanie,
he & alle his companie, — Austyn....
þat Ihesu criste suld þam here
for whom þei mad þer praiere.
Whan he com befor þe kyng,
Saynt Austyn mad a [pre]chyng — [*Worm damage in P.*]
....prechyng
& said Saynt Gregore tille him sent — ......he sent
for him & his amendment,
& somond him forto come
to cristes lawe, þe lawe of Rome.
He teld him þe incarnacion — ..hym of..
& siþen of his passion;
þat Ihesu þoled wondes fyue
& died & ros fro dede to lyue;
& steih tille heuen god & man,
tille our kynde þe blis he wan;
& how he is fulle of mercie,
& tille ilk a man redie — ....synful man.
þat in gode hope him wille calle,
tille his blis he bringis alle. — ....brynge vs.
Whan þis prechyng was alle done,
tille him said þe kyng sone,
"Faire er þi wordes & suete
& þe hotes þou dos vs hete, — .þy byhestes þow vs byhete
& þi god is mylde of mode;
as þou said I vnderstode.
Bot for ȝe er ȝit so newe
& non of vs ȝow neuer knewe,
þerfor ȝit I ne may
leue our forfadres lay — Leten...
þat we long on haf leued,
& tille our godes þer in cheued,
& ȝours ȝit er not iknowe,
þerfor we salle bide a throwe;
& ȝe er of so fer cuntre
& als pilgrimes seme ȝe,
vs þis new lawe to preche;
& if it be sothe þat ȝe teche
& among vs wille lende,

I salle not be ȝow vnhende.
Takes ȝour wonyng whore ȝe wille
& þat ȝow falles to haf in skille,
[87ra] & alle þo þat ȝe may wynne
tille þat lawe þat ȝe begynne,
I grant ȝow my wille fre
if it be certeyn þat I may se."
Þe kyng þam granted at þer comyng
& þe cite to mak þer biggyng;
Doroberma þat cite hight,
now Canterbirie is þe name right. Þat Caunterbury now cald ys.
He did þam haf suilk purueiance
þat felle vnto þer sustenance; .neded for þer.
to preche þe folk he warned nouht
bot do as þam gode þouht.
To þe cite þei com singand,
þe croice befor, men bare in hand;
a table þei brouht þam bituex,
þeron purtreite a crucifix;
& þe letanie þei sunge
with o voice & o tunge.
Þerwith þei a faire anteme .þey seide...
Ihesu criste for to queme:
"Deprecamur te Domine in omni misericordia tua
vt auferatur furor tuus & ira tua
a ciuitate ista & de domo tua
sancta quia peccauimus Alleluya."
(Of mercie, Lord, we pray þe,
do þi wreth fro þis cite,
& fro þi holy house alsua,
for we haf synned, Alleluya.) .our synnes we synge.
[*L adds:*] Alleluya ys forto seye
Make me saf God er y deye
[I]n þat tyme þat I now rede, [*Capital om. in P.*]
þe date was, as sais Saynt Bede,
fyue hundreth ȝere & fourscore
& foure ȝeres mo before.
In þis date was an emperour,
Maurice he hight, þat bare þe flour.
[*L adds:*] Þre & fifti ȝer Emperour had he ben
Syn Augustus was Emperour sen
Þys Maurice þat y of telle her

He Rengned on and twenti ȝer
I telle ȝow now of hym story
ffor in his tyme was seint Gregori

In þetende ȝere as regned he,
Saynt Gregore tok his dignite
& was pape þrittene ȝere, ...þrytty.
sex monethes & ten daies sere;
in þis tyme com Saynt Austyn.
Befor had Sessons wonned herein
a hundreth & fyfti ȝere,
& were heiþen ilkon pleynere ..heþene al plener
[87rb] sen Vortiger tyme, þat Hengist cam,
tille Saynt Austyn brouht cristendam.
Seynt Austyn had þer wonnyng
long ar he cristend þe kyng, Good while er....
& ȝede to preche ouer alle aboute.
To his prechyng many gan loute;
þei sauh his life faire & clene ....honeste..
& euer mylde withouten tene;
many myracle þei saw him wirk.
Bot þat tyme was þer no kirk,
bot a chapelle without þe toun
sen tyme of þe Bretoun,

[*L adds:*] Syn þe Romains hadde þys lond
Was þe Chapel þat þey þer fond

þat chapelle was of Saynt Mertyne.
Oft þe folk with Saynt Austyne
went þider, þe faith to lere, .þyder wiþ hym....
matyns & messe forto here.
Tille þe kyng wele vnderstode
þat his lawe was certeyn & gode,
he did him cristen & alle hise
& was gode siþen tille godes seruise.
A kirke he ordeynd in þat cite
in þe name of þe trinite;
right as Saynt Austyn wild,
alle his wille þe kyng fulfilled.

[*L adds:*] Þe kynedam of sire Ethelbright
Vntil Humber was his right

At London anoþer kyng gan wonne,
Ethelbrightis sister sonne,
Saberk was his name;
Dam Ricula hight his Dame.

Of þis halfe Temse was his empire,
of Estsex he was alle sire;
bot alle þe kyngdom þat Saberk helde
acheued vnto Ethelbright schelde.
Þre men of religioun .holy men..
with Saynt Austyn had renoun: ...had gret.
[*L adds:*] & for godnesse wel ys to wyten
Þer names of þo þat ar writen
Sir Mellite hight þe ton,
Sir Iuste was lufed of manyon,
Sir Laurence hight þe þrid;
alle were bisshopes als bitid.
Mellite was bisshop London ..bischop of.
þat was þe se of Breton;
þe est Sessons within a lite
wer cristened þorgh Mellite;
[87va] sai Ethelbright did him wirke Sire....
Saynt Paule mynstire to be his kirke.
Sir Iuste was bisshop in þat estre
þat we Inglis calle Rouchestre; .we on...
before it had name selly ..hadde a..
in Bretons, Dorciberny;
bot þe Englis whan þei cam, ...þey first came
Roffa, þei cald it after a name,
& siþen for Rof, Rofcestre teld;
Sir Iuste þat bisshopriche held.
Ethelbright þorgh grace him grewe,
wrouht him a kirke of Saynt Andrewe.
Laurence was bisshop after Austyn;
he did him doun & Laurence in.
Saynt Austyn to preche ȝede,
in Ihesu werke to wele spede,
clerkes ordeynd, kirkes did make
þat þe paiens did doun schake.
Whan he had alle þat coste
brouht to cristendom almoste,
toward Roucestre he tok his way,
godes word forto say.
Beside Rouchestre in þe lond
southest, a folk he fond .þethen a...
þat to godes word gaf no tente,
ne no grace in þam hente,
bot þer he stode þam to preche,

þer saluacoun forto reche. & þer sauacion.teche
Behynd on his cloþes þei heng Byhynd hym.....
righ tailes on a streng.
Whan þei had don þat vilenie,
þei drofe him þien with maistrie;
fer way þei gan him chace,
tailes þei kast in his face.
Þis holy man god bisouht
for þei him þat vilanie wrouht,
þat on þam & alle þer kynde,
tailed alle men suld þam fynde;
& god granted alle þat he had, ...bad
alle þat kynde tailes had.

[*L adds:*] Tailles hadde & tailles haue
ffro þat vengaunce non may þem saue

For þei with tailes þat gode man schamed,
for tailes þe Englis kynd is blamed;
[87vb] in many sere lond is said,
of þo tailes we haf vpbraid. .....vmbreyde
Whan þis gode man was ascaped,
þat schame to haf þat kynd is schaped,
tille a valeie he fled þo files.
Fro Rouchestre is fyue miles ..hit ys manie.
bituex tuo valeys to þe northwest.
At a hille he gan rest,
werie he was for fer gon,
so were his felawes ilkon
& þe grete hete þam greued.
Als þe folk þat misleued & þe..misbileued
had don him so foule despite,
boþe he þouht & said fulle tite
þat he wild mak him alle ȝare
fro þat wikked folk to fare.
Bot Ihesu criste wild it nouht;
he spak tille him for he so þouht,
"Leue alle þi þouht ilk a dele Let al þat....
& traiste on my help wele;
þou ert my seruant & pa[i]es me. [*Worm damage in P.*]
Þi dedes, þi þouht, wele I se. .þought & dede wel y hit.
Of my grace to þe I grante;
þat þou dos, I hold couenante."

[*L adds:*] Heuen ys open to þe redy
And for wham þou askest merci

Whan Saynt Austyn had sene & herd
god of heuen þat him ansuerd,
he þanken him of his grace, .þanked...swete grace
& kneled doun in þat place
& kiste þe erþe fele siþe;
he grette for ioy, so was he bliþe.
Whan he had long praied & grette,
doun in þe erthe his staf he sette;
þer where he saw þat sight, .right as he sey..
he fitched his staf doun right, .pighte..þer doun vpright
& þer of þe erþe water sprong
þat is now a riuere long
þer neuer befor was non sene.
No men wonand þer had bene,
for no man mot lyue no duelle
withouten riuere or water of welle;
& for þer was non beforn,
was þe cuntre waste & lorn.
[88ra] Saynt Austine gladded his felawes
of godes sight & his sawes,
& for he had sene þere
þe sight þat he sawe neuer are,
Chernel ha cald þat ilk stede, .he....
for he sawe god & herd his bede.
(Cerno is on Inglis, "I se";
El is Ebrow, "god salle it be."

[*L adds:*] Do to gyder Cerno & El
Þat ys called Cernoel

Cernel, þis word may be trod, [*L om. four lines, to 14617.*]
"I sawe," or "I se god.")
Saynt Austine did it write
þat he sawe god, wele is to wite.
Whan þe Englis & Sessons, .Englische men..
first kynges & þe barons, .þe kynge þen..
had resceyued þe bapteme
& childre als cristned in creme,
mykelle ioy Saynt Austine mad
& þanked with herte glad. .þanked god...
Toward Wales, Bretons he fond
ageyn þe Englis defended þer lond
ageyn alle þe Englis powere.
Monkes, chanons, & seculere, Monke Abbote..
þorgh Gurmund þe Englis had it wonne,

& ouer þe Bretons riden & ronne,
& into Wales did þam chace,
þer þei wonned, biggand a place.
Þo religious whilom wer here,
þore wonned in stedes sere; Þen woned þey þor...
of þo ilk religious
fond Saynt Austine many a hous,
monkes, abbotes, without vitaile,
þat lyued on þer trauaile.
Seuen bisshopes fond he þere
þat in Wales wonnand were;
an archbisshop of more degre,
at Kerlion was þan þe se;
at Bangore als was an abbaie
of blak monkes, bot non graie;
tuo þousand þer was þare lote, ...lot
þer abbot hight sir Dynoth. ....Dynot
Þise monkes at þer auys .two þousand at here deuis
were departed in seuen partis;
[88rb] þre hundreth were in a couent, ...euere in o.
vnto labore set & sent;
bot on to lyue had þei nouht
bot þer trauaile þat þei wrouht. .by þer....
Saynt Austine for þer bisshop sent,
to wite his wille, to him þei went.
He said he was of Rome legate
& of Englond primate.
"Þerfor ȝe auh þorgh reson ..oughte..
of me resceyue þe benyson
& be bowand vnto me."
Alle þei said, "Þat suld not be;
oure primate of Kerlion is.
He is our hede & salle vs blis.
He is confermed of þe courte of Rome,
we stand at non oþer dome; .nyl stande....
& for Englis men sake
ageyn vs auh to take, .þe oughte we..

[*L adds:*] Þaw a party reson hit wolde
Ageyn þe Englische we oughte holde

for þai cached vs out of our fees ..us chased....
& wonne with wrong in our cuntrees;
& we Bretons er cristen men
& þei er of þe lawe paien

& now conuerted late are;
our vilanie for sothe it ware ..certes..
forto be to þam sugette,
& leue him þat has vs gette.
Þo we hold oure enmys ...for oure.
þat has þam brouht to suilk pris.
We wille noiþer of þam no þe
comon with alle, no blissed be."
Saynt Austine said no more;
þer wikked wille him forþouht sore. .yuel wil þem ouer þoughte.
Tille Ethelbright he turned ageyn
& teld how þei had desdeyn .telde hym....
to bouwe on to þe Englis blode ..ought....
or tille any þat wild þam gode.
Þe kyng wrathed þer withalle
& said tille Austine, "Fond I salle
þat our kynd þat now ere heires
salle do þam bouwe, maugre þeirs!"
He sent his sonde also quik
vnto þe north to Kyng Ekfrith, ...Ekfrik
[88va] & bad him com with alle hise
þat tille him did any seruise,
& teld how þei of Kerlion
& of Bangore, without reson,
has despised alle þer kynne

[*L adds:*] ffor þem forsaken seint Austyn
Ne til hym nold bowe on none wyse
But al for vs gan hym despise
He sente aboute for alle þer kynde

of Englis þat þei mot fynde.
At Leicestre mad þei samnyng ....somonynge
of souht & north, ilk a kyng; .southe.....
terme þe set to mak þam ȝare
forth into Wales to fare.
Brochiuayl with Bretons helde,
of Laicestre he bare þe schelde.
He had don þe Bretons somoun
þorgh þe cuntre fro toun to toun
ageyn þe Englis for to go,
bot þe Bretons were to fo. ....al to fo
Brochiuayl was disconfite;
tille a wod he fled fulle tite
& his men wer slayn alle doun,

Kyng Elfrik wan þe toun.
Monk & hermyte, ilk a taile,
þat had þer hope on Brochiuayle,
alle wer þei don to suerde,
lewed & lered mad ferde. ...al so ferd
Þo monkes þat were at Bangore ....of.
bisouht þe kyng with hert sore
þat he wald haf of þam mercie,
& of þe kirke saue þe clergie.
Þei praied alle, boþe monk & clerke,
chanon, heremite, man of werke,
riche & pouer, alle bare fote;
for þer praier fond þei no bote.
Þe Englis on þam wer fulle feloun,
þe ouerhand had, felle als leon;

[*L adds:*] Monk ne clerk wolde þey non spare
ffor þe byforn vnbuxom ware

on preste & clerk mad þei no kepe
þan þe woulf dos of þe schepe.
Ouer mykelle was þer ire
of so fele to mak martire,
tuo þousand & tuo hundreth mo,
so mony of þam did þei slo. .manie.....
Siþen said þei þat alle wild wend,
Bangore destroie & bring tille end; .to struye....
[88vb] bot ȝit ȝei said þei wild abide
to purueie þam whan þei suld ride.
To Canterbiri com Saynt Austine,
þer he died & mad his fine.
He died are Saynt Gregorie,
a ȝere before, sais þe storie;
þe date of criste to telle fro,
sex hundreth ȝere & four mo, ...fyue.
in his lyue was ordenance; ...was his.
in his sted, Bisshop Laurance.

[*L adds:*] When seint Gregore passed his lyue
Þe date was sex hundred ȝer & fyue

Whan Ethelbright had regned here
in Kent, sex & fifti ȝere,
he was biried sollemly
& Dam Berk is laid him by;

[*L adds:*] Twelf ȝer after seint Austyn
Lyued Ethelbright er he made hys fyn

þe date of criste þus fele to neuen — ....mene
sex hundreth & sextene. — ...euen fiftene
Ethelbright sonne hight Edbald;
right faith wild he not hald.
His wikkidnes is to mene,
to Iuste & Mellite did he tene,
he & Segbert sons þre,
& to ffrance did þam fle.
Edbald þorgh a vision
knew þat he had misdon, — He knew wel he had.
& þorgh þe Bisshop Laurance,
he had on criste gode affiance.
Þre of Segebert sonnes were slayn,
þe bisshopes com to lond agayn.
Bretons of Wales herd how
þat þe Englis þer monkes slow;
þei gadred þam to conseil
for to venge þat tirpeil.
Þre noble men wer in þe cite,
þo þre mad a grete semble;
þo þre wer alle kynges
& of þe Bretons lordynges.
Bledrik of Cornwaile was sire
& lord of alle Deuenschire;

[*L adds:*] Als þe water of Ex rennes
ffro þe hed þer men hit kennes
Vnto þe se þer hit gos yn
Longe helden hit þe Bretons kyn
Euere til Adelston cam
He dide þat kynde mykel scham

of North Wales, Kadwan was kyng,
of south Wales, Margadu was lordyng;
alle was þeirs vnto Seuerne
biside þe hille of Maluerne.
[89ra] Bot Athelston þorgh force & eie
drofe þam biȝond þe water a weie. — He drof byȝonde þe water of Weye
Bledrik, Margadu, & Kadwan
gadred oste of many a man;
Englis, Sessons, þei assailed,
& þe Englis þam sore trauailed.
Elfrik was wonded, þat he dred, — ...þe deþ he.
in feld he gaf bak & fled;
fele of his were þer slayn,

& he escaped with grete payn.
Sir Bledrik of Cornwaile
was slayn in þat bataile;
no wonder þof him ille bitide, ..þey hym yuel.
he had no merci þat merci cride;
of þe monkes I told beforn,
withouten mercie wer þei lorn.
Sir Kadwan & Margadu
gadred ostes & boste blew;
to Leicestre boþe þei went
& held þer a parlement;
þorgh comon conseile of olde & ȝing,
þei ches Kadwan þer kyng. [*Brown ink has been spilled in P; the text is conjectural for seven lines.*]

Þan bolded fast þe Bretons,
& Kadwan sent his somons ...aboute somons
to þe Englis kynges in alle cuntres
on þis half Humber þat held þer fees;
bot þei wild to him cheue,
on oþer halue he suld þam greue.
Þei sauh it was non oþer bote,
þei com & felle Kadwan tille fote;
þat is to say, mad him feaute,
& he þer aller chefe to be. ...alder chef schuld.
(I hope alle com þam þat wo
for þe monkes þei did slo.)
Kadwan said he wild passe Humber,
Elfrik for to bring to komber; .to struye & to comber
Northumbirland he wild destroie
& alle þer kyng for him noie; ...kynde for þem schold noye
oiþer in bataile he suld him slo
or do him fle þe reame fro.
Elfrik herd his manace,
how to wo he wild him chace.
[89rb] He gadred togidir his barons .assembled..
þat Englis wer & Sessons,
grete ostes wer on ilk side.
Wise men þer were did þam abide
& ilkon said his auis
þat frendes had on boþe partis:
"If þis kynges togidir smyte,
þe sorow to fele wille not be lite;

[*L adds:*] Non of vs schal neuere more
Þe grete los ageyn restore

þerfor I rede we fond to abate
þis kynges wrath þat now is hate." ..wrathes þer ire &.
So þei did als þei red,
fro on tille oþer so wele þei sped
þat þei boþe granted þe pes;
to mak it siker, ostage þei ches.
Alle þer rightes forto saue, ..Richesse..
þei set þe lond wilk it suld haue: ....what ilk...
fro Humber north, Elfrik suld be,
Kadwan fro þien þe south cuntre. ..þeþen al...
Þus was departed ilk a schelde
& þe pes fulle wele helde,
for neuer was luf of lordynges
so mykelle as bituex þo kynges. ..as was...

[*L adds:*] Þat þet on hadde þey hadde hit bothe
Noþyng mighte make þem loþe

Wifes þei toke boþe at a terme, ...þer loues to ferme
tuo sonnes þei had þer luf to ferme. ..had þey at o terme
Elfrik sonne hight Eadwin,
Kadwan sonne hight Kadwalyn;
in o ȝere were þei born.
For þe pes suld not be lorn,
did þei þer sonnes togider ȝeme
þat þe ton þe toþer suld queme;
in on þei wer clad & fed,
of o maistre lered & led.
Armes to bere, wapen to welde, [*Transp. L*]
whan þei were waxen of elde [*Transp. L*]
& þamself with witte kouþe lede,
scheld to bere & ride on stede;
into Bretayn did þam send
faithly þer luf to amend, ffor whi þer loue schulde more.
for þer was Kadwan kynde,
conquest of Maximian we finde;
þer were þei knyghted boþe togidere
& duelled þer tille þei com hidere.
[89va] Whan tyme was þer fadres suld deie,
be messengers þei herd saie;
ouer þe se þei had passage
& resceyued þer heritage.

Frendes þei were þe first tuo ȝere
als þer fadres lufed here,
& held þer londes als þei lay ......or lay
departed bi þer fadres day:
Edwin fro Humber Northwarde,
þe south was Kadwalyns parte.
Bot Kadwalyn had mo cites ...mo & betere.
& larger londes of rent & fees
þan Edwin had be mykelle þing;
þe south, þerfor, was chefe kyng
& croune bare ouer ilkon, ...ouer þem.
& alle þat oþer suld bere non.
At Kadwalyns corounment
alle kynges tille his feste went.
Sir Edwyn him þare biþouht,
Kadwalyn of a bone bisouht
& praied him þat he mot be,
with leue, crouned in his cuntre;
þis bisouht þe Kyng Edwyn
to haf leue of Kadwalyn.
Conseile, said Kadwalyn, he suld take;
as conseile gaf, so suld men make.
"Bot I salle wite what is to don,
& þou salle haf an ansuere son." .....answere right.
Afterward, no while was, .no þrowe ne.
þei mette at þe water of Duglas
to conseile þer and to wite
how þat þing best mot site.
Bituex þam was þe water, I wene,
& messengers ȝede ay bituene.
Many skilles forth were kast
how it mot be mad stedfast;
as Kadwalyn of his hors light, ...doun lyght
a heuynes & grete vnmyght
on Kadwalyn gan it lepe,
þat nedely behoued him slepe. .nede most he þer right.
Brian kept him as he lay,
his kosyn, & had grete affray ..þat was in..
[89vb] of þat þat Edwyn had bisouht
þat neuer ore bifore was wrouht;
& now wille grante suilk a foly
to low his state þat ore was hie;
& as he his lord kepte,

ouer his hede sore he wepte,
þat with þo teres þat he lete,
mad he his lord hede wete. ..þe kynges hed al.
For sorow & sobbyng Brian quoke
þat his lord þerwith woke
& biheld Brian fast; & he...
þe kyng had wonder & was ogast.
"Brian," he said, "what tiþing now?
What eiles þe, whi gretes þou?"
"No wonder," said Brian, "þof I grete.
Ʒe ere in wille ȝour wirschip lete. ......to lete
In no kyng tyme here beforn
was þe kroune so mykelle lorn
als it is now in poynt to be.
How it salle turne, wele I se.
Of our ancessours, ilk a Bretoun,
of alle holy had þei þe croune; Byfore alle oþere bere...
& now I hope it salle not so, ...drede hit schal nought.
þat are was, now salle be tuo. .or was on....
Þe hole croune þat are had on,
if it be tuo, I telle it gon.
Þise Englis salle haf so grete pride
þat wo salle wax on ilk a side;
for þer kynde rises on heght,
þat non of ours dar with þam feght.
Sen Malgo tyme was no kyng
þat mot of þam wynne any thyng,
& now is Edwyne so wele with þe,
croune to bere þer non suld be;
& I se ȝe þink nouht
what þei tille our kynd haf wrouht.
Slouh þe Kyng Aurelius Þey slowe...
& so þei thynk þat þei salle vs,
& certeynly wele þei may;
Bretons powere gos fast away.
Sen Arthure died here beforn,
þe scheld of Bretayn has bien lorn."
[90ra] Þe kyng listend what Brian said;
in his herte fulle wele it laid.
"For þyng þat þou has greten sore,
so ne salle it tide no more; .schal hit tyde neuer.
þat hole was, hole salle bileue,
þe right croune salle I not reue." . hole coroune non schal me .

Tille Edwyn he sent bode hastife
þat as he wille in luf haf life, — . als he wolde his loue & .
he suld no more þerof speke;
þe croune wild neuer breke. — . . wolde he . .

[*L adds:*] Ne his conseil wolde nought consent
To suffre non oþer corounement
Hit were neyþer reson ne lawe
Þat on was by elde dawe
& now schulde be gyuen to two
So for hym schuld hit neuere go

"It salle be hole þat now es,
for me salle it neuer be les;
no here no lenger wille I lend,
in to Wales wille I wend."
Edwyn was felle & proude,
tille his message he said o loude, — . . messager . . . .
"Salle I neuer him eft biseke
ne þerfor beuwe ne be meke. — . . bowe . . .
Suilk frenschip I salle haf here, — . ffraunchise . . . .
& als he has, þe same manere."
Kadwalyn said bot he left, — . . but ȝyf . .
with force it suld be him reft.
On þis manere parted þei boþe,
neuer frende bot euer wroþe.
Edwyn þeron was fulle brym;
to Ȝork he ȝede & crouned him.
Als Kadwalyn was in Wales,
tille him of þis teld men tales — Of þys was teld hym many .
þat Edwyn for his despite
did croune him so tite. — . hym Croune al . .
Whan Kadwalyn herd it say,
to Humber with oste he toke þe way
& on Edwyn gan to renne,
men to slo, tounes to brenne.
Edwyn he þouht disherite
& if he myght, his hede of smyte.
Bot Edwyn was grete of wille,
he wild fle not for dede no ille; — . wolde nought fle for drede ne .
nouþer wild he treus ne pes,
batail he wild & þerto ches.
With Kadwalyn so hard he mette,
Kadwalyn fled at þe first sette

[*L adds:*]	Toward þe southe he wolde haue fled
	But Edwyn his weye wyþ sperd
[90rb] into wodes him to hide;	[*Transp. L*] & Cadwalyn fley hym byside
for Edwyn lette his way þat tide,	[*Transp. L*] . busches & wodes hym for . .
bi outen pathes þat he fond	. sties & paþes . . .
he fled in to Scotlond;	So he fley . . .
& euer Edwyn after fleih,	
Kadwalyn grete peyn dreih;	. . . he drey
a schip he toke, to Ireland went,	
bot Edwyn mot him nouht hent,	
bot suyth into þe south did haste,	. schop hym swyþe wiþ alle .
Kadwalyn londes to waste.	
[*L adds:*]	Casteles dide he bete right doun
	Contres destruied toun by toun
	Al his lond he þorow ȝede
	Til alle he dide sorewe & drede
Of Brian sister men him told,	
at Wircester scho was in hold;	
Edwyn þien hir toke,	. þere hure out .
to ȝork he sent hir to loke;	
with his wife scho was seruant,	
maiden gentille & auenant.	
[I]n þe kynges courte, Edwyn,	[*Capital om. in P.*]
was a clerk couþe of deuyn;	
for in Spayn was he born,	ffer . . . . .
of chances he couþe telle beforn.	
He knewe alle foules crie	
& inouh of astronomie;	. couþe y now . .
Pellith hight þat ilk clerk.	
He serued Edwyn of gode werk,	
for Kadwalyn myght for wele no wo,	. . myghte neuere . . . .
no tyme in hauen to schip go,	
ne in þe se hidirward ride,	
felle it neuer so gode a tide,	
þat ne þis clerk deuyn	. þys ilke . .
teld it euer tille Edwyn.	Als swiþe teld hit . .
He know alle maner roune	. knew . . .
& many a coniurisoune,	. . manere .
& many chances couþe discrie	
þorgh quantise & clergie.	By sciences & artȝ of .
Kadwalyn was oft on flote	
with many faire schip on schote,	

& wele wynd gan him dryue, .wel þe....
vp in þis lond to aryue;
& euer com Edwyn him biforn
þat his trauaile was euer lorn,
& alle þorgh þis clerk engyne ..was þorow þe clerkes.
þat warned euer Edwyne. ..ay þe Kyng.
[90va] Kadwalyn had sorow & site
þat he was ay discomfite,
& many oþer sore it ment
þat out of lond with him went;

[*L adds:*] & fur ȝeden lond & lyth
Þat wyþ hym byde many wo sith

to þam he said he wild wende
to Litelle Bretayn to seke frende.
"With Kyng Salmon wille I speke;
he may me help my bale to wreke.
He ȝernes me to se & haue,
som of myn may he saue."
He sailed day & on þe nyght, ..al day....
vmwhile boþe wrong & right,
tille he com vntille an ilde,
Gernet, a litille land wilde.

[*L adds:*] No lond nyster ferrere west
Þer þe sonne goþ to rest

Bituex Bretayn & Corwaile ...Cornewaille
is þat ilde withouten faile.
No while ne was he þore & bynne a while þat he cam.
þat þe kyng euelid sore,
þe feuere agew þat him wele hatte, ..agu ful sore hym.
bot sone he chared & wele suatte.
Venyson he ȝarned to ete,
he myght with non oþer mete.
Þe kyng comanded to Brian,
he had non oþer leche man,
þat he suld gete him venyson
els his euelle suld bring him doun.

[*L adds:*] But ȝyf þat y som venison haue
No þyng so sone may me saue
Hit ys no tale wher of hit be
But þat þou mightest gete hit me
Brian hadde ful gret longyng
ffor to saue his Em þe Kyng

He toke þo men þat were wonte
go to chace & ȝede to honte;
þei sauh dales & ȝorgh þe lynde,   . soughte þe dales & þe playnes
[*L adds:*] Þey soughte busche & montaynes
& þorow mores & þorow lynde
fond þei nouþer herte no hynde,
wilde boore, ne buk, ne doo,
ne hare, ne conyng, foune, ne roo.   . . Cony ffowen no Ro
Þan had Brian sorow inouh
& said, "How myn eam fare nouh   . . . schal myn Em fare how
þat I may no venyson fynde?"
Bot he did as a man fulle kynde:
he schare a pece out of his thee,
lard it & roste as felle to be,   & lardid & rostoid. . . .
& dight it for þe kyng fulle wele;
& he ete it ilk a dele
& passed wele þat age,   . . . þo þat hache
so suete mete neuer ete he.   . . . . or et.
[90vb] Whan þe kyng felte him of myght,
þer schippes alle to se he dight
& aryued vp at a toun,
Achidalet, þe name Bretoun.   . was þe . .
[*L adds:*] ȝyt men seyþ after þe flod
Men knowes þere þe toun stod
Þe kyng welcomed Kadwalyn
& oft pleyned his mykelle pyne.   . . compleyned . . .
[*L adds:*] & his in to make soiour
He dide hym haue at grete honur
He hight him he suld in a stounde
help to bring Edwyn to grounde.
"Bot certes, grete meruaile I haue
þat grete Bretayn may þe not saue.   . . . . ȝe nought.
Fulle wele kept it Belyn,
Maximian, & Constantyn,
& Lucius did cristen be.   . . dide vs . .
Arthure is ded, wele I se;   But Arthur . . . may men.
þe les neuer a fote of land,   Þey lore . . . . .
myn heritage I hold in hand;
so wild þat þou did þin   So woldy . . . .
egayn þe Englis paen Edwyn."   Ageyn . . . .
Cadwalyn said, "Sir Salmon,
our kynges conquested long is gon.   . kynde conqueste is longes.

Wite þou wele þo conqueroures
were myn ancestres & ȝoures,
& vengeance felle on fele of þo
þat of þer blode com no mo.

[*L adds:*] On riche men hit a veniaunce
Childre to gete þat haue no chaunce
Þenne goþ heritage out of kynde
When nought of þe blod men fynde
Þen schul men gyue hit for good
To þem þat han hated al þe blod

Lucius þat brouht vs cristendam,
non heire of his body cam.
Aliens had after him .had hit..
þat tille our kynd were fulle brym.
Constantyn & Maximian,
non haire of þam ne ran, .heir of þer body.
ne Arthure, þe noble kyng,
of his body com no þing;
ne of Conan ne Vortapus,
ne Malgo, ne Caricius;
of alle þise, heire was non. ....com þer.
Bot out of kynd it is gon,
& god wild þat þei non had,
in alle synnes þer lyfe þei lad; Þat synfully þeir lyues.

[*L adds:*] Þey vsede alle manere synnes
ffor synful lyf oure kynde blynnes

ne god wille no more þei be
kepers of þat dignite.
Gildas writes & sais þe same,
þan am I nouht forto blame." Þer fore am....
[91ra] Alle þe wynter þer he lay
& purueid him fro day to day
folk & schippes for to gete,
opon þe se to haf a flete,
in þat þei mad purueiance.
Brian said he wild o chance
wend tille Englond priuely,
if he Pellith mot com by. ..by sleyghte mighte..
"For als long as he is on lyue,
in Englond may we neuer aryue,
for he kan telle þorgh his arte
whider we wille & to what parte."
Brian auentured him alle in drede,

bot god him gaf wele to spede;	
a Barbflete to schip he went,	At Barbeflet....
at Southampton hauen he hent;	
fair cloþes ne wild he were	
bot dight als a beggere.	.dightym al lyke to..
A schorte staffe did he make	
as palmers in handes take,	
square gronden, scharp euenlike,	[*Transp. L*]
did he þerin a fulle gode pike.	[*Transp. L*]
He feyned him croked many tyme	
als he had long bien pilgryme.	....ben a.
He lened him as he were werie	.let hym al he had ben.
& spired after þe kyng priuelie;	.al wey spirde.
[*L adds:*]	After þe kyng he spird vmwhile ffor non hoped til hym no gyle
so quayntly about he wond,	
þe kynges kourte at ȝork he fond.	
He did him among þe poraile	
with bagge & burdon of þer entaile;	
with þam he stode, with þam he went,	
& as his iȝe oside glent,	But euere his eye o syde he.
he saw his sister with a bacyne,	
water for to fecche þerin;	
& Brian stirt forþe in hir way	
& stilly said what he wild say.	
[*L adds:*]	When scheo hym knew sche gan to grete He seide þy gretyng I rede þou lete ffor ȝyf any man me aparceiue ffro þe deþ may y nought weyue Þer fore þou lete now al þy mone & drawe vs by oure self al one
Þei ȝede out of þe pres a lite	
þat non of þam mot se no wite.	..ne scholde hem se ne.
He asked after þe clerk Pellite,	
with þat he com þer als tite.	
"Lo," scho said, "he comes here,"	
& teld him alle Pellith manere.	
[91rb] "Haf gode day," said Brian.	
"Do þin erand as þou bigan."	
Toward Pellit he gan hie;	
of him com neuer his iȝe.	ffro hym ne lefte he neuere..
Pellit among þe pouer ȝede	
als he suld haf bette þer nede,	

to & fro als a fole,
& Brian folowed him on hoole,
& amang þe most pres   .right in al þe..
among þam alle, Pellit he ches.
His staffe priuely vp he warp   ..ful sleyly...
& put þe long pike so schap   ......scharp
agayn þe herte in at þe bak.
He felle doun, no worde he spak.
[*L adds:*] Cried he neyþer wo ne way
But ded he was & þer he lay
Brian lete þe staffe lig þere   .lefte his staf right.
& ȝede beside als nouh ne were,   .drow o syde as nought..
[*L adds:*] & as queyntely as he might
O drey he held hym out of sight
among þe pouer hid his face;   ...he hidde..
sleih he was & had faire grace.   & sleyly wroughte &...
Alle þat day he skulked,
among þe pouer folk he hulked.
Whan nyght com he was fayn,   .þe nyght cam he was ful.
his gate he toke south agayn;   .wey he tok to þe south.
boþe nyght & day fast he spedde   What day what night ful...
þat tille Oxenford he redde.   ...algate he.
Þan com þe folk withouten ses
about Brian forto pres,
þe Bretons alle & of Cornwaile   ...& þe of.
& of Wales þe pedaile,   ...cam gret.
& askid him wheþen he cam,   Þey frayned hym faste when..
whider he wild & to wham.
[*L adds:*] & what nede ys now in hande
Þat Cadwalyn comeþ nought to lande
"Where Cadwalyn, we pray þe telle,   And where he ys....
whedir he salle com or duelle."
"Certes," he said, "within a throwe
ȝe salle vnderstond & knowe
þat Edwyn salle not dur abide,
bot a mischance him betide.   But ȝif....
Warnysch ȝour castels, do mak tours;
for ȝow salle sone com socours."
Of alle þe moste he wist þer wille,   ...grete....
þerfor fulle boldly & stille,
he did vitaile þe toun wele,
defensable with bretask & pele.
[91va] He sent his eam a messengere

& teld him on what manere
he had slayn þe clerk Pellite,
& stored Oxenford to his profite.
Of þat bode þe kyng was paid;
his wendyng was not delaied,
nyght & day mad him redy,
ten þousand had to his nauy, ..he hadde til..
what of his, what of frendes ..hise owen & of.
þat Salmon with him sendes.
Whan þat he was alle ȝare, When Cadwalyn...
tille he were forþe, grete was his care.
At Toteneis he gan vpryue,
glad was þe folk he was olyue.
Grete sorow mad Edwyn
þat slayn was his clerk Pellyn.
Penda, kyng of Lyndeseie,
how Brian did he herd seie;
grete force of folk Penda did fet
Kadwalyn forto withset;
Oxenford he seged about,
bot Brian held him without.
Whan Kadwalyn was aryued on land,
tille him com smert tiþand
þat þe Kyng Penda .an Englische..
biseged Brian & was his fa.
Kadwalyn was alle enired,
to rescue Brian he desired.
Alle þat he myght he hasted, As faste as he...
iorneis to mak, folk he tasted,
& whan he was þe toun nehi,
he bad þam rest þat were weri.
"Restes ȝow for ȝour trauaile, Rest ȝou now...
þe smertlier ȝe may assaile."
Þe folk of þe toun was glad ...Oxenforde were.
& grete ioy Brian mad;
ioy he had he was so nere, Gret ioie þer was....
& more of his grete powere.
Cadwalyn was felle of herte,
þe sege he assailed smerte.
Long had he bien born bak,
þe fellier on þam he brak; .hertiloker....
[91vb] he doutid noiþer dede no dynt,
many man þer was tynt. Þat tyme was many a man þer.

Felli wer þei holden waken, Hertly....
Penda, maugre his, was taken
& smertli don in hold; ...in syker.
for no raunson mot he be sold,
ne for no man loþe ne leue
bot he wild to Kadwalyn cleue
& hold of him his heritage
with feaute & with homage. & don hym feaute &.
Whan Penda had to Kadwalyn
obligid him & mad his fyn,
more luf to mak & bate strife,
Penda sistere he toke to wife
& wedded hir on cristen lawe.
To gode mot no man Penda drawe;
Penda was euer ille in dede, Ay was Penda yuel..
so sais þe boke of Saynt Bede. As telleþ.....
Kadwalyn þanked his barons
& nameli þe Bretons; .nameliche of..
alle þer trauaile & þer ille
þat þei tholed for him with wille, ..had þoled wiþ gode.
alle he suld auance þer lore
þat þei lost for him before,
& alle þo þat did him noie,
þam gan he fast destroie.
He passed Humber with folk inouh,
tounes he brent & men slouh.
Edwyn his comyng herd say,
how he spared non in his way;
he gadred alle his retenance,
knyghtes, squiers, & sergeance,
& alle oþer þat of him helde,
& come alle to Hatfelde;
þider samned boþe partis
þat long had bien enmys.
Penda, þat ilk Sareȝin, ..schrewe þe.
he com to help Kadwalyn. To helpe he com wyþ.
Edwyn was hardy & bolde,
auht & fourti wynter olde;
he was slayn, his sonne him with,
a gode knyght, was kald Offrith.
[92ra] Elleuen ȝere was Kadwalyn kyng ...Edwyn.
or he toke cristenyng,
& þerin tuo wyues he toke

or he þe paien lawe forsoke.
Guenburh þe first hight so,
with hir had he childir tuo,
Offrith & Eadfrith þus þei hight,   Offriht.....
boþe were þei knyghtes wight;
Ethelbirge hight þe toþer,   Dame Ethelburgh...
þe kyng of Kent was hir broþer;
Ethelbriht hir fader was
þat we befor red in pas.
Saynt Bede sais of þis Edwyn
sen he forsok þe lawe Sareȝyn,

[*L transp. two couplets.*]

he was cristened on Pask day   So god a Cristen kyng was non
at ȝork, forsok peaen lay;   In al þis lond als he alon
so god a cristen kyng was non   He was Cristned o þe Pasche day
in þis lond als he alon;   At ȝork fursok his Paen lay
sex hundreth ȝere þe date was þo
& passed seuen & tuenty mo

[*L adds:*] Emfled his doughter born
Sche was Cristned a ȝer byforn

whan he our cristendom gon take.   ..þe Cristendam þoughte.
Þe Kirke of ȝork he did first make,
bot long are it were brouht to ende,
he was slayn with folk vnhende;
bot Saynt Oswald, þat gode man,
he ended þat Edwyn bigan.
Edwyn was sex ȝere
cristen kyng in þis lond here.

[*L adds:*] What cristen what heþen þral
Seuentene ȝer he Regned in al

Þat ȝere þat he was slayn,   .selue ȝer Oswy..
his cosyn Osri in þe same payn,
þe ȝeres of criste sex hundreth wore
& þretty ȝere & þre more,
þe ferþe day in þe Idis   ...þat ys y..
of Octobir, who so it bidis.

[*L adds:*] Þer he lay a chapel ys wrought
& ȝit ys þer folk þat þyder han sought

Now of Kadwalyn salle we say:
he slouh þe Kyng Orkenay, ...of Orkeneye
Sir Kadan, & Sir Gabaon,
þe Scottis kyng was þe ton,
& many oþer lordes mo,

for whilk was mad mykelle wo. .wham..ful mykel.
Kadwalyn had neuer mercy
of Edwyn kynd he mot com by.
[*L adds:*] Man & woman he slow al day
& childre þat in þe Cradel lay
[92rb] Alle he slouh, alde & ȝong,
þat tille Edwyn told any tong;
ȝyt of Edwyn was left on quik,
his eame son þat hight Osrik
þat resceyued þe heritage; .rescowed..
bot litille held he it in age,
Kadwalyn wrouht him so wouh,
his tuo kosyns & him he slouh.
[*L adds:*] Þowh al he hadde Crysten feyþ
To þo Crysten he dide ouer leyþ
Þat ȝong & olde al ȝede to ded
ffor o man þat hym mys bed
Saynt Bede blames Kadwalyn,
of wille he calles him barbaryn.
(Barbaryn is Sareȝin strange,
to merci neuer wille turne ne change.) ..þat wil nere turne..
For alle þe world so ferd he,
o lyue wild he late non be;
þe slauhter lasted so grete stounde,
vnneþis a cristen man men founde
bot turned to þe lawe paien
þat are was wont to be cristen, ...brought...
vnto þe tyme of Saynt Oswald,
þe fayth agayn he he hald; Þat þe feiþ ageyn dide.
vnto þe reame he had right,
of wille fre & gentille knyght. And was ful fre...
He sent for þe Bisshop Aidan
of Scotlond, þat gode man; ..was þat..
þat bisshop com his folk to preche,
þer cristendom fro paen to reche. ...Paen reche
Of Oswald Saynt Bede telles,
many of his miracles spelles;
of on to telle, mikelle I charge
how he vnto þe pouer was large.
Pouer folk spired & men þam told
where Oswald suld Paske hold.
On Pask day in tyme of mete,
þe pouer gadred, gode to gete;

right als þe borde was laid,
þe cloþes spred, þe grace said,
þei serued þe kyng in a siluer dissh
(what maner mete, I ne wote iwis).
His ambner stode him before .aumener stod þe kyng.
& said so many pouer were þore,
"& ȝit com on ilk a side,
of our almos help to bide." .ȝoure almes...
[92va] Þe kyng toke þat he suld ete
& brak þe dissh with alle þe mete,
bad him departe amang þam alle
þe siluer, as best wild falle. Boþe mete & syluer as hit..
Aydan sauh how he it brak,
þerfor tille þis word he spak: .til hym....
"Neuer þat hand rote ne elde, Nere mote.....
bot hole withouten end it welde."
Non oþer it is bot as he seid, & so hit ys right als..
at Peterburgh in schryne is leid,
at þe abbay in þe kirke;
þe Kyng Penda did it wirke.
Oswald was sib Edwyn beforn,
of Acha his sister born; ....was Osewald.
þerfor, Kadwalyn wild not ses
bot on Oswald werre pres, .faste on..gan.
to Scotland he chaced Oswald;
for Kadwalyn had more folk & bald,
Oswald fled & gaf him place
so þat Kadwalyn left his chace;
his folk him þouht trauailed sore,
bot Penda þat tyme was þore.
He bad him folow, Oswald to take,
or do him þe lond forsake.
Whan Oswald wist þe certeyn
þat Kadwalyn turned ageyn,
ageyn Penda wild he stand;
for him ne wild he be fleand.
In a felde Oswald gan bide
& stand to chance what mot betide. To bide þe bataille what so.
Heuen felde þe name is kald
for þe luf of Saynt Oswald.
In þat feld, a croys he lift
& bad þam not be oglift ..þem alle...
to com & knele befor þe croys,

"& pray Ihesu, alle with a voyce,
þat he þis day stand vs by
ageyn Penda his enmy,
þat with wrong vs anoies
& þe cristendom destroies." .our Cristen men.
Alle þey did as he bad,
praied Ihesu þat his blode schad
[92vb] on þe croice for mannes nede,
ageyn Penda wele to spede. ..wel þat day.

[*L adds:*] Alle were þey of gode repentaunce
& wel y schryuen for alle chaunce

Sien þei dight þam to bataile Syn þey...þe.
& Penda gan þam fast assaile;
his oste was mykelle & wide spred, ...gret...
nere were þei slayn & Penda fled.
He scaped with mykelle pyne
& pleyned him to Kadwalyne,
& said bot he venge him wold,
of him suld he neuer hold. ....namore.
At þat tyme, þus it left
vntille þei samned ostes eft; ....þer hostes.
þe bataile was beside Thirwalle ....Þyrlwal
þat som tyme closed þe North alle. .whilom..Northende.
Þer was many miracle schewed
þat witnes lered & lewed. .witnesseþ boþe...

[*L adds:*] Þe cros dide þere many merueilles
Halp man & best of þeir trauailles

Ȝit Kadwalyn & Penda
þouht to wirk Oswald wa;
þei gadred ostes, þis enmys,
& com on him in tuo partys;
in a stede hate Maȝerfelde,
þer schewed Oswald his schelde,
þer he said he wild abide;
grete folk was on ilk a side. .were þer batailles on eyþer.
Oswald wist he suld þer die
& mot skape on no weie; .mighte nought scape by..
in his fallyng he said on hie,
"Of alle þe saules, Lord haf mercie!" ..our....

[*L adds:*] Þat was þe laste werde he seid
& fel doun & þer he deyd

Of þo men þat þis word herd,
a biword in alle þe cuntre ferd:

"God haf our saules, quod Oswald!"
Þis biword was long tald.

[*L adds:*] Þys þey seide at ilka rage
& longe had þey hit in vsage
Þis word witnesseþ wel seynt Bede
Þat longe was vsed in many lede

Bot nyen ȝere was he kyng,   Nyne wynter...
& auht & þretty was he ȝyng;
þe date of criste was þan redy,
sex hundreth ȝere tuo & fourty.
Þise wikked men þat him slouh   ..kynges...
did hang his lymmes on a bouh;
a tre þei did set þerfore,
handes, armes, did þorgh bore.   ..þey dide..
His hede hang a ȝere to mone,
bot Oswi, his sister sonne,   ...broþer.
[93ra] was kyng, & toke þe hed hyngand
& biried it at fferneland;
of an ilde it is þe name,
to Durham hous longes þat same.
A quene was lady of þo landes,
scho did tak þe armes & handes;
þe ton scho biried vnder molde,
þe toþer kept in siluer & golde
in Saynt Peter Kirk to hold.
For þe quene þe toun was told   & after þe Quen....
Bebba, for þe quene it kald;   ....hit is.
a nyce name for soþe I hald,
& for it was so nyce a name,
I trow þei changed it for schame.
Or þat tyme hight it Metehamstede,
Peterburgh, þat semely sede.
Long after Oswald was dede,
holy kirke mykelle peyn bede,
for þat þat he þerin wrouht,   ffor al þat he þer inne had.
with strange was alle doun brouht;   .stronge men....
preste & clerk slouh alle doun,   ...þey slowe right.
waste was left ilk a toun,   Þat al was wast ner ilk..
& þe godes away born;
tille Oswy com, nere alle was lorn.

[*L adds:*] & for he was his broþer sone
Hym fel to haue þe Regione

Þo þat þer were, conseile helde   .....þey held

& bitauht Oswy þe schelde.
Oswy sauh þe folk alle pouere
& þe lond at no recouerere, ...recouere
þe powere of Kadwalyn mykille, ...was mikel
& Penda poyned him as a prikille.
He sauh his powere was nought
if Kadwalyn on him souht; ..werre on..
leuere him were in luf to bowe
þat no mo of his folk men slowe. .þey namo of his men.
[*L adds:*] Þan in werre bere hym ouer heye
& euere be on þe werre partye
To Kadwalyn his sonne he sent ...sonde..
þat he wild com to parlement;
he com þider alle with leue.
Kadwalyn wild him not greue;
[*L adds:*] He gaf hym boþe seluer & gold
ffor Cadwalyn schold ben hym hold
he resceyued his homage
& restored his damage; .som restored of..
þusgate was þe pes granted
& in luf long hanted.
[93rb] Bot Oswy mykelle kynde had .Cadwal...
þat oft conseiled him & rad
for to werre on Oswy;
þei claymed of his grete party. ...hys land..
Bot Oswy defended als a man, ..defended hym...
of him neuer nouht þei wan. So þat of hym neuere þey ne.
Ane Alfrith claymed of his right, On Alfriche....
ouer Humber com with him to fight, ..he chased hym þorow.
on þis half he fled him fra;
he com & pleyned to Penda
þat he wild him mayntene And preied he...
ageyn Oswy þat was so kene,
& if he mot þat lond wynne, .þe lond þat he might of hym.
his parte suld be þerinne. He schulde haue his part.
Penda said he durst nouht,
for Kadwalyn at on was brouht .Cadwal & Osewy were al saught
with Oswy as þe partis ches. [*Om. L*]
"Bot I salle salle fond som quayntes .fonde i schal by som.
[*L adds:*] Of Cadwalyn to haue grauntise
if I may gete his leue; & ȝif.....
with ȝow to hold, I salle him greue."
Sone at þe Whitsontide, Þan fel hit...

Kadwalyn wild no lengere bide;
at London he set his coronment,
alle his barons þider went
forto be at his fest,
south, northe, west, & est;
bot Oswy þat tyme not kam .þider cam nought þo Osewy
(I ne wote for whi no wham). ....what hit was ne why
Whan Penda perceyued, he mad grete faire
why þat Oswy was not þare;
to Kadwalyn he mad pleynt ...made his.
& said Oswy was fals & feynt,
"þat he com not for þi somons
to þi courte as oþer barons.
Alle ere comen, ilk a Breton,
& Englis, & ilk a Sesson. .ilkan Englische & Saxoun
Bot Oswy tok þi somons in veyn;
to com to courte he has disdeyn."
Þe kyng excused him curtasly.
"He has som grete encheson why;
perauenture he has sekenesse ..haþ som.
or oþer greuance þat makes him stresse."
[93va] "Nay," quod Penda, "it is not so!
Þou sees not what Oswy wille do;
in þis tyme of þi coronment,
into Saxone has he sent
after soudeours, was me told, ..as was..
to venge þe dede of Oswold.
Whan he sees tyme þat he may,
on þe to renne he wille assay;
bot & þou wille gif me leue, .Cadwalyn wil þou...
I salle him bring to mischeue,
þat ouþer salle I do him fle,
or quik or dede bring him to þe."

[*L adds:*] Seide Cadwalyn þus may hit make
Neþeles y schal conseil take

Kadwalyn kald Bretons him about
& did Penda go without,
& þe Englis euerilkon
so þe Bretons were alon.
Kadwalyn said, "Lordes alle,
sais now what wille best falle
of þis þat Penda has bisouht,
whedir is it to do or nouht." Wheþer hit is god....

Þan spak Sir Margadu, .spak first..
lord of Southwales, for þer pru.
"Long is sen þis wo was gunnen, .hit is þys was by gonne
& ȝit is not alle ouer runnen ..is hit....
bituex vs & þe Englis kynde,
& non wote how it wille ende. .ȝit wot non how hit wyl bynde
How so bituex þam be strife or stresse,
euer to noye vs ere þei fresse;
be þei beneth, be þai aboue,
vs wille þei neuer loue,
ne þer treuth ne wille þei hold;
to do felonie þei er bold. ..a felonye ar þey ful.
Haf þis in þi herte streite
þat þei haf don vs grete desceite
so fele tymes here beforn,
& also oft has þou suorn
þat þou suld bring þam heþen, ..scholdest ȝit...
bot þin othe is ay bineþen;
sen þou sees þat þou may nouht
haf þi dede with þi þouht, ffulfylle.....
ne perchance is not þi wille,
suffre þe ton þe toþer spille.
[93vb] Suffre þe ton þe toþer schende
& entermet þe at non ende. Ne entremet þe at neyþer.
Penda is Englis & not gode
& Oswy is of Englis blode;
mak of þam no maner iangle, .we þer of no..
soffre þe ton þe toþer strangle. .þe dogges ech oþer.

[*L adds:*] Suffre hem eyþer on oþer renne
& ilkon oþer robbe & brenne

So may þe lond of þam be quite [*Transp. L*] & þorow meschaunce of fight or flyt
þorgh mischefe of fight & flite." [*Transp. L*] Þys lond mai happe of þem be quit
Þe Bretons spak at a braid:
"Sir Margadu, þou has wele said.
At þis conseile alle we hold
as Sir Margadu vs told.
Penda," þei said, "do what þou wilte;
to Kadwalyn it is no gilte."
Penda proudly tok his leue;
of þouht he forto greue. Oswy algate wold he.

[*L adds:*] He gadred gret host on his side
& Penda cam wyþ ful gret pryde

He purueied oste fulle hastifly, .sembled his...
fulle felly to werre on Oswy; ffersly to struye sire.
Oswy sone herd seie
how Penda wild on him lyue & deie.
He douted sore his wikked res
& sent to Penda for þe pes;
& if he wild þerto grant,
he wild gyue him couenant, .wolde hym gyue in god.
gold & siluer at his myght,
his lond to haf withouten fight.
Penda said he wild not leue,
he suld him chace, þe croune reue.
With Oswy was holy man, ..was an..
his name was Bisshop Aydan; Bischop he was his name.
wo him was whan he it herd [*Om. L*]
þat Penda ageyn Oswy misferd. [*Om. L*]
He praied god for þer nede,
ageyn Penda, Oswy to spede.
"Se, se, Lord, his wikkednesse! Louerd þou quenche..
His grete powere þou mak it lesse,
& suffre vs neuer to fele þe smerte,
þe felonie of his wikked herte."
Whan Oswy sauh no luf wild send,
at his powere he wild defend; But at...moste hym fende
he gadred oste on his side
& Penda com with grete pride.
At a day bataile was sett,
boþe ostes togider mett;
[94ra] a gode hope Oswy was in
þat he suld þe maistrie wyn.

[*L adds:*] He tristed wel y þe Holy Gost
& Penda tristed on hys grete host

Þe smote togider bitterlike ...so bitterlyke
þat ilk side fond oþer quike; .eyþer....
þat werre bigan, þe wars had, He þat hit gan þe worse he.
Penda partie alle to schad.
His grete oste ȝede alle doun
& slayn was feloun; ..was þere þat.
fulle wele he sped þat gaf þat dynt,
Penda life & saule was tynt.
Þe ȝere þat he to dede ȝede,
þe date was, as sais Saynt Bede,

sex hundreth ȝere, fifty & fyue,
þat day Penda les his lyue.
Opon Tuede þe bataile was,
þritty dukes slayn in þat pas; .....plas
of Penda side euerilkone,
for whilk many mad mone. ...was mad.
Wilfrith his scaped þat pyne, Wolfrith his sone...
com & told Kadwalyne, & cam & told hit to.
& he gaf him his heritage Cadwalyn gaf...
& he tille him mad homage.
Kadwalyn þat kept þe lond,
a trewe iustise þe folk him fond; ...men hym.
he regned foure & fourty ȝere.
[*L adds:*] What in pes & in wer
He died at London, þei laid him þere;
[*L differs:*] At Londone wax he syk & deyde
Þe Bretons þere his body leyde
& forto haf menyng of him,
how he was noble, meke, & grim,
of koper þei did mak a knyght,
a hors of kopir alle dight,
set him þeron in kynges wede
als he was wont to ride on stede;
þer biside laid his body, ..þey leyde..
aboun at a ȝate fulle hie Abouen..gate..
in London toward þe west;
long it stode streitly fest. ...þer wel y fest
Biside þei set a chapelle
of Saynt Martyn, a faire iuwelle;
þus þei did grete nobley, ..dide for..
his dedis forto mene & sey.
Cadwaldrus was after Kadwalyn
his fader, & Penda kosyn.
[94rb] Penda kosyn, his sister sonne
Kadwalyn wedded, I did ȝow mone.
Cadwaldre was a gode kyng
& lufed god of alle þing.
In his tyme failed þe corne,
was non als it was beforne; ffor þer was non as..
of þat defaute com grete dere
& grete hunger ouer alle here; .....was here
þre dayes to go if þei mot drie
or þei fond any mete to bie

ouþer in burgh or cite,
or vpland in any cuntre,
bot if þei any bestes toke,
or fissh in ryuer or in broke,
or any leues or rotes seth
þat hang on hege or on heth.
Alle was els turned tille faile,
myght no man lif on his trauaile.
If þis mischefe com ferly sore, ..meschaunce...
3it þer was anoþer more:
so grete a manqualme com þerwith,
for dede mot non vnneþis haf grith. ffro deþ vneþe might non..
Þorgh roten ayer & wikked wyndes,
in alle stedes men died grete myndes; ....dide..

[*L adds:*] Now 3ede þey vp right hol & fer
Now fel þey doun ilk oþer ner
Etynge spekynge fel þey doun
& goynge boþe in feld & toun
ffader Moder Eam & broþer
Gentil & bonde & alle oþer

vnneþis in tounes was any lefte
þat mot tille þe lond efte. Of Bretons þat mighte....
Þe vengeance was so ferly grete,
it spared non, bot alle þorgh schete;
so fele lay dede in ilk way,
þei fond non quik in erþe þam to lay. Þat þe quyke ne mighte hem on erþe.

[*L adds:*] 3yf any had leyd a cors in pyt
Hym self fel þanne ded þer myt

So mykelle was þer sorow & drede,
left hous & land, away þei 3ede.
What for moreyne, what for dere,
fo þer were þat myght lyue here.

[*L adds:*] Of his long lyf can noman seye
Þat ses his frend sodeynly deye
Þat ses his neighebur brenne hym by
To saue hym self he ys bysy

Cadwaldre, kyng of þis lond,
ouer alle so mykelle wo fond,
to Litelle Bretayn for sorow he fled;
þat were o lyue, with him þam led.
Alayn he hight, þat þan was kyng,
þat fayn was of his comyng.
Whan þe Bretons hþen went, ...heþen.

þer fair wonnyng mykelle þei ment
[94va] & said it was a vengeance strong;
agayns god þei lyued wrong.
"Now salle we lese þis lond þorgh synne
þat our kynd has welte with wynne."
Þat lered were, þis psalme þis sunge   .....þey songe
& verseild it with o tunge.
"Deus auribus nostris" hate þat psalme
þat þei said for þat qualme;
at a verse þat is þerin,
pleynt to gun þei bigyn: Pleynyng to god þus gan þey gynne
"Vendidisti populum tuum sine precio,"
toward þer schippes þei song so.   ....songen hit.
"Dedisti nos tanquam oues escarum
& cetera per totum psalmum."   [*L om. the last three words.*]
To schip went Cadwaldres,
with him þe Bretons þat he ches;
with sory & herte fulle brym,   .sorwful chere & herte.
oft mad þei pleynt tille him,
"Wo tille vs, synnfulle þat are,
þat for our wikkednes þus fare.   ....we þus.
With synne we wrathed god alle myght,
& þorgh his we lese our right.   ..his wraþe....
Lord of mercy, we praye þe,
space of penance gif vs fre;
of þis grete wrath þou stynt,
þof we synnfulle, our lond haf tynt.
Grante þo gode men þat þou ches
þat our kynde not alle it les.
We se þi vengeance more may do   ....ȝit more..
þat þe Romeyns mot neuer com to,
ne oþer strangere þan were þei
myght non bring vs ore away.
Out of mesure synned we,
als wele to þin as to þe,
þat we ne are worþi ageyn be kald
to penance, ne our lond to hald.
We wild no mercy whan tyme was,
now schewes þi wraþe þat grete trispas;   .schewest vs wraþe for þat.
now we fynd þou kan right deme.
Whan we had tyme, we wild not queme;   While....nolde þe queme
oft we fauht to fend our land,
þou gaf vs þan þe ouerhand.   & ay þou gaf vs þe heyer hand

[94vb] Þou gaf vs grace to wynne þe pris
alle tymes of our enemys. Al wey...
Now is it for nouht we fynd,
we lese alle rote & rynd. ..hit al by...
We pray þe, Lord sufferable, ...to be suffrable
& turne our grete to ioye stable ...sorewe...
& com ageyn, if þi wille be,
on our lond to serue þe."

[*L adds:*] Now may þe Romayns come ageyn
Þe Scottes & Peytes þat dide vs peyn
& þe tricherous Saxons
Þeyr tricherye vs euere mones
Þys voyde land schul þey now take
Voide of vs mighte neuere þey make
Al þer strengthe dide vs nought fle
But godes wrathe þat serued we

Suilk sorow & suilk mone
mad þe Breton euerilkone
to Cadwaldre þer cheftayn
as þei schipped to Lesse Bretayn.
Whan þer flote to lond was laid,
þe Kyng Alayn beforsaid,
resceyued him with gode wille,
with him to beleue stille, Preynge wyþ hym to leue.
& alle þo þat with him wore,
tille he wild, suld duelle þore. While.....
Þan was þis lond waste left
manqualme, hunger, þe folk reft. Moryne & hunger þe folk had.
Elleuen þhere, þus writen þei fond, Enleuen ȝer....
was here non to tile þe lond, ..no folk might...
bot right fo of þe Bretons .ful fewe...
& als fo of þe Saxons;
alle folk with tempest vnkynde
was slayn, non mot men fynde.
Whan þis tempest sessed was,
fele ȝeres passed hard pas;
þe Sessons vnto Sessoyne went,
þei were fayn & þider ment. & þey....went
Þei aryued in Northumberland,
þe most of þer kynd þer þei fand;
fro Scotland vnto Cornwaile,
alle þe lond gan þei taile;
Logres it hight a fulle gode throwe,

for Loqerin þat we Inglond knowe.   ...we in..
Bot Bretayn was, bi olde tales,
Ingland, Scotland, & Wales,
alle a land & a name   .o land al was o.
(of þis mater I told þe same).
Was non here þat letted þer way
no þer takyng wild withsay,

[*L adds:*] ffor of þe Bretons were left but fo
Or any þat were yborn of þo
& þo skulked to wodes & fennes
To Cornewaille þey fledden hennes

[95ra] for Bretons in to Wales fleih;   In to Walys þey fledden also
of þer kynd was nouht þat deih.   .Bretons kynde were left namo
At þis tyme þat I here mene,
þe Bretons passid out alle clene, ...quit &.
& þe Englis þer biggyng   .Englische made her þeyr.
& chese þam of þer kynd a kyng.
Þer Sessons þat hider camen,   Þyse Saxons...
luf & pes þei held samen;
þe lond to tile, ouer alle þei souht,
cites, kastels, tounes wrouht,
mad houses, tiled þe felde.
Þer vsages & þer lawes helde;
þat þei in Sessoyne held before,
þe same wild þei haf þore;
þe tounes names on þer langage
held þei after þer linage;
þe erldomes & þe baronyes,
on þer vsage mad parties;

[*L adds:*] & somme þey helde on Bretons manere
Longe had þey seyn hit byforn here

of pes þe mad gode sikernesse,
þe lond to tile with more & lesse.
Whan þe Englis were oueralle spred,
in fele stedes fostred & fed,   ...stored..
& þe folk was wele mored
& þe lond wele stored,   ...bettere a stored

[*L adds:*] Hit was er a wel good þrowe
As mannes in wyt may þat wel knowe

Cadwaldrus him biþouht
þat to Bretayn for hunger souht;
bi passagers he herd wele say
þe venomouse heyre was away.

Gretand he praied Kyng Alayn	
to gete his kyngdam agayn,	
& als he had bisouht him so,	
on þe nyght a voyce com him to	
& said, "Leue at my biddyng,	..lef now...
tille it be schewed tokenyng;	....wyþ toknyng
of Bretayn god has purueied þis,	....ordeyned.
þat it is gyuen to þe Englis;	& gyuen hit haþ...
þe Bretons kynd salle no more	
in þat lond mak wonnyng þore	
tille þat tyme com þat is auysed,	
þat Merlyn beforn prophetised.	..til Arthur prophetysed
He said þe folk of Breton,	
or domesday salle it be don,	
[95rb] þat þei salle haf þis lond agayn	
whan filled is þe terme certayn."	
He bad him he suld go to Rome	
to þe pape & take his dome.	
"Þe to asoyle, penance to drie,	
among þe payntes salle þou lie.	
Þe prophecie salle not falle	
tille Bretons bring þi bones alle	
out of Rome to þis Bretayn;	
þan salle þei haf þe lond agayn.	
It salle betide suilk a waies	
als Saynt Metodie saies,	
þat many holy bones of pris	
þat now in fertre lis,	.y þys tyme...
salle men tak & away lede	
out of þe fertres for paien drede;	
& so salle his bones be brouht,	
what tyme be, wite we nouht."	..hit schal be...
Cadwaldrus, whan he þis herd,	
als a man in duale he ferd;	
[*L adds:*]	Stoneyed he was a wel god þrowe Er þan he couþe hym self y knowe
at þe last, þer of he brak	
& to Kyng Alayn he spak,	
& teld him what þe voyce said,	
what tokenyng for him was laid.	
Grete ferly had Kyng Alayn;	.wonder...
he ȝerned forto wite þe certayn.	& wilned faste to...
His wise clekes he did calle,	..clerkes he dide forþ.

& did þam seke þer bokes alle
to wite what þe prophecies
ment & said in sere parties,
if þei acorded tille þat selcouth
þat Cadwaldre said with mouth.
Þei souht þe prophecies of Aquile,
at Chestre was it said suld be.
Sibile sawes forþe þei laid
& also what Merlyn said, — .what þe Clerk Merlyn had.
& þe sawes of Sophonie;
non of þam wild not lie, — Of whiche non ne wolde.
þe voice & þer bokes ilkone, — [*Transp. L*]
bot þei acorded alle tille one; — [*Transp. L*]
non seid sere forto blame, — ..seer..
& þe voice said þe same. — But as þe vois þey seide..
[95va] Alayn said tille Cadwaldre kyng, — To Cadwaladrus seide Aleyn þe.
"I conseile þe fulfille þat þing.
Sen god of heuen has set it so, — ....haþ seid hit.
his wille I rede þat ȝe do."

[*L adds:*] ffor couetyse of no lond
To don his wille ne schaltow wond

Cadwaldre bad Iuor, his sonne,
& Iny, his neuow, wend & wonne
in Bretayn & maynten eft
þo þat were of Bretayns left,
"þat þei ne lese þat ore was myn,
my fredam for no barbaryn." — Þeyr fredam...
(A barbaryn is, sais Saynt Bede,
þat has no mercy for no nede.) — Ne had neuere merci...
Cadwaldre alle þe world forsoke,
to god & to penance him toke;
to Rome went Cadwaldrus — ..þen wente.
vnto þe Pape Sergius
þat resceyued him with wynne
& tille him he schroue his synne;
with wille of herte he myght of mene, — ....þat he myght.
& þe pape asoiled him clene.
In langore lay he many a day
& died þe tuelft Kalend of May;
þe date of criste was euen in lyne,
sex hundreth ȝere, foure score & nyne,
& his soule went to blis;
þe body at Rome in fertre is.

Blisse we god þat grace him gaf, Þanke......
þise verses er his epitaf:
"Culmen opes sobolem pollencia regna triumphous
Exuuias proceres castra menia lares
Queque patrum virtus et que congesserat ipse
Cadwal armipotens liquit amore dei ..liquid..
Vt petrum sedemque petri rex cerneret hospes
Cuius fonte metas sumeret almus aquas."

[*The following four lines are evidently an interpolation in P and omitted in L.*]

Explicit historia britannie transposita in linguam maternam per Robertum.
Incipiunt Gesta Anglorum super petrum de
Langtoft transposita per eundem R. Mannyng.
[95vb] Now haf I told of þe Bretons,
of kynges & som barons,
how þei mayntend þis lond
siþen Brutus first it fond Syn Brutus tyme þat...
vnto Cadwaldrus tyme.
Þerof Bretons leue we to ryme
& now of Inglis wille we telle.
Sen þe Bretons here gan duelle
þat toke þe lond þorgh godes heste,
þer tyme we kalle þe Inglis geste.
Alle is cald geste Inglis
þat on þis langage spoken is;
Frankis spech is cald romance,
so sais clerkes & men of France.
Pers of Langtoft, a chanon
of þe hous of Brdlyngtoun, Schauen y þe hous of Brydlyngtoun
on Frankis stile þis storie wrote, On Romaunce al..he.
of Inglis kynges for him we wote. ...as we wel.
He wrote þer dedes as þei wrouht, ...alle þat..
after him in Inglis I it brouht;
of his menyng, I wote þe way,
bot his faire spech I can not say.
I am not worþi open his boke,
for no konyng þeron to loke,
bot forto schew his mykelle witte,
on my spech þat is bot skitte, ..spekynge....
how he was quaynt in spech & wys
þat suilk a boke mad of pris,
& gadred þe stories alle tille one

þat neuer ore was mad for none.
Whan he first bigan his werk, .Peres....
he bisouht a holy clerk
to gyue him grace wele to spede,
þat holy man hight Saynt Bede;
for in his bukes mykelle he fond,
he mad fyue bokes of Inglond.
I salle praie him þat ilk wais
als he holy & curtais, ..ys corseint &.
he gif me grace wele to say
& rightly þis in ryme lay,
þis story þat is said of Pers, ...þorow Peres
þat alle be paied þat it hers. Amen.

The Chronicle

PART II

[96r] [I]n saynt Bede bokes writen er stories olde, [*Capital om. in P.*]
sex hundreth & four score & nien ȝere mo er tolde
sen þat Ihesu criste of Marie was born,
& þe Kyng Cadwaldre þis lond had alle lorn. ....forlorn
For Englis & Sessons he went to Lesse Bretayn .þe Englisch & Saxoynes...lytel.
to speke with his cosyn, his name was Kyng Alayn,
& fro þien he went vnto þe courte of Rome
for to tak his penance & of his synnes dome. ....ydone
Whan he was asoyled of þe Pape Sergie,
he died & was biried in Rome solemplie. ......Toumbe.
In þe ȝere after, nouþer lesse ne more, ...next after....
kom his & his kosyn Ini & Iuore. Cam Cadwaladres sone & cosyn...
In schip out of Irelond in Wales gan þei vpryue;
þorgh out Chestreschire werre gan þei dryue.
Had þei no styntyng bot þorgh alle þei ran, ...wiþstandyng.þurgh out...
vnto Wynchestre alle þe lond þei wan. Right to Wynchestre.....
In Westsex was þan a kyng, his was Sir Ine. ......his name...
Whan he wist of þe Bretons, of werre ne wild he fine.
.......werre wolde nought.
Messengers he sent þorghout Inglond
vnto þe Inglis kynges þat had it in þer hond,
& teld how þe Bretons, men of mykelle myght, .telde hem.......
þe lond wild wynne ageyn þorh force & fyght. .....þurgh werre force & right
Hastisly ilkone þe kynges com fulle suythe,
bolde men & stoute, þer hardinesse to kiþe. fful bolde.......
In a grete Daneis felde, þer þei samned alle,
þat euer siþen hiderward Kampedene men kalle.
Of alle þo Inglis kynges þat þan comen wore, ...þat þyder þen..
Sigbert, Kyng of Estsex, in elde was he more, ...for elde men toke byfore
he bigan to speke tille alle þe chiualrie: And he...first til...
"We be comen alle of kynde of Germenie .....þe kende..
þat chaced has þe Bretons here of þer kythe. ......out of..
Now ere þei comen to clayme it & mykelle force þam with;

oiþer bihoues vs defend it or ȝelde vp our righ.
Eyþer vs byhoues....hem vp our right
I rede we chese a hede þat vs to werre kan dight,
Þerfore chese we an heued......
& to þat ilk hede I rede we vs bynde, ..þat ilke chef hed.....
for werre withouten hede is not wele we fynde." .to werren.....y.
Þe barons ȝede to conseile & teld it siþen on hie.
"Ine Kyng, kyng of Westsex, was a knyght worþie .Kyng of.he ys...
forto gye vs alle þat now er comen here." .gouerne.......
Ine toke þe feaute, displayed his banere, ..þer feufte.þen his.
& went to þe bataile in a fulle faire grene
þat is vnder Kampedene, a medew I wene.
[96v] Iuor & Ini were disconfite þat day; Boþe Iuor......
þe Iris & þe Wals with þam fled away. ....Walsch men wyþ hem þey..
Alle were þei nere slayn, & þo þat þer left
fled vnto Wales vnto þer schippes eft.
Whan þise Bretons tuo were fled out of þis lond, ...boþe were...þe feld
Ine toke his feaute of alle þat lond helde.
At þe fiftend day, þei samned at Southamptoun;
with ioy, alle at ons þei went tille Snawdoun. ....to Swanton
On Iuor & Ini þat tapised bi þat side, Now Iuor..aspied...
to purueie þam a skulkyng, on þe Englis eft to ride.
.leyen an enbuschement......
Bot Ine had þe Englis euerilkon at wille,
bot Segbert of Estsex at home left stille; ......he lefte.
he was of grete elde & myght not trauaile. ...so gret.he...
Bot Iuor & Ini þe Englis gan þam assaile;
þe Englis were bolde & drofe þam to þe sand.
Þe fled out of Wales away tille Ireland. Þey.......
The Englis kynges turned, þei mot do no more,
bot soiorned þam a while in rest a Bangore, ...at.
þat ilk a kyng of reame suld mak him alle redie. [*Transp. L*]
.....Roiwme schulde..redy
At þe Paske after, þe Kyng Ine gart crie, [*Transp. L*] ....Ine dide gie a gy
home forto wend to childe & to wife,
to visitte þer londes, to solace þer life.
Ine, kyng of Westsex, for his wife sent, ...he sente
vnto Malmcestre þe quene tille him went; ......so wente
dede him toke & he died, als it salle do vs. [*Transp. L*]
Ine þe kyng had a sonne, his name Adellus; [*Transp. L*] ....was Hedellus
sorow & site he made, þer was non oþer rede, Wo & sorewe he......
for his sonne & heyre þat so sone was dede. ...& his Eyr.....
Ine was kyng of Westsex sex & þritty ȝere;

fulle wele he ȝemed þe lond fro wo & fro wehere. ....wer
Iuor & Ini oft did he þam chace, ...eft he dide þem.
in his tyme to rise had þei neuer grace;
tuenty grete batailes Ine ouerkam. ...Kyng Iny.
Þe quene withouten childe, non heyre of hir nam.
..deide wyþ childe...hure nam
Ine went to Rome als in pilgremage;
Adelard, his cosyn, he gaf his heritage. Til Athelard his.....
Þe pape him asoyled in treuth stedfast;
whan he had don his penance, he ȝald to god þe gaste.
......to god he ȝald his gast
Adelard of Westsex was kyng of þe empire,
of Noreis & Surreis, guyour of ilk schire.
He ne suffred neuere wrath to be aboue
bituex kyng, baron, þat ne he mad ay loue.
.kyng & baron but euere he made loue
[97r] Alle þe Bretons he ouercome þat wild him assaile,
& in his þirtende ȝere force gan him faile; ...þrettenþe..þen gan..
tille Vttred, his kosyn, a stiffe knyght in stoure,
he gaf his kyngdom & died in langoure. ..al his Kynedam....
He ligges at Bathe, for þider was he born; .lyþ in toumbe at......
þe holy man, Saynt Bede, died a ȝere beforn.
Henry of Huntyngton, sen þat day & þat ȝere,
to write Inglis gestes, fond he non his pere.
A bisshop of Lincoln, Alisandre he hight,
praied him to write þe gestes þat were right; He praied....stories...
þerfor þis Henry is cald a compiloure.
He wrote þe Englis gestes whilom of honoure,
þus wrote to þe bisshop Henry þe same. ..he to þe bischop þys Henry in same
He sais þis lond hight Bretayn þat now has oþer name, .seyde......haþ oure.
Inglond now is cald for Inglis men, we fynd; ..ys hit cald.....
þe folk þat is þerin, it is of diuers kynd.
He sais þis lond has suffred so many tyme wo,
fiue sorowes he writes, withouten oþer mo. Of fyue......
Þo ilk fiue sorowes he calles fiue woundes .....calleþ hem..
þat ere not ȝit haled, ne salle be many stoundes. ....furgetene.....
Noþeles þe clerk Merlyn sais certeyn ....seiþ þys for.
þat Bretons at þe last salle haf þis lond agayn
whan Cadwaldre salle calle with him þe Kyng Konan;
what tyme it salle falle, ȝit wote no man. .....ne wot..
Now of fiue sorowes þat ȝit not endid are, ..þyse fyue......
Henry in his writyng telles what þei ware.
The first of þise fiue was þorgh Romeyns .firste wounde.....þe Romayns

þat wan it of Casbalan into þer demeyns.
Grete treuage þei toke of þis lond here,
þre þousand pounde of gold to paye ilk a ȝere;
& four hundred ȝere lastid þat ilk wo, ... wynter. þat wo
þei mad þe lond fulle pouere, þe folk did þei slo.
Þe toþer sorow of þis lond, mykelle gan it greue;
þe Scottes & þe Peihtes togider gan þei cheue
to waste alle Northumberland, þe godes away þei ledde,
þat men with þe bestes in feldes þei þam fedde.
Þe þrid sorow of þis lond com þorgh þe Sessons ...... þorough Saxons
þat ten siþes aryued vppon þe Bretons,
& siþen were chaced ageyn aw with maistrie, ... al..
& eft aryued on þam here þorgh quantise of spie. .... of a spie
At þe last þei chaced out þe Bretons so clene,
away vnto Wales þer kynd is, I wene. Into Walys & Cornewaille.....
[97v] Þe Englis of þis lond þe lordschip þei toke
& haf it ȝit in þer hond, þe Bretons forsoke.
Þe ferthe sorow of þis lond com þorgh þe Danes;
þe folk of þe north slouh, destroied þer wanes. & slowe þe Northerne folk...
Siþen wan þei alle þe south, maistrie þei schewed,
& laid þer Dangilde on lered & lewed,
& left þe Inglis þe lond on a forward dere
to pay ilk a hede a peny to þam bi ȝere. .. for ilkan heued......
Þe fift sorow þer after com whan William conqueroure
þat aryued on þis lond, Harald he slouh in stoure,
& barons oþer inouh þat died in þe feld,
þe lond lese þe armes, changed is þe scheld. And þe landes armes. y þe.
Siþen he & his haf had þe lond in heritage
þat þe Inglis haf so lad þat þei lyue in seruage.
He sette þe Inglis to be thralle þat or was so fre.
He þat bigan it alle, in þe geste may ȝe se.
Henry of Huntyngton testimons þis title; ... recordeþ in his.
þe Kyngdom of Westsex, he sais it was not litelle
whan Adelard died þerfro & Vttred þerto went.
Vttred, in his first ȝere, messengers he sent ...... out he.
for kynges & barons vntille his parlement;
in stede þer he it sette, þei wist what it ment. .... wiste wel...
Bot Eadbald it withsaid, kyng of Lyndesay; Sire Edbal he wyþseyde him...
he was of þe Bretons kynde, he stode of him non eye.
Vttred wrathed him þerfore & ran on him fulle tite,
& tuys þorgh batale in felde was Eadbald disconfite;
ȝit wild he not be war þer bi, so proude he was in herte,
tille he was wonded þe þrid tyme & died also smerte.

Biried he is at Repyndon & in þe kirke he lis. ....Repyngdoun......
(He þat wille not bowe, in skille I hold him vnwis.)
Many tymes on Vttred, Bretons bataile souht;
Vttred was so valiant, he gaf of þam right nouht. Bot Vtred...of hem gaf he..
He regned fiftene ȝere & died alle to rathe; Vtred........
he ligges biried als a kyng in þe toun of Bathe.
After Vttred regned Sibriht his kosyn;
he luffed wele þe Bretons, þat com tille ille fyn. ....Iuel.
He bare him so tille his barons þat noiþer ȝong ne olde
wald vnto him bowe ne bliþeli of him holde. Wolde nought til hym......
What did þe barons alle with þis fole Sibriht?
Chaced him fro his reame & chese anoþer knyght;
Kynewolf, of þe kynred of Adelardes blode,
a while lufed þe Inglis & wele with þam stode. Þat whilom loued.......
[98r] Sibriht, þat schrew, as a lordan gan lusk;
a suynhird smote he to dede vnder a thorn busk. ...hym to deþe....
Kynewolf toke þe kyngdom, for better mot not falle,
& siþen toke þe feaute of þe kynges alle
as his ancestres had it beforhand. ..þre auncestres had..
Bot of Kent & Lyndesay & Northumberland, Boþe.....of.
þise þre kynges geynsaid it hym, ...ageyn seyd..
& Kynwolf to þo þre bare him so brym; ...þem alle þre....
so wis he was in dede, of body so valiant,
with dynt of suerd & drede, he mad þam recreant. .....dede....
Kyng was Kynwolf sex & tuenty ȝere;
he was neuer wedded to womans daungere,
no childe had he neuer his heritage myght to wende,
bot welth inouh to welde vntille his lyues ende.
At Wynchestre he lis, þider men him bare; ..þer he lys & þider...
fulle frely he lyued here, his soule with god it fare.
Whan þe Kyng Kynwolf had don his endyng,
Brittrk, his kosyn, þei lift him to kyng. Bryttryk.......
Offa, kyng of Lyndsay, a faire douhter had; .þe Kyng.....he hadde
Brittrik hir wedded & quene home hir lad. ..spoused.....
Whan he had regned foure ȝere, one ryued vpon his right,
a duke of Danmark, Kebriht he hight.
Britrik had a stiward, his name was Herman;
Kebriht he kept at Humber & on him he ran. ......þer on hym ran
Hard was þe bataile als þei togider stynt;
Herman was þer slayn, þe duke gaf þe dynt.
Ageyn to Danmark Kebriht gan schake
þat þe Kyng Kebriht ne myght him ouertake;
So þat..Brittrik might hym nought.

he mot not venge Herman of Kebriht þat him slouh,
....Kybright of Herman.he.
he did his ost turne agayn & had sorow inouh.
In his elleuent ȝere, com folk þat misleued,
aryued on Brittrik & sore þei him greued. .vpon..sore hym agreued
Þore Brittrik bare him so in þat ilk bataile,
þe dede ȝede Danes to, þe Noreis gan him vaile.
To deþe ȝede þe Danes Wo þe Norreys...
Edburgh hight þe quene þat I ore of ment;
scho purueied a poyson to þe kyng sonne of Kent.
Hatred before was, Saynt Bede herd, I say,
ffor eld hate byfore hand as..herde hit seye
biten þe kyng of Kent & þe kyng of Lyndsay. Bytwene a Kyng.......
Eilred of Lyndesay alle Kent he wasted;
þe kyng after, I say, to hate often he tasted.
Wherfore..afterward to greue hym ofte..
Þe was of Lyndesay als I ore told; Þe Quen....y ȝow er.
scho purueid þat poyson þorgh hatered of old.
[98v] Brittrik, hir lord, þat scho nouht wiste, .hure owen....nought ne.
vnwarned drank þerof a drauht als him liste.
He lyued bot a moneth, þerof gan he die; Þenne lyuede he bute..for....
at Teukesbiri in toumbe his body did lie.
Sibriht þat I of told þat þe lond had lorn,
þat a suynhird slouh vnder a busk of thorn, ...hadde slayn.....
had a kosyn hight Egbriht whilom exiled was
þorh þe Kyng Brihtrik (I ne wote for what trispas). ....cas
Þis ilk Egbriht was norised at Paris .....in ffraunce at.
in Charlemayn courte, sire of Saynt Dinys. ..cour was lord...
Ailrik was his fader, a duke of faire fame,
lord of Wicombe, of Redynges, & of Tame.
His moder was Sibriht sister, þat was a fole kyng.
Þat Brittrik was dede, him com tiþing; ....Egbright herde.
he toke leue at Charles & com tille þis lond;
among his riche kynde, gode frendes he fond.
What þorgh lowe of lond & olde auncestrie, ..lawe.....
wan he þe regne of Westsex alle pleynerlie.
Gat he þe Reome..wyþ sleiþe al priuely
Whan he pleynere seyseyn in þat his eam had lorn
þat his fiue ancestres had holden beforn,
þorghout þe south to þe north he had for grete nyth;
if any Breton were fonden, holdand lond or lyth,
þat he suld voide þe lond, if he his life wild saue.
Many fled to Lynday socour forto haue, ...Lyndeseye...

to þe Kyng Bernewolf þat was Breton, ...a Breton
& he withsaid his feaute þat he suld haf don.
Bituex þise tuo kynges a werre bigan;
slayn was Bernewolf & with him many man. & slayn was sire.....a man
Vnder Elendoune þe bataile was smyten;
men syng in þat cuntre, fele ȝit it witen,
"Elendoune, Elendoune, þi lond is fulle rede
of þe blode of Bernewolf þer he toke his dede."
After þat bataile, Egbriht, þus herd I say,
seised Kent & Estsex, Southsex & Surray,
& alle þe grete lond fro Douer to Grymsby. .also al þe lond....
Wilaf, Bernewolf sonne, þerwith had envy;
he wild haf venged his fadere if he had haued myght,
bot he fond no force agayn þe Kyng Egbriht;
if he wild ouht haue after, after his fader decesse, ...haue after...
nedly him bihoued com tille Egbriht pes.
At þe last he com & mad þe kyng homage;
Egbriht for his curteisie gaf him his heritage.
[99r] Egbriht of alle þe lond had þe regaute, ...regalte
fro Douere vnto Tuede, alle was his fee. ......of his fe
Wilaf with him he led, Wales forto se.
Bangore with force þei toke þat cite; & Bangor al wyþ.....
þe Walsch men it sauh, it mot no better be; ...þat seye hit mighte...
þei com befor Egbriht & mad him feaute.
Sone after þe wyntere, whan þe somer bigan,
þe kyng & his meyne went to Burgh Konan.
It was on Whitsonday in tyme of slepyng,
kom messengers of þe north & teld Egbriht þe kyng
þorgh ffrithbald, a lord of þe northende, .a Knyght Sire ffrethebald.....
& said, "Sir Egbriht, our chefe kyng to tille lende, ...to wham we holly.
suffre not Sir ffrethebald long to lede þis pyne.
His folk beside Tuede es slayn & kast þer ine. [*Line order in L is 268, 266, 267.*]
He is now in poynt his regne forto tyne;
þorgh þam of Danmark, þis lond wille þei wyne,
.þe Danes of...þey þenke wynne
& if þei Sir ffrethebald haf now ouercomen,
þe to þere remenant of þe north son salle þei nomen.
Þat oþer remenaunt......haue nomen
Sir, for þis hie feste & for þe trinite, ...holy.....
suffre vs nouht to lese for defaute of þe." ...to be lorn in...
What did Kyng Egbriht withouten any somons,
& withouten askyng of erles or barons?
He hied him þider suyth, & whan he com to Tuede,

he sauh suylk oste of paiens þat alle he was in drede;
. sey such ost of Paynymes......
neuerþeles at Karham was þe bataile gyuen.
Þe kyng was narow holden, his folk alle to dryuen;
... straite holdes .. was al ..
tuo dukes & tuo bisshopes foreuer toke þer leue.
Þe kyng was alle affraied, þer dede gan him greue;
þe kynges folk was litelle, it had no dure. .....& hadde ..
On þe nyght he fled away þat non suld him se;
myght he neuer noure fynd a restyng place, ...nowhere....
right vnto Donkastre þe Danes gan him chace.
Whan he wend haf passed þo þat gan him dryue,
þan were aryued in Humber þritty schippes & fyue,
ilkon with folk inouh redy to bataile.
"God wate," said þe kyng, "now comes me trauaile!"
Dardan hight þe cheftayn of þat company,
Sadok sonne, of Danmark Kyng Danesry. ....Kyng of Denescherye
Þer pauillons had þei sette beside þe water of Done;
Egbriht gadred partie & ȝared him fulle sone.
Listen now how Ihesu criste for his mykelle mercy .....of his grete .
agayn þe fals paiens þe cristen stode he by.
[99v] Sibriht, duke of Brailes, Egbriht sister sonne,
he com his eam to socour fro fer þer he gan wonne.
Yward, þe gode Westreis, Edald þe vauasoure, Þider wente þe.....
Wilaf, kyng of Merce, he com to þat stoure;
Harald of Donsmore, his lord þider led,
Berald of þe Marche, of strength non he dred.
Haldayn of Donkastre was chosen þat ilk day
to bere þe kynges banere ageyn þe paien lay.
Bot Hakon, Hernebald sonne, of best he bare þe voice:
in stede of kynges banere, he did him bere þe croice
in wirschip of Ihesu & of his passion;
þe paiens were so ferd þei myght haf no foyson.
Þe ferth day of Septembre in þe heuest tide, ...heruest .
at Donkastre mot men se manyon to batale ride,
þat to þe Kyng Egbriht alle were þei gyuen
for þer heritage þer to die or lyuen.
Þei hewe on þe paiens as men of wille gode,
þe paiens ageyn þam fulle stifely þei stode; ...our Cristen ful...
þei fauht alle þat day ne left þei not þe nyght.
....ilke day þey lefte nought þat .
Wilaf, þe kyng of Merce, was slayn in þat fight,
& Berald of þe Marche, & þe Duke Vttre, . Berard.... also Sire Vttre

lord of Cirencestre, þat night slayn was he. Þe noble Duk of……
Alle þat nyght þe kynges folk fulle ille were þei led;
manyon was slayn & wonded hard bisted. . were þer slayn & manion . .
Right in þe mornyng in aldermost nede, …. . þer moste .
com þe kynges sonnes tuo, als criste wild it rede,
out of Germinie with folk inouh of myght,
Adelwolf & Ethelbert, knyghtes boþe fulle wyght.
Was neuer in alle his lyue þer fadere ore so glad
als whan he sauh his sons tuo, þe paiens force to sprad.
Adelwolf his fader saued at þat ilk iorne,
& Ethelbert in þe felde, his fader lete he se
how Dardan for his lance doun to þe erth went
& smote his hede of, his fader to present.
Harald of Donesmore vppon Done him mette;
Vibrand, Dardanes broþer, with suerd so him grette Wybrond. . . . he . .
þat þorghout his armes Wibrand alle to hewe; . . al his harneys. . . .
sone with þe Danes gamned þam no glewe. So þat wyþ . . . þer . .
Þat perceyued Haldayn þat bare þe croice on hie, [*Transp. L*]
sex & þritty paiens enbussed priuelie. [*Transp. L*] . . . . were busched .
He tok his suerd in hand, þe croyce lete he falle,
& medeled him in þe pres among þe barons alle.
[100r] Before þe kyng & his sons he rimthed þam þe way; ……. remede hem . .
many wer þe paiens þat Haldayn did slouh þat day. …… dide þer deye
Bituex vnderon & noen was þe feld alle wonnen, . vndern . þe Noon . . . . .
for alle þat wild abide were ouer riden & ronnen. . . þe false Danes were. . . .
Þe kyng with þe maistrie went in to þe toun;
þe pris he had wonnen in vertew of cristes passioun.
Whan he had done þere alle þat he suld do,
he went vnto Wynchestre his conseile gaf him so.
Vnto þe somerestide, þer gan he lende,
fyue & þritty batailes had he brouht tille ende.
He felt hym heuy & ferly seke, his body wex alle seere;
. felde hym take wyþ siknesse his. . . .
his childre he wild auance tille he o lyue were. . . . . . while. . . .
Tille Adelwolf gaf he Westsex, hede of alle þe thede,
lordschip ouer alle þe londes bituex Douer & Tuede. …… Berewyk . .
Ethelbert held Estsex, Southsex, & Kent,
for homage & feaute tille Adelwolf it went . . . . . Athelwold . .
Whan Egbriht had feffed his sons in londes seere, ……. landes þer
now in his last ende of fyue & þritty ȝere,
at Wynchestre he died & þer his body is laid.
Was neuer þe lond so ȝemed, þe folk so þan said.
…… als manie a man hit seyd

Fyue childir he had, knyghtes douhty of handes,
& alle were þei kynges in diuers landes.
Adelwolf of Westsex, after his fadere dede,
at Chestre sette his parlement, his tenantȝ þerto bede. ......barons..
He sent for alle þe kynges fro Berwik vnto Kent,
& þei with fulle gode wille alle vnto him went
& mad tille him feaute withouten any chest,
& cleymed him for þer chefe of West & of Est,
of North & of South in length & in brede,
fro Kent vntille Berwik als lastes alle þat thede.
He was first of Inglond þat gaf god his tiþe Kyng Athelwolf was þe firste.....
of isshue of bestes, of londes or of liþe.
Siþen he went to Rome as man of holy wille,
his sonne & he alle þat ȝere with þe pape duelled stille.
Þe toþer ȝere next after his duellyng, ...next folowyng...
he went home bi France & spak with þe kyng;
þe kyng him his douhter, hir name was Iuwet, ..gaf hym.....Iuet
fulle wele on Sir Adelwolf was þat maiden sett.
He brouht hir Inglond & siþen lyued tuo ȝere; ..hure til......
he lies at Wynchestre beside an autere. Hys body lyþ.....
Þre þousand marke he gaf with testament fulle right
to Petir & Paule of Rome to susteyn þer light.
[100v] After Adelwolf, his sonne, hight Edbalde,
to ȝere & a half þe regne gan he halde.
Of him in Holy Kirke men said euelle sawe: ......an yuel.
his stepmoder, Iuwet, he weddid agayn þe lawe;
of his body was no force, non for him wild murne.
Bot þus I fond in my boke, he lies at Schirburne.
Þe date of criste to neuen þus fele were gon, ...nemne...þer gon
auht hundreth euen & sexti & on.
After Edbalde com Ethelbert his eam,
Adelwolfes broþer, of Egbrihtes team.
He did him coroune kyng, he was a noble man,
& in his first ȝere, paiens on him ran,
right at Wynchestre ageyn þam gan he stand; ....hym gan þey stonde
þe kyng þam bataile & did þam fle þe land. ..þer gaf hem bataille......
In werryng & in wo he regned fyue ȝere;
men biried him at Schireburn, Edbald fulle nere.
Þe date of Ihesu criste was writen in þis lyue,
auht hundreth wynter, sexti & fyue.
After Ethelbert com Elfrith, his broþer
þat was Egbrihtes sonne, & ȝit þer was anoþer:
Elfride þorgh heritage toke him þe coroune

& gaf Alfride, his broþer, Surray to warisoune.
Tille Elfride oure kyng com tiþinges starke
þat fyue kynges & fyue erles wer comen of Danmarke
þat wild on him renne & reue him þe coroune;
with alle þer grete folk þei lay in Aluertoune. ....people....
[*L adds:*] Norhumland was taken & don destruccioun
Al was þeires vntil 3ork Þe land vp & doun
Þe kyng & his broþer þat hight Alfrede
gadred folk togider als men þat had nede
& com to þe bataile with fulle egre herte;
þe Danes stode þam ageyn with bataile fulle smerte.
In þe passion tyme was þe first bataile;
nene was þat ilk ȝere, grete was þer trauaile. Nyne were.......
Þe toþer ȝere, þe þrid day after Halwethurs tide, ...þe Halythurstyde
þe Danes, þorgh godes grace, were on þe wers side, ...help.....
for slayn were þei alle, erle & baron.
Þe kyng did mak at 3ork a faire procession
& þanked Ihesu criste with hert fulle mylde
þat ageyn þe paiens his lond myght schilde. Þat he.......
Elfride had a kosyn þat kyng was of schelde, ...elde
Northfolk & Southfolk of Elfride he helde,
þat was Saynt Edmunde þe croune þat tyme bare.
A duke of Danmark, his name was Inguare, A Duk cam out of.....
[101r] Vbbe, an erle of Huneis, with þat Inguar kam
vppon Saynt Edmunde, Northfolk he nam.
Edmunde sent his messengers, of pes þam bisouht;
Inguar sent bode ageyn þat pes wild he nouht, .sente hym bode......
bot if he ȝald him þe lond, þan he suld haf pes;
þat wild not Saynt Edmunde, þe bataile he ches. ....raþer he ches
He atired him to bataile with folk þat he had, .ordeined........
bot þis cursed Danes so grete oste ay lad .þyse.....þey.
þat Edmunde was taken and slayn at þe last.
Fulle fer fro þe body lay was þe hede kast; ..fro þer þe......
þe body son þei fonde, þe hade was in doute. ..sone men founde þe heued...
Vp & doune in þe felde þei souht it aboute
to haf knowyng þerof, alle þei were in were, ...þey were al in a wher
tille þe hede himself said, "Here, Here, Here!"
Þer þei fond þe hede is now a faire chapelle,
Oxen hate þe toun þer þe body felle; Hoxene hatte now......
þer where he was schotte, anoþer chapelle standes In þe stede þer he.....
& somwhat of þat tre þei bond vntille his handes.
Þe tone is fro þe toþer moten a grete myle; ......about...
so fer bare a woulfe þe hede & kept it a grete while

vnto þe hede said, "Here," als I befor said;
fro þe woulf þei it toke, vnto þe body it laid. ....token hit & to þe...
Men sais þer he ligges þe flesch samen ȝede, .seyþ ȝit þere....to gydere.
bot þe token of þe wonde als a rede threde. .a tokne...þat like ys a..
Now lies he in schryne in golde þat is rede; ....ys so red
seuen ȝere was he kyng, þat tyme þat he was dede. ..had he be.......
In þe ȝere after, right in þe tyme of May,
Oseth, þe Danes kyng, com Inglond to affray.
He aryued at Berwik in þe water of Tuede,
priue help of þe Scottes he had at his nede,
& com fast toward þe south, grete powere he led.
Elfride & his broþere out of ȝork fled;
þei praied god specially þat he wild þam saue
& ageyn þe Danes, help inouh to haue.
At þe poynt of þe bataile displayed his banere;
þe kyng ȝede to þe kirke, his messe forto here.
Bot Alfride, his broþer, ȝede to þe bataile;
he was ouer hardy, þe Danes he gan assaile.
Discomfite was Alfride within a litelle throwe;
þe kyng herd þat telle þat his side ȝede lowe. ..þen herde telle.....
He dight him to þe bataile, his folk to socoure.
God did faire miracle for Elfride þat houre,
[101v] for non of þe Danes askaped with þe life,
bot þe Scottes kyng þat mayntend þat strife
opon Elfride ran als traytoure inferd. ..he ran as.ful ferd
Elfride he wonded with dynt of a suerd; Elfred þat.......
sex ȝere was he kyng, with werre weldid þe scheld;
fulle gode was his endyng, he ligges at Driffeld.
Þof alle þat he werred in wo & in strife,
þe foure & tuenty houres he spended in holy life:
þe first .viii. houres in preyere alderbest; In þe firste eyghte....
þe toþer .viii. houres in slepe & in rest;
In þe oþere eyghte he slep & hadde his rest
þe þrid .viii. houres he studied how he myght
mayntene þe lond with lawe, his folk hald to right. .his landes lawes.....
Haluendele his godes he gaf to godes werkes,
sustened abbeis, norised pouer clerkes; .Relygions &.pore.
did reise vp kirkes þat were fallen doun, He dide.......
& alle þat him serued he brouht to warisoun. .....he gaf hem.
Þe ȝere of cristes birth was auht hundreth euen
& þus many mo, sexty & elleuen.
Alfride, his broþer, a gode clerk was he one, .þat was his.......
of body so douhty in Inglond was none, So doughti man of bodye in...

he resceyued þe coroune after his broþer dede;
strong were þe batailes þe Danes on him bede.
Tuo & tuenty batailes he wanne þe first ȝere;
þe Danes so many tymes aryued on him here, ...fele siþe....
þat he so many slouh, a duke had envie ...manie of hem.....
& eft aryued on þis lond with fulle grete nauie.
Rollo was his name, a knyght fulle douhty,
þat Alfride wend wele haf lorn þe seignory. ffor wham þat Alfrid haue lost..
Whan þei com to bataile, ilk oþer gan askie; ...to þe....aske
Alfride vnto Rollo sone gan him alie,
so many douhty dyntes was bituex þam tueye; ....were.hem beye
wele þei did togidere, better may no man seye.
God þorgh his grace þat day so wele sped Alfrid þorow godes grace.....
þat Rollo asked cristendom at þe Kyng Alfred.
Þorgh þat cristendom, þo þat were so wroþe, ..holy.þey þat er were.
at Haly Kirkes fayth, alle on were boþ. ....þey boþe
Rollo was kald Roberd whan he was baptiȝed
þorgh þe Kyng Alfride als he had deuised.
Now is Roberd cristen, he dightes his nauie
& ferde ouer þe see & conquerd Normundie;
duke þan was he cald þorgh conquest of hond. ....his hond
Alfrid he left stille here in Inglond.
[102r] ȝit anoþer Danes kyng in þe norþ gan aryue;
Alfrid it herd, þidere gan he dryue. Sire Alfrid þat herde seye &....
Hauelok fader he was, Gunter was his name;
he brent citees & tounes, ouer alle did he schame.
Saynt Cutbertes clerkes þo Danes þei dred, ...þo Danes so..
þe toke þe holy bones, about þei þam led; ......wyþ hem þey.
seuen ȝere þorgh þe land wer þei born aboute,
it comforted þe kyng mykelle whan he was in doute.
Whan Alfred & Gunter had werred long in ille, ...wiþ.
þorgh þe grace of god Gunter turned his wille;
cristend wild he be, þe kyng of fonte him lift, [*Transp. L*]
Crysten men þey wolde be....þem.
& þritty of his knyghtes turnes þorgh godes gift. [*Transp. L*]
Þo þat first were foos & com of paien lay, ...þat leued on..
of cristen men haf los & so þei wend away. ...þey haue þe.....
Bot I haf grete ferly þat I fynd no man [*L om. 519–538; the Havelok interpolation is below at 538*.]
þat has writen in story how Hauelok þis lond wan:
noiþer Gildas, no Bede, no Henry of Huntynton,
no William of Malmesbiri, ne Pers of Bridlynton
writes not in þer bokes of no Kyng Athelwold,

ne Goldeburgh, his douhtere, ne Hauelok not of told.
Whilk tyme þe were kynges, long or now late,
þei mak no menyng whan, no in what date.
Bot þat þise lowed men vpon Inglish tellis,
right story can me not ken þe certeynte what spellis.
Men sais in Lyncoln castelle ligges ȝit a stone
þat Hauelok kast wele forbi euerilkone,
& ȝit þe chapelle standes þer he weddid his wife,
Goldeburgh, þe kynges douhter, þat saw is ȝit rife,
& of Gryme, a fisshere, men redes ȝit in ryme
þat he bigged Grymesby, Gryme þat ilk tyme.
Of alle stories of honoure þat I haf þorgh souht,
I fynd þat no compiloure of him tellis ouht.
Sen I fynd non redy þat tellis of Hauelok kynde,
turne we to þat story þat we writen fynde.

[*L has the following instead of 519–538 of P*.]

Forþ wente Gounter & his folk al in to Denemark
Sone fel þer hym vpon a werre styþ & stark
Þurgh a Breton kyng þat out of Ingeland cam
& asked þe tribut of Denmark þat Arthur whylom nam
Þey wyþseide hit schortly & non wolde þey ȝelde
But raþer þey wolde dereyne hit wyþ bataille y þe felde
Boþ partis on a day to felde come þey stronge
Desconfit were þe Danes Gounter his deþ gan fonge
When he was ded þey schope brynge al his blod to schame
But Gatferes doughter þe Kyng Eleyne was hure name
Was Kyng Gounteres wyf & had a child hem bytwene
Wyþ wham scheo scapede vneþe al to þe se wiþ tene
Þe child hym highte Hauelok þat was his moder dere
Scheo mette wiþ Grym atte hauene a wel god marinere
He hure knew & highte hure wel to helpe hure wiþ his might
To brynge hure saf out of þe lond wyþinne þat ilke night
When þey come in myd se a gret meschef gan falle
Þey metten wyþ a gret schip lade wyþ outlawes alle
Anon þey fullen hem apon & dide hem mikel peyne
So þat wyþ strengþe of þeir assaut ded was quene Eleyne
But ȝyt ascapede from hem Grym wyþ Hauelok & oþer fyue
& atte þe hauene of Grymesby þer þey gon aryue
Þer was brought forþ child Hauelok wyþ Grym & his fere
Right als hit hadde be þer owen for oþer wyste men nere
Til he was mykel & mighti & man of mykel cost
Þat for his grete sustinaunce nedly serue he most
He tok leue of Grym & Seburc as of his sire & dame

And askede þer blessinge curteysly þer was he nought to blame
Þenne drow he forth Norþward to kynges court Edelsie
Þat helde fro Humber to Rotland þe kyngdam of Lyndesye
Þys Edelsy of Breton kynde had Orewayn his sister bright
Maried to a noble kyng of Norþfolk Egelbright
Holly for his kyngdam he held in his hand
Al þe lond fro Colchestre right in til Holand
Þys Egelbright þat was a Dane & Orewayn þe quene
Hadden gete on Argille a doughter hem bytwene
Sone þen deyde Egelbright & his wyf Orewayn
& þerfore was Kyng Edelsye boþe ioyful & fayn
Anon þeir doughter & here Eyr his nece dame Argille
& al þe kyngdam he tok in hande al at his owene wille
Þer serued Hauelok as quistron & was ycald Coraunt
He was ful mykel & hardy & strong as a Geaunt
He was bold Curteys & fre & fair & god of manere
So þat alle folk him louede þat anewest hym were
But for couetise of desheritison of damysele Argille
& for a chere þat þe kyng sey scheo made Coraunt tille
He dide hem arraye ful symplely & wedde togydere boþe
ffor he ne rewarded desparagyng were manion ful wroþe
A while þey dwelt after in court in ful pore degre
Þe schame & sorewe þat Argille hadde hit was a deol to se
Þen seyde scheo til hure maister of whenne sire be ȝe
Haue ȝe no kyn ne frendes at hom in ȝoure contre
Leuer were me lyue in pore lyf wyþoute schame & tene
Þan in schame & sorewe lede þe astat of quene
Þenne wente þey forþ to Grymesby al by his wyues red
& founde þat Grym & his wyf weren boþe ded
But he fond þer on Aunger Grymes cosyn hend
To wham þat Grym & his wyf had teld word & ende
How þat hit stod wyþ Hauelok in alle manere degre
& þey hit hym telde & conseilled to drawe til his contre
Tasaye what grace he mighte fynde among his frendes þere
& þey wolde ordeyne for þeir schipynge & al þat hem nede were
When Aunger hadde yschiped hem þey seilled forþ ful swyþe
ffulbut in til Denemark wyþ weder fair & liþe
Þer fond he on Sire Sykar a man of gret pouste
Þat hey styward somtyme was of al his fader fe
fful fayn was he of his comyng & god help hym bihight
To recouere his heritage of Edulf kyng & knyght
Sone asembled þey gret folk of his sibmen & frendes
Kyng Edulf gadered his power & ageyn þem wendes

Desconfyt was þer Kyng Edulf & al his grete bataille
& so conquered Hauelok his heritage saunȝ faille
Sone after he schop hym gret power in toward Ingelond
His wyues heritage to wynne ne wolde he nought wonde
Þat herde þe kyng of Lyndeseye he was come on þat cost
& schop to fighte wyþ hym sone & gadered hym gret host
But atte day of bataille Edelsy was desconfit
& after by tretys gaf Argentille hure heritage al quit
& for scheo was next of his blod Hauelokes wyf so feyr
He gaf hure Lyndesey after his day & made hure his Eyr
& atte laste so byfel þat vnder Hauelokes schelde
Al Northfolk & Lyndeseye holy of hym þey helde

[*L resumes the text as in P*.]

Sone after com an erle, Alfden hight þat hunde, ...a Danisch Erl....
aryued vp with Inguar þat slouh Saynt Edmunde,
vpon þe Kyng Alfrid werre son began.
Bot þorgh þe gode northeren, slayn wer ilk a man;
sex & fifty batailes Alfrid ouercam.
After nyen & tuenty ȝere, þe dede him hiþen nam, ...deþ.hennes.
& sex monethes mo, þus þe story said.
At Wynchestre in toumbe in þe Abbay is he laid;
[102v] þe date þat certeyn es in boke writen here,
nouþer more no lesse þan nien hundreth ȝere.
After þis Alfride kom Edward þe olde; .þe noble Alfred....
faire man he was, & wis, stalworth, & bolde. ....men tolde
At London at Saynt Poules toke he þe croune
& purueied his parlement of erle & baroune. An assingned a.....
He seid vnto þam alle þat purueied suld it be ......ordeyned...
þat in alle þe lond suld be no kyng bot he;
.no Kyng schuld be y þys lond but alone he
þe smale kynges of þe lond alle were þei comen,
of Scotland, of Wales, of Kombirlond þei nomen,
Inglis & Danes, & þe gode Norreis,
duke, erle, & baron, & oþer knyghtes curteis.
Þei said in þat parlement þorgh conseile of alle
þat Edward felle best be chefe, oþer suld non falle.
Now is Edward chosen kyng at þer parlement
& þe lordschip of þe lond alle tille him went.
ffourtene childre he gate opon tuo wifes,
sex sonnes & auht douhtres, þo were faire lyues:
Athelstan, Edwyn, Edgar, Edmond, Edred, Edwy.
Hilde was his douhter, was kald Hilden Lady.
Elfled & Saynt Eadburgh þat lyued holy life; [*L differs*:]

Elfled þat oþer sister þat þurght wyt & queyntyse
Halp hure broþer mayntene þe lond in god assise
Seint Edburgh was þe þridde þat liuede holy lyf
þe ferth Octouian Mary þat emperoures wife. ..Marie Octouian þe..
Þei passed of þis world whan þei were right ȝonge;
what þer names were I kan telle no tonge. .alle þer.....wiþ no.
In Edwardes tend ȝere, aryued vp in Kent
þre kynges & sex dukes þat out of Danmark went;
in to Lyndsay brouht þei him tiþng ......tydynge
& purueied oste & dight him als a douhty kyng.
He assembled his host & schop for þeym..noble.
At Teteford in Northfolk his banere was displaied;
þe þre kynges were slayn, þe toþer were affraied
þat þei went to þer schippes, so hard he sette his chace,
Edward had þe maistri & þanked god his grace.
He com neuer to bataile þat he ne had þe maistrie;
foure & tuenty ȝere was he kyng, & þorgh no folie,
neuer in his lyue a fote of lond he les.
Scotland & Cumberland & Wales he had in pes,
Cornwaile, Lyndsay & Kent, Dorsette & Surreie. [*Om. L*]
He ligges at Wynchestre, þe soth it is to seie, [*Om. L*]
þe date of god, nien hundreth & four & tuenti mo. ..was nyne......
Whan dede his lyfe sundred, þe folk for him was wo.
When he was bured at Wynchestre þe.....
After Edward þe olde regned Athelstan
þat was his eldest sonne & a noble man.
[103r] Þe baronage & þe clergie were somond to Kyngeston;
þer wes his fest holden & gyuen him þe croune. .was........
Þe next ȝere after his coronment, ...folowyng after þe.
þe Walsh men þat luf no pes on him ran & brent.
Bot Athelstan þe maistrie wan & did þam mercie crie,
& alle Northwales he set to treuage hie:
tuenti pounde of gold be ȝere, thre hundreth of siluer clere,
& þer to fyue hundreth kie ilk ȝere to his lardere. ....þousand kyn by ȝere...
Siluer for Southwales, not a ferþing noke; But he nolde of Southwalys take...
oþer treuage he sette, a þousand kie he toke. But oþer..þem sette.....
Þe ferth ȝere of þe regne, Owald, a werreoure,
Constantyn, of Scotland kyng was & traitoure,
Onwer, kyng of Wentland, þese þre with þer powere
werred on Athelstan with oste fulle austere.
Bot Athelstan þorgh godes grace so with þam fore .....so wente hem byfore
þei were fayn to ask pes & feaute þei him suore.
Þe tend ȝere of his regne sen he was crouned kyng, ...after his corounyng

of Edwyn his broþer bifelle suilk a þing: .....a wonder þyng
at London in his courte with wiknes men him fond. ......yuel...
Athelstan did him bynd both fote & hond
& kast him in tille Temse whan it was most brym;
to chastise alle oþer, he tok vengeance on him.
At myn vnderstandyng, he wild take no mede As men þat tyme tolde he....
þat was ateynt of wikkednes, his broþer to dede ȝede.
Constantyn of Scotlond þat I are of spak,
brak his feaute sone (of treson it is lak) ...ful sone..hit ys a.
& alle folk of Danmark with Constantyn held
& slouh our Inglish men, wasted toun & feld.
Athelstan herd say, he went to Beuerlay ..hit seye....
& praied to þe Bisshop Ion, in fertre þer he lay,
þat he wild bede his bone vntille þe Trinite,
& he suld gyue his kirke franchise & fe
to haf & to holde, als he was kyng leale;
of him haf þei chartre seled with his seale.
Siþen he went to Durham & gaf Saynt Cutbert
londes & liþes with chartir aperte;
þe bisshop of his gift holdes his fe. .....ȝit haldes al..
Siþen he went to bataile, Constantyn to fle;
Constantyn he reymed & did vnto stresse ....put hym tyl destresse
& wan þe lond ilk dele & wasted alle Cathenesse,
& his son ȝolden vnto his ostage;
siþen he turned to London & his baronage.
[103ᵛ] Athelstan in Scotland a selcouth ded he one, ...wonder dide he on
he smote depe at Donbarre an elne in þe stone.

[*L adds:*] Þey seyn ȝit at Dunbarre þat Athelston so smot
An elne dep y þe ston many man hit wot

At þe feste of our Lady, þe Assumpcion,
went þe kyng fro London toward Abindon;
þider out of ffrance fro Charles, kyng of fame,
com þe of Boloyn, Adulphus was his name, Cam þe Erl......
& þe Duke of Burgoyn, Edmunde sonne, Reynere.
Þe brouht Kyng Athelston present withouten pere;
fro Charles, kyng sanȝ faile, þei brouht a gonfaynoun
þat Saynt Morice in bataile befor þe legioun, ...bar in....
& scharp lance þat thrilled Ihesu side, & þe...þyrlede..
& a suerd of gold; in þe hilte did men hide
tuo of þo nayles þat war þorh Ihesu fete
tached on þe croyce, þe blode þei out lete, Were tached to þe......
& som of þe thornes þat don were on his heued,
& a fair pece þat of þe croyce leued ....cros was leued

þat Saynt Heleyn sonne at þe bataile wan
of þe soudan of Askalone, his name was Madan.
Þan blewe þe trumpes fulle loud & fulle schille;
..þey faste trompe boþe loude & schrille
þe kyng com in to þe halle þat hardy was of wille.
Þan spak Reyner, Edmunde sonne, for he was messengere.
"Athelstan, my lord þe gretes, Charles þat has no pere.
He sendes þe þis present & sais he wille him bynde
to þe þorh Ilde, þi sistere, & tille alle þi kynde." .ȝonge Hilde þy......
Befor þe messengers was þe maiden brouht;
of body so gentille was non in erth wrouht,
.fetoures so fair in erthe was þer non ywrought
no non so faire of face, of spech so lufly;
scho granted befor þam alle to Charles hir body,
& so did þe kyng & alle þe baronage. ..dyde þenne þe.....
Mykelle was þe richesse þei purueied hir passage ......to þeir.
& led hir vnto ffrance, spoused forto be.
Athelstan leues stille & passed not þe se. But Athelston he lefte stille.....
[I]n þe ȝere after þat Ilde wedded was, [*Capital om. in P.*]
Constantyn of Scotlond did ȝit more trispas. .þe Scottische Kyng dide more.
He brouht þe Kyng Anlaf, aryued vp in Humbere,
seuen hundreth schippes & fiftene, so fele were þe numbere.
Athelstan herd say of þer mykelle oste;
he & Edmunde, his broþer, dight þam to þat coste.
At Brunesburgh on Humber þei gan þam assaile;
fro morn vnto euen lasted þat bataile.
At þe last, to þer schippes þe kyng gan þam chace,
alle away þei fled, þat was of godes grace,
[104ʳ] bot þe most partie algate was slayn; ....natheles..
þat with þe life fled, I trowe þei were fulle fayn.
& þe fewe þat fledde wyþ þe lyf y.....
Whan þe Kyng Anlaf sauh his folk lorn,
he fled vnto Danmark þer þere he was born.
At þe Pask after, he ryued in þe south
at a hauen of Sandwich in þe portis mouth. Atte toun of...hauenes.
Whan he was aryued, þe folk was affray ......in afray
& com vnto Wynchestre þer þe kyng lay. ffor he cam vntil.....
He brouht with him a deuelle, a hogge geant; ......an huge geaunt
wele haf ȝe herd telle, he hight Colibrant.
Of wham we haue herd telle his name was.
Anlaf sent messengers vnto Athelstan
& bad him ȝeld þe lond or fynd anoþer man ...fighte for þe......
to fight with Colibrant þat was his champion.

Who felle to haf þe lond, on þam it suld be don.
Athelstan tok a day, a parlement did make,
if any ageyn Colibrant þe bataile durst take.
He fond no man þat durst, for non had myght
with Colibrant alone in bataile to fight.
Þan praied Athelstan to criste & sore wepe, ...& ful sore he wep
& god sent him tokenyng on nyght als he slepe
þat he suld fynd a palmere orly at morn ......erlich y þe morn
at þe south ȝate, alone as he was born,
& if he wild praie him for Ihesu cristes loue, .ȝif þou wilt......
he wild do þe bataile & þei suld be aboue. .....þou schalt..
Þat was Guy of Werwik as þe boke sais;
þer he slouh Colibrant with hache Daneis. .slow he..an hache.
Anlaf turned agayn (I trowe him was wo),
he & alle his to schippe gan þei go.
God delyuerde Athelstan of many hard affaies; ......frayes
sextene ȝere was he kyng & seuentene daies.
Siþen at Gloucestre, dede euelle him toke, Syn after..þe deþ...
bot quik he out went, so sais my boke.
(Pers can not say where he lies,
bot as I herd telle, I say myn auys.)
Men say he was fonden in þe north cuntre
at Hexham now late, I wene soth it be.
Þe date whan he died, of god men tellis by,
When he deide þe date of crist was writen redely
nien hundreth wynter & fulle fourty.
After Athelstan, þe kyng was Edmunde his broþer;
þe northren did him desceit & ches þam anoþer,
one Anlaf þei ches & crouned him for kyng.
Alle þe northende was in his kepyng
[104v] & alle þe south ende tille Edmunde þei drouh.
Vpon þe fals Norreis Edmunde wan inouh,
fyue cites he wan þat þei held for þers
þat whilom was ancestres fro heires vnto heires. ..were his auncestres....
Lyncoln, & Derby, & Southampton, Notyngham & Derby & Lyncoln toun
Lycestre, & Stamford, þise fyue wan Edmon,
& yit þe Kyng Anlaf so hard gan he chace .ȝit þat kyng so....
þat he asked cristendom opon godes grace,
boþe he & Reynald, was Guthefrides sonne.
He exilde þam out of þe north þer þei wild wonne
& gaf to Malcolme, kyng of Scotlande, ..hit vntil....
þat he suld be him leale bi se & bi sande. ....land
The fifte ȝere of his regne, he went to Canterbiri,

þe feste of Saynt Austine to hold it fulle myri.
A thefe of his courte was outlawed late; Þer cam a þef......
þe kyng knew him fulle wele, he mette him in þe gate.
Whilom he serued in his panterie
& was outlawed for a felonie. .þer he was....
Þe kyng tok þis pantelere & strangled him right þore
..caughte þat trethour &....
& he wonded þe kyng dedely fulle sore.
Seuen ȝere was he kyng & seuen monethis mo;
at Gloucestre is he laid, þe pantelere did him slo. .Glastyngbury........
Þe date was nien hundreth, fourty & seuen;
þis was þe selcouthest cas þat haf herd neuen. ...wonderest þyng þat y..nemene
Edred after Edmunde had þe coroune;
vpon þe Pask day at London toune,
siþen of alle his barons he tok feaute,
bot þe northeren men held him no leaute.
Eylrike of Danmark for kyng þei him ches
& forsoke Edrede, þer were þei les. ...as false men & les
Edrede with powere vntille þe north went;
alle þe toun of Ripon he wasted & brent. Ripon & al þe Contre he...
Northumberland was in affray for Edred comyng;
þei did doun Eylrik, þe Danes kyng, Þat þen dide.....
& went out of þe lond with his rascaile,
was he not so hardy at stand to bataile. .....to bide þe.
Alle þo Norreis þat had bien so fikelle, .þe false Noreys.....
pes forto haue þei glosed him fulle mykelle;
þer londes & þer rentes were at his wille.
He gaf Saynt Cutbert þerof, ȝit þei hold it stille.
Alle þe regne holy was þat tyme in his hand,
& erles & barons þat wer in þe land,
[105r] so wele were þei chastised, alle com tille his grith
þat þe pes of þe lond þe sikered him alle with. ......þey sykered...
Auht ȝere was he kyng, his daies alle filled;
at Wynchestre he lies, so himself willed. ..was he leyd as..
Þe date, nien hundreth fifty & fyue, ..was Nyne....
whan þat Kyng Edred passed of þis lyue.
After Sir Edred was his broþer Edwy;
he resceyued þe croune of þe seignory. ....& al þe.
So foole a man of his life non was seene;
þe hie men of þe lond conseild þam bituene .gret.......
to do doun Edwy at a parlement
& tille his broþer Edgare gyf þe tenement.
Saynt Donstan þe bisshop was at his coronment, ...corounyng

& of alle his ancestres was neuer better kyng.
He was boþe gode & wys in alle his dedis
& right vnderstandyng to help at alle nedis.
[*L adds:*] ffoles couþe he chaste right dom to gyue
And penaunce for þer trespas þat wel wolde nought lyue
Mikille he wirschiped god & serued our Lady;
þe Abbey of Rumeye he feffed richely ...Romeneye..
with rentes fulle gode & kirkes of pris;
he did þerin of nunnes a hundreth ladies. .putte......
Edgare forto fle lichery of lyfe,
his barons gaf him conseile forto take a wyfe,
Elfled þe faire, þe dukes douhter Ormere.
He gate of hir Saynt Edward þat is þe martere.
Dame Elfled died sone, ȝit wild he luf mare;
he tok bittere Estrild, dukes douhter Orgare; ..Dame Estrilde þe...
of hir lord Edgar had scho sonnes tueye:
Edmunde, þat in his tende ȝere at Peterburgh gan deie,
Eylred was þe ȝongest & Estrild fulle dere,
wo was in his tyme as ȝe may after here. Mikel wo.......now.
Edgar, þer fader, had alle Ingland.
He went to Kerlion, þe Walschmen he band ..in to Walys....
with homage & feaute in right & in lawe.
Kymak, kyng of Scotland, he com for fyne awe, Kymal...cam for..
& Malcolme of Combirland was at his wille; ....he cam wiþ hem in fere
Maccum, kyng of þe Iles, Dufnald fitȝ Omere,
Macoun þe Kyng of Iles & Dufnald fitȝ Ormere
Sifreth & Huwalle, Iacob & Iuthille,
he did þam mak feaute als right was & skille.
Siþen he went aboute, kirkes vp to raise,
abbayes forto help, were fallen in miseyse.
He gaf to Crouland in þe abbot tyme, Gountere,
þre myle of seignorie about his autere. ...lordship..heye.
Auhten ȝere Edgar regned kyng & sire;
he lies in tombe in þe abbey of Glastenbire. Hys body in a toumbe ys leid at.
[105v] Of Edgar þe kyng, þus fond I writen;
Pers telles þe same þing, at his boke may ȝe witen.
Sen four & tuenti ȝere þat he in erth was laid,
an abbot of Glastebiri, Edward his name is said, ...Glastyngbury.....
he did mak a toumbe Edgar in to lay,
bot it was ouer litelle in alle maner way.
Þei brak in tuo his schankes to mak þe toumbe mete;
þe blode was boþe warme & fresh þat of þe schankes lete.
Þe abbot wex alle blynd þat did his bones breke.

Þe Bisshop Owald herd of þat miracle speke, ..Osewald.....
reustat at þe toumbe, he tok vp þe bones; Reuested atte þe.......
in a fertre þam laid, a riche for þe nones. ...he þem leyde.....
Þe date was nien hundreth sexti & þrittene;
he was a holy man þorgh miracle was sene. ....man of lyf...hit.
After Edgare was Edward his sonne ..þe Kyng cam...
regnand in alle þe lond als his fader was wonne;
Saynt Dunstan corouned him bifor þe baronage
& oþer bisshopes inouh; fulle ȝonge he was of age.
A gode man he was & stalworth knyght als stele;
in Ingland neuer before was kyng lufed so wele .....Kyng þat liued..
ne of þe folk strange non honourd so mykelle. .....was non honoured..
Þe right lawes did he loke for fals men & fikelle,
boþe riche & pouere he ȝemed in euenhede;
non suld do oþer wrong for couetise no drede.
Estrild, his stepmoder, scho þouht on felonie;
tille wikked men scho spak Edward to aspie;
þei did als scho þam bad & wrouht þam seluen wouh.
At Koruesgate þorgh desceit Edward Kyng þei slouh.
Þre ȝere was he kyng, þe story þus me said;
his body at Westmynstere in fertre is it laid. ...Wynchestre.....
Þe date was nien hundreth sexti & sextene;
þat was alle forwondred, for his dede come tene. .tyme....his deþ fel gret.
Unto Kyngeston þe first wouke of May,
com Saynt Dunstan opon a Sonenday, Þyder cam.....
& of alle þe lond, erle & baroun, .so dide of al..boþe...
to Eilred, Edgar sonne, bitauht him þe coroun.
Saynt Dunstan hette him wele, in sorow his life to lede;
in alle his life ilk dele of suerd he mot him drede.
Saynt Dunstan tille him spak wrothfulle wordes of eye;
how þei of his mouth brak, listen I salle ȝow seye:
"Eilred," said Dunstan, "þi broþer Edward was slayn
þorgh þi moder Estrid, þerof scho was fulle fayn, ...Estrild.....
[106r] for slauhter of þi broþer has þou þe coroune.
Wele weld it salle þou neuer, þou has it þorh tresoune.
Þof alle Edgar þe gate, Estrild þi moder ware;
to þe reame has þou no right bot þorgh slauhter care.
...hastow....treson & care
For þe luf of þe, þi broþer did scho slo;
þerfor þou & þine salle weld it with wo,
& sone after þi daies, þe reame salle men se
gouerned þorgh aliens kynde & euermore fro þe."
Whan Dunstan had þus said bifor alle þat were þore

& taken had his leue of barons lesse & more,
Eilred þe ȝonge kyng toward London ȝede.
A rede cloude in þe skie about Ingland gan sprede;
so mykelle blode it rayned, þe erth wex alle rede.
Þe folk was affaied & alle heuy als lede. ..were al affrayed & woxe...
Þe toþer ȝere next of his coronment, ...after his.
þe Danes vp aryued, Souhampton þei brent
..aryued o þys land & Southamptoun..
& robbed Cornwaile, þe folk were alle anoyed [Transp. L]
þat with Norwais Kerlion was destroied; [Transp. L]
.ȝer wyþ Norweye Men Kerlion..
þei com to London & brent þe cite. Þe Danes come......
Eilred & þe barons þat were of his meyne
with þe erle of Herford held contek & fight;
þat þer heritage defend, þei ne myght.
Als alle þis sorow & wo was in þe gynnyng,
died Saynt Dunstan; men herd þe angels syng.
Iustyn & Godemunde of Danmark, dukes riche,
aryued in Southfolk & brent Ipsewiche, ...al ȝepeswiche
men & women slouh & robbed þorgh þe lond;
tille þei com to Mideweie, cuntre non þei fond. ....Medeweye encountre non..
With þe erle of Kent þei countred at Medeweie;
þe maistrie of him þei wan, þei did his folk alle deie.
......þey slowe his men al day
Þe lerid & þe lewid þat wonned in þe south
sauh werre on ilk a side, þei wer in þe woulfes mouth.
Ten pounde of gold bi ȝere for þe pes þei gaf;
to Iusty & Gudmund þei tok alle riffe & raf. .Iustyn....boþe...
To schip þei turned & went & charged þam fulle wele,
aryued in Danmark with robberie ilk a dele.

[*L adds:*] Þen wente þe Kyng Eylred forto haue lyued in pes
ȝit cam a fflute ouer flod & on his lond gan pres
Northfolk al þey toke & many tounes brent
& seysede Lyndeseye þe Contre þurgh out schent
When þey had slayn & Robbed al Northumberland
Þey lode þer schipes & ledde þat Pylage to þer land

[*The second scribe begins in L, fol. 80r.*]

In to Wales þat coste went Eilred pitously
forto gadre him oste if he mot haf maistrie.
In þat ilk tyme as he to Wales went,
tuo outlandes kynges on þis lond hauens hent.
To outlandiche....haueþ he hente
Anlaf of Norway, of Danmark Kyng Suane,

aryued in þis lond, to many wer þei bane. .....navies..bathe
Þer ostes boþe at ons vnto London nam;
þe toun was warned wele & wist þat þei cam.
[106v] Folk inouh redy was gadred to þe cite,
þei went egrely & did þo kynges fle;
fro London þei wer dryuen & com to Southampton.
Man & beste þei slouh, destroied þe cuntre doun.
Eilred myght nouht to stand þam ageyn;
for pes he þam bisouht to gyf þam a certeyn.
ffyue þousand pound of siluer þe Danes kyng toke;
þe went to þer schippes & to Danmark schoke, ...þe schoup
& many of þo Danes priuely were left
& busked westward forto robbe eft.
Wilton had þei taken, Southampton also,
Cornwaile & Wales bouwed þam vnto;
þe cuntre of Dorseth, lond & tenement,
alle had þei wasted fro Seuerne vnto Kent.
Eilred on a stound þe told of þat wo; ....þey told hym...
four & tuenti þousand ponde he gaf a way to go, ...gaf þem....
to haf pes in his lyue, þe lond no more schende; ....lond þey scholde no..
þe Danes tok þe siluer, to Danmark gan wende. ...þat gold..hom þey.
Four & tuenti wynter lasted þis sorow, ...dured hym..
if he had pes at euen, he had non at morow,
for so hette Saynt Dunstan, he suld alle his lyue
with werre his lond welde & with his suerd stryue.
Now has Eilred nede of help & socoure;
for boldenes he wild him bynd to som berde in boure. .help.........
Fulle fo frendes he had & fele foos inowe;
vnto þe duke of Normundie he went for to wouwe. ....ouersee to wowe
He wedded þe dukes douhter, faire Emme þe Blaunche;
þre bouwes of þam spronge, þe ton es holy braunche.
Tre twystes of....is an holy.
Edmunde Irenside was eldest of þo þre;
[*L adds:*] ffor dowȝtynesse of his dede þat name þenne lawȝtte he
þe to high Edward, þe þrid Alfrid hight he.
[*L differs:*] Þat oþer hiȝt Edward þat now liggeþ in Shryne
Þe þridde hiȝt Alfrid þat suffred muche pyne
Þorgh of Sir Richard, duke of Normundie, Thurw conseil of.....
Eilred ȝede þorgh his lond priuely to spie
euerilkon þe Danes & smertly bounde, .of þe Danes ful smertly were þey.
or smyte of þer hedes ay as men þam founde;
þus had Eilred þe lond at his wille.
Bot þe duke died sone & þat felle him fulle, ...ful hym ful ille

þan was Eilred socoure sone away went;
tiþing com to Danmark þat he þe Danes schent.
Suane, þe Danes kyng, þer with had enuy;
to aryue on h Ingland he dight his nauy. ..vp Engelond..hym gode.
Whan he was aryued, he sent fulle baldely
messengers to Eilred als tille his enmy;
[107ʳ] þis was his message: his Danes wild he venge,
ageyn him in bataile to renne & to renge.
Eilred our kyng his help had he lorn .Kyng of þis land.....
of þe duke of Normundie þat dede was beforn.
Suane, þe Danes kyng, was of so grete strength
þat he destroied þis lond in brede & in length;
fyue wynter holy lasted þat werre
þat neuer Eilred, our kyng, durst negh him nerre; ......neyhe hym ne derre
noiþer bi north no bi south com him neuer help.
Wo was alle his comforth, of sorow mot he ȝelp;
þritty þousand pounde vnto Suane he sent,
pes to haf his lyue, & þei to Danmark went. ....lif tyme &....
Now is Kyng Suane went tille his cuntre;
Eilred sent for Edrik to be his owen priue.
So fals a traytour in erth was non as he;
of Lincolne he gaf him þat cuntre schire. ..schire Duk by þe Kyng was he
Þe duke said vnto þe kyng, "Sir, I salle ȝow say, Edrik seide........
for to saue ȝour lond wele a fulle siker way,
do mak þre hundreth schippes opon þe sees koste
to kepe þam of Norweie & þe Danes oste,
& if þe folk þerin be trewe vnto þe,
doute þe of non enmys þat comes vp on þe." ......comeþ by þe se
Þe sent to seke many a schip wright .Kyng sente......
to þe toun of Sandwiche, þe nauie forto dight.
Whan Edrik it wist þat þe schippes wer redy,
he sent to Norweie his lettres priuely
vnto þe Kyng Anlaf tille Inglond to com.
Anlaf & Sir Thurkille aryued vp in þei nom;
...Turkil to Engelond þe wey þey nome
Anlaf & Thurkille aryued vp in Kent;
alle about þei robbed & tok þat þei mot hent. ...robbed & refte & tok....
Þe folk of þe cuntre to þis conseile þei ches:
to gyf þam four hundreth pounde forto lyue in pes.
Þe Danes tok þat siluer & turned eft ageyn,
& voided þe cuntre, þe folk was fulle feyn.
Bot in þe ȝere after, obowen Grimsby, ...aboute Grymmesby
eft þei gan aryue þorgh sonde priuely,

þorgh fals Edrike þat þam þider hasted;
Lincolne & Lyndeseie þei stroied & wasted.
Fals Edrike went, pes with þam to make,
fourti þousand pounde he did þam take ..... þe Danes take
þat non in alle þe cuntre more suld be piled,
bot euer was Eilred fouly begiled.
[107v] Whan þe kyng wende haf pes in his lyue,
Suane of Danmark at Sandwyche gan aryue . þe Kyng of Denemark....
& brouht hider with him his sonne þat hight Knoute;
þe folk vntille Humber to Suane gan þei loute.
Alle was þorgh Edrik þat mykelle was to blame;
he was þe kynges conseiloure & did him mykelle schame.
Ane erle in þe north, Vttred men kalde, .. was in .. Vutred men hym .
he com vnto Gaynesburgh, of Suane for to halde;
forto lyue in pes & werre forto fle, ... loue & pees þe werre ..
he com vnto Suane & mad him feaute.
Of þe north Suane had a partie, þe south he desired;
ostes tille him his sonne fast þei atired. ... & to his sone .. hem .
Knoute went to þe north, Suane in to þe south;
þan was Eilred in þe wolfes mouth.
Suane toward Oxenford went fulle smertly
& in þat ilk toun did he krie a krie
þat alle þat him serued & of his meyne ware,
man, woman, & childe suld þei alle forfare.
Þey scholde destrue man & child & womman al .
Kastels suld þei bete doun, kirkes suld þei brenne, ... churches...
boþe cite3 & tounes þat þei mot se or ken.
Of þe toun of Wynchestre feaute had he at wille;
siþen he went to London, þat hated he fulle ille.
Þe bode com to þe kyng þat soiorned þerin . word.......
þat þe Kyng Suane þe toun wild he wyn.
A Danes erle with þe, Kurkille he hight,
. Danysche erel was with oure Kyng Turkil he .
he halp our kyng defend þe toun at his myght.
Kyng Suane gaf assaut þe walles to assaile;
mykelle folk he les & tynt his trauaile. Michil of his ... & lost ..
Four & tuenti þousand in Temse alle at ones
wer dronkled of Danes, þe Deuelle haf þer bones. . drenched.......
Suane turned fro London alle þorgh felonie
& went to Wallyngford to mak his maistrie.
Siþen he ȝede to Bathe & sette þe toun on fire;
Achelmare tille him felle, an erle of Deuenschire,
Achelmare with feaute to Suane he him bonde;

fro Wellis vnto London alle felle to his honde.
Suane toward Danmark sped him fulle fast [*Transp. L*]
& ostage of London he had at þe last. [*Transp. L*]
Ilk cried on oþer, "Now is Suane kyng
ouer alle Inglond & Eilred has no þing."
Eilred is so reymed of his tresorie, ... destrued ...
his wife & his childre he sent to Normundie.
[108r] Þe bisshop of London, he hight Sir Alphanie,
led Edward & Alfride & Emme þat was ladie.
In þe wynter after, Eilred went ouer þe se
vnto Nomundie with his wife to be. Riȝt in to Normandie with Emme....
Whan þe Duke herd say þat Eilred þider cam,
with mykelle nobley ageyn Eilred he nam, ... aȝen hym þe wey..
resceyued him curtasly & said, "Lefe & dere,
my lond is at þi wille tille þe socoure is here." ...... whiles þy self ert.
Þe date a þousand was & mo bi fourty ȝere The date of Ihesu a ..... xiiii.
þat Eilred & his childre soiorned with Duke Richere.
Now comes Suane eft ageyn with cristes malison,
þe lond leid to taliage so mykelle on ilk a toun
.. hey leide to tallage so gret on eche..
þat noiþer erle no baron of alle þer heritage
myght not lyue þeron to gif þer taliage;
treuage als he asked of Saynt Edmunde þing,
. he axed of al þat was seint Edmondus þe Kyng
þe corsaynt & þe kirke he thrette for to brennyng,
.... churche he þretnede þowr.
& bot he had his askyng, þe lond he suld destoye. .... destroie
To Gaynesburgh he kald þe barons forto noye;
he said befor þam alle of Saynt Edmundes lond ..... þat whilom was seynt..
he wild haf treuage or brenne alle þat he fond.
Alle was wele tille euen after þe soupere;
he ȝede about & plaied with þo þat were him nere.
.. & romed aboute with.....
He sauh out of þe firmament an armed knyght com doun;
þat was Saynt Edmunde, cruelle als a leon, . was as seynt.....
suerd girded & lance in hand, þan gan Suane to crie,
With swerd gird & ....
non sauh bot he one, he said, "Now salle I die!
Non hym saw but he alone......
Help, knyghtes, if ȝe may, I may no ferrer go. .... ferther.
I se Edmunde with me wroþe, I wote he wille me slo!"
With þat word he felle doun dede as any stone,

lyfe & saule to helle, & flesch, blode, & bone. . . . ȝede to . . . . . .
Now is Suane dede & wonnes with Sathanas;
þe Danes ches Knoute to kyng of Danmark þat he was, ... his was
& Inglond he seised for his fader conquest.
Grete taliage laid he þeron bi esten & bi west;
þe folk wild not suffre to be treuwageres, ... suche truwagers
bot sent after Eilred bi certeyn messengeres
& praied him to com home, þe croune ȝeme & take;
þe lordschip of Knoute kyng wild þei alle forsake. . . . Knouthe þe Kyng wil . . .
Eilred sent tille Inglond Sir Edward, his sonne,
with his letter sealed & þanke wild he þam conne
& blithely tille Inglond wild he com agayn,
if he myght on þam troste þat þei were certayn.
[108v] Alle þe comons of þe lond with letter þam bond,
& ilkon sette his seale þerto with his own hond
þat if he wild com ageyn þe lond forto were,
neuermore to Danes kyng faiþe suld þei bere.
Whan he wist þer wille, he hied hider suythe;
. Eilred wiste þus þer . . hied hom swyþe
þei resceyued him fulle faire & were of him blythe. . . . . . . were glad & .
With him, alle þei said þei wild lyue & deie,
alle holy þe lond bot þei of Lyndseie. . holiche al þe . . . . .
Eilred þer lege lord, him þei alle forsoke Lyndeseye þer liche lond Eilred þey . .
& þer hede Kyng Knout þei þan toke.
. to be þer Kyng & hed Knouthe to þem þey .
Now rises Eilred & gadres oste stark . . . . . an host riȝt stark
& chaces Kyng Knoute in tille Danmark. . chaced Knouthe þer Kyng riȝt in to .
Whan þe Danes were out þat timbred him his tene, ... þen wrek Eilred . .
Lyndeseie he destroied quite alle bidene. . . . þowrout al .
It was þam self to wite þei lete of him so lite;
þe wrong was alle þairs, þe kyng did bot right.
Whan þe kyng wende þat pes suld forþe go,
þe fals Erle Edrik bigan eft a wo: . . . . bygan of nywe wo
tuo olde gentille men Edrik did forfare;
þe ton hight Sigiferd, þe toþer Sir Morgare.
For couetise of þer londes & seignorie þat þei helde . . . . . & lordschip . . .
& for þei were a partie smyten into elde, ... woxen . .
þe fals Edrik did lede Sigiferdes wife
vnto Malmcestre, hir name was Aldife.
Edmunde Irenside, Eilredes sonne,
þat euer in þis lond stille wild he wonne,
of þis ilk treson he herd oft speke, of þus grete tresons . . of wel spekon

& of fals Edrik fayn wild he him wreke. .....wolde he wrekon
He toke Sigiferdes wife withouten his fader leue
..fro Edrik þis womman withoute...
& wedded hir at þe kirke, Edrik forto greue.
Whan he had hir wedded, he went also quik ....ywedded Edrik wente al quyc
& oute of alle þo londes he kast þe Erle Edrik
of alle þat tenement þat boþe þe brethres ware
þat longed to Sigiferd & to Sir Morkare.
Now is Eilred oure kyng fallen in sekenes;
he lies at Euescham, his abbay it es.
His eldest sonne, Edmunde, knyghtes gode he sekes;
fro Douere vnto Wales, þe folk tille him mekes,
& þe Erle Edrik he gadred mykelle pride, ...gadreþ to hym gret.
knyghtes & sergan3 on Lyndesay side,
forto slo Edmunde þorgh tricherie. .awreke on Edmund þourw som.
Bot Edmunde es wele warned of his felonie;
[109r] Edmunde bi messengers þe erle he diffies.
Edrik in tille Danmark to Knoute sent spies
for to com tille Inglond sone suld he assay,
aryued þat he ware of 3ole þe tuelft day.
Knoute bi his sonde Edrik ageyn grette;
to aryue he suld fonde þe day þat he him sette.
Comen is Knoute to cuntre, to ride he him hastis,
man & woman to slo, he robbes & wastis. ..womman child to.....
A gode erle of Warwik was don to þe suerd
þorgh þat fals Edrik als he did Sigiferd.
Eilred was led to London & seke gan þer lie;
Edmunde praied him of help priuely bi spie.
Londreies inow com tille Edmunde
& wastid alle & brent Leicestre alle doun.
Bot þe fals Edrik did his quantise ....dede ay..
þat Edmund with Knoute mette in non wyse.
Knoute & Edrik þei seised þorgh tresoun,
Bokyngham & Bedford, þe toun of Huntyngtoun,
Lincoln & Notyngham, þe toure of Northampton; ....toun..
siþen went to Donkastre & vntille Aluerton, .þey wente.....
& alle Northumberland it was at þer wille.
Edmunde & þe erle Vctred þat tyme held þam stille; ....Vttred.....
to London vnto Eilred hasted þei þer weie,
for bodword men brouh, þe kyng suld sone deie. ...bro3te.....
Whan Edrik wist Edmond to London was gone, ..wiste þat.....
his londes & his rentes he seised eft ilkone.
Eilred at London endid his life; ...sone eyndid..

auht & þritty wynter he regned with strife.
Þat tyme he died in peyn & in wo,
þe date was a þousand & sextene mo. .date of Ihesu a....
Now is Eilred biried þat mykelle wo bade; .....muche wo abed
þe clergie & þe baronage samned at a reade .....gedere on on red
& com to Southampton & corouned Sir Knoute.
Þe burgeis of London were wroþe & stoute, ...London þer of wex...
& said þei [su]ld fond to felle Knoutes pride; [*P has a blemish*.]
..þey scholde.....
þei corouned for enuy Edmunde Irenside.
Þerof were þei paied, alle þe north cuntre; .were wel apaied al...
þe com alle to London to mak him feaute.
Knoute gadred him an oste, on Edmunde he ran,
& Edmunde on him ageyn as a douhty man,
& trauailed sore, Knoute neuer he blanne. ...Knouth þe Kyng neuer he ne blen
Whan wend haf left, Edmunde biganne; .Knouthe wente..þan..
[109v] tuo ȝere þei werred with many trauailes. ...trauailled þus with meny werres
In þo tuo ȝeres were sex grete batales;
in þe sex batailes was many a man slayn.
At þe last þei acorded; þe lond was fulle fayn.
Edmunde of þe lond had þe haluendele;
he regned bot tuo ȝere, no more his tyme felle.
He lies at Glastenbire toumbed, as I wene,
þe date of criste a þousand & mo bi auhtene.
Whan god had don his wille of Edmunde Irenside,
Knoute vnto London com with grete pride.
He asked þe barons in þat parlement
if he schewed a þing oþer waies he ment,
.Edmund hadde y schewed eny þyng or y ment
if Edmunde þe kyng whan to acorde went,
In his laste wil owþer þan when þey furst to acord went
if he saued to his heyers eiþer lond or tenement. or if........
Ilkon said þat Edmunde þe kyng
spak no word þerof at þer sauhtillyng. ....in his departyng
Wharfor þe barons granted him ilkone, .alle þe...echeone
Knoute to be corouned & haf it alone. ....Kyng &...
Whan Knoute had resceyued boþe þe seignories,
he parted þe lond in foure parties.
Alle þe West cuntre him seluen he held,
fals Edrik gaf he Lyndeseie, of Lyncoln þe scheld;
vnto þe erle Thurkille he gaf Estangle;
Northfolk & Southfolk ficacie men iangle; ...þat fikays haþ men.
to þe Erle Vctred, Northumberland he toke, ...Vttred...

þe pes to mayntene, þe suore alle on þe boke. ..for to.þey swour....
Þan toke Kyng Knoute alle his homages
þat cleymed to hold of him þer heritages.
Edmunde had a sonne & childre no mo;
þorgh Edrikes conseile, Knoute did him slo,
& tok quene Emme & wedded hir to wife;
thorgh Edrikes conseile, scho scorted his life.
Thurw conseile sche schorted Edrikus.
Knoute on a day bi his wife satte,
of Edrikes treson scho warned him of þat.
"Listen me, Lord Knoute, if it be þi wille, List to me.......
how he betraied my lord & my sonne fulle ille. ...my furst......
Whilom Eilred my lord he him bitraist to ȝow,
Furst he trayed Eilred..falsly to ȝow
& my sonne Edmunde þorgh treson he slouh, & siþþe.......
& if he regne long, he salle haf þe same. .....ȝe schul haue..
He was neuer with no man þat he ne did him schame."
Þe kyng on on þe morn went to London, .Kyng on þe morwe...
his ȝole forto hold was his encheson.
[110r] Knoute þouht on þat tale þat his wife him told
& siþen ateyned Edrik þorgh treson of old; .suþþe he...falsnesse..
þe ferthe day of þe fest, no lenger it was,
Edrik was hanged on þe toure for his trispas.
Þan said þe quene þat Edrik þe giloure
had not fully dome þat felle to traytoure. ..fulle....a traitour
"Traytours with runcies suld men first drawe." ..hurdels....
"Ȝa, Dame," said þe kyng, "bot he salle haf þe lawe:
þat his body salle hang in colde & in hote,
schame tille alle his kynd þat it sees & wote."
Knoute of his body gate sonnes þre,
tuo bi tuo wifes, þe þrid in iolifte.
Bi þe first had he Suane, he was eldest broþer; ..furste wif.......
bi Emme þe second wife, Hardeknoute anoþer.
Harald he had geten on his playeng; ......wilde pleyng
Knoute lufed him best, he was his derlyng. ...best & was..
Olaf in Norweie regned fulle stoute
& bare him ouer strange to þe Kyng Knoute.
Knoute com with his kythe þat kant was & kene
..with power þat wiȝtty was..
& chaced him out of Norweie quyte & clene; ......quytly..
þan was he kyng of Danmark, Inglond, & Norweie.
Danmark was his heritage, he conquered þe toþer tueie.
Malcolme, þe Scottis kyng, þat tyme died he;

Mathithade, his broþer, resceyued þe regaute. Mathelhade.....
Knoute as for his chefe he tok his homage;
of þe kyngdom of Inglond he had þe heritage. ffor of Riȝt of.....
Knoute vnderstode wele he mot not long lyue;
his sonnes in his lyue his londes wild he gyue.
Suane gaf he Norweie, Olaf he chaced oute;
Danmark, his heritage, he gaf tille Hardeknoute.
He assigned Harald to Inglond to had it in fee, ..to Harold Engelond in fee
þus he gaf his londis tille his sonnes þre.
Seuentene ȝere was he kyng þorgh conquest & desceit;
at Westmynstere he ligges in a toumbe purtreit.
.Westmoster he liþ y buried in tombe vnder led
A þousand was þe date & sex & þritty
whan Knoute kyng died, so sais þe story.
Harald was curteys & strong, of body auenant;
to be þer kyng & hede, þe lond was wele ogrant. ....lond ȝaf hym grant
Hardknoute of Danmark payd not withalle ...gladed not.
þat he suld bere þe coroune, for he was born thralle.
He gadred of Danes folk right inouh
& did him toward þe se & tille þis lond drouh.
[110ᵛ] Whan he was aryued, he sent to Harald
& said þat a bastard no kyngdom suld hald
bot if þat he it wan with suerd or with lance,
..he wan hit with dent of swerd or.
of tirant or of saraȝin, þorgh douhtynes of chance,
& if he wille þe lond ȝeld & to þe pes chese,
"For he is my broþer he salle not alle lese, ..is of myn kyn.....
& if he wille þorgh bataile, þerto wille I stand,
& bataile bituen vs wille not be semand."
Harald was fulle, a loue day he toke .was ful wys.....
to here what þe barons þam boþe wild loke.
Vnder Southamptoun was þer assemble, ...þere assemblie
of Harald & Hardknoute what suld bituex þam be;
for þei were breþer, þe luf was more sene.
Þe barons portiond þe lond euen þam bituene: ..partid.....
Harald tille his parte suld haf alle þe northende
& alle þe southside tille Harknout suld wende;
...suthside to Hardeknoþ schulde so leynde
to þat ilk lokyng boþe þei consent, .þis ordynance...
in luf þei departed, Hardknout home went.
In þat tyme þat Harald & Hardknout held partie,
died þe Duke Roberd þat regned in Normundie.
William was his heire, resceyued þe heritage, .Bastard was.....

þat we kalle þe Bastard þat sette vs in seruage. . was oure Conqurour & sette . . .
Richard was Roberd fadere, þe duke þat died beforn,
Emme þe quene, his douhter, of þe whilk was born
. oure queyne . . was of wham was y bore
Alfred & Edward, Hardknoute þe þrid, . . Seynt Edward & . . .
þe tuo first of Eilred, of Knoute Hardknoute tid. . . . . by tidde
Alfred & Edward þat of Eilred kam . . Edward confessour . . kyng . .
wer with Duke Roberd, now ere þei with William.
Dwelled with . . & now dwelleþ with .
Þo childre tok to rede to com vnto þis lond
to speke with þer moder, at Wynchester þei hir fond.
Alfrede was eldest, non mot his wille withhald;
to London he wild alle gate to speke with Kyng Harald.
Godwyn, an erle of Kent, met with Alfred,
him & alle his feres vntille preson þam led; . . . . men & feres . . . .
of som smote of þer hedes, of som put out þer iȝene, ... eye
sex hundreth at Gildford did Godwyn slo & pyne. . . . . . . sle & deye
Alfred he was led to þe abbay of Elyng, ... Ely
bifor Godwyn himseluen þei did his iȝene out þring.
. . . þe putte out boþe his eye
He lyued bot þre daies & ȝald to god þe gaste;
þe bode com to his moder, scho did Edward in haste . word . . . .
wende to Normundie for drede of Alfred pyne, . . . aȝen for . . . .
to William, hir broþer sonne, was Edwardes kosyne. . . Bastard . . . & was . .
[111r] Edward told William of Alfred alle þe case
& praied him of help, for he dred harder pase,
& if he myght conquere Inglond þat was his speyre. . . . . . Engelond to him sur
Edward sikerd him wele to mak William his heyre
& bond him with skrite, his seale hyngand þer bi, . obleschud hym . . . . honged . .
& William hette him wele to help him sikerly.
Now duelles Harald þe kyng among his baronage;
tille Emme, Hardknoutes moder, he did a grete outrage,
his broþer a foule despite, himself vileyn skandre. & to his . . . . . . sklandres
He chaced hir out of þe lond, & scho went vnto fflandres
vnto þe Erle Baldwyn, for scho was of his kynde.
He resceyued hir fulle faire, inouh he did hir fynde
to brige into Danmark þer Hardknout was kyng. Riȝt sone into . . . . .
Of Inglond & of Flandres brouht men him tiþing
how Kyng Harald chaced his moder of lond;
what skille he had & whi, Herdknout ȝerned to fond.
Now Hardwnout toward Flandres dightes him day bi day.
. Hardeknoþ into.diȝtteþ . . . .
Þat tyme at Westmynstir, Harald sore seke lay,

died & was þer laid, als my boke me told;
fyue ȝere was he kyng & sex & fifty old.
Þe date of criste þan was a þousand & fourti;
Harald for his trespas ȝit felle a vilany. ....ȝut fel hym..
Now is Kyng Harald dede þat whilom was so stoute;
þe barons sent Flandres vnto Hardeknoute ..sent til...
& praied him com to lond, þe coroune if he wild take,
if he wild vnderstond, non oþer kyng wild þei make.
Whan he wist þer wille, he hasted him þider suiþe;
þei gaf him þe coroune & were of him fulle bliþe.
He studied how he myght venge his moder despite;
he did Harald body do drawe vp also tite
..lat drawe Harold of þe erþ sone aftur as tid
& þorgh þe podels it drouh þat foule were & deppest,
.lett hym be drawe þurw fen & podeles þat fulest were..
& siþen in to Temse his body did he kest; .....his dede body kest
þat fischid in Temse on þe nyght, whan þei þer nettes vp wond,
.fisshers of Tamyse aftur whan.....
þe body of Harald in a nette þei fond;
þei durst it not forth schewe, for þe kyng wer þei ferd.
Som frendes he had þat biried it in kirkeȝerd.
..hadde he fewe þey..in a chirche ȝerd
Hardeknout did charge þe lond in suilk treuwage
þat noiþer erle no baron myght lyue for taliage,
so þat alle þe comonalte had him ageyn herte, ...peple....
þat were to him so fre forþouht it sore & smerte.
....byforen so fre forþowȝt them...
Hardknoute wex fulle wroth toward Godwyn of Kent
for his broþer Alfred þat he slouh & schent,
[111v] & to þe Bisshop Alfrik þat was his conseilere. .....was Godewyne.
Þei dred þe kyng folle sore, for he was fulle austere.
Þe elrle had frendes, to acorde þei gaf him þe weie;
.Eril of Kent hadde fele frendis..þey ȝaf awey
þe erle was fulle quaynte, did mak a riche galeie
with fourscore armed knyghtes in suilk apparaile dight
þat so riche armes was neuer sene with sight,
& ilk knyght bare on his arme be redy acounte
also mykelle brent gold as sextene vnce amounte.
Withouten alle þis a hundreth knyghtes he toke,
befor þe kyng & þe barons, he suore on þe boke
þat neuer Alfred his broþer þorgh him was dede,
no blynfeld, no slayn bot þorgh Haraldes rede. Ne blynfolded ne.....
Þei said he did inouh, þe erle alle vplift; ....þey alle.

þe kyng forgaf his wraþe, resceyued his gift.
In Saynt Edwardes life it sais he was forsuorn; ......þat Godewyn..
[Lines 1321–1340 of P appear in L after 1625 of P. The variant readings are given here.]
bifor Edward himself he strangled & was lorn,
& I salle telle þat tale or I ferrer go,
how falsnes brewes bale with him & many mo.
In Saynt Edward tyme, þe erle suld with him ete;
a seruitour þer was þat serued at þe mete.
He stombled at a chance & felle on his kne, ...ful doun on his o kne
þorgh þe toþer schank he ros & serued in his degre. ......& serued forþ...
"A ha," said þe erle, "had þat schank ne bien,
þou had liggen þer stille, þe risen suld not haf sene." .....þe risyng schold not haue be.
"God wote," said þe kyng, "so is it with me nouh,
& I had my broþer Alfred þat þou slouh. ....yuel slow
Þof I had stombled þorgh myn vnmayn, ...myn owen.
he suld haf bien my schank & reised me agayn."
"Þan hopes þou," said þe erle, "þat for me was he dede?
I praye god if it wer so, I strangle of þis brede,"
& putte a morselle in his mouth with þat ilk worde.
Bifor þe kyng & þam alle, he strangled at þe borde;
þe kyng biheld him a stound & sauh no repentance.
He bad drawe away þat hound, god has taken vengeance. ....þe hund for god haþ..
Whan Harknout & þe erle wer at an assent, *[P and L correspond again with this line.]*
þorgh alle his lond, þe kyng his sonde sent
forto reise þe treuage þat on þe lond was sette;
Pader & Thurston to þat office were fette.
Þe folk of Wircestre ageyn þe treuage spak;
bituex þam & þe messengers broþefulle wordes brak. .....wretful.out.
Pader & Thurston þer hedes þer þei left;
þe kyng burd send oþer to ask treuage eft. ..by howede to seynde...his truwage.
[112r] Þe kyng sone herd say his messengers were slayn;
toward Wircestre he com with myght & mayn .þe toun of.......
& comanded alle þo þat euer lufed him wele,
alle Wirecestreschire spare it neuer a dele,
noiþer man no beste, no manere, no no toun. ..ne best ne lordschupe ne..
Þe cite of Wircestre þei brent euen doun, .hed....brend hit al.
alle þei wasted quitely & slouh þe folk fulle ȝerne.
Bot þo þat fled with þer godes to þe ilde of Seuerne

& þat wer in þe ilde duelled þer for drede .þo þat weren.......
vntille þe kyng turned & his wrath ouer ȝede.
Right als Hardeknout had left alle þat folie,
com Edward, Eilred sonne, out of Normundie,
& Hardeknoutes broþer on his moder side,
right heyre of þe lond þorgh grace þat may betide.
Edward was welcom tille Hardeknoute þe kyng;
he bad his wille suld be als his in alle þing. .....be do as....
Here now of Hardeknoute how he endid his life:
tille a duke of Danes he gaf his douhter to wife;
þe bridale was holden at þe maner of Lambithe.
After mete in þe haule, þe kyng mad alle blithe;
in alle his ioy makyng among þam ilkone,
he felle dede doun, colde as any stone.
Þei bare him to Wynchester & biried him þore;
tuo ȝere & a half he regned & no more.
A þousand was þe date & tuo & fourty.
(I trowe it was for vengeance he died so sodenly.)
Alle þe baronage at Pask afterward ...of þe lond at Ester.
com to Wynchester to coroune Kyng Edward
als he þat had gode right vnto þe regalte,
in Inglond was non so right heyre as he.
Whan he had regned fyue & wele was aboue, ...v ȝer &...
Suane, þe kyng of Danmark, sent to him for loue
& praied him for his nauy to help him with summ.
Bataile was gyuen in þe se ageyn þe Kyng Magnum ....Magoun
þat was kyng of Norweie, with wrong gan him trauaile.
Edward sent him fifty schippes to help at his bataile.
For alle þe help þat he had, Magnus on him so ran ....Magon....
& chaced away Suane & Danmark on him wan.
He..Swane þe Kyng & Denemark of hym wan
Bot þis ilk Magnus lyued þer no longe, ...Magun..not.
eft Suane, þe Danes kyng, his lond did vnderfonge,
& eft vntille Edward Suane sent ageyn
& praied him bituex þam þe pes wer certeyn.
..þat pes were bytwyxt þem for euer.
[112v] Edward him granted opon suilk a wise
þat neuer þe Dangilde for ne non of hise ....ne neuer for non..
suld be chalanged for man of Danes lond, ..more chalenged...Danysche blowde
& Suane, kyng of Danmark, to þat conant him bond;
.....vnto þis couenant stowde
þus was þe pes granted with skrite on boþe sides
& þe Danes gilde forgyuen þat neuer eft bitides.

In þis Edwardes tyme, a riche erle þan was
þat hight Godwyn of Kent (I red him ore in pas). ......rede nov forþ in pas
He had a sonne, Harald, heyre of his tenement; ....hi3t Harold....
Engle his wife he drofe away & held in peyrment. ...Harold drof.....
Egyne, þat was an abbes, out of hir hous had,
maugre hire wille, in hordom his life with hir lad.
Ageyn þe Kyng Edward & of his to wynne, [*Transp. L*] ......his lond..
Godwyn þe erle to werre wild bigynne. [*Transp. L*]
.his fader to werre þan wolde he.
Harald & Lofwyn, þise were his sonnes tueye;
douhty knyghtes þei were, after salle we seye. ....but here after...
Godwyn sent for frendes, knyghtes he had inowe;
þe kyng was at Gloucestre & þiderward þei drowe.
Whan Edward perceyued, his herte was in studie
how þat werre bigan on him so sodanly.
Þe kyng 3ared his folk on haste, alle þat he myght;
þe erle in his askyng had no maner right.
Wherfor þe erle of Ba did Gowyn vnderstand ....Bathe dide Godwyn.
to leue alle his werre & take þe lawe of land. .....& stonde to....
"At London at þe benke schewe þer þin askyng, ...benche he seyde....
alle þat lawe wille, þou wynnes it of þe kyng."
The kyng com to London with lawe to mote in benke;
men sauh on þe kynges side þer was no gile no wrenke,
& for he had þe treuth, on his side were þe mo,
& Godwyn perceyued wele, on his side were bot fo; ....not so
þerfor Godwyn & his fro London went away.
He stode vntille no more, defaute he mad þat day, ...no lawe.....
þerfor was þe dome gyuen þorgh þe iustise
to exile þe Erle Godwyn, his sonnes, & alle hise.
Godwyn went to fflandres vnto þe Erle Baldwyn;
at Bristow in tille Ireland schipped Harald & Lofwyn.
Whan þe erle was exiled, his sonnes tille Irland ouer,
.....& his sones in Irlond were.
William þe Normant aryued vp at Douer .Bastard þe.....
in luf & in pes to speke with Sir Edward;
he had bien in his courte whan his happe was more hard.
......when hit was wyth hym..
He resceyued him with ioy & with herte fulle glad;
to se þe lond about, þe duke with him he lad.
[113r] Whan he had soiorned long & was in wille to go,
gode giftes he him gaf or þat he went him fro,
so þat alle of his were paied of þer parte; ...þe dukes men were apaid..partye
with ioy alle ageyn þei went to Normundie.

Þis Harald & Lofwyn þat out of lond were dryuen,
with grete oste of Ireland at Chestre vp aryuen;
Dorseth & Somerseth þei robbed & did wo,
of knyghtes & sergan3 þei slouh þritty & tuo.
Whan þei had so robbed þat þam þouht inouh,
þei went ageyn to schip & saile vp drouh;
toward þe south side turned þei þar flete,
þar fader & þei o chance togider gan mete;
Godwyn & his sonnes at Sandwych hauen hent.
Lettres tille his frendes for help about sent,
of socour & conseile bisouht þam pitously;
of many had he grante to ask for him mercy.
Whan þe kyng wist þat þei had taken land,
for þe barons he sent þat were his wele willand,
& for þe longe duellyng of barons in þe way,
Godwyn þat non wist aryued in Surray.
Þe kyng also suiþe ta bataile mad him 3are; ...sone to....
Godwyn he diffied & alle þat with him ware.
Godewyn he sette not by ne noun þat...
Grete wer þo parties þat ferd in to þe felde;
Eldolf, bisshop of Bath, þe pes mayntend & helde.
Bot god & sir Eldolff þe pes...
Eldolf, þe gode bisshop, com with his clergie .Buschupe of Bathe com...
& said to Kyng Edward, "Sire, we þe mercy crie
for þe Erle Godwyn þat wille 3eld him to þe.
His sonnes er at þi wille & alle þat with þam be."
Þe barons said, "For þare sake, for þam þan praye we.
Þare trespes we vndertake opon alle our fee," .trespas......
& þe erle com himself, mercy forto craue.
Þe kyng for his curteysie granted þam pes to haue
& gaf him ageyn boþe rent & lond.
Harald & Lofwyn to þe pes þam bond,
bot Suane, þare broþer, þat died in Lumbardie,
for he slouh his cosyn, he fled þorgh folonie. ....þowr felonye
He went to þe holy lond to do þerfor penance
& died þer for colde in Lumbardie o chance.
The kyng wedded a wife þat Godwyn douhter was;
scho soiorned at Romeneie for hir fader trespas.
Þe erle bisouh þe kyng to tak hir home ageyn; ..by so3tte.......
þe kyng granted þat þing to mak pes alle pleyn.
[113v] Þe erle vnto þe kyng bare him siþen so wele
& his sonnes boþe tille him war trost als stele;
siþen in alle his courte were non so wele him with,

þei halp him at þare myght to maynten pes & grith.
On þe Wissonday at Burgh in Lyndeseie, ..Whitsonday....
com bode to þe kyng & þus gan þei seie .tydyng to.....hit.
þat þe Duke Siward had taken in his balie
Machog, þe Scottes kyng, þat wild þorgh traitourie
haf traised Edward þe kyng; þat in þe north was rife,
þerfor Machog les þe reame & his life. ..lost..& al so his.
He gaf it to Malcolme þat was of Cumberland;
þorgh gift of Edward, he seised it in his hand.
Malcolme mad homage tille Edward our kyng
þat he & alle his age of Ingland suld hold þat þing.
.....heirs of hym schulde...
Griffyn, kyng of Wales, þat ilk self ȝere
was proued traitoure fals & þat bouht he fulle dere;
opon þe tuelft euen, Griffyn his hede les, ..next twelfthe.....
to Gloucester was it brouht befor þe kyng at des. ....at his des
Edward had a kosyn in preson at Hungarie;
Edmunde, his broþer sonne, was þer þorgh tricherie.
Þe kyng sent to frendes for him alle aboute;
for praier, at þe last, þe childe was laten oute.
Home vnto Inglond þe childe tille Edward cam
& for þat childes luf, forgeten was William;
....loue al most for geten was Duk.
þouht he not of þe trouth þat he to William plight,
for to mak him his heyre if he þe lond haf myght.
Neuerþeles to William he ȝeld him wele his bone;
of þis no more to speke: þe childe died right sone.
Algar, an erle of Kent, þat tyme exiled was.
(My boke sais with wrong: he did no trespas.)
He went in to Wales to Griffyn, Griffyn sonne; ......Griffyn Griffynes.
þese tuo a werre als Walsch men er wonne. ..werred þe Kyng as....
Whan Edward herd say, he samned alle his oste; .....sonned...
Harald, Godwyn sonne, led þam bi þat coste.
At Herford in Wales, þe ostes þer mette
& dight on boþe parties in batailes to sette.
Harald & his Inglis biheld þe erle Algare;
þam forþouht fulle sore þat he suld þore misfare. Hem ouerþoȝt......
Þis wald þe Inglis conseile, if þei mot Algare saue, .was........
for him þei suld biseke þe kynges pes to haue.
Þe Inglis com to þe kyng þer he was in place
& specially Harald, he had þe kynges grace.
..by Harold þey hadde for Algar þe grace
[114r] On þe erle Algare had þe kyng mercie [*Om. L*]

& forgaf Sir Griffyn also for curteisie. [*Om. L*]
Whan þat Kyng Edward wend to lyue in pes,
Griffyn, kyng of Wales, eft he mad a res.
He com vnto Herford & slouh þe Bisshop Ligere,
spared noiþer preste no clerk, to dede alle ȝede in fere,
kirkes & houses brent, nouht þan wild he spare;
þer þe Inglis had bigged, he mad it wast & bare.
Malcolme, of Scotland kyng, ȝit on Inglond ran;
þe kyng had him auanced, he was an vnkynd man.
Northumberland he brent & wasted þat he fond;
kirkes non wild he spare of Saynt Cutbertes lond.
Þe bisshop sent to þe kyng, for socour him bisouht; ......of help hym.
whan Malcolme herd it say, no more skaþe he wrouht.
Þe kyng did samen his men to abate Griffyns pride
& Harald þam bitauht ageyn þe Walsch to ride.
"Do him vnto þe suerd withouten iugement [*Transp. L*]
..swiþe vnto þe deþ with outyn eny.
if ȝe may Griffyn take bityme at any went." [*Transp. L*]
& if he Griffyn take myȝtte....
Harald went to Wales, his was fulle fre, ...his warrant...
& whan he com þer, Griffyn was passed þe se ......was ouer..
vnto Irlond; þan comandid Harald
þo londes to destroie þat Griffyn þer gan hald,
his tounes forto brenne, þe houses doun to breke,
& destroie þat kynde þat ouht to him couth speke.
Harald þe Walschmen did þam ilkon suere And Harold..eche on dede swere
þat to Kyng Edward faythe þei suld alle bere;
siþen to Rotland he went & exiled Griffyn þore,
him & alle his heyres for þat tyme euer more. .....fro....
Griffyn com ageyn whan Harald home was went,
þe folk priuely of Wales mad þer a parlement;
þei said þat Sir Griffyn with right he was outlawed
& Edward of Inglond had þam so gate awed, ...so geten by wed
þei said, "We wille no more, his vengeance is ȝit hote."
..þe wolde be trewe to hym þere....
Þei toke þer Sir Griffyn & of his hede þei smote
& sent it Kyng Edward & presentid him with þat,
right at Glastenbiri, at his mete þore he sat.
Griffyn had tuo breþer, Bleoth & Ruthe Walan; ......Riche Walan
þo tuo were with þe kyng whan he on Griffyn kan.
......whan Harold on Griffyn ran
Þerfor vnto þam tuo he gaf Griffyns feeȝ;
for south Wales holy, þei mad þe kyng feauteȝ.

Harald to Wales went vnto Portastiche;
wrightes he did make haules & chambres riche,
[114v] whan Harald or þe kyng wild com þider eftsons ..was as kyng wold come..
in þe tyme of gese to tak þam venysons. ...of grece..þe.
Karaduk, Griffyn sonne, he fordid þo wones;
he com þider on nyght, þe wrightes slouh at ones,
& alle þat he mot gete, he robbed & reft,
peny no penyworth, no þing he no left.
[I]n þat ilk tyme þat þis was beten doun, [*Capital om. in P.*]
Harald tille his fader went to Southampton,
for Dunstan, Agilet sonne, wild greue Sir Godwyn;
....wol greue his fader Godewyn
for Gospatrik was slayn, þei blamed him þerin. [*Om. L. A later hand has pencilled the line in the right margin.*]
My boke tellis nay, Godwyn did him no dere; ..me telliþ þat Godewyn....
it sais þe Quene Egyn þe blame suld scho bere,
scho did slo Gospatrik withouten any skille.
Tostus of Cumbirland retted Godwyn þer tille;
Tostus of Cumbirland, he was chefe iustise,
ageyn þe erle Godwyn, he gert sette assise; .....dide do sette.
Gospatrikes dede on Godwyn wild he venge.
Harald souht Tostus to leue þat ilk chalenge;
he praied him for luf, in pes lat him be stille,
& kisse & be gode frende in luf & in a wille. ......in pes..o.
Tostus wild not leue bot held on his manace,
& Hareld tened withalle, of lond he did him chace. .Harold........
Tostus ouer þe se went to Saynt Omere,
his wife & his meyne, & duelled þer þat ȝere
with þe Erle Baldwyn, þe wynter alle plenere;
his londes he were gyuen to Morkar fitȝ Richere. Here londes here were.....
Þe gode Kyng Edward to London turnes he,
þe feste of ȝole to hold with grete solempnite.
At Saynt Petir mynstere þat he did sette & wirke,
..Peteres churche þat..make & sette
on Saynt Steuen day he did halow þat kirke. ....churche
Þe kyng fro day to day he heuyed more & more;
nerhand his endyng, sekenes greued him sore.
Þe nyr his eyndyng day sikenesse...
Þe barons befor him kald & said vnto þam alle,
"Tille Harald, Godwyn sonne, þe regne wille best falle."
Me meruailes of my boke, I trowe he wrote not right,
Men meruailleþ of my writyng..my bok nys..

þat he forgate Wiliam, of forward þat he him hight;
..for gatyn William Bastard of þat he hadde..
neuerles þe forward held, what so was in his þouht.
Naþeles forward he him huld......
I wote wele criste it wild þat Edwardes wille wer wrouht.
Who so lokes his life & redis his vision, Hoso lokeþ......avision
what vengeance ordeynd was on Inglond to be don;
of princes of þe lond it sais of þam þis sawe
þat þei dred no þing god no ȝemed euenhed of lawe.
.dredeþ no þyng of god..euene þe.
[115r] Bot felawes vnto þefes to robbours of ilk cuntre,
þar wilkednes was fulfilled, venged behoued it be.
.wikkednesse is fulfuld & venged most..
Prelates ne no prestes, non of þam lyued wele; ....fewe of...
þe did not goddes hestes bot brak þam ilk a dele: Þey..........
licheros lif þei led & þouht it in þar breste,
holynes did away, of þe kirke gaf þei leste.
Holy lif was put away of churche þey recched.
Edward god bisouht þat it suld be forgyuen
& amendid with penance, & þerof clene be scryuen ....y shryven
of þat þat þei had don, & þat þat suld betide,
to warne þam þerfro & fle it on ilk side.
Bot þis was ansuere ageyn, a day þer in salle falle,
..answere agayn ȝif was vnto seynt Edward
þare wiknes is fulfilled, þer in ere waxen hard. .wikkednesse...þey beþ wexen.
God has sette þat ȝere a day þer in salle falle;
þe Inglis salle go to suerd, to pyne þar soules alle.
....to þe swerd to peyne þere..
Dede & fire salle fede þe scheperdes & þare schepe;
þis vision is ȝit to drede, þink & gif gode kepe.
I trowe it is ouergone þorgh William conqueroure.
He com & slouh ilkone þo wikked men in stoure
& sette vs in seruage, of fredom felle þe floure;
þe Inglis þorgh taliage lyue ȝit in sorow fulle soure.
Now is Edward dede þe soner for þo affrayes;
þre & tuenti ȝere, sex moneþes & seuenten dayes
he regned in þis lond; þe date of god þan wex
a þousand, I fond, sexti ȝere & sex.
[*L follows here with the passage at 1321–40 of P.*]
After Saynt Edward, Harald kyng þei ches ..Edward days....
þorgh conseile of þam alle, & he þe scheld les. ....þe schuld al les
In right & in lawe, þe barons held him trewe,

neuerles his falshed brouht vs sorowe alle newe. Naþeles.......
Tostus þat was exiled þorgh Harald, ore I told,
.his broþer...þourw Harold as y er.
he com out of fflandres, brouht an oste fulle bold;
fro Sandwich to Lincolne Tostus ran,
tresore alle & bestes, he robbed ilka man. Of tresour on & oþer he...
Þat herd Harald, fulle kene he was & kof;
with folk out of þe south, toward þe north drof.
Tostus herd it say, þe best wild he do;
to Malcolme, þe Scottis kyng, Tostus alied to.
Tostus tok his leue, aryued in Norweie,
& how þe gamen ȝede, lithe I salle ȝow seie. ...game.lusteþ & y schal seye
In Norweie was a kyng, my boke tellis sua,
Saynt Onlaf broþer, Harald Heruegra. ....Aruagra
He aryued in Tyne, bot sone he went ageyn ..vp in Tyme.....
& smote in tille Humber, his flete alle pleyn, ...Humbre with....
[115v] in an arme of Ouse vnder Ricalle lay; ......Richal he.
on Saynt Mathew euen on a Wednesday,
Edwyn & Morkare, tuo lordes Kumberland, ...of Cumberland
to Harald & Tostus þei gaf bataile on hand; ..Aruagra &......
Harald of Norweie had folk right inouh.
[*Line order differs in L. The P lines have been combined.*
L has 1651, 1650, and adds here:]
And Tostes hadde mychel kyn al folk þey slow
A hundreth & fifty þe toþer side alle slouh;
A hundred & fyȝtty to Ȝork ostages þey ladde
Harald & Tostus vndir Ricalle so sped, Harold Norwey &...þus þey.
a hundreth & fifty to Ȝork ostage þei led.
Nouht þien fulle fer to þam com a tiþing .for þan ful sone to....
þat Harald was comand, neuly was mad kyng. ...newely of Engelond..
Of þat ilk tiþing Tostus was affraied,
& Harald Heruegra, I trow, was no þing paied.
.þat oþer Harold Haruagar was noþyng wel apaied
Þorgh a mede þei passed vnto Staunford brigge,
þar loges & þare tentis vp þei gan bigge.
Whan Harald þider cam & sauh alle þar manere,
tille þam smertly he nam, displaied his banere. ..schortly..displaynge..
In þe mornyng it was, he mette with his enmys,
& alle þe day þei fauht, at euen he had þe pris.
Harald & Tostus boþe to dede ȝede .Haruagra.....þey.
þorgh Harald þe ȝong kyng, of wham I salle rede.
Listen & I salle rede why þe misauentoure

on Harald side gan sprede þorgh William conqueroure. ..siþþe.....
The duke of Normundie, William is his name,
Wolnoth, Haraldes broþer, he had in prisoun at Kame,
& his neuow, Hakon, in preson was him with. [*L om. 1668–1671*]
(I ne wote for what reson, so fer out of þer kith.)
Harald, whan he was ȝonge, he went vnto ffrance,
þe cuntre forto se & for to here of chance.
Alle his mishappyng felle, he com in to Pountif,
As Haroldis mys schapyng fel.....
to Richere þat was erle, men told it fulle rif.
To Richard þat Erel þat y tolde of ful riȝt
Þis lord of Pountif, Richer le fitȝ Iȝoun,
he tok þis ilk Harald & did him in presoun.
Þe bode of him sone kam to þe duke of Normundie;
þe duke went to Pountif & toke him with maistrie
& brouht Harald home & seid þorgh curteisie, ...to his court....
"Harald, haf now þin eyse in alle my seignorie." .....& alle þyne be murye
Now has Harald his eyse at reson in alle þing;
þe meyne in alle þing plesed him next þe kyng. ..gan hym plese. William..
William & Harald went þam for to paly, ...on a day þey wente for to pleie
tales togider þei tald, ilk on a gode palfray.
Whan þei had wele riden þat þam þouht right lang, ...longe
þei lighted & abiden biside a water stank. ....strong
[116r] "Harald," said William, "listen to my resoun, William seide to Harold listeþ...
what right þat I haue of Inglond þe coroun ....to þe croun
after Edwardes dede, if it so betide
þat god haf ordeynd, so I after him abide.
Whan þat we were, Edward þe kyng & I, ...were ȝonge.....
he was in my fader courte exiled, I ne wote whi,
out of Inglond; þan suore he to me,
if he þe coroun mot wynne, his heyre suld I be.
Þerof he mad me skrite, his hote to mak leale,
....a bond his othe to make al leal
& for to sikere his dede, set þer to his seale.
Harald, whan þou ses tyme, do þi help þerto;
I salle delyuer þ broþer & þi neuow also,
And y..þy broþer þy nevew & alle þe oþere.
& Marie, my douhter, to wife I wille þe gyue.
A man I salle þe make richely forto lyue,
or my chefe iustise, þe lawes to mend & right. .be my..my.....
Þi sistere I salle gyue a riche prince of myght."
"Sire," said Harald, "I salle, if þat I may,

help þe þe coroun to hald & euer I se þat day.
..croune to þe to ȝif if y se euer..
My broþer delyuer þou me, my neuow þou me grante,
..þenne deliuere me.....
& hold þi certeynte & salle hold couenante." ..þis in certeinte y schal..
Þe presons forth were fette tille Harald or he foore;
Þey weren fet forþ til Harold þes hostes with honour
to hold þat he had hette, on þe boke he suore.
Now gos he home, Harald, & has ouercomen his tene;
þe othe þat he suld hold, it is forgeten clene. .hest...halden he haþ..
Edward is dede, allas; messengers ouerwent ....þe while messegers beþ went
to William, Harald was þorgh comon assent
And tolde þat Harold was þurw þe..
was corouned nobly & for kyng þei him helde,
Coroned Kyng in Engelond &..hym held
bot þe duke of Normundie, to William felle þe schelde.
Ac to þe Duk..aftur fel..
Þe duke wrote to þe kyng in luf withouten loth, ...loue & noþyng wroþ
bisouht him ouer alle þing þat he wild hold his oth
& ȝeld him þe coroun of Inglond ilkadele,
or Marie to warisoun, wed hir & ioy it wele;
..his dowþttour haue to wif with warson & ioye here.
& if he wild not so, he suld mak him oknowen
he suld wynne it, fordo in right as for his owen.
.hadde his truthe fordo & make þis lond..
Harald wrote ageyn & seid he neuer þouht
Marie to wedde certeyn, þe lond hight him nouht,
& if he wild it wynne with dynt als duke hardie,
he suld fynd þerinne Kyng Harald redie.
Ȝit is Halald, I say, regnand in myght & mayn;
Riȝt hadde Harold some seyen regnyng....
þe kyng of Norway in bataile has he slayn.
Þe duke forgeten is he of þing þat Harald hette.
..for to geten his riȝt of þat þat Harold heyt
Now is he in þe see with saile on mast vpsette;
[116v] toward þis lond þei drouh to auenture his chance ....þem of.
with Normandes inouh of fflandres & of ffrance. .....& men of.
He had redy sailyng þat to þe lond him ledde,
& at his riuyng, þe lond non him forbedde. ...aryvyng þe land hym forbedde
His folk went vp to lond, himseluen was þe last; Ac to lond his folk went....
to bank ouer þe sond, plankes þei ouer kast. .þe bank ouer þe lond....
Als William þer on suld go, he stombled at a nayle, ...chanel

in to þe waise þam fro, he tombled top ouer taile.
...wose he ful doun & tumbled top &.
His knyghtis vp him lyft & did him eft atire, ...nywe.
William was oglyft, his helm was fulle of myre;
William was not paied, þat falle mad him ofright.
He stode alle dismaied, þan said tille him a knyght,
"Discomfort no þing þe, so faire happe neuer þou fond; ......help neuer ȝe.
stoupe & þou may se, þi helm has wonne lond.
& stoupe now & y se þyn..taken.
Þat þe lond is þin, þi helm schewes it þe.
Forsuorn is Haraldyn, he salle no dure." ..Harold..neuer y þe
Whan William alle was dight & to þe boun, ..was nywe diȝt..bataille bone
redy with him to fight, he fond Harald fulle sone.
He fond fulle wele & sone þat Harald nouht ne slepe;
to proue with dede to done, fulle wakand on him lepe.
...dede of dont ful wakant to hym he.
To bataile haf þei mynt, Harald & William, ...ment...
bot non stode Harald dynt þat bifor him kam;
þe rouht of þare rascaile he did it rere & ryme,
Normanȝ & Flemmyng taile he kutted many tyme.
To while þat he was fresch, þei fond him fulle austere;
þei felt of his pruesse als knyght did his deuere, ...þat dede..
for he was ouer prest & egre to assaile,
he wild haf no rest tille he myght trauaile. .....whiles...
Allas for for Sir Harald, for him was mikelle reuth;
.for sir Harold...muche ruthe
fulle wele his awen suld hald if he had kept his treuth.
He hadde holde his owyn if.....
Bot þat he was forsuorn, mishappyng þerfor he fond,
suld he neuer els haf lorn for William no lond,
ne bien in þat bondage þat brouht was ouer þe se; Ne we ben.........
now ere þei in seruage, fulle fele þat or was fre.
But siþþe were in seruage þat by fore were.
Our fredom þat day for euer toke þe leue;
for Harald it went away, his falshed did vs greue. ....was our myschiffe
He was so fer in presse, so fele wer him about,
him befor alle þei ches þat he suld not skape out.
Normanȝ & Burgolons with lance, suerd, & mace
bare Sir Harald doun; allas, he had no grace. Was sir Harold dented doun.....
So douhty knyght of dede was non of noiþer sides; [*Transp. L*]
þore to dede he ȝede als man forsuorn betides. [*Transp. L*]
Ther....forsworen man ofte mystydes

[117r] Nien monethes beforn kept Harald þe regalle,
bot þat he was forsuorn, þerfor he lost alle.
Out of þe stoure þat stode tuo man [a]skaped ware, [*A letter has disappeared in P.*]
..stokes þer stond..askaped warde
of Sir Haraldes blode, Eadwyn & Morkare.
Þei tok þe Quene Edith for doute of treson,
was Kyng Edwardes wif, led hir to Kelion. ....Kairlion
Wele was scho þer to hold priue soiorne. .þenne was......
Eadwyn & Morkare to London gan þei turne,
vnto þe Londreis þei told þat þei had fonden an hayre,
was Edmund kosyn, þe kyng; þe Londreis wer in speyr
him for þar kyng vplift, his name was kald Edgar.
....wolde vp lifte his name was.
For William þei wer oglift & said, "Þat we ne dar, ...aferd......
for slayn is Kyng Harald, & in lond may non be
bot he of William hald for homage & feaute."
Morkar recleymed es, as es þe faukon fre,
& Eadwyn com to pes, he mot no better se;
þe burgeis of London þar conseile wild it nouht [*Om. L*]
to gif Edgar þe coroun þat for heyr þei brouht. [*Om. L*]
William þe Conquerour to London has he þouht,
þer þe bataile was stoure, an abbay wild he haf wrouht;
....doun..by hym was.
þer he & Harald mette, þer standes þe kirke, [*Om. L*]
for blode þat þer was gette, to praie þei suld not irke. .....sched......
[*L adds:*] ffro peyne þem to lette þat þey com neuer in myrke
To London com William his ȝole feste to hold, ...Cristemasse..
his barons with him nam, knyghtes þat wer bold. .harneys..he nam his....
Wardeyns of tour & toun, & oþer þat ne wold,
þar landes les alle doun, for tynt wer þei told;
to Frankis & Normanȝ for þar grete laboure,
to Flemmynges & Pikardes þat wer with him in stoure,
he gaf londes bityme, of whilk þer successoure
...by tymes whuche was þere gret socour
hold ȝit þe seysyne with fulle grete honoure.
& holdeþ þem ȝut y sesed here heires with..
Fair grace William fond, his chance fulle wele him satte,
þe reame of Inglond so graciously he gatte.
Þe Archbisshop Stigand, of Inglond primate,
þat tyme was suspended, þe pape reft him þe state,
& abbot & prioure, men of religion,
& oþer men of honour, archdecane & person,

wer priued of þar office, of woulfes had renoun,
for lichorie, þat vice, wer many als don doun.
Þe archbisshop of Ʒork com with deuocioun,
þorgh William praiere com to London toun.
Bifor þe barons brouht, he gaf William þe coroun; ...was broȝt.....
to chalange was he nouht, Sir Stigand was don doun. ....noȝt for Stygand...
[117v] Whan William was coruned kyng so solemply
& had taken homage of barons bi & bi,
he turned ouer þe se vnto Normundi;
Dam Helienore, quene was sche, scho bare him company.
Whan he had duelled þore, at Pask he com ageyn,
& Dam Helianore, with many knyght & sueyn,
to London alle þei went, þe courte holy alle pleyn.
For þe archbisshop þei sent, messengers ȝede tueyn.
Elred, þe archbisshop of Ʒork, had þe se;
þe kyng him bisouht als clerk of dignite,
"To coroune Helianore, þat biseke I þe."
Þe bisshop corouned hir þore bifor þat faire semble.
Whan þe folk had bien at þe coronment ilk dele,
boþe þe kyng & þe quene, þe barons paied wele. ....liked hit.
Þe kyng & þe clergie ordeynd þat ilk seele
þe pes to ȝeme & gyue with lawes trewe als stele.
Edmunde & Edwyn, Harald sonnes of Kent,
alle Somersetschire þei wasted & brent; ..wasted robbed &.
Sir Adinoth þei slouh, & alle þat þei mot hent.
Whan þei had frauh inouh, ageyn tille Ireland went.
...y frawȝt þer schupes to Irland agayn þey.
Þe Erle Robert Comyn þe west had to welde, ...northe...
[*L adds:*] At Burghe in Cumberland his parlement he huld
Þe barons of þe Northe on þis Robert gan beld
þat non vnto William for no þing suld þam ȝelde.
[*A leaf has been lost in L, lines 1834–1913 of P.*]
Whan þat Kyng William þo tiþinges herd say,
to þe toun of Durham fulle fast he toke þe way;
þe bisshop to him said, & told to him fulle tite,
þat þe Norreis purueied to do him a despite.
For þat ilk tale þat þe bisshop told,
þe Komyn had his bale, his lif was lightly sold;
þe lond of Saynt Cutbert he did serch þat nyght.
William alle apert his oste redy he dyght,
at þat þei mot fynd, to suerd alle þei ȝede,
& or Roberd wist or þouht on suilk a dede,
ore was his hous on fire þer Sir Robert lay

& brent Roberd to dede; bi þat it was day.
Now is þe Komyn dede, his haires has alle lorn;
William þam it forbede þat held his londes beforn.
Now William has soiorned & slayn alle his enmys,
& to þe south is turned als kyng þat wan þe pris.
Tiþynges com him fulle stoute þat a grete oste & stark
with Harald & with Knoute, þe kyng sonnes of Danmark,

[*Two lines have been crossed out and repeated at top of the next leaf.*]

[118r] were aryued in Humbere, & an erle Turkille
with folk withouten nombere, þe Norreis felle þam tille.
Comen is þe erle Edgar with alle þo of his kynde;
Sir Wolnoth, he is þar þo with þat he mot fynde,
Marlesuayn, Turkille sonne, & Suane, a douhty knyght,
of Scotland, Gospatrik with þam at alle his myght.
Þe Normans in þe south wer in so grete affray,
of kastels & of touns þei com out alle day;
to ȝork ran ilk a man to rescet in þat toun
þat no Danes man þe walles to breke doun.
Sir William Malet was wardeyn of þe cuntres,
Sibrigh þe Gaunt was set with him to kepe þe fees;
þise tuo brouht tiþng þe wer comen bi þat coste,
þerfor William þe kyng did turne ageyn his oste
& suore a grete othe þat he suld neuer spare
noiþer lefe no lothe northeren what so þei ware.
William turned ageyn & held þat he had suorn:
alle mad he wasteyn, pastur, medow, & korn,
& slouh boþe fader & sonne, women lete þei gon.
Hors & hondes þei ete, vnneþis skaped non.
Whan þe Danes herd þat William held his oth,
þat he with þe Norreis so ferd, spared lefe no loth,
fulle quantly þei sent to William messengers.
Of pes þei mad present to turne ilkon þer pers
ageyn to Danmark go, with his wille & his leue,
þat he suld no mo slo, ne þei suld him not greue.
Now duellis William eft, fulle bare mas many wone;
of gode men er non left bot slayn er ilkone.
Clerkes vnneþis þei lete to kirke olyue to go;
horses & hondes þei ete for hunger & for wo.
Grete synne did William þat suilk wo did wirke,
so grete vengeance he nam of men of Holy Kirke
þat not did no wem tille him ne no trespas;
fro ȝork vnto Durhem no wonyng stede was.

Nien ȝere, sais my buke, lasted so grete sorowe;
þe bisshop clerkes tuke, þar lyues forto borowe,
Saynt Cutbertes bones of fertre toke þei out.
With þam þei fled at ons in sere stedes about,
þat vengeance burd be don, als tellis Saynt Edward.
He sauh in a vision þat vengeance suld falle hard
of prestes & of clerkes, of princes of þe lond,
of god ne of his werkes þei dred not þat þei fond.
[118v] Saynt Cutbertes clerkes in hidnes euer ȝede,
at Geruans set þer merkes, a house þe gan vpspede.
ȝit Northermore þei ȝed vntille Bethlyngton,
at Toghalle was þe þrid & þer restid þam doun;
þe ferth was holy Eland, þer þe se it withdrouh,
þei ȝede on þe sand to þat ilde wele inouh.
Whan þei wer þerinne, of non had þei doute;
þe flode bigan to gynne & klosed it aboute.
Siþen dred þei no þing of thefe ne of feloun
þat were with the kyng, Norman no Burgoloun.
Þe kirke of Geruans þat ilk tyme was brent,
Durham þe same sans alle to fire went.
Þe croice & þe rode, right as criste vs bouht,
tille askes alle it ȝode, þe fire spared nouht.
Þe Normans did it alle in þe guyse of theft;
þe godes þerof stal, no þing þei ne left.
Whan William vnderstode how his men ferd with alle,
of Holy Kirke þe gode his serganȝ robbed & stal,
he comandid alle his to mende þat trespas
in alle maner wise as it ore feffed was,
& on þe same asise serued & alowed [*L resumes after gap*.]
....assises..sowed
of alle þe franchise þat it are was dowed.
Bot of þat wikkednes þat men suld haf wroken
was noiþer more no lesse of þer penance spoken.
Þe bisshop brouh þe bones ageyn vnto þe se ..broȝt þe holy.....
tille Durhames wones þer þei wer wont to be. ..Minstre......
William þe Conquerour changis his wikked wille:
out of his first errour repentis of his ille,
& of his crueltes he gynnes forto assuage
& gaf ageyn þo fees of whilk he toke ostages.
Gospatrik com tille hand & left of his manage, ...meynage
& William Comberland gaf him in heritage. ..al Cumberland..to.
Gospatrik ȝed alle þorgh his dedis forto praise,
þe kastelle of Bamborgh þe walles he did vpreise.

Malcolme, þe Scottes kyng, þerwith had envie
þat Gospatrik of suilk þing bare his state so hie,
dight him to Combirland, destroied about aywhare;
ilkon he slouh at hand, þer godes away bare.
Many with him he led & did þam in seruage;
in Scottland was alle spred mykelle of þat lynage.
..where wide spredde muchel of þere.
On þis Gospatrik, William gan affie;
he dight also quik & went Normundie. ..suffred hym be al quyt & dede hym to.
[119r] Malcolme in Kumberland dos þat he may tille ille;
Gospatrik his willand lates him haf his wille. .hym suffred to do al..
Þre þousand pounde Malcolme sent tille Gospatrik tresorie,
to William comyng þat went suld suffre his folie.
Til William come aȝen scholde...
Litelle wend William of his trecherie.
A message tille him nam vnto Normundie, .messenger til hym com..
teld William eueridele of Malcolme robberie;
for siluere þat he toke, suffred þe folk to die. [*Transp. L*]
Gospatrik did not wele, mayntend his partie; [*Transp. L*]
William also suiþe dight him tille his nauie. .als tid to Hamptoun had..
William has hauen nomen & is at Southampton;
When he had hauen take sone..
þo þat with him er komen, erle, knyght, & baron, ...aryved Eryl...
went tille Comberland fulle suiþe opon haste,
þe cuntre þat þei fand alle was wilde & waste.
Malcolme fled beforn in mountayns & in playn;
he wend for neuermore William suld com agayn.
No more did Gospatrik þat did him þat disceit, ..wente Gospatrik.....
bot comen is William quik & sekes þam fulle streit.
Bi a side of Scotland, Malcolme flies fer in,
bot William Malcolme fand in þe toun of Abrenethyn;
þer is Malcolme taken & ȝolden to preson.
Siluer was not forsaken, was giffen for his raunson;
to take he bed inouh, for at his wille he was.
William, to do his prowe, forgaf alle his trespas;
Malcolme with skrite him bond his heires of his lynage,
to hold of Inglond for feaute & homage.
Whan þe pes was siker, þe kyng turned fulle suiþe;
Gospatrik þat suffred biker, he reft boþe lond & liþe.
..so ferde byfore he refte hym...
Cumberland him reft, his oþer londes als,
þe lif ouer mykelle him left, for he was traitour fals.

Siþen to Durham went, þer he destroied þe see;
...he wente þere he had destrued þat.
þe bisshop he bisouht Saynt Cutbertes bones to see.
Þe bisshop opned þe schryne, þe bones þei vp raised; ..vpened.......
þe kyng wepte with his ine, þat sight mykelle he praised
& siluer grete plente opon þe altere laid;
þer franchise gaf þam fre, þe whilk þat þei of said.
Þe kastelle did he wirke of his tresore alle,
& Saynt Cutbertes kirke closed with a walle.
Siþen he bad þam turne to 3ork & þer abide,
for þer he wild soiorne alle þe Whitsons tide.
At 3ork did he crie his pes suld holden be
þat non did felonie bi land no bi se;
siþen he ȝede to London, þat cite set to grith,
& to þe lawe alle bondon ilk man in his kith. .sette þe lawe al aboute.....
[119v] Chefe iustise he sette þe sothe to atrie,
for lefe no loth to lette, þe right lawe to guye,
þe wronges to amend & maynten þe right,
ageyn þe fals defend þorgh dome of iustise sight.
That tyme þat I of say of William þe kyng,
þre monkes of Lyndsay ȝede to seke wonyng.
Þe first, Dan Aldwyn, þe toþer, Elwyn hight he,
Þat on Dan Aldewyn hiȝt þe furste of alle þre
[*L adds:*] Þe secounde Dan Lewyn was þus told my bok to me
þe þrid hight Reynfride, þus told my boke to me.
..Dan Reynfred hiȝt religious men ful meke
[*L adds:*] To 3ork schire large & wid þey wente wonyng to seke
Hughe le fitȝ Galdre, of 3ork he was schirue, ...Shyreve
he resceyued alle þre & heberd þam bileue.
...þem þre & herborwed þem y fere
After þer soiornyng whan þat þei suld wende,
he praied þam of alle þing, as gentille men & hende, Þey prayed of alle......
to haue saf condite vnto þe new kastelle,
& Hugh did as he hight, led þam sauely welle; ...as so tid....
fro þe new kastelle vnto Geruans þei ȝede,
þer duelled þei non seel, to Durham gan þam spede. ...no while.....
Whan þei to Durham com to þe Bisshop Waltere,
þer þei bigan a home of religiouse manere. ..gan an home make...
A closter þei bigan, þe bisshop þo þat wrouht, ...& þere þo..
hired ilk a man & alle paied & bouht. Þey hured eche....þey paied..
Or it wer alle ent, þe werke þat þei did wirke, ...eynded......
þei ordeynd a couent to ministre in þat kirke.

"Help, Lady," said Waltere, "of þe þan is þis house,
þat are was prouendere, now is religiouse."
To ȝorke þe com ageyn & wrouht þer worschiply
cloistre with couent pleyn, a kirk of our lady.
Whan it was wrouht tille ende, þe monkes alle þre ...broȝt......
to Whitby gan wende þat standis on þe see;
þer wirke þei wild an abbeye wele to preise,
in wirschip of Saynt Hilde, a kirke þei did vp reise.
Þus wrouht þise monke þre þorh þe Holy Goste, ..þes monkes.....
abbayes in sere cuntre þat wikked men did waste, ...contres.....
& many a gode man to holy lif did calle ...wilde......
þat þorgh þe lawe paien men left & lete doun falle.
At London is William, at Lundreis takes leue; ....& of þe toun takeþ.
to þe parlement he nam at Paris to Lowis cheue.
Þe Duȝe Pers of ffrance were þat tyme at Parys;
to William felle þar chance, he mad conquest of pris:
þe toun wan of Terwenne, þe castelle of Malbis,
his auncestrie whilom when left it þorgh folis;
whan William with þe lawe had seisen pleynerly, ...seised hit pleynly
siþen he gan him drawe toward Normundy,
[120r] þe lond to visite & to comforte his frendes.
He restid bot a lite, a sonde þe Inglis him sendes;
....litil þe Englysche tydyng..
þe erle of Surrey sent Hacon, Henry sonne. ....is sent Haucon..
He to William went & praied him ȝit eftsonne
to com tille Inglond or els alle he lesis,
ageyn him wille men stond & partie tille him chesis; ....þem.
William was in wehere whan he herd þat tiþing.
In his auhtend ȝere als he regned kyng, ..viii.....
at Wynchestre he held his parlement ilk ȝere, ...þat ilke.
& þer men him teld who was his aduersere:
of Northfolk, þe erle Roger, men said of him treson;
for praier or for pere, þei did him in prison. ....paynge men dide...
Vnto þe Marche gan long an erle, Wolnot he hight;
þe kyng with mykelle wrong did him slo þat knyght. ...medlyng....slee..
Abowen Wynchester was schewed tille alle þat þer ware,
to lewed men & lerid, to kirke as þei him bare,
miracle faire & myrie whan þei laid him in pitte.
William of Malmesbirie witnes it in his writte.
Siþen in his þrid ȝere, he tellis þer of a chance:
of Durham, Bisshop Waltere was smyten þorgh with a lance;
in Gatesheued it was, & þo þat suld be schent,
þo did þat trespas, Sir Liolfes kynde of Kent;

þe Erle Liolf was slayn for þe bisshop dede.
My boke sais certayn þat he gaf neuer þat rede;
þerfor Kyng William did fleme alle þat kynde,
þar landes fro þam nam þat men mot knowe & fynde.
Siþen in his ferþe ȝere he went tille Aluerton.
No man wend in erþe drede of no felon;
on warned him of a þing þat Malcolme, with poysoun,
A man ȝut warned........
schuld begile þe kyng with som þat lufed tresoun.
.haue giled William Kyng.....
William sent his sond, his eldest sonne Roberd,
if he mot vnderstond or any suilk of herd. .....of eny treson.
Roberd about did spie if Malcolme wild haf wrouht,
bot alle it was a lie, þat þing was þeuer þouht.
..was mad a lye suche treson was non.
[I]n his auhtend ȝere þat William was regnand, [*Capital om. in P.*]
..xviii.....
extendours he sette forto extend þe land, He sente out certeyne extentours....
erldam & baronie, how mykelle felle to þe schelde;
knyght & sergeancie als, how mykelle þei helde;
how mykelle lond & rent Holy Kirke had to a prowe. [*Om. L*]
Alle þei did extend to witte þe verrey valowe,
& William wist of alle what it suld amounte,
of lordyng & of thralle, þe extente þorgh acounte.
.Lordschupe & alle oþer þe...
[120v] Roberd Courthose, his sonne, he gaf alle Normundie
to hold as it was wonne als heyre of ancestrie.
William passid þe se, þer of he mad þe skrite,
of ffrance to hold þat fe, of oþer tenement alle quite.
His oþer sonne, William, Inglond assigned he, ...William Rous...
& alle þat of him cam, with chartre mad he fre.
His sonne Henry was sire of Wales with chartre streite,
of alle Loncastre schire vntille Bromsthueite.
Ade, his douhter dere, he lufed hir als his life,
þe erle of Plesance, Steuen, weddid hir to wife,
& Kyng Steuen on hir gate, þat withouten reson,
of þis lond had þe state & conquered þe coroun.
His douhter Custance was wedded to Bretayn,
with Williams ordenance, vnto þe Erle Alayn.
Tuo ȝere & a half he duellid in Normundie
& in þat lond self at Kame gan he die.
At Saynt Steuens Kirke þei laid him with honoure;
himself did it wirke, he was þar fondoure.

Tuenty ȝere had he þe land & nien moneth streite;
þe date was a þousand & fourscore & auhte.
The conquerour is laid at Kame, dede in graue;
þe Courthose beforsaid Normundie salle haue; Robert Curthose....
to William þe rede kyng is gyuen þe coroun,
at Westmynstere tok he ryng in þe abbay of Londoun.
..he had þe regalye.....
Whan he had alle plenerly seisyn of þe lond,
þe barons & þe clergy ageyns him he fond;
þis was þare comon sawe in burgh & cite,
þe Courthose with þe lawe suld þare lord be. Robert.....þe kyng.
"He is broþer eldest, þe coroun salle he bere.
He is of body best þe reame forto were." & bold man of...lond..
What did þe grete lordynges, erles & barounes?
Kastels & oþer þinges seised, maners & tounes; ..holdynges sesed...
þe kyng had fulle grete þouht, his reame ageyn him ros;
frendes fast he souht to venge him on his fos.
Þis sorow & þis drede lastid him þre ȝere;
.drede lestid hym longe þre ȝer al in wo & wher
of pes ne myght he spede bot euer in þer dangere.
His frendes gan him rede to go to þe kyng of ffrance
to conseile him in þis nede, to abate þat distance;
for þis Kyng William dight him vnto schip,
his frendes with him nam vnto Kyng Philip.
Vnto Kyng Philip he schewed ilka dele
.þe Kyng Philippe of France he schewed hit..
how his barons gan kip, ageyn him did not wele. ...with þer wit aȝenst....
[121ʳ] "Þerfor I am comen to wite at ȝow, our heued,
þe londes þat we haf nomen, to whom þe salle be leued,
& at ȝour iugement I wille stand & do,
with þi þat it be ent, þe strif bituen vs tuo."
Philip said bliþely & sent his messengers
tille Inglond to þe clergy, erles, barons, þer pers,
& askid if þei wild stand to þer lokyng. ....Kyng Philippus.
Þe Duke Roberd fulfilled, so did William þe kyng.
Þe barons wrote ageyn, at his demyng þei ches;
þei held his dome certeyn for he was prince of pes.
Philip was fulle wis, with scrite he bond þam boþe;
he said þan his avis, "Kisse & be not wroþe."
At þe first þei kiste as frendes felle to be.
"Of ȝour fader biqueste, dome þan salle ȝe se."
Doun þei sat on benke among þe Duȝe Pers;
Philip gan him thnke & said on þis maners, .bygan hym beþenke.....

"William þe Conquerour, his ancestres & he,
held with grete honour Normundie in fe
of alle kynges of ffrance, & so did he of me,
for alle oþer distance with homage & feaute.
Alle Inglond he wan þorgh his vassalage
& Harald Kyng ouer ran þat did William outrage;
þerto had he no right, no non of his lynage,
þat William wan with myght is told non heritage.
We se alle day in place þing þat a man wynnes,
it is told purchace whedir he it hold or tuynnes,
Whe seieþ hit is purchace wheþer hit be lond or Innes
& þat comes of grace or of conquest bigynnes.
He may tille he has space gif it withouten synnes,
..suche ȝyven al þat he has purchas..
heritage þat lyues & leues to þe eldest sonne.
Purchaced þing men gyues woman weddyng to mone,
or tille a man is strange for his seruise eftsone. ....estrange for longe seruice.
Heritage salle men not change on purchace wise to wone.
.....but purchas as..
Roberd, þorgh our assent, þe heritage to þe lies,
& þou, William, salle hent þe purchace at our avis;
...schalt hente Engelond...
þus ȝour fader ȝow sette als man of lawe was wis.
His dede ne wille we lette, be þe martir Saynt Denys." ......I swere by..
Whan Roberd sauh & wist how þe conseile ȝede,
to þe Holy Land him list & þider gan him spede.
Whan he com at Marsille & ouer þe se suld wend,
Philip sauh his wille & after him gan send;
þe bode was sent to rathe, þe messenger com ouer sone;
for soth it was gret skathe his passage was fordone.
[121v] The rede Kyng William felle a faire chance: ....hym fel a ful fayr.
to Saynt Poules he cam withouten greuance,
for erles & barons bi sond he forsent .....sonde for þem sente
& alle at his somons to parlement went. ....þey wente
He schewed on & oþer þat bated was þe strife
bituex him & Roberd & were in luf of life, ..& his broþer &.....
with chartre wele wreten & selid certeyn,
& wele it was to witen no chalange ageyn.
Wherfor he þam hight if þei to luf wild drawe,
þe coroune at his myght to maynten with lawe,
& þat he so suld, þe barons had affiance,
his kastels þei him ȝolde with alle þe purtenance.
[I]n þe ȝere folowand at þe someres tide, [*Capital om. in P*.]

Roberd com to þis land, at Douer gan vp ride.
Whan herd say, with luf tille him he sped, .William hurde hit seye......
& with grete noblay tille London him led.
Within þo auht daies com William þis tiþing:
þe north had fele affraies þorgh þe Scottis kyng,
þe cuntre gan assaile, þe folk forto schende.
Roberd gaf him consaile þider samen to wende,
....þat þey scholde þider wende
with þider þei ferd, William & Roberd. Wiþ ost þider.....
Malcolme, whan he it herd, fled for ferd .....he fled away..
& William toke him þere, his folk slouh ilk man, [*Transp. L*]
& als þei were fleand vnto Louthian. [*Transp. L*]
Malcolyn & his herde þey fledde to ton Louthþan
So ferd þei him found, þei obliged þam to gyue .harde........
fourti þousand pound at his pes to lyue;
opon þat he suore to hold of him his fe
& or William fore tok homage & feaute. .þere William of hym tok boþe...
To London William turnes & had alle his wille,
& Malcolme soiornes in Scotland with ille. ..hym scornes...mykil ille
Whan he was at London, a haule he did vp wright,
first þouht & founden, for chambre was it right. .þat hit was fonded.....
Roberd leue has taken & went to Normundie;
to Wales is William schaken, estres to spie.
It felle in tyme of þe ȝere at Saynt Brice feste
þat he had regned here nyen ȝere at þe meste,
ros in Northumberland suilk a sorow hard: ...a sorwe sory.
Malcolcolme ȝede robband & his sonne Edward. Malcolyn ȝede.....
Þat herd an erle, Roberd, he ȝared him to bataile.
With Malcolme & Edward, he gan þam assaile;
þat bataile was hard, fo men has no frith, ...ful hard for falshede haþ..
slayn was þat coward & his sonne him with. ..Malcolyn coward.....
[122r] Þe folk þat ascaped on Malcolme side
to Scotland þam raped & puplised it fulle wide;
þei mad parlement & toke þam to rede, [*Transp. L*]
Malcolme to god was went & Edward his sonne dede, [*Transp. L*]
& corouned Dufnald, Sir Malcolme broþer.
His sonnes þei ne wald þe ton no þe toþer.
ffor Malcolyns to sones þey ne tok noþer on ne oþer
Of Malcolme þat man, left tuo sonnes ware,
þe ton hight Dunkan, þe toþer Edgare.
Dunkan sauh his eam had his heritage;
þer he wist bote of beam, he went þat viage ...bote to ben he...
to William þe rede kyng þer he was in Wales;

what tid of þat þing, he told him alle þe tales. .by tidde of his þyng......
"Myn heritage I craue of þe þat is my heued. Dokan seide myn.........
Help me it to haue þat Dufnald has me reued."
With scrite, vnto William Sir Dunkan him bond,
& to þe heirs þat of him cam for þe coroune of Scotlond.
Inglis & Normans þe kyng did somoune
to wend with Sir Dunkan & do Dufnald doune
& seise Dunkan þer in, als heyr of heritage,
to hold & alle his kyn, of Inglond for homage.
Whan corouned was Dunkan & þe fest ent,
Inglis & Norman to Kyng William went.
Dufnald, þat is put oute, alle about wendes
in fele stedes aboute & gadres his frendes
& conseiled with þam þis cas þat alle suld þei go
& spie where þe kyng was, Dunkan if he mot slo.
Slayn haf þei Dunkan & eft corouned Dufnald;
of Kyng William wild þei no more hald.
Þe kyng was in affray, he myght not tent þerto;
with Roberd þe Moubray, his coroune he wild fordo.
Roberd wild haf reft William alle his right,
þe coroune his kosyn left, & gif it him þorgh myght.
William is war of þis, þorgh for Roberd he þretis
.....þurghe force on Robert precys
& takes him maugre his, his kastelle doun betis.
Better were Roberd in pes haf holden him stille
þan layn in prison sperd & at his fomen wille.
.lyge..stret his men were beton ille
In Wyndesouere is he leued, sorow þan is his pyne; ..he is leyd.....
þat hewis ouer his heued, þe chip falles in his ine.
....hed hit falleþ þus in ryme
Þe next ȝere þer bi, William to Wales went;
þe Walsch men did foli, his lond robbed & brent. ....schent
Þerfor William ne wold vnneþis leue on olyue,
þat boþe ȝong & old alle ȝede to þe knyue;
[122v] neuer bifor in Wales was don so grete greue, ...was suche vengeance ȝyve
bi dounes & bi dales, þar folk at suilk mischeue.
Sen þis greuance hard, þe slauhter & þe drede,
fulle sone afterward, þe kyng to Ȝork ȝede.
Þider com Edgar, was Malcolme sonne,
& Sir Dunkan broþer þat slayn was þorgh tresonne,
& schewed to William þat heyre he was of kynde,
of Malcolme he kam, righter salle non fynde. .Malcolyns bloud......
"Wherfor I ȝow biseke, help me þe lond to haue,

& I with wille fulle meke 3our seruise salle I saue."
William vnderstode þat he said reson
& was next of blode, & Dufnald did treson.
He dight an oste fulle stoute with Edgar forto leue,
Dufnald to dryue oute or his hede him reue.
Eustace of Ferers þat oste suld guye; ......he gye
of Scotland þei him brouht, Dufnald forto spie,
[*Line order in L is 2247, 2250, 2251, 2248, 2249*.]
Wiþ Edgar & his peris Dufnald for to spye
& seised Edgar in alle, as right was þerto;
to William for þe regalle, he did þat he suld do.
Edgar & his peres þe chaced day bi day; So fast on hym þey so3t & chaced...
of Scotland þei him brouht for euer & drof away.
Edgar was Maldes broþer, men kald þe gode quene,
3it sais on & oþer so gode has here non bene.
Whan William had his wille of Scotland & of Wales,
to riche men was he grille, of pouer held no tales. ......of poure tok he..
Clerkes of Holy Kirke he chargis greuosly;
þei were bisie & irke on þer rentes to lyue by.
Of alle his wikked werkes, þese me þouht þe meste,
þat seuenten kirkes he mad tille his foreste .seventyne churches fordide for his.
[*L adds:*] Kirches seuentyne he dide þem beton doun
to his nywe forest bydene tenement churche & toun
þat neuer ere non was sen þe cristendam; ..suche er non....
he did grete trespas of Holy Kirke so nam. ..ri3t gret.þat of....
Wele tuelue 3ere kept he þis lond,
& how he died here, selcouthly I fond,
& if 3e wille lithe, I salle telle it 3ow. ...wol me listen.....
His dede com him suythe meruellosly, se how.
.deþ com ful swyþe & meruaillich ynow
On a Thurday at nyght, at euen he 3ede to reste;
..Þursday..þe kyng 3ede to his.
to hunte þer he had tight in his new foreste. ..a morwe he ti3t....
On slepe sone he felle, þe sueuen bifor him ran; ...he ful þis sweuene...
him þouht in his chapelle he was withouten man,
ne non he sauh no herd, & he biheld aboute,
þe dures were so sperd, he myght in no stede oute. .dores.....nawr oute
So grete hunger him cam & mete had ne none,
ne he ne wist to wham þat he mot mak his mone.
His hunger was so grete, he wend haf waxen wode;
opon þe rode he schete & ete it als it stode.
[123r] Whan he had eten þat, 3it him hungred eft,

þe Mariole þer scho sat, of hir no þing he left.
Whan he was turned & went out of þat affray,
for a bisshop he sent at morn whan it was day.
Sir Ode of Wynchestere, so þat bisshop hight,
he told him of alle þe estere þat him mette þat nyght;
þe bisshop gan it rede, "God is þe turned grym;
ouþer in word or dede has þou greued him. .....ȝe haue y wraþed.
Þerfor alle þat þou may, to penance tak þou space,
þat neuer on Friday to wod þou go to chace;
þe riuer salle þou forsake on Friday ilka dele.
Þat penance I þe take, Sir Kyng þou kepe it wele."
Sir Ode þe bisshop es with leue went him fro;
þe kyng herd his messe, to gamen þan wild he go.
His penance was forgeten, he asked for his archere,
....he clepeþ forþ his archers
Walter Tirelle was haten maister of þat mister. ..he hiȝt was....
To triste was he sette forto waite þe chance;
with a herde þei mette, a herte þerof gan lance, ...to an hert he gan to lance
Walter was redi, he wend haf schoten þe herte;
þe kyng stode ouer nehi, þe stroke he lauht so smerte.
Þus died William þe kyng on þis ilk manere;
Sir Ode herd þat tiþing, fulle mournand was his chere.
At Westminstre is he laid at Saynt Petir Kirke, .Wynchestre.......
in a toumbe purtraid, þe bisshop did it wirke.
Þe date a þousand was & a hundreth mo.
Forgif him his trespas, Ihesu, þat lete þe slo.
[*Line order in L is 2301, 2310–23, 2302–9, 2324; L is in the same order as P thereafter.*]

Þat tyme in Scotland was a mayden ȝeng,
as I red biforhand, Malcolme douhter, þe kyng.
Malde hight þat mayden, many of hir spak, ...of here gode.
fair scho was, þei saiden, & gode withouten lak.
A douhter had Saynt Margrete þat in Scotland lis,
of þat douhter sute com Malde þat was of pris,
...swete als com Maud þat was Emperys
& Dunkan & Edgar þat I red biforn.
Maldes breþer þei war, of Margrete douhter born.
.....Malcolynes wyffes yboren
After William, men cald þe rede kyng, [*This line in L follows 2301 of P.*]
Henry þe coroun nam, his broþer þat was ȝing.
Þe bisshop, Maurice, Henry corouned he,
þat tyme he did þe office, of London kept þe se.

Roberd þe Courthose to þe holy lond was went;
a Breton, daþet his his nose, for Roberd þider sent.
. Brutoun þat þis þyng nolde for . . .
A Breton sent þat sond, he did for treson, ... he dide hit . .
& Roberd com to lond withouten oþer reson;
[123v] þat did Roberd trauaile for nouht, he was a file,
noþeles þe erle of Cornwaile kept his wif þat while;
Charles douhter scho, lord of Ceȝile, . . sche was þe Lord . .
Dame Edith, bright as glas, Roberd þouht no gile . . briȝt of fas but Robert . . .
bot com on gode manere tille his broþer Henry.
He wife þat soiorned here, he led to Normundie. His wif . . . .
Henry wedded Dam Molde þat kyng was & sire; . . þis gode Mold . . . . .
Saynt Anselme, men tolde, corouned him & hire.
Þe corounyng of Henry & of Mald þat may
at London was, solemply on Saynt Martyns day.
The bisshop of Durham, Kandolf he hight,
of falshede to mak a gleam, þe wrong vnto þe right,
for he & oþer fele sent vnto Roberd;
þat stound suld he not spele sen he þat tiþng herd.
. stynte schold he noȝt siþþe þat he tydyng hurde
Roberd purueid him stille & com whan he wild,
"Þe folk is alle in wille, þe lond þe to ȝeld."
Þorgh messengers fals, Roberd gadred oste;
Henry was warned als & did kepe þe coste.
To þe fiue portes he sent & het þam in couenant
þat aliens suld non hent hauen of Normant.
. . . . hauene hent neyþer no normand
Þer sikernes was fast of þe fiue portes & þe kyng,
Henry dight him on haste to þe toun of Hastyng,
a kastelle did vp sette, his oste longe þer lay;
þei wend Roberdes flette suld haf comen bi þat way.
Þe bisshop þouht treson, forwarned was Henry,
he went to Southampton, with him alle his clergy; . . . . he & al his clergy
þe maistres of þe portes for gyftes tille him toke,
þe kyng & his force for Roberd þei forsoke.
A hundreth schippes & fiftene went to Normundie . . . & fiȝtty . . .
to help & to mayntene þe Duke Roberdes partie.
Roberd mad him alle preste, þe wynde gan him dryue;
þe first day of herueste at Portesmouth gan he ryue.
Toward Wynchestre þam dight, his folk forto eyse,
in token þat he had myght, a kastelle he did reyse.
To erles & barons lettres he sent aboute,
for riche rewardons to Roberd gan loute; . . . . . þey gan route

fulle fele suilk he fond þat with Roberd held,
of Inglis of þis lond agayn Henry bare scheld.
Roberd bi his letter his broþer gan diffie;
him þouht his partie better of him to haf maistrie.
Bot gode Anselme þat kept of Canterbirie þe see,
before þe barons lept, kried, "Pes, per charite!" ...he wepte & cried...
[124r] Þorgh conseile of Anselme þat wild þe comon prowe,
ilk auailed his helme & to conseile drowe;
þe parties were fulle stark, neuerlesse þorgh praiere, ...naþelese..
Henry þre þousand mark gaf to Roberd bi ȝere. .a þousand......
Þus gate was þat werre pesed withouten lore;
.was þis comsyng of werre peised withoute more
þat noiþer partie com nerre, I blisse Anselme þerfore.
....nyr y blessed be Anselm.
In couenant of pes men may wele witen,
bituex þam, noþeles, a skrite enselid & writen.
Als Anselme þe strif gan pes of þe duke & þe kyng, ...had pesed þe Duk...
com Reberd de Beleyse þorgh his ouerwenyng .Robert de Bloyse...
& passed hider ouer þe se & in to Wales went.
He gadred grete mayne of alle þat he mot hent; ...meyne......
þe Frankis tille him felle & alle þe Walsch fulle fikelle,
þe kastelle Arondelle he seised & als of Tikelle,
cites, burghes, & tounes ageyn Kyng Henry;
at Burgh in Schrobschire, to werre mad him redy. ......he made a cry
Alle Schrobschire held with Roberd de Beleyse;
Henry lift vp scheld, his kastels did he sayse,
þe walles did doun felle, þe tours bette he doun;
in þritty daies to telle, Roberd was taken in toun.
Within dayes þritty, taken he was þorgh spie
& led to Kyng Henry, don had he felonie, ...for don he had.
& his broþer Arnald, for with Roberd he fore;
as for traytours bald þe lond boþe forsuore.
Now is Henry venged of his traytours
& lord of mykelle þing & riche man of tresours.
Mald, þe gode quene, gaf him in conseile
to luf his folk bituene & leue alle his tirpeile,
bere him tille his barons þat held of him þer fees,
loue hym with his Barons with burgeys of Citees
& to lordes of tounes, tille burgeis of citees. .....þat holdeþ of hym þere fees
Þorgh conseile of Dame Malde, a kynde woman & trewe,
þer ore was hatred alde, now gynnes luf alle newe.
.erst was hard & cold now..be nywe
Now luf þei fulle wele, þe barons & þe kyng;

þe kyng dos ilk a dele in skille alle þer biddyng. ....reson...
Bot Henry þink it stark þat he is charged so
to gyue þre þousand mark & bonden be þerto. ..þe thousand.....
Þorgh conseile of his barons, he sent to Duke Roberd.
(What was his respons writen, I ne sauh no herd.) ....y say noþer writen..
Tuo gentille men, of blode þe best of Normundie,
Henry gaf gyftes gode to hold on his partie.
Whan Henry wist þer wille bi messengers priue,
an oste he purueid stille & passed ouer þe se;
[124v] he þouht to compas ille, þe same tille him did he, ...chace hym ille......
now salle Roberd fulfille þat he tok in his cuntre.
Whan Henry was ryued þer þer he wild ame, ...aryved þere þat...
þorgh power did he dryue Roberd out of Kame.
Bayone rent & fe sone had he lorn; Boþe...Robert had sone.
þe best of þat cuntre tille þe kyng wer suorn.
Roberd fele siþes at þat comyng les
boþe londes & liþes or he mot haf þe pes,
if he ne were þorgh help of William de Martayn, ʒif hit ne.......
& Roberd de Beleyse halp him with myght & mayn;
þise tuo went to ffrance & fonden at Parys,
als it was þar gode chance, Sir Philip sonne Lowys;
for Roberd þei bisouht of socour & mercie.
Sir Lowys failed nouht, his help was him redie;
Lowys wrote his letter vnto þe Kyng Henry
þat þei acorded better for his luf specially;
þe bisshop of Parys þe pes þan formed he,
if þei at his auys boþe wild paied be. ....wolde yformed.
"Roberd salle cleyme alle quite to Henry bifor vs here
þre þousand mark be skrite þe Henry gaf bi ʒere, Þe....þat....
þat Roberd ne non of hise salle ask Henry þe kyng
þis dette on non wise, peny no ferþing." .....noþer peny..
Whan þis barette was ent, þe bisshop tok his leue
& Henry home went, to no mo wild he greue. ..hamward went for.....
Þe londes wild he nouht ʒeld þat he of Roberd wan,
bot haf þam he wilde & hold for any man. ......holde þem...
Sen þat Henry was gone, Roberd went to ffrance
to Sir Lowys on one & told him þat greuance, ...a noun &....
& Sir Lowys þerfore bad him tille Ingland go
to praye Henry restore þo tounes he tok him fro.
Roberd tille Ingland kam & bisouht þe kyng
þo fees he fro him nam, restore ageyn þat þing;
Henry ansuerd nay, þerto were him lothe ..hym nay þat were hym ful.
& Roberd went awith, with William was he wrothe.

..went away with Henry...

Whan he sauh þat Roberd for wroth turned so sone
& no þing ansuerd bot to wend was alle bone,
Henry mad him ȝare & after him fulle suiþe
to Normundie to fare & se what he wild kiþe,
& duelled þer a ȝere biside Roberd, his broþer,
þat noiþer werre, wo did þe ton to þe toþer.

.nawre werre ne were by twyxt on & þat oþer

In alle þis ilk chek of Roberd & Henry,
bituex þam wex contek, þe kyng & þe clergy;

. Waxed a gret contek bytwext þe....

[125r] þe kyng, in þe courte of þe lay, þe clerkes wild iustise.
Saynt Anselm said him nay, he wild on non wise;
þe kyng on gan hald to haf þam at his dome, ..þer on gan.......
Saynt Anselm þerfor appeld vnto þe courte of Rome. ...hym called vnto....
Whan he had sped his nedis & fro þe courte comen,
þe kyng for oþer dedis to Normundie was nomen.
Anselm duelled nouht, bot sone ouer þe se
to þe kyng tiþing brouht what þerof suld be. .....what dom...
Þe bisshop schewed him skille þat he mayntend þe ille,
þe kyng consentid þertille & gaf Anselm his wille.
Þorgh Anselm maytenyng was þe contek ent; ..mayntenyng....
he tok leue at þe kyng & home to Inglond went.
Þe kyng his retenanȝ alle tille him he drouh

..al his retenance til hym faste drow

of Inglis & Normanȝ & gadred folk inouh.
Whan he had samned his oste of folk fer & nere,
he seged bi þat coste þe kastelle of Tenkere,
whilom Wiliam Mortayn þerof lord was;
þe Courthose is vnfayn, him þenk it a trespas,
þerfor þe duke him dight as man of grete value.
Roberd Beleyse with myght þe sege þei wend remue;
þe Mortayn, befor spoken, with his nevow, Reynere, William Morteyn......
þe sege þe wend haf broken, þei com with þer powere.
Þe kyng sauh þat þei kam, his trompes did he blowe;
to þe bataile he nam, Roberd side ȝede lowe. ...he hym nam....
Roberd side ȝede doun for he bitrayed was:
his owen men did treson, þe kyng him tok, allas.
Now taken is Roberd & brouht vnto prison ...Robert Curthose....
at Corue, his kastelle, sperd depe in a dongeon.

.Corff in þe castel hous ful fast...

William þe Mortayn he skapes with no gile;
fettered he is certayn, Roberd of Stoteuile,

& Sir William Crispyn with þe duke was led
togider prisoned in, ȝeres & dayes þam fed. .in to prison...yfed
Þe kyng þam þerin mete & cloth inouh ..fond þem þere in mete...
þat neuer þei were otwynne vntille ded þam slouh.
Often I haf herd told of þis Duke Roberd,
so gode knyght no so bold was non in alle þe werld
ageyn þe Saraȝins in bataile forto go;
now he ligges in pynes, sorow wille him slo. ..ligges & pynes....
Why felle him suilk chance & þis ilk mishap?
For of godes ordinance he forsoke þe schap. ......þat was schape
Godes grace he forsoke for ȝernyng of þis lond;
Þe kyngdom of Ierusalem forsok for coueytise...
vengeance þerfor he toke, at his endyng he fond.
[125ᵛ] At Coue is Roberd dede; þe maner of his endyng .Corff........
my boke it me forbede to telle þerof no þing.
A hardy knyght was he, ouer alle bare þe pris.
At Ierusalem Cite opon godes enmys,
Godferay Bolion said, þat many man it herd,
"More my triste is laid on þe Duke Roberd
& I had grete nede ageyn þe saraȝines to go,
& better suld he spede þan a hundreth mo;
take him þe kepyng, þe coroun of Ierusalem,
for seke is þe kyng, of him is no bote of beem."
.sik þan...þer nys no bote but on
Þe þrid day of Aduent bifor cristes messe, ...cristemesse
þe kyng a seknes hent, þe dede him tok alle fresse.
Þe folk of þat cite to god mad orisoun
at þe temple domine with gode deuocioun.
Who þan were worþi þe coroune forto haue,
ageyn þe paemy þe cristendam to saue?
Godfrey & Roberd, & lered men & lewed,
& god þer praieres herd & to þam alle schewed:
a brightnesse com fro heuen & on Roberd light,
þre tymes alle euen þat alle sauh it with sight;
þris, þat alle mot se, þe light on Roberd toke. ......briȝtnesse þat on..
Vngracious man was he, þris he it forsoke;
þorgh conseile of som of hise, refused he þat present,
þei said, "On oþer wise he salle haf auancement."
Godfrey was oglift, to Roberd spak fulle tite,
"Withouten any essoyne, vengeance salle falle þe not lite!
....schal falle smert
[*Line order in L: 2512, 2513, 2511, 2514*.]

Forsakes þou godes gyft, þou dos him grete despite."
Þus sayd Godfrey of Bolyon, his hert was fulle of site;
Godefray of Boloyne seide with ful sore hert
forsoth vengeance he fond, of criste þe grace he les,
for couetise of þis lond, his mischeue he ches. ...... myschance..
Of Roberd is no speyre to mak of parlement,
his broþer Henry is heyre of alle his tenement; ... is his heyr of lond &.
of alle Normundie withouten geynsayng,
als heyr of ancestrie, Henry seysed þat þing.
Sone þan was it told vnto þe kyng of ffrance
þat Roberd lif was sold þorgh treson & mischance.
Whan Lowys herd þat sawe þat Roberd was so dede
ageyn right & lawe, tille Henry he misbede;
for traytours of men Inglis to Lowys þam bond,
þei hight him forto wisse how he mot haf þis lond.
.hiȝt for seye & wyse þat he myȝt...
He trowed to þer conseile, at Douere he gan vp ryue;
it had bien wroþerheile if he ne had went belyue.
of his purpos he gan fail he turned aȝen ful bliþe
[126r] Þe kynges kosyn Thebaut, & Randolf Gobion, ..sone Tebaud & on..
to gyf Lowys assaut samned at Chilyngton. ....þe sembled..
Of Wales þei had inowe þat Sir Lowys gan chace
& of his men þam slowe, to rest þei had no space;
vnto þe se side chaced þei Sir Lowys, Riȝt in to þe......
he durst not abide no turne Thebald his vis.
To schip ilkon þei went, fulle on lond leued, ...but som on lond by leued
mot þei Lowys hent, he suld haf lorn his heued.
Whan Henry herd telle þis, of þat gode cheuysance,
of of þe toþer Inglis þat conseild Lowys of ffrance & of þe oþer......
þat suld haf bien his owen & mad þe chance ouer grim,
......had ordeyned þe chance ful.
& þei wer fulle wele knowen þat wild haf tresond him,
how Gobion was certeyn, Thebaut, his neuow stoute
...truwe & certeyn & Tebaud...
turned Lowys ageyn, of lond þei chaced him oute.
Siþen with grete nobley & with mykelle honoure,
Henry toke his way toward þe emperoure,
to þe emperour of Almayn, his douhter to gyue; .....Maud his...
Malde hight þat mayden, a fayrer mot non lyue.
Þat mayden moder hight Mald, þe gode quene;
lady to maynten right, sen sho was, has non bene. ....& as gode as myȝt.
Now has Kyng Henry þorgh þis weddyng

grete power & party ageyns a lordyng. .....oþer lord & kyng
Now Henry Kyng leue nam at þe Emperour Henry
..þe Kyng his leue nam...sir.
& his sonne William & went to Normundy. & als his......
He gaf William, his sonne, with skrite & f seele fulle fre
.....al Normandy in fee
to hold als it was wonne, alle Normundie in fe;
..as hit was wone by scrit & seal ful free
to Thebaud of Plesance left with him of his meyne,
& vntille Inglond eft he turned ouer þe se.
In his seuentend ȝere þat he regned kyng,
Malde þe quene, his pere, in god scho did endyng.
.his queyne & fere..made hure.
At London at Saynt Poules, in toumbe is scho laid;
criste þan haf hir soule, mensk of hir men said.
.....muche gode of here is.
If any man wille witen & se of hir storie, ...& knowen...
at Westmynster writen er þei redilie. ..hit is writen & fynde hit þere al redy
Now es þe kyng sory, hir dede dos him fulle gram;
he gos to Normundy to his sonne William.
Tuo ȝere he wonnes & faire courte þer held,
vntille boþe his sonnes þer moder dede he teld,
& in þe þrid ȝere, þe kyng to Inglond went.
His sonnes & þer powere anoþer tide þei hent;
þei toke anoþer tide, allas, it was ouer hard,
& dronkled bi þe se side, boþe William & Richard.
þe drenched....his sones William..
[126ᵛ] Tuo erles & þer wyues with þam dronkled were, ...hem drenched.
& many oþer lyues in þe se left þere. ....were left al.
William Bigot þer felle, Roberd Maudut þat hight,
& Sir Geffrey Ridelle, & Othes þat was his knyght.
Þise men wer of gode þat dronkled alle in fere, ...dronched...
to lyue non ne ȝode bot on was marinere.
Þe bodies with þer godes wer costen vp on þe sond; ......cast vpon..
after an ebbe of þe flode, euerilkon þei fond.
Tuo sonnes were our kyng born þat his heires suld be
& boþe ere þei lorn, forsoth þat is pite.
To lond com þe kyng after þat passage .Londoun com.....
with many grete lordyng of his baronage;
Godefrey of Louayn, þe duke þat was douhty,
bi messengers tuayn sent to Kyng Henry ...he sent after..
for his douhter, Adelayn, þat wele was þan of age.
Sir Henry mad þe fyne & mad þe mariage; ......mad was..

þe may, withouten vice, his weddyng was wele dight, ...vis here weddyng...
& Malde, þe emperice, is heyre of Henry right.
Þe Emperour Henry þat Mald has to wyue,
scho had no child him by Mald in alle his lyue;
þan died þe emperour, Henry for Mald sent,
...Emperour Henry & Maud til Engelond went
as emperice with honour, Mald tille Inglond went.
....þe kyng for Maud had sent
Henry was alle glad of his douhter comyng;
nouht long siþen scho had praier for weddyng. ....araied hure..
Þe gode erle of Aniowe of Mald herd he say,
fulle richely, to trowe, tille tok his way; ..y trowe til Engelond...
he ryued vp at Douere & dight him eft alle bone.
......richely he was by gone
Whan alle were wele ouere, to London com he sone;
þe erle so wele sped tille our Kyng Henry
þat his sonne suld wed, & Mald was alle redy.
...schal wedde Maud & sche was redy
Þe emperice was dight as lady felle to be;
with hir went many a knyght tille Aniowe, þat cuntre.
Þe erle, þis lady gent gaf Henry, his sonne,
alle his tenement þat his eldres was wonne. & al his faire..he to haue was.
Whan þe fader had ent alle at his auys, ...had mad eynde al after gode.
to þe holy lond he went & died on godes enmys.
Henry, his sonne, & Molde, þat held þe seignorie,
a sonne þei had fulle bolde & his name Henrie. .....& als was yhote.
Siþen had þei anoþer þat þei cald William,
þat was Henry broþer, boþe of Mald cam.
Hir fader þe kyng loued þo childre so And Maudis fader.......
þat he wild for no þing þe sight of þam forgo.
[127r] Þe kyng went at þe last vnto Normundie
& praied his douhter fast to bere him companie
& hir sonnes, boþe Henry & William;
þei were him nere, boþe gladly with him þei nam. ...noȝt loþe.....
Henry regned here þritty ȝere & fiue
& þre moneþes sere in þis feble lyue, ...more in þis wrecchede.
þe dede euele him toke, he died at his day;
þe body did þei loke þat long abouen erþe lay.
On bere lay Kyng Henry, on bere biȝond þe se,
þat non wist certeynly who his heyr suld be.
Of Mald som had þe speyre, þe erle wif of Aniowe,
hir son Henry, & heyre of him, was maste to trowe.
So long he lay on bere for doute of his lynage,

tille men þe soth mot here who suld haf þe heritage,
els I ne wote for wham his biriyng suld men schonne,
tille Steuen of Plesance cam þat was his sister sonne;
Steuen com for þe nons, þis lond to haf he þouht.
After were Henry bones to Redynges Abbay brouht; Aftur hym.......
his bones did he lay in a toumbe of honour,
it was his owen abbay, þerof he was foundour.
Henry is at his reste, his soule at cristes wille,
& Steuen wille do his beste, in Inglond leues he stille.
Thebaud, Steuen broþer, es erle in his cuntre;
of o side ne of oþer, no þing deles he. ..þyng noþer of oþer of no side medleþ.
Henry of Aniowe takes conseile at frendes;
with Malde þat is so trowe, to Saynt Denys he wendes,
& his sonne, Henry, þat men held of gret pris;
þei gaf him Normundie bifor þe Kyng Lowys
& tille his heyres for ay to hold of þe kyng of ffrance,
& on þe toþer day men teld him of a chance
Riȝt in þat oþer day was told þem..nywe.
þat Gerard of Peiters, þe erle Marchis had fet;
Aniowe with þer souders was alle biseged & set.
Whan Henry herd telle, he tok leue at Lowys, .þe Eril Henry herd hit......
bot Mald scho gan duelle at þe castelle, Sir Amys,
þat was duke of Gaynes, Henry cosyn þorgh right. ...of Gyans....
To suffre Henry paynes, he hette him alle his myght.
Also þe Duke Henry with his fadere ȝede,
with help of Normundie, þe better mot he spede.
Bot William, Henry broþer, died & þan was wo;
þe werre with alle þe toþer lasted fiue ȝere & mo.
In alle þis ilk tirpelle wex Steuen a fulle wise man;
þorgh quantise & conseile þe coroune of Inglond wan.
[127v] Þe date of Ihesu pundred, þat men tellis bi, ...a numbred....
[*Transp. L: 2654 and 2655 are on one line and reversed.*]
a þousand & a hundred & sex & þritti. .....sexty ȝer &.
On Saynt Steuen day, withouten any conquest,
þe barons on gode aray at London mad þei feste;
þorgh conseile of ilkon, þai gaf Steuen þe coroun.
Heyre was he non no þertille had resoun;
þe emprice sonne, Henry, he had right þertille,
bot right ȝede þer forby þe barons did no skille. ....forþ by þe....
Bot sen his corounyng, tille Oxenford he fore
& þer Steuen þe kyng bifor þe clergie suore
þat if a bisshopriche, vacant wer þe se, ...fal & vacant...
þe kyng no non of his suld chalange þat of fe,

with wrong no with right, of non þat fro him cam,
so help him god alle myght & þat halidam.
Anoþer oth not lefte þe clergie did him karke ....charge
þat wodes ne foreste, withouten palaised parke,
..&. wiþouten & paleysed parkes
þe comon folk suld queme on & oþer in fere; ...scholde comyne.....
þe kyng no man suld deme in courte for wilde dere,
..scholde no man deme.....
clerk ne lewed man for no wilde beste,
for comon þe folk it wan, wod open & forest.
. be comyn þe peple wolde þurw alle.
Þe þrid poynt þei wild, to suere he was dryuen,
þat þe Danegelde for euer suld be forgyuen,
& of of ilk a hide tuo schillynges þat he toke & of ilk an......
suld neuer eft betide, he suore þat on þe boke,
Þat hit schulde neuer more by tide......
ne costom no seruise of þing þat he forgaf, & noþer custume.......
þat noiþer he no hise suld chalange rif no raf.
Of som poyntes he spak & suore vnto þe clergie,
þat ilk ȝere he it brak, þe kyng in som partie.
Whan wrathed Steuen with Dauid of Scotland Thenne wraþed.....
þat wild not tille him cheuen no bowe vnto his hand.
Dauid vnto Mald had mad his homage;
Steuen was in defaut, to Dauid did outrage.
Bot Henry, Dauid sonne, þat his heyr suld be,
contek for to schonne, to Steuen mad feaute. .& strif to schone....
Steuen sauh his skille þat Henry did resoun,
with alle þat longed þer tille, he gaf him Huntyngtoun.
Henry of Huntyngton, he wrote þe gestes olde
& sais in his sermon þat newe ere now tolde. ......nov are nywe.
A bisshop of Lyncoln, Alisaundre he hight,
þat non suld be forholn, he praied him if he myght.
In Alisaundre tyme kam, & Henries þe compilour, ...& in Henres..
ros þe ordre of Sempyngham þorgh Gilbert þe confessour.
.... Symprynghan....
[128r] Saynt Margrete story sais Dauid of hir kam,
of Dauid, Kyng Henry, of Henry com William; .Kyng Dauid com Henry....
of William, Alisandre, & Alisandre of him
þat wedded Kyng Edward sistir, þat was þe Scottis grim;
.......to Scottis harm
þis is þe genelogie fro Saynt Margarete, þe quene,
of kynges, bi & bi, in kynde þat has bene. .kyng by kyng by & by in....
Now of Steuen to speke turne we eft ageyn;

our tale wille we not breke bot telle forth þe certeyn.
At Pask in London þe kyng his feste held .Estertid in Londoun toun.....
with erle & baron, with knyght þat was of scheld. .Eril Duk &.......
Was non þat þider ȝode þat holden was of pris
þat he ne had gyftes gode of Steuen þat was wys.
After þis fest, praised Steuen with alle his here, ...y pesed.....
þe castellis he seised þat he hat neuer ere, ...hadde..
& Baudewyn of Beduere he flemed fro toun & felde.
A kestelle with powere ageyn þe kyng held, .castel......
þe kastelle tille him toke, Baudwyn had it lorn.
Here how þe kyng forsoke his oth þat he had suorn:
in Huntyngtonschire, þe kyng in þat forest
a moneth lay to spire for wod & wilde beste;
forsters did somoun, enquered vp & doun,
whilk men of toun had taken his venysoun,
& who þat was gilty þorgh þe foresters sawe,
mercied was fulle hi & don & fulle grete awe.
Merced he was ful heye & put in...
Þus he brak his avowe þat he to god had suorn ....oþ.....sworen
for a buske or a bowe þat he forgaf beforn.
Opon þis ilk syn, to Normundie he went;
þoserganȝ he fond þerin, he exiled þam & schent
þat had kept þe land þorgh Mald, þe emperice,
þat were hir wele willand were putt out of office.
Siþen he went to ffrance & com vnto Parys
& þer acordance bituex him & Lowys, .mad þer.....
& gaf it Eustace, his sonne, alle Normundie in fe
to hold, as it was wonne, of Lowys for feaute. ...þe wone was..by feaute
Þe kyng for his seruise confermed his gyft,
& on þis ilk wise, Eustace to duke was lift.
Þe þrid ȝere of his regne, he com to Ingland;
Bedford he biseged & wan it to his hand.
Siþen dight him to Scotland & mykelle folk him with
& slouh alle þat he fand for luf of Kyng Dauid,
for he mot neuer drawe Dauid tille homage.
Dauid did bot lawe, Mald had his seruage,
[128v] tille Mald with alle his myght, for lefe or for loth;
for scho was heyre þorgh right, to hir he held his oth.
He sauh he myght not spede & Dauid com no nerre;
to Wales suiþe he ȝede & on þam gan werre.
Steuen stoutly deles in stedes þor he kennes .....þere he comes
þat ageyn him holdes kasteles, on þam raþely rennes;
in Herford fulle stoutely his gannok has vp set. ....had Stephen Gannok..

With Roberd fitȝ Henry, Steuen so with him met
þat Bristow kastelle & toun, whedir he wild or non,
& Slede with alle þe honour & oþer sex ilkon, He sesede with.......
Carro, Lodelow toun, Schrobesbiri, & Warwik,
Dunford, & Maltoun, Steuen wan þam ilk a stik,
& þo þat þe casteles kept, in penance þei soiorned
þat eft not on him lept, to Wynchestre he tourned.
At Wynchestre he spires, his frendes drawes tille him,
..agayn hym spires.....
for folk of fele schires agen him turnes grim.
Whan Dauid of Scotlond herd þe soth sawe
þat Steuen was duelland in þe south grete þrawe, ...dwelland...a gret thrawe
þe folk ferly mykelle ageyn him þei ros, & þat þe.......
& Dauid herte gan tikelle þat him wex fele fos. ......to hym wext..
Fulle son at Rokesburgh his parlement he helde;
þe folk did somon þorgh of tuenty wynter elde ....al þurghe....
& gaf þam sonde at wille in Inglond forto fare,
man & beste to spille, non ne suld þei spare.
Southward þe Scottis hasted, bifor þam bare alle doun,
alle þe cuntre wasted vnto Aluertoun.
Whan þe Kyng Dauid Aluerton had sene
& wend wele at his grith alle Inglond had bene,
þe Norreis so þam defendid ageyn þo þat he brouht;
whan Dauid alle had spendid, of þam wan he nouht.
Liste how Dauid les his spence & his trauaile .....spences...
& whilk on him gan pres to renne on his rascaile. .....perce.....
The Archbisshop Thurstan, a gode clerk wele in age,
herd þe Scottis com, ilkan of Dauid baronage,
forto destroie Inglond & set it in seruage.
Thurstan sent his sond tille a bissh sauuage, ...buschupe sauage
Rauf of Orkeney, noble of lynage, ...noble man..
þat he suld tak þei wey opon his kostage þat scholde take þe wey...
& do þe Scottis deie & þer pride asuage.
Whan Rauf herd him so seie, he dight him to þat rage.
Þise were þo þat nam, als in þe geste it sais:
of Almarle, Erle William, & Walter de Gounteis;
[129ʳ] Roberd de Brus þer cam, & Gilbert de la Say,
& his sonne Adam, & Roger de Moubray;
Walter Spek was in þat stoure, gode knyght at alle nedes;
þe boke tellis grete honoure of his douhty dedes,
of monkes & chanones he did mak abbeis,
wis man in þe lawe, knyght gode & curteis.
William Peuerelle com als, he was of þe west,

ageyn þe Scottis fals, a gode man with þe best.
Þise were þe barons þat com of þe north ende
þat Rauf mad somons, ageyn Dauid to wende;
þise men lift þer standard þat stoute was & grim
ageyn Dauid wandelard & disconfite him. ..þe wanlard...
Said Rauf tille ilkon or þei ta bataile went, ...þey to..
"Of þe Bisshop Thurston haf I comandment
þe clerkes for to tech for þe londes nede,
þe lewed also to preche & comforte þam to dede.
3e wite wele a remenant & for soth 3e kenne [*Om. L*]
þat Inglis & Normant be now ons men. [*Om. L*]
3our ancestres conquered alle ffrance quitely; .....queyntely
were þei neuer ferde of frankis men hardy.
...3ut aferd of ffranceys þat huld þem.
[*L lacks a folio: lines 2800–2877.*]
Poyle with alle þe recchesse & Akres als þei wonnen,
þorgh þer douhtinesse þe lond þorgh þei ronnen;
siþen wan þei Inglond þat is so plentyuous,
& now er þise bot mansbond, rascaile of refous.
On 3our fadres þink þat were staworth in stoure,
for þise ne salle 3e blenk bot hold vp þer honoure.
Go we with gode wille & here I 3ow assoyle
of alle 3our synnes ille, granted of þe apostoyle,
þat 3e haf said or þouht or don, þat is schryuen;
in criste þat vs alle bouht, be it 3ow forgyuen.
Þerto my benyson tille alle þat go bliþely,
in þe name of þe fadere & þe sonne & spiritu sancti."
Dauid of Scotland hasted to þe bataile.
Walter Spek ros on hand, þe folk to forme & taile;
he bad þat non alone breke out of þe rengaile.
William of Almarle acordes to þat consaile
to while þat þise men bold with þer folk gan daile;
Sir Robert de Brus, þe old, to Dauid gan trauaile.
Here now of þe Brus, how he Dauid gan saile
with word þat was irus, if it mot out auaile:
"Dauid, my lordyng, land I hold of þe
& als of Steuen Kyng, for hamage & feaute.
[129v] Leue alle þis foly þat þou here bigynnes;
þin heyres salle it by & þou no thyng wynnes,
& loke þat þou not lese of lond þis ilk day.
Þe best I rede þou chese, þi lif saue if þou may,
for Inglis & Normant er stalworth men in stoure;
it is folk valiant, ouer alle þei bere þe floure,

for neuer mot þou fynde Inglis kyng giloure;
to þe & to þi kynde haf þei don honoure,
londes haf þei gyuen to þin ancessoure.
If trespas be misdryuen & do þin owen socoure,
& I wille mak amendes, tak a day of loue;
if þou ne wille, þou spendes & we salle be aboue.
Þou may haf þi wille if þou to loue chese,
& if þou turne tille ille, non wote who salle lese.
Wherfor, my Lord Dauid, do bi gode conseile;
tak ȝow pes & grith & late be þis tirpeile,
& late not now be spoken of þe mishap,
for eft it wille be wroken with a hardere klap."
Dauid listend Roberd, to pes fulle eth to drawe.
Bot on þer was ansuerd & sturbled alle þer sawe,
William, his neueu, a man of proude wille,
& said, "Roberd þe Bru, traytour hold þe stille!"
Roberd said him nay, traytour was he non.
"Dauid, haf gode day, myn homage now is gon."
He smote his hors with spors & fleih fro þat rascaile
& comandid his trompors to blow vnto bataile.
Rauf of Orkeney cried, "Inglis, go now, go
& do þise Scottis deie, þei waken vs euer wo!"
Þe Normans wer alle glad, þorgh schet þam als þe ro;
þe Inglis did as he bad, bifor þam stode bot fo.
Almerle his banere sprad & oþer barons mo,
mikelle blod þei schad of folk þat þei gon slo.
Dauid away fled þat bigan alle þat þro.
Here how a squier sped, sen Dauid fled þam fro:
a hede þat was of smyten þat þis squier fond,
priue, þat non suld witen, in an orfreis it wond
& sette it on a spere in an orfreis vnbiweued,
& said, "Lo, here I bere Dauid Kyng heued!
Þis is þe hede þat was of Dauid, þe Scottis kyng."
Þe Scottis said, "Allas, þis is a grete encumberyng!"
Þe Scottis þat stode fer fro & þe hede biheld,
fulle wightly gan þei go, flehand out of þe feld.
[130r] Wolgryn & Dufnald for euermore þei left,
of knyght no squier bald, on lyue non þei left.
Þe Scottis whan þei cam, bestes oueralle þei toke,
hors & nete alle samen bifor þer oste þei schoke;
þei did it for a wile, þorgh & þorgh toun
to put bestes in perile, our folk to bere doun.
Our men herd it say, þei were warned beforn,

in ilk strete & way þei ordeynd an erþe horn.
Whan þe com, þam blewe, þe bestes ageyn fled;
þe Scottis men doun thewe, for roryng wer þei dred.
Þe bestis þorgh þam ȝede & ouer þer rascaile ran,
þe Inglis after, with dede, & slouh þam ilk a man.
Þis was at Kouton More þat þe erþe hornes blewe;
þer þe Scottis misfore, men telle þe tale ȝit newe.
Sir Henry, Dauid sonne, þe romance sais so þere, [*L resumes*.]
his dedis were more to mone þan sex þe best þer were;
our barons had þe pris, with þam held þe right,
þe Scottis side doun lis, þei þanked god alle myght.
Þe moneth of heruest was Dauid disconfite;
þe next ȝole, alle preste, Steuen dight him fulle tite
& tille Scotlond went & tok he Kyng Dauid,
& tille Inglond him sent, his sonne Henry him with. .....& his....
A sonne had Steuen þe kyng, Eustace was his name,
in armes gode gynnyng, of pruesse had he fame.
..a gode by gynnyng he had & of prowesse a name
Lowys douhter of ffrance Eustace tok to wife;
Steuen for þat chance was more stouter in strife. ......stinter & stiff
Alisander þat was bisshop of Lyncoln schire,
(I ne wote for what trespas) þe kyng tille him had ire.
Sleford & Neuwerk þe kyng reft him þo tueyn,
at Wynchester þorgh conseile he had þam boþe ageyn.
Þat ilk tyme so felle, Mald þe emperice com to lond;
.....þat Maud com to Londoun
þe castelle of Arondelle open ageyn hir fond.
Whan Steuen vnderstode Mald was in Arondelle,
with mykelle folk & gode bigeged þat kastelle.
.muchel folk by seged he þat same.
Mald þouht of þis stoure, scho biþouht hir straite,
& douted dishonoure þat mot com þorgh disceite;
scho did hir to Bristow & duellid oþer half ȝere,
& þider fro Aniowe com hire a messengere
& told to Mald here þat scho fulle wele trod: ....trowed
hir lord lay on bere, his soule bitaken god, ...by tawȝtte to.
& Henry hire sonne had þe heritage
to hold as it was wonne, don was his homage.
[130v] Mald in Bristow lettres fast sendes .is in...sche sendes
bi messengers trowe forto procore frendes;
to burgeis &citeȝ þe wardeyns alle scho freistes ....freyssches
& to lordes of feeȝ þat scho on treistes; ....on wel tristes
of help scho þam bisouht in right & leaute,

þat þei failed hir nouht, for heyre þe wist hir be. ...... verray heir is sche
Þe barons said scho had right in hire askyng;
son was þe contek schad bituex þam & þe kyng. Sone was noȝt þe.......
Ilkon on his side to bataile purueid him
þat power had to bide most was stoute & grim.
Þe powers þoȝt to abide for þey were...
Sir William of Almarle wex a stoute sire, ... Arundelle.. ful..
he ȝerned to haue alle Lyncolnschire,
ageyn Gilbert þe Gaunt reised his banere;
Gilbert was valiaunt, ageyn him fulle austere.
& Gilbert was roillant ageyns hym auster
Gilbert had þe erledam þat tyme of heritage;
bituex him & William was don many outrage.
Of Gilbert first to telle, to William did he wouh:
he did brenne Helwelle & William broþer slouh;
þe castelle of Bitham to Gilbert ȝolden was,
it longed to William þat tyme felle him þat cas. at Londoun to ... ful in..
William of Almarle þat tyme northward rode; .. Arundel....
þe castelle of Hundmanby he cast doun alle o brode.
Sir Eustace le fitȝ Ion at þat dede was,
more him þan ilkon þe wited þat trespas. .... þey wyted..
Who so was wroþe or oþer biforn for any chance, ... with oþer....
his enmy, þe toþere, tok þan his vengeance.
Þo þat lufed werryng mad parties ay bituen;
som held with Steuen þe kyng & som with Mald þe quene,
for erles & barons þat were of Maldes kynde
souht citeȝ & touns, þe kyng if þei mot fynde.
Hir frendes fulle fast waited aboute & woke,
& Mald, at þe last, Kyng Steuen scho toke
& led him to Bristow & did him þer in hold,
in prison, I trowe, þorgh þe quene Mold. .... þat hiȝt Dame .
Þan þe riche & pouere & alle comonly
for Berwik to Douere held hir for lady.
Whan þe lond gan hir loute & alle was at hir wille,
þan bare scho hir ouer stoute & wild vnto no skille,
[*L adds:*] ffor þer womman is hed sche is a wykked wed
Mesure is þer noun leued to don non euen hed
for or þat ȝere was gon, scho bare hir so stoute
þat þe Lundreis ilkon, of London drof hir oute.
Mald þorgh þe Lundreis fro London is katched; ...... is sche chaced
with hors & herneis Bristow has scho latched. ..... haþ sche cacched
[131r] What for ire & tene & alle in euelle wille,
scho stokked Kyng Steuen, & þer did scho ille. . schulked..... Mold ful .

Now turnes eft Mold to Wyncester fulle stoute, ...Wynchestre..
& Steuen out of þat hold quantly skaped oute.
Roberd went hir with, Maldes half broþer, ...þat was Moldes..
& þe Kyng Dauid of Scotland was þe toþer.
At Wynchester gan scho duelle, biseged þe castelle;
þe Londreis herd it telle & ȝared þam fulle welle
with gode aparaile of alle þat þei mot gete,
þe sege þei gan assaile & tok hir at þe mete.
Roberd þer was taken in to þe Londreis hand,
bot Dauid was wele waken, he fled fast to Scotland;
alle þorgh Chestreschire he fled to Louthian. .....vn to lond
A preste was with hire þat Mald from þam wan.
Mald & Roberd Louelle tille Oxenford þei fled
& seised þe castelle & Steuen fast him sped, ..þere.....hom fledde
& gadred him an oste & went vnto Wilton,
& did reise in þat coste a stalworth donion.
Mald wist þat fulle wele, hir barons þider sent,
& Steuen left ilka dele & to Northampton went.
William Marschalle o chance was taken at þat turne; ....iourne
he gaf for his delyuerance þe castelle of Schirburne.
Folk biȝond þe se þat were of Steuens kynde,
tille him com grete plente & oþer þat þei mot fynde.
Steuen with his power tille Oxenford gan schake;
his sege he set plener, þe castelle forto take.
Þe emperice it held, was it þe wynter tide, Maud þe...al in...
þe snowe lay in þe feld, þe water frese biside; .sege....þe freres faste.
þe lady had defaute boþe of mete & drynk,
& scho dred þer assaute, hunger was at þe brynk.
.drewe his assaute & hunger was at.
Scho asked hir conseile what was þer of to rede, ...best to rede
"Steuen wille vs traueile & famen vs to dede." ....or famyne vs to deþe
Non ne couth ne wild conseile on no partie, ...of hure parte
bo þe castelle to ȝeld & ask þe kyng mercie; But....& crie...
þat ne wild scho nouht, hir herte was so stoute.
Bot here now how scho wrouht & how scho passed oute.
A fulle selcouth rede tok at hir owen herte; ....sche tok....
scho left for life no dede, ne colde þat was so smerte.
Sone after mydnyght þat crowe suld þe cok,
in þe snowe for syght, scho ȝede out in hir smok;
ouere þe water of Temse þat frosen was with iys,
withouten kirtelle or kemse, saue kouerchef, alle bare vis.
.....kerechiff al bar ywis
[131v] To Walyngford scho wan, & þer scho left a while,

þe way scho ȝed & ran, on length it is ten mile;
& Steuen þe castelle wan of þam euer ilkon,
þei ȝelded it ilk man wham Dam Mald was gon.
. ȝulden þem . . when Dame Maud . .
In þis tyme had Steuen regned auht ȝere in alle,
lered & lewed were euen & pere & paringalle, ... parvigalle
so þat knyght & squiere, if þei powere mot make,
of Holy Kyrke pleynere tok þat þei mot take.
Þe pape þan herd þe pleynt, he sent hider a legate;
at London þei wer atteynt, decre was mad for þate:
ȝif any lewed man laid hand opon clerk, ... a clerc
or with ille on ran þat of corun had merk, . . yuel ouerran þat wiþ croune . .
he suld not escape þorgh bisshop granted fre;
of non bot of þe pape myght he assoyled be.
Þe kyng it was herd & chastised his meyne . . say hit was hard . . . .
& oþer afterward left of þer nycete. . euer þere afturward . . . .
Ther after half a ȝere þe clergie had gode pes,
þat noiþer wo no werre non on þam gan pres. . . here ne þere . . . . .
Bot Geffrey of Maundeuile þe Kyng Steuen him reft
his baronie þat while, robberie with Iob was left; . . . . for robberie þo . .
þe abbay of Rameseie bi nyght he robbed it,
þe tresore bare aweie with hand þei myght on hit. . . he bar . . . þat þey myȝt . .
Abbote & priour & monke þei did out chace,
of Holy Kirke a toure to theft þei mad it place.
. . churche . . þey made of þat place
Roberd þe Marmion þe same wayes did he;
he robbed þorgh treson þe kirke of Couentre.
Here now of þeir schame what chance bifelle,
þe story sais þe same soth as þe gospelle.
Roberd þe Marmyon he lepe vp on his stede, ... worþeþ . . . .
[*L lacks four leaves: lines 3019–3237*.]
þorgh Couentre þat toun vnto þe kirke he ȝede.
He comandid his men to dryue out þe couent,
þe godes him biken þat þei mot tak or hent.
Whan þei had inouh, als mykelle as þei mot lede
þat þei of herneis drouh, to go þei gan þam spede.
He turned his bridelle with querte, he wend away haf gone;
þe dede him smote to þe herte, word spak he neuer none.
Geffrey of Maundeuile to fele wrouh he wouh;
þe Deuelle ȝald him his while with an arowe on him slouh;
þe gode bisshop of Chestre cursed þis ilk Geffray,
his lif out of þis estre in cursyng went away.
Arnulf, his sonne, was taken als thefe & brouht in bond

befor þe kyng, forsaken & exiled out of þis lond.
[132r] Þe marschalle of þam alle, Helys of Saynt Omere,
to ded þan gon he falle doun of his destrere.
Þe maistir of þer pedaile þat kirkes brak & brent,
& abbeis gan assaile, monkes slouh & schent,
was born in Pikardie & his name Reynere,
in suilk felonie gadred grete auere.
He had what he wild & was of wendyng ȝare
& had a schip wele filled, ouer þe flode to fare;
þerin was wif & childe & tresore wikly wonnen.
So com a tempest wilde, his schip had alle ouer ronnen;
þe maryner was ogast þat schip þat wild not go,
lotes did þei kast for whom þei had þat wo.
Þe lote felle on Reynere & on his wif also;
þris kast at tymes sere felle it on þam tuo.
Þe schip man wist wele þe tempest þat þam smote,
for þam com ilk a dele, he did þan tak a bote
& did þam alle þerin, Reyner & his gode,
& whan þei were otuyn, þer schip ferd on þe flode.
Reyner & his wif doun tille helle þei sank;
for his wikked lif, þe Deuelle ȝald him þat þank.
In his tende ȝere, a hatrex wex alle hote,
þe kyng fulle austere ageyn Sir Hugh Bigote;
þe kyng did not wele, with þe wrong he wrouht,
amendes he mad som dele, bot of þe most right nouht.
Rauf, þe erle of Chestre, & þe kyng were wroth;
in his elleuend ȝere, þe wend haf acorded both
in alle maner of þing þat Rauf felt him filed.
Bot here now how þe kyng, Rauf þe erle begiled:
vnto Northampton, Rauf to courte kam,
þe kyng, þorgh treson, Rauf þer he nam
& held him tille he ȝald of Lyncolne þe castelle,
& plenerly haf he wald þe rentis þat þerto felle.
Þe tuelft ȝere of his regne, at ȝole he held his feste
at Lyncolne, as in signe þat it was his conqueste.
Sone after þat feste þat he þer seysen toke,
þe courte, moste & leste, tille Arundelle þei schoke.
Þat þe kyng was gone, Rauf herd sone say;
to Lyncoln forth on one, Rauf þan tok his way
& reised a mangnel to kast vnto þe toure;
þe burgeis wer fulle felle, þei ȝald him hard stoure.
Þe gyour of his oste at þat saut was slayn,
& Rauf for alle his boste fulle fast fled agayn.

[132v] The ȝere next on hand ȝede þe kyng of ffrance
to þe holy land with his purueiance.
Þe emperour with þo kynges went withouten grace,
þo & oþer lordynges mad þe grete manace,
vpon godes enmys forto tak vengeance.
Þei sauh þe payens of pris of so grete purueiance,
þe cristen turned for drede withouten dynt of lance.
Bot here how þe poraile spede, god gaf þam fair chance.
Þe poraile þat went þider þat had no spendyng,
þei suore þer oth togider to lette for no þing
to wend vnto Spayn, & tuo citeȝ þei wan;
þe saraȝins was þer wayn & slouh þam ilk a man.
Þei ȝede fro lond to lond & non ageyn þam stode;
þe better grace þei fond þe ferrer þat þei ȝode.
Hidere com þat tiþand tille oþer lordes many mo
how mykelle grace þei fand þat durst þe saraȝins slo.
Þe lordes mot haf schame whan þei herd it telle,
þat dred for godes name, at home þei ȝede to helle.
In his sextend ȝere, Steuen þat þe lond auht,
Mald scho died here, hir soule to god betauht,
& hir sonne Henry to lond was he comen.
Þe barons & þe clergy tille him alle þe nomen,
& with þe Kyng Steuen þei held parlement
þat Henry & he euen acorded or þei went;
with skrite was set þe pes & ordeynd þorgh baroun
þat Steuen tille his dises of Inglond suld bere coroun,
& his gyft certeyn be holden stabilly;
to Normundie ageyn suld turne þe Duke Henry,
& Ingland alle holy, after Steuen þe kyng,
suld turne to þe same Henry withouten geynsaiyng;
& if þat Henry die or Steuen mak his deses,
Henry heyr we seie salle haf þe lond in pes,
coroun forto bere as heyr & eldest sonne,
his heritage to were in right als it was wonne.
So þat Steuen þe kyng, no non of his heyres,
for heritage no þing salle chalange for þeires,
þis dede was enseled, bitauht þam of Saynt Poules,
þat wrong were not deled for drede of lif & soules.
Now wendes Duke Henry vnto Normundie,
seysine has plenerly of alle his cheualrie,
& Steuen leues here, Inglond is his balie.
After in his þrid ȝere, Steuen fulle seke gan lie,
[133r] & in þat grete languour endid he his life.

Ninetene ȝere þe honour he kept in werre & strfe;
at ffeuersham he lis, at a heuen in Kent,
in an abbey of prịs he founded with lond & rent;
& Mald þe emperice, þer þan is scho laid,
þat serued þer office, to me so þei said.
Þe date a þousand right, a hundreth & fifty,
þat Steuen to dede was dight, now comes þe secunde Henry.
Now is Steuen dede & lies at ffeuersham;
þe barons þair red & after Henry nam.
To London þei him brouht with grete solempnite;
þe popille him bisouht þer kyṇg forto be.
Þe day of Saynt Liger was Henry corouned kyng,
Thebald of Canterber gaf him þe coroune & þe ryng.
Þis Henry was Mald sonne, þe erle wif of Aniowe,
þe emperice was wonne & right heyre forto trowe,
for Henry douhter scho was & his heyre þorgh sight.
Now comes hir sonne in pas, Henry, hir heyr þorgh right.
Henry has four sonnes & douhtres has he tuo,
as þe story mones, þese ere þe names of þo:
Henry & Richard, Erle Geffrey & Ione;
ilkon afterward was kyng & quene bot on.
Geffrey was no more bot erle of Bretayn,
& Dame Helianore scho we quen of Spayn.
Dame Ion was ȝongest & lady of Ceȝile,
þer fader, kyng richest lyuand in alle his while.
Þis ilk Henry is told Henry þe scecunde,
so riche a prince in wold, in þis lond siþen non funde.
Aniowe & Normundie alle holy he held,
of Gascoyne þe seignorie bowed vnto his scheld.
Ilk a knyght & squiere, clerkes were to him suorn,
þan was his chancelere, Thomos, of London born.
Saynt Thoma fader, I fynd, hight Thomas Beket,
in London of noble kynd & maste of alle was let.
A riche man he was, mot spend þre hundreth poun[d].

[*The leaf is damaged and letters are lost*.]

Ersdeken, his sonne Thomas of Caterbiri þat [stound],
in alle manere cause, he souht þe right in skille,
to gile no to fraude wild he neuer tille.
Þe ersebisshop þat was, þat tyme died he;
þe erresdeken Thomas was sacred in his se.
Wele mayntend he Holy Kirk & alle þe dignite,
with þe lawe to wirke mayntend þe ordine;
[133v] if any man mad pleynt of clerk for hastiuenesse,

or if þei were atteynt in oþer wikkednesse,
Thomas suffred nouht cleke to be alle schent,
ne to þe lay courte be brouht to tak þer iugement,
bot tille Holy Kirke of whom he bare þe merke,
& at þat lawe to wirke if he were ordeynd clerke.
Þe kyng for þat cheson wrathed with Thomas.
Here now þe reson whi þat wreth first was.
Clerkes often tide misdo blithely
for deynoushede & pride, & for þer state is hy;
þei passe mesure & right forto haf þer wille,
& whan þei ere in myght, wille þei kepe no skille,
for þei wille vnderfong a fulle gre emprise
& susteyn it with wrong, with sleiht & quantise.
Þo þat felt þam greued of þer wikked dedis,
to lordes þat þei to cheued pleyned þei most nedis.
Þat suilk was not lees, it com to þe kynges ere;
he comandid his pes to lered & lewed þat were,
& if a clerke men founde in his lond þat reft
þorgh slauhter or wounde or þorgh oþer theft,
men suld schewe his gilte in þe courte of lay
& þer be saued or spilte, bot Thomas said him nay.
Thomas said þe kyng þat othe suld he wele loke
þat he suore at þe gynnyng whan he þe coroune toke,
"Þorgh god I þe forbede to chalange any clerke
in lay courte, for no nede of Holy Kirke has merke,
ne þe franchise fordo þat it ouh to halde,
bot tille þat courte com to of whilk he is membre calde."
Þis was at Clarendoun þat Thomas gaf respouns,
& siþen to Narthamptoun Thomas com eft sons,
delyuer his clerkes fro dome, bot no grantise was.
[Wh]erfor to þe courte of Rome þan kalled Saynt Thomas.

[Damage to the leaf affects six lines.]

[T]homas toke þe way & passed ouer þe se;
þe Kyng Henry herd say, his messenger sent he.
[.......hop] Rogere of Ȝork þan kept þe se;
[...............his] powere corouned forto be.
[.....oynt] also with wrong þei mad alle mirie,
tille Thomas felle it to þe kirke of Canterbirie.
Whan Thomas it wist, he did mak a cursyng;
Roger he cursed first þat corouned þe ȝong kyng,
& alle þat wer him with or in his courte wer sene,
saue þe kyng had grith, his childre & þe quene.
[134r] To Thomas þe kyng bisouht þe bisshop to assoile,

bot Thomas wild nouh bot þorgh grace of þe apostoile;
wherfor þe kyng wex wroth & Thomas did exile,
his kynred lefe & loth he did fleme & reuile.
Þe kyng suld haf no plight þat Thomas so was dede;
he said bot tille a knyght þat Thomas him misbede,
& if he had had men as he wend of renoun,
þei suld haf venged him of suilk a clergioun.
Foure kyngtes it herd withouten any more;
to Canterbiri þei ferd & slouh Thomas right þore.
Who so wille wit þis chance, his lif & his languour,
& how þe kyng of ffrance did him grete honour,
& how þe pape sent his bulle with a legate,
& how or he went he serched alle þe state,
& how at Pountney þe angelle to him said,
& how alle his kynde exile was on þam laid,
& how þe apostoile laid on þam grete payn
or he wild þam assoile þat had Thomas slayn,
& how for Holy Kirke he suffred passion,
& how god dos wirke in schrine þer he is don,
open his boke & se, for þer in ere þei writen
meruailes grete plente þat fele of vs ne wite[n]. *[The page has been cut and repaired with loss of a letter.]*

Comen is tiþing þe bisshop slayn is he
& þe ȝonge kyng is went ouer þe se.
Of Almarle, Erle William with þe kyng was þen,
tuo castels he nam, open þe Frankis men;
of Almarle in þe castelle þre lordes he toke,
of messengers fulle snelle he sent hider to loke.
Vntille Inglond of fflandres men fulle ille,
in warde or in bond, in prison leue þei stille.
Þe fader, Kyng Henry, in herte had he payn
& anguised greuosly þat Thomas was so slayn;
William, þe Scottis kyng, þerfor was fulle blithe
þat Henry had ille likyng, werre on him gan he kithe.
Burgh his way beforn he sesed þat kastelle;
Mulgard þorgh him was lorn, Prudhow saued welle.
His way left he nouht tille he com tille Alnwik;
þer was he taken & brouht to Richemunde also quik.
Richard þe Moruile, knyght of gode renoun, *[L resumes.]*
Richard Comyn þat while with him com to þe toun.
com þat tyme wiþ hym in to þat ilk.
Þe Northren so wele stode in treuth to þe Kyng Henry
þat gyftes he gaf þam gode & þat was largely,

[134v] so þat alle þe toþer com vntille his grith,
of lordes on & oþer & fayn to hold him with.
Contek in countes alle was peysed wele,
baret of baron feeȝ forgyuen ilka dele.
Þan was Inglond in pes & charite
& alle in Henry, gracious kyng & fre. ...Henry hond....
In his nientend ȝere of his regalte,
Henry his sonne, his pere, was ȝit ouer þe se;
to Henry...power gaff þat tyme was....
þe kyng sister of France Henry alied him to.
Here of a desceyuance þei conseild him to do: .nov of a distance þey....
þe Erle Philip of fflandres gaf him in conseile, ...Henry..
& Thebald of Plesence egged to þat tirpeile,
ageyn his fader to rise, þer he had no right;
þe kyng of ffrance & hise hight him alle his myght.
Whan þe fader wist þe sonne wild werre on him,
I blame him not if him list turne ageyn fulle grim;
for þam of Scotlond he sent, William & Dauid his broþer,
Aftur þe kyng of Scotlond.......
tille blithely þei went & with þam many oþer. Til Henry........
Þe erle of Leycestre þe oste alle did he guye,
of werre he was þer maistre, dight þam to Normundie.
Owȝwer was he þe.....
Whan þei were vp aryued, þei fond þer þar chance;
þat reame was biseged with þe power of ffrance. .þe toun of Roone was......
Henry chaced his sonne þorgh force fro toun to toun; ......fro þe toun
þe kyng of France eftsonne left tent & pauilloun, ...swiþely....
Philip of Flandres fleih & turned sonne þe bak,
& Thebald nouht ne deih, schame of þam men spak.
.Tebaud noȝt þere dowȝtty schame....
Fro toun to toun of reme þe Frankis did þei fle,
.þe toun of Roone þe Freynsche...
ouer tok it to ȝeme & saued þat cite; Oure men tok.......
our Inglis duelled þer vnto þe pes were pleyn, Þe Englissh host dwelled......
þo þat þer were beforn wild no more com ageyn.
So þat þe Freynsche þat þere were wold....
In þe moneth of May our Inglis of was ȝare ......Englisshe host was þare
vpon þe first day tille Inglond forto fare. ....prest til...
Fulle sone þe ȝong kyng with gode man þat wer gayn ....men...
purueid his wendyng, & Richard fitȝ Alayn,
þe Duke of Peiters, & þe erle of Bretayn,
þise & oþer pers to sauhtillyng did þer payn;
þise on knees gan falle bifore þe kyngis face,

for luf þei praied him alle to grante þe kyng his grace. ....grante of his.
"3our wrath him forgyue, þe trespas to amend, ..3ore sone...for to.
in pes with 3ow to lyue & at 3our conseil descend."
Þe sonne cam also suiþe & cried his fader mercy;
þe kyng þerof was bliþe, forgaf him gentilly,
[135r] & he with scrite & oth mad obligacion
þat for leue no loth, þorgh conseile of treson,
suld werre on him begynne bi water ne bi lond, ..hym non giffe.....
ne his pes breke no tuynne, þe sonne þertille him bond.
...to breke þe sone þer to hym.
In alle þis sauhtillyng bituex þe fader & þe sonne
com þe Scottis kyng & asked Henry a bone,
of grantise of grace to haf his seignorie;
bifor alle in þat place, he gaf it him bliþely.
Þan wer boþe þe kynges brouht alle tille euen
& pesed in alle þinges, þanked be god of heuen.
Þan said Sir Henry, nedes burd him wende .....by howed..
to France & Normundie to witte a certeyn ende.
At Parys wild he be at þer parlement,
þer wille wald he se to what þei wild consent.
At þe Du3epers þe sothe wild he wite
& on what maners & wharto he suld lite,
& whedir þei wild to werre or þei wild nouht,
or alle in luf sperre þat þing þat þei had wrouht.
He sauh wele bi signe he drouh fast tille elde;
long myght he not regne ne on his lif belde,
wherfor Henry said he wild or he went
þat þe summe wer laid of his testament.
Liste & I salle rede þe parcelles what amountes,
if any man in dede wille keste in acountes.
Sex þousand marke tille Acres did he fend .....þere dide he send
ageyn his comyng þidere bi marchand3 so he wend;
fifty þousand marce had he lent abbeis ...also he lent til.
þat wer in pouerte, vp þam forto reise;
alle þat was gyuen & befor hand lent
þat was not in cofre whan he mad testament,
of þat þat was in cofre & in his cofines, ...coffiners
he mad his testament als did oþer pilgrimes. ....as men doþ ellis wheres
To Waltham 3ede þe kyng his testament to make,
& þus quathe he his þing for his soule sake.
To Temples in Acres he quath fiue þousand marke .þe Templers.......
& fiue þousand to þe hospitale for þei were in karke.
To þe folk þat duelled Acres forto fende, ...in Acres þem.defende

oþer fiue þousand marke he gaf þam to spende. ....despende
Tille oþer houses of þe cuntre fiue þousand marke he gaf,
tille heremites & tille seke men & oþer of suilk raf,
tille monkes & to chanons þat were in Inglond,
fiue þousand marke resceyued þei of his hond.
[135v] To þo of þat religion þat were in Normundie,
fiue þousand mark vnto þer tresorie, ...he gaff to þere croisery
& to meselle houses of þat same lond,
þre þousand mark vnto þer spense he fond. .hondred...despens..
To ladies of habite, Vilers & Mortayn, ...in Vilers..
he gaf tuo hundreth mark (I trowe þei were fayn). ....ful fayn
To þo religiouses þat were in Gascoyne,
he gaf a þousand mark withouten essoyne. ......eny assoyne
To þam of ffounȝ Eberard þer his body lis,
he gaf tuo þousand mark þo ladies of pris.
To þe ladies of Bretayn men calle Seynt Suplice,
he gaf a hundreth mark to mend þer office.
To þe houses of Chartres, tuo þousand mark bi counte, ..hous of Charterhous.....
& þre þousand mark to þe ordre of Grant Mounte.
To þe ordre of Cisteaus, he gaf tuo þousand mark,
þe ordre of Clony, a þousand to lay vp in arke,
þe ordre of Premonstere, tuo hundreth mark þei had,
to þe ladies of Markayne, a hundreth mark þei lad;
to þe houses of Arroys þat ere biȝond þe se,
tuo hundreth mark þorgh testament gaf he.
To women of Inglond of gentille lynage, .poure wommen.....
a hunderth mark of gold to þer mariage. iii hondred marc.....
To gentille & tille oþer þat were in Normundie,
a hundreth mark of gold þei had to þer partie.
To gentille women of Aniowe of non auancement,
a hundreth mark of gold vnto þam was sent.
Withouten þis testament þat he did writen [*After two lines of fol. 110v in L, the scribe inexplicably skips 115 lines. A later hand notes the omission here*.]
& þe grete tresore tille Acres was witen,
& þat he lent religiouse to bring þam aboue,
fourty þousand mark he gaf for gode loue.
Whan þe Kyng Henry had mad his testament,
he dight his oste redy & to Parys went;
fro Derwent to Douere þat best wer worþi,
with [....]went þei ouere, atired richeli. [*A hole in the P MS has been repaired with letters lost*.]

Þa[......]nd þe folk in Paris þat þei wele herd,
with so fayre folk of pris neuer no prince ferd.
Of þe kyng of France he asked amendment;
þe Duȝepers for chance, þei ros with on assent
& in þer conseile kaste þer chance on ilk side;
þei acordid at þe laste þat pes mot beste betide.
Whan pes was set certeyn bituex þo kynges tueye
& Normundie þorgh seþen, tille Inglond he tok þe weye.
[136r] In þe ȝere afterward, at midsomer men teld,
þe kyng in Oxenford his parlement held.
Bi his writte he sent after Kyng William;
William dight him & went, tille Oxenford he cam
& suore to Kyng Henry, þe next Assumpcion
þat was of oure lady, suld com to Ȝork his toun
& bring þider his clergie, of Scotlond þe barons.
He did so certeynlie þe day of his somons;
þer þei mad ilkon homage & feaute,
not to þe fader alle on, bot tille his heir suld be,
& obliged þam with scrite, hyngand ilk a seale,
þat þer dede was perfite & his homage leale;
& þe kirke of Scotland to Canterbirie, our se,
obliged þam & band as to þer primalte;
& if þe Scottis kyng mistake in any braide,
of treson in any thyng ageyn Henry forsaid,
þe barons & þe clergie in on wer alle schryue.
Vnto Kyng Henrie ageyn, William suld be gyuen,
& if it so betide þat any thefe or feloun
fle fro Inglond side to Scotlond regioun,
bot he mak þam to wite whi þat he is comen,
þat þe courte may him quite o chance if he be nomen;
if he be els funden for thefe tald & hent,
tille Inglond brouht alle bunden & þer haf iugement.
Als if it so be of Scotlond skape a thefe
& tille Inglond fle als a felon grefe,
bot if he to þer baylifes mak his sikernesse,
þat þei wille him maynpis if he wer cald to stresse;
if he folowand were souht for þat felonie,
ageyn to Scotland be brouht & þer hanged hie.
Whan þis þing was grant, Henry dred disceite;
he wild þat his couant were holden stable & streite.
He sesed fiue castels & held þam in his wage,
foure erles & sextene kynghtes þerfor in his ostage;
ilkon of þo knyghtes had a barony,

þei & alle þer rightes were don in his mercy.
Whan Henry for his owen had holden þat seignorie
& þe dede was knowen þorghout Albanie,
þe castels & ostagers he ȝald þorgh curteysie,
& with William with chartre bond him tille Henrie
þat he & his heires & alle þer progenie
of Scotlond suld hold of Henry certeynlie,
[136v] & of alle his heires, & com to þer crie,
& homage & feaute to mak þam redie.
Whan þis was set & stabled & pes cried on hii,
Henry, þe ȝong kyng, ȝede to Normundie
& died þer þat ȝere & biried solemplie.
Whan þis ȝong kyng was dede & laid in graue,
fro Ierusalem com tiþng þat help burd it haue.
What tyme in Ierusalem wad dede a douhty kyng,
was blode non of his teme bot a mayden ȝing;
Baldewyn þe meselle his name so hight,
noble kyng & lele & wele ȝemed his right;
neuer in his lyue he lese a fote of lond.
Þe saraȝins gan him dryue, þei were him euer fleand,
for foule meselrie he comond with no man;
saraȝin with maistrie neuer nouht of him wan.
With him was a knyght & vnder him chefetayn
& namecouth of myght, William of Aquitayn.
Whan Badwyn was dede, he weddid þe mayden ȝing;
þorgh þe cristen rede, William was chosen kyng.
For þis bold Baldewyn, cristen men gan morne;
gode hap had þe saraȝin ageyn on vs to turne.
Þe saraȝins on vs cam, our cristen force gan felle,
so þat Kyng William no langere þer durst duelle.
Bode com to þis lond for help & socour;
Kyng Henry he fond & schewed him alle his stour,
how þe fals soudan destroied alle þe lond,
slouh ilk cristen man, or els in prison bond,
"Þerfore I pray to ȝow, haste þat ȝe wer comen;
bi þis is Acres now biseged or alle nomen."
Whan þe kyng it herd, he wept with his ine,
þe cristen so misferd, þe saraȝins did so pyne.
He said, "My sonne, myn heyre, þat was corouned late,
of his lif was in speyre, he myght haf taken þe gate.
Bot now is he dede, myn heyre þat bare coroune,
þerfor I kan no rede, I doute me of tresoune;
for if I were of lond, þe werre suld sone bigynne,

aliens suld sone fond our heritage to wynne.
Richard my sonne is knyght, with me wild he go;
sone suld we lese our right if we were fer þerfro.
Fayn I wuld purueie for Acres, þat cite,
ordeynd wer som weie how it mot saued be."
William tok his leue at our Kyng Henry,
giftes wele to leue he had richely.
[137r] He went to þe kyng of ffrance & schewed him his resons;
þorgh þer ordenance þe Duȝepers gaf respons.
Bifor Sir William þe Duȝepers gaf ansuere:
"It er bot tuo kyngdams on þis half Grece to were,
ffrance & Inglond, þise tuo regions,
& er in diuerse lond & in sere bandons.
Henry in Inglond wonnes & has tresore inouh;
Richard & Ion, his sonnes, fulle felle & wille non bouh,
& if þat ȝe were gone & we went with ȝow,
þat Richard & Ion wille waken vn mykelle wouh.
Bot whan Kyng Henry & his sonnes wille go,
we salle be redy forto wend with þo."
William went ageyn vnto Ierusalem;
of þise kynges tueyn was ȝit no bote o beame.
Henry for his trespas did fulle grete honour [*L resumes after a gap on fol. 110v; cp. line 3352 of P.*]
to þe martir Saynt Thomas for mercy & socour.
Sex ȝere siþen lyued he in wo & sorow soure;
he went ouer þe se & lay in grete langoure,
in grete sekenesse & hard he lay in Normundie.
Tille him com his sonne Richard, forsoth fulle kyndelie,
& whan Henry suld die, Richard þorgh blissyng bond,
he suld his cheualrie vse in þe Holy Lond.
"I salle leue þe inouh forto do with alle."
"Fader," he said, "for ȝow certes þider I salle."
Whan he had regned here & felt of fele assaies
foure & tuenty ȝere, sex monethes & tuelf dayes, xxxiiii ȝeres.....
no more of him to seie, he died sone afterward.
He ligges in an abbeie men calle þe Founȝ Eberard.
A þousand & a hundred þe dete, fourscore & nyne, ...date...
so many ȝers it pundred whan he passed þis pyne.
So muche was numbred when Henry...
[I]n a moneth mirie, Septembre þe gynnyng, [*Capital om. in P.*]
Baudwyn of Canterbirie com to coroune þe Kyng
Richard, at Londoun opon a Sonenday
at Westmynstre tok þe coroun, of Ȝork Bisshop Geffray

. Wynchestre was þat bar þe Croys of . . .
was sent after þat tyde, him felle to be þe toþer; He was . . . . for hym fel . . . .
opon þe fadere side, he was Richardes broþer.
Richard his pallion bi messengere did com
& his confirmacion fro þe courte of Rome. . . . wiþ outen eny gate to .
Comen er to Kyng Richard boþe erle & baroun
þat had þe lond in ward þorghout þe regioun,
knyghtes & burgeis, sergan3, als was resoun,
homage to mak alle weis þat felle vnto þe coroun.
[137v] Þe pes did he crie & purueied warnisoun; . . . . warisoun
þe sara3ins þorgh maistrie haf won Acres toun.
Inglis & Normant knyghtes, for rewardoun, ... guerdons
with Richard ere in couant ageyn sara3ins feloun.
His fader left him inouh penyes, grete foysoun . . . . ynow of seluer . .
þat he þe way not widrouh opon his benisoun. . . . . no3t withdrow . . .
Þe kyng of ffrance was went to Saynt Denys to holde
his priue parlement, & þer one him it tolde . owyn priuey . . . was hym y tolde
þat Richard priuely his purueiance did gynne,
opon þe paemy þe lond Surrie to wynne; . . . . lond of Surry forto .
to Paris turned þe kyng for þat ilk sawe,
& þer a samenyng, his barons þider gan drawe. . made þere . . . . . to .
He bisouh i þam alle to conseil at þat nede, . by so3tte þem . . . . . .
what help mot best falle for þe sara3ins drede,
& teld þam an outrage, þat "Richard þe kyng
wille stele þis viage withouten my wityng."
Loke how Kyng Philip said vncurteisly! . . . . . ful envyesly
(Daþet haf his lip & his nose þerby.) Dared haþ . . . . . hym by
Forto þat parlement com Richard messengers ffor anon to þat . . . .
þat to Philip wer sent & to þe Du3epers;
þe names of þam þat cam was þe erle of Peiters,
of Almarle, Erle William, & an Erle Rogers,
Lucas de Lucie, & Roberd de Coynguers;
þise grete Philip of ffrance & alle his conseilers. Þey grette wel Philippe . . . . . .
The erle of Almarle said, "Richard, our Inglis kyng,
his luf is tille 3ow laid & luf is his gretyng,
þat 3e wille tak to herte þe grete noyse & crie
fro Acres þat comes so smerte, lorn is so doelfullie.
Our cristen men ere lorn, þe sara3ins alle aboue;
þerfor Richard beforn praies 3ow for loue.
For him þat on þe croice died for mankynde, ... vs & al .
bes boþe at a voice, in one 3our wille be mynde
Beþ . . on voys in wil & in on mynde
to help þe cristen men þat Ihesu criste bouht,

ageyn þe oste paen þat him lufed neuer nouht.
Richard him atires, his wille þerto is fest;
so mykelle he þider desires þat he may haf no rest.
If ȝe of him haf help & he for ȝow socour,
alle þis world salle ȝelp of ȝour grete honour."
Whan þe Duȝepers herd þe bodword of Richard,
to Philip þei ansuerd, "His sond ȝe salle reward.
He bedes ȝow luf inouh, ȝe þank him of his sond;
so noble bot on of ȝow is non be water no land.
..a man nys non but ȝe by water ne by.
[138r] Richer kyng is non in þis world bot ȝe,
no valianter of bon in cristendam als he.
Large er þo londes þat his eldres wonnen,
þe dedes of þer hondes þorgh reames er ronnen;
siluer he has inouh, his fader has him fonden.
Knyghtes to do his prouh with skrite tille him er bonden
to whom Acres salle be ȝolden also tite. ..with worschupe Acres.....
His felauschip to fle, to god ȝe do despite."
Pilip sent ageyn to Richard curteyly; Philippe....curtesly
bode bi þo certeyn said often grant mercy Þo by bode ful. & seide...
& þanked him his gode wille & his noble sond,
& he wild fulfille & at his myght suld fond,
& sent Richard to say þe next Marche folowand
he suld tak þat way, if wynde wild with him stand,
at Marsile to aryue, if he of lif had space,
& if þe wynde wild dryue þorgh myght & godes grace.
He praied Richard þe kyng & alle his men of gode
to leue for no prechyng þat way þat þei ne ȝode.
Whan Richard had conceyued þat Philip þer to stode,
his mobles on siluer reised þorgh Inglond alle his gode.
.noblis & seluer...of...
Rentes & som feeȝ he comandid to selle
þat burgh no citeȝ of taliage suld non telle;
þe tende suld be nouht, no þe tuende non make.
.entent was to take noȝt of þe lond ne taillage make
Þe bisshop of Durham bouht Saberg with þe wapentake;
þe bisshop of Wynchestre at þe kyng he bouht
tuo maners tille his estre, & Richard wisly wrouht,
for he wele vnderstode of taliage was grete drede;
it suld neuer do gode ne þerwith alle suld spede,
......þerwiþ schuld be no gode spede
namely to þe Holy Lond þider he þouht to go;
in taliage non he bond, ne robbed, ne did wo.

He sent to þe Scottis kyng þat he suld com & do
& mak pes for þat þing þat he was halden to.
Þe moneth of Nouembre after Alhalwemesse,
þat wele is to remembre, com Kyng William alle fresse,
batand to Canterbiri & þer ȝald him his fee.
of Scotlond to Canterbury . . gaff hym . .
Kyng Richard, our sire, homage & feaute
he mad for alle þo landes þat he of Inglond held,
& tille þe pes he standes þat bowes tille his scheld;
ȝit of penyes rounde to Richard gan he bede,
sexti þousand pounde to mende his misdede,
& Richard on þis wise forgaf it William so
to saue þat seruise þat Malcolme was wone to do
[138v] vnto þe Inglis kynges as right was & skille,
& do alle þe comynges whan bodword com þam tille
to London forto com whan parlement suld be,
als custom was wonne, & tak þer his liuere;
& Richard als quik ȝald to Kyng William
Rokesburgh & Berwik þat he in his hand nam. . . . . . to hymward nam
William tok his leue, his way to Scotland ches;
wele mot William cheue & alle þat lufes pes.
Kyng Richard ȝit duellis & purueis him to fare
& mykelle þing sellis, siluer forto ȝare.
Wardans sette he stable, trewe men at his myght,
þat neuer lufed fable bot mayntend pes & right.
Sire Huge of Durham, bisshop & man worþi,
an oþer Sir William, bisshop of Ely, . . clerc . . . . .
þise suld kepe þe lond & þe dignites.
Iustises tille þam he bond to kepe þe lawes & feeȝ; . . . . pees
Huge Bardolf fulle fers, William Marschalle his pere, ... fere
Geffrey le fitȝ Pers, William dela Bruere,
þise were mayntenours to sustene þe coroun
& rightfulle gouernours þe folk in feld & toun. . riȝtfully to gouernoure . . . . . .
Now has he brouht to stalle, his lond stabled redy,
& now with his folk alle he wendis to Normundy,
& þer he purueis him tille Acres & Sully, ... Surrye
on godes enmys grim he gadres gode party.
In þe cite of Rouhan his ȝole feste he held . . coste of Rohane . . . . .
with many douhty man & knyghtes gode of scheld.
Þe Monenday þat felle to be next after þe tuelft day,
þe kyng of France & he at þe riuer of Saynt Rymay
held a parlement, gode sikernes to make
þat boþe with on assent þe way suld vndertake;

ilkon sikered oþer with scrite & seale þerby,
togidere suore þam breþer, wherfor þe clergy .þey swour þem þere...
gaf a grete cursyng on whilk of þam so brak, ...side of þem..
bigan a wikked þing þat euelle bituex þam spak.
Now is Philip certeyn, he gos to Saynt Deny
& Richard turnes ageyn to dight his nauy.
He serches ilk coste of alle his seignorie;
þe guyours of his oste, þise wer withouten lie:
þe ersebisshop of Anxus, Danȝ Guard of renoun, ...Angers.Gydar..
with anoþer bisshop, Bernard of Bayoun,
& Richard de Cameuile, & Roberd du Sabloun,
& William de ffortiȝ was lord of Oleroun;
[139r] þise gouerne þer nauie, now ere þei in þe se,
toward þe paemie þidere þei ȝerned to be. ..cost of Panye þere....
Richard said þam his wille, "Mariners if ȝe moun
aryues in to Marsille with godes benisoun."
Þis was þe first woke of þe Passion.
As I on on boke gan loke, þe oste, clerke & baron .y on bok.......
wer sailand in þe se toward Marsille, þat toun,
help þam þer þei wild be, criste & Say Simioun. ......god & Seynt.
Þei had in þer route a hundreth schippes & ten,
bot god þei had no doute ne no defaute of men.

[*L adds:*] Shupmen þey had y nowe þat couthe wel þere mestere
Man ne þurfte þey knowe but god ne haue dangere

On þe fifte day changed þer wynde,
reft þam þe right way, to wend þe wer blynde; ....þey were al.
þe right se of Bretayn þer out were þei went
in to þe se of Spayn wer dryuen in a torment
among þe saraȝins, bot god þat grace þam lent ....god grace þere..
saued þam alle þo tymes fro þer encumberment;
ten schippes wer dryuen þorgh ille auisement, ...þere yuel assent
þorgh a tempest ryuen, þe schipmen held þam schent;
on þer was on depe kroken & alle to rent, ...to depe broken & so was al..
þe nien god gan kepe þat grace he þam sent.
Eft god þei bisouht to saue þam in þat cas,
sauely to hauen be brouht for luf of Saynt Thomas
þat for Holy Kirke suffred martirdam, ...churche þoled.
& god for þam gan wirke; her how a voice cam.
A schip þer was of London, richely atired,
a hundreth þer in fondon to serue god desired. ..þere were in....þey.
Biside þam on þer schip com a bisshop doun,
þe mast in hand gan kip with croice & paillioun,
& a kyng þe sihi, of gold schone his coroun. ...þey sey.....

Anoþer bisshop þam bi, þe first said his sermoun,
þan said þe ersbisshop to Londreis wordes suete:
"I am Thomas, ȝour hope, to whom ȝe crie & grete,
Martir of Canterbire, ȝour bale salle I bete.
Seynt Edmunde þe martire, his help I ȝow hete,
..Kyng & Martir his help he wil ȝo lete
þe bisshop, Saynt Nicholas, whos help is ay redie
to schipmen in alle cas whan þei on him crie. ......aske hym mercy
We þre haf þe ward of god & our ladie,
þe schippes of Kyng Richard to kepe & ȝow þam bie."
After þis biheste þat Thomas to þam said,
sone alle þe tempest in a throwe was laid;
þise nine schippes gan ride þer wyld wynd þam driue,
þei ne wist to what side ne what hauen in to riue.
[139v] At Leons Sur le Rone was Philip & Richard;
þei spak & mad þer mone what hauen þe mot toward.
In alle þe cuntre þorgh so grete folk mot men se
þat nouþer cite ne burgh myght þei in herberd be.
Philip toward Gene his oste did alle go,
& Richard oste bidene at Marsille left alle þo;
to mete on a while þe trompes blowe alle clere.
Batand fro Ceȝile com him a messengere
fro þe quene, Dam Ione, his awen sister dere; .....þe kynges suster.
bifor þam euerilkone he told Kyng Richere,
"Dede is Kyng William þat regned in Ceȝile
þat Ione þe lady nam, he lyued bot a while; .Iohans to quene nam he regned...
þat erle is of Tancre, Geffrey, a douhty knyght, ..þat is of Tancrede....
& valiant man of dede & to þe coroun has right,
he regnes after him & late had þe coroune;
to Ione he is fulle grim & haldes hir in prisoune."
Herfor Kyng Richard wrathes him & sais,
"Dight vs þiderward our busses & galais! Swythe diȝt...schupes..
Mi sister I wille out wyn or I ferrer go.
Bot he bigyn, Ceȝile he turnes fro,
& bot he wille with pes acorde in reson,
it salle rewe him þat res þat he to Ione has done."
Þe date was a þousand, a hundreth & ninetie
þat Richard was sailand toward paemie.
Þe seuent day of heruest in þat ilk ȝere
þat I rakend last writen abouen here, ..rekened....
þat Richard turned to Gene, & whan he com to lond,
Philip was mykelle to mene, Richard seke him fond.
Bot mykelle he comfortid him & siþen tok his leue;

toward Ceȝile fulle grim, þe kyng he þouht to greue.
. Sisile a pilgrym þe Kyng....
Whan his flete was alle at Tibre euerilkone,
þe pape a cardinalle sent, Sir Octobone.
(What Richard spak & he, conselle is & was,
to me it is priue, I sauh it in no pas.)
Þer duellid Richard schip þre daies to gesse;
bi þat was Kyng Philep risen of his sekenesse
& was in Ceȝile arriued at Meschyne,
& after in a while, com Richard euen as lyne, ...as blyne
þe day of þe croice in þe heruest tide.
Right als godes voice had ordeynd him to ride, . as gode wolde.....
were þo schippes nine þat Richard wend haf lorn,
in þe hauen of Meschyne ariued litille beforn;
[140r] it was a godes grace þat þat ilk nauie
ariued in þat place þer Richard suld lie.
Thre days in þat cite duellid Kyng Richard;
to þe kyng of Tancre he sent his letter hard
to deliuer his sister Ion out of his prison.
Men mad tille him grete mone, it was without reson.
"Bot he deliuer hir me with luf at my praiere,
þat tyme salle he se, scho salle be bouht fulle dere!"
Þis kyng of Tancrede, he was a wys knyght;
he sauh it was to drede & he did not alle right.
He sauh Richard anired & his mykelle myght,
his folk ariued & tired, & ay redy to fight.
He sent his sister Ione with mykelle honeste,
with his barons ilkone to Mischines, þat cite.
Philip was curteise, ageyn Dame Ione he ȝede,
tille hir broþer paleise with grete honour did lede.
An ilde was þer biside þat a saraȝin held,
trouage he gaf bi tide to cristen men þei teld.
"Allas," said Richard, "þat euer it suld so be
þe cristen þorgh forward suld grant a saraȝin fre."
A water þat closed it in, þat flum was de la fare, ...felon....
þe wonnyng of þe saraȝin, þat ilde hight Labamare.
Kyng Richad it wan & tille his sister it gaf; . Richard........
þe saraȝins ilk man he slouh, alle rif & raf.
Anoþer ilde biside, men cald it Griffonie,
Richard þat ilk tide, he did þam alle out flie.
Þe wonyng of þat ilde, Richard gon þam reue;
was non of þam so wilde þat lenger durst þer leue.
Whan þe folk þis herd, þe burgeis of Meschyn

þer ȝates ageyn him sperd & wild not lat him in;
wherfor þe contek on þis maner it cam,
& for þei did þat chek, an oth he suore to gram.
Bot þe kyng wild mende þat þei did him þere;
..Kyng Tancred wold a mende þat....
a þing he suld sende to do, als lawe it were,
fulfille þe testament of Kyng William þat was,
þat tille his sister ment for dowerie, þat trespas,
"& bot he ȝald it alle þat is writen þerin
with luf, els I salle with werre fond him to wyn." ....fonde hit..
Whan þe kyng of France herd þo tiþinges
þat so grete distance was bituex þo kynges,
conseil gan he take þat he suld be partie,
a gode acord to make forsoþe fulle fayntlie.
[140v] Noþeles þe kyng of Tancrede did fulle curteisly;
to Kyng Richard he ȝede & said he was redy
þe testament to fulfille of Kyng William,
& þat his men fulle ille vnskilfully nam.
"Alle þat was reson, I wille amend it wele,
& tille þi sister haf don plenerly ilka dele,
alle þat me felle to do of Williams testamet. ....testament
Witnes I tak hir to, hir seluen in present."
Hir seluen, Dame Ione, acorded with his sawe.
"Of þe testament alone, he has don alle þe law,
alle þat felle to me, bot ȝit I ask anoþer
þat fallis vnto þe Kyng Richard my broþer.
Of my lordes witeword, witnes þer of haf I: ...questword.....
of gold þer is a borde & tretels þer bi, ...tresteles..
of siluer oþer vesselle, gilte fulle richeli, ..þer is a vessel...
& ȝit anoþer iowelle faire & worþi,
a pauillon of honour with riche atiffement .....mykel atierrement
to serue an emperour at a parlement.
Þis quath my lorde þe þat tyme he suld die,
þe soth forto say & witnes wille not lie."
"Dame," said Tancred, "of trestels & borde,
fulfille I salle in dede þe kynges witworde." .....my lordes quethword
Fourti þousand vnces of gold he bede þe kyng, ... Tancred bad..
& Richard tok þe pundes withouten more sayng.
"Bot þis," he said, "I saue þat Arthure, my cosyn,
Tancred douhter salle haue & alle þat now is þin;
of Bretayn Arthure is als erle of heritage,"
& he granted to þis, confermed þat mariage.
Als þise tuo kynge wore about þis forward,

at Meschyne righ þore, þe kynges moder Richard, ..riȝt.....
ariued at þat riuale, brouht him busses þritti, ...Ryvaile..vessels.
charged with vitaile, with gode men & douhti,
of fflandres, þe Erle Philip, a lorde of honour,
of Helianore schip he was hir gouernour.
Elianore brouht þer a fair maiden ȝing,
þe kynges douhter of Nauere, to Richard þe kyng.
Hir name was Berengere, faire woman of age,
was þer non hir pere, of no heiere parage. .noun fonden here per of noun..
In Cipre of þat may was mad þe mariage
at Kyng Richard pay þorgh conselle of baronage.
Whan þei were trouth plight & purueied þe sposage,
Helianore forth hir dight to Rouhan hir menage,
[141r] bileft Dame Berengere at Richardes costage;
Dame Ione kept hir dere, þei lyued als birde in cage.
Þe kynges sustere kepte here dere at mury as bryd..
Whan pes was alle certeyn of Richard & Tancrede,
to þe cite of Kateyn in pilgrimage þei ȝede
to þe fertre of Saynt Agace, Richard mad offeryng ..ferther seynt Agesse...
& praied hir of grace to duelle þat with þe kyng.
.....þere to dwelle with Tancred..
Alle þre dayes tide Richard mad soioure;
þe barons bi þat side did him grete honoure.
Whan Richard suld wend, he tok leue at Tancreȝ;
Tancreȝ was fulle hend, conueied him tuo iourneȝ,
gaf him four schippes grete & were of way beforn, ...on wey.
þe tuo charged with whete, þe toþer with oþer corn,
To charged..& to of oþer.
& fiue oþer galeis with alle þer apparaile.
Richard was curteis, þanked his trauaile, ...gret availle
& Richard at þat turne gaf him a faire iuelle:
þe gode suerd Caliburne þat Arthur luffed so welle.
Þan said Sir Tancrede vnto Richard our kyng,
"God þat saues at nede boþe þe olde & ȝing
kepe þe fro mischance & fro þe fals enmys
þat er with Philip of France euer ageyn þi vis.
Bi Hugh of Burgoyn he sent a letter vnto me
þat I suld or þou went be bitraied þorgh þe, ...haue ben traised by.
& if werre or wo had risen vs bituen,
þe & þine to slo, with me he suld haue bien.
Þe soth þan schewes it þat my sawe is trewe.
Sir, haf here þis writ & schewe him alle newe;
if he it geynsay, I wille proue it on him."

Tancred went his way & Richard wex fulle brim. ....al grym
Richard tok his leue, Sir Roger turned & went,
& Richard gan him greue, to Philip þe letter sent.
Þe nauie com on a stounde to Meschyns þat cite;
biforn him he founde his sister & his meyne. Byfore Philipe þey fonde.....
Richard with Philip dele wild he nouht;
Philip bote on his lyppe & perceyued Richard þouht,
whi þat it ment, Philip gan aspie.
A wiles to Richard sent, how long he wild þer lie
Sone to Richard he sente......
& what tyme he had tight forward his nauie, ...had y ment...
his sege to sette & dight to help þe cristen crie. [*Om. L*]
Richard ansuerd þertille & said, "It is foly
to schewe conseil & skille þat not is to affie,
& þhit þer owen writte þer dede dos certifie. .ȝut þyn owen.....
Me þink in myn inwitte it semed traytorie."
[141v] Þan spak Philip ogrefe said, "I wote what þis menes: ...on greff & seide.....
þat was a fals brefe & forged wele it semes ...ful fals þeff & forseide...
for my sister Aleyse þat is now forsaken,
for on of mor richenesse of Nauer þou has taken.
It salle not so, Richard, I wille þe gif a gyue:
..noȝt be so Richard a gift y wil þe.
þou salle hold forward if þou wost þat I lyue." ....if y mote lyue
Whan Richard vnderstode þat Kyng Philip had suorne,
bifor þe clergie he stode & proued it on þe morne
....stoude he seide at eue & morwen
þat his fader Henry þat ilk Aleyse had knowen,
"A childe scho him by þat he held for his owen. ...had hym by......
A mayden childe it was & now dede is it;
þis wer a grete trespas agayn myn owen inwitte,
so febli forto wirke, for drede of godes awe,
ageyns Holy Kirke, tille Aleyse forto drawe.
I, Richard, haf maugre & I Aleyse take, ...if y Aleys þen.
whan my fader & she suilk samenyng gan make."
Þan said Kyng Philip tille alle þo of ffrance,
"Of gile þis is a trip of Richard desceyuance;
Gisors, my gode cite, with alle þe purueiance, ...appurtenance
Richard I gaf it fre to mak þis aliance
of him & hir, þo tuo þat er now in distance,
ten þousand mark & mo þat now er in balance,
& I betraised of alle; bi god þat alle may auance, [*Om. L*]
I salle bring him to stalle bot he mak me acquitance." [*Om. L*]
Now said Kyng Richard, "Þe manace late alle be;

Nay sir seide Richard þy manas...
þou salle haf reward of Gisors, þi cite,
þe tresore ilk a dele þat þou me bitauht,
for me salle haf wele alle þat þou euer auht." ..þou schalt haue......
Þe barons suffred nouht þe kynges to be wroth,
luf & pes þei souht þat þei acorded both;
Richard ȝald him his right, his tresore & his toun,
þorgh witnes & sight of clerk, erle, & baroun,
his sistir forto marie where god wild loke; ......wolde hire lok
to mak certeyn partie, Richard a quitance toke. ..cler partie....
After þe acord, sone Philip dight him forward,
to boote mad him bone & tok leue at Richard; .schupe he made.......
þe wynde was in his saile, tille Acres gan him driue,
bot litille was his trauaile tille Richard gan ariue.
Whan Philip tille Acres com, litelle was his dede;
þe Romance sais grete skam, who so þat pas wille rede.
...gret schame who so wil hit.
Þe Romancer, it sais, Richard did mak a pele, .romance......pile
on kastelle wise, alle wais wrouht of tre fulle welle;
[142r] in schip he did it lede to reise vp bi þe walle,
& if him stode nede, to couere him with alle. ....to nede to socore...
He reised it at Meschines, of werre tiþing he herd,
for þe ilde of saraȝins þer ȝates ageyn him sperd.
Þe romance of Richard sais he wan þe toun;
his pele fro þat forward he cald it mate Griffoun.
Tancred he was wys, he did Richard wille,
to Philip turned his vys so þat he held him stille. ..he turned his wyle......
[*L adds:*] Richard mad hym suche a mes in Meschins Citee
Þat Philipe praied hym pes on knees pur charitee
The romance of Richard seis plenerliche ilk a del
Þis acordes in som weis to þat romance riȝt wel
Now is Philip on flete, Kyng Richard ȝit duellis;
hes pele þat he vpsette, eft ageyn it fellis. His pile...he takeþ hit doun &.
For wrath first of Tancrede, Richard vp it reised,
if he had turned to nede his folk forto haf eised.
Bot whan þei were mad frendes þorgh sight baroun, ...siȝt of.
Tancred to him sendes, praied him take it doun,
þat no man for envie eft ageyn him held,
ne þorgh non oþer harie to do him reise his schelde. ....hatrie......
Now purueies him Richard ilk a day alle preste;
tille he be forward, he may haf no reste.
Acres þan is his triste opon þe saraȝin feendes,
....tryyst for þideward he wendis

to venge Ihesu criste, þiderward he wendes.
..for Ihesu Crist vpon þe sareȝins fendes
Þe kynges sister Ione & Dame Berenger,   ...Iohne & his wif..
formast of ilkone, next þam his chanceler,
Roger Mankael þe Chancelere so hight,   .Mankdel....
his tide felle not wele, a tempest on him light.
His schip was doun born, his self gan þer deye;
þe kynges seale was lorn with oþer busses tueye.   ....schupes.
Dame Ione þe fre to Ihesu scho bisouht,   ..his suster fre....
in Cipres scho mot be to hauen sauely brouht;
þe mayden Berenger, scho was alle ofright   .ȝonge quene.....
þat nouþer fer no nere, þe kyng scho sauh no sight.
Tuo busses wer forfaren þat in þe tempest brak,   .vessels.......
þe godes attached waren to þe kyng of Cipres, Isaac.
Þat þat askeped þat drede & to Cipres wan,   Tho þat skaped......
Isaac did þam lede to prison, ilk a man.
Whan Kyng Richard herd of þat mischuos tide   ......myschance fultide
& how his schippis misferd, he turned vnto þat tide;   ....to þat side
tille Isaac lettres sent bi Roberd of Thornham,
Sir Steuen with him went, anoþer knyght, William.
"Praie him for god aboue als I am his pilgrime,
ȝeld it me with loue þat he holdes of myne,
my godes þat he has þare, my men deliuere of bond,
& destorbe not our fare, we salle to þe Holy Lond;
[142v] & if he wille nouht deliuer me my þing,
fulle dere it salle be bouht, bi Ihesu heuen kyng."
Þe messengers kamen to þe Kyng Ysaak;
Ysaak tille alle samen þis ansuere he spak:
"Messengers, wherto chalange ȝe my þing
& what haf I do to with Inglis tayled kyng?   ....þe Englisse tailled.
Þe godes þat be fonden on my lond o chance,
tille him I am not bonden to mak deliuerance.
It is my profit, to myn I wille þam holde."
Þei went ageyn fulle tite, to Kyng Richard alle tolde.
Whan Kyng Richard herd say Ysaak respons,
"Turne we þiderward & delyuer our prisons,
& so it may betide þei salle dere abie
my þat þei hide, my men in prison lie."   my godes þat þey nov hide.....
Now he changes his weie, tille Acres may he nouht;
many þerfor gon deie, I schrowe Isaak so wrouht.   .....schrewe...
It was Isaak to wite, tille Acres he com no nerre,
þe skaþe on him gan bite þat Richard turned þe werre.
Whan Isaak had tiþand, emperour of Griffons,

þat Richard drow to land, with him alle his barons,
he did gadre an oste of Cipre & Griffonie
& com vnto þat coste to waite Richard nauie.
Richard was perceyued, þei were renged redie,
& how þer pencels weyued, son he mad a crie.
"Arme we vs, I rede, & go we hardilie, Aryue vs y rede....
& we salle mak þam schede & sondre a partie!"
He was first þat stirte to lond out of the boote,
armed & suerd girte bot an axe he smote. ...gerd but wiþ....
With þat axe he hewe, þe Griffons mad him weie;
many to dede he threwe & to grounde doun leie.
His maryners gan vp riue about in stedes seere,
þe Griffons þei gan driue bifor þam alle plenere,
þe Kyng Isaak fleih, his men had no foyson;
at þat tyme he ne deih, his partie ȝede doun. ...al wey his partye went al.
Richard cried on hie, "Londreis, folowes me!
Loke ȝe be me nehi, fulle gode giftes gete ȝe.
Take we þis emperour þat getis þise Griffons,
falle salle þis honour for hold of our prisons." ..his honur.....
Isaak had a spie þat warned him ay beforn
to tak þe mountayn hie & bide þer tille þe morn.
Whan þe euen cam, Richard dred tresoun;
agen to þe water he nam, did set his pauilloun,
[143r] þe godes þat þam gan falle geten at þat iorne,
felawes were þei alle als forthely as he. .....ferforthe..
Ysaac sauh his vow tille & Saynt Symeoun, Ysac made his mone til god...
what falle þerof or how, þe morn he suld com doun
.so fel þer of sone þe morn he wold..
with schelde & lance in hand to saue his regioun,
to mak þe Inglis fleand þat had robbed his toun;
if he of his mot take ouþer erle or baroun, ȝif he or his......
his prison suld he wake, þat wer deppest donioun, In prison...ȝe in þe depe.
for patriarke no pape, for bulle ne pardoun, ..ne for pape...for.
þerof suld he not scape withouten grete ransoun. þerout ne scholde he....
In tentis Richard rested alle þat ilk nyght;
his men wer wele gested with brede, wyne, & light.
On þe morn he ros & went to Lymosoun,
a cite large in clos, þe folk were fled þe toun.
Griffons þei it held, þei wer scaped away;
vitaile inouh at weld þei fond of corn & hay; ...wille......
Isaac did it store to hold for tuo ȝere.
Ariued were þer bifore Dame Ione & Berengere.
Þat tuo barges mot lede, of þat ware did he fille, ...of whete þey dide.

tille his siþen he ȝede & warned þam fulle stille, .his host siþþe.....riȝt.
in þe mornyng to rise, þe tyme at þe day sterne,
þe emperour & hise to seke, þei suld alle ȝerne.
His barons euerilkone be þat tyme wer dight;
þe kyng formast to gone, þe way he led þam right.
Was non in tente ne toun behind him durst be, ...by hym þen derste.
bot Bernard of Bayoun þat was kepand þe se.
Richard rode stilly neihand þe emperour;
he gaf a bold crie whan he bigan his stour.
Þe tentes doun he hew, Isaac to reuile,
& for non him knew, askaped he þat while.
Bare in serke & breke, Isaac away fled; Bothe in......
it was not told a leke þat non of his þien led.
..noȝt worþ a lek...þem þen ledde
Richard alle ouer ran & toke alle þat he fond;
a faire þing þer he wan, þe baner of þe lond.
Som of þam were gode, to Richard gaf bataile,
bot alle to dede ȝode & lost alle þer trauaile;
taken were a partie, bot maste of þam were slayn.
Als man þat wan maistrie, Richard turned agayn,
to Lymoson þam led, his fest he did þer crie, ..þem ledde & his weddyng gan.
Berenger wild he wed & þer soiorne & lie.
Þe þrid day of þe fest, Sir Bernard of Bayoun
newed eft þer geste, þe quene he gaf þe coroun.
as spekeþ þe gest he gaf þe quene..
[143v] To þat sollempnite com lordes of renoun
þat weddyng forto se for grete affeccioun;
of Ierusalem cuntre þe gode Kyng Guyoun,
Gaufrey, his broþer was he, & Aunfrey of Turoun,
Reymoun of Antioche, of Triple þe Erle Bumoun,
ffrere Ruffyn Delmount & þe Duke Leoun;
þise mad Richard homage, douhteli kneland doun. ....mekely knelant.
Ageyn þe saraȝin lynage þat leues on Mahoun,
alle þei same þis same þat ȝare þei were & boun ..seide þe same......
to die in Ihesu name with gode douocioun ....deuocion
þat for vs suffred schame & died þorgh passioun.
"We trowe it is our frame, his resurreccioun."
Richard said his skille, "Lordynges þis is resoun
bituex vs, if ȝe wille mak obligacioun
þat I be ȝour aller broþer & ȝe in my bandoun, ...alle ȝore......
þat non faile oþer ne consent to resoun."
Þei granted alle þerto, kyng, erle, & baroun,
& who þat wille not so gaf him þer malisoun. ......he gaf...

Also suiþe Richard "has armes" did crie
& his oste did parte to þo þat couth it guye. ...as armed did he.
Þe noble Kyng Guyon tok of his cheualrie
oþer lordes of renoun, assigned þam þer partie.
Whan Isaac herd seie what help Richard was comen
& how to stop his weie parties had þei nomen,
of his men most worþi at þam conseile gan take;
þe best he mot go bi acord with Richard make.
Þo messengers camen, þe conseil þat he ches ...& enformed his pes
bifor Richard alle samen & enformed his pes,
..þe samen þey conseilled þat he ches
"Ȝour wille wille he alle do & be at ȝour mercy."
Richard ansuerd þerto, "I grante it bliþely."
Þan com þe emperour bifore Kyng Richard.
"Þat I did dishonour, Sir, haf it to no reward; .....haue ȝe no.
þe dede þat I did ille, my foly it was.
I praye þe with gode wille, forgyue me þat trespas;
þi man wille I be bi water & bi land,
þis reame to hold of þe & bowe vnto þi hand.
Þo men þat I did take to prison þe toþer morn,
amendes I wille make & bring þam þe biforn;
þi godes þe biken or þe valow verray ..ȝe schal han þem al redy par ma fay
þat þi dronkled men tynt þe toþer day,
& with þe wille I go als felawes in ferd. ....in þe feld
A hundreth knyghtes mo, armed & gird with suerd,
...& mo armed with sper & scheld
[144r] & four hundreth to bote, squieres of gode aray,
& fiue hundreth o fote to whilk I salle pay .foure. on fote suche as schal þe.
ilk day þer wages to þo ilk plenere,
knyght, squier, & pages þe termes of tuo ȝere.
My douhter & myn heyre to loke hir I þe grante ......ordeyn....
þat þou be in speyre I salle hold conante." ....no dispeir þat y nel..
Richard curteise was þat sauh bede suilk loue, ...say hym...
forgaf alle þe trespas, wirschipid himself aboue; .hym...& worschuped hym.
tent & pauillon tille Isaac did he signe,
wirschipped him at reson right as himself was digne.
Whan þe day was ent, to rest men wer alle laid,
Isaac gan repent þat he to Richard said;
fulle stille away he went (þat was a theues braid).
A messenger he sent þat þus to Richard said,
"Isaac wille not grante to oblige him to þe, ...to be y bunde..
no to be þi tenante, his body bonden be, ...ne his lond y..
ne to suilk seruage his heyrs disherite,

ne ȝeld at terme & stage rent mykelle no lite."
"O Deuel!" said þe kyng, "þis is a foltid man.
Whan he with trechettyng bi nyght away so ran, ...trechiryng.....
þei red him alle a mysse þat conseil gaf þerto.
Wenes he our men Inglisse forto treccher so?" ......trechere.
Now gos Kyng Richard his purueiance to make,
how & whiderward he hoped Isaac take.
To þo lordes þat camen als Bumund & Sir Guye,
& þe toþer alle samen, he toke galeis tuenty
& busses þat were gode, o hundreth of þe moste .Shepes......hey mast
to fare opon þe flode to waite wele bi þat coste,
eft bi Cipres side Isaac to aspie
if he toke any tide out of lond to flie.
Richard south þe lond with gode folk & hardie; .soȝtte.......
þe tounes þat þei fond, þei felle to his mercie.
Roberd of Thornham bare him nobilly;
bi þe se side he nam & wan it per maistrie, al þat side.....by.
þan turned he to þe kyng after his conquest.
Þei mad þan a samenyng to go toward þe west;
þe cite of Nichoci þei wan & were þer in,
& anoþer þerbi, a toun men calle Cherin.
Doun of þe kastelle mote Isaac douhter cam
& felle Richard to fote, gretand þat doole him nam.
.....gret doel to here sche.
"Lord Kyng," scho said, "on me þou haf mercie!"
& Richard hand to laid, lift hir curteislie ..his hand..&..vp.
[144v] & sent hir tille his wife & tille his sister Ione,
& þer scho led hir life with þo ladies ilkone.
Þe castels & þe godes, tounes stored wele, ...þe side tounes he astorred.
vitaile vnto þer fode, Richard toke ilk dele. .to þere nede....
Sir Guy & Bumund þei com as þei ȝede,
þe ne tynd ne fond ne were at no dede; Þey ne sey hym ne fond newhar...
Roberd bisouht þe kyng to turne toward Bufnet
& þer ouer alle þing his sege þer to set.
"In alle Griffonie ne es so strong a toure,
& þat ȝe wille þer lie, it is to ȝour honoure." .if ȝe...hit shal be..
Richard also suiþe to Bufnet he ȝede,
his maistrie gan he kiþe, engynes dight to dede.
Whan þei were alle dight stalworþely & fast,
boþe day & nyght vnto þe toure he kast.
To while þat Kyng Richard was kastand to þe toure,
Statin, his stiward, spak to þe emperoure On Statyn þat was Styward..his lord..
als his mete he sat & was his seruitoure, Als at.......

"Forto amend þour stat I wille conseiloure, Sire . . ȝore estat . . be ȝore .
Sir Kyng Isakin, I am þi vauasoure. . Emperour Ysaac . . . .
My name is Statin, I wille be no traitoure.
I haf kept þi land; I se þat dishonoure
is now þe nerhand þorgh þis conquerour, . . to ȝo neyhand þurw Richard .
þat an Inglis kyng, a wys werreoure. þat is . . . a ful . .
Loke þou lese no þing for þi fole erroure,
ne þe lond be not lorn þat þin ancessoure . . . . . . þat þurw . .
so wele kept biforn als noble gouernoure.
Go & mak his pes or he do þe more stoure,
& þou to þi deses may haf þe frute & floure." . . . . . . haue þyn honur
Þan said Isaac tille him, "Ert þou his mayntenour?"
Fulle broþely & brim he kept vp a trencheour . iresly & grym . . . . .
& kast it at Statin, did him a schamfulle schoure,
his nese & his ine he carfe at misauentour. . nose plat als þe chyn . . by .
Statin vp he stirte, him þouht þerof grete schame, . a side he sterte . . . . .
"Sir, þou has me hirte, þerfor þou ert to blame!"
Als so suiþe he ȝede vnto Kyng Richard
& schewed him alle þat dede of Isaac þe coward.
"Sir, be my socoure & venge myn outrage!"
Richard did him honoure & he mad him homage.
Statin wele þan lete, he ȝalde him alle þe honour
of Baaf & Bufnet þat he of Is Diendamour,
. Baiff & of Bufnet Canddre & Danndamour
castels & citeȝ þat he he of Isaac held, ... he of Ysac .
baronies & feeȝ he ȝald him ilk a scheld.
[145ʳ] Þe grete lordes Inglis þat þe werre had gonnen . . . . by gonnen
wer fulle glad of þis, Cipres so sone was wonnen.
Beside of Saynt Andrew was an abbay,
Cape þe name men knew, & þerin herd þei say
þat Kyng Isaac was priuely hid þer in; . þe Emperour Ysaac . . . . .
to Richard so þei spak, he went him out to wynne.
Isaac tiþing herd Richard com him to seke;
ageyn Richard he ferd, to fote he felle fulle meke
& said, "Sir, mercy! My life þou saue it me.
Do not þat vilany fettred þat I be;
in prison þou me do bot nouht in bondes bynde.
I pray ȝow it be so for schame of my kynde."
Said Richard, "Þou salle haue at þin owen deuys; . . . . haue riȝt . . . .
þi life I salle þe saue." Isaac he did vp rise.
"O dele," said þe kyng, "þis is a fole Briton!" . deuel . . . . . . fool .
He spak no maner þing for regne to gif raunson,
. . no more þyng for to ȝyf his .

ne no þing him bisouht, he was of kynges blode, ...he by þoȝt.....
bot for prison bisouht als fole þat couth no gode.
Now er his aneus wrouht of siluere wele ouer gilt; [*Om. L*]
daþet þat þerof rouht, his was alle þe gilt. [*Om. L*]
Taken is he to loke to Berenger & Ione, ...to Richard wiff & to his suster.
& þei him vndirtoke, þo ladies euer ilkone.
To Statin gaf Richard þe cite in kepyng
& bad him be stiward als ore was with þe kyng.
.mad hym þer of styward to holde of hym..
For Isaac did him schame his lord suld be, ...þat schold haue.
þei cald him þis toname, Statin þe Nasee.
He changed þe tounes name & called hit...
Now is Cipres lorn fro Isaac & hise
& to Richard suorn for his valiantise.
Þe mene folk comonly, fulle gode men & wise, .men & folk al......
com to his mercy, doand him seruise, ...& dide þere.
þat bies woule & wyne & sellis with conant. [*Transp. L*]
"Do com," said Statyn, "burgeis & merchant, [*Transp. L*]
& knyght & squiere, & mak þam ȝour tenant,
citeȝ & tounes sere, hosbond & sergant,
& tak of þam homage as custom is & haunt."
To do þat ilk seruage, þe folk said, "We graunt
& þerto half our þing for to haf þo lawes ..ȝif half.....oure.
þat Samuel, þe gode kyng, gaf bi olde dawes ..oure olde kyng....
& sikred it with skrite, hyngand set his seale,"
.sikered hit with Scrit & sette þer to þere.
& Richard gaf it so quite þat þei suld him be leale.
..for ȝaf hit quyt so þey wolde..
Now has Kyng Richard of Cipres þe seignorie,
what with nesshe & hard wonne þe maistrie.
[145ᵛ] To Statin þe Nasee did he grete curteisie,
alle Cipres gaf him fre ageyn his vilanie,
with a suerd to holde of Richard heyres alle,
Inglis kynges tolde to whom þe chefe salle falle. To..scholde......
Statin þe reame nam in þat ilk conaunt
þat Roberd of Thornham, if þe kyng wald him graunt,
with him forto duelle to maynten þe pes,
þe foles forto felle þat rise wild in res.
Now leues Roberd with Statin Nasee
tille tiþing be more herd or pes better be, ...pees þan sikerer.
with þe kynges leue þe lond to iustise,
his enmys to greue þat ageyn him wild rise.
His wille has Richard sped in Cipres fer & nere

& Isaac forth is led with Ione & Berengere
at Triple to soiourne, & þer þei mad a crie
tille Acres forto turne alle holy þer nauie;
bihynd left non of hise, bot alle with him þei nam
bot he þat was iustise, Roberd of Thornham.
Now er alle on flote, god gif þam grace to spede,
with douhty folk to note whan þei com to dede. ....nede
At none þe toþer day þei sauh fer in þe se [*Transp. L*]
a grete busse & gay, fulle hie of saile was he; [*Transp. L*] ..schupe........
þe weder was fulle soft, þe wynde held þam stille,
þe saile was hie o loft, þei had no wynde at wille.
In Philip nauie of ffrance a pencelle þei put oute,
his armes on a lance ouer alle þe schip aboute.
So mykelle was þat barge it myght not lightly saile,
& so heuy of charge, & þe wynde gan faile.
To wite what þei were went a marinere; ....Messenger
respons þei gaf him þere, þei wer men of mistere, Answer þey ȝaf......mester
fro Antioche were went vnto Kyng Philip,
"& for vs has he sent & his is þis schip."
[*L adds:*] Þe maryners by huld hit eche to Kyng Richard þey told
Þe Prince of Antioche he ȝede þe schup to byhold
Said þe Kyng Richard, "Sir, Prince if þou be, ...þat þou go
bityme turne to meward, for I wille speke with þe." .com aȝenward for....þo
Þe prince com fulle sone, Sir Richard did he calle, ..com aȝen sone.....
"Do dight & mak ȝow bone, þe schip ere saraȝins alle;
tille Acres þei þam rape, venom for our men lede,
& if þei vs ascape, þe cristen may þam drede!"
Þan cried Richard on hie, "Now batale vs belyue, ...enbataille we vs blyþe
þorgh help of oure ladie þat schip salle alle to ryue.
Ilk man þat may wynne tok to his partie; .....tak...
to set chalange þer inne salle no man be hardie." ....so hardy
[146r] Þe kynges owen galeie, he cald it Trencchemere, ...trenchemer
þat was first on weie & com þe schip fulle nere;
oþer were þer inowe þat þer after drouh,
bot he com with a suowe þat þe schip to rof. ....suche a swow.....
Þe schip cast crokes out, þe galeie to þam drouh;
þe kyng stode fulle stout & many of þam slouh.
Wilde fire þei kast þe kyng to confound,
his schipmen were fulle wrask, els had he gon to ground;
....wrast ellis had go to grunde
þe kyng abaist him nouht bot stalworthly fauht,
alle to dede he brouht þat his galeie ouer rauht.
Þe galeie þer þorght schete & þe kyng was gode;

þe schip þat was so grete, it dronkled in þe flode. ......hit drenched...
Þei teld fiueten hundred sara3ins þat drenkled were, ...drenched þere
fourti & sex wer sundred, & alle þo were saued þere;
.....& þey y saued were
þe summe couth no man telle of gold þat was þer in
& oþer riches to selle, bot alle mot þei not wyn.
Þe venom alle þei hent, in þe se cast it away,
þe folk it mot haf schent þat about Acres lay.
Armour þei had plente & god besquite to mete; .....bred bysquyd..
it sanke son in þe se, half myght þei not gete.
Richard bade, "Hale vp hie 3our sailes þer god vs lede.
Our men at Acres lie, of help þei haf grete nede."
Þe date was a þousand, a hundreth nienti & one.
Fro Cipres he was sailand, a toun he wan, Acon.
Als grace of god wild be, þe wynde gan him dryue;
þe euen of þe Trinite vnder Acres Richard gan aryue. .vigilys of.......
Dame Ione & Berengere bifor him fond he eft;
Isaac þe emperere at Triples was left.
Þe folk of Griffonie, whan Richard was gone, ...was went
to Statin had envie, a monk þei ches ilkone ....by assent
þat Isaac cosyn was & corouned him for kyng;
þei did a foule trespas, it was vnsemly þing.
Statin wild þei greue, mispaied was Roberd;
he said þei salle mischeue whan he þat tiþing herd.
Night & day þei woke, Roberd & Statyn;
þorgh force þe monke þei toke & brouht him to Cheryn,
3it he skaped out, þe monke, of prisoun.
Þei cried "has armes" about Roberd fro toun to toun.
Þe folk whan þei were comen to Statyn & Roberd,
eft þe monke þei nomen, at Cheryn þei him sperd; ....ferd
opon þe þrid day þe folk he did somoune,
lered men & lay, fre & bond of toune,
[146v] a quest þan wild he take of þe monke þat bare þe coroune.
His abite he gan forsake, his ordre lete alle doune,
& 3it anoþer sawe of behoues be spoken: ....þer of be howeþ..
ageyn þe comon lawe þe prison has he broken.
Som chesons þei cast & som for him said, ...men seide
bot here now at þe last what dome was on him laid.
Said Sir Roberd, "Monk þou was whilom;
for wirschip of þe werld, forsoke þou alle & som.
To god þou mad a vow in þi professioun,
his traitour ert þou now, þou did him a tresoun;
for þe worldes blisse þou left þin habite,

& now þou wost for wisse of boþe ert þou quite.
We toke þe als robboure in þis ilk cuntre;
þou reft þe kyng his honour þat felle not vnto þe.
To Cheryn, þat ilk toun, þider was þou led
& þer þou brak prisoun & away þou fled;
eft we did þe take, in prison we þe bond.
Þat lawe I salle þe make þat is Richard lond. ....is in..
Galwes do ȝe reise & hyng þis cheitefe! .....henges on þis þeff
Better him were weth eise in clostre haf led his life, ...wiþ ayse.....liff
þe seruise of his song recorded & lered,
þan chalange with wrong þat Kyng Richard conquered,
& þi messe songen & serued god alle myght
þan to be hongen in þi frendis sight."
Now of þis olde monk & þis new kyng
þat was not worth a fonk, don has his endyng; .....flonk....
þe folk was alle pesed, to Statyn wild þei cheue.
Of Statyn þat was sesed Roberd toke his leue
with ricchesse inouh þat he to Acres led,
& teld Kyng Richard how of alle þat he had sped.
"Þe folk of Griffonie a monk þei chese to kyng,
sib Isaac, a partie had mad a chalangyng; Sub to Ysac in party he made..
in Cipres wer þei comen, þer maistrie gan þei kiþe,
& we ageyn þam nomen & tok him als suiþe;
to Cheryn we him led & þer he brak prisoun.
Eft we toke him fled, brouht him ageyn to toun;
& after þat he was fled we broȝt....
þe courte opon him sat, þe quest filed him & schent
......quest vyle hym schent
for trespas, of þat he tok iugement."
"Allas for vilenie," said Richard þe kyng,
"þat a kyng suld so die, hanged for no þing. ...scholde deye so for eny.
Roberd, þou ert to blame, þou did ageyn resoun.
Certes, þou has don schame tille alle þat bere coroun."
[147r] "Sir," said Roberd, "þer of is not to speke.
Late alle þis be sperd; on godes enmys þe wreke.
Siþen Philip hider cam, he gaf neuer non assaut;
it wer mykelle scham to mak suilk a defaut.
A partie has þou sped, þanked be god alle myght,
ȝit salle þou mak þam dred or com a fourtenyght.
Do reise vp þin engyns & wyn of þam þise dikes;
I trowe þe saraȝins our comyng mislikes."
Richard als suiþe did reise his engyns;
þe Inglis wer þan bliþe, Normans & Peteuyns.

In barges & galeis he set mylnes to go;
þe sailes, as men sais, som were blak & blo,
som were rede & grene, þe wynde about þam blewe.
A selly sight to sene, fire þe sailes þrewe; .selcouþ siȝt to se þe fir...
þe stones were of ryues, þe noyse dredfulle & grete,
.stones al of ryves.....
it affraied þe saraȝins as leuen þe fire out schete. ....in lemes....
Þe noyse was vnride, it lasted alle day; ...vnliþe....
fro morn tille euentide þerof had many affray.
To while þei had wondryng of þis þat þei ne knew,
Þe whiles þat þey made.......
stode Richard, our kyng, þe chyne in tuo he hew
& sesid þe saraȝin dikes maugre þam euerilkon;
now þe saraȝins mislikes, to Mahoun mad þei mone,
our cristen wer fulle fayn, þe sauh Richard þerin; [*Transp. L*]
...ful fawe þat Richard was withinne
þe dikes wer alle drawen with iren chynes þrin. [*Transp. L*]
Þe diches þat were drawen with yren cheynes twynne
"Certes," said þe soudan þat was in Acres toure,
"þis is a kyng, a man, þis is a werreoure; .kyng cristen is a man þat is..
me þink els a wonder bot he salle do grete wo.
He salle sched vs o sonder, fro Acres salle we go;
if he forth haf grace as he now bigynnes,
hiþen salle he vs chace & alle þis lond he wynnes." Hennes..........
Þe bisshop of Perouse com to Kyng Richard,
"Sir, ouer meruailouse our duellyng here is hard.
Sir, here biforn of men haf we told
fourti þousand lorn for hungre & cold.
Þe hungre was so grete & þe cold so stark
þat a quarter whete was at tuenty mark;
for ten mark men sold a litille bulchyn, ...solde altel with tyne bolechoun
litille lesse men told a bouke of a motoun. ...solde a body of.
Men gaf fiueten schillynges for a goos or a heen ..fiȝtty.......
for þe grete lordynges bouht to seke men. þat þe......
An ay bi it selue for fiue schillynges was bouht,
a pere for penyes tuelue or þei had it nouht.
[147v] Þe comon of þe oste bouht þam hors flesch,
or mules or assis roste, or haf bien mete lesse. Oure Mules & asses.....
Many grete mishappes, many hard trauaile
haf comen vs hard clappes whan þei gan vs assaile."
He told to þe kyng many hard chance
þat tellis here no þing bot alle in þe romance.
He tellis in þe romance, sen Acres wonnen was,

how god gaf him faire chance at þe bataile of Cayfas.
Siþen at Naȝareth at þe Assompcion messe,
at Assur he did to deth þe saraȝins more & lesse;
siþen at Iaphet was slayn Fauuelle, his stede; .....Favel..
þe romance tellis grete pas þer of his douhty dede.
Bot þe bisshop sais vnto Kyng Richard
how þam felle oþer wais so many woes & hard,
"Bot, Sir, we here wele telle ȝe ere so trew a kyng,
our folk þat here duelle ȝerne ȝour comyng;
ouer alle now is said, 'His comyng þank we god,
our hope is on him laid & fulle wele is it trod,'
þat ȝe salle wele spede to schorten our soiorne
& mend our grete nede, to ioy þat it mot torne.
Ȝour wille is euer so gode & ȝour treuth so treist,
ȝour douhtynesse of blode þe saraȝins salle freist.
Now Ihesu for þat croice þou þoled on passioun, ...þat he þolede..
here our sinfulle voice & grant ȝow wynne þe toun."
Whan Kyng Richard herd þe cristen had suilk pyn,
fulle soft he him ansuerd, wepand with his ine.
"To criste for me biseke þat he gyue me þat grace
þe cristendom to eke, þe saraȝins to chace."
And to þe cristen eke þes sarsyns þat we.
Richard also suiþe did set his pauilloun;
his maistrie sone gan kiþe, he dight him to þe toun.
Now ere þe dikes wonnen opon godes enmys
& sautes has bigonnen þorgh whilk he getis pris,
so did Kyng Philip with sautes on þam gan pres,
bot for a forgetilschip Richard & he boþe les.
..envye of worschupe Richard....
Philip left his engynes withouten kepyng a nyght;
þat perceyued þe saraȝines, with fire brent þam doun right.
For he com on þe morne, assaut he wild haf gyuen, When he.........
his engyns fond he lorne, brent, & tille askes dryuen.
Richard said his avis, blamed him for þat dede,
"A werreour þat were wys, desceyt suld euer drede,
wele more on þe nyght þan opon þe day;
in mirke withouten sight wille enmys mak affray." ....asay
[148r] Richard lent him of hise, Acres for to assaile; ..som of.....
Philip withouten fayntise did alle his trauaile.
Þe to kyng & þe toþer assailed it so hard
þat þe soudan broþer cried pes opon forward.
Alle þei went to here what þe soudan wild say;
þe folk com alle in fere with þo kynges tueye.

Þis was þe sarazins sawe: "Þe toun ȝeld ȝow we wille; ...Soudans.......
if ȝe grant vs þe lawe, I salle say ȝow þe skille.
Late vs alle out com, þis is þe first we chese,
þat non be slayn ne nom, ne life no lymme lese; ....ne no man lyme ne.
& if þat we wille take a baron of ȝour oste, .with þat wel wille......
& cristen kyng him make to regne bi þis coste.
Him þan wille we say who is moste valiant,
if ȝe consent þat way, þe marchis of Mounfraunt." ....Montfrank
Richard was hastif & ansuerd þat stund, ...hym þat stonde
"Certes þou lies, cheitif, & as a stinkand hund!
Here ere a þousand mo more worþi haf pris .....& more.to haue.
þan he þou tellis fro þat ilk traitoure Marchis. ....vs to þilke..
It salle auaile him nouht þat he ȝour soudan sent!
I se þat he has bouht þe lond with his present,
þov he þis lond haþ boȝt with sonde of..
& þis lond is oure & our right wonyng,
for our ancessoure here of was he kyng .crist oure...is heir &.
& ȝe ere our enmys, þe cristendam to spille, ...þe cristen men..
& now is þe marchis turned to ȝour wille. .....mys turned al to..
I rede out of þis oste þe marchis go his gate.
Bi god þat myght has moste, he may go to late!
..almyȝtty most he may go ȝut..
If he þorgh traytorie salle be at ȝour deuys,
I salle do him hang hie or drawe with runcys."
.......ellys be drawe with ropys
Said þe kyng of ffrance, "Richard whi art þou wroth?
What is ȝour distance þat he is þe so loth, ...þat Markys....
& he is gentille knyght, of kynges blode comen;
if he with vnright ouht of þin haf nomen,
he salle at þi wille mak alle þin amendes
& late alle be stille þat þou him defendes."
Said þe Kyng Richard, "Sir, at ȝour honoure,
in þat ilk forward he ȝelde me my tresoure
þat my fadere Henry gaf to þe Holy Lond. .....me til þe..
He toke it wikkedly out of þe Hospitelers hond,
fourti þousand pounde, & if he ȝelde it me,
we salle fare & founde als frendes falle to be." ......frendys scholde be
Sir Philip stille he stode, worde ne spak he more;
in þat same way þei ȝode right als it was ore.
Aboute þere iourne þey...þey dide ȝore
[148v] Richard asked þo landes þat þe cristen wan ......crysten byfore.
out of þe sarazins handes & chaced þe soudan;
þe sarazins wild not ȝelde so mony londes sere, ...many londes þere

ne þe kynges ne wilde acorde in oþer manere.
[*L adds:*] Wherfor þe Sarsyns til Acres agayn were sent
Þe kynges diȝtte þere engynes & to þer assaut went
Oft tille our Inglis men was schewed a mervaile grete: Sone til........
a darte was schot to þem, bot non wist who it schete.
In þe schaft was purtreit (þorgh þe Holy Goste, trowe I)
"In nomine patris," it said, "et filii et spiritus sancti."
Was neuer cristen man couþe perceyue þe certeyn,
ne wist what tyme no whan it passed out eft ageyn;
it com fro þat tureile þat Richard had doun smyten. ...þe tourel.....
Alle þe saraȝins conseile in þe schaft was writen,
& alle þer ordinance Kyng Richard it wiste;
it was a fulle faire chance schewed þorgh Ihesu criste.
Richard mad þankyng to Ihesu for þat sond
& for þat schewyng, to wirschip him suld he fond.
To Philip & Richard þe saraȝins said þei wild
in a gode forward þe toun to þam ȝeld;
of Ierusalem, þe land þei said he suld it haue,
þerto tuenti þousand of cristen men to saue.
Þei treistid not þer tille, bot þei did it in dede;
þe kynges with gode wille vnto assaut ȝede. .....to þe assaut þey.
Richard had minoures þat myned vndere þe walle,
a pece with a grete cours at ons felle doun alle; .pyce...tour.....
þe Frankis bare þam stoute, þe myned boþe & cast
vnto a toure, Maudut, & wan it at þe last. ...sanȝ dout......
Þe saraȝins som þei slouh & som for drede fled;
at þat tyme, wele inouh þe Frankis manly sped;
þe Inglis at þer triste bifor þam bare alle doun,
& Richard, als him liste, þe way had redy roun. ....made redy & rom
Now has Richard entre & Acres taken es; ...entred....
þe saraȝins com fulle fre & offred him grete riches.
Unto Philip of France þe Frankis mad a crie,
"Þi worschip to auance, com in als kyng hardie,
com in as lord of fe, for hedeles ere þei hopped,
& slayn alle may þou se þat þi way stopped;
.alle beþ slayn þat þou maist se....
& now is Acres taken þorgh Richard þe conquerour."
His banere held þam waken, was put of o toure;
..y splaid & waken was put out in a.
Kyng Philip did also, his baner was forth laid,
& righ it felle þerto for no man him withsaid. as riȝt ful þerto.....
Þe erle of Ostrece cam & put his banere out .Erel of Hostry......

& Richard asked þorgh wham þe erle bare him so stout.
..wondred of þam þe Eril....
[149r] Kyng Richard þorght hatie, after þe erle sent ..in hastie....
& asked, "Of what seignorie holdes þou lond & rent
þat þou has put out here þi baner for maistrie,
among kynges baneres, withouten auowrie?"
"Sir," said þe duke, "I am now comen here
þise saraȝins to rebuke & slo at my powere.
Mi lond I hold with right at no mans dome
bot of god alle mygh & Saynt Petir of Rome." ....myȝt & of....
"If þou to non þat lyues," said Richard, "þou cheue ne bowe,
þi lond men salle gife tille one þat may it vowe."
Grete scathe afterward in a litille þrawe .striff.....
com tille Kyng Richard for þat envios sawe.
Now haf þe cristen won Acres þat was lorn,
þe sararins ouer ron with force & doun born. .Sarsyns beþ.......
Þe folk was mykelle & strong, of mete þei had grete nede;
þam burd departe þer þrong, þat lond mot þam not fede.
Þey most departe........
Þei parted þe oste in tuo þorgh comon acordance, ...ordynance
Richard wille was so, so was Philip of ffrance.
A castelle was þer biside, fro Acres a iorne,
grete scaþe it did bi tide to þe cristen in þe cuntre;
þat castelle hight Pilgrym, of alle it bare þe flour,
þe saraȝins kept it þat tym for þer chefe warnistour. ....chif socour
Þat castelle was fulle strong & ille for to wynne;
þe saraȝins kept it long, þei wer inow þer in.
Philip went him þidere þat castelle to conquere;
þe Frankis alle togider did nouh whan þei com þere. .....noȝt....
Richard oste forth ran & grace bifor him fond;
auht iornes he wan within þe saraȝins lond.
Philip þat þer lay, to spede had he no grace;
it was not worþe an ay, his dede no his manace.
Richard herd it say, he dred an oste mot skip
behind & stop his way bituex him & Philip,
"& if þe soudan ros opon Philip of ffrance,
& I were þan in clos withouten cheuisance,
so myght it in a while þe gode torn tille ille.
A man salle ay drede gile, þe gode is not at wille."
..scholde drede gile þat he noȝt soudeynly spille
Richard his oste did turne, tresore he had inouh;
nouht wild he soiorne, to Philip fast he drouh.

Whan Kyng Philip herd þat Richard was comand,
how faire hap with him ferd, so fer wan in þe land
& wiþ hov faire hap herde so fer wynnyng..
þat Richard turned ageyn, his marschalle teld him why, & hov Richard.......
& said Philip certeyn, "Our dede is not worþi; þen seide.......
[149v] our dede has bene nouht sen we hider camen.
To turne haf I þouht tille Acres alle samen;
if Richard hider com, wynne it bifor vs alle, ...he wold wynne....
þat we þis sege nom, schame it wille vs falle. ....furst nom.....
Þan salle men doute vs lesse, men se we do no dede;
þe saraȝins our pruesse not so mykelle wille drede."
Now is þe oste Frankis tille Acres alle went,
& comen ere þe Inglis with pauilloun & tent
& loged þam right wele, ouer alle þer þam þink;
inouh þei had catele & plente mete & drynk.
Whan þei had alle eten & watches mad alle preste,
to gete þat þei had geten, Richard ȝede to reste.
Þat castel for to geton but Richard went..
Orely on þe morn, his messe he ȝede to here,
to Ihesu of Mary born þis was his prayere:
"Lord Ihesu," he said, "als so verrayly
as my luf is on þe laid & on þi moder Mary,
help me to venge þi dede of þis saraȝins kynd
þat gaf conseile & rede þe to bete & bynd,
& namly on þat blode þat com of fals Pilate
þat wist sakles þou stode whan he on þi dome sate. ..gultelis........
Ihesu, for þin honour, if it be þi wille,
I ask þe now socoure, my ȝernyng to fulfille." .....myn help..
Richard at godes bord his messe had & his rightes.
Here now swilk a word he spak to his knyghtes:
"Of þis Kyng Philip haf we no maner of help;
togidir I rede we kip þat men of vs ȝelp. ....skippe....may ȝelp
I vowe to Saynt Michael & tille halwes þat are, ...to alle halwes..
þat for wo ne wele hiþen ne salle I fare,
ne tille Acres go tille þe castelle be taken,
þat Philip went fro, for vs has it forsaken.
Suþþe Kyng Philip went hit fro & for....
For his awen defaut, with vs he has envie.
Go we to þe assaut þat god vs alle condie." ....gye
Þe dikes were fulle wide þat closed þe castelle about
& depe on ilk a side with bankis hie without,
was þer non entre þat to þe castelle gan ligge
bot a streite kauce, at þe end a drauht brigge

with grete duble cheynes drauhen ouer þe gate, ...was drawen...
& fyfti armed sueynes, porters at þat ȝate. ....were porters þer ate
With slenges & magneles þei kast to Kyng Richard, ...oþer gyles.....
our cristen, bi parcelles, kasted ageynward; ..oþer whiles casten to þem.
ten sergeanȝ of þe best, his targe gan him bere,
þat egre wer & prest to couere him and to were.
[150ʳ] Himself as a geant þe cheynes in tuo hew;
þe targe was his warant þat non tille him threw.
Right vnto þe ȝate with þe targe þei ȝede
fightand on a gate, vndir him þe slouh his stede.
Þer for ne wild he sesse, alone in to þe castele,
.....sece on fote he fawȝt riȝt wel
þorgh þam alle wild presse, on fote fauht he fulle wele,
& þurw þam gan he prece alone in to þe castel
& whan he was withinne & fauht as a wilde leon,
he sondred þe saraȝins otuynne & fauht as a dragon.
....atwynne & fly forþ als..
Withoute, þe cristen gan crie, "Allas, Richard is taken!"
Þo Normans were sorie, of contenance gan blaken;
to slo doun & to stroye neuer wild þei stint,
þei left for dede no noye ne for no wounde no dynt;
þat in went alle þer pres, maugre þe saraȝins alle,
& fond Richard on des fightand & wonne þe halle. ...at þe deys fiȝttyng....
No body bot he alone vnto þe cristen cam .....vntil oure cristen.
& slayn he had ilkone þe lordes, bot þre he nam.
With þo þre o lyue his messengers went; ...þat were on lyff..forþ.
tille Acres gan þei dryue, to Philip mad present.
Now is grete honour comen to Inglis men
þorgh Richard þe conquerour, his douhtynes we ken. .....dyntes wel þey.
Kyng Philip of ffrance fulle gretely is he noyed
þat Richard had suilk chance, þe castelle had destroyed.
Þorgh spie þe soudan wist þat Philip was no payed; ....noȝt.
no gamen him ne list bot held him alle dismayed.
To Philip a letter he sent, þe Soudan Saladyn,
anoþer to Richard went, þat brouht a saraȝyn;
þus þan gan he seye, als it wer for þer prowe,
"Vnto þe kynges tueye þe soudan gretes ȝow
& sais, for seuen ȝere god þan were þe trewe; .....so ȝe wol be truwe
if ȝour god be so clere & of so grete vertewe
as ȝe preche oft tide, for sothe ȝe schew & seie, ...soþ ȝe precheȝ..
we saraȝins on our side be þat tyme salle purueie
þat þis lond salle be ȝours, & we bicome cristen
withouten mo stours or blode spillyng of men,

& haf alle þat ȝe wan withouten gansaying." ....gayn saynge
Þerto ansuer gan Philip þe kyng ..gaf Philipe þe Fransche.
& said, "Þer men bedis skille, skille men ouh to take;
þo þat wille not þat tille, skille salle þam forsake." ....þer til skil...
"Allas," said Richard, "þat euer it suld be couth
or spoken efterward, said of cristen mouth,
for a saraȝins sawe contreued of fals quayntise,
a cristen man suld him withdrawe fro Ihesu criste seruise.
a man....& leffe cristes.
[150v] Alle ere we hider comen, Ihesu criste to serue;
þe way for him we nomen, for him to lyue & sterue.
His childre ere we alle, of god our fader biforn; ....boren
þis lond suld to vs falle þer our fader was born.
..schal vs falle þat oure fader has forloren
Ihesu was born here & alle our first lynage;
we ere his childre dere, we clayme þis our heritage
þat þise paen hondes our ancestre haf reft,
& þorgh hard woundes, of þam salle reyme it eft. ......wol ref hit.
Bot if þei wille with pes þis lond ȝeld vs alle quite,
þei salle þan haf reles, of fayth gode respite;
if þei at no certeyn wille ȝeld it vs with pes,
we salle wynne it ageyn þat þei bifor vs les.
Þat dos not his deuere with dede no with rede, He þat doþ noȝt.......
hastely þis ȝere falle him þe ferynges dede."
on hym mot falle þis ȝer þe fyuerouse deþ
Philip vnderstode Richard wild not consent
þat ilk couant forth ȝode þat þe soudan sent.
..couenant for ȝede þat þe Souden by letre.
Philip held him stille & bigan to smyle
(men sais þat comes of ille & þinkyng som gile); ......& is tokne of.
noþeles, day & oþer he purueied priuely,
of mast, saile, & roþer he dight his schip redy.
Oft he sent for leue vnto Kyng Richard,
sekenes gan him so greue þat he mot wende homward.
He was in poynt to ȝelde þe gaste & sone to die; [*Transp. L*]
for euel he ne myght him welde, in bed behoued him lie. [*Transp. L*]
Sen oþer wais ne myght vaile, þan said Richard for wo,
"Philip now wille me faile & alle gate wend me fro.
Conant holdes he non þat he to Ihesu hight,
with body & soule alon to venge him at his myght;
sen Ihesu he wille not venge, ne hold his vowe no þing,
he salle him chalenge þe day of his endyng;
if he wille go or duelle, as he wille, I wille wele.

Þe despite þat is to telle, to god is don ilk dele."
Fulle oft biforhand bituex þam was distance
for wynnyng of þe land þat Richard wan þorgh chance. ...diuerse lond.....
Haluendele asked Philip as for first conant
& for felawschip of Cipres conquerand;
of þat Philip of France, for he suld haf grantise,
mad Richard a quiteclamance fro him & alle hise, ..a couenant fro....
& neuer þorgh no destresse suld clayme þer of no right;
Þat neuer....chalenge þer of riȝt
Philip with grete mekenesse his trouth þerto plight,
Gascoyn & Normundie suld ȝeme at his powere ....ȝyven...
withouten vilanie tille his comyng were nere.
[151r] Philip tok his leue withouten more essoyne;
his suld alle to cheue tille Sir Hugh of Burgoyne, .host schulde cleue.....
alle þe Frankis oste Sir Hugh had in kepyng.
Now sailes fro þat coste, home wendes Philip þe kyng
..forþ þe cost hamward...
in þe se sailand, he lendes toward Lumbardie;
þe erle of Ostrice wendes with him companie.
.Eriles host Austre wendiþ in his.
Richard stille he leues, þe lond he wild more se,
& Saladyn he reues þe flom of Cisare.
At þat ilk flom Richard gaf bataile;
greuance had he som, here now of his trauaile.
In Antioche, in Acres, in alle þo ilk cuntres
he set wardeyns wacres to kepe alle þe entres, ...wakres...þo.
siþen toward Cayfas displaied his banere,
& euer his nauie was in þe se biside not fere. ....by sides hym noȝt fer
Richard his his spie on Soudan Saladyn; .had his....
som said he suld lie at þe toun of Ioppyn. ....Iospyn
To Ioppyn whan he cam, þe soudan was not þere;
þe flom þe soudan nam, Richard forto affere.
Saladyn priuely was bussed beside þe flom
& spied strete & stie what Richard suld com; ..aboute streytely what tyme...
þat he suld not pas ne mo man of his oste, ...ne no....
þe water stopped was þer passage suld be moste.
Saladyn did stoppe þe dikes kank & bro .....bank & broo
þat non suld ouer hoppe, ne man ne hors suld go;
þorgh þat enbussement þat was so priuely, .buschement y leid þat...
Richard suld be schent if þat way he com by.
Richard fast him drouh toward Cisare
to witte where or how þe best passage mot be.
Whan Richard þider cam, he sauh þer was tregette,

passage non he nam, þe forthes wer withsette. Passing....fordes were forset
Richard beheld aboute, of gile he dred him neid;
of saraȝins a grete route þe lond was vmbeleid,
& alle þat suerd mot bere or oþer wapen weld, ...wilde
were sette Richard to dere, enbussed þorgh þe feld. ......on eche a side
He said, "Ihesu, mercy, & þi moder dere,
wherefore we com & why, now we fynd þam here." ffor whom.........
Whan he sauh he ne myght passe on non wise,
in þre parties to fight, his oste he did deuise.
Sir Iames of Auenu, he had þe first eschele,
was non of his vertu in armes did so wele.
Gentille of norture & noble of lynage,
was non þat bare armure þat did suilk vassalage; ....suche vyage
[151v] of werre & of bataile he was fulle auise,
þer wisdom suld auaile was non so trewe als he,
pere had he non in þe lond þer he was born.
He praied þe kyng on one he mot be first biforn,
& he gaf him þe vamward þe saraȝins oste to cleue,
& he at Kyng Richard foreuer þan toke his leue.
Þe kyng withoute essoyn suld be in þe midde,
& þe erle of Burgoyn he suld haf þe þridde.
With were þe templers & þer fraternite, With hym were.....
fals in alle maners, so tellis þe stori me.
On þe toþer side, þe of of þe saraȝin, ...þe host of..
in þe vamward suld ride þe Soudan Saladyn,
paien most worþi of alle þe lond of his kyn, ...& most of..
so told me þe stori þat I fond writen in.
In þe secund turbe was Maister Coradyn, ...warde was sir..
lord of Damas, his fader was Safadyn,
soudan so curteys, neuer drank no wyne,
þe same þe romans sais þat is of Richardyn, ...romance seis was..
& ouer þe þrid pas was maister, Sir Melchyn,
lord of Bandas, & Sir Matifasyn, .was of Blandas...
lord of Galile & þe stede þat chayn þe lord...of þe stede of Caym
& sire of þat cuntre þer Abel was slayn.
Iames of Auenue, he was verray pilgryn, ...truwe pilgrym
he gan first remue þe croice mad on his bryn. ..hym furst......brym
On þer first eschel he smote in fulle hastif
& þorgh þam ilka del als grehound or mastif,
tuys withouten encumbre, with suerd in his hand
he slouh withouten numbre, bifor him mot non stand.
Biside com a saraȝins bituex him & a bank,
Sir Kalaphes Duryns, he smote of Iames schank.

Þan spak Iames þo, a kosyn, "Help, Richard!
...þo nov help me Cosyn Richard
Fulle fer ert þou me fro, kast þe now to meward. ......haste....
Þi sister sonne am I, þou eam & I cosyn, ...þou myn Em & y þy.
þi fader, Kyng Henry, in þe castelle Constantyn,
my moder þan gate he opon Dame Auelyn,
Countas of Marche was sche, & or I ȝit do my fyn,
my dede salle I venge on Kalaphes Duryn."
With a gode suerd of Lorenge he smote þorgh þe saraȝin,
Iames lese þer his hand & died in þat pyn;
on þe morn men him fand & þe frere Baudwyn,
a frere of þe hospitalle, þe erles sonne Paulyn,
was lord of Morian alle & of Mount Modyn. ...Moravalle &...
[152r] Whan Richard herd say þat Iames was slayn,
he wend for dole to dey, he com as a wode man
& Saladyn sauh him cam, þer of fulle wele he lete;
ageyn Richard he nam, togider gan þei mete,
a kyng & a soudan of alle þe world þe beste.
Richard tille him ran, a stroke on him he fest;
he smote him in þe helm, bakward he bare his stroupe,
þe body he did ouerwhelm, his hede touched þe croupe.
....ouer heluyn þe hed...
He felle doun with þe dynt, bot son he ros vp light, ...a ros vp ful riȝt
herneys nouht ne tynt bot eft on hors fulle wight.
.noȝt he ne tynt but liȝt on his hors..
Richard at þat turne þe flom he wan fulle wele,
for saraȝin ne wild he skurne þat were of his eschele.
.no Sarsyn wolde skorn......
Fourti þousand paien, what drenkled & what slayn,
& a þousand cristen, so was þe tale certeyn;
for soth þe þrid eschele fulle hard was bisted,
þe templers ilk a dele failed & þien fled.
Þe erle bakward was born, & alle þe Frankis men
fulle nere had þei bien lorn, bot þei cried, "Help, cristen!"
Þe erle bigan to crie, "Turne & help vs, Richard,
or els salle we die þat ere in þis rereward!" ......beþ.þis warde
"Sir," said Kyng Guyon, "turne ageyn, I rede,
Frankis & Burgoillon els alle gos to dede!
Þe Soudan Saladyn has þam nere conquered,
þe templers, magre myn, fals þei er & ferd.
If þei had standen nere, þe myght haf wonnen pris;
non dos þer deuere bot Raynald þe Marchis."
Said þe Kyng Richard, "If þe duke be taken,

it salle be þam hard bot þei haf him forsaken."
Þe flom sone he left, ageyn toke his gate;
þe duke from þam he reft, welnere he com to late.
Þe duke at þat bataile lost sex & þritty knyghtes,
þre hundreth of pedaile, a hundreth sergeanȝ at rightes;
þe duke alle þese les, & þo þat were olyue,
Richard for alle þe pres, sauely did þam vp ryue.
At þat tyme Richard þere many a man slouh he,
þe kynge sonne of Dare, he smote in tuo his the.
Þe Soudan Saladyn he was fulle vnfayn;
he fled with mykelle pyn vnto þe mountayn.
Richard has þe pris at þe flom of Cisare,
þe saraȝin force doun lis, Ihesu we þank þe.
Þise saraȝins were so fesid þat fled was Saladyn,
& Cisare has he sesid, Iapht & Ioppyn, ...sesed & Iaphet..
[152v] Cades & Ascalon, alle has Kyng Richard,
vnder him Kyng Guyon had þam alle in ward.
Þe duke was in a cas, his wondes wer so grym
þat his leche was in ille hope of him,
& Richard was fulle dred þe leche mot him not saue;
tille Acres þei him led, better hele to haue.
In þer way, ilk dele þei fond voide als hethe,
þe toun of Mount Carmele, þe toun of Naȝareth,
þe strong castelle Pilryn þat first wonne was. ...Pilgrym....
Alle tok Ricardyn, Caloyn & Kayfas,
ilkon þise þei seised, tome alle þei fond; .þus þey seide toom...
seke were þer heised, heled þam of wound.
Syk men were þey raised & heled were..
Þe soudan to Richard sent to speke togider in glath,
for þe pes it ment & of no maner wrath,
ne no þing suld it greue vnto þe cristiente.
Þe barons said, "Bi leue, welcom mot he be."
Saladyn come þider þat day þat he sette,
þe barons wer togider, þe kyng & þam he grette.
"Sir," said Saladyn, "þi god has grete powere.
Er alle þise cristen þin þat þou kepes here?"
"Þise Inglis," said Richard, "in my kepyng þei are;
þe Frankis haf oþer ward, with þe erle of Burgoyn þei fare."
"Bot þei be of þi faith, els do þei wrong;
þei stand alle to gode graith whan þou ert þam among,
.standeþ al to godis griþ.....
& þou ert comen fro ferne & riche kyng is of fe.
....of fer a Riche Kyng art þou..

If þou pes wille ȝerne for þe & þi meyne,
& trewe for seuen ȝere, I consent þertille,
if þou has þat manere to do euenhede & skille."
"Certes, Saladyn," said þe Kyng Richere,
"to mak partie ageyn myn, ȝit ha þou gode powere, ...ȝut hauest þou..
& for þe pes to seke has þou no mystere.
Þertille to mak me meke, my herte is ȝit in wehere;
þou has power inouh, wherto askes þou pes,
& my wille wille not bouh to grante þat þou ches.
If þou þe lond wille ȝeld, þerof is to speke,
& siþen if þou wild þi lay forsake & breke
& take our bapteme of funte as childre ȝing,
I salle gyue þe a reame & do þe coroun kyng."
"Sir," said Saladyn, "þank I auh ȝow conne ....y þe came
þat þou me profers of þin & has non enchesonne;
if I myght þe paemie iustise þam ilkone
& non had seignorie bot I myself alone,
[153r] þan I trow my þouht myght acord to þin. Þat y þurw my.....
Bot now dar I nouht; my broþer Safadyn
is riche of tenement, his sonnes strong & stith, .richer..& so..stiff
þer wille wille not be went, ne lete þer lond ne lith. .wil wol...ne leve....
Wild þe bicom cristen, fulle eth I were to drawe,
bot I dar not for þam alle one to leue our lawe."
Richard said, "Par fay, go now & conseile þe,
& bi þe þrid day þat salle haf certeynte.
Bi þan I salle þe say how þat it salle go,
of pes to haf þe way, or werre, on of þe tuo."
Listen now a gile of Sir Safadyn, ..of a gile...
contreued a wikked wile on his broþer Saladyn.
Now wendes Saladyn þer his oste gan lie;
his broþer Safadyn his comyng did spie.
He sent to Kyng Richard a stede for curteisie,
on of þe best reward þat was in paemie,
bad him bi þat ȝere token ware him for tricherie, And bad..þat tokne..of.
said Saladyn was fulle foken, on him may non affie. ....fikul.....
"He sais behind þi bak, in strange companie,
wordes þat er to lak, he dar þe wele diffie;
if he & þou alone myght ȝow togider alie,
he myght withouten mone of þe wynne þe maistrie;
& Sir, if þou be suilk als men of þe crie,
rebuke him for þat ilk of þat auauntrie.
If I may þe auaile of hors or armurie,

for soth I salle not faile to mende þi partie."
Bot or þat day felle to stand þat þer acorde suld be,
....scholde stonde þat...lye
had Richard herd tiþand out Normundie. ....out of.
Þe folk out of France to Normundie were comen;
to Richard desceyuance his londes haf þei nomen.
Bot he com right son Normundie to fende,
his right bes nouht doun soner þan any wend.
..wol be for don ȝe sonner þat..
Wherfore to som of his he schewed þam þe skille,
to treus on alle wise him burd grant þertille. ......by howed..
Under þe mount Thabor in a faire medue;
boþe þe parties wer þore to conseile for þe treue.
"Sir," said Saladyn, "is it þi wille to say
þis day is myn & þin, chese þou now what way."
For Safadyns sawe Richard had enuie,
wherfore a gode þrawe he stode in a studie;
þat sawe þat he þer said, so wele it was of leten,
in boke it was vplaid, ȝit is it not forgeten.
[153v] Richard þis ansuerd to Saladyn for treu,
for þo men þat it herd wrote vs þat word alle new.
"Treus þou askes a þrowe for tuo ȝere or þre;
þo men þat þe knowe say þou skornes me. ...þou knowes....
Þe folk of paiemie þe word þer of fer gos, Of þe peple of.......
of alle þat seignorie þorghout, þin is þe los,
in armes is þer none þat to þi renoun reches.
Wherfor þou has gone & of þi pruesse preches ....& þy bost aboute.
þat if þou me mot mete bi our seluen tuo,
my lif I suld forlete or my hede for go;
& if þou wille it proue þat þou ert so worþi,
a stede tille our behoue, here is on alle redi.
Now for þi grete valow, I ask þe a bone
þat or we grante trew, fight we als so sone
þat on non oþer side body so bolde to be,
on fote ne hors ride to socour me no þe;
& whilk of vs is doun & mad is recreant,
cleyme & accioun he lese & þe remanant .by riȝt accion he lese al þat.
of þat ilk land þat cristen euer auht
þat þei held in þer hand of god þat þam it tauht."
Þan said Saladyn, "If þou fynd any man,
cristen or saraȝin, þat what tyme or whan ....hurde what...
I mad auancement with þe alone to fight, ..eny avantement.....
bot I to bataile went for my reames right,

here I salle þe gyue alle myn heritage,
& als long as I lyue to be in þin ostage." ......to ben þyn.
Þe Maister of þe Temple com procurand þe pes,
"No more of þis to demple, tak þat þat ȝe first ches."
...þis Comple takeþ þat ȝe..
Saladyn for alle hise hette to hold conaunt ..al þis he hiȝt...
seuen ȝere at his deuise, & Richard þerto graunt
þat ilk a cristen man suld hold & haue certeyn [*Transp. L*]
alle þat he þer wan & no þing ȝeld ageyn. [*Transp. L*]
Now is it in forward alle pesed & wele ent; .....al paised & al valent
now turne Kyng Richard, tille Acres is he went.
After Kyng Guyon & for his sonne he sent,
of Antioche, Reymon, him also he ment; ..Region....
Aunfrey of Turoyn, he was þer present;
of Triple, Erle Bumoun fulle suiþe þider glent;
Sir Ruffyn broþer, Leoun, alle þise held parlement.
Kyng Richard his resoun said þam how he was schent;
Philip did him tresoun, destroied his tenement,
"For to stanch his foysoun, homward haf I ment. [*Om. L*]
[154r] Normundie alle doun, mykelle þer of is brent
& slayn blak & broun of alle þat he mot hent. ....may be.
I wille of þat feloun take vengement
þat so fordos my coroun if grace be to me lent.
Wherfor, ȝe lordynges, ȝe ere me lefe & dere,
I take in ȝour kepynges þe londes þat we wonne here;
þe freres of þe hospital & þe temple also, ...& of þe templers.
biseke þam I salle þat þei help ȝow þerto.
Now haf I don & said & tauht ȝow þat I may,
my hope is on ȝow laid, lordynges haf gode day."
The prince of Antioche, & þe Kyng Guyon,
Bumunde, erle of Triple, & Aunfrey of Turoun,
þise had in þer ward cite, kastelle, & toun
þat þe Kyng Richard wan of saraȝin feloun;
& Isaac þe emperour takes his liuerisoun,
with freres mad soioure in temple dominoun.
.þe freres mad sorwe in þe temple dongeon
His douhter with þe quene was for hir warisoun,
& so felle it to bene, hir fader lese þe coroun;
& as Richard home went toward þis regioun,
or he were taken or hent or holden in prisoun,
he gaf his sistere þat while vnto þe Erle Reymoun,
lord of Saynt Gile, a man of grete renoun.
I fond in my boke what skille ne for whi .fond noȝt in.......

þat he his folk forsoke & ȝede so priueli
Aufrice to aspie, him were better haf left; Austrice.......
þer in þorgh felonie was he robbed & reft,
taken with enmys & holden in prisoun.
I kan not say þe pris was gyuen for his raunsoun;
in prison was he bonden, as þe romance sais,
in cheynes & lede wonden þat heuy was of peis.
Anoþer pyne he had, if it may be trod,
with iren nayles sad, it sais his fete was schod.
Þerfor þe pape of Rome cursed þam wroþerheile, ...with ille heil
alle þat did þat dome or þerto gaf conseile.
His moder, Dame Alienore, & þe barons of þis land
for him trauailed sore & brouht him out of band.
Whan he of bond was brouht for raunson þat was riche,
his moder so bisouht, he aryued at Sandwiche;
to Canterbire fulle euen he souht to haf his bote,
miles he ȝede seuen to Saynt Thomas on fote.
With fulle riche offeryng he wirschipped Saynt Thomas;
his praier did him bryng out of his hard cas,
[154v] þanked god & him, so wele for him had schaped
þat of his anguys grim so lightly was escaped.
To while þat Richard was biȝond þe se in hold,
Ion did him trespas, his rentes tok & sold,
Iohan his broþer dide trespas his rentes...
his castels sesed & brak, bigan a grete distance,
& neuer no word spak of Richard deliuerance,
bot als a kyng of lond, Ion bare him fulle stoute;
þerfor Richard wele fond with dome to chace him oute
..wil stonde with..bere..
& deme him als anoþer for his vnkynd folie.
To Kyng Richard, his broþer, Ion mercy gan crie;
þer moder þam bisouht for to be at one,
of trespas þat he had wrouht, Richard forgaf it Ion
& said, "Þi misdede be in þi mynsyng ....be euer in þy myndyng
euer more to drede eft to do suilk þing;
& I wille neuer more on þi trespas þenk
if þou repent þe sore þat þou did suilk a blenk."
Richard to London wendes to hold parlement,
for his barons sendes & þei alle to him went.
At Westminster ilkone parlement þei held; .Wynchestre....
to þam he mad his mone & þus to þam teld:
"Lordynges, of my chance wele ȝe auh to wite,
& þat þe kyng of ffrance wille me disherite;

for þat I was bistad biȝond þe se in hold,
þerfor Philip is glad & beres him fulle bold;
my castels he takes & seises my citeȝ,
destruccion he makes of rentes & feeȝ.
Wherfore, barons dere, sais me a gode certeyn, . . . seieþ to . . . .
& how & what manere my lond to gete ageyn."
Þan spak þe Erle Rogere as a man fulle wys,
"Erles with þar powere, barons þat er of pris,
knyghtes gode & wight, sergeanȝ alle in ferd, ... hurde
þise salle alle be dight & help þe with þer suerd.
Bisshopes & parsons, burgeis of citeȝ,
& riche merchandes eftsons salle help with þer mone. . . . . þere mene
Abbay & priorie & oþer religions
for vs salle pray & crie in þer affliccions.
Better is holy bede of man þat right lyues,
& standes vs in more stede þan alle þe gode he gyues."
. til vs more . . . þo þat vs .
Þe comen wele was paied of þat conseilyng
þat it were not delaied, so was Richard þe kyng.
Now wille Kyng Richard alle his lond extende,
merschalle & stiward þerfor about dos sende,
[155r] & homage & feaute he askes & releue; . . . . . axed nywe & releff
þe barons er fulle fre to do as to þer chefe.
Now has þe kyng wele sped & comen ageyn to London,
& penies with him led & spendyng has he fondon.
His purueance with hym led his . . . .
His barons alle aboute fast tille him drowe
with hors & armes stoute, þer com tille him inowe.
Richard wendes to schip, he wille no lenger duelle;
þe boste of Kyng Philip fayn þan wild he felle.
Ariued is Richard at Depe in Normundie.
[*L ends here, the last line on fol. 131v.*]
He lay þer half a ȝere estres to aspie,
& whan he sauh he might on his folk affie,
his werre ordeynd & dight to þo þat couþe þam guye,
to Gascoyne þat he were, fulle smertly he gan hie.
Cursels, a castelle, þere he wan with maistrie;
þe sergeanȝ þat it held wer in poynt to die,
to prison þei þam ȝeld, bot mercy gan þei crie;
ȝit he tok a pray þorgh quayntise & spie,
Burreȝ he wan þat day, boþe hous & seignorie;
at þe Dangu þat nyght he tok his herbegerie.
To Cursels Philip had tight with alle his companie,

he ne wist it ʒolden was tille he com so nehi.
Whan he wist, he fled þat pas, to Gisors tok þe stie.
Richard perceyued þis, þat Philip to Gisors fled,
he comanded his Inglis þat after fast þei sped;
þei com Philip so nere þat he cried, "Tak þe kyng!"
Bot non so hardi were to smyte him for no þing.
Me þouht Kyng Philip inouh was disconfite
whan he & alle his trip for nouht fled so tite.
Pauillon & tent Philip bihynd him left;
to Richard was it sent, [n]o þing þerof reft, [*An erased letter*.]
for mykelle lete þei ligge, þerof mad þei no force;
Philip vnto þe brigge þei chaced him of Gisors.
On þe brigge were alle þe vamward & þe rere,
vnder þam þe brigge gan falle doun in to þe riuere.
Philip & his meyne in þe water lay;
schame him was to fle & so him com þat day.
A knyght, a bourdour, Kyng Richard hade,
a douhty man in stoure, his name was Markade.
He sauh Kyng Philip als he lay in þe water,
"Sir Kyng, rise vp & skip, for þou has wette þi hater;
þou fisshes not worþe a leke, rise & go þi ways,
for þou has wette þi breke, schent is þi hernays."
[155v] Þe brigge was brode & long, boþe of tre & stones;
whan so mykelle þrong was þer on at ones,
sex hundreth mot men se, so fele fallen þer were,
of whilk þritty & þre did þer endyng þere.
Richard comanded alle gate þat Philip suld men saue,
for no þing suld þei late bot help þat lif mot haue.
Of Mount Morice, Mathi, a baron renome,
Sir Alayn of Russie, Sir ffouke de Geffre,
þise grete were alle taken & þer knyghtes þam bi.
Makade held þam waken & tok of þam tuenti;
þe prisons he had in ward, for he was gode & trewe.
Now turnes Kyng Richard to se his lond, Aniowe.
Sen þis ilk tyme bifore or afterward,
I know no more to ryme of dedes of Kyng Richard.
Who so wille his dedes alle þe soth se,
þe romance þat men redes, þer is þe propirte;
þis þat I haf said, it is Pers sawe,
als he in romance laid, þerafter gan I drawe.
The ferth day formest next Palme Sonenday,
þe tyme, as I gest, Richard ʒede to play.
Þorgh a cuntre, men calle it Lymosin,

þe castelle manaced he þat Philip had þer in.
Richard com ouer nere þe castelle to aspie;
þat sauh an alblastere, a quarelle lete he flie
& smote him in þe schank; for þat stroke, allas,
it bigan to rank, þe querelle envenomed was.
Siþen on þe nyent day died Kyng Richard;
he ligges at an abbay men calle Founȝ Ebrard.
He regned nien ȝere & sex monethes mo,
maugre þe alblastere þat þus Richard gan slo.
I wene it hate Chahalouns, or it hate Galiard,
ouþer þe castelle or þe toun þer smyten was Richard.
A thousand & a hundred þe date, nienti & nien,
þat Richard fro vs sundred, dede he was with pine.
Now is Kyng Richard dede & laid in stone;
non heire was afterward bot his broþer Ion.
His broþer, Erle Geffrey, right heire felle to be,
bot after Richard day, Ion tok þe dignite, *[Lines 5044–5045 are*
or Arthure his sonne if he had had his lif. *probably transp.]*
Bot Ion was þe enchesonne & moued þer a strif.
Tiþing here we say þat Ion wille wedded be;
þe erle of Aquiley, his douhter takes he,
[156r] Eliȝabeth þe gent, fair lady was sche,
tuo sons of þer descent, tuo douhtres, ladies fre.
The Ersbisshop Hubert, of Canterbire þe se,
com with gode hert to do þe solempnite
at Westmynster, þorgh assent of erle & baroun,
(to þat I ore ment, Hubert gaf þe coroun)
& enoynted he was als kyng þorgh resoun.
Ion did ay trespas, men fond in him enchesoun;
he lyued in wo & strife & in tribulaccoun.
He was of licherous life, þorgh what his nacioun
partie ageyn him ches & wild haf born him doun.
Normundie he les at his confusioun;
in þe court of ffrance he was cald a feloun
for Arthure dede, þat chance, his broþer sonne Geffroun,
erle was of Bretayn þat to þis lond had right
for to haf bien cheftayn, if Ion his dede had dight.
(My maister nouht he wrote, to write he me forbede;
noþeles, wele I wote, siþen þe child was dede.)
Ion had right þertille, þe lond to haf in ward,
þat Arthur suld bi skille haf bien heyr next Richard.
Arthure sister ȝing, for dole þat maiden suete,
for sorow scho mad endyng, hir name was Margarete.

Now þe bode is gon to ffrance, Arthure is dede,
& somond haf þei Ion, to Philip courte him bede
to tak his iugement of þat felonse,
his dede to him þei ment, Arthurs þe Bretaynie.
Ion dred þat wendyng, to ffrance wild he nouht;
wherfor Philip þe kyng on londes souht,
Tolouse & Tolousan seised, & Normundie,
þorgh slauhter of þat man, Ion les þat seignorie.
What dos þe Kyng of ffrance? Atires him gode nauie,
tille Inglond o chance to wynne it with maistrie.
He wend haf wonne þis lond as he did Tolousan;
þe cuntre sone he fond in his berd redy ran,
þe Walsch & oþer inow with þam of Peuenese,
þe Frankis men þei slow, Philip was fayn to fle.
Now is Philip fled, here wan he bot lite,
& Ion northward him sped, his lond for to visite;
vnto Scotlond he sent after Kyng William.
To Lincoln William went & Ion ageyn him cam
withoute þe toun a myle & in þe wyntertide;
þe day of Saynt Cecile þer parties gan abide.
[156v] Homage he did him suere & feaute in fere
þat faith he suld him bere at alle his powere.
Boke þer was non fette, ne non þer after fore,
Hubert his croice doun sette & William þeron suore.
(Þis is þe same Hubert þat þe saw of nam
þat translate Saynt Gilbert in þe hous of Sempyngham.)
Now Hubert is dede, our sire, & to god is gon;
þe prioure of Canterbire sendes to Kyng Ion,
bisouht him of leue to mak eleccoun,
to chese þe suld cheue a man of gode ronoun.
Ion wrote to þe couent, bisouht þam alle holyche
þat þei wille mak present to þe bisshop of Norwyche;
of som he had grantise his wille forto do,
& som said oþerwise þat it suld not be so.
Alle þe priour side, þe suppriour þei ches,
oþer for enuie & pride, þe voice of many he les.
Þe priour said, "Þis day þe suppriour chese we."
Þe toþer side said, "Nay, þe kynges praier salle be."
With him of Norwiche grete partie gan hald,
wherfor boþe holyche to Rome þe parties cald.
Monkes fourtene with him of Norwyche held,
in a voice alle bidene vnto þe kyng þe teld
& suore him in leaute how so euer bitid,

Norwyche he suld be ersbisshop sacrid.
Þise monkes stoute & stark to spede wele þei wend;
þe kyng þre hundreth mark gaf þam forto spend.
Now er þei alle on gate, vnto þe courte þei cam,
eleccion þorgh hate it falles to no fram.
To þe pape of Rome þei mostred þer resoun,
þe pape at his dome þer elites quassed doun;
eft he bad þam chese a man of gode renoun,
or þei suld þer voice lese of alle þer eleccioun.
Now is þer voice alle laid to Norwyche partie,
bifor þe pape þei said, "Norwyche is most worþie."
Þe pape wild not consent, he quassed þer elite;
þe monkes alle were schent, suspended þam als tite.
Þe pape þei felle biforn, mercy gan him crie,
vnto þe kyng þe suorn to maynten his partie.
Þe pape þam assoled & set þam vp at des;
so þei were conseiled, of Langton, Steuen, þei ches.
Þise monkes were dismaied for Steuen of Langton;
þe pape þerof was paied, mad þe confirmacion.
[157r] Maister Steuen of Langton ersebisshop salle be,
þe kyng casten doun, who was wroth bot he.
Whan þe kyng vnderstod þat his clerk was forsaken,
for soth þan was he wode & Maister Steuen taken;
þe clergie of þat schire so euelle he þam led,
þe monkes of Canterbire fro þer cloister þam fled
& gaf it to Brabans, þe cloister, in kepyng;
þorgh conseil of Sathans wrouht þer Ion þe kyng.
Þe pape sauh out of cours þe wikkednes of Ion,
him & his fautours he cursed euerilkon
& enterdited þis lond þat messe was non said;
a ded man, if men fond, in kirke ȝerd was non laid.
He was a fole of lif & vsed lichorie;
both mayden & wif alle wild he ligge bie.
What did þe baronage & burgeis of cite?
Distroied & did outrage of castelle, toun, & fe;
about þei gan him chace & hunted him als hayre,
long had he no space to duelle no wele fare.
Many men of his kynde sauh him so abaued;
for him þei fauht with mynde & oft so was he saued.
Als þis wo was lastand in cursyng perilouse,
Kyng William of Scotland did his douhter spouse
to þe erle of Boloyn, & whan Ion it wist,
withouten any essoyn, north alle gate him list;

son he wan Berwik, a castelle he þouht to reise,
he cast þe groundwalle þik, his folk he þouh þer eise.
William he þouht to greue for þat grete despite
þat he withouten leue his douhter gaf marite.
Edenburgh & Rokesburgh vp þat he asked quite,
& his sonne Alisandere for ostage ȝeld him tite.
Bot þe Kyng William alle þis ageynsaid;
in conaunt þat þei nam, with pes alle was it laid.
Of William has Ion þe pris; toward þe south he drouh
& rennes on his enmys & dos þam schame inouh,
& his enmys on him, & destroyed alle his feȝ;
ilkone tille oþer were grim þorgh tounes & citeȝ,
so þat Holy Kirke, & alle þe ordineȝ,
& bisshop wo he wike, & clerkes of digniteȝ,
þei reue þam prouendes þorgh power þat þei haue,
& no man þam defendes no wille þam help no saue.
Oft was þe pleynt mad vnto þe pape,
þe maufesours ateynt & cursed ouer þe nape;
[157v] þe pape of þer erroure had fulle grete pite,
he sent to þer socoure tuo legates ouer þe se.
At Douere þei gan ariue, Pandolf & Durand,
to London gan þei driue, þe barons þer þei fand;
þorgh Pandolf prechyng þer werre was brouht tille ende.
Þe barons & þe kyng were mad felauhes & frendes,
asoiled & alle on euen, bot þe kyng an oth suore
he suld him venge on Steuen whider so euer he fore,
& of þo fourtene monkes where men mot þam finde,
be beten alle fonkes or in prison þam binde.
Pandolf & Durand did com forth, þe ersbisshop
& þe monkes forth þei fand, Ion said þei suld hedeles hop.
Pandolf proued þe kyng, in his disputeson,
he mayntend wrongfulle þing & wild to no reson;
he proued þorh wisdam in ilk manere cas
þat þe kyng misnam & did grete trespas.
Alle gate þe kyng he pesed so þat þe werre was ent
& ilk a clerke sesed ageyn to haf his rent;
Pandolf tok his leue & to Rome went.
(I trow on him gan cleue many riche present.)
Now is Pandolf gone & Steuen ersbisshop es,
assoiles Kyng Ione of alle his wikkednes.
Ion has sonnes tuo bi Eliȝabeth þe quene,
& tuo douhters also, fairere were non sene.
Henry was eldest, heyre of alle his þing,

& Richard ȝongest, of Almayn chosen kyng;
Isabelle, fair as floure, þat neuer childe had,
ffrederik þe emperour, emperice home hir lad;
þe erle of Leycestre þe toþer weddid here,
& Ion regned in þis estre, kyng auhten ȝere.
At þe abbay of Suynesheued þer he drank poyson;
at Hauhe his lif he leued, so say men of þat toun.
A þousand & tuo hundred þe date was, & sextene,
his tyme was alle forwondred & endid alle with tene;
at Westmynstere euen es Ion laid solempnely.
Þe Ersebisshop Steuen corouned his sonne Henry,
a gode man alle his lyue, of pouer men had mercie;
clerkes þat wild þryue, auanced þam richelie,
kirkes wild he dele prouendis þat wer worþie,
to clerkes of his chapele þat wele couth syng & hie.
Henry Kyng, our prince, at Westmynster Kirke,
þe erlys douhter of Prouince, þe fairest may o lif,
[158r] hir name is Helianore, of gentille norture,
biȝond þe se þat wore was non suilk creature,
in Inglond is sche corouned, þat lady gent;
tuo sonnes, tuo douhteres fre, Ihesu has þam lent.
Edward & Edmunde, knyght gode in stoure,
of Laicestre a stounde was Edmunde erle & floure.
Vnto þe Scottis kyng was maried Margarete;
of Bretayn, Beatrice ȝing, þe erle had þat mayden suete.
ffaire is þe werk & hie in London at Westmynster Kirke
þat þe Kyng Henrie of his tresore did wirke;
grace god gaf him here þis lond to kepe long space,
sex & fifty ȝere withouten werre in grace.
Bot sone afterward failed him powere,
bot his sonne Edward was his conseilere;
our quene þat was þen, Dame Helianore his wife,
þe gode erle of Warenne, Sir Hugh, was þan olife.
Sir William of Valence, Sir Roger Mortimere,
Ion Mauncelle, þe clerke, & an erle, Richere,
& oþer knyghtes inowe of biȝond þe se
to þe kyng drowe, auanced wild þei be.
Edward suffred wele his fadere haf his wille;
þe barons neuer a dele said þe kyng did ille,
aliens to auaunce ouþer in lond or rent.
To mak disturbaunce, þei held a parlement;
of þe aliens ilk taile þe lond voided clere.
To þe kyng & his consaile þei sent a messengere;

þe kyng sent þam ageyn, his barons alle þei grette,
at Oxenford certeyn þe day of parlement sette.
At þis parlement rested þat distaunce,
for þer was it ent, aliens to auaunce.
Þe kynges state here paires þorgh conseil of baroun,
to him & his heyres grete disheriteson;
of wardes & relefe þat barons of him held,
þer he was ore of chefe, tille him no þing suld ȝeld;
& oþer þat held of þam þer þe kyng felle be partie,
nouht of þat suld claym of alle þat seignorie;
tille ilk a lordyng suld ward & relefe falle,
bot tille þe kyng no þing, he was forbarred alle.
Þe kyng perceyued nouht of þat ilk disceit;
þe chartre was forth brouht with wittnes enseled streit,
ne no men þat were strange in courte suld haf no myght,
ne office to do, no chance withouten þe comon sight.
[158v] Þis þei did him suere als he was kyng & knyght,
þat oth suld he were & maynten wele þat right.
The kyng was holden hard þorgh þat he had suorn,
his frendes afterward, þo þat wer next born,
þe com to him & said, "Sir, we se þin ille,
þi lordschip is doun laid & led at oþer wille.
We se þis ilk erroure, nouht þou vnderstode;
it is a dishonoure to þe & to þi blode.
Þou has so bonden þe, þei lede þe ilka dele;
at þer wille salle þou be, Sir, we se it wele.
Calle ageyn þin oth, drede þou no manace,
nouþer of lefe ne loth þi lordschip to purchace.
Þou may fulle lightly haf absolucioun,
for it was a gilery, þou knew not þer tresoun.
Þou has frendis inowe in Inglond & in ffrance;
if þou turne to þe rowe, þei salle drede þe chance."
Þe kyng listned þe sawe at þat consail wild do;
þe barons had grete awe whan þei wist he wild so.
Þei tok & sent þer sond after Sir Symoun;
þe Mountfort out of lond was whan þis was don.
A message þei him sent, þe Mounfort son home cam;
þe barons with on assent to Sir Symon þei nam.
Þei teld him þe processe of alle þer comon sawe,
& he, as fole alle fresse, fulle eth þerto to drawe.
Withouten his conseile or þe kynges wittyng,
to maynten þer tirpeile he suore ageyn þe kyng,
þe statute forto hold in werre & in pes,

þe poyntes þat þei him told, þerfor his life he les.
Hardely dar I say he did aperte folie,
als wys men þis way here first þe toþer partie.
Sir Symon was hastif, his sonnes & þe barons,
sone þei reised strif, brent þe kynges tounes
& his castels tok, held þam in þer bandoun;
on his londes þei schok & robbed vp & doun.
Þo þat þer purueiance of Oxenford not held,
with scheld & with lance fend him in þe feld.
In alle þis barette, þe kyng & Sir Symon
tille a lokyng þam sette, of þe prince suld it be don.
An oth suore þei þare to stand to þe ordinance,
ouer þe se to fare bifor Philip of ffrance;
at his dome suld it be withoute refusyng,
þerfor went ouer þe se Sir Henry our kyng.
[159r] Þe quene wild not duelle, to þe kyng gan hir hie;
þus my boke gan telle, scho tok grete vilanie
of þe Londreis alle whan scho of London went;
whi þat it suld falle, I ne wote what it ment.
Bot whan þe kyng of France had knowen certeynly
þat þe purueiance disherite Kyng Henry,
he quassed it ilk dele þorgh iugement;
þe kyng was paied wele & home to Inglond went.
Whan Sir Symon wist þe dome ageyn þam gon,
his felonie forth thrist, samned his men ilkon,
displaied his banere, lift vp his dragoun;
sone salle ȝe here þe folie of Symoun.
The erle did mak a chare at London þorgh gilery;
himself þer in suld fare & seke he wend to ly.
Sexti þousand of London, armed men fulle stoute,
to þe chare were fondon to kepe it wele for doute.
Þer þe bataile suld be, to Leaus þai gan þam alie,
þe kyng & his meyne were in þe priorie.
Symoun com to þe feld & put vp his banere;
þe kyng schewed forth his scheld, his dragon fulle austere.
Þe kyng said on hie, "Symon, ieo vous defie!"
Edward was hardie, þe Londres gan he ascrie;
he smote in alle þe route & sesid him þe chare,
disconfited alle aboute þe Londreis þat þer ware.
Edward wend wele haf fonden þe erle þer in,
disceyued ilka dele, he went & myght not wyn.
To whille Sir Edward was aboute þe chare to take,
þe kynges side, allas, Symoun did doun schake.

Vnto þe kynges partie Edward turned tite;
þan had þe erle þe maistrie, þe kyng was disconfite;
þe soth to say & chese, þe chares gilerie
did Sir Edward lese þat day þe maistrie.
Þe fourtend day of May, þe batail of Leaus was,
a þousand & tuo hundreth, sexti & foure in pas.
Þe kyng of Almayn was taken to prisoun;
of Scotlond, Ion Comyn was left in a donioun;
þe erle of Warenne, I wote, he scaped ouer þe se,
& Sir Hugh Bigote als with þe erle fled he.
Many faire ladie lese hir lord þat day,
& many gode bodie slayn at Leaus lay.
[159v] Þe numbre non wrote, for telle þam mot no man
bot he þat alle wote & alle þing ses & can.
Edward þat was ȝing, with his owen rede,
for his fader þe kyng, himself to prison bede;
for þe kyng of Almayn, his neuow was ostage.
In prison nere a ȝere was Edward in cage;
aboute with Sir Symoun, þe kyng went þat ȝere,
cite, castelle, & toun, alle was in þe erles dangere.
It was on a day Edward þouht a wile,
he said he wild asay þer hors alle in a mile.
He asayed þam bi & bi & recreied þam ilkone,
& stoned þam alle wery, standand stille as stone.
A suyft stede þer was a lady þider sent;
Edward knowe his pas, þe last of alle him hent,
asaied him vp & doun, suyftest he was of alle;
þat kept him in prisoun, Edward did him calle,
"Maister, haf gode day, soiorne wille no more.
I salle ȝit, if I may, my soiorne trauaile sore!"
Þe stede he had asaied & knew þat he was gode,
in to þe watere he straied & passed wele þat flode.
Whan Edward was ouere graciously & wele,
he hoped haf recouere at Wigemore castele.
Edward is wisely of prison scaped oute;
felaus he fond redy & mad his partie stoute.
Þe erles sonnes wer hauteyn, did many folie dede;
þat teld a knyght certeyn to þe erle als þei boþe ȝede.
The erle ȝede on a day to play him with a knyght
& asked him on his play, "What haf I be sight?"
Þe knyght ansuerd & said, "In ȝow a faute men fynde
& is an ille vpbraid þat ȝe ere nere blynde."
Þe erle said, "Nay, perde I may se right wele."

Þe knyght said, "Sir, nay, ȝe vnneþis any dele,
for þou has ille sonnes, foles & vnwise;
þer dedes þou not mones ne nouht wille þam chastise.
I rede þou gyue gode tent & chastise þam sone,
for þam ȝe may be schent, for vengeance is granted bone."
Þe erle ansuerd nouht, he lete þat word ouer go;
no þing þeron he þouht tille vengeance felle on þo.
Euer were his sonnes hauteyn & bold for þer partie,
boþe to knyght & sueyn did þei vilanie;
for lefe ne for loth, folie wild þei not spare,
wherfor wex with þam wroth Sir Gilbert of Clare.
[160r] Sir Gilbert herd say of þer dedes ille,
of non þe had ay to stynt ne hold þam stille;
þer of Edward herd say þat Gilberd turned his wille,
to Gilbert tok his way, his luf to tak & tille.
Sone þei were at one, with wille at on assent;
his luf fro Munfort gon, I telle Symon for schent.
Treuth togidere þei plight, Edward & Gilbert,
ageyn Symon to fight for ouht þat mot be herd.
Mercy suld non haue, Symon no his sonnes,
no raunson suld þam saue, for doute of drede eftsones
schent is ilk baroun, now Gilbert turnes grim;
þe Mountfort, Sir Symoun, most affied on him.
Allas, Sir Gilbert, þou turned þin oth!
At Stryuelyn men it herd how god þer for was wroth.
The erle sonnes vp & doun, of parties mad þei bost,
towhils at Northamptoun þise kynges gadred ost.
Symon sonnes it left, to Killyngworth þei went
& þer þe soiorned eft, þer rioterie þam schent;
suilk ribaudie þei led, þei gaf no tale of wham,
towhils Sir Edward had seisid alle Euesham.
Þe fift day it was after Lammesse tide,
& writen is in þat pas, at Euesham gan þei ride.
In the aldernext þat þe bataile was of Leaus,
þe gynnyng of heruest as þe story scheawes,
com Symond to feld & þat was maugre his;
or euer he lift his scheld, his wist it ȝed amys.
He was on his stede, displaied his banere;
he sauh þat treson ȝede, doun went his powere.
He sauh Sir Edward ride, batailed him ageyn,
Gloucestre þe toþer side, þan wist þe erle certeyn
his side suld doun falle; tille his he said sone,
"God haf our saules alle, our dayes ere alle done!"

Edward first in rode & perced alle þe pres,
þo þat him abode, þer lyues alle þei les.
He mad his fader quite of prison þer he lay,
deliuerd him als tite with dynt of suerd þat day.
Hard was þat bataile & ouer grete þe folie,
so scharply gan þai assaile, so mykille folk gan die;
stoutly was þat stoure, long lastand þat fight,
þe day lost his coloure & mirk was as þe nyght.
Þe lif of many man þat ilk day was lorn,
þat þat it first bigan, wrotherhaile wer þei born.
[160v] Now is þe bataile smyten, Sir Symon is þer slayn;
his sonnes, als ʒe witen, died on þat playn;
his membres of þei schare & bare þam to present.
Sir Hugh Despenser þare als he to dede went;
Sir Rauf, þe gode Basset, did þer his endyng;
Sir Pers of Mountfort fet his dede at þat samenyng;
Sir Guy Baliol died þore, a ʒong knyght & hardy,
he was pleyned more þan oþer tuenty;
þise & many mo died in þat stoure.
Þe kyng may sauely go & maynten his honour;
pris þan has þe sonne, þe fadere maistrie.
Þei went Northampton, so wild Kyng Henrie.
At þe parlement was flemed barons fele;
þe Countas of Leicestre, hir sonnes wild no man spele,
oþer lordes inowe of erles & barouns,
to þe wod som drowe & som left in prisouns.
To say longly or schorte, alle armes bare,
Almerik or Mountfort depriued was þare,
& þe tresorie þat he had in kepyng
& gaf þat ilk bailie tor þe Mortimere sonne ʒing.
A legate, Ottobon, þe pape hider sent
to mak þe barons on þorgh his prechement.
Þe quene com out of ffrance & with hir alle þo
þat for þer purueiance were exild to go,
saue Ion þe Maunselle, he died biʒond þe se;
als chance for him felle, þe toþer welcom be.
A thousand & tuo hundred, & sex & sexti,
þat þat er fled & sundred, þo rise ageyn Henri,
for after þe takyng of Kilyngwoth castelle,
þe flemed ageyn, þe kyng ros eft fulle rebelle;
for þe men þat were fled, disherited of þer londes,
to purches þam þei sped, now ilk of þam so fondes.
Robert of fferers he robbed boþe & slouh

bi nyght in stede sers & tille his felawes drouh;
of þam was þer non þat lufed Kyng Henry.
To Chestrefeld ilkon þe com vngraciously;
þe kyng did þam spie with gode men of renoun,
com on þam priuelie, assailed þam in þe toun.
Þe barons fauht ageyn, þei wist of no socoure;
many of þam wer slayn & som passed at honour,
þat was þe gode Deyuile, he did wele his deuere;
þat stoure he held a while & passed quite & clere.
[161r] In þe monyng eft bigan a new stoure.
Robert fferers þer left Baudewyn þe Vauasoure,
lord of Chestrefeld, þise myght not lightly fle;
þer side alle doun held, taken were þer meyne.
Robert of Wollerton (I trowe for som trespas),
he had grete renoun, on Kene hanged he was.
Þis douhty Deyuile, his name was Sir Ion,
of Axholm to þe ile he scapid himself alon;
for to robbe & reue, þer he held his haunt.
He wild spare ne leue burgeis no merchaunt,
& whan he dred him ouht for ouercomyng of mo,
toward þe south he souht als he were non of þo
bot as a passand man felawes forto seke,
so often away he wan & vmwhile cheke bi cheke;
þus did þe Deyuile more þan half a ȝere
& gadred him þat while inouh of powere.
Whan þei wer inowe on whilk þei mot afie,
to Lyncoln þei drowe & þer þei suld relie;
þe tuelft day of Aprile whan þer power was grete,
& went alle at o wile, in to Lyncoln þei schete.
Þorghout þe Iuery þei robbed þam & slouh,
þe cofres with tresory þe braken, & awey drouh
þe chartres & þe scris þat noied cristen men
þat lay for vsure in pris, elleuen als for ten,
were casten in fire & brent, in podels vilaynly
of Iues slayn & schent, a hundred & sexty.
Whan Sir Edward herd þat þei had Lyncoln taken
& þe Iuerie misferd, þer tresorie ouerschaken,
he sped him þider in haste with hilled hors of pris;
he com & fond alle waste, away were þo enmys.
Þei went to þe Ilde of Hely vnto Sir Hugh Pecche;
þei manned þam so boldely, on þam had non entre.
Edward lete not wele þat he with þam not mette;
to Kilyngworth Castele he went þe sege to sette.

Fro midsomeretide to þe Apostle Saynt Thomas,
þe fled mayntend þer side, þe castelle holden was
for alle þat þider went, Sir Edward & ilkon,
vntille þe pape sent his legate, Ottobon.
Whan þis legate was comen, of som he was bisouht;
in forward out þei nomen, els wild þei nouht.
Sir Henry of Hastyng he ȝald it bi his wille,
ouer alle maner þing life & lymmes haf stille,
[161v] & alle þer tresorie þat þerin was fonden,
withouten vilenie vnto þe pes bonden.
Þis legate, Ottobone, mad a cursyng hard
of þam euerilkone þat brak þat afterward,
& som of þer heyres so hard charged wore,
& ȝit many it peyres & som has satled sore.
Þan went þis Ottobone þorghout þe cuntre
& quaynted him with ilkone, lewed & ordine,
& many of þam wer mendid of folies þorgh his dome,
& he þe better spendid als he went to Rome.
Sir Edward vnto þe ilde he went, of Hely,
with many man fulle wilde, to bataile redy.
Edward alle aboute he spied in to ride;
within had þei no doute, defendid on ilk side,
so ageyn Edward þei held it half a ȝere;
þei sauh þe sege so hard, þei sent a messengere,
þei ilde forto ȝelde at his owen biddyng
if he þam saue wilde ageyn Henry our kyng.
Edward was curteys & man fulle of mercy;
with hors & herneys he went to Kyng Henry.
Right in alle þis fare wex an euel chek:
ageyn Gilbert of Clare þe kyng was in contek.
Sir Edward was witnes whi þe wrath suld be,
bot ȝit to me it es for soth als priuete.
Þe men þat were in þe ilde of þis contek herd;
þe conseiled þam a while & siþen to London ferd
to Gilbert of Clare & mayntend his powere,
with him bileft þei þare a quarter of a ȝere.
Men in hert it kast þat were of gode avis,
it myght not long last, suilk werre & partis;
þe partis conseile hent, messengers þei ches,
vnto þe kyng þei sent for a finalle pes.
At þe last right nede, pesed behoued it be,
so þat ilk man ȝede with pes to his cuntre.
Edward als so quik toward þe north him sped,

þe castelle of Alnewik he tok & with him led
þe gode Lord Vescy þat was so trew a knyght;
to kepe þat seignory, he tok tille on þat myght.
Sir Edward com to London þer was his fader Henry;
on knes he felle to grounde & praied for þe Vescy.
Þe kyng was fulle curteis, forgaf him ilk a dele,
þe lord of Kilyngworth als þat tyme sped wele.
[162r] His body did þe saue withouten prisoun,
his londes forto haue, he gaf þe kyng raunson.
Right als þis werre was ent & þe lond in state,
þe pape his bulle sent hider vnto þe legate
& comanded him to preche þorgh alle þe lond,
þe saraȝins do grete wreche þe cristen forto schond.
Vnto þe kyng of ffrance was sent anoþer legate
þat teld him of þat chance; whan Lowys herd of þat,
himself þe first was croised on his flessh;
forto wend þat pas, his wille was euer fressh.
Sir Henry of þis lond was þat ilk wille;
his sonne þer to him bond, his fader mot leue stille;
Sir Edward toke þe croice for his fader to go.
Ihesu, þou grant him voice to venge him on þi fo!
A þousand tuo hundred mo, & sexti & ten,
Sir Edward forto go, he gadres him douhty men.
The next Letenes tide, Sir Lowys went his way;
no langere wild he bide for þyng þat men mot say.
With erles & barouns, with knyghtes gode of plight,
als suilk prince of renoun felle to haf þorgh right,
he hied him fulle ȝare toward þe Grekis se,
þank god his gode fare whan he schipped suld be.
Withouten any hune, þe wynde gan him driue
vntille þe lond of Tune, & þer he gan vp ariue.
Þe saraȝins to destroie, fulle nobilly he gan,
þe cristendam mot it noie, þe dede of suilk a man.
Long dured he nouht siþen he comen was,
bot þat god wille haf wrouht els his dede, allas.
The next heruest folowand, Edward was fulle ȝare;
bi Rome he went þat land, with þe pape spak he þare.
Siþen in Ceȝile alle þe wyntere he lay,
þe somer com in a while, & he went on his way
in þe se sailand to Tune, & whan he com to lond,
tiþing com him vntime, Sir Lowys dede he fond.
Þer duelled he no more, tille Acres went our kyng;
þe cristen þat þer wore wer fayn of his comyng.

Grete folk of ffrisland þat to Acres were comen,
tille him þei were willand, for lord þei alle him nomen.
Þe oste was spred fulle wide about Acres þat lay,
alle paemie þat tide was in grete affray;
of men of armes bold þe numbre þei ame,
a thousand & tuo hundred told of cristen men bi name.
[162v] Þe lond þei suld haf wonne þorgh powere þat þei had
bot if treson had gonne & þorgh disceit bien lad.
Mykelle was þe drede þorgh out paemie
þat cristendam at nede mot haf suilk cheualrie;
þe soudan was in wehere þe cristen had suilk oste,
Sir Edwardes powere ouer alle he dred moste;
þerfor day & night he was in grete studie
on what manere he myght Edward slo þorgh spie.
Ther es a stede of wynne, þei calle it Haut Assise,
men norise childre þer inne on merveilous wise,
euer in ioy & blisse in alle þat þei may do,
þei wene it salle neuer misse ne oþer dede com to;
þei faire right als dos foles, þei do as men þam say,
þe childir of þo scoles, þei þink to lyue ay.
Þe soudan of þo in cloþes of gold him clad,
tille Edward suld he go & do as þe soudan bad.
A letter þis fole tok, bad him for nessh or hard,
þeron suld no man loke bot only Sir Edward.
Envenomed knyfe he bare also priuely
þat non þer of were ware who so stod him by.
Bi þam self alone in chambir suld þei be,
so bad þe soudone, "Schewe him his priuete
& whan þou sees leysere þat he ne perceyue þi witte,
with þe knyf him to with þe knyfe him to smite."
Comen is þe saraȝin to speke with Sir Edward,
clad in cloþes fyn, himself is a mosard.
He said he wild speke with þe kyng priuely,
conseile non to breke no telle it alle on hii.
Sir Edward granted wele, tille his chambre him brouht;
of treson neuer a dele no þing þeron he þouht.
Þe letter in his hand laid, enselid & in silke bounde,
þe envenomed knyfe out braid & gaf Edward a wounde.
(To, I wene, he lauht als his romance sais.)
A trestille Edward rauht þat heuy was of pais,
þe saraȝin so he smote in þe hede with þat treste
þat brayn & blode alle hote & iȝen alle out gan brest.
Now for Edward woundes þe cristen ere sori

þat within so stoundes ere chances fallen selli.
His surgien him tolde if he suld him saue
& his lif holde, reste behoued him haue;
þat was a mischance þat þer hede doun lay,
& þe kyng of ffrance died þat oþer day.
[163r] Anoþer ȝit more stark, þe pape þat tyme was dede,
& þe patriark, þe legate, liggis in lede.
Þe kyng of Nauer hight his help to Sir Edward;
in Ceȝile þe dede him dight als he was þiderward.
To god his father foundes, mad his testament,
Sir Edward of his woundes was in grete tourment.
After þe martynmesse þat he died here,
he regned more ne lesse þan sex & fifty ȝere.
At Westmynstere he lis toumbed richely,
in a marble bis of him is mad story;
sen þat he was dede, god has schewed his life.
Edward with his rede in his lyue tok a wife,
þe kynges douhter of Spayn, Da Helianore fulle ȝing;
of hir fairhede was fayn, Edward, our ȝong kyng.
In Acres of hir is born a mayden childe, Dame Ione,
was non fairer biforn of Inglis als scho one.
A þousand & tuo hundred þe date, sexti & tuelue,
Sir Edward help is sundred, o lyue is bot him selue.
Þe day of saynt Edmound þat martir is & kyng,
Sir Henry at Londoun in god mad his endyng.
Þat tyme his sonne Edward was in paemie,
his chance felle þer so hard þat home behoued him hie,
for alle his help was dede, als I said beforn.
Þis lond behoued haf hede, his heritage in born;
þe date of criste pundred þes fele ȝeres to mene,
a þousand & tuo hundred, sexti & fourtene.
In þe ȝere folowand þat I rekened here,
Edward com to land als prince of grete powere;
þe next Sonenday after þe Assumpcioun
of Mari moder & may, Sir Edward had þe coroun
in þe kyrke of Westmynstere at þe abbay sollempnely.
Þe bisshop of Canterbere, Robert of Kilwardeby,
corouned Edward þore biforn alle þe clergy,
& Dame Helianore corouned quene & lady.
Was neuer at Saynt Denys feste holden more hii,
ne was of more pris, ne serued so redy.
Was neuer prince, I wene, þat I writen of fond,
more had treie & tene þan he had for his lond,

in Scotlond & in Wales, in Gasconie also,
if ȝe liste alle þe tales þis storie tellis ȝow to.
Pray we alle to god of myght & his modere Marie,
grante him conquere his right, Gascoyne & Normundie
[163v] þat þe kyng of ffrance chalanges falsly!
Help him to þat chance, moder of mercy,
& Thomas þe martire, Saynt Ion of Beuerle;
Saynt Cutbert be þer fere, he trestes on ȝow þre.
To while in Gascoyne es þe pes ȝit alle certeyn.
We salle leue þat pas vnto we com ageyn
& telle ȝow oþer tales of Edward curteisie,
& of Leulyn of Wales & his beryng hie,
of Dauid, his broþere, & of his felonie;
Resamiraduk anoþere, how he did folie;
how þe contek was laid of Scotlond þat first gan;
how eft þei mad a braid & on Inglond ran;
of Madok, þe Morgan, of þer nyce ribaudie;
of Ion Baliol, no man, & of his treccherie;
& of his Duȝe Pers, togider þei gan alie,
I schrowe alle þer maners þat lufes þer partie.
A þousand & ii hundred, sexti & fiftene,
þe date of criste so pundred whan Leulyn gan þis tene.
The next ȝere folowand of Edward coronment,
Leulyn of Walsland into ffrance he sent,
þe Mountfort douhter to wedde, hir frendes alle consent.
Almerik hir ledde to schip, now er þei went;
now þei saile & rowe to Wales to Leulyns.
A burgeis of Bristowe charged was with wynes,
he ouertoke þer schip & asked wheþen þei ware;
he said with Kyng Philip to Wales wild þei fare.
What did þis burgeis? Desturbled his wendyng,
þe may & hir herneis did led vnto þe kyng;
þe mayden Edward toke, als he was fulle curteys,
in saufte did hir loke & þanked þe burgeys.
Whan Leulyn herd say, to werre sone he bigan;
for tene he wende to deie þat taken was his leman.
Edward wex fulle grim whan he wist he was risen,
sone he hasted him to mak þam alle ogrisen;
þe Walssh wer alle day slayn, now rewes þam þer res,
& Leulyn is fulle fayn to pray Edward for pes,
gyues Edward for his trespas fifti þousand mark,
& þertille bonden was with scrite & oth fulle stark
to com tuys in þe ȝere vnto his parlement.

Þe may on þis manere with Leulyn home scho went
& held his heritage in pes as he did ore,
mad was þe mariage at Snowdon biside Bangore.
[164^{r}] In þe ȝere seconde after his corounment,
new statute þe fonde, to Westmynstere þei ment.
Þe nex Paske folowand, Edward sent his brefe
to Leulyn for his land, to com als tille his chefe.
Leulyn had despite of Edwardes sonde,
bot werred also tite on him with nyth & onde.
Edward raised scheld, after his men alle sent
þat seruise of him held, manly tille him went
& ran on Sir Leulyn & alle his folk him with,
& maugre boþe his bryn was fayn to com to grith.
Dauid at þat while was with Edward þe kyng,
ȝit auanced he þat file vntille a faire þing,
to Frodesham with þe fe & alle þat longed þer tille,
to Leulyn forgaf he alle his euelle wille.
Now is Leulyn bonden eft to Sir Edward;
if he with faute be fonden, I trowe it falles him hard.
Now turnes Edward ageyn to London, his cite,
& wille wite certeyn who schent has his mone;
of clippers, of roungers, of suilk takes he questis,
olde vsed traitoures ilk at oþer hand kestis.
Ilk thefe oþer out said, ilk a schrewe oþer greues,
of fele wer handes laid & hanged þer as theues.
Edward did smyte rounde peny, halfpeny, ferthyng;
þe croice passed passed þe bounde of alle þorghout þe ryng.
Þe kynges side salle be þe hede & his name writen;
þe croyce side, what cite it was in coyned & smyten.
Þe pouere man ne þe preste, þe peny prayses no þing;
men gyf god þe lest, þe feffe him with a ferþing.
A þousand & tuo hundred & fourscore ȝeres mo;
on þis mone men wondred fist whan it gan go,
was mad anoþer statute þat non erle no baroun,
no oþer lord stoute, ne fraunkeleyn of toun,
tille Holy Kirke salle gyue tenenement, rent no lond,
fro þo þat now lyue into þe dedis hond
without leue of þe kyng or of his consaile.
Þe encheson of þis þing may mykille auaile,
for freres of þe croice, & monk & chanoun,
haf drawen in o voice his feeȝ to þer almoyn
þorgh whilk drauht his seruise is lorn & laid doun,
þat is tille him & hise in disheritsoun;

not for þi he wille þat alle religioun
haf & hold in skille þat gyuen is at resoun
[164v] þe londes þat þei haue now in possessioun.
His seruise he wille now saue þat non be þorgh tresoun,
ne no baron so bold to selle þam lond ne gyue,
for myght þei, as þei wold, no man suld bi þam lyue.
Men here biforn haf gyuen þam out of skille;
it lies now waste & lorn, half may þei not tille.
A þousand & tuo hundred þe date, fourscore & tuo;
on Leulyn has men wondred, no gynnes Dauid to thro.
For now bigynnes Dauid to wax a werreour;
with Leulyn gan he kith to be þe kynges traytour.
Þei mad a samenyng & did als þei were wonne
to disherite þe kyng & his ȝongest sonne;
on his londes þei ran & robbed ilk a toun,
brent & slouh ilk man, his kastelle bette þei doun.
Sir Edward herd wele telle of his grete misdede,
þer power forto felle it cacchis him to spede.
He sent north & south after his baronage;
sone it was fulle couth þat Leulyn did outrage,
atired þer wendyng toward þe Marche right sone.
Leulyn ageyn þe kyng, & Dauid, were alle bone
to maynten forth þe werre & susteyn þer treson;
þe entres did þei sperre & held þam in Snowdoun.
In Wales it is fulle strong to werre in wynter tide,
for wynter is þer long whan somer is here in pride.
Þat was to þam grete pyne þat werryng vndertoke,
& Snowdoun did Leulyne wele to kepe & loke;
þe kyng knowe no side how he mot com þerinne,
nouþer go no ride, ne how he suld it wynne.
A water in Snowdoun rennes, Auber is þe name,
an arme of þe se men kennes, þe depnes may non ame;
þe kyng controued þer ouer a brigge forto make,
& of Leulyn to couere, Snowdoun forto take.
Botes he toke & barges, þe sides togidere knytte,
ouer þe water þat lage is fro bank to bank rauht itte;
þei fleked þam ouerthuert, iustely forto ligge,
ouer þe water smerte was so ordeynd a brigge.
Whan þe brigge was ent at Inglis men pay,
withouten auysement þe brigge þei wild asay,
sent þei non bifore to wite how þei mo passe,
þerfore had þei lore for non avisement wasse.
Forth went knyght & sueyn & fote men alle in fere;

þe Walsch com þam ageyn, did our men alle arere,
[165r] þat turnyng þer vnthank as heuy was þe charge,
vnder þam alle sank, bothe batelle & barge.
Þe gode men þat were lorn on our Inglis partie,
þe Clifford first biforn Sir Roger did folie;
William of Lyndeseie & Ion Le fitȝ Roberd,
Sir Lucas of Tame, þise grete þer misferd
& alle þer squierie & oþer þat with þam nam,
alle drenkled þorgh folie & faut of wisdam.
A man þat oste salle lede & controues no quayntise,
how he disceit salle drede, scaþe vmwhile salle rise.
Had þei had a spie among þe Walssh oste
& warned þam priuelie þat þei were bi þat coste,
þei had bien men lyuand þat þer to dede went
þat folie tok on hand withouten avisement.
That tyme þat þis crie com of þise barouns,
com Sir Ion Vescy fro þe kyng of Aragouns,
brouht fote folk inouh of Baskles & Gascouns
þat þe Walsh men slouh, raumpand as leouns.
Þorgh mountayn & more þe Baskles ȝe þer weie,
oure nesch & hard þei fore & did þe Walsch men deie;
þei passed alle þe Marche, Snowdoun þei wan in,
of tounes þei mad þam parche & souht after Leulyn.
Dauid couth non oþer, þe folowed þam so streite,
bot fled fro his broþer, skulkand with disceite.
Sir Roger þe Strange & Sir Reynald þe Gray,
þei ne wold turne ne change bot spied þer Leulyn lay.
Leulyn in a wod a bussement he held;
biside a more a mod quayntly was he teld.
Sir Roger lay biside with priue folk & stoute
& spied tyme & tide whan he suld issue oute.
Leulyn wend no gile had bien þer so nere,
he went to play a wile with fo of his banere.
Sir Roger was perceyued whan Leulyn out cam,
þer pencels þei weyued tille Sir Leuly he nam.
"Traitoure!" said Rogere, "what salle þe werre auaile?
Now I find þe here, wele set is my trauaile.
Tuys ert þou forsuorn, & tuys þi feaute broken,
tuys was þou doun born & for pes eft spoken.
Þis is þe þrid tyme þat mykelle þou him misbede.
Daþet who þe kyme, for þou has souht þi dede;
salle þou neuer þi lyue do Inglis man more wo.
Hastilie þe schryue, þi hede þou salle forgo."

[165v] Sir Roberd Body, a knyght, his suerd best bote,
doun sone he he light & Leulyn hede of smote.
Now is Leulyn forsuorn & his hede of smyten;
his heritage is lorn fro his heyres, ȝe wyten.
More þan a ȝere beforn þat he lauht þis schame,
a douhter was him born, Wencilian hir name;
in hir credille ȝing tille Inglond scho cam,
þorgh conseile of þe kyng, was brouht to Sempyngham
& þer was scho inne four & fifty ȝere,
norised with wynne, nunne & seculere.
Now haf we new tateles, dede is Wencilian,
Leulyn douhter of Wales þat on Inglond ran.
Hir dede was mykelle ment for scho was fulle curteys
among þe ladies gent, þe los of hir so seys.
Þe seuent day of Iuny, Whitsoneuen þat tyme,
died þat lady bituex vndron & prime.
Þe date of criste pundred þus many ȝeres euen,
a þousand & þre hundred, þritty ȝere & seuen.
Hir cosyn, Dame Gladous, of Dauid douhter born,
a nunne of Sixille hous, died a ȝere beforn.
(Of Wencilian wrote I here next Leulyn story;
scho was his douhter dere to bere him company.)
Now skulkes Dauid aboute to wynne it ilk a dele.
His heritage þat is oute, he wenes fulle wele,
alle þat Leulyn held, lond & tenement,
holy to haf þe scheld þorgh heritage descent.
With lordes þat were nehi, he held his parlement;
at ȝole, at Denebeghi, after þam alle he sent
to fend þe Walschrie with him at þer powere;
to him þei gan alie & ros fulle austere.
Whan þe kyng herd say þat Dauid werred on him,
to Wales he went his way fulle scharply & fulle brim.
Edward did him chace, fulle febilly he defendes;
to rest had he no space, his tyme he tynes & spendes.
Þe euen of Saynt Morice was taken Sir Dauid,
als a fole nyce he brak þe kynges grith;
his hede þei of smyten, to London was it born,
þe dede body þe britten on four quarters torn;
þe quarters wer sent to henge at four citeȝ,
so is he worth be schent who so traytour beȝ.
Leulyn & Dauid haf born grete honour
and Snowdon com to grith, ilk castelle & toure
[166r] to þe kyng is eschete als to chefe of alle;

þe lordes þat er grete þe cheued as tenaunȝ salle.
Þe kyng þorghout þe lond he did crie his pes
& with þe lawe þam bond, als skille wild he ches.
Wardeyns gode he sette to stabille þe lond & mende;
iustise þat þe lawe gette, to vnkonand þei kende.
Whan alle was don & ent þat felle to conqueroure,
to London he went, a while to mak soioure.
He sent to his barouns, a parlement to hold,
þei com at his somouns; in parlement he þis told:
to Gascoyn bihoued him go & þat hastilie.
Tiþing com him þerfro, þer was contek & crie;
þider bihoued him nede to set þat lond in pes,
for foles haf no drede þat long is iustiseles.
A þousand & tuo hundred & fourscore ȝere & sex,
on Wales many on wundred, for more wo ȝit þer wex.
Edward wele has sped of alle þing þat has bien,
tille Gascoyn with him led Dame Helianore, our quene.
Þe gode erle of Cornwaile þis lond had in kepyng.
In luf & pes sanȝ faile went Edward our kyng
& spak with þe kyng of ffrance at Paris as he went.
Þan felle a fair chance, þei wer at on assent;
forth he gan him hie, tille Gascoyn is he comen.
Þe rightes he did attrie of þo þat wrong had nomen,
rightfulle dome he gaf on foles for þer misdede;
no man he ouerhaf bot alle þorgh lawe ȝede.
To while Sir Edward gos to Gascoyn forto apese,
Wales to werre vp ros þorgh conseile of a Rese;
on Reseamiraduk, of Wales a lordyng,
our Inglis did rebuk & werred on our kyng.
I kan not telle ȝow whi þat werre was reised olofte;
men said þe wrath & cri com þorgh þe Lord Tiptofte.
Þe kyng herd þat pleynt, vnto þe Rese he sent
a letter enselid fulle quaynt, for þe pes it ment.
He praied to hold him stille tille his tocome mot be,
& he suld do his wille in alle þat skille mot se.
His pleyntes he wild here in skille at lordes sight,
& if he baron were, he suld haf fulle gode right.
Þis Reseamiraduk, als fole & vnwise,
his letter gan rebuk, sette it at light prise;
þe skaþe þat he myght do with slauhter or prison hard,
alle he brouht þam to þat longed tille Edward.
[166v] A þousand & tuo hundred þe date, forscore & nine;
on our men þei wondred, in Wales did þam pyne.

Whan Edward had bien in Gascoyn þre ȝere,
ageyn he & þe quene on lond ryued vp here.
At his comyng he fond of clerkes & men of pleynt,
& iustise of þe lond of falsnes was atteynt.
For giftes, som iustise lete þe lowe doun go,
& som on oþer wise did wrong to þe coroun;
þe first iustise in benk, Sir Thomas of Weland,
for falshed & for wrenk, he forsuore þe land;
he went ouer to ffrance & com neuer ageyn.
His clerkes stode to chance, passed for a certeyn,
þei wer out of þe tour delyuerd for mone;
þer held þei long soiour, bot penies mad þam fre.
Opon þis forward or þei wer out gon,
to serue Kyng Edward, neuer more suld þei non.
Sir Elys of Bekyngham, to do lawe him was lefe;
Sir Ion of Metyngham, he left þe iustise chefe;
Sir Rauf of Heyngham, þe wrong oft he ches,
he departed with gram & þe benk les;
Sir Adam of Stretton, fulle hard was he led,
nouht without encheson, I lay my gloue to wed,
for gold & siluer strong he gaf so grete plente,
bifor þe kyng it song "Placebo domine."
With wrong alle it cam, with gile salle gyuen be.
"Dilexit," Sir Adam, gilerie & falste.
Thise iustise er atteynt of falshed & folie,
now comes a new pleynt to destroie þe Iuerie;
þe kyng dos enquere of þer wikked dedes,
so many þer were, dome on þam salle nedes.
For þam þe kyng dos sette his priue parlement;
þei said þorgh þer rescette, þe cristen men were schent.
Þe barons alle said, alle holy þe clergie,
þe lond þei wild voide of þat herisie.
I wene þe kyng alegid þei were of his tresour,
noþeles he wild haf briggid þer fals leue & erroure.
For þe penie fiftend, þe Iues wild he fleme;
þe clergie said at þe end, "We grante it as ȝe deme."
Þe lerid & þe lay granted þat þei said
& assigned a day þat taxe to be laid;
þe dettes þat men þam auht, þer stedes & þer wonyng,
wer taxed & bitauht to þe eschete of þe kyng.
[167r] Þe Reseamiradic was taken þat ilk ȝere
in Wales, þorgh a spie, for alle his powere.
Whan þe kyng herd it seie, to Ȝork he did him lede,

schames dede to deie als traytour for his dede.
First was he drawen for his felonie,
& as a thefe þan slawen, on galwes hanged hie.
Now is non of age of his ancestrie
may haf his heritage to whom it salle alie.
A þousand & tuo hundred, fourscore & elleuen,
on Wales men ȝit wondred, þe pes not ȝit euen.
The next ȝere folowand, Acres was assaled;
þe cristen myght no stand, of help alle þam failed
& þe cite lorn, & alle don to þe suerde
þat were cristen born, þe lewed & þe lerid.
Whan þe pape had tiþing it was in saraȝins handes,
he gaf Edward our kyng þe tende of alle þe landes;
Inglond, Scotlond & Wales, Ireland þerto was laid,
þan mot he fille his males, no man him withsaid.
Holy who salle spare, if it nede stode,
whan þo þat hedes are do þerto no gode.
Þat ilk ȝere þe quene died in Lyndseie,
at Westmynster, I wene, his body did þei leie.
A litelle þer biforn died Margarete,
þe heyr of Scotlond, born of Alisander biȝete;
wherfor Sir Edward, for þat maiden dede,
hied him Northward, his barons he asked rede.
In þe north, at Norham, he wanissed þe castelle,
þe barons þider cam & conseild þat best felle;
þei brouht þe cronykles þat were in Scotland,
þe olde chartres & titles þat wer in abbays hand,
of ilk a bisshop se & ilk a priourie
þat were of dignite, of olde ancestrie,
examend þam & cast ilk amountment.
Þei said alle at þe last þorght of on assent,
of Inglond suld þei hold þorgh right & skille;
ſo wild þe feffementes ald & þei granted þertille.
Þis was certified & sikere on ilk side;
it myght not be denied for þing þat mot betide.
Þis conseild Sir Antoyn, þe bisshop of Durham,
þat non eft mad essoyn, þe kynges right to clame.
[N]ow wex þe Scottes wode, now haue þei nythe & onde, [*Cap. om.*]
who of þat fals blode ouh to be kyng of þe londe;
[167v] þat was right heire is dede, on þat side is no mo;
þorgh blode & right rede, to Dauid salle it go.
Dauid of Huntyngton was Kynges Wiliam broþer;
tille his heires, þorgh reson, of William is non oþer;

of William now is non, Dauid heire salle be,
& his heirs of him gon salle haf þe regalte.
Dauid had douhtres þre, were gyuen to þre lordynges
þat claymes þe regalte: Baliol, Brus, Hastynges.
Þis ilk þre barons þorgh descent of blode
haf right & resons to þe coroune fulle gode;
þise þre ȝald þer right vp to Sir Edward
tille it wer atried þorgh sight whom it felle afterward.
Sir Edward is seised in Scotland ilk a dele,
þise þre barons pesid & hold þam paied wele.
Now com þis barons eft & ask iugement
to whom it salle be left þorgh comon assent;
þe kyng wille bot wele, þe lawe alle vnderstandes.
Þe hie folk, ilk a dele, he did com of boþe þe landes,
Scottis & Inglis, he said to þe wisest,
"Gyue now gode dome of þis, whilk of þise may best
to resceyue þe coroune, Scotlond forto ȝeme,
þat þe right go not doune & best may ȝow alle ȝeme."
What for þe kynges sawe & skille þei vnderstode,
& þorgh þe londes lawe & descent of blode,
þe triours alle þat caste & put þer saw tille on:
"We say with word stedfaste, we chese Baliol, Ion.
Sir Ion þe Baliol es a man þe reame may saue
& nere of blode & flessh þe heritage to haue
for euer, we vnderstond, tille him & alle hise,
holdand of Inglond for homage & seruise."
Our kyng, Sir Edward, held him wele payed;
he did þam no more hard ne langer was delayed,
disseised himself of alle & ȝald it to Sir Ion;
bot Ion his homage salle mak or he be gon.
Saynt Steuen day it felle þat Ion mad his homage
at þe newe castelle, listnes þe langage:
"My Lord, Lord Edward, þe kyng Inglis
& chefe lord of þe Scottis,
I, Ion Baliol, þe Scottis kyng,
I bicom þi man for Scotlond þing
with alle þe purtenance þertille
þat to þe reame longes with skille,
[168r] þe whilk I hold & salle þorgh right
clayme to hald at alle my myght,
heritagelik of þe
& of þin heires þat after þe be
of Inglond, with lif & lymme,

for erthly worship þat I nymme,
ageyn alle þo may lyue & deye
& with þam hold in luf & eye."
On þis maner þe kyng it toke,
his right forto saue & loke.
Þis was at þe newe castelle,
on Saynt Steuens day it felle;
a þousand CC. fourscore & þre
þe ȝers o Ihesu wer whan þis felle to be.
Our kyng, gode Edward, þorgh Scotlond ferd;
as he com howard he souht Saynt Cutberd
& mad þer his offryng, siþen com to Beuerlay
& offred þer fair þing, to London his way.
On fele þinges he þouht & wex heuy als lede,
how chances on him souht & þat þe quene was dede.
His solace was alle reft þat scho fro him was gon,
ne no sonne him left bot ȝing Edward alon.
He was tendre & ȝing, of him had he no speyre,
himself in ille likyng, & had no waxen heyre
þat mot kepe þe coroune if he of lond went.
He drouped þerfore doune & said þe lond were schent
if he tille Acres ȝede, in perile sulle alle be;
of þe child wer drede, þe lond als wele as he.
In þinkeng of alle þis, þe batailed in þe se,
Normans & Inglis were slayn grete plente;
þe Normans þat day les for þer powere was nouht.
Þe portes had als þei ches, schippes inow þam brouht,
to Douer & Germne cam, & vnto Wynchilse,
to Romeneye & Schorham, & to Peueneshe,
to Gipwiche & Sandwiche, & to Southamptoun.
Alle þe portes were riche, Irays & Bayoun;
þe fiue portes, þorgh powere, þe se had so conquerd
þat Normans alle þat ȝere durst not be sene for ferd,
þorgh þe lond of ffrance was said fulle sone.
Philip herd þat chance, how þe Inglis had done,
& alle how it bigan & alle þe skille why
þat þei togider ran & we had þe maistrie.
[168v] Sir Edward, god him saue, he is in grete longyng,
a where he mot haue þat auenant is & ȝing,
þat wer of hie parage, suilk on wild he take,
his euenhed in mariage, gentille gendrure to make.
His herte gaf tille Dame Blanche, if hir wille wer þerto
& Holy Kirke wild stanche sibred bituex þam tuo.

Hire þan wild he wedde forto saue þe pes,
in luf þat þei þam ledde, in werre þat nouþer les.
For Blanche, his cosyn, he sent how it mot be
to mak a mariage fyn, Philip sister was sche,
& als vnto þe pape for to wite þe certeyn
what þe clergie wild schape whan þe courte were pleyn.
Edward messengers vnto þat mayden sent
to wite of hir maners, to se hir body gent;
þei com vnto þat may & sauh hir contenance,
so fair lady þat day was not in alle France.
Whan þei had sene þat sight þei com & teld our kyng,
"Creature non myght be fayrer bi no þing,
fro Rome hiderward, fayrer non was."
Enamoured bicom Edward of Dame Blanche, allas!
Blanche did write stille, a letter Philip sent,
hir herte & hir wille, alle wist he what scho ment.
A þousand & CC. fourscore & fourtene,
ȝit salle Edward be encombred þorgh Dame Blanche schene.
Oft had þe parties spoken of þis mariage
& teld boþe þer avis to messengers of passage.
Philip & Dame Blanche granted þe aliance,
noþeles of a branche þer was a disceyuance.
How þe granted þertille þei tald bi a messengere;
þe fourme of þer skille þei said on þis manere:
"Edward, without essoyn, salle gyue Philip þe kyng
alle holy Gascoyn without disturblyng.
After þe forty dayes of þat feffement,
Philip without delayes salle gyue þat ilk tenement
tille Edward & tille Blanche & þer heirs of þam comen,
if it be so no branche in wedlaike of þam be nomen;
if Blanche ouer lyue Edward, scho salle haf hir lyue
Goscoyn afterward, ageyn þat non salle stryue,
& after Blanche desces, withouten gaynsaying,
salle turne to þe heires in pes of þe Inglis kyng."
To þat ilk scrite Edward set his seale
þat his gift was perfite & with witnes leale.
[169r] Whan alle was spoken, wist not Sir Antoyn;
fulle sone it had bien broken & Philip fro Gascoyn.
Philip seysed Burdews þorgh Sir Edward scrite,
þe toþer, as so say deus, ȝald þam also tite.
What did Kyng Philip whan alle þis was ent?
To Paris gan he skip & held his parlement,
& Charles, his broþer, with him com he þidere,

þe erle of Artous þe toþer, þre fals men togidere.
Þise þre ageyn Edward mad a compassement,
for Normand & Pikard, to courte after þam sent;
þo þat were in þe bataile, þat on þe had lorn,
þat portes gan assaile, as I told biforn,
Edward þei cald & teld þat he was mayntenoure.
Þe robbed he alle, held as a resceyuour;
of suilk felonie Edward in courte þe cald,
did non þat curteisie þat þer for him wild hald.
Of þat fals controueyng gaf þei iugement,
depriued þei our kyng of alle þe tenement
of londes of Gascoyn, þat neuer more suld he
for no maner essoyn eft chalange þat fe,
bot of þe kyng of ffrance holden suld it be.
Edward kepe þi chance, þei haf bitraised þe!
Men sais in þe courte of France among þe Deȝe Pers,
with right he leses his chance þorgh faut þat not apers;
þer may ne write be brouht to wynne ageyn his right,
bot þorgh force be souht þorght dynt of suerd & fight.
Edward sore it ment whan he wist þat tirpeil;
for Sir Antoyn he sent to com to his conseil,
& for þo barouns þat were his wele willand,
for conseil & resons & chance þat was comand.
Sir Antoyn first bigan, spak hastily & wilde:
"Sir Kyng, þou was a man, be not now hold a childe!
Þou suld do right nouht without þe comon sight
þat may of scaþe be wrouht ageyn þe reames right.
Do ȝit be, be consaile, þou salle not it repent,
bot som þat may not auaile, þi wille to suilk es went.
Þi manace drede þei more in hastynes suorn
þan if þi reame alle wore in poynt forto be lorn."
"Sir Antoyn," said þe kyng, "I wite þis no man
bot myn vnconyng, þis folie myself bigan."
"Sen þou has don amysse at þin vnconyng,
we may not faile at þis to help þe in alle þing,
[169v] & if þou þink to wynne Gascoyn ageyn, þi lond,
hastily bigynne Philip to folow; þou fond
þou may not ligge & slepe as monke in his dortoure,
þou salle rise vp & lepe & stirre vnto þe stoure,
& gete þe frendes fele þorgh gifte of mone;
tresore may þou non spele of lordes biȝond þe se.
Þe kyng of Almayn & þe duke of Boloyn,
þe to help were fayn, & þe erle of Burgoyn,

þe kyng of Aragoun & þe erle of Sauuay,
þise er redy boun to help þe nyght & day.
Whan þou of þise ert sikere to þe þorgh aliance,
þan is tyme to bikere with þe kyng of ffrance."
Whan Antoyn his resons to þe kyng said þus,
þan spak þe barons: "Sir Kyng, listen tille vs.
Forsoth ilk lordyng whilk Sir Antoyn has said
disherited is þorgh þe kyng, chalanges þam of neid.
He has spared non þer he mot fynd encheson,
þat he disherites ilkon of castelle & of toun;
þerfore we rede ȝe sende to þe kyng of Almayn,
& ȝour londes to defende, & reue Philip his wayn,
& to þe kyng of Aragoun & tille alle þe toþer.
Be calle þam of tresoun, Philip & Charles, his broþer,
bynd ȝow alle togider to lyue & to deie.
We se nouþer whidere þou may haf sikerer weie;
siluer may þou non spare of þo þat with þe be,
for Philip is euer ȝare & has so grete pouste."
To þat ilk consail þe kyng acorded to;
Sir Antoyn wille trauail þe message forto do.
Þe ersbisshop of Deuelyn, he was chosen his pere,
a baron bold & fyn, Sir Hugh Despensere;
of Krawecombe, Sir Ion, a clerke gode & wys;
now is Antoyn gon to procure þe partys.
Þe Almanȝ alle wer lefe be suorn to þe Inglis,
& þer kyng was chefe in wille to do alle þis,
& bisshop & baron alle þei had gode wille;
with obligacion, þe Inglis suore þei tille
be helpand þe Almanȝ in alle maner of nede;
boþe to hold couenaȝ, with scrite enselid þe dede.
Now Antoyn is of lond, god saue him & his pers.
Edward sendis his sond, to France messengers,
ffrere Hugh of Malmcestre was a Iacobyn,
& William of Gaynesburgh was a Cordelyn.
[170r] Alle þise passid þe se, so com þe erle of Artoys,
in prison did þam be a seuenyght in Caleys;
to Paris siþen þei cam & þer fond þei þe kyng.
Þe letter forth þei nam to trowe þer sayng,
þis letter of credance þei schewed in his present.
Here now þe acordance what þer sayng ment:
Sir Hugh was man of state, he said as I salle rede,
"To prince & to prelate men salle loute & drede,
& for lord dere his biddyng salle men do,

to lesse & more in fere haf fayth & treuth also;
& for our lord Edward þat god him saue & se,
we tok þis trauaile hard, his bode to bere to þe.
He settes þe terme & stage bi vs, whan & why
þat he has don homage for Gascoyn plenerly,
in forward formed in pes as was þer acordance;
as ȝour ancestres ches, of Inglond & of ffrance,
þei mad a pes final aftere þer contek.
Þou has broken it alle & don him many ille chek.
Now at his last goyng whan he to Gascoyn went,
ȝe sette a certeyn þing at ȝour boþe assent,
& þat suld holden be, euer withouten ende;
þou brak þat certeynte wikkidly & vnhende.
Ȝit he biddes þe se how wrong þou wilt him lede.
Bituex him & þe was mad a priue dede,
of Gascoyn certeyn was þat feffement
forto feffe him ageyn in þat tenement;
þi seisyn is wele knowen, þe days has þou plenere
to restore him his owen, he sent to þe Duȝe Pers.
As lawe wild & right, & couenant was in scrite,
ȝeld it, þou has no right, with wrong holdes it in lite
ageyn alle maner skille, & ȝit þou ert so grefe,
for whilom þou wrote him tille & cald him in þi brefe,
þi kynde faythfulle & leale, of Gascoyn noble duke,
þerto þou set þi seale, þat right wilt þou rebuke;
neuer siþen hiderward suilk speche vnto him touched.
Wherfore our Kyng Edward in þouht fulle wele has soucheḍ,
þou holdes him not þi man, no þing holdand of þe,
ne he þinkes neuer for þan to mak þe more feaute.
He hopes to wynne þat land with dynt of douhty kyght;
of god he claymes holdand & neuer of no right.
At þis tyme is not els of Sir Edward to seye,
bot of Edmunde þat duellis with him als breþer tueye,
[170v] forbi any oþer with him wille hold & be.
He is his lord & broþer, he certifies þat to þe
þat no man in þis werld he lufes so mykelle no dredis,
ne with him is non herd so mykille may help at nedis,
for he sees so wele ȝour grete controued gile
ageyn his broþer ilk dele compassed in a while,
reft him his heritage, sais on him felonie.
He ȝeldes vp his homage, forsakis þi companie,
& þerto alle þe londes þat he held of þe,
& ȝeldes vp alle þe bondes of homage & feaute

saue þe right þat may falle of ancestres olde
vnto þer heires alle to haf & to holde.
We er pouer freres þat haf nouht on to lyue;
in stede of messengeres, saue condite vs gyue
þorgh þi lond to go in þin auowrie
þat non vs robbe ne slo for þi curteysie."
The respons were redy þat Philip did þam bere.
A knyght fulle auerty gaf þam þis ansuere:
"Þe conantȝ þat wer sette in nessh & in hard
Kyng Philip has þam gette fro þat tyme hiderward.
Bot þorgh þe kyng Inglis & þorh his maryners,
þe conantȝ ere gan mis in many stedes sers.
Homage vp to ȝeld, lordschip to forsake,
so Philip it wild, on þat wise we it take.
As ȝe haf mad present, þe kyng vouches it saue."
Þe messengers went, condute he did þam haue;
þei hed redy wendyng, at Douer þei toke lond
& sped þam to þe kyng, at London þei him fond.
Whan Edward þer respons knowe & what þei ment,
for clerkis & barons son after he sent,
& eft, þam alle biforn, teld þam alle þe chance
how Gascoyn was lorn þorgh þer gilerie of France.
"Withouten help of ȝow, wyn it may I nouht;
to saue þe londes prow, to ask þis haf I þouht.
I ask half þe godes to haf of þe clergie,
& saue ȝour oþer fodes to maynten my partie."
Marchant & burgeis to þe sext be laid,
he wild on no weis þat it were geynsaid;
þe barons alle plenere in þe tende him seised,
so in þat self ȝere it suld be payed & reised.
Þe lond fulle hard was sette in þat ilk laying,
noþeles we ere in dette at nede to help þe kyng
[171r] & praye god for his right, boþe foles & wys,
to saue him day & nyght ageyn his enmys.
If þei þat tyme had wonnen & venquised Sir Edward,
& þorgh þis lond wonnen, Normanȝ & Pikard,
þe Kirke of Inglond fulle ille þei suld haf said,
& had alle gon to schond, þe clergie ille bisted,
þat neuer bisshop ne person, ne riche prouendere,
ne erle ne baron, ne knyght ne squiere,
ne burgeis of cite, merchant ne frankeleyn
þat euer had bien fre, bot seruage leyn,
for alle þis þraldam þat now on Inglond es.

Þorgh Normanȝ it cam, bondage & destres,
& if þei now powere had of vs, wite ȝe wele
streiter we suld be lad bi þe tend dele.
Better vs is to giue & saue vs fro disceite
þan with our fomen lyue in seruage so streite.
The kyng þis pay has nomen & in cofres has;
Sir Antoyn home is comen fro Almayn þer he was.
Þe bisshop of Deuelyn don has his endyng,
Sir Hugh gode hele is in & comen is to þe kyng;
þe ersdeken of Richemunde to þe pape is sent;
Sir Ion of Crawecombe with him is he went,
þe pape forto telle þe sothe how it was
& in his dome to duelle who did moste trespas.
Toward Portesmouthe þe kyng fast drouh,
to werre as he wele couthe, he ordeynd whilk & how,
first to be cheftayn, to Gascoyn forto go.
Sir Ion of Bretayn, formast on of þo,
Sir Ion Sayn Ion, he knewe wele þat cuntre;
Roberd Tiptoft anoþer on, his sonne salle with him be;
Sir Laurence of Sauueye also he was þare.
Þei aryued alle o weye at Burgh sur la Mare.
Þiderward as als he went, Sir Henry þe Lacie,
þe kyng eft for him sent, I salle telle ȝow whi.
In Wales is a schreward to werre risen on,
for he wend Sir Edward ouer þe se wer gon.
Snowdon gan he hald als his heritage,
& prince þei him cald, þat bastard outrage.
Þe Inglis men he slouh & robbed alle þer þing,
þe castelles doun drouh þat longed tille þe kyng.
Þis tiþing com him eft how Wale him bitrayed,
þerfor is Gascoyn left & þerat werre delayed.
[171v] Schortly forto say, to Snowdon has he tight
& in Abretonway a castelle vp he dight,
& þer he held his ȝole with fele of his baronage;
of Gascoyn was dole þat he left þat viage.
Fro ȝole vnto þe Pask werred Sir Edward;
grete trauaile it askes, colde & greuance hard,
þorgh pite mykille he les & reufulhed of herte,
for þe folk he with him ches wer first auster & smerte;
þat Wales mot haf bien wonnen if he had don þam tille,
& þorghout Gascoyn ronnen if he had don þam skille;
if he had don so wele, gyuen þam alle þer lyue,
þer wynnyng ilk a dele þat þei mot reyme & gyue,

holdand in warantie of him & of his heyres,
chef of þat seignorie to þam & to þeirs,
for soth Wales had bien wonne at þat dynt
& Gascoyn had bien seen wonne þat is tynt.
For þe pes to haue, he mad so long a trayne
þe knyghtes mot þam not saue þat were in Aquitayne,
for Charles wan Riouns, þorgh fight had he þe pris,
& fettred þe Gascouns, led þam to Paris.
Saynt Seuere was ȝolden þorgh force in couenant;
Burdeus wild þei no wolden had Frankis & Normant,
þan ȝede ilk a Pikard scornand & makand ryme.
Lorn is now Edward Gascoyn in alle his tyme.
Þe Inglis wend haf help of þe kyng of Aragoune;
of Edward had þei mad ȝelp, & his broþer Edmoun,
& of þe erle of Lincoln þei wend þei suld com þider,
bot alle þei wer forholn & failed þam alle togider.
To while our Inglis alle wer in tribulacioun,
Wales, wo mot it falle, ros eft þorgh tresoun.
Bot after þe Pask tide, þe kyng so on þam ran,
maugre alle þer pride, Snowdon on þam wan;
siþen in Angleseie did set his pauilloun,
komand in his weie, cried pes in ilk a toun,
tille alle þat pes wild haue, pes he wille gyue,
& lyue & lymme suld saue þo þat in pes wild lyue.
Bot þe erle of Gloucestre so had him misborn,
Southwales þat was his estre, þorgh Morgan had he lorn.
(I ne wote whi it was bituex him & Morgan,
ne how com þat trespas þat Morgan on him ran.)
Tille Edward, our kyng, wild Morgan not be gode,
bot Maddok mad werryng & cald him prince of blode,
[172r] was taken þorgh consaile & led to Londoun;
now is Maddok wroþerhaile, don in þer prisoun.
Þorgh Edward long trayne Gascoyn is born doun;
non defendes his chayne bot only Bayoun.
If he bi tyme had gon þorh help of his Gascons,
þer suld haf standen non, Philip no Charlons.
He suld haf wonnen Saynt Seuer & Rions,
Tolouse & Tolousan, Burdeus with his somons.
Wales, wo þe be, þe fende þe confound!
Scotlond (whi ne mot I se) be sonken to helle ground.
Was neuer in þam both terme set ne stounde
þat þei discorded wroth, þe pes non in þam founde;
in Wales, said beforn, alle day is mischance,

& Gascoyn now is lorn þorgh treson of ffrance.
What did Ion Baliol þat Edward did auance,
bot falsly as a fole bigan a disceyuance;
þorgh conseile of hise, he sent vnto þe pape
& controued a quantise, a new falsnes did schape,
& said Scotlond suld be, þorgh right & olde setnesse,
holden of his fe & of non els þat es,
& Edward of Inglond þorgh force & myght
in his homage him bond ageyn his wille & right.
"We ask ȝow grace of þis, assoyle him of þat othe
þat he did, maugre his, to wrong was him lothe,
bot he mot quitely go in world where he fore
& frely passe him fro, fro whom þat he to suore."
Þe Pape Celestyn, of non avisement,
with letter bulled fyn assoyled to Scotlond sent.
Whan þis bulle was brouht home bi messengres,
a vileynie þaim þouht to mak þam Duȝe Pers,
desherite Edward of alle his seignorie,
of Ion Baliol musard suilk was his curteysie.
For Edward gode dede
a wikked bounte,
þe Baliol did him mede;
turne we ageyn to rede,
a Maddok þer left we
& on our geste to spede.
Now is Morgan ȝolden & Maddok he bendes,
þe kyng comen to London bi consail of his frendes;
tuo cardenalles of Rome þe pape hider sent,
to Paris boþe þei come to þe parlement.
Þei said, luf to mak, þe pape wild entermet
þat non ageyn oþer take tille tyme þat he had set.
[172v] Þise cardinals so bond Edward & Philip,
nouþer suld werre bi lond, no in water bi schip,
bot hold þam stone stille in pes at þer cuntre;
þat nouþer of þam did ille, þe pape wild iustise be;
þise kynges stille þei left at þe papes request.
Þe Normanȝ com now eft & mak a newe gest.
Als pes was mad of partie þorgh cardinals þat com ouer,
þe folk of Normundie aryued vp at Douer,
& men of Caleis camen with þam, wele I wene,
to brenne þe toun alle samen & slouh men þrittene.
Þe wardeyn herd it telle of þe castelle biside,
a monke of a celle bare him wele þat tide.

Þei sette so wele þer wardes & stifly samen stode
þat Norman3 & Pikardes left boþe hede hode.
A monke þer was, I wene he slouh tuenti,
þer hedes quyte & clene he laid þam bi & bi.
A monk was of þat celle, þei slouh him, Dan3 Thomas;
a saynt he, men telle, with Norman3 slayn he was.
I wene þat þei 3ede, mykelle not þei wonnen;
þe Frankis þat mot spede to schippes fast ronnen.
After alle þis fare, þe cardinals went þer weie.
What ansuere þei bare, þe soþe can I not say;
noþeles of fele þis was þe comon sawe,
þer folk alle sulle þe spele & fro werryng þam drawe,
Edward & Philip, & late þe folk ouer wend,
& passage haf in schip to londes forto lend
in þe sufferance of pes tille þe acorde wer ent;
þe Inglis þerto ches if Alman3 wild consent.
To while þise cardinals trauaild for þe pes,
here of a wikhals, how he bigan a res.
Thomas Turbeuile was taken at Rions;
at Paris he duelte a while in hold with oþer prisons.
To þe prouest he spak & bed him his homage
his oth þat he ne brak, he left in his ostage
& hise childre tuo & suore him his leaute;
tille Inglond suld he go to spie ilk a cuntre,
tille þe kyng suld he say þat he of prison fled.
He wist non sikerer way for socour tille him sped.
Þe prouest als tite to Thomas þerfor him bond
& granted him with scrite tuo hundreth pounde of lond,
& Thomas trouht him plight & suore on þe messe,
of Inglond alle þe right & Wales more & lesse,
[173r] & of Scotlond alle þe men þat were of pris
suld enclyn & falle to Philip fit3 Lowys.
Now gos þis Thomas his treson to purchace,
bot how Edward was warned þorgh godes.
Thomas tille Ingelond com to kyng & said
bi nyght he skapid of bond, of prison þer he was laid,
for his luf to haue, suilk perille on him drouh,
& þat he vouched saue for his luf wele inouh.
Þe kyng tille him þerfore did grete curteysie,
wynnyng for his lore he gaf him largelie.
Now gos Turbeuile & serchis day bi day
to do þe kyng a gile how & whan he may.
He serchis alle þe coste where were best comyng

to bring in Frankis oste for to tak our kyng.
Whan he had serched alle & knew ilk a coste,
his man with þe cardinalle he sent to þe prouoste;
þe prouest mad grete ioye for þat ilk sond,
"It turnes bot tille þe boþe, if godes grace may stond."
Þe clerke þat wrote þe lettere to Thomas Turbeuile,
he þouht forto do bettere þan Kyng Edward to gile;
tille on þat was priue, þe kynges conseiloure,
þe clerk lete him alle se, þe dede of þat traytoure.
Whan Thomas was perceyued, his lettres wer away;
þe kynges courte he weyued for he dred to deie.
A seruant þer was þat wist whan Thomas fled,
fulle sone after Thomas better pas he sped;
opon þe þrid day at a toun hamelet,
Thomas was his pray as he to mete was set.
Now Thomas taken es & to London brouht;
grete was þe wikkednes þat Thomas had wrouht.
To þe iustise he said he wild speke with þe kyng
of his traytours neid to warn him of a þing.
Thomas þerfor was don to prison eft ageyn,
to þe kyng als son þe sent bode certeyn.
At Malmesbirie þe kyng with his moder was
whan him com tiþng of Turbuile Thomas;
he teld þe kyng ilk dele, Thomas wild speke with him
& warn him he suld wele whilk wer his traytours grym.
His moder, Helianore, abated þer grete bale.
"Sonne," said scho, "neuer more trowe ȝe traytours tale;
suilk traytours als he for hate wille mak a lie
þorgh þe whilk mot be vengeance & felonie.
[173v] Sonne, on my blissyng, trowe þou not his sawe,
bot late him haf endyng als a traytour þorgh lawe."
Þe kyng wrote his lettere agayn to þe iustise
þat he wist non bettere bot do him to iuwise,
for alle þat he has said be don vnder fote,
tille þis werld be, it is ȝit no tyme to mote.
Now þe Turbeuile has his iugement;
drawen is a while on London pauiment
& siþen was he hanged as thef for treson;
faire grace Edward fanged in his tribulacioun.
Now is þis wikhals dede þorgh vengeance
& þe cardinals gon er in to France,
oft for þe pes with Philip mad bergayn;
vnto þat conseil ches þe kyng of Almayn,

clerkis bituex þam sent hidir to Edward.
What þer conseil ment, þe distance so hard,
þe wrath was so grete bituex þise kynges tuo,
vnnethis acorde þei schete bot þus with mykelle wo.
To Kaunbray suld þei send men þat were of gode
þat þer greuance kend, þe distance vnderstode.
Clerkis & lewed men suld deme at Kaunbray
& trie þe soth & ken in whom þe wrong lay,
to what manere of pes þe parties wille descend,
& who þe wrong first ches, þat partie suld amend.
To þo ilk resons þe Inglis wer assent,
bisshopes & barons were gode of þo þat went.
To while our men were out forto mak þe pes,
men of armes stout þe kyng to Gascoyn ches.
Sir Edmound, his broþer, þe first was redy;
of Lyncoln þe erle anoþer, Sir Henry þe Lacy;
Sir William þe Vescy, wys man & bold baroun,
& oþer lordes worþi þat were of gode renoun;
sex & tuenty baners of Inglond alder best,
of armes þat knewe þe maners to werre were alle prest.
In Inglond were left als douhty as þo,
of þam þe kyng toke, eft to Scotlond wild he go;
þe Scottis kyns withsaid, he auht him non homage,
now þenkes he mak a braid for þat grete outrage.
Of Marche þe first day, at þe new castelle,
our kyng þer he lay his purueiance so fel,
to Scotlond forto go to wite whi & what wise
þer kyng & oþer mo withsaid him his seruise.
[174r] A þousand & tuo hundred, fourscore & sexten,
on þe Scottes has many wondred þat bigan þis tene.
Sir Roberd Roos of Werk with þe Scottis fled;
he set so ille his merk þat neuer eft he ne sped,
þe kyng his castelle sesis & held þer his Pask day;
him & his þer esis & alle þat feste þer lay.
Þe Scottis did first mys, þei wakend alle þat wouh;
tuo schippis of our Inglis, þe folk þer in þei slouh.
Sir Edward herd it telle & dight him to Berwik,
no stounde wild he duelle bot seged it also quik.
What did þan Sir Edward, pere had he non like,
opon his stede, Bayard, first he wan þe dike.
In Pask weke it was, þe Friday þei it wan,
in þe non tyme felle þis cas þat slayn was ilk a man
þat were in Berwik, fourti þousand & mo,

was non of þam left quik bot alle to dede ȝede þo.
Of þe Inglis sanȝ faile bot o knyght dede, I wote,
Sir Richard of Cornwaile, a Flemmyng him smote;
right out of þe rede haule schot was a quarelle,
fire þei fest on it alle & brent it þat it felle.
Þe wardeyn of þe castelle sauh þer chance fulle hard;
vntille mercy he felle & ȝald him tille Edward.
William of Duglas ȝalde him also tite;
Symon ffreselle þer was, he wild haf don dispite.
He wend haf had fulle light, Edward at his wille,
bot þanked be god alle myght, his prison leues he stille.
Þe erle of þe Marche, Patrik, lord of next cuntre,
he did no maner wik, þe kyng gaf him his gre.
Sir Gilberd Vmfreyvile wholom was with þe kyng;
Sir Robert Brus þat while ageyn him did no þing;
golde & siluer þei fonde & oþer metalle plente.
Now has þe Baliol a stounde lorn issu & entre,
& on þe fairest toun þat was in his pouste,
of ricchesse it had renoun þat felle to a cite.
Now is Berwik born doun, abaist is þat cuntre.
(Ion, gete þi coroun, þou losis þi dignite!)
Now dos Edward dike Berwik brode & long
als þei bad him pike & scorned him in þer song:
Pikit him & dikit him . on scorne said he. [*In margin*:] Couwe
He pikes & dikes . in length as him likes . how best it may be
& þou has for þi pikyng . mykille ille likyng . þe soþe is to se.
Withoute any lesyng . alle is þi heþing . fallen opon þe,
[174v] for scatred er þi Scottis . & hodred in þer hottes . neuer þei ne the.
Right als I rede . þei tombled in Tuede . þat woned bi þe se.
Now is Edward left Berwik forto dike;
þe Scottis er risen eft, Inglond to bisuike.
Þe gadred þam an oste, fourti þousand & mo
þat com bi anoþer coste þe Inglis forto slo;
þise were hede & meste þat led þat meyne:
Rosse & Meneteste, Assetelle, þise erles þre.
Corbrigge is a toun, þe brent it whan þei cam,
tuo hous of religioun, Leynercoste & Hexham,
þei chaced þe chanons out, þer godes bare away,
& robbed alle about, þe bestis tok to pray.
Whan þei had slayn & brent, robbed toun & feld,
to Dunbar alle þei went als þer vnhap wild;
þe castelle sone þei toke & þer þar pauilloun.
Þe erle Patrik men s[cho]ke, it was his owen donioun.

Edward herd it say þat Dunbar was so taken,
his folk was sone on way with sege to hold þam waken.
In alle þis ilk goyng, so com þe cardinalle
fro Kaunbray to þe kyng with ansuere of alle,
& fro þe kyng of ffrance, hereafter salle ȝe here.
Þise men mette him o chance & com with him in fere:
Sir Amys of Saueye, an erle of grete renoun,
anoþer com in his weye, Sir Otes de Grauntsoun;
þise fro Cipres cam & tille our kyng þam sped.
Whan þe saraȝins Acres nam, passand away þei fled,
how of þise ilk traytours þat Holy Kirke had schent,
felle misauentours or þei fro Dunbard went.
[I]n þe moneth of May at Berwik was Edward; [*Capital om.*]
þe first Tuesday com him tiþinges hard
þat þe erles of Scotlond had reysed baner oloft
& brent & slayn with hond Exham & Larnercost,
& Dunbar had þei seised þat standes on þe se;
þe erle Patrik was fesed, þat tyme þerin was he.
Edward also quik sent þe erle of Warenne
& þe erle of Warwik, an oste did þam bikenne.
A douhty erle in stours, Sir Hugh Despensere,
barons & vauasours, knyghtes & squiere,
& fote folk inowe þat wele couth of barete,
to Dunbar þei þam drowe, þe sege þer to sette.
Þei tirede þam to kest smertly to þe assaute;
þer to þei were alle prest, in þam was no defaute.
[175r] Þe Scottis þat were withinne þe hoped of socoure,
þe Baliol suld þam wynne out of þat soioure.
Þe Scottis now þei þenk of gile & quantise,
how þei mot do a blenk tille Edward & hise.
A knyght was þam among, Sir Richard Seward,
tille oure faith was he long & with Kyng Edward;
tille our men he com tite & said þe Scottis wilde
þre dayes haf respite & þan þe castelle ȝelde;
to þe Baliol suld þei send þer castelle to rescue.
"Bi þat bot he vs mend with for ȝow to remue,
þe castelle ȝe salle haue without any delay;
ostegers ȝe to haue our Inglis toke þat day."
A messengere þei sent to telle alle þe maners,
to þe Scottis he went & said as ȝe may here.
He com to Baliol Ion & tille alle þe oste,
bifor þam euerilkon, he spak þise wordes boste
right as Sir Richard tauht him for to say:

"Þi men er biseged hard in Dunbar with grete aye.
Whan þei fro Ingland cam, Dunbar þe toke tille hold;
to Berwik tiþing nam & tille Sir Edward told.
Edward þider sent folk, a grete partie,
doun Sir Richard went & spak to þam lufly.
Many of þam he knewe, so fair spak & so suete,
for þre days trewe þe Inglis him hete.
Whan our company wist of trewe certeyn,
tille 3ow þei bad me hie, ilka knyght & sueyn,
þis bodword to telle vnto þe treus is hote
þat 3e ne rest ne duelle for 3it no man wote.
To morn in þe none tide whan þei ere at þe mete,
þider 3e alle salle ride, a faire pray salle 3e gete.
Whan þei of þe castelle se þat 3e com so stoute,
þei ere of wille fulle fre to issue on þam oute;
þe Inglis wille not wene þat 3e be comand now,
of þo 3e salle mak clene, lap þam bituex 3ow
þat þei neuer eft rise to do 3ow more trauaile.
I knowe non oþer wise what way may 3ow auale.
Armes now 3ow alle þat non him withdrawe!
How it may best falle, I haf 3ow said þe sawe. *[In margin:]* Couwe
Whan 3e haf þe pris . of 3our enmys . non salle 3e saue.
Smyte with suerd in hand . alle Northumberland . with right salle 3e haue
& Inglond 3it alle . for werre salle . be tint for þis drede.
Scotte neuer bigan . vnto Inglis man . to do so douhty dede,
[175v] þer on þat grene . þat kynrede kene . gadred als þe gayte,
right als I wene . on som was it sene . þer þe bit bayte."
For þis mannes sawe þe route of rascaile
tille armes gan drawe & dight þam to bataile.
Richard, þat first gaf rede to þat consaile,
he sauh þam, rif & raf, comand ilka taile;
also suiþe he 3ede doun to þe Inglis men.
"I se an oste to spede, comand bi batailes ten,
& 3it me þink þer mo þat er neghand nehi;
if 3e wille, I wille go & do þam hold o drehi."
"Nay," said þe Inglis men, "we trost not on þi tunge;
þe castelle we salle biken, Sir Vmfrey Boun þe 3onge,
þat non salle passe out, nouþer þe ne þou."
Þe Inglis, armed stout, toward þe Scottis drouh;
þer stedes broched þei fast, þat myght formast he 3ede.
Þe Baliol was agast for he stode tille no dede;
for soþe at þe first, in poudre as dos þe chaf,
fleand fast þei þrist & fled, boþe rif & raf.

Was neuer non of þam þat bode wik no gode,
bot Sir Patrik Graham a while to bataile stode.
He was a man douhty, bot slayn he was fulle sone;
ten þousand & fyfti & four þer were so done.
Was neuer in no bataile so mykelle folk misferd
with so litille trauaile þat man sauh ne of herd. *[In margin:]* Couwe
Þe Scottis had no grace . to spede in þer space . for to mend þer m[i]sse,
þei filed þer face . þat died in þat place . þe Inglis rymed þis.
Oure fote folk . put þam in þe polk . & nakned þer nages.
Bi no way . herd I neuer say . of prester pages.
Purses to pike . robis to rike . & in dike þam schouue,
þou wiffin . Scotte of Abrethin . kotte is þi houue.
[T]hise erles þat I of red þat in þe castelle were *[Illuminator errs: S for T.]*
sauh þer folk not sped bot slayn alle þer here.
Whan our men out camen to þo þat left þer stille,
þei com out alle samen & ȝald þam tille our wille.
Opon þe toþer dai, Edward þider cam;
þe prisons of þer pray, alle þat euer þei nam,
were brouht him bifore, þre erles, þre barons,
& mo be fiue score, knyghtes & lordes of touns;
þise wer in his wardes, & auht & tuenti mo,
tuo clerkes, tuo Pikardes ȝit were among þo.
To þe toure of London þe þre erles were sent
& þe barons bondon also þider went;
[176r] tille oþer castels about þei sent tueye & tueye,
in aneus for doute, ilk on on his hakneye;
in kartes oþer were sent with aneus on þer fete,
þus in sorow it ent, þer gamen turned to grete.
Þorghout Inglond men said of þam schame
& þer þei were in bond, men scorned þam bi name. *[In margin:]* Couwe
Þe Scottis . I telle for sottis . & wrecchis vnwar,
vnsele . dyntis to dele . þam drouh to Dunbar.
Now is tyme to telle of þe Duȝe Pers
þat in Scotlond duelle, wille mak þer parti fers.
Ȝit held þe kyng of ffrance Gascoyn with outrage
for þat mischance of Blanche mariage;
for þat abatement, he chalanges it þorgh right,
Edward þidir had sent many a hardy knyght;
þat while þei were werand in Gascoyn euer ilkon,
þe clergi of Scotland egged þer Kyng Ion.
His barons did also for þe comon prow;
to ffrance suld he go, þe bisshop of Saynt Androw,
þer nedes forto mone, to procure an aliance

of þe Baliol sonne & Charles douhter of ffrance,
& if it myght þat weys be brouht to certeynte,
þe Scottis & Franceys togider suorn suld be,
Inglond to destroye fro Tuede vnto Kent.
Þe Frankis, withouten noye, hauen mot þei hent
in Tuede at þer wille, whan þei wild com or go
Northumberland to spille, þe folk to robbe & slo.
Right sone afterward, þe stiward of Scotland
com to Kyng Edward & brouht vntille his hand
erles & barons, bisshopes plenerly,
knyghtes, lordes of tounes, & alle com to his crie.
Kyng Ion & his sonne withouten lond or rent
er now led to London to bide þer iugement.
Now is Scotland hole at our kynges wille,
& Ion þe Baliole at London leues stille.
Right as Merlyn spak had Edward þe kyng
Scotlond als Albanak had at þe gynnyng. *[In margin:]* Couwe
Þe Walsh & þe Irish . tille our men Inglysh . halp douhtily
þat we þe Scottis had . & to prison lad . & com tille our crie;
now is alle ent . & home ere þei went . þe Iris & Wals.
God gyue at þe parlement . þe Scottis be alle schent . & hanged bi þe hals .
Edward now þenk . þei did þe a blenk . brent Hexham,
þe croice & þe rode . brent þer it stode . or þei þien nam;
[176v] now has þou myght . gyf þi dome right . þer dede is wele sene.
Els wille þei eft . on þo þat er left . bigynne newe tene;
men may merci haue . traytour not to saue . for luf ne for awe,
atteynt of traytorie . suld haf no mercie . with no maner lawe.
Ion þe Baliol . no witte was in þi pol . whan þou folie þouhtis;
to leue þe right scole . þou did als a fole . & after wrong wrouhtis;
for boule bred in his [boke] . whan he tynt þat he toke . alle his kyngdome,
for he has ouerhipped . his tippet is tipped . his tabard is tome.
Priue pride in pes es nettille in herbere, *[In margin:]* Exemplum
þe rose is myghtles þer nettille spredis ouer fer;
þe Baliol so ferd with þe Duȝe Pers.
His reame, as ȝe herd, he lost þorgh conseilers;
first he was a kyng, now is he soudioure
& is at oþer spendyng bonden in þe toure.
Edward now he wille þat Scotlond be wele ȝemed
& streitly in skille þorgh wise men demed,
þat non slo ne brenne ne eft ageyn him rise.
Sir Ion of Warenne, he is chef iustise;
Sir Henry Percy kepes Galweye.
Þise tuo had baly of þis londes tueye.

To Berwik cam þe kynge eschekere,
Sir Hugh of of Cressyngham, he was chancelere;
Walter of Admundesham, he was tresorere,
for iustise with him nam to mak þe lawe clere.
Forto norise pes, his benk he did þer crie,
shireues, balifes he ches þat office couþe guye;
of Inglis men trewe þat lufed alle þe right
he mad wardeyns newe & gaf þam alle his myght
þat Frankis no Flemmyng power suld non haue
bot forto selle þer þing, merchandise to saue,
þat to þe pes þam toke & com vnto his mercy,
he did þam suere on þe boke to com vnto his crie,
homage & feaute mad him with þer hand
at his wille to be bi se & bi sand.
Þo þat þe werre bigan & kid it so couth
were taken ilka man & sent in to þe south.
Oure men ere in Gascoyn to werre on þer enmys;
þe gode Bisshop Antoyn þer he bare þe pris.
His dedes ere to alowe for his hardynesse,
he did many on bowe in þat lond þorgh stresse;
his boldhede did þam wynne & com vnto his crie.
Were it now to gynne, we wan it not lightly.
[177r] Þise Duȝepers . com to þe freres . þam for to schriue, [*In margin:*] Couwe
þe iugement . ageyn þam went . to schorte þer liue;
Cambinhoy . beres him coy . þat fendes whelp,
þer with craft . he has þam raft . it may not help.
Þe trulle þe drenge . on se þei lenge . þe fendes tueye,
þe hold þam fer . & dar no ner . þan Orkeneye.
Andrew is wroth . þe wax him loth . for þer pride,
he is þam fro . now salle þei go . schame to betide.
Þou scabbed Scotte . þi nek þi hotte . þe deuelle it breke;
it salle be hard . to here Edward . ageyn þe speke.
He salle þe ken . our lond to bren . & werre bigynne;
þou getes no þing . bot þi riuelyng . to hang þer inne;
þe sete of þe Scone . is driuen ouer Done . to London led.
I hard wele telle . þat bagelle & belle . be filchid & fled.
Now tels Pers . on his maners . a grete selcouth.
He takis witnes . þat it soth es . of Merlyn mouth,
a wondere were . tuo watres þer er . togidir gon,
& tuo kyngdames . with tuo names . now er on;
þe ildes aboute . alle salle loute . vnto þat lond
of whilk Edward . is iustise hard . þat so þam bond.
He sais he has wonnen . & þorgh ronnen . many landes;

alle salle þei loute . tille him for doute . & dede of handes,
he sais Scotland . is in his hand . for now & ay.
At myn inwitte . it is not ȝit . alle at our fay.
He sais Merlyn . in his deuyn . of him has said
þat þre regions . in his bandons . salle be laid,
Scotland & Wales . þise er his tales . þis lond al on
was Brutus wayn . & cald Bretayn . first Albion.
I calle þerto . it is no so . þei er o sundere;
þat he has spoken . it is now broken . with mykelle wondere.
A prophecie . sais he salle die . & whan he is ouere,
after þat day . Scotlond may . haf gode recouere.
Ȝe haf wele herd . þe Brus Roberd . was Scottis kyng
wele tuenti ȝere . in gode powere . mayntend þat þing.
Als he it left . ȝit wille þei eft . rise fulle austere;
it is not alle . brouht to stalle . for no powere.
Þat Pers said . me þink it is laid . þe pes so trewe,
now ilk ȝere . bi tymes sere . þei gynne alle newe.
Ihesu so meke . I þe biseke . on croice þat was wonded,
grante me þat bone . þe Scottes sone . alle be confonded.
Atte Seynt Edmond toun þe parlement was sette,
bisshop & baroun, þe clergie alle þer mette;
[177^{v}] þe baronage holy þer þei gan alle samen,
þe kyng alle þe clergie, praied þam bi name,
if þei wild at þer myght help him bi þat weye,
als þei bifore hight in Westmynster Abbeye,
"Of help I haf grete nede, my werre is not alle ent;
to wite what ȝe me rede, I set þis parlement,
þis lond forto saue, my were to mayntene."
Þe tuelft penie to haue þei granted alle bidene,
& of merchandie þe seuent penie to haue
vnto his tresorie þe barons vouched saue.
Forto gyue answere, Roberd of Wynchelse
studied how he mot were alle his primaute.
He sent to þe kyng tuo bisshops of renoun
& schewed þat spiritualle þing þorgh pouert ȝede alle doun.
Afterward he ȝede himself to þe kyng
& said, "Sir, god forbede to greue þe ony þing.
Sir, I schewe þe here for alle Holy Kirke
þat no man has powere þerof to deme no wirke
withoute þe pape of Rome, godes vicarie.
He salle at his dome set it lowe & hie.
He has mad a statute þat vs hard byndes,
of forfeture of frute & rent þat vs fyndes,

þat tende ne tuende half no partie,
þorgh gift to non salle lende bot in his auowrie.
Opon þat he giffes a solempne cursyng
tille þo þat þeron liffes without his wittyng."
"Sir clerke," said þe kyng, "þou has said folie!
Hote is dette þing þer treuth has maistrie.
Bot if þe bulle vnfolden were red among vs here,
ȝour hote salle be holden als dette in þat manere;
þou & alle þin salle help me as ȝe hight.
Ȝour hette wille I not tyne, bi Ihesu in Marie light!"
"Sir," þe bisshop said, "fulle gladly we wille
þat our godes be laid ȝow to help at skille.
Þorgh leue of þe pape þat has of vs powere,
ȝour clerke ȝe þider rape with our messengere.
Whan þei had schewed him alle our state & ȝour askyng,
with his leue we salle help ȝow at his biddyng."
"Certis, Sir Bisshop, terme ne wille I sette
to conseile with þe pope for þing þat þou me hette.
Bot if þou wilt haf now respite in þis cas,
of ȝour hote conseile ȝow with þe clergie þat þou has,
[178r] for ȝour hote is dette als to me.
At Saynt Hillari messe at Westmynster salle be;
no lenger may I lette, me comes on ilk half werre,
of þat þat ȝe me hette gyues me þan ansuere."
"Sir," þe bisshop said, "of þis we pray þe,
þat no wikked braid of minystres þat be
tille vs, ne non of ours, ne nouht of our lay fe
be taxed with non of ȝours, grante it per charite."
"Sir Bisshop, drede þe nouht, þou salle no þing tyne;
scaþe salle non be wrouht þorgh no man of myne.
Sir Bisshop, I pray þe & þou alle holelyche
þat ȝe pray for me þorghout ȝour bisshopriche."
Ilk bisshop tille his se, whan it was don, þei went
for þe kyng & his meyne forto pray þei sent.
Þider to Saynt Edmoun com þe tresorere,
Walter of Langtoun þat had bien messengere,
with þe cardinalle forto enforme þe pes;
nouþer of som no alle ne wist what þei ches.
Bot þo þat were priue, oþer myght not witen;
tille my maister no me was not told no writen.
Ȝit com afterward oþer messengers
tille our Kyng Edward with luf & faire maners
þat contek suld not skip eft þorgh no treson

bituex him & Filip for þe lond of Gascon;
þe cardinalle was wys, ordeynd how it suld be.
Þe kyng at his auys sent messengers þre:
Sir Waltere of Langton, Sir Hugh Despensere,
Ion of Berwik was boun þe þrid messengere;
þise wist þe certeyn of alle þe kynges wille.
God bring þam wele ageyn & saue þam fro ille!
Of þe barons of Scotland at þe parlement
were non had ȝit in hand no gyuen iugement;
þo þat þorgh right dede were worþi
& atteynt, þorgh þe kyng did þam merci.
With Wales did he so & þei were neuer trewe;
whan he had most to do, þei mad him sorow newe.
Þe day of Saynt Hillari þe kyng set þam bituen;
at London certeynli his parlement to haf bien,
was brouht him þis tiþing comen fro Kaunbray,
of pes to speke no þing bot werre fro day to day.
Wherefor þe kyng wille fonde forto purueie him
trewe men bi water & londe for doute of treson grim.
[178v] He sent his day to hold of parlement þat he sette,
þe certeyn wite he wold what þe clergi him hette.
Þe bisshop of Canterbire fulle bold his ansuere was,
for him & alle his schire he vouwed to Saynt Thomas
þat no kirke of hise taliage suld non gyue,
ne do to non seruise towhile þat he mot lyue,
"without þe papes leue þat has of vs powere."
Tille his partie gan cheue þe Bisshop Oliuere;
he turned not forbi for leue ne for loth.
Þe kyng vnto þe clergi was þerfor fulle wroth
& said with euel wille despite he suld him do.
Þe bisshop said þertille, "I am redi þerto."
"Nay, Sir," said þe kyng, "þou ert not so worþi,
ne I wille for no þing be so fole hardi."
Tille þo was he so hard, out his pes did þam deme,
bot sone afterward som gan him queme.
Som of þe bisshops said þat help behoued him haue,
at skille þei wild be laid his right forto saue
& Holy Kirke defende, "Saue it & vs fro schame."
Þe bisshop of Ȝork so kende & wild do þat same;
he granted for to gyue þe fifte penie to þe kyng
in his werre wele to lyue & saue þer oþer þing.
In alle þis grete gram of þe clergi & þe kyng,
of fflandres, þe Erle William sent him a tiþing;

þorgh his conseilers a sauhtillyng wild he schewe,
with þre lordes pers of Blankmonte & of Kewe,
þe þrid messengere a lord of grete honoure
þat was þe tresorere, of fflandres resceyuoure,
of Hanaud þe erle, first bigan & alle his Henners,
þe Duke Ion of Braban with þe Holanders;
þise praied þe Erle William for þer aller sake
þat þei tille Edward nam, þe aliance to make.
Þise sent þis men & said þat þer conseile so ches,
"Þei wild tille vs be laid in gode lufe & pes
þat our merchantʒ mot go forto bie & selle
with luf withouten wo & at ʒour hauens duelle."
If he wild ageyn France reise werre & baners,
þe Flemmynges wild þat chance to be his souders
ageyn Kyng Philip & his Duʒe Pers
þat with wrong wild skip & reue him þo maners
þat þe Kyng Arthu gaf Sir Beduers,
in Gascoyn alle þoru to his botlers,
[179r] þe whilk Kyng Henry, & now his sonne Edward,
his ancestres holy haf had it afterward.
Þise teld to þe kyng alle þer lordes wille
& for þis tiþing leue ʒit þe prisons stille.
ffor þise ilk chances þat I haf of tolde
was no deliuerance of þe Scottis bolde,
nouþer as Saleberi no at Saynt Edmundes toun,
was non ʒit at þe wiri ne ʒolden for raunsoun.
Of many foule mischeue com him tiþing þikke,
bot on þer was oure greue & þat him þouh most wikke.
Þe tiþing is so nowe his courte it dos to blaken,
þe soth ilk on þei knew, Sir Ion of Saynt Ion is taken.
He kept his castels, his vitaile, his mone,
vndere þe kyng seales þe chance, listnes me.
Þe Wednesday next at euen befor Kandilmesse,
a spie did Sir Ion leue þat Frankis oste non was,
namely in þat pas þat he suld lede þam bi;
he lied, þat Iudas, ten þousand were redi.
Sir Ion mad him prest, he trost þat losengere.
His bataile was formest, displaied his banere
& passed alle þe pas þat þei alle so dred;
biside enbussed was fiften hundred, sped
in foure grete escheles, alle to batail sette.
Þe first he disconfet wele, þe toþer with him so mette
Sir Ion fulle hardely to fight did his peyn

& bad Sir Henry Lacy þat he suld turne ageyn.
"Þis oste is grete biforn, I rede þat ȝe fle!"
Þer vitaile was alle lorn, herneis & þer mone,
Sir Iames of Beauchamp wonded & may not stand;
in a water stampe he was dronkled fleand.
Sir Ion þorgh þam brast (bifore ȝe herd me neuen),
was taken at þe last & his knyghtes elleuen,
& of his squierie, gentille men auhtene;
þer pride & þer folie, I trowe, on þam was sene.
Boste & deignouse pride in ille avisement
mishapnes often tide & dos many be schent;
þe proude Kyng Pharaon þat chaced Israel
dronkeld euerilkon & godes folk went wel.
Sodom & Gomor, fulle vile synne þat stank,
boþe for euer more doun tille helle þei sank.
Dauid, þat simple was, slouh þe grete Golie;
Iacob sonne, Iudas, solde Iosep for envie;
[179v] Lucius þe emperour was slayn for couetise;
Arthur had dishonour for wronges many wise;
Modred, a fole aperte, was slayn licherie;
Cadwaldre for pouerte fled fro Bretanie;
Harald þis lond les for he was forsuoren;
Leulyn brak þe pes, his hede he lost þerforn.
Allas, non with oþer chastised ȝit wille be!
Edward, do turne þe roþer & fare ouer þe se,
& socoure þo þat are ȝit in Gascoyn left,
ne late þam not misfare, ne þer powere be reft.
Saynt Thomas salle be þi help & þi socoure,
Saynt Ion of Beuerle, Cutbert þe confessoure.
Bot þou haf help of god þorgh praiere of som saynt,
I telle not worþe a cod, for alle þi faire is faynt.
On þo þat god lufes lest mishappenyng salle falle,
þat kepe not his bihest, þei ere vngraciouse alle.
It sais in a storie (þe Bible may not lie)
þat god god gaf þe maistrie to þe childre of Mathatie;
þe Bible sais bot seuen þe were & no mo,
seuen thousand euen ageyn alle durst þei go;
þei wer stedfast & traist, lufed god & held his lawe,
folie wild þei no fraist ne to no falshede drawe;
god lufed þam & þei him, he halp þam at þer nede;
ensample I rede ȝe nym þat ȝe may so wele spede.
Þe date was a þousand, þre hundred alle bot þre;
Edward tok on hand fflandres forto se.

After þe Haly Þorsday, þe kyng sent his sond,
messengers of way for barons of þe lond,
for bisshopes þat þei kende, & oþer þat þei found
þat ilk ȝere mot dispende of londes tuenty pound,
suld com þer he was & with him mak þer frette,
or with his body pas tille Gascoyn als he sette.
Þe barons & of hise said þei suld not so
suilk a newe seruise to reise ne to do,
"For our state it apeires without any reson
& tille alle our heires grete disheriteson."
Þe barons were alle in ire & spak for þat tirpeile;
þe bisshop of Canterbire þei praied him of conseile.
Þe bisshop knewe þe right, þe wille of boþe what ment,
als Holy Kirkes knyght he com to þe parlement.
The kyng spak for his prow whan þei were alle sette:
"I am castelle for ȝow, toure, hous, & rescette,
[180r] & ȝe als naked berd loken in pauilloun
þat to fight is ferd, or ȝate þat first is doun.
My lond of Gascoyn is lorn þorgh tresons;
I may not cast essoyn bot folow my somons.
I haf mad a vowe to leue for wele ne wo.
At my nede now with me behoues ȝow go;
salle non finde encheson þorgh quantise to say,
bot þat ȝe be alle boun with me to wende þat way."
Þan ansuerd Sir Roberd, bisshop of Canterbire,
"Sir, ert þou not ferd of wreche of godes ire
þat þou wilt werre bigynne without amendment,
ageyn god don synne, ageyn Holy Kirke has went?
I rede þou mak amendes of þat grete misdede,
praye god þat alle defendes als Holy Kirke wille rede,
& bot þou do, Sir Kyng, as I conseile þe,
I salle mak cursyng on alle þat passe with þe."
After þe ersbisshop, þe erle marschalle, Rogere,
bifor þe kyng ros vp & spak tille him austere.
"Of þis we ask respite, oure conseile to take,
noþeles also tite I say for þe comon sake."
He said for þe barons þat non of þer homage
suld passe for somons bot at þe kynges costage,
ne non of þer powere to passe þe se suld grante
without conseile of pere & costage in conante.
Þe kyng his wordes toke wraþefully tille herte;
for ire nere he quoke & ansuerd him fulle smerte.
"Sir Erle, I comand þe þat þou be þe ton,

for þou salle wende with me whedere þou wille or non
or þin office forgo of þe marschalcie;
respite I gyue no mo bot mak alle redie."
Þe erle, "Wend I nouht so sone myn office lete.
I haf not ȝit so wrouht to haf maugre þe grete."
Out of þe courte he went, duellid he no while.
Þe kyng for on sent, Sir Geffrey Geneuile,
& of þe marschalcie presented him þe ȝerde,
bad arme him priuelie, & priues alle herde.
Now tille armes þat may als þei suld lyue or deie,
þei hoped þe toþer day þe barons resteie;
þe erle wist it sone, in him was no defaute,
þe barons were alle bone to mak þe kyng assaute.
Right als þe parties togider suld haf smyten,
Sir Antoyn was wys, he did þe kyng to witen
[180v] what perille salle betide if þei & his barons
& werre togidere ride als enmys felons;
to þe barons he ȝede & praied þam to bowe.
"Þe kyng to ȝow has nede, help him if ȝe mowe;
if him com any scaþe, tinselle of seignorie,
tille ȝow it wille be waþe; leues alle þis folie."
The barons at þe last tille Antoyn gaf ansuere
of þing þat þei wild ask, bad him þe copie bere,
& said to Saynt Albans þider wild þei com
to parlement alle at ans & stand to right dome.
If he & his conseile to þam wild him meke,
þei wild him auaile & do þat he wild biseke.
Sir Antoyn turned ageyn & schewed him þer assent
if he wild hold certeyn þe day of parlement.
Þe kyng wild not, þider ouer þe se wild he fare
to wite where & whidere þe ferd his frendes þare,
withouten rede of mo in schip to Flandres went;
non erle wild with him go, for baron non he sent.
His folie was þe more þat he non with him toke;
suilk tiþing sauh he þore, fulle fayn fro Brigges schoke.
Now is Edward ariued in Flandres bot with fo;
with his barons he striued, with him wild non go.
A kyng þat striues with hise, he may not wele spede;
whore so he restis or riues, he lyues ay in drede.
His vitaile he has purueid in Brigges forto be;
his wynes were þer leid & warnised þat cite.
God þat wote alle þing what is don or whi,
he saue Edward our kyng þore þorgh his merci!

Bituex þe kyng of ffrance & þe Erle William
was þat tyme a distance, a wrath bituex þam nam;
þe prouest of þe toun, a wik traytour & cherle,
he þouht to do tresoun vnto his lord þe erle.
To Philip priuely a letter did he make,
if he had oste redy, Brigges mot he take;
com what tyme he wild, þe toun suld he wynne,
þe comon he suld him ȝelde & Edward þerinne.
Edward mot he haue if he wild him rape,
þe toun he suld so saue þat he suld not ascape.
Of þis whan Philip herd, oste he did sone ȝare.
Þat tyme þat he forth ferd, he [herd] not of his fare. *[Letters blotted.]*
Þe preuest with þe burgeis [þat d]ay to conseile ȝede;
Edward herd it say, of gil[erie a]s som drede
[181r] & oþer were perceyued, þat þer ȝede disceite;
bot ȝit was it not reyued, so Edward þouht him streite.
A child of þat land, þat knew not Sir Edward,
Edward sauh him stand þe Fle þe Flemmynges to reward;
fast he gan behald þe samenyng of Flemmynges.
Edward child cald & asked him tiþinges,
"Sonne, what hers þou say of burgeis of cite?"
He said, "Sir, grete aye þat þe Inglis here in be,
& for þe Inglis sake tille it wille falle hard,
for þe Frankes hope take þe toun & Sir Edward."
Sir Edward also sone þer gile gan he knowe,
dight him to bataile bone, his trumpes did he blowe.
Þe Flemmynges vndirstode þe kyng warned was,
þe cheynes & ȝates gode þei sperd þat non mot pas;
þe Walsch without þe toun, euerilkon þei lay,
þat was þe enchesoun for fight & for affray.
Whan þei þe trumpes herd þat he to bataile blewe,
& saw þe ȝates sperd, þan gamened þam no glewe.
"Ouh for Saynt Dauy, þe Flemmyng wille him gile!"
Þe kest alle suilk a crie þat men mot here a myle;
fire & brondes þei nam in houses of þer gatis,
& ouer þe water suam & set fire on þe ȝatis;
maugre þe Flemmynges, on þam þe ȝatis þei brent,
cheynes þei hew & rynges, & tille Sir Edward went
& fond him alle redy armed on his stede.
Was no cheyne so hie þat he ne sprong ouer als glede
& comandid ilk man to schip suiþe to go;
þorgh þe Flemmynges he ran & manyon did slo.
His stede was blak as rauen, þei kald his name Feraunt;

he rode vnto þe hauen & said he wild to Gaunt.
Vnneþis fro þat felons ascaped he þat wo,
if he had had his barons, he had not gyuen of þo.
Þe kyng of Almayn had hight him his help;
he mad a fals trayn, of him is not to ȝelp.
He sent Edward to say help him mot he nouht;
werrand on ilk a way his enmys on him souht.
(Allas, þat a kyng es fals ageyn his pere!)
Edward dred him no þing bot was ay glad of chere.
An erle þer was of Bare, he werred fast on France;
þe Walsch with him war ȝare forto do mischance,
þer markettis, & þer faires, & [þer ca]stels reft; [*Blotted*.]
now alle þe cuntre peir[es], vnneþis ouht þei left.
[181v] Philip on his partie did þe erle grete tene;
alle þat he mot com bie, he robbed alle bidene.
Þe bisshop of Durhem trauailed day & nyght,
of strife to felle þe stem, þe pes to mak alle right,
bot Philip was ay hard, his ansuere euer so light.
His wist þat Edward had bot litelle myght;
has he had his erles, his barons with him lad,
of alle þe Frankis cherles þe maistrie suld he haf had.
A man þat beris him stoute whan þat he suld bowe,
in chance if þat he loute, he findes foos inowe.
Listnes now þis pas whi þat I þus said,
in wham defaut was þat þertille may be laid.
Gestes þat er olde, writen of many man,
þritti reames men told þat Kyng Arthur wan.
He parted his wynnyng tille his men largely
þat nouþer erle ne kyng wille withsitte his cry;
þei were at his wille were he neuer so hie,
boþe of gode & ille at alle his nede redie.
Oure kyng, Sir Edward, ouer litille he gaf,
tille his barons was hard, ouerhipped þam ouerhaf.
He wild not be so hende, so large, no so fre;
þerfor þei lete him wende alon ouere þe se.
Þorgh þat wendyng alon, nere he had bien schent;
it was to mak of mone þat non erle with him went.
Þorgh tiþing brouht bi tide, þe Scottis wist of þis;
ilk Scotte on his side mad þerof ioy & blis.
Þe rascail of þer route bigan to werre alle newe;
now Edward is oute, þe barons be not trewe.
Þe suffred, as it sais, þe Scottis eft to rise,
& William þe Walais, þer hede & þer iustise,

þorgh fals concelement, William did his wille;
our castels has he brent, our men slayn fulle ille.
Sir Hugh of Crissengham he did nycely & mys:
þe tresore with him he nam, sperd it in his coffris,
& wild gif no wages to þe folk þer ware;
þerfor ȝomen & pages home gan alle fare.
Whan Sir Ion of Warenne þe soth vnderstode
þat þe Waleis gan brenne, an oste he gadred gode
& went to Striuelyne agayn Waleis William.
Bot þe erle with mykelle pyne disconfite away nam,
& þat was his folie, so long in his bed gan ligge
vntille þe Waleis partie had vmbilaid þe brigge.
[182r] With gauelokes & dartes, suilk ore was non sene,
myght no man þam departe, ne ride, ne go bituene,
þore first þam tauht how þei did Fawekirke;
alle gate þe brigge he rauht, of nouht our men were irke.
Whan þe erle herd say þe brigge how William toke,
he douted to die þat day, þat bataile he forsoke;
þe Inglis were alle slayn, þe Scottis bare þam wele;
þe Waleis had þe wayn als maistere of þat eschele.
At þat ilk stoure was slayn on our side
god men of honour þat wald to þe bataile bide,
Sir Robert of Somervile & his eldest sonne,
he held þe stoure a while for dede ne wild he schonne,
& knyghtes & sergeantȝ, noble men fulle couth,
of prowes fulle valiantȝ boþe bi north & south.
Sir Hugh of Cressyngham in armes nouht ne deih,
for ridyng lauht he skam, out of his sadelle he fleih;
his stede ouer him ran, he lay vnder his fete.
Þat sauh þe Scottis man & þerof wele he lete,
he & oþer inowe þat Sir Hugh wele knewe.
(I wene þei quik him flouh & his lymmes to hewe.)
Sir Marmeduk of Thuenge in þe felde bare þe flour,
with þe Scottis gan he menge & stifly stode in stour;
fightand he couerd alle weys þe castelle of Striuelyn,
maugre þe Waleys, Sir Marmeduk went in.
After þis bataile, þe Scottis sent ouer þe se
a boye of þer rascaile, quaynt & doguise,
to Flandres bad him fare þorgh burgh & cite,
of Edward whore he ware bring þam certeynte,
& whan he com ageyn, he teld þam þis tiþing
þat sothly & certeyn dede was Edward þe kyng,
& to þat stede he ferd þer he was laid in graue;

þe Scottis, whan þei it herd, more ioy ne bad þei haue.
To werre þan ros þei eft, tille god þei mad a vowe
þat no þing suld be left þat myght to Inglond prowe.
Mercy suld non haue, tille alle þei suld do wo,
kirke suld no man saue bot brenne þerin & slo.
In Northumberland þer first þei bigan
& alle þat com tille hand þei slouh & ouer ran.
To fflandres tille Edward tiþinges men him sent
þat Scottis com in hard, "Þe north is nere alle brent
& more salle ȝit be lorn bot if we haf socoure.
Nouht standes þam biforn, toun, castelle, ne toure."
[182v] Þe kyng for þo tiþinges was noyed greuoslie;
to conseil þo lordynges he cald þat wer him bi.
Whan þei had alle cast þer conseil vp & doun,
þe kyng was at þe last avised on þis reson
þat nede behoued him grante to clerke & baroun,
& hold þam þe conante of ilk peticioun.
Bi letter he þam sent & grantid þer askyng,
alle þat reson ment of ilk maner þing.
Bi letter & bi mouth he praied þam of socoure
& þat he myght & couth þat were to þer honoure,
he granted at þer wille if þei wild socoure him
ageyn þe Scottis ille þat bere þam now so brim.
The bisshop of Canterbire þerof payed was he,
for him & alle his schire þis gift gaf fulle fre;
to saue þe pape statute þat þem bihoued defende,
of Holy Kirkes frute he gaf þe kyng þe tende,
gadred with clerkis hand & kept to þat viage,
wendand to Scotland, biteched it þe baronage,
þe lond forto saue & Holy Kirkes dignite.
Þis grantid he þam to haue, Roberd of Wynchelse,
þe clergie of þe north þe fifte peny suld gyue,
whan þe barons ferd forth in pes þat þei mot lyue,
& grantid þamself at þe first gynnyng
whan þe kyng asked half of alle þer moble þing.
Now er at on assent þe barons & þe clerkis;
þe Scottis hold þam schent, of þer conseil now herkis.
Þe Scottis vnderstode þat holy þe clergie
were alle in wille gode to help þe kynges partie,
& þe barons also in luf with him wild dele,
for he had grantid þerto þe chartre forto sele;
& after þat selyng alle suld þei come,
þe barons & þe kyng, & tak of þam hard dome.

What did þe Scottis þo bot þis conseil þei ches:
to Striuelyn suld þei go in manere of pes,
Sir Marmeduk biseke, his wrath forto asuage,
& to þam mak him meke for luf & for ostage;
þei suore þer cristendam, if þat he wild com oute,
withouten any gram, tille þei wild loute,
boþe loude & stille, in nesch & in hard,
& to pes with gode wille ȝeld þam tille Edward.
Sir Marmeduk out cam, he trosted on þer fayth;
to him & his þei nam and smertly did þam grayth
[183r] toward Dun Bretayn & him in prison þer sperd.
His frendes were vnfayn for non wist how he ferd;
þei did þat treson, if þam felle any chance,
for him þei mot eftson of þers mak deliuerance.
Þe clergie of þe south mad a disputesoun
& openly with mouth assigned gode resoun
þat scathe ne mot bifalle, ne forto wrath þe pape,
"Bot for him & vs alle myght it better schape."
In alle þis spekyng com þe tresorere
fro Edward, our kyng, to schewe þe chartere here.
He spak vnto þe clergie: "Ȝe barons þat here be,
þe kyng fulle curteislie gretis ȝow wele bi me
& sais þat he wille Inglond alle ese,
& þat ȝe ask in skille, ȝour hertes forto pese,
þe chartre of franchise conferm it ȝow he salle,
& of þe first assise, as his fader gaf it alle."
Þe chartre was red on hi in Westmynstere & schewed
ilk poynt, bi & bi, to lerid & to lewed.
Þe bisshop of Canterbire, in comon alle o liche,
schewed it in ilk schire, alle his bisshopriche.
Whan þei þe chartre in alle had schewed day bi day,
Sir Roger, þe Erle Marschalle, of Herford þe Erle Vmfray,
at Ȝork þei tok on hand þer parlement to sette;
þe hie folk of þe land þer alle togidere mette.
Þe Erle Ion of Surray com with grete powere;
of Gloucestre, stoute & gay, Sir Rauf þe Mohermere
& his wif, Dame Ione, whilom Gilberdes of Clare;
þo banerettis ilkone fro Douer to Durham ware.
At þe kirke of Saynt Petir þe day of Saynt Agnes,
þe bisshop on his mitere, of Carlele, it says,
he stode vp in pulpite þe office forto do;
þer chartre he red it bituex þe erles tuo,
& cursed alle þo þat þe chartre brak

or stroied, or did ouht fro ony poynt þerin spak.
After þis sentence gyuen, tille armes alle þat myght,
was it no lenger dryuen, to Scotlond alle þam dight;
in alle Northumberland þer þe Waleis had bene,
alle was in þe kynges hand, þe Scottis wer non sene.
In alle þis nesch & hard, euer lasted þe distance
bituex Kyng Edward & þe kyng of ffrance,
bot [it w]as delaied tille a day certeyn [*Letters are missing*.]
of right dome set & saied how pes mot be pleyn;
[183v] þei consentid boþe, þorgh conseil of þe pape,
to pese þam tuo wroþe, with sight he wild schape
þorgh mariages, was hopyng of þe pes,
þat were þe certeyn stages þat boþe parties ches.
Þe kyng on suld haue, a may was in spekyng,
tille his sonne suld men saue Philip douhter ȝing.
In alle þis ordenance, our kyng sent messengers
þat kewe þe greuance, wyse men, barons, pers,
vnto þe courte of Rome, þe pape to schew þat cas,
how wondere chances come & who did most trespas,
of Inglis & Frankis who was most culpable,
in þe pape leues alle þis to mak mende & mak alle stable.
To while Pape Boniface duellid opon þis
to gyue dome þorgh grace to mende boþe þer mys,
þe kyng tok his consaile & home to Ingland went,
gode wynde in his saile Ihesu criste him lent.
Þe erles of Scotlond þat atteynt wer of treson,
þe kyng himself willand deliuerd þam fro prison;
þise were of þer gest, as I kan names fynde:
þe erle of Menetest was of Edward kynde;
þe erle of Ascetelle, Sir Ion þe Comyn,
Badenauh sonne, I telle, & þretty of þer couyn.
Alle þise, & wele mo atteynt of traytorie,
þe kyng lete þam go of his curteisie
withouten siluere or golde or any oþer treuage;
þer penance was þei suld go in pilgrimage.
Here of þis wikked hals þat our kyng gaf leue:
to France þei ȝede, þo fals, to Philip wild þei cheue,
bisouht him of socoure & auancement;
to maynten þam in stoure, þei mad hir þer present,
Scotlond of him to hold euer withouten ende
if he in luf wold as lord vnto þam lende.
Philip gaf respons & bad þam go þer way.
"Ȝe ere foles Bretons, disceit is þat ȝe say!

Þe pape me defendes with bulle þat bindis hard;
to renne on þo landes þat longes tille Edward
to whils þat oure trewe duellis on iugement,
for me salle neuer be newe, no fals compassement."
Confused, þei went away, þat fals companie;
þei failed of þer pray, to hauen gan þei hie
& hired þam a schip, gaf siluere largelie;
to Scotlond gan þei skip, þe wynde was þam redie.
[184r] Edward vnderstode þorgh oft heryng say
how þe fals blode compassed tene & tray.
He mad his pilgrimage to Saynt Thomas of Kent,
siþen north on his viage to Beuerley he went.
Bifor Saynt Ion he woke a nyght or he þien nam,
to Ȝork þe gate he toke & souht Saynt William;
Saynt Cutbert he souht to help him at his nede,
siþen he dred him nouht, northward als he ȝede;
northward in his weie, he held his parlement,
to speke & to purueie, to be of on assent,
to Scotlond forto go to take vengement
of þam his folk did slo, destroied his tenement,
& how þei were alle lorn þat com to þat couent;
for þei were forsuorn, vengeance on þam went.
Þe date was a þousand, þre hundred alle bot one;
at ffoukirke in Scotlond, Scottis escapid none.
On þe Maundeleyn day, a litelle bifor Lammesse,
of Scotlond & Galway com mykelle folk alle fresse;
of þe Marche & þe Ildes a spere þei suld bring.
Þei com, þe lond to schilde, to ffaukirke in þe mornyng;
our Inglis men & þei þer togidere mette,
þer formast conrey þer bakkis togidere sette;
þer speres, poynt ouer poynt, so sare & so þikke,
& fast togidere ioynt, to se it was ferlike.
Als a castelle þei stode þat were walled with stone,
þei wende no man of blode þorgh þam suld haf gone.
Þer folk was so mykelle, so stalworth, & so clene,
þer foyntes forward prikelle, nouhut wild þei wene,
þat if alle Inglond, fro Berwik vnto Kent,
þe folk þerin men fond had bien þider sent,
stength suld non haf had to perce þam þorghoute,
so wer þei set sad with poyntes rounde aboute.
Þe kyng sauh þam comand so sadly in þe mede,
his folk he did withstand & dight þam alle to dede;
siþen he to þam said, "Go we þer god vs spede!"

Þer lances alle forth laid & ilk man broched his stede,
þei sauh kynges banere, raumpand þre lebardes;
þer hors folk alle plenere, þei fled as fals cowardes,
þe fotefolk left alon if þei wild stand or fle.
Help had þei non of þam þer hede suld be;
þus þe Waleis wrouht & said þan þis bi skille,
"To þe renge ere ȝe brouht, hop now if ȝe wille!"
[184^{v}] Þer scheltron sone was shad with Inglis þat were gode;
pite of non þei had, bot alle to dede ȝode.
Als fleihes doun þei fleih, ten þousand at ones;
to stand non ne degh bot felle doun als stones.
Bituex prime & none alle voide was þe place,
þe bataile slayn & done alle within þat space.
Was no man Inglis maynhed no dede þat day
bot a templer of pris, Sir Brian þe Geay,
maister templere he was on þis half þe se.
He folowed þe Scottis pas, whan þe bigan to fle,
fer in tille a wod, men calle it Kalenters;
þer in a mire, a mod, withouten help of fers,
slouh þei Sir Brian alon withouten mo.
(Allas, þat douhty man þat he so fer suld go!)
Þe Walsch folk þat tide did nouþer ille ne gode;
þei held þam alle biside, opon a hille þei stode,
þer þei stode þat while tille þe bataile was don.
Was neuer withouten gile, Walsh man no Breton,
for þei were euer in wehere, men so of þam told,
whilk was best banere, with þat side forto hold.
Saynt Bede sais it for lore, & I say it in ryme:
Walsh man salle neuer more luf Inglis man no tyme.
After þis bataile, þe kyng turned ageyn;
ouer þat fals pedaile he ordeynd a wardeyn
þat held þam in suilk awe þei durst no more rise;
þorgh smerthed of þe law, he did þam iustise.
He ȝared his his wendyng, to London gan him rape;
þider him com tiþing, lettres fro þe pape,
& bad þat he suld take þe kyng sister of ffrance,
for Gascoyn pes to make þorgh þat aliance,
not Dame Blanche, þe suete, þat I first of spake,
bot Dame Margarete, gode withouten lak.
Þe papes maundement he resceyued curtasly;
bi tyme þat it were ent, he dight þerto redy,
in purueiance of alle as he had most to don.
So com þe erle marschalle baitand to London;

of Herford, þe Erle Vmfray also com he þidere,
& oþer barons of nobley, & alle samned togidere.
Þe erle for þam alle with luf bisouht þe kyng
of poyntis behoued falle, do þam at þer praying.
"Withoute any delay, do mak þe purale
be a certeyn day, Sir, þat pray we þe."
[185r] Þe kyng wild his myght, delaied it were alle weys,
noþeles semand bi sight his ansuere was curteys.
He schewed þe Erle Rogere þe papes mandement,
he myght on no manere do nouht or it were ent;
bot he suore on his fayth, & certeynly þan hete,
whan it were don in grayth, þe weddyng of Margarete,
to mak þe purale it suld not be delaied;
with suilk men suld it be þat þei suld hald þam paied.
So faire with his respons, so faithfulle þei bisemed,
boþe erles & barons his wordes alle þei quemed.
Þe Erle Vmfray þat was, for euer tok his leue;
þe dede him slouh, allas, tille his pers it gan greue.
The pape þan sent his bulle vnt Philip of ffrance;
þe curte of Rome fulle has ordand aliance
þat þe Kyng Edward suld wed Margarete,
& in þat ilk forward þer werryng suld þei lete
foreuer in Gascoyn of alle maner of skille.
Without any essoyn, Philip grantid þertille;
Philip for þat may mad purueiance redy
with folk of gode aray, to Douer com in hy,
& þer oure Inglis men resceyued fulle miry;
þe barons alle with blis brouht hir to Canterbiri,
& as þe courte of Rome had ordeynd þat spousale,
right opon þat dome he wedded hir sanȝfaile.
Robert of Wynchelse, þat corseynt is verray,
did þat solempnite opon a Wednesday
next þe lattere fest þat is of our lady.
Þe Wednesday formest, þe kyng had fulle grete hy,
for on þe morn he went his way toward Scotland.
With ille auisement he did, & þat he fand,
whan he was in þe Marche, he samned his oste;
þan was it bot a parche & litelle with þe loste,
for himself alone toke þat viage,
help asked he none of alle his baronage;
þat was for þe purale þat he had þam hette,
he wild not do þer gre þat terme þat he sette.
Þe Scottis wist þat wele & schewed him þe vis;

þer side was ilka dele in poynt to wynne þe pris.
Boldely þei bed bataile with visage fulle austere,
þe kynges side gan faile for he had no powere;
ferrere mot he nouht Scotlond forto se,
þat tyme no þing he wrouht bot spendid his mone.
[185v] Þe Marche vnder wardeyn he left als it was ore;
vnto þe south ageyn he went & did no more.
Whi þat he not sped þis skille mot it be,
with hauelon þam led to mak þe purale.
The kyng after þe Pask his messengere sent
for þe bisshopes askis to com to þe parlement;
for erles & barons, at London suld it be,
four kyghtes be somons chosen in ilk counte.
First þe nemnid alle þo þe purale suld make,
þat þorgh þe reame suld go, þe boundes forto stake.
Whan it wer brouht tille ende & stabled & sette,
to gyue þe penie tuentende, þe kyng þer þei hette.
Þis was þe toþer roson men þan suld þei ȝare,
for þe lond of Gascon to Rome forto fare
to wite at þe pape why he mad delay;
þe tyme he wild not rape, no set a certeyn day
þat Edward suld haue þe lond of Gascoun,
his seignorie to saue als it was resoun.
Now was þis þe þridde of þat parlement,
for chance þat him bitidde, þe kyng þus þam bisent.
"I praie ȝow in þis nede to help me with ȝour oste;
þe Scottis on me bede, I wild abate þer boste."
To maynten his partie, þei hete to help him wele;
he aiorned þam to relie in þe north at Carlele.
After midesomers tide, þorgh comon ordinance,
no lenger suld þei bide bot forth & stand to chance.
Norreis & Surreis þat seruise auht þe kyng
with hors & herneis at Carlele mad samnyng;
þe erle marschalle, Rogere, no hele þat tyme not haue,
he went with his banere, Sir Ion þe Segraue,
to do alle þo seruise þat longed þe office tille
& mayntend alle þe prise þer he sauh lawe & skille.
Þe Quene Margerete with childe þan was sche,
þe kyng bad hir not lete bot com to þe north cuntre
vnto Brotherton on Wherfe, þer scho was
& lighter of a sonne, þe child hight Thomas.
Whan þe kyng herd say sho had so wele farn,
þider he went way to se hir & hir barn,

& with hir he soiorned tille sho was purified
þan eft agayn he turned & tille his ost hied.
Þe quene with hir sonne at Cawod leues she
tille tyme com eftson, on Ouse fulle ese.
[186r] At Karlele is þe kyng with erles & barons;
þer þei mad spekyng to renne on þer felons,
bot som of þam þat ware, conseild oþer manere,
þorgh pastours forto fare for bestes to lardere;
men said, "Þer were inowe in mores & in medis
& if ȝe wille, we mowe of bestis do gode nedis."
Þe cuntre herd it seie, þe folk of ilk a schire
had þer bestis aweie þorgh mede & þorgh mire
þat no strange man knewe ne myght so go;
þer to þe rayne bigan & flowand bank & bro,
it ran doun on þe mountayns & drenkled þe playnes.
Sir Edward sauh þo paynes and tok þe gate agayn;
þe more h forsoke, þe fote men ilk a flok,
a pouere hamelete toke, þe castelle Karelauerok.
In alle þis grete pres praied þe kyng of ffrance
þe Scottis suld haf pes þorgh Edward sufferance;
vnto þe messengere þat Philip to him sent,
he gaf þe treus a ȝere & þan to London went.
ffeyntise, liþt duellyng, on mornes long to lie,
surfeyte in euenyng & luf of licchorie,
affiance of feloun, of enmys haf pite,
wille without resoun, conseile of wise men fle,
wynnyng forto hold, & gyue not largely,
þe Bretons, men of told, forsoke suilk party.
Of Arthure, men say þat rede of him in pas,
alle tymes in medle euer more first he was,
mornyng & euenyng sobre & honest,
felons þat wild him greue, or enmys þat mad chest,
als he was worþi had he iugement.
Had he of non merci, for praiere no present,
at conseil & at nede he was a skilfulle kyng;
so curteis of non, men rede, ne prince of more praysing,
was non in cristendam als he was in his tyme,
ne suilk on ȝit non cam þat man may mak of ryme.
I told ȝow þis resoun & for ensample sette,
if þe kyng wild haf don þe purale als he hette,
þorghout Inglond, enselid & with scrite,
bi tyme had mad þat bond & drawen it not o lite,
it had bien his heires prowe, þe lond had bien alle his

long tyme or now þat now in auenture is.
Þe date a þousand was & þre hundred euen;
at Lincoln þe parlement was in Lyndesay & Kesteuen.
[186v] At þe Pask afterward his parlement set he,
þe gode Kyng Edward at Lyncoln his cite;
at Sant Katerine hous þe erle marschalle lay,
in þe brode gate lay þe Brus, erle was he þat day;
þe kyng lay at Netilham, it is þe bisshopes toun,
& oþer lordes þer cam in þe cuntre vp & doun.
Erles & barons at þer first samnyng
for many maner resons pleyned of þe kyng
þat þe purale did not als he suld,
ne þer chartre gaf fre, þe poyntes vse ne wuld,
ne suffre þam to hold þat þe chartre of spake,
þorgh mayntenours bold þe poyntes alle þei brake.
ȝit þei said him tille, his ministres wasted þe lond,
tak þing out of skille & pay not with hond;
& ȝit þei mad pleynt of his tresorere
þat fele þinges atteynt, "He mayntend þorgh powere,
fordos vsages olde & lawes of þe chekere;
of many has it bien tolde, to þe we pleyn vs here
him forto remue þorgh comon assent.
Assigne it for more prow at þis parlement
þat can þat office guye & do þe right vsage,
þat no man thar eft crie for wrong & outrage."
Þe kynges ansuere was smert & said, "I se þhe wille
þorgh pride of hert reuile me with vnskille,
& so lowe me to chace, myn officers to change
& mak þam at ȝour grace, þat were me ouer strange!
It is non of ȝow þat he ne wille at his myght
haf sergeanȝ for his prow withouten oþer sight.
Salle no man put þorgh skille his lord lowere þan he,
ne I ne salle no wille to while I kyng salle be.
If any of myn mad strife or tak þing not right,
stiward or balife, schewe þer wrong þorgh sight,
þat wrong I wille so mende, if þat it be atteynt,
þat non thar com no sende to courte to mak eft pleynt.
Þe chartre þorgh resoun & þe purale,
þei fordo my croune if þei granted be,
þe whilk ȝe salle & ouh to maynten with me;
to mak it lesse no louh ne peired salle it be.
Of þis I grant to morn þat ȝe trie þis þing,
with sex & tuenti suorn, if I to ȝour askyng

may acorde right wele þe coroune forto saue,
dismembred not a dele, ȝour askyng salle ȝe haue.
[187r] Anoþer, I am withoute of penie in tresorie.
Mi lond withouten doute salle help me a partie."
The wisest of þe clergie with erles & barons
togider went to trie of þer peticions;
þo sex & tuenti ȝede þat were suorn þertille,
of ilk doute & drede þei said & set þe skille.
Discharged wille þei be of þe grete oth þei suore
perille forto fle, þe poyntes were so store;
þe sent ageyn & said, "To kyng it was no haunte
of certeyn sette & laid to trechet þer conaunte,
no tille prince no kyng it is no maner told
to mak eft lokyng, ne deme þat dere was sold.
Sir, fairere þe wore graunte vs þi curteysie
þan parties pinched more, þe auantage set so hie;
þat þou may gyue with right whan þou wille & how,
þat salle not be þorgh sight demed of lesse þan þou.
Put þe not so louh to deme þi power fre;
ȝeld vs þat þou ouh & we salle luf þe,
& serue þe we wille alle at þin avis,
& help þe at skille to renne on þin enmys."
He sent þam bode ageyn, schortely to say & here,
þer prayere was in veyn, to ese þam in no manere.
His wille & his auise þat he asked certeyn,
þei ȝede be partise, disputed þer ageyn;
þe parties wer so felle altercand on ilk side
þat non þe soth couth telle whedir pes or werre suld tide.
Bot god þat is of myght & may help whan he wille,
for for boþe þe parties dight & put þam in þis skille
þat or Michelmesse þei suld reise to þe kyng
þe fiftend penie, no lesse, for þer chartre selyng,
& for þe purale set with certeyn bounde
þorgh þe lond suld be delaied no lengere stounde.
On þat þei grantid & abated alle þer þro;
whan þe kyng wild þam calle, to Scotlond suld þei go.
Ȝit our messengrs for Gascoyn were at Rome,
foure lordes fulle fers, to here þe papes dome.
Þe foure at Rome ware to areson þe pape,
þe right forto declare, & for þe parties so schape
to whom þe right suld be of Gascoyn euer & ay,
& þorgh his decre þe pes pronunce a day.
Þe Pape Boniface tok Philip messengers

& ours in o place, sette þam to mete als pers,
[187v] & preched to þam alle als þei sat in fere.
"Lordyng, þus salle falle as I salle say here.
Men say in ȝour tuo londes ere men of grete resoun
& wele vnderstondes & knowes þer enchesoun;
þo ilk men so wise suld go & enforme ȝour kynges
withouten mo iustise or trauaile of oþer lordynges;
þerfore gos ageyn & tille ȝour kynges say,
bot þei with luf certeyn acorde in euen way,
& if þei ne do, be Saynt Petir of Rome,
our courte salle ordeyn so on þam so hard dome,
at þe next feste þat comes of Saynt Andrew,
þat þei & alle þer geste þat dome salle doute & rew."
Þe messengers þei ȝede, bare þei with þam no more;
I turne ageyn to rede of þe parlement we spak ore.
The kyng gaf his sonne at þe parlement
Wales in to wonne & Chestreshire to rent,
Mustrelle & Pountif þat er biȝond þe se.
Prince he was vp rif & erle also was he,
of him þat held þer londes, þei mad him alle homage.
To Scotlond now he fondes to redy his viage
with þritti þousand Walsh redy at his banere,
erles & barons als, boþe knyght & squiere.
Alle com to Carlele to conseil how were best
to passe þe Scottis se wele to tak toward þe west.
His fader also ȝede & chese þe est side,
at Berwik opon Tuede his oste did þer bide.
Als þei were alle plenere to counseil & to schape,
so com a messengere fro Boniface þe pape,
þe bisshop of Spolete with a newe ordinance.
Anoþer him gan mete, comand fro þe kyng of France.
(I herd neuer telle for what maner discert;
þeron I most nede duelle tille it come out aperte.)
Þe kyng has þe letter in hand to trowe þat þei said;
þe werryng in Scotland now is delaied & laid.
Ho com to Linliscow & did þer crie his pes,
& teld his barons how þat nede behoued him ses;
siþen he & his sonne turned toward þe south,
þe Marche, als it was wonne, keped wardeyns couth.
Þe turned to London, of þe treus to speke,
& feythly þerto bondon, on no manere to breke;
vnto þe terme fortold of Saynt Andrew messe,
þe pape did him hold with gode sikernesse.

[188r] Þe pape set þat terme, for his hopyng was
þe pes þei suld afferme for drede of hardere kas.
Kyng Philip of ffrance had Erle William,
a cheson for a chance (I ne wote whi it cam),
Charles to William hette he suld him sauely lede
vnto þe parlement, sette ageyn withouten drede.
Whan William was comen & wende no tresoun,
sone was he nomen & don in prisoun;
now is þe erle þus schent, bondon in iren & stele.
Philip to fflandres sent & sesid it ilk a dele,
& mad suilk wardeyns in his name to be
destroied at þe geyns, þat þei mot fynd or se,
defoules þer wyues, þer douhtres lay bi,
þer lordes slouh with knyues, of fo had þei merci.
Þe tounes spak of þis, þe folk gadred aboute;
to renne on þe Frankis þei samned gret route.
Þei folowed on þam hard þorghout þat cuntre
þat Frankis & Pikard alle were fayn to fle;
þo þat fleih, þei ferd vnto þe kyng of ffrance.
Þe kyng he it herd, tak he wille vengeance
of knyght and of burgeis, an oste he did relie,
bitauht it þe erle of Arteys þat oste forto guye.
He did þer no prow, he was first was doun.
A foule herlote him slowe (trut for his renoun!)
& oþer withouten numbir, þer names I may not telle.
Alle þei ȝede tille encumbir & er went to helle;
of Huneys er þei clene, Pikard & Burgoilloun,
of Bascel & Viene, of Braban & Bretoun;
þat tyme no at anoþer had þe Frankis no foisoun.
Þei & alle þe toþer, þe Flemmynges laid þam doun;
þat schame has ȝit non ende, no þat vpbraidyng,
þat on ffrance salle lende for falsnes of þer kyng.
Now salle we turne ageyn tille our owen lessoun;
whan Charles courte is pleyn, I gyue it my malisoun.
Þe date was euenlik a þousand, þre hundred & tuo,
whan þe erle of Karrik turned þe Scottis fro.
Sir Vmfrey Boun þe kyng his wife wedded þat ȝere,
Edward douhter þe kyng, Eliȝabeth þat clere.
In alle þise spekynges, men ȝede þat were wise,
bituexen þise tuo kynges þat no contek suld rise,
bot contene forth þe trew vnto þe Paskes terme
fro þe Saynt Andrew, so long þe pes to afferme.
[188v] Of þis þe kyng of ffrance praied Sir Edward

þat with his sufferance & leue in forward,
suffre þe Scottis to go, þat men þat he for sent;
þe kyng tille alle þo gaf leue & þei alle went.
ffor perille of suilk goynges, þe kyng purueid to go
Sir Ion of Hastynges, he was first of þo,
& Sir Emery þe Brette, to Goscoyn forto wende
to bide þe terme sette, þe treus how it suld ende.
Þe Inglis men were wone to wery long trayne,
of bataile better cone, lite was alle þer payne;
dishonour haf þei ay of þer long respite.
I spak þis for a day þe Scottis assailed þam tite,
our men in Scotland with sautes sodeynly;
þe Segraue myght not stand, Sir Ion tok þe gayn stie.
His sonne & his broþer, of bedde als þei woke,
& sextene knyghtes oþer, þe Scottis alle þam toke.
Sergeantȝ wele þritty alle ȝald þam þat while,
on þei slouh smertly, Sir Thomas de Neuile.
Sir Rauf, þe coffrers, þat tyme was tresorere;
he was on of þer pers, his lif was alle in wehere.
He bed grete catelle his lif forto saue,
Sir Symon þe ffreselle þat ilk catelle suld haue.
Symon was austere, to Rauf spak fulle grim,
þat mad þe tresorere, "Þou has desceyued him
& me, & many mo, fro our wages ȝede quite.
Sir Rauf, þou resceyued þo bi taile & bi scrite,
þou did vs more trauaile, ilk man þou reft his wage;
now salle I wite þe taile & put þe in þe arerage.
Of preste þou has no merke, albe ne non amite,
bot laced in a hauberke þat is no clerkis abite.
For alle þo clerkes of Rome þat sing in kirk or rede,
þou salle haf þi dome als þou serued in dede."
A boye, for fulle pautenere, he had a suerd þat bote;
he stirte vnto þe cofrere, his handes first of smote,
& fro þe body his heued, a dynt þan did þe cleue,
his werryng so he leued, at armes he tok leue.
In alle þis mykelle frape wex a grete distance
of Boniface þe pape & þe kyng of ffrance;
þe kyng said & did crie þe pape was heretike,
vsure, & symonie, & synne sodomike,
errid mislyuyng, haunted maumetrie,
wastid kirkis þing, & lyued in bugerie,
[189r] & was worþi to schende, boþe soule & lyf
to die withouten ende, þis mad þe kyng vp ryf.

Pape Boniface herd telle of þat crie,
he did bifor his face com holy þe clergie
to conseil what were best for þat vilanie
þat þei ageyn him kest, said on him heresie.
Þis conseile alle þei said, "Late it ȝit rest & slepe;
þis fame of ȝow is laid, þo wise men þat were ȝepe
wite if he wille avowe alle his wikked sawe,
or amend & bowe, þeron behoues vs drawe."
Þe pape on þat couenaunt he said he wild so wirke
þe amendis, if he wild graunt to god & Holy Kirke,
& if he wild nouht com to amendement,
alle France suld be brouht tille encumberment
þorgh comon enterdite & þorgh croiserie,
als lond þat is alle quite fro god on ilk partie.
After salle ȝe here þe ende of þis folie;
turne we tille our matere & on our gest to hie.
Þe date a þousand was, þre hundred mo bi þre;
þe kyng did grete trespas, diffamed þe papes se.
In þe next somerestide, Sir Edward had haste,
no lenger wild he bide Scotland forto waste.
Conseil he had of on, a brigge he suld do wrihte,
botes & barges, ilkon with flekes mak þam tighte,
þe Scottis se to passe if þat he had nede;
þer passage neuer ore wasse, he rode ouer on his stede.
Þe Scottis sauh him com, fleand fast þei ȝede,
mores & mountayns nom bifore þei dryue for drede.
Þe kyng did parte his oste to sprede in parties sere.
West alle bi þat coste ȝede þe erle of Huluestere;
þe kynges oste, at gesse, in þe est mad lardere
of tounes & hamelesse, of granges & garner;
more & mede did rynce, wod & playn he brent,
þe same way þe prince destroied þer he went.
So fer northward he ferde þe Scottis to chace,
of Inglis no man herde þat euer kyng had þat grace,
so fer baner to bere & suilk oste forto lede,
no wasted with no werre, þe cuntres gan þam drede,
saue Kyng Athelstan þat wastid alle Catenesse;
siþen was no man þat so fer mad stresse,
þe tounes, þe countes, þe foreyns alle aboute
to þe kyng felle on knes, his powere did þam loute.
[189v] Vnto his pes þam ȝald, feaute did him suere,
treuly with him to hald, non armes ageyn him bere.
Be þat þe werre was ent, wynter was þer ȝare;

to Dounfermelyn he went, for rest wild he þare.
For þe quene he sent & scho did dight hire chare,
fro Cawod scho glent to Dounfermelyn to fare.
Þe lord of Badenauh, ffreselle, & Waleis,
lyued at theues lauh, euer robband alle weis;
þei had no sustenance þe werre to mayntene,
bot skulked opon chance & robbed ay bituene.
Þei com vnto þe kyng for pes, if it mot tide,
opon þer askyng he iorned þam to bide;
men dred for þat iorne þei suld haf had þe pes,
for eft þan suld men se bigyn alle new þe res.
In þat ȝere, it sais, þe pape had grete despite
þorgh þe Columpneis, cardinalles of habite;
þei were born in Rome, alle þe Columpneis,
þat kynde bare þe blome, riche men & curteis.
Men said alle þat kynde had whilom þe dignite;
if clerke of þam myght fynde, pape suld he be.
Þus þan was þe sawe whilom in þat cite,
þe pape fordid þat lawe, þe skille can I not se.
Cardinals were þei, þe pape did þam doun
& exiled þam awey, & mad distructioun
of londes & feeȝ, þer kastels doun he cast,
& alle þer digniteȝ ne lengere suld þei last.
Grete was þat linage & many to þam cheued,
& of þat ilk outrage þe felt þam sore agreued
þat þe pape did þam reuile; of þo in Rome þat wore
went vnto Ceȝile þore help þei fond wele more.
Þe kyng of ffrance þidere sent þam help inouh;
þer kynde & þei togidere vntille Anayne þei drouh,
þer þe Columpne kynde, þe pape forsoth þei toke,
tresore þat þei mot fynde with þam away þei schoke.
Tuo days þe pape withouten mete lay;
þe þrid day com grete frape & conged him away.
Of alle þat grete tresoure þat euer he biwan,
als bare was his toure as Iob þe pouere man.
Men sais he gaf pardoun, assoiled þam of pyne,
þat with deuocioun brouht him brede or wyne.
Grete pite it was þat þe hede of cristendam
suld for any trespas take so foule a scham.
[190r] Wele I wote alle frayed he went fro þat cite
vnto Rome mispayed to þe papes se.
He cursed þe kyng of ffrance & alle þat with him held
þat did him þat mischance, ageyn him reised scheld.

He lyued bot þre days & died sone, þei said,
þe soner for þat affrays, at Petir Kirke is he laid.
Now haf we bulle certeyn, a newe Pape Benet
þat calles þer ageyn þat Boniface set,
assoyles alle bi name þo robbours þorgh grace
þat did despite & shame to Pape Boniface.
Who may now in Rome haf any sikernesse
þat þer is hiest dome & ȝit vncerteyn es?
Þat Boniface bond with sentence so brim,
eft men Benet fond þat he assoiled him.
He is fole þat affies in þe courte of Rome;
comes a noþer & bies & fordos þat dome.
"Pur quante posse dare," what þing & how mykelle.
"Pur fare & defare," Rome is now fulle fikelle.
Turn we now oþer weys vnto our owen geste
& speke of þe Waleys þat lies in þe foreste.
[I]n þe forest he lendes of Dounfermelyn; [*Capital I om.*]
he praied alle his frendes & oþer of his kyn,
after þat ȝole þei wilde biseke Edward
þat he mot him ȝelde tille him in a forward,
þat were honorable to kepe wod or beste,
& with his scrite fulle stable & seled at þe lest,
to him & alle hise to haf in heritage,
& non oþer wise als terme, tyme, & stage,
bot als a propire þing þat were conquest tille him.
Whan þei brouht þat tiþing, Edward was fulle grim
& bitauht him þe fende als his traytoure in lond;
& euer ilkon his frende þat him susteynd or fond,
þre hundreth marke he hette vnto his warisoun
þat with him so mette, or bring his hede to toun.
Now flies William Waleis, of pes nouht he spedis,
in mores & mareis with robberie him fedis.
Here now how þei sped, þe Scottis in his mercie:
þe ffreselle first fled out, taken on þer partie,
tuo ȝere out of kith in strange reame suld be,
þe þrid suld he haf grith ageyn to haf his fe;
þe toþer alle suld haue boþe lif & lymmes
& þer tenement saue bot raunson of þam nunnes;
[190v] raunson suld þei gyue after þer folie
& in his pes to lyue & haf þer manauntie.
Siþen in þe Lenten tide he went to Saynt Andrew,
about on ilk a side did crie his pes alle new.
Þe bisshop of Glascow þe clergie alle out ches,

þe best men & trew, & com vnto þe pes;
þe kyng was so curteis he granted þam þer wille
saue þe amendes, he sais, raunson for þer ille,
& suld be bot right bifor þe baronie,
& at þe comon sight of alle þer clergie.
After þe Pask sone þe kyng did mak alle ȝare
þat his oste were bone to Striuelyn to fare.
Whan þei were alle comen, þei ȝede about to se
how it mot be nomen & þe engynes set suld be;
thrittene grete engynes, of alle þe reame þe best,
brouht þei to Striuelyne, þe castelle doun to kest.
Tuo knyghtes were þerin þe castelle had in warde,
Sir William of Depplyn, Sir William Olifarde,
& tuenti of honour without page & portere,
& a frere prechoure, a monke, þer conseilere;
þer was within þrittene maydens & ladies
& no mo men to mene þat felle to telle of pris.
An engyn had þei þerin & profred forto kast;
þe ȝerde brast in tuyn, to help mot it not last.
Þe engyns with oute to kast were þei sette,
wallis & kirnels stoute, þe stones doun bette.
Þe kyng did mak right ȝare an hidous engyn,
þe name þei cald Ludgare, or Lurdare of Striuelyn.
Whan þei kest þerto, þe walle þorghout þei clef,
& non oþer did so, bifor him alle doun dref;
þre monethes & þre days þe sege so long þei teld,
fulle & hard affrays had alle þo þat it held.
Sore þei were trauailed & socour com þam non
& alle þer store failed, þer mete was nere gon;
tille þe kyng þei sent, þei wild be at his wille,
bot he wild not consent, he þouht to do þam ille.
So long was þe trayne or it wer brouht to stalle,
it were to me grete payne forto telle it alle.
I wote wele, at þe last alle com þei oute,
withouten conaunt cast, tille his mercy gan loute.
Boldely þei camen & schewed þam to his face,
felle it to gode or grame, þei did þam in his grace.
[191r] Þe castelle now is ȝolden, þe kyng dos wardeyns wise
to kepe þe lond & dres, þe folk forto iustise;
þe lond was so wast he mad þer no soioure,
tille Inglond in hast he turned with honoure.
Þe moneth of Septembre ȝolden was Striuelyn;
Edward may remembre þe trauaile & þe pyn,

with many grete encumbre of in hard stoure.
At Brustwik opon Humbre þer he mad soioure.
Sir Ion of Warenne þat ilk tyme gan deie,
his body was redy þen in graue forto leie.
After þe enterment, þe kyng tok his way
to þe south, he went þorgh Lyndesay.
He spired as he ȝede who did suilk trespas,
brak his pes with dede tille he in Scotlond was;
of suilk suld be spoken, if men of þam pleyned,
þo þat þe pes had broken, if þei mot be atteyned.
Wise men of gode gaf ansuere to þe kyng
þat suilk foles ȝode, it was certeyn þing.
"Þorgh þe lond is don suilk grete greuance,
bot it be mendid son, a werre may rise o chance.
Þise contekours whidere þei assigned a stede þat es
& þer þei com togidere & mak a sikernes
þat þei salle alle go to whom or where þei wille,
to robbe, bete, or slo ageyn alle manere skille;
þei profere a man to bete for tuo schilynges or þre,
with piked staues grete, beten salle he be,
in feire & markette þei salle seke him oute.
Alle þe lond is sette with suilk foles stoute;
if a chapman wille not leue of his merchaundie,
in his hous for tene þei do him vilenie,
or els he be at one largely to gyue of his,
els þei salle him ilkone bete him þat he pis.
For men of suilk maners, bot þer be som iustise,
sone in fo ȝers, perchance a werre salle rise."
Þe kyng herd alle þe fame, þe pleynt of ilka toun,
& gaf þam a newe name & cald þam trailebastoun.
Þe date was a þousand, thre hundred mo bi fiue;
suilk men þorgh þe land he did þam tak bilyue.
The kyng þorgh þe lond did seke men o resons
& with þe iustise þam bond to site on trailebastons;
som þorgh quest þei demed be bonden in prisons,
& þo þat fled þei flemed als þe kynges felons.
[191v] Som men out þe kast of lond was holden wrong,
fals couenantȝ þei brast þorgh powere holden long,
& som gaf raunson after þer trespas,
als þe dede was don, so þe amendes was.
Bot men did amend suilk folie openly knowen,
non suld þam defend ne dur wonne in þer owen.
(A, Ihesu, whan þou wille, how rightwis is þi mede,

þat of þe wrong has gilt, þe endyng may þei drede!)
William Waleis is nomen þat maister was of theues;
tiþing to þe kyng is comen þat robberie mischeues.
Sir Ion of Menetest sewed William so nehi,
he tok him whan he wend lest, on nyght, his leman bi.
Þat was þorght treson of Iak Schort, his man,
he was þe encheson þat Sir Ion so him nam.
Iak broþer had he slayn, þe Waleis þat is said,
þe more Iak was fayn to do William þat braid.
Selcouthly he endis, þe man þat is fals,
if he trest on his frendes, þei begile him als.
Begiled is William, taken is & bondon,
to Inglond with him þei cam & led him vnto London.
Þe first dome he fanged, for treson was he drawen,
for robbrie was he hanged, & for he had men slawen;
& for he had brent abbeis & men of religion,
eft fro þe galweis, quik þei lete him doun
& bouweld him alle hote & brent þam in þe fire.
His hede þan of smote, suilk was William hire,
& for he had mayntend þe werre at his myght,
on lordschip lended þore he had no right,
& stroied þore he knewe in fele stede sers,
his body þei hewe on foure quarters
to hang in foure tounes to mene of his maners
[*In margin*:] Couwe de Waleys
in stede of gonfaynounes & of his baners.
At London is his heued . his quarters ere leued . in Scotland spred;
to wirschip þer iles . & lere of his wiles . how wele þat he sped,
it is not to drede . traytour salle spede . als he is worþi.
His lif salle he tyne . & die þorgh pyne . withouten merci;
þus may men here . a ladde forto lere . to biggen in pays,
it fallis in his i3e . þat hewes ouer hie . with þe Walays.
Of William haf 3e herd how his endyng was,
now of Kyng Roberd to telle 3ow his trespas.
Als Lenten tide com in cristenmans lauh,
he sent for Ion Comyn, þe lord of Badenauh,
[192r] to Dounfres suld he come vnto þe Minours Kirke.
A spekyng þer þei nome, þe Comyn wild not wirke
ne do after þe sawe of Roberd þe Brus;
away he gan him drawe, his conseil to refus.
Roberd with a knyue, þe Comyn þer he smote,
þorgh whilk wounde his lyue he lost, wele I wote.
He 3ede to þe hie autere & stode & rested him þore,

com Roberdes squiere & wonded him wele more.
For he wild not consent to reise no folie
ne do als he ment to gynne to mak partie
ageyn Kyng Edward, Scotland to dereyne,
with werre & batail hard reue him his demeyne,
Sir Ion wild not so, þerfor was he dede.
Bot Roberd wild do, & oþer þat gaf him rede,
þat he suld go to Scone & mak redy þe se,
& whan it were alle bone, to tak þe dignite;
þe garland Roberd toke þat whilom was þe right,
þe lond forto loke in signe of kynges myght.
Primatis, bisshopes tuo, þo with croice & ryng,
& an abbot mo of Scone þat dubbid þe kyng,
erles, barons inowe mad him þer feaute.
With oth he did þam bowe at his wille to be,
& alle Inglis men did he woyde þe lond
þat þei mot fynde or ken in stede þer he þam fonde.
Now goes þe Brus about, werre he þinkis to hold;
þe Inglis þe kacched out, to þe kyng þe told.
Edward þan he toke folk with his banere;
þe erle went, of Penbroke, his name was Sir Eymere,
& oþer men fulle gode, barons & barons pere,
at tyme wele þei stode & did þer deuere.
Þe date was a þousand, þre hundred mo bi sex
whan þe werre of Scotland þorgh þe Brus eft wex.
In þis ȝere, als I told, at þe Whitsonen day,
þe kyng his fest suld hold at Westmynster fulle gay.
His sonne, Edward þe Prince, & fiftene for his sake,
þre hundred of þe prouince, knyghtes wild he make;
it was þe kynges costage, for ilk a knyght was gest.
Also þei mad mariage of som þat were þe best;
þe ȝong erle of Warenne with grete nobley was þare,
a wif þei him bikenne, þe erles douhter of Bare;
þe erle of Arundelle his londes lauht he þan
& toke a damyselle, William douhter of Warenne;
[192v] ȝong Sir Hugh was þare, þe Spensere, stoute & gay,
Gilbert douhter of Clare wedded he þat day.
It is not to wene bot certeynly to witen,
ioye inouh is sene þer suilk a fest is smyten;
in alle Bretayn was nouht siþen criste was born,
a fest so noble wrouht aftere no biforn,
out tak Carleon þat was in Arthure tyme;
þer he bare þe coroune, þerof ȝit men ryme.

The prince after þe fest sone his leue toke
with iolif men of gest, toward þe north he schoke
to chace Kyng Robyn where he myght him fynde
þat slouh þe gode Comyn, destroie him rote & rynde.
His fader Edward north mad his iorne,
him toke a sekenes hard, at Laynercost lay he;
bot Ihesu þorgh his myght, blissed mot he be,
reised him vp right & passed þat hage.
Þer after ros hard schoures in Scotlond of þe clergie,
bisshops, abbotes, & priours þei had misborn þam hie,
& alle þat fals blode þat often was forsuorn
þat neuer in treuth stode sen Ihesu criste was born.
Sir Eymere of Valence lay at Saynt Ion toun,
in his alience with many erle & baroun
of Scotlond, þe best were þan in his feith;
þer þei gan alle rest tille þei herd oþer greith.
Sir Robert þe Brus sent to Sir Eymere
& bad he suld refus ilk a pautenere,
þe traytours of hise þat him had forsaken;
þei suld to þe iewise whan þei þe toun had taken.
Þe toþer day on þe morn com þe Brus Roberd,
þe toun wist it beforn þorgh spies þat þei herd.
Sir Eymere wild haf gon out, Sir Ingram Vmfreyuile
preid him forto lout tille it were none þat while.
"If we now out wende & leue þe toun alone,
þei gete þe faired ende & we be slayn ilkone.
Bot do crie þorgh þe toun þat non, for wele no wo,
in stete walk vp & doun, bot to þer innes go."
Whan þe crie was cried, walkand was non sene
bot to innes hied as þer no man had bene;
þe Scottis perceyued wele þei durst not issheu oute,
it neghed nere metesel, þan ros vp alle þe route.
At þe hie midday went þe Scottis men,
tuo myle was þer way to þe castelle of Metfen.
[193r] Whan þei to Metfen cam, þei dight þam to þe mete;
þan said Sir Ingram, "If we go now, we þam gete!
Dight vs now ilkone, go we god vs spede.
Leue not þe toun alone, þe way I salle ȝow lede."
On Saynt Margarete Day Sir Ingram & Sir Eymere
com on þam þer þei lay, alle dight to þe dynere;
þer vaumward was sone dight, our Inglis had mervaile
þei were so sone at þe fight & redy to assaile;
þe Inglis þorgh þam ran & had þe fairer side,

þe Scottis ilk a man, þe lordes durst not bide.
Here now a contreuore þorgh Roberdes avis:
abouen þer armore did serkis & surplis,
alle þe fled on rowe in lynen white as milke,
for non suld þam knowe þer armes whilk were whilk;
our men þat wild haf dede bare þam forth fulle stoute,
Sir Eymer had no drede, he serchid þam alle oute.
At þe first comyng, he slouh Sir Eymere stede,
þat did Robert þe kyng, & turned bak & ȝede.
Sir Eymer had inowe þat horsid him ageyn.
Robertes men þei slowe, þe numbre vncerteyn,
þan bigan þe chace & drof þe Kyng Robyn;
to reste had he no space long to duelle þerin.
Þe ffreselle þer he fled, sone after was he fonden;
now taken he is & led vnto þe toure of London,
þer his dome he feyng als traytoure salle ȝe witen:
first drawen, & siþen heyng, & his hede of smyten.
Allas, it was to mene his vertuȝ & his pruesse,
so fele in him were sene þat perist for falsnesse!
His hede vnto þe brigge to sette was it sent,
þe body lete þei ligge & som þerof þei brent.
Here now þe grete despite & þe vilenie
þat to þer bak gan bite of Scotlond þe clergie.
Þe bisshop of Saynt Andrew & þe abbot of Scone,
þe bisshop of Glascow, þise were taken sone,
fettred on hakneis, to Inlond ere þei sent
on sere stedis, it seis, to prison mad present.
Lewed men & clerkis þat did werre mayntene
als theues bare þei merkis, hanged alle bidene;
Cristofore of Seton, many man him sauh
hanged for treson of Ion of Badenauh;
hanged als þe ffreselle, & in þe same stede,
þe erle of Ascetelle þei bed þe same bede,
[193v] saue he was not drawen, þat poynt was forgyuen,
bot alle with schame slawen, þorgh treson þerto dryuen.
Allas, þat ientille blode com to so ille fyne,
& alle for falsnes ȝede to schemes dede & pyne;
& wele I vnderstode þat þe Kyng Robyn
has dronken of þat blode, þe drink of Dan Waryn.
Dan Waryn he les tounes þat he held,
with wrong he mad a res & misberyng of scheld;
siþen in to þe forest he ȝede, naked & wode,
als a wilde beste ete of þe gres þat stode.

Þus of Dan Waryn in his boke men rede.
God gyf þe Kyng Robyn þat alle his kynde so spede!
Sir Robynet þe Brus he durst noure abide,
þat þei mad him rescus bot in more & wod side;
towhile he mad þis trayne & did vmwhile outrage,
come Arthure of Bretayne & asked his heritage.
Holy Richemond schire he cleymed þat þorgh right,
Kyng Edward, our sire, him ansuerd fulle light.
He had so light ansuere þat Arthure toke his leue.
(God schilde vs fro þe werre þat non with oþer greue!)
Whan Arthur was gon, þe kyng did alle anoþer,
he gaf it to Sir Ion, Sir Arthures broþer,
holdand of him in fe, als whilom was vsage,
of Sir Edward fre & of alle his linage.
Þe duke of Bretayn with fulle heuy chere
passed ouere ageyn, fulle light ansuere had here.
Now of Kyng Robyn salle I ȝit speke more
& his broþer Tomlyn, Thomas als it wore,
& of Sir Alisandere, þat me rewes sore,
þat boþe com in skandere for dedes þei did þore.
Of arte he had þe maistrie, he mad a coruen kyng
in Cantebrige, to þe clergie, or his broþer were kyng.
Siþen was neuer non of arte so þat sped,
ne bifore, bot on, þat in Cantebrigge red.
Robert mad his fest for he was þore þat tyme,
& he sauh alle þe gest þat wrote & mad þis ryme.
Sir Alisander was hie Dene of Glascow,
& his broþer Thomas ȝed spiand ay bi throw
where our Inglis men ware, not in clerke habite,
& non wild he spare, bot destroied also tite;
þorgh þe Kyng Robyn þei ȝede þe Inglis to spie.
Here now of þer fyn þam com for þat folie.
[194r] A sergeant of Galweye, his name was Makedowel,
on Askwednesday whan messe was don ilk del,
sursaute he þam mette als þei fro kirke cam;
þer way he þam withsette, smertly þore þam nam.
He did þam fettre wele, streitly & right hard,
& sent þam to Carlele vnto Kyng Edward;
þe kyng wele paied was, he sette iustise of lawe,
demed þe Brus Thomas boþe to hang & drawe,
Sir Alisander þe same, & after þer hangyng,
boþe bi o name hede þam bad þe kyng.
Þe Pape Boniface wrote in his sexte boke

what clerke felle to haf grace for what cas men him toke,
whilk clerke for what trespas where men suld him saue,
& where he taken was, what habite on suld haue;
& if he were atteynt als thef þorgh felonie,
of suilk þe pape mas pleynt & writes to þe clergie;
& if þe decretal ne were ordeynd for þis,
þe clerkes ouer alle ne rouht to do amys.
Þe date a þousand was, þre hundred & seuen;
þe clergie for þat cas held þam more in euen.
After þe Paskes wele þat þise men were þus schent,
þe kyng at Carlele held his parlement;
fro Rome a cardinalle þe pape þider sent
to wite þe sothe alle, þe mariage long of ment;
if þe prince mot haue þe kynges douhter of ffrance,
þe acorde & pes mot saue þorgh þat aliance;
& at þe parlement was a grete spekyng,
for þe clergie it ment of Holy Kirkes þing.
Erles & barons ilkone it forsuore
(for what manere resons ȝit wot I no more),
bot of þe last ende of þer grete counsaile,
to London suld þe sende men þat myght auaile
to speke & purueie whilk suld ouer þe se,
þe sothe to Philip seie & sette a certeynte
of þat mariage how & whan suld be,
& bate alle oþer outrage, for Gascoyn do feaute.
Of alle þe poyntes spoken þe parties bifore had said
neuer suld be broken, on payne þeron was laid,
& whan þe parties wold mak a finalle pes,
god grante it þam to hold þe conant þat þei ches.
Ȝit gos Kyng Robyn forth in his rioterie,
ne com not ȝit his fyn, to ende of his folie.
[194v] Bot Sir Ion þe Waleis taken was in a pleyn
þorgh spiyng of Norreis men þat were certeyn,
fettred on a hakeney & to London led;
to bring him sone on wey, þe iustise þerto sped.
Als his dedes was, þeron þei gaf þe lawe,
for som of his trespas first þei did him drawe;
siþen for oþer theft þei hanged him, men witen,
siþen lete him doun eft & his hede of snyten,
& born to London brigge fulle hie with outheys,
biside his broþer to bigge, William þe Waleys,
þat neuer had pite of Inglis man no weys,
bot brent toun & citeȝ, kirkes, & abbeys;

chanon, monk, & ffrere alle passed þorgh his suerd,
was no man so dere, to dede þei ȝede in ferd.
Blissed be þou god, þat þou in erth cam,
þi word is wele trod, I say it bi William;
þou said with suerd þat smote, with suerd suld be smyten.
Bi þe Waleis it bote, þe vengeance ȝe may witen.
A, Ihesu, fulle of myght, þat alle þe world salle deme,
may no man lyue so right, no so wele him ȝeme,
no so stalworth be, ne so douhti of dede,
þat has powere to fle þe dede þat is to drede.
Adam first gan synne, did þat god forbede,
alle we were him inne whan he serued þe dede;
siþen he & we alle com of him & Eue,
þorgh þe dede salle falle, be we neuer so leue.
Þe hardy Kyng Belyn þe cite of Rome wan,
& siþen Constantyn & Maximian;
Arthure wan alle ffrance, slouh þe emperour of Rome;
þise of suerd ne lance douted dynt no dome.
Þise kynges men dred, & alle þe world þam knewe,
for alle þer grete boldehed, þe dede ȝit doun þam threwe.
Where ere, ere now, alle þise, where ere þei bicomen?
Þise hardy men & wise, þe dede þam has alle nomen.
Among alle þise hardie may Edward, our kyng,
be sette fulle solempnelie & mad of grete praisyng;
sen þe dede of Arthure, in Inlond was þer non
þat so wele stode in stoure ageyn his foos ilkon.
Þis was Edward, Kyng Henry sonne, þe last,
tiþing haf we hard, þe dede him doun has kast.
Now may men sing & say, in romance & ryme,
Edward is now away, right has lorn his tyme.
[195r] Sir Ion of Badenauh, who salle venge þi dede?
Þe prince is heire þorgh lauh þat to þe coroun him bede.
He has mad his vowe to stroie þe Kyng Roby
þat in Dounfres slowe Sir Ion, þe rede Comyn.
His dede whan it felle, here þe date I salle ȝow neuen,
of criste a þousand ȝere, þre hundred & seuen;
in þe moneth of Iuly, euen þe seuend day,
toward Scotlond to hie, at Burgh bi Sandeȝ he lay.
His tyme was no more sette here to regne in landes;
he died at a hamelette, men calle it Burgh bi Sandes.
Þe body þat nyght þer lay, þe soule at cristes dome;
þe pape, þe toþer day, wist it in þe courte of Rome.
Þe pape on þe morn, bifor þe clergie cam

& teld þam biforn, þe floure of cristendam
was dede & lay on bere, Edward of Inglond.
He said with heuy chere, in spirit he it fond,
fiue ȝere he gaf pardoun of peyns to be fre,
þat for him with deuocioun said Pater & Aue.
To Waltham þei him brouht, baronage & þe clergie,
for monethes for him wrouht his seruise solempnelie;
þei bawmed his body, tresore wild þei non spare,
þe pouere þei gaf party, his soule bettere to fare.
Four & tuenty ȝere, auht monethes & fiue daies
noblie regned he here bi profe & gode assaies.
Fro Waltham befor said, to Westmynster þei him brouht,
biside his fadere is laid in a toumbe wele wrouht;
of marble is þe stone & purtreied þer he lies,
þe soule to god is gone to þe ioye of paradis. Amen.
Now most I nede leue here of Inglis forto write,
I had no more matere of kynges lif in scrite;
if I had haued more, blithly I wild haf writen.
What tyme I left þis lore, þe day is for to witen:
Idus þat is of Maii left I to write þis ryme,
B letter & Friday bi ix þat ȝere ȝede prime.

Expliciunt gesta Britonum & Anglorum in lingua materna per Robertum Mannyng transumptus Anno christi Millesimo CCCmo tricesimo viii Idus Maii . littera dominicali D prima ix tempore Regis Edwardi tercii a conquestus xi.

Notes
Glossary

ABBREVIATIONS

ALMA: *Arthurian Literature in the Middle Ages.* Ed. Roger Sherman Loomis. Oxford: Clarendon Press, 1959.

Arnold: Ivor Arnold, ed. *Le Roman de Brut de Wace.* Paris: Société des Anciens Textes Français, 2 vols., 1938, 1940.

Bede: *Historia Ecclesiastica Gentis Anglorum.* Trans. Leo Sherley-Price. Penguin Classics, 1955. *Bede's Ecclesiastical History of the English Nation.* (Introduction by Dom David Knowles) Everyman's Library, 1954.

Brunner: Karl Brunner, ed. *Der Mittelenglische Versroman über Richard Löwenherz,* Wien und Leipzig: Wilhelm Braumüller, 1913.

Furnivall:[Edition of Ch1] Frederick J. Furnivall. *The Story of England by Robert Manning of Brunne, A. D. 1338.* 2 vols. Rolls Series 87, 1887.

Hearne: [Edition of Ch2] Thomas Hearne, *Peter Langtoft's Chronicle (As Illustrated and Improv'd by Robert of Brunne) From the Death of Cadwalader to the End of K. Edward the First's Reign.* Oxford, Printed at the Theater, M.DCC.XXV. [1810 edition in Hearne's Works, vols. 3 and 4.]

HRB: Geoffrey of Monmouth, *Historia Regum Britanniae.* Trans. Lewis Thorpe. Penguin Books, 1966.

L: Lambeth MS 131. Lambeth Palace Library, London [variant text to line 4973].

Light: David Anthony Light. "The Arthurian Portion of the 'Roman de Brut' of Wace: A Modern English Prose Translation with Introduction and Notes" (Ph.D. diss., New York University, 1970).

MED: *Middle English Dictionary.* Ed. Hans Kurath, et al. Ann Arbor: University of Michigan Press, 1952–.

OED: *Oxford English Dictionary.*

P: Petyt MS 511, Vol. 7, Inner Temple Library [base text]. *Chronicle* Part I, Ch1: ff. 1–95v; Part II, Ch2: ff. 96r–195r.

Pers: Peter of Langtoft (as RMB always names him).

R: Rawlinson MS D.913 [variants for lines 12550–699 in Ch1].

RMB: Robert Mannyng of Brunne.

Stepsis: [Edition of Ch2] Robert Peter Stepsis, "An Edition of Robert Mannyng of Brunne's Chronicle of England" 2 vols. Ph.D. diss., Harvard University, 1967.

Wright: Thomas Wright, ed. *The Chronicle of Pierre de Langtoft, in French Verse, From the Earliest Period to the Death of King Edward I.* 2 vols. Rolls Series 47, 1866, 1868; repr. Kraus, 1964.

NOTES TO PART I

[The following line numbers are those of the edition of Ch1 in P. Additions and variants in LR correspond to the line numbers of P. A lost leaf at the beginning of L left a stub in the margin preserving a few initial letters; consequently, if L originally had a different arrangement in the prologue (ll. 1–198), there is no surviving clue. For the Latin captions appearing throughout the text, see Furnivall's edition of Ch1, *passim.* The captions in the two MSS (PL) are mostly identical and generally appear in the same place with relation to the lines in the text. I doubt that these Latin embellishments were in Mannyng's original version of the work, but they may have been added in the first professional copy. Many of the comments in the following notes are suggestions for further exploration, not necessarily firm conclusions. The reader who is interested in pursuing the sources in more depth may find that other interpretations can be elicited, or in some cases, explanations of erroneous or ambiguous readings of the MSS.]

100: RMB is probably referring to the Middle English version of Thomas' "Tristrem" here rather than the famous French version by a poet at the court of Henry II. A brief description is in "English Rimed and Prose Romances" by Robert W. Ackerman in *ALMA*, 514–16. The romance dates from ca. 1300.

111: The MS is equivocal for *heuyed;* Furnivall reads it *henþed* and emends to *henyed,* both unrecorded. RMB's use of *heuyed* elsewhere supports this reading.

145–62: This reference to Dares may be misplaced: the passage would be more logically located after l. 200, which is, incidentally, at the beginning of f. 2r c.2. The captions here clearly separate these lines from the matter preceding and following.

145ff.: Dares the Phrygian was frequently cited as a literary source, but later scholars have concluded that his "Excidio Trojae Historia" was a late Roman forgery. The work appears in several MSS of *HRB* as a prologue, e.g., National Library of Wales MS 13210D. See B. F. Roberts and Daniel Huws, "Another MS of the Variant Version of the 'Historia Regum Britanniae,' " (1973), 147–52. See also Nathaniel E. Griffin, *Dares and Dictys: An Introduction to the Study of the Medieval Versions of the Story of Troy* (1907). E. B. Atwood convincingly argues for RMB's use of a different source; see note for 320–726 below.

163–65: RMB quotes Geoffrey's assertion that he had translated *HRB* from "Breton" speech. RMB regularly refers to that language throughout, but makes no distinction between "Breton" and the "Welsh" of his own time. Geoffrey himself left the matter uncertain, confounding scholars searching for his sources.

167–70: Robert of Gloucester, half-brother of the Empress Matilda, is here given credit for instigating the translation by Geoffrey. This comment may provide a clue to the type of *HRB* MS that RMB used, for many of the surviving MSS are grouped together when they include this dedication to Robert of Gloucester. The passage here appears before the translation of *HRB* by Wace begins (at l. 727), indicating that RMB consulted a source other than Wace for his prologue. See Thorpe, 39–40, n. 7. The classification of MSS and works associated with *HRB* is discussed by Julia C. Crick in *The Historia Regum Britannie of Geoffrey of Monmouth,* 4:119–20; see also Crick's *A Summary Catalogue of the Manuscripts,* vol. 3 (1988). The dedication to Robert of Gloucester appears in so many MSS, however, that identification of a MS that RMB might have used (based on this dedication alone) would be almost impossible. See also Robert A. Caldwell (1954) on College of Arms MS Arundel XXII, p. 646.

177–78: Mayster Wace wrote in "romance" or "made romance"? The different meanings intended by the word "romance" evidently did not trouble RMB. He is referring here to a work written in French ("Frankis") to distinguish it from Geoffrey's "Latyn." Hundreds of works written in French had been called "romances" in the sense of *genre* in the two centuries after Wace translated *HRB*. In the second part of his *Chronicle* [Ch2], RMB frequently refers to one or another work as "the romance," indicating that it is a specific work (unnamed) used as a source. The account of the reign of Richard I, for example, has several references of this kind that suggest a well-known and widely circulated historical poem. In his epilogue to Ch1, RMB explicitly states that "Frankis spech is cald romance" (15917).

181: A word or two may be missing from this line: probably it should read "vnto þe tyme of Cadwaladres."

202f.: RMB's biblical references here are not specific, but he may have followed some version of the genealogy provided for Brutus by Nennius, in the work usually entitled *Historia Brittonum*. Nennius was probably a late reviser of an anonymous work. The citations of Gildas in *HRB*, Wace, and RMB are also references to this work, which survives in thirty-five MSS; the oldest version (ca. 828–29) in Harley MS 3859, according to the editor, is perhaps the second edition. See John Morris, *Nennius: British History and The Welsh Annals* (1980). See Nora K. Chadwick, "Nennius and the 'Historia Brittonum,' " in *Studies in the Early British Church* (1973), 37–39. Fifteen MSS, none earlier than the twelfth century, attribute the work to Gildas. RMB might have had a later genealogy (possibly in French) as his immediate source, however, as the long discussion in ll. 201–428 (augmented by reference to the Bible) could not depend entirely on what remains in the surviving Nennius texts.

213ff.: See Sarah M. Horrall's account of the sources of biblical lore available to the author of *Cursor Mundi* in "For the commun at understand" (1989), 104ff. This contemporary work uses a wide range of "what may be loosely termed theological or catechetical sources" (p. 103); the narrative differs greatly from the version in RMB's *Chronicle*: compare the long passage on Noe and his sons (l. 1625 in *Cursor Mundi*, Morris ed., 1:102).

284: The MS reading in L probably reflects a confusion of *f* with long *s* in an earlier copy. P is doubtless correct: *vndersette*. Another notable example (15283) is *Offrith* (or *Offriht* in L), who is Bede's *Osfrid* (Bede 2:20).

294: The spelling of *Dardanum* is capriciously altered in the lines following, sometimes to conform to the necessities of rime. The PL scribes both seem to be uncertain when a name first appears, but a more consistent spelling is usually adopted when the name is used repeatedly.

320–726: The Troy story: RMB's actual source was a version quite different from the "Excidio Trojae Historia" attributed to Dares. (See n. 145 above.) RMB drew some of the details from the anonymous *Compendium Historiae Trojanae-Romanae*. See Elmer Bagby Atwood, "Robert Mannyng's Version of the Troy Story" (1938), 5–14. See also *Excidium Troiae* by Atwood and Virgil K. Whitaker (repr. 1971); the episodes RMB used are outlined on pp. xxxi–xxxiii. The recent study of RMB's version by Margaret J. Ehrhart, *The Judgment of the Trojan Prince Paris in Medieval Literature* (1987) discusses his sources at length, especially on pp. 65–68.

324: *MED* cites this line and 4935 in Ch2 for *mynsing* (i.e., remembrance, memory) and has only one other reference (ca. 1400) with a different meaning. The word is *mynsyng* here in 324L but *myndyng* in Ch2 4935L.

438: The two lines added in L here are nearly identical to 453–54 in P, where L repeats them.

439f.: See note to line 145. The story of Jason is dealt with summarily here, but several MSS of RMB's sources include it as a prologue. Gaimar also evidently included an account of Jason, according to his "Epilogue," in the lost earlier book of his history. See Alexander Bell, "The Epilogue to Gaimar's 'Estoire des Engleis' " (1930), 55.

449: This line in P is faulty; L is doubtless correct.
727: *HRB* and Wace begin with this line. RMB follows Wace faithfully hereafter except as noted.
800: Wace (at l. 80) has "E Postumus fu sis surnuns," but the MSS vary: Portemus, Porimus, Postomius, Pollemius; Pollinius is in Wace MS F (BL Addit. MS 32125, Anglo-French, 13th C.).
846–47: Logically, *fader* instead of *modere* should be in l. 847 though PL agree. The father's death is described in detail at 850ff.
1000: Antigonus says that the Greeks should keep trying. The shift to direct quotation is awkward, but the version in L is not more effective.
1067–68: L now reads "to on fede" and "ȝelde for nede." A later hand has added *on* and *for* above the line. Furnivall notes several alterations of this kind, since he was using L as his base MS. See his edition pp. 7 (nn. 3, 7), and 13 (n. 12) for earlier examples, and the note for 2229–30 below. I have not noted these gratuitous additions in L since they are generally irrelevant to the base text in P.
1274–76: See Arnold, p. 792, Wace 578–80. L adds two lines from Wace.
1363–4: See Wace ll. 667ff. RMB inserts the Latin "prayere" and the attribution to "Ouide."
1416: Wace has "E les montaines d'Azare" (712).
1495: See Arnold, p. 794, note l. 809. Wace names the character Humbert; he is Himbert in *HRB* (Thorpe, p. 67) and Numbert in Laȝamon, l. 712; compare *Laȝamon: Brut,* vol. 1 (ed. Brook and Leslie, 1963).
1573–77: This passage is rewritten from Wace 886–89. The second of the two lines added in L at 1574 is not in Wace.
1577ff.: Wace has *Suharz* at 901, 908 for P's Suard (1577) and Suhard (1584, 1592). L has *Swerd* consistently.
1732: See Arnold, p. 794, note l. 1053. The Wace MSS vary for this line.
1821: RMB uses *trip* with two different meanings. Here it is "trick" or "contrivance" as also in Ch2 3848; in Ch2 4992, he means "troop." In the Ch2 examples he was searching for a mid-line rime for "Philip."
1826: *MED* has *elboue* (n.) from OE elboga (elbow), but RMB is not cited; *elboulyne* (some kind of cord or string) is cited from a document dated 1345–49 and *elbowelines* from 1346 (E.1, p. 52). The context here suggests a unit of measurement, which is interpreted as *cubyte* in L.
1982ff.: The sense of this passage implies that Humbert fought Albanak, who had a son engaged in the battle. The L variant is closer but probably should read: "þat was a childe [of? or called?] Albanak." RMB has rewritten the passage in Wace (at 1300ff.). In *HRB* (2:1, Thorpe, 75), the three sons of Brutus were Locrinus, Kamber, and Albanactus; the passage in RMB's version has become confused by later scribes or RMB misunderstood the source; however, compare 1942–43, where the sons are correctly named.
2009: The word *ȝened* probably should be *ȝerned* in P, but possibly *for* should follow.
2155ff.: See Arnold, p. 796, note to line 1526 for comments on the place-names.
2166–86: The list of names for the sons and daughters of Ebrauk originated in *HRB*, 2:8 (Thorpe, 79; Thorpe's translation is based on the edition of *HRB* by Griscom from CUL MS 1706). The names were somewhat transformed by Wace, who preferred his French version (beginning at 1540), and further altered by RMB or his scribes. Wace's version may have been rearranged to preserve the rime. The more than two hundred MSS of *HRB* demonstrate a remarkable variety of different spellings for Geoffrey's characters.
2211: *Preyed* (L) and *pered* (P) probably should be *peyred,* i.e., he was impaired or had failed in health.
2217–20: *HRB* cites the prophets Haggai, Amos, Joel, and Azariah (2:10). Wace has "Amos, Aggeus e Iohel" (1626).
2223: *Rudhudibras* (P) or *Rehudybras* (L) is *Ruhundibras* in Wace (1608, 1627), Rud Hud Hudibras in *HRB* 2:9 (Thorpe, 80). Wright notes: "The scribes [of Langtoft] appear to

have blundered very much over this name" (p. 32). RMB's spelling (in L) matches Langtoft's MS B: Rehudibras.

2229–30: RMB's lines in both PL have lost some of their force. In *HRB* (Thorpe, 80) "the eagle spoke"; in Arnold's text, Wace has "uns aigles, ço dit l'on, parla. . ." and Langtoft has "un egle parla" (Wright, 32). (Variant Wace MSS for l. 1617 have "un angel" [C], "un ange" [G], "uns Angleis" [R].) Somehow "Aquile" has become personified in P, while L has lost the eagle altogether: "Awhileon spake þanne & prophesied." Furnivall notes that *egle* has been inserted in this line in L by a later hand (p. 80, n. 11). See note 15857 below.

2270: Geoffrey's Cordelia is Cordeille in Wace (1672ff); in the B MS of Langtoft, she is Gordeil (Wright, 34) but Cordeylle (or Cordeyle, Cordylle, Cordelle variously) in other MSS.

2334: *Hennis* could be read *Henuis* or *Heunis;* the duke appears again at 2375 as *Hewyn,* which is Langtoft's name, translated by Wright as *Hernuin* (p. 36) from some *HRB* MS that has "Hernuinis dux Cornubiæ." Wace mentions him once with the name *Hennim* (l. 1893). The variant reading in L at 2334 could be *Henmeis,* possibly corrupted from *Henweis* in an earlier MS. At 2375, L avoids the name with *When.* Thorpe's translation of *HRB* calls him *Henwinus.*

2442: The long addition (in L) to Lear's soliloquy is in Wace 1917ff. In Langtoft's account, most of the details in RMB's lines 2435ff. are entirely omitted: the events concerning Cordelia's rescue of Leir are reduced to a few lines (Wright, 36–39).

2570: Compare ll. 3456 [Ch1] and 2527, 4913, 5424, 6392 in Ch2, and 3674 in *Handlyng Synne.* Howard Naish interprets the meaning of *wroþerheile:* "disastrously." Scribes who did the variant MSS of all RMB's works regularly attempted to change this misunderstood term.

2603: The line readings in PL are identical; probably the phrase "in his tyme" was intended.

2621f.: See 2627; L is correct: *Ferreus* was eldest. The two lines added in L at 2626 are in Wace (2146–47).

2657: See Arnold, p. 798, note to line 2195 and introduction, p. xxxiv. Arnold uses this line in his classification of the Wace MSS: "group b1" has four barons, "group a1" has five. *HRB* has "Regnum quinque regibus submissum est," but names only four. (Thorpe, 88: Cloten, Pinner, Rudaucus, Staterius). Since Laȝamon says four, he evidently used a different type of Wace MS from the one RMB translated. However, in 2665–68 RMB names only four: Statere, Pincere, Rudak, and Cloten. To arrive at five, we could add Cloten's son Donwal Douhty (Wace: Dumwallo Molmuz, l. 2214). See Arnold, p. 798, note to line 2305 on Dyfnwal Moel Mud, who appears in ancient Welsh texts, but ultimately derives from *HRB.* In Thorpe's translation, Dunvallo Molmutius comes from Gildas (p. 89, *HRB* 2:17).

2696–98: The additions in L appear in a somewhat different arrangement in Wace (2235–41), a typical embellishment. Omission in P is probably the scribe's choice in an attempt to shorten the text.

3010: This line is probably corrupt: *nouhted* does not make sense as a verb. The line in L is also doubtful, but *nought* may mean "none of them."

3065–66: See Arnold, p. 799, note for line 2613; in 3063, RMB names the road "Fosse." This detail is found in the "variant" version of *HRB.* See Hammer's edition 3:76–78. Other details which differ among the *HRB* MSS are identified in Robert A. Caldwell, "Wace's *Roman de Brut* and the Variant Version of Geoffrey of Monmouth's *Historia Regum Britanniae*" (1956), 675–82.

3464: Compare Ch2 337: *rimthed* (P), *remede* (L) with Ch1 3464 *rimethed* (P), *rempede* (L). *MED* derives *rimthed* from OE rymþ and *rempede* from OE rempan (citing Ch1 3464 as the only reference). The meaning differs: ME rempen (v.) means to hasten, go at once. For ME rimthen (v.), *MED* cites both of RMB's lines, meaning to make room, clear a way. One other citation (dating from 1440) is also given. Hearne's edition misreads *rincthed* in Ch2 337.

3625: Pantaleus is Partholoim in *HRB* (Thorpe, 100). Thorpe notes that "Partholoim is a confused memory from Nennius, *Historia Brittonum* (par. 13)." Wace has Pantalous (3275) and RMB closely translates Wace in this passage. See Arnold, p. 799, note for line 3275.

3684f.: See Arnold, p. 800, note for line 3348. The list of "schires" where the "Marchenlawe" was still observed in his time is RMB's addition. Differences between the MSS are slight, but may indicate that the reviser of L had some legal interests. Note that L preserves the rime which is faulty in P.

3690: *Siluius* is from Langtoft. See Wright's note (1:52, n. 2) on the name; he is *Sisillius* in *HRB* (2:16, Thorpe, 87) and *Sisillus* in Wace (3353).

3706: The confusion of *c-t* probably affects both MSS here. Furnivall reads the last word of this line in L as *bastardie,* but it is possible to interpret the word in both MSS as *bascardie.*

3909: The P scribe has combined two lines; the correct version is in L. Probably P should read: "In all his time he was hende / in alle godenesse his lyf gan ende."

3910–15: See Wace ll. 3611ff. The burial at *Aldburgh Castel* and the reference to *Glud* (or *Klud* in L) are RMB's additions.

4008: *Archinaul* is close to Wace's *Archinal* (3711); he is *Archmail* in *HRB* (3:19). The long list of rulers in *HRB* and Wace presents the same kind of rhetorical embellishment RMB employs in the earlier genealogies, e.g., at 380–410. Many of Geoffrey's names are simply invented to provide a color of historicity. The controversy about Geoffrey's sources (especially the origin of names) has exercised many scholars: see Thorpe's introduction, 18ff. and his notes. Very little has been added to his analysis that would identify any other authentic historical figures since Thorpe's translation appeared.

4019: The necessity of rime (with *Redion* in the line following) suggests that the word *fon* was a compromise for *fonk. Fon* is given in *MED* as an OE verb (to seize, grasp), or a number (OE hwon, little, few). Compare RMB's use of *fonk* in Ch2 4276 (L: flonk) and Ch2 5184 *fonkes* (meaning something worthless or contemptible).

4115–56: RMB expands Wace's lines 3821–46. The L addition at 4124 may have been in his text but omitted in P, an instance of shortening. It is clear, however, that the scribe of L (or the reviser whose text was copied here) made extensive changes in the "Cesar" story; most of the variation between P and L for the major section between 4119 and 5262 could be attributed to the work of the reviser. See note for 4862–71 below.

4154: The comparable line in Wace (3846) is "D'aler conquerre les lointains" (rime: "Romains"). *MED* cites this line (from P) from OF lointain, meaning distant, remote. (L.6, p. 1155; one other citation is given, dated ca. 1500). Evidently RMB could not translate Wace's term, for it appears in the P version with dubious spelling, perhaps because of the rime with *Romeyns* in 4153. L recasts the whole line and changes the meaning.

4275: Compare Ch1 12973 and Ch2 3835. This is a typical phrase which is always changed in L, perhaps because it was unfamiliar to the L scribes. In 4275 "gyf þe a gyue" (P) is "truage schol we þe gyue" in L. In 12973 PL are the same: context interprets the word as "gift"; in Ch2 3835 "gif a gyue" in P is "a gift y wil þe gyue" in L. Here, *gyue* as a noun seems to have some further meaning than merely a gift in P, while in L (and also in *Handlyng Synne*) the scribes do not recognize the phrase as it was probably originally written.

4317: The *c-t* confusion in *Ignartet* (P) or *Ignarcet* (L) is not easily resolved. *HRB* has *Gueithaet* and Wace "E Guertaet les Suthgualeis" (l. 4004).

4499–504: The comparable passage in Wace is ll. 4177–82. The addition in L at 4502 corresponds to the sense: Caesar is bribing the French with no subtlety.

4559: RMB's use of *kemse* (to rime with *Temse*) may be an unusual metaphor: the word means a shirt or undergarment, derived from OE cames, or OF chemyse (originally Latin *camisia*). Here it seems to suggest "the ship's shirt" as a figurative expression. In Ch2, 2989, *kemse* is translated from Langtoft's *chemyse* and means a garment, "kirtelle or kemse."

4585: The P version, *snarled* from OE snearu (ME snarlen, v., entangled) is probably correct. *Swerued* in L is possible but not preferable. Compare Wace 4252–59 with RMB's version in 4578–90.
4637: P: rengid route; L: rengede route. *MED* (R.3, p. 435) cites this line from L and suggests "[?read: on route]," which might be an appropriate emendation if the MSS differed. The line means that the Bretons are in total disarray: "als wode." Possibly *route* is an error from an earlier MS, but *MED* (R.6, pp. 860–63) distinguishes five different nouns for *route.*
4748: Furnivall reads *Temnace* with the *m* as an expansion, but gives *Tenuace* for P in a note. The name is from Langtoft (p. 58, MS B: "Tenuace l'autre estoit . . ."). He is *Tenuantius* in *HRB* (Wright's note, p. 58) or *Tenvantius* in Thorpe's translation, and *Tenuancius* in Wace (4841).
4862–71: Furnivall notes (p. 172, n. 10) the differences between P and L as indicated in the text. (These lines are omitted in L.) He says that P "follows the Wace MS du Roi 73 . . . and then the MS du Roi 27, that De Lincy printed." Arnold's edition lists Bib. Nat. ff. 1450 and 1416 [H and J] as the base text and variant text respectively for De Lincy's edition (pp. viii–ix). Arnold's MS J has another omission (Wace 10563–86) corresponding to the omission in Ch1 at 11138–58 (see note below). After 4871 (of P), the passage in L is evidently a lengthy repetition in error. As the text indicates, the passage following P's l. 4871 is out of order as well: it appears on f. 21v, c. 2 of L.
4938ff.: See Arnold's note to Wace, p. 800, l. 4552, concerning the differing accounts in Wace MSS for Caesar's activities in this passage.
5222–61: The passage from L following 5261 is an interpolation; see Wace ll. 4816–56 for the correspondence to 5218–61 in P. Furnivall notes that the long passage in L is "an expansion at will of two lines in Geoffrey of Monmouth, lib. iv. 10." (p. 185, n. 4). Very likely the reviser who was responsible for the text copied in L consulted another authority to find the historical details in this long interpolation. Though much of the matter is irrelevant (or perhaps was irrelevant to Mannyng), the account provides a major illustration of the way in which "history" grew during the century after RMB wrote. See note 4115–56 above.
5262ff.: The prophecy of Taliesin (*Teselyn* in P, *Telesyn* in L) is an addition by Wace. Geoffrey's book (iv.11) has only a sentence mentioning the birth of Christ. Arnold's note (p. 802, l. 4856) refers to the *Historia Brittonum* as the source, and *Vita Merlini* to identify Taliesin in the sixth century. See Robert H. Fletcher, *The Arthurian Material in the Chronicles* (1906), 91, n. 5; Fletcher discusses the similarity between Taliesin and Merlin.
5316: The & at the end of the line in P is not marked for correction. L is probably correct.
5367–75: This passage is expanded from Wace 4956ff.; 4959–62 of Arnold's edition are lacking in Wace MSS DL and in RMB's text. See note 6145–46.
5494–95: These lines translate Wace 5074ff. See Furnivall's notes 10–11, p. 196.
5534: In *HRB*, *Karpenhuelgoit* is "Kaerpenhuelgoit, now called Exeter" (4:16, Thorpe, 122). Wace mentions *Essecestre* in l. 5199, but does not have Geoffrey's name for the town. How the city becomes *Oxenford* in RMB's ll. 5532 and 5535 is a mystery.
5561: The four lines added in L are partly an interpolation. Wace does not include the comment that Vespasian helped in the conquest of Ireland. (Compare Wace 5148–52). Furnivall's note (p. 199) refers to *HRB* 4:16, saying that "Geoffrey . . . implies this" (i.e., that Vespasian helped the king win Ireland). Thorpe's translation merely says: "They sent their troops over to Ireland" (p. 122). Furnivall's *HRB* source may be different, or he extrapolates from it, perhaps to justify the reading in L.
5601f.: This is a reference to the account in *HRB* 4:17 (Thorpe, 123). For l. 5597, Wace has only "Si apele l'on Vestinaire" (5184). See Furnivall, 200, n. 7. Thorpe refers to the discussion of Geoffrey's source in J. S. P. Tatlock, *Legendary History of Britain* (1950), 20.
5654: *Danuan* (P) or *Dunian* (L) is *Dunian* in Wace 5225; Furnivall misreads L as *Duman.* He is *Duvianus* in *HRB* (Thorpe, 124) and *Dunyanus* in Langtoft.
5662–5671: A *flamen* was a priest of pagan Rome, but RMB seems to confuse priests with

temples here. See *MED* (F.2, 602) for the definition. Wace does not include these details about the British; RMB vaguely identifies a Latin source in 5664. Compare *HRB* 4:19 (Thorpe, 125) and Wace 5245f.

5784–85: The two lines repeated in P at the top of f. 35v c. 1 appear with some slight variations: "Getan modere was a Romeyn / of men of gode knyght & sueyn."

5910: L is correct about the number of legions; Wace has: "Tramis i unt treis legiuns" (5477), but Wace MSS [CS and M] differ. In *HRB* 5:4 (Thorpe, 128), "the Senate sent Allectus as legate, with three legions."

6034–36: Wace (5594) has *Coel* as "cuens de Gloëcestre," but three of Arnold's Wace MSS [CSF] give Colecestre. The spelling used in 6036, 6044, and 6048 reverts to Wace's *Choel* in 6050, 6070, 6072ff.

6138: *Leonyn* corresponds to *Joelin* in Wace (5715) or *Leonin* in other Wace MSS [CSFGR]. In *HRB*, he is *Iolinus* (Thorpe, 133). The names of the wise Roman uncles differ in L (6138–48), probably in error.

6145–46: Wace here adds a comment on the story of Helen's retrieval of the cross in Jerusalem (5720–24). Several Wace MSS omit this detail, and two MSS lack Wace's ll. 5719–30: Durham Cathedral MS C.IV.27.1 [D] and Lincoln Cathedral MS 104 [L]. Because of provenance and similarities such as this one, we might suspect that RMB's source belonged to the DL MS tradition of Wace. See note to 5367–75 above.

6166: For the Wynchestre destination in L, Furnivall notes: "R. Brunne follows Geoffrey" (p. 220, n. 5). Compare Thorpe, 133: "he marched to meet Trahern not far from Winchester." Wace has: "Trahern a Porcestre turna" (5745) as in P, but see RMB's line 6171 which is translated from Wace's line 5749: "A Wincestre d'illeuc alout." The precise translation in P has been altered in L (or its immediate source).

6389–92: The line order in P is closer to Wace 5975–79; the version in L is evidently a revision.

6471–73: It is perhaps possible that RMB used the repetition here as a poetic device, but more likely that the version in L is closer to the original. The P scribe may have tried to cover up a blunder. Note the different spellings of *myrk-mirk* and the obvious attempt to supply a rime word in *rayne.*

6489: The change of scribe in P occurs after the first three words in line 6489; the second scribe repeats them in error and then has a problem fitting the rest of the line in the space.

6532: *Saxins* in P is a rare substitution: this MS usually has *Sessons,* but the pagans Melga and Guanis are referred to as *Saracens* in the preceding passage (6484, 6488, 6494). The second scribe, who writes this passage (from 6489), perhaps used a word that was not in his source MS.

6541: The P MS has *fleuh,* an unusual spelling for *flouh* (i.e., flayed). L has *slowe* here, which may reflect an earlier error of misreading *f* and long *s,* though the effect of these words is the same: death.

6688–94: The comparable passage is in Wace 6243–49. The four lines added in L are rather freely translated and redundant.

7226: *OED* has *throd* as a form of *thro* (v.) (i.e., to grow, thrive). Perhaps *þrod* was already obsolete when L changed it to *kynde.* In P, the phrase is redundant: "þrod to þriue"; compare Ch2 5768 where *to thro* means to grow up, thrive.

7326: The reference to *Lindesai* (RMB's own territory) actually comes from Wace: "En Lindesie, e granz aveirs" (6842). The change to *Kent* in L is inexplicable. *HRB* also has Lindsey (6:11): "To their leader Hengist he gave many lands in the neighbourhood of Lindsey." (Thorpe, 157).

7410–16: See Arnold's note to line 6917 (804–5) on Thwancastre. The passage in Wace (6912–24) is closely translated.

7428–32: The second scribe in P was evidently having some difficulty in these lines. But the reference to *Ingge* (or *Inge* in L) is not clear. RMB seems to be referring to a legendary character for whom England was named in some other source. Wace does not have 7426–

32 of P: he introduces Hengist's daughter as "Ronwen ot nun, si ert pulcele" (6931); however, the four lines added in L (7432) may have been in RMB's text. See note for 14173–214 below.

7745–83: RMB's account of the Saxons' treachery is based on Wace (7231–60), considerably rearranged and expanded. Wace's account is also highly dramatic and effective.

7960: The only instance of the crossed *d* character in this MS occurs in this line: *saið*.

8057f.: The dragon fight and the explanation are not in *HRB*, but Geoffrey's book vii, the prophecies of Merlin, follows this passage in many MSS. See Julia C. Crick, *The Historia Regum Britannie of Geoffrey of Monmouth* (1990), 4:7–8 and 4:64–65 for a list of MSS which include the "Prophecies" as a separate item. (Thorpe translates the last paragraph of book vi and all of vii, pp. 169–85). Wace has a different version in ll. 7519 (discovery of the sleeping dragons) to 7582, where *HRB* 8 begins. RMB (8057–158) follows Wace, but the passage is expanded from 64 lines to 102; e.g., 8099–108 are expanded from only two lines in Wace. Langtoft has no details of the dragon fight. (Compare Wright 1:114.)

8082–84: This brief flight into alliteration is RMB's embellishment. Neither he nor Laȝamon could resist the dramatic possibilities of this scene; compare RMB's line "flammes of fire com of þer mouht" (8078) with Laȝamon: "fluȝen of heore muðe . fures leomen" (Caligula MS, Brook and Leslie edition, 1:412). Wace has: "E des geules flambes jeter" (7530), but most of the passage represents RMB's expansion.

8101–5: Blase, Tholomer, and Sir Auntayn are not in Wace; however, the disclaimer in 8109–10 is RMB's substitute for Wace's lines 7539–42, where Wace declines to translate Geoffrey's "prophecies" because he did not understand them. (See Arnold's note for added lines in Wace MSS, p. 400, n. 7542). RMB's immediate source ("Blase boke") is not easily found. Perhaps he knew the French prose work, "Les Prophécies de Merlin" (ca. 1272–79) in which Merlin and his scribes set down the prophecies (edited by Lucy Allen Paton, *MLA*, 1926). See C. E. Pickford, "Miscellaneous French Prose Romances" in *ALMA*, 352–54. The scribes are Blaise, Maistre Antoine, Bishop Tholomer, and Maistre Petronne. Note that L (8103) has the spelling *Amytayn* for P's *Auntayn* (Antoine?); the P MS could be read *Amitayn*, or possibly an earlier copy may have been misread. A clerk called Amytans appears as an adviser to Arthur in a late fifteenth-century Scots poem, "Lancelot of the Laik," based on part of the French prose "Lancelot," where the adviser is not named. See R. W. Ackerman, "English Rimed and Prose Romances," in *ALMA*, 491–93. Blaise is cited as an authority in several works; he was evidently a Welshman, Bleheris, "a story-teller of pre-eminent artistry and power," according to Roger Sherman Loomis. Blaise was "an omniscient source for the early history of Arthur and Merlin" (*ALMA*, 58).

8203–10: Compare Wace, 7622–32; some revision may have been done in both of RMB's MSS.

9655: RMB rimes *flegh* and *begh* here; the expression "bi bank and begh" means that Arthur pursued Colgrine everywhere. The alteration in L is probably the work of the reviser. See *MED* (B.5, p. 1088): *bough,* (e).

9792: RMB adds this line identifying *ffiskertoun*. Compare Wace 9187, and note in D. A. Light, p. 120 for other references: "Fiskarton is about five miles from Lincoln." (M. Pelan, *L'Influence du "Brut" de Wace sur les romanciers de son temps,* 1931.)

9875–904: The comparable passage in Wace is 9271–300; the P version is a rearrangement of Wace's description, but L has rewritten and expanded it, possibly from a different source. See D. A. Light, note p. 122. A brief list of the terms used to describe armor ca. 1300 is in H. R. Loyn, ed., *The Middle Ages: A Concise Encyclopaedia* (1989), 36.

9904: Compare the two lines added in L to Wace 9299–300: "Alques fu luncs e alques leez / Mult ert en busuine dutez." These lines are omitted in two Wace MSS [DL], however. Possibly the reviser of L's exemplar consulted a different Wace MS than the one RMB translated. See note for lines 6145–46 above.

9930: The six lines added in L are not a direct translation of Wace, but the passage in 9322–37 (one of Wace's famous examples of repetition) contains most of the same matter. See

Lesley Johnson, "Robert Mannyng's History of Arthurian Literature" (1991) for several examples of RMB's "reworkings of Wace's virtuoso passages" (p. 134, n. 11). From this point in the *Chronicle,* there is a marked increase in the number of additions in the L MS (or omissions in P). Whether the additions were in RMB's text or not is debatable, but one may conjecture that most of them were, and that the P MS reflects the scribe's attempt to shorten the work and save his labor. Compare the parallel passage in MS R at 12550–699 where P's omissions are very clearly demonstrated. R. H. Fletcher, *The Arthurian Material in the Chronicles* (repr. 1958), has an exhaustive list (pp. 204–8) of passages showing differences in RMB's version from that of Wace. His analysis is based on Furnivall (Ch1) in L and the Le Roux de Lincy edition of Wace, which differs from the edition of Arnold.

10056: The second line added in L is strange. Perhaps the L scribe (or the reviser) was anticipating 10057. Compare Wace 9447–48: "Escot en l'eue s'enbatirent / Par les illes se departirent."

10090: L adds two lines; compare Wace at 9487. RMB abridges 9477–87. See Light, note p. 126, concerning Wace's changes to *HRB* here.

10211–18: RMB adds these lines, evidently from another source; compare Wace 9604–5. In 9605, Wace has "Piram, un sage chapelein. . . ."

10247: The various names for Genoyre in the Wace MSS are in Arnold, p. 808, note to line 9645, where he gives fifteen variants in comparison with others in *HRB*. None of them have precisely the same spelling as in PL. Tracing the type of *HRB* MS that Wace might have used has exercised many scholars. For an excellent review of the controversy over the "Variant Versions," see Julia C. Crick, 4:13–18. Using proper names as a clue to identification of a possible source MS is obviously futile when so many variants appear.

10314: See Arnold's note (p. 809, note to line 9708) on "Rumarek Kyng of Wentland" and note 10922 below.

10333–34: The P scribe has added *in pes* at the end of 10333 in smaller script, evidently a correction to line 10334 but not so marked. The reading in L is probably correct and is the justification for the text as shown in 10334.

10359f.: See Light's notes (132–33) for references on the round table. The account in Wace is "the earliest known mention of a round table in connection with King Arthur." Compare Wace 9751f.

10390: The eight lines added in L correspond to Wace 9783–88, but out of order. Arnold notes differences among the MSS of Wace on p. 515.

10391f.: Wace's lines (9791–99) have been much expanded: 10391–420 are added in P; the additions in L at 10404 and 10418 may have been in RMB's original translation.

10415–20: RMB may have been referring to the French prose "Vulgate Cycle" here. See Jean Frappier's chapter in *ALMA*, 295–318. There are five romances dated in the early thirteenth century.

10433: *Sichelyn,* king of Norway, appears in Wace (9807) and in *HRB* as *Sichelm* (9.11, Thorpe, 223). The name of the king is omitted in L; either the reviser recast this line or the revision may be the result of a misreading in a prior MS.

10706: "He toke him bir" means that he gathered strength. See *MED* (B.3, p. 877): bir(e), (n.) 3b, where this line is quoted from L for *byre.*

10763–75: RMB adds this passage (see Wace 10144–46). The lines added in L after 10764 and 10774 are probably interpolations. See the references in note 8101–5 and 10415–20 above. Lesley Johnson, "Robert Mannyng's History of Arthurian Literature" (1991), 142–44, has a useful discussion of this passage, with additional references on French prose narrative.

10804: The two lines added in L are in Wace at 10183–84, but omitted in two of the Wace MSS [GR]. The P scribe evidently found them objectionable.

10818–28: RMB expands and rearranges this passage from Wace 10190–200; the lines added in L after 10826 more or less represent Wace at 10199–200. At the top of f. 48 in L, ll. 10819–20 are repeated in error with a slightly different reading.

10879ff.: The list of kings and other dignitaries at Arthur's feast begins at 10249 in Wace, with some variations in spelling. See Arnold, p. 538, for variants in the Wace MSS.

10906–12: Wace has a different arrangement of this list of names (compare 10274–88): 10910 is Wace's line 10286 ("Ne vuil jo mie faire fable") which provides RMB with an excuse to skip Wace's lines 10275–84: "to rekne þam alle it is fable." RMB needed *fable* for a rime with *table*.

10922: *Reumarek* (10922L) comes from an earlier passage (10314). In Wace 9710, he is "Rummaret de Wenelande." See J. S. P. Tatlock, *Legendary History of Britain* (1950), p. 475, n. 34, for a detailed account of this character. (See also note to line 5601 above.) The P version in 10922 (*Kynmare*) is inexplicable. There may have been a garbled line in the MS which was P's source. Compare 10896 where *Kinmare* is "kyng of Canterbiri."

10937–52: This passage is based on Wace 10329–36 with several additions; RMB has attempted to imitate Wace's stylistic repetition here.

11022–26: This passage differs in Wace (10408–18), but the version in L is also different from both P and Wace. The variants in the Wace MSS do not account for the added lines in L. The reviser may have borrowed some of his descriptions from later French romances that were not available to RMB. Compare L's expansion and embellishment in 9879–90.

11138–58: RMB has an abridged version of Wace (10540–88); see Light, note p. 150: "This celebrated passage does not occur in seven MSS [of Wace]." But it is included in Arnold's edition for reasons explained on pp. xlix–l of his introduction. The MSS lacking the passage are Arnold's HABPNTD. (On p. 553, Arnold notes that MSS PDLFHABNT lack 10543–588.) The differences in these MSS are in Arnold's notes to these lines. The passage has Wace's detailed embellishment of the activities at the feast, based ultimately on *HRB* 9:13–14 (Thorpe, 228–29). See note for lines 4862–71 above. Wace MS J has a number of variants here, and 10563–86 of the base text are missing. Wace's use of both the Variant and Vulgate versions of *HRB* may be reflected in these later passages of the *Brut*. See the discussion in Neil Wright, *The "Historia Regum Britannie" of Geoffrey of Monmouth: The First Variant Version* (1988), especially pp. lxxvii and cii–civ.

11158: L is probably correct; it is impossible to deduce what P means.

11171–94: This passage reveals an attempt to render Wace's repetition (in 10598–620), or at least to imitate the form of the French. RMB was not especially successful, but the attempt is notable. Ten of the Wace MSS omit 10601–20 [PDLCFHABNT]. The six lines in L at 11185f. are probably a revision of RMB's version.

11523: P has *bares* and L has *þe bars*. The meaning could be "barriers" since the next line suggests that treachery may be expected. Light's translation of this part of Ohel's speech (Wace 10916–17) has: "Cross Burgundy, cross France, cross the Alps; take Lombardy!" (p. 158) The barriers would be the Alps, but something has been lost in RMB's translation.

11532: The last word in the first line of the L addition probably should be *wel* to rime with *ilkadel*.

11543–48: These lines are not in Wace and they are conspicuously out of order here. They are in *HRB* at the beginning of 9:15 (Thorpe, p. 230) but out of context. Dubrice (last mentioned at Arthur's coronation), Arthur's uncle David, and the reassignments of bishops appear in *HRB* just before the envoys from Rome arrive at Arthur's court, which would place them at ca. l. 11190 in RMB's text. Furnivall includes these lines in parentheses but makes no comment (pp. 412–13).

11570–606: The P version is abbreviated, while L has lines that are probably closer to RMB's original. Much of Wace's embellishment in the passage (10980–11040) has been omitted. Arnold's variant MS notes (p. 574) indicate that Wace MS J lacks 10985–86 and 10993–11004.

11661: The word *þoute* is quite clear in the MS but is evidently an error. The word *route* in L is doubtless correct.

11689–90: RMB (or his scribe) runs the names together: compare Wace, "Vint Marcel e Luces Catel / Cocta e Gaius Metel" (11115–16).

11769: Compare Wace 11228: "Boelines sachent e halent," and the descriptive passage (in 11205–32). RMB does his best with it, but the nautical terms lacked some necessary English equivalents. According to Light, this famous description of the departure of the fleet includes a number of terms not found elsewhere in twelfth-century French literature. For *boulyne* and *bouspret* (in L) see *MED* (B.5, p. 1100). The six lines added in L at 11798 are in Wace (11234ff.). See Light's translation and notes, pp. 163–64.

11879: Compare Wace 11317–18. Arnold notes that these lines naming the giant are lacking in six of the MSS and are inserted in the text in two different places in the MSS where they do occur. He comments that if the lines are an interpolation in Wace, there is still no way to account for the source; the giant's name is not in *HRB* (Arnold's note, p. 811).

12036–44: The word *lothyn* has inspired some notice as a link to line 1095 in the alliterative *Morte Arthure;* see J. L. N. O'Loughlin's article in *ALMA*, p. 523, n. 1. In RMB's description of the giant, Dinabroke, we find *broþen* in P and *lothen* in L. At 12042, P has *lothelik.* Both words are obviously employed to accommodate the rime. Since the P version is at least as authentic as the appearance of *lothen* in L, the connection is doubtful. The *Morte Arthure* poet's language is ultimately from Lincolnshire: in this matter of diction, we probably have an example of local idiom rather than any direct influence of RMB on the later poet.

12070: The word *etild* is not in *MED*, nor does the passage in Wace account for it: "Artur senti le cop pesant, / S'espee tint, leva le brant. . ." (11503–4). The reviser of L's copy found a term to interpret the intention: *peyned,* meaning that he took pains to, made an effort.

12128ff.: Wace has the story of *Rithon* (at 11563ff.) which is derived from *HRB* 10:3 (Thorpe, 240). He is Retho, whom Arthur killed on Mount Arvaius. Wace includes the unusual word *urle* in 11578, and "El munt d'Arave le venqui" in 11588. The progressive confusion of names appears in l. 12156: P has *mounte de Rame* and L has *Derane.*

12179: In both MSS, *Ostun* or *Hostun* is written with a stroke over the *u* for the nasal, either *m* or *n.* Compare 12792, 12798, 12806, 12954: in 12792 *Oscom* rimes with *som* in P, while L has *Oston,* the only instance where the word is spelled out. In 12953–54 the rimes are *thrum-Hoscum* for P and *þrom-Ostum* in L, with *Ostum* abbreviated. The scribes were probably more concerned about the eye-rime than precise spelling of the word.

12200–208: Compare Wace 11641–46. Furnivall notes (p. 438, n. 7) that RMB "follows the Arsenal MS of Wace" in 12205–8 (Arnold's MS R). See Arnold, pp. 606–7, for the MS variants.

12469: P evidently errs in this line, as he refers later to "Sir Yder" (12473, 12475, 12479ff.). The reading in L is correct, but see 12715, where "Yder sone" appears again but is not named.

12550: The fragment in MS R begins with this line. The differences in the three MSS in this part (12550–699) demonstrate that R was another copy of RMB's text in the North East Midland dialect as represented in the same MS tradition by P. These MSS may be nearly contemporary. The revision in a different dialect found in L is illuminated by the differences in line readings where PR differ from L. Differences in RMB's text as compared to Wace are also demonstrated: there are many lines in LR that are not in P nor in Wace. In comparison to Arnold's edition of Wace (especially after 12023), it appears that RMB has rearranged the text, but his changes may have come from a different Wace MS. Arnold switched to a different base MS at l. 12000 for reasons explained in his introduction; the change is noted on 2:624. (It is doubtless a coincidence that the fragment of Ch1 in MS R begins at this juncture.) The base MS for the rest of Arnold's edition is Durham Cathedral MS C.IV.27.1 [D]. The parallel lines in R also reveal that P has abridged this part of his text, for LR have several lines added at 12570 that are translated from Wace (see ll. 12023–36) but omitted in P. It is at least possible that PR descend from the same source MS, and the L revision was based ultimately on a MS that was also a descendant of the PR MS source. There is another possibility: could P have been a copy from the complete R MS? To answer this question, one must take into account the P scribe's omissions in order to shorten his text and his frequent alterations of the diction within the lines he was copying. Because of P's omissions, it would not be possible for R to have used P as exemplar.

12566: P errs, possibly an attempt to cover up another error, and omits the added line in LR; the rimes are disturbed, indicating clumsy revision in P from 12566 to 12570.

12869: *Correie* is probably RMB's word and the L line is misread from the beginning. Compare 7414: "Castelle de Correie" (P) and "Castel de Correye" (L). *MED* refers *correi* to *conrei* (in C.5, p. 528, where four references to RMB's *Chronicle* appear).

12900: This line and 12905 are identical in P, while L has slight differences: *doughti* for *gode* in 12900 and *godnesse* for *gode dedis* in 12905. The comparable lines in Wace are 12398–99 and 12403.

12945–48: Compare 13271–74. This curious repetition suggests that RMB may have used a disarranged Wace MS. Comparable lines in Wace begin with "Lucius fud d'Espaine nez" (12451), but the repetition is missing: it would be at ca. 12840, just before RMB's line, "He knewe wele Sir Wawayn" (13275).

12973: See note for line 4274 above.

12983: Compare 12954 and L variants in both lines: *Ostum* (Autun). Evidently P confuses *c-t* here. See note for line 12179.

13169: The L scribe added 13178 here in error, then crossed it out and added it correctly nine lines later: "Wel holpe his men þat about him war."

13197–98: *Boloyne* in 13197 is an error in P, but *Babilloyne* is correct in L. Wace has *Buluine-Babiloine* (12743–44).

13382: The roman numerals here are rare; the only other instances in this MS are in the hand of the second scribe. Compare ll. 6497 *xxx* and 7420 *xiii* (L: *sexten*).

13449, 13454: *Chinnun* is the probable reading in P, but *Chimuin* is possible, closer to L's *Chymoun*. Furnivall reads *Chinnun* for P (p. 486, n. 3); Wace has *Chynon* in 12996 and 12997.

13472: L has two crossed-out lines (f. 59v c. 2) mid-column, evidently a correction done by the scribe as they are also bracketed; the lines are 13677–78 (f. 60v c. 2).

13592–97: RMB adds the details about the burial from Langtoft (Wright 1:220.); compare Wace 13148–49. From l. 13400 on, RMB frequently augments Wace's account by reference to Langtoft's version of the events.

13687: See Arnold's note for Wace 13253, p. 812. The Wace MSS differ: nine have Camble as in Arnold's edition. Light's note (p. 204) refers to other authorities on the river Tamar at the border of Cornwall. In *HRB* the river is the Camblam or the Camel (Thorpe, 259–60).

13693–98: RMB takes these lines from Langtoft (1:223, ll. 18–23) as noted by Furnivall (2:495). The duel of Arthur and Modred is not in Wace. Hamel, *Morte Arthure: A Critical Edition* (1984), in her note for l. 4226, quotes RMB's lines "following Langtoft." The resemblance of this passage in RMB's account and in *Morte Arthure* at this point is not sufficient to justify regarding RMB's *Chronicle* as a source for the passage in the alliterative poem, though Langtoft might have been a source.

13721–37: These lines are much changed from the passage in Wace (13275–93). The two lines added in L at 13722 may be interpolated. The list of names in 13727–32 is in *HRB* 11:2 (Thorpe, p. 261) and in Langtoft (1:224) but not in Wace. The date of Arthur's ending (542) is correct in L: "Cinc cenz e quarante dous anz" (Wace, 13293). See Light, 205, for other references concerning Arthur's departure to Avalon.

13896–903: This passage is based on Wace 13430–45; the lines added in L at 13896 and 13902 are in Wace, which P omits, evidently to shorten the text. The Wace MSS have many variant readings, chiefly omissions.

13945–50: Wace has a somewhat different version (13495–99); the four lines added in L (after 13948) may have been based on discoveries after RMB's time.

13953–59: This passage is ultimately based on *HRB* 11:10 (Thorpe, 265). Langtoft has an allusion (1:230.)

13973–82: Mannyng attributes this passage to Bede, but it is not in the *Eccl. Hist.;* see Furnivall's n. 1, p. 506 and n. 2, p. 510. *HRB* 11:9 includes a tirade similar in tone to RMB's brief homily.

14004–24: RMB has rewritten and expanded this passage from Wace (13547–74); the line order in L is closer to Wace's version. The arrangement in P may be an attempt to cover up an omission of the six lines after 14004 which are in the correct order in L.

14047–56: Wace has only a few random lines in this passage (13577–82). RMB's account of the sparrows, however, follows Wace closely (13592–624). For 14083–84, Wace has "La cité as muissuns nomer" (13621). Neither *moshon* (P) nor *mischeroun* (L) are in *OED* or *MED.* RMB may have invented a word or adapted Wace's term, or the scribes have misinterpreted. See the note for 13385 in Arnold's edition (p. 813) and other references there cited: "la ruse de Gormond pour prendre Cirencester est mentioneé avant Wace par Gaimar dans son *Estoire des Englés*" (p. lxxx). Gaimar attributes the siege of the city to Cerdic. Arnold adds: "Miss Houck a proposé une ingénieuse explication de l'équation Cirencestre-Cité as moissons (*Brut,* 13617–24). Elle part de Kaer Ceri, Cité des blés pour arriver à Cité as moissons (récoltes), d'où par un malentendu, Cité as moissons (moineaux)" (p. 813). The reference in Gaimar is at ll. 856–63 (see Bell's, ed. of Gaimar's history, 1960, pp. xiv–xv), with *muissuns* in l. 858. The story in the *Anglo-Saxon Chronicle* attributes the capture of Cirencester to Ceawlin in 577 (see Arnold, pp. 305–6).

14107–219: Most of this passage is lacking in Wace: see 13643f. RMB names his sources in 14121–24. Langtoft deals with the seven kingdoms (1:230–32), saying he found the account in Gildas: "Gildas, en ses estoryes, pur veir, nous ad counté." RMB has much expanded this passage. The attribution to either Gildas or Nennius is doubtful, however. See Furnivall, p. 512, n. 8 and p. 513, n. 3. See R. William Leckie, Jr., *The Passage of Dominion: Geoffrey of Monmouth and the Periodization of Insular History in the Twelfth Century* (1981), especially pp. 65–69.

14173–214: RMB attributes the account of Engle and Skardyng to Thomas of Kendale (14202) and the detail that Engle had "nien" ("nynetene" in L) sons is from "Maistre Edmunde" (14205). None of this matter is in Wace; however, for the naming of the land, Wace devotes several lines (13643–52). At (or after) 14214, RMB (or a later scribe) has probably omitted some lines that would explain the reappearance of the *Inge* legend here. Compare ll. 7428L and 7429 for RMB's earlier attempt to discredit the story: here he says he never found "in boke writen ne wrouht" (14215) any support for the idea that *Inglond* was named for *Inge.* See R. M. Wilson, *The Lost Literature of Medieval England* (1970), 39–40.

14234–320: Wace has a very brief comment (at 13676) on the loss of Christian faith and follows immediately with the mission of Augustine (13683). RMB has evidently rewritten the account from Bede, 2:1, with additions.

14240–50: The added lines in L (at 14240 and 14250) may be interpolated, but were probably in RMB's original version. Bede's tale of St. Gregory and the English children is in *Eccl. Hist.* 2:1. At 14330, the more specific reference to Bede may reveal a meticulous scholar's hand in revision, but the "fifte capitle of þe boke" (P), or the "secounde boke" (L) concerns events of AD 616, the death of Ethelbert and other matters. See the table of genealogies of the Kentish kings in the Everyman edition of Bede, p. xxiii, where the ancestry of Ethelbert is given from Nennius and the *Anglo-Saxon Chronicle* as well as Bede. (RMB's version is in ll. 14333–42). See Arnold's note for line 13683 (p. 814) for a comparison of *HRB* and other sources, and the Bede references. For Wace 13694, Arnold quotes the passage from Bede, 2:5 in Plummer's (Latin) edition.

14317–541: The arrival of "Saynt Austyne" in Kent and the events thereafter are in Bede 1:25 and 1:32ff. RMB follows Bede as he says in 14330. Wace has only a few lines (13693ff.) for the events of Augustine's mission compared to RMB's account. At line 13713, Wace has Augustine go to *Dorecestre* (not *Roucestre* as in 14541 and 14568 of RMB), but the variant Wace MS C has *Roucestre* (BL MS Cotton Vitellius A. x.) here and also at Wace's line 13747. The "righ tailes" episode (14550) is briefly told in Wace, beginning at 13723: "A ses dras destriés li pendeient / Cues de raies. . . ."

14340–41: Furnivall reads *Irumeryk* in L; possibly the scribe misread his source MS that had *Irmineryk* (as in P) which is correct in Bede. The minims in *um* or *mi* can be confusing. He is named *Eormenric* in Nennius and the *Anglo-Saxon Chronicle.*

14457–460: These lines are in red ink in P and touched up with red in L.

14465ff.: This passage is from Bede 1:23. The date should be 582 for the beginning of the reign of Maurice; L is correct on the twenty-one year reign, but Bede says Maurice was the fifty-fourth *successor* to Augustus. In l. 14473, P is correct: thirteen years, six months and ten days.

14481–502: RMB follows Bede in 1:26. After 14502, he follows Bede 2:3 to l. 14532.

14626: This line may be misplaced. The passage would be more logical if 14626 came after line 14630. Compare Furnivall's punctuation of this passage on p. 530: "Ageyn al þe Englische poer, / Monke, abbote, & seculer." (L, ll. 15273–74, Furnivall's numbers).

14699ff.: The spelling of *Brochiuayl* is consistent in PL but the name is *Brochinal* in Wace (only in l. 13889). Furnivall notes some Wace variants (p. 533, n. 3) that are not given in Arnold's list (p. 726). (Furnivall was using the edition of Le Roux de Lincy, of course.) In *HRB*, this character is *Brochmail* (11:13; Thorpe, 267).

14731–59: This passage is not in Wace; the death of "Saynt Austine" is in Bede 2.3 and the death of "Ethelbright" in 2:5.

14913–50: RMB has much expanded Brian's speech: see Wace 14079–98. The six lines added in L are in Wace (14094–98).

15070–72: Wace's name for the town is transformed here from "A Kidelet ariva dreit. . ." (14225) to *Achidalet.* The two lines added at 15070 in L replace 14226–28 in Wace: "Ki a cel tens cité esteit / Entre Dinan e la marine / Encore i pert bien la ruine." The two lines added in L at 15072 are in Wace (14231–32).

15075–109: RMB has added this passage from Langtoft (Wright 1:246–48). Compare Wace 14235–37.

15249–52: These four lines are from Bede (2.20) according to Furnivall (p. 554, n. 3), but the marriage is also recorded in Wace (14388–90), probably based on *HRB* 12:14 (Thorpe, p. 280). The Penguin and Everyman editions do not have Penda's marriage in 2:20.

15268–311: This passage differs from Wace, though he alludes to the battle of Hatfelde (Helfelde) in 14407. The substance of the account is in Bede 2:20, and a briefer version in Langtoft (p. 252: MS B: Halfeld). In *HRB*, the site of the battle is Hevenfeld. Compare *HRB* 7:10 (Thorpe, 277).

15326–72: Bede's opinion of the barbarous Cadwalyn is in 2:20; the events of Oswald's reign are in Bede 3:2–3, 6. Compare 15327–30 with RMB's second definition of *barbaryn* (also attributed to Bede) at 15877–78.

15413–60: This passage is not in Wace (see 14483ff). The account is based on Bede 3:9; the proverb in line 15433 and the account of the mutilation are in Bede 3:12.

15599–608: These lines are not in Wace. Bede deals with Bishop Aidan in several chapters of book 3; the context of this passage is perhaps extrapolated from 3:16 where Aidan invokes God's vengeance on Penda. The account of the battle and the death of Penda is in Bede 3:24 [AD 655]. At 15627, RMB gives the exact date.

15691–748: Only a few of these lines are in Wace. The source is in *HRB* 12:15 (Thorpe, 280–81). Langtoft has a very short version of 15717ff., Cadwaldre's pleynt (pp. 258–60). It is impossible to determine whether the eight lines added in L at 15748 were RMB's original lines.

15761: The P MS clearly has *þhere* and L has *ȝer,* though Furnivall read P as *yhere.* In either reading, the error is doubtless in P.

15800: From this point to the end of his *Chronicle*, Part I, RMB expands and abridges Wace freely. Wace, however, included several passages that RMB omitted (e.g., 14757–74); the remainder of RMB's text after 15905 is, of course, not in Wace. Part of the text from 15814ff. is provided in abbreviated form in Langtoft (pp. 260–64), but see Wace 14775ff. The passage in Wace (14843–58) is also given in truncated form in Langtoft (p. 262), but not in RMB's text. Arnold says Wace's ll. 14839–58 are missing in MS H (p. 777).

15857: See Thorpe, pp. 282–83 (*HRB* 12:17–18) for comments on the variant texts of *HRB* in this account. As before, *Aquile* is personified (see note for 2230 above). The phrase, "what Merlyn said" (15860) reveals that Geoffrey's *Prophecies,* though rejected by Wace, were known to RMB; however, Langtoft's MS B was probably RMB's immediate reference: "Les lineys [*sic*: MS A has livers] Aquile e Sophon les prophez" which Wright translates as "The books of the eagle which prophecied at Sephou" (pp. 262–63). Wace may also have influenced RMB here: "Se cuncordot as diz Merlin / E Aquile le bon devin / E a ço que Sibille escrist" (14813–15).

15895–900: Every other line in P is in red.

15896: In L, a later hand corrects to *menia castra lares.*

15901–4: These four lines fill up the remainder of c. 1; they may have been the source of the confusion about two separate works in the MS which is asserted in the early catalogs of the Petyt collection. See the general introduction to this edition.

NOTES TO PART II

The following notes to the text of Ch2 refer to Thomas Wright's edition of Langtoft. Though Mannyng referred to Langtoft in several passages in Part I of his *Chronicle* [Ch1], his major source was *Le Roman de Brut de Wace* (ed. by Ivor Arnold, 2 vols. Paris: SATF, 1938, 1940). As the text notes for Ch1 indicate, RMB's occasional reliance on Langtoft applies mainly to some of the later passages, where he also consulted Bede. Scholars concerned about the Wace MSS have discovered that both the "Vulgate" and "Variant" versions of Geoffrey's *HRB* were used, particularly in the later parts of Wace's poem. It may be possible that some of RMB's references to Bede were in the Wace MS which he used for his translation; if so, he may have depended less directly on Bede than his frequent references would suggest. Identification of such a MS is nearly impossible, however, and would require a different kind of approach than the present edition affords.

Part II [Ch2] begins with the second of Langtoft's three books at p. 278 of Wright's ed., vol. 1. Langtoft's books are printed as a single work in the edition, paginated accordingly. This division of Langtoft's chronicle was suggested by M. Dominica Legge, who credits the arrangement originally to Gaimar (see her *Anglo-Norman in the Cloisters* [1950], especially 70–74, and also *Anglo-Norman Literature and its Background* [1963], 278–80).

For his edition, Wright used four of the Langtoft MSS:

A. British Library, Cotton Julius A. V [base MS]
B. British Library, Royal A. XI
C. British Library, Royal 20. A. II
D. College of Arms, Arundel LXI

For the text of the history of Edward I (book three), Wright also includes a few variants from College of Arms MS Arundel XIV [E], which is discussed in his preface to vol. 2 (vii–viii). Wright also there describes Cambridge University Library MS Gg. I.i [G], which has a different version of some of the political songs but contains only the portion of Pers' work covering the years 1272 to the end of 1296. He also discusses the contents of Bibliothèque Nationale, Paris MS F.Fr. 12154, which has two versions of Langtoft's work: one of these covers Pers' text for the years 688 to the end of 1296; the other is a separate complete text but they stem from different MS traditions.

A reliable analysis of these MSS and eleven other Langtoft MSS (some of them briefly mentioned by Wright) is by Thomas M. Smallwood, "The Text of Langtoft's *Chronicle,*"

(1977), 219–30. Jean Claude Thiolier has published an "Édition Critique et Commentée" with the title *Pierre de Langtoft: Le Régne D'Édouard Ier* (1989), which includes detailed descriptions of all the MSS listed by Wright and Smallwood, as well as some other MSS which he regards as sources for Langtoft's text (35–142; his summary of MS sources is on 150–51). Thiolier presents a partially edited text based on MS E and the 642 lines in MS F (Oxford, Bodleian Fairfax MS XXIV).

In Smallwood's analysis, however, MSS EF "represent a separate independent revision" of Langtoft's original work (p. 224), while Thiolier regards MSS EF as the first version of Langtoft's work and disagrees completely with Smallwood's analysis. I do not find any merit in Thiolier's arguments for the primacy of MSS EF. The evidence Smallwood presents to support his classification of the Langtoft MSS seems to me to be quite convincing.

Among the MSS of Langtoft, only MS B (BL Royal A. XI) has a substantial body of readings that are clearly related to Mannyng's translation, as indicated in the variant notes to Wright's edition. There is a close concurrence of the spellings of proper names, for example, and much of the diction in Mannyng's text appears in the French spelling found in this MS. Since MS B has not been printed, however, I have relied on Wright's notes for its contents; further study of the Langtoft MSS would probably reveal more information about Mannyng's source MS. The purpose of identifying such a source MS, of course, would be to illuminate doubtful readings in Mannyng's text as much as possible. There are occasional variant readings in the other Langtoft MSS (noted as appropriate) which suggest that the MS tradition represented in B had some variables and that this MS was not the actual source Mannyng used; the type of MS, however, that survives in B has sufficient resemblances to Mannyng's text to provide useful comparisons.

For establishing a text of Mannyng's *Chronicle* in Part II [Ch2], the only complete source is Petyt MS 511, Vol. 7 [P]. The Lambeth MS 131 [L] has only the first 4973 lines of the P text in Ch2. It is revised in a different dialect and shows that the text has been altered in many passages. The chief addition in L is the "Havelok" interpolation, which appears at l. 538 after omission of P's ll. 520–38.

Thomas Hearne, who first edited this part of the P MS in 1725, has been consulted for readings in lines that are not clear and on MS pages that have evidently been damaged since Hearne's edition was prepared. His numerous errors are not listed separately, however, since a careful reading of P and comparison with L (and Wright's notes for Pers' MS B) have provided most of the corrections for the text as presented here. Unfortunately, many of Hearne's errors have been repeated in Wright's notes, as well as in virtually every later study of Mannyng's *Chronicle.* Hearne's pioneer edition includes a great many interesting comments that he (the premier antiquarian of his age) thought worth printing. Many of his perceptions seem quaint, but in some instances Hearne's judgments now appear to be at least as sound as those of later scholars. It is recommended that doubtful readings (so marked in the following notes) in this new edition be compared to Hearne's edition, particularly for references to those instances in which later studies have quoted Hearne's work, including the citations in *OED* or *MED*. Many of the unusual words appearing in Hearne's edition are misreadings of the MS, though it is not always possible to discover what the P scribe intended either. The following notes include discussion of some of these strange words in an effort to illuminate RMB's intentions and the scribe's possible or probable misinterpretations and errors.

Though Hearne had three of the Langtoft MSS available, he used them only for occasional notes. He also knew of L but did not use it for variant readings. Some of Hearne's misreadings have been corrected in citations for Ch2 in the *Middle English Dictionary,* based on reinterpretation of what the P MS preserves as well as the editors' conjectures.

Other sources for materials used by both Langtoft and Mannyng have helped to illuminate some sections of the text. The major section on Richard I, for example (at ll. 3485ff.), has some useful parallels in the nearly contemporary "romance" of Richard, as it appears in the edition by Karl Brunner (1913). Earlier (now lost) versions of this work (perhaps in French) probably included some of the matter in Langtoft's source, though the MSS edited by Brunner differ from Langtoft and Mannyng in significant ways. An earlier edition of this "romance" was published by Henry Weber, *Metrical Romances of the Thirteenth, Fourteenth, and Fifteenth Centuries* (1810) under the title "Richard Coeur de Lion," with Gonville and Caius College, Cambridge MS 175-96 as base text. Weber's edition is cited by Robert Peter Stepsis in his dissertation. See the introduction to this edition for further information on the sources and authorship of the "Romance" RMB cites.

The following line numbers apply to the text for P:

67–68: P has transposed these lines; L is correct.

109–10: Several references to Henry of Huntingdon indicate RMB's great admiration for the twelfth century author of the *Historia Anglorum,* in which the "fiue sorowes" theme is an organizing principle. Though RMB is translating Pers here (Wright, 1:286–90), it is clear that he had a thorough acquaintance with Henry's history. A recent appraisal of Henry of Huntingdon is in Nancy F. Partner, *Serious Entertainments: The Writing of History in Twelfth-Century England* (1977).

196: P errs: L correctly has *Brittrik,* and P's confusion continues to l. 197. Compare l. 191: Herman is Britrik's steward, killed by Kebriht (194). In Pers (MS B), the name is confused: *Rebrith;* MS D has *Kebrike.*

205–6: Pers does not cite Bede here, and RMB has expanded this passage (Wright, 1:294). RMB seems to be reviewing notable events recorded in Bede (v.24) with an eye to Henry of Huntingdon's account as well.

241–42: Wright (p. 296, n. 18) says the "Ellendune" song is from Henry of Huntingdon, in Latin verse. RMB translates Pers (p. 298).

290: Pers' line is: "fiz le ray Sadok de la Danascherie" (MS B, 1:300) almost exactly as we have it in L. In MS C: "de Daneschery."

297: The first letter in this line has been misread by Hearne and changed in L. It is "Y" for "Yward," as in Pers' MSS BCD: "Iward" (1:302, n. 3).

337: See note for 3464 in Ch1 where the same words appear (*rimethed* in P, *rempede* in L). *MED* cites Ch2 337 *rempede* as the only reference; *rimthed* (from OE rymþ) has a different meaning.

385–56: Most of the dates within the text are supplied by RMB from captions or rubrics that appear in Pers' MSS. It is possible that he was using an earlier version of the B MS type which had the captions in the text. In this instance, Wright notes that RMB has the wrong date: it should be 860. Perhaps "& on" is added in P for a rime with "gon."

411: Wright says "Robert of Brunne has misunderstood this line" (1:310, n. 14). MS B: "Fu neef cenz cel an. . . ." Wright's translation is: "Was repeated nine times that year. . . ." Wright's expectations of Mannyng's adaptation of Pers were frequently disappointed.

416: The last two letters in this line have disappeared, but there is no doubt of the scribe's intention: *schilde,* as also in L. The rime in the following line is an error in P, but correct in L: *elde.*

436–44: Stepsis discusses the possible source for these added lines in his introduction (p. xl). William of Malmesbury, *Gesta Pontificum Anglorum* (Hamilton, ed., Rolls Series 52, 1870) includes the story, but it was widely known in RMB's time. See M. Dominica Legge, *Anglo-Norman Literature and its Background* (1963), pp. 83–84.

455: Wright quibbles about RMB's translation: "Al Pount de la Bataille" or "Battle-Bridge" is in Pers' line (1:314).

466–519: Both MSS have indications of editing: P condenses and L translates and amplifies. Probably neither MS accurately represents RMB's intentions. For l. 490, e.g., P is obscure and L omits the important words "wend wele." The sense is that Alfride feared Rollo would take the seignory from him. Since this portion of the text immediately precedes the "Havelok" interpolation in L, substantial editing (or tampering) in L is likely.

505–7: Pers has: "Gounte pere Havelok de Danes ray clamez" (MS B, 1:318) which is the only mention of Havelok in his text, and the conflict between Gunter and Alfred follows (to 518). All the matter in 519–38 of P and, of course, the interpolation in L is added. Wright notes: "Gunterus is, of course, the Guthrun of authentic history" (1:318, n. 1).

521–22: RMB lists the historians he knew and admired; these lines provide clues to his sources for several passages. Gildas died ca. 540, and William of Malmesbury died ca. 1143, Henry of Huntingdon shortly after 1154. See Antonia Gransden, *Historical Writing in England, c.550–c.1307* (1974) for bibliography and evaluations of all these early historians.

538ff.: The "Havelok" interpolation is discussed in the introduction to this edition. Various commentators on the "Havelok" matter have printed the text of L, and no two of them are identical; moreover, the various opinions on the source of this addition to the L MS are based on somewhat slender evidence. Among the earlier presentations of this section are the version printed in Walter W. Skeat's edition of *Havelok the Dane* (EETS 4, 1868), pp. xi–xiii, based on the edition for the Roxburghe Club by Sir Frederic Madden (1828); this version also appears in Sisam's revision of Skeat (1915). The recent edition by G. V. Smithers, *Havelok* (1987) has a different transcription (pp. xxii–xxiv) with several variations from Skeat-Sisam, mostly misreadings. Smithers includes a table of "characters" appearing in the various versions of the story (on p. xxxi), partly following the table given in Sisam's revised edition of Skeat (p. xix); Smithers adds comparisons for the "Anglo-Norman Brut" and a short prose chronicle called *Le Petit Bruit* attributed to Rauf de Bohun. See the earlier study by Edward K. Putnam, "The Lambeth version of *Havelok*" (1900), 1–16. Several words in the MS have variously been misread, and accordingly printed; the following list could still be challenged:

l. 3: *þourgh* seems to have the *o* crossed out, leaving the scribe's intention: *þurgh.*
l. 9: *schopè* is the usual spelling in this MS, but the *o* may seem to be an *e* here, as well as in ll. 73 and 76: a sloppy *o* might appear to make the word read *schep.*
l. 27: *Seburc* corresponds to the spelling of this name as it appears in other versions of the tale, but the last letter appears to have been written over an erasure.
l. 44: *anewest* is the correct word, sometimes misread as *auewest.*
l. 45: *desheritison* is the customary spelling in this MS (and also in P), while earlier transcribers have invented the term *desheraison.* I believe that this invented word cannot be justified, though the MS leaves the possibility of some slight doubt.

The peculiarity of Madden's version is transcription of thorn [þ] as *th,* followed by Skeat-Sisam. Smithers has ignored the usual expansion of *ll* (written with a slash) to *-lle,* for several occurrences of the words *bataille, wille,* and the name of *Argille* (or *Argentille* in l. 78). Hearne's curious misreading, *Hanelok* in all occurrences, was corrected by Madden-Skeat with the note: "*Hanelok* in Hearne, throughout, but undoubtedly *contra fidem* MSS [*sic*]" (Skeat p. ix, n. 2). Since Hearne did not offer any alternate readings from the L MS in his edition of P, he was evidently unaware that the Havelok story in L differed. Madden made the discovery when he was attempting to verify Hearne's edition. Madden's judgment of the passage is sound: "the Lambeth MS . . . does not correspond with the [Hearne's] edition, but has evidently been revised by a later hand, which has abridged the Prologues, omitted some passages, and inserted others. The strongest proof of this exists in the passage before us, in which the Lambeth MS. entirely omits the lines [519–38] of Rob. of Brunne respecting the authenticity of the story of Havelok, and in their place substitutes an abridged outline of the story itself, copied apparently from the French chronicle of Gaimar." (Quoted in Skeat, p. xi.)

566: Wright notes: "It may be remarked that Pierre de Langtoft appears to have taken the account of the marriage of the princess Hilda from William of Malmesbury" (1:326, n. 10). This note is appended to a later passage (for MS C at RMB's l. 634). Langtoft's mention of *Hilde* is translated here: "Hilde fu une des feylles, dit Hildene levedye" (1:320).

567: The version in L follows Pers' account (1:320). The names of Edward's children differ in the various Langtoft MSS.

568: This line in PL is obscure. Pers has: "La quarte ad le emperour Octavyan marye" (1:322), meaning that the emperor married Edward's daughter. Either RMB mistranslated or PL followed a source that assumed "Mary" was the name of the fourth daughter.

569–70: RMB is translating (or interpreting): "Passez sunt les autres hors de ceste vye" (1:322), the second line probably added for the rime.

631–32: These lines and the two added in L (redundantly) are not in Pers' text for the MSS Wright edited, though differences among them suggest RMB may have had a source that included them.

705–8: One of RMB's tidbits from local tradition appears here; compare ll. 797–98 for another: *Crouland* is in the neighborhood of Bourne, RMB's birthplace. Henry of Huntingdon, Archdeacon of Lincoln, also mentions Edgar's benefactions. See Stepsis' note (for 803–4), p. 446.

801–12: RMB perhaps knew the tale from a different source, though he follows Pers closely here. Wright says the account is from William of Malmesbury (1:340, n. 11).

811: P has *reustat* which is probably a misunderstanding of an unfamiliar word; L is correct. See *MED* (R.4, p. 634) citing this line: "[read: reuest F revestuz]" i.e., arrayed in ceremonial vestments. This word also occurs in *Handlyng Synne* (l. 9062): "þe prest hym reueste to begynne messe."

828: In L, a later hand has written a gloss below: ?"Corffeston," and in 830, "Wynchestre" is scratched out and an illegible word inserted above.

859–60: The line order in L agrees with Pers (1:344–46); however, these lines are both on the same line in P and transposed in L. The P scribe evidently discovered that he had omitted a line and adapted his text to cover the error.

874: RMB adds the figure, "in þe woulfes mouth" interpreting Pers line, "Pur pees aver saunz guere par trowe se lyaynt" (1:346). See l. 984.

878: Pers has the added lines in L (1:346–48). There is no apparent reason for the omission in P; it is probably another example of P's condensation of the text.

879: The second hand begins in L at top of f. 80r. The differences in the PL MSS are chiefly attributable to the obviously revised character of the L MS. In particular, the L scribes rarely attempt to preserve the internal rimes found in P, though some of the unusual words and strange spellings in these mid-line rimes are certainly attributable to the scribe of P. The characteristic letter forms of the second hand in L suggest that the folios hereafter were written somewhat later than the first 79 folios.

944: P tacks on *schire* at the end of the line but does not mark it as a correction; probably the word belongs after *Lincolne* as in L. Both MSS have questionable lines here: 943–44L is "So fals a traitoure in erthe was non as þeis Edrik was he / Of Lyncoln schire Duk by þe kyng was he."

956–57: P has a careless redundancy here; the repetition of names suggests an error, but they occur in both MSS.

1007–8: The transposition in L agrees with Pers (1:356).

1021: The correct date is in L: 1014, given in a caption in Pers' text (1:358).

1030: Pers' line is: "Vers Gaynesburge s'en va fere convocacioun" with a variant [MS C]: "pur fer destruccioun"; Wright remarks that "Robert of Brunne's translation is curiously paraphrastic here" (1:358, n.13).

1062–72: RMB has rewritten Pers' account, emphasizing the failure of Lindsey to accept Eilred (1:360). *Liche lond* (1063L) is probably an error. The MS could read *leche,* but the phrase makes no sense. Stepsis reads *liche lord* for L, but the P reading is doubtless correct.

1105: Wright quibbles: "It was the country, and not the earl, which was put to the sword" (1:364, n. 1). Pers has: "Le counté de Warwyk mys est à l'espeye." Possibly RMB's source was defective.

1118: Compare 1163. Pers' MSS differ: Wright's MS A has *Uthrede,* while CD have *Huctrede* and MS B has *Vctred.* The *c-t* confusion affects L in both lines. The character *Edryk* (or *Eyrike* in MS D) is in Pers' text for l. 1163, i.e., a different beneficiary for Northumberland.

1128: The use of "at a reade" (L: "on on red") evidently means that a council was held for the purpose of crowning Knoute; the rime is disturbed in P, however, and L (as given) is not clear.

1145–46: RMB here includes a caption from Pers: "Anno Domini millesimo XVIII" actually refers to the events following (1:366). Edmund Ironside is recorded as king only for part of 1016, from April when Æthelred died to the autumn of the same year when Edmund was defeated at Ashingdon by Cnut. Pers' text is faithfully translated in this passage and the error is his (or a scribe's). See F. W. D Brie, ed. *The Brut* (1906, p. 119).

1150–52: The lines in L are somewhat more precise; Pers has: "Et fist une demaunde molt covertement / Si ly rays Emoun à lur acordement / Salvayt à ses freres terre ou tenement" (1:366). L may be revised here.

1170: The differences in PL here indicate that L may be corrected from the source or that P is attempting to cover an error.

1204–12: Wright translates "Macbeth" in 1204, though his MSS have Makethad [A], Mathecade [B], Macherad [C], Machecade [D] (1:370, n. 6). RMB's Mathithade (P) and Mathelhade (L), illustrate the recurring confusion of *c-t* in all these MSS. To compound confusion, Wright emends *f[r]ere* and translates "brother" though the traditional Macbeth was not Malcolm's brother. Compare note for 1483.

1211: Doubtless *had* is an error for *haf* in P.

1213: RMB's judgment of Canute ("þorgh conquest & desceit") is not in Pers' text (1:370).

1223–64: The preliminary leaf in MS P has the same text as these lines (on f. 110v). The minor differences are discussed in the introduction to this edition.

1264: "William Bastard" is the epithet used in all the MSS in Wright's edition (1:374, n. 5). L consistently uses this term, while P usually explains it by modification.

1294f: Wright notes the source of this account in Florence of Worcester, "who is Langtoft's authority" (1:376, n. 4). See Gransden (1974), pp. 143–44, on the attribution of authorship for Florence.

1321–40: This passage, placed after 1625 in L, is not in Pers' text, but there is a gap in corresponding lines at 1593–1625 in the MSS (compare 1:378 and 398 in Wright). The passage may have been in a Pers MS now lost or in one of the MSS Wright did not include in his edition. Since the account is an addition, it would be more logically located as it is in L (after 1625). Stepsis traces the story of Godwin's death to *Estoire de St. Edward le Rei* (ed. Luard, Rolls Series 3, 1858), ll. 3277–3311. Nancy F. Partner (1977) says that Henry of Huntingdon also "tells the anecdote of Godwin choking to death at King Edward's table after challenging God" (p. 26, referring to Huntingdon, 193–96).

1400f: Wright notes that it was Harold's brother Sweyn who seized the abbess whose name was Eggyve [MS A], Edgyve [BD] or Edigne [C] (1:382, n. 11).

1414: "Ba" would seem to be an unfinished word, since L has "Bathe." Pers' MS B, curiously, has "de Baa" (1:384, n. 6). Compare 1457 where MS B has "L'evesqe Edolf de Baa" (1:388, n. 1). The explanation may be that l. 1414 alludes to a new town in Gascony named *Baa* for Robert Burnell, bishop of Bath and Wells. See Michael Prestwich, *Edward I* (1988), p. 310.

1483: RMB spells the name as Pers does in MS B; he is Mathethe [MS A] or Mathoge [MS D]. Wright notes, "Of course, this was the king commonly called Macbeth" (1:388, n. 17). See note 1204–12 above.

1518–19: These lines, omitted in L, have no precise counterpart in Pers' text, but the forgiveness of Griffyn (1519) is apparently added to establish the Welshman's ingratitude as evidenced in the lines following (see 1:392).

1554: The name of *Ruthe Walan* could be read *Ricche Walan* in P; L has a correction for the last word from *Waleyn* to *Walan,* probably to conform with the rime. Wright gives *Ruthwalan* for his MS A and no variants, but identifies him as *Rhywallon* (1:395).

1571: Quene Edith (L: Ediþ), sister of Harald, is Pers' *Eggyve* [MS A] or *Edgyve* [BCD]. See 1774: she is "la rayne Egith" in Pers [MS B]. The internal rime, *Godwyn* (l. 1570), may explain the alteration in her name (*Egyn*) in l. 1571, but this is an extreme instance.

1594–1625: Compare 1321–40 above. Pers has two lines: "Le duk de Normendye ublyez avayt / Du couenaunt q'il fist nul ly mentyvayt" (MS B, 1:398). RMB names his source for this passage in l. 1598, evidently a life of St Edward, which may be *Estoire de Seint Edward le Rei* (ed. Luard); Stepsis cites ll. 3711–65 in this work.

1612–14: The confusion in these lines is a scribal error in P.

1629: The reference to Harald's perjury here and *passim* may be based partly on the account in Henry of Huntingdon; see Nancy F. Partner (1977), p. 26 and her note to Huntingdon, 197.

1642: *Tyne* is Pers' word (1:400); in L, *time* is not capitalized, possibly meaning "timely."

1646–53: Pers has eleven lines in this passage, including the line added in L (at 1648). P is confused in 1649 and 1651 where Pers' lines are: "Cent et l. hostages ount en lur postez / De Everwyk mès nul n'ount de ilokes menez" (MS B, 1:400).

1668–71: The omission of these lines in L is inexplicable; see Wright, 1:402, for the comparable passage. From 1626 on, the L version has been much edited and rewritten down to the lost leaf (at 1834).

1682–85: RMB rewrites his source for dramatic effect. The rime word *paly* (for "play") is a simple transposition of letters, but *stank* (1685) is probably a scribal misinterpretation. Pers' line is: "A sun park ly mene et desuth un lay" (1:402). See l. 7010: *stampe*. The rime is corrupt in P (*lang-stank*) while L has *longe-strong*. *Stank* and *stampe* are from OF estanc according to *MED* (S.13, p. 587), but *stampe* is a unique citation for the meaning in l. 7010, where an internal rime for *Beauchamp* was needed.

1710–22: RMB rewrites and combines some of Pers' sixteen lines (1:404). The passage has evidently been revised in L, much to the detriment of the verse pattern. Pers' repetitive end-rime (*laisses* ending here in -ent, and the preceding passage in -ay for twenty-five lines) made the translator's task difficult. The modified verse pattern with a mid-line rime is notable in this part of Ch2, at first undertaken rather haltingly but later emphatically. A few of the earlier examples in Ch2 are: south-comforth (937–38); hider-Humber (973–74); baron-þeron (1025–26); felle-helle (1041–42); sonde-fonde (1101–2); Warwik-Edrik (1105–6).

1732–42: RMB adds this anecdote; Pers has nothing comparable (1:406). Stepsis suggests the probable source was William of Malmesbury, *Gesta Regum Anglorum* (see his introduction, p. xl). RMB names William as his source for a later episode; compare l. 2039.

1743–69: RMB completely rewrites this passage; Pers has only twenty lines, some of them translated here, but in a different order (1:406–8).

1786–91: The text in P is from Pers (1:408); 1789–90 are one line in Pers, while 1791 and the line added in L are lacking.

1803–11: RMB adds the details concerning Stigand. Pers names the archbisshop Alred (l. 1808; MS B, 1:410).

1817: RMB follows MS B: "Elianore la reine." She is "Malde" in Pers' MS A, "Malade" in MS D (1:412).

1870: Wright notes that RMB has mistranslated Pers here: "The meaning of the original is clear, that the women were subjected to every kind of shameful outrage before they were killed" (1:416, n. 10). Pers has: "Tue pere et fiz les femmes sunt livrez / Ad vilaine mort n'est nul eschapez."

1871: The first half of this line may be in error; compare 1880–81, where the internal rime is preserved (*lete-ete*).

1890–93: RMB adds these lines, perhaps from the life of St. Edward. Compare note for 1321–40.

1985–87: These lines are altered; L has probably been revised. Pers has: "Cel houre de Lindesey iii moynes oy nomer / Le secund ad à noun Elwyn et Aldwin le primer / Reynfrid fu le tierce qe vount quere habiter" (MS B, 1:426). The line added in L at 1987 is not in Pers' text, but l. 1988 might have suggested the idea to the reviser of L.

1988: The sheriff's name varies in the Pers MSS: "Huge le fiz Bardryk" [A], "Hugo le fitz Galdrik" [B], "Hugo le fiz Baldrik" [CD] (1:426, n. 13).

2029: L is correct; Langtoft has "le viii an" (1:428).

2039: RMB identifies his source; Stepsis provides the reference to William's *Gesta Regum Anglorum* (ed. T. D. Hardy, 2:428).
2040: RMB's translation is misleading here; Pers has "Le terce an après cele dure vengaunce . . ." (1:430).
2098–2110: RMB adds the details of William's encounter with Philip; Pers has only four lines (1:434).
2129–41: RMB expands seven of Pers' lines, adding 2130–33 and recasting the rest (1:436).
2170–71: The line order in L is closer to Pers'; "Louthþan" in L should be "Louthyan" (*y* and *þ* are sometimes similar in this MS).
2190–99: Pers has only four lines here (1:440); RMB adds identification of the principals.
2227: RMB adds a favorite proverb. The variant line in L is inexplicable.
2246–53: The line order in L is somewhat closer to Pers' arrangement and is more logical (1:444). Note internal rime in P: 2247–51, 2248–49; P has repeated half of line 2247 in 2251. The variant line in L is probably correct for 2247.
2259: The redundant lines added in L are not in Pers.
2298: L agrees with Pers on Wynchestre (1:448). P and L frequently disagree on Winchester and Westminister.
2332: This line in L is difficult: "Robert purueid hym ire & stil to come when þey wolde." The word *ire* is possibly an abbreviation for *lettre,* i.e., "letter and style," but this interpretation is not more logical than the sense in P. Some manipulation is suggested in P to provide the internal rime *stille-wille.*
2475–76: Pers has: "Aunz et jours ilokes le fet le rei garder / A vestir le trove à beyver et manger" (MS B, 1:458).
2478–85: RMB adds these lines, providing a judgment of Robert that Pers does not have. The same matter at 2510ff., however, is from Pers (1:460).
2487: RMB translates Pers' line: "Recorder la maner mon lyvre me defent."
2511–14: The line arrangement in L is closer to that of Pers (1:460).
2520–35: RMB rewrites Pers' account and changes the order of events; the exigencies of rime seem to be strained in both versions (1:460).
2527: *Wroþerheile* is attested in all of RMB's works and usually altered to some other expression by other scribes. Compare ll. 4913, 5424, 6392 (in Ch2), 2570, 3456 in Ch1, where L retains the word with different spelling, 3674 in *Handlyng Synne* (MS H changes it to *wroþer in helle*).
2529: The scribe of L was doubtful of the name of the town. After *at* is a substantial blank space, then the word *toun* is added at the end of the line. He may have been using a faulty source, or perhaps he thought *Chilyngton* was an error. Pers [MS B] has the same word as in P.
2552–53: The scribe of P has garbled these lines; L is doubtless correct.
2690–2703: RMB adds this passage; in 2703, acknowledging the digression, he promises to stick to the story. He is essentially repeating the citation of his source in ll. 91–97.
2696: Since RMB was intimately acquainted with the works of Wace, he may be referring here to Wace's *Vie de Saint Margrete.* See Stepsis' note (p. 454 for his ll. 2708–21).
2744: The word *gannok* has conjectural etymology; see *MED* (G.1, p. 27) for references and other later citations.
2747: L is evidently in error; Pers has: "Et Slede of le honur et altres chastels sys" (1:472).
2773: Pers has: "Maunde par messagers à l'eveske salvage," translated as "the wild bishop" by Wright (1:474–75). Possibly RMB avoided translation of Pers' rime word because he was attempting to keep the *-age* rime (see lines 2770–77). These lines are virtually identical in P and L.
2800–2877: The missing leaf in L disappeared before the folio numbers were added to the MS. The previous leaf (104v) is much damaged (smudged), and f. 105r has a large blot.
2811: P abbreviates "spiritu sancti" here but it is spelled out in this way at 4426.
2832: This phrase (from AF jour damour) appears first at l. 1231: a day appointed for a meeting between rivals to arrange reconciliation.

2840: Evidently part of this passage has been omitted; see Wright (1:479), where Pers' added comment is translated: "The king looks at him, the tear of weeping falls from him. They would have been reconciled then, but for a meddler . . ." who is William, the nephew (l. 2842).

2866–80: RMB rewrites this passage and adds details, including the "erþe horn" (2871: "tunniers," MS B) and the locale (2876). Wright quotes RMB and remarks, "The whole of this part of the narrative is rather obscure, and the very paraphrastic translation of Robert of Brunne, with apparently some independent information, preserved to his time by tradition, only partially clears it up" (1:480, n. 9). Stepsis suggests that Langtoft may have used the *Vita Thurstini Archiepiscopi;* see his note (for 2889, p. 455) where part of this work is quoted.

2913: The word *noȝt* in L is a correction above the line.

2933: J. A. W. Bennett (1986) comments on this passage (p. 96) in RMB's account, noting the similarity to part of the Peterborough chronicle entry for the year 1140. Pers' version differs somewhat: see 484–86.

2943: The two lines added in L are not in Pers' text (1:486); they express a rather unlikely comment for Mannyng. Possibly they were added by the reviser of L, but note the internal rime: "hed-leued."

3001: *Corun* evidently means *croune* as in L; perhaps a tonsure?

3018: The four missing pages in L are simply blank leaves: ff. 107rv and 108rv. The text resumes on f. 109r with the line corresponding to 3238 in P.

3019–23: RMB translates this passage with graphic details. At 3024, Pers has: "En retornaunt la resne fu ferus à quoer" (MS B, 1:490).

3036: Hearne has misread *Reynere* as *Reyuere* here (and in 3044, 3048, 3050) but he is *Rayner* (or Reyner, MS B) in Pers' text (1:492).

3052: The P scribe probably meant *hatred* for *hatrex* but was anticipating the next word, *wex.*

3074–81: A group of lines with identical or similar rime words is unusual for RMB, though Langtoft's typical *laisses* are obviously the model here. The text translated has the same rimes here: Fraunce, apparaunce, Alemaunce, manance [*sic*], etc. (1:494), and Pers stretches his stanza for a total of fifteen lines (to RMB's 3088), then adds another *laisse* (to RMB's l. 3111): nomé, comaundé, richeté, etc. The effort of conforming to Pers' pattern is abandoned here in favor of the usual couplets, but RMB still keeps the internal rime.

3081–87: Wright comments, "Robert of Brunne has much misunderstood his text here" (1:494, n. 8). RMB actually followed his text as he understood it; Wright's translation is often at variance but not necessarily more accurate. In these lines, it is possible RMB was following a different Pers MS.

3115: RMB is translating Pers' line: "En le terce an après chet en maladye." The logic would be improved by moving *after* to follow *ȝere,* but the internal rime (with *here* in 3114) would be lost. The sense is that Stephen enjoyed his *balie* only three more years before he fell ill.

3117ff.: The scribe makes a number of careless errors in this passage: *strfe* (3117); *heuen* (for *hauen,* 3118); *red* (for *rede,* 3125, and *gaf* is probably omitted in this line); *we quen* (for *was quene,* 3129); *scecunde* (3142); *Thomos* (3147); and *Thoma* (3148); *Caterbiri* (3151); *cleke* (3160); *gre* (for *gret,* 3170). None of these peculiarities can be explained as changed diction for the sake of preserving internal rime. They are simply errors, perhaps because the scribe was tired or sleepy. The MS is often carelessly written and rarely shows any attempts to correct errors, but this passage presents one of the most error-prone sequences of lines in the entire work.

3118–24: RMB augments Pers, who has only the first line: "Sun cors à Faversham entoumbez en l'abbye" (MS B, 1:496). Stepsis (pp. 456–57) notes that the burial of Stephen is from Henry of Huntingdon, VIII:39. In line 3121, RMB implies that he had information from a contemporary source, which would be impossible. See Stepsis' note for his lines 3140–41.

3129: The identification of Thebald is found only in Pers' MS B (2:2).

3150–51: Letters supplied in these lines (in brackets) are from Hearne, who may have transcribed the MS before the leaf was damaged (possibly the letters were lost when the MS was repaired or rebound). The damage at 3192–94 is not emended in Hearne's edition, but he adds Pers' lines in a note (p. 130 in the 1810 ed. of Hearne's *Works*). In 3221, Hearne has *witen* at the end of the line.

3156–65: RMB expands six lines from Pers (Wright, 2:4). He was evidently aware of other accounts of the conflict between Henry and Becket.

3189–94: Hearne provides the letters within brackets. See 3150–51 above. RMB is making a close translation in this passage; in 3192–94, Pers has: "Le erceveske de Everwyk son noun fu Roger / Et sun fiz Henry le fyst corouner / Et oynder en rays le regne govern-er" (2:6, with MS B variants). RMB probably added the last part of l. 3194 to provide a rime.

3221: See note for ll. 3150–51.

3226–9: Wright comments that RMB's translation is "in language not very intelligible." Pers' lines are: "Al chastel d'Aumarle barouns prist-il trays / En Engleterre les meyne ses sunt les deus Flandrays / Ke morent en prisoun pur lur fez malvays" (with MS B variants, 2:8). An edition with the whole text of MS B might indicate other differences.

3227: Wright's comment about RMB's unintelligibility in this passage may be somewhat justified. The word *snelle* (swift, prompt, from OE snel) was misread in Hearne's edition (p. 132) as *suelle.* This is the only instance of *snelle* in RMB's works, and was doubtless employed (correctly) to provide the rime with *castelle* in 3226.

3239: L has rewritten this line and lost Richard Comyn, an important character. Perhaps this change has some relevance to the fact that the previous four folios are blank in this MS. The P MS follows Pers' text here (2:16).

3263: L is correct and probably reflects RMB's translation. Pers has here: "La cité de Reme assegé trovayt" (MS B, 2:12). MS A, however, has "Roanne" here and "Roan" at 3268 ("Reme" in MSS BCD), suggesting that the text in L may have been corrected from a different Langtoft MS. Note the internal rime, *reme-ȝeme:* P does not present a simple error.

3347: L is correct; Pers has "treys C."

3352–3466: The gap of 115 ll. in L (after two lines at the top of f. 110v) may provide a clue to the line arrangement of the source MS, but is otherwise inexplicable. The folios in this part of the L MS have 37 or 38 lines (sometimes including rubrics); if two leaves of an exemplar were skipped, each page would have had about 28 or 29 lines, recto and verso. The note concerning the missing lines is in the right margin, by a later (but not much later) hand.

3359–60: These damaged lines are translated from Pers: "Sunt of le ray alez atyrez richement / Dunt parmy Parys est dit communement" (2:18). Stepsis emends 3359 with "[þe kyng]" and 3360 "þa[n sa]id" (p. 189). Hearne avoids emendation: 3359: "With. . . . .went"; 3360: "þa. . . . . .nd"; Stepsis' emendation of "sa]id" can be justified only by the line in Pers' text.

3370–97: The legal terminology in this passage has been rewritten and clarified by RMB, but the translation is substantially the same as in Pers' text (2:18–20).

3413: Pers adds nine lines here, not translated by RMB, concerning Henry's dealings with the lord of Galway, Rouland, and David, brother of the king of Scotland (2:20–22).

3416–17: The scribe nods: *tiþng* occurs elsewhere, but *wad* is an error for *was;* 3417 has a capital *W* (for *what*) but *þat* would make better sense.

3467: RMB strangely translates Pers' line: "Henry fiz l'emperyce fet molt graunt honurs" (2:24). There is no mention of a "trespas" but the following lines indicate that RMB was interpreting the events. The hagiography on Thomas' life appearing before the early fourteenth century may have influenced RMB's version. Pers' next line, "Al fertre saint Thomas où sovent gist en plurs," RMB has in 3469.

3478: L has the correct reading: thirty-four years.

3512: RMB adds a favorite exclamation not in Langtoft. The interpretation in L suggests that the scribe misunderstood or the meaning had changed.

3528–44: RMB generally follows Pers here but expands his eleven lines (2:30), perhaps from another source. Stepsis (pp. xlff.) has explored the probable sources of the additions RMB made to Pers' account and concludes that the Middle English romance of *Richard Coer de Lion* (ed. by Weber) accounts for some of them, but RMB's immediate source was probably "the lost ancestor" of that romance (p. xliii).

3576: Pers' text has *Xvj* (=16) (2:32); PL both have *sexti.* Wright notes: "According to Roger de Hoveden king William paid ten thousand marks sterling" (n. 4).

3630: L adds two lines for Pers' lines: "N'ad nul endrait de sai mestre de garçoun / Chascun a gens assez ke sevent lour escoun" (MS B, 2:36).

3639: Pers' line is: "Une fu là naeez de Depe verraiment" (MS B, 2:36). Wright translates: "One was there sunk, a ship of Dieppe truly" (2:37).

3700–20: RMB's version of this passage is rewritten from Pers' fifteen lines. "þe Kyng of Tancre" (3708, 3713) is a misreading of Pers: "Le ray Tankrede" (2:42).

3725: P has "þat flum was de la fare"; L has *felon* for *flum.* Both are evidently misunderstandings of Pers' line: "En le flum de la Fare derechef" [MSS BCD]. MS A has "En le floum de [la] Fare rychement entrayt" which Wright translates: "Entered the river of the Faro in rich array" (2:42). *MED* (F.1, p. 404) quotes this line and identifies *Fare* as the Strait of Messina, and gives only one other reference (Mandev., c.1400).

3747: Compare 3700–3720. Here, Pers has: "le rays Tankrede" (2:44).

3789: Pers has: "Bernerger demort ne pas cum hostage" (2:48).

3793: Confusion of *c-t* may go back to earlier MSS of either RMB or the source MSS of PL. Pers has "Agate" but "Agace" rimes with "grace" in RMB's next line in P. L follows P with "Agesse" and does not struggle with the internal rime, repeating "grace" as in P. Wright does not note differences among the Pers MSS; he simply translates "Agatha" (2:49).

3820: Pers has: "Ilokes ad trové sa soer et sa amye" (MS B, 2:50); RMB translates the last word as "his meyne" while Wright has "his sweetheart."

3835: A typical phrase for RMB is *gif a gyue* (L: *a gift*). Compare ll. 4275, 12973 in Ch1 and notes for those lines.

3837–46: RMB writes with more candor and delicacy than Pers of this affair, who has: "La lay de saint eglise trop serrait blemye," omitting 3842. The difference in emphasis is achieved by using Richard's own words.

3848: *Trip* in this context evidently means "a trick" but see 4992 where it means "troop." Pers' line for 3848 is "En le ray Richard ne quiday descaivaunce" (2:52). In 4992, Pers has "tut sun hoste" (2:118). RMB needed a rime for *Philip* in 3847 and also in 4991. The word *trip* occurs also in Ch1, 1821, there meaning "a trick"; *OED* has two nouns and suggests a relationship to OF treper, triper (v.) with one of the meanings "to make a false step or mistake."

3850–56: Pers has nine lines here, including (but rewritten) 3853–54 omitted in L. The version in L at 3855 is somewhat closer to Pers: "Nai sir dist Richard lesset ta manaunce" (2:52).

3870–80: RMB adds this passage, citing his source, "þe romance of Richard" (3877). The four lines added in L (at 3880) may have been in the original, but are more likely the work of the reviser. The sense of the passage suggests that RMB was supporting Pers' account with the added details, though they are somewhat redundant. RMB follows Pers closely at 3881ff. (2:54). Capitalization has been normalized in the text, though the P scribe uses capital *R* in 3870–71, but not in 3877. L consistently has lower case here. Capitals generally do not have much significance in either MS.

3893: Pers has: "Sa soer et sa amye" again translated by Wright as "his sweetheart" (2:54–55). L anticipates the wedding to come.

3895–3945: RMB has paraphrased and rearranged this passage, probably using another source. Pers has thirty-two lines, mostly in a different order (2:54–56).

4101–23: Pers has the same end-rime (-our) throughout this passage (2:66–68). RMB embellishes his sixteen lines but manages to keep the same end-rime for most of it.
4112: The L scribe writes *knyf* then crosses it out and writes *trenchour.*
4122: Pers' version is "Baffe et Buffenet, Candare et Dendamur" (2:68).
4144: RMB may be adding a touch of irony here, or at least a pun.
4155–56: The line order in L is closer to Pers' text (2:70).
4165–66: RMB's colloquial expression translates Pers' line: "Et par graunt conqueste Cypre ad saisye" (2:70).
4179–4230: RMB has rearranged and expanded this passage. Many details are not in Pers' version and were probably drawn from another source. Pers has forty lines, including the lines added in L at 4198 (2:70–74).
4209: The name of the *galeie* has somehow been adapted from the name of the captain: *Aleyn Trenchemer* appears in Brunner's edition (2488–2626) and is an active participant in the sea battle.
4213: MS P has a *c-t* confusion for *crokes,* misread by Hearne (his ed., p. 170); L clearly has *crokes.*
4232: Wright supplies a rubric from MS B (2:74) with the name of the town, *Acon;* in MS C it is *Actu.* Wright assumes that *Acres* is meant, as in l. 4234. RMB incorporates the rubric in his text, perhaps finding it convenient for the rime with *one* in 4231.
4301–68: RMB evidently used another source for this passage; Pers has only fourteen lines. The arrangement suggests that Langtoft abridged the details, as was customary in his work (2:78–80). The comparable passage in Brunner's ed. has many echoes suggesting that RMB used a "romance" similar to (but probably of earlier date than) the version Brunner edited. Compare, for example: "Kyng Richard out off hys galye / Caste wylde ffyr into þe skye / And ffyr Gregeys into þe see" (2643–45); "Ffoure sayles were þertoo / ȝelew and grene, rede and bloo / Wiþ caneuas layd wel al aboute / Fful schyr wiþinne and eke wiþoute / And al wiþinne fful off ffeer / Off torches maad wiþ wex ful cleer" (2659–2664). See the introduction to this edition for further references on this work.
4303: *Mylnes* is obscure; *MED* (M.4, p. 475) cites this line for the definition "a military engine devised by Richard I"; the only other citation for this use is Brunner: "A melle he made. .þe. . Stones. . Grounde. .neuere whete no grote But rubbyd als þey were wood." (Brunner, 2656 with parts of ll. 2666–69). This citation is somewhat misleading since the lines intervening between 2656 and 2666 pertain to the confused *ryues* in RMB's l. 4307.
4307: Pers has: "Les aletz en movent les molées Le Ryns." Wright quotes Hearne's note explaining the source of the "odd stones" from the river Rhine and translates, "weighty stones" (2:80, n. 5). The explanation may be simpler than either Hearne or Wright perceived, but it is possible that RMB was misreading his source MS. *Rynes* probably should be read *ryues,* since L has *ryves,* but the meaning is still obscure. Perhaps it means river stones (i.e., from the edge of a river), or possibly broken stones (from *ryue,* the verb). Langtoft's MSS BCD all have "Le Ryns," according to Wright. Brunner's passage is less obscure than RMB's, but interpretation is still difficult: "Wiþ strenges off wyr þe stones hang / Stones þat deden neuere note / Grounde þey neuere whete no grote / But rubbyd als þey were wood" (2666–68). There are several variant readings indicated in Brunner's edition for these lines (p. 226). The expression "als þey were wood" (l. 2668) may mean "as if they were crazy" (i.e., *wode*), for in the following lines (see RMB's 4307–9) the "romance" indicates that the purpose of the apparatus to was to frighten the *Sareȝynes* (Brunner, 2674–80).
4324: Compare 4340. RMB makes very selective use of the information in the Bishop's tale, including the details he preferred, and finally refers his reader to the "romance" for more of the "hard chance" (4339). Brunner's ed. says "þe erchebysschop of Pyse" (2693) told Richard a "doolful tale" (2697ff.) which differs considerably. The original version of the "romance" reflected variously here has probably been rearranged in both RMB's version and the one edited by Brunner. The passage beginning at 4324, however, has some striking details in common with Brunner's ed.: "A quarter off whete men vs solde / Ffor

syxty pound off ffloryns tolde / Ffor ffourty pound men solde an oxe / þouȝ it were but lytyl woxe / A swyn ffor an hundryd ffloryn / A goos ffor halff mark off gold ffyn / And ffor an hen to syke þynges / Men gaff of penyes ffyftene schillinges / And for an ay penyes vnleuene / And ffor a pere syxe or seuene. . . / þerwiþ þe more and þe lasse / Bouȝte hem fflesch off hors and asse / þey myȝte haue non oþir þyng. . ." (pp. 237–38, ll. 2853–62, 2873–75). The differing sums in this list are of little importance since the order of the items is similar in both versions.

4345: *Fauuelle* could be read as *Fanuelle,* but both L (*Favel*) and Brunner's ed. of the "romance" of Richard confirm the spelling as in the text. Compare Brunner 2334 (*Fauell*) and 5507 (*Fauuel*).

4368: A word regularly changed by RMB's later scribes: *forgetilschip* also occurs in MS O of *Handlyng Synne: forgytelscheppe* (for l. 2558). The other *HS* MSS have various modifications for this unfamiliar term: *rechelesshepe* (B); *ȝetylede* (C); *ientylnesse* (D); *rechelessnesse* (F). In this line in Ch2, L has "envye of worschupe," which is a rather imaginative reinterpretation.

4380–4423: For this passage, Pers has only ten lines, including the two added in L at 4422 (2:82). RMB adds the entire account of the "Marchis of Mounfraunt." This character appears in Brunner's ed. (2713) accompanying Saladyn.

4404: Either *runcys* (P) or *ropys* (L) could be correct, but which was RMB's original word is not clear.

4444: Pers has "la thour Maldite"; L is evidently in error.

4481–84: Compare the version in Brunner's ed. at 6305–20 on the seige of "Castel Pylgrym."

4549–50: The version in L is more logical; P has miscopied both lines.

4640: *Wacres* (or *wakres* in L) is a word designed to rime with *Acres,* meaning *watches* in this context, derived from OE wæcce. See 4513 for the expected spelling. Probably *wacres* is not an error but a deliberate modification.

4643–61: Pers' account is much rearranged in this passage (2:96–98).

4680: RMB adds this line. Wright notes: "Robert wrote after the Templars had been condemned and proscribed" (2:100, n. 1). The Templars' trial was in 1312.

4691–92: Pers has: "Seygnur de Galilée et del leu où Kayn / Tua sun frere Abel par feloun engyn" (2:100). *Chayn* in P is an error.

4694: Pers has "Se signe [MS B] de la croyce et prent sun chemyn" which Wright translates: "Signed himself with the cross and takes his way" (2:100–101).

4700ff: Pers must have the credit (or blame) for this improbable speech. James, mortally wounded, recounts his ancestry whilst asking for help (2:100–102).

4712: Pers' MSS BCD have *Morian;* RMB adds *alle* for the rime with *hospitalle.*

4736: Pers has: "Les freres od les croices tapisent cum futys" (MS B, 2:104). Compare ll. 4680, 4728.

4773–82: This passage in Pers differs; RMB adds Richard's qualification of the role of Burgoyn (compare 2:106).

4837–40: RMB includes a hint that he was drawing on some other source: "in boke it was vplaid" by "þo men þat it herd" (i.e., the speeches in this passage). Since he does not refer to the "romance" here, we may deduce that he had another history with eye-witness accounts. See note, ll. 4906–24 on other sources.

4861: *MED* (B.1, p. 539) cites Langtoft for this line: ". . . m'en alay avauntant . . ." and suggests "?a boast"; L has a rather ambiguous (and abbreviated) word which probably should read *avantement.* The readings in both P and L could have been altered from an earlier MS.

4866: RMB (or a scribe) invents *demple* to rime with *Temple.* The word is cited in *MED* (D.2, p. 964) with the L variant, *comple,* as "Prob. error for camplen." Neither word appears elsewhere in RMB's works.

4869–71: P has the same line order as Pers here; RMB adds 4871 (2:112).

4874: Pers has "Raymound"; the "Region" in L may be corrupt, though the line is logical as given.

4880–90: RMB rewrites Pers' five lines (2:112), converting them to direct speech.
4896: The version in L is curious and probably altered. Pers has: "Al Temple entre freres demoraunt à mesoun" (MS B, 2:112).
4905: P clearly has Aufrice; Pers' MS B has Ostrice (2:114). Evidently L is correct here.
4906–24: RMB expands and rewrites Pers' account, perhaps drawing from the "romance" (cited in 4909); however, the Brunner edition does not have these details. RMB had some other historical version. See Brunner's introduction, pp. 49–51, for a discussion of the earlier (and later) fictional and factual "Literarhistorisches" and their editions which include accounts of the reign of Richard I.
4941: The preference of L for parlements at "Wynchestre" suggests support for the provenance of the MS in an area of more interest to the scribe. Pers has *Westmouster* [MS A] and *Weymouster* [MS B] (2:116). Compare line 4939, where London is clearly indicated as Richard's destination.
4973: This is the last line in L, f.131v. The blank pages following in the MS probably were intended to be used, but the scribe simply stopped here.
4992: See note for l. 3848 on *trip*.
4995–5008: RMB expands and dramatizes this passage from eight lines in Pers (2:120). Wright adds this note: "Marchades was the commander of the Routiers in Richard's service, and had the reputation of being a great joker."
5010: The number differs in Pers' text: "l. et iij" (2:120).
5020–24: RMB modifies Pers' account here and adds 5023–24. Pers acknowledges a source, however: "Voyse et lyse sun liver ke est enromauncez" (2:122).
5025–42: RMB draws some of the details of Richard's death from another source, but generally follows Pers' account (2:122). In 5037, RMB seems to have some doubt, either about his source or the facts. (Stepsis notes that Richard died at "Castel Gaylard," p. 464). See Brunner's ed., l. 7208. For a better account of Richard's death, see John Gillingham, "The Unromantic Death of Richard I" (1979). The idea that Richard went to the Limousin for "recreation" (i.e., "to play," 5026) is clearly at variance with the facts. RMB and Pers (who has only eight lines) have used some account that may have come from a source based on conjecture. RMB's disavowal of responsibility for accuracy of the tale (in 5023–24) suggests that he knew of different versions which he could not verify.
5044–45: These lines are evidently transposed; the scribe has preserved the end rime (*lif-strif*) in 5045–46, perhaps by altering his source.
5050: Pers does not mention John's children. See 2:122.
5065: Pers has: "Mon mestre me suspende à dire en moun sermoun" (2:124). Evidently the "master" is Pers' mentor, not RMB's. The following lines are closely translated by RMB also.
5073: A word may be missing at the end of this line or the scribe misspelled *felonie* which rimes with *Bretaynie.*
5094–96: RMB alters Pers' lines to accommodate the information in 5096.
5152: *Mynde* is needed for the internal rime with *kynde* but the meaning of "fauht with mynde" is not clear. Pers has: "Combatent pur le rays, par ount il est salvez" (2:130).
5160: Pers' MS B has: "sa fidle preist marit" (2:130).
5170: *Wike* is an error for *wirke,* riming with *kirke.*
5176: The word *tuo* is followed by *a legates* in the MS. Probably the *a* should have been cancelled, but it is not so marked.
5200ff: The P MS is dim for the remainder of f. 157v. Hearne's readings have been consulted here.
5204–9: RMB expands Pers' three lines, doubtless using another source. Wright notes that John was buried at *Wircestre* (as in Pers' MS D); the other Pers MSS that Wright edited have *Wyncestre* (2:134, n. 2). RMB adds the information in 5206, but Stepsis notes that "it is not true" (p. 465, n. for his l. 5237). The date in 5207 is translated from a rubric in Pers' MS B.
5302–4: RMB is commenting on Pers' lines: "A son issir de Londres les Loundreis verrai-

ment / Le fesaynt plus despyt ke nul home entent" (MS B, 2:140). Line 5304 is added.

5312: Wright notes that this line occurs only in Pers' MS B: "La grande folie qe li quens emprent" (2:140, n. 18).

5317–34: RMB rearranges and augments Pers' eleven lines; 5333–34 are drawn from a Latin caption in Pers' MS B with the spelling "Leaus," though Pers [MS A] also uses "Lewes" in his text (2:143).

5349–64: RMB adds this passage from another source. Pers has only two lines here: "Sire Eduuard de prisoun sagement alayt / En soccour et ayde les marchyz assemblayt" (2:144). Stepsis suggests (on p. 465, n. ll. 5380–92) Nicholas Trivet's *Annales* (ed. Thomas Hog, English Historical Society, no. 23 [London, 1845], 264) as a possible source. See Antonia Gransden, *Historical Writing in England: c.550–c.1307* (1974), 501–7. The *Annales* were probably written ca. 1320 (Gransden, p. 504 and n. 167), but if RMB were in the midst of his translation in 1320, he could have drawn from some other source also available to Trivet, several of which are listed by Gransden.

5365–5424: Pers has a much shorter version of these events, only twenty-five lines, including a two-line caption in MS B (RMB's 5403–6) omitted in the other Pers MSS (2:144–46). Probably RMB's source is the same as the one he employed in the preceding passage (5349–64); the circumstantial details and direct quotation imply that he had an authoritative reference and was not merely elaborating Pers' account.

5397–99: RMB mistranslates Pers here: "Taunt cum les reis [MS B] poer assemblaynt / Fu Norhaunton pris les barouns là lessaynt / Symon fiz le counte et gens ke ly suaynt / Cum soz et chaitifs à Kenelworth alaynt" (2:144). Stepsis discusses the meaning in a note (for his ll. 5428–30, p. 466): "Northampton was taken by the barons, who left Simon's sons in charge of it; it was not the place where Edward prepared his army." The meaning might be improved by adding *to* at the beginning of l. 5399. Pers' following comments leave no doubt of his disdain for Simon's sons.

5419–24: RMB expands two ll. in Pers (2:146) and rearranges the account to 5437, probably depending on another source as well. Part of this passage may have been drawn from an eye-witness account in that source. The first words in l. 5424 are clearly *þat þat*, probably an error for *þo þat*.

5442–44: Pers' line begins "Almeryk de Mounfort." Perhaps the scribe was having difficulties with his source. Some letters in this passage have been worked over in darker ink. The *r* in *tor* is a letter added in error, probably by the scribe. Compare Wright, 2:146.

5472: *Kene* is the spelling in Pers' MS D; the other MSS have *Chene* (2:148, n. 12).

5474–92: RMB adds details and rearranges Pers' thirteen lines (2:148–50). The assault on Lincoln's Jews occurred about the time of RMB's birth.

5495: RMB translates from two lines in Pers: "As chivas covers ad maundé ses amys / A Nicole se haste . . ." (2:150).

5573: The word *hune* is clearly used for the rime with *Tune* in 5574. See *MED* (H.5, p. 908), *hone*, n. (2), where this line is cited with the correction for Hearne's reading ("hime [read: hune]") and the source: "Prob. Celtic; cp. OIr. on, oin . . ." meaning delay, hesitation.

5574: "Time" (Tunis) is various in Pers' MSS (2:154) and may have been repeatedly miscopied. MSS AD have "Tunes," MS C has "Temes." Compare 5583: the scribe again writes "tune" or "time"; the MS could be read either way. In both lines, the word is not capitalized, but a location is clearly indicated in the context. The mid-line rime in 5584 is *vntime* which complicates the problem of possible misreading in an earlier MS.

5592: Pers' text has: "Deus c. mil par ayme" [MSS BCD] (2:156) which Wright translates as "two hundred thousand."

5601–7: RMB rewrites three lines in Pers' account (2:156). In the passage following (to 5629), RMB rewrites the dramatic narrative from sixteen of Pers' lines, indicating that he used another source (5625). Lines 5626–28 are drawn from a caption in Pers' MS B, omitted in the other MSS: "Ici le rei Edward occist le Sarazin de un tresel qe vint à li en message par treson del soudan." Wright comments: "This rubric . . . reads like the title to an illumination in a MS" (2:158, n. 4).

5607: A word may be lacking here: should the line read "on of þo"? Probably the scribe has picked up *of þo* from the previous line. The comparable line in Pers' text begins: "Un de cel escole le soldan prent . . ." (2:156).

5616: The first half of this line may be lost. The MS has the line exactly as shown in the text with no indication that the scribe caught his error.

5625: RMB seems to be alluding to a "romance" of Edward I, but possibly the line has been altered from *þe romance,* meaning the account of Edward in Pers' French text.

5639–40: These lines may be transposed, but a line could be missing. Pers has: "Sir Edward par ses playes est en graunt torment / Le ray Henri sun pere ad fet sun testament." The passage in 5640–55 may also be out of order. A possible arrangement would be 5640, 5639, 5651–52, 5654, 5653, 5641–45, 5646–50. Except for the transposition in 5639–40, Pers and RMB are more or less in the same order (2:160).

5647: The scribe has faltered: RMB intended "Dame Helianore."

5650: Wright includes a long introduction to the account of Edward's reign that appears in his MS A (2:162–64). At line 5651, the date is given in a caption; the other Pers MSS have various brief passages evidently intended as prologues. At the end of this introduction in MS A, the patron of Pers' work is named: "De noster rays Eduuard Scaffeld li requist / Recorder la geste escotez cum il dist" (2:164). Thea Summerfield has identified *Scaffeld* as the sheriff of Northumberland, John Sheffield, who was appointed to his post in 1305. He was a partisan of the bishop of Durham, Anthony Bek; Summerfield suggests that he commissioned Langtoft to write the chronicle at the instigation of the bishop during a period when Bek was in disfavor with Edward I. See "Context and Genesis of Pierre de Langtoft's *Chronicle*" (1994), pp. 321–32. Michael Prestwich, *Edward I* (1988) discusses the relationship of Bek and Edward at length, pp. 69ff. See T. M. Smallwood, "The Text of Langtoft's *Chronicle,*" (1977), especially p. 225. Smallwood uses the "rhetorical introduction" here as one key to the various types of Langtoft MSS. A modern edition accounting for all of them might help to identify RMB's sources more precisely.

5653ff: RMB follows Pers generally in this passage, but the specific lines translated are mainly from his usual source, a MS of the type represented in MS B. The difficulties in the MS tradition are reflected to a certain extent in Wright's notes. RMB probably also used an independent source augmented by his own personal knowledge, since the events of Edward's reign were within his own lifetime. Line 5653 is the beginning of Pers' third book, the story of Edward I's reign, appearing separately in several of the MSS. Historians still regard Langtoft's account as a primary source for this period. Antonia Gransden (1974) refers to M. Dominica Legge's *Anglo-Norman Literature,* (1963) on the division of Pers' books: "he imitated Gaimar's general scheme." Gransden disapproves of the "romantic" tradition (i.e., its fictional basis) in Langtoft's work, but adds: "Nevertheless Langtoft managed to give a fairly accurate record of contemporary affairs" (pp. 479–82).

5686: "Resamiraduk" is "Dresamiraduk" in Pers' MS B, "De ray Sameraduk" in MS C. The name is variously spelled thereafter. Compare ll. 5915, 5971, and note for 6341 below.

5698–5718: RMB is evidently following another source here; Pers has only eleven lines. On 2:162–70, Wright provides alternate readings for Pers' MS E beginning with the introduction to the history of the reign of Edward I through the passage ending at l. 5712 of RMB's text, then decides that it was not "necessary to collate MS E further" (2:170, n.13; see his preface, 2:vii–viii). MS E is the famous Arundel MS XIV, containing Wace, Gaimar's "Histoire des Engleis" (ed. Bell, 1960), the "Lai of Haveloc," and Langtoft's third book. See T. M. Smallwood's analysis (1977) of Pers' MSS, and his articles on the murder of Comyn (1975) and "The Prophecy of the Six Kings" (1985) for more information on MSS EF.

5716–17: These lines are evidently transposed, though the rimes are preserved for 5715–18. Langtoft does not mention the marriage at Snowdon.

5737–46: RMB rewrites Pers' passage (2:172–74) concerning the new coinage. He is rather more emphatic in his condemnation of the debasers of the money supply than is his exemplar. He describes the actual coins and has a somewhat different view of the use of money than Pers does.

5748: Hearne suggests that "fist" should be "first" (p. 239), but the MS is not ambiguous. There is no comparable line in Pers' text (2:174).

5762–66: RMB adds these lines.

5768–5801: RMB's account differs markedly from Pers' version, though the source may have been a different Pers MS. Only a dozen of RMB's lines match Pers' text in this passage. From line 5650 on, RMB's differences from the texts printed in Wright's edition increase. Wright frequently blames RMB's "imperfect understanding" of Pers' text, but it is also possible that the translator simply had a different version before him, one that may itself have been corrupt. See Wright, 2:178, n. 1. Since this part of Pers' text (his third book) appears separately in several of the surviving MSS, one would have to compare those that Wright did not collate for his edition in order to be sure whether RMB was adding to his source or mistranslating. M. Dominica Legge has theorized that Langtoft revised his work; which MSS might reflect the revision, however, are not clearly identified. In her early article, "A List of Langtoft Manuscripts, with Notes on MS Laud Misc. 637" (1935, pp. 20–24), Miss Legge suggests some directions that might be explored, but this article should be compared with Smallwood's, "The Text of Langtoft's *Chronicle*" (1977). In Miss Legge's *Anglo-Norman Literature and its Background* (1963) is the following: "[Langtoft's] chronicle originally terminated before the end of Edward I's reign. His first version ends on a note of triumph ... [after the betrayal of William Wallace]. This state of affairs did not last, and the end was revised several times, probably by Langtoft himself, on a bitterer and bitterer note, until the final version terminates with the expression of misgiving, only too well founded, about the future when Edward II came to the throne" (p. 279, *passim*). Until a new edition of Langtoft's work appears with some exploration of those parts which Langtoft may have revised, it is impossible to discover the content of the MS which RMB used as his immediate source. There is also ample evidence that he made significant changes to Pers' text based on his personal knowledge of the events.

5819: Pers' MS A has "Baskles e Gascons" as in RMB. MS B has "de bachelers e garsçons" (2:180, n. 6).

5829–46: RMB adds these details. Pers has only two lines: "Leulyn est trové covert en busons / Perduz ad la teste n'ad mister de chaperouns" (MS B, 2:180).

5842: *Kyme* is obviously invented for a rime with *tyme* (5841). The word is related to OE cuman or cyme (i.e., arrival, encounter). The meaning of this line is not clear, however, for *daþet* is an imprecation.

5849–66: RMB adds this passage, clearly from personal knowledge. The year 1337 is the one just before he says he completed his translation. (See the rubric at the end of the MS.) His residence at the Gilbertine houses is attested in *Handlyng Synne* (l. 60) and at the beginning of this MS (Ch1, l. 141). Thorlac Turville-Petre, "Politics and Poetry in the Early Fourteenth Century: The Case of Robert Manning's *Chronicle*" (1988, pp. 1–28), cites this passage as revealing one of the circumstances of the relationship of the Gilbertines and the three Edwards: "Daughters of royal captives were confined in Gilbertine nunneries; in 1283 Gwenllian and Gwladus, children of the princes Llywelyn and David, were sent to Sempringham and Sixhills" (p. 6).

5915: See n. to l. 6341.

5935: *Lowe* means "law" here: Pers has: "Les uns avaynt par douns les la lei [MSS BCD] besturné" (2:184).

5952: Stepsis points out that RMB is ironically using "Placebo domine" from the first words of Psalm 114. See p. 468, n. to his l. 5983.

5954: For this line, Pers has: "*Dilexit quoniam* fraude e fauseté" (2:186).

5971: See note for l. 6341. Here, the MS could be read *Beseamiradie,* but probably the mid-line eye-rime governs: *spie* (5972).

5989: Pers has: "Tute saint Eglise quant nul esparnye" (2:188). RMB may have misunderstood the line, or P errs in omitting a word.

5991–92: RMB localizes the queen's death; "his body" is probably a scribal error.

5995–6010: RMB expands this account from seven of Pers' lines (2:190). He may have followed a later, possibly revised, Pers MS. See M. Dominica Legge (1963, p. 279), for theories concerning Langtoft's own revisions to the later parts of his work and n. 5768–5801 above. In *Anglo-Norman in the Cloisters* (1950), 70–71, Miss Legge discusses the chronicles of Bridlington and evidence drawn from "the monastic chronicles of the whole kingdom," probably the sources referred to in this passage, especially in 5999–6003. See Michael Prestwich (1988, pp. 363ff.) for details: in March 1291, Edward consulted the abbot of Evesham and "probably some thirty others" to provide information from the monastic chronicles. Bridlington, where Langtoft was a canon (according to RMB), evidently had a substantial library of historical works. See J. A. H. Murray, introduction to his *Thomas of Erceldoune* (1875), pp. xxxii–xxxvi, for a discussion of the "prophecies," mostly in later MSS such as Lansdowne 762 which bears the title: "Brydlington." (RMB alludes to Erceldoun in Ch1, l. 94.)

6006: The first word in this line is clearly *fo* but *so* may be intended.

6049–66: Pers presents Baliol's "homage" in prose from MS A (2:192–94); Wright notes many variations among the MSS. It appears to be a precise copy of a legal document.

6070: The scribe has omitted a letter or a stroke over the *o:* he meant *homward.*

6073–82: RMB adds several lines in this passage revealing Edward's feelings. Lines 6073, 6075, 6078, and 6080 are not in Pers' text (2:194); they are perhaps from a different MS version or altered. How RMB became privy to these intimate feelings he attributes to the king would depend on some other account written by someone who knew him well.

6087: "Germenie" in Pers' MSS BC, "Gernemue" in MSS AD; Wright translates: "Yarmouth" (2:197).

6098: The first two words are not logical; perhaps the line should begin "and whom" or "& where"; the first possibility is better, meaning a woman who might be his wife.

6117–18: Stepsis says RMB has mistranslated here: "Edward, not Blanche, sent the letter showing his feelings" (p. 468, n. to his ll. 6148–49). Perhaps *to* has been lost at the beginning of 6117, but the meaning has certainly been altered as well. Compare 2:198 in Wright. See also Prestwich's biography of Edward (1988), pp. 380–81 and 483.

6120: Here, as in 6024, RMB supplies the foreboding. Pers has three lines for 6120–26 (2:198).

6140–41: Pers' MSS [AB] differ: "A Philipe [B] ad saisi Burdeaus of quant ke apent / Par lettre sire Edward Gascoyne á li se rent" (2:198). Wright supplies the second of these lines from MS B as it is missing in MS A. Stepsis comments that *fro* may be an error, or that *Philip* should be *Edward* in 6140 (p. 468, his n. 6171). These lines are important to reveal the actual events: Philip was using Edward's "scrite" as an excuse to seize Gascony.

6142: Pers has: "Pur veir en Deu ws dye encontre leur talent" which Wright translates "For truth I tell you in God, against their will" (2:198).

6229–80: RMB abridges Pers' text somewhat, omitting some of the redundancy in his source (2:206–10).

6261: The last word in this line should be *knyght.*

6313: The scribe has used the abbreviation for *per-* here, which would yield *perrouendere;* the intention is obviously *prouendere,* or a prebendary. RMB also uses this word at 2003. The "riche prouendere" is not in Pers' text.

6313–22: RMB rewrites this passage; Pers has thirteen lines with more emphasis on the threat of French rule, e.g.: "Li Frauncays orgullous à si bas nus menerait" (2:214).

6341: The rubric beside this line in the MS begins "Resamiraduk," but he is not named in the text; compare 5686, 5915, 5919, 5971. RMB is scarcely translating: Pers uses the abbreviation *Rese* in some of the same lines (Wright, 2:184, nn. 2, 6, 10).

6350: More confusion of *c-t:* Pers' MSS have Abyrconeway [A], Abbrettounwaye [C], Abreconewaye [D]. Wright does not include a variant for MS B (2:216, n. 8).

6400–409: RMB rewrites and condenses this passage; he is modifying Pers' indignant condemnation of Edward's enemies (2:220–22).

6422–28: RMB differs from Pers: "Fist à Jon Bayllof tel est la bounté / Dount li rays

Eduuard / Du ray Jon musard / Est rewerdoné / De Escoce sait cum pot / Parfurnyr nus estot / La geste avaunt parlé" (2:222). The demands of the verse form may account for these differences. Wright prints these lines in a tail-rime stanza, for which RMB slightly changes the content. Later, these short "songs" are sometimes drawn from different sources in RMB's text. In the introduction to vol. 2, Wright defines "ryme cowée" or tailed rime: "It consists of two lines rhyming together, and then a shorter line with a different rhyme, then two lines rhyming together again, followed by another short line which rhymes with the preceding short line. These short lines were the tails; they most commonly rhymed in pairs, so as to form a series of verses formed of stanzas of six lines each, resembling some of our ballad poetry; but we find sometimes in this form of verse several tail-lines rhyming together" (pp. viii–ix). The actual arrangement of these lines in MS P has been reproduced in the text rather than in stanzas as Wright printed them from Pers' MSS.

6448: The expression probably should be "hede & hode"; Wright translates Pers' lines: "their hats remained with the heads of some of them" (2:225). The soldiers lost their heads and their helmets or hoods of mail.

6479–6529: RMB rewrites this account, evidently following a different source but not rearranging the order of events (on 2:226–28). Pers has twenty-nine lines. The traitor Thomas Turbervile was the subject of a popular song that may have been known to RMB. See the collection in Isabel S. T. Aspin, ed., *Anglo-Norman Political Songs* (1953), number V, "Thomas Turberville." This song is dated 1295–97 and appears in BL Cotton Caligula MS A.xviii (first half of the fourteenth century). For 6515–24, RMB certainly had additional data; Pers does not mention the queen mother's advice to Edward.

6480: The last word in this line, *grace,* has been omitted in error. Pers has: "Escotez ore coment la grace Jhesu Krist" (2:226).

6527–28: Compare note for l. 8181.

6549–56: RMB condenses this passage; Pers has thirteen lines followed by another tirade against "les fels mastyns," Edward's enemies (2:230–32), which RMB omits. Parts of this passage are also omitted from Pers' MSS BD. The last line in Pers' text echoes words in the "songs" at 6713 ("nakned þer nages") and 6824 ("þi riuelyng"): "For soul les rivelinges et la nue nage" (2:232).

6555: The word *kyns* is probably an error for *kyng.*

6562–76: RMB rewrites this passage; Pers merely summarizes the action (2:232). In 6575, Pers has "Quatre mil de Escoce," a more likely figure.

6590–97: RMB omits or modifies several of Pers' lines, including a comment on Robert Brus: "Vers le rays Eduuard tynt tuzjours sa fealté / Encountre les Escoz amour l'ad moustré" (2:234). One of Pers' lines is omitted between 6590–91: "Kant Berwik fu prise dedenz estayt trové . . ." which is necessary to explain where the treasure was found (in 6591).

6599–6604: This song, introduced with the line, "Et par mokerye en Englays rymeyé," is given in English in Pers' text (2:234–36). Wright inserts RMB's lines 6601–2 in his text as they are lacking in the Pers MSS.

6612: Hearne reads *Leynertofte* but the scribe's intention is probably "Leynercoste" here. In 6634, the MS has *Larnercost,* but the letter *r* was perhaps *y* in the MS the P scribe was copying. Pers' MSS vary and probably have also been misread: Lanercost [AB], Lavertoft [C], Lavertost [D]. Wright converts *u* to *v,* so these should probably be Lauertoft and Lauertost; accordingly, Lanertoft and Lanertost may have been miscopied. Misreadings of *u-n, c-t, f-s* are persistent in all these MSS. In 8128, the scribe probably intends *Laynercost.*

6613–30: RMB abridges Pers' twenty-three lines, omitting some of his irrelevant judgements (2:238).

6618: Letters are blotted: *schoke* is Hearne's reading.

6683–88: Pers has the first part in French and 6687–88 in English (2:244). RMB translates closely, adding words only to improve the rime.

6703–4: Pers adds six more lines of contumely against the cowardly Scots (2:246). RMB shares his opinions, but does not dwell on them at length.

6709–10: RMB omits an eight-line digression in Pers' text (2:246–48).

6711–16: The first two lines of this "couwe" are not in Pers' text and the rest varies among the MSS. Instead of 6716, Pers' MS A has: "Thay token ay tulke / The roghe raggy sculke / Rug ham in helle." MS E has another variant: "How ferd the wreches thenne / The devel I them bikenne / That ragged sit in helle" (2:248, n. 7). MS B: "Thou wiffin / Scot of Abrenityn / cloutid is thi honne," and MS D: "Wiffyn / Scot of Abernithin / Clut es ty honne" (n. 10). Unfortunately, the Wright edition is misleading for ll. 6715–16 because the ending rime words should be *schouue* and *houue* (i.e., *schouve, houve*), misread by Hearne and accepted by Wright in his notes. These lines are cited in *MED* (H.5, p. 1016); the citation for *schouve* in *MED* (S.6, p. 767) is somewhat misleading, however: "Songs Langtoft (Petyt) p. 277" is given as reference, but obviously Hearne's ed. of RMB's Ch2 is the actual source. (The key to sources in the *MED* for "Songs Langtoft" refers to Wright's edition of *The Political Songs of England,* Camden Society, 1839.) The variants cited by *MED*, however, evidently come from other MSS of Langtoft: "[vrr. syonne, sonne, souue]." T. M. Smallwood cites these lines in his discussion of "The Text of Langtoft's *Chronicle,*" (1977, p. 220) as one of the aspects distinguishing the groupings of the MSS. See Richard M. Wilson, *The Lost Literature of Medieval England* (2nd ed., rev. 1970), pp. 201–8.

6716–17: Pers has ten lines here that RMB omits; they are an expression of Pers' delight at the Scots' defeat in the battle of Dunbar (2:250).

6735–36: RMB's version of this very short "couwe" closely matches Pers' text, which is also in English (2:252).

6765–78: The last two of these lines is in English in Pers' text (2:254–58). RMB revises little here except in line 6774. In 6777, Pers' English line has: "For boule bred in his bok / Wen he tint that he tok / Wiht ye kingedome." The word *bok* was evidently omitted in P in error. RMB and Pers have virtually identical lines for 6778. Red strokes have been added to the punctuation in the P MS here (f. 176rv) and on f. 177r.

6771–73: The line order is disturbed in the MS but marked for correction with "a" and "b" (f. 176v).

6778: Pers and RMB are applying a contemporary epithet; see Ronald McN. Scott, *Robert the Bruce: King of Scots* (1989), 30: "John Balliol ... pilloried to posterity as Toom Tabard, the Empty Jacket." Scott does not provide a specific reference for this bit of lore, but it may have come from our text.

6783: *Soudioure* may be an error for Pers' *sojourner* (2:258), giving a totally different meaning to this passage. See *MED* (S.11, p. 283 [f.]), a unique reference identified (on p. 281) as "?error."

6792–93: According to Pers, Sir Hugh was the treasurer and Walter was the chancellor (p. 260). This confusion may be a scribal error in P; however, compare 6911–12, where "Walter of Langtoun" is identified as *tresorere.* The name Walter applies to two different people in Pers' text; compare 2:274 for his lines on Walter de Langetoun, the treasurer, corresponding to RMB's lines 6911–12. According to Michael Prestwich (1988), John Langton was the chancellor and Walter Langton the treasurer (pp. 526–28), but these offices were held at various times; the confusion could be in either Pers' or RMB's accounts or possibly both.

6813–26: RMB follows Pers' French through 6816, then inserts his own version adding ll. 6817–18. His ll. 6819–26 are quoted in full by Wright (2:262); 6825–26 are from Pers, who resorts to English in 6823–26 (2:260–64), with a slightly different reading. Wright does not note any of RMB's differences after 6826, but they are not substantial. RMB's source may have been a revised Pers MS or an independent literary version of this "couwe."

6817: The meaning of this line is obscure and *trulle* and *drenge* do not occur elsewhere in RMB's works. Very likely *trulle* means "troll" from Scandinavian mythology; *dreng* is OE from ON: a man or warrior, also possibly a creature. From the last part of the line, they are two fiends from the sea.

6826: *MED* (F.2, p. 555) cites *filchid* from "Songs Langtoft" but the origin of the word is uncertain. Compare Wright, 2:264.

6827ff.: The first line is added by RMB and he continues to use the "couwe" form, though Pers resumes his usual *laisses* at 6828 (2:264–66), with seventeen lines riming. The passage is redundant in both versions to 6852, probably due to the difficulties of the rime form and the allusive nature of the context. RMB is offering a commentary on Pers' text and sometimes disagrees with Pers' sermon: the opinions at 6839–52 are not in the MSS Wright edited, but RMB's source may have differed. Compare note 5995–6010 above. Wright comments that RMB "wrote at a later date, when the hopes here expressed were overthrown, and the Scots were again troublesome" (2:268, n. 1). If RMB had access to a late MS, this may be one of the passages Langtoft himself revised.

6950–53: RMB adds these lines. Pers identified Oliuere as bishop of Lincoln (as in 6946); possibly RMB had other information about the bishop's defiance of Edward.

6967–71: Pers has these lines after RMB's line 6982 (2:280).

6987: *As* is an error for *at.*

6988: Stepsis' definition of *wiri* (OE were, dat.) is "the money value of a man's life," indicating (in this context) that no one was "priced for ransom." *OED* is not entirely helpful, but there is a suggestion of a connection with *wergeld.* Probably *wiri* was needed for the rime with *Saleberi.*

7010: See note for ll. 1682–85 on *stampe.*

7025: Pers' line is: "Et Modred demaglé par sa reverye" (MS B, 2:284).

7025–48: RMB rewrites this long exhortation to Edward (2:284–86) from Pers, who employs direct address to the king only in lines 7030–36. The rest is simply a short sermon with little reference to Pers' passionate speech. Stepsis (p. 473) refers to 1 Maccabees 2 as the source of the biblical citation (in 7041–46), which is not in Pers' text.

7065–66: RMB adds this figure; Pers has: "Et ws [*sic*] la barbicane i portez pavillion" (MS C, 2:288). Wright indignantly remarks that RMB has "marvellously misunderstood this line" (n. 5). On the other hand, it is likely that RMB chose to use a metaphor of his own instead of Pers'. Lines 7064 and 7067 are translated faithfully.

7122: *þe ferd* may mean "they fared" together, but *ferd* as a group of companions may have been the intention, which suggests that something has been omitted.

7123–30: RMB rewrites and rearranges Pers' text (2:292). The blame is the barons' according to Pers, while RMB thinks that Edward erred in his dealings with them.

7146–48 and 7189–90: The blots (probably of binding glue) may have been inflicted on the MS during the rebinding in 1850; they occur on facing pages of the MS. Since Hearne made his transcript before 1725, the letters in brackets are supplied from his reading.

7150–80: This episode is added by RMB, evidently from another source.

7152: "þe Fle" is an obvious scribal error, not marked for correction.

7189–90: See note for 7146–48.

7194: *OED* cites *stem* in this line: "only a single instance of the word has been found" (sense 1b) between the OE period and the sixteenth century. See *MED* (S.14, p. 652).

7199–7200: RMB adds this proverb.

7201–14: RMB emphatically blames Edward for the "defaut"; Pers begins with: "Escotez la defaute en qi tut pecchayt" (2:296); thereafter, RMB writes his own version. Though Pers acknowledges that Edward gave too little to his barons, he still considers that the king was affronted by their refusal to help him.

7220–39: RMB rewrites this passage and adds details of the battle. Pers does not have 7235–37 (2:298).

7235: The reference is to the battle of Falkirk (1298) in which the Scots were defeated. Compare Thomas of Erceldoune (Thornton MS, l. 360) variants: *fowse kyrk, faw chirch, fawkyrke* (ed. J. A. H. Murray [1875], 21).

7249–52: RMB omits some of the grisly details; e.g., for "en menues corayes son quir escorchez" (7252), he says only that Sir Hugh was flayed. Pers has "Du ribaudaile d'Escoz sun cors fu demaglez" in the preceding line (2:300). RMB also omits the reason for this savagery: "En despit ly roys ki clerk il fu clamez," but this line is also omitted in Pers' MS B.

7271–86: Pers has a much longer passage here (2:302). RMB has rearranged and abridged it.
7321–24: RMB omits part of Pers' lines that explain what the debate was about: "Tant com les clers du su devaient compasser / Ke par la disme grande [MSS BC] ne pussent mal aver / Ne la pape offendre . . ." (2:306).
7331–32: Pers has: "La chartre des franchises ws [*sic*] voet confermer / E de la foreste l'assise amender" (2:306), which is more logical than RMB's *first assise* in 7332.
7342: Wright notes: "Joan Plantagenet, widow of Gilbert earl of Clare, Gloucester, and Hertford" (2:306, n. 11).
7346: The meaning of this line might be improved if *mitere* were taken as an error for *minstere,* but the MS clearly reads *mitere.* The rime with *Petir* is only slightly faulty.
7357: Hearne's reading is in brackets.
7363: Pers has: "Ly rays Edward avera cele dont fu parlance" (2:308).
7366: *Kewe* is an error for *knewe.*
7388: Probably *hir* should be *him* in this line.
7414–59: RMB adds the comment in 7414 and the date. His translation follows Pers' line order but the details are augmented, possibly from a different Pers MS (2:312–16); RMB probably had personal knowledge of the events.
7428: *Nouhut* might be read *nonhut;* more likely the word *nouht* is intended.
7431: The first word should be *strength.*
7445: Pers has: "Com mousches i morurent c. mil par coup d'espé" (2:314).
7452–56: The location of the battle at the wood of *Kalenters* and the details in this passage are added by RMB. Compare Wright, 2:314–16.
7460–64: RMB adds these lines. His distrust of the Welsh is at least equal to Pers' hatred of the Scots. For 7463, Stepsis identifies the quotation from Bede in *Hist. Eccl.* v.23. Chapter 23 concerns "The present state of the English nation and the rest of Britain [AD 725–731]" and includes the comment: "The Britons for the most part have a national hatred for the English." (Leo Sherley-Price, trans., Penguin Classics, p. 324). RMB's opinions may have been reenforced by his reliance on Henry of Huntingdon, who based his historical account on Bede. See Nancy F. Partner, *Serious Entertainments: The Writing of History in Twelfth-Century England* (1977): "[Henry] simply echoes Bede in condemning the Britons for irreligiousness" (p.25). Partner's discussion evaluates the opinions of the English about the Britons (Welsh) and refers to the "five plagues" which RMB employs at the beginning of Ch2 (ll. 109ff.).
7469: The first *his* should probably be *him.*
7513: Edward's haste in leaving his new bride is from RMB's reading of MS B: "En le jour [MS B] après. . ." (n. 3, 2:320). The other Pers MSS have *iver* or *yver,* the winter following. The error is in MS B.
7534: The second word should be *knyghtes;* Pers' MS B has: "Quatre chivalers de countez" (2:320).
7535–60: RMB rewrites and augments Pers' twenty-two lines, probably using another source or a revised Pers MS (2:322). Few of the lines are directly translated.
7555–58: Wright objects to RMB's translation: "The original. . .states that Segrave was sent as a substitute" (2:322, n. 14). The difficulty could be remedied by replacing "went" with "sent" in 7556. Pers has: ". . . Roger deshaité se sent [MS C: se assent] / Sir Jon de Segrave en soun lu present."
7580: *Paynes* may have originally been *playnes* as in 7579, but perhaps another meaning is intended.
7587: Pers has: "Demore e traine feynte e lung matinez" (2:326). The word *liþt* is a form of the verb *lithen,* meaning to be comfortable, or easy, painless. See *MED* (L.5, p. 1116), v. (2).
7610–17: RMB rewrites four of Pers' lines (2:328) and adds the details in lines 7613–16, probably from personal knowledge.
7633–34: Pers has: "Ly reys Edwarde respount irusement de quer / Jeo vey ke par orgoyl me voulez reviler" (MS A, 2:330). The error in *þhe* should be *þe.*

7688: Pers names the "foure Lordes": "Le cunt de Nichol," "Le counte de Sauveie et Hughe le Despenser," "Sir Jhon de Berewike" (2:334).
7711: Pers has *Mustroyle* [MS A], *Moustroille* [C], *Moustroylle* [D]; Wright translates *Montreuil* (2:337).
7712: The rime with *Pountif* prompts *vp rif* here, suggesting an emerging nobleman, as in *vp risen.* The word *rif* is not given in *MED* in any appropriate sense.
7737–45: Pers has a more circumstantial account of the betrayal of William by Charles, the king's brother. RMB translates only seven of Pers' thirteen lines (2:338).
7760: *Trut* elsewhere appears as *prut* or *tprut;* see *Handlyng Synne,* l. 3016. *OED* has one other reference (from ca. 1440). Though the word does not appear in the MSS edited by Wright, it occurs in a Langtoft revision (MS F: Fairfax 24, f. 4) according to *OED.*
7761–64: Pers names seven victims and includes specific details about their mutilation in eleven lines, beginning with "ly quens d'Artoys" (2:340). RMB's line 7761 seems to be based on Pers: "Et banerez sanz numbre des quels n'ad [MS B] mencion," but the reason for omitting the names Pers supplied is not clear.
7768–72: RMB abridges Pers' fourteen lines (2:342).
7773–74: The scribe has confused the relationship by copying *þe kyng* in error in 7773; evidently *þe ȝyng* was intended. Pers has: "Li quens Umfrei de Boun [MSS BC] cel an à femme prist / La filye al reys Edward Elizabeth est dit" (2:342).
7777: "Contene" may be an error for "contenue"; Pers has: "Continuer la trewe ke pees se tenist" (2:342).
7797: The MS has "Rauf þe Coffrers" for Pers' "Ralf ly Cofrers," as if the title were a proper name in both.
7811–14 and 7819–21: RMB's translation of Pers' text differs; Wright notes RMB's lines but without his usual comments on inadequate translation (2:346. nn. 1, 6).
7850: Hearne and Stepsis misread *Huluestere* as *Hulnestere;* he is *Hulvester* in Pers' text, translated *Ulster* by Wright (2:348).
7859–60: RMB adds this comment; compare l. 631 and Ch1 l. 14773 on Athelstan.
7877–7923: RMB rewrites and expands this passage from Pers' briefer account (2:350–52).
7921–22: RMB employs a curious translation: Pers has "Pur quanqe [MS B] posse dare à graunt et à petit / Par fare e defare [MS B] Rome nous derit" (2:352). The first line begins "Pro quante" in MS A. Was RMB correcting his source MS? Wright translates: "For however much he may give to great and to little, Rome mocks us by doing and undoing." Stepsis remarks that the alteration "cleverly changes the meaning . . . to produce a more bitter and cynical statement on the Papacy than is in Langtoft" (p. 476, n. for ll. 7950–51). Compare note 8251 below on Pope Boniface.
8005–24: RMB has rearranged this passage. Pers managed to rime fourteen lines with *-aunce* (2:360), a task that his translator evaded by using couplets, but he retains the mid-line rime.
8024: RMB attributes the naming of *trailebastons* to Edward while Pers is more oblique: "Traylebastouns sunt nomez de cel retanaunce." See Antonia Gransden's summary of Langtoft's treatment of Edward's actions (*Historical Writing in England I* [1974], 479). Michael Prestwich (1988) discusses the matter on pp. 285ff.
8037–59: RMB rewrites Pers' nineteen lines, adding 8042–49, probably from personal knowledge (2:362). These events occurred in 1305 (l. 8025), when RMB was presumably engaged in writing *Handlyng Synne.*
8051–52: See note for 8181.
8063–70: These lines are bracketed in the MS. RMB's "couwe" differs: Pers has for 8063–64: "A Loundres est sa teste / Du cors est fet partye / En iiij bones viles / Dount honurer les ylles / Ke sunt en Albanye." Pers does not have lines 8065–66; for 8067–68 he has English lines very close to RMB's version (2:364).
8069–8102: Pers writes this entire passage with lines riming in *-er* (2:364–66). RMB rearranges the lines and rewrites the account, omitting some of Pers' details and adding his own version of the events. The major change is in 8070–80, concerning the murder of John

Comyn. T. M. Smallwood discusses the revised Langtoft account in "An unpublished early account of Bruce's murder of Comyn," *The Scottish Historical Review* (1975), from College of Arms MS Arundel XIV [Pers MS E] and Bodleian MS Fairfax 24 [F]. RMB's version is not based on this revised account; the source for his very brief passage is perhaps local hearsay. The murder of an important Scottish nobleman by the aspiring king was much discussed and reported widely in other contemporary accounts. See R. McN. Scott, *Robert the Bruce* (1989), p. 73 (and *passim*) and references there provided. See also Michael Prestwich, *Edward I* (1988), pp. 498–505.

8121: The unusual expression *out tak* evidently means "except for." Pers has: *forpris* (2:368).

8128: See note, l. 6612 above. The scribe may have copied *Laynertost* from his source MS. Pers' MSS here have *Lanercost* [AB], *Lavertost* [C] (Wright, 2:370, n. 1). The several references to Lanercost suggest that some version of the chronicle of that house was available at least to Pers and perhaps also to RMB. Scott (1989) draws on *The Chronicle of Lanercost, 1201–1346,* trans. Sir Herbert Maxwell (Glasgow, 1913) for his retelling of the Bruce story, including the episode of Comyn's death. See Antonia Gransden (1974), pp. 494ff.

8140: The P scribe has picked up the second half-line of 8141, then finished with the correct words as shown in the text. The MS actually reads: "& bad he suld refus . þat him had forsaken . ilk a pautenere" (f. 192v). For this passage, Pers has: "Maunde à Sir Emer par ses bassatours / Rendre luy la vile deliverer les traitours / Ke wayvez luy avoyent à lour deshonours" (2:370).

8145–84: RMB has rearranged and rewritten a short passage in Pers' text, evidently using another source (2:370–72). Stepsis notes that some of the details are also given in Nicholas Trivet's *Annales* (pp. 409–10), but says "the account is too skimpy to have been a source" for Mannyng (n. for 8174–95, p. 477). Trivet's work and the Lanercost chronicle are discussed together in Gransden (pp. 501–7) as sources for the events of this period.

8181: The internal rime *feyng-heyng* seems to be a scribal variation for the identical *fanged-hanged* in 6527–28 and 8051–52. These spelling distortions are only justified by considering the rimes.

8191: The "fettred" men were sent from Scotland to *Inglond,* probably not to *Irlond.*

8202: The usual phrase is *schames dede,* a shameful death.

8203–4: Wright notes: "The reference . . . is to the history of Fulk fitz Warine, the celebrated outlaw under king John" (2:372, n. 10). Stepsis adds: "Either the romance in Anglo-Norman prose of *Fouke Fitzwarin* ed. L. Brandin (Paris, 1930), which was composed before 1314, or the original, lost, poetic version of the romance, on which the prose is based, written between 1256 and 1264" could have been the source (n. 8238, p. 477).

8225–40: RMB has cleverly used Pers' lines (2:374) to allude to his acquaintance with the Bruce brothers. Pers has seven lines, including 8226–27 and 8235–36, but RMB differs entirely in the emphasis. In 8225, for example, Pers has: "Du fols rey Robyn qe voet plus parler"; RMB decides to "ȝit speke more," and adds 8228–34. In 8229, "coruen kyng" is probably corrupt: A. B. Emden, *A Biographical Register of the University of Cambridge to 1500* (1963) notes in his article on Alexander that " 'corven kyng' . . . makes nonsense in its context. It would seem more probable that the 'arte' of which he had the mastery was intended to mean 'the seven liberal arts' and that 'corven kyng' is a scrivener's mistaken rendering of the unfamiliar term 'commencyng,' meaning 'a commencement feast' " (p. 100).

8250: This line is obviously corrupt: does it mean that both Thomas and Alexander were to be beheaded?

8251: The reference to Boniface's "sexte boke" is from Pers (2:374). The title is *Liber Sextus,* "an analysis of the principal ecclesiastical legal developments from 1234 to his own time" (i.e., from his birth in 1233, and his papacy 1294–1303). *The Middle Ages: A Concise Encyclopaedia* ed. by H. R. Loyn (1989), p. 57. The context here may refer to Boniface's bull *Clericos Laicos* as well.

8256: *Mas* should probably be *mad.*

8259–60: These lines may be transposed. Pers has 8260, then the rubric for the date follows in MS B (2:376, n. 2).

8290: The last word should be *smyten* as in 8299.

8301–27: RMB has written his own version of this passage, translating only a few of Pers' lines (2:378–80), possibly following a revised Pers MS. The elegiac tone and allusions in both versions are similar. Wright notes that three lines (not precisely translated) occur only in MS B (2:380, n. 7). The device of alluding to earlier kings and emperors (8309–14) is another structural scheme employed by Henry of Huntingdon. See Nancy F. Partner (1977), pp. 27–28.

8327: The scribe failed to add *-n* to the last word in the line. Pers has: ". . . le rei Robin destrure" (2:380).

8330–52: Pers has eighteen lines, most of them translated by RMB, and adds five lines which RMB omits. Line 8347 is evidently in error: Edward reigned 1272–1307, correctly given as thirty-four years in Pers (2:382).

8352ff.: RMB closes with his short apology to the reader. "B letter" in the last line should be "D"; it is correct in the rubric following.

THE GLOSSARY

Preface

Table of Manuscripts and Sources Cited and Abbreviations

Ch1: Robert Mannyng of Brunne, *The Chronicle*, Part I, folios 1–95v [PL]

Ch2: Robert Mannyng of Brunne, *The Chronicle*, Part II, folios 96r–195r [P] [L: folios 72r–131v]

L: Lambeth MS 131 (Lambeth Palace Library, London) [Part I: ll. 199–15946; Part II: ll. 1–4973]

LALME: *A Linguistic Atlas of Late Mediaeval English* (Angus McIntosh, M.L. Samuels, Michael Benskin, eds. 4 vols. Aberdeen, 1986)

P: Petyt MS 511, vol. 7 (Inner Temple Library, London) [Base text for the edition of *The Chronicle*] [Part I: ll. 1–15946; Part II: ll. 1–8358; LALME LP 38]

R: Rawlinson Miscellany D.913 (Bodleian Library, Oxford) [Part I: ll. 12550–12699]

RMB: Robert Mannyng of Brunne

Manuscripts cited for *Robert Mannyng of Brunne: Handlyng Synne,* ed. Idelle Sullens, Medieval & Renaissance Texts & Studies, vol. 14 (Binghamton, 1983).

A: Ashmole MS 61 (Bodleian Library, Oxford) [ll. 3799–3912; LALME LP 71]

B: Bodley MS 415 (Bodleian) [ll. 1–12638; LALME LP 6620] [Base MS]

C: Cambridge MS Ii.4.9 (Cambridge University Library) [ll. 147–2988; LALME LP 621]

D: Dulwich MS XXIV (Dulwich College Library, London) [ll. 1–2894; LALME LP 4646]

F: Folger MS V.b.236 (Folger Library, Washington, DC) [12582 ll.]

H: Harley MS 1701 (British Library, London) [12597 ll.; LALME LP 6630]

O: Osborn MS a.2 (Yale University Library [Beinecke], New Haven) [ll. 2501–12371; LALME LPs 471, 484, 521]

S: "Simeon": Addit. MS 22283 (British Library, London) [ll. 9899–10818]

V: "Vernon": Eng. Poet MS A.1 (Bodleian) [ll. 9899–10818; LALME LP 7630]

W: Westminster Diocesan Archives MS H.38 (ff. 146v–147r) [ll. 3657–3676; not cited for the edition]

Sources for the Glossary

Previous glossaries for Mannyng's works have helped, in varying degrees, to establish a basic word list. The remarkable capability of a computer to locate a word in the text still requires that one must first know the word itself in order to begin the search for examples. To the following sources especially I owe a debt of gratitude.

(1) Frederick J. Furnivall, *The Story of England by Robert Manning of Brunne, A. D. 1338* (2 vols. RS, 1887). Furnivall's edition of Ch1 included a glossary (2:769–846) with the head note: "The Old French is from Burguy; the Anglo-Saxon mainly from Bosworth; The Gothic &c. from Stratmann." At the end of the introduction in vol. 1, Furnivall credits Sidney J. Herrtage for "help with the Indexes and Glossary" (p. xxiii). The word list is for his base manuscript L, and includes definitions of the most minimal sort. The etymologies are also minimal and citations are confined to one or two examples from the text, with an occasional amplification for unusual terms.[1]

(2) Thomas Hearne, *Peter Langtoft's Chronicle (as Illustrated and Improv'd by Robert of Brunne)*... (2 vols., 1725; reprint 1810). Hearne's edition of Ch2 does not have a glossary, though some words that were of particular interest to him are included in notes in his introduction and at the foot of the pages where they occur. Many of his random notes cite sources in Latin. Since Hearne's edition of Ch2 has been the only one available in print, except for Stepsis' unpublished dissertation (1967), his readings (right or wrong) have been regularly cited by later scholars. In Walter W. Skeat's edition of *Havelok the Dane* (1868), 105–56, for example, a word list for "Havelok" is provided which derives in part from Hearne's edition; this selection of words is chiefly useful to support the dialectal identity of "Havelok" as a North East Midland work.[2] Skeat included a number of examples common to RMB's *Chronicle* [Ch2] and the text of "Havelok" in Laud Misc. MS 108; Skeat comments that RMB, "a Lincolnshire man, approaches nearer to the present poem [Havelok] than any other writer" (p. 135). Thus, the use of RMB's language to support the glossaries in many other Middle English editions has depended on the editions of Hearne and Furnivall, including the citations to his works in *OED* and *MED*.

(3) Robert Peter Stepsis added a word list to his dissertation (*An Edition of Part II of Robert Mannyng of Brunne's Chronicle of England* [1967], 479–620), but did not include line references. The etymologies are chiefly derived from the *OED* as only a few of the fascicles of the *MED* were available to him in 1967. The words listed are from manuscript P, Stepsis' base text for Ch2. Some of Stepsis' definitions are conjectures based on the context where the words appear and are sometimes fanciful, but I have found his word list useful in compiling the basic body of information.

(4) George Howard Naish's dissertation ("Handlyng Synne and Medytacyuns" —1936) includes an admirable glossary for *Handlyng Synne* and additional notes

[1] Furnivall was one of the chief instigators of the project that eventually became the *New English Dictionary* and its successor, *The Oxford English Dictionary*. He began gathering citations in 1858. The glossary for his edition of Ch1, which appeared almost thirty years later (1887), may have benefitted to a certain extent from the word-searches of Furnivall and his collaborators. See William Benzie, *Dr F. J. Furnivall: Victorian Scholar Adventurer* (1983), especially pp. 87ff. on the beginnings of the dictionary project.

[2] See Angus McIntosh, "The Language of the Extant Versions of 'Havelok the Dane,'" (1976), 35–49.

for various unusual words keyed to line numbers. His citations are comprehensive, based on his edition of manuscript B and variants for manuscripts CDHSV. Many of the variants are also included as footnotes to the text where they differ from B. Naish also included approximately seventy words he found in the citations from the "Bowes MS" (now Osborn MS A.2 [O]) which were in James Orchard Halliwell's *A Dictionary of Archaic Words* (originally published in 1847). Naish cites the 1889 edition with the title *A Dictionary of Archaic and Provincial Words, Obsolete Phrases, Proverbs, and Ancient Customs from the Fourteenth Century* where the editor's name is given as Halliwell-Phillips. After Halliwell plundered the Osborn manuscript for "archaic words," the manuscript disappeared until it was acquired in 1957 (with the Osborn manuscript collection) by the Beinecke Library at Yale University. Naish's glossary and additional notes have been indispensable; he employed the *OED* for etymologies, definitions, and various other distinctions in the use of words in *Handlyng Synne*, and analyzed the language as far as possible based on comparisons to the texts in the Hearne and Furnivall editions of RMB's *Chronicle*.

(5) Hubert Gburek's dissertation, "Der Wortschatz des Robert Mannyng of Brunne in *Handlyng Synne*" (1977), is based on Harley MS 1701 [H] which was the base text for Furnivall's editions of *Handlyng Synne*. Gburek's word list is exhaustive, including every citation for every word in the manuscript. The other apparatus includes a list of words in *Handlyng Synne* recorded for the first time in English, a list of words recorded for the last time, and "hapaxlegomena" [*sic*], which is mainly comprised of scribal peculiarities in manuscript H. Gburek's choice of manuscript H for this study is discussed in the introduction to this edition of the *Chronicle* (see n. 67). Gburek's variant readings are from manuscripts ABCDFO. I have consulted Gburek for a few additional references to lines in *Handlyng Synne*. His etymologies and definitions are, of course, in German.

(6) The *Middle English Dictionary* (*MED*) has had some minor alterations in plan since the first appearance of fascicles for the letters E and F in 1952. Quotations from Middle English texts were based originally on those assembled for the *Oxford English Dictionary* (*OED*, published in twelve volumes, 1933); my desk reference is *The Compact Edition of the Oxford English Dictionary* (2 vols., 1971), which has the complete *OED* in reduced facsimile. This reference has been used for the last letters of the alphabet, i.e., beyond the *MED* fascicles already published, with some occasional citations in earlier parts of the *OED* when a comparison to the *MED* was necessary.

The dates of the manuscripts have some effect on the diction, for they extend over a long period in which the language was rapidly changing. Some of these dates are modified from the approximate dates given in *MED*: P (?a1400, probably early in the last quarter of the fourteenth century); L (a1450, perhaps later); R (?a1400; the fragment is nearly contemporary with P); B (probably ca. 1400); H (a1400 or a little later); F (not dated, but other parts of the original undivided manuscript may be ca. 1400)[3]; A (a1500); C (a1450); D (a1425); SV (ca. 1390, but in dispute); O (ca. 1450 to possibly 1460, the year of the death of William Bowes of Streatlam, perhaps the original owner); W (?1393, as indicated by a note in the manuscript, according to Horrall, but likely copied in part ca. 1400 or later). These dates are based on the list in the *Middle English Dictionary: Plan and Bibliography* (1954 revision, p. 58). LALME generally uses the same dates listed in *MED*. For various reasons which are explained in the introduction to this edition of *The Chronicle*, the conjectural dates above are somewhat adjusted, partly based on paleographic considerations. We can be reasonably sure that P is a copy of an exemplar in the language of Lincolnshire, made about the middle of the fourteenth century but done by scribes at least one generation after RMB completed the work in 1338.

MED qualifies its dates as within twenty-five years earlier when they are preceded by *a* = *ante*. These dates were established during 1946–49 based on whatever information was available to the *MED* editors at that time; subsequently, many studies have appeared which refine these conjectural dates, particularly on the basis of paleography. (See the *MED* "Plan," p. 18.) The copy of *Handlyng Synne* in B, which must have been done by ca. 1400 since so many other copies derive from it (FH and perhaps A and W), is in a hand with the paleographic characteristics of other early fifteenth-century manuscripts, a beautiful secretary script.

The words included in the glossary comprise a selective list, derived from the sources given above. There is, of course, a possibility that I may have missed some of RMB's diction; however, absolute completeness based on such a vast amount of material was not my primary objective. Because the glossary originally included a great many line citations discovered during a computer search, I found that it was necessary to limit the citations for any one word form to a maximum of five (i.e., words with identical spelling and representing a specific part of speech—noun, verb, etc.) The citations could have been limited further, but confining the interpretation to only a few alternatives would be a disservice to the reader. The choice of deciding which interpretation of meaning applies in the context is open: wherever a word is found, whether the line reference is specifically cited or not, the reader can make his own application of the meaning.

The purpose of this glossary is to record the manuscript evidence for the language itself: in theory, one could discover as much as has survived of RMB's original work. The edition of *The Chronicle*, however, is not merely a late twentieth-century reconstruction of what the various scribes might have retained from that original, since only an autograph manuscript would preserve the au-

---

[3] See the description of the undivided F manuscript in the introduction. The first part, *Handlyng Synne* and *Medytacyuns*, is not analyzed in LALME; the second part ("Mandeville's Travels") is now in the Princeton University Library; the third part ("Piers Plowman" C-text, with the "Estorie del Evangelie" and the "Assumption of the Blessed Virgin Mary") is Sterling MS S. L.v.17 in the University of London Library. See LP 7780 and LP 7650 in LALME for this last part, in the dialect of South Worcestershire. A summary description of the whole manuscript is in N. R. Ker, *Medieval Manuscripts in British Libraries* (1969), 1:376–77.

thorial text. The order of citations, therefore, is based upon the relative dating of the manuscripts of the works rather than on the order of RMB's composition: he says that he began *Handlyng Synne* in 1303 and finished the chronicle in 1338, but none of the surviving manuscripts were made in his own time and the copies of all the *Handlyng Synne* manuscripts and manuscript L of *The Chronicle* are dated much later. What we have is a record of the changing language with a reflection of much of RMB's own Lincolnshire lexis from the early fourteenth century which remains in spite of probable alteration in intermediate exemplars.

The order of citations is as follows: Ch1 and Ch2 from P with variants for manuscripts LR as applicable, then *Handlyng Synne* (from B), with variants for manuscripts ACDFHOSVW when they represent significant differences from B. This arrangement is necessary because *The Chronicle* is the most reliable source for RMB's language in a Lincolnshire dialect, and P is the oldest manuscript preserving any of his work. The index (or key) word is chosen from the text of Ch1 or Ch2 whenever possible, or from *Handlyng Synne* if the word appears only in that text. One might question the value of including examples of words ending in *e* and more examples without the *e:* the scribe's habits are demonstrated, while recording his variable spelling. It is easy to perceive a pattern of scribal habits by scanning an entry for a word with multiple examples. The glossary also includes many examples drawn from manuscript L (as alternate readings for P) which do not appear in the side-notes for L in the text. These are mainly minor spelling variations which do not affect the sense of the text in any direct way but are significant to demonstrate the differences in the L manuscript.

In most citations, the texts of P for *The Chronicle* and B for *Handlyng Synne* are sufficient to identify RMB's vocabulary, though there are hundreds of instances in which a word from one work does not appear in the other. For other dialectal distinctions in P, see LP 38 in LALME (3:253–54). *Handlyng Synne* manuscript B is a translation to the South East Midlands dialect of Hertfordshire (LP 6620 LALME, 3:180) near the border of Buckinghamshire. For these texts, the dialect is not necessarily more important than regional usage and varying diction, often dictated by poetic considerations. Many of RMB's terms were peculiar to Lincolnshire and, judging from the changes made in later copies, were evidently unfamiliar to scribes in other areas.

Generally, the index words are given in the order of noun, verb, adjective and adverb (in a single entry where the root is the same), with an occasional separate entry for participial forms and the gerund. These verbal derivatives may demonstrate other meanings that have been lost in later stages of development of the language. The alphabetization governs the order to some extent: a strict adherence to the arrangement used in *MED* would not be economical for this glossary. The context readily distinguishes adjective from adverb, but identical forms are common for nouns and verbs. I have omitted the devices supplied in modern dictionaries for analyzing phonology. These distinctions can be found in *MED* for all instances where phonology might be important. Similarly, distinction of capital letters and lower-case forms in the manuscripts has been ignored, following the practice of the scribes themselves. Erratic capitalization in PL is the rule. Most of *The Chronicle* scribes did not bother to capitalize the first words in a line of verse, and even proper names regularly begin with a lower case letter. Some of the capitals seem to be included for purely decorative reasons.

Scribal variations in the manuscripts presenting texts of the same work (either *Handlyng Synne* or *The Chronicle*) are possible clues to words Mannyng may have used that have been changed in some of the later manuscripts. Consequently, a variant manuscript reading might retain the word he originally used. With only two manuscripts and a fragment for *The Chronicle,* however, we have very limited evidence. In *Handlyng Synne,* the two copies (FH) from B also have evidence of some occasional editing by the scribes; where variants are given for these manuscripts, it is clear that the changes are scribal. Though the diction in FH is usually identical to that of B, the syntax (especially in H) is frequently altered. The spelling preferences in FH may sometimes appear to be substitutions, but the scribes were merely exercising their editorial prerogatives. In F, for example, *i* is usually preferred to B's *y;* moreover, F regularly corrects one of B's idiosyncracies, *w* with the following vowel omitted, by adding *o* or sometimes *u.*

Among the hundreds of examples of identical words in BFH, only those few which are examples of unusual or otherwise unattested diction have been included in the glossary. Words in the other *Handlyng Synne* manuscripts which represent substitutions or other significant variations, however, are added, usually at the end of the entry. Some of the variants may not reflect other exemplars; they could simply be scribal choices or misunderstandings. It is notable that manuscript O, probably the latest of all the manuscripts, has many readings of unusual terms which are closer to those in BFH than to the text of CD or SV. Undoubtedly the exemplar of O derived from one quite similar to the BFH text that was translated to a northern dialect.

The copyists had reasons for deliberately changing (a) words that they did not understand, or (b) terms that seemed archaic or were otherwise unfamiliar, or (c) words they assumed to be errors (and which often actually were errors as attested in P and B), or (d) words which were altered to cover up the copyist's errors. The wide variety of different words surviving in the *Handlyng Synne* manuscripts containing excerpts or fragments (particularly CDSVO) reflects considerable alteration, apparently progressive, that occurred during the century or more after RMB wrote.[4] The whole corpus of manuscripts represents the work of many scribes, not just copies of texts written by one author.

The etymologies in *OED* and *MED* are generally the same, though *OED* provides much more exploration of the ultimate sources of the language. I have cited only the proximate root derivations in this glossary; the most likely immediate source is given, and very few words in RMB's vocabulary are traceable to earlier European tongues. His OE, ON, and either OF or Anglo-French (*MED*'s AF) roots account for almost all of the diction. For AF, words occurring in

[4] The list of notes in my edition of *Handlyng Synne,* 317–75, includes many variant readings that are not repeated in this glossary. The line readings of the manuscripts given there have a different purpose and do not present RMB's diction in the systematic fashion this glossary employs. The reader should consult the *Handlyng Synne* notes for more detail concerning specific line references cited here.

Manuel des Pechiez [MP] are cited whenever possible, since this was RMB's acknowledged source for *Handlyng Synne* and has a nearly contemporary vocabulary. Langtoft is cited in some entries, especially when RMB's diction is very similar. The objective was to differentiate RMB's language and isolate his words from the mass of the other *MED* citations. Whenever it was possible, citations used in *MED* and *OED* are among the examples because they are a key to more precise etymologies or definitions in the dictionaries.

For Wace and Langtoft, RMB's chief sources in *The Chronicle,* specific quotations of some of the passages RMB translated are given in the text notes for Ch1 and Ch2; this information might be used for other etymologies if needed. The great variety of different manuscript spellings makes Langtoft's work less useful for this purpose. Another difficulty arises from our lack of a comprehensive edition of *Manuel des Pechiez:* the only reference is Furnivall's parallel text in his EETS edition of *Handlyng Synne.*

Coinages or spelling distortion for the sake of rime are discussed in the introduction to this edition. Manuscripts P (especially in Ch2) and BFH were written by scribes who were very conscious of eye-rime. The words cited in *MED* or *OED* with references *only* to Mannyng's works are marked [◆] in the margin (before the index words) in this glossary. Whether these are otherwise unattested words in Middle English depends on the possibility that examples may be discovered in other manuscripts eventually. It is also possible that other citations for these words escaped the editors of *MED* and *OED* and that they will appear in new editions of known Middle English texts. Whether the words appearing only in RMB's works are discovered elsewhere or not, we should consider that Mannyng was one of the earliest writers of a substantial body of Middle English verse employing an extensive vocabulary, and that his direct influence on the language in the later fourteenth century was proportional to the dissemination of the manuscripts. The *Chronicle* was not copied by many scribes and, so far as we know, *Handlyng Synne* was copied only in translations.

Other contemporary works discussed in the introduction to this edition are also preserved in late manuscripts and various dialects. The strong influence of the East Midlands dialect on the speech of London, however, and the eventual development of standard English has been remarked by many scholars. Though many manuscripts written in the later fourteenth century preserve other dialects, the dialect RMB used was one that persisted, markedly affecting the language of other authors.[5] The scholars who attempt to trace a direct influence from RMB on later works, such as the English prose *Brut* or the *Morte Arthure,* are responding to the lexis that persisted to the end of the century, but not necessarily drawn from RMB's poetry.

---

[5] The historian Harry Rothwell, commenting on the importance of London in the early fourteenth century, points out that "the native element . . . had been strongly reinforced from the provinces, so strongly from the East Midlands that Londoners' speech was permanently affected" (*English Historical Documents, 1189–1327* [1975], 3:8). In a note to this statement, Rothwell says that the influence was "from a southern dialect to East Midland, neither a southern nor Northumbrian but a Mercian dialect destined to become the standard English" (n. 3).

Alphabetization

There are some necessary rearrangements of the vocabulary to accommodate the texts. I have not followed *MED* in these matters, but the reader who needs to find additional information may consult the "Plan" for *MED* cited above.

(1) ȝ - yogh appears after the letter *g*.
(2) *IJ* are both transcribed as *i*, but words which would have *j* as initial letter in modern pronunciation are listed separately after *i*.
(3) *Sh-sch* are alphabetized as if they were all spelled *sch* [see *MED* S.2, p. 187 for explanation].
(4) *þ* - thorn is alphabetized among the words with initial *th-* .
(5) *V* is the initial letter for *u* (*u* usually appears in other than the initial positions); words which would have *V* as initial letter in modern pronunciation are listed after *U*.
(6) *Sc-sk* are cross-referenced as appropriate.
(7) *C-K* are usually cross-referenced, but both should be consulted as necessary: a word may appear in a different form as the sole example with a different initial letter.
(8) *I-Y* are alphabetized interchangeably since *Y* does not have the modern phonetic value; in RMB's manuscripts, *y* is simply an alternate to *i* and is usually used to avoid too many minims in a sequence. (In *Handlyng Synne* the *y* often seems to be merely decorative.) The confusion of *þ* with *y* is not a major problem in the *Chronicle* manuscripts, though neither appears regularly dotted to indicate a difference between them.

Omissions

This glossary is necessarily selective. As mentioned above, the line citations have been limited to no more than five for any one word form, i.e., with identical spelling. The reader must choose the definition applicable to the context in many instances. A grammatical analysis of pronouns represented in the dialects of the many different scribes is not included, but the student of dialect will, of course, make his own choices based on whichever text he is studying. Analysis of any short passage in the text will provide ample data for the customary pronoun usage of the scribes.[6] Since pronouns are considered a reliable clue to dialect in manuscripts of this period, I did not think it necessary to do more than identify the dialect itself. The analyses in LALME cited in the list of manuscripts above include the pronouns. A few of the pronouns, however, i.e., *þar, þare, þer* are included in the glossary to differentiate them from adverbs spelled identically.

This glossary could not go beyond the language of the surviving manuscripts to establish a firmly authenticated word list representing *only* Mannyng's actual vocabulary. What survives in the manuscripts is filtered in various ways, by spelling and dialectal differences, by the changes in the language, and by the idiosyncratic

---

[6] The personal pronouns in P are very like the modern forms: *I, þou, ȝe, he, hire (hir), þam, ȝow, his, my, mine,* etc., with some few variations that are not dialectally significant.

editorial procedures of the scribes. But this glossary does give us some choices by comparison among all these diverse manuscripts: if an unusual word appears in both *The Chronicle* and *Handlyng Synne,* it is probably Mannyng's own word. If a word appears only in one of the late copies and no vestige remains in manuscript P, it may plausibly be considered a later contribution by a scribe. Curiously, the variant readings in the fifteenth-century Norfolk MSS of *Handlyng Synne* [CD] and the later northern O manuscript do not preserve many words that also appear in the Lincolnshire manuscript P of the *Chronicle,* the manuscript that is probably at least a quarter of a century earlier than any other manuscript containing his work. There is a huge gap between what must have been the original language of *Handlyng Synne* and the considerably altered diction of all the fifteenth-century manuscripts, though the words that recur constantly in all of them provide strong surviving evidence of his lexis. We must be grateful for the version of the *Chronicle* that remains in P. What we can hope to learn from the vestiges of what Mannyng originally wrote is here and should invite further study.

ABBREVIATIONS FOR THE GLOSSARY

See MED for abbreviations of unusual or rare language sources.

adj.	adjective
adv.	adverb
conj.	conjunction
ger.	gerund
n.	noun
v.	verb
pl.	plural
ppl.	past participle
pres.p.	present participle
p.	past tense
fig.	figuratively.
HS	*Handlyng Synne*
MP	*Manuel des Pechiez*
RMB	Robert Mannyng of Brunne
AF	Anglo-French (= Anglo-Norman)
L	Latin
OE	Old English
OF	Old French
ON	Old Norse (as preserved in 13th-century Icelandic)

The key [index] word is derived from the examples in the entry. Sigla for the variant MSS are given at the head of the preface, above.

A

abaist, obeist v. [OF abaissier, abessier] frighten, astonish; cast down, upset **Ch1** 4634, 10690, 11890 abaist P abaischt L; 5005, 5371 obaist P abaischt L; 7774 obeist P abayscht L; 3797 abeised P abesed L; 3125 obessed P obeysed L; 12745 abaiste; 13396 bessed P baysche L; 1628 abate P abesen L; **Ch2** 4217, 6595 abaist; **HS** 5642 abashed *O* abayste

abate v. (1) [see batand] [from abaten] abase; reduce in numbers, stop; cease strife **Ch1** 4475, 4797 abate; 1628 abate P abesen L; 565 abate P bate L; 2986, 6089, 6125 bate; 2423, 3000, 8414 abated; 2390, 4520 abatid P abated L; 2404 abatid P abyde L; 2405, 4520, 6118, 13422 abatid; 4516 bated; 4368 abatid P bated L; **Ch2** 1532, 2101, 7548 abate; 2152 bated; 8276 bate; 6515, 7685 abated; **HS** 3938 abate; 4508 bate *HO* abate; 9940 wlates *S* bateþ *V* bates

abate v. (2) [OF batre] beat wings; fight, argue **Ch1** 1673, 9114, 13070 abate; 3512 batid; 4368 abatid P bated L; 3000, 8352, 8414 abated

abatement n. [OF] lessening; loss; impairment **Ch2** 6741 abatement

abaued, abawed ppl. [from OF abauir] confused, disconcerted **Ch2** 2619 abauen; 5151 abaued; **HS** 9543 abawed

abbay, abbey n. [OF abbeie] community of monks or nuns; house they occupy **Ch1** 6947, 8796 abbay; 8613 abbey; 10848 abbeie; 14641 abbaie; **Ch2** 546, 1259, 3010, 5665 abbay; 774, 3119 abbey; 796, 2011 abbayes; 476, 2784, 3310, 8053 abbeis; 6000 abbays; 2008, 6858 abbeye; 3480 abbeie; 8294 abbeys; **HS** 1996, 2098, 3156 abbey; 8946 abbeye

abbas, abbes n. [OF abbesse (MP)] the woman superior of a convent **Ch2** 1402 abbes; **HS** 8265 abbas

abbot n. [OE abbod, OF abbat] superior of monks in an abbey **Ch1** 10086 abot P abbotes L; 8592, 9146 abbotes; 14644 abbot; **Ch2** 797, 1804, 8092 abbot; 3012 abbote; 8132 abbotes; **HS** 1917, 2088, 4022, 8545 abbot; 10023 abbotes

abeyte, bayte v. [ON; cp. OE bætan] bite; torment, excite; be excited, enamoured **Ch2** 6688 bayte; **HS** 181 abeyted *C* lustely steryd; 5990 beyte; 10910 bayteþ; 6782 byte *O* bayt-ede

abesen v. [see abaist, abate]

abyde v. [see bide, v.] [OE abiden] remain, expect, endure; wait for **Ch1** 1098 abyde; 2568, 3755, 7883, 9060, 15425 abide; 5185 abide P stonde L; 6284, 12341 abide P abyd L; 5008 bide P abide L; 2483, 3433, 8312, 9062 abode; **Ch2** 1685 abiden; 340, 1689, 2533, 5090, 8211 abide; 2915 bide P abide L; 5416 abode; **HS** 2501, 4289, 9850, 9967, 11881 abyde; 5605, 12198 abode; 11386 abyt; 7913 abyde *O* stande to

abie v. [see bie, v.] [OE abycgan] redeem, buy, pay for **Ch1** 3454 abie P abye L; **Ch2** 3927 abie; **HS** 3613, 7287, 8744, 9320 abye; 3838 abeye; 2450 abye *C* abyen

abite n. [see habite]

abomynable adj. [OF, L] disgusting, nauseating **HS** 6520 abomynable

aboue, aboun, abowen adv./prep. [OE abufan] above, up; more, superior to **Ch1** 2413 aboue P alone L; 2284, 3785, 5922, 7098, 9254 aboue; 8074, 12483 abouen; 5048 up P abouen L; 5661 vndere P abouen L; 9896, 10707, 11172, 13378, 15648 aboun; 5661 vndere P abouen L; 13290 aboun P abouen L; **Ch2** 83, 696, 2833, 3523, 4048 aboue; 963 obowen P aboute L; 2036 abowen; 2619, 3688 abouen; **HS** 285, 1148, 4616, 9944, 12523 aboue; 4131 aboue *O* abown; 7029 aboue *O* abowne; 9131 aboue *F* on *O* apon

about adv./prep. [OE onbutan, abutan] encircle, in all directions; round about; throughout; everywhere; concerning **Ch1** 641, 1129, 4914, 7529, 9075 about; 4846, 5758, 6714, 8166, 11080 aboute; **Ch2** 798, 3775, 4964, 7950, 8097 about; 432, 2936, 5324, 6831, 7861 aboute; **HS** 1516, 3406, 5467, 8057, 8868 aboute

abreggyd, abbregged v. [OF abregier] reduce, diminish **HS** 1776 abreggyd; 11956 abbregged

accioun n. [AF] an act, deed **Ch2** 4856 accioun P accion L

acheued v. [see cheve, v.] [OF achever] obtain **Ch1** acheued 14510

acyse n. [see asise, assise]

acord n. [OF] reconciliation, agreement **Ch1** 2624, 3216 acorde P acord L; 4763 acord; 5219, 5552, 5555 acorde; 5226 acordes; **Ch2** 3746, 3865, 4024 acord; 1151, 3683, 4823, 6461, 8266 acorde; **HS** 246 acord *C* be attoun *D* haue forȝeuenesse

acord v. [OF acorder] agree; show, prove **Ch1** 6304, 9371 acorde; 5226 acordes; 2225, 2335, 5551 acorded; **Ch2** 1309, 3683, 4422, 7702 acorde; 4797 acord; 2815 acordes; 1142, 2417, 3057, 3860, 6207 acorded; 3365 acordid; **HS** 5510 acord; 10735 acordeþ

acordance n. [OF] agreement, harmony **Ch2** 2727, 6228, 6237 acordance; 4477 acordance P ordynance L; **HS** 2003 acordaunce *C* cor-dawns

acount n. [AF acunte (MP)] record; computation **Ch1** 7102 acountes; **Ch2** 1313, 2063 acounte; 3307 acountes; **HS** 4782, 4839, 6749, 10893, 11390 acounte; 1205 acuncte

acounted v. [AF acunter (MP)] to count; to

amount to **HS** 6323, 6393 acounted; 11948 acounteþ

acountir n. [see encounter]

acountours n. [from AF acunter, v.] one who keeps accounts or records **HS** 5410 acountours

acouped v. [OF acouper] accused of an offense **HS** 11454, 12408 acoupe; 12574 acouped; 3434 acouped *O* acombryde; 4690 acouped *O* blame; 11079 acouped *O* calde

acquitance n. [OF aquitance] remission, repayment, release from an obligation **Ch1** 1203 aquitance P acquitaunce L; **Ch2** 3854, 3864 acquitance; **HS** 10820 aquytaunce

acursed v./adj. [see curse, v. and cursed, adj.] [cp. OE cursian] to be condemned, declared outcast **HS** 1714, 2165 acursyd; 3390 acursed

addre n. [see neddre]

adray n. [see aray] [AF derei] confusion, disturbance **HS** 4672 adray *F* arai *O* disary

adred v. [see dred, n./v.] [OE adræden, ofdrædd] frighten; to be frightened **HS** 734, 2256 adred; 5641 adrad; 2245 adred *D* aferd; 5468 adred *O* for drede

aduersere n. [OF adversier] an enemy, adversary **Ch2** 2031 aduersere

affere v. [OE afæran] to make afraid, terrify **Ch1** 7676 afere; **Ch2** 4646 affere; 1781 oglift P aferd L; **HS** 4861, 8994, 9059, 9254 aferd; 2245 adred *D* aferd; 4409 afered *O* dout

afferme v. [OF afermer, L affirmare] agree to; ratify or confirm **Ch2** 7738, 7778 afferme

affiance n. [OF affiaunce] confidence, trust **Ch2** 2158, 7589 affiance; **HS** 385, 12076, 12630 affyaunce

affie, afie v. [OF afier] trust, have faith **Ch1** 3763, 4306 affie; 3760, 5886, 6580, 13095 affied; 12560 afied P affied LR; 2442L, 12032L affye (om. P); **Ch2** 1934, 3828, 4814, 4975 affie; 5483 afie; 7919 affies; 5394 affied; **HS** 10248, 10501 affye; 4114 truste *O* affaye do

affynyte n. [OF] kinship; alliance **HS** 7380, 7381 affynyte

affliccions n. [OF afliciun] misery, distress, sorrow **Ch2** 4958 affliccions; **HS** 309 afflycyouns; 1430, 1794, 10462 afflyccyun

affray n. [OF effrai] riot, disorder **Ch1** 12126 affray; 8937L affray (om. P); **Ch2** 1858, 2218, 4310, 4376, 5590 affray; 679 affray P in a fray L; 747, 2218, 5590, 7164 affray; 1622 affrayes; 2165 affraies; 7910, 7978 affrays; 701 affaies P frayes L; **HS** 1822 affray *C* a raye; 2154 affray *D* fray; 7836, 8051, 9857 affray

affray v. [OF effraer] attack, terrify **Ch1** 3283, 3462 affraid; 3409 affreide P affrayed L; 7696L affraye (om. P); 8937L affrayed (om. P); 14014 affraied; **Ch2** 448 affray; 280, 576, 1654, 4308 affraied; 856 affaied P affrayed L; **HS** 2241 afrayd

affryght v. [see ofright] [OE afyrhtan, afyrht] to be frightened or terrified **HS** 8767, 10559 affryght

aforced v. [OF efforcier, aforcer] to force, compel **Ch1** 5773 aforce P enforce L; 10390L aforced (om. P); 11795 aforced; **HS** 3665 aforcede *O* a forsyd *W* aforsed

aforn adv. [see fore, forn]

agayn, ageyns adv./adj./prep. [OE ongean, ongan, agen] against; before; opposed to **Ch1** 1588, 3150, 5353, 7831, 8008 ageyn; 2538, 3467, 4909, 7692, 9393 agayn; 2210, 4614, 7680 agayn P ageyn L; 5335, 6711 ageyns; 5703 amang P ageyns L; 9105 agayn P ageyns L; 9059 agayns; 6626 ageyns P geynes L; 13016 ageyns P þer gayns L; **Ch2** 1612, 1831 ageyn P agayn L; 1720, 2096, 4501, 7742, 8320 ageyn; 1951, 3073, 3994, 7580 agayn; 2089, 2549, 3844 ageyns; **HS** 245 aȝeyne; 524 aȝeyn; 10634 agayn; 2532 aȝayn; 18, 328, 478, 8103 aȝen; 578, 2126, 3758, 7827, 11075 aȝens

agast ppl. [see gast, ogast] [from OE gæstan] frightened **Ch1** 6475 agast P agaste L; 7678 agaste P agast L; 10295 agast; 14910 ogast P agast L; **Ch2** 3042 ogast; 6702 agast; **HS** 5468 agast

age n. (1) [AF age (MP)] being elderly **Ch1** 870, 2143, 4041, 6098, 6967 age; **Ch2** 818, 2584, 3783, 5977 age; **HS** 1112, 1664, 5052, 7670, 7675 age

age n. (2) [see hache, hage: ague]

ageynsaid, aȝenseyþ v. [see geynsay] [OE ongegn + secgan; cp. L contra-dicere] deny, refuse, oppose, contradict **Ch1** 4894 agaynsaid P agaynseide L; **Ch2** 175 geynsaid P ageynseyd L; 5163 ageynsaid; **HS** 646, 12314 aȝenseyþ; 6433 aȝensseyþ

ageynward adv. [OE ongegnweard] backward **Ch1** 387 agaynward P ageynward L; **Ch2** 4542 ageynward

agher conj. [OE ægþer] either **HS** 3293 agher *F* awer *O* oure; 10551 agher *SV* sum wher

aght n. [see auht, ouht] [OE æht] possessions **HS** 2456 aght GLOSS BH gode *C* frawth *D* auȝt; 4139 aght GLOSS BH gode; 6042, 6375 aght

aglyft adj. [see oglift]

◆ **agraunte** v. [see ogrant] [OF agraunter] to acknowledge, grant **HS** 4164 agraunte

agreue v. [see greue, ogrefe] [OF agrever] to injure, disturb, harass **Ch2** 200 greued P agreued L; **HS** 490 greue *C* agreve; 9080 sore agreued *O* sorowe & grewyde

agryse, agrisen, ogrisen v. [OE agrisan] frightened, horrified, dismayed **Ch1** 980 agrysen P agrisen L; 2946 at gros P agros L; 8418 gros; 9476 grisen P agrysen L; **Ch2** 5710 ogrisen;

HS 8772 agryse; 707 agresyn *C* agreuyd

aȝenchar v. [OE aȝen + cearran] retreat; repent **HS** 2062 aȝenchar *C* ageyn chare *D* bryngiþ hym in car

ay, ey n. [OE æg] egg **Ch2** 4333 ay P ey L; 4490 ay

ay, aywhere, aywhore, ouerwhere adv. [OE æȝhwær, ahwær] ever, everywhere, anywhere **Ch1** 107 ouerwhere; 717L aywhore (P differs); 2629 ay; 2948, 5608 aywhere; 3006 ai whore P ay where L; 3265, 5855, 8594 ay whore; 8462 aiwhere P aywher L; 6186 aywhare; 14890 ay; **Ch2** 7186, 7195 ay; 1930 aywhare; **HS** 5580, 8314 aywhore; 7981 aywhare; 2795 awher *D* euere *F* auȝwer *O* euer; 2927 euerywhore *O* ay qwore; 3074 alway *O* ay; 12212 eurywhere *O* ay qware; 1066 ay GLOSS B euere; 3609 ay GLOSS B eure; 6467 aywhore GLOSS H euermore

aye, awe, eye n. [see eye, eie] [OE ege; ON *aga] fear, terror; respect; anger **Ch1** 2866 aye P eye L; 4919, 6264, 12924 awe; 14773 eie P eye L; **Ch2** 790, 2719, 3843, 6773, 7467 awe; 5384 ay; 6662, 7156 aye; 150, 839, 6062 eye; **HS** 1358, 4908, 6729, 9075, 12106 awe; 38, 566, 2710, 6047, 11150 eye; 2020 eye *D* awe; 2613 awe GLOSS B drede; 3236 awe GLOSS BH drede

aiere n. [see eyre, n.]

aioynte ppl. [OF ajoint, ppl.] allied, connected **HS** 11492 aioynte *O* enyonte

aiorned v. [OF ajorner] order to appear in court **Ch2** 7550 aiorned

ayr n. [see heyr]

ayse v. [see ese]

aywhare, aywhore adv. [see ay]

aknowe, oknowe ppl. [see knowe] [OE oncnawan] admit, confess, acknowledge **Ch1** 8549 oknowe P aknowe L; **Ch2** 1718 knowen; **HS** 8383 aknowe

akton n. [OF aqueton] jacket worn over the armor **Ch1** 9882 acton P aketon L; 11182 aktons P

albe n. [OF aube, albe, ML alba] ecclesiastical garment **Ch2** 7807 albe

alblaster n. [AF alblastre, OF arbaleste, arbalestier] crossbow; missile shot from a crossbow; archers **Ch1** 1034, 6133, 14022 alblastes P arblastes L; 13022 alblastes; 3407 alblastis; 2922 alblast schotes P arblast schutes L; 3479, 3508, 11732 alblasters P arblasters L; 12888 alblastrers P arbalasters L; **Ch2** 5030, 5036 alblastere

alderbest, alderlaste adj. [OE alre-, superl.] best of all, last of all **Ch1** 1773 alderbest; 4650 alderlaste; **Ch2** 471, 6551 alderbest

aldermost, aldernext adj. [OE alre-] most of all; the very next **Ch1** 5122 aldermost P alder meste L; 6649 aldermast P alderworst L; **Ch2** 319 aldermost; 5405 aldernext; **HS** 1680 alþernest

ale n. [OE ealu] beer, ale; drinking in company **Ch1** 7468, 7484 ale; **HS** 47, 4548, 5971 ale; 6546 [MS *O* interpolation ll. 25, 78] ale

alegid v. [OF alegier; AF aleger (MP)] claimed, charged; mitigate, relieve **Ch2** 5963 alegid; **HS** 1775 aleggyd; 11955 alegged; 11946 allegeþ

alehous n. [OE ealu-hus] tavern **HS** 4540, 5978, 6564, 6602 alehous

alepy adj. [OE anlepig; cp. hleapan; short form of onlepi] a single **HS** 9151 alepy

algate adv. [ON phrase; cp. OI alla gotu] nevertheless, always, yet; by all means, altogether **Ch1** 260 alle gate P algate L; 2786, 4708, 5554, 6539, 8908 algate; 3610, 3658, 4782, 4796, 7757 alle gate; 2786 algate P alwey L; **Ch2** 673 algate P natheles L; 1254, 5191, 7236 alle gate; 4612 alle gate P algate L; **HS** 837, 1529, 7067, 8424, 12415 algate; 1529 algate *D* also; 7266 algate *O* some dele; 9086 euer *O* algates

aliance n. [OF] alliance or treaty; bond of marriage **Ch1** 10750 aliance; **Ch2** 3850, 6970 aliance

alie v. [OF alier] form an alliance, engage in combat; attack; marry; join, associate **Ch1** 5335, 13294 alied P relied L; 6293, 6581 alied; 12559 alied PR allied L; 13096, 13757 alied; **Ch2** 492, 4817, 5317, 5978 alie; 1637, 3250 alied

alien n. [OF] foreigner, stranger **Ch1** 3184 aliens P straungers L; 6766, 6793, 13834, 15093 aliens; 6693L alien (om. P); **Ch2** 2337, 3446, 5239, 5246 aliens

alyght v. [see light, v.]

alyue adj. [see olife, oliue]

alle, aller, alþer n./adj./adv. [OE æl, eal] all, every; everyone, everything **Ch1** 894, 951, 14804 allere P alder L; 5410, 6018, 6064 alle; 7522 alle lost P alder lest L; **Ch2** 4, 809, 2055, 4844, 8301 alle; 6969, 4013 aller P alle þore L; **HS** 662, 1263, 1990, 6159, 12081 al; 6733 all; 18, 3887 alle; 1803 alþer

Almanȝ, Almaygne n. [AF Almaun; OF Almaigne] Germans, Germany **Ch1** 252 Almaygne; 2003, 8821 Almayn; 2201 Almayne; **Ch2** 6213, 6217, 6462 Almanȝ

almes n. [OE ælmesse] charitable gift **Ch1** 15360 almos P almes L; **HS** 3444, 5694, 6625, 6958, 11017 almes

almes dede n. [OE ælmes-dæd] deeds of mercy; works of charity; gift **HS** 1481 almasdede; 5162 almes dedes; 6624, 7116, 7181 almes dede

◆ **almoyn** n. [AF almoigne] possession, tenure **Ch2** 5756 almoyn

aloyne v. [OF aloignier] remove **HS** 9365 aloyne *O* allone

alone, al onely adj./adv. [phr: al one] solitary; without companions **Ch1** 780 alle one P alone L; 1736 alane; 1127, 1130 alon; 6915 alone; **Ch2** 3377 alle on; 4817, 4861, 5613 alone; 5474, 6076 alon; **HS** 108, 697, 870, 4005, 11013 alone; 7392 allone; 6827 allonely; 10131 al only; 11748, 12332 al onely

alose v. [see los] [OF aloser] to praise, honor **Ch1** 10774 alose; 7418, 11100 alosed; 9021 named P alosed L

aloute v. [see loute] [OE alutan] to submit or surrender **Ch1** 3528 loute P aloute L

alowe v. [AF alouer; cf. L adlandare] recognise; grant **Ch1** 11498 alowed; **Ch2** 1914 alowed P sowed L; 6809 alowe

als adv. [OE ealswa] also, as **Ch1** 183, 1923, 3748, 5452, 9399 als; 2138 as P also L; 3724 als P also L; 4849 also P als L; 5937 als P as L; 9015 also; **Ch2** 692, 2413, 3775, 4448, 8287 als; 2648, 3282, 4093, 4887, 8110 also; 4117, 4852, 5543 als so; **HS** 369, 9579, 10155, 12177 also; 622 als; 2748 als GLOSS B also

alsaume adv. [ON allir saman] one and all **HS** 9090 alsaume *O* all samene

alstyt, als tite adv. [see astyte] [OE alswa, phr.] immediately, as soon as **Ch1** 8063 als tite; **Ch2** 5126, 5418, 6473 als tite; 5724, 6583, 8238 also tite; **HS** 6784, 6950 alstyt

altere n. [see autere]

◆ **altercand** ppl. [L alterc-ari] quarreling **Ch2** 7677 altercand

ambner n. [see aumener]

ame, ayme v. [OF aesmer] to guess, reckon, count; intend, aim **Ch1** 744, 4411, 4691 ame; 4628 amed; 13408L ame (om. P); **Ch2** 2404, 5591, 5790 ame; **HS** 7025 ayme *O* name; 9037 kan ame *O* can name

amend v. [see mende] [OF amender, L emendare] to reform; remedy a fault; make reparation **Ch1** 2428 amend P haue mended L; 3198 salle amend P schal amenden L; 3865, 6638 amendid P amended L; 692, 2428, 3902, 5091, 7324 amend; **Ch2** 1982, 3280, 4100, 6542, 8035 amend; 1609 amendid; **HS** 768, 3656, 5368, 8632, 12242 amende; 2337 amendede

amendes n. [OF] reparation, retribution **Ch2** 2832, 3055, 4409, 7077, 8034 amendes; 7832 amendis

amendment n. [OF amendement] correction, reparation; redress, restitution **Ch1** 9108 amendment; **Ch2** 3362, 7075 amendment; 7833 amendement; **HS** 2545, 3502, 5308, 10939, 11984 amendement

amerous adj. [OF] in love, enamoured **HS** 7989, 7990 amerous

amysse, amys adv. [see mys] [ON phrase; cf. OI a mis, OE mis-don] faulty, wrong, improper **Ch2** 4061, 6179 amysse; 5408, 8258 amys; **HS** 348, 11280 amys; 3351 amys *O* omyse; 6546 [MS *O* interpolation l. 66] amyse

amite n. [OF amit, L amictum] a linen scarf **Ch2** 7807 amite

among, amang adv./prep. [OE gemong] amid; within, between **Ch1** 53, 367, 2552, 5703, 13409 amang; 5905, 7298, 8567, 13408 among; 7094 amonge; 1190L amanges (om. P); 5698 omang; **Ch2** 226, 2120, 3635, 4778 among; **HS** 948, 1550, 2513, 3297 among

amount v. [OF amonter, AF amunter (MP)] amount to; have meaning; be equal to; match **Ch1** 7101 amountes; **Ch2** 1314, 2062 amounte; 3306 amountes; **HS** 7762, 9696, 11138, 11389 amounte; 4480 amountede; 6324 amounted; 11947 amounteþ

◆ **amountment** n. [prob. OF] sum total, amount **Ch2** 6003 amountment

anamorde, enamoured adj./ppl. [OF enamoure] amorous, in love **Ch1** 9244 anamorde P enamured L; **Ch2** 6116 enamoured; **HS** 8172 anamourd

ancessoure, ancestres n. [OF ancessour, auncessor] family, forebears **Ch1** 943, 1461, 7084 ancessoure; 3945 ancestres; 6634, 6668, 6681 ancessoures; 4278 ancessoures P auncessours L; 6797 ancestre; 7262, 7267 ancessours; **Ch2** 173, 718, 2798, 6275, 6982 ancestres; 2830, 4107, 4398 ancessoure; 4593 ancestre

ancestrie n. [OF ancesserie] forebears **Ch1** 11470 ancetrie P auncetrie L; **Ch2** 227, 2019 auncestrie; 2065, 2519, 5977, 6002 ancestrie

anele v. [OE elen] administer extreme unction **HS** 11276 anele

anelyng ger. [see anoylyng] [from OE elen] anointing; extreme unction **HS** 11241, 11258, 11282 anelyng

aneus n. [OF aneaus, pl. of anel] rings as fetters **Ch2** 4143, 6730, 6731 aneus

anewest adv. [OE on nea-wiste] near, nearby **Ch2** 538L [Havelok interpolation, l. 44] anewest

angel n. [AF aungle (MP)] celestial servant; angel or messenger **Ch1** 7962, 14286, 14296 angels; 14288 angelle; **Ch2** 866 angels; 3214 angelle; **HS** 1406 aungelys; 1796, 2497, 10058 aungel; 12156 aungeles

angreþ v. [ON; cp. OI angra] angered, resentful **HS** 3986 angreþ

angrily adv. [from verb] resentfully, fiercely **Ch1** 2027 wrothfully P angrily L; 3730 egrelike P angerly L

anguys n. [OF angoisse, anguisse] trouble, misery **Ch1** 4784 anguys P anguisse L; **Ch2** 4924 anguys; **HS** 11964 angwys

anguised v. [OF anguissier] grieved, troubled **Ch2** 3231 anguised

anired v. [OF eniré] angered **Ch1** 15219 enired

P anired L; **Ch2** 3715 anired

ankere n. [OE ancor, OF ancre] ship's anchor or mooring **Ch1** 1303, 3659 ankere; 11767 ankres; 11791 ankers

anoye v. [see noye, v.] [OF anoier] disturb, offend; injure, vex **Ch1** 2050 dispite P onoy L; 15399 anoies; **Ch2** 859 anoyed; **HS** 918 anoyd; 1855 noye *C* anoye

anoylyng ger. [OF enoilen, v.] sacrament of extreme unction **HS** 844 anoylyng *C* holy anoynt *D* anoyntyng

anoynt, enoynt v. [OF enoindre, enoint] to consecrate; use healing ointments **Ch2** 5055 enoynted; **HS** 7418 anoynt; 11632 anoynte

anoyntyng ger. [from OF enoindre] consecration, anointing **HS** 11991, 11992 anoyntyng; 11990 anoyntyng *O* ane oyntynge

anon, anone adv. [OE on an(e)] at once, instantly; shortly, soon **Ch1** 1261 anone; 5163 on one P anon L; 7399L, 7587L anon (om. P); **HS** 313, 1859, 6879, 9407, 11727 anone

ansuere n. [OE ondswere] reply; decision, solution **Ch1** 2320 ansuere P answere L; 4271, 4738 ansuere; **Ch2** 1612 ansuere P answere L; 3455, 3918, 6456, 7486, 8224 ansuere; 6865 answere; **HS** 1077, 1770, 3671, 5455, 10185 answere

ansuere v. [OE andswerian] reply; defend a charge **Ch1** 2315, 5108, 6838, 7882, 9351 ansuerd; 7214 ansuerd P onswered L; 4204 ansuere; 4179 ansuered; 5181 ansuerde; 8031 ansurd; **Ch2** 4580 ansuer; 2434, 3827, 4360, 7090, 8216 ansuerd; **HS** 197 answeryd; 512, 2406, 5524, 7402, 7624 answere; 12581 answered

anteme n. [L, OE antefen] musical composition based on a scriptural text **Ch1** 14455 anteme

apayed ppl. [see paye, payd, v.]

apayrment n. [see apeyre] [AF] deterioration **Ch1** 2389 apayrment P þe peirement L

aparaile, apparaile n. [OF apareil] rigging, war equipment **Ch1** 2368 aparaile P apparayl L; 653, 2417 apparaile; 7632 apparaile P porayl L; **Ch2** 1311, 3801 apparaile; 2956 aparaile

aparseyue v. [see perceiue]

apechid v. [prob. from AF *anpecher] accuse **Ch1** 4884 apechid

apeyre, peire v. [AF ampeirier, OF empeirier] harm, injure, diminish **Ch1** 2388 apeyr P apeire L; 8200 peire; **Ch2** 7057 apeires; 8601 paired; **HS** 3938 apeyre *O* payre; 1518 apeyryn

apere v. [from OF aparoir] to appear; be visible **Ch2** 6162 apers; **HS** 1858, 8200 apere

aperyng ger. [from OF aparoir] semblance **HS** 2341 aperyng *D* schewyng

apert, apertly adj./adv. [OF apert] open, in view; clearly, plainly **Ch1** 2002, 13994 apert; 2453 apertly P apertely L; **Ch2** 1841 apert; 624, 5287, 7025, 7726 aperte; **HS** 9192, 12459 apert; 2715, 10325, 11523, 12400 apertely; 203 apertely *C* redyly; 400 apertlye *C* of gret peryll; 1217 apertly *D* a gret party; 7906 gret *O* aperte; 10346 penyblely *H* peynybly *O* benyngly *SV* ful apertely

apes n. [OE apa] ape; a simian **Ch1** 11188L apes (om. P)

aportenance n. [see apurtenance]

apostle n. [OE, OF] apostle of Christ; a missionary; preacher, evangelist **Ch1** 5461 apostels P þapostles L; **Ch2** 5501 apostle; **HS** 3515, 8319 apostle; 7223, 11264 apostole; 11718 apostoles

apostoile n. [OF] the pope as successor to Peter; the papacy **Ch1** 7646 apostole P apostoylle L; **Ch2** 2807 apostoyle; 3201, 3216 apostoile

appeld v. [OF apeler, L appellare] appeal to a higher authority **Ch2** 2447 appeld

appetyte n. [OF apetit (MP)] desire for food **HS** 7236 appetyte

apples n. [OE æppel] fruit; sphere, orb, ball **Ch1** 287 apples; 288 appilles P apples L; **HS** 12381 appul

appryse n. [AF aprise (MP)] learning, instruction **HS** 3950 appryse GLOSS BH lernyng

apurtenance n. [AF apurtenaunce] right, privilege; possessions **Ch1** 7364 purtenaunce P strengþe L; 5678 aportenance P aportynaunce L; 10442 apurtenance P appurtynaunce L; **Ch2** 3849 purueiance P appurtenance L

aqueyntaunce n. [OF acointance] fellowship **HS** 5791 aqueyntaunce

aquitance n. [OF] compensation; redemption **Ch1** 1203 aquitance; **Ch2** 3854 acquitance; 3864 aquitance; **HS** 10820 aquytaunce

ar adv. [see ere, adv.]

aray n. [AF arrai] condition, preparation; clothing, dress **Ch1** 9338 aray; 11737 aray P array L; **Ch2** 2657, 4041, 7504 aray; **HS** 6116 aray; 1822 affray *C* araye; 4672 adray *F* a rai *O* disary

aray, array v. [OF areer, areyer] arrange, prepare; draw up an army; equip, dress; furnish, procure **Ch1** 4964 renge P arraied L; 4966 set P arrayed L; 7310 dyght P arrayed L; **Ch2** 538L [Havelok interpolation, l. 47] arraye; 2593L araied (P differs)

archeflamyn, archeflame n. [see flamin, flamme]

archer n. [OF archer, archier] user of bow and arrow; hunter **Ch1** 3478, 5435, 6133, 6690, 12887 archers; **Ch2** 2290 archere P archers L

ardawe felde n. [see ere, eryn; feld] [prob. from ON *ar-daga, a day's plowing] a plowed field **Ch1** 1890, 3663 ardawe felde P eryed feld L

arely adv. [see orly] [OE ærlice, arlice] early in the morning **Ch1** 8987 arely P erlik L; 12638 arly P erlik LR; 12953 arly P erlyk L

arerage n. [OF arrierage] arrears, short in accounts **Ch1** 13441 arrerage; **Ch2** 7806 arerage

arere v. [see arysen, v.] [OE aræran, OF areren] withdraw, retreat, force back **Ch1** 1648 go obak P arere hem L; **Ch2** 5802 arere

areson v. [AF aresunier] inquire; urge **Ch2** 7689 areson; **HS** 7764 aresoned *O* resawyde

arysen v. [see rise, v.] [OE arisan] rise, raise up **Ch1** 6476 risand P arysen L; **HS** 7950, 8421 aryse; 7875 aros; 3344 areyse; 1870 *D* a rere (B differs); 7651 areysen *O* rase

aryue v. [see ryue, v. (2)] [OF ariver] reach the end of a journey **Ch1** 42, 2959 aryued; 2981 ariued; 4654 ryue P aryue L; 6182, 6870 ryued P aryued L; **Ch2** 122, 540, 1638, 3262, 6442 aryued; 505, 964, 1102, 3551, 4234 aryue; 3624 aryues; 3699, 3974, 4973 ariued; 3868, 5177, 5574 ariue

ark n. [OE arc, L arca] chest, coffer **Ch1** 2908 ark; **Ch2** 3341 arke; **HS** 4988, 4990, 5011, 5024 ark; 5020 ark *O* warke

arme n. [OE earm] arm, limb; tributary of a river **Ch1** 1836, 3823, 7946, 9374, 15442 armes; 1993, 12413 arme; 5360 arme P þarmoure L; **Ch2** 1313, 1644, 5790 arme; **HS** 701, 1476 armys; 2325, 9117 arme; 3314 armes

arme v. [OF armer] take arms, prepare for war **Ch1** 1168, 9110, 9130 arme; 4329 armes; 5941, 8220 has armes; 472, 2707, 4963, 7702, 9332 armed; **Ch2** 4017, 4246 has armes; 3939, 7100 arme; 1035, 3942, 5315, 6700, 7173 armed; 6681 armes; **HS** 1757 armede

armes n. [OF] weapons; men of arms: warriors **Ch1** 1539, 2683, 5342, 6622, 8860 armes; 8211 armis; **Ch2** 138, 2887, 4845, 5441, 8170 armes; **HS** 4375, 10541, 10659 armes

armour n. [OF armure] weapons **Ch1** 4612, 7737 armour; 5060 armoure; 8741 armore P armure L; 11885 armour P armure L; 12100 armure P armes L; 12383 armure; **Ch2** 4227 armour; 4670 armure; 4821 armurie; 8168 armore; **HS** 3438 armour *O* harnes

arowe, arewes n. [OE arewan] missile shot from a bow **Ch1** 4990, 13543 arowes; 6718, 6726, 10292 arwes; 8200L (P differs) arewes; 11395 arowe; **Ch2** 3027 arowe; **HS** 1372 arwys; 8517, 8521 arewes

arrogaunce n. [OF, L] pride, haughtiness **HS** 3119, 3121 arrogaunce

arsoun n. [OF arson] saddle bow **Ch1** 13174 arsoun

arte n. [OF art] craft; skill; science, knowledge **Ch1** 2831, 15119 arte; 5627 artes; 15016L artȝ (P differs); **Ch2** 8229, 8231 arte; **HS** 8154 artt

asch n. [OE æsc] the ash tree **Ch1** 12118 asch

aschamed, oschamed ppl. [see schame] [OE asceamod] disgraced **Ch1** 1831 oschamed; 2343 aschamed P schamed L; **HS** 6571, 12017 ashamed

aschore adv. [phrase: on shore] on shore **Ch1** 717 aschore P ay whore L

ascrie v. [OF escrier] shout, attack **Ch1** 4607 ascried P asemblede L; 4989, 8398 discried P ascried L; 5881 ascrie P descrie L; **Ch2** 5322 ascrie

asise n. [OF assise] trial, judgment; ordinance; practice; manner, character; proper order; company, fellowship **Ch1** 232, 5659 assise; 4711 asise P assise L; 9316 asise; **Ch2** 1914 asise P assises L; 1575, 5601, 7332 assise; **HS** 342, 1490, 5343 asyse; 2911, 4831, 5045, 8803, 9811 assyse; 3213, 6570, 12179 acyse; 804 asyse *C* syse; 2852 asyse *C* gyse; 3833 acyse GLOSS B maner *A* gyse *F* asise *O* assyce

askape, escape v. [see skape] [AF aschaper] escape; free oneself **Ch1** 370, 1997, 5949, 6221, 9346 ascaped; 1050, 5331 ascape; 6029 ascapid P ascaped L; 740 escaped P ascapede L; 217, 1171, 8457 escaped; 9086, 13281 escape; 13303 eskaped; **Ch2** 463, 1772, 3986 askaped; 2190, 7179 ascaped; 3905 askeped P skaped L; 4924 escaped; 7416 escapid; 4204, 7144 ascape; **HS** 6716 askape; 8044 ascaped; 10675 eschape

aske v. [OE ascian, acsian] demand, request **Ch1** 1063, 2870, 4729, 7498, 8491 asked; 969, 1207, 3632, 5987, 9251 ask; 5173 askes; 8138 aske; 6978, 7506, 8207 askid; 15179 askid P frayned L; **Ch2** 604, 1348, 2981, 4524, 7330 ask; 4787, 4965, 6354 askes; 1027 asked P axed L; 496, 2290, 4419, 5368, 8214 asked; 7532 askis; 2112 askid; **HS** 162, 617, 2829, 6614, 11644 aske; 194 askyde; 3574 askyþ; 1936 askede *C* speryd *D* aspyed

askes, asshen n. [OE æsc] ashes **Ch2** 1907, 4372 askes; **HS** 3286 asshen *O* aske

askyng ger. [OE acsung] inquiry, request **Ch1** 2872 askynges; 4218, 7070 askyng; **Ch2** 274, 1029, 2912, 6891, 7874 askyng; **HS** 153, 2108, 2426, 4820, 12086 askyng

asper, asperly adj./adv. [OF aspre, adj.] harsh, cruel; cruelly **Ch1** 4604 asperly; 13042L asper (om. P)

aspie v. [see spie, v.] [AF aspier] stealthy observation, scouting **Ch1** 1532 spied P aspied L; 13758 aspied; **Ch2** 826, 3823, 4069, 4974, 5029 aspie; 51 tapised P aspied L; **HS** 508 parseyuyd *C* aspyẹd; 1936 askede *C* speryd *D* aspyed

assay n. [AF assay (MP)] trial, test; effort **Ch1** 3997 þe saies P þer assayes L; 4241, 4551, 8394, 9339 assay; 5066 assais P assayes L; 6845 assay P fray L; **Ch2** 3477, 8348 assaies; 4376 affray P asay L; **HS** 1428 asay

assay v. [AF asaier, essaier] test, try; determine **Ch1** 1000 fraist ȝitt P assay eft L; 2279 asked

P assaied L; 5804 assaid P assayed L; 6310 stande to P assaye L; 7444 asaied P aysed L; 10649 assay; **Ch2** 1099 assay; 5350, 5798 asay; 5355, 5359 asaied; 5351 asayed; **HS** 416 fraystys GLOSS BH asayþ; 487 fondyþ *C* asayth

assaile v. [OF assailier, assaler] attack **Ch1** 1006 asaile P assaile L; 477 assayle; 9253 assailes; 1419, 3207, 5893, 7607, 9341 assaile; 3730 assail; 3764 assailled; 4326 saile P assaille L; 3379, 7619, 8498 assailed; **Ch2** 56, 458, 1754, 5420, 8164 assaile; 4379, 5462, 7790 assailed; **HS** 4208 asayle; 4973, 5009 assayle *O* sayl

assaut n. [OF] armed attack, seige **Ch1** 1044, 1637, 5023 assaut; 1029, 1032, 3413, 4978, 9332 assaute; 8221 assaute P assaut L; **Ch2** 997, 2529, 4295, 4371, 4534 assaut; 2977, 6643, 7104 assaute

asse n. [OE assa] domesticated ass **Ch2** 4336 assis P asses L; **HS** 5606 asse

assemble n. [OF assemblee] gathering, meeting **Ch1** 1643L þassemble (P differs); 6938 a semble P asemble L; **Ch2** 1233 assemble P assemblie L; **HS** 9399 assemblee

assemble v. [OF assembler] congregate, meet; gather together **Ch1** 3151L, 5543L assembled (P differs); 5765 gadred P assembled L; 4607 ascried P asemblede L; **Ch2** 574 purueied P assembled L

assent n. [OF] consent, approval; mutual agreement **Ch1** 3297, 4103, 7727, 8809 assent; **Ch2** 1341, 3363, 5909, 7629 assent; **HS** 1048, 1324, 2404 asent; 1838, 10535 assent

assent v. [OF assentir] consent, agree to; condone **Ch1** 6956 consented P assented L; 4783L assent (om. P); **Ch2** 6543 assent; **HS** 8401 asente; 2166 *C* cente (B differs)

assigne v. [OF assignier, L assignare] allocate; convey, bequeath; entrust **Ch1** 4965L assigned (P differs); 11082 signed P assigned L; **Ch2** 7630 assigne; 1211, 2068, 4020, 8009 assigned; 4049 signe

assoyle, asoyle v. [OF assoiler] absolve, forgive **Ch1** 15829 asoyle P assoille L; 15886 asoiled P assoillede L; **Ch2** 3200, 3217 assoile; 2806, 6413 assoyle; 5181 asoiled; 9, 79 asoyled; 5129 assoled; 7913 assoyles; 3003, 6418, 7918 assoyled; 5196 assoiles; **HS** 11952 asoyle; 11612 assoyle; 8877, 10831, 10854, 12616 asoyled

assone, alsone adv. [see sone]

asswyþe adv. [see suyth, swyþe] [from OE as swiðe] as quickly as possible, immediately **Ch1** 3376 also suyth; 8905 als suythe; **HS** 4101 asswyþe *O* also swyþe; 4512 asswyþe *O* als sone; 5211 and asswyþe *O* also swythhe

astate n. [see state, estate] [AF astat] state, condition **HS** 3332 astate *O* avaintte

astyte adv. [see alstyt, als tite] [prob. from ON titt, tiðr] at once, immediately **Ch2** 1294, 7084, 8238 also tite; **HS** 1800, 11733, 12247 astyt; 4726, 6950 alstyt; 264 astyte *C* anoun; 3153 astyt *O* tytte; 6557 astyt *O* full tyte; 6784 astyt *O* all so tytte; 3193 astyt GLOSS B anone; 8453 astyte GLOSS B anoun

astronomie n. [L astronomia] science of astronomy; divination **Ch1** 276, 8918 astronomye; 7828, 10854, 15004 astronomie

asuage v. [see suage] [OF assuagier] mitigate, relieve; appease **Ch1** 888 asuage; **Ch2** 1922 assuage; 2776, 7309 asuage

asundere, osundere adv. [see sonder, v.]

atache v. [OF atachier, AL attachiare] fasten up; attach property **Ch1** 11770 atache P atached L; **Ch2** 3904 attached

ateynt, teynte ppl. [from OF ateindre, ataindre] accused, convicted; guilty **Ch1** 5107 teynte; **Ch2** 612, 5174 ateynt; 1182 ateyned; 2999, 3159, 5934, 7643, 8255 atteynt; 8004 atteyned; **HS** 3064 ateynte; 12496, 12635 ateynt

atent n. [see entent, tent]

◆ **atiffement** n. [see tyffe, v., tyffure, n.] [OF] trappings, decoration **Ch2** 3763 atiffement P atierrement L

atire n. [from OF atirier, v.] apparel, adornment, dress **Ch1** 4678 atire P atyr L; 7454 hatir P atyr L; 7491 hatire P atir L; 8231 atire; **HS** 4581 atyr; 3454, 7027 atyre; 1407 atyre *D* tyr

atire v. [see tired, v.] [OF atirier] dress, equip, prepare for battle **Ch1** 2090, 2493 atire P atyre L; 6453 attire P atyre L; **Ch2** 1736 atire; 3529, 5079 atires; 982, 3359, 3645, 5779 atired; 427 atired P ordeined L; 3716 tired; 6643 tirede; **HS** 3337 atyre; 8841 atyred

atrie v. [OF atrier] try, investigate **Ch2** 1980 atrie P trie L; 5910 attrie; 6024 atried

aturne v. [see turne, v.] [OF aturner] yield allegiance **HS** 5503 aturne

atwynne adv. [see otuyn, otwynne]

auaile v. (1) [prob. from AF valoir] help, benefit, be profitable; succeed, prosper **Ch1** 2087, 8391 auaile; 2250 auaile P vaylle L; 2828 auaile P auayle L; 3943 auaile P auaille L; 6477 auailed P nauaillede L; **Ch2** 2819, 4395, 5837, 7118, 8272 auaile; 2361 auailed; 6680 auale; **HS** 561, 839, 3172, 10321, 11402 auayle; 9479, 10683 vayled; 10677 auaylede; 10979 vayleþ; 2342 avaylede *C* it helpeth *D* it avaylede; 5180 auoyde *O* avayle; 10882 auayleþ *O* vayles

auaile v. (2) [OF avaler] lower; sink, descend **Ch1** 12074 availed P valede L; **Ch2** 2361 auailed

auance, auaunce v. [OF auancer (MP)] promote, advance **Ch1** 2040, 6968, 7142, 10441 auance P auaunce L; 4974 auentour his chance P auaunce L; 2406 auanced P auaunsed L; 5130 auanced P auaunted L; 7802 auanced P auaunced L; **Ch2** 348, 3853, 4452, 6405 auance; 5239, 5246 auaunce; 1527, 5212, 5236, 5730 auanced; **HS** 3120, 10963, 10990, 11002 auaunce; 3087 auaunced; 880 auaunsyd *C* awansyd man; 3936 auaunssed *O* avaunced; 5518 vaunsed

auancement n. [see auantement] [OF auauncement] promotion, preferment **Ch2** 2509, 3350, 4861, 7387 auancement; **HS** 5521, 11010 auauncement; 7398 auaunsemente; 5516 vaunsemente

auantage n. [OF] superiority, profit **Ch1** 7332 auauntige P auauntage L; **Ch2** 7666 auantage; **HS** 2396 auauntage

auante, auaunte v. [OF avanter] to boast, brag **HS** 3115 auaunte *O* rose; 3118 auaunte þe of *O* rose þe; 8309 auaunte *O* avante; 8312 auaunte

auantement n. [prob. from AF auanter (MP)] boasting **Ch1** 11425 auauntement; **Ch2** 4861 auantement (?auancement) P avantement L; **HS** 4580, 8302, 8318, 11669 auauntement

auantour n. [OF] braggart **Ch1** 10486 auauntour; 12315 auantours P auauntours L

auaryce n. [OF] greed, miserliness **HS** 5330, 5342, 10135 auaryce; 5970 auarys

auarous adj. [OF avarus] greedy, miserly **HS** 5578, 6063 auarous

auaunce n. [from OF auancer, v.] boasting, ostentation **Ch1** 4974L auaunce (P differs); **HS** 4581 auaunce

auauntrie n. [from OF avanter, v.] boasting **Ch2** 4820 auauntrie

auctorite n. [OF] legal power; authenticity **Ch1** 13978 auctorite; **HS** 168, 1240, 3550, 8319, 12170 autoryte

auenant n./adj./adv. [from OF auenir, v.] becoming, honorable; agreeable, attractive, handsome, appropriate **Ch1** 4683, 7938, 11981 auenaunt; 5486 auenant P auenauant L; 6459 auenant P auenauntest L; 6890, 6892, 7489, 9151 auenant; 7426 auenaunt P fair & semly L; 11391 auantlike P auenauntly L; **Ch2** 1217, 6098 auenant; **HS** 12121 auenaunt; 3233 auenaunt GLOSS BH hauyng *O* þare avante; 3436 auenaunt *O* avaunte

auenture n./adj./adv. [see misauentour, perauenture] [OF aventure] chance, fortune, danger; in jeopardy **Ch1** 1557, 2931, 5592 auenture; **Ch2** 7608 in auenture; **HS** 6661, 7305 auenture; 8940 auentours

auenture v. [see auntre]

auere n. [AF aver, aveir] possessions, wealth **Ch2** 3037 auere

◆ **auerty** adj. [from OF avertir] wise, prudent **Ch2** 6282 auerty

aught, auh, auht v. [OE æht, agan, ahte] own, possess; owe, ought **Ch1** 1914 auht P laught (error) L; 1975, 3577, 4085, 6586, 8419 auht; 5145 awe P aughte L; 7016 auh P owen L; 10780 auht P aughte L; 14251, 14655, 14664 auh P oughte L; **Ch2** 4793, 4943 auh; 3092, 3858, 4857, 5969, 7553 auht; **HS** 806 oghte *C* owest *D* owe; 1013 oghte *C* awte *D* owyn; 1641 oghtyst *C* owe *D* owist; 2591 oghte *C* owen *D* owyn; 3652 oghte *O* aught

auht, auhte numeral [OE eahta, æhta] the number eight **Ch1** 3685, 5663, 12846 auht P eyghte L; 6082, 13977, 15274 auht; **Ch2** 386, 1124, 2994, 4488, 8347 auht; 2083 auhte; **HS** eyghteþe *O* aghte

auhten, auhtend numeral [ON *ahtandi] eight, eighth, eighteenth **Ch1** 12885 auhtend P eyghteþe L; **Ch2** 799, 5204 auhten; 1146, 7013 auhtene; 2029, 2056 auhtend

auis n. [OF avis] sight, view, scrutiny; information, knowledge, counsel, opinion, decision **Ch1** 1152, 1197, 2711, 7837 auys; 523, 4032 auyse; 610 deuys P auys L; 5034 vys P auys L; 7542 vis P auis L; 5211, 5456, 12276 auys P auis L; **Ch2** 706, 2419, 2604, 6922 auys; 2117, 4373, 5537, 6122, 7671 avis; 4671, 7675 auise; **HS** 2341, 3980, 8472, 11651 auys

auise v. [OF aviser] examine, decide; advise, counsel, confer; take aim at **Ch1** 523 auyse P auys L; 855, 15821 auysed; 11915, 12509 auised; 1886 auysed P auised L; **Ch2** 7278 avised; **HS** 9704 auysed

auise adj. [from OF aviser, v.] wise, prudent, discreet **Ch1** 4032 auyse; 12274 avise P auise L

auisement n. [OF] caution, attention; inspection, observation; advice **Ch1** 1671 auysement P auisement L; 13277 auisement; **Ch2** 5800, 5816, 6417, 7514 auisement; 5798 auysement; 3637 auisement P assent L

aumener, ambner n. [OF] alms distributor; servant at a meal who distributes food **Ch1** 15357 ambner P aumener L; **HS** 5575 aumenere; 6837 aumener

auntre, auenture v. [OF aventurer] happen; take a chance, attempt **Ch1** 1072L auntres (om. P); 2039 auntred; 3242 awnterd P (L differs); 4974 auentour P auaunce L; 8527L auntre (P differs); 8529 auenture P auntre L; **Ch2** 1728 to auenture

auowe, avow n. [see vow, n.] [from OF avouer, v.] oath, promise **Ch2** 2720 avowe P oþ L; **HS** 2888 vow *D* avow

auowe v. [OF avouer] take oath; promise, maintain, approve **Ch2** 7829 avowe; **HS** 1677, 7648 auowe; 2891 auowede; 7655 auoweþ

auourie, auowery n. [OF] protection, patronage, permission **Ch1** 3299 auowri P auowery L; 3630 auowery; 5822 auourie P avowerye L;

Ch2 4464, 6279, 6878 auowrie
auoutours n. [OF avoutre] an adulterer **HS** 4936 auoutours *O* vanatours
auowtrye n. [OF avout(e)rie] adultery **HS** 7359 awoutrye; 8983 auowtrye
auster, austere adj./adv. [OF austere] stern, harsh, severe, grim **Ch1** 5380, 13226 austere P auster L; 6404 austerly P hastely L; **Ch2** 602, 1308, 3053, 5874, 7801 austere; 6356 auster
auter, altere n. [OE alter, OF auter] altar **Ch1** 1368 autere P auter L; 1370, 7256, 13767 autere; 11861 altere P auter L; **Ch2** 1970 altere; 376, 798, 8079 autere; **HS** 6488, 9958 auter; 2286, 9966, 10755, 11100 autere; 1564, 1576 autyr
autoryte n. [see auctorite]
away adv. [OE on weg, aweg] out, away; to a distance **Ch1** 102, 861, 2436, 6881, 8905 away; 4717 away P aweye L; **Ch2** 44, 282, 672 away; 3011 aweie; **HS** 721, 2153 away; 346 doun awey; 1176, 12625 awey; 11221 aweye
awe v. (1) [from ON *agan] inspire with fear, to awe **Ch2** 1549 awed; **HS** 1593 awys GLOSS BH feryþ *C* owes; 10290 aweþ
awe, awen v. (2) [see owne]
awe v. (3) [see aye, owe]

B

bachelere n. [OF] a youth; novice knight, squire **Ch1** 898, 2674 bachelere; 4698, 7207 bachelers; 7582, 10542 bachilere
bacyn, basyn n. [OF bacin] basin, helmet **Ch1** 10695, 11188 bacyn P basyn L; 15141 bacyne P bacyn L; **HS** 351 bacyn
bagbely, bagge, bely n. [see sloppe] [ON; cp. OF bague] bulging bag **Ch1** 15138 bagge; **HS** 501, 511 bagge; 502 bely; 503 bagbely *C* bagge
bagelle n. [OIr bachal, from L baculum, staff] a pastoral staff **Ch2** 6826 bagelle
bayte n. [ON beita] lure, temptation **HS** 5339 bayte
bayte, beyte v. [see abate, v. (1) and (2), and abeyte, v.]
baytynges ger. [from OE bætan, v.] bothering; reproofs **HS** 10902 baytynges *O* bettynge
bak n. [OE bæc] back of the body; from the rear, at the back **Ch1** 1174, 1674, 7117 bak; 8372L bak; 1807 bakkes; **Ch2** 8188 bak; 7422 bakkis; **HS** 705, 2384, 2390, 7815, 9287 bak
bak, bakward adv. [OE on bæc] away, toward the rear **Ch1** 4619, 4995, 6731, 12991, 13306 bakward; 4616 go bak P abak L; 8372 bak; **Ch2** 8174 bak; 4719, 4729 bakward; **HS** 5029 bakward
bakbiter n. [OE bæc, from bak-biten, v.] defamer, slanderer **Ch1** 2798 bakbiteres; **HS** 1523, 1526 bakbyter; 4218 bakbytere; 1515 bakbyterys; 3530 bakbyteres; 10244 bakbyters
bakbytyng ger. [from OE bæc] slander **HS** 3557, 11645 bakbytyng; 1030, 1528 bakbytyngge
bakward adv. [see bak]
balance n. [OF] in balance; in jeopardy **Ch2** 3852 balance; **HS** 5665, 9432 balaunce
bale n. [OE balu, bealo] destruction, disaster; misery, misfortune, trouble **Ch1** 438L bale (om. P); 453, 1239, 4125, 11516, 15032 bale; **Ch2** 1324, 1839, 3653, 6515 bale; **HS** 1740, 2354, 6002, 10166, 10942 bale; 8745 bale GLOSS H sorow
balie, baillie, baly n. [OF bail, bailie] captivity; wall of a city; office, control, management; protection, custody, dominion, power; a prison **Ch1** 2807, 11217 balie P baillye L; 4105 baile P baylle L; 4407, 5186 bailie P baillye L; 10951 baily P bailly L; **Ch2** 1482, 3114 balie; 5444 bailie; 6790 baly; **HS** 1443, 3072, 3076, bayly; 3939 baylye
balife, baillif n. [OF] a court official **Ch1** 4543, 6157 bailifs P baillifs L; 8594 bailifes; 10718 bailifs; **Ch2** 3394 baylifes; 6796 balifes; 7642 balife; **HS** 5499 bayle *O* baylȝes; 6795 baylyues *O* balȝes
balle n. [prob. OE *beal] orb, sphere **Ch1** 571, 590, 597, 601 balle
band [see bynde, v. and bond, n.]
bandon, baundon n. [OF] power, command; being under control of someone **Ch1** 2379 baundon P baundoun L; 5261L (add, l. 48) baundon; **Ch2** 3458, 6838 bandons; 4013, 5291 bandoun
bane n. [OE bana, bona] death, destruction **Ch1** 8216 bane; **Ch2** 884 bane P bathe L
baner, banere n. [OF] ensign; combat company **Ch1** 2998 baneres; 8331 banere P baner L; **Ch2** 40, 575, 2852, 5834, 8099 banere; 3990, 4457, 6633, 7857 baner; 4464 baneres; 6551, 8062 baners; **HS** 3406, 7651 baner
banerettis n. [OF baneret] high ranking knight **Ch2** 7344 banerettis
bank n. [see benk, bro] [ON; cp. OE benc] hill, river bank; earthwork **Ch1** 1838, 3540, 4941, 6001 bank; 3384 bankis; 4599 bankes; 9655 bank & begh P (L differs); 11764 bi bro bi bankis P by banke & brymme L; **Ch2** 1733, 5794 bank; 4536 bankis; 4651 kank (error) P bank L; 4699 bank P bonk L; 7578 bank & bro
banne v. [OE bannan; ON banna] curse **HS** 3513 banne; 9180 banned; 366, 368 curse *CD* banne; 1247 malysun *C* bannyng *D* maleys; 3760 curse *O* ban
bapteme n. [OF bapte(s)me] baptism; Christianity **Ch1** 14619 bapteme; **Ch2** 4791 bapteme; **HS** 200, 9501, 9660 bapteme; 12269 baptem
baptise v. [OF and L] baptize; to be baptized **Ch1** 5639 baptiste; 5646 baptise; 5656 bap-

tiȝed; **HS** 9517, 9691, 9703 baptysed; 9694 baptyse

barbaryn n. [OF] foreigner, heathen **Ch1** 15328, 15329, 15876, 15877 barbaryn

bare v. [see bere, bare, born] [OE barian] to uncover, expose; lay waste **Ch1** 4623 bare P bar L; **HS** 9462 bareþ

bare adj. [OE bær] uncovered, exposed **Ch1** 2692, 6521 bare; **Ch2** 1525, 1878, 3987, 7900 bare; 2989 bare P bar L; **HS** 2327, 3342, 5419, 6792, 11219 bare

barehede, bareheued adj./adv. [phr.: bar-hed, bar-heved] bareheaded **Ch1** 3224 barehede; 10081 bareheued

barelle n. [OF baril] barrel; an urn **Ch1** 3588, 3590, 3593 barelle

bares n. [prob. OF barre, n.] barricade **Ch1** 11523 bares P bars L

baret, barette n. [OF barat] struggle, battle; strife, turmoil **Ch1** 2894 baret P barette L; 2978, 6089 barette P baret L; 8415 baret; 11506, 12984 barette; **Ch2** 3245 baret; 2424, 5295 barette; 6641 barete

barfote adj. [OE bærfot] barefoot, shoeless **Ch1** 8533, 10081, 14719 barefote; **HS** 3825, 3833 barfote

barfreis n. [see berfreis]

bargayn n. [OF bargai(g)ne] trading, negotiation; agreement **Ch1** 8406 bargayn; 13884 bargayn P bargayne L; **Ch2** 6531 bergayn; **HS** 196 ȝyfte *C* barganye

barge n. [OF] sailing vessel; war ship; river craft, boat or raft **Ch1** 4283 bargis; 5833L barges (P differs); 11776L barges (om. P); **Ch2** 4193, 5804 barge; 3975, 4303, 5793, 7844 barges

barlykke n. [OE bærlic] grain; meal of barley **HS** 10118 barlykke

barme n. [OE bearm] lap **HS** 9632 lap *O* barme

barn n. [OE bearn] child **Ch2** 7564 barn; **HS** 2818 chyld *D* barn

baron n. [OF baroun] nobleman ranking below an earl and above a knight; feudal tenant **Ch1** 3987, 4732, 6231, 7345 baron; 4051 baroun; 3027, 4670, 4843, 6324, 7663 barons; 3803, 3866, 6522, 8175 barouns; 7777 barouns P knyghtes L; **Ch2** 1947, 3245, 5013, 5763 baron; 3491, 3963, 8136 baroun; 552 baroune; 2094 barounes; 1628, 2089, 3979, 5961, 8093 barons; **HS** 3091, 9374 barons; 6793 barouns

baronage n. [OF barnage] the nobility; peers; body of nobles, retainers **Ch1** 6099 baronage; **Ch2** 589, 1271, 3786, 5777, 8343 baronage

baronie, barony n. [OF] body of barons; baron's domain **Ch1** 15799 baronyes; **Ch2** 2058, 3009, 7955 baronie; 3402 barony; 4124 baronies

barred adj. [OF barrer] closed barrel head **Ch1** 3594 barred

bastard, bastardye n./adj. [OF] degenerate, false; illegitimacy of birth **Ch1** 905 bastardye; 2813 bastard; 3706 bascardie P bastardie L; **Ch2** 1224, 6344 bastard; 1243L, 1264L, 1429L, 1595L bastard (P differs)

baston n. [OF bastoun] a type of verse, stanza **Ch1** 89 baston

batale, bataile n. [OF] warfare; an attack; body of warriors **Ch1** 4318, 5883, 6174, 8371 batale; 713, 1005, 1623, 5041, 9336 bataile; 7304, 7322, 8127 bataille; 3518 batile; 1635, 5320 batailes; 9340 batayle; 13611 batails; 12846 batailes P batailles L; **Ch2** 308 batale; 1140 batales; 201, 1647, 2480, 5520, 7788 bataile; 5333, 7003, 8084 batail; 75, 346, 1511, 6694 batailes; **HS** 2845, 10535, 10598 bateyle; 4974, 7539 batayle; 4988 were GLOSS B bateyle

batale, bataile v. [OF bataillier] fight; line up an army for assault **Ch1** 3614, 5333 bataile; 4364 batailed P beot hem doun L; 5434 batailed P batailled L; **Ch2** 4205 batale P enbataille L; 5411, 6083 batailed

◆ **batand** ppl. [from OF batre, ppl. batant] come speedily, without delay **Ch1** 1702 abatid P hasted L; **Ch2** 3571, 3670 batand; 7478 baitand

bate v. [see abate]

batelle n. [OF batel] small boat **Ch2** 5804 batelle

bath n. [OE bæþ] bathing pool; bath water **Ch1** 2244 bath; 2237, 2243 bathe; 8699 bathes; **Ch2** 882 bane P bathe (?error) L; **HS** 1265, 10330 baþ; 11040 bath

bathed v. [OE baþian] to bathe or wash **Ch1** 8701 bathed

bathyng ger. [from OE baþian] a bath **Ch1** 2243, 13825 bathyng

bawmed v. [OF embausmer] to embalm **Ch2** 8345 bawmed

beam, beem, beme n. [OE beam] ray of light; the cross; trumpets; relief from misfortune **Ch1** 8920 beam P bem L; 10191 bemes; 11142 sounes of bemes P blewe trompe L; **Ch2** 2199 bote of beam P bote to ben L; 2495 bote of beem P bote but on L; 3466 bote o beame; **HS** 2235 beme *CD* bem

become v. [see bicom]

bed n. [OE bedd] a bed **Ch1** 643, 2645, 7945 bed; 617, 640, 7975 bedde; **Ch2** 4610, 7231 bed; 7793 bedde; **HS** 696, 2230, 3264 bed; 1696 bede; 7037, 8392, 12553 bedde

bede n. [OE gebed] prayer, request; rosary beads **Ch1** 13432 bedis; **Ch2** 4959, 8198 bede; **HS** 4033 bed; 3465, 9006, 12182 bedes; 4299 bedys

bede, bed v. [see bidde, misbede] [OE beodan, bead] offer, give, promise; invite; challenge to battle **Ch1** 305 bad P bed L; 3978, 9153 bed;

2883, 6491, 11523, 13505 bede; 4737 bedis; 9390 beede; 5459 bed P profred L; 6986 beed P bed L; 11402 bad; **Ch2** 360, 3575, 4047, 5344, 8326 bede; 1958, 6467, 7523, 8198 bed; 3535 bedes; 4581 bedis; 3769 bede P bad L; 827, 1340, 4813, 7259, 8250 bad; 1127 bade P abed L; **HS** 2746 bede; 12182 bad; 7489, 10067 bedde

bedel n. [see bailif] [OE bydel; OF bedel] minor official **Ch1** 6157 bedels P bedeles L

bedene adv. [see bidene]

bedrede n./adj. [OE bed-reda] confined to bed **Ch1** 8847 bedered; 9418 bedrede

beem n. [see beam]

befalle v. [see bifalle]

befor, biforn adv. [see fore, forn] [OE beforan] formerly, previously **Ch1** 1061 aforn P byforn L; 6634 befor P byfore L; 7452, 8173, 9037 before; 7948 bifore; **Ch2** 1770, 2870, 3799, 5864, 8144 beforn; 2308, 3820, 5993, 7007, 8338 biforn; 3278, 6723, 7011, 8277 bifore; 3820 biforn P byfore L; **HS** 304, 859, 2718, 4227, 5534 before; 9425, 9632, 10114, 11942, 12632 byfore; 5379 beforn; 10129, 10490 byforn

beggere n. [OF begart; MDu beggaert] mendicant **Ch1** 15126 beggere

begh n. [OE bog, boh] bough; fig.: everywhere out of doors **Ch1** 9655 bank & begh P (L differs)

begyle v. [see gile] [OF guiler] dupe, outwit; cheat **Ch1** 2880 begile P bygile L; **Ch2** 970, 3059, 8049 begiled; 2051, 8048 begile; **HS** 2653 begyle; 8732 begyled; 8374 bygyles; 1626 begyle *C* gyle; 2384 begyle *C* false *D* falsyn; 3152 begyle *O* gyle; 4602 begyle *O* gylys

behete v. [see bihest, beheste]

behetyng ger. [from OE behatan] a promise **HS** 11227 behetyng

beholde, biheld v. [see hold, hald] [OE behealdan, beheold] look at; watch; to esteem, regard **Ch1** 1798 beholde P byhelde L; 1561, 1889 behelde; 3054, 6856, 8917 beheld; 1885, 3162, 5022, 8755 biheld; **Ch2** 4659 beheld; 1339, 1512, 2270, 2862 biheld; **HS** 8135 behold; 3122, 11462 beholde; 2186, 9397 holde; 3270 beheld; 7030, 8515 byheld; 12183 byhelde

behoue n. [OE to . . . behofe] for someone's benefit; in the interest of **Ch1** 2416 behoue P byhoue L; 2681 bihoue; 6414 behoue; **Ch2** 4850 behoue; **HS** 1166 behoue

behoue v. [OE behofian, bos, bod] to be necessary, required, unavoidable **Ch1** 1810 behoued P byhoued L; 1071, 3504, 4349, 5002 behoued; 8276 behoues; 14896 behoued P most L; 4782 bos P byhoues L; 8961 bos P byhoueþ L; 4404 bod P byhoued L; **Ch2** 33 bihoues; 4253 behoues P behoweþ L; 7070, 7830 behoues; 1603, 4610, 5656, 6955, 7730 behoued; 250, 5899, 7289 bihoued; **HS** 4833, 9554, 10844 behoueþ; 129, 3237 behouyþ; 6466 behouede; 11602, 11605 behoued; 1645 behouyþ *C* muste; 9622 byhoueþ *O* aghte; 9941 byhoueþ *SV* most; 10086 behoueþ *S* mot *V* moot; 11367 most *O* behoues

behouely adj. [OE behoflic] necessary, beneficial **Ch1** 8648 behouely P byhouely L

◆ **behowe, byhowe** v. [OE hawian, ?behogian] to inspect, take an interest in **Ch1** 10947 behowe P byhowe L

beyte, bayte v. [see abeyte]

bekyr n. [see biker]

beknede v. [OE beknian] point to **HS** 6207 beknede

belayd v. [see vmbeleid]

belde v. [OE beldan] grow strong, flourish **Ch1** 5943 belde; 8437 belde P egrely L; **Ch2** 1832L beld (P differs); 3303 belde; **HS** 9729 belde

beleue, byleue n. [see leue, n. (1)] [cp. OE gelefa] faith, doctrine **HS** 8149 byleue; 378 beleue *C* trost; 494 beleue *C* thowth; 560 beleue *C* I trost; 562 beleue *C* trowed *D* beleue; 564 fayþ GLOSS B beleue; 578 beleue *C* feyth *D* trouþe; 860, 868 beleue *D* trouþe; 4248, 4649, 8278 beleue *O* trowth; 9896 beleue *O* treuthe; 9906 beleue *OSV* trouþe; 9910 beleue *O* trowþe *SV* trouþe; 9949 beleue *O* trowthe *SV* treuþe; 9954 beleue *O* trowe *SV* trouþe; 10000 beleue *O* trowthe *SV* þouht; 10522 beleue *SV* trouþe; 8262 beleue *O* faythe

beleue v. [see leue, v. (2)] [OE gelefan] have faith in doctrine **Ch1** 9355 leue P byleue L; 5403 leued P bileued L; **HS** 355, 372 beleue; 552, 556 beleue *D* trowe; 562 beleuyst *C* trowest *D* trust; 659 trowst *C* leue; 859 beleuede *C* leuyd *D* trowedyn; 869 beleuyn *D* leuen; 1605 beleue *D* leue; 2647 beleuyþ *C* trowe *D* telle *O* trowys; 4976 beleuede *O* lefyd; 7743 beleuede *O* lewyd; 9519 beleue *O* trowes; 9867 beleue *O* leffe; 9947 beleue *O* trowe *SV* leeue; 9965 beleueþ *O* trowes *SV* troweþ; 9984 beleue *OSV* trowe; 10028 beleue *O* trowe *SV* leue; 10385 beleued *O* hopped *SV* hoped; 10576 beleuede *SV* leeuede; 10627 beleue *F* ne leue *O* leve *SV* con; 10633 supposeþ *O* hopes *SV* leeueþ; 12335 byleue *O* trowe

beleuyng ger. [from OE gelefan, v.] faith **HS** 547 beleuyng *C* trowth *D* trowyng *F* þe leuing

bely n. [see bagbely]

belyue adv. [see bilyue]

belle n. [OE, L] gong; church bell; musical instrument **Ch1** 10192 bellis; 11145 belles; 14236 belle; **Ch2** 6826 belle; **HS** 4259 belle; 4278 bell; 4775 belles

beme n. [see beam]
bemene v. [see bymene]
benam v. [see bynime]
◆ **bendeles** n. [OF bendel] narrow ornamental bands **Ch1** 9895 bendeles
bendes v. [OE bendan] to overcome; to submit to **Ch2** 6429 bendes
beneth adv. [see bineth]
benison n. [OF] grace before eating; formal blessing **Ch1** 6858 benyson P benisoun L; 6993, 14656 benyson; 7509 benison P benisoun L; **Ch2** 2810 benyson; 3500, 3624 benisoun; **HS** 4710, 4735 benesoun
benk, benche n. [ON] court of law; seat, throne **Ch2** 5937, 5948, 6795 benk; 1418, 2120 benke; 1416 benke P benche L; **HS** 3576, 5439 benche
berd n. (1) [OE beard] beard; fig.: face to face with, oppose **Ch1** 12040, 12155 berde; **Ch2** 5082 berd
berd, birde, bryd n. (2) [from OE byrd, brid] bird; lady **Ch2** 910 berde; 3790 birde P bryd L; 7065 berd; **HS** 4006, 7481, 7490, 7492 bryd
berdede adj. [from OE beard, n.; cp. OF barder] bearded; fig.: a lascivious man **HS** 3211 berdede bukkes
bere n. (1) [OE bera, *beora] a bear, beast **Ch1** 11806, 11818 bere; **HS** 4038, 4056, 4079 bere
bere n. (2) [OE gebære, gebæru] clamor, commotion **HS** 9067 bere
bere n. (3) [OE ber; AF bere (MP)] a bier, coffin; litter **Ch1** 9470, 9495, 9520 bere; **Ch2** 2620, 2624, 2903, 8339 bere; **HS** 6239, 8038, 8040, 11034 bere
bere v. [OE beran] carry away; bring back; bear arms or a crown; to give birth **Ch1** 546, 1891, 4286, 7747, 12163 bere; 13429 bere P carie L; 1371, 2663, 4377, 7909, 9594 bare; 1482, 6549 bare P bar L; 4624 bore; 899, 2430, 4935, 7978, 12991 born; 4842 born P boren L; 207 beren; 7854 beres; 795, 10274 borne; **Ch2** 302, 1571, 2827, 4292, 7864 bere; 4946, 6815 beres; 176, 1198, 4073, 7707, 8194 bare; 89, 1220, 4516, 5658, 8134 born; 1246 born P ybore L; 2309 born P yboren L; 4590 born P boren L; **HS** 610, 3073, 7760, 10186, 11786 bere; 701, 1448, 2977, 6733, 10659 bare; 573, 3189 bore; 2752 bers; 2681 beren; 3499 beryn; 638, 1516 berys; 3056 berst; 4179 beryþ; 4278 berþ; 7640 bereþ
berfreis n. [OF berfrei] movable towers used in a seige **Ch1** 1029 berfreis P berfreys L; 5966 barfreis P engyns L
bergayn n. [see bargayn]
berye v. [see birie]
beryng ger. [from OE beran, v.] bearing, demeanour **HS** 10649 beryng
besaunt n. [OF, L] gold coin of Byzantium; silver coin used in western Europe **HS** 6854, 6954 besaunt; 7008 besauntes
besege v. [from OF siege, sege, n.] beset, afflict; beseige a city, castle **Ch1** 1026 besege; 3296 seged P byseget L; 4931 bisege; 3399, 5051, 5939, 7832, 9227 biseged; 6558 biseged P byseded L; 5758 beseged; 8199 beseged P byseced L; 13602 bised (error) P byseged L; **Ch2** 2643, 2954, 3263, 3438, 6662 biseged; 2897 bigeged (error) P byseged L; **HS** 3810 besegede
besette v. [see biset]
beside adv. [see biside]
besouht v. [see biseke, seke]
besquite n. [OF bescuit, biscuit] flat cakes of unleavened bread **Ch2** 4227 besquite P bred bysquyd L
bessed, baysche v. [see abaist] [OF baissier] lower, put down, embarrass **Ch1** 4634 abaist P bayscht L; 13396 bessed P baysche L
best adj./adv. [OE betst] the best; comparative term **Ch1** 255, 1212, 6237, 9243, 10999 best; 1289, 4658, 7198, 8274 beste; **Ch2** 303, 1636, 4812, 6600, 7717 best; 2633 beste; **HS** 890, 1234, 3249, 7934, 11157 best; 2818, 3561 beste
beste, bestis n. [OF] beast, foul creature; animals, cattle **Ch1** 207 11807, 13336 beste; 3742, 3755, 3773, 8232 best; 468, 2134, 6883, 7244, 13253 bestis; 954, 11186, 13958, 15669 bestes; **Ch2** 890, 1353, 2761, 8208 beste; 2874, 6614, 7576 bestis; 120, 368, 1633, 2872, 7572 bestes; **HS** 3597, 4806, 8712 beste; 6768 best; 5990, 8690, 8709 bestes
bet, bette v. [OE betan] relieve need **Ch1** 15156 bette P bet L
betake, betauht v. [OE betæcan] give, grant or bestow; deliver, commit, surrender; **Ch1** 595 betaght P bytok L; 2492, 13743 bitauht; 6465 bitaght; 6467 bitauht P bytaughte L; 6855 betauht P bytaught L; 6864 bitaught him P bitaughtym L; 11963 bitauht P taught L; 12123 bitech P bytake L; **Ch2** 836, 1533, 3110, 3857, 7935 bitauht; 2903 bitaken P by taw3tte L; 3093 betauht; 7292 biteched; **HS** 10892, 10936 betecheþ; 481, 2455 betaght; 1246 beteche *D* betake; 1272 betaghte *C* 3oue *D* betakyst; 10920 betake *O* beteche
◆ **betas, bytas** n. [cp. OI beiti-ass, and biti (crossbeam)] a sail yard **Ch1** 11796 betas P bytas L
bete n. [from OE beatan, v.] beating of a drum **HS** 8996 bete
bete, bette v. [OE beatan] beat, knock down; flog, punish **Ch1** 8960 bete; 10180 betes; 8602, 12441 beten; 11430 bete doun P bere hem doun L; **Ch2** 989, 3653, 4520, 8020 bete; 1566, 5184, 8014 beten; 2223 betis; 2378, 5774, 7972 bette; **HS** 2358, 4615, 6829, 7130, 11149 bete;

7132 bet; 7023 beten
beteche, bitech v. [see betake, betauht]
beþenk v. [see biþouht]
betid, betides v. [see bitid]
betyng ger. [from OE beatan] beating, punishment **HS** 6729 betyng
betoknes v. [see token]
betraied v. [see bitrayed, betraised]
betrowþe v. [see trouht, trowþyd] [from OE treowþ] to promise to marry **HS** 1705 betrowþe *C* trewth ply3th *D* truþe
bette v. [from OE betera] remedy a need **Ch1** 15156 bette P bet L
better adj./adv. [OE betera] better; comparative term **Ch1** 2215, 4772 bettir; 2087 bettire; 1260, 2852, 5441, 7874, 9141 better; 1206, 5011, 8366 bettere; **Ch2** 770, 2417, 5518, 7324, 7788 better; 6496, 6522, 8346 bettere; **HS** 912, 1768, 4216, 6830 better; 1538 betre; 6355 bet; 6356 beter; 10081, 10980, 10982 bettre
betuen adv./prep. [see bituen]
betuex adv./prep. [see bituex]
beute n. [AF beaute (MP)] beauty; physical attractiveness **Ch1** 6087 beute; **HS** 3045 bewte; 12617 beute
bewent v. [OE bewenden] to turn about **Ch1** 1583 bewent P bywent L
bewreye v. [from OE wregan] accuse, betray; reveal, divulge **HS** 11506, 11520, 11622, 11624, 11648 bewreye *O* wry; 3533 bewreyþ *O* wryes; 3608 bewreye *O* wray; 12028 bewreyest *O* wryes; 11455 forwreye *O* furthe wry; 5644 bewreyyng *O* wereand
bycche n. [OE bicca] female dog; a contemptuous expression **HS** 500 bycche; 8956 bych
bicom, become v. [OE becuman] to become; come to, arrive at, reach; to be suitable, proper; to happen **Ch1** 3648, 8953 bicom; 5462 bicom P bycome L; 4216, 5789 com P bycome L; 6957 bicome; **Ch2** 4577 bicome; 4801, 6052, 6116 bicom; 8315 bicomen; **HS** 3876, 5818, 5821 become; 7494, 8254 bycom
bidde v. [see bede] [OE biddan, beodan] pray, plead **Ch1** 3375 biden; 4734 bides; 5100, 7240 bid; 15310 bidis; 7471 bidis P haldes L; **Ch2** 6245 biddes; 6705 bode; **HS** 4289 byd; 4952, 11810 bydde; 4613, 6438, 11411 byt; 249, 274, 1262, 4029, 12182 bad
bidding ger. [OE biddan] command, order, demand **Ch1** 895 biddyng; 5201 praiere P biddyng L; **Ch2** 2393, 5525, 6231, 6892 biddyng; **HS** 4960, 9078, 10944, 12372 byddyng; 1092 byddyng *D* entent
bide v. [see abide] [OE bidan] stay, remain; delay **Ch1** 2684 bide P byde L; 1550, 3480, 4784, 5556, 9335 bide; 3375, 4613, 11896 biden; 9660, 12015 bode; 12014 bod P abod L; **Ch2** 3954, 5568, 6760, 7552, 8166 bide; 2915 bide P abide L; **HS** 1933, 5044, 9746 byde; 11984 abydeþ *O* bydes for
bidene, bedene adv. [source obscure] completely, forthwith, altogether **Ch2** 1068, 3668, 5112, 7192, 8194 bidene; 2259L bydene (om. P); **HS** 2575 be dene GLOSS B rewe
bie, bouht v. [OE bycgan, becgan] pay for; atone for; redeem **Ch1** 632 bye; 8729, 8959, 10533, 15666 bie; 6637, 10533 bouht; **Ch2** 3658, 6973 bie; 4155, 7920 bies; 1906, 2809, 3916, 4333, 4396 bouht; **HS** 96, 2459, 5793, 9477, 10869 bye; 5949, 9820 byeþ; 364, 1193, 5299, 6480 beye; 1787 boghtyst; 3856, 10897 boghte; 5298, 8304 boght; 6904 yboght
bifalle v. [see falle] [OE befeallan] happen; become; enter into; belong to **Ch1** 1172 felle P bifel L; **Ch2** 7323 bifalle; 606 bifelle; **HS** 2134 befallyþ; 2724 befalle; 9418 byfalle; 1761, 3567, 7853 befel; 2660 befelle
♦ **bigate** n. [see gate, n. (2)] [ON gata] a side road, byway **Ch1** 9989 bigate P bywey L
bi3ete ppl. [see gate, v.] [OE bigetan] begotten **Ch2** 5994 bi3ete
biggen v. [ON; cp. OI byggja] build; dwell; erect tents or lodges **Ch1** 8606 bigged; 448, 452, 1878, 8610, 3655 bigged P bygged L; 14630 biggand; **Ch2** 1657, 8292 bigge; 534, 1525 bigged; 8067 to biggen; **HS** 3427, 9449 bygge; 9462 bygge *O* lage
biggyng ger. [from ON byggja] settlement, building **Ch1** 1894 biggyng; 332, 5787 biggyng P byggynge L
bihalued v. [from bihalve, adv.; cp. OE on ... healfe] surrounded **Ch1** 9795, 9959 bihalued P byhalued L
biheld v. [see beholde]
byherd ppl. [from OE herian] praised, extolled **Ch1** 10378 wele herd P wel byherd L
bihest, beheste n. [see hest] [OE behat] a promise **Ch1** 4920 biheste; 4923 hotes P byhestes L; **Ch2** 3659 biheste; 7038 bihest; **HS** 4203 beheste
byhete v. [OE behatan] to promise **Ch1** 4503 hette P byhet L; **HS** 3510 behete; 10657 byhete *O* hyghtes *SV* bihotest; 11211 behete *O* hyghtes
byyng ger. [from OE bycgan] purchase, buying **HS** 5962 byyng
biken v. [from OE cennan] make known; entrust, grant, commit **Ch1** 2772 bikenne P bykenne L; 7033 biken P bykenne L; **Ch2** 3021, 4037, 6698 biken; 6638, 8112 bikenne
biker n. [obscure; cp. MDu bicken] battle, skirmish; quarrel **Ch1** 7376, 9500 biker P byker L; 9113 bikere; 12596 biker P byker (v.) L; **Ch2** 1963 biker; **HS** 7915 bekyr; 9834 byker; 1178 *D* bekyr (om. B)
bikere v. [obscure; cp. MDu bicken] to skirmish;

make assault or war **Ch1** 12596 biker (n.) P to byker L to biker R; 12659 to bikere P byker L biker R; **Ch2** 6192 bikere

byles n. [OE byl; ON, cp. OI kyli] boils **HS** 6644 byles *O* kyls

bileue v. [see beleue, v.] [OE belæfan] leave, remain; to give up possessions **Ch1** 4741 leue P byleue L; 5999 bileued P leued L; 14945 bileue P byleue L; 15413 left P byleft L; **Ch2** 3789, 5536 bileft; **HS** 3318, 4560 beleue

byleue n./v. [see beleue]

bilyue, belyue adv. [from OE phr. bi live] quickly, eagerly **Ch1** 1574L blyue (om. P); **Ch2** 1989 bileue; 2527, 4205 belyue P blyþe L; 8026 bilyue; **HS** 7782, 8859 bylyue; 5619 belyue *O* als swyth

biloke v. [see lok, loke] [OE beluken] shut in, lock up, enclose **Ch1** 3174 biloke P bylok L; **HS** 1868 lokun *C* loke *D* be loke

bymene, bemene v. (1) [see mene] [OE bemænan] lament, complain; moan, grumble **Ch1** 2338, 12165 ment P byment L; **HS** 5122 bemene; 10751 pleynede *SV* bimenede

bymene, bemene v. (2) [OE mænan] intend, mean, signify **Ch1** 8982 mene P bymene L; **HS** 6636 bemene

byn, bynne adv./prep. [OE binnan] within; during a certain time **Ch1** 7351L bynne (om. P); 9559L byn (P differs)

bynde v. [see bond] [OE bindan] bind; impose allegiance, captivate; join **Ch1** 428 byndes; 1812 bynd P bynde L; 5741, 13886 bond; 15554 ende P bynde L; 8454 bonden; **Ch2** 788 band; 438, 1055, 3594, 5562, 8028 bond; 910, 6203 bynd; 6875 byndes; 1005 bonde; 1979, 6728, 7745, 8049 bondon; 2395, 3922, 4056, 6784, 8029 bonden; 919, 5623 bounde; **HS** 1315, 1790, 10585, 11593, 12250 bynde; 8058, 10587, 10609 bonde; 1816 ybownde; 3932 bownde; 5184, 12562 bounde; 8777 ybounde

byndyng ger. [from OE bindan] fettering **HS** 10678 byndyng

bineth, benethen adv./prep. [OE beneoþan] beneath, in; subordinate, powerless **Ch1** 4531, 12544 bineþen; 6661 beneþen; 6819, 8034 beneth; 8543 bineth; 9249 benethen; **HS** 684 beneþyn; 2538 beneþen; 8584 byneþen; 11926 byneþe

bynime, benam v. [see nam, v.] [OE beniman] deprive, rob, take away **Ch1** 2660 benam P bynam L; 11343 haf P bynime L; **HS** 2910 to make hym lese *C* benemyn hym *O* to do hym lese

bir, byre n. [ON] strength **Ch1** 10706 bir P byre L

byrde v. [see burd, bord]

birie v. [OE byrigan] entomb a corpse; bury **Ch1** 7675 birie; 3876 berid; 1706, 9003, 13457 beried; 1945, 5245, 8815, 13430, 14743 biried; **Ch2** 155, 394, 1127, 1371, 3414 biried; **HS** 1563 beryd; 3370 byryed; 8730 berye; 9136 byrye

biriels n. [OE byrgels] tomb; memorial **Ch1** 8616, 8911 biriels

biriyng ger. [from OE byrigan] entombment; funeral **Ch1** 13592 birieng P byrying L; **Ch2** 2626 biriyng

birne v. [see bren, v.]

bis n./adj. [OF bysse, bise] fine linen; dark fur for trimming garments **Ch1** 612 bys; 4697 bis P bys L; Ch2 5644 bis; **HS** 6638 bys

bisege v. [see besege]

biseke, besouht v. [OE besecan, besohte] beg, entreat, pray **Ch1** 117 besoght; 8119 besoght P bisoughtym L; 3102, 4912, 5772 besouht P bysought L; 5152 sekes P bisekeþ L; 547 beseke P biseke L; 5081, 6650 biseke P byseke L; 5645, 8577, 9205 besouht; 1358 souht P bysoughte L; 5209 bisouht P sought L; 6126, 6266, 7691 bisouht P bysoughte L; 6130 bisouht P preied L; **Ch2** 1515, 2240, 4888, 6851, 7927 biseke; 1474, 3507 bisouh P byso3tte L; 423, 1530, 3127, 5505, 7481 bisouht; **HS** 260 seke *C* beseke; 784 besechyþ *C* besekys *D* besekiþ; 1961 beseche *C* pray; 2946 besecheþ; 3855 besoghte GLOSS B preyd; 10373 beseche; 10480 bysoghte *SV* preyed

bisemed, besemed v. [from ON suma, OE seman] seem, look; to be suitable **Ch1** 153 besemed; **Ch2** 7493 bisemed; **HS** 7934 beseme *O* fall

bisent v. [from OE sendan] sent a message to **Ch2** 7546 bisent

biset v. [see set] [OE besettan] occupy; fig: surrounded; encumber; beseige a stronghold **Ch1** 5819 bisete P biset L; 6088 besette P byset L; 6349 sete P byset L; 7612 biset P byset L; 10513 sette P bysette L

biside, beside adv./prep. [OE besidan] nearby; there, away; moreover **Ch1** 499, 1097, 3408, 7730, 8796 beside; 7750 besidyn; 2997, 8586 biside; 13454 bisid; **Ch2** 266, 376, 4127, 4647 beside; 1685, 2975, 4479, 5830, 8350 biside; **HS** 64, 1764, 5982, 6005 besyde; 973, 6869, 8506, 10329, 11754 bysyde

bisie, bysyly adj./adv. [OE bisig] anxious, earnest; occupied, diligent **Ch2** 2257 bisie; **HS** 8783 bysy; 9483, 10731 bysyly

bisight, besight n./v. [see sight]

bysmere n. [OE bismer] disgrace; ridicule **HS** 7401 bysmere

bistad, bestedde v. [ON; cp. OI stadd-r] hard pressed, beset **Ch1** 12054L bystad (om. P); **Ch2** 4945 bistad; 318, 4727, 6312 bisted; **HS** 3364 bestedde

bisuike v. [OE beswican] betray, deceive, cheat

Ch1 11156 suoke P byswok L; **Ch2** 6606 bisuike

bit n. [OE bite] bite of a sword, a blow **Ch2** 6688 bit

bite, bete v. [OE bitan] bite; cut, slash; slander, offend **Ch1** 8356, 13253 bite; 8082, 13034 biten; 5147L byte (P differs); 11580L byte (om P); 3378 byte; 3004, 4358, 4376, 7786 bote P bot L; 8356, 9128, 11816, 12104 bote; **Ch2** 3932, 8188 bite; 3822, 5845, 7811, 8300 bote; **HS** 3554, 6647, 6782, byte; 5112 byt; 7516 byten; 5275 bete

bitech, bitauht v. [see betake]

biþouht, beþenke v. [OE beþencan] ponder, reflect, consider **Ch1** 5816, 14875 biþouht P byþought L; 12900 think P byþenke L; 4253 biþouhtis P byþoughtest L; **Ch2** 2898 biþouht; 5816 bithouht; **HS** 151, 2057, 2147, 10829 beþenke; 4045 beþoghte

bitid, betyde v. [OE phr. be tidan] happen, befall **Ch1** 10762 betid; 1124, 1618 betid P bityd L; 3394 betid P bytidde L; 4816 betides; 4796, 5038, 7956, 8630, 9209 betide; 14516 bitid P bytydde L; 14785 bitide P bitid L; **Ch2** 5113 bitid; 4480 bitide; 7546 bitidde; 1362, 2677, 3386, 6008, 7107 betide; 1396 bitides; 1769 betides; **HS** 386, 459, 1969, 3022, 5325 betyde; 3895, 11742 betyd; 4391 betydde; 8957 bytydde; 1467 betydde *CD* þat tyde; 3354 befel *O* betyde; 5043 tyde *O* betyde

bityme, betymes adv. [see time, n.] [OE tidan; phr.: to timan] in good time, promptly **Ch1** 14040 bitymes P by tyme L; **Ch2** 1535, 1798, 4200 bityme; **HS** 4236, 4920 betyme; 5510 betym; 7096 by tymes; 11293 be tyme

bitrayed, betraised v. [see traist] [from OF trair, traiss-] betrayed, committed treason against **Ch1** 5004 betraist P bitraischt L; 7773 be traist P by traischt L; **Ch2** 1174 betraied; 1175 bitraist P trayed . . . falsly L; 2468, 6347 bitrayed; 3810 bitraied P ben traised L; 3853 betraised; 6160 bitraised; **HS** 3360, 11835 betrayd

bitter adj./adv. [OE bitter, -lice] harsh to the taste; cruel, harmful; disagreeable **Ch1** 8356 bitterly; 8951 bitter; 15617 bitterlike; **Ch2** 782 bittere; **HS** 1740, 11526, 11570 byttyr; 1470 byttrer; 1244 byttyrly

bituen, betuene adv./prep. [OE betweonum] between, among **Ch1** 1268, 1713 betuene; 2054, 2323, 3689, 6091 bituene; 4115, 5490, 6913 bituen; 362 betuen P bytwyxten L; **Ch2** 1230, 2109, 2932, 3811, 6933 bituen; 766, 1236, 2387, 7234, 7872 bituene; 206 biten P bytwene L; **HS** 4085, 5165, 6691 betwene; 8205, 12032 bytwene; 5786 betwe

bituex, betuex adv./prep. [OE betwix] between **Ch1** 1714, 4125, 5737, 7959, 8877 bituex; 516, 711, 1416, 5438, 7327 betuex; 856 betuex P bytwyxt L; **Ch2** 84, 237, 2153, 6920, 7447 bituex; 7776 bituexen; **HS** 1120, 1821, 2323 betwyxe; 3881 betwyx; 9284 bytwyxe; 10049 bytwyx

biwan v. [from OE winnan] acquired, won **Ch2** 7899 biwan

biword n. [cp. L pro-verbium] a proverb, saying **Ch1** 15432, 15434 biword

biȝond adv. [see ȝon]

blak n. [OE blæc] the color black; a black object; black spaces on a game board **Ch1** 11158 nek (error) P blek L; 6471L blak (P differs); **HS** 11871, 11875 blak

blak adj. [OE blæc] black in color, pale, livid **Ch1** 2944 blak; 6970 blake; 14642 blak P blake L; **Ch2** 4304, 4882, 7177 blak; **HS** 1387, 10146, 11548, 11736, 12603 blak; 4887, 8696 blake; 10210, 10234 blakkere

blaken v. [OE blacian] become pale, be frightened **Ch2** 4554, 6991 blaken

blame n. [OF] blame, sin **Ch2** 1571 blame; **HS** 610, 1282, 10852 blame

blame v. [OF blamer] rebuke, scold, accuse; censure, belittle **Ch2** 975, 4116, 4291 blame; 1569, 4373 blamed; **HS** 32, 1052, 2007, 8640, 12364 blame; 8553 blamed; 8633 blameþ

blan v. [see blynne]

blast n. [OE blæst] blast of wind or breath, blowing a trumpet **Ch1** 1156, 1157 blaste; 12118 blest P blast L; **HS** 2968 blast

blaunchette n. [see oblaunchre]

ble n. [OE bleo] bright of complexion **Ch1** 14282L ble (om. P)

blede v. [OE bledan] to bleed; to suffer wounds **Ch1** 4339 blede; **HS** 5302, 10549 blede; 9111 bledde

bleynt v. [see blenk]

blely, blelyche adj./adv. [see blythe]

blen v. [see blynne]

blenk, blynk n. [ON blekkja, blenkja, v.] deception; guile; blink of light **Ch1** 1072 blenke P blenk L; 1230 blenk; 6931 blenk P blenke L; **Ch2** 4938, 6648, 6769 blenk; **HS** 4186, 6588 blynke; 6298 blenke; 4450 blynke

blenk, blenche v. [OE blencan; ON blekkja] to evade, glance aside; to awake; deceive, cheat **Ch1** 1520 glent P bleynt L; **Ch2** 2805 blenk; **HS** 428 blenkys; 3575 blenche; 5675 blynke; 4170 blynke *O* synke

blent v. [see blynd, adj.] [OE blendan] to make blind **Ch1** 4516L, 6974L blent (P differs); 12106 blent; **HS** 3407 blent; 8894, 12164 blynde; 12158 blyndeþ

blesse, blisse v. [see blis, n.] [OE bletsian, bledsian] to bless; cross oneself; give thanks; be blessed **Ch1** 137 blissid; 14676 blissed; 14660 blis; 15893 blisse; 5575L blessed (P differs);

Ch2 2365 blisse P blessed L; 8129, 8297 blissed; **HS** 758 blessyd; 2741, 9838 blessed; 3877 blesse; 3482 blessedyst; 3591 blessede; 7955, 8196 blys; 8228 blesseþ; 12059 blyssed

blessyng ger. [from OE bletsian] divine sanction; invocation **Ch2** 3473, 6519 blissyng; **HS** 1294, 1961, 5807 blessyng; 9839 blyssyng

blewe v. [see blowe]

blyche adj. [see briche]

blynd adj. [OE] to be blind; be deluded **Ch2** 809 blynd; 3632, 5370 blynde

blynde v. [see blent]

blynfeld v. [OE geblind-fellian] to strike blind **Ch2** 1318 blynfeld P blynfolded L

blynne, blan v. [OE blinnan] stop, turn aside **Ch1** 2056, 13597 blynne; 2248 blyn P blynne L; 8233 blynne P lynne L; 13081 blan; 15104L blynnes (om. P); **Ch2** 1137 blanne P blen L; **HS** 747, 1733, 3734, 10278, 12562 blynne; 3737 blynne GLOSS B leue; 9065 blan

blis n. [OE] happiness, good fortune; prosperity **Ch1** 3228, 5219 blisse; 4429, 5268, 14296, 14414, 15891 blis; 7088 blis P blys L; 8179 blis P blisse L; **Ch2** 7216, 7506 blis; 4261, 5603 blisse; **HS** 24, 106 blysse; 3892, 6332 blys

blis, blisse v. [see blesse, blisse]

blysful adj. [from OE blis, n.] happy, prosperous **HS** 1409, 8833, 12272 blysful

blythe, bliþeli adj./adv. [OE bliþe] pleased, cheerful, happy **Ch1** 848 blythe P bliþe L; 2498 blythe P blyue L; 4923, 13821 blythe; 7309 blithe P blyþe L; 8167, 8172, 14592 bliþe; 124 blythely; 13560 bliþely P gladly L; 3800, 3984 bleþely; 9200 blethely P bleþely L; 9621 bliþeli P bleþely L; **Ch2** 1292 bliþe; 1060, 1368 blythe; 3232 blithe; 164 bliþeli; 2810 bliþely; 1053, 2110, 3166, 3259 blithely; 8355 blithly; **HS** 5620 blyþe; 6679 blythe; 803 blelyche *F* bleþliche *C* gladly *D* redily; 46 bleþly; 5767, 11336, 11495 bleþely; 6728 blethly *F* gladli; 6906 gladly *O* blythly; 1084 blely *F* bleþeli *H* bleþly; 11787 blelyche *F* bleþeliche *O* blytely

blode n. [OE blod] blood, bloodshed; lineage, descent **Ch1** 2603, 4348, 6435, 9015, 12084 blode; 2654 blude; **Ch2** 167, 855, 3418, 6390, 8204 blode; 2239L bloud (P differs); 1393 lond P blowde L; **HS** 671, 1835, 6086, 10031, 10652 blode

blody adj. [OE blodig] bloody **Ch1** 3168 blody; **HS** 705, 710, 5287 blody

blome n. [ON; cp. OI blom] flower, blossom; fig.: superiority, eminence **Ch1** 4130, 10346, 12444 blome; **Ch2** 7880 blome

blowe, blewe v. [OE blawan] to blow, exhale; blow a horn **Ch1** 1156, 10191 blowe; 1157 blowen; 11142, 11816, 14790 blew; 4694 glewe P blowe L; 1814, 3493, 4293, 10457, 13471 blewe; 13019 blowand; **Ch2** 2847 blow; 2466, 3669, 7160 blowe; 649, 2872, 7154 blewe; **HS** 3274 blowe

bobaunce n. [OF] ostentation, boasting **HS** 994 bobaunce *C* thyngis *D* ryot; 3302 bobaunce *O* bobans; 4580 bobaunce

bode n. [OE boda] message, command, news **Ch1** 1516, 3396, 4924, 8850, 14947 bode; **Ch2** 993, 1262 bode P word L; 424, 1676, 3546, 5071, 7673 bode; 1481 bode P tydyng L

body n. [OE bodig] body, corpse; a person **Ch1** 1800, 3113, 5483, 7687, 9067 body; 3718, 7489, 8236 bodi; 3738, 6491 bodis; 7970, 12968 bodies; 15133 body P bodi L; **Ch2** 830, 1294, 4853, 5551, 8345 body; 4330 bouke P body L; 5340 bodie; 2576 bodies; **HS** 841, 1581, 3370, 11624, 11988 body; 7464, 9149 bodyes

bodyly adj./adv. [from OE bodig] in the flesh, bodily **HS** 1380, 1596, 3116, 10003 bodyly; 9983 bodyly *SV* bodiliche

bodword n. [ON] message, news **Ch1** 9673 bodword P bodeword L; 14391 bodword P message L; **Ch2** 1120, 3533, 3580, 6671 bodword

boke n. [OE boc, bec] volume of writings; an authoritative source; the Bible **Ch1** 230, 1752, 5564, 8101, 10517 boke; 146, 167, 721, 1731 buke; 7960, 8104, 15940 bokes; 15939 bukes; 836 cast lotes P loke þer bokes L; 7857 lotes caste P bokes kest L; **Ch2** 547, 1283, 3220, 5302, 8251 boke; 1886 buke; 1, 523 bokes; **HS** 44, 1366, 2718, 4926, 12114 boke

bold, bald, boldely adj./adv. [OE beald, bald] brave, fearless; overconfident; aggressively **Ch1** 2991, 4467, 5039, 5374, 7663 bolde; 1760, 3759, 6680, 8414, 9383 bold; 8415 boldest; 3489 baldere; 5374 boldere; 2558, 5911, 6526 baldest; 11523 baldlie; 914 boldelyer P boldeloker L; 1005, 5943, 7114 boldly; 2634, 4974 baldely; **Ch2** 1631, 2479, 4946, 5763, 7622 bold; 24, 550, 2607, 4853, 6986 bolde; 2865 bald; 927 baldely; 5498, 7523, 7987 boldely; **HS** 759, 4193, 5542 bold; 1454, 11865 bolde; 2256 bolder; 2499 boldly; 11864 boldely; 6623 boldlyere

bolden, bolded v. [OE bolden, balden] to become bold **Ch1** 3009, 14795 bolded; 3377 boldid P boldede L; 12585 bolded PL boldid R; 12683 bolden; 7597 boldeli bolded P baldely bolded L

boldhed n. [from OE beald] boldness, audacity, courage **Ch1** 12959 boldhede; **Ch2** 6811 boldhede; 8314 boldehed

boldnes n. [from OE beald] courage **Ch2** 910 boldenes P help L

bole n. [see bulle] [ON; OE *bula, bulluc] male bovine **Ch1** 474, 476, 494, 496, 504 bole; 482, 502 boles

boles hide n. [ON, OE] bull's hide cut into thongs for the measurement of land **Ch1** 7398, 7401 boles hide P boles hyd L

bolled, bolned v. [ON; OI bolgna] become distended, swollen **Ch1** 8090, 9585 bolned; **HS** 8871 swal *O* bolnyde; 10213 swolle *O* bolnede *SV* bolled; 10241 swollen *O* bolnede *SV* bollen

bolte n. [OE bolt] bolt for a crossbow **HS** 8304 bolte

bolued, belewed v. [OE belgan, bolgen] roar, bellow **Ch1** 8082 bolued P belewed L

bond, band n. [see bynde] [ON band] a serf; pledge, promise, obligation; fetters, restraints; domination; imprisonment **Ch1** 2823 bond; 3036 treuh P bond L; 3044 othe P bondes L; 5575L bonde (P differs); 8951, 11289 bandes; **Ch2** 1269 bond P obleschud L; 3030, 3913, 4917, 6734, 7606 bond; 4916 band; 4135, 6274 bondes; **HS** 3932 band; 7368 bond; 10216 bandes; 10618 bondes; 12006 bonde; 12010 bande

bondage n. [AF] feudal tenure or service; vassalage, subjection **Ch2** 1760, 6318 bondage; **HS** 2203 bonddage; 5755 bondage

bone, boun n. (1) [OE ban] a bone of the body **Ch1** 1753 bone P bon L; 1841, 3589, 6761, 8236 bone; 2258 bon; 8815, 15832, 15841 bones; **Ch2** 1042 bone; 3538 bon; 510, 811, 1000, 1967, 2630 bones; **HS** 661, 10540 bone; 4864 boun; 8689 bones

bone n. (2) [ON] boon, favor; prayer, request **Ch1** 5990, 14876 bone; **Ch2** 619, 1502, 3289, 5376, 6852 bone; **HS** 8971, 9123, 10417, 10483 bone

bone, boun adj. [ON] ready; armed; willing **Ch1** 1637, 10657 boune P bone L; 4719 boun; 1804, 2859, 4951, 7558, 9194 bone; **Ch2** 2596, 3866, 5780, 7958, 8088 bone; 1744 boun P bone L; 4007, 6190, 6924, 7072 boun

boneryte n. [OF bonerte] graciousness, kindness **HS** 1928 boneryte GLOSS B godenesse *C* bonoture *D* honoryte

bord, burd n. [see burd, behoue, v.] [OE bord] plank; side of a ship; table, altar **Ch1** 4584 burdes P bordes L; 2920, 9157, 10361 burde; 2924, 4382, 9190, 15353 borde; 11770 bordes; **Ch2** 4525 bord; 1338, 3760, 3767 borde; **HS** 2389, 4709 bord; 4715 burd; 12126 borde

bord v. [see burd, bord, v.]

bore n. [OE bar] male swine **Ch1** 8154 bore P bor L; 15055 boore

bore v. [OE borian] pierce, penetrate **Ch1** 4624, 15442 bore

borewe n. [see burgh]

◆ **borghgage** n. [OE borgh + OF gage] pledge of responsibility **HS** 9583 borghgage *O* borowage

◆ **borghgang** n. [OE borgh + gang] act of assuming sponsorship; surety **HS** 9589 borghgang *O* borowgange

borowe, borue v. [OE borgian] pledge security; borrow; protect, save **Ch1** 8959 borowe P borewe L; **Ch2** 1887 borowe; **HS** 364 borue; 3460 borwe; 5547, 10124, 11563, 11954, 12332 borowe; 6990 borowed; 10709 borowe *V* borwe

bos, bus v. [see behoue, burd] [from OE behofian] be necessary, required **Ch1** 1276 bos P most L; 4782, 11396, 11397 bos P bihoues L; 8961 bos P byhoueþ L; 11389 bus vs P we moste L; 12541 bus P bos L

bost n. [AF] bragging, boastful speech; praise of someone else; pride, arrogance; threat **Ch1** 8652 bost; 981, 1578, 4920, 6292, 9429 boste; 14790 boste P bostes L; **Ch2** 5397 bost; 3073, 4972, 7015, 7548 boste; 4846 pruesse P bost L; **HS** 1901, 3473, 4580, 4696 bost; 5160, 7426 rous GLOSS BH bost

boste, bostful, bostly adj./adv. [from AF bost, n.] arrogant, proud **Ch2** 6660 boste; **HS** 3050, 7155 bostful; 12517 bostly

bosum n. [OE bosm] the embrace; the breast **Ch1** 7748 bosums P hoses L; **HS** 4891, 6654, 12454 bosum

bot, but conj./adj./adv./prep. [OE butan, bute] but; except; apart from; merely, only **Ch1** 5438, 7263, 7721, 8149 bot; **Ch2** 213, 5826, 6824, 7357, 8294 bot; **HS** 494, 1381, 6990, 8731, 12629 but

bote n. (1) [OE bat, batas] ship, boat **Ch1** 5399, 5400 bote P bot L; 11899 bote; 7620, 13547 botes; **Ch2** 3047 bote; 3866 boote P schupe L; 3941 boote; 5793, 7844 botes

bote n. (2) [OE bot] good, profit, advantage; remedy **Ch1** 4772, 6867, 9996, 10743, 14720 bote; **Ch2** 4041, 4919 bote; 3466 bote o beame; 2199 bote of beam P bote to ben L; 2495 bote of beem P bote but on L; **HS** 3445, 3772, 9594, 11190 bote

bote v. [see bite, v.]

botelere, botlers n. [OF boteillier] servant in charge of wine; the cup-bearer of a king **Ch1** 10786 botelere P boteler L; 10932 botilere; 12628 botelere; 13074 botelere P botyler L; **Ch2** 6980 botlers

botened v. [OE botian] to be cured **HS** 9233 botened *O* ryghtede

botenyng ger. [from OE botian] relief **HS** 11036 botenyng *O* ryghte tynge

boterie n. [OF] wine cellar **Ch1** 11074 boterie P botelerye L

bouh n. [see bouwes]

bouke, bukke n. [ON bukr, OE bucca] male animal, buck; fig.: lascivious man **Ch1** 1320 buk P bukke L; 15055 buk; **Ch2** 4330 bouke

P body L; **HS** 3211 bukkes

boule n. [OF boul] deceit, trickery, falsehood **Ch2** 6777 boule

boulyne, bouspret n. [OF boelines (Wace); cp. MLG bochspret, Du boegspriet] nautical terms: bow-line, bowsprit **Ch1** 11769 boulyne (2) P bowlyne on bouspret L boun adj. [see bone, adj.]

bounde n. [OF bonde] boundary **Ch2** 5742, 7683 bounde; 7536 boundes

bounte n. [OF] goodness, virtue, distinction **Ch1** 5419, 6102, 6066 bounte; **Ch2** 6424 bounte; **HS** 5849, 7803 bounte

bourd n. [OF borde, bourde] story, jest, game **Ch1** 4696 burdis P bourdys L; 7476 bourd; **HS** 8671 bourd; 4629 bourdes; 4663 bourdys; 9265 bourd *F* tale

bourded v. [OF bourder] make a sharp answer **HS** 8670 bourded

bourdour n. [OF] a wit; entertainer **Ch2** 5001 bourdour

boure n. [OE bur] chamber, bedroom **Ch1** 5485L bour (om. P); **Ch2** 910 boure

bouweld v. [OF esboeler] to disembowel **Ch1** 3383 bouweld P bowaylled L; **Ch2** 8055 bouweld

bouwes, bouh n. [OE bog, boh] bows, limbs of a tree **Ch1** 15440 bouh; **Ch2** 914 bouwes P tre twystes L; 2721 bowe

bowaille n. [OF boele, bouele] bowels, entrails **Ch1** 4348 bowes (?error) P bowaille L

bowe n. [OE boga] weapon; longbow, crossbow **Ch1** 1007, 1519, 1522, 1788 bowe; 1764, 3411, 13022 bowes; 6133L bowes (om. P)

bowe, bouh v. [OE bugan] yield, submit, kneel **Ch1** 895, 3979 bowe; 8246 bowand; 12570 bowed L bouwed R (om. P); 14681, 14686 bouwe; 14958 beuwe P bowe L; 14657 bowand P bowynge L; 11277 bewe P come L; **Ch2** 156, 2683, 4469, 6810, 8094 bowe; 898 bouwed; 3145 bowed; 3574 bowes; 3460, 4788 bouh; **HS** 1078, 3000, 3018 bowe; 1082 bowyng; 5836 bowande

bowmen n. [OE boga + men] archers **Ch1** 13870 bowmen

bray v. [AF braier (MP)] wail; howl, bellow **Ch1** 3460 bray P braye L; **HS** 4883 braye

braid, breyd n. [OE gebrægd, gebregd] trick, fraud; attack; uproar **Ch1** 1134, 2302, 12742, 15579 braid P breyd L; 10659, 12998 braide; **Ch2** 4053, 5688, 6556, 6902, 8046 braid; 3382 braide; **HS** 11869 breyde

braid, breyde v. [see vpbraid] [OE bregdan, bredan] rush, attack; draw a sword **Ch1** 10659 braide P brayd L; 12090 braid P breyd L; **Ch2** 5624 braid; **HS** 673 vpbreyde *C* breyde *D* vpbrayd; 676 vpbreydyng *C* breyden; 1889 vpbreyde *C* breyd *D* vpbreyde

brayn n. [OE brægen] the brain **Ch2** 5628 brayn; **HS** 5032 harnes GLOSS H brayn

brak, breke v. [see brast, v.] [OE brecan] break, wreck; break out **Ch1** 398, 1829, 5347, 12578, 15845 brak; 1450, 3633, 5425, 6835 breke; 2022, 8263, 12101 broken; 3639 kroken P broken L; 6213 put P breken L; 12570 breke L broken R (om. P); 13078L breke (om. P); **Ch2** 840, 3034, 4266, 7349, 8002 brak; 809, 2814, 4790, 5620, 7734 breke; 4254, 5839, 6240, 6842, 8274 broken; 7622 brake; 5488 braken; **HS** 1834, 1842, 5030, 10060 brak; 1673, 4864, 8255, 9906 breke; 1718 brekst; 11223 breken; 2163, 11345 brake; 8678 broke; 4638 broken; 1033, 1867 brokun

branche n. [OF] branch, twig; line of ancestry **Ch1** 11204 branches P braunches L; 8931 branches; **Ch2** 914 braunche; 6124, 6132 branche; **HS** 9113 braunche

bras n. [OE bræs] brass, bronze **Ch1** 1436, 2240 bras; 2696L bras (om. P); **HS** 7129, 7131 bras

brast, brest v. [see to brast] [ON breste, brast; OE berstan] break, fall apart, burst **Ch1** 2258, 5945, 8063, 8361 brast; 11872, 11973 braste; 1829 brak P brosten L; 2823 brist P brest L; 3496 brest; 2948 brosten; 13070L brest (om. P); **Ch2** 7011, 7970, 8032 brast; 5628 brest; **HS** 10612, 11878, 12252 breste; 9297, 12196 brast; 8870 blaste *O* braste; 10680 to braste *S* brak *V* barst

◆ **bre** n. [OE breaw, breg; cp. OHG brawa] the bank of a stream **Ch1** 10169 bre

brede n. (1) [OE bread] bread, pastry; food **Ch2** 1336, 3968, 7902 brede; 4227L bred (om. P); **HS** 838, 5606 brede; 9957, 10071, 10364 bred

brede n. (2) [OE brædu] breadth, width; space; unit of measurement **Ch1** 1955, 6602, 7405, 9054 brede; 3071 o brede; **Ch2** 365, 934 brede

brede v. [OE bredan] breed, beget; nurture **Ch1** 10044, 10048 brede; **Ch2** 6777 bred

brefe n. [OF brief, bref] letter, message **Ch1** 937 brefe P bref L; 939 brefe P lettre L; 4209 brefe; 5958 brefis P lettres L; **Ch2** 3832, 5721, 6254 brefe

brek n. [OE bræc, brek] breach in a military formation **Ch1** 14046 brek

breke n. [OE broc, brec] breeches; armor for the thighs **Ch1** 9880L breche (om. P); **Ch2** 3987, 5006 breke

breke v. [see brak, v.]

bren, birne v. [OE brinnan; ON brenna] to burn, set afire **Ch1** 2248 birne P brenne L; 3738, 4757, 4897 brenne; 1040, 2572, 5415, 7306, 8818 brent; 7034 bren; 7288 robbe P brenne L; 9894L brent (om. P); 11904 bren P brenne L; 15690L brenne (om. P); **Ch2** 989, 1032, 2923, 7268 brenne; 6823 bren; 592, 1314, 4370, 5774, 8294 brent; 1028 brennyng; 1354 brent P brend L; **HS** 484, 1581, 2534, 3278, 6416 brenne; 1448, 1734, 2515 brennyng; 12456 brenþ; 3278 brende; 1575, 3279 brent; 2536 brende *CDO* brent; 3281, 9779 brende *O* brynte; 6546 [MS *O* interpolation, l. 48] brennes; 2496 brennyng *C* brent; 2528 brennyng *O* bretynyd; 2526 ȝenand *CDH* brennand *O* gaynande; 4489 brennyng *O* brade; 1572 brennyng *C* brennand

brennyng ger. [from OE brinnan] burning **HS** 2575, 2578 brennyng

brennyngly adv. [from ON brenna] ardently **HS** 7204 brennyngly *O* brymandly

brest n. [OE breost] bosom **Ch1** 1806, 9128 brestes; 3007, 3168, 4623, 11959, 13111 breste; 3507 breste P brest L; 4344 breste P brynyes L; 7756 brest; **Ch2** 1606 breste; **HS** 946, 1538, 3658, 11478, 11760 brest

brest v. [see brast, v.]

bretask, bretaxes n. [OF bretesque, bretasce] seige-tower, defensive structure on a wall, barricade **Ch1** 1040 bretasks P bretaxkes L; 14030 bretaskes kirnelles P bretaxed & carneled L; 15192 bretask P bretaxes L

breþer n. [see broþer]

breþerhede n. [from OE broþer] fraternal relationship **HS** 4207 breþerhede *O* brethirschep

brewe v. [OE breowan] harm, injure **Ch1** 1239, 11516 brewe; **Ch2** 1324 brewes; **HS** 1704 byttyr bale *C* brewyth . . . bale; 1864 brewe . . . bale *C* brewen *D* brewyn; 2354 brewyþ; 6002 brewede; 10942 breweþ

briche adj. (1) [OE bryche] helpful, useful **Ch1** 3111, 11164 briche; **HS** 4930 *BFH* blyche (?error) *O* briche

◆ **bryche** adj. (2) [OE bryce] frail, humble **HS** 5821 bryche GLOSS H logh

bryd n. [see berd, birde, n. (2)]

bridale n. [OE bryd-ealo] wedding feast **Ch2** 1367 bridale

bridelle n. [OE bridel] horse bridle; control, authority **Ch1** 10659, 13166 bridelle; 13048 bidelle (error) P bridles L; **Ch2** 3024 bridelle

brigge n. [OE brycge] bridge, gangway **Ch1** 3060, 3062, 11774 brigges; **Ch2** 1656, 4996, 5796, 7236, 8185 brigge; 4538 drauht brigge; **HS** 5259, 5261, 5268 brygge; 1385, 1391, 1427, 1467, 1472 bregge

brigge v. [from OF abregier] restrict, curtail **Ch2** 1277 brige; 5964 briggid

bright adj. [OE breht, bryht] giving light, shining; of vivid color; fair **Ch1** 3004, 3364, 3594, 4451, 8920 bright; 7932 light P bright L; **Ch2** 2321 bright P briȝt L; 538L [Havelok interpolation, l. 31] bright; **HS** 5651, 10207, 10229, 11537, 12601 bryght

brightnesse [OE beorhtnes] radiance, brilliance **Ch2** 2504 brightnesse; **HS** 1409, 12600 bryghtnes

brim n. [see bro, bank]

brim adj./adv. [prob. blend of OE breme and grim] grim, fierce, savage **Ch1** 4895, 14965 brym; 912 brym P grym L; 13698 brim P grym L; **Ch2** 5876, 7286, 7917 brim; 176, 609 brym; 3816 fulle brim P al grym L; 4112 broþely & brim P iresly & grym L; **HS** 8574 brym *O* bryme

bryn n. [ON brynja; cp. OI brynn] brows, eyebrows **Ch1** 12040, 12077 bryne P bryn L; **Ch2** 4694 bryn P brym L; 5728 bryn

brink n. [?ON *brink] shore coast; bank of a stream; edge **Ch1** 4579 brinke; 10015 brynk; 10185 brinkes; **Ch2** 2977 brynk

bring, brouht v. [OE bringan, brohte] bring, fetch; lead, take **Ch1** 5651, 6269, 7558, 8002, 9097 bring; 14414 bringis; 813, 1215, 4556, 6884, 9249 brouht; 8663 brouhtes; 176, 3897 broght; **Ch2** 4036, 6490, 7419, 8286 bring; 4922 bryng; 973, 2251, 3781, 5621, 8343 brouht; **HS** 2076 bryngyþ; 9852 bryng; 2290 bryngge; 5172, 12015 brynge; 3738 bryngyst; 8402 bryngst; 3400 brynth; 3006 brynþ *H* bryngeþ; 11273 bryngþ; 1943 broght; 1129, 12524 broghte; 2714, 6243, 8294 broght

brysl adj. [prob. from OE *brysol] ?frail; bristly, enraged **HS** 8574 brysl (?brist) *F* brisk *O* brosell

britten v. [ON; cp. OI brytja] cut up, cut apart **Ch2** 5882 britten

bro n. [OE bru] brow, forehead; brow of a hill; bank of a stream **Ch1** 11764 bro bi bankis P banke & brymme L; **Ch2** 4651 kank (error) & bro P bank & broo L; 7578 bank & bro; **HS** 8063 brous

broched v. [OF brochier] spurred; charged into action **Ch1** 12601 broched PL brochid R; **Ch2** 6701, 7436 broched

brode adj. [see brede, n.] [OE brad] wide, broad; spacious **Ch1** 2806, 4532, 8311, 9137 brode; 1955 brede; 2895 broth P brod L; **Ch2** 2927, 5007, 6597, 7614 brode

broke n. [OE broc] small stream **Ch1** 6003, 7603, 7606, 15670 broke; 6001 brokes

broke v. [see brak, v.]

brond n. [OE brond, brand] firebrand, torch **Ch1** 8972 brond; 8926, 8982 brondes; **Ch2** 7169 brondes

bronston n. [OE bryn-stan] burning sulphur **Ch1** 14064, 14069 bronston P brymston L

brothe, broþely, ◆ **broþefulle** n./adj. [ON breþr; cp. OI braðr] rash, hasty; violent, angry **Ch1** 2895 broth P brod L; 4895 brothe & brym P wroþ & brym L; 12040 brothen P lothen L; **Ch2** 1346 ◆ broþefulle P wretful L; 4112 broþely P iresly L; **HS** 8063 lothly *O*

brothly
broþer, breþer, breþryn n. [OE] brother, brothers **Ch1** 46 broþire; 294, 2594, 6416, 8208, 9009 broþer; 911, 1995, 2653, 3443, 6965 breþer; 7008 breþere; **Ch2** 330, 771, 2923, 5826, 8045 broþer; 452 broþere; 1235, 1554, 2309, 3610, 6264 breþer; 1087 brethres; **HS** 280, 302 broþyr; 10590, 10632, 10704 broþer; 3562 breþer; 1689, 3170 breþren; 1964 breþryn
brouk v. [OE brucan] enjoy **Ch1** 6353 brouk; **HS** 6146 broukeþ
broun adj. [OE brun] brown; dark **Ch2** 4882 broun
brous n. [see bro]
brouse v. [OF brisier; OE brysan] injure, damage **Ch1** 12569 sette P brouse LR
brunyes n. [from OE byrne] cuirass, coat of mail **Ch1** 13286L brunyes (om. P)
brusse, brusche n. (1) [see busk, n.] [OF broce] brush, weeds; a bush **Ch1** 8224 brusche; 12463 brusse P busch L
brusse, brusche n. (2) [?OF brosser] charge, encounter **Ch1** 13031, 13032 brusse P brusche L
◆ **bugerie** n. [OF bougrerie, bugerie] fornication **Ch2** 7820 bugerie
buk, bukke n. [see bouke]
◆ **bulchyn** n. [see bole] a young bull **Ch2** 4329 bulchyn P bolechoun L
bulle n. [see bole, n.] [OF bulle, L bulla] papal edict, message **Ch2** 3212, 5554, 6883, 7393, 7911 bulle
◆ **bulled** v. to denounce by letter under the pope's seal **Ch2** 6418 bulled
burble v. [?ML or OF; cp. L bullare] bubble, swell **HS** 10214 burble *O* popyll *SV* welleden
burd, bord v. [see behoue, bihoue, bos] [from OE bihofian] must; it is necessary **Ch1** 4282 nedeli borde P nede byhoued L; 8272 nede bord P nede he mest L; 8337 burd me P oughte L; 11414 bord P byhoued L; 12203 bord P moste L; 12961, 13724, 14027 burd; **Ch2** 1890, 3416 burd; 4476 burd P most L; 3294 nedes burd P nedes byhowed L; 1348, 4830 burd P byhowed L; **HS** 4073 byrde GLOSS BH moste *O* brude; 7839 neded *O* burd; 7840 shuld ha *O* burde; 10827 shuld *O* burde; 10895 shal *O* burde; 11557 oughtest *O* burde
burdon n. [OF] a pilgrim's staff **Ch1** 15138 burdon
burdoun n. [OF] the bass part of a song **Ch1** 11031 burdoun
burgeis n. [OF] freeman, citizen, inhabitant of a town **Ch1** 1930 burgeis P burgeys L; 3422, 4051, 8607, 9147, 14267 burgeis; **Ch2** 1130, 1786, 3493, 5700, 7757 burgeis; 5706 burgeys; 2389 burgeis P burgeys L
burgh, borewe n. [OE burg] town, city, village **Ch1** 3058, 7586, 10288, 10611 burgh; 11166 burghes P burwes L; **Ch2** 260, 2090, 3558, 3666, 7259 burgh; 2374 burghes; **HS** 1315 burgh; 12528 borewes
Burgolon, Burgoilloun n. [OF Burguignon] a Burgundian **Ch1** 10380 Burgolon P Burgoiloun L; **Ch2** 7763 Burgoilloun
burne n. [OE burna] stream **Ch1** 8050 burne P borne L; 10194 burne
burnessid ppl./adj. [from OF brunir, burnir] burnished, polished metal **Ch1** 3594 burnessid P yburnuscht L; 4451 burnissed P burnusched L; **HS** 1409 bryghtnes *D* bernys
burte v. [from OF bourden] joust, clash **Ch1** 4582, 13038 burte
bus v. [see behoue, bos]
busk, busch n. [OE busc] bush, woods, grove, thicket **Ch1** 3384 buskis P buskes L; 3540 bank & busk; 9693 busk P busche L; **Ch2** 170, 216 thorn busk; 2721 buske or a bowe
busk v. [see busse, v.] [ON; cp. OI buask] hurry; get ready **Ch1** 934 bussed P busked L; 5018 busked; 9075 busked P ybusched L; **Ch2** 896 busked
buskyng ger. [from busk, v.] preparation **Ch1** 8863 buskyng P buschyng L
busse v. [from OF embuissier, enbuschier] ambush; conceal troops **Ch1** 984 busse P enbusche L; 1665 busse P busche L; 1112, 1113, 9667, 12753 bussed P busched L; 934 bussed P busked L; 6208 busched P enbusched L; 4976, 9679 bussed P enbusched L; 12658 bussed P enbusched L buschid R; 13686 busshed; **Ch2** 334 enbussed P busched L; 4647 bussed; 4662, 7002 enbussed
bussement n. [from OF enbuschement] military ambush; place of concealment **Ch1** 987, 4981, 6213 bussement P enbuschement L; 4993 enbussement; **Ch2** 5829 bussement; 4653 enbussement P buschement L
busses n. [see cogger] [OF buce, busse] cargo or merchant ships **Ch1** 5833 busses coggers P barges & balyngers L; **Ch2** 4188 busse; 3680, 3777, 3898, 4067 busses; 3680, 3898 busses & galais P busses & schupes L; 3903 busses P vessels L

C

cables, kables n. [AF] heavy rope used on a ship **Ch1** 1041 cables; 2950, 10963, 11765 kables
cached v. [AF cachier] grasp, seize; drive, pursue **Ch1** 14665 cached P chased L; **Ch2** 2946 katched P chased L; 5776 cacchis; 8098 kacched; **HS** 6376 caght
cage, kage n. [OF] enclosure, prison **Ch1** 1335 cage P gage L; **Ch2** 3790, 5346 cage; **HS** 4006

kage

caitife, caytifte n. [AF caitif, caitive] wretch, miserable person; captivity **Ch1** 945 caytifte P cheytifte L; 11942 caitife P cheytyf L; **Ch2** 4269 cheitefe P þeff L; 4392 cheitif P kaytif L; **HS** 733, 739 kaytyff; 1422 caytyuys; 943 caytyf *C* wreche

calle v. [see cleped, clepyn]

can, con v. [see con, conne]

candell, kandel n. [see kandelstyke] [OE candel] a candle, taper **HS** 6546 [MS *O* interpolation] (l. 30) candell; (ll. 38, 58) kandell; (ll. 40, 42) kandels

cante adj. [see kant]

care, kare n. [OE caru] grief, sadness; pain, misery **Ch1** 564, 6818, 14233 care; 6520 care P kare L; 3176L, 8521L kare (P differs); **Ch2** 846 care; **HS** 1106 care; 3929, 10706, 11220 kare

carfe, karf v. [OE ceorfan] cut, slice **Ch1** 4536 coruen; 7402 karue P carf L; 7621 karfe P carf L; 11084 kerue; **Ch2** 4114 carfe P carff L; 5882 corn (error: ?torn); 8229 coruen kyng (error: ?commencyng); **HS** 1156 karf *C* cuttyt *D* carf

careful adj. [OE carful] sorowful **HS** 706 soruful *C* careful

carol n./v. [see karol]

carping ger. [from ON karpa] quarreling, foolish talk **Ch1** 11362 carping P ianglyng L

carponters n. [AF] carpenters **HS** 9168 wryghtes GLOSS H carponters

carte, karte n. [OE, ON] a cart, wagon **Ch1** 6739 carte; **Ch2** 6731 kartes

cas, kas n. [OF] state of affairs; event; plight **Ch1** 434, 2485, 2810, 4704, 7980 cas; 3488 kas P cas L; 6652, 13549 caas; **Ch2** 218 trispas P cas L; 738, 2925, 4922, 6574, 8260 cas; 1265 case; 7738 kas; **HS** 1287, 1377, 7826, 8816 cas; 327, 5787, 8476, 10558, 12297 kas

cast v. [see keste, cast]

castel, kastelle n. [OE, AF] fortress; stronghold; a tower on a ship **Ch1** 2950 kastels P casteles L; 8222, 9212, 9396 castelle; 6381, 7025, 8263, 9210 castels; 8380, 13959, 14029 kastelle; 13478 kastellis; **Ch2** 1927, 2897, 4893, 5774 kastelle; 989, 1859, 2095, 2377, 7887 kastels; 2743 kasteles; 4549, 5500 castele; 2709 castellis; 2711 kestelle P castel L; 2750 casteles; 529, 2895, 6048, 7962, 8156 castelle; 6346 castelles; 4085, 5291, 6729, 7222 castels; **HS** 3437 castels; 3812 casteyl; 3822, 7644 castel

catel, katel n. [AF chatel, OF catel] goods, property, wealth **Ch1** 5676, 10099 catelle; 1873 kataile; **Ch2** 4512 catele; 7799, 7800 catelle; **HS** 1106, 1125, 9465 catel; 3371 kateyl; 5747, 10684 katel; 11218 katele *H* kateyl; 10249 gode *SV* catel

cause n. [see kauce, caucieȝ] [OF cause, L causa] matter of concern; legal action **Ch2** 3152 cause

cause v. [OF causer] cause an effect, produce, make **HS** 576 make *C* dost *D* cause; 991 settyst *D* cause; 1532 ȝeueþ *D* causith

celere n. [OF celer, L cellarium] underground chamber **Ch1** 2062 celere P seler L

cely adj. [see sele, selli] [OE selig] happy, worthy **HS** 1410 cely

celle n. [OE cell, OF celle] a hermit's cell, dwelling **Ch2** 6446, 6451 celle; **HS** 171, 4024, 4036 celle; 4067 cele GLOSS BH godely (error)

centiner n. [OF centiner] officer commanding a hundred men **Ch1** 3509 milleners & centeners P mylers & centaynes L; 13005 be centiners & millers P by milers & by centeners L

certeyn n. [from OF certain, adj.] fact, truth; tribute, fee; confidence **Ch1** 2362, 8812, 9312 certayn; 15385 certeyn; **Ch2** 892, 4597, 4949, 6107, 6940 certeyn; **HS** 8501, 9171 certeyn

certeyn, certeynly adj./adv. [OF certain] fixed, assured, determined; definitely **Ch1** 605, 1359, 3638, 6702, 8882 certeyn; 821, 4461, 4915, 6140, 7648 certayn; 3434 certeyns; 2836 certaynli; 3361 certayne; 520 certanly P truely L; **Ch2** 1721, 3613, 5244, 6242, 8284 certeyn; 1054, 2045, 2473 certayn; 2621, 5305, 8117 certeynly; 2057L certeyne (om. P); 3375, 3409 certeynlie; 6934 certeynli; **HS** 225, 597, 2831, 7732, 9223 certeyn; 7438 certeyne; 10597 certayne; 8241 certaynly; 591 certeynly *C* trewely; 1704 certeyn *C* sekyr; 2889 certeynly *O* sekyrly

certeynte n. [OF certainete] pledge, agreement; true report **Ch1** 1146, 8045 certeynte; **Ch2** 528, 1705, 6244, 7260, 8274 certeynte; **HS** 8219 certeynte

certes adv. [OF] certainly; indeed **Ch1** 5154 certes; 14670 forsothe P certes L; 8646 certis; **Ch2** 3476, 4317, 4392, 4783 certes; 6893 certis; **HS** 215, 752 certys; 2557, 12045 certes

certifie v. [OF certifier] state as true, make an affirmation **Ch2** 3829 certifie; 6007 certified; 6266 certifies

chace n. [OF] hunting of game; pursuit or attack on an enemy **Ch1** 1507, 8746, 15380 chace; **Ch2** 577, 2285, 8177 chace

chace v. [see chase]

chaf n. [OE] refuse of grain; straw **Ch2** 6703 chaf

chaffare n. [OE *ceap-faru] goods, wares; bargaining **Ch1** 10972L chaffare (om. P); **HS** 2593, 5795, 7887 chaffare; 2940 chaffare *C* ware

chayne, chyne n. [OF] fetter; spiritual bond; a sign of office; lock of a drawbridge **Ch1** 8535,

8546 chyne P chayne L; 8454 chynes P cheynes L; **Ch2** 4316 chynes P cheynes L; 4691 chayn (?error) P Caym L; 6394 chayne; 4539, 4545, 4910, 7162, 7172 cheynes; 4312 chyne; 7174 cheyne; **HS** 12196 chayne; 12199 cheyne

chalange n. [OF] false or malicious accusation; an injury **Ch1** 4186, 4199, 14179 chalange; **Ch2** 1577, 2155 chalenge; 4208 chalange

chalange v. [OF chalengier] accuse; treat unjustly; lay claim to **Ch1** 3452, 4187 chalange; 8834, 8854 chalanged; **Ch2** 1393 chalanged; 1811, 2665, 3219, 4272, 6158 chalange; 4616 chalenge; 5677, 6196, 6741 chalanges; **HS** 5407 chalange

chalangyng ger. [from OF chalengier] slandering; accusation; rebuking **Ch1** 4755, 8853 chalangyng; 11493 chalangeyng; **Ch2** 4282 chalangyng

♦ **chalans** n. [OF] barges **Ch1** 10058 chalans

chalys n. [OF chalice, calice] cup for sacramental wine **HS** 9489 chalyce; 10061 chalys *O* clathes

chambir, chambre n. [OF chaumbre, chambre] room, bedroom; king's audience room **Ch1** 3827 chambre; 7138 chambire; 7451 chambir P chaumbre L; 10911, 11007 chambir; 9880 chambres (?error) P iaumbers L; 13961 chambres; **Ch2** 2179, 5621 chambre; 5613 chambir; 1559 chambres; **HS** 1943 chamber; 2233 chambre; 4749, 4750 chaumbre

chambirleyn n. [AF chamberlain (MP)] personal attendant; chief officer in the king's chamber **Ch1** 10967 chambirleyns; **HS** 6995 chamberleyn

champion n. [OF] defender, protector **Ch1** 14176, 14177, 14190 champion; **Ch2** 685 champion; **HS** 9843 champyons

chance n. [see ochance] [OF] occurrence, event; luck or fate; exploit, adventure **Ch1** 1204, 4716, 6310, 7173, 9367 chance; 5406 chances P chaunces L; 4064 chance (error) P chaunge L; **Ch2** 1671, 2292, 4342, 5678, 7872 chance; 5630, 6074, 6985, 7368 chances; **HS** 132 chauncys; 386, 1565, 6406, 9624, 11824 chaunce

chancelere n. [OF] officer of the king's exchequer; secretary **Ch2** 3147, 3895, 6792 chancelere; 3894 chanceler

change v. [OF] vary; replace, exchange **Ch1** 1926 charged P chaunged L; 4074 change; 3222, 4077 changed; 4064 chance (error) P chaunge L; 9291L chaunge (om. P); **Ch2** 2137, 5828, 7635 change; 138, 3631 changed; 1920 changis; 3929 changes; **HS** 480, 1134, 7548, 8112, 9977 chaunge

chanon n. [AF canun, canon; CF chanoine] minor order of priest; clergyman under canon rule **Ch1** 188, 14718, 15919 chanon; 10853, 14626 chanons; **Ch2** 2784 chanones; 3324, 6613 chanons; 8295 chanon

chapele n. [OF] place of worship **Ch1** 12167, 14489, 14491, 15651 chapelle; 11861 chapelle P chapel L; **Ch2** 435, 437, 531, 2269 chapelle; 5214 chapele; **HS** 9343 chapel

chapelet n. [see croket]

chapitille, capitle n. [AF chapitel (MP)] chapter of a book; a chapter of monks **Ch1** 7124 chapitille P chapitel L; 14330, 14331 capitle P chapitre L; **HS** 3573, 7838 chapytyl

chapman n. [OE ceapman] merchant, dealer **Ch2** 8017 chapman; **HS** 5546 chapmen

char n. (1) [OE cier, cer] task **Ch1** 8686 char P chare L

chare, chaiere n. (2) [OF char] chariot; chair, throne **Ch1** 10985 chaiere P chayer L; **Ch2** 5313, 5316, 5323, 5327, 7867 chare; 5331 chares; **HS** 7759 chayere; 5017 chayer *O* schayer; 5029 chayer *O* scharere

chare v. [OE cerran, cearrian, cierran] to turn, trick; change condition **Ch1** 11524 chares P chars L; 15044 chared; **HS** 2062 aȝenchare *C* ageyn chare *D* bryngiþ hym in car

charge n. [OF] cargo, load; fig.: duty, care **Ch1** 3721, 4286 charge; 4284 charges; **Ch2** 4194, 5803 charge; **HS** 423, 2794, 3739, 10186, 11986 charge

charge v. [OF chargier] load, burden; entrust **Ch1** 11775 charge; 738, 1429, 3623, 8072, 12768 charged; 1222 charge P chargen L; 1926 charged P chaunged L; **Ch2** 1301 charge; 877, 2394, 3778, 5513, 5700 charged; 2256 chargis; 2668 karke P charge L; **HS** 2790, 6544, 6823, 7611, 12463 charge; 1422, 2709, 5606, charged; 1630 chargyd; 4572 chargeþ; 1258 bad *D* chargid; 4684 chastyed *O* charged

charite n. [OF] benevolence; love; formula used in prayer **Ch1** 3219, 11949 charite; **Ch2** 2359, 3246, 6905 charite; 3880L charitee (om. P); **HS** 2257, 3863, 7155, 10231 charyte; 1942, 5611, 7892, 10371, 10415 pur charyte

charme n. [OF] spell; verse for incantation **HS** 521, 533 charme

charmed v. [OF charmer] cast a spell upon **Ch1** 9314 charmed

chartre, chartir n. [OF] document granting rights or privileges; document attesting an agreement **Ch1** 5828, 5831 chartre; 5822 chartire P chartre L; 11651 chartere P chartre L; **Ch2** 624 chartir; 622, 2069, 2154, 3407, 7682 chartre; 7326 chartere; 5489, 6000 chartres; **HS** 5362 chartre; 9802, 9817, 9835 charter

chase, chace v. [OF chacier] to hunt animals; pursue, expel or attack an enemy **Ch1** 5417 exilde P chaced L; 5713, 7594, 15377 chaced; 5893 chaced P chased L; 6295, 6842, 7178,

7615, 15598 chace; 4783 chaces P dryueþ L; 1504 chasant P chasand L; **Ch2** 284, 2530, 4322, 5877, 8125 chace; 31, 2250, 4996, 6613, 7017 chaced; 2946 katched P chaced L; **HS** 11938 chace

chaste adj. [OF] pure, virginal **Ch1** 11111 chaste; **HS** 1551, 1883, 3027, 7461, 7547 chaste; 7368 chast

chastise v. [AF chastier (MP)] punish, discipline someone **Ch2** 610, 5374, 5375 chastise; 757, 3004, 7029 chastised; 772L chaste (om. P); **HS** 1489, 3787, 4829, 8898, 11148 chastyse; 3525 chastyd; 294 downcaste *C* chaste; 958 chastyd *C* warnede; 4684 chastyed *O* charged; 4870 chastyed *O* chastys; 6978 chasteþ *O* fenndes

chastysement n. [from AF chastier] reprimanding; punishment **HS** 4854 chastysement; 5038 chastysement *O* schatymente

chastysyng ger. [from AF chastier] admonishing; punishment **HS** 4828, 4900 chastysyng; 4858 chastysyng *O* chestiment; 4866 chastysyng *O* chastyng

chastyte n. [AF chastete (MP)] purity **HS** 1678, 7550 chastyte

chaungable adj. [OF] untrustworthy **Ch1** 2442L chaungable (om. P)

chaunsel n. [OF chancel] area of a church with altar, choir **HS** 8808, 8886 chaunsel

chaunsfullyche adv. [from OF chance] perhaps **HS** 10683 chaunsfullyche *SV* happyliche

chefe n. [OF chef, chief] head, leader, ruler **Ch1** 938, 4210 chefe P chef L; **Ch2** 364, 1205, 4170, 5722, 6214 chefe; 6362 chef

chefe adj. [from OF chef, n.] highest in rank, power; preeminent **Ch1** 14138, 14140, 14142 chefe P chef L; **Ch2** 264, 1574, 2574, 4482, 6050 chefe; 352, 6788 chef; **HS** 3404 chef

chefetayn n. [OF chevetai(g)ne] ruler, governor; captain **Ch1** 2738 cheftanes P cheuentaynes L; 3522 cheiftayns P cheftayns L; 4175 cheftayne P cheftayn L; 5769 chieftayn P cheftayn L; 6369 chieftayn P cheuentayne L; 6413 ceiftane P cheftayne L; 6547 cheftan P cheuentayne L; 6777, 8955 cheftayn; 12946 chefetayn P cheuentaigne L; 13192, 13377 chefetayn; 13214 chefetayns; **Ch2** 289, 5064, 6333 cheftayn; 3425 chefetayn

cheyne n. [see chayne]

chek n. [OF eschec] strife, incident; delay, evil deed, blow; check as a term in chess **Ch1** 1816 chekkes; 8440 chek P chekke L; 11157, 11229, 12528 chek; 4955 chek hasarde P chek ful harde L; 14045 chek P check L; **Ch2** 2442, 3736, 5529, 6240 chek; **HS** 2699, 7771 chek

cheke n. [OE cece, ceoce] cheek; fig.: alongside **Ch1** 1816 chokes (error) P chekes L; **Ch2** 5480 cheke bi cheke

cheke v. [OE ceocian] choke, strangle **Ch1** 12358 chekid P cheked L; **HS** 3191 cheke *F* scheke *O* schake

cheker n. [OF eschequer, escheker] chess board; exchequer **Ch1** 10146 cheker; 11154 chekere P cheker L; **Ch2** 7627 chekere

cheltroun n. [see scheltron]

chepe v. [OE ceapian] bargain; to buy, sell **HS** 2940 chepe

cherche n. [see kirk] [OE cir(i)ce; ON kirkja] body of christians; a church **Ch1** 2596, 5651 kirk P chirche L; **Ch2** 1607, 3013 kirke P churche L; **HS** 928 cherche *C* kyrke; 2163 kyrk GLOSS B cherche; 3210 cherche *O* haly kyrke; 3818 cherche *A* chirch *O* kyrk; 834, 2276, 4260, 12565 cherche; 3835, 4576, 9492, 10602, 12195 cherche *O* kyrke

chere n. [OF chere, chiere] manner, behavior; look or expression; frame of mind; friendliness **Ch1** 1366, 3974, 7096, 9322 chere; **Ch2** 2297, 7186, 8223, 8340 chere; **HS** 4042, 5155, 5677, 8536 chere

cherisid v. [see chirest]

cherle n. [OE ceorl] churl, low fellow **Ch2** 7137 cherle; 7198 cherles; **HS** 8694, 8700 cherles; 10646 cherle

ches n. [OF escheks, esches] chess game **HS** 1044 ches; 4310 chesse

ches, chose v. [OE ceosan] to choose **Ch1** 227, 2549, 4459, 7839, 9141 ches; 1254, 1895, 3949, 5714, 8311 chese; 5927 chese P chesen L; 920, 1291, 5930 chosen; 3271 chose; 5714 chese P chose L; 6526 ches P chose L; **Ch2** 426, 2114, 4025, 6542, 8280 ches; 34, 1227, 4281, 5331, 7719 chese; 2027 chesis; 301, 3428, 5200, 6209, 7534 chosen; **HS** 214, 4019, 11000, 11020, 12483 chese; 1655, 6309 ches; 1040 chees; 4490, 10605 chose

chesyng ger. [from OE ceosan] act of choosing **Ch1** 2833 chesyng; **HS** 10997 chesynge

cheson, chesun n. [see encheson] [AF enchesun (MP)] reason, cause **Ch1** 270, 6647, 8013, 9030 cheson; **Ch2** 3164, 7740 cheson; 4255 chesons P enchesons L; **HS** 5649 chesun; 2955 encheseoun *C* cheson

cheste n. (1) [OE ceas, ceast] strife, quarrelling; a dispute **Ch1** 4745 cheste; **Ch2** 363, 7596 chest

cheste n. (2) [OE cest, cist; L cista; ON kista] coffer, box **HS** 2620, 6091 cheste

cheteryng ger. [ME chiteren, v.] chattering **HS** 355, 359 cheteryng

cheualrie n. [see chiualrie]

cheue v. [see mischeue] [OF chever, chiever] execute, attain, accomplish; be faithful to, recognize **Ch1** 14799 cheue; 14426 cheued P ycheued L; **Ch2** 118, 2015, 4630, 6946, 7386 cheue; 2683 cheuen; 3173, 5888, 7889 cheued

cheuisance n. [OF] fulfillment; nourishment

Ch1 842 cheuisance; Ch2 2536 cheuysance; 4494 cheuisance; HS 7216, 7217 cheuysaunce
chide v. [OE cidan, cidde] scold, speak in anger; quarrel **Ch1** 7884 chide; **HS** 1970, 3474, 3492, 3520, 6890 chyde; 2008 chydyn; 11238 chyden; 11385 chyt *O* chydes
chydyng ger. [from OE cidan] quarreling, scolding **HS** 1901, 3527, 6836 chydyng
child n. [OE cild] son; infant, youth **Ch1** 831, 2103, 3724, 6149, 6898 child; 2168 sons P children L; 3169 son P child L; 795, 1982, 4675, 8500, 11878 childe; 799 chylde; 1942, 4087, 5781, 7243, 14268 childre; 3453, 7522, 8123, 10608, 15282 childir; 929 childere P children L; 929, 2016, 3302, 5290, 7880 childere; 7347, 14243 childer; 1942, 8589 childire; 7159 childire P children L; **Ch2** 2589, 5066, 6082, 7562 child; 63, 988, 3040, 5201, 7559 childe; 357, 5606 childir; 348, 1012, 3199, 6469, 7040 childre; **HS** 352, 710, 3805, 10059 chyld; 700, 1507 chylde; 1227 chyldyr; 2883, 4861 chylder; 6081, 7996, 9601 chyldren
chyldhede n. [OE cildhad] early youth **HS** 7660 chyldhede
childeles adj. [from OE cild, n.] without offspring **Ch1** 8504 childeles
chyme n. [OF chimbe, var. of cimbe, cimble] cymbals, set of gongs or bells **Ch1** 3998 chyme P chume L; 11145 chymes P chymbes L; **HS** 7130 tympan *O* chyne
chyn n. [OE cin] the chin **Ch1** 1816 chynnes; 12356 chyn; **Ch2** 4114 ine P chyn L
chyne, kyne n. [OE cine] crevice, gully, ditch **Ch1** 1716 kynes; 13418 kynnes P chynes L
chirest, cherisid v. [OF ch(i)eriss-, ch(i)erir] hold dear; to esteem **Ch1** 2325 chirest P loued L; 8643 cherisid P cherisched L
chiualrie, cheualrie n. [OF chevalerie] band of mounted warriors **Ch1** 301 chyualrye; 6100 knyghtes P chiualrie L; **Ch2** 29 chiualrie; 3113, 3474, 4019, 5596 cheualrie
choys n. [OF chois] selection, election **HS** 11021 choys
cyrcumstaunces n. [OF] aspect of a situation **HS** 12431, 12441 cyrcumstaunces
cite n. [OF] capital city, cathedral town **Ch1** 732, 2749, 5680, 8841, 12794 cite; 446 citees; 3258, 4045, 7037, 7170 citeȝ; **Ch2** 861, 2090, 4893, 6594, 8309 cite; 717, 2374 cites; 508, 2389 citees; 990, 2908, 3558, 5883, 8294 citeȝ; **HS** 177, 878 cytee; 1927, 10787 cyte
citolles n. [OF] stringed instruments **Ch1** 11144 citolles P sitoles L
clad v. [OE *claþian] put on clothing; be clothed, dressed **Ch1** 5891, 8887, 11105, 11113 clad; 6982 cled; **Ch2** 5607, 5618 clad; **HS** 3382 cladde; 5729 clad
clap, klap n. [OE clæppan] blow; stroke of bad fortune **Ch2** 2839 klap; 4338 clappes
clarioun n. [OF clarion] trumpet **Ch1** 11144L clarioun (P differs)
clay n. [OE clæg] earth, soil **HS** 11089 clay
clawe n. [OE clawu] claw, talon **Ch1** 8084 clawes; 11818 klawes; **HS** 12199 clawes
clawe, klawe v. [OE clawan] scratch **HS** 4283 klawe; 4285 klawyþ
cleyme n. [OF] demand, request; right, title **Ch1** 13636 cleyme P to cleym (v.) L; 13638 cleym; **Ch2** 4856 cleyme
cleyme, clayme v. [see quyt clayme] [OF clamer] demand; be entitled to; quit **Ch1** 6155 cleymed; 4506 claymed P cleymed L; 15490 claymed; 11473 cleyme; **Ch2** 364, 1166, 8215 cleymed; 32, 4592, 4625, 6056 clayme; 5252 claym; 6020, 6262 claymes; 2420 cleyme alle quite; **HS** 9568 cleme
clene adj./adv. [OE clæne] pure, empty; wholly, entirely **Ch1** 1714, 8055, 8249, 8341, 14485 clene; 14260 clene P cler L; 2324, 3804 quyte & clene; 8249 clene P klene L; **Ch2** 125, 1200, 1709, 6450, 7763 clene; **HS** 325, 1542, 4350, 8284, 11545 clene; 4794 clenly
clennes n. [OE clænness] purity, chastity **HS** 1888, 6516 clennes; 2046 clennesse
clense v. [OE clænsian] purge; drive out **Ch1** 6356 clens; **HS** 98 clense; 12270 clenseþ
cleped, clepyn, calle v. [OE clypian, cleopian] give a name, call, give a title **Ch1** 3748 cal; 297, 5564, 6520, 7951, 9107 calle; 3816 calle P caldit L; 315, 3746, 5293, 8787, 9240 cald; 270, 1906, 4108, 7974, 9193 called; 2158, 2160, 4071 calde; 3684 callede; 1958L cleped (om. P); 5664 sais P calleþ L; 7466 callis; 13993 kalled P cald L; 15276, 15391 kald; **Ch2** 103 calles P calleþ L; 7912 calles; 95, 503, 3729, 5061, 7276 cald; 2290 asked P clepeþ L; 2447 appeld P called L; 107, 3336, 4201, 5269, 8334 calle; 3185 calde; **HS** 80 clepyn; 441 klepyd; 1267 clepede; 138 clepyd *D* callyd; 232 clepyn *D* callyn; 354 clepyn *C* holden *D* callyn; 1151, 2070 clepyd *CD* callyd; 2582 callyn *CD* clepyn *O* callys
clere adj./adv. [OF] pure, bright; shining, gleaming; loudly, clearly; illustrious **Ch1** 3033, 7822 clere; 3892 clere P cler L; **Ch2** 595, 3669, 5241, 6794, 7774 clere; **HS** 2285, 5923, 9828, 10324, 12428 clere
clergy n. [OF] clerical status; learning, scholarly method; doctrine **Ch1** 302, 6762 clargie P clergie L; 7827 clergie P clergye L; 8591 clergie; 9005 clergy; **Ch2** 589, 1458, 5137, 6856, 8343 clergie; 2089, 2343, 3095, 5667 clergy; 6744, 6940, 6961 clergi; **HS** 1202, 5512, 8814, 10021, 11608 clergye
clergioun n. [OF clerjon] disparaging term for a minor clerk **Ch2** 3207 clergioun
clerk n. [OE clerc; OF; L clericus] member of

the clergy; ecclesiastic; notary; writer **Ch1** 147, 5654, 6773, 7429, 14723 clerk; 204, 8622 clerke; 166, 721, 835, 8804 clerkes; 5652, 11030 clerkis; **Ch2** 105, 1523, 2672, 5135, 6498 clerk; 3163, 5234, 6890, 8252 clerke; 476, 1880, 2256, 5940, 8258 clerkes; 3000 clerk P clerc L; 6294, 7291, 7808, 8193 clerkis; **HS** 81, 421, 5749, 8825, 11598 clerk; 37, 832 clerkys

cleue, clyue v. (1) [OE clifian] adhere to, cling **Ch2** 5194 cleue; 4630 cheue P cleue L; **HS** 2578 cleuede; 8326 clyue; 7902 clyue *O* slefe

cleue, clefe v. (2) [OE cleofan] split, cut apart **Ch1** 4382, 13330 clouen; 7990 cleues; 10695 clefe P claf L; 10708 clefe P clef L; 12114 klafe P clef L; 1585 clef; 12381, 13169 clefe; **Ch2** 4675, 7813 cleue; 7975 clef; **HS** 5474 cleue; 1574, 1820, 5283 cloue; 1828 cloue yn *C* partyd on

clymbe v. [OE climban] climb, ascend **HS** 2120 clambe; 7279 clumbe; 8324 clymbe

clippers n. [from ON; cp. OI klippa, v.] one who clips coins **Ch2** 5737 clippers

clipte, clyppyng v. [OE clyppan] embrace; snatch, seize **Ch1** 11818 clipte; **HS** 3881 clypte *O* halsede; 3884 clyppyng *O* halsynge

close, clos n. [OF clos; ML clausum, closum] in trouble, surrounded; enclosure, encampment **Ch1** 3330, 4056, 5742, 9215, 14005 clos; 4049 close P clos L; 12752 klos P clos L; **Ch2** 3970, 4494 clos

close, klose v. [from OF clore] close up; fortify; obstruct a passageway **Ch1** 994, 1698, 4048, 7417, 8389 closed; 14020 klosed P closed L; **Ch2** 1901 klosed; 1973, 3725, 4535 closed; **HS** 8711, 10746 closed

clostre n. [OF] monastery, convent **Ch1** 7007 clostire; **Ch2** 1998 closter; 4270 clostre; 2005 cloistre; **HS** 8650 cloustre

cloth n. [OE claþ] garment; cloth for a table **Ch1** 1800 cloth; 618 clothes; 3163, 6970, 6982, 15125, 15354 cloþes; **Ch2** 2476 cloth; 5607, 5618 cloþes; **HS** 1148, 2552 cloþ; 3380, 4700 cloth; 6023 cloþes

clothe v. [from OE claþ, *claþian] to dress, put on clothing **Ch1** 6971 cloth; 7116 clothe

cloþyng ger. [from OE claþ] dressing **Ch1** 910 clothyng; 7292, 9315, 11114 cloþing; **HS** 3323, 5703, 7614, 11035 cloþyng

cloude n. [OE clud] a cloud **Ch1** 6471 cloude; **Ch2** 854 cloude

cod n. [OE codd] seedpod, shell **Ch2** 7036 cod

code n. [OF; L codex] a body of laws **HS** 2184 code

cof adj. [see kof]

coffrer n. [OF coffrier] treasurer, officer of the king's household **Ch2** 7797 coffrers; 7812 cofrere

cofre, cofines n. [OF cofre; L cophinus] box, chest, coffin **Ch2** 3313 cofre; 5488, 6323 cofres; 3314 cofre & . . . cofines P coffiners L; 7224 coffris; **HS** 6184, 6194, 6199 cofre

cogges, coggers n. [AF cogge] military ship **Ch1** 5833 busses, coggers P barges & balyngers L; 11776 galeis cogges P cogges barges L

coy adj. [OF, from L quietum] quiet, reticent **Ch2** 6815 coy

coife n. [OF] a skull-cap **Ch1** 10696 coife P coyfe L

coyned v. [OF coignier] to mint metal, make coins **Ch2** 5744 coyned

cok n. [OE; OF coc] a cock, rooster **Ch2** 2986 cok; **HS** 7278 cok

cokewold n. [see kokewold]

cold n. [from OE cald, ceald, adj.] coldness of temperature, season; chills **Ch1** 3640 colde; **Ch2** 4326 cold; 1189, 1471, 2985, 6354 colde; 2391L cold (P differs); **HS** 1154, 9155, 9176, 9571 cold; 6901 colde

cold adj. [OE cald, ceald] cold **Ch1** 3884 cold; **Ch2** 1370 colde; **HS** 1146, 9111 cold

colde v. [OE *caldian] grow cold, be chilled **HS** 9398 colde

cole n. [see kole]

colour n. [OF colur (MP); L color] pigment; visible color; paleness **Ch1** 2490, 7490 colour; 9315 colore; 10703, 11105 coloure; 11086 colours; **Ch2** 5422 coloure; **HS** 1413 colours; 1397, 3222 kolour; 5472 colour

com v. [OE cuman] approach, arrive; attain, obtain **Ch1** 1061 comand P comynge L; 4625, 4959, 8123 comand; 8639 come; 8224, 8810, 9378 com; 8153, 10152 coms; 8028 coms P comeþ L; 8349, 9154 comen; 12788 cam; **Ch2** 224, 1563, 5715, 6756, 8307 com; 832, 6432, 7368, 8214 come; 27, 402, 5909, 7743, 8040 comen; 4499, 6168, 6677, 7724 comand; 288, 1023, 5956, 6899, 7920 comes; 950 comes P comeþ L; **HS** 179 com; 395, 1423, 3171, 4301, 10043 come; 358, 374 comyþ; 573 comun; 2502 cum; 2766, 2774, 3920, 3946, 12617 cumþ; 9949 comes; 3035, 6143, 8192 cam; 3836 camme

comand v. [OF comander] command, order, demand; prescribe **Ch1** 966 comande; 9148 comand; 2509, 3074, 9197 comanded; 4885, 4967, 8223, 9312 comandid; 6370 command; **Ch2** 1538, 1912, 2847, 3557, 7175 comandid; 1351, 4988, 5011, 5555 comanded; 7091 comand; **HS** 555, 1069 comaundyd; 907 comaundede; 1601, 3793 comaundyþ; 11165 comaundeþ; 6527, 7555 comoundeþ; 9972 comounded; 11729 comounde

comandment n. [AF comandement (MP)] order, request; instruction **Ch1** 7685 comandment; **Ch2** 2793 comandment; **HS** 14 comaundementys; 147, 240 comaundement; 1001, 7559

comoundement; 11155 comaundemens
comete n. [OF, L] a comet **Ch1** 8918 comete
comyng ger. [from OE cuman] arrival; approach **Ch1** 8641, 9234 comyng; **Ch2** 747, 5933, 6489, 8173 comyng
comfort n. [see discomfet] [OF] assurance; trust; gratification **Ch2** 938 comforth; **HS** 4032, 4069, 6925, 8570, 12047 cumfort
comfort v. [OF, L] strengthen; reassure; aid, support **Ch1** 3775 comfort; 8299, 8985 comforted; **Ch2** 2795 comforte; 3691 comfortid; 512 comforted; **HS** 2244 cumfortyd; 6997, 8481, 11863 cumforted
comlyng n. [OE *cymeling, OHG chomeling] stranger, foreigner, visitor **Ch1** 8447 comlyng P comelyng L; **HS** 2157, 2160 cumlyngys
◆ **commare** n. [OF commere] godmother **HS** 9873 commare
◆ **commatres** n. [L commater] godmothers **HS** 1695 godmodrys *D* commatres
comon n. [OF comune] commonwealth, town; people, folk **Ch1** 3940, 4725, 12862 comon P comunes L; 1190 comoun; 3932, 4666 comune; **Ch2** 4335, 7142, 7335 comon; 1055 comons; 2673 for comon P by comyn L
comon, comune adj. [from OF comune] owned jointly; shared **Ch1** 2788, 3061, 3297, 6764, 8809 comon; 7353 comune; **Ch2** 1711, 2670, 4477, 6457, 7551 comon; 4961 comon wele; 7956 comon sight; **HS** 10 commune; 7438 comoun; 10436 comune
comon, comone v. [OF comunier] deal with, associate with **Ch1** 14676 comon P comune L; **Ch2** 3423 comond; **HS** 6552 comone
comonalte n. [OF comunalte] people of the country **Ch1** 123 comonalte; **Ch2** 1303 comonalte P peple L; **HS** 5964 comnalte
comonly adv. [from OF comune] jointly, in common; frequently **Ch1** 7079, 8079 comonly; **Ch2** 2940, 4153 comonly; **HS** 691, 888, 932, 1733, 2945 comunly; 5723 comunlyche; 7552, 7553 comounly; 893 comunly *C* comely
company n. [OF compaignie, cumpainie] army, host; companionship **Ch1** 3103, 4312, 5752, 7210, 8279 company; 5752 company P compaygnie L; 5838 companyes P compaignies L; 8317 companyes; 1476 companye; **Ch2** 289, 1815, 5866, 6669 company; 2613, 4634, 6272, 7397 companie; **HS** 66 companye; 1718, 1869, 3866, 4028 cumpany
compas n. [OF] a circular area **Ch1** 4531, 8814, 10372 compas
compas v. [AF cumpasser] devise, plan; scheme, plot **Ch1** 6931 compasse; 4521 compassid P schopen L; 8692, 8696 compast P compassed L; **Ch2** 2402 compas P chace L; 6270, 7402 compassed
compassement n. [OF] scheming; a plot **Ch2** 6147, 7396 compassement
compilour n. [OF] historian, chronicler **Ch2** 2694 compilour; 95, 536 compiloure
comple v. [see demple]
comsyng ger. [from OF comencier] beginning; undertaking **Ch2** 2364L comsyng (om. P)
con, konne, couþe v. [OE cunnan, ppl. cuþ, cuð] to know, to be able to **Ch1** 8, 957 cone; 695, 3501, 7238, 9307 kan; 78, 6814, 8043, 9258 can; 1752 kan P can L; 2035 kons P cones L; 7960 con P kone L; 10474 konne P kone L; 7901 kone; 18, 2215, 5562, 8871, 13789 couth; 88, 4354, 7459, 9142 couthe; 8355 couht; 1680, 11734, 12054, 13063 kouth; 15000 couþe; **Ch2** 528, 705, 5342 can; 34, 570, 4908 kan; 1052, 4793 conne; 7788 cone; 4018, 4223, 4583, 5214, 5778 couth; **HS** 55, 595, 3081, 8931, 11762 kan; 4445 couthe; 377, 1485 can; 5979, 7891 cun; 55 kun; 6532 cone; 1169 kone; 11895 konne; 5096, 8898 cunne; 3536 kunne; 793 canst; 10622 kanst; 9658 kunnat; 2261, 4449, 12174 coude; 3554 koude; 2860, 4901, 7693, 8105, 11197 couþe; 9594, 11557 coudest; 2135 kone *C* knowe *D* knawe; 9662 kunne *O* can; 9622 kone *F* to knowe *O* to cone; 11814 kunne *O* ken *SV* con; 11890 kunne . . . shewe *O* ken & knaw
conand, connyng, kunnyng ger. [from OE cunnan] craftiness, knowledge **Ch1** 3106 konand P konnynge L; 5802, 10183 conand P connynge L; 15928 konyng P conninge L; **HS** 3077 cunnyng; 7134 kunnyng
conant, cunnaunt n. [see couant, couenaunt]
conceyue v. [from OF concevoir] observe, realize; conceive a child **Ch1** 794, 7949, 9326 conceyued; **Ch2** 3555 conceyued; **HS** 10012 conceyued
concelement n. [OF] hiding of activities **Ch2** 7221 concelement
concorde n. [OF; L concordia] harmony **Ch1** 2766 concorde
condie v. [OF conduire] guide, accompany **Ch2** 4534 condie P gye L
condite, condute n. [OF conduit] grant of safe passage **Ch2** 1992, 6278 condite; 6290 condute
conferme v. [OF confermer; L confirmare] to endorse, ratify, approve **Ch1** 2748, 14661 confermed; **Ch2** 7331 conferm; 2730, 3774 confermed; **HS** 9830, 10032 conferme; 12120 confermed; 9836 confermyng
conferment n. [OF cunfermement (MP)] confirmation **HS** 9854 conferment
confessour n. [OF, L] confessional priest; one who avows Christian faith **Ch2** 2695 confessour; 7034 confessoure
confirmacion n. [OF] ratification of election **Ch2** 3490, 5132 confirmacion; **HS** 9813, 9815 confyrmacyoun; 9797, 9893 confyrmacoun;

9839 confyrmacoun *H* confermacyoun
confound v. [AF confoundre, L confundere] harass; rout, defeat **Ch1** 11518 confoundes; **Ch2** 4215, 6399 confound; 6852 confonded; **HS** 1735 confunde; 8222, 11904, 12060 confoundeþ; 2522, 11966 confounded
confused ppl. [L confusum, ppl. of confundere] frustrated **Ch2** 7397 confused
confusioun n. [L and OF] discomfiture, humiliation, perdition **Ch2** 5060 confusioun; **HS** 1748, 7427, 9195 confusyun; 1478 confusyown
conged v. [OF congier] dismissed **Ch2** 7898 conged
conyng, cony n. [OF conin] a rabbit; rabbit fur **Ch1** 15056 conyng P cony L; 10972L conyng (om. P)
conisance n. [OF conissaunce] an emblem, badge **Ch1** 5366 conisance P conisaunce L
coniure v. [L, OF] charge, conjure **HS** 3597, 12224, 12589 coniure
coniurisoun n. [OF] magic formula, a spell **Ch1** 8783 coniurisoun P coniurysoun L; 15014 coniurisoune; 8786 coniurisouns
connyng, cunnyng ger. [see conand]
conquere v. [OF conquer-re] conquer, subdue; win tribute **Ch1** 3099, 4146, 4553, 6684 conquere; 4132, 5221 conquerd; 4165, 5167, 6682 conquered; 5709, 12156 conquerde; **Ch2** 4485, 5676 conquere; 502, 6191 conquerd; 1202, 2798, 4272, 4735 conquered; 4622 conquerand P conquerant L
conquerour n. [OF conquereor] title of a victorious ruler **Ch1** 1438, 2530 conquerour; 6669 conquerours; **Ch2** 2122, 4104, 4455, 4564 conquerour; 135, 5893 conqueroure
conquest n. [OF] forceful subjugation; defeat of an adversary; victory **Ch1** 5143, 6796 conquest; 6367 conquest P conquered L; 4555, 5141, 5222 conqueste; **Ch2** 503, 1045, 1213, 2656, 4075 conquest; 3065 conqueste
conrey, correie n. [AF cunrei, correie] detachment of troops; battle arrangements **Ch1** 3317,- 4651, 8305 conrey; 12869 correie P conreye L; **Ch2** 7422 conrey
consciens n. [OF; L conscientia] the mind; moral sense **HS** 627, 645 ynwyt *C* consciens
conseil n. [OF conseil, L concilium] meeting, conference; plan; adviser, advice, instruction **Ch1** 533, 917, 1063 counselle; 1189 counseil; 1199, 1259 counseile; 1505 rede P conseil L; 2569, 6258, 8471, 9380 conseile; 5746 consele; 2208 conseyle; **Ch2** 3281, 4025, 6168, 7579, 8076 conseil; 959, 1448, 2508, 6407, 7827 conseile; 3695, 3786 conselle; 6173, 6691 consaile; 6207, 6430 consail; **HS** 194, 1196, 3652, 7642 cunseyl; 1128 cunsel; 5417 cunsayl; 3658, 3662 cunseyl *W* cunsel
conseil v. [AF cunseiler, L consulere] advise, teach; consult, deliberate **Ch1** 1065 counselle; 1195 counseils; 3172, 6240, 7046, 9241 conseile; 2057, 2867, 9045 conseiled; 3336, 4527, 5441, 6236 conseild; 3934 counseild; 10296 conseld P conseilled L; **Ch2** 2101, 4803, 6894, 7147 conseile; 7276, 7717, 7825 conseil; 2537, 3251, 5998, 6009, 7571 conseild; 2214, 5130, 5534 conseiled; **HS** 1756 cunseylde; 1504 entycedyst *C* cowncellyn
conseilyng ger. [from AF cunseiler] consultation **Ch2** 4961 conseilyng
conseiloure n. [AF cunseiler] adviser; king's council member; confidant **Ch1** 3279 conseiloures; 4302 conseilere; 5326 conseiloure; 7833 conseilours; 9296 conselors; **Ch2** 976, 4100, 6497 conseiloure; 1307, 5230, 7966 conseilere; 3518, 6782, 6963 conseilers; **HS** 4280 cunseyler; 5409, 5422 cunseylours; 6180 cunseyleres
consent v. [OF consentir] give assent; approve of, connive with **Ch1** 1259, 6129, 6990 consent; 6077, 7501 consentid; 6956 consented P assented L; **Ch2** 1239, 4390, 5697, 6462, 8081 consent; 2453, 7359 consentid; **HS** 1675, 8332, 11175 consent; 5403 consente; 9041 consented; 1875 consentyþ; 11193 consenteþ
consentour n. [OF consenteor] an accomplice **HS** 7621 consentour
constable n. [OF conestable] chief executive officer; governor of a castle **Ch1** 3472 constables P conestables L; 6381 constables
constablie, constablerye n. [OF constablerie] office of a constable **Ch1** 4408 constablie P constablerye L
contek, cuntek n. [AF] strife, conflict, dissension **Ch1** 2800 contake P contak L; 2785, 7738, 12527 contek; 11230 contek P cuntek L; **Ch2** 863, 2443, 3244, 5530, 7776 contek; **HS** 7447, 7772, 7789, 9021 cuntek; 995 cuntek *C* fyȝttyngis; 2700 cuntek GLOSS BH debate
contekour n. [AF] rioter, brawler **Ch2** 8009 contekours
contenance n. [OF cuntenaunce] bearing, outward appearance; manners **Ch1** 8889, 9180, 9316 contenance; **Ch2** 4554, 6111 contenance; **HS** 2940 *C* (add) cowntenauns
contene v. [OF contenir] contain; persist, last **Ch1** 5574 contend P contened L; **Ch2** 7777 contene; **HS** 7005 conteyneþ
contre, cuntre n. [OF contree] country, district; land **Ch1** 690, 5757, 6606, 8823, 12793 contre; 7103 contre P lond L; 8824 contres; 308, 1486, 5598, 9039, 12182 cuntre; 1925, 7819, 8592 cuntres; **Ch2** 870, 2011, 4001, 5515, 7753 cuntre; 878L, 746L contre (om. P); 4639, 7858 cuntres; **HS** 178 cuntree; 1856, 3899, 10562, 10740, 10788 cuntre
contrarye v. [OF contrarier] contradict **HS** 2042

D contrarye (B differs)

contrariosly adv. [from OF contrarios, adj.] spitefully **Ch1** 12313 contrariosly

contred v. [see countre, v.]

contreue v. [OF controver] plot, conspire; plan, invent **Ch1** 7044 contreue P contreoue L; 8871 contreue; 14058L contreued (om. P); **Ch2** 5811 controues; 4585, 4808 contreued; 5791, 6269, 6408 controued

contreuore n. [OF controveure] stratagem **Ch2** 8167 contreuore

contrycyun n. [OF, L] remorse **HS** 12325 contrycyun; 12577 contrycoun

controueying ger. [from OF controver] falsehood, contrivance **Ch2** 6155 controueying

conueie v. [AF conveier] to guide, accompany **Ch1** 12631 conueie PR conueye L; **Ch2** 3798 conueied

conuerted v. [OF, L] convert to Christianity **Ch1** 14669 conuerted

cop, coupe n. [OE cuppe, OF cope] drinking vessel, bowl, goblet **Ch1** 1356 coppe; 7453 coupe; 7473 cop; 11171 coupes

cop schotin adj. [from OF cope] drunk **Ch1** 7450 cop schotin P cuppe schoten L

coper, koper n. [OE, from L cuprum] copper **Ch1** 15643 koper P coper L; 15644 kopir P coper L

copple n. [OF cople] a pair of verses, a couplet **Ch1** 102 copple

coppled v. [OF copler] to join verses into couplets **Ch1** 88 coppled

corage, korage n. [OF] bravery; strength; lust **Ch1** 5295L corage (P differs); **HS** 406 corage; 9722 korage

coraious adj. [OF] valiant, brave **Ch1** 11345 coreious P coraious L; 11534L coraious (om. P)

◆ **Cordelyn** n. [OF corde, var. of cordele] a Franciscan friar **Ch2** 6222 Cordelyn

cordes n. [OF corde] cord; a nautical line; stringed instruments **Ch1** 1041, 2950, 10963 cordes; **HS** 4775 cordes

corn n. [OE] grain; crop of cereals **Ch1** 449, 1873, 2888 corn; 1062, 10273, 15661 corne; **Ch2** 1869 korn; 3800, 3972 corn; 5882 corn (error: ?torn); **HS** 5380 corn; 5991, 10100 corne

corner n. [OF] a point of land; enclosed place; nook or recess **Ch1** 10149 corners; 10151 cornere; **HS** 5823 noke GLOSS B a corner

cornerd v. [from OF corner, n.] angular, pointed **Ch1** 10146 cornerd

coroun, croun n. [AF coroune (MP)] monarch's crown; top of the head; tonsure of a cleric; fig.: the realm, royal status **Ch1** 1174, 2743, 6994 croun; 5013, 6888, 7144, 9011, 14923 croune; 3899 coroun; 14946 croune P coroune L; 8966 crowne; 11757 crowne P coroune L; 14916 kroune; **Ch2** 836, 1716, 4898, 6596, 8326 coroun; 399, 1220, 4251, 6079, 8122 coroune; 7646 croune; **HS** 998 corowne; 1447, 5272 crown; 3285, 3478 croune

corounalle n. [AF coronal] circlet, head ornament **Ch1** 9894L corounal (P differs); 11008 corounalle P coronal L

coroune, croune v. [OF coroner] crown a sovereign **Ch1** 3805 coroned; 3898 corounde; 6204, 6546, 8801, 9017 croune; 2234, 5253, 6044, 6392 crouned; 11008 crouned P corouned L; **Ch2** 389, 1376, 1822, 3484 coroune; 4792, 5936 coroun; 817, 1712, 2312, 3441, 5667 corouned

coronyng ger. [from OF coroner] ceremony of coronation **Ch1** 6010 crounyng; 5261L (add, l. 42) coronyng; **Ch2** 2326, 2662 corounyng; 605 crouned P corounyng L; 769 coronment P corounyng L

coronment n. [OF] coronation of a sovereign **Ch1** 6989 corounment; 8808 crounment P coronement L; 14873 corounment P coronement L; 15509, 15531 coronment; **Ch2** 1824, 5719 corounment; 591, 769, 857, 5695 coronment

correie n. [see conrey]

cors n. [OF] a body, corpse **Ch1** 4452L, 15686L cors (om. P); **HS** 945, 983 cors

corsaynt n. [OF cor-seint] saint's body, relic; a holy person **Ch1** 6031 corsayntes P corseynt3 L; 13949 corsayntes; 15942 holy P corseint L; **Ch2** 1028 corsaynt; 7509 corseynt; **HS** 8742 cors seynte; 11094 corseynt; 9231 corsent *O* saynte

cosin n. [OF] relative; kinsman **Ch1** 3913, 6535, 7544 cosin; 1683, 2614, 4706, 8456, 12312 cosyn; 13742 cosyne; 4109 cosyns; 13777, 13992, 15656 kosyn; **Ch2** 78, 1469, 3771, 5863, 6105 cosyn; 1779, 1494, 2528 kosyn; 1264 kosyne; 12, 4701 kosyn P cosyn L; **HS** 9455 cosynes; 9456 cosyne

costage n. [OF] expense, cost, spending **Ch1** 2400, 6624, 6810 costage; 11643 costages; **Ch2** 2775 kostage; 3789, 7086, 7088, 8109 costage

coste, cost n. (1) [OE] way, means; expense **Ch1** 1050 coste P cost L; 6660 coste P costes L

coste, koste n. (2) [OF] shore, coast **Ch1** 1050, 2688, 6183, 8718, 9227 coste; 3253 costes; 1286 costestes (?error) P costes L; 4941 bank P cost L; 7293, 8166 cost; **Ch2** 947 sees koste; 668, 1864, 3936, 6491, 7850 coste; 3603 cite P coste L

costen v. [see keste, cast]

couant, couenant, cunnaunt, conant n./adj. [OF covaunt, covenant] treaty, agreement, promise **Ch1** 2019 conount P couenaunt L; 2383 conant P coueinaunt L; 3045 conant P couenaunt L; 3312 conaunt P couenaunt L; 5188, 5487, 7723, 8885 couenant; 8551 conant; **Ch2** 1705 couenante; 1394 conant P couenant L; 4046, 7088, 7280 conante; 4155, 4602, 4613, 4621, 8280 conant; 7662 conaunte; 6283, 6286 conantȝ; 4867, 5164, 7986 conaunt; 3399, 3498 couant; 2236, 2366, 6251, 6369 couenant; 7831 couenaunt; 8032 couenantȝ; 4624 quite clamance P couenant L; 7413 couent; **HS** 198, 1646, 2362, 4673, 12505 cunnaunt; 2199 cunnaunte *C* connawnt *D* comenaunt; 2458 cunnaunte *C* cunnawt *D* cunnaunte; 3435 couenaunt *O* commanente; 3510 cunniaunt *O* conande; 5504 cumnaunt *O* connande; 5548 cunnaunt *O* conande; 5960 cunnaunt *F* couenauant; 11210 cunnaunt *O* conande; 3234 couenaunt (adj.) GLOSS B semely; 6316 cunnound *O* cownande

coueyte v. [AF coueiter (MP)] to covet, long for **HS** 182 coueytyd *C* desyred; 1106, 1672 coueyte; 2103 desyred *C* ȝernyd *D* coueytid; 2904 coueyte *O* ȝem; 2944 coueyte *O* ȝerne

coueytous adj. [see couetise]

couent n. [OF] convent, monastic group **Ch1** 14647 couent; **Ch2** 2001, 2005, 3020, 5101, 7413 couent; **HS** 3570 couent

couere v. (1) [OF covrir] cover, protect, conceal **Ch1** 7147 couerde; 11399 couere P keuere L; 13543 couere; **Ch2** 3874 couere P socoure L; 4544 couere; **HS** 11518 couered; 12460 couert

couere v. (2) [see recouere] [OE acofrian] to recover **Ch1** 6727, 6818 couer; 8848 couer P couere L; 11399 couere P keuere L; **Ch2** 5792 couere; 7255 couerd; **HS** 10548 couerd

coueryng ger. [from OF covrir] cover, shelter **HS** 9169 coueryng

couetise n./adj. [OF] covetousness, greed **Ch1** 2785 couetise P couetyse L; 2551, 4227 couetise; 4013 couetos; 4489 couettouse; 4516L coueytous (om. P); **Ch2** 824, 1075, 2515, 7023 couetise; 2484 ȝernyng P coueytise L; **HS** 1987, 2912, 4598, 5327, 5341 coueytyse; 5420, 6004 coueytus; 5577, 5976 coueytous

couyn n. [OF covin, covine] confederates, fellows; company **Ch2** 7380 couyn; **HS** 9033 couyne; 3005 couyne GLOSS B cumpany

countas n. [AF] wife of a count or earl **Ch2** 4706 countas

counte n. (1) [see acounte] [AF] valuation **Ch2** 3338 counte

counte n. (2) [AF] territory ruled by a count; a county court **Ch2** 7534 counte; 3244, 7861 countes; **HS** 8915 counte

countre n. [OF acontre] combat, encounter **Ch1** 6508 countre P encountre L; 11489 a countir P encountre L

countre, acountir v. [see encountre] [OF] to meet in battle, attack, charge on **Ch1** 13191 contred P countred L; **Ch2** 871 countred

coupable, culpable adj. [OF coupable] guilty, blameworthy **Ch1** 13527 coupabille P coupable L; **Ch2** 7369 culpable; **HS** 4551, 7331, 8345 coupable; 618 fals tale *D* tale culpable; 1328 coupable *C* cowntabyl *D* culpaple

cours n. [OF cours, cors, L cursus] way, course **Ch2** 4442 cours (?error) P tour L; 5141 cours; **HS** 2529 cours

court n. [OF; AF curt (MP)] court, entourage, body of councilors; the papal Curia **Ch1** 7066 court; 4724, 5254, 6910, 9151, 11168 courte; 15136 kourte; **Ch2** 1478, 5061 court; 7, 1691, 4287, 6500, 8336 courte; 7498 curte; **HS** 1074 curt; 5424 courtes; 6261 courte; 9224, 12116 court

courte, couert n. [from OF covrir, v.] shelter, place of refuge **Ch1** 14385 courte P couert L

couth adj. [see con, conne] [OE cuþ, ppl. of cunnan] well-known, familiar **Ch1** 10177 couth P couþ L; **Ch2** 5778, 7732 couth; **HS** 3067 couth

couward n. [see coward]

coward, cuhard n./adj. [OF co(u)arde] recreant, villain; fool; timid, cowardly **Ch1** 1676 couward; 2814 cuhard P coward L; 3448 cowerde P cowardȝ L; 4459 cowardes; 4971 coward; **Ch2** 2189, 4118 coward; 7438 cowardes; **HS** 12039 coward

cowardyse n. [OF] cowardly behavior **Ch1** 9091L cowardyse (om. P); **HS** 10923 kowardyse

couwee, kowe n. [OF co(u)e, ppl. of co(u)er] tail-rime verse **Ch1** 85, 89 couwee; 88 kowe; **Ch2** [marginal annotations in P, not necessarily in RMB's original:] 6599, 6683, 6710, 6735, 6764, 6813, 8062 couwe

craft n. [OE cræft] skill; trade, occupation; trickery **Ch1** 6937L craft (P differs); 9260 craftes; 13341 crafte P craft L; **Ch2** 6816 craft; **HS** 1202, 3949, 5051, 8255, 10629 craft; 7169 craftes; 12058 crafte

crake v. [OE cracian] to break, crack **Ch1** 5013 crake; **Ch2** 3639 kroken P broken L

craue v. [OE crafian] beg, ask, demand; long for, desire **Ch1** 649, 1274, 7272, 8561 craue; 5985L craue (P differs); **Ch2** 1464, 2202 craue; **HS** 1117, 2823, 5596, 10514, 11802 craue; 7241 kraue

creatour n. [OF] God; fig.: the communion elements **HS** 3874, 10308, 10815 creatour

creature n. [OF] being; a created thing **Ch2** 5218, 6114 creature; **HS** 3779, 11534 creature; 8250, 11531 creatures; 9902, 11317 creatours

credance n. [OF] letter of credence: certifying trust **Ch2** 6227 credance

♦ **crede, krede** n. (1) [?cp. crouden: OE crudan, cread] crowding, thronging **Ch1** 11016 krede

P crede L
crede n. (2) [OE creda] confession of faith **HS** 4247, 9707 crede
credille n. [OE cradol] cradle for a baby **Ch2** 5851 credille
creme n. [OF cresme, OE crisma] baptismal cream; chrism **Ch1** 14620 creme; **HS** 9502 creme
crepe, crept v. [see krepe]
creuesse n. [OF crevace] fissure **Ch1** 13418 creuesse P creuesses L
cry, crie, krie n. [OF cri] shout, call; outcry, noise, tumult; decree, summons **Ch1** 5940, 8398 cri; 4989 crye; 1649, 11702, 13607 crie; 3357, 9644, 15003 crie P cry L; 4290 cry; 6520 kry P cry L; 3840, 7583, 9111 kri; 3758 kri P cry L; **Ch2** 3410, 4451, 5898, 6802, 7168 crie; 5918 cri; 7206 cry; 986 krie; **HS** 709, 1648, 4958, 6669 cry; 10907 crye
cry, crie, krie v. [OF crier] shout, cry out; decree, summon **Ch1** 6520 kry; 7583, 9094 krie; 5365 krie P crie L; 3460, 7141, 8529 crie; 2740, 14217 crie P crye L; 1257, 4329, 5941, 8220, 8368 cried; 14786 cride; 13313 criand P criynge L; **Ch2** 986 krie; 62, 593, 3652, 5127, 6795 crie; 2848, 3412, 4246, 4989 cried; **HS** 333, 1568, 2512 crye; 8314 cryde; 6901 kryyng
criyng ger. [from OF crier] shout, cry; lamenting **Ch1** 8399 criyng; **HS** 2521, 6939 cryyng
crist n. [OE Crist, ult. Gr.] Christ; used in combinations **Ch1** 8599 crist; 185, 5260, 6768, 8369, 10122 criste; **Ch2** 3, 293, 691 criste; 2496 cristes messe P cristemesse L; **HS** 9517 cryst
crystal n. [OF] piece of crystal used for foretelling the future **HS** 353 crystal
cristen adj./n. [OE Cristen] a Christian; pertaining to Christianity **Ch1** 5635, 6767, 7648, 9066, 15304 cristen; 6020, 6769, 8371 cristen men; **Ch2** 294, 518 cristen; **HS** 57 crystyn; 2614 cristen; 5242, 3872 crysten; 869 crystynmen; 4323, 7750 crystenman
cristen v. [OE cristnian] to baptize, christen; give a name **Ch1** 14620 cristned; 6019 cristened; **Ch2** 515 cristend; **HS** 9610 crysten; 9636, 9686 crystene; 9522 crystened
cristendom n. [OE] Christian faith; being baptized; Christianity **Ch1** 5509, 6833 cristendam; 5643, 6771, 7574, 13906, 15297 cristendom; 10120 kristendom; **Ch2** 496, 722 cristendom; 2501, 5576, 5596 cristendam; **HS** 2400 crystyndom; 2748, 5246, 9503, 11714 crystendom; 4661, 8165, 9509 crystendam
cristenyng ger. [cp. OE cristnung] baptism **Ch1** 15278 cristenyng; **HS** 9503 crystenynge; 9662 crystenyng
cristiente n. [OF crestiente] Christian faith; the body of Christians collectively **Ch1** 5637 cristiante; 9021 cristiente; **Ch2** 4769 cristiente; **HS** 232 crystyanyte; 11244, 11712 crystyante
croice, croys n. [OF crois] cross for crucifixion; gibbet; sign of the cross **Ch1** 8804 kroces P croces L; 14393 croyce; 14450, 15403 croice; 15393, 15395 croys; **Ch2** 1906, 5094, 5755, 8091 croice; **HS** 3869, 3880, 4759 cros; 7752 croys; 7491, 7871 croyce; 7850 crouche
croised v. [OF croisier] to make the sign of the cross **Ch2** 5559 croised
croiserie n. [OF] crusade, expedition **Ch2** 7835 croiserie; 3327 tresorie P croisery L
croke, kroke n. [OF crok, ON krokr] crook, hook, prong **Ch1** 1812 krokes P crokes L; **Ch2** 4213 crokes; **HS** 1473 crokys *C* hokys; 2515 crokes *D* hokys; 2525 croke *D* hook; 2527 kroke *D* hook
croked adj. [OE crocod] crooked, crippled **Ch1** 15131 croked
croket n. [AF] an ornamental curl of hair **HS** 3207 croket GLOSS BH a chapelet
cronykles n. [see kronykles]
croppe n. [OE crop, croppa] fig.: entirely, the entire plant **HS** 9809 croppe & rote
crote n. [prob. Scand.; cp. Norw. dial. krota] a bit, residue, clod **Ch1** 2096 ilk a crote; **HS** 2602 eury grote *O* ylke crotte
croun n. [see coroun]
croupe n. [OF crupe, croupe] rump, haunches of an animal **Ch2** 4720 croupe
crowe v. [OE crawan] cock's crow **Ch2** 2986 crowe; **HS** 7278 crowe
crucifix n. [AF] a painting or image of Christ crucified **Ch1** 14452 crucifix; **HS** 3879, 3882, 3885, 3890 crucyfyx
cruelle adj. [OF cruel] pitiless; austere, stern; fierce **Ch1** 4777 cruelle; 5119 ouer cruele P cruel L; **Ch2** 1036 cruelle
cruelte n. [OF] heartlessness **Ch1** 5129 cruelte; **Ch2** 1922 crueltes; **HS** 1462 *D* cruelte (B differs)
◆ **crusse** n. [from OF croissir, v.] crash; a shattering, crushing **Ch1** 2918 crusse P crusche L; 4612 crusse
cuhard n./adj. [see coward]
cumbraunce n. [see encumbraunce]
cuntek n. [see contek]
cuntre n. [see contre]
cuppe n. [see cop]
curs n. [OE] a curse, malediction **HS** 6139 curs
curse, kurse v. [see banne, warye] [OE cursian] to curse, condemn; utter a malediction; (ppl.:) wretched **Ch1** 6818 cursed; **Ch2** 428, 3028, 4913, 5174, 7907 cursed; **HS** 9090 cursed; 9122 cursedest; 1244 kurse *C* banne *D* waryen; 1248 cursyþ *C* bannyth; 1288 waryyþ *C* bannyth; 1290 waryyþ *C* acursed *D* warye; 2029 cursyd *C* cursed *D* acursyd; 3760 curse *O* ban; 3763

curse *O* ware; 7972 kurse *O* wery
cursednes, kursednes n. [from OE curs] misfortune; evil fate **HS** 3476 cursydnes; 7228 kursednes *H* cursednes *O* werydnes
cursers, kurserys n. [from OE curs] those who curse **HS** 1297 kurserys *D* waryerys *H* cursers
cursyng ger. [from OE cursian] condemnation; excommunication **Ch2** 3029, 3611, 5153, 6879, 7080 cursyng; **HS** 1251 cursyng *CD* bannyng; 1268 kursynge *D* waryed; 1286 waryyng GLOSS B cursyng *F* cursyng; 1300 kursyng *D* waryyng; 1304 kursyngge *C* bannyng *D* waryyng; 6552 cursyng *O* cursynge
curtays, curteis adj. [AF curteis (MP)] with courtly or refined manners; gracious, considerate **Ch1** 4096, 7081 curtais; 5634 curtays; 7122 curteis; 9167 curtaise; 11351 curteise; 7569L curteys (P differs); **Ch2** 558, 2785, 3802, 5549, 7953 curteis; 3719, 4047 curteise; 4687, 5527, 5705, 5857, 7486 curteys; **HS** 590, 6838, 7076, 7181, 11296 curteys; 8634 kurteys
curtaisly, curteisly adv. [from AF curteis] graciously, considerately, kindly **Ch1** 3125, 3629, 5288 curtasly; 6782 curtaisly; 12142 curteisy P worschipfully L; **Ch2** 3545 curteyly P curtesly L; 3747 curteisly; 4082, 7328 curteislie; 7475 curtasly; **HS** 6829, 7077 curteysly
curtasie, curteysie n. [AF curteisie] courtesy, kindness **Ch1** 495 curtasye; 2290, 2678 curtasie; 2476 curtasy; 3093 curtasi; **Ch2** 252, 1678, 4167, 6154, 7382 curteisie; 3406, 6422, 7665 curteysie; **HS** 2661 curtesye; 5862, 10780 curteysy; 5058, 6080, 6828 curteysye
curtene v. [OF curtiner] surround with curtains; conceal or hide **Ch1** 641 curtene P cortine L
curtynes n. [AF curtines (MP)] curtains to set off an altar **HS** 9345 curtynes *O* courchyffes
custom, custum n. [OF] traditional practice; customary rent or service; habit **Ch1** 457 custom P custume L; 4695, 7467, 11053 custom; 6548 custon P custume L; 7315 custome; **Ch2** 2678 costom P custume L; 3582, 4159 custom; **HS** 849, 932, 3872 custum; 464, 2369, 7605 custome
customer adj. [OF coustumier] be accustomed, be in the habit **HS** 8809 customer
custummable adj./adv. [OF] customary, regularly; habitually **HS** 3768, 4416, 3543, 3501 custummable; 2668 comunly *C* custamablye; 3513 custummable *O* customably
cutt v. [see carfe, karf]

D

day n. [see dawe]
dales n. [OE dalu, dæl; ON dal-r] valley, glen, dell **Ch1** 6153, 8462 dounes & dales; **Ch2** 2233 bi dounes & bi dales
dalf v. [OE delfan, dalf] dig a hole or ditch **Ch1** 13947 dalf; **HS** 11089 dalf
damage n. [AF dammage (MP)] injury, loss **Ch1** 4510 damage; **HS** 5796 dammage
dame n. [OF dame, L domina] a lady, woman of rank; a title **Ch1** 291, 372, 515 dam; 14506 dam . . . dame; 366, 1959, 3676, 5550, 9398 dame; **Ch2** 1815, 2324, 2993, 3671 dam; 781, 2390, 4915, 6120, 7474 dame; **HS** 519, 4598, 4607 dame
damyselle n. [AF dameisele] a maiden; an unmarried woman **Ch1** 763 damyselle; 6444 douhtres P damysels L; **Ch2** 8114 damyselle
dampnable, damnable adj. [AF dampnable (MP)] blameworthy, reprehensible **HS** 3767 damnable; 8346 dampnable; 12094 dampnale
dampnacion n. [OF] condemnation, consignment to perdition **Ch1** 13796 dampnacion; **HS** 214 damnacyun; 5236, 5250, 11432 dampnacyoun; 10163 dampnacoun
dampne v. [AF dampner (MP)] condemn, blame, censure **Ch1** 4731, 5093 dampne; **HS** 1342 dampne; 3423 damned; 5681, 12541 dampned; 7224 dampneþ
dangere, daungere n. [AF daunger] control, possession; risk, peril **Ch1** 2420 dangere; **Ch2** 180 daungere; 2099, 5348 dangere; 3630L dangere (om. P)
dangilde, danesgilde n. [see gild] [ON] land tax levied by the Norman kings **Ch2** 1392 dangilde; 1396 danesgilde; 2675 danegelde
dar, dur, durst v. (1) [see þar] [OE durran, dear, dorste] to dare, venture; be under obligation or necessity **Ch1** 1127, 4781, 7394, 9114 dar; 2804, 5126 dare; 9725 dar P dur L; 1550 durst P dirste L; 2857, 3530, 6990, 8828, 14097 durst; 11980 durste; 3755 durst P durste L; 11284 dur; **Ch2** 1781, 4798, 5287, 6818 dar; 7921 dare; 8036 dur; 689, 1299, 3432, 7042, 8166 durst; **HS** 1399, 4325, 8387, 11642, 12392 dar; 832, 7649, 8276 dur; 1277, 3814 durste; 7852 durst; 2249 darst þou *C* þe thar *D* þar þe
dar, dur, durst v. (2) [OF durer, L durare] to last, endure, survive **Ch1** 6189 dur; 6624 suffre P endure L; 7236 þorgh P dur L; 8617 doure P dure L; 3245 dured P durede L; 5734 dured; 13645 dure; **Ch2** 905 lasted P dured L; 1743 dure; 5577 dured; **HS** 6529, 7190, 7197 dure; 2208 dure *D* endure
darte n. [OF dart] javelin or spear; metal-pointed missile **Ch1** 1765, 1788 darte; 2927, 3001, 3411, 4990, 6729 dartes; 11716L dartes (om. P); **Ch2** 4424 darte; 7233 dartes
date n. [L datum] a point in time; date of a document; historical date **Ch1** 185, 1744, 5692, 6032, 6410 date; **Ch2** 385, 709, 2654, 5929, 8329 date; 3481 dete P date L
daþet exclamation [OF dahait, de(s)hait] used in imprecations and curses **Ch2** 2315 daþet P þat

L; 3512 daþet P dared L; 4144, 5842 daþet

daunce n. [AF dance (MP)] a dance; group of dancers **HS** 4695, 9126, 9219 daunce; 4685 daunces

daunce v. [OF dancer, danser] to dance **HS** 9011 daunce; 9064, 9079 daunsed

daungere n. [see dangere]

daungerous adj. [AF dangerus (MP)] domineering, overbearing **HS** 7249, 8624 daungerous

daunte v. [AF danter (MP)] subdue, defeat; intimidate; fondle or caress **Ch1** 4487 daunte P adaunte L; **HS** 2960, 8118, 8423 daunte; 4880 dauntede

dawe, day n. [OE dæg, dagas] day; phrase: o dawe = kill **Ch1** 1210, 3269, 5274, 6914, 8803 day; 1311, 2955, 5080, 6167 days; 457, 3086, 3570 dawes; 1845, 13918 o dawe; 8510, 12394 of dawe; 2787 be old dawe; 3680 be þat dawe; 8502 drawen P brought of dawe L; 8510 of dawe P to drawe L; 3086 ȝeris & dawes; 5202 haf gode day; 1410 daies; 8590 dayes; **Ch2** 49, 740, 3701, 4890, 6933 day; 6249, 6668, 7897, 7909 days; 1623, 2380, 2475, 5414 dayes; 4162 dawes; **HS** 89, 95, 1145, 4150 day; 3250 days; 10208 dayes; 10485 haue gode day; 1035 o dawe GLOSS B to þe deþ; 1070 doun o dawe *C* don of dawe *D* be slawe; 2124 to dawe; 2172 o dawe; 4110 adawe

debate n. [OF debat] quarrel, dispute **HS** 2700 cuntek GLOSS BH debate; 4140 vnsaght GLOSS B at debate

debonurere adj. [OF debonaire, deboneire] kind, courteous **HS** 5800 debonurere *H* dubonure

deceyue v. [see deseyue]

deces, decesse n. [see deses]

decre n. [OF decree] a papal decree, command **Ch2** 2999, 7692 decre; **HS** 4641, 7379, 8721 decre

decretal n. [L and OF] a papal decree **Ch2** 8257 decretal

ded, dede, deth n. (1) [OE deþ] death; a dead man **Ch1** 1524, 1701, 4809 dede P ded L; 2979 dede P deþe L; 217, 261 deth; 2031, 4638, 4852, 5198, 6095 ded; 796, 1946, 3500, 6481, 9250 dede; 3424, 3895, 4404, 6007, 8120 dede P deþ L; **Ch2** 170, 1576, 2265, 5430, 7434 dede; 2477, 3033 ded; 832 dede P deþ L; **HS** 949, 1215 ded; 1316, 1373, 1524, 3660 deþ; 1704 ded GLOSS B deþ; 2053 ded GLOSS BH deþ; 2333 ded *C* gost; 9920 deþ *O* dede *SV* deþ; 2349 ded knyght *C* gost

dede n. (2) [OE ded] deed, action **Ch1** 1867, 2844, 4500, 6927, 8975 dede; 21, 66, 3119, 9293 dedes; 193, 3203, 8292, 10406, 15654 dedis; **Ch2** 2875, 4118, 5576, 7810, 8303 dede; 2783, 5020, 5957, 6809, 8287 dedes; **HS** 90, 1479, 4444, 7412, 12442 dede

ded, dede adj. [OE dead] dead **Ch1** 1843, 3583, 5694, 9391, 15540 dede; 2713 ded P dede L; 5702, 6987 ded; 1524, 9491, 12541 dede P ded L; **Ch2** 1622, 2486, 3443, 5635, 7449 dede; 5144 ded; **HS** 537, 2228, 9205, 10363, 11735 ded

dedly, dedely adj./adv. [OE deadlice] as if dead, like death; mortally **Ch1** 2642 dedely P dedlyk L; 13452 dedely; **Ch2** 734 dedely; **HS** 27, 1640, 4243, 8359, 11539 dedly

def and doumbe adj. [OE deaf, dumb] unable to hear or speak **HS** 5907 def and doumbe

defly adv. [from OE deaf] refusing to hear; not listening **Ch1** 5179 defly P deflike L

defaute n. [OF] failure; sin, neglect **Ch1** 1061 defaut; 5056, 5093, 9333, 15663 defaute; **Ch2** 272, 1423, 3630, 6644, 7103 defaute; 2685, 4296, 4533, 7202 defaut; **HS** 404, 3741, 4828, 5395, 11762 defaute; 9654 defaute *O* vnkonnynge

defend v. [OF defenser] to defend, forbid, protect; to fortify **Ch1** 924, 7831 defende; 2890, 3521, 4320, 6689, 8297 defend; 4354 defend P fende L; 4833 defended; 5526 defended P fended L; 2465, 9914, 11814, 12396, 13257 defendid; 9057 fendid P defended L; **Ch2** 33, 864, 996, 1983, 8036 defend; 6200, 6957, 7289 defende; 2766, 5522 defendid; 4410, 5172, 5877, 6394, 7393 defendes; **HS** 3753 defendyng; 6570, 8229 defendeþ; 8721 defended; 12349 defendest; 11282, 11485 defende

defens n. [OF] defending by fighting; resistance; fortification **Ch1** 6124, 9214 defens; **HS** 11105, 11156 defens

defensable adj. [OF] ready to fight **Ch1** 3471 defensables; 12206, 15192 defensable

defie, deffie v. [see diffie]

defoule v. [OF defoler] violate, rape **Ch2** 7749 defoules; **HS** 7638 defouled

degyse, doguise adj. [see desguise, v.] [OF desguise] strangely dressed **Ch1** 14171 diuers P degyse L; **Ch2** 7258 doguise

degre n. [see gre] [OF] step, platform; rank, social condition **Ch1** 410 degre; **Ch2** 1328 degre; **HS** 7556, 7689, 8878, 10063, 11602 degre

deye, die v. [ON] to die **Ch1** 846, 6083 died P deide L; 847 deied P deide L; 6490, 8360, 9245, 10847 die; 2686 dey P deye L; 3701 die P deyde L; 3772 deid; 9002 deied; 8094 diede; 1078, 3504, 5970, 7018, 8848 deie; 4750, 5251, 5780 died; 5087 die P deye L; 8120 dye P deye L; 15590 deie P deye L; **Ch2** 213, 1038, 3104, 5420, 7238 die; 784, 3930, 5708, 6203, 7997 deie; 4714 dey; 67, 1283, 3093, 6712, 8334 died; **HS** 768, 3168, 12032 deye; 6222, 9207 deyde; 2194 deye *C* qwelle

deignouse adj. [from OF desdeigne] disdainful **Ch2** 7015 deignouse

deih, degh v. [OE deih, deȝh, dought] be strong, capable, courageous **Ch1** 1566, 3787, 5011 deih; 7440 dought; 8410 douht P dought L; 13668 douht P doughte L; **Ch2** 3267 deih P dowȝtty L; 3948, 7247 deih; 7446 degh

deyne v. [see deme] [OF deignier] consider, condescend to speak **Ch1** 5517 deyned P dedeyned L; **HS** 6785 deyneþ *F* demeþ *O* domes

◆ **deynoushede** n. [from OF desdeigne] arrogance **Ch2** 3167 deynoushede

dekene n. [see ersdeken, subdekene] [OE deacon, AF dekene (MP)] a deacon **HS** 1051, 8843, 8879, 9269, 11016 dekene

delay n. [OF] postponement; pause in a battle; stop in a journey **Ch2** 6655, 7483, 7541 delay; 6130 delayes; **HS** 5353, 6899, 11789 delay

delay v. [OF delaier] postpone; obstruct, prevent; procrastinate **Ch1** 9458 deleyd P delayed L; 15198 delaied; **Ch2** 6044, 6348 delayed; 4962, 7684, 7728 delaied; **HS** 196 delayde; 6994 delayed

dele, deyl n. [OE dæl] division, part, share; amount, degree, extent **Ch1** 3406, 4778 dele; 176, 1271, 5305, 7120, 8984 ilka dele; 4059, 5348, 6253, 8209 ilk dele; 6934, 7016 som dele; 1454, 3606, 4778 neuer a dele; **Ch2** 1352, 6320, 7652 dele; 878, 2104, 3752, 5867, 7522 ilka dele; 628, 1824, 4086, 6270, 6513 ilk dele; 3055 som dele; 1942 eueridele; **HS** 1438 adeyl; 2119, 3276, 12628 ychedeyl; 5748 ychedel; 7881 echedeil; 11550 echedeyl; 116 euerydeyl; 1226 euerydel; 4476 eurydele; 7061, 9948, 12244 eurydeyl; 3237, 4377, 10348, 11893 sumdeyl; 7265 sumdele

dele v. [OE dælan] to share, distribute; to part, divide; distinguish; to act, behave **Ch1** 4798, 6443 dele; 11618 deilde P deled L; **Ch2** 3821, 5213, 6736, 7303 dele; 2635, 2742 deles; 3111 deled; **HS** 238, 3374, 5228, 6343 dele; 6953, 7008 delt

delectabyl adj. [see delytable]

delycyus adj. [OF] delightful, choice **HS** 4604, 6640 delycyus

delycyuslye adv. [from adj.] luxuriously **HS** 6618 delycyuslye

delyt v. [OF delitier] be delighted, have pleasure in **HS** 2664 delyt yn *O* ioy of; 2654, 3085, 3431, 7222, 12536 delyte; 8129 delyteþ

delytable adj. [OF] delightful, pleasant **HS** 1398 delytable *C* delectabyl *D* delectable

delite n. [OF] delicacy, luxury **Ch1** 9185 sightes P delites L; **HS** 2659, 3139 delyt; 10144, 12555 delyte

delyuer v. [OF delivrer] to save, give relief to **Ch1** 2985 delyuer P deliuere L; 4789, 8249, 8568 delyuer; 5605 deliuer; 5864 delyuere; 6594 deliuerd; **Ch2** 701 delyuerde; 1697, 1704, 3188, 3926 delyuer; 3709, 3711, 3915 deliuer; 3913 deliuere; 5418, 7376 deliuerd; 5941 delyuerd; **HS** 2284, 11237 delyure; 8282 delyuer; 10414 delyuerd

deliuerance n. [OF] being freed, escape **Ch2** 2969 delyuerance; 3922, 4928, 6986, 7320 deliuerance

deme v. [OE deman] judge, condemn; rule **Ch1** 8477, 15737 deme; 154, 4852 demed; **Ch2** 2671, 4931, 6539, 7664, 8301 deme; 6786, 7668, 8029, 8248 demed; **HS** 145, 1497, 1500 deme; 9433 demed; 1490 deme *CD* demyn; 10220 (B differs) *V* couþe þenne deme; 6785 deyneþ *F* demeþ *O* domes

demeyne n. [OF demaine, demeigne] possession, territory; control, rule **Ch1** 3544, 6376, 7585 demeyns; 6085 demeyn P demayne L; 7422 demeins P demaynes L; 3186 demeyns P (L differs); 4671 demeyns P demeynes L; 12287 demeyng (error) P demeynes L; **Ch2** 112 demeyns; 8084 demeyne

demene v. [OF demener] manage, control **Ch1** 2190 demene P demeyne L

demyng ger. [from OE deman] judgment, trial **Ch1** 8490 endyng P demyng L; 12287 demeyng (error) P demeynes L; **Ch2** 2114 demyng; **HS** 1496 demyngge *C* dom

demones n. [ML demon, dæmon (ult. Gr.)] evil spirit; incubus **Ch1** 7974 demones

◆ **demple** v. [prob. error for camplen] to fight, wrangle **Ch2** 4866 to demple P comple L

dented v. [see dynt, n.] [from OE dynt, n.] strike blows **Ch2** 1767 bare down P dented L

departe v. [see partid] [OF departir] divide, estrange **Ch1** 2276, 4476, 5037, 15363 departe; 2323 departe P depart L; 4744 departed P parted L; 7110 departe P parte L; 222, 230, 1598, 3886, 6998 departid; 383, 1310, 2055, 3389 departed; 7524 depart P departed L; **Ch2** 4476, 7234 departe; 1240, 5948 departed; **HS** 3371 departede; 6226, 11396, 11560 departed; 1832 departyd

departyng ger. [from OF departir] departure **Ch2** 1154 sauhtillyng P departyng L; **HS** 9393 departyng

depe adj. [OE deop] having depth, at a depth **Ch1** 1175, 1786, 2062, 8035 depe; 6468 deppest; **Ch2** 632, 2471, 3639, 4536 depe; 1295, 3964 deppest; **HS** 1387, 5260 depe

depeynt ppl. [OF depeindre, depeint, ppl.] portrayed, painted **HS** 8741 depeynte; 11093 depeynt

depnes n. [OE deopnes] depth, deep water; the sea **Ch1** 10148 depnes; **Ch2** 5790 depnes; **HS** 2487 depnesse

depriued v. [ML & OF] exclude from; depose **Ch2** 5442, 6156 depriued

dere n. (1) [OE deor] wild animals, deer **Ch1**

1506, 2789, 2791, 10838 dere; 6342 deere; 2794 dere P der L; **Ch2** 2671 dere

dere n. (2) [OE daru, *dearu] harm, injury, difficulty **Ch1** 2789, 8789, 11827, 15663, 15689 dere; **Ch2** 936L derre (P differs); 133, 1570 dere; **HS** 4105, 9158 dere; 719 greuusnesse *C* dere *D* care & dred; 1769 dere *C* dred *D* dere

dere v. [OE derian] to harm, injure **Ch1** 6803, 7552, 8765, 8789 dere; 4586 dered; 7853 deres; **Ch2** 4662 dere; **HS** 2759 deryþ; 7162, 7639 dereþ; 1804 dere GLOSS BH desese; 2638 dere GLOSS B harme; 3529 deres GLOSS B harmyþ

dere adj./adv. [OE deore] precious, beloved; costly **Ch1** 1228, 3127, 5200, 6637, 9323 dere; **Ch2** 785, 1019, 4592, 7664, 8296 dere; **HS** 336, 1787, 3909, 6596, 9320 dere; 2450 fuldere; 3838 ful dere *O* full sare

dereyne v. [OF derainier] challenge, fight, claim **Ch1** 4208 dereyn P dereyne L; 12226 derayne P dereyne L; 12297 dereynt; **Ch2** 8083 dereyne

derk n. [from OE deorc, adj.] darkness, murk **HS** 2164 myrk GLOSS BH derk

derk adj. [OE deorc] threatening weather **Ch1** 6471 myrk P derk L

derlyng n. [OE deorling] beloved person **Ch2** 1196 derlyng

derwrþely adj./adv. [OE deorwyrþe] worthy, excellent, splendid **HS** 5077 derwrþely *F* derworþli *H* derwrþly *O* dere worthy hede; 11288 derwrþely *F* derworli *H* derwurly *O* dere worthely

des, deeȝ n. (1) [OF de, dis, dice] dice **Ch1** 11150, 11332 deeȝ P des L; **HS** 1043 *C* dyse (B differs)

des, dese n. (2) [AF deis] dais, raised platform **Ch1** 9159 des P dees L; 11195, 11061 des; **Ch2** 1493, 5129 des; 4558 des P deys L; **HS** 9389 des; 6620 dese GLOSS H on table

desceyuance n. [AF] treacherous action, lying, trickery **Ch2** 3251 desceyuance P distance L; 3848, 4826, 6124, 6406 disceyuance

desceit, disceit n. [AF] treachery, lying **Ch1** 1024 desceyt; 2880, 7014 desceite; 4996 disceite P deseit L; 5717 fehtes P deseites L; 5979, 9281, 10596 disceite; 6911 sleiht P deseit L; 7014 desceite P deseyte L; 8454 desceite P deseit L; 12632 desceit PR deseite L; 12771 descent P deseit L; **Ch2** 712, 828, 1213 desceit; 1952, 5255, 5594, 5811, 7392 disceit; 2899, 3398, 5826, 6321, 7149 disceite; 4374 desceyt; **HS** 3815, 12500 deseyt

descend v. [OF descend-re] fall; inherit **Ch1** 6679 descend P desende L; **Ch2** 3281, 6541 descend

descent n. [OF] lineal descendant; lineage **Ch1** 12771 descent; **Ch2** 5050, 5870, 6021, 6036 descent

desdeyn, disdeyn, dudeyn n./v. [OF desdeigne, desdeignier] being scornful, contemptuous **Ch1** 2316, 14680 desdeyn; 4224, 5182, 5710 disdeyn; 5517 deyned P dedeyned L; 9452 dudeyn P dedeyn L

deseyuable adj. [AF] deceptive **HS** 472 deseyuable

deseyue, deceyue v. [AF decevoir] be false to; cheat, rob **Ch1** 2710, 13110 disceyue; 5348 desceyued; **Ch2** 5326 disceyued; 7802 desceyued; **HS** 414 deseyue; 469 deseyuyþ; 2650 deseyue *C* dysteyne *D* disceyue *O* dyssafe; 12053 deseyued; 12607 deceyued

desert n. (1) [OF] deserving; merit; worthiness **Ch2** 7725 discert; **HS** 3335, 6681 desert

desert n. (2) [OF] wilderness **HS** 7905 desert

deserue v. [OF deservir, L deservire] to be worthy **Ch1** 7366L deserue (P differs)

deses, deces n. [see dysese, n.] [OF deces] death; an end **Ch1** 3950, 13810 deces; 3694 deses P deces L; 7553 decese P deses L; **Ch2** 249 decesse P deses L; 3099 dises; 3104 deses; 6135 desces

desese v. [from OF deces, n.] to harm **HS** 1804 dere GLOSS BH desese

desgyse, dysgyse v. [see deguyse, adj.] [OF desguiser] dress strangely **Ch1** 4697 in þer quantise P hem desgysede L; **HS** 3323 dysgyse; 3330 dysgysed; 3398 dysgyse *O* dysgysythe

desherite, disherite v. [OF desheiter] to dispossess, deprive **Ch1** 5305 disherite P deserite L; 5834 disherited P desired L; 14975 disherite; **Ch2** 4057, 4944, 5306, 5772 disherite; 6421 desherite; 6198 disherites; 5455, 6196 disherited

desheriteson, disherison n. [OF desheritaison] deprivation of land or privileges; despoiling of lands **Ch1** 3211 disheriteson P desherytysoun L; 10225 disherison P desheritison L; **Ch2** 5248, 7058 disheriteson; 5758 disheritsoun; **HS** 4383 desherysun; 5364 dyserytsun *F* deseritsun *H* dysheresun

desire n. [OF] yearning; wish; passion, lust **Ch1** 2904, 3039, 7842, 8121 desire; 8421L desir (P differs); **HS** 3409, 3453, 7618, 7995 desyre

desire v. [AF desirer (MP)] wish or want; yearn **Ch1** 8633 desire; 4809, 9168, 14250 desired; **Ch2** 981, 3646 desired; 3530 desires; **HS** 1451 desyrede; 2103, 7614 desyred; 2682 desyreþ

desyryng ger. [from verb] wishing, craving **HS** 5333 desyryng

despise v. [from OF despisier] have contempt for **Ch1** 7518 dispisid P despised L; 11563 dispise; 14693 despised; 14693L despise (om. P); **HS** 3319, 11672, 12569 despyse

despite, dispite n. [OF despit] insult, contempt,

scorn; offended pride **Ch1** 498 despyte; 703, 2046, 2050 dispite; 2317, 3428 despite; 8733L despit (om. P); **Ch2** 1273, 2512, 4618, 5159, 8187 despite; **HS** 3051, 6558, 6783, 6949 despyt; 8567 despyte

destorbe, desturble v. [OF destorbler] frighten, stir up **Ch1** 1100 desturble; 3311 destorbled P letted L; **Ch2** 3914 destorbe; 5703 desturbled; **HS** 9006 dysturble; 4735 dysturblede; 1214 desturblyst *D* lett; 1713 desturble *C* strobyll; 1725 desturble *C* distrobyll *D* stourblyst; 1876 dysturble *C* strobyll *D* distourble; 4717 sturbled *O* dystrubyd; 4735 dysturblede *O* distrubyd; 11068 dystourbleþ

destrere n. [OF destrier] war horse **Ch2** 3033 destrere

destresse n. [see stresse] [OF destresce] anxiety or hardship; compulsion **Ch1** 3320 stresse P destresse L; 3444 stresse P destres L; 9923 destresse; 11973 destrisse; **Ch2** 627 stresse P destresse L; 4625 destresse; 6318 destres; **HS** 2908, 6556, 7316 destresse

destroy v. [OF destruire] ravage, devastate **Ch1** 706 destroye; 718, 786, 3294, 9239 destroyed; 5420 destroyed P destruyed L; 1506, 4762 destroie; 8158 distroye; 6767 distroies; 3743 distroid; 2571, 4841, 7568 destroied; 13806 distroied; 15400 destroies; 4192 destroied P destruyed L; **Ch2** 1539, 2772, 5575, 5956, 8126 destroie; 1029 destoye P destroie L; 1011 reymed P destrued L; 6751 destroye; 988L destrue (om. P); 130, 1930, 3435, 7412, 8238 destroied; 1966 destroied P destrued L; 4566, 5167 destroyed; **HS** 917 destroyd; 1856 dystroye; 4758 destruye; 8079 stroye

destruction, distructioun n. [OF and L] devastation, ruin **Ch1** 339 destruction; 439 destructon P destructione L; 3212 destruccion P destruccioun L; **Ch2** 404L destruccioun (om. P); 4948 destruccion; 7886 distructioun

deth, death n. [see ded, dede, n.]

dette n. [OF] something owed in goods, money, tribute; an obligation **Ch2** 2423, 6306, 6884, 6897 dette; 5969 dettes; **HS** 6244 dette

deuel n./adj. [OE deofol] Satan; demon, evil spirit, fiend **Ch1** 2138 deueles P þeues L; 11324 deuel; 13999 deuele; **Ch2** 681, 1000, 3027, 3051, 6821 deuelle; 4059 deuel; 4139 dele P deuel L; **HS** 216, 1735, 12585 deuyl; 2455, 6041, 11868 deuel; 6200 deueles; 767 deuylweye *C* ful harde weye; 9674, 11081 deuel weye

deuere n. [AF dever] duty; doing one's duty **Ch2** 1753, 4599, 4738, 5465, 8102 deuere

deuyn, diuinour n. [OF devin, devinour] a prophet, philosopher; theology, prophecy, divining **Ch1** 5262, 15000 deuyn P deuin L; 6773 deuyns P deuynes L; 7978, 8029 deuyne P deuyn L; 7993 diuinours P dyuinours L; **Ch2** 6837 deuyn; **HS** 2788 deuyne; 11418 deuyn

deuyne v. [OF deviner] to plot **Ch1** 8046 deuyned P diuined L

deuys n. [OF devis, devise] intent, desire; design **Ch1** 224, 545, 610 deuys P deuis L; 311 dyuise; 1283 deuyse P deuise L; 3792 deuise P deuis L; 7723 deuis; **Ch2** 4137, 4403 deuys; 4868 deuise; **HS** 11792 deuys

deuyse v. [OF deviser] observe, spy out, make ready **Ch1** 8620 deuyse P diuise L; 14224 deuysed P deuisede L; **Ch2** 500 deuised; 4666 deuise; **HS** 9518, 9540 deuysed

deuocioun n. [L and OF] piety; awe, reverence, prayer; worship **Ch2** 1808, 2499, 7902, 8342 deuocioun; 4008 douocioun P deuocion L; **HS** 4736, 5309, 10412 deuocyoun; 8514, 9008, 12185 deuocyun

deuoutely, deuowt adv./adj. [OF] reverent; pious; faithfully **HS** 4719, 11257 deuoutely; 10720 deuowt

deus exclamation [OF dieu, L deus] Oh, God! **Ch2** 6142 deus

dyffamacyun n. [OF difamacion] evil report **HS** 7428 dyffamacyun

diffame v. [OF difamer] dishonor, speak evil; disgrace **Ch2** 7840 diffamed; **HS** 6572 dyffamed; 8307 dyffame; 11642 dyffamest

diffie, deffie v. [AF deffier] reject; challenge, denounce **Ch1** 5880 deffie P defye L; **Ch2** 1097 diffies; 1455 diffied P sette not by L; 2356, 4816 diffie; 5321 defie

dight v. [OE dihtan, dihte] prepare; adorn, equip; rule **Ch1** 613, 2193, 4495, 6462, 13011 dight; 2030 dightes P dightest L; 4542 dighted; 4957 dyght; **Ch2** 34, 952, 4954, 6350, 8159 dight; 1841 dyght; 501, 1281 dightes; 4422L dyȝtte (om. P); **HS** 947 dight; 1404, 9020, 12011 dyght; 3294, 6319 dyghte; 742 ydyght *CD* dyȝt; 1413 cast wyþ *D* dyȝt with; 3188 ydyt GLOSS BH stopped *O* es dytte

digne adj. [OF digne, L dignus] worthy, suitable **Ch1** 1342 digne P dygne L; **Ch2** 4050 digne; **HS** 3903, 5718 dygne; 1584 dygne GLOSS B wrþ; 9904 wrþy *SV* digne; 11995 weyl *O* dygnely

dignite n. [OF] worth, esteem; rank **Ch1** 2750 dignyte; 6119, 6407 dignite; 14472 dignite P dignete L; **Ch2** 1821, 3156, 5044, 6596, 8088 dignite; 3593 dignites; 5170, 7888 digniteȝ; **HS** 3401, 3935, 10966, 11128 dygnyte

dike n. [OE and ON] trench, ditch; fosse or wall **Ch1** 1047 dyke P dyk L; 1716 dykes; 5736 dike P dik L; 6597, 6736, 8224 dike; **Ch2** 6715, 6572 dike; 4299, 4313, 4365, 4535, 4651 dikes; 4316 dikes P diches L

dike v. [OE dician] dig a ditch **Ch2** 6597, 6605

dike; 6599 dikit; 6600 dikes

dymynucyun n. [L; AF diminuciun (MP)] lessening of sin **HS** 12422 dymynucyun

dyn n. [see dunede, v.] [OE dyne] loud noise; clamor **Ch1** 9777 dyn P dene L; 11307 dynne

dyne v. [AF diner (MP)] to eat, dine **HS** 7311 dyne

dyner n. [OF] a meal **Ch2** 8162 dynere; **HS** 4302, 4309, 7322 dyner; 7294, 7295 dyners

dynt n. [OE dynt] blow of a weapon; stroke; shot of a bow **Ch1** 1007, 4638, 9964, 12381, 15623 dynt; 7788 dint; 10752 dynt P dint L; 7786 dintis; 4832, 8429 dyntes; **Ch2** 178, 466, 1749, 4721, 8312 dynt; 6736 dyntis; 493 dyntes; 4564 douhtynes P dyntes L; 1225L dent (om. P)

diocise n. [ML; OF diocise] a bishop's diocese **Ch1** 5680 diocise P dyocise L

disceyue v. [see desceiue]

discert n. [see desert, n. (1)]

discharged v. [OF deschargier] free from an oath **Ch2** 7659 discharged

dyscyples n. [OE discipul; OF desciple] disciple of Christ; follower **HS** 857 dyscyplys; 4082 dyscyples

discomfort, discomfeture n. [OF desconfiture] defeat; cause of defeat **Ch1** 1001 discomfite P desconfit L; 1016, 2929, 4456 discomfite; 5593 discomfeture P disconfiture L; 1607 discomfite had P desconfyted (v.) L; 8488 discomfeture; 9134 discomfite; 13646 disconfeture P at desconfiture L; **Ch2** 538L [Havelok interpolation, ll. 8, 77] desconfit; 43, 152, 2882, 4991, 5330 disconfite; 459 discomfite

discomfite, disconfite v. [OF desconfit, desconforter] defeat, rout; be dismayed, discouraged **Ch1** 2096 discomfet P destruyed L; 7319 discounfet; 5877, 9115 discomfet; **Ch2** 1740 discomfort; 5324 disconfited; 2791, 7230 disconfite; 7004 disconfet; **HS** 4982 scumfyghte *F* scunfiȝte *O* discomfyte; 4986 dyscumfyte

discord v. [OF descorder] disagree, quarrel **Ch1** 3796 discordid P discorded L; 7011 discord; **Ch2** 6402 discorded

discorde n. [OF descorde, L discordia] a quarrel **Ch1** 4115 discorde

dyscrecyoun n. [OF] perception; ability to discern **HS** 10168 dyscrecyoun; 10169 dyscrecoun

discrie, descryue v. [see ascrie] [OF de(s)crier, descrivre] describe; announce, declare **Ch1** 4989, 8398 discried P ascried L; 5881 ascrie P descrie L; 9612 discrie P descrye L; 11829 discried P descried L; 15015 discrie; **HS** 11629 dyscrye; 8415 descryue; 1416 descryue *C* dyscrye

disdeyn n. [see desdeyn]

dysese, deses n. [OF disease, desaise] misfortune; misery **Ch2** 4110 deses; **HS** 8098 were GLOSS H dysese

dysgyse v. [see desgyse]

dishonour n. [AF deshonur (MP)] disgrace, shame, indignity **Ch1** 944, 6145 dishonoure; 6113 dishonour P desonour L; **Ch2** 2899, 4103, 5266 dishonoure; 4030, 7024, 7789 dishonour; **HS** 11480 dysonour

dismaye v. [OF desmaier, from esmai, n.] be alarmed, upset; frightened **Ch1** 3410 dismeide; 3461 dismaid P dysmayed L; 4420, 14013 dismaied; **Ch2** 1739, 5131 dismaied; 4568 dismayed; **HS** 5221 dysmaye

dismembre v. [OF desmembrer] cut off the limbs **Ch2** 7652 dismembred; **HS** 668 dysmembre

dysonoure v. [OF deshonorer] disgrace, treat irreverently **HS** 11553 dysonourest

disour n. [OF diseor] story teller, entertainer **Ch1** 75, 11149, 11185 disours; **HS** 8305 dyssour

dispende v. [see spend] [OF despendre] spend, waste, consume **Ch1** 6639 dispendid P spended L; 10605 spended P despended L; **Ch2** 3221 spende P despende L; 7052 dispende; **HS** 6228 despende; 52, 4594 dyspende; 1199, 4313, 6086 dyspendyþ

display v. [AF despleier] raise a banner **Ch2** 40, 455 displayed; 575, 4641, 5311, 5409, 7000 displaied; 1659 displaied P displaynge L

dispise v. [see despise]

dispoiled v. [see spoiled, v.]

dysport n. [AF] diversion, entertainment **HS** 4111, 6926 dysport

disputed v. [OF desputer, L disputare] engage in controversy **Ch2** 7676 disputed

disputeson n. [OF desput(a)ison] formal debate; controversy **Ch2** 5187 disputeson; 7321 disputesoun

disseised v. [AF disseisir] dispossessed; refl.: surrendered dominion **Ch2** 6045 disseised

dissh n. [OE disc] platter, bowl **Ch1** 15355, 15362 dissh; **HS** 2830 dysshe; 5828 dysshes

distance n. [OF destance] disagreement, discord **Ch2** 2101, 3744, 4619, 7355, 7815 distance; 3251 desceyuance P distance L; 5245 distaunce; **HS** 995 dystaunce

dysteyn v./adj. [from OF desteindre] to disguise one's purpose **HS** 469 deseyuyþ *C* dysteynyth *D* disteynyn; 472 deseyuable *F* desteinable *C* deceyuabyl *D* dysteynable; 2650 deseyue *C* dysteyne *D* disceyue *O* dyssafe

dystyncte v. [L distinctus, OF destin(c)ter] distinguish, discern **HS** 11596 dystyncte *O* dystynse

distroye v. [see destroye]

disturbance n. [from OF destorbler, v.] conflict,

agitation **Ch1** 8027 disturbance P desturblaunce L; **Ch2** 5240 disturbaunce
disturbe v. [see destorbe, desturble]
disturblyng ger. [from OF destorbler] disorder, trouble **Ch2** 6128 disturblyng; **HS** 8818 dystourblyng
dytours n. [OF diteor] accuser **HS** 1335 dytours *C* cowrs *D* doctourys
diuers adj./adv. [OF divers(e)] various kinds, ways; differently **Ch1** 2954 diuerse; 1496 dyuers P diuerse L; 2688, 3253 diuers P diuerse L; 3553, 3635, 4074, 8873, 10396 diuers; 4868 diuerse; 4869 diuersly; **Ch2** 100, 358 diuers; 3458 diuerse; 4620L diuerse (P differs); **HS** 8420, 10574, 11426 dyuers; 7329 dyuers *O* diuerse
diuinours n. [see deuyn, n.]
doelfulle, doelfullie adj./adv. [from OF doel, n.] sad, sorrowful; grievously **Ch1** 6744 doelfulle; 6699, 11952 doelfulli P delfully L; 7774 sodenly P deolfuly L; 10112 dolefully P deolfoly L; 13938 dolefully; **Ch2** 3522 doelfullie; **HS** 2515 sorowfully *CD* dolfully *O* dulefully
dog n. [OE docga] cur; worthless person; a term of contempt **Ch1** 15576L dogges (P differs); **HS** 5098, 5099 dogge; 8766 dogges; 8956 dog
dogh n. [OE dah, dag] dough for pastry **HS** 10106, 10107, 10109 dogh
doguise n. [see degyse]
dole n. (1) [OE dal, gedal] charitable gift **HS** 6936 dole
dole, doel, doole, doyle n. (2) [OF doel, del, dol] sorrow, mourning, pity; lamentation **Ch1** 861 dole P deol L; 2030 doole P dol L; 6839 doel; 8956, 11940 dole; 10638 doele; **Ch2** 4080 doole P doel L; 4714, 5069, 6352 dole; **HS** 7074 doyle; 6912 doyle GLOSS BH sorwe
dome, dom n. [OE dom] judgment, punishment; justice **Ch1** 506 dom; 570, 2596, 5255, 8138 15828 dome; **Ch2** 1186, 2446, 4467, 5517, 8312 dome; **HS** 1073, 1589, 6694, 9165, 11456 dome
domesday n. [OE domesdæg] the day of last judgment **Ch1** 8619, 15824 domesday; **HS** 8658 day of dome
domesman n. [from OE dom] a judge, arbiter **Ch1** 525 domesman; **HS** 1489, 1492 domus men
dominoun, domine n. [OF, ML] precinct **Ch2** 4896 dominoun P dongeon (?error) L; 2499 domine P dominion L
dongeon, donion n. [OF donjon] fortress; underground prison **Ch2** 2471 dongeon; 2965 donion P dongeon L
doo n. [OE da] female of the fallow deer **Ch1** 15055 doo
dore, dure n. [OE duru] door **Ch2** 2271 dures P dores L; **HS** 5016, 6096 dore
◆ **dormers** n. [?OF dormeor] ?sleepers, ?stealthy persons **HS** 1343 dormers *C* lyȝeres *D* demerys
dortoure n. [OF dortour] dormitory of a monastery **Ch2** 6183 dortoure
douary, dowerie n. [AF dowarie] life interest of a wife or widow **Ch1** 6437 dowerie P dowarye L; 7504 douary P dowarye L; **Ch2** 3740 dowerie
doufe, dowue n. [ON dufa] a dove **Ch1** 11019 doufes P douues L; **HS** 219, 304, 8832 dowue; 284 dowuys
doughter n. [see douhter]
douht v. [see deih, degh, doute]
douhter, doughter n. [OE dohtor] daughter **Ch1** 2016 douhter P doughter L; 766, 1224, 2289, 6248, 8980 douhter; 345, 7424, 7536 doghter; 278 doghters; 349 doghteres; 353 doghtres; 741 douhtere; 2167, 2358, 6444 douhtres; 2267, 2275, 6446 douhters; 2045 douthter P doughter L; **Ch2** 1698, 2306, 3132, 6748, 8265 douhter; 5198 douhters; 5220 douhteres; 5050, 7749 douhtres; **HS** 242, 1257 doghtyr; 2857, 3706, 9036, 9117, 9128 doghter; 198, 204, 208 douȝtyr
douhty, doughty adj. [OE dohtig, dyhtig] bold, brave, strong **Ch1** 1433, 2674, 3254 douhty P doughti L; 2677, 4040, 5136, 6798, 9019 douhty; 2700, 4096, 4659, 6337, 9293 douhti; 1278, 3276, 13704 douhtiest; 13010 douht; **Ch2** 357, 1768, 3417, 5566, 7456 douhty; 3778, 8303 douhti; **HS** 3806, 4375 doghty; 4416, 10541 dughty; 4992 doughty
douhtily, douhtilike adv. [from OE dohtig, adj.] bravely, vigorously **Ch1** 1634 douhtily P doughtyly L; 5793 douhtily P doughtyly L; 9954 douhtilike P douhtilyke L; **Ch2** 4005 douhteli; 6765 douhtily
douhtynes n. [from OE dohtig, adj.] valor, strength, bravery **Ch1** 2840, 12976 douhtynes P doughtines L; **Ch2** 2801 douhtinesse; 1226, 4564 douhtynes; 4356 douhtynesse; 915L dowȝtynesse (P differs)
doun, down adv. [OE dune, adune] to a lower place; downward **Ch1** 492, 2257, 4413, 6747, 9364 doun; 6800 dounward; 13286 donward; **Ch2** 327, 1354, 3647, 6393, 8314 doun; 432, 2207, 4252, 6080 doune; **HS** 818, 3387, 4036, 6523 down; 10786, 12515 doune
doune n. [OE dun] hill; open country **Ch1** 6153, 8462 dounes; **Ch2** 2233 dounes; **HS** 6113 doune
dounriht adv. [OE dune, adv. + OE rihte, adv.] straight down; outright **Ch1** 1776 dounryght; 6327 dounriht; **HS** 1373, 12060 down ryght
doute, doughte n. [OF dote, doute] uncertainty, perplexity; anxiety, fear or respect **Ch1** 896, 4396, 5019, 9361, 13813 doute; 4915, 7530

dout; 8991 douht; **Ch2** 431, 1774, 2624, 6938, 7658 doute; **HS** 462, 4960, 7924, 9569, 11506 doute; 2773 dowte; 1815 drede *C* dowte *D* douȝtte; 3311 doute GLOSS B drede

doute v. [OF doter, douter, L dubitare] be in doubt, fear **Ch1** 6479, 12004 douht; 896, 2793, 2846, 7381, 8977 doute; 7440 dought; 4890 douted; 15235 doutid; **Ch2** 950, 3444, 3630, 4507, 7706 doute; 2899, 7238, 8312 douted; **HS** 857 doutyde *H* douted; 8249 douten; 8276, 10944 doute

doutous adj. [OF dotos, doutous] undetermined **Ch1** 13718 doutous P dotouse L

dowed v. [see douary] [OF doer, douer] to endow **Ch2** 1915 dowed

dowerie n. [see douary]

down caste v. [OE dune, adv. + ON kasta, v.] overthrown, defeated **HS** 294 down caste; 7510 down kast

dowue n. [see doufe]

dragon n. (1) [OF dragon, L draco] a dragon **Ch1** 289, 8923, 9022, 11813, 13252 dragon; 8059, 8076, 9024 dragons; 8125, 8129 dragoun; **Ch2** 4552 dragon; **HS** 1747, 1752, 1865 dragun

dragon, dragoun n. (2) [OF dragon] battle standard; banner design; helmet ornament **Ch1** 9024 dragons; 9028, 9896, 13133, 13177 dragon; 12843 dragoun; **Ch2** 5320 dragon; 5311 dragoun

drauht, draught n./adj. [prob. OE *dreaht; cp. OE dragan] pulling, a tug; move in chess; pulled up **Ch1** 475 draght P draught L; 1828 drow . . . a drauht P draught L; 4390 drauht; 11155 drauhtes P draughtes L; 12384 drauht P strok L; 12116 drauht; **Ch2** 212, 5757 drauht; 4538 drauht brigge

drawe, drouh, drauhen v. [OE dragan] pull, tug, draw **Ch1** 858 drouh P draught L; 679 drogh P drowe L; 682, 1468, 4341 drowe; 952, 1725, 5279, 8768, 13149 drawe; 7499, 8656, 8778 draw; 10171 drawes; 7569 drauh; 1828 drow; 679 drogh; 1322, 2444, 4713, 7618, 9139 drouh; 4292 drawe P drowe L; 4391, 7610, 8502, 9067 drawen; 4713 drouh P drough L; 6049 drouh P wyþdrow L; 7767 droh; **Ch2** 715, 1222, 4498, 6331, 7894 drouh; 1295 drouh P drawe L; 1294, 3506, 4404, 5282, 8288 drawe; 3934 drow; 2752 drawes; 4316, 5756, 6526, 7606, 8199 drawen; 4539 drauhen; 4969, 5236, 5440, 5484, 6642 drowe; **HS** 5429, 8764, 8800, 9290 drawe; 644 draghst; 11256 draghest; 3582, 3810, 3831, 4471 drogh; 703, 713 drawyn

drecche v. [OE dreccan] injure, kill; vex **Ch1** 1440 drecched; **HS** 8153 drecche; 9856 drecched

drecchyng ger. [from OE dreccan] trouble, harm **Ch1** 7966, 8868, 11509 drecchyng

drede n. [cp. OE ondrædan] fear, terror **Ch1** 861, 3295, 5127, 11824, 13098 drede; 4113, 8649 dred; 7798 drede P dredde L; **Ch2** 178, 1263, 4445, 6685, 8172 drede; **HS** 101, 1390, 5470, 7406, 7571 drede; 3236 awe GLOSS BH drede; 3420, 8285 drede *O* doute; 5468 adred *O* for drede; 10559 drede *SV* doute

drede, dred v. [see adred] [OE drædan] to become frightened **Ch1** 883, 1270, 4540, 7161, 9373 dred; 966, 1670, 6950, 9306, 13719 drede; 3267 dred P dredden L; 2792 dredes; 5062 dredis; 6516 dreded; **Ch2** 300, 1893, 5477, 7186, 8313 dred; 1601 dred P dredeþ L; 1617, 3714, 4936, 6230, 8304 drede; 6267 dredis; **HS** 165, 1815, 5320, 7571, 11710 drede; 7711 dred; 7910 dredde

drede, dredful, dredfully adj./adv. [from OE drædan] horrible, fearful; frightening **Ch1** 2913 drede; 12116L dredful (om. P); **Ch2** 2873, 4759 dred; 4307 dredfulle; **HS** 7848 dred; 1388, 2496, 10224 dredful; 3272, 11679 dredfully

dref, dryue, drogh v. [see drawe] [OE drifan] chase, pursue, drive **Ch1** 1586 dref; 1864, 3190, 4293, 5523, 6885 dryue; 6532 dreue P drof L; 1408, 6482, 13329 dryuen; 7516 cast P dryuen L; 1654, 2084, 4560 drofe; 3935 drof; 4783 chaces P dryueþ L; 13306 dryuen P dryue L; 9378 dryuand; 12113 drafe P dref L; **Ch2** 14, 2405, 3020, 4562, 7848 dryue; 57 drofe; 1401 drofe P drof L; 2251, 2945, 8177 drof; 7976 dref; 889, 1438, 3634, 7352, 8200 dryuen; 3661, 3867, 3946, 5178, 5573 driue; 6825 driuen; **HS** 4054, 6248, 6953, 9435 dryue; 2703 dreue; 4481 dreuyn; 5618, 8570 drofe; 3812 drogh *A* droff *F* drouȝ *O* held; 9301 to drofe *O* to rafe

dreynte v. [see drenge, v.]

dreme n. [see mette] [OE and ON] a dream **Ch1** 1394, 1396, 1401, 11822 dreme; **HS** 446 dreme; 379, 423, 431 dremys; 7602 þoght *O* dreme

dreme v. [see mete, mette, v.] [OE dream and ON] to dream **HS** 389 dreme *C* mete; 391 dreme *C* mete *D* metyn; 454 dremede *C* dremdyst *D* drem (n.); 464 dremyn *C* dreme; 7580 dremyng *O* in mette (n.); 11976 dremed

drenge, dreynte, drenkeled, dronkend v. [OE drencan] to drown **Ch1** 2002 dronkend P dreynte L; 993, 995, 1998 dronkend P drenkled L; 1175 dronkend P drowned L; 9788 dronkeld P drenkled L; 10182 drenkled; 11873 dronkled P drenkled L; **Ch2** 6817 drenge; 4220 dronkled P drenched L; 4221, 4725, 5810, 7579 drenkled; 7018 dronkeld; 1000, 2569, 2574, 4038, 7010 dronkled; **HS** 12520 dreynt

drery adj. [OE dreorig] melancholy, sorrowful **HS** 4027 drery
dres v. [OF drecier] set in order, place; arm oneself **Ch1** 10670 dight P dressed L; **Ch2** 7990 dres; **HS** 4298 dresse
drie, dreih v. [OE dreogan and ON] suffer, endure, bear **Ch1** 741 drye P dreye L; 15665 drie; 14988 dreih P drey L; 15829 drie P drye L; **HS** 3299 drygh GLOSS BH suffre; 3545 drye GLOSS BH suffre; 8099 drye GLOSS H suffre
drye adj. (1) [OE dryge] withered; arid, bare **HS** 3506, 9112, 11927 drye; 1031 drye *D* dreyȝe
drie, drehi adj. (2)/adv. [ON; cp. OE dreogan, gedreog, gedreoh] lasting, tedious; kept at a distance, far away **Ch1** 1038L a drey (om. P); 5017 o drehi P a drey L; 5955 o drie P a dreigh L; 8778 odreih P o drey L; 11904L drey (om. P); 15166L o drey (om. P); **Ch2** 6696 o drehi
drynke n. [OE drenc] a drink **Ch1** 3956, 7073, 7657, 8901 drynk; 5052 drink; 11088 drinkes; **Ch2** 2976, 4512 drynk; 8204 drink; **HS** 2363 dryng; 6606 drynke; 6519, 6563, 7222 drynk
drynke v. [OE drincan] to drink **Ch1** 3449 drink P drynke L; 7470 drink; 7437 drinke; 7473 drinkis; 7479, 7485, 9172 drank; 7119 drunken; **Ch2** 8204 dronken; **HS** 4570 drynke; 390 drynkyn; 3184, 9150, 9377 drank; 6679 drunke; 6546 [MS *O* interpolation] (l. 8) drynkes; (l. 33) drynke
drynkere n. [OE drincere] a drunkard **Ch1** 3955 drynkere
drinkheille n. [see wassaille] [prob. ON phrase] "drink to your health" **Ch1** 7472 drinkhaille P drynk hayl L; 7475 drinheille P drynk hail L; 7478, 7485 drinkheille; **HS** 6546 [MS *O* interpolation, l. 78] drynk ale
drynkyngge ger. [from OE drincan] drinking **HS** 1029 drynkyngge
dronkend v. [see drenge, dronkeld, v.]
drope n. [OE dropa] a drop of liquid **HS** 6744, 6748, 8426 drope
droppe v. [OE dropian] to fall in drops; sprinkle **HS** 6672 droppe
drunke, drunkenes n./adj. [from OE druncen] the effects of drinking **Ch1** 7093 drunken P dronke L; 7074 drunken; 3958, 7495 drunkenes P dronkeness L; **HS** 6604 drunke; 6608, 9720, 9721 drunkenes; 6546 [MS *O* interpolation] (l. 100) drounken lewe; (103) drounken lewyde; (76) dronkenes; (93, 111) dronkennes; (56) dronkyne; (86) dronken; (97, 106, 108) drounken
duale, dwale n. [OE dwala] in a daze, trance **Ch1** 8942, 15844 duale P dwale L
dubbid v. [OE dubbian, OF adober] to create a knight; to invest with rank **Ch1** 6722 dubbid P dobbed L; 10475 dubbid; **Ch2** 8092 dubbid
duble adj. [OF] twice the amount; two aspects **Ch1** 8429 dubled P double L; **Ch2** 4539 duble
duche n. [OF duchee] realm of a duke **Ch1** 3122, 3132 duche
dudeyn n. [see desdeyn]
duelle, dwelle v. [OE dwellan, dwelian] reside, remain; wander; deceive **Ch1** 160, 1227, 2066, 6358, 8868 duelle; 7720 dwelle; 5814 duelle P reste L; 739, 2511, 4541, 7825 duelled; 3550, 3564, 13463 duellid; 8161 duellid P dwelt L; 5470 duellyng; 11977 duellis; 2419L dwelt (P differs); 12304 duelles P dwellyng L; **Ch2** 2645, 4350, 5301, 6974, 8178 duelle; 1271 duelles; 1878, 3587, 3881, 6264, 7395 duellis; 370, 1357, 1816, 2450, 5585 duelled; 2078, 3697, 3707, 7097, 7371 duellid; 2755 duelland; 6466 duelte; **HS** 65 duellyd; 172, 4491, 7921, 12002, 12258 dwelle; 1742 wonyng *D* duellyng
duellyng, dwellyng ger. [from OE dwellan] delay, tarrying; habitation **Ch1** 3547, 4908, 6284 duellyng P dwellyng L; **Ch2** 371, 1452, 4324, 7587 duellyng; **HS** 6655, 11978 dwellyng
duȝepers n. [OF doze per(s), duze pers] twelve peers; any famous knight or noble **Ch1** 1597 duȝperis P dosze peres L; 10928 duȝepers P dusze pers L; **Ch2** 3298, 3455, 3533, 6813 duȝepers; 2016, 5691, 6420, 6737, 6977 duȝe pers
duke n. [OF duc, L dux] hereditary nobleman **Ch1** 3121 duke; 13243, 15630 dukes
dunede v. [OE dynian] echoed **Ch1** 10677 stonyed P dunede L
◆ **dunhede** n. [from OE dun, adj.] ?darkness, dun-colored; ?thinness **HS** 10138 dunhede *FH* dunhede *O* donhede *SV* honeste
dure n. (1) [OF] endurance **Ch1** 13563 dure P duree L; **Ch2** 281 dure
dure n. (2) [see dore]
dure v. [see dar, dur, durst v. (2)]
dwale n. [see duale]
dwelle v. [see duelle]

E

eam n. [OE eam] uncle **Ch1** 4746 eame P eem L; 4091, 14000 eam P em L; 5199 eme P eem L; 6134 eames; 6294 eem; 5157, 6306, 6535, 15193 eam; **Ch2** 229, 296, 387, 2198 eam; 4703 eam P em L
ebbe n. [OE ebba] ebb of a flood, flow of water **Ch1** 10172, 12015 ebbe; **Ch2** 2577 ebbe
ech, eche pronoun [see ilk, ilka]
edefie v. [OF edifier] to transform **Ch1** 6431 herberw P edefie L
edge n. [see egid, adj., egged, v.] [OE ecg] edge of a sword **Ch1** 4713 edge P egge L; 4871L (add, l. 8) egge
eere, ere n. [OE eare] the ear **Ch2** 3174 ere; **HS**

4763 eere; 6932 ere

eft adv. [OE eft, æft] once more, again; back, afterwards **Ch1** 1051 eft P efte L; 1239, 5413, 6665, 7989, 8606 eft; 6703 ageyn P eft L; **Ch2** 1389, 3641, 5400, 7664, 8290 eft; **HS** 254, 799, 1546, 8056, 9227 eft; 12167 efte

eftsone, eftsons adv. [OE eft and sona] after, immediately; afterward **Ch1** 1859 eftsons P eftesones L; 1920 efton; 4548, 5798, 7604 eftsons; **Ch2** 2136 eftsone; 2025, 3265 eftsonne; 7320, 7568 efton; 1560, 3187, 4956 eftsons; 5392 eftsones; **HS** 1267 eftsonys; 6118, 7676, 9656 eftsones; 9694 eftsone

egged v. [ON eggja] to urge, entice, incite **Ch2** 3253, 6744 egged; **HS** 1509 eggyst

egid adj. [OE ecged] sharpened **Ch1** 7746 egid P egged L

egle n. [see erne]

egre, egrely adj./adv. [OF egre, aigre] sharp, sour, bitter; aroused **Ch1** 1640, 4392, 5385, 9064 egre; 1006 egrily P egrely L; 3437 egre P egrely L; 3711 irouslik P egreliche L; 3730 egrelike P angerly L; 8396 egrely **Ch2** 407, 1754, 4544 egre; 888 egrely

egred v. [OF aigrier] to arouse, incite **Ch1** 9957 egred

eye n. [see awe] [OE eage, ege] the eye **Ch1** 3420L, 6727L eye (om. P); 6730, 11946, 15140, 15154 iȝe P eye L; 4169 egh P eye L; 7680, 9175, 11224, 13025 ie P eye L; 6836 ine P eyne L; 11445, 12084 ine P eyen L; 12078, 12332 ine P eyn L; 3371 ine P eyene L; **Ch2** 1969, 2227, 3439, 4114, 4360 ine; 1257 iȝene P eye L; 1260 iȝene; 5628 iȝen; 8068 iȝe; **HS** 2833, 4269 ye; 3575 eȝe; 4914, 8134 eye; 428 eȝyn; 671 ygne; 2972 eȝen; 3978, 6666 yne; 8869, 9141 ye *O* eghe; 10214 yen *O* eghen *SV* eȝen

eile v. [OE eglian] to be ill **Ch1** 14912 eiles P eilest L

eyr n. [see heyr]

eyre n. (1) [OF air] vigor, haste **Ch1** 1484 eyre

eyre, ayer, aiere, heyre n. (2) [OF air] the atmosphere; climate **Ch1** 500 eyr; 7963 eyre; 8076 aiere; 15679 ayer; 15810 heyre

eyghte, eyghteþe numeral [see auht, numeral] [OE eahtoða] the number eight; eighth part **Ch1** 7564L eyghte (om. P); 5663 auht P eyght L; **HS** 2635 eytþe *CD* eyȝtande *O* aghtande; 11619 eyghteþe

eise n./v./adj. [see ese]

eke v. [OE eacian, eken] to increase, add on **Ch2** 4362 to eke

eke adv. [OE eac, ec] also, moreover, likewise **Ch1** 1811L & eke (om. P); **HS** 1170, 4227, 10304, 10812, 11004 eke

ekename n. [ON; cp. OI auka-nefni] nickname, epithet **HS** 1532 vyle ekename *C* nyth name *D* sclaundrous name *F* unkede name

elbous n. [OE elboga; cp. elboulyne] ?a unit of size **Ch1** 1826 elbous P cubyte L

elde n. [OE eldo, ældo] maturity; adulthood; old age **Ch1** 756, 3115, 4099, 6223, 7938 elde; 3740 held P elde L; **Ch2** 28, 55, 1076, 3302 elde; **HS** 1126 eld; 1093, 1163, 2807, 6439, 9730 elde

elde, eldest adj. [OE eldra] older, oldest; aged **Ch1** 7237 elde; 227, 2117, 5292, 6942, 7581 eldest; 4038 heldest P eldest L; **Ch2** 2391 alde; 588, 1253, 2052, 2134, 7243 eldest; **HS** 3873 elder; 2993 eldest

eldere, eldres n. [from OE eldra, adj.] older persons; parents **Ch1** 6106 eldere P elder L; **Ch2** 2603, 3539 eldres

eleccioun n. [AF eleccioun] election, choice, selection **Ch2** 5099 eleccoun; 5118 eleccion; 5122 eleccioun; **HS** 11019 eleccyone; 10996, 10997, 11068, 11080 eleccyoun

elite n. [OF elit, ppl. of elire] one elected to office **Ch2** 5120 elites; 5125 elite

elleuen, elleuend, enleuene numeral [OE endleofon, endleofta] the numeral eleven; the eleventh in order **Ch1** 6093 elleuen; 6456 elleuen P enleuen L; 7564L enleuene (om. P); **Ch2** 5979, 7012 elleuen; 199 elleuent; 3057 elleuend; **HS** 11785 elleuenþe

elne n. [OE eln; elne, gen.] unit of measure; an ell **Ch2** 632 elne

els, elles adv. [ON, OE elles] also, otherwise **Ch1** 82 ellis; 1676, 4928, 5156, 6700, 9199 els; 1360L elles (om. P); 3504 or P elles L; **HS** 106, 5530, 8888, 10916 elles; 1548, 4856 ellys; 603 ellys *C* ell

elswhere adv. [ON, OE] in another place **Ch1** 1206 elles where; 8611 elswhere; **HS** 2060 ellyswhore; 2078 ellyswher; 9320, 11824 elleswher

emperice n. [OF emperesse] consort of an emperor; a woman ruler **Ch2** 2587, 2724, 2974, 3120, 5202 emperice; 2307 of pris P emperys L

emperour n. [AF empereur (MP)] ruler of an empire **Ch1** 2593, 3529, 4368, 5449, 6144 emperoure; 3526, 5063, 5763, 6112, 13223 emperour; **Ch2** 2544, 3764, 4895, 7023, 8311 emperour; 2543, 4098 emperoure; 4236 emperere; **HS** 3089, 10954 emperours; 5813, 5895, 11318 emperour; 9164 emperoure

emprise n. [OF enprise] undertaking, task, enterprise, exploit **Ch1** 11894 emprise; 5810 grete empris P grete emprises L; **Ch2** 3170 emprise

empty adj. [see void] [OE æmetig] empty **HS** 7855 empty

enamoured adj. [see anamorde]

enbataille v. [OF embataillier] to array for

battle **Ch1** 4987 renged P enbatailled L; **Ch2** 4205 batale P enbataille L

enbussed v. [see busse, v.] [OF enbuschier] placed in ambush **Ch1** 4976 bussed P enbusched L; **Ch2** 334, 4662, 7002 enbussed

enbussement n. [OF enbuschement] concealment, ambush **Ch1** 4981 bussement P enbuschement L; 4993 enbussement; 6213 bussement P enbuschement L; **Ch2** 52 skulkyng P enbuschement L; 4653 enbussement P buschement L

encheson n. [see cheson] [OF enchaison from L occassionem] cause, excuse; pretext, occasion **Ch1** 4017 cheson P þencheson L; 3542, 4853, 6366, 8420, 15526 encheson; **Ch2** 1180, 5754, 6197, 7071, 8044 encheson; 5056, 7164, 7698 enchesoun; 4794, 5046 enchesonne; **HS** 1524, 2440, 7592, 10301, 12421 enchesun; 7765 enchesoun; 9035 enchesoune; 228 enchesun *D* cause; 1322 enchesun *C* cause; 2955 enchesoun *C* cheson

encoumbraunce, combrance n. [from OF encombrer] hindrance, temptation, trouble **Ch1** 8133 combrance; **HS** 11504 cumberaunce; 12620 cumbraunce; 1020 cumberaunce *C* fondyng *D* encoumbraunce; 2218 myschaunce *C* comerawnns

encountre n. [see countre]

encumbre, komber n. [OF] impediment, nuisance, trouble **Ch1** 14808 komber; **Ch2** 4697, 7995 encumbre; 7762 encumbir; **HS** 7787 encumbre; 12522 cumbre

encumbre v. [OF encombrer] hinder, burden; destroy, ruin **Ch1** 12052 encombire P combren L; **Ch2** 6120 encombred; **HS** 11082 encumbred; 7466 cumbren; 9754, 11983 cumbred; 5376 acumbred

encumberyng ger. [from OF encombrer] oppression, subjugation **Ch1** 8949 encomberyng P encombrynge L; **Ch2** 2861 encumberyng; **HS** 2191 cumbryng; 2766 cumberyng

encumberment n. [OF] trouble, affliction, misfortune **Ch2** 3636, 7834 encumberment; **HS** 2148 cumbrement *D* encumbrement; 2469 combrement; 8402 cumbremente

end n. [OE ende] result; completion, conclusion; death **Ch1** 324, 1655, 3672, 5228, 8237 ende; 2856, 3235, 5504, 6615, 9159 end; **Ch2** 346, 3295, 5179, 7389, 8271 ende; 4538, 5966 end; **HS** 123, 1436, 4862, 7813, 6687 ende; 9179 end; 8895 endes

ende, ent v. [OE endian] come to an end; cease; to die **Ch1** 15554 ende; 2461 endes; 3066 endes P endeþ L; 3231, 3875, 4745, 5689, 12201 endid; 11570 ent; **Ch2** 7786, 8282 ende; 8047 endis; 109, 1365, 3116, 5208 endid; 2000, 2604, 6143, 5553, 7865 ent; **HS** 9198 ende; 841, 2252 endys; 6414 enden; 7376 ended

ending ger. [OE endung] the end; extremity; death **Ch1** 7354 ending; 765, 2522, 3948, 5244, 8490 endyng; **Ch2** 185, 1591, 4276, 5654, 8069 endyng; **HS** 823 endyngge; 4796, 6507, 9672, 11242, 11436 endyng; 10495 endynge

endles adj. [OE endeleas] perpetual, everlasting **HS** 6687, 6690 endles; 1080, 2627, 6673 endeles

endyte v. [AF enditer] write or compose; to condemn **HS** 1337, 5987 endyte; 9048 endyted

endytement n. [AF] indictment, accusation **HS** 8917 endytement

enemy, enmy n. [AF enemi (MP)] adversary; hostile person, foe; evil spirit **Ch1** 1072, 1276, 8214, 8449, 9201 enmy; 1607, 2708, 6313, 7380, 9013 enmys; 7048 enmys P enemys L; 2620 enuyous P enemys L; 2712L, 6391L enemis (om. P); 6717 enmyes; **Ch2** 928, 2931 enmy; 950, 1848, 3078, 5496, 7672 enmys; **HS** 3836, 6594, 7474 enmy; 3364 enmys; 10256 enemy

enforme v. [OF enformer] to guide; negotiate **Ch2** 4026 enformed; 6913, 7699 enforme

engyn n. [OF] assault machine, contrivance; ability, cleverness **Ch1** 1039, 3401, 5424 engynes; 5966 barfreis P engyns L; 8695 engyns; 8715 engyn; 9283 engyne; 7836 engine P engyns L; 15023 engyne P engyn L; **Ch2** 4299, 4301, 4372, 7971 engyns; 4094, 4369, 7960, 7961 engynes; 7969, 7973 engyn

enginour n. [OF engigneor] builder of fortifications; military strategist **Ch1** 1037 enginours; 4527 engynoure

engynous adj. [OF engignous] clever, cunning **Ch1** 11798L engynous (om. P)

enired v. [see anired]

enoynt v. [see anoynt]

enpaired v. [OF empeirier] damaged **Ch1** 10209 enpaired

enquere v. [OF enquerre] investigate; to question **Ch2** 5957 enquere; 2716 enquered; **HS** 8919 enquere

ensample n. [AF ensample (MP)] example, illustration; specimen **Ch1** 3905, 8574, 8582 ensample; 2439 forbisen P ensample L; **Ch2** 7046, 7603 ensample; **HS** 329, 1661, 5571, 9194, 9253 ensample; 6938, 10024 ensamples

enseled v. [OF enseeler] sealed **Ch1** 11617 we seilde (error) P wel enseled L; **Ch2** 3110, 5256 enseled; 2367, 5623, 5920, 6218, 7605 enselid

ensens n. [OF] incense **HS** 11106 ensens

ensense v. [OF encenser] to fumigate with incense **HS** 11100 ensensed; 11103 ensense

entaile, entale n. [OF entaille] form, outline, appearance; kind **Ch1** 10134, 15138 entaile P entaille L; 14256 entale P entaille L

entamed v. [OF entamer] to open a wound **Ch1** 12077 entamed

entent n. [see tent, n.] [OF] purpose, aim or object; opinion, idea; attention **Ch1** 174 entente; 4280, 4803 entent; **Ch2** 3559 þe tende P þe entent L; **HS** 977, 1795, 4487, 10160, 10844 entent

enterdite n. [OF entredit, L interdictum] papal sentence or decree **Ch2** 7835 enterdite

enterdited v. [OF entredire] to sentence **Ch2** 5143 enterdited

enterement, enteryng n./ger. [OF enterrement] burial, funeral **Ch1** 6096L þenterement (om. P); **Ch2** 7999 enterment; **HS** 6390 enteryng *O* berying

♦ **enterlace** n. [cf. OF entrelacier; enterlace, ppl.] intricate rimes **Ch1** 86 enterlace

entermet v. [OF entremetre] intercede, meddle **Ch1** 7391 entirmet P entermet L; 12285 entirmet P entremet; 15572 entermet; **Ch2** 6433 entermet

entyce v. [see tyce] [OF enticier] to tempt, lure, induce **HS** 1504 entycedyst *C* cowncellyn

entycement n. [OF] temptation **HS** 2146 entycement *C* tysment

entyrludyes n. [OF entrelude] entertainment; a play **HS** 8995 entyrludyes

entre n. [OF entree] entrance; admittance, access **Ch1** 1056, 1087, 3358, 5915, 9285 entre; 1052 entries P entres L; 5031 entres; **Ch2** 4449, 4537, 5498, 6592 entre; 4640, 5782 entres; **HS** 4708, 12149, 12152 entre

envenomed v./adj. [see venom] [from OF venim] to put poison on something; having poisonous properties **Ch2** 5032, 5611, 5624 envenomed

enuy n. [AF enuie (MP)] ill-will, hatred; spite, malice; one of the deadly sins **Ch1** 776 enuye; 7591 enuy; **Ch2** 925, 1132 enuy; **HS** 1345, 3640, 3917, 7151, 10114 enuye

enuyous adj. [AF enuius (MP)] having hatred, enmity, ill-will **Ch1** 2553 enyous P enuiouse L; 2620 enuyous; 4490 enuyouse; **HS** 3954, 3976, 4082 enuyus; 8623, 10242 enuyous; 3986 enuyus *O* invyusly men; 3988 enuyus *O* invy es; 3990 þe enuyus *H* enuyus man *O* þe envyus

epitaf n. [OF epitaphe, L epitaphium] an epitaph **Ch1** 15894 epitaf

ere n. [see eere, ere; heyr]

ere, erst, are adv. [see or, ore] [OE ær, ærest] first; before, formerly **Ch1** 1938 are P erest L; 6218 ere P er L; 9992 ar P er L; **Ch2** 1947, 2826, 3456 er; 2003 are; 2579, 3135, 3169, 3220, 3344 ere; 2260 ere P er L; **HS** 654 ar *D* or; 1223 erwhyl *D* er qwhyle; 1820 er *O* are; 3281 before *O* ayre

eren, eryn n./adj. [see iren]

erend, arend n. [OE ærend] prayer, petition; mission to deliver a message; purpose, intention **HS** 1012 erende; 4814, 7684 erand; 7640 erandes; 365 erend *C* herden *D* arende; 1944 erend *C* erdyn

eryn, eryed v. [see feld, n.] [OE erian] plowing **Ch1** 1890, 3663 ardawe felde P eryed feld; **HS** 2446 ere *C* tyl *D* eryn; 2448 eryn

erytage n. [see heritage]

erle, erelle n. [OE eorl] nobleman below the rank of king, prince, duke, emperour **Ch1** 8433, 9145, 9391, 13237 erle; 9341 erle P erl L; 8203 erelle; 8799 erles; 9298 erls; **Ch2** 539, 1504, 3519, 5043, 7081 erle; 756, 7494, 7533 erles; **HS** 10631, 10645 erle; 3091, 6793 erles

erledom, erledam n. [OE eorldom] territory of an earl **Ch1** 9223 erledam; 15799 erldomes

erly adv. [see arly, orely] [OE ærlice] early; early in the morning **Ch1** 1336L erlyk (P differs); **HS** 1064, 7225, 12184 erly

ermyte, ermytage n. [see heremite, hermitage]

erne n. [OE earn] eagle; image of an eagle, as on a banner **Ch1** 10044, 10048, 10137 ernes; 13221 egle . . . herne

ernest n. [OE eornest] in seriousness **HS** 1292 ernyst *D* sclaunder; 3481 ernest

erre v. [OF errer] roam; go astray; deviate **Ch2** 7819 errid; **HS** 473, 9524, 12365 erre

errour n. [OF] false opinion; heresy; deviation from truth, wisdom or good judgment **Ch1** 5266 erroure; **Ch2** 1921 errour; 4106, 5175, 5265, 5964 erroure; **HS** 1181 errour; 5421 errours

ersdeken n. [OE ercediacon] administrative officer under a bisshop or archbishop **Ch2** 3155 erresdeken; 3151, 6327 ersdeken

erth n. [OE eorþe] the earth **Ch1** 203, 2062, 7854, 8671, 12384 erth; 10677, 11820, 12058 erthe; 10955, 12766, 13950 erþe; **Ch2** 327, 656, 855, 943, 8297 erth; 2049, 2619 erþe; **HS** 660, 2269 erþe

♦ **erþe horn** n. a contrivance for making a noise underground **Ch2** 2871 erþe horn; 2876 erþe hornes

erþly adj. [OE eorþlic] worldly **HS** 831 erþly

erth molde n. [OE] this earth **Ch1** 442 erth molde

escape n./v. [see scape, skape, ascape]

eschekere n. [OF eschequier] session of the king's exchequer **Ch2** 6791 eschekere; 7627 chekere

eschele, aschelle n. [OF] detachment of soldiers **Ch1** 4965 aschelle P bataille L; 12838, 13000 eschele P eschel L; 12879 eschelle P eschele L; 13065 eschel; **Ch2** 4685 [Langtoft: eschele] turbe P warde L; 4695 eschel; 4667, 4724, 4727, 7240 eschele; 7003 escheles

eschete n. [OF] confiscated property reverting to the king **Ch2** 5887, 5970 eschete

ese n. [OF aise, eise] comfort, pleasure; rest,

leisure **Ch1** 3548, 6288, 7039, 7337, 7840 ese; **Ch2** 1680 ease; 4270 eise P ayse L; **HS** 1098, 6060, 7740, 10453 ese
ese, ayse v. [OF aaisier] provide comfort, soothe **Ch1** 84 aysed; 7444 asaied P aysed L; **Ch2** 4766 heised P raised L; 6566 esis; 7329, 7674 ese; 3884 eised; 5158 eise
ese, ayse, eyse adj. [OF aise, ppl. of aaisier] easy, comfortable **Ch1** 1888 eyse P esyest L; 1896 eyse P ayse L; 5489, 5609, 6343, 7820, 9619 ese; 3142 eise P eyse L; 6339 ese P ayse L; **Ch2** 7568 ese
esement n. [OF aaisement] comforts **Ch1** 10863 esement P aysement L
esquaymous adj. [OF escoymous] fastidious **HS** 7250 esquaymous
essoyn n. [OF essoigne] excuse; offering an excuse **Ch1** 11720 essoyne P want L; **Ch2** 4677, 5156, 6127, 7068, 7502 essoyn; 2511, 3333, 4629 essoyne
ester, estyr n. [see pask, pasch]
estre n. [OF estre: to be, used as noun] country, city; events, location, conditions **Ch1** 5230, 6170, 6895, 8608, 13763 estre; 3944 estres; **Ch2** 2281 estere; 3029, 3562, 5204, 6386 estre; 2181, 4974 estres; **HS** 10593 estre GLOSS BH a toune
ete v. [OE etan] to eat, consume **Ch1** 3756, 7437, 9172, 9248, 9807 ete; 10374 eten; **Ch2** 1325, 1871, 2275, 8208 ete; 2276, 4513 eten; **HS** 3182, 5385, 6679, 12382 ete; 390 etyn; 10840 eteþ
eth adj. [OE eaþe, eþe] easy, at ease **Ch2** 2840, 4801, 5282 eth
◆ **etild** v. [unrecorded: ?error] **Ch1** 12070 etild P peyned him L
etyng ger. [from OE etan, v.] eating **HS** 6539 etyng
euangelyst n. [OF euangeliste] St John: writer of the gospel **HS** 3626 euangelyst
euele, yuel n. [OE yfel] wickedness, moral evil; illness **Ch1** 4521 foly P yuel L; 3213, 4590, 4771 ille P yuel L; 5184, 15050 euelle; 6081, 8131 euelle P yuel L; **Ch2** 607 wiknes P yuel L; 2618 euele; 703, 3612 euelle; 4610 euel; **HS** 368, 470, 2478, 12586 euyl; 695 euyl *C* aungyl (?error); 2553 euyl *CD* ille; 3923 euyl *O;* 3038, 3044, 3424, 7158, 11691 euyl *O* yll
euele adj./adv. [see ille] [OE yfel] wicked, depraved; sinful, harmful, painful **Ch1** 2758, 4421, 4589, 5629, 5836 ille P yuel L; 2799 wikly P euele L; 3455 wikke P yuel L; 3929 yuel men P schrewes L; 4243 litelle P euele L; 7096 euel; 7354 iuelle; **Ch2** 381 euelle P yuel L; 1332L yuel (om. P); 2948, 5137, 5732 euelle; 3001, 3637 ille P yuel L; 5529, 6949 euel; **HS** 2724, 4240, 6369, 9443, 11557 euyl; 7405 euel; 1896 wykkyd *D* euyl; 2073 wykkyd *C* euyl; 3971 euyl *O* ill; 4953 foly *O* euyle; 6560 euel *O* yll; 9653 euyl; 10172 ylle *SV* vuel *O* wyke
euelid v. [OE yfelian] fell sick **Ch1** 15042 euelid P iueled L; **HS** 8033 euyld
euen, euenyng, euentide n. [OE æfen] evening **Ch1** 2434, 5544, 5546, 9320 euen; 1313, 5533 euentide; **Ch2** 670, 1661, 3955, 5879, 6995 euen; 4310 euentide; 7588, 7595 euenyng; **HS** 7290, 10609 eue; 376, 505 euen; 9420 euentyde
euen, euenly adj./adv. [OE efen, efn] level, smooth; equal, fair, just; average; exactly **Ch1** 382, 4653, 5224, 6410, 8978 euen; 4258, 7405 euenly; 5129 euenlike P euenlyk L; 6737 euen like P euene y like L; **Ch2** 386, 1236, 3292, 4919, 5209 euen; 7771 euenlik; **HS** 64, 105, 1589, 11194, 12148 euene; 1574 euyn; 5670, 7611, 7623 euen; 1590 euene lyke; 6360 euenly; 1616, 2489 euene *C* ȝeuen
euenhed n. [from OE efen, adj.] fairness, justice, equality **Ch2** 823, 4782 euenhede; 1601, 6100 euenhed; 2943L euenhed (om. P)
euer, euere adv. [OE æfre] always, ever, continually **Ch1** 210, 1564, 3559, 6802, 9310 euer; 7294, 8969 euere; 546, 2318, 6697 for euer; 13722L for euere & ay (om. P); **Ch2** 84 ay P euere L; 970, 1703, 2099, 5603, 7899 euer; 279, 1762, 4676, 6041, 7501 for euer; **HS** 154, 493 euere; 1549 euer; 3755 eure; 229, 1402 for euere; 6050 foreure; 2328 euer after; 694 euer *C* alwey; 1066 ay GLOSS B euere; 2927 euerywhore *O* ay qwore
eueridele n./adv. [from OE æfre + dæl] all, everything **Ch2** 1942 eueridele; **HS** 4476 eurydele
euerilkon, eurychoun pronoun [from OE æfre + ælc] everyone, one and all **Ch1** 1565, 4569, 5368, 6220, 7285 euerilkon; 7779, 8220 euerilkone; 4352 alle P eueryche L; 14572 ilkon P euerichon L; **Ch2** 53, 2992, 4313, 5142, 7163 euerilkon; 530, 3693, 4146, 5512 euerilkone; **HS** 2603, 6988 eury; 7434, 8978 eurychone; 107 euerychone; 4860, 5090, 10773, 10188 eurychoun; 10019 eurywham *O* euer ylke qwame *SV* eueriche mon
euermore adv. [OE æfre + mare] always, ever afterwards **Ch1** 287, 718, 2780, 5103, 8665 euermore; 5989 euer mare; **Ch2** 850, 1545, 2864, 4936, 7020 euermore; **HS** 646, 1399, 11992 euermore; 2144, 12039 euermor; 9803 eure more
examine v. [OF examiner] investigate; to test **Ch2** 6003 examend; **HS** 9625 examyne
excuse v. [AF escuser (MP)] exonerate, absolve; forgive or pardon **Ch1** 10124, 15525 excused; **HS** 2385 excuse; 6967 excusede; 12363 excused
executour, sekutour n. [AF executur (MP)] an agent; executor of a will **HS** 1220, 6236, 6309,

6412 executours; 6366 executur; 6496 executour; 1187 exekutour *C* executour; 1182, 1183 sekutour

exile n. [OF] banishment **Ch2** 3215 exile

exile v. [OF exilier] to banish or condemn someone **Ch1** 5417 exilde P chaced L; 3636 exilde; 4848 exile; 5112 exille; **Ch2** 1425, 3202 exile; 1428, 2723, 3031, 1504, 1544 exiled; 5448 exild

extend v. [L extendere] survey, assess land **Ch2** 2057 extend P extente L; 2061 extend; 4963 extende

◆ **extendours** n. [AF estendour] surveyors **Ch2** 2057 extendours P extentours L

extente n. [AF extente] assessed value of land, revenue **Ch2** 2063 extente; **HS** 6076 extente

F

fable n. [OF] fiction; fanciful narrative **Ch1** 10360 fable; 8025, 13528 fabille

face n. [OF] face **Ch1** 3168, 7208, 9290, 14286, 15167 face; 7192 faces; **Ch2** 657, 3278, 6712, 7824, 7987 face; **HS** 304, 10200 face; 10207 faces

facounde n. [OF faconde] fluency, eloquence **Ch1** 9304 facounde

fade adj. [OF] pale, dull in color **HS** 3219 fade

fader n. [OE fæder] parent; priest, confessor **Ch1** 280, 2083, 6054, 7862, 8834 fader; 331, 901, 2410, 5569, 8144 fadere; 8210 fadir; **Ch2** 325, 1045, 2604, 4589, 8127 fader; 247, 2648, 4413, 5435, 8350 fadere; **HS** 1, 142, 3003, 3838 fadyr; 4879, 4915, 6282 fader; 12162 fadres

faderles adj. [OE fæderleas] without a father **Ch1** 8500 faderles

fay, fey, feyþ, faith n. [AF feid, fei, fai, from L fidem] religious system, belief; loyalty **Ch1** 5863, 9188, 14493 faith; 3850 feche þe bere (error) P faiþ bere L; 13897 feith P feyþ L; 14381 faith P feythe L; 15338 fayth P feiþ L; **Ch2** 4037L par ma fay (P differs); 498, 4596, 6232, 7315, 7489 fayth; 1058 faiþe; 1543 faythe; 4777, 5092 faith; 4803, 6836 fay; 8137 feith; **HS** 564 fayþ GLOSS B beleue; 4010 feyþ; 5411 fey; 10575 fay; 7749, 9946 feyth

faythfulle, feythly adj./adv. [from AF feid] loyal, trustworthy **Ch1** 3783 rihtfulle P feyghtful L; 5097L, 6415L feyþful (P differs); 7328 ffeithfully P ffeyþfullike L; 8213 feitfully; 14852 faithly; **Ch2** 6255 faythfulle; 7493 faithfulle; 7734 feythly

faile n. [see sanȝ faile] [OF faille] neglect; failure, error; scarcity, lack **Ch1** 4224, 5874 withouten faile; 15673 faile; **HS** 885 wyþoutyn fayle; 1621, 2241, 7220;, 7367, 11401 wyþoute fayle

faile v. [OF faillir] fail in expectation, performance; be at fault or lacking **Ch1** 1552, 2847, 5158, 6190, 8733 faile; 1544, 3380, 5311, 8538, 15661 failed; 3765 failled; **Ch2** 86, 4194, 4822, 6180, 7524 faile; 2415, 4728, 5982, 7598, 7980 failed; **HS** 547 faylyþ; 9695 fayleþ; 1674, 2580, 3642, 4858, 7914 fayle

fayn, feyn v. [OE fæȝnian; cp. OF feindre] to be joyful, welcoming; disguise, conceal, pretend **Ch1** 197, 5925, 6843, 7991, 15696 fayn; 781 fayne; 7441 fain P fayn L; 3831 feined P feyned L; 5378 feyne; 8872 fened P ffeyned L; 15131 feyned; **Ch2** 1082, 3243, 4972, 5648, 5712 fayn

fayn, feyn adj./adv. [OE fægen] joyful, happy; eager, willing **Ch1** 758, 2960, 6079, 6889, 15770 fayn; **Ch2** 842, 3331, 4972, 6188, 8046 fayn; 962 feyn; **HS** 5798 feyn

faynte, feynt v. [from OF feint, adj.] to be cowardly, weak; to fade **Ch1** 2490 feynt; 8282 faynte; 13320 feynt P feynte L

faynt, feynt adj. [see feyn, v.] [from OF feindre, v.] weak, cowardly **Ch1** 4486 faynte P feynte L; 10704, 15518 feynt; **Ch2** 7036 faynt; **HS** 11774 feynte; 4914, 12495, 12636 feynt

fayntise, feyntise n. [OF] deceit, hypocrisy, faint-heartedness **Ch1** 1591, 4608, 7118 fayntise P feyntise L; 7295 fayntise; **Ch2** 4378 fayntise; 7587 feyntise; **HS** 5129, 12267 feyntyse; 11791 feyntys

fayntlie adv. [from OF feint, adj.] deceitfully **Ch2** 3746 fayntlie

faire, fare n. (1) [OF afaire] affair, event **Ch1** 15515 faire P fare L; 4829L fare (P differs); **Ch2** 7036 faire; 2603 tenement P faire L

faire, feyre n. (2) [OF feire] a fair; gathering of buyers and sellers **Ch2** 7189 faires; **HS** 9448 feyres; 9449 feyre

faire, fair, feyr adj./adv. [OE fæger, fægre] good, lovely, sweet; beautifully, neatly; fluently **Ch1** 103, 617, 679, fayre; 194 feyrere; 762, 6227 feyre; 517, 544, 600 fayrest; 1350, 3364, 6932, 9164, 11455 faire; 3717, 4668, 7302, 7762 fair; 300, 2008, 2369, 3778, 7210 fairest; 3718 fayr; 5808 fairer; 1655, 2076, 2856, 12776 fairere; 2014 fairere P fair L; 6335 faire P god L; 4025 fare; **Ch2** 41, 657, 2148, 5730, 7493 faire; 1800, 2305, 3781, 5049, 6667 fair; 3361 fayre; 2545, 6115 fayrer; 6667 fair spak; 5198, 7665 fairere; 5216, 6593 fairest; 5650, 8165 fairer; **HS** 1241, 1475, 9252 feyr; 3063, 12146 feyre; 1915 fayre; 1000, 3220, 4212 feyrer; 1392, 4434 feyrest; 2663, 3512 feyr spekyng

fairhed, feyrhede n. [from OE fæger, adj.] physical beauty **Ch1** 692 fairehede; 9163 fairhed; **Ch2** 5648 fairhede; 8148 faired (?error: fairer); **HS** 3047, 12610 feyrhede; 3244 feyrhede *O* fayrnes

fallace n. [OF] deceit, guile **HS** 2778, 2779 fallace

falle n. [OE feall] falling from a horse **Ch1** 10675 falle

falle, felle v. [see befalle] [OE feallan] drop, fall, sink; to happen; to suffer misfortune; to sin **Ch1** 1952, 3380, 5677, 7411, 10673 felle; 3874 fel; 5124 fals P falleþ L; 3412, 3447, 4604 fellid; 4342, 4639 feld; 5770 felled; 2833, 6449, 7990, 8014 falles; 2369, 7848 fallen; 4771 fallis; 1251, 2408, 4582, 7354, 9370 falle; 5124 fals P falleþ L; **Ch2** 3960 falle P fel L; 3758, 8068 fallis; 3221 fele; 3882 fellis; 1620, 2182, 4080, 6024, 8329 felle; 108, 1612, 3033, 6275, 8308 falle; 2227 falles P falleþ L; 5118, 5734 falles; 477, 1089, 5009, 5630, 6602 fallen; **HS** 49, 1477, 3002, 5724, 10934 falle; 914, 7589 fal; 75, 1120, 6406, 10744 fyl; 919 fel; 4704 fell; 6661 fyll; 1635, 7211 falþ; 1700 fallyþ; 3448 fallys; 11414 falleþ; 8597, 8677 falles; 681 fallyn

fallyng ger. [from OE feallan] a fall; descent from rectitude **Ch1** 8024, 15429 fallyng; **HS** 8553 fallyng

fals n./adj. [OE fals, L falsum] deceit, fraud, treachery **Ch1** 1569, 4139, 7044, 9044, 15518 fals; 7998 fals (adj.) P fals (n.) L; **Ch2** 294, 1082, 3807, 4521, 8133 fals; 340L, 744L 751L false (P differs); **HS** 371, 1220, 2636, 11229, 12636 fals; 6259, 6260 false; 7880 fals *O* wrange

falsdom n. [from OE fals, adj.] deceitfulness **HS** 2746 falsdom

falsen v. [OF falser] to deceive, pretend; forge documents **HS** 5362, 12018 false; 11198, 11224 falsen

falshed n. [from OE fals, adj.] treachery, deceitfulness **Ch2** 2329, 7044 falshede; 1629, 1763, 5938, 5955 falshed; **HS** 644, 2714 falshede

falsly adv. [from OE fals, adj.] with guile, treacherously **Ch2** 5677, 6406 falsly; 1175L falsly (om. P); **HS** 2083 falsly; 9469 falsle; 11077 wrongly *O* falsly

falsnes n. [from OE fals, adj.] deceitfulness, treachery **Ch1** 5917, 7120 falsnes; **Ch2** 1324, 5934, 6408, 7768, 8202 falsnes; 8184 falsnesse; 1182 treson P falsnesse L; **HS** 1498 falsnesse; 2085, 2086, 2708 falsnes

falste n. [OF falsete] treachery, dishonesty **Ch2** 5954 falste

fame n. [OF] reputation, good name; rumor; behavior **Ch1** 266, 1386, 3602, 6321, 7482 fame; **Ch2** 221, 635, 2887, 7828, 8023 fame; **HS** 1519, 2075, 4713, 10961, 12363 fame

fame v. (1) [OF famer] defame, slander **HS** 3653 fame; 8307 dyffame *O* fame

famen v. (2) [OF afamer] to starve someone **Ch1** 5314 famen P enfamyn L; **Ch2** 2979 famen P famyne L

fang, fong v. [see vnderfong] [OE fon] grasp, seize, capture; take the throne; take a prisoner **Ch1** 242 vnderfang P gan fonge L; 2909 fong P fonde (?fonge) L; 5621 gan fong; 13123 vpfange; **Ch2** 6528, 8051 fanged; 8181 feyng; **HS** 1471, 7802, 11931 fonge; 11980 fangeþ; 1020 cumberance *C* fongyng (?fondyng) *D* encoumbraunce

fantome n. [OF fantosme, L phantasma] illusion **HS** 2239, 7157 fantome

fare, faire n. [see faire, n. (1)] [OE faru, fær] a journey; proceeding **Ch2** 3914, 5150, 5572 fare

fare, fore v. [OE faran, feran, ferde] travel, go, proceed **Ch1** 500, 3048, 6461, 8717, 12172 fare; 10814 far; 2796, 5953, 6412, 7936, 10937 ferd; 92, 2480, 7085, 9219, 12475 ferde; 10809 faren; 5559, 7809, 10197 fore; 5858 farde P sayled L; 13877 farde P ferde L; 7809 fore P foor L; 13896L for (om. P); 7454, 8011 farand; **Ch2** 184, 2439, 4776, 7030, 8346 fare; 502, 2168, 7855 ferde; 1456, 3209, 4132, 5534, 7755 ferd; 603, 2382, 2697, 5182, 6415 fore; 7563 farn; 1706 foore; **HS** 4177, 6135, 10913 fare; 3981, 9813 farþ; 1221 vare *CDFH* fare; 9276 ferd; 4885, 5494, 6135 ferde; 9388 farand; 2832 fore GLOSS BH dede; 2939, 7970 fare GLOSS B go; 3818 ferde GLOSS BH ȝede *O* wende; 5015 fore GLOSS BH ȝede

farre adv. [see fer, fere]

fast adj./adv. [see rotefast, stedfast] [OE fæst(e)] fixed, secured; stable; faithful; tightly, firmly, immovably **Ch1** 477, 3660, 4568, 7075, 11381 fast; 1158, 4959 faste; **Ch2** 451, 1835, 4655, 6454, 7847 fast; **HS** 945, 1261, 1749, 2510, 6253 faste; 8058, 8777, 8948, 9215, 10587 fast; 1157 ȝorne GLOSS B vaste

fast, fest v. (1) [OE fæstan; ON festa] fix, make firm or stable; to attack, inflict injury; secure with fetters **Ch1** 8004, 11766 fast; 15650 fest; 14064L feste (om. P); **Ch2** 3529, 4718, 6580 fest; **HS** 1473 fastyd; 10611 feste

faste v. (2) [OE fæstan] abstain from food **HS** 271, 1773, 9732, 10790, 11667 faste; 3181 fastede

fastyng ger. [from OE fæstan] refusing food **HS** 310, 2021, 5162 fastyng

faucoun, faukon n. [OF faucon] peregrine falcon **Ch2** 1784 faukon; **HS** 8647 fauchoun; 10924 faucoun *O* fauchoun

fauht v. [see feht, feiht, fight]

faute n. [see defaut] [OF faute, faulte] lack, scarcity, deficiency **Ch1** 1030 with faute P y þe faut L; 1061 defaut P faute L; 4416L faute (P differs); **Ch2** 5810, 6162 faut; 5369, 5734 faute; **HS** 4900 faute; 3993 defaute *F* faute

fautours n. [OF fauteur] followers **Ch2** 5142 fautours

Fauuelle n. [OF fauvel, favele] name of a tawny horse **Ch2** 4345 Fauuelle

fawe v. [OE fægen] change color **Ch2** 4315 fulle

fayn P ful fawe L

feaute n. [OF feaute] homage; loyalty, obligation **Ch1** 4522, 14147 feaute; 6362 feaute P fewte L; **Ch2** 48, 1961, 3376, 5091, 8276 feaute; 40 feaute P feufte L; 1557 feauteȝ

feble adj./adv. [OF] weak, infirm; ineffective, powerless **Ch1** 11322, 13797, 13900 feble; 8289 febille; 14231 wakest P febleste L; **Ch2** 2617 feble P wrecchede L; 3843 febli; 5877 febilly; **HS** 6116, 8137, 8819, 10962 feble; 7253 febel

febylnes n. [from OF feble, adj.] weakness **HS** 406 febylnes

feblyng ger. [from OF feble, adj.] becoming weak **HS** 408 feblyng

fecche v. [see fet, fette]

fede v. [OE fedan, fedde] supply with food; nourish **Ch1** 1067, 5901, 7116, 7215, 7242 fede; 438 fedde; 15804 fed; **Ch2** 1616 fede; 120 fedde; 7940 fedis; **HS** 5387, 6623, 9915, 10796 fede; 6640 fed; 7274 fedde; 6755 fedest

fedirhames, feþerhames n. [OE feþerhama] plumage, wings **Ch1** 2252 fedirhames P feþerhames L

fedres, feþeres n. [OE fed(d)er, pl. feth(e)ren, fedres] feathers **Ch1** 10052 fedres P feþeres L

fee n. [AF fee] estate, land, property; feudal obligation **Ch1** 667, 7350 fee P fe L; 1926, 6763, 8593 fees; 1930, 2516, 4166 fee; 2153 feeȝ P fe L; 4543 feeȝ; 6121 feeȝ P fes L; **Ch2** 620, 2067, 2406, 4453, 6903 fe; 254, 1211, 1463, 3571 fee; 1863, 1923, 2388, 2433 fees; 1556, 3245, 4124, 4948, 7887 feeȝ; 5167 feȝ; **HS** 1110, 11717 fee; 6031, 6334, 6810 fe

feffe v. [AF feffer, feøffer] endow, invest with an estate **Ch1** 8210 feffid P feffed L; 10793 feffed; **Ch2** 5746, 6248 feffe; 353, 774, 1913 feffed

feffement n. [AF] an estate; charter of conveyance of an estate **Ch2** 6006 feffementes; 6129, 6247 feffement

fehte, feihte n./v. [see fight]

feie v. [OE fegan] to put off, delay **Ch1** 13320 feie

feihter n. [see fighters]

feyn v. [see fayn, v.]

feyng v. [see fang, fong, v.]

feynt v./adj. [see faynt]

feyrnes n. [see fair, feyr] [OE fægernes] brightness; eloquence; justice **HS** 2299 feyrnes; 7026 feyrnesse; 3244 feyrhede *O* fayrnes

feith n. [see fay, faith]

felawe n. [ON felagi] companion, loyal friend **Ch1** 143, 1524, 2553, 3085, 8274 felawes; 7754 felawe; 5935, 7474 felaw; 7768 felau; 7745 felaus; 13155, 13184 felauhes; **Ch2** 1602, 3958, 4039, 5458, 5479 felawes; 5364 felaus; 5180 felauhes; **HS** 1550, 1614, 2320, 3607, 10766 felawe; 10747 felaus

felawe v. [from ON felagi, n.] to associate with **Ch1** 5716 folowed P felawed L; 6425 fleand P felawed L

felawrede n. [from OE felaw + rede] companionship; a comrade **HS** 4034 felawred; 1650, 1880, 11397 felawrede; 7371 felaghrede

felawshepe, felaushepe n. [from ON felagi] community, company **Ch1** 10 felawschip; 7762 felichip P felawschip L; **Ch2** 3544 felauschip; 4622 felawschip; **HS** 60 felaushepe; 4206 felawshepe

feld, felde n. [OE] flat, open country; a pasture; battleground **Ch1** 502, 2696, 6173, 8407, 15793 felde; 8752, 14054 feld; 1890, 3663 ardawe felde P eryed feld L; **Ch2** 25, 432, 1456, 2710, 7253 felde; 137, 2863, 3598, 4662, 6615 feld; 4039 ferd P feld L; 120 feldes; **HS** 997, 1125, 3269, 4062, 8516 feld; 9900 feldes

fele v. (1) [OE felan] to feel; to be aware; to touch **Ch1** 2460, 2461 fele; 3178 felid; 7941, 8320, 12101 felte; 8700 felt; **Ch2** 347, 1753, 3058, 3172, 7890 felt; **HS** 3965 felyst; 7912, 8489, 8556 fele; 2329, 4436, 8861 felte; 7014, 9155 felt

fele v. (2) [OE feolan] to reach, advance on enemies **Ch1** 5744 fele; 13887 felt P felde L; **Ch2** 3477 felt

fele adj./adv. [OE fela] many, much, a great extent; large amounts; often, greatly **Ch1** 91, 4055, 8260, 9588, 15804 fele; **Ch2** 240, 1761, 3477, 6073, 8059 fele; **HS** 5265, 5680, 7758, 8063, 8884 fele; 385 mochyl *C* fele

felle, felly adj./adv. [OF fel] cruel, angry, fierce; wickedly, violently **Ch1** 8066, 9206, 9730, 10730, 15231 felle; 5768 felly P ffellyk L; 15588 felly P fersly L; 15237 felli P hertli L; 15234 fellier P hertiloker L; **Ch2** 3071, 3460, 7677 felle; **HS** 3218 felle; 9122 fellyche; 3149 felleche *O* felonly

felle v. [see falle, v.]

felon n. [OF] wretch, wicked person, traitor **Ch1** 1276L feloun (om. P); 4487 felon P folet L; 5707 felons; 15622 feloun; **Ch2** 2049 felon; 1902, 4718, 4894, 5061, 7589 feloun; 7108, 7570, 7596, 8030 felons; **HS** 412, 1314, 2111, 3556, 4189 felun; 9844 felons; 3644 tresun *O* felon

felon, felons adj. [OF felun] false, wicked, base, hostile **Ch1** 484 felons P felenous L; 1980 felon P lyþer L; 2627, 4768, 5124, 7713, 13693 felon; 14721 feloun; **Ch2** 3393 felon; 7108, 7179 felons; 5073 felonse (?error); **HS** 1075, 4198 felun; 1344 feloune; 8522 felons

felonye n. [OF] deceit, treachery, crime, betrayal **Ch1** 2761, 7149 felonye; 2878, 3335, 4723, 6591, 8855 felony; 3931, 6020, 15608 felonie; 5839 felonyes; **Ch2** 732, 1977, 4906, 5685,

8255 felonie; 1469 folonie P felonye L; **HS** 1351 felony; 1311 felonye; 1456 felunnye; 3130 felonnye; 5986, 7152 felonye; 7596 felonye *F* folie *O* foly; 10900 felonye *O* velany

felonli, felonlik adv. [from OF felun, adj.] cruelly, wickedly, savagely, treacherously **Ch1** 489 felonlike; 1642, 8351 felonly; 4991 felonli P felonlyk L; 3000 fersliere P felonloker L; 9528 felonlik P felonlyk L; **HS** 1359 felunsly *C* folyli; 3149 felleche *O* felonly; 5248 felunly; 4119 felunleche; 5614, 7783 felunlyche

fen n. [OE fen, fennas] swamp, slough **Ch1** 1887, 9215 fen; 15782L fennes (om. P)

fende n. [OE feond] foe, enemy; Satan, a devil **Ch1** 1331, 1339, 14282 fende; 11965 feende; 7495 feend P fend L; 1334, 7280, 7975 fendes; **Ch2** 3891 feendes; 6399, 7935 fende; 6815, 6817 fendes; **HS** 4, 8235, 10256, 11876 fend; 1754, 7480, 12590 fende; 5265, 10936, 10950 fendes; 1572 fendys; 1280 fende *D* deuyl; 1432 fend *F* deuel; 2600 fendys *C* deuyll; 3186 fende *O* dragon; 11502 fendes *O* deuyls; 11904 fend *O* deuyll

fende v. [see defend, v.] [OF defendre] defend, excuse **Ch1** 1574, 4273, 5925, 6851 fend; 6391, 7024, 8325, 9342 fende; 5526 defended P fended L; 6693 fende P fendeþ L; 4354 defend P fende L; 5526 defended P fended L; 8325 fende; 9057 fendid P defended L; 12310L fende (om. P); **Ch2** 3320, 4827 fende; 5294, 5873 fend; 3308 fend (error) P send L; 3892 wendes P fendes L; **HS** 7420, 9834 fende

fens n. [from OF defens] defense **Ch1** 1047, 8523 fens

fer, fere, farre adv. [see ferne] [OE feor, feorran] far; at a distance, afar **Ch1** 276, 2254, 5858, 7104, 8941 fer; 1092 farþere P ferrer L; 1694 feire P fer L; 3346, 4384 fere; 7758 ferer; 5749 fulle nere P fer & ner L; 5846 fer P ferþer L; 5959 fer & hend; 9930L farre (P differs); 12286L ferrer (P differs); 15038L ferrere (om. P); 4611 ferweis P (om. L); **Ch2** 440, 1764, 4702, 6780, 7855 fer; 4642 fere P fer L; 4779 ferne P of fer L; 1323, 3087, 3681 ferrer; 2458, 4179 fer & nere; 7525 ferrere; 1039 ferrer P ferther L; **HS** 6113, 7806, 5895 fer; 6843, 8676 fere; 337, 798, 2405, 2884, 3653 furþer; 6173, 12194 ferþer; 9247 ferþere; 7342 ferþest

ferd, fere n. (1) [OE phr., for ferd] being afraid; fright **Ch1** 6194 for ferde P for ferd L; 14712 ferde P ferd L; 1992, 6683 ferd; 6881 pouerte P fere L; **Ch2** 306, 1299, 4736, 6092, 7066 ferd; 2172 ferd P harde L; 2799 ferde P aferd L; 465 in ferd P ful ferd L; 1781 oglift P aferd L; **HS** 12194 ferd

ferd, fere n. (2) [OE ferd, fyrd] army, host; companion; together in a company **Ch1** 7203 fers P feres L; 5436 in fere P y fere L; 7214L feres (om. P); 7763 in fere; 12614 fers P pers LR; **Ch2** 1256 feres; 7454 fers; 4039 in ferd P in é feld L; 4953, 8296 in ferd; 8296 in ferd; 1523, 2574, 4382, 5091, 7695 in fere; 791L, 1989L in fere (P differs); 2557, 3595 pere P fere L; 5680 fere; **HS** 1924 pere *C* fere; 2247 frere *CD* fere; 2603 sere *C* fere *F* þere *O* sere; 5058 yn fere

ferd, fere v. [OE gefæran] frighten someone, be afraid **Ch1** 6685 fere; 7676 afere P fere L; **Ch2** 4248 sperd P ferd L; **HS** 484 drede *C* ben ferd; 1593 awys GLOSS BH feryþ *C* owes; 3589 aglyfte GLOSS BH feryd

fere adj. [AF fer] healthy, strong **Ch1** 9515 fere

ferynges adj. [see feuere]

ferly, ferlik n. [OE, ON ferliki, monster] astonishment; a wonder, strange event **Ch1** 1233, 8675 ferly; 5576, 5595 ferlik; 4349 ferly P (L differs); **Ch2** 519 ferly; **HS** 10773, 11086 ferly; 9384 ferlyke; 1823 wndur *C* merueyle *D* ferly; 3865 ferly GLOSS BH wndur; 7485, 8211 ferly GLOSS H wundyr; 3707, 12232 wndyr *O* ferly; 10614 wunder *O* ferle

ferly, ferlik adj./adv. [OE færlic, from fær] strange, marvelous, wonderful; astonishing **Ch1** 1702, 3114, 6054, 6086 ferly; 1440 ferly P (om. L); 14337 ferlike; **Ch2** 347, 2756 ferly; 7424 ferlike; **HS** 5620, 5713, 9137, 9294 ferly; 11975 wnder *O* so ferly; 3483, 4107 wndyrly *O* ferly

ferne adv. [see fer, adv.] [OE feorran, fyrn] from afar, far away **Ch1** 4983, 8315, 9013, 10389 ferne; **Ch2** 4779 ferne P of fer L

ferme n. [OF] a lease of land **HS** 2409 ferme

ferme v. [see afferme, conferme] [OF fermer] to confirm; strengthen **Ch1** 14838 ferme; **HS** 9896 ferme

fers adj./adv. [OF] bold, valiant; violent **Ch1** 5329, 6526, 10730, 11721 fers; 5119L fers (P differs); 6115L fers (om. P); 3000 fersliere P felonloker L; 13094 strong P fers L; 15588 felly P fersly L; **Ch2** 3595, 6738, 7688 fers; **HS** 2574 feres

ferth, fourþe numeral [OE feorþa] fourth **Ch1** 793, 7268, 8094, 8803, 12871 ferth; 6779 ferþe; 12057, 14139 ferthe; **Ch2** 129, 1183 ferthe; 307, 568, 599, 1898, 5025 ferth; 2048 feré; **HS** 1057 fourþe; 2751, 4243 vourþe

ferþing n. [OE feorþung] a silver coin worth a quarter of a penny; a "noke": the smallest amount or nothing **Ch2** 2423, 5746 ferþing; 5741 ferthyng; 597 ferþing noke; **HS** 5770 ferþyng; 5812 a ferþyng noke GLOSS B a corner

fertre n. [AF fertre] tomb, shrine **Ch1** 15838 fertre; 15840 fertres; 15892 in fertre P fertred

(v.) L; **Ch2** 618, 812, 830, 1888, 3793 fertre
ferweis adv. [see fer, adv.]
fesed v. [OE fesan] put to flight **Ch2** 4753 fesid; 6636 fesed
fest, feste n. [OF feste] feast, celebration **Ch1** 299, 7264, 7468, 15511 fest; 1769, 4665, 5504, 6010, 9153 feste; 4685 fest day; **Ch2** 728, 1792, 3066, 6566, 7705 feste; 590, 1183, 2708, 3995, 8233 fest; 271 hie feste P holy feste L; 633 fest of our lady; 1587 feste of ȝole; **HS** 805 festys; 815, 6987, 12146 fest; 6017, 9373, 11099 feste
fest v. [see fast, v. (1)]
fet, fette, fecche v. [OE fetian, later feccan, feccean] seek, look for; catch **Ch1** 1620 fette P yfet L; 3562, 6991, 7845, 8225, 8669 fet; 8315, 9638, 11627, 14004 fette; 14596 fitched P pighte L; 8941 fecched P feightit L; 12348L foched (om. P); 15142 fecche P feche L; 3850 feche þe bere (error) P faiþ bere L; **Ch2** 1706 fette P fet forþ L; 2642, 5430 fet; 1344, 5093 fette; **HS** 2590, 7797 fet; 1206, 10619 fette
fete n. [see fote, n.]
fettre v. [OE gefeterian] shackle, bind **Ch1** 8452 fettred P fetered L; **Ch2** 8245 fettre; 2473 fettered; 4134, 6368, 8191, 8285 fettred
fetowur n. [see surfeyte, surfeture]
feuere, ◆ feuerynges, ferynges n./adj. [OE fefer, fevre; OF fievre from L febris] fever; sudden death **Ch1** 3895 ferynges dede P ◆ ffeuerynges deþ L; 15043 feuere agew P feuere agu L; **Ch2** 4600 ferynges dede P fyuerouse deþ L; **HS** 6960, 6968 feuere; 7001 feuer
fewe adj. [see fo, adj.]
ficacie adj. [see fikelle] [?from OE befician, deceive] treacherous, crafty **Ch2** 1162 ficacie P fikays L
fift, fifti, fiften numeral [see fiue]
fight, fehte n. [OE feoht] hostile engagement; war **Ch1** 5717 fehtes; 7710, 8066 fight; 10604 faute P fight L; **Ch2** 8164 fight; **HS** 4917, 5371, 7475 fyght
fight, fauht v. [OE feohtan, feaht] to fight, struggle, quarrel **Ch1** 2945 fight P fighte L; 3282, 4351, 8325, 12086 fight; 1562, 3441, 5322, 8413, 12053 fauht; 8409, 8990 fouht; 476, 483 faught; 8077 fauhte; 8154 feihtand P fyghtyng L; 8740 feiht; 14928 feght; **Ch2** 4550 fauht P fawȝt L; **HS** 1758, 3365, 9846 fyght; 3756 fyghte
fighter, feighter, feihter n. [OE feohtere] warrior, combatant **Ch1** 7547 feihters P fighters L; 8427L fighteres (P differs)
figure n. [OF, L figura] shape; likeness, image **Ch1** 9261 figures P vigures L; **HS** 3780 fygure
fikelle, fykyl adj. [OE ficol and facne] crafty, false, wicked **Ch1** 3798 fikille P swykel L; 4493, 5872, 8899 fikelle P fykel L; 10485 fikelle P fykele L; 5515, 7072 fikille P fykel L; **Ch2** 4814 foken P fikul L; 751, 822, 2372, 7922 fikelle; **HS** 2643, 5224, 5948, 8136, 8365 fykyl
filchid v. [origin uncertain] take as booty **Ch2** 6826 filchid
file n. [OE fylen, v., ON fyla] wretch, fool, rascal; ?a wench **Ch1** 14567 files P fyle L; **Ch2** 2318, 5730 file; **HS** 8373 fyles; 4541 ylka fyle GLOSS B eury mayde gerld GLOSS H maydgerle
file v. [OE fylen] to defile, discredit, reject **Ch2** 3058, 6712 filed; 4287 filed P vyle L; **HS** 8662, 7192, 12569 fyle; 8731, 12277 fyled; 9547 fyled (?error) B *O* fulfyllede
filette n. [OF filet] trimming, edging **Ch1** 12144 filette P fylet L
fylle n. [see fulfille, v.] [OE fyll] plenty **HS** 6645 fylle
fille v. [OE fyllan] to fill up; satiate, satisfy; come to an end **Ch1** 8224 fille; 2387, 6736 filled; **Ch2** 3975, 5988 fille; 759, 3039 filled; **HS** 2895, 7260 fyll; 6758 fylle; 3250 fyllyd; 6210 fylde; 8064 fylden
fylþe n. [OE fylþ] defilement, obscenity **HS** 3681, 6581, 7564 fylþe; 7566 fylþes; 10086 fylþe *F* foli
fyne n. [OF fin, L finis] end, conclusion; death; agreement **Ch1** 2256, 3673, 6096, 6402, 15246 fyn; 13715, 14734 fine P fyn L; **Ch2** 2585, 5252, 8201 fyne; 162, 4706, 8240, 8282 fyn; **HS** 663 fyn GLOSS BH ende
fyne, finalle adj. [OF fin] excellent, superior; valuable, honorable, pure **Ch1** 180, 8626, 11530 fyne; 4302, 11746 fyn; **Ch2** 790 fyne; 5618, 6106, 6210, 6418 fyn; 5540, 8279 finalle; 6239 final; **HS** 4967, 7864 fyn; 8748 fyne
fynde, fand, fond v. [see fond, v.] [OE findan] discover, encounter, determine **Ch1** 5563 find; 1236, 4182, 7166, 10252, 14694 fynde; 3748, 7295 finde; 1159, 4028, 6830, 8521, 9392 fynd; 1241, 4433 founde; 5524L founden (P differs); 4, 785, 1439, 5601, 6879 fand; 167, 1019 fonden; 13954 fondon; 839, 1897, 5903, 6508, 9122 fond; 845, 1327, 5220, 8041, 8064 fonde; **Ch2** 3646, 4968 fondon; 5183, 7071 finde; 36, 2047, 5369, 7882, 8125 fynde; 5838 find; 99, 1723, 4664, 6197, 7748 fynd; 92, 1252, 3690, 6292, 8340 fond; 1949, 2735, 3089, 4710, 7514 fand; 920, 3176, 6402 founde; 2172, 7051 found; 6591, 8096 fonde; 232 fonden P founde L; 431 fonde P founde L; 707, 1778, 3921, 5734, 8179 fonden; 3820 founde P fonde L; 3646, 4968 fondon; 7200 findes; 6876 fyndes; **HS** 383, 1102, 1544, 11423, 12113 fynde; 5305 fyndeþ; 5134 fynst; 10114 fyndes; 2042 fyndyn; 8774 fond; 79, 1810, 5616, 10588 fonde; 5933, 9221, 10771 founde; 1815, 2425 fownde;

2596 founden
finger n. [OE] finger **Ch1** 3166 fingers P fyngres L; **HS** 6671, 10243 fynger
fire n. [OE fyr] a conflagration; wild fire: Greek fire **Ch1** 2247, 8122, 8430, 8923, 10694 fire; 1372 fyre; 8078 fire P fyr L; 1039 wilde fire; **Ch2** 1003, 1905, 4370, 6580, 8055 fire; 4215 wilde fire; **HS** 1736, 2601 fer; 2492, 2493 ferys; 1598, 2271, 2495, 2565, 5297 fere; 7546, 10104, 12446, 12454, 12526 fyre
fyrmament n. [OF; L firmamentum] the heavens; the sky **HS** 219, 285, 2491 fyrmament
first numeral/adj./adv. [OE fyrst] first in a list; the earliest; first in rank **Ch1** 13, 1927, 4611, 8696, 12531 first; **Ch2** 146, 1248, 4210, 6967, 8305 first; **HS** 147, 2113, 9501, 11907, 12299 fyrst; 403, 827, 3011 ferst
fysycyene n. [OF fisiciien] healer **HS** 1183 fysycyene
fisch, fissh n. [OE fisc] fish; fish as food **Ch1** 6883, 10840, 10861 fisch; 10150, 10153 fisches; 15670 fissh; **HS** 7285 fysshe
fisch v. [OE fiscian] to catch fish **Ch2** 1297 fischid P fisshers (n.) L; 5005 fisshes
fisshere n. [OE fiscere] a fisherman **Ch2** 533 fisshere
fyste n. [OE fyst] the fist **HS** 6213, 9301 fyste
fitched v. [OF fich(i)er] drive a stake **Ch1** 14596 fitched P pighte L
fithelers n. [OE fiþelere] a fiddler, entertainer **Ch1** 4000 fithelers P fythelers L
fithels n. [OE fiþele] fiddles **Ch1** 11144 fithels P fyþeles L
fiue, fift, fiften numeral/n./adj. [OE fif, fifta] five, fifth, fifteen, fifteenth; fifty **Ch1** 3781, 3813 fiue; 4977 fyue; 233 fyften; 850, 3021, 6330, 8712 fiften; 8590 fiftene; 4436 fiftend; 5693 fyfti; 49, 186 fifty; **Ch2** 102, 2336, 4042, 6724, 8347 fiue; 135, 5403 fift; 727, 3631, 6959, 7295 fifte; 7002 fiften; 159, 666, 2346, 5693, 8107 fiftene; 49, 7682 fiftend; 4221, 4331 fiueten; 543, 1284, 3122, 5642 fifty; 5713 fifti; **HS** 72, 1137, 2738, 4898 fyue; 1307, 1309 fyþe; 2755, 11491 fyfþe; 66 fyftene
flamins, archeflamyns n. [L flamen] a temple of the pagan Britons; the chief priest of the Britons **Ch1** 5663L flamins (om. P); 5664 flamyns; 5667 archeflamyns P arche flaminus L; 5668 archeflame P chef flamee L; 5670 flamyns P flamins L
flamme, flaume n. [AF flamme (MP), flambe] blazing dragon's breath; a flame **Ch1** 8078 flammes; 11811 flaume; **HS** 5923, 5924 flamme
flammyng, flaumand v./ppl. [AF flaum(b)er] to blaze; gleam **Ch1** 8970 flaumand; **HS** 7028 flammyng
flax n. [OE fleax] flax, tinder **Ch1** 14064 flax
fle, fleih, fled v. [OE fleon] retreat, run away, flee **Ch1** 1168, 3199, 6178, 9131, 14294 fle; 716, 2929, 5391, 8821, 13516 fled; 992 fled P flowe L; 13998 fled P flemed L; 1574 fle P fles L; 4428, 9654 flegh; 437 fledde; 11286 flees; 5387, 6541, 8373 fled P fledde L; 8377 fleh P ffley L; 3010, 5712, 8374, 15388 fleand; 3013, 8374, 13399 fleand P fleyng L; 6425 fleand P felawed L; 5389 fledden; 14987 fleih; 12396 fleand P wyþdrawande L; **Ch2** 392, 1611, 3544, 7007, 8304 fle; 44, 1356, 4753, 6628, 8169 fled; 2171 fleand P fledde L; 3422, 3962, 6704, 7010, 7847 fleand; 2863 flehand; 2963 sped P fledde L; **HS** 439, 1854, 4239, 7920, 10682 fle; 8946 fled
flees n. [OE fleos, flies] fleece of a sheep **Ch1** 441 fleeȝ; 445 flees
fleh, fleih v. [OE fleogan and fleon] fly, move swiftly away **Ch1** 1565 fleih P fleyghe L; 1406 flie P fley L; 7710, 8280, 13026 flie; 2251, 6718 flie P fleye L; 6975 flie P flye L; 8076, 8228 fleih P fley L; 8430 fleh P fleye L; 5010, 9961, 14987 fleih; 10694 flegh P fley L; 11810 flegh; 11808 flouh; **Ch2** 3730, 4070, 5030 flie; 1954, 7939 flies; 2846, 3947, 7248, 7445, 7755 fleih; **HS** 218 flye *D* fley a flyȝe; 9185 flye; 11871 fleyng *O* fleghande; 7483 fleyng *O* fleande; 322 fleye; 1273, 1860, 7486, 7492 fleygh
fleih, flie n. [OE fleoge] flies, flying insects **Ch1** 2605 flies; **Ch2** 7445 fleihes; **HS** 218 *D* flyȝe (B differs); 10924 flye; 10925 flyes
◆ **fleked** v. [from ON fleki, n.] to cover with hurdles **Ch2** 5795 fleked
flekes n. [ON fleki, flaki] a frame of wattles, a hurdle **Ch2** 7844 flekes
fleme v. [OE fleman] banish, expel, put to flight **Ch1** 4507, 13998 fled P flemed L; 4853 flemed; **Ch2** 2046, 3203, 5965 fleme; 2710, 5437, 5454, 8030 flemed
flesch, flessh n. [OE flæsc] meat; of the flesh; in bodily form **Ch1** 206 flesche; 11324L flesche (om. P); 1841 flesh; 1753, 3589, 6761, 10861, 13712 flesch; **Ch2** 4335 flesch; 5559, 6040 flessh; **HS** 92, 181, 7283 flesshe; 703 flesh; 661, 1620, 7578, 11665, 12514 flessh
flesshly adj. [OE flæslic] made of flesh; physical nature or appetites **HS** 1641, 1682, 2010, 4157 flesshly; 7684, 7724, 8430, 8510, 10145 flesshe-ly
flete n. [see flote]
fleuh v. [see flo, flouh]
flycche v. [see flit] [OF flechier] turn away, divert **HS** 1712 flycche *C* flyt *F* flitte
flie v. [OE flygan, causative of fleon] put to flight, shoot a missile; rout a foe **Ch1** 1142 slone P flayd L; 13356 lete flie P let flye L; 3199 did þe fle; **Ch2** lete he flie
flyght, flite n. [OE flyht] flight **Ch1** 2253, 4428,

4479 flight; 15578 flite P flyt L; 3011L flyght (P differs); **HS** 284 flyght

flynte n. [OE flint] hard stone to make a fire **Ch1** 8430 flyntes

flit v. [ON flit, ppl.] flee **Ch1** 3474, 13122 flit P flitte L

flyte v. [OE flitan] to chide, rebuke; quarrel, taunt **HS** 3149 flytes GLOSS BH chydyþ; 3770 flyte GLOSS BH chyde; 7758 flytte GLOSS BH chydde; 6546 [MS *O* interpolation, l. 93] flytte; (l. 94) flyttynge (ger.)

flo, flouh v. [OE flean] to flay, skin; shave **Ch1** 6541 fleuh P slowe L; 12131 flo P flow L; 12138 flouh P flowe L; 12150 flo; **Ch2** 7252 flouh; **HS** 7630 flos

flode n. [OE flod] river, stream, sea **Ch1** 738 flude; 1404, 3450, 4573, 7559, 10164 flode P flod L; **Ch2** 1901, 2577, 3049, 4220, 5360 flode

flok n. [OE floc] flock, group **Ch1** 12175 flok P folk L; **Ch2** 7581 flok

flom, flum n. [OF flum] river, stream, flood, the sea **Ch2** 4636, 4646, 4647, 4741, 4751 flom; 3725 flum P felon L; **HS** 9550 flum

flore, florth n. [OE flor] floor **HS** 2233, 2820 flore; 6184 florth

flote, flete n. [OE flota, OF flote] fleet of ships, afloat **Ch1** 1479, 1484, 1733, 2928, 15017 flote; 1533 flete P fflute L; 2980 flote P fflute L; 2917 flotes P fflutes L; 2915, 4549, 8839, 13517, 15112 flete; 1487 flotes P flute L; 3011 flote P flyght L; 6502 flete P nauye L; **Ch2** 1444, 1643, 3693, 3881 flete; 2341 flette; 4185 on flote

flour n. [OF flour, OE flur] blossom, flower; flour for bread, powder; fig.: the best, greatest **Ch1** 3778, 3782, 6409, 11094, 13224 flour; 3860, 11582 floure P flour L; 8339 floure; **Ch2** 1620, 2827, 4110, 5222, 8338 floure; 4481, 7253 flour; **HS** 1395 flourys; 1414, 3504 flours; 998, 10108 floure; 3031, 3221, 5003, 9986 flour

flowe n. [from OE flowan, v.] flood; high tide **Ch1** 992L in flowe (P differs); 4573 flowe P se L

flowe v. [OE flowan] to flow, run **Ch1** 10173 flowe; 11863 flowes; 10164, 10167 flewes P flowes L; **Ch2** 7578 flowand

flowred, flurshede v. [from OF florir] to flourish; rhetorical: flowery **HS** 881 florysyngge; 905 flurshede *C* flowred *D* floreschedyn; 3065 flurshyd *O* flowrede

fo, fa, fomen n. [OE fa, fah, adj.: hostile] the devil, an enemy; foe, opponent **Ch1** 4791, 8295, 8358, 8443, 9361 fo; 3378, 5003, 5051, 5743, 13602 fos; 6599 foos; 3528, 4811, 6207, 7372 fomen; 15218 fa; **Ch2** 911, 7200, 8320 foos; 2757 fos; 2188, 2225, 6322 fomen; **HS** 6155, 7773, 11325 fo; 6280 fos

fo, fewe adj. [OE fa, var.: fah] few in number **Ch1** 1014, 1250, 2409, 6801, 7776 fo P fewe L; 1672L, 6029L fewe (P differs); 1669 fo; 4079 fo P þe L; 12608 fo PR (L differs); **Ch2** 674L, 1300L fewe (P differs); 1911, 1421, 2851, 5834, 8022 fo; 1604 non P fewe L; **HS** 8720 fo GLOSS BH fewe; 2451, 4299, 6302, 8715, 10761 fewe

fode n. [OE foda] supplies, provisions **Ch1** 6391, 6882, 8802 fode; 910 fude P fode L; **Ch2** 4086 fode; 6300 fodes; **HS** 5065, 5099, 6486 fode

foyntes n. [OF foine] a type of spear **Ch2** 7428 foyntes

foyson, foson n. [OF foison] power, strength; abundance **Ch1** 1587, 8088 foson P foysoun L; 4636 fosons P fuysons L; 8678 fosoun P fuysoun L; 13616 foysoun P fuisoun L; **Ch2** 306, 3947 foyson; 3499, 4880 foysoun; 7765 foisoun; **HS** 5808 foysun

foken adj. [see fikelle] [OE facne, fæcne] deceitful, false **Ch2** 4814 foken P fikul L

fold n. (1) [OE fald] a sheepfold **HS** 4848 foldes; 5522 folde

fold n. (2) [OE fald] phrase: many fold; manifold; many times, often **HS** 114 many a folde; 7466, 9010 many fold; 6902 many folde; 8420 folde

folde v. [OE fealdan] to fold, bend, twist; to be folded **Ch1** 3474, 10969 folde; 11380, 11617 folden; 11608 tong o fold

fole n. [OF fol] a fool **Ch1** 15157 fole; 17, 4923 foles; 2029 foole P fol L; 3903 folis P folyes L; **Ch2** 765 foole; 165, 4142, 5282, 6776, 7919 fole; 4174, 5373, 5900, 7392, 8016 foles; **HS** 667, 2939 folys; 7917, 8373 foles; 11145 fole; 9020 foles *O* felows

fole, folehardy adj. [OF fol] foolish, stupid, imprudent **Ch1** 1381 wele P fole L; **Ch2** 223, 4106, 5925 fole; 4139 fole P fool L; 6952 fole hardi; **HS** 4868 fole; 665, 1243, 8405, 9715 fole hardy; 7347 folehardye

foly n. [OF folie] stupidity, foolish acts, nonsense; sinfulness, lechery **Ch1** 1688, 4786, 5364, 7592, 8528 foly; 3762, 9095 folie; 4521 foly P yuel L; 7389 foly P ffolye L; **Ch2** 2822, 3827, 4031 foly; 580, 1939, 5686, 7014, 8282 folie; 2229 foli; 2019 folis; 5517 folies; **HS** 156, 3500, 9059, 11145, 12305 foly; 176, 1665, 4120 folye; 2804 foly *C* falsely; 3031, 3499 folyys; 8944 folys; 3680 fylþe *F* folie *O* foly

foly, folily adj./adv. [OF] unwise, rash, foolish **Ch1** 5008 foly P (L differs); 2396 fouly P folyly L; **Ch2** 5365 folie; **HS** 1649, 1985, 2812, 2961 foly; 1199 folylyche *D* folyly; 2831 folyleche *C* folily *D* folylyche; 2967 foly *O* foule; 7698 foule *O* foly; 1359 felunsly *C* folyli

folk n. [see fotefolk] [OE folc] common people

Ch1 648, 2246, 5436, 9364, 11016 folk; 1928 outen folk P straunge folk L; 12851 hors folk P horsmen L; **Ch2** 821, 1345, 4071, 6754, 8099 folk; **HS** 1403, 1744, 4981, 10205, 12521 folk

folte n. [OF folet] a stupid, silly person, a fool **Ch1** 4487 felon P folet L; 7125, 13782 folte P folt L; **HS** 8303 folte

folted adj. [from OF folet] stupid, foolish; insane, unwise; false, wicked, impious **Ch1** 4011, 4019, 7132 foltid P folted L; 7123, 9705 folted; **Ch2** 4059 foltid; **HS** 5839 folted; 3426 foul *O* foltyde

folow, folue v. [OE folgian] to follow; pursue or attack **Ch1** 8275, 8381, 12833 folow; 1568, 2580, 3510, 5716, 9070 folowed; 1576 folowes; 7617 folwed; 12546 folowes; **Ch2** 6182, 7068 folow; 3949 folowes; 5825, 7452, 7753 folowed; 2160, 3396, 5579, 5695, 5721 folowand; **HS** 1510 folue; 7228, 7340 foloweþ

fond, founde v. (1) [OE fundian] go, travel, proceed **Ch1** 4465 fonde; **Ch2** 1102, 6939 fonde; 5639 foundes; 7714 fondes; 2412 fonden; 4416 founde; **HS** 2939 fonde

fond, found v. (2) [OF fonder; L fundare] endow, establish; found an institution **Ch1** 1436 fonde; 3534 fond; 5231 funded; 14137 fonden P founden L; **Ch2** 3329, 3548, 7936, 8340 fond; 5720 fonde; 3119 founded; 2179 founden P fonded L; 3541 fonden; 5316 fondon; 5639 foundes

fond v. (3) [see finde] [OE fandian] try, test, prove, attempt; tempt **Ch1** 2845, 6200, 6252, 7709, 8764 fond; 3183, 4756 fondes P fandes L; 2466, 7115, 7695, 7855 fonde; 7751 fondis; 7859 fond P fondyt L; 8200 fondit; 4819 fondid; **Ch2** 1280, 3742, 4072, 4434, 4930 fond; 5186 fand; 6937 fonde; 5456 fondes; **HS** 487 fondyþ; 7274, 10567, 12005 fonde; 5983 fondes; 175 temptyd *D* fondyd; 4535 fondyþ *O* fyndes; 8550 tempte *O* fanden; 8557 tempteþ *O* fandyde

fondement n. [OF, L fundamentum] foundation **Ch1** 8034 fondement P ffundement L

fondyng ger. [OE fandung] trial, testing, tempting **Ch1** 6683 fondyng; **HS** 5865 fondyng; 1020 cumberaunce *C* fondyng *D* encoumbraunce; 7496, 7806, 8447 temptyng *O* fondynge; 7498, 8520 temptyng *O* fondyng; 7532, 8430, 8562 temptynge *O* fandynge; 7524 fleshely temptacoun *O* fleche fendynge; 7886 temptacyun *O* fondyng; 8286, 8288 temptyng *O* foundynge; 8510 flesshely temptyng *O* foule fondynge; 8522 sterynges *O* fondynges

fong v. [see fang, v.]

fonk n. [cp. OHG funcho, MDu vonke] spark of fire; fig.: something worthless, contemptible **Ch2** 4276 fonk P flonk L; 5184 fonkes

font n. [OE] baptismal water receptacle **Ch2** 515 fonte; 4791 funte; **HS** 4667, 9727 fonte; 9516 font stoun; 9785, 9793 font stone

forbarre v. [AF forbarrer] stop, prevent, forestall; shut out **Ch2** 5254 forbarred; **HS** 106 forbarre; 7358, 7468, 10937 forbarreþ

forbede v. [OE forbeodan] to prohibit; stop, restrain, deny **Ch1** 636 forbedes; 1509, 2341 forbed; 1537, 9272 forbede; 5531 forbed P furbed L; 9041 forbede P furbed L; **Ch2** 1731 forbedde; 1847, 2487, 3182, 5065, 8305 forbede; **HS** 237, 5151, 9070, 12359, 12385 forbede; 1063 forbedyþ; 2612 forbed; 8933, 9942 forbedes; 4641, 8113 forbode; 8997 forboden

forbere v. [OE forberan] endure pain, tolerate; be patient **Ch1** 13692 forbere P (L differs); **HS** 1078, 5089, 5378 forbere; 2014 forber

forbi adv. [OE foran + be] by, also, to that place; away, aside, past **Ch1** 4237 forbi P forby L; 4572 forby; 7077 bifor P forby L; **Ch2** 530, 6265, 6947 forbi; 2661 forby P forþ by L; **HS** 10760, 11660 forby

forbysen n. [OE forebysen] story, proverb, example **Ch1** 2439 forbisen P ensample L; **HS** 4153 forbysen *O* for syn; 7240 forbysyn *H* prouerbe *F* forbisin *O* forbysen; 7673 a prouerbe *O* a bysen; 8085 prouerbe *O* forbysyn

force, fors n. [OF force] power, authority; dignity, physical strength; fortitude **Ch1** 1656, 4640, 6176, 8678, 9203 force; **Ch2** 32, 2345, 3264, 4474, 6411 force; **HS** 3684, 10833, 10839 force; 2296, 3365, 4202, 10293, 11368 fors

force v. [OF forcer] exert force, compel; fortify **Ch1** 925 force P enforce L; 4494 forced þem P forcedem L; 5373 aforce P enforce L; **HS** 3665 aforcede

◆ **forcelesse** n. [?error: blend of forcelet and forteresse or forceresse] a stronghold **Ch1** 7041 forcelesse P forceresses L

forcelet n. [AF] fortified place, a castle, stronghold **Ch1** 7408 forcelet; 5024, 7373 forcelete; 4775, 5975 forceletes; 7040 forcelettes

fordo, fordid, fordon v. [OE fordon] destroy, annihilate; devastate, pillage; to be destroyed, perish **Ch1** 206, 3078 fordid P fordide L; 2130 fordid P fordede L; 8070 fordid; 5129, 8156 fordo; 13790 fordid P furdude L; 11419 fordo P furdo L; 90, 8598 fordon; 6769 fordone; **Ch2** 2219, 3184, 7646 fordo; 2147 fordone; 4884 fordos P fordoþ L; 7627, 7920 fordos; 1562, 7884 fordid; **HS** 296, 8338, 11850 fordo; 1326, 1715 fordost; 7078 fordoþ; 104 fordoun; 3950 fordedyst; 884, 886 fordede *C* dystroyed; 1350 fordo *C* to don awey; 9798 vndoun *O* fordone

fore, forn, aforn adv./prep. [see before] [OE foran, forne] before, formerly, previously **Ch1** 4749 or P forn L; 1061 aforn P byforn L; 2507L aforn (P differs); 7431 fore; 7690 are P

fore L
fore adv. [OE for] forward in time; farther **Ch1** 182 forer; **Ch2** 5093 fore; **HS** 1528 furþ *C* for *D* forth; 2234 furthe *C* forth *D* foor
foreyn adj. [OF forain] foreign, alien **Ch1** 1650 þer foreyn men P þerfore men L
foreyn n. [from OF forain, adj.] alien; a privy, outer room **Ch2** 7861 foreyns; **HS** 7437 foreyne; 6407 foreyne O priuay
foreris n. [OF forrier] forager, one who collects provisions for an army **Ch1** 12732 foreris P fforreyers L
forest n. [OF] woodland, wilderness; a king's park **Ch1** 6342 forestes; 10838 forest; **Ch2** 2259, 2667, 7924 foreste; 2673, 2714, 7925, 8207 forest
foresters, forsters n. [OF forestier] gamekeeper; hunter **Ch2** 2716 forsters; 2718 foresters
forfadres n. [see fader] ancestors **Ch1** 9752 forfadres P auncestres L; 14424 forfadres
forfare v. [OE forfaran] to perish, be destroyed; to kill, ruin **Ch1** 108 forfare; **Ch2** 988, 1073 forfare; 3903 forfaren
forfet v. [from OF forfet, n.] offend, transgress, to sin **Ch1** 3079 forfetid; **HS** 1728 mysdo *C* forfet *D* mysdede
forfeture n. [OF forfeture] punishment for crime; penalty **Ch1** 4674 forfetore P forfeture L; **Ch2** 6876 forfeture
forgat, forȝete v. [OE forgetan] to forget **Ch1** 2059, 3139 forgat; 5032 forgat P furgat L; 6588 forgat P forgete L; 8209 forgetis; 1445 forget P forgete L; 676, 2488 forgate; 13559 forgete P furgete L; 2355 forgeten; **Ch2** 1499, 1709, 2290, 4838 forgeten; 1595 forgate P forgatyn L; **HS** 5143, 7585 forget; 4598, 6633, 6753, 6965, 9763 forgete; 5966, 6998 forgat; 9769, 10839, 11464 forȝeteþ; 4482 forȝetyn; 11386 forȝyt; 10862 forȝat; 1944, 6321 forȝate
forged v. [OF forgier, forger] counterfeit a document **Ch2** 3832 forged P for seide L
♦ **forgetilschip** n. [prob. from OE forgeotul] an act of negligence or carelessness **Ch2** 4368 forgetilschip P envye of worschupe L; **HS** 2558 rechelesshepe *C* ȝetylede *D* ientylnesse *F* rechelessnesse *O* for gytelscheppe
forgyue, forȝeue v. [OE forgefan] pardon, absolve, excuse **Ch1** 6352 forgif P forgyue L; 9037 forgyuen P furgaf L; **Ch2** 2301 forgif; 3280, 4032 forgyue; 1320, 2721, 4048, 5549, 5732 forgaf; 1396, 2675, 2809, 3245, 8199 forgyuen; **HS** 587, 1016, 2206, 3912, 5194 forȝeue; 3910, 4482 forȝeuyn; 5995 forȝyuen; 9765, 12072 forȝyue; 3544 forȝyfþe; 12070, 12088 forȝyfþ; 3847, 12097, 12111 forȝaf; 3901 forȝaue
forgyfnesse, forȝeuenes n. [OE forgyfennes] remission or pardon of sin; forgiveness **Ch1** 5987 forgyfnesse P forgyuenesse L; **HS** 598 forȝeuenes; 603 forȝeuenesse; 4510, 11436 forȝyfnes; 9338, 11421, 11766, 12102, 12630 forȝyuenes
forgo v. [OE forgan, foreode] surrender; abandon, forfeit **Ch1** 15028L furȝeden (om. P); **Ch2** 2611, 5844 forgo
forhede n. [OE forheafod] the forehead **Ch1** 10698, 12075 forhede
forhele, forholn v. [OE forhelan] to conceal, hide **Ch2** 2693, 6376 forholn; **HS** 570 forhelyst *C* for hele *D* for hile; 1949 forhelyþ; 2047, 8317, 11709 forhele; 11879 forhale; 5962, 11376, 11867 forhole; 3177 forholne; 12453 forholen; 3694 forhole GLOSS B hed; 3695 forhole *F* hole; 2150 hele *C* forhele; 2428 forhelyst *D* kepist
forlayn v. [OE forlicgan, forlegen] commit adultery or rape **Ch1** 7976 forlayn; 11969 forlayn P furlayn L; 13498 forlayn P forleyn L
forlate, forlete v. [OE forlætan] forsake, neglect, lose **Ch1** 3586 lete P for let L; **Ch2** 4848 forlete; **HS** 3778 forlate *O* to hlate; 9764 forlete
forlore, forlorn v. [see lorn] [OE forleosan] lose, be deprived of; ppl.: wasted, ruined **Ch1** 104, 9265 forlorn; 1456 lorn P forloren L; **Ch2** 4 lorn P forlorn L; 4590L forloren (P differs); **HS** 9128 forlorn; 860 forlore *C* lorn *D* forlorn; 1207, 2559, 3190, 12625 forlore
formast adj./adv. [OE formest; cp. forþmest] first of all **Ch1** 1777, 3476, 4326 formast P formest L; 4965 formast; **Ch2** 3894, 3980, 6334, 6701, 7422 formast; 5025, 7000, 7512 formest; **HS** 5272 formest
forme n. [OF fourme, L forma] physical shape, state; figure **Ch1** 9288 forme; **Ch2** 6126 fourme; **HS** 3600, 12512 fourme; 10055, 10078 forme
forme v. [OF furmer] to shape, create **Ch2** 2418, 6237 formed; 2419 paied P yformed L; 2813 forme; **HS** 3780 furmede; 11544 formed
fornycacyoun n. [L; AF fornicaciun (MP)] adultery, lechery **HS** 7353 fornycacyoun; 8982 fornycacyun
fornome v. [OE forniman] destroy **HS** 7504 fornome *O* ouer nomyn
forres n. [prob. from OF furrer, forrer] furs **Ch1** 10971 forres P forours L
forrour n. [OF forreure] a furrier **Ch1** 12133 forrour P furour L
fors n. [OE for] ditch, furrow **Ch1** 12554 fors P fores L foris R
forsaid ppl. [OE foresægd] above named **Ch1** 15754 beforsaid; **Ch2** 3383 forsaid; **HS** 267 forseyde *C* iche
forsake v. [OE forsacan, forsoc] repudiate,

betray; disown, deny; abandon **Ch1** 2045 forsakes; 6658, 6809 forsake; 2033 forsaken; 607, 3861, 6758, 14000, 15879 forsoke; 15292 forsok; **Ch2** 1050, 2286, 4252, 4790, 6287 forsake; 2512 forsakes; 6272 forsakis; 1957, 3833, 4532, 5135, 8141 forsaken; 128, 1063, 2507, 4258, 7592 forsoke; **HS** 202, 2131, 4668, 10865, 12389 forsake; 154, 262, 4665, 9991, 12388 forsoke; 2738, 2739 forsakþ; 266, 1746 forsakyn

foresent ppl. [OE forsendan] sent forth **Ch1** 7431 foresent

◆ **forset** n. [cp. OE forsettan, v.] defensive move **Ch1** 2884 forset

forset v. [OE forsettan] to stop or block **Ch1** 1811, 1821 forset P forsetten L; **Ch2** 4658 withsette P forset L

forsoth, forsoþe adv. [OE forsoþ] indeed; in truth **Ch1** 115, 307 forsoth; 11286 forsoþe; **Ch2** 2514, 3472, 5532, 6195, 7895 forsoth; 3746 forsoþe; **HS** 686, 1347, 7347, 9405, 12470 forsoþe

forspoken v. [OE forspecan] ?spoken of before **HS** 1034 of spokun *C* forspekyth *D* forspoken

forsuore, forswere v. [OE forswerian] lie under oath, commit perjury; to renounce **Ch1** 8001 forsuorne P fursworn L; **Ch2** 2383, 5938, 8269 forsuore; 1321, 1771, 5847, 7414, 8133 forsuorn; 7027 forsuoren; **HS** 2762 forswere; 2698, 2791 forswore

forth v. [see fore, adv.] [OE forþian] finish a task; complete; go forward **Ch1** 13666L forthe (om. P); 1728 furth P went L; 4652 forth P wente L; 10424 forth P forþ L; 10574 forþe P forþ L; **Ch2** 4602 forth ȝode P for ȝede L; 7552 forth; **HS** 938 furþ; 8708 go furþ *O* gange on; 3951 furþeryd

forth, furþ adv. [see fore, adv.] [OE forþ] on, forth, forward **Ch1** 69, 1430, 3507, 5217, 9334 forth; 3486, 4146, 5744 forþer; 2724, 5375, 6991 forþe; 11140 forþe P forþ L; **Ch2** 2703, 3788, 4487, 5185, 8281 forth; 1071 forþe; 1398 ore P forþ L; 4632 forth P fro L; **HS** 926, 938, 1237, 5905, 9064 furþ; 6183 forth; 2234 furthe; 744 forward *CD* forth; 798 furþer *CD* forth; 337, 800, 2405, 2884, 3653 furþer; 6173, 12194 ferþer; 9247 ferþere; 7342 ferþest

forthely adj./adv. [from OE forþ] earnest **Ch2** 3958 forthely P ferforthe L

forþenke, forþouht v. [OE forþencan] regret, bewail, begrudge; made sorry, angered **Ch1** 2702, 2344, 12003 forþouht P ouer þoughte L; 4840 forþenkes P forþynkes L; 7111 forþenkes P ouer þynkes L; 7281 forþinkes P ouer þynkes L; 10800 forþouht P forþoughte L; 12003 forþouht; **Ch2** 1304, 1513 forþouht; **HS** 1142 forþoughte; 6908 forþynkeþ; 6909 forþynkest; 6918, 10847 forþynke; 3933 forþynke *O* euer thynk; 3964 forþynkyst *O* ouere thynk

forthes n. [OE ford, poss. influenced by ON] a ford in a body of water **Ch2** 4658 forthes P fordes L

forþy adv./conj. [OE] on that account; therefore **Ch1** 3300, 3651 forþi; **HS** 7685, 9651, 11212 forþy

fortold ppl. [cp. L prae-dicere] predicted **Ch2** 7735 fortold

forward n. [OE foreweard] agreement, treaty, promise **Ch1** 4901 forward P forewarde L; 14375 forwarde P foreward L; 14380 forward P foreward L; **Ch2** 1595, 3775, 4436, 6237, 7928 forward; **HS** 957, 4090, 4671 forward

forward adv. [from OE foreweard, adj.] forth, onwards; hereafter **Ch1** 967 hiþen forward P heþen forward L; 7342 forward; **Ch2** 133, 3825, 3865, 3890, 7428 forward; **HS** 744 forward *CD* forth; 4830 forward

forwarned ppl. [cp. OE warnian] informed beforehand **Ch2** 2342 forwarned

◆ **forwondred** ppl. [cp. OE wundrian] anticipated strange events **Ch2** 832, 5208 forwondred

forwreye v. [OE forwregan] to accuse, denounce **HS** 11455 forwreye *O* furthe wry

foson n. [see foyson]

foster v. [OE *fostrian; cp. OI fostra] nourish a child; maintain, educate **Ch1** 3665 fostered; 10424 fostred; 15804 fostred P stored L

fote, fete n. [OE fot] the foot; measure of distance; on foot: to walk **Ch1** 6866 men of fote; 8171, 12850 fotemen; 13231 foteman; 3481, 3482, 10573 on fote; 8533 bare fote; 7368, 8527 fote; 10147, 12286 fote P fot L; 1129, 1820, 9129, 12091 fete; **Ch2** 581, 608, 3421, 6523 fote; 4042 o fote P on fote L; 4550, 4854, 4920 on fote; 4080, 4132 to fote; 643, 4912, 6731, 7249 fete; 5801, 7581 fotemen; **HS** 3446, 3842 fote; 671, 1468, 11578, 11726 fete; 3313 fet

fotefolk n. [OE] infantry, foot soldiers **Ch1** 10958 fote folk P fot folk L; **Ch2** 5819, 6641, 6713, 7439 fotefolk

fouche, fourche n. [OF forche, fourche] a fork; fig.: the crotch **Ch1** 1820 fouche (?error) P fourche L

foule n. [OE fugol, fuglas] birds; domestic fowls **Ch1** 4690, 10043, 13182, 15003 foules

foule v. [OE fulian] to befoul; pollute **HS** 5991 foule

foule adj./adv. [OE ful] filthy, soiled; vile, indecent, sinful **Ch1** 1172, 2049, 5881 foule; 1778 fule P foule L; 2396 fouly P folyly L; 8451 fouly; **Ch2** 970 fouly; 922 fulle P ful ille L; 1273, 3423, 4240, 6989, 7904 foule; 1295 foule P fulest L; **HS** 1592, 4955, 7447, 8629,

12537 foule; 1874, 10235 foul; 3017 fowle; 7758 fouly; 6759 fouler; 7429 foulest; 7698 foule *O* foly; 7760 foule *O* lothly; 8718 fouly *O* vylany; 12319 foul *O* vile

found v. [see find, fond, v.]

foundour n. [AF fundur] founder, builder of a city or institution **Ch1** 10851 foundoure P foundour L; **Ch2** 2081 fondoure; 2631 foundour; **HS** 2583 foundur

foune n. [OF feon, foun] fawn, deer **Ch1** 15056 foune P fowen L

four, fourtene, fourty numeral/adj. [see ferth, numeral] [OE feower, feower-teoþa, feowertig] **Ch1** 823 four; 208, 1933, 4117, 7599, 12873 foure; 249 fouretene; 6408 fourtend P fourtenþe L; 2119, 2658, 4034, 5617, 12948 fourty; 2763, 4686 fourti; **Ch2** 115, 3134, 5853, 6708, 8347 four; 189, 1158, 3208, 5334, 8061 foure; 563, 5111, 5660, 6119 fourtene; 5333 fourtend; 710, 1021, 1373, 3355 fourty; 968, 1285, 3769, 4222, 6607 fourti; **HS** 409 voure; 2492, 4082, 7996 foure; 2002 furty; 7821 fourty

fourme n./v. [see forme]

fourscore numeral/adj. [from OE feower] eighty, four times twenty **Ch1** 2597, 4284, 6033 foure score; **Ch2** 2, 1311, 3481, 5901, 6561 fourscore; 5929 forscore

fourtenyght n. [OE, ME feowertene niht] fourteen days, two weeks **Ch2** 4298 fourtenyght

fraied adj. [see affraye] [from OF affraien, v.] frightened **Ch1** 12329 fraied P frayed L; **Ch2** 7905 frayed

frayned v. [OE frægn] inquire, ask **Ch1** 15179 askid P frayned L

fraist, freist v. [ON; cp. OI freista] to test; ask, attempt **Ch1** 1000 fraist P to assay L; 1822 fraist P sayed L; 8277 fraiste P frayst L; 6845 assay P fray L; **Ch2** 2908 freistes P freyssches L; 4356 freist; 7044 fraist; **HS** 416 fraystys GLOSS BH asayþ

frame n. [ON; cp. OI frami] benefit, profit; advantage, help **Ch1** 2463, 7158, 10095 frame; **Ch2** 4010 frame; 5118 fram; **HS** 675, 4423, 5804 frame

frame v. [OE fremian, framian] benefit, profit; do good **Ch1** 10902 frames; **HS** 5, 4250, 9758 frame

♦ **frame** adj. [from OE framian, v.] strong; effective **HS** 4250, 9612 frame

franchise n. [OF] rights, privileges, immunities, freedom, social status **Ch1** 962, 3078, 4228, 5905, 6694 franchise P fraunchise L; **Ch2** 620, 1915, 1971, 3184, 7331 franchise; **HS** 8596, 8804, 8924, 9494 fraunchyse

frankeleyn n. [AF frankelein] landowner, gentleman of a town **Ch1** 6446 frankeleyns P frankelayns L; **Ch2** 5750 fraunkeleyn; 6315 frankeleyn

♦ **frapaile** n. [OF frapaille] rabble, camp followers **Ch1** 12817 frapaile P frapaille L

frape n. [OF frap] multitude; a blow; commotion, disturbance **Ch1** 993, 1142 frape; 9688, 12607 frap P frape LR; **Ch2** 7815, 7898 frape

fraped v. [OF fraper] to strike, beat **Ch1** 10012 to fraped

fraude n. [OF] dishonesty, treachery **Ch2** 3153 fraude

frauht v. [cp. MDu vrachten, vracht] loaded, full **Ch2** 1831 frauh P yfrawȝt L

frawth n. [see auht] wealth, cargo **HS** 2456 aght GLOSS BH gode *C* frawth *D* auȝt

fre, frely adj./adv. [OE freo, freolic] lavish; generous, gracious; at liberty **Ch1** 955, 3090, 4269, 9127, 14439 fre; 3907 free; 878, 1202, 4252, 6696 frely; 4247 freli; **Ch2** 141, 1761, 3850, 6316, 8341 fre; 184, 6416 frely; **HS** 678, 3525, 4574, 8906, 11360 fre

fredom n. [OE fredom] liberty **Ch1** 888, 3075, 4320, 5925, 15876 fredam; 958, 4258 fredom; **Ch2** 1620, 1762 fredom

frend n./adj. [OE freond; cp. OE fremede, fremde (strange, remote) in variant MSS] friend, ally **Ch1** 1478, 3190, 5229, 6385, 7360 frende; 1245, 2462, 3144, 5775, 7400 frendes; 6230, 7502 frendis; 3924 freendis; 6385 frende P fremde L; **Ch2** 226, 1300, 3885, 6430, 8048 frendes; 1579 frende P frendes L; 7936 frende; 4274, 5273 frendis; **HS** 8236 frend; 2452 frende; 2251, 3371 frendys; 6302, 10935 frendes; 6459, 9875 frend man; 7681, 9875 frend *O* fremmede

frere n. [OF] monk; member of a religious brotherhood; comrade, brother **Ch2** 4004, 4711, 7966, 8295 frere; 4887, 4896, 5755, 6277, 6813 freres; **HS** 688, 2247, 4307, 10404, 11859 frere; 6179 freres

frese, frosen v. [OE freosan] cold; freezing **Ch2** 2975 frese; 2988 frosen

fresse, fresshe, fresly adj./adv. [OE fersc, OF fres, fresche] new; lively, vigorous, bold; suddenly, recently **Ch1** 1564 fresse P fresche L; 808, 1653 fresh; 3319, 3443, 4348, 5589 fresse; 4625, 6343, 13261 fresch; 4994 fresly; **Ch2** 808 fresh; 1752 fresch; 2497, 3570, 5282, 7418 fresse; 2908 freistes P freyssches; 5560 fressh; **HS** 10068, 11093 fresshe

frest, fryste v. [OE *fyrstan; rel. to ON fresta] to lend money on credit **HS** 5507 frest *O* fryste

frette n. [OF fret] a payment made to secure peace **Ch2** 7053 frette

frith n. [OE friþ] peace of the nation **Ch2** 2188 frith

frith v. [OE friþian] to grant peace; protect **Ch1**

8618 frithe P ffryþe L
frog n. [OE frogga] a frog **Ch1** 1778 frog P froge L
frost n. [OE, ON] freezing weather **HS** 9154 frost
frounte n. [OF front] foremost rank of an army **Ch1** 3332 frounte
frow adj. [?ON; cp. OI fra-r, OS frah] unreliable **HS** 2305 frow
froward adj. [OE fromweard] perverse, contrary **HS** 4517 froward
frusse n. [OF fruis, frois] clash; attack, violent charge **Ch1** 8300, 12464 frusse P frusch L; 13031 frusse P frusche L; 2917 frusse P frosche L
frussed v. [OF fruissier] crush, smash together **Ch1** 2950 frussed P to frusched L; 3008, 5968 frussed P fruschte L; 1174 to frusshed P furfrusched L; 12442L fruscht (om. P)
frute, fruyt n. [OF fruit (MP)] profit, benefit, reward; offspring **Ch1** 31, 1383, 1891, 3860 frute; **Ch2** 4110, 6876, 7290 frute; **HS** 914 frutys; 1414, 2102, 2132 fruyt; 2881 frute
ful, fulle adj./adv. [OE ful] filled to capacity; entire; completely; as intensive particle with verbs or adverbs: very, quite **Ch1** 3788, 7348, 7762 ful; 448, 1122, 6342, 7713, 9186 fulle; 1488, 2419 fully; **Ch2** 2438, 3227, 4801, 5527, 5783 fulle; **HS** 96, 1059, 6199, 10029, 12328 ful
fulbut adv. [OE ful] head to head, directly **Ch1** 13105L fulbut (P differs); **Ch2** 538L [Havelok interpolation, l. 64] fulbut
fulfille v. [see fille, v.] [OE ful-fyllan] to fill up; cover; endow; satisfy, accomplish **Ch1** 1396, 7342, 8421, 9309 fulfille; 797, 8442 fulfilled; 7004, 7070 fulfild; 9155 fulfillid; **Ch2** 2403, 3548, 3739, 4524 fulfille; 1603, 1613, 2113 fulfilled; **HS** 1092, 1610, 11266 fulfyl; 2822, 5778 fulfylle; 6395 fulfyll; 6398 fulfylde
fultide adv. [OE ful + tide] eventually **Ch2** 3907 tide P fultide L
fultyt, fulle tite adv. [OE ful] immediately **Ch1** 9135 fulle tite; **HS** 2660 fultyt GLOSS B sone; 7235 fultyte
funte n. [see font]
furgh n. [OE furh] a furrow **HS** 2448 furgh *D* forw
furþ, furþer v./adv. [see fer, farre, forth]

G

gadre v. [OE gadrian, gædrian] assemble, gather; hoard; summon **Ch1** 1990, 3254, 4545, 5752, 9061 gadred; 3611 gadred P gadered L; 1604 gedred; 8168, 8193 gadird; 4543, 6600, 8595 gadre; 6501 gadir P gadred L; 11566 gedir P gedere L; **Ch2** 292, 1221, 2960, 5398, 7751 gadred; 1093 gadred P gadreþ L; 880, 3935 gadre; 1065, 2213, 3602, 3935, 5566 gadres; **HS** 992, 6088, 6117, 11770 gadere; 7094 gadre; 1032 gaderyþ; 2622, 5579 gadered; 6095, 7598 gadreþ; 6099, 12436 gadereþ; 6473, 6475 gederdest; 1556 gadryþ; 6068, 6070 gadren; 6119 gadred
gaderyng ger. [OE (ge)gaderung] a meeting; an army, assembly **Ch1** 4316 gaderyng P garderynge L; **HS** 1003, 4644, 6564, 7264, 11135 gaderyng; 8372 gederyng
gadlyng n. [OE] rascal, scoundrel **HS** 769 gadlyng
gaf v. [see gif, gyue]
gay adj. [OF] merry; carefree; wanton, lascivious; glittering, ornate **Ch1** 661, 11024 gay; **Ch2** 4188, 7342, 8106, 8115 gay; **HS** 2972, 3332, 5068, 8892 gay
gayn, geyns adj./adv. [ON, cp. OI gegn] ready, the quickest way **Ch1** 6626 ageyns P geynes L; 3348 gaynere P geyner L; 12807 gayn; **Ch2** 3274, 7792 gayn; 7748 geyns
gayne v. [ON gegna] to avail, help **Ch1** 3362 gayne P non ageyn L
gaynsay, geynsay v. [see agaynsay] [OE gegn + secgan] to deny, refuse, oppose **Ch2** 175 geynsaid P ageyn seyd L; 3815 geynsay; 6302 geynsaid
gaynsaying, geynsayng ger. [from OE gegnsecgan, v.] denying, opposing refusing **Ch2** 2518 geynsayng; 3103 geynsaiyng; 4579 gansaying; 6135 gaynsaying
gayte, goot n. [OE gæt] a goat **Ch1** 11251 goot P got L; **Ch2** 6687 gayte
galeie n. [OF galie, galee] galley; seagoing vessel **Ch1** 11776 galeis; **Ch2** 1310, 4209, 4213, 4218 galeie; 3680 galais; 3801, 4066, 4303 galeis
galle n. [OE gealla, galla] gall, bitterness **HS** 1470 galle
galweis, galwes n. [OE galga, gealga] gallows; cross for crucifixion **Ch1** 3417, 3419 galwes P galewes L; **Ch2** 4269, 5976 galwes; 8054 galweis
game, gamen n. [OE] pleasure, delight, sport **Ch1** 3108, 3232 gamen P game L; 9, 4869, 11127 gamen; **Ch2** 1639 gamen P game L; 2289, 4568, 6732 gamen; **HS** 47 gamys; 3088, 3481, 4069, 9303, 11572 game; 2001 game *D* gamyn; 9091 gaume *O* gamene
gamen v. [OE gamenian] play, be merry **Ch1** 4002 gamen; **Ch2** 7166 gamened
gan v. [see gyn]
gannok n. [?OE] camp; ?stronghold **Ch2** 2744 gannok
gannokerys n. [from gannok] [unattested] ?taverner, alehouse keeper **HS** 2453 tauuarsyns (?error: kauersyns) *C* theuys also *D* gannokerys
gaped v. [see gaspand]

garland n. [OF garlande] string of flowers **Ch2** 8089 garland; **HS** 998 gerlaund
garner n. [OF grenier, gernier] grain storehouse **Ch2** 7852 garner
garnysons n. [see warnistour]
gart, gert v. [ON; cp. OE gearwian] made to do; caused **Ch1** 2146 gert P dide hym L; 6927 gart do P had don L; **Ch2** 1575 gert P dide do L; 62 gart; **HS** 4478 made *O* gart; 10433 dedest be *O* garte *SV* dudest; 12161 made *O* garte
gashadles n. [see gate] [from ON gata and OE sceandan, shadel] crossroads **Ch1** 10808 gashadles P grete routes L
gaspand, gaped v. [ON; cp. OI geispa] gape, open the mouth wide **Ch1** 3771 opind P gaped L; 12357 gaspand P gapyng L; 12359 gapid P gaped L
gast, gost n. [OE gast, gæst] ghost, spiritual being, devil **Ch1** 8653, 8654 gost; 11974, 12764 gaste P gast L; **Ch2** 80 gaste P gast L; 1261, 4609 gaste; 2010, 4425 Holy Goste; **HS** gost 220; 11246 gostes; 142 gaste; 1160, 5482, 8262, 9533, 9679 gast
gast v. [see agaste, ogaste] [OE gasten] terrified **Ch1** 11382 gast
gate, ȝate n. (1) [OE geat, gæt] gate, entryway, doorway **Ch1** 3565, 3567, 4083, 4438 ȝate P gate L; 4783 ȝate; 3580, 3582, 4437, 14437 gate; **Ch2** 4539 gate; 694, 4540, 4547 ȝate; 3734, 3876 ȝates; 7169 gatis; 7170, 7171 ȝatis; **HS** 3832 ȝates; 4040, 4730, 5604, 6643, 12192 ȝate
gate, gatte n. (2) [ON gata] path, road; way, manner, method **Ch1** 2606 stretes P gates L; 3344 gate P wey L; 3772, 5038, 6791, 8201, 9143 gate; 12807 gate P weye L; 7879 ȝates; 3231, 3772, 5794, 7949 þusgate; **Ch2** 730, 3442, 4548, 5117, 7614 gate; **HS** 2212 gate GLOSS B maner *C* algate (?error) *D* gate; 2489 wey *CD* gate; 4655 weyys *O* gate; 8042 wey *O* gatte; 8483 wyse *O* gatte; 4039, 4729, 5603, 6142, 12183 gate GLOSS B wey; 6644, 6857 gate GLOSS BH wey; 5590 gat GLOSS BH wey; 12191 gate
gate v. [see gete, gate, v. (1)]
gauelokes n. [OE gafeluc] javelins, spears **Ch1** 11716L gauelokes (om. P); **Ch2** 7233 gauelokes
geant n. [OF geant; OE gigant] monster; fabulous creature; a man of great strength or size **Ch1** 1794 geante P geaunt L; 1384, 1775, 1845 geantȝ P geauntȝ L; 11851, 11888 geaunt; 11860, 12128, 14192 geant; 1750 geauntes; 1757, 8667, 8693 geantȝ; 1467, 1691, 1751, 1832, 1835 geant P geaunt L; **Ch2** 681 geant P geaunt L; 4545 geant
geyn adj./adv./v. [see gayn]
geynsaying v. [see gaynsaying]
gelde n. (1) [see gilde]
gelde n. (2) [OF geldon] company of foot soldiers **Ch1** 13871 gelde
gelous adj. [OF jalos, gelos] envious, possessive **HS** 1123, 1893 gelous
gelusye n. [OF jalosie, gelosie] solicitude; suspiciousness **HS** 1889, 1897 gelusye
gender, gendre v. [OF gendrer] beget a child, procreate **Ch1** 7229 gendre; 7225 gėnderand P gendryng L
gendrure n. [OF gendreure] children, offspring **Ch1** 7243 gendrure; **Ch2** 6100 gendrure
gent adj. [OF] high born, of noble birth or character **Ch1** 2193, 2899, 3718, 5469, 7451 gent; 3138 gente; **Ch2** 2602, 5049, 5219, 6110 gent
gentille adj. [OF] noble, kind, gracious; of noble birth **Ch1** 2187 ientilere P þe gentilest L; 6745 gentile; 463, 3109, 5483, 7423, 10779 gentille; 7194 gentille P faire L; 4259, 6457 ientille; 6444 ientille P gentil L; 13938L gentil (om. P); **Ch2** 656, 1073, 4669, 6100, 7013 gentille; **HS** 669, 3039, 3335, 8720, 10652 gentyl; 8692 gentyle
gentilly adv. [from OF gentil] graciously, kindly **Ch1** 7209 gentilly; **Ch2** 3283 gentilly
gentrye n. [from OF genterise] good breeding **HS** 669 gentrye
gerlaund n. [see garland]
gert v. [see gart]
gese n. [see goos]
gesse n. [from gessen, v.] guess; for instance; supposition **Ch2** 7851 at gesse; **HS** 1953 at gesse GLOSS B hap; 11331, 11803 at gesse
gesse, gest v. [MDu gisse, gessen] perceive, suspect, estimate **Ch2** 3697 to gesse; 5026 as I gest; **HS** 103, 3762 gesse; 10170 to ges
geste n. (1) [OF] heroic poem, story, chronicle; jest; expedition, heroic action **Ch1** 38, 6537 gest; 5223, 15914, 15915 geste; 98, 5227 gestes; 460, 9629, 13973 gestis; **Ch2** 142, 2778, 3998, 6428, 7923 geste; 6440, 7838, 7923, 8234 gest; 94, 96, 2690, 7203 gestes; 3998 gestes P gest L; **HS** 2843, 4746 geste; 2476 gestys; 4368, 10712 gestes; 11380 story *O* geste
geste n. (2) [OF] noble family, race, kindred **Ch1** 1770, 4666, 7467, 8800 geste; **Ch2** 7377, 8124 gest; 7706 geste; **HS** 6018 geste
geste n. (3) [ON] a guest **Ch1** 9617 gestis; **Ch2** 8109 gest; **HS** 360, 1940, 9374 geste; 5927 gestes; 10296 gest
gested v. [from ON geste, n. (3)] to provide with food or entertainment **Ch2** 3968 gested
gestours n. [from OF gesten, v.] entertainers, jesters **Ch1** 11147 sangsters P gestours L
get n. [OF] mode; manner of singing **Ch1** 3993 get

gete, gate v. (1) [ON geta; OE bigetan] to acquire, buy; earn; beget children **Ch1** 668, 3924, 5053, 6756, 8838 gete; 592, 2290, 7392, 8963 getes; 357, 806, 5840, 7978 geten; 2565, 4274 getis; 11489 getis P getes L; 905, 2115, 2817, 6892, 7927 gate P gat L; 292, 293, 319, 378 gatte P gat L; **Ch2** 1564, 3950, 4228, 6674, 8148 gete; 6824 getes; 4366 getis; 563, 780, 1191, 2074, 4705 gate; 1195, 3957, 4514 geten; 845 gate P begat L; **HS** 1494, 1621, 6242 get; 3362, 6818, 7584, 12152 gete; 603 getyst; 4784 gest; 7205 getest; 8339 gete; 3809, 5109, 7996, 9874 gat

gete, gette v. (2) [ON; cp. OI gæta] watch over, protect; guide, rule **Ch1** 644, 13012, 14672 gette; **Ch2** 3951 getis; 5892, 6284 gette; **HS** 10173 gete

getyng ger. [from v. (1), OE bigetan] begetting a child **HS** 8338 getyng

gettours n. [OF getour] braggarts, bullies **HS** 761 gettours

gyblot n. [AF gybelot (MP)] a giblet; fig.: a gratuitous addition **HS** 4274 gyblot *F* gilloc (?error) *O* gyblot

gyf, ȝyue v. [see gyue, gyf, gaf, v.]

giffer n. [from ON gefa, OE gyfen, v.] the giver **Ch1** 513 gyffere; 10254 giffer P gyuere L

gyffyng, ȝyuyng ger. [from ON gefa, v.] giving **Ch1** 11193 gyffyng P gyuyng L; **HS** 6835, 7088 ȝyuyng; 11989 ȝeuyng

gift, gyue, ȝyft n. [OE gift] gift, reward, bribe **Ch1** 693, 1300 gyft; 3719, 4137, 4520, 8803, 11193 giftes; 4026, 5750, 6360 gifte; 5762, 11192 gyfte; 4275, 12973 gyue; **Ch2** 516, 625, 1487, 6138, 7288 gift; 2512, 2730, 3100 gyft; 6185 gifte; 3835 gyue P gift L; 1435, 3452, 3950, 5935 giftes; 2344, 2395, 2707, 3241 gyftes; **HS** 36, 196, 3685, 8147, 11006 ȝyfte; 5626, 12288 ȝyft; 5514 ȝyftes

gilde, gelde n. [ON] phrase: Danes gilde, a land tax levied for defense against the Danes or as tribute **Ch2** 2675 Danegelde; 1392 Dangilde; 1396 Danes gilde

gilden, gilte adj. [OE gylden] golden, overlaid with gold **Ch1** 287, 445 gilden; **Ch2** 3761 gilte; 4143 gilt

gildes n. [ON gild] associations **Ch1** 14130 gildes P gyldes L

gile n. [OF guile] trick, plot, lie; treachery **Ch1** 2302, 2631 gyle; 535 quante gyle P quynte wyle L; 13980 gile; **Ch2** 1419, 3153, 4807, 6488, 7460 gile; 4541L gyles (P differs); **HS** 486, 2779, 3070, 8401, 11728 gyle; 2784 gyle *C* fals

gile v. [OF guiler] to deceive, beguile, trick **Ch1** 1821 gyle; 6932 gile; **Ch2** 6496, 7167 gile; **HS** 7820 gyle; 362 gylys *D* begylys; 1626 begyle *C* gyle; 2384 begyle *C* false *D* falsyn

gilery n. [OF guilerie] deceit; stratagem, treachery **Ch2** 5272, 5331, 5954, 6296 gilerie; 5313, 7148 gilery; **HS** 4913, 5977 gylerye; 6612 gylrye

giloure n. [OF guileor] deceiver, traitor **Ch2** 1185, 2828 giloure; **HS** 5975 gylour

gilt n. [OE gylt] offense; sin, crime; a debt **Ch1** 2561, 15584 gilte; 4449, 8549 gilt; **Ch2** 3178 gilte; 4144, 8038 gilt; **HS** 1295, 4168, 8141, 11617 gylt; 3848 gylte

gilty adj. [OE gyltig] culpable; guilty of an offense **Ch2** 2718 gilty; **HS** 6607, 12382 gylty

gyn n. [OF gin] inventiveness, cleverness; skill **Ch1** 4536 gyn P gynne L; **HS** 503 *C* gyn (B differs)

gynne, gan v. [OE ginnan] to begin, start **Ch1** 201, 2412, 7571 gynne; 12784 gunne P gonne L; 1874 gynnyng; 2490, 5523, 6556, 7477, 9344 gan; 1387 gyn; 2411 gynnes; **Ch2** 1901, 3503, 6812, 8082 gynne; 1922, 2391, 5768 gynnes; 4809, 5420, 5748, 6946, 8305 gan; 4125 had gonnen; **HS** 72, 959, 5028, 9729, 12190 gan; 452, 3274, 4973, 7859 gun; 598 mote be here *D* must gynne

gynnyng ger. [from OE ginnan] starting point, first part **Ch1** 1616, 2386, 4532 gynnyng; **Ch2** 865, 3181, 3483, 5406, 7297 gynnyng; 2887 gynnyng P bygynnyng L

gyour n. [see guyour]

gird, girte v. [OE gyrdan] wrap; encircle with a belt; fasten a sword; equip; strike off **Ch1** 1800 girt P gyrt L; 6002 gird of P (L differs); **Ch2** 1037 girded P gird L; 3942 girte P gerd L; 4040 gird P armed L

girdille n. [OE gyrdel] a belt **Ch1** 3163 girdille P girdel L; 10708 girdille; **HS** 684 gerdyl

gysarmes n. [OF gisarme] a battle axe **Ch1** 11716L gysarmes (om. P)

gyse n. [OF guise] custom, manner; fashion **Ch1** 5937 wise P gyse L; **Ch2** 1908 guyse; **HS** 3328, 3403 gyse; 3214 newe gyse *O* sarsyn gythese; 3215 gyse *O* gythes

gysyng ger. [tr. from AF duner (MP)] giving, disposing **HS** 3373 gysyng (?error) *F* gising (?error) *O* gyffynge

gyue, gyf, gaf, ȝeue v. [ON gefa, OE gyfan] render, grant; to give in marriage **Ch1** 1219, 1276, 1623, 2275, 4275 gyf; 224, 2236, 5892, 9380, 15893 gaf; 1816 gaf P gef L; 852 gaff; 3034, 5516, 5822, 8284, 9098 gif; 1972, 2358, 2698, 3044 gyfen; 1975 giffen; 2429 gyffen; 2596 gifes P gyueþ L; 12924 giffe; 12915 giffes; 693 gyfen P gyuen L; 2197 gyuen; 3191, 3290, 4448, 8556 gyue; 3719, 3862, 3905, 8211 gaue; 14780 gaf bak; **Ch2** 1026, 1617, 3835, 4140, 7225 gif; 768, 892, 960, 5746 gyf; 78, 1556, 4061, 6979, 8346 gaf; 1957 giffen; 6879 giffes; 2135, 4960, 5713, 6900 gyues; 620, 1701, 4361,

6130, 8019 gyue; 277, 1424, 3385, 4908, 7351 gyuen; **HS** 1611 gyue GLOSS BH kepe; 324, 1124, 4387, 6739, 6914 ȝaf; 1921 ȝyf; 530 ȝaff; 423, 3685, 4361, 5082, 8147 ȝeue; 5550, 6270, 8329, 11806, 11974 ȝyue; 1162, 7086, 11555 ȝyfst; 1707 ȝeuys; 10293 ȝyues; 2955, 3380, 5736 ȝaue; 8331, 10833 ȝyueþ; 1200, 12288 ȝyfþ; 7131 ȝyfþe; 7642, 10975, 11004 ȝyuen; 15, 1053 ȝeuyn; 1638 ȝeuen; 9316 take *O* gyf

gyues n. [AF gyves] shackles, leg bonds **Ch1** 1129 gyues

glad, gladly adj./adv. [OE glæd] joyful, merry, gay **Ch1** 603, 3802, 7448, 9322, 15227 glad; 4664, 7073 glade; 7146 ioyfulle P glad L; **Ch2** 323, 2592, 4126, 4946, 7186 glad; 2615, 6887 gladly; **HS** 373, 1778, 2872, 6867 glad; 987, 1346 gladly; 7041 gladde

glade v. [OE gladian] to cheer, encourage, comfort **Ch1** 7095, 12898 glade; 1280 gladdes P gladeþ L; 11558 gladed; 14605 gladded; **Ch2** 1219 payd P gladed L

◆ **gladhede** n. [from OE glæd, adj.] joy, gladness **HS** 12467 gladhede

gladyng ger. [from OE gladian] rejoicing, merry-making **Ch1** 7449 glading; **HS** 9379 gladyng; 380 gleteryng *C* glederande *D* gladyng

gladnes n. [from OE glæd, adj.] happiness **HS** 3991 gladnes

glas n. [OE glæs] glass **Ch1** 2075 glas; **Ch2** 2321 glas; **HS** 5262, 9344 glas

glath n. [ON] joy **Ch1** 3232 gleth P glathe L; **Ch2** 4767 glath

gleam, gleme n. [OE glæm] flash of light; radiance **Ch2** 2329 gleam; **HS** 380, 424, 2236 gleme

glede n. [OE gled] a spark **Ch2** 7174 glede

glederande adj. [see glesyng, gleteryng]

gleyue n. [OF glaive] lance, spear **Ch1** 2709, 13109, 13112 gleyue

gleman n. [OE gliwman, gleoman] minstrels, entertainers **Ch1** 9706 glewman P gleman L; **HS** 4770 glemen; 4737 glemennes

glent n. [cp. ON *glent] glimpse **Ch1** 12428 glent

glent v. [ON *glent] glanced; struck a blow; dodged, flinched **Ch1** 1520 glent P bleynt L; 10008, 10669, 12379, 12670, 15140 glent; 12081 glente; **Ch2** 4876, 7868 glent; **HS** 6186, 7043 glent

glesyng adj. [from OE glisian] glistening, shining **HS** 424 glemys *C* glydande glemys *D* glasyng glemys; 2525 glesyng *C* glysynd *D* grysly *O* gleterande; 2972 glysyng eȝen *C* gre glederande *O* eyen glesande; 4460 glesyng *O* glysand

gleteryng, glederande, glyder v./adj. [see glesyng] [blend of ON *glitra and OE gliddrian] flash, sparkle, glitter; strike a glancing blow; clash **Ch1** 4334 glidre; 13188L glyder (om. P); **HS** 380 gleteryng *C* glederande *D* gladyng (?error); 1408 gleteryng *C* brennyng schyre *D* schyning; 2236 shynyng *C* glyden; 424 glemys *C* glydande glemys

glew v. (1) [OF gluer] to stick things together **HS** 9029 glew

glew v. (2) [OE gliwian, gleowian] to make merry, be joyful; please **Ch1** 4694 glewe P blowe L; 9617 to gle P (L differs); **HS** 9029 glew

glewe, gle n. [OE gliw] entertainment, sport, joy, pleasure **Ch1** 1771 glewe P trompes & pypyng L; 11141 glew; 11148 glew P murþe L; **Ch2** 332, 7166 glewe; **HS** 1911 glew; 4738, 4773 gle

glyde v. [OE glidan] to glide, slide **Ch1** 2966 ride P glyde L

glift v. [see glent, oglift] [from ME gliffen] glanced upward **Ch1** 3371 glift P glyfte L

glose n. [OF glose] gloss; commentary **HS** 12099 glose

glose v. [OF gloser] comment, describe; flatter, deceive **Ch1** 5873 glosed; 2313 glosand P glosyng L; **Ch2** 752 glosed; **HS** 3411 glose

glosand, glosyng ger. [from OF gloser] deceit, flattery **HS** 2907 glosyng *C* glosene *O* glosynge

glotony n. [OF] vice of gluttony; drunkenness **HS** 1032, 4603, 6517, 10142 glotonye; 6756, 7203 glotony; 6546 [MS *O* interpolation, ll. 14, 26] glotony

glotun n. [OF gloton] glutton or drunkard **HS** 7214, 7246, 12246, 12319 glotun

gloue n. [OE glof; ON] pledge for a wager **Ch1** 10630 gloue; **Ch2** 5950 gloue

gnaisted v. [ON *gnasten, OI gnastan] gnashed the teeth **Ch1** 1817 gnaisted

gnapped v. [cp. MDu cnappen; imitative] snapped **HS** 10215, 10243 gnapped *O* nypped *SV* nymped

gnawe, gnogh v. [OE gnagan] gnaw, bite, chew **HS** 3580, 3581 gnogh *O* gnow; 3584 gnogh *O* gnew; 9291, 10216 gnawe

god n. (1) [OE] the deity; a pagan god **Ch1** 2430, 4270, 5642, 7651, 9353 god; 1742, 2070, 5689, 7653, 8482 godes; 13652 godis; 7255, 7278, 8368 goddes; **Ch2** 1147, 2282, 3863, 4858, 8218 god; 412, 2483, 3091, 4525, 7074 godes; 1605 goddes; **HS** 2, 200, 3107, 7738, 9247 god; 6162 goddes

goddoghter n. [OE goddohter] a god-daughter **HS** 9710, 9740 goddoghter

gode n. (2) [OE god] goodness; welfare, benefit; charity; wealth, goods **Ch1** 2238, 3602, 5442, 7801, 8697 gode; 152, 838, 4927 gude; 931, 1620, 3288, 5445, 8485 godes; 933, 1246 gudes;

Ch2 468, 1911, 4142, 6705, 8005 gode; 119, 1356, 3021, 4085, 6888 godes; **HS** 595, 1167, 6485, 10708, 11213 gode; 2770 godes
gode adj./adv. [OE god] excellent; skilled, beneficial; well, very; effectively, zealously **Ch1** 922, 2198, 4133, 6223, 8587 gode; 130, 842, 3675, 5435, 9241 gude; 5752 god; **Ch2** 311, 1617, 5572, 6846, 8348 gode; 4227, 7040, 7242 god; **HS** 7, 1479, 2106, 6418, 12639 gode
godes n. [from OE god, n. (1)] goddess **Ch1** 1367, 7272 godes
godfadrys n. [OE godfæder] godfathers **HS** 1688, 1692 godfadrys
godhed n. [OE godhad] the nature of god; divinity **Ch1** 2286 godhed; **HS** 11546, 12304 godhede
godmodrys n. [OE god-modor] godmothers; ?a godparent **HS** 1694 godmodrys; 1695 godmodrys *C* tweyn of kyn *D* commatres
godnesse, godenes n. [OE godnes] merit, virtue; excellence; generosity **Ch1** 3602 of gode P godnesse L; 3909L godnesse (om. P); **HS** 62, 1204, 5530, 6429, 11138 godenes; 104, 11332 godenesse
godsone n. [OE godsunu] a godson **HS** 9710 godsone
gold n. [see gilden, gilte] [OE] objects made of gold; gold color; money **Ch1** 618, 2443, 3588, 4451, 10354 gold; 441, 3290, 4513, 11171, 15452 golde; **Ch2** 114, 1314, 3347, 4223, 5951 gold; 445, 6591, 7383 golde; **HS** 1408, 4999, 6334, 6810, 7028 gold; 10742 golde; 6201 goldrynges
golsoght n. [ON; cp. OI gulu-sott; OF iauniȝ (MP)] jaundice **HS** 3977 iawnes *O* golsoght; 3979 iawnys *O* iavnys
gonfaynoun, gomfaynoun n. [OF gonfanon] banner, battle standard, pennant **Ch1** 12844, 13148 gonfaynoun; 13222 gomfaynoun P gunphanoun L; **Ch2** 639 gonfaynoun; 8062 gonfaynounes
goos, gese n. [OE gos] goose, geese **Ch2** 1561 gese P grece L; 4331 goos
goot n. [see gayte]
gospelle n. [OE gospell] gospel **Ch1** 9311 gospelle; **Ch2** 3017 gospelle; **HS** 2441, 2815, 9269, 11465 gospel; 4346 gospelle; 4843 gospell
gost n. [see gast, gost, n.]
gostly adj./adv. [OE gastlic, gastlice] spiritually; like a devil; devoutly **HS** 983, 2372, 3736, 11316, 12165 gostly; 1534 gostlych
gouler n. [see oker]
gouernayle, gouernaunce n. [OF governance] authority or power to rule **HS** 1194 gouernayle *C* lokyng *D* kepyng *F* gouernaunse *H* gouernaunce
gouerne v. [OF governer] rule, command, control **Ch1** 6123 gouerne; **Ch2** 39 gye P gouerne L; 850 gouerned; 3621 gouerne; **HS** 451, 5060, 10967 gouerne
gouernour n. [OF] ruler; head of a religious institution; military commander; ship captain **Ch1** 918, 2736, 3511 gouernoure; 3050, 5301, 5705 gouernour; **Ch2** 3598 gouernours; 3780 gouernour; 4108 gouernoure
gourdus n. [AF gourd] cucumber plant; ?watermelon **HS** 2105 gourdus *C* growndis *D* turcus *H* gourdys
grace n. [OF] favor, honor; virtue from grace; good fortune; kindness; grace before a meal **Ch1** 133, 1167, 4864, 11520, 14288 grace; 4866 graces; 15354 grace P graces L; **Ch2** 74, 1767, 3290, 5228, 8252 grace; **HS** 26 gracys; 850, 1457, 4337, 9755, 12061 grace; 4719 graces
gracious, graciously adj./adv. [OF gracios] merciful, benevolent; fortunate; wealthy; happily **Ch1** 7226 graciouse; **Ch2** 3247 gracious; 1801, 5361 graciously; **HS** 5805, 10779 gracyous; 12079 gracyously
graie adj. [OE; WS græg, A greg] grey monks; Franciscan friars **Ch1** 14642 graie
graith n. [see grith] [ON, cp. OI greiði] order, governance, control **Ch2** 4778 gode graith P Godis griþ L; 7316, 7490 grayth; 8138 greith; **HS** 9945 greyth
grayþe v. [ON, cp. OI greiða] prepare, arrange, dress **Ch1** 7203 dight P greyþed L; 12147 redy P greyþe L; **HS** 7252 greyþe
gram n. [OE grama] rage, hostility; dispute **Ch2** 3736, 5948, 6961, 7312 gram; 7988 grame
gram adj. [OE gram, grom] hostile **Ch2** 2562 gram
◆ **gram** adv. [from adj.] angrily **Ch1** 12321L gram (om. P)
grant n. [OF grant] consent, permission; promise **Ch1** 1793 o grante P graunt L; 2020 graunte; 7937 o graunt; 2384, 3046 grant; 5487 grant P graunt (v.) L; **Ch2** 1218 ogrant P grant L; 1449 grante
grant v. [see ogrant] [OF granter] permit, allow; admit, consent, promise **Ch1** 967, 1281, 3649, 7396, 9181 grante; 521, 549, 970, 4488 graunte; 3820, 8884 graunt; 8550 grant; 1101, 3305, 6452, 9106, 15485 granted; 593, 2872, 5456, 5826, 7813 graunted; 7399 grantid; 7500 grauntid; 5175 grantes; 6954 grant P graunte L; **Ch2** 3724, 4358, 4830, 5564, 7649 grant; 1704, 3279, 4028, 5676, 8280 grante; 4160, 4172, 4868, 7832 graunt; 7665 graunte; 658, 1395, 4015, 5621, 7953 granted; 7281, 7304, 7685 grantid; **HS** 1773, 4340, 7247, 11224, 12345 graunte; 2555 graunt; 191 grauntyde; 8256, 9737 graunted; 570 grauntys; 6419 graunteþ; 468 grauntyd *CD* ȝouen; 2989 graunte *C* ȝef *O* gyfe
grant merci interjection [AF grant merci (MP)]

thank you **Ch1** 551, 2289, 3126 grant mercy; 13184 grant mercies P graunt mercis L; **Ch2** 3546 grant mercy; **HS** 6986, 10475 graunt mercy

grantise n. [OF grantaison] concession; warrant **Ch1** 671, 778, 7221, 9819 grantise P grauntyse L; 5658 grauntise; 15504L grauntise (om. P); **Ch2** 3188, 3290, 4623, 5103 grantise

graue n. [OE græf] grave, burial place **Ch1** 4442, 7698, 8515, 8910, 13435 graue; **Ch2** 2084, 3415, 7263, 7998 graue; **HS** 6387, 9133 graue; 8688 graues; 3263 graue *O* graffe

graue v. [OE grafan] to dig; bury a corpse **Ch1** 6600, 8038, 8051 graue; **HS** 10601 graue

grauers n. [OE grafer, græfere] digger, miner **Ch1** 8039 grauers P mynours L

gre, grece n. (1) [see degre] [OF gre, greis] a step, stairs; order of descent; a fall **Ch1** 23, 361 gre to gre; 10656L gre (om. P); **HS** 1564 þe gre *C* þe degre *D* a gre; 3710 gre *O* degre; 4637 gre; 2414 a grece *C* gre *D* degre; 3726 grece *O* gre; 3579 grecys; 6522, 6524 greces; 7279, 8324 grece

gre n. (2) [OF gre] pleasure, favor, wish; prize **Ch1** 486 gree P gre L; 12532 gre P pris L; **Ch2** 6588, 7520 gre; **HS** 6574 gre

grechaunde v. [see grete, v. (2), grucchyng, v.]

gredy adj. [OE grædig] greedy **HS** 6876 gredy

gref, grefe n. [AF gref] distress; trouble, pain **Ch1** 13546 grefe P gref L; **Ch2** 3831 ogrefe P on greff L; **HS** 2133, 11194, 12341 gref

gref, grefe adj. [see greue, ogrefe] [OF grief] troublesome, onerous **Ch2** 3393, 6253 grefe; **HS** 3713, 10269, 11125 gref; 5400, 11374, 12153 grefe; 9513 greff; 7567 greue

grehond n. [OE; WS grighund] a greyhound **Ch1** 11173 grehondȝ; 11252 grehunde

◆ **greilles** n. [OF graille, graisle] a military wind instrument; ?a fife or bugle **Ch1** 3493 greilles P greyles L

gremiand adj. [from OE gremian, v.] offensive, obnoxious **Ch1** 13831 gremiand P gremande L

grene n. [from OE grene, adj.] a field; the village green **Ch2** 41, 6687 grene; **HS** 4655 grenys

grene adj. [OE grene] the color green; livid **Ch1** 4347, 14094 grene; **Ch2** 4305 grene; **HS** 1393 grene

grene v. [OE grenian] to grow green, to flourish **HS** 8663 grenes

grepe, grope v. [OE grapian, gripan] grip; dig out **Ch1** 8051 groupe P groupes L; 12107 grapte P groped L; 8051 groupe P groupes L; **HS** 5171, 12299 grope; 2325 grepe *C* grope *D* grypyd

grennyng adj. [from OE grennian] grinning **HS** 4460 grennyng

gres, gresse n. [OE græs] grass, weeds **Ch1** 4347 gresse P gras L; 10862 gresse P gres L; 10841 gres; **Ch2** 8208 gres; **HS** 5991 gresse; 8663 gres

gretand, gretyng ger. [from OE gretan, v. (2)] weeping, lamentation **Ch1** 3165, 6838 gretand; 11950 gretyng; **Ch2** 4080 gretand

grete n. [from OE gretan, v. (2)] weeping, sorrow **Ch1** 15746 grete P sorewe L; **Ch2** 6732, 7096 grete

grete v. (1) [OE gretan, grætan] to greet, honor; attack **Ch1** 5165, 7205, 9176 grette; 6869 grete P gret L; 7456, 7749 grett; 7465 gretis; **Ch2** 3518 grete P grette L; 330, 1101, 4772, 5243 grette; 652, 4572 gretes; 7328 gretis; **HS** 4184 grete; 4191, 10620, 11468 grette

grete v. (2) [OE gretan] to weep, lament **Ch1** 3585 grete P gret L; 5365 grete P grede L; 9007 grete; 14943 greten; 14912 gretes; 14592, 14593 grette P gret L; 6838 gretand; 3165 gretand P gretynge L; **Ch2** 3652 grete; 4080 gretand; **HS** 11579 grete; 5721 grette; 715, 8427 grete GLOSS B wepe; 5721, 10494 grete GLOSS H wepte; 2521 wepyng *O* grett; 5716 gretande *F* grechaunde; 10970, 11573 wepyng *O* grettande

grete adj./adv. [OE great] great, large in size **Ch1** 495, 729, 993, 6476, 7426 gret; 564, 1294, 5236, 9309, 15680 grete; 6159, 6176 gretter; 7571 greteli P gretly L; 7607 gretli; 9238 gretly; **Ch2** 75, 1272, 2371, 5951, 8314 grete; 2147 gret; **HS** 1478, 2800, 12442 gret; 3584, 8871 grete; 296 gretlye; 3343 gretlych; 2012, 4084, 8345, 12327 gretly; 617, 8813, 9527, 10177 gretter; 3270 gretoun *O* grette ane

gretyng ger. [from OE gretan, v. (1)] a greeting, salutation **Ch1** 4808 gretyng P gretynge L; 12283 gretyng P message L; **Ch2** 3520 gretyng

greuance n. [OF grevance] offense, misery; resentment, punishment **Ch1** 4794, 9366, 15528 greuance; **Ch2** 2149, 2429, 4638, 6354, 8007 greuance; **HS** 3997, 8811 greuaunce; 790 chaunce *D* greuaunce

greue n. [AF gref] grievance, wrong **Ch2** 2232 greue

greue v. [OF grever] injure, oppress; harass, offend **Ch1** 2863, 3206, 5821, 9354, 15586 greue; 6401L greued (om. P); 7708, 8700, 14573 greued; **Ch2** 117, 2425, 4608, 6870, 8218 greue; 200 greued P agreued L; 1591, 3172 greued; 2283 greued P wraþed L; 5739 greues; **HS** 38, 490, 2397, 5428, 10036 greue; 2683 greuyþ; 6093 greues

greuous, greuosly adj./adv. [see agrisen, agros] [AF grevous] bitter, tedious, hard; oppressive **Ch1** 1242 greuous; 8401 greuous P grysly L; 4238 greuosli P greuously L; 5088 greuosly; **Ch2** 2256, 3231 greuosly; 7275 greuoslie; **HS**

9744 greuus; 11071 greuous; 1037, 2679, 3733, 5505, 9782 greuusly; 6737 greuuslyke
greuusnesse n. [from AF grevous, adj.] injury, grief **HS** 719 greuusnesse
grew v. [see grisen, gros] [cp. MDu gruwen, MLG gruwen, growen] to be terrified **Ch1** 8418 gros & grew
grewe v. [OE growan, greow] to grow **Ch1** 2941, 7900 grewe; 10168 grewes; **HS** 7516, 9156 grewe
griffon, Gregeis, Griffonie n. [OF Grifon] Greeks, Greece **Ch1** 158, 711, 989, 1008, 1160 Gregeis; 868, 1310 Gregeys; 432, 621, 899, 1464 Grece; **Ch2** 3933, 3943, 3951, 3971 griffons; 3456 Grece; 3729, 3935, 4091, 4237, 4281 Griffonie
griffoun n. [see mate griffoun]
grille, gryl adj. [see seme] [OE; cp. gryllan, v.] fierce, cruel **Ch1** 4534 semegrelere P semeþ griller L; **Ch2** 2255 grille; **HS** 5600 gryl
grim, grymly adj./adv. [see brim] [OE grimme, grimlic] fierce, cruel; angry, dangerous **Ch1** 912 brym P grym L; 5151, 6297 grim P grym L; 15642 grim; 3209, 8065, 8401, 8562, 14194 grym; 8067 grimly P grym L; 11880 grimly P grisly L; **Ch2** 2282, 2753, 5168, 6938, 7934 grim; 2282, 4757, 6514 grym; 3816, 4112 brim P grym L; **HS** 782, 2523, 3663, 7783, 10265 grym; 12597 grymly; 1386 grymly *CF* grysly; 5600 gryl ne grym
gris n. [OF] grey fur, fur trimming **Ch1** 611, 11175 gris P grys L
grisen, gros v. [see agrisen, grew] [OE; cp. agrisen] shudder, quake, feel horror **Ch1** 2946 at gros P agros L; 8418 gros & grew; 9476 grisen P agrysen L; **Ch2** 5710 ogrisen; **HS** 7876 gros GLOSS BH dredde *O* grose; 10222 grys *O* gryse *SV* grise
grysly adj./adv. [OE grislic] horrible, dreadful, hideous, fearful **HS** 666, 692, 1822, 9057 grysly
grith n. [OE from ON griþ] peace of a nation, stability; pardon, clemency **Ch1** 2747, 3631, 4483, 7435, 15678 grith P gryþ L; **Ch2** 757, 2765, 3199, 5728, 7944 grith; 4778 graith P griþ L; **HS** 10657 gryþ; 11560 gryþþe *O* gyrthe; 12091 gryþ *O* gyrthe; 12062 (caption in *O*) gyrthe
gronden v. [OE grindan] to grind; sharpen a weapon **Ch1** 15129 gronden
grope, groupe v. [see grepe]
grote n. [see crote]
ground n. [OE grund] foundation; land, earth; ground **Ch1** 3753, 8150 ground; 1375, 3947, 5323, 8072, 13289 grounde; **Ch2** 4216, 6400 ground; 3944, 5548 grounde; 5158 groundwalle; **HS** 3387, 9779, 11852 grounde
gruchande, grucchyng v. [OF gruchier] grumble, complain **HS** 1085 gruchande; 10121 grucceþ; 3489 grucchedyst *O* gorched; 3492 grucchyng *O* gorchande; 5716 gretande *F* grechaunde
guerdons n. [see rewardon]
guye v. [OF guier] lead or guide; drive; rule, govern, manage **Ch2** 1981, 3260, 4976, 6796, 7758 guye; 4534 condie P gye L
guyour, gyour n. guide, ruler, military commander **Ch1** 3351 giours P gyours L; **Ch2** 82 guyour; 3072 gyour; 3616 guyours
gulardous n. [AF goliardeis] a buffoon **HS** 4705 gulardous
gultelis adj. [from OE gylt, n.] innocent of guilt, sinless **Ch2** 4522 sakles P gultelis L
guttys n. [OE guttas] entrails **HS** 702 þarmys GLOSS BH guttys

Ȝ

ȝa, ȝe, ȝis, ȝo adv./conj. [OE ȝe, ON ja] yes **Ch1** 2308 ȝis; 7955, 14301 ȝa; 14298 ȝa P ȝe L; **Ch2** 1188 ȝa; **HS** 5906 ȝo; 2321, 2549 ȝe *C* ȝa; 11671 ȝe; 8241, 10475, 12587 ȝee; 11052 ȝys
ȝald v. [see ȝeld]
ȝare n./adj./adv. [OE ȝeare, ȝearwe] ready, readily **Ch1** 890, 3047, 9196, 12171, 15203 ȝare; **Ch2** 1454, 3038, 5571, 6206, 7973 ȝare; **HS** 1963 *C* ȝare (BFH differ)
ȝare v. [OE ȝearwian, ȝearwede] to prepare, get ready **Ch1** 8518 dight P ȝared L; **Ch2** 3588, 7145, 7539 ȝare; 292, 1412, 2186, 2955, 7469 ȝared
ȝate n. [see gate] [OE geat, gæt] path, road; a gate **Ch1** 1912, 3577, 5313, 9216 ȝate; 3565, 15648 ȝate P gate L; 5952, 7879 ȝates; **Ch2** 7066 ȝate; 3734, 3876, 7162 ȝates
ȝe pronoun [see ȝow, ȝour]
ȝede, ȝode v. [see go, went] [OE gan, gon, gangan, eode, eodan] went **Ch1** 480, 1430, 5507, 8754, 15621 ȝede; 3204 ȝedis; 2328, 5582 ȝed; 1403 ȝode; 3053 ȝode P went L; 4618 ȝod P ȝoden L; 13726 ȝede P ȝed L; **Ch2** 918, 2467, 4440, 6371, 8174 ȝede; 1896, 1926, 2991, 5408, 8236 ȝed; 1038 ȝede P romed L; 1907, 3554, 4418, 7444, 8006 ȝode; **HS** 507, 2336, 2510 ȝede *C* went; 522 ȝede *C* went *D* gan to gon; 1371 ȝede *C* wentyn; 1809 ȝede *C* went *D* come; 9224 ȝede *O* come; 10419 ȝede *SV* eode
ȝeld, ȝald, ȝolde v. [OE ȝeldan, gieldan] to yield, give; repay; perform a vow; allow; return **Ch1** 14010 ȝeld; 1068, 3246, 6168, 7102, 9935 ȝelde; 2038 ȝeldes P ȝeldest L; 5061 ȝeldes; 10782, 11974 ȝald; 5288, 5561, 10755 ȝalde; 5991 ȝalde P ȝolde L; 9396 ȝold; 6640 ȝolde; 4866, 5186, 5994, 9127 ȝolden; 12764 ȝeldand P ȝeldyng L; 13657 did P ȝald L; **Ch2**

684, 2426, 4595, 6252, 7670 ȝeld; 1833, 4412, 5525, 6652, 7928 ȝelde; 6272, 6274 ȝeldes; 2993 ȝelded P ȝulden L; 2159 ȝolde; 629, 2924, 3543, 4985, 6988 ȝolden; 80, 1261, 3051, 6023, 7863 ȝald; 4121, 6583 ȝalde; **HS** 1209, 2216, 2808, 4342 ȝelde; 5482 ȝald; 12017 ȝolde; 2532 ȝeldyst; 6424 ȝoulde; 4839 ȝylde; 12163 ȝeelde; 5650 ȝelde *O* gyfe

ȝeldyng ger. [from OE ȝeldan] yielding **Ch1** 5465 ȝeldyng

ȝelle, ȝelp v. [OE gellan, ȝelpan, ON gella] shout; cry out **Ch1** 9697, 12033 ȝelp; 7357 ȝelpe; 10049 ȝelle; **Ch2** 938, 3532, 4528, 7182 ȝelp; **HS** 4894 ȝelle

ȝelp n. [OE gelp] complaint **Ch2** 6374 ȝelp

ȝelugh adj. [OE geolu] yellow **HS** 3450 ȝelugh; 3980 ȝelgh; 3448 ȝelugh (2) *O* ȝallande, ȝalow

ȝeme n. [OE gemen] care, heed; attention **Ch1** 7023 ȝeme; **HS** 458 heyd toke *D* ȝem took GLOSS D keep; 5084 ȝeme nymes *O* he menes

ȝeme v. [OE geman, ON geyma] to heed, observe; keep, preserve; govern **Ch1** 2011, 6056, 10718, 14843 ȝeme; 9218 ȝemed; **Ch2** 1049, 3269, 4627, 6033, 8302 ȝeme; 72, 823, 1601, 3420, 6785 ȝemed; **HS** 1306, 4823, 9910, 11322, 12637 ȝeme; 10998 kepe *O* ȝeme

ȝenand ppl. [OE genian] gaping **HS** 2526 ȝenand

ȝenkþe, ȝenþe n. [see ȝouth]

ȝepe adj. [OE ȝeap] bold; proud **Ch2** 7828 ȝepe

ȝer, ȝere n. [OE ȝer, gear] year **Ch1** 49, 850, 3639, 8118, 15625 ȝere; 1746 ȝere P ȝer L; 436 ȝeere; 790, 3086 ȝeris; 1883, 5479 ȝers; 4034, 10762 ȝeres; **Ch2** 11, 1021, 3248, 6846, 8358 ȝere; 1140, 2475, 5659, 5747, 5861 ȝeres; 3482, 6068, 8022 ȝers; **HS** 66, 810 ȝer; 835, 1965, 2589, 10299, 11099 ȝere; 6975 ȝers; 2573, 6077 ȝeres

ȝerd n. [OE ȝerd, geard] rod, staff; ship's yardarm; arm of a seige engine; church yard **Ch1** 11766 ȝerd; **Ch2** 7099, 7970 ȝerde; 5144 kirke ȝerd; **HS** 4862, 4999, 8680, 8918 ȝerd; 2612 cherche ȝerd

ȝerne v. [OE geornan] desire; wish for **Ch1** 625 ȝern P ȝerne L; 1953, 5454, 6196, 8379, 9012 ȝerne; 2938, 5854, 6908, 8442, 15850 ȝerned; 635, 15033 ȝernes; 8898, 15045 ȝarned P ȝerned L; **Ch2** 4350, 4780 ȝerne; 1280, 2917, 3622 ȝerned; **HS** 452, 7356 ȝerne; 5346, 6645, 6742 ȝerned; 5059 ȝerne GLOSS BH desyre *O* lere; 1451 desyrede *C* ȝernyd *D* askyd; 2103 desyred *C* ȝernyd *D* coueytid

ȝerne, ȝorne adv. [OE georne, ON gjarn] eagerly, quickly; earnestly **Ch1** 1677, 4982, 7922, 9399, 13764 ȝerne; 7400 ȝern; **Ch2** 1355, 3978 ȝerne; **HS** 1157 ȝorne GLOSS B vaste [i.e.,: fast] *C* with skorn *D* hym beforn

ȝernyng ger. [from OE geornan] desire; yearning **Ch1** 9309, 14104 ȝernyng; **Ch2** 2484, 4524 ȝernyng; **HS** 7613 ȝernyng; 5333 desyryng *O* ȝernyng

ȝif conj. [OE gif] if, whether **Ch1** 3753, 6512, 7876, 8184, 8200 ȝif; 3032, 4553, 5036 if P ȝif L; 2562, 3199, 4241, 4979, 8730 if P ȝyf L; **Ch2** 3000 ȝif; 3963 if P ȝif L; **HS** 75, 9467, 9989, 10266 ȝyf

ȝyue, ȝif, ȝaf v. [see gyue, gif, gaf]

ȝing, ȝeng, ȝong adj./n. [OE ȝeong, geong] young; a young person **Ch1** 783, 1974, 4087, 7487 ȝing; 7428 ȝinge; 1224, 2364, 15436 ȝyng; 1797 ȝenge; 3138 ȝeng P ȝong L; 6965 ȝenge P ȝonge L; 7160 ȝeng; 834, 4151, 8195, 11972, 13944 ȝong; 4679, 6745 ȝonge; 2560, 6417 ȝongere; 1965, 2271, 2299 ȝongest; **Ch2** 2311, 3427, 4791, 5224, 7364 ȝing; 2302, 3274, 3413 ȝeng; 163, 2231, 3274, 5648, 8115 ȝong; 569, 818, 1670, 3223, 6698 ȝonge; 785, 3140, 5200, 5772 ȝongest; **HS** 3883, 4899, 6540, 8429 ȝyng; 1127, 1133, 1666 ȝung; 4433 ȝunge

ȝit, ȝet, yit adv. [OE get, giet] yet, moreover; again, still **Ch1** 719, 1051, 1348, 2015, 8133 ȝitt; 1692, 3732, 6103, 10534, 14092 ȝit; 10520 ȝit P ȝut L; **Ch2** 108 ȝyt; 128, 1286, 3466, 6672, 8314 ȝit; 1286, 1799 ȝit P ȝut L; 721 yit; **HS** 248, 2282, 4290, 5299, 11845 ȝyt; 686 *C* ȝet (BDFH differ)

ȝole n. [OE geol, ON jol] yule; the Christmas season **Ch1** 10206, 10207 ȝole; **Ch2** 1100, 1587, 3064, 5872, 7927 ȝole; **HS** 814, 815 ȝole; 4652, 9179 ȝole nyght

ȝoman n. [OE guma, gome] yeoman; farmer **Ch1** 736 ȝoman; **Ch2** 7226 ȝomen

ȝon, ȝonder adv./adj. [OE geon] beyond; at a distance **Ch1** 4189, 4197, 11998, 12540 ȝon; 4171 ȝone; 11997 ȝonder; 4171 ȝondere; **HS** 5893 ȝone *F* ȝonder

ȝong adj./n. [see ȝing, ȝeng]

ȝorne adv. [see ȝerne]

ȝoten v. [OE geotan] poured, put **HS** 6765 ȝoten *O* gyttyn

ȝouth, ȝenkþe n. [OE geoguþ] youth; a young man **Ch1** 3957, 4751, 6105, 10270, 11128 ȝouth; 1932 ȝouth P ȝonkþe; 7460 ȝouthe; 5287L ȝougþe (P differs); **HS** 4909, 7677, 11604 ȝouþe; 2807 ȝunþe; 5050 ȝenþe; 6439 ȝyngþe; 7669 ȝenkþe *O* thoghte

ȝow, ȝe, ȝour, ȝours pronoun [OE ge, eow, eower] you, yours **Ch1** 23, 1080, 3176, 5864, 9093 ȝow; 6817 ȝowe; 7746, 7755 ȝou; 221, 1668, 3160, 6636, 8817 ȝe; 7533, 7757 ȝee; 134, 1273, 4231, 7765, 9391 ȝour; 5454, 7748 ȝoure; 6663, 6666, 6676 ȝourself; **Ch2** 840, 2240, 4572, 6888, 8329 ȝow; 142, 1535, 3950, 5821, 8069 ȝe; 946, 2241, 4013, 6974, 7701 ȝour; 3280, 4100 ȝour P ȝore L; 4577, 6904 ȝours;

HS 11, 61, 1178, 4360, 8898 ȝow; 329, 765, 5488, 6052, 11223 ȝe; 766, 4360, 5489, 6300 ȝour; 897, 952, 6301, 10800 ȝoure; 6052 ȝours; 1177, 3152 ȝowself; 6301, 10802, 11224 ȝeself; 8898 ȝoureself

H

habite, abite n. [OF (h)abit] dress of a religious order **Ch1** 6975, 6980 abite; 6952 abite P habite L; 6996 habite; 8887 abite P habyt L; 11545 habite P abyte L; **Ch2** 2261, 3330, 7878, 8237, 8254 habite; 4252, 7808 abite

hache n. (1) [OF] a Danish axe **Ch2** 698 hache

hache, hage, age, agew n. (2) [OF ague] illness, acute fever **Ch1** 15043 feuere agew P agu L; 15065 age P hache L; **Ch2** 8130 hage

haf, has, haue v. [OE habban] take, hold, keep; possess; and auxil. **Ch1** 132, 1215, 4180, 8545, 9321 haf; 955, 4009, 6233 haf P haue L; 487, 1265, 6586, 9270, 10257 haue; 98, 1132, 2309, 4075, 9100 has; 1391 has P hast L; 911, 1928, 2053, 7196 haf P han L; 6635 haue P han L; 1291, 1587, 2435, 8202, 9399 had; 2429 had P hadde L; 12802 hadde; 12309 haf P ha L; 12348L ha (om. P); 12759 haden P hadden L; **Ch2** 106, 4806, 5362, 7604, 8355 haf; 249, 1515, 4869, 6862, 8254 haue; 98, 1340, 4846, 5768, 8327 has; 846 has P hastow L; 20, 1330, 4824, 5224, 8045 had; 5001 hade; 1300, 1309 had P hadde L; 2709 hat P hadde L; 4037L han (P differs); 247, 8355 haued; **HS** 38, 470, 523, 1118, 1242 haue; 546, 7062, 7910 ha; 2834 a; 100 hast; 3684 hase; 4835, 6151, 6552, 11708 has; 304 haþ; 373 hauyn; 2929 hauen; 6075 han; 171, 3118 had; 136, 418, 7061 hadde

hage n. [see hache]

haile n. [OE hægel] hail **Ch1** 13028 haile

hayre, hare n. (1) [OE hara] a hare **Ch1** 5127, 7594, 11252, 15056 hare; 10972L hare (om. P); **Ch2** 5149 hayre

haire, heire, her n. (2) [OE her, hær] hair **Ch1** 4025, 4028 heire; 10082 haire; 11934 haire P her L; 14274 hide no haire P huyde ne her L; **HS** 3201, 3226, 9156 her; 4298 heer

hakneye n. [OF haquenee] small saddle horse **Ch2** 6730 hakneye; 8191 hakneis; 8285 hakeney

hakse adv. [ON; cp. Dan. harsk] ?fiercely **HS** 3672 *O* hakse (?error: harsk) (B differs)

hale n. [see halle, haule, n.] **hale** v. [OF haler] haul, draw up **Ch1** 11769 hale; **Ch2** 4229 hale

halewe, halow v. [OE halgian] sanctify, honor, observe **Ch1** 5674 halowed P halewode L; 7268 halow; **Ch2** 1589 halow; **HS** 820, 893, 910 halewe; 834 halewyd; 930 halewyþ; 921 halewede; 4680 halwed; 8615, 9342 halewed

halewys, halwes n. [OE halga] saints, martyrs **Ch2** 4529 halwes; **HS** 144 halewys *D* seyntis

half n./adj. [OE] half part; quantity; a side, extent **Ch1** 805, 3639, 4304, 6608, 8135 half; 3379 halfe; 1392 half P halue L; 5072, 8448 halue; 2688L halues (P differs); **Ch2** 380, 2952, 4161, 6299, 7451 half; **HS** 921, 1581, 2823, 6766, 9070 half

haly adj. [see holy]

halyday n. [OE haligdæg] holy day **HS** 802, 979, 12179 halyday

halidam n. [OE haligdom] sacrament **Ch2** 2667 halidam; **HS** 2725 halydom; 3669 halydam *W* haly dam

halle, haule n. [OE heall, OF hale] public room; hall for entertaining; pavilion, tent **Ch1** 5485L halle (P differs); 7452 halle; 9157 in halles & hales; 13961 halles; **Ch2** 650, 4558 halle; 1368, 2178, 6579 haule; 1559 haules; **HS** 3297, 5878, 5911, 5928 halle; 3425, 3437 hallys

halp n./v. [see help]

hals n. [see wikhals] [OE hals, heals] the neck, throat **Ch1** 3161 hals P nekke L; **Ch2** 6768 hals; 7385 wikked hals; **HS** 2122 nekke *C* hals *D* nekke; 2688 hals GLOSS B necke GLOSS H nek; 11559 nekke *O* hals

halsed v. [from OE hals, n.] embraced **Ch1** 7940 halsed P clipte L; **HS** 3881 clypte *O* halsede; 3884 clyppyng *O* halsynge (ger.)

haluendele n./adj./adv. [OE phrase, healfan dæle] half, in two parts **Ch1** 10719 halfendele P haluendel L; **Ch2** 475, 1143, 4621 haluendele; **HS** 1582 haluyndele *C* halfe *D* halfyndel; 1588 haluyndele *C* halfe *D* half; 2824 haluyndele *C* halfedel *D* halfuendel; 7708 haluendele

hamelet n. [OF] a small village **Ch2** 6503 hamelet; 7582 hamelete; 7852 hamelesse; 8334 hamelette

hancel n. [OE handselen] omen, augury **HS** 369, 373, 378 hancel

hand, hond n. [OE] the hand; in phrases with adverbial relationships **Ch1** 688, 2052, 3544, 7453, 9192 hand; 638, 6334, 8107 hande; 1418, 3168, 7154, 8950, 15450 handes; 7754, 10752 handis; 4832 honde; 1602, 7170 hond; 597, 2025, 2937, 7453 in hand; 1199 on hand; 1384 in honde; 1557, 2378 to hand; 5575, 5613 at hand; 1612 beforhand; 2495 biforhand; **Ch2** 1487, 3011, 4697, 6000, 7727 hand; 20, 1056, 3325, 5752, 7624 hond; 1006 honde; 357, 438, 4420, 5740, 7812 handes; 3540 hondes; 173, 3312 beforhand; 2303, 4619 biforhand; 335, 1487, 3648, 4858, 5623 in hand; 1591, 4104 nerhand; 3983 neihand; 1647, 2813, 3074, 5816, 7339 on hand; 1924, 7270 tille hand; 1931 at hand; **HS** 1068, 1175, 2702, 8040, 9143 hand; 8132, 9215 hande; 2121 hond; 83, 10334 honde; 9285 hende; 11149 handes; 3328 yn hand; 2050 to hande

handel v. [OE handlian] to handle, manipulate,

deal with **Ch1** 1815 handeled; **HS** 89, 99, 101, 105, 129 handyl; 6580 handleþ

handlyng ger. [from OE handlian] discussion; management **HS** 80, 83, 94, 7580, 7889 handlyng; 7692, 7718 handelyng

hang, henge v. [OE hangian, hon; ON hanga] to hang, execute **Ch1** 3421 hanged P hongeden L; 3453 henge; 3596 hang P henge L; 8535 heeng P heng L; 9029 hang P heng L; 9863 heng; 11444 hange P henge L; 14549 heng P henge L; 15440 hang P henge L; 15443 hang; 15445 hyngand P hengand L; **Ch2** 1189, 4404, 6824, 8061, 8248 hang; 1184, 3397, 4290, 5740, 8289 hanged; 1269 hyngand P honged L; 3378, 4163 hyngand; 4269 hyng P henges L; 4274 hongen; 5883 henge; 8182 heyng; **HS** 2121 hyng *C* hynge *D* heng; 2125 hyng *C* hynge *D* hong; 2688, 9211, hange; 2074 hangyþ; 11979 hangeþ; 1472 honge; 11559 hangþ; 12328 hyng; 2064, 5207 hanged

hangyng ger. [from OE hangian] execution, hanging **Ch2** 8249 hangyng

hap, happe n. [see mishap, vnhap] [ON hap] chance, fortune, luck **Ch1** 2960, 6593, 9501 hap; 2442 happe P help L; 15577L happe (om. P); **Ch2** 3430, 4500 hap; 1431 happe; 1740 happe P help L; **HS** 5616 hap; 1953 at gesse GLOSS B hap

hap, happe v. (1) [from ON hap, n.] to happen **Ch1** 5429 to wyn P happede L; **HS** 132 happyd *D* han falle; 1727 be *C* happe to ben; 6385 happede for *O* fell so

happed v. (2) [cp. lappen; OF happer] to wrap up **Ch1** 8902 happed

happyliche adv. [from ON hap] luckily, by chance **HS** 10683 chaunsfullyche *SV* happyliche

hard n. [see nesch, nesshe] [from OE heard, adj.] misfortune, affliction, difficulty **Ch2** 4166, 5609, 6044, 7355 hard

hard adj./adv. [OE heard, hearde] harsh; tough, brave, difficult **Ch1** 1057, 7612 harde; 1805, 3388, 3884, 4900, 6635 hard; 1578, 7352 herd; 1984 herd P faste L; 7348 herd P harde L; **Ch2** 721, 3071, 4338, 5734, 8245 hard; 3004 herd P hard L; 1266 harder; 2839, 7738 hardere; **HS** 1492, 4518, 6406, 9018, 11678 hard; 5374, 11824 harder; 3634, 7316 hardere

hardy adj. [OF hardi] bold, rash, brave **Ch1** 467, 1575, 4149, 5369, 6732 hardy; 2835, 3475, 3759, 4633, 7584 hardi; 4364, 8971 hardie; 3471, 13952 hardiest; 2704, 8206 herdy; **Ch2** 458, 2799, 5431, 6742, 8316 hardy; 1722, 4071, 4452, 5322, 8317 hardie; 4990, 6952 hardi; **HS** 2607, 3592, 4919, 5545 hardy

hardily adv. [from OF hardi, adj.] courageously, boldly **Ch1** 1673 hardily P hardely L; 7313 hardlie P hardyly L; 8397 hardeli; **Ch2** 3939 hardilie; 5287, 7005 hardely; **HS** 1333, 3735, 4777, 7319, 8779 hardyly; 2803 hardely; 204 hardely *C* baldely

hardynesse n. [from OF hardi, adj.] bravery, valor, daring **Ch1** 873, 1563 hardynesse; 3313, 8436 hardynes; 3710 hardinesse; 1688, 3765 hardines; 4615 hardynes; **Ch2** 24 hardinesse; 6809 hardynesse; **HS** 4204 hardynesse

hare n. [see hayre, hare]

◆ **harie** n. [from OE hergian, v.] hostility **Ch2** 3888 harie P hatrie L

harm n. [OE hearm] loss, ruin; injury, wrong; bad fortune; sin, deceit **Ch1** 12414 harme; 1024, 6623, 7020 harmes; 6516L harmes (P differs); **Ch2** 2699 grim P harm L; **HS** 2326, 5122, 9139 harme; 3422 harm; 10542 harmes

harneys n. [OF harnois, harneis, harnes] body armour, equipment, weapons **Ch1** 4348, 12020 herneis; 6871 herneys P harneys L; 8142, 10824 harneis; **Ch2** 331 armes P harneys L; 2947, 3023, 5704, 7008, 7554 herneis; 5006 hernays; 4722, 5528 herneys; **HS** 3432 harneys; 4600 harnyse; 1448 eryn *C* harnes; 3438 armour *O* harnes; 10338 shone & hys hosen *SV* hernes *O* hose hys schone

harnes n. [ON hjarni] brains **HS** 5032 harnes GLOSS H brayn

harpe n. [OE hearp] stringed musical instrument **Ch1** 11143 harpes; **HS** 4747, 4757, 4760 harpe

harpours, harpers n. [OF harpour, OE hearper] harp player **Ch1** 76 harpours; **HS** 4750 harpers

hasard n. [OF] game of chance with dice; fig.: misfortune **Ch1** 4955 chek hasarde P chek ful harde L; 11151 hasard

hasardour n. [OF hasardeor] gambler, gamester **HS** 1042 hasardour

hasardrie, haȝardrie n. [OF hasarderie] playing the game of hazard **Ch1** 11332 haȝardrie P hasardrie L

haste n. [OF haste, heste] haste, eagerness, impatience **Ch1** 2987, 4958 haste; 4875, 5310, 6582 hast; **Ch2** 7992 hast; 1262, 1948, 2339, 5495, 7841 haste; 4461 þorght hatie (?error) P in hastie L; **HS** 141, 1262, 1744 haste; 1159, 5481, 9609 hast

haste v. [OF haster] to hurry, drive **Ch1** 8962 hast; 3729, 7021, 9237, 9368 haste; 2694, 4499, 7991, 13287, 15221 hasted; 1702 abatid P hasted L; 6507, 7807 hastid; 1027 hasted P hastede L; **Ch2** 3437 haste; 4702 kast P haste L; 965, 1291, 2762, 2812, 5710 hasted; 1103 hastis; **HS** 4492, 11387 haste

hasty, hastif adj./adv. [from OF haste] eager, rash; swift, urgent **Ch1** 4719 hastif; 6789 hasty; 14947 hastife; **Ch2** 4391, 4695, 5289 hastif

hastyly, hastely adv. [from OF haste] speedily,

eagerly, suddenly **Ch1** 6317, 9194 hastily; 6404 austerly P hastely L; 15587 hastifly; **Ch2** 23 hastisly P hastely L; 4600 hastely; 5844, 5897 hastilie; 6179, 6182 hastily; **HS** 227, 777, 5747, 11394 hastely; 6898 hastylye; 961 hastyly *C* hastely *D* stedefastly

hastynes, hastiuenesse n. [from OF haste] rashness, hastiness **Ch1** 5090 hastifesse P hastynesse; **Ch2** 3158 hastiuenesse; 6175 hastynes

hat, hate v. [see hight]

hate n. [prob. from OE hatian, v.] hate or fear; extreme anger **Ch1** 4476, 4817, 7532, 8202, 13689 hate; 3925 hete P hate L; **Ch2** 6517 hate; **HS** 1337, 3788 hate

hate v. [OE hatian] to hate, loathe; despise, scorn **Ch1** 3933, 7346 hate; 1210 hates; 2406, 3871, 4519, 6214, 7534 hatid; 2642, 2999, 4811, 6933, 8351 hated; 9521 hotid P hated L; 11429 to hate . . . haf hated P hat . . . han hated L; **Ch2** 208 hate; 992 hated; **HS** 10895 hate; 3104 hatyþ; 5108, 5111, 11530 hateþ; 3539 hatys; 4233, 9939 hates

hate adj. [see hote]

hater, hatren, hatir n. [see atire] [OE hæteru, hatian] clothing, garments, attire **Ch1** 7454 hatir P atyr L; 7491 hatire P atir L; **Ch2** 5004 hater; **HS** 5583 hatren

hatred n. [from OE hate + ræden] hate; the sin of wrath **Ch1** 8877, 13690 hatered; **Ch2** 205 hatred P hate L; 210 hatered; 2391 hatred P hard L; 3052 hatrex (error); **HS** 11980 hatrede

hatren n. [see hater]

hatte v. [see hytte, hight] [OE hatian] have a fever, become hot **Ch1** 15043 hatte

hauberk, hauberions n. [OF hauberc; cp. OE healsbeorga, OF hauberjon] coat of mail, chain or plate armor **Ch1** 3223, 8361, 9881, 10291 hauberk; 3373 hauberkes; 2698L hauberks (om. P); 4344 hauberk P brunyes L; 11181 hauberions P (om. L); **Ch2** 7808 hauberke

hauelon n. [OF havellon] deception, guile **Ch2** 7530 hauelon

hauen n. [OE hæfen] harbor, port, bay; refuge **Ch1** 622, 1312, 4587, 7706, 15124 hauen; 1286, 5814 hauens P hauenes L; 2481 heuen P hauene L; 4294 hauen P heuen L; 6693L hauenes (om. P); **Ch2** 1446, 2337, 3900, 6752, 7398 hauen; 882, 6974 hauens; 678 hauen P hauenes L; 3118 heuen

haukes n. [OE hafoc, ON haukr] hawks **HS** 3086 haukes

haunces v. [cp. OF hauncier] lift up, raise **HS** 12442 haunces

◆ **hauncenhede** n. [cp. haunce, v.] presumption, pride **HS** 5164 hauncenhede *O* hauntehede

haunt n. [OF hant] habitual use, customary practice; dwelling place **Ch1** 1905, 4057, 6548 haunte P haunt L; 1749 hauntes; 4684, 11313, 11852, 12010 haunt; **Ch2** 4159, 5475 haunt; 7661 haunte

haunte v. [OF hanter] practice habitually; use, observe custom **Ch1** 2133, 3306 haunted; 15486 hanted; **Ch2** 7819 haunted; **HS** 1028, 3092, 5546, 7226 haunte; 569 hauntys; 751 hauntyn; 1017 hauntyst; 851 hauntyn *C* halwed *D* han *H* haunted; 7794 hauntyng; 2024 haunte *C* hawnthe *D* vse; 2971 haunte *C* awntyn; 7450 vsen *O* haunttys

hauteyn adj. [OF hautain] proud, arrogant **Ch2** 5365, 5379 hauteyn

hay n. [OE heg, hig] hay; mowed grass **Ch1** 10862 hay; 14068 hay P hey L; **Ch2** 3972 hay

hede, heued n. (1) [OE heafod] chief, head of a body **Ch1** 949, 3856, 6813, 8289, 12162 heued; 6002 hede P heued L; 1818, 7152, 9129, 13332 hedes; 47, 2746, 4025, 9395 15443 hede; 7138, 12907 hede P hed L; 9012 hede P heued L; 10666 iren P hed L; 12113 hede P nekke L; 15445 hed; **Ch2** 134 hede P heued L; 431 hade P heued L; 328, 1492, 4720, 5658, 8290 hede; 920, 1257, 1347, 5990, 6450 hedes; 645, 2106, 2535, 7813, 8063 heued; 2227 heued P hed L; **HS** 2180, 3292 hed; 318 hede; 3312 hedes; 3225 heuedys; 5272, 9675 heued; 3277 heued *O* hede; 4493 hed *O* heued

hede n. (2) [from OE hedan, v.] heed, notice; attention to **Ch1** 4981L, 8287L hede (P differs); **Ch2** 8250 hede; **HS** 2950, 7206, 12189 hede

hede, heued adj. [from OE heafod] principal, leading; valuable **Ch1** 10850 hede kirke P heued kyrke L; 14146 hede toun P hed toun L; **Ch2** 1064 hede; **HS** 9510 heued synne

hede hode n. [from OE heafod] leadership **Ch2** 6448 hede hode

hedeles, heuedles adj. [from OE heafod] decapitated **Ch1** 1076 hedeles P hedles L; 6518 heuedles P hedles L; **Ch2** 4453, 5186 hedeles

hedelynges adv. [from OE heafod] headlong **HS** 6546 [MS *O* interpolation, l. 55] hedelynges

hedyr adv. [see hider]

hedys v. [see redis]

hege n. [see heþ, hethe]

heght n. [see hie, adj./adv.] [OE heahþu, hyþe] height **Ch1** 973 heght P heighte L; 4533 heght P heyght L

heire, her n. [see haire]

heire, here, eyr n. [AF heir, aire] heir, one who inherits **Ch1** 402 heyre P heyr L; 761, 2372, 2523 heyre; 2268 eire; 2654 here P eyr L; 2262, 3702, 4766, 6226, 13740 heire; 4177 heires; 11456, 11457 ayre; 6218 ere; 3892 ayr P heyr L; 6242 heir; 3113 heire P heyr L; **Ch2** 1787, 2686, 3105, 5068, 5994 heyr; 1243, 5043,

6017, 8326 heire; 1152 heyers; 1778 hayre P heir L; 3377 heir; 76, 1693, 2739, 4045, 5199 heyre; 70 heyre P eyr L; 718, 2578, 3408, 6016, 7607 heires; 1545, 2640, 3108, 5513, 6361 heyres; 2205, 6131 heirs; 4057 heyrs; **HS** 1182, 2026, 6477 eyr; 9444 eyre; 6284, 6280 eyres

heyre v. [from AF heir, n.] to inherit **Ch1** 12974L heyre (om. P)

heised v. [?from OE hean] raised **Ch2** 4766 heised P raised L

heiþen n./adj. [ON, OE hæþen] pagan, heathen **Ch1** 14478 heiþen P heþene L

held, heldest n. [see elde]

hele n. [ON] health, good fortune **Ch1** 8898 hele; **Ch2** 4760, 6326, 7555 hele; **HS** 1402, 5227, 7012, 11042, 11475 hele

hele v. (1) [OE hælan] cure, make whole **Ch1** 4434, 4656, 8467 hele; 8704 heled; **Ch2** 104 haled; 4766 heled; **HS** 10570, 11472, 11851 hele

hele v. (2) [OE helan, helian] to cover, conceal **HS** 2150 hele *C* forhele; 12480 heleþ

helm n. [OE helm] helm of a ship or warrior; armor **Ch1** 2709, 3223 helme P helm L; 4987, 8348 helm P spere L; 3004, 3373, 4334, 9759, 11768 helmes; 4380 schelde P helm L; 5433, 8348 helm; **Ch2** 1737, 1741, 1742, 4719 helm; 2361 helme

help n. [OE] assistance; support, rescue **Ch1** 1020, 1594, 4399, 6196, 8256 help; 2442 happe P help L; **Ch2** 450, 1266, 3416, 5657, 7893 help; **HS** 840 help; 971, 1612 helpe

help v. [OE helpan] provide aid, support **Ch1** 1712, 2036, 4676 halpe; 1632 helpes; 2516, 4480, 6828, 9270, 12034 help; 5148, 6808, 8404, 12095 halp; 7098 hulpen P holpen L; **Ch2** 996, 1479, 2411, 6765, 7045 halp; 772, 2667, 3826, 5678, 7970 help; 6217 helpand; **HS** 548 helpyþ; 752 helpe; 5673, 8787, 10719 helpeþ; 5686, 6736 halpe; 1480, 4118, 10665, 11636 hylpe; 10718 holpe

helples adj. [from OE help, n.] helpless **Ch1** 10088 helples

hende adj./adv. [OE gehende] courteous, noble, gracious, kind; near, convenient **Ch1** 10532 hend; 1220, 5288, 7628, 8326, 9369 hende; 323 heende P hende L; 5959 hend P hende L; 8727, 12218 hender; **Ch2** 3798 hend; 1991, 7211 hende; **HS** 280, 2886, 5134, 7173, 10747 hende; 2976 wrote or kende *C* ferre or hende; 5028 handys *O* hend

henne, hennes adv. [see heþen] [OE heonon] hence, away from **Ch1** 15782L hennes (om. P); **Ch2** 544, 4322 hiþen P hennes L; **HS** 4499 henne; 1854 henne *CD* hens; 602 þedyr *D* hens; 7063 fro henne *O* from hythen

hent v. [OE hentan] seize, catch, grasp, take **Ch1** 988, 1835, 6593, 10670, 15124 hent; 2481, 5359, 12082, 14546 hente; **Ch2** 882, 1830, 3390, 5539, 6752 hent; **HS** 5619, 9104 hente

hepe n. [OE heap] pile of refuse, money; heap of corpses **Ch1** 5971 hepes; **HS** 6068 hepe; 2300 muk hepe

hepe v. [OE heapian] heap up, gather **HS** 11688, 12416 hepe

herber n. [OF herbier] garden; bower with flowers **Ch1** 6915 herber; **Ch2** 6779 herbere

herber, herberwe v. [from OE herberwe, ON herbergja] to entertain, lodge, shelter, protect **Ch1** 5608 herberd P herborwed L; 6431 herberw P edefie L; 7436 herber P herberwe L; 13583 herberwed P herbergwed L; **Ch2** 1989 heberd P herborwed L; 3666 herberd P herborwed L; **HS** 10297 herbere

herbergerie, herborue n. [OF herbergerie, cf. ON herbergi] lodgings; home **Ch2** 4983 herbegerie; **HS** 10113 herbergerye; 1938 osteyl GLOSS B herborue

herbes n. [OF erbe, L herba] plants, vegetation **Ch1** 13957 herbes

herde n. [see hyrde, n.] [OE heord; ON] flock; herd of animals, game **Ch1** 853 herde; **Ch2** 2293 herde; **HS** 5559 herd

here n. [OE] an army, host; crowd of people **Ch1** 4829, 5995 here; **Ch2** 31, 2708, 6718 here

here, herd v. [OE heran] to hear, listen; consent; understand **Ch1** 7347, 7983, 8634, 9202, 10986 here; 7743 heres P hereþ L; 7826 here P hereþ L; 669, 3149, 6839, 9350, 10938 herd; 169, 2639, 5180, 6872, 7086 herde; **Ch2** 5288, 6228, 7673, 7941, 8240 here; 1634, 2998, 5775, 6710, 8144 herd; 7100, 7856 herde; 6826, 8322 hard; 7155 hers; **HS** 46, 1864, 6722, 10480, 11426 here; 2763, 3174, 9067, 10642 herd; 698, 3828, 4886 herde; 499 heyr; 4259 heryþ; 4555, 10082 heren; 10467 heres

heremite, ermyte n. [OF] hermit **Ch1** 11546 heremyte; 14718 heremite; 14709 hermyte; **Ch2** 3323 heremites; **HS** 263, 1762, 8447, 12171, 12247 ermyte; 1799 ermyt

herfore adv. [OE her, adv. + for, prep.] therefore, for this reason **Ch1** 707 herfore; 6824 þerfor P herefore L; **Ch2** 3679 herfor; **HS** 6837, 11755 herfore

heresie, eresye n. [OF (h)eresie, L haeresis] heresy; opposition to Christianity **Ch1** 5673 heresie P eresyes L; **Ch2** 5962 herisie; 7826 heresie; **HS** 9678 heresye; 10022 eresye

heretike n. [OF eretique, L hæreticus] a heretic; a rascal **Ch2** 7817 heretike

heritage n. [OF] inheritance **Ch1** 908, 2655, 6053, 9015, 13639 heritage; **Ch2** 139, 3446, 4592, 7931, 8214 heritage; 1166 heritages; **HS** 2026, 5055, 9479 erytage

heritagelik adv. [from OF heritage] by right of inheritance **Ch2** 6057 heritagelik

herk v. [prob. from OE hercnian] to listen **Ch1** 8069 herk; **Ch2** 7300 herkis; **HS** 5750 herk; 5017 herkenyng *O* harkynand

herlote n. [OF herlot] rascal, scoundrel **Ch2** 7760 herlote

hermyn n./adj. [OF ermin] ermine fur **Ch1** 11068 hermyne P eremyn L; 11187 hermyn

hermitages n. [OF] hermitage **Ch1** 13431 hermitages P heremytages L; **HS** 4005, 7506 ermytage

herne n. [see erne]

hert n. [OE heorot] male of the red deer, stag **Ch1** 855, 1320, 15054 herte; 853 hertes; **Ch2** 2293, 2294 herte

herte n. [OE heorte] heart; the mind; will, intention **Ch1** 589, 2913, 6820, 9206, 15231 herte; 1640, 1893, 3759, 8650, 9171 hert; **Ch2** 407, 1410, 4786, 6101, 7089 herte; 415, 2513, 5052, 5537, 7634 hert; 7330 hertes; **HS** 111, 2104, 3497, 4152, 7576 herte; 8544, 10826 hert

hertely, hertiloker adj./adv. [cp. OE geheortlice] devout, willing; angrily, violent **Ch1** 1358 herte fulle P hertly L 12241L hertely (om. P); 15234 fellier P hertiloker L; 15237 felli P hertly L

hertles adj. [OE heortleas] cowardly; half-hearted **Ch1** 11322 hertles P herteles L

heruest n. [OE hærfest] harvest season **Ch1** 11269 heruest; **Ch2** 2882, 3687, 3701, 5406, 5579 heruest; 2349 herueste; 307 heuest P heruest L; **HS** 813 heruyst; 816 heruest

hesils n. [OE hæsel] the hazel bush **Ch1** 9075 hesils P þornes L

hest n. [see hete, bihest] [OE hæs] command, decree, law; vow, promise **Ch1** 6354 hete (error) P heste L; 13974 hestis P heste L; **Ch2** 1605 hestes; **HS** 899 hest

hete n. [OE hæte] heat; fig.: lust **Ch1** 6348, 10260, 14573 hete; **HS** 2128, 6672, 7451, 9155 hete

hete, hette v. [see hight]

heþ, hethe n. [OE hæþ, ON] heath, moor; wasteland **Ch1** 8745 hii hilles P heþ L; 15672 hege . . . heth P heg . . . heþ L; **Ch2** 4761 hethe

heþen, hiþen adv. [ON; cp. OI heðan] hence, from here **Ch1** 967, 6660 hiþen P heþen L; 12543 hiþen; 14478 heiþen P heþene L; 15565 heþen; **Ch2** 544, 4322 hiþen P hennes L; 4530 hiþen; **HS** 8583 heþen

heþenesse, haiþenes n. [OE hæþenes] pagan country **Ch1** 13848 haiþenes P heþenesse L

heþing n. [ON hæþing] mockery **Ch2** 6602 heþing

hette n. [see hote, n.]

heu, hew n. [see hu, heu, hew]

heue, hoff, houe v. [from OE hebban] to lift up; to wait; halt **Ch1** 5328, 12404 houed; 9995 houe P ryde L; **HS** 9579, 9705 heue; 1690 hoff; 9727 hefe; 1685, 9502 houe

heued n. [see hed, hede, n. (1)]

heuen n. [see hauen] [OE heofon, heofen] heaven, paradise; the sky **Ch1** 137, 284, 2286, 5649, 14409 heuen; **Ch2** 2504, 3293, 3916 heuen; **HS** 24, 1372, 4358, 5727, 11396 heuene; 7054 heuen

heuenyng ger. [ON hefning] vengeance **HS** 9770 heuenyng

heuy adj. [OE hefig] massive, weighty; slow, slothful **Ch1** 4286 heuy P gret L; 8677, 8953 heuy; 11785 heuy chere P sadness L; **Ch2** 347, 4194, 5626, 5803, 6073 heuy; 8223, 8340 heuy chere; **HS** 2268, 5130, 5177, 10121, 11977 heuy

heuyed v. [OE hefigian] to make heavy, weigh down **Ch1** 111 heuyed; **Ch2** 1590 heuyed

heuynes n. [OE hefignes] physical heaviness, weight **Ch1** 14894 heuynes P heuinesse L; **HS** 4269 heuynes

hewe n. [OE heow] color, brightness; pigment **Ch1** 150, 11102 hewe; **HS** 9157, 9229 hewe; 5884 hewe GLOSS BH colur; 8726 hew *O* thewes

hewe v. [OE heawan] cut down, cut off **Ch1** 2649, 3383, 4345, 5030, 9799 hewe; 2698L hewen (om. P); 3769 heu P hew L; 6560, 8505 to hewe; **Ch2** 311, 3943, 8060 hewe; 3985, 4312, 4545, 7172 hew; 7252 to hewe; 2227 hewis; 8068 hewes

hide v. [OE hydan] to conceal; protect, shelter **Ch1** 1123 hid; 3382 to tapise P to huyden L; 1717, 5976 hide P hyde L; 13659 hid P hyd L; 8745, 13772 hide P hyde L; **Ch2** 642, 3928 hide; 4129 hid; **HS** 2502, 3416, 4464, 8788, 9419 hyde; 33 hydde; 2077, 4077, 8343, 11916, 12457 hyd

hide n. [OE hid] skin; animal hide; a land measure **Ch1** 7398, 7401 hide; 14274 hide no haire P huyde ne her L; **Ch2** 2676 hide

hider adj./adv. [OE] hither, to this place or time; this way and that **Ch1** 2425, 4901, 5652, 5706, 6162 hider; 1928, 5910, 6621, 6788, 7250 hidere; 5520L hyder (om. P); 7216 hidere P þennes L; 7641 hidire; 12105 þider P hider L; 12688 here & þare P hyder & þyder L hider & þyder R; **Ch2** 973, 2998, 3227, 4295, 6431 hider; 3088 hidere; 6533 hidir; **HS** 1801, 7846, 12592 hedyr; 6701 hyder

hiderward adv. [OE hiderweard] to or toward this place or time **Ch1** 9836 hiderward P hydeward L; 15009 hidirward; **Ch2** 26, 6115, 6257, 6284 hiderward

◆ **hidnes** n. [from OE hydan, v.] secrecy **Ch2** 1894 hidnes

hidous adj. [AF hidous] terrible, huge, ugly **Ch1** 3744 hidous P hydous L; 13690L hydous (om.

P); **Ch2** 7973 hidous; **HS** 1419, 12603 hydus; 10223 hydous

hye, hy n. [stem of OE higian, v.] haste **Ch1** 5261L hye (om. P); **Ch2** 7504, 7512 hy; **HS** 4288 hy

hie v. [OE higian] to hurry **Ch1** 4938 hie; 4652L hyed (P differs); 5307, 6187, 6961, 10035, 12477 hied; 12369 fast hieng P gret haste L; **Ch2** 4977, 5656, 6670, 7838, 8332 hie; 275, 1059, 5571, 7566, 8152 hied; **HS** 5078 hy; 12233 hyed

hie, hye adj./adv. [OE heh, heah] high, lofty; proudly, arrogantly **Ch1** 283, 2676, 5010, 8745 hii; 10136, 12809 hi; 9074 hiie; 1405 hie P hey L; 2097 heiere P heyer L; 3110, 6180, 9911, 10165, 13008 hie; 3057 hegh; 3061, 6466, 6617, 6719, 6783 hei; 2097, 7891 heiere; 7010, 11000 hiest; 11929 hie P hy L; **Ch2** 766 hie P gret L; 271 hie P holy L; 37, 333, 3949, 4205, 5321 on hie; 5620 on hii; 4229, 5225 vp hie; 594, 1929, 4404, 6874, 8235 hie; 3412, 5669 hii; 3784 heiere P heir L; 3167 hy; 3784 heiere; 7916 hiest; **HS** 1218, 1615, 3497, 3908 hy; 358, 1004, 1898, 6733, 6776 hye; 1395 heghe; 2427 an hii; 10999 hyghe; 3102 hegh; 3300, 7309, 9003, 11099 hygh; 3056 hyy; 3934 hygher; 820 hyest; 10063 heghest

hyght, heght n. [OE heahþu, on hyþe] height, stature; altitude, depth; high situation; excellence **Ch1** 973, 5615, 8071, 12091, 14927 heght; 4533, 5022 heght P heyght L; 7080 heiht; 1302 hyght P vpright L

hight, hette, hate v. [OE hatan; cp. OI heita] to give a name, be called; command; promise, vow; threaten **Ch1** 264 hyght P hight L; 581 hett P hyghte L; 585, 8267 hight P highte L; 772, 3676, 6354, 9072, 13236 hight; 591, 1740 hette P het L; 1736 hete P hyght L; 9108, 13923 hette; 2209 hatte; 4503 hette P byhet L; 5499 hat; 5654 hiht P highte L; 5761, 6306 het; 5874 hette P hight L; 751, 2997, 5232, 8843, 9294 hate; 6368 hate P hote L; 9294 hate P hat L; 9295 hate P heyghte L; 10487 hette P hyght L; 10537 hate . . . hight P hat . . . hight L; 12810 hate P hatte L; **Ch2** 2336 het; 3654, 6668, 7549 hete; 837, 1707, 4867, 7741 hette; 6671 hote; 93, 1398, 2034, 5637, 7562 hight; 436 hate P hatte L; 2291 haten P hiȝt L; 5037, 5118 hate; 2525 hight P hiȝt L; 2607L yhote (om. P); **HS** 1464, 10546 hyght; 2095, 4008, 8170, 9040 hyghte; 222, 8035 het; 1197, 2339, 2340, 8179, 8185 hette; 8183 hat; 5949 heteþ; 10590 hyght *O* was calde; 10594 hyght *O* hyghte *SV* heet

hille n. [OE hyl] hill, mountain, elevation **Ch1** 283, 1610, 4984, 5025, 8749 hille; 1416, 3059, 8320, 10297, 11910 hilles; 3262 hille P hul L; 5022 hille P hilles L; 7841 hille P hil L; 8174 hillis; 1784 hilled (error) P hilles L; **Ch2** 7458 hille; **HS** 2269, 10743 hyl; 7136, 10739 hylles; 2300 muk hepe *D* muk hyl; 2301 muk *D* muk hil; 6546 [MS *O* interpolation, l. 92] muke hyll

hyle v. [see hele, v. (2)] [ON, ?OE *hyllan] to cover, bury, clothe; protect **Ch2** 5495 hilled hors; **HS** 4268, 9176 hyle; 11123 hyleþ; 1148 wrye *C* hylle *D* hyl; 11769 hyle *O* ill

hilte n. [OE] handle of a sword, dagger **Ch1** 9887 hilte

hynde n. [OE hind] female red deer **Ch1** 1357, 1374, 15054 hynde; 4687 hyndes

hyng v. [see hang]

hippes n. [OE hype] hips **Ch1** 10003 hippes

hyrde n. [OE herd] herdsman **HS** 4052, 4074 hyrde; 8679 hyrdes

hire v. [OE hyrian] hire a workman for wages; to rent, pay or bribe **Ch1** 3144 hired P waged L; 13626 hired P huyred L; **Ch2** 1999 hired P hured L; **HS** 920 herede; 5404 hyredest; 5954 hyre; 6362 hyred

hirte v. [see hurte]

hiþen adv. [see heþen]

hytte v. [OE hyttan, from ON hitta] strike, attack **Ch1** 15043 hatte; **HS** 5274 hytte

hodred v. [LG hudern; cp. MnE dial. houder] to huddle together **Ch2** 6603 hodred

hogge, huge adj./adv. [OF ahoge, hogge] great in size; monstrous **Ch1** 11807L hugely gret (P differs); **Ch2** 681 hogge P huge L

hold n. [OE] stronghold; kingdom, domain; possession **Ch1** 1183, 5071, 9279 holde; 3022, 3551, 3883 hold; 12419 holde P hold L; **Ch2** 2938, 2951, 4945, 6466, 6663 hold; **HS** 1896, 7017 hold; 6475, 10613, 12272 holde

hold, hald v. (1) [OE haldan] grasp; capture, seize **Ch1** 282, 1340, 3275, 4324, 5955 hald; 591, 3685, 4072 halde; 8128 haues P halde L; 1192 halden; 4378, 5808, 6314 helde; 812, 2393, 4514, 8115, 14053 held; 7471 bidis P haldes L; 7362 holdin; 7671 holdes; 1922 hold P holden L; 4997 holden; 2124, 3326, 5711, 7144, 8551 hold; 2432, 4925, 5384, 6074, 7664 holde; 2783 held P helden L; 2825 holdes P holdeþ L; 3320 hald P to holdem L; 5431 holden P halde L; 12257 heldid P helded L; 13286 helde P held L; **Ch2** 156, 1776, 3836, 6055, 8280 hold; 164, 2729, 3501, 4169, 6276 holde; 351, 2123, 3638, 4568, 8260 held; 474, 2217, 5109, 6343, 7864 hald; 380, 978, 3184 halde; 48, 1075, 2059, 2758 helde; 625 holdes P haldes L; 2743, 3912, 4613, 6252 holdes; 230, 1367, 3100, 5261, 8031 holden; 232 holdand P haldynde L; 3568 halden; 3678 haldes; 6042, 6361, 8221 holdand; **HS** 2442, 5330, 11109 hold; 795, 1678, 3140, 7398, 11269 holde; 4847 holdes; 2658 halde; 1746, 11051 helde; 5000,

8851, 9632, 11880 held; 5380 haldest; 1009, 4671 haldyst; 965 hylde; 1186, 4321, 5330, 12053 halt; 1226 halt *C* holdyth *D* holdiþ; 2658 halde *D* calle *CO* telle; 7884 halt *O* lette; 5340 haldyng; 6534 holden; 795 holde *C* halowe; 802 holde *C* halow *D* halewe

holde v. (2) [shortened form of biholden] behold **HS** 9397 holde

hole n. (1) [OE hol] hole, pit; cavern **Ch1** 473 hole; 4584 holes; **HS** 10739 holes; 10746 hole

hole, hoole n. (2) [from OE hol, adj.] the whole **Ch1** 14945 hole; 15158 on hoole P ay on hool L

hole v. (1) [from OE hol, n.] to shell nuts **Ch1** 14062 holed P holede L

hole v. (2) [OE holian] to pierce; dig a hole; undermine **Ch1** 3404 to hole P to perce L; 6735 holed P holede L; **HS** 10743 holed

hole, holle adj. (l) [OE hol, adj.] hollow **Ch1** 8058 holle P hole L

hole adj. (2) [OE hal] whole; healed **Ch1** 8020, 9515, 9522 hole P hol L; 14923, 14945, 14951, 15368 hole; **Ch2** 6761 hole

holy, haly adj. [OE halig] holy, divine, sacred; consecrated, hallowed **Ch1** 5641, 5651, 6773, 7644, 8264 holy; 8512 haly P holy wryt L; 2596 holy kirk P holy chirche L; **Ch2** 510, 2012, 3013, 4959, 5751 holy; 2010, 4425 holy goste; 2605, 3565, 4413 holy lond; 2143, 2314, 3075 holy land; 1883, 2256, 3643, 6629, 7832 holy kirke; 498 haly kirkes; **HS** 1 holygost; 8552, 11051, 11302 holy; 142 hely gaste *H* holy gost; 1160, 5535 hely gast; 1642 holy cherche

holy, holike adv. [from OE hal, adj.] wholly, all together; unanimously **Ch1** 2873, 4562, 7988, 13775 holy; 1733 holy P holyke L; 2586 holy P holyk L; 3858 holike P holyke L; 4034 holy P fully L; 12282L holy (om. P); **Ch2** 755, 1818, 4182, 6855, 7824 holy; 1062 holy P holiche L

holyleche, holyche adv. [from OE halig, adj.] devoutly; together **Ch2** 5101, 5110 holyche; 6907 holelyche; **HS** 3142 holyleche *O* halyly; 11420 holyche *O* haly

holynes n. [OE halignes] sanctity, sinlessness; religious rites **Ch2** 1607 holynes P holy lif L; **HS** 1948, 8601 holynes; 1954 holynesse

hom, hame, homward n./adv. [OE ham] house; shelter, palace; native town or land; the grave; homeward **Ch1** 2334 hom; 2152, 3670, 5235, 7722, 10479 home; 10200 hamward; 11044, 12328 homward; **Ch2** 54, 1049, 1546, 6324, 7373 home; **HS** 1129, 5716, 9199 home; 4061, 7904, 7921 hom; 9691, 11502 hame; 925, 2850 homward

homage n. [OF omage, homage] acknowledgment of feudal allegiance **Ch1** 2815, 3616, 3845, 4522, 13640 homage; 3043 homage P omage L; **Ch2** 251, 1488, 2125, 4159, 7713 homage; 1165 homages; **HS** 216 omage *D* seruage

hond n. [see hand]

honde, hunde n. [OE hund] dog, mongrel; as a term of abuse **Ch1** 8445, 8447, 8450 honde; 6561, 13107, 13182 hondes; 7594 hunde P hound L; 12930, 12931 houndes; **Ch2** 539 hunde; 4392 hund; 4696 grehound; 1871, 1881, 4593 hondes; **HS** 5104, 5109 hound; 3086, 6649 houndes; 5107, 10909 hounde

honeste n. [OF] reputation; honor; splendor **Ch2** 3717 honeste; **HS** 10138 dunhede *O* donhede *SV* honeste

honeste adj. [OF] honorable, noble, worthy **Ch1** 9152 honeste; 300 fairest & mest P most honeste; 9152 honeste; **Ch2** 7595 honest

honour n. [OF] worship; reward, distinction; domain **Ch1** 725, 1628, 3587, 4443, 7189 honoure; 1417, 3032, 5104, 9335, 10852 honour; 2352 honor; 4277 honoures; 6136 honours; 467 honoure P honur L; **Ch2** 96, 535, 2080, 4411, 7992 honoure; 1805, 3117, 4523, 5464, 7965 honour; **HS** 3873, 5392, 9429, 12608 onour; 6417 onours; 3178 wrshepe *O* honour

honour v. [OF honerer] to honor; show respect for; worship **Ch1** 5458, 7071, 7167 honoured; 8616 honoure; 8642 honourd; **Ch2** 821 honourd P honoured L; **HS** 1058 honoure; 10015 wrshepe dede *O* honouryde *SV* honourede; 854 wrshepe *D* honoure; 1301 wrshepyþ *C* honowur *D* honouriþ

honorable, honorablie adj./adv. [from OF honour, n.] worthy of respect or distinction; reverently, devoutly **Ch1** 2381 honorable P honurable L; 4439 honorablie P honurabloker L; **Ch2** 7929 honorable; **HS** 10601 onourably *O* honorabylly *SV* honorabliche

honoryte n. [unrecorded; poss. error] **HS** 1928 boneryte *C* bonoture *D* honoryte

honte v. [see hunt, v.]

hook, hokys n. [see croke, kroke, n.]

hop v. [see hoppe, v.]

hope n. [OE hopa] trust, confidence; expectation **Ch2** 3652, 4352, 4758, 4890 hope; **HS** 1709, 2696, 4364, 8458, 11057 hope

hope v. [OE hopian] expect; trust **Ch1** 1891, 8080 hopid P hoped L; 3832 hopid P hopede L; 226, 946, 4391, 7182, 9116 hope; 2036 halpe P hope L; 4888, 6209, 8410 hoped; 10440L hoped (om. P); **Ch2** 7158 hope; 1335, 6261 hopes; 5362, 4064, 6645, 7102 hoped; 7361 hopyng; 7737 hopyng (ger.); **HS** 2691, 4238, 7807 hope; 8069, 10450 hoped; 5465, 6969 hopede; 8330 hopeþ

hoppe v. [OE hoppian] to dance, leap; fig.:

hedeles hopped: beheaded **Ch1** 1076 hedeless hoppe P hedles hop L; 12988L hopped (om. P); **Ch2** 7442 hop; 4453, 5186 hedeles hopped; 4652 ouer hoppe; **HS** 9225 hoppyng; 9218 hoppyng (ger.)

hordom n. [OE horedom] fornication; prostitution **Ch2** 1403 hordom; **HS** 1602 hordam; 1844, 2033, 7638 hordom

hore n. [OE] whore; term of contempt **Ch1** 13481 hore; **HS** 2928 hore

horn n. [OE, ON] animal horn; musical instrument, a bugle; apex of a bishop's mitre; arrangement of a woman's hair **Ch1** 1155, 1161, 1320 horn; 2696L horn of brass (om. P); 10192 hornes; **Ch2** 2871 horn; 2876 hornes; **HS** 3226 hornys; 11116 horn

hors n. [OE] a horse **Ch1** 1704, 4657, 7795, 10648, 12271 hors; 10658, 10661 horses; 11538 hors P horsed L; **Ch2** 1871, 2867, 4821, 5528, 7554 hors; 1881 horses; 4335 hors flesch; 7438 hors folk; **HS** 3432, 4582, 4600, 4616 hors; 3086 horssys

horsed v. [OE horsian] to provide a horse; mounted on horseback **Ch1** 10653, 12837 horsed; **Ch2** 8175 horsid

hoses, hosen n. [OE hosa, hose] leg coverings, hose **Ch1** 7748 bosums P hoses L; **HS** 3831, 10335 hosen

hospitale n. [OF ospital] hospital, especially of the order of knights hospitallers **Ch2** 3319 hospitale; 4711 hospitalle

hospitelers n. [from OF ospital] order of knights hospitallers **Ch2** 4414 hospitelers

host n. [see oste]

hostage n. [see ostage]

hote, hette n. [see hest] [OE hat] vow, promise; command **Ch1** 4923, 14418 hotes P byhestes L; 5762 hote P hot L; 6354 hete P heste L; **Ch2** 4867, 6886 hette; 1694, 6882, 6884, 6897 hote; **HS** 2801 hote GLOSS BH a vow

hote adj. [see hatte, v.] [OE hat] hot; excited, fresh **Ch1** 2237 hate bathe P hote bathe L; 2241, 4994, 7137, 8513, 12076 hote P hot L; 8877 hote; **Ch2** 1189, 1550, 3052, 5628, 8055 hote; **HS** 2271, 2493, 4494, 6580, 11040 hote

hotte n. [OF hute] shed or hut **Ch2** 6603 hottes; 6821 hotte

houre n. [see oure, n.]

hous, housyng n. [OE hus] dwelling **Ch1** 141, 3863, 8231 hous; 1847, 5425, 8230, 8610, 15793 houses; 10863 housyng; **Ch2** 1402, 4982, 5864, 7064, 8018 hous; 1895, 2002 house; 1524, 3322, 7169 houses; **HS** 1124, 4020, 8657 hous; 1424 hows; 1451, 6351 house; 1407 howsys *C* howsyng *D* housis

housel n. [OE husel] holy communion, the Eucharist **HS** 842 housul; 7306, 10258, 10261 housel

housel v. [OE huslian] administering communion; partake of the Eucharist **HS** 10064, 10180 housel; 10079 housele

houue n. [OE hufe (i.e.,: houve)] hood, cap **Ch2** 6716 houue

hu, heu, hew n. [OF hu, heu, hou] clamor, shouting **Ch1** 5996 hu P hew L; 11702 hu P heu L

huche, hucche n./v. [see rolle] [OF; cp. whicche] money chest, coffer; box for relics **HS** 6230 hucche *F* whicche; 9807 rolle *O* huche; 9809 rollyng *O* hochynge (?ger.); 9811 rollyng *O* huchynge

huge adj. [see hogge]

hulk v. [from OE hulc, n., a hiding place] hide; lie concealed **Ch1** 8174 hulk P hulke L (n.); 8745 hulk P in hulk L (n.); 15170 hulked

hund n. [see honde]

hundred, hundreth n./adj./numeral [OE and ON] one hundred; a hundredth part **Ch1** 1499, 4550, 6033, 6760, 7066 hundreth; 4977, 5282, 5693, 7701 hundreth P hundred L; 7778 hundirth; 8313 þousand P hundred L; 12885 hundred; 10063, 10524 hundrethes; **Ch2** 386, 2493, 4744, 5334, 7937 hundreth; 115, 2655, 4221, 5592, 8330 hundred; 3329 þousand P hondred L; 3347 hunderth P hondred L; **HS** 76 hundryd; 10481 hundred; 2279, 9927 hundyrsyþe; 10477 hunder syþe

hune n. [?Celt.; cp. OIr on, oin] hesitation, tarrying **Ch2** 5573 hune

hunger n. [OE hungor] starvation; a period of famine **Ch1** 1060, 3640, 5061, 7622 hunger; 5065, 5075, 5079, 10607 hungere; **Ch2** 1881, 2272, 2977 hunger; 4326, 4327 hungre

hunger v. [OE hyngrian] be hungry, crave **Ch2** 2276 hungred; **HS** 6680 hungrede

hunt, honte v. [OE huntian] to hunt game **Ch1** 15052 honte; **Ch2** 5149 hunted

hurd n. [OE hord] hoard; store of treasure; place of safekeeping **HS** 1556, 4912, 6070, 6168, 11770 hurd

huresons n. [see hore] [from OE hore] bastard son; term of contempt **Ch1** 3448 huresons P hore sons L

hurte, hirte n. [OF hurt; cp. hurte, v.] wound, injury **Ch1** 4877, 12087 hirte; 12087 hirte P hirt L

hurte, hirte, hurteld v. [OF hurter] to injure; collide, crash **Ch1** 1818 hurteld P hurtlede L; 4581, 13037 hurte; 11297 hirte P hirt L; 13548 hirte; 2918 hurtyng (ger.) P hortlyng L; **Ch2** 4116 hirte; **HS** 3746 hurt

husbond, hosband n. [OE husbonda, from ON] male spouse; farmer, steward, tenant **Ch1** 2275 husbondes P hosebandes L; 6509 husband men P husbonde men L; 8587 hosbondes; 10114 hosband; **Ch2** 4158 hosbond; **HS**

1149, 1706 husband; 1732, 6314, 10562 husbund; 1972, 1974 husbundys; 6352, 7770 husbonde; 2445 husbandes; 4868 husbunde man; 10423 housbund; 10534, 11754 husbond

I[Y][J]

ydel adj. [OE idel] vain, sinful **HS** 11136, 12554 ydel

idelnes n. [OE idelnes] idleness **Ch1** 11321, 11329 idelnes; **HS** 608, 658, 5047 ydylnes; 756 ydylnesse; 3094 ydelnesse; 5063, 10120, 10121 ydelnes

ydyt v. [OE gedihtan] adorn; arrange **HS** 3188 ydyt GLOSS BH stopped *O* es dytte

ie, eye n. [see eye]

iys n. [OE is] frozen water **Ch2** 2988 iys

ilde, yle n. [OF ile, isle; AF ildle] island, isle **Ch1** 271, 1315, 4189, 7613, 15037 ilde; 3662 ilde P ylde L; 7619 ilde P yle L; 1979, 2004, 5474, 5813, 13814 ildes; 5842 ild; **Ch2** 1356, 1899, 3721, 5497, 5533 ilde; 5474 ile; 792, 8064 iles; 6831, 7419 ildes; **HS** 1741 yle *C* ilede; 1743 yle *C* ylde; 1746 yle *C* ile

ylyche, ylyke adv. [OE gelice] the same way, alike, equally **HS** 2644, 4336, 7464 ylyche; 12261, 12264 ylyke

ilk, ilka, ech adj./pronoun [OE ælc, ilca] each, every; the same one **Ch1** 171, 1813, 4712, 6058, 9374 ilk; 156, 1036, 1554, 8770 ilka; 1056 ilk P ylkan L; 6845 ilk P ylka L; 3317 alle P ilke L; **Ch2** 82, 1490, 4207, 5542, 7997 ilk; 874, 1633, 2875, 5522, 6806 ilka; 2840 ech; 1024, 1999 ilk P eche L; **HS** 5503, 6359, 6361 eche; 2518 ache; 4541 ylka; 182 þeke *C* ych; 4948 yche *O* swylk; 464 euery *C* ilke; 1430 euery *C* ich; 12337 same *O* ylke; 178, 2352, 5781, 7719 yche

ilkadele, ilk dele n. [from OE ilca] every part, everything **Ch1** 926, 2845, 6352, 7120, 8984 ilkadele; 8209 ilkdele; **Ch2** 878, 2104, 4728, 5326, 7746 ilkadele; 628, 1824, 4761, 5307, 6513 ilk dele; **HS** 192 euerydel *C* il del; 554 euerydeyl *C* ildel

ilkon, echon pronoun [OE] each one, all; every, everyone **Ch1** 477, 1095, 5130, 6462, 9377 ilkon; 929 ilkone P ylkone L; 1812 ilkon; 1009, 3590, 4429, 6533, 9337 ilkone; 1299, 1599, 1604 ilkan; 1565, 1724, 4569, 6220, 7285 euerilkon; 8220, 8235 euerilkone; **Ch2** 1155 ilkone P echeone L; 1542 ilkon P eche L; 23, 1369, 3894, 5168, 8269 ilkone; 2771 ilkan; 287, 1875, 3402, 5503, 8320 ilkon; 919, 2577, 4313, 5142, 7936 euerilkon; 53, 3693, 3979, 5512, 7163 euerilkone; **HS** 1174 echon; 147, 1802, 10720 echone; 559 echoun; 4182 echon *O* ilkone; 9549 echoun *O* ylkane

ille, yl adj./adv./n. [see euyl] [ON] abstract evil; evil conduct, sin **Ch1** 838 ille P wykke L; 966, 1082 ille P ylle L; 1179, 2756, 3918, 7155, 14363 ille; 2758, 4421, 4590, 4771, 6351 ille P yuel L; 3929L yl (om. P); 13846L ille (om. P); **Ch2** 317, 2807, 4483, 5373, 7982 ille; 162 ille P iuel L; 922L ille (om. P); **HS** 247, 2275, 2896, 8637, 11813 yll; 1059, 3040, 8481, 10204, 12614 yl; 8092, 10172 ylle; 6560 euel *O* yll

ymage n. [AF ymage (MP)] image, likeness **Ch1** 1333, 1353, 1399 ymage; **HS** 3224, 8741, 11554 ymage

yn, innes n. [OE in(n)] lodging, inn **Ch1** 9155, 10959 innes; **HS** 1940 yn

incarnacion n. [OF, ML incarnacioun] the incarnation of Christ **Ch1** 1862 incarnacioun; 13736, 13841 incarnacoun; 14405 incarnacion

ynceste n. [L incestus] incest **HS** 7370 ynceste

inche, vnche n. [OE ynce] inch **Ch1** 9888 inche P vnche L

incubi n. [L incubus] demon who deludes women **Ch1** 7974 incubi demones

inerly, interly adv. [from OE innera, adj.] inwardly **Ch1** 3167 inerly P inderly L; 10645 interly P inderly L

inke n. [OF enque] ink for writing **Ch1** 11613 inke & penne

inouh, inowe, ynogh, ynow n. [OE genoh, genog] enough; many people, a great deal **Ch1** 87, 896, 4342, 9507, 12713 inowe; 3093, 4471, 7386, 9260, 14021 inouh; 1321, 9605 inowe P ynowe L; 680 inogh; **Ch2** 137, 1319, 1958, 4512, 5482 inouh; 1408, 4211, 4970, 5483, 8175 inowe; 4484, 5083 inow; **HS** 6440, 7300 ynogh; 7069 ynow; 8719 ynowe

inouh, inowe, ynogh, ynow adj./adv. [OE] enough, sufficient; very much; plenty **Ch1** 867, 3403, 6812, 7065, 12013 inouh; 1037 inowe; 3115 inouh P inough L; 755, 2297, 2889, 9179, 11592 inouh P ynow L; 11605 inouh P ynowe L; 584 inogh; **Ch2** 182, 1729, 3459, 5166, 8118 inouh; 3499 inouh P ynow L; 911, 5439, 6641, 7200, 8093 inowe; 1109, 6086 inow; **HS** 1460, 1750, 6682, 8520, 9308 ynogh; 2306, 2862, 7218, 10814 ynow

ynspyracyun n. [OF inspiracion] divine guidance or communication **HS** 7747, 8541 ynspyracyun

instede prep./adv. [from OE in + stede, n.] in place of **Ch2** 304, 6278, 8062 in stede

inwitte n. [OE] conscience; mind, reason, understanding **Ch1** 15806L in wyt (om. P); **Ch2** 3830, 3842, 6836 inwitte; **HS** 7667, 7974, 11456 ynwyt; 627, 645 ynwyt *C* consciens *D* inwit; 632 ynwyt *C* wytte *D* inwit; 8806 my wyt *O* myne inwytte

ypocrysye n. [AF ypocrisie (MP)] hypocrisy, trickery **HS** 3197, 11486 ypocrysye

ypocryt n. [AF ypocrite (MP)] pretender to goodness or piety **HS** 3140, 3154, 3194 hypocryt; 3145, 12504 ypocryte; 3150 ypocrytes

ire n. [OF ire, L ira] anger, rage, violence **Ch1** 1835, 3712, 4221, 4526, 14725 ire; 5615 ire P sorewe L; 3925 niht and hete P ire & hate L; 10703 ire P yre L; **Ch2** 2891, 2948, 7059, 7074, 7090 ire; **HS** 1266, 7708, 8049, 10103, 12072 yre; 3705 ire

iren, eryn n./adj. [OE iren] made of iron; fig.: strong, like iron; iron chain, weapon **Ch1** 4569, 4593 iren schod; 9516 irne; 9880, 9904, 10666 iren; **Ch2** 4316, 4912, 7745 iren; **HS** 1448 eryn; 9344 eren

irke, yrken v. [?Celtic] to be weary; bored **Ch1** 10912 irke P yrke L; **Ch2** 1791 irke; **HS** 1117 wexyn sone sad *C* yrken *D* orkyn

irke, yrk adj. [prob. Celtic; cp. OI arcoat] tired, reluctant **Ch2** 2257, 7236 irke; **HS** 4344 yrk; 4543 yrk GLOSS BH slogh

irus, irouslik adj./adv. [OF irus, iros] wrathful, irate; irascible **Ch1** 4005 irous; 3711 irouslik P egreliche L; **Ch2** 2819 irus; 4112 broþely & brim P iresly & grim L; **HS** 7153 irus GLOSS H wreþful; 10238 yrous *SV* tyrauns

issue, issheu n. [OF] exit; outcome; progeny **Ch1** 5027 passe (v.) P issue L; 9285 issheu P issue L; **Ch2** 368 issheu; 6592 issu

issue, issheu v. [OF issu, ppl. of issir] come or go out **Ch1** 3438 issued P isseden L; **Ch2** 5832, 6676 issue; 8153 issheu

ywar adj. [see ware, adj., vnwar] cautious, wary **HS** 4201 ywar

iwis, ywys adj./adv./n. [OE gewis] certainty; indeed, surely **Ch1** 15356 iwis P ywys L; **Ch2** 2989 bare vis P ywis L; **HS** 3030, 6678, 9541, 10379, 11743 ywys

I as J

Iacobyn n. [OF] a Dominican friar **Ch2** 6221 Iacobyn

iambe leue n. [cp. OF iambes levees] head over heels **Ch1** 13216 iambe leue P turnde þem ouer L

iangle n. [OF] idle speech, gossip **Ch1** 15575 iangle

iangle v. [AF iangler (MP)] to chatter, talk idly, gossip **Ch1** 4066 iangle; **Ch2** 1162 iangle; **HS** 4547, 8904, 9261 iangle; 1005 ianglyst; 5593 iangland

ianglere n. [AF ianglere (MP)] idle talker, boaster **HS** 9312 ianglers; 9316 ianglere

ianglyng ger. [from AF iangler] chattering; quarreling **Ch1** 11362 carpyng P ianglyng L; **HS** 4540, 9258 ianglyng

iaumbers n. [AF iamber] leg armor **Ch1** 9880 chambres P iaumbers L

iawnes n. [see golsoght] [AF iauniz, OF jaunice] jaundice **HS** 3977 iawnes *O* golsoght; 3979 iawnys *O* iavnys

ientille adj. [see gent, gentille]

ientylnesse n. [from ientil, adj.; see forgetilschip] **HS** 2558 rechelesshepe *C* ȝetylede *D* ientylnesse *F* rechelessnesse *O* for gytelscheppe

Iew, Iuerie n. [OF juif, jui; AF iuerie] a Jew; the Jewish community **Ch2** 5487 iuery; 5494, 5956 iuerie; **HS** 2597, 7728 Iew; 720 Iewys; 9531 Iewe; 4194, 9525, 9528 Iewes

iewele, iuelle n. [OF juel] jewel, treasure; a present, bribe **Ch1** 8892 iuels; 612, 658, 666, 679 iuels P iueles L; 15652 iuwelle P iuwel L; **Ch2** 3762 iowelle; 3803 iuelle; **HS** 6204 iew-eles; 9424 iuelles

iewise n. [see iuwise]

iogelour n. [AF jogelour] juggler, minstrel, harper **Ch1** 4001 iugelours P iogelours L; 9702 ioguloure P iogelour L; 11139 iogelours; **HS** 1041 iogelour *C* iugalurye *D* iogelour; 3687 iogolours

ioye n. [AF ioie (MP)] bliss, happiness **Ch1** 325, 1277, 1606, 1899, 8641 ioye; 4661, 5268, 6347, 8098 ioy; **Ch2** 50, 1437, 4354, 5603, 7264 ioy; 6493, 8118, 8352 ioye; **HS** 376, 1404, 2739, 7159, 12119 ioye; 2860 ioye *C* hym mery

ioye v. [OF ioir] rejoice, enjoy **Ch1** 3894 ioyed P reioysed L; **Ch2** 1717 ioy P ioye L; **HS** 1991 ioyed; 12116 ioyeþ

ioyfulle, ioyous adj. [from AF ioie, n.] glad, happy **Ch1** 7146 ioyfulle P glad L; 7321 ioiefulle P ioly L; 5686, 6332, 8463 ioyfulle P ioyful L; 11801 ioyfulle P ioiful L; 5621L ioyous (P differs); **HS** 2872 glad *O* ioyfull

ioynt n. [OF] part, sequel **HS** 5092 ioynt; 11492 a ioynte *O* enyonte (v.)

ioynt v. [OF joindre, ppl. joint] combine, fasten; enjoin **Ch1** 5739 ioynt P yioynt L; **Ch2** 7424 ioynt; **HS** 10868 ioyneþ *O* ioynes; 11788 ioyneþ *O* enyones

ioly, ioliff adj. [OF joli, jolif] vigorous, youthful, lusty; happy **Ch1** 7321 ioiefulle P ioly L; **Ch2** 8124 iolif; **HS** 1727 ioly; 1127 iolyff

iolifte, iolyte n. [OF jolifte] gaiety, illicit behavior **Ch2** 1192 iolifte; **HS** 3402 iolyte

iorne, iurne n. (1) [see soiorne] [OF jornee] a day; a day's work; combat, enterprise; journey **Ch1** 7849, 15222 iorneis P iornes L; 13320 fight P iourne L; **Ch2** 325, 3957, 4479, 7875, 8127 iorne; 3798 iourneȝ; 4488 iornes; 2968 turne P iourne L; **HS** 1952 iurne; 7730 iurnes

◆ **iorne** n. (2) [from AF journer, v.] postponement **Ch2** 7875 iorne

iorned, aiorned v. [AF ajourner] to postpone **Ch2** 7874 iorned; 7550 aiorned

iorneid v. [OF jornoiier] to travel **Ch1** 3355 ioneyd P iourneyed L; 13513 iorneid P ior-neyed L

iowelle, iuelle n. [see iewele, n.]

iuelle adj. [see euele, adj.]

iugelour n. [see iogelour]
iugement n. [OF] a sentence; decision; a trial **Ch1** 4724, 4887, 8491 iugement; **Ch2** 1534, 3161, 5307, 6525, 7597 iugement; **HS** 1497, 3757, 5324, 10254, 12094 iuggement
iugge n. [OF juge] a judge **HS** 5639 iugge
iugged v. [AF juger] bring to judgment **HS** 5408 iugged
iuggyng ger. [from verb] a legal decision **HS** 5403 iuggyng
iuste v. [OF juster, jouster] to joust **Ch1** 4341 iusted P iustede L; 5893, 11121 iusted; 8427, 12498 iuste; **HS** 4636 iuste
iustely adv. [from OF just, adj.] exactly **Ch2** 5795 iustely
iustyng ger. [from OF juster] tilt in a tournament **HS** 4625 iustyng
iustours n. [OF jouster] tilter in a tournament **Ch1** 7547L iustours (P differs)
iustise n. [OF] fairness; punishment, vengeance; a judge, arbiter **Ch1** 6107 iustis P iustise L; 1252, 3903, 6161, 15638 iustise; **Ch2** 1424, 1700, 4184, 6521, 8286 iustise; 3594 iustises; **HS** 3404, 4832, 6569, 7976 iustyse; 6795 iustyses; 1311 iustyse *C* dom
iustise v. [OF justicier] try, punish; rule, govern **Ch1** 2224, 4097, 6357, 9138 iustise; 10245 iustised; **Ch2** 2444, 4177, 4795, 7990 iustise
◆ **iustiseles** adj. [from OF justise, n.] lawless **Ch2** 5900 iustiseles
iustiser n. [OF justicier] a ruler; judge **Ch1** 2215 iustiser P iustyser L; 12875 iustisere P iustiser L
iuwelle n. [see iewele]
iuwise, iewise n. [OF juise] sentence, punishment; damnation **Ch2** 6522 iuwise; 8142 iewise; **HS** 6778 iuwys; 7796 iuwyse

K

kables n. [see cables, n.]
kacche v. [see cache, v.]
kage n. [see cage, n.]
kaynard n. [prob. AF] a sluggard **HS** 8303 kaynard
kaiser n. [OE casere] lord, ruler; emperour **Ch1** 11639 kaiser P cayser L; 13075 kaisere
kandelstyke n. [see candell, n.] [OE candel sticca] candle holder **HS** 9381, 9383, 9385 kandelstyke
kandilmesse n. [OE candelmæsse] feast of the purification of Virgin Mary **Ch2** 6995 kandilmesse
kant, cante adj. [cp. MDu kant] bold; fierce, cruel **Ch1** 1882 cante P kant L; **Ch2** 1199 kant P wiȝtty L
kare v. [see care, n.] [OE carian] to be troubled **HS** 11541 kare
kareyne n. [AF careine] corpse; carcass **HS** 8766, 8778 kareyne
karf v. [see carfe, v.]
karke n. [AF; cp. CF charge] trouble, need **Ch2** 3319 karke
karke v. [see charge, v.] [AF; cp. CF chargier] be burdened with; impose on **Ch2** 2668 karke P charge L
karole, carole n. [OF carole] circle of stones; dance in a circle; song **Ch1** 1771 carols P caroles L; 8753, 8785 karole P carole L; 13780 karolle P carole L; **HS** 4685, 8991, 9004 karolles; 985, 3460, 9020, 9057 karol
karole v. [AF caroler, karoler (MP)] to perform a dance, sing in a carole **Ch1** 1773 carolde P karoled L; **HS** 9046 karolle; 9075 karolleþ; 9091 karolde; 9255 karolle; 9109, 9142 karolland; 9047 karollynge (ger.)
karte n. [see carte, n.]
kas n. [see cas, n.]
kast v. [see keste, cast, v.]
kastel n. [see castel, n.]
kataile, katel n. [see catel, n.]
kauce, caucieȝ n. [AF caucie] path; highway or causeway **Ch1** 3060 cauceiȝ P causes L; 3071 kauceȝ P causes L; **Ch2** 4538 kauce
kauersyns n. [AF cauersins (MP)] money-lenders, usurers **HS** 5555 kauersyns *O* cauersynes; 2453 tauuarsyns (error) *C* theuys *D* gannokerys
kechyn n. [see kichyne]
keye n. [OE cæg] a key **HS** 6196 keye
kemse n. [OE cemes, from L camisia] undergarment; ?shirt; fig.: a ship's sail **Ch1** 4559 schippes kemse P (L differs); **Ch2** 2989 kemse
ken, kenne v. [OE cennan; ON kenna] to know, recognize, make known; tell, teach, announce **Ch1** 78, 2104, 4068, 7477 ken; 3158, 4189 kenne; 8189 kennis; 8655 kennys; 6818 couer P kenne L; 7429 ken P kenne L; 659 kende; 1117 knew P kende L; **Ch2** 528, 990, 4564, 6823, 8096 ken; 6538 kend; 2796 kenne; 5892, 6958, 7051 kende; 5790 kennes; 2742 kennes P comes L; **HS** 2976 kende; 2967 kenne GLOSS B knowe; 7142 kenne GLOSS BH teche
kene adj. [see kant] [OE cene] bold, fearless; eager **Ch1** 5733, 8481, 15498 kene; **Ch2** 1199, 1634, 6687 kene
kennyng ger. [from OE cennan] teaching, a warning **Ch1** 2452 kennyng
kepe n. [from OE cepan, v.] attention, concern **Ch1** 2452 kepe; 4690 kepe P kep L; **Ch2** 1617 kepe; **HS** 431, 4264, 5523, 9316, 10891 kepe
kepe v. [OE cepan] care about, desire; remain, stay; maintain **Ch1** 465, 2061, 4088, 6163, 9201 kepe; 2965 keped; 3695, 4093, 6414, 7646, 11338 kept; 289, 471, 1115, 9234 kepte; 6421 had P kepte L; 7293 kepis P kepes L;

9216 kepes; **Ch2** 948, 3169, 5316, 6160, 7990 kepe; 192, 1770, 4482, 5356, 7291 kept; 3982 kepand; 4774, 6789 kepes; 7732 keped; **HS** 3680 kepyþ; 10903 kepeþ; 4052, 7194, 11824 kepe; 2571 kepte; 978 kepe *D* holdyn; 1611 gyue GLOSS BH kepe

keper n. [from OE cepan, v.] ruler, guardian **Ch1** 6813 keper P kepere L; 8494 kepere; 15106 kepers P keperes L; **HS** 1566, 1577 wardeyns *C* keperis

kepyng ger. [from OE cepan, v.] defense, government; guard; provision **Ch1** 6393, 6901, 7159, 9331, 14257 kepyng; **Ch2** 714, 2494, 4147, 4775, 5905 kepyng; 4886 kepynges

kerchyues n. [see kouerchef, n.]

kerres n. [ON] marsh, bog **Ch1** 13956 kerres

keste, cast v. [ON; cp. OI kasta] throw, shoot, scatter; utter a cry or threat; calculate; build, decorate **Ch1** 1032, 1782 6003, 9071, 11125 kast; 518, 1036, 4169, 7587, 9258 kest; 492, 1701, 3659, 6692, 9171 cast; 1649 kest P cast L; 10366 kast P cast L; 6719, 7857 caste; 11123, 12814 keste; 7859 kestyng; 2552 kestis; 10138 kestes; **Ch2** 266, 1086, 4712, 7971, 8322 kast; 2927, 4213, 5158, 6003, 7986 cast; 3307 keste; 3364 kaste; 2576 costen P cast L; 1296, 6643, 7168, 7826, 7975 kest; 5738 kestis; 6037 caste; 5134, 5491 casten; 4097 kastand; 4542 kasted P casten L; **HS** 826, 2267 cast; 2104, 8869 caste; 1233, 11362 kest; 10142, 11701 keste; 6545, 11726, 11809 kaste; 6214 kyste; 1413 cast *D* dyȝyt

keuiles n. [OF keville, ML kevilla] fastening for ship's rigging **Ch1** 11770 keuiles P kyuiles L

kichyne, kechyn n. [OE cycene] a kitchen **Ch1** 11071 kichyne; **HS** 5913 kechyn

kid v. [see con, couth]

kie, kii, ky, keyn n. [OE cu, cy] cows, cattle **Ch1** 4686 kii P ky L; **Ch2** 596, 598 kie P kyn L; **HS** 504, 546 ky; 516 keyn

kyme v. [cp. OE cuman, v. and cyme, n.] arrival, coming **Ch2** 5842 kyme

kyn n. [OE cyn] race, tribe, clan; family **Ch1** 1362, 4185, 13637 kyn; 1388, 6825 kyn P kynde L; 7521 kin P kynde L; 14343, 14693 kynne P kyn L; **Ch2** 2209, 4683, 7926 kyn; 1648 folk P kyn L; **HS** 1684, 7371, 10666 kyn

kynd, kynde n. [OE cynd] characteristics; race, family, by lineage **Ch1** 14, 2669, 4249, 7165, 15553 kynde; 427, 4073, 5614, 6110, 7052 kyndes; 1160, 3749, 4026, 6677, 8520 kynd; 7360 kind; **Ch2** 100, 126, 1190, 3149, 4519 kynd; 150, 2238, 4136, 5151, 8210 kynde; **HS** 433, 2884, 4152, 6770, 7373 kynde; 8634 kende; 3012 kynde GLOSS BH fadyr or modyr

kynde, kyndly adj./adv. [OE gecynde, gecyndelice] kind, courteous; innate, natural **Ch1** 10418L kynde (om. P); **Ch2** 2390 kynde; 3472 kyndelie; **HS** 1172, 5314, 5692, 8659, 10762 kynde; 5098, 5104 kyndere; 4841, 11957 kyndly

kindled v. [ON; cp. OI kindelen] set afire **Ch1** 14070 kindled

kyndnes n. [from OE gecynde, adj.] good will **Ch1** 2476 kyndnes

kynes n. [see chyne, n.]

kyng n. [OE cyning] monarch; ruler **Ch1** 7321, 8195, 15591 king; 447, 1512, 4055, 6204, 9019 kyng; 4311, 9466 kingis; 6484, 10913 kyngis; 195, 2657, 4314, 6642, 8710 kynges; **Ch2** 206, 1316, 4239, 6156, 8219 kyng; 147, 2124, 4141, 6925, 8030 kynges; **HS** 447, 2351, 4742, 9355 kyng; 12280 kynge; 4926, 12114 kynges

kyngdom n. [OE cyningdom] sovereignty; dominion; territory of a king **Ch1** 2509, 3936, 4021, 5965, 6908 kyngdam; **Ch2** 88, 144, 1206, 1224 kyngdom; 6777 kyngdome; 3456 kyngdams; 6830 kyngdames; **HS** 2823, 9394, 9432 kyngdom

kynred n. [OE cynrede] family, lineage **Ch2** 167, 3203 kynred; 6687 kynrede

kyngriche n. [OE cyning-rice] kingdom **Ch1** 14141 kyngriche

kip v. [see skip, v.] [ON; cp. OI kippa, MDu kippen] seize, grasp **Ch1** 638 kippe P kyp L; **Ch2** 2105, 3648 kip; 4528 kip (?error) P skippe L

kirk n. [see cherche] [ON kirkja] church **Ch1** 2596 kirk P chirche L; 5651, 8264, 9156, 14488 kirk; 5675, 7637, 8596, 8602 kirkes; 7916, 9029 kirke; **Ch2** 155, 1084, 3380, 5751, 8243 kirke; 2005, 3156, 7809 kirk; 2997, 5665 kyrke; 1607, 3013 kirke P churche L; 477, 2259, 3034, 5213, 8294 kirkes; 7820 kirkis; 1300, 5144 kirkeȝerd; **HS** 2163, 4544 kyrk; 927, 970, 1038 cherche *C* kyrke

kirnel, karnele, carnel n. (1) [OF crenel] battlement, embrasure **Ch1** 1033 kirnels P karneles L; 5953 kirnels P karnels L; 6691, 14022 kirnels P carneles L; 14030 kirnelles P carneled (v.) L; **Ch2** 7972 kirnels

kirnels n. (2) [OE cyrnel] nuts **Ch1** 14062 kirnels P kerneles L

kirneld, carneled v. [from OF crenele, ppl.] to fortify with battlements **Ch1** 9470 kirneld P corneled L; 14030 kirnelles (n.) P carneled L

kirtelle, kyrtyl n. [OE cyrtel] tunic, gown; cloak **Ch2** 2989 kirtelle; **HS** 5706, 5729, 5870 kyrtyl

kisse, kys v. [OE cyssan] to kiss, embrace **Ch1** 3227, 5218 kisse; 1370, 14591 kiste; 6701 kissed; 7480, 7488, 7940, 9375 kist; 7474, 7476 kissand; **Ch2** 2117 kisse; 2118 kiste; **HS** 7680, 8118 kys; 7694, 7828, 8115 kysse; 3871, 2878 kesse; 7686 kessest; 2718 kest; 3860, 3874 keste; 2954 kystyst

kyssyng ger. [from OE cyssan] kissing **HS** 7683, 8106, 8121 kyssyng

kith, kythe, kyþ n. [OE cyþ, cyþþu] native land, country; kinsmen **Ch1** 6825 kyth P kyþ L; 8329 kith P kuythe L; **Ch2** 1669, 1979, 7943 kith; 31 kythe; 1199 kythe P power L

kithe, kiþe, kid v. (1) [OE cyþan, cydde] to make known, tell, show; appear **Ch1** 1617, 5407, 9142 kid P kyd L; 6591 kiþe P kyþe L; **Ch2** 24, 2439, 4094, 4283, 4364 kiþe; 3233 kithe; 6805 kid; **HS** 9928 kyþe; 34 kydde; 2078, 7482, 8344, 11450 kyd

kith v. (2) [from OE cyþ, n.] become acquainted **Ch2** 5770 kith

klap n. [see clap, n.]

klawe n./v. [see clawe]

klose n./v. [see close]

knaue n. [OE cnafa] boy, servant; a low-born man **Ch1** 736, 3689, 6091, 7934, 10258 knaue; **HS** 1688, 1719, 5528, 5881, 6082 knaue; 8687 knaues

kne n. [OE cneo] the knee **Ch1** 7455 kne; 7748 the P kne L; 3818, 5164, 7850 knes; 8536 knees P knes L; 12093 knees; **Ch2** 1327 kne; 5548, 7862 knes; **HS** 4880 kne; 952 knees *D* kneen; 1473, 3187, 11467 knes

knele v. [OE cneowlian] kneel **Ch1** 3177 knelid P kneled L; 6859, 14590 kneled; **Ch2** 4005 kneland P knelant L; **HS** 3869 kneled; 3878 knelede

knelynges ger. [from OE cneowlian, v.] act of worship or respect **Ch1** 1368 knelynges

knyfe, knyue n. [OE cnif; ON knifr] dagger **Ch1** 3498 knyf; 2647, 5359, 6923 knyfe; 7756 knife; 3006 kyues (error) P knyues L; 7746 kniues P knyues L; 7794 kniue; 11183 knyues; **Ch2** 2231, 8077 knyue; 5611, 5616, 5624 knyfe; 5616 knyf; 7750 knyues; **HS** 1025 knyff; 4489 knyues; 4494 knyf

knight, kniht n. [OE cniht] noble warrior; soldier; a chess piece **Ch1** 1213, 4096, 6859, 9120, 11155 knyght; 1492, 3143, 5134, 6100, 9193 knyghtes; 4603 knyghte; 7302, 7448, 7460 knight; 4354 knyhtes; 7445, 12238 knightes; 10267 knyghtis; 8206, 8211 kniht; 7421 knihtes; **Ch2** 1753, 2488, 5369, 6649, 8109 knyght; 1736 knyghtis; 1793, 3402, 4743, 5569, 7963 knyghtes; **HS** 1374, 2222, 3308, 3366 knyght; 4610 knyghtes

knyghted v. [from OE cniht, n.] to be dubbed a knight **Ch1** 6390, 14855 knyghted

knyghthede n. [cp. OE cnihthad] knighthood; army **Ch1** 4130 knyghthede; 6390 knyghted P men of armes L

knyghtschip n. [from OE cniht, n.] prowess, courage **Ch1** 13817 knyghtschip

knytte, knyt v. [OE cnyttan] fasten by a knot; tie, bind up **Ch1** 7403, 11765 knyt P knytte L; 8110 knytte P knyt L; 9714 knytte; **Ch2** 5793 knytte; **HS** 3187 knyt; 7599 knytteþ

knyue n. [see knyfe]

knokked v. [OE cnocian] beaten **HS** 11678 knokked

knottis n. [OE cnotta; ON, cp. OI knottr] knots; fig.: a riddle, mystery **Ch1** 8110 knottis P knottes L

knowe, knawe, knegh v. [see aknowe, oknowe] [OE cnawan] know, recognize, be aware of, perceive, understand **Ch1** 142, 1517, 2951, 5230, 7052 know; 872, 4425, 7909, 9101, 10948 knowe; 169, 1453, 4412, 8897, 11101 knew; 149, 2650, 5857, 10854, 13472 knewe; 4267, 10368 knawe; 1117 knew P kende L; 9712 knewe P knew L; 14164 knowen P knowe L; 14427 iknowe P knowe L; 9321 knowen; **Ch2** 730, 3986, 5272, 6491, 7151 knew; 6552, 7251, 8313 knewe; 2047, 4842, 5354, 5787, 8170 knowe; 2539, 3405, 5305, 6249, 8035 knowen; 5020 know; 7698 knowes; 2560 witen P knowen L; **HS** 128, 2547, 9600, 11340, 11683 knowe; 3003, 8951 knewe; 70 knew; 8791 knowne; 9212 knawe; 2135 kone *C* knowe *D* knawe; 9622 kone *F* to knowe *O* to cone; 10379 knowe *O* hope *SV* trouwe; 1441 knegh *C* sey *D* saw; 10450 hoped were *SV* kneuh; 11676 knegh *F* kneuȝt *HO* knew; 12254 knoweþ *O* kennes

knowyng ger. [from OE cnawan] understanding, perception, recognition **Ch1** 166 knawyng; **Ch2** 433 knowyng; **HS** 5898 knowyng

knowlache n. [from OE cnawan] friendship; recognition **HS** 5786 knowelache; 5890 knowlache

knowleche v. [from OE cnawan] to acknowledge **HS** 10309 knowleche

knowlegyng, knoulachyng ger. [cp. OE cnawelacing] acknowledgement **Ch1** 10580 knowlegyng P knowlechyng L; **HS** 11346 knoulachyng

kof, kofe, cof adj./adv. [see cante] [OE caf] eager, bold, courageous **Ch1** 1882 kofe P cof L; **Ch2** 1634 kof

koke n. [OE coc] a cook **HS** 7251, 7255 koke

kokewold, cokewold n. [OF cucuault] a cuckold; husband of an unfaithful wife **HS** 1894, 1895 cokewold; 6288 kokewold

kole, cole n. [OE col] coal **HS** 1449 kole; 10740 coles

kolour n. [see colour, n.]

komber v. [see encomber, v.]

konand, konnynge [see conand, adj.; connynge, ger.]

kon, kons v. [see con, konne]

korage n. [see corage, n.]

kornstak n. [see corn] [OE] a stack of corn or

corn husks **Ch1** 14068 kornstak P corn stakkes L

kosyn n. [see cosin, n.]

kote, cote n. [OF] tunic, coat; an overgarment with heraldic arms **Ch1** 9882L cote of armes (om. P); **HS** 3046, 3358, 3373, 3390 kote

kotte v. [?OE geclutod] ?patched, ragged **Ch2** 6716 kotte [poss. error for klotte; cp. Langtoft MS B: clut, MS D: cloutid]

kouerchef, kerchyue n. [from OF cuevre-chief, courchief] head covering **Ch2** 2989 kouerchef P kerechiff L; **HS** 3447 kerchyues; 8887 kercheuers

kowardyse n. [see cowardyse, n.]

kowe n. [see couwee]

kracchid, cracchyng v. [cp. MDu cratsen, ME cracchen, v.] scratch, scrape with claws **Ch1** 8084 kracchid P cracchyng L

krede n. [see crede, n. (1)]

krepe, crepe v. [OE creopan; cp. OI krjupa] to crawl, proceed stealthily **Ch1** 8174 krepe & hulk P crepe L; 9742 crept P crep L

kri, krie n./v. [see cry, crie]

kristendom n. [see cristendom, n.]

kroke, kroces n. [see croke, n.]

kroken v. [see brak, crake, v.]

kronykeles, cronykles n. [OF cronicle] chronicles, histories **Ch2** 5999 cronykles; **HS** 9243 kronykeles

L

laboure n. [OF labor, L] work, toil **Ch1** 14648 labore; **Ch2** 1796 laboure

lady, leuedy n. [OE hlæfdige] lady, woman; term of respect **Ch1** 560, 695, 2284, 2899, 5478 lady; 375 lady P leuedy L; 620 lady P lauedy L; 1330 ladie P lefdy L; 3138 lemman P lady L; 500, 541, 598 ladyes; 3978 ladies; 10965 laddes (error) P ladies L; 10127, 11004 ladies P leuedys L; 11084 ladies P ladys L; **Ch2** 566, 2547, 3674, 5049, 7511 lady; 776, 3330, 4146, 5050, 7967 ladies; 1014, 3657, 4206, 5339 ladie; **HS** 143, 438, 854, 7257, 11459 lady; 775 leuedy

ladde n. [?ON] a youth; servant **Ch1** 5800, 5999 ladde; **Ch2** 8067 ladde

laght v. [see lauht, v. (2)]

laghter n. [OE; cp. WS hleahtor] merriment **HS** 9271, 9297 laghter

lay n. (1) [OF lai] song, lay **Ch1** 3996 laies P layes L; 9700 laies; **HS** 4752 layes

lay n. (2) [see lauh, lawe] [OF lei, var. of loi] law, religion, faith; the lay court **Ch1** 7259, 7388, 7508, 14424, 15292 lay; **Ch2** 2444, 3161, 4250, 4790, 6903 lay; **HS** 801, 2623, 4254, 8915, 12384 lay

lay adj./n. [OE, cp. læg] unlearned; ignorant person **Ch2** 4250, 5967 lay

lay v. [see leye, lie, v.]

layþ adj. [see loth, adj./adv.]

laying ger. [from OE lecgan, v.] taxing **Ch2** 6305 laying

lak n. [ON lak-r] defect, fault, sin; blame, need **Ch1** 152, 5861, 7187 lak; **Ch2** 614, 2305, 7474 lak; **HS** 2383, 4221, 5543, 8297, 12604 lak; 7454 lakkes

lak v. [?from ON lak-r, n.] be inadequate, deficient; to abuse, disparage **Ch1** 6934 lak P lakke L; 12314L lak (P differs); **Ch2** 4816 lak; **HS** 3538 lak; 4084 lakk

lake n. [OE lacu] a lake **Ch1** 10131 lake

lame v. [from OE lama, adj.] to maim **Ch1** 1832 lamede P lamed L

lance n. [OF] spear, javelin **Ch1** 1007 lance P spere L; 1542, 3766 launce P spere L; 4975, 10668, 12408 lance; 3003, 3483, 8361, 12398, 13029 lances; 3496 lances P speres L; 12051 launce; **Ch2** 327, 1225, 3961, 5294, 8312 lance; 7436 lances

lance v. [OF lancier] thrust, throw a dart **Ch1** 3411 lanced P launced L; **Ch2** 2293 lance

land, lond n. [OE] the country; territory **Ch1** 12, 687, 2855, 4949, 8830 land; 30, 44, 268, 307 lande; 231, 2599, 4183, 6817, 10751 landes; 6524 landis; 755, 2120, 5213, 6602, 9041 lond; 786, 2465, 6441, 8042, 13492 londe; 5113 londis; 1939, 2954, 5844, 7871, 8983 londes; **Ch2** 392, 1977, 4033, 5580, 8026 land; 358, 2047, 4419, 6833, 8333 landes; 474, 1529, 4070, 6305, 8090 lond; 6012 londe; 1212 londis; 1075, 2830, 5076, 6790, 8113 londes; **HS** 1110, 2032, 2701, 9801, 11717 land; 1254, 1284 lond

lang adv. [see long]

lange, langage n. [OF] language; words, speech **Ch1** 125 lange; 169, 1496, 4066, 8842, 12210 langage; 3553 langage P language L; **Ch2** 6048 langage; **HS** 8096 langaged (adj.); 9907 long *O* langage *SV* prolonge

langour, langore n. [OF langer, langueur] sickness, infirmity **Ch1** 3874 langour; 9434 langoure P langoryng L (ger.); 15887 langore P langour L; **Ch2** 88, 3470 langoure; 3116, 3210 languour

languysced v. [OF languiss-, stem of languir] grow weak, fail in strength **Ch1** 8849 languest P languisched L; 9419 languysced P languissed L

lap v. [see vmbilapped] [from OE læppa, n.] enclose, surround **Ch2** 6678 lap

lappe n. [OE læppa] lap **HS** 9632 lappe *O* barme

lard v. [OF larder] prepare meat for roasting **Ch1** 15062 lard it P lardid L

lardere n. [AF; cp. CF lardier] supply of meats in storage; fig.: carnage **Ch2** 596, 7572, 7851 lardere

large v. [from OF large, adj.] to enlarge, increase

Ch1 7233 largid P larged L; 8071 larged
large adj./adv. [OF] generous, liberal; at large; plentiful; many **Ch1** 3720, 3907, 5634, 6101, 8566 large; 1187, 4137 largely; 3090 largest; **Ch2** 1987L large (om. P); 3539, 3970, 7211 large; 3241, 7205, 7591, 8019 largely; 6486, 7399 largelie; 5794 lage (?error); **HS** 5338, 6543, 6824, 11945, 12464 large; 5569, 8967, 11211 largely; 6827 largelye
largesse n. [OF largece] liberality, generosity; abundance **Ch1** 874, 3092 largesse; **HS** 7025 largesse *H* largenesse; 6834, 7071 larges
lasch n. [prob. imitative; cp. lashen, v.] crash, violent fall **Ch1** 12117 lasch P lasche L
last n./adj./adv. [OE lætest, latost] latest; last, most recent; immediately before; finally **Ch1** 30, 2251, 3158, 4644, 8735 last; **Ch2** 106, 1142, 4256, 6004, 7985 last; 3365 lastes; **HS** 601, 825, 3048, 10768 last; 4064, 5684, 7341, 8472, 12455 laste
last v. [OE læstan] to endure; continue **Ch1** 8619, 9245 last; 7677, 7858 laste; 4226 lastes; 1324, 2956, 3415, 5882, 8085 lasted; 7327 lastid; 436, 710 lastand; 12951L lastynge (P differs); **Ch2** 5538, 7888, 7970 last; 366 lastes; 115 lastid; 2098 lastid P lestid L; 670, 1886, 2651, 4309, 7355 lasted; 905 lasted P dured L; 5153, 5421 lastand; **HS** 272, 1774, 2373 laste; 3058, 3722 lastyþ; 7174 lastyng
lat, late, latte v. [see let, lete, v.]
late adv. [OE] tardy; recently, lately; slowly, reluctantly **Ch1** 1743, 5510, 6684, 7193, 9115 late; **Ch2** 525, 708, 3441, 4402, 4742 late; **HS** 1064, 4507, 5915, 6858, 12184 late; 7051 latter
lattere adj. [OE lætra] following after **Ch2** 7511 lattere
lauh, lawe n. [see lay, n. (2)] [OE lagu] law, rules; custom, system of faith; territory ruled by law **Ch1** 22, 3678, 6830, 8509, 15290 lawe; 458, 1926, 3569, 5623, 15794 lawes; 7570 lauh; **Ch2** 382, 2020, 4384, 5945, 8287 lawe; 822, 1700, 3594, 4161, 7627 lawes; 227 lowe P lawe L; 5935 lowe; 7870, 8171, 8326 lauh; **HS** 549, 2842, 7625, 9352, 11192 lawe
lauht, latched, laght, lawȝtte v. (1) [OE læccan] catch, ensnare; seize, latch on to **Ch1** 1827, 3578, 4086, 6721, 8698 lauht P laught L; 7785 laght; 13641 lauht; 1976, 4086 lauht P laughte L; 10187 latche P take L; 13336 kacches P lacches L; **Ch2** 915L lawȝtte (P differs); 2295, 5849, 7248, 8113 lauht; 2947 latched P cacched L; **HS** 6041 laght; 8146 laft *O* be laste
lauht, lagh, louh v. (2) [see laghter, n.] [OE hlæhhan] laugh at, deride **Ch1** 6335, 8674, 10710 louh P low L; 9178, 9518, 11317, 12119, 14299 louh; **HS** 4191 lagh; 9281 laghhe; 11557 laghe; 3068, 11556, 11571 laghyng; 9271, 9303, 9309 logh; 9277 low
lauour n. [OF laveoir] pitcher; ?bowl **Ch1** 11188 lauour P (om. L)
lawe n. [see lauh, n.]
leale, lele adj. [OF leal] honest, loyal; virtuous; legal **Ch1** 5829 leale P leel L; 6415 lele P trewe & feyþful L; 10880 lele P lel L; **Ch2** 621, 3379, 4164, 6138, 6255 leale; 3420 lele
leaute n. [OF] loyalty, allegiance **Ch1** 12526 leaute; **Ch2** 742, 2910, 5113, 6469 leaute
lebard, libard n. [OF] leopard; as a heraldic emblem **Ch1** 11188L lepards (om. P); 13251 libard P lubard L; **Ch2** 7437 lebardes
leche n. [OE læce] physician or surgeon; a leech **Ch1** 8872 leche; 7662 leches; 13341 leche craft; 15048 leche man; **Ch2** 4758, 4759 leche; **HS** 10569, 11806 leche
lechery, lichorie n. [OF lecherie] adultery, fornication **Ch1** 11992 lecherie; 11327 licherie; 11986 lichorie; 4016L lecherie (om. P); **Ch2** 777 lichery; 1807, 5145 lichorie; 7025 licherie; 7588 licchorie; **HS** 175, 1003, 8100, 12402, 12535 lecherye; 1844 lechery
lecherous adj. [OF lecheros] lascivious **Ch1** 4012 licheros P lecherous L; **Ch2** 1605 licheros; 5058 licherous; **HS** 7990, 11665 lecherous
lechour n. [OF; AF lechur (MP)] lascivious person **Ch1** 11334 rioterie mystere P lechours mester L; **HS** 7622, 7633, 7641 lechour; 8350 lechoure; 1032, 2193, 5537, 7633, 10235 lechours
lede, led n. (1) [OE lead] metal, lead; fig.: heavy, weighed down; a lead coffin **Ch1** 8953 lede; **Ch2** 856, 4910, 5636, 6073 lede; 1214L led (om. P); **HS** 11736 led
lede n. (2) [OE leod, from læden, v.] people, country, lands **Ch1** 1429, 7241, 13720, 14252 lede; 15434L lede (om. P); **HS** 9219 lede; 10572 ledes
lede, led v. [OE læden] conduct, lead, bring; take away by force **Ch1** 931, 1429, 3352, 6814, 9085 lede; 933, 5411 led P lad L; 639, 2334 ledde; 730, 1013, 3084, 7171, 9051 led; 12760 laden P ladden L; 7805 led P ledde L; 7920 lad; 8291, 12899 ledis; 9292 ledes; **Ch2** 255, 1651, 4180, 7530, 8285 led; 1403, 1433, 6320, 6766, 7197 lad; 119, 1730, 5698, 6104 ledde; 265, 1077, 4203, 5973, 8160 lede; 3988, 3995 led P ledde L; **HS** 774, 3142, 6109, 9145, 12190 lede; 4586, 4954, 5161, 6442 ledes; 1807, 3363, 10785 ledde; 5354 ledest; 5636 led
ledere n. [OE lædere] leader, lord **Ch1** 1465 ledere; 3360 leders; **HS** 1803 ledere
lefe, leue n. [OE leof] beloved person, sweetheart, wife, friend **Ch1** 2914 wyf P lef L; 10715 lefe P lef L; **Ch2** 1019, 1873, 2738, 3203, 5381 lefe; 3285 leue
lefe, leue adj. [OE leof] beloved, dear **Ch1** 1228, 3852 leue P lef L; 5717 lefe P (L differs); 9323

leue; **Ch2** 3285 leue P leff L; 1019, 3203, 4885 lefe; **HS** 934, 1340, 2417 lef; 4382, 9514 leff; 7958 leef; 12154 lefe; 1614, 4411, 7568 leue

lefe, leuere adv. [from OE leof, adj.] would rather; sooner; willing **Ch1** 14382 leue P lef L; 953, 2555, 4497, 8387, 10618 leuere; 6490 leuer; **Ch2** 1867, 1981, 5270, 5945, 6213 lefe; 6947, 8308 leue **HS** 33, 1973, 2811, 7723, 11232 leuer; 2279 leure; 1289 wyle gladly *C* arn lefe

left v. [see leue, v. (3)]

leg n. [ON; cp. OI leggr] leg; the shank **HS** 3314 legges; 4638 leg

legate n. [OF] ecclesiastic having papal authority **Ch1** 14653 legate; **Ch2** 2998, 3212, 5445, 5557, 5636 legate; 5176 legates

lege adj. [AF lege, liege] lawful; entitled to feudal allegiance **Ch1** 7349 lege louerdes P lige L; **Ch2** 1063 lege lord

legion n. [OF legion, L legio] a Roman legion; organized band of armed men **Ch1** 3557, 5985 legion; 5706, 5765, 5910 legions; 6163L, 6592L legions (om. P); 6530 legiouns; **Ch2** 640 legioun

legysters n. [OF] lawyers, legal advisers **HS** 5410 legysters

leie adj. [OE, cp. læg; from leah, n.] fallow, uncultivated ground **Ch1** 6880 leie P leye L

leye n. [OE, cp. A leg, WS lieg] flame of a fire **HS** 6674 leye *O* flawme

leye, lie, liggen v. [OE licgan, gelegen; ON liggja] lie down, bow, fall; remain, belong to, pertain to **Ch1** 1716 ley; 1955, 3831, 5428, 8590, 15830 lie; 196, 4036 lys; 1151, 1950, 4260 lis P lys L; 14149 lis; 3791 lise; 5566, 5690 lies P lys L; 4230 lien P lyuen L; 291, 1843, 5323, 7850, 9230 lay; 945, 6488 layn; 5631, 7698 ligges; 5971, 7382, 13491 ligge; 7371 lig P lyg L; 7698 ligges P lygges L; 12361 lig P ly L; 13491 ligge P lyn L; **Ch2** 1107, 3115, 4092, 4809, 7587 lie; 183 lis P lys L; 376 lies P lyþ L; 1330 liggen; 4537, 4995, 5146, 6183, 8186 ligge; 384, 2138, 5766, 7924, 8351 lies; 404, 2619, 4226, 5633, 8335 lay; 2225 layn P lyge L; 89 ligges P lyþ L; 760 lies P was he leyd L; 1214 ligges P liþ L; 916L liggeþ (P differs); 155, 2306, 3118, 3334, 5643 lis; 160, 529, 2481, 3480, 5034 ligges; 5636 liggis; **HS** 537, 1582, 2009, 3822, 4943 lay; 10041 laye; 7377, 8513, 9716, 11932, 12204 leye; 10547, 12208 leyn; 1165, 3428, 5260, 7430 lygge; 4602, 7844 ly; 1375, 4411, 8753, 7662 lye; 1653 lyst; 2587, 11114 lyþ; 1831, 6030, 7948, 11110 lys; 4355 lyen; 8784, 9131, 12140 lyggyng; 1668 lyggyng *C* leuyng *D* lyȝing; 524 to lygge *C* ly down *D* to stente; 1626 lygge *CD* lyn

leih, lie n. [OE lyge] falsehood, a lie **Ch1** 3786 leih (v.) P lye L; **Ch2** 2055, 3616, 6517 lie; **HS** 2834 lye; 4166 lye GLOSS B lesyng

leih, ley, lay v. (1) [OE lecgan] give, put, set; situated, recorded **Ch1** 984 leye; 72, 184, 2052 layd; 2524, 3408, 4083, 8112, 9395 laid; 12089 laid P leyd L; 556 layd P yleyd L; 2239 ley P leye L; 2349 said of P leyde on L; 2705 ley P leye L; 2713 ley P leyen L; 2908 leyd; 3792, 5273 leid; 6861 laid P layde L; 3181, 6880, 8515, 9989, 14863 lay; 7640 laid P leyd L; 7754 leih; 8909 leie; 4413 laied P leyd L; 10660 laide P layd L; **Ch2** 442, 3415, 4518, 6301, 8350 laid; 6316 leyn; 430, 805, 2630, 3341, 4226 lay; 812 laid P leyde L; 2226 leued P leyd L; 5992, 7998 leie; 7132 leid; **HS** 1068 leydyst; 1154, 5598, 9451, 10676, 12414 leye; 2389, 4486 leyd; 5565, 9101, 10438 leyd; 7168, 8040, 9432, 11696 leyde; 10438 *V* leyd *S* leide (B differs)

leih, lye v. (2) [OE, WS leogan] speak falsely, deceive, slander **Ch1** 2230 lied; 3800 lie P lyes (n.) L; 6493, 13723 lie; 3786 leih P lye L (n.); 8075 leih P ley L; **Ch2** 3766, 7039 lie; 4392 lies; 6998 lied; **HS** 1346, 2662, 3512, 11487 lye; 11734 lyest; 11749 lyest *O* legh; 12400 lyeþ

leysere n. [OF leisir] spare time, opportunity, occasion **Ch1** 2725 leisere P leyser L; 12406 tome P leyser L; **Ch2** 5615 leysere; **HS** 836 leysere

leke n. [OE] a leek; "not worth a leek": of no value **Ch1** 12690 leke PLR; **Ch2** 3988, 5005 leke

leman, lemman n. [OE leof + man] lover, mistress; beloved **Ch1** 2932, 2961 leman P lemman L; 3038, 3042, 3084, 11108, 11135 lemman; 3138 lemman P lady L; 10804L lemmans (om. P); **Ch2** 5708 lemman; 8042 leman; **HS** 4613 lemman; 208 hys owne *C* lemmam *D* his wyf

leme, leuen n. [OE leoma] gleam of fire light **Ch2** 4308 as leuen P in lemes L

lemed v. [from OE leoma, n.] flame, blaze; shine as lightning **Ch1** 2943 leuende lyght P lemed lyght L; 8921 lemed P lemede L; 8922 lemyng (ger.)

lend v. (1) [see lenge, v.] [OE lendan] arrive; dwell, stay **Ch1** 3024 lende P wende L; 622, 4236, 6997, 7549, 14433 lende; 3642 lend P lende L; 8829 lend; 9510 lenged P lendend L; **Ch2** 345 lende; 6460 lend; 4633, 7925 lendes

lend, lene, lent v. (2) [OE lænan] give, allow; pay **Ch1** 4523 lende; 1305, 3653, 4409, 9109, 12398 lent; 6593 hent P lent L; **Ch2** 6878, 7390 lende; 3310, 3312, 4884, 5220, 7374 lent; 8058 lended; **HS** 3112, 9788, 10250 lent; 5366 lente; 6986 lentest; 4679 lene; 2401 to lene *C* lene *D* to relene; 4677 lenyþ *F* leueþ *O* leuyse

lende, lenede v. (3) [OE hleonian] to lean,

recline **Ch1** 6997 lende; 15133 lened P let L; **Ch2** 264, 7768 lende; **HS** 12181 lenede

lenge v. [see lend, v. (1)] [OE lengan] dwell; remain, linger **Ch1** 9510 lenged P lendend L; **Ch2** 6817 lenge

lene v. [see lend, lent, v. (2)]

lenger comp. adv. [see long, lang, adj./adv.]

length, lenkþe n. [OE lengþu, lengoþ] duration; distance, linear extent, height **Ch1** 1826, 8691 length P lengthe L; 1955, 8691 length; 9054 lengthe; 3071L lengþe (P differs); **Ch2** 365, 934, 2991, 6600 length; **HS** 3720 lenþe; 2982 lenkþe; 5049 lengþe; 7670 lenkþe *O* longhte

length v. [cp. OE lengthu, n.] prolong **Ch1** 5977 length P lengþe L

lent v. [see lend, v. (2)]

lenten adj./n. [OE lenten, lencten] spring; the season of Lent **Ch2** 7949, 8071 lenten tide; **HS** 2021 lentyn; 3819 lenten tyde

lepe, lept v. [OE hleapan] jump, spring; skip, hop **Ch1** 7380, 8903, 14895 lepe; 9082 lepe P lep L; 13344L lep (P differs); 4699 skipped P lepen L; **Ch2** 1747, 3018, 6184 lepe; 2751 lept; 2359 lept (?error) P wepte L; **HS** 12552 lepe; 425 lepys; 6036 lope; 11910 lopen

lepes n. [OE; infl. by hleapan, v.] a jump, leap **Ch1** 3849 sunder leps P sonderlypes L; **HS** 9226 sundre lepes

lepy adj. [shortened form of onlepi] single; ?a little **HS** 9151 lepy *O* lytell

leprous adj. [see meselle] [OF lepros, L leprosus] afflicted with leprosy **HS** 11568 leprous

ler adj. [see tome, voyde] [OE gelær] of vessels: empty, having no content **HS** 7854 ler vessel *O* tome wessell; 7865 ler *O* tome

lere n. [see lore] [from OE læran, v.] teaching **HS** 3522 lere

lere v. [OE læran] learn; teach **Ch1** 2, 260, 4263, 6937, 8114 lere; 276, 885 lered; 4263, 7460, 7462 lerid; 5350 lerid P lered L; 6622 lere P lereþ L; 10386L lere (om. P); **Ch2** 8064, 8067 lere; 4271 lered; **HS** 3172, 5036 lere GLOSS B teche; 597, 1201, 2377, 11905 lere; 3956 leryþ; 5672 lers; 8622 leres

lered, lerid adj. [see lewed] [from OE læran] educated, wise, literate; a cleric **Ch1** 6 lerid; 15418 lered; **Ch2** 132, 2502, 2995, 3175, 4250 lered; 873, 2037, 5967, 5984, 7334 lerid; **HS** 8822, 10812 lered

lerne v. [OE leornian] be instructed, be educated, learn **HS** 3750, 4913 lerne; 3078 lernyd; 11602 lerned; 1053 lerenyd (ppl.) *H* lerned; 11627 lerned *O* lerde; 422 techyþ *D* lernyth

lernyng ger. [OE leornung] learning; knowledge **HS** 3950 appryse GLOSS BH lernyng; 2093 techyng *C* they teche *D* lernyng

les n./adj. [OE leas] falsehood; false, deceitful **Ch2** 744 les; 3174 lees; **HS** 1525, 1656, 2198, 4931, 6384 les

lese, lees v. (1) [see lose, v.] [OE leosan; cp. forleosan] lose; spoil, destroy; renounce **Ch1** 368, 1555, 3406, 6428, 8576 les; 715 lees; 3505, 4206, 5430, 6647, 8298 lese; 8399 lees P les L; 1456 lorn P forloren L; 148, 1245, 3502, 6350, 9365 lorn; 10390L lese (om. P); 12704 les P lore L; 15258 lost; **Ch2** 581, 1627, 4368, 5416, 8205 les; 138, 1228, 3421, 4106, 5339 lese; 272 lese P be lorn L; 2026 lesis; 6162 leses; 931, 2406, 3235, 4730, 8324 lorn; 4372 lorne; **HS** 2075, 10898, 11024, 11161, 12484 lese; 12139 lese *O* lettyn; 2083, 3321 tyne GLOSS BH lese; 9456 tynes GLOSS B lest; 9628 loste; 996 lost *D* lorn; 2942, 3326 lost *O* lorne; 12016 lostest *O* lese; 12154 lesseþ *O* lettes; 9480 lest; 1511, 4792, 5901, 8304 lore; 664 lore *C* schent; 2058 lore *C* lorn *D* forlorn; 5788 ylore; 5992 lorne

lese v. (2) [OE lesan] loosen; absolve **HS** 11591 lese; 11986 leseþ

lesyng n./ger. [OE leasung] lying; a falsehood **Ch1** 10485 lesyng P (om. L); 9355 lesynges; **Ch2** 6602 lesyng; **HS** 618, 636, 2651, 3544, 3547 lesyng; 1527 lesyngge; 3542 lesyngys; 4166 lye GLOSS B lesyng; 616 fals þyng *C* þi lesyng *D* fals lesyng; 2656 maken lesynges *C* leȝen *O* makes lyes; 2661 vse as *C* lyȝe *D* lyȝen also *O* lyes as

lesse v. [from OE leas, adj.] diminish, lessen **Ch1** 2403 to lesse; 2421 lessed P lessede L

lesse, lest compar. adj./adv. [OE læssa, læst] smallest in size or extent; lowest, humblest **Ch1** 247, 3597, 5604, 6776, 8765 lesse; 1410, 5604 less; 2559, 8775 lest; 2326, 2955, 4862, 7008 leste; **Ch2** 11, 548, 1917, 4507, 7682 lesse; 5 lesse P lytel L; 1607, 3067 leste; 5746, 7037, 8042 lest; 4336 mete lesse; **HS** 1231, 2072, 2678 les; 135, 541, 3173, 5501, 9815 lesse; 2256 lasse; 3205, 4349, 7607, 11555, 11850 lest; 6777, 7357, 11614 leste; 5536 last

lesson n. [OF lecon] a subject; a sermon **Ch2** 7769 lessoun; **HS** 422 lessun; 11427 lessoun

lest n. [see lust, n.]

letanie n. [OF] litany of the saints **Ch1** 14395, 14453 letanie

lete, late, lette v. (1) [OE lætan] grant, leave, permit; give up, omit **Ch1** 2430 lete P leet L; 1839, 3180, 7096, 8961, 14914 lete; 283 lette P leet L; 7466 letis; 809, 4774, 6975, 7323, 11950 lete P let L; 5787, 14266 lette; 1002, 1194, 7051, 8569, 9352 late; 1225, 2402, 5982, 7889, 8661 lat; 5172 lat P let L; 5115 laten; 7822 laten P lat L; 13278 let; 497 latte P late L; 11451 leue P late of L; 15133 lened P let L; **Ch2** 335, 2013, 5030, 7250, 8290 lete; 1578, 3734 lat; 1294 did P lat L; 2141 lette; 3149 let; 4837 leten; 1937 lates; 1497 laten; 2837, 3855,

4385, 6459, 7827 late; **HS** 7, 2365, 8428, 10493, 12096 lete; 3103, 4411 latyþ; 520, 2388, 8559, 12404 late; 2839 haue late *CD* a lettyn; 4381, 5722, 11503 lette; 1010 lettyst; 10299 latest; 3478, 3103 lettyþ; 4826 lateþ; 7896, 10312, 12405, 11509 letteþ; 4413 lettede; 797 leue *C* leuyn *D* letyn; 1600 late *C* leue; 2094 leue *C* blynne *D* letyn; 7884 halt *O* lette; 9273 held *O* lete; 9296 y lete *O* me thoghte; 10493 lete *V* lette

lete, lette v. (2) [OE lettan] hinder, delay; neglect **Ch1** 3311 destorbled P letted L; 2356 leten; 5514, 5751, 8961 lete; 11539 lete P lette L; 10594 lette; 11297, 12467, 13533, 15781 letted; 13466 lettyng (ger.); **Ch2** 1981, 2141, 3083, 6899 lette; 5499, 7560 lete; **HS** 1198, 4381, 8858 lette; 1007 lettyst; 10996, 11146 letteþ; 3948 lettyddyst; 1438 lettyng (ger.); 1214 desturblyst *C* lett

leþer n. [OE leþer] leather; skin of a person **HS** 502 leþer; 3450 leþer GLOSS BH skyn

lettre, letter n. [OF] an alphabetic character; personal or official communication; document **Ch1** 4201 lettre P lettres L; 4279, 4799 lettre; 2906, 4215, 7694 letter; 4799 lettere; 4451, 13470, 13473 lettres; 5958 brefis P lettres L; **Ch2** 1052, 3708, 4569, 5623, 8358 letter; 954, 2352, 3909, 6499, 7470 lettres; 4602L letre (om. P); 6495, 6521 lettere; **HS** 2975, 2977, 7038, 10082, 10979 lettre; 9388 lettres

lettred adj. [from OF lettre] learned, literate **HS** 7895 lettred

leue n. (1) [see lefe, n./adj.] [OE leafa] belief, faith **Ch1** 8541 leue; 15756 beleue P leue L; **Ch2** 5964 leue

leue n. (2) [OE leaf] leave, permission, authority **Ch1** 631, 2518, 4153, 8160, 15537 leue; **Ch2** 225, 3285, 5753, 6892, 8217 leue; **HS** 1642, 1995, 2398, 8795, 11614 leue

leue v. (1) [OF alever] relieve **HS** 9535 leue ȝoure *O* refe ȝou

leue v. (2) [OE lefan, lifan] to believe, have faith **Ch1** 1338, 14425 leued; 2824 witte P lef L; 7277, 7279 leue; 4741, 9355 leue P byleue L; 5403, 5999 leued P bileued L; **Ch2** 6996, 7069 leue; 4006 leues; **HS** 149, 5218, 7289 leue; 2079 leuys; 7743 beleuede *O* lewyd

leue v. (3) [OE læfan] stop; omit, remain; leave, abandon **Ch1** 60 leues; 759, 1515, 5113, 6846, 14364 leue; 3855 leuid P leued L; 5303, 6812, 8290, 12161 leued; 67, 3869, 5548, 6121, 8774 left; 1524 leued P lefte L; 5850, 8504 lefte; **Ch2** 646, 2226, 2534, 8063 leued; 1415, 2387, 4802, 5682, 8160 leue; 662 leues P lefte L; 2134, 3114, 4175, 6762, 7567 leues; 45, 1565, 3668, 6847, 7527 left; **HS** 54, 3820, 5317, 9706, 12043 leue; 3278, 9676, 10314 leued; 3752, 9547, 10377 left; 8005, 9371, 4385, 7492, 9078 lefte; 797 leue *C* leuyn *D* letyn; 1973 leue *C* lete *D* to letyn; 2094 leue *C* blynne *D* letyn; 9257 leueþ *O* leffe

leue, lyue v. (4) [see lyue, n., olyue, adj.] [OE leofian, leofode] to live, be alive, survive, dwell **Ch1** 878 lyfe; 848 lyffed; 598 lyffande; 864 lyfed P lyuede L; 964, 4236 lif P lyue L; 3192, 4276, 5336, 8557, 15590 lyue; 1247, 4640, 6696, 9367 lyf; 2848, 8149 lyf P lyue L; 4230 lien P lyuen L; 4247, 5446 life P lyue L; 216, 2592, 5617, 6902, 8093 lyued; 6027 leued; 6899 lyfed; 13078, 13451 liffed; 13712L lyuende (P differs); **Ch2** 310 lyuen; 5206 leued; 3452 leue; 960, 2257, 4588, 5752, 8302 lyue; 2134, 4469, 4959, 7130 lyues; 6880 liffes; 184, 1261, 3790, 5057, 7909 lyued; **HS** 500, 3249 leuyd; 1839, 2046, 4032 leue; 1415 leuyng; 1706 leuand; 10527 lyuand; 5414, 5553, 11440 lyue; 8388, 9457, 10400 lyueþ; 1708 leuys *C* is leuande *D* is lyuand; 2229 leuyng *C* leuand *D* lyuende; 1966 leuyd *C* dwellyd; 1400 leue *C* dwellyn *D* luyun

leued adj. [from OE lef, n.] leafy **HS** 9054 leued wode

leues n. [OE leaf] leaves, foliage **Ch1** 15671 leues

lewed, lowed adj./n. [see lered] [OE læwede] a layman, non-clerical; uneducated; unable to read Latin **Ch1** 6, 84, 131, 14712, 15418 lewed; 7427 lewid; **Ch2** 527 lowed men; 873 lewid; 132, 2037, 2995, 5516, 7334 lewed; 6539, 8193 lewed men; **HS** 833 lewyd man; 43, 6311 lewed men; 3084, 8822, 10090 lewed; 477 lewdman; 10901 lewed *H* smert *O* lowde

liche n. [cp. oliche] [OE lic] a body, dead or alive **Ch2** 1063 lege lord P liche lond (?error) L; **HS** 11123 lyche *O* lyes ches (?error)

liche adj./adv. [see like, liche]

licherie n. [see lechery, n.]

lyd n. [OE hlid] cover of a tomb; a lid **HS** 1811, 6197 lyd

lie n. [see leih, lie, n., lesyng]

lye v. [see leih, lye, v. (2)]

lie adj. [from OE lyge, n.] false, mendacious **Ch1** 10399 lie P lye L; **HS** 10025 lye GLOSS B fals

lier, lyere n. [OE leogere, legere] liar, deceiver **Ch1** 8005 liers P lyeres L; **HS** 1343 dormers *C* lyȝeres *D* fals demerys; 3629, 4935, 12415 lyers; 4225 lyere

lyff n. [see lyue, lyf, n.]

lift v. [ON, cp. OI lypta] to raise, pick up; restore, erect **Ch1** 6361, 7128 lifte; 6857, 15393 lift; **Ch2** 186, 4082 lift; 1736 lyft; **HS** 1811, 3590, 9785 lyfte; 12440 lyftes

ligge v. [see leye, lie, liggen, v.]

light n. [OE leht, leoht] light, illumination **Ch1** 1658, 5676 light P lyght L; 2943 lyght; 8086, 8921 light; **Ch2** 378, 3968 light; 2506 light P briȝtnesse L; **HS** 2627, 5436, 5727, 11311, 11916 lyght

light adj. (1) [OE, from leht, leoht n.] light, easy, trivial; swift, active **Ch1** 74 lightest; 118, 125, 1904 light; 11048L lightere (om. P); 12368 wyght P lyght L; **Ch2** 5926, 7195, 8217, 8224 light; **HS** 2034, 4605, 5181, 11816, 12246 lyght

light adj. (2) [OE leoht] bright, clear **HS** 10208, 10230 lyght

light v. (1) [OE lihtan] emit light, shine **Ch1** 8927 lightend P lightened L; **Ch2** 2504 light

light, liht v. (2) [OE lihtan] alight, dismount, arrive **Ch1** 3481, 5398 light; 14358 lyght; 8928, 13738 lighted; 7932 liht P (L differs); **Ch2** 1685 lighted; 3299 lite; 2504, 3896, 5846, 6886 light; **HS** 3386 lyght; 580, 3844, 6034, 9961, 11319 lyghte; 3859 alyght

light, lightly adv. [OE leohtlice] brightly, clearly; easily, wantonly **Ch1** 646, 2356, 4474, 5196, 8793 lightly; 4469 lightli; 5902 leihtly P lyghtli L; **Ch2** 1839, 4193, 4924, 5469, 6812 lightly; 4721, 6585, 8216, 8224 light; 7562 lighter; **HS** 1647, 3711, 8559, 10898, 11496 lyghtly; 7350 lyghtlyere

lyghtnyng ger. [from OE lihtan, v.] flash of light **HS** 9158 lyghtnyng

like, liche adj./adv. [see oliche, olyke] [OE gelic; ON, cp. OI likr] similar, equal, suitable; exactly **Ch1** 1336, 2159, 6737, 8923, 9300 like; 9880L liche (om. P); 10832 liche P yliche L; 11086 liche; **Ch2** 444 als P like L; 1063L liche (P differs); 6571 like; **HS** 11550 lyk; 10218, 10247, 10600, 12298 lyke; 2237, 5888 lyche

like v. (1) [OE lician] to please; approve, wish, choose **Ch1** 620, 1381 likand P lykynge L; 4421 likand P lykande L; 2899, 3977 liked; 4794 likes; **Ch2** 1825 paied P liked L; 6600 likes

likynd, lykned v. (2) [from OE gelic, adj.] to compare, be equal to **Ch1** 3604 likynd P lyknede L; 3945, 10832 likned P lykned L; 8925 likned; **HS** 3976 lyknyd; 4760 lykned

likyng ger. [OE licung] feeling of pleasure, delight, obsession **Ch2** 3233, 6078, 6601 likyng; **HS** 4741, 6626, 7032, 12620 lykyng; 12436 lykyngge

lykkede v. [OE liccian] to lick **HS** 6650 lykkede

lyknes n. [OE gelicnes] appearance, shape **Ch1** 1330, 1755, 7970, 9289, 9298 liknes; **HS** 284, 4173, 7481, 9977 lyknes; 8840 lyknesse

lyme, lymme n. (1) [OE lim] limb of the body; a member **Ch1** 2139 lym; 5988 lyme; 1756, 8583 lymes; 153, 8903, 10130, 15440 lymmes; 3749, 3750, 7362 limes; **Ch2** 4386 lymme P lyme L; 6059, 6384 lymme; 5508, 7252, 7945 lymmes; **HS** 1320, 3635, 11927 lyme; 5083, 5085 lymes; 4130 lemes

lyme n. (2) [OE lim] birdlime; fig.: something that entraps, sticky **HS** 2137 lyme

lynage, lyne n. [OF linage, lignage] race, family; ancestry, descent **Ch1** 10250 lyne; 942, 2656, 3635, 4256, 6037 lynage; 4230, 5806 linage; 5329, 8589, 13806 lynages; **Ch2** 1933, 2128, 3346, 4006, 4669 lynage; 7889, 8222 linage; **HS** 2880, 3034, 4205 lynage

lynde n. [OE lind] woods; open spaces in forests **Ch1** 4688 lyndes; 15053 lynde

lyne n. [OE line] ship's tackle; "euen as lyne": straight, directly **Ch1** 11763 lynes; 4653 lyn P lyne L; **Ch2** 3700 lyne

lion, leon, lyoun n. [OF lion; OE lea, leon] a lion **Ch1** 1588 lyon; 5125, 11026 lion; 11188L lyouns (om. P); 11814 leon P lyoun L; 13251, 13335, 13696, 14722 leon

lip n. [OE lippa] a lip **Ch1** 8782 lippes; **Ch2** 3512 lip; 3822 lyppe; **HS** 4183 lyppes

list, liste v. (1) [OE lystan] wish, desire, choose to; be pleasing to **Ch1** 698 list P lyst L; 7479, 8773 list; **Ch2** 2143, 3257, 4568, 5156 list; 212, 4448 liste; **HS** 6446 lyste

liste, luste, listen v. (2) [see lithe, v. (2)] [OE hlystan] listen to, attend to, hear **Ch1** 2 listene; 124, 1443, 6905 listen; 2168, 4566 listen P lystneþ L; 3171 listen P list L; 2308 listen P lyst L; 1454, 7903, 8984, 12350, 14941 listend; 2556 listend P lystned L; 454, 4126, 6909 listes; 3542, 11040, 11216 liste; 2176, 6630, 14057 listens P lystneþ L; 11410 listens P leste L; **Ch2** 2768, 3306, 5674 liste; 2264 lithe P listen L; 2840 listend; 1639 lithe P lusteþ L; 293, 840, 1664, 4807, 6194 listen; 1173 listen P list L; 1686 listen P listeþ L; 6048, 6994, 7201 listnes; 5275 listned; **HS** 9582 lyste; 48, 2941, 4307, 11640 lestene; 5897 lestnede; 8705 lystened; 12518 lystenede; 3126 lestenyþ O herkyn

lite n. (1) [from ON hlita, v.] delay; expectation **Ch1** 3151 lyte P lite L; 5767L lyte (om. P); 8736 lite P lyte L; **Ch2** 6252, 7606 lite; **HS** 5049, 5354, 11384 lyte

lite n. (2) [see litelle] [OE lyt, adj.] small amount, little; short time **Ch1** 1062 litelle P lite L; 1641, 4577, 5438 lite; **Ch2** 1069, 2511, 4058, 5085, 6252 lite; 2023 lite P litil L; **HS** 528, 3553, 4391, 6999, 9260 lyte

litelle, lytel, luytel n./adj./adv. [OE lytel] small, short **Ch1** 1062 litelle P lite L; 3306, 4243, 6264, 7123, 7931 litelle; 2809, 3966 lytelle P litel L; 2808, 4627, 5250, 5807, 8780 litille; 4381 litille P lite L; 11297 litelle P lytel L; 14061L luytel (om. P); **Ch2** 5 lesse P lytel L; 144, 1940, 3869, 5993, 7417 litelle; 3704, 4329, 4471, 6710, 7209 litille; **HS** 6962, 5066, 6903, 10890 lytel; 91, 2004, 4405, 7049, 7327 lytyl

lyth n. [ON; cp. OI lyðr] land, property; country, people **Ch1** 15028L lond & lyth (om. P);

Ch2 232 lyth; 368, 1963 liþe; 624, 2409 liþes; 4800 lith
lithe, lyþe v. (1) [OE liþian] alleviate, assuage **Ch1** 13084 lithed P leþed L; **HS** 2280 lyþe
lithe v. (2) [see liste, listen, v. (2)] [ON; cp. OI hlyða] listen, hear about **Ch2** 1639 lithe P lusteþ L; 2264 lithe P listen L
lyþer, lyþerly n./adj./adv. [OE lyþre, adj.] wicked persons; evil; treacherous **Ch1** 1980 felon P lyþer L; 2899 liþerly P lyþerly L
liþt adj. [OE liþe] gentle; dwelling in ease **Ch2** 7587 liþt
littere n. [OF liter] a portable bed; litter **Ch1** 9469 littere
lyue v. [see leue, lyue, v. (4)]
lyue, lyf n. [see olife, olyue] [OE lif] existence; living creatures; in this world; life on earth **Ch1** 185, 2112, 3122, 6884, 7893 lyue; 207, 278, 8297, 8550 lyues; 793, 2131, 2288, 5988, 8583 lyfe; 1103, 1560, 3586, 5616 lyf; 5289, 6696 lyues (gen.); 1400 lyfes (gen.); 8959 lif; 8238, 9035, 9268, 10130 life; 7775 liues; **Ch2** 323, 1208, 2865, 6133, 8078 lyue; 564, 1887, 2571, 5416 lyues; 586, 777, 1042 lyfe; 837, 1321, 1598, 2072, 4386 life; 3210, 3442, 6059, 7798, 8354 lif; 6814 liue; 940 lyue P lif tyme L; 674 life P lyf L; 182 lyues (gen.); **HS** 740, 1236, 1439, 5139, 11940 lyff; 3160 lyf; 1082, 2618, 3632, 5138, 12242 lyue; 5065 lyues
liuere n. [AF livere] retinue; badge or uniform of retainers or servants; feudal rights **Ch1** 2388, 2389, 10385 lyuere P liuere L; 3089 lyuere; **Ch2** 3582 liuere
liuerison n. [OF livreison] provisions, allowances **Ch1** 2380 liuerison P lyuersoun L; 7324 liueresons P liuersons L; **Ch2** 4895 liuerisoun
lo interjection [OE la] "behold!" **Ch1** 1627 lo
lodesman n. [cp. OE lod-man, lad-man] leader, director **HS** 9029 lodesman *O* halderman
lofe n. (1) [OF] a ship's spar, tackle **Ch1** 11796 lofe P loof L
lofe n. (2) [OE hlaf] a loaf **HS** 5617, 5622, 5657, 5667, 10757 lofe; 10350 loues
loge n. [OF] lodging, building; tent **Ch1** 1659, 4420, 4609 loges P logges L; 4426 loge; 4613, 9082 loges; **Ch2** 1657 loges
loged v. [OF logier] encamped, housed **Ch1** 3664, 4322, 4941, 6182 loged P logged L; 9080 loged; **Ch2** 4511 loged
logh adj. [see lowe, louh, adj./adv.]
lok n. [OE loc] a lock, fastening **HS** 6198 lok
loke n. [see loke, v. (2)] [OE locian] appearance **Ch1** 2449 loke
loke v. (1) [ON; cp. OI loka] lock up, fasten; guard **Ch1** 948, 2970, 3230, 9280 loken; 12102 stoken P loken L; 1056 loked; 2908 lokyn P loken L; 4110 loked P loken L; 1087, 5823, 7164, 9133, 12824 loke; 9797 luke; **Ch2** 7065 loken; 2619, 3227, 4145, 5706, 6064 loke; 4045 loke P ordeyn L; **HS** 11838 loken; 1538, 6023, 9093 loke; 1868 lokun *C* loke *D* be loke
loke v. (2) [OE locian] see; take care; consider, decide; decree **Ch1** 168, 627, 649 luke; 633 luke P loke L; 1053, 1790, 2026, 7295, 8278 loke; 4753 loke P lok L; 9178 luke P lout L; **Ch2** 822, 3180, 4106, 5610, 8090 loke; 1598 lokes; 3863 loke P lok L; **HS** 122, 1589, 4350, 7685, 11335 loke; 1818 lokede; 6763 loke GLOSS BH kepe; 8775 lokede *O* soghte
loking ger. [OE locung] gazing; decision, ordinance; supervision **Ch1** 919 lokyng; 7030 kepyng P lokyng L; **Ch2** 1239, 2112, 5296, 7664 lokyng; **HS** 2215, 8134, 8410 lokyng
lomb n. [OE lamb] young sheep **Ch1** 1588 lomb; 10972L lomb (om. P)
lond n. [see land, n.]
long, lang adj./adv. [OE lang] tall, deep; a long time, at length **Ch1** 51, 241, 2063 lang; 159, 5284, 6223, 9060, 14598 long; 2511, 7404 longe; 3202 long P longe L; 1718, 7316, 13675 lenger; 11478, 15508 lengere; 3532, 4424 langere; 8247 langer; 8621 langest; 6899 lengest; 10186 long P lange L; 15086 long P longes L; **Ch2** 1684 lang; 265, 1207, 5784, 6650, 8264 long; 1387, 1452, 2340 longe; 1183, 3732, 4971, 6899, 7842 lenger; 3432, 5568, 6044 langere; 7684, 7888 lengere; 6044 langer; 5441 longly; **HS** 3058, 7819, 10381, 11284 long; 9266, 11037 longe; 507, 1794 longge; 3827 lang; 729, 892, 1933, 2334 lenger; 2982 lengere; 1225, 11651 langere; 2542, 3435, 10281, 10667 langer; 3226, 3442 syde GLOSS BH long
long, lang v. [cp. OE long, lang, adj.] belong to, pertain to; suitable to **Ch1** 241 lang P longe L; 2447 longe P lange L; 2838, 5677, 5680, 5965 longed; 11595 langes; **Ch2** 2034 long; 6817 lenge; 1088, 2689, 5731, 6346, 7557 longed; 6054, 7394 longes; **HS** 2033, 2038 longe; 2912 longyþ; 5511, 8290 longeþ; 7858 longede *O* langede; 9494 longeþ *O* falles
longyng n. [OE langung] desire, yearning **Ch1** 8706 longyng; **Ch2** 6097 longyng; **HS** 5866, 6615, 7117, 7531, 12130 longyng; 9933 longynge
lope v. [see lepe, v.]
lord, louerd n. [OE hlaford] king, noble, ruler; spouse **Ch1** 583, 3116, 6057, 7130, 9348 lord; 131, 3422, 6763, 8810, 12525 lordes; 7266 lord P louerd L; 8520 lordes P lordynges L; 8171 lordis; 7457 lauerid P lord L; 7349 louerdes; **Ch2** 211, 1063, 3620, 5750, 7639 lord; 1646, 3090, 4560, 5439, 8166 lordes; 3765, 3779 lorde; **HS** 1617, 3410, 4329, 5510, 12071 lord; 8715 lordes
lordan n. [OF lordin] wicked person; low fellow **Ch2** 169 lordan

lordyng, louerding n. [OE hlafording] master, ruler **Ch1** 903, 3616, 4370, 5715, 6618 lordyng; l, 429, 4307, 8555, 12545 lordynges; 2054 lordynges P lordes L; 7776 lordings P lordes L; 7733 louerding; **Ch2** 2549, 2820, 5253, 5915, 6195 lordyng; 2094, 3077, 4890, 6019, 7700 lordynges; 2063 lordyng P lordschupe L; **HS** 2195, 3098 lordyng; 2998 lordyngys; 5409, 6620 lordynges

lordschip n. [OE hlafordscipe] rule, government; sovereignty, dominion **Ch1** 36, 286, 4100, 4475 lordschip; 4892 lordeschip; **Ch2** 127, 350, 1050, 5270, 8058 lordschip; 798 seignorie P lordship L; 1353L lordschupe (om. P); **HS** 2209 seynorye GLOSS H lordshyp

lore n. (1) [OE lor] loss of property, money; loss in battle; damage **Ch1** 3644, 6632, 7636 lore; **Ch2** 2364 lore P more L; 5800, 6486 lore; **HS** 2460, 5549, 6045 lore

lore n. (2) [OE lar] narrative, story; instruction, learning **Ch1** 4787, 6943 lore; **Ch2** 7463, 8356 lore; **HS** 745, 2941, 4013, 5564, 7998 lore; 2693 lore GLOSS B techyng

lorn v. [see lese, lose, v.]

los n. (1) [OF] reputation, fame; praise, renown **Ch1** 3088, 5430, 9214, 10378, 12744 los; **Ch2** 518, 4844, 5858 los; **HS** 868, 1522, 4648, 9964 los; 1050 los *CD* loos; 1350 gode los *C* good name

los, lost n. (2) [from OE losian; ON los] loss, failure, defeat **Ch1** 5334, 9697 tynselle P los L; 12519 losse P los L; 13546 tinselle P lost L; **Ch2** 7516 loste; **HS** 2462 losse

lose, lous adj. [ON lauss, louss] free, loose **HS** 10626 los; 10586 lose; 4806, 5098 lous

lose v. [see les, lese, v. (1)] [OE losian] to lose, be dispossessed, deprived **Ch1** 3208 sped nouht P lostest L; 3406 les P lostey L; 2736 tynt P lost L; 6301 lose; 6373, 7986 lost; **Ch2** 6596 losis; 1771, 3992, 4743, 5422, 7028 lost; 490 lorn P lost L; 998 tynt P lost L; 1485 les P lost L

losed v. [see alose] [OF los, lous, aloser] praise **Ch1** 10350 losed

losengere n. [OF] flatterer, liar **Ch1** 2797 losengeres P loȝengeours L; **Ch2** 6999 losengere; **HS** 3503 loseniours; 3507 loseniour

losengrye n. [OF losengerie] flattery, deceit **HS** 3511 losengrye

lost n. [see los, lost, n. (2)]

lote, lot n. [OE hlot] object used to wager; choice made by lot **Ch1** 7247 lote; 836, 7239, 7859, 8003, 8010 lotes; **Ch2** 3043 lotes; 3044 lote; **HS** 4021 lot

loteby, ludby n. [from OE *lotian] lover, paramour, concubine **HS** 1732 ludby *C* loteby *D* lotebyȝe; 2930 ludby *C* loteby *O* lottoby

loth, layþ n. [OE laþ] injury, misfortune; evil; hate **Ch1** 14382 laith P leythe L; 15326L leyþ (om. P); **Ch2** 1714 loth P wroþ L; 1981, 2738, 3285, 5381, 6947 loth; **HS** 4966 loth; 6780 loth GLOSS BH harm

loth, lothly adj./adv. [OE laþ, loþlic; ON] hateful, unpleasant, evil **Ch1** 2026 lothely P loþliche L; 3852 lothe P loþ L; 10715 lefe & lothe P lef & loþ L; 11807 vgly P lothly L; 12116L loþly (om. P); 12042 lothelik; 13830, 15241 loþe; **Ch2** 1867, 6414 lothe; 1873, 3203, 4406, 6819 loth; 2615L loþe (P differs); **HS** 934, 3020, 4382, 5758, 8999 loth; 3578 loþly; 8066 lothly; 8063 lothly *O* brothly; 563 layþ GLOSS BH fowl

loth v. [ON, OE laþian] be hateful or distasteful to; hate **Ch1** 6970 loth P loþe L; **Ch2** 2434 lothe; **HS** 3461 lothes; 686, 752 loþys; 4534 loþyth

lothen adj. [ON; cp. OI loðiun] hairy, shaggy **Ch1** 12040 broþen P lothen L

loude adj./adv. [OE hlud] as in loud noise, cry, songs **Ch1** 6470, 13723 loude; 14956 o loude; 7711 loud; **Ch2** 649 loud; 7313 loude; **HS** 3050, 4712, 5475, 6413, 10069 loud; 1131, 1568 loude; 2859 *C* al on lowde (B differs)

loue, luf n. [OE lufu] love, desire **Ch1** 77, 3634, 6304, 8244, 9247 luf; 1218, 2664, 2961, 9249, 15790 luf P loue L; 3714, 3789, 6079, 7327, 8542 loue; **Ch2** 592, 2162, 4518, 5386, 7702 luf; 6972 lufe; 1499, 1714 luf P loue L; 84, 695, 1380, 3524, 4047 loue; **HS** 1064, 2710, 6828, 7683, 11214 loue

loue day n. [AF jour damour] day for a meeting for reconciliation **Ch2** 1231 loue day; 2832 day of loue

loue, luf v. [OE lufian] to love **Ch1** 588, 2288, 5297, 6969, 9257 luf; 2293, 2326, 9253 lufes; 2307 loues; 8213 louedis P louedest L; 8644 louand; 6645 lofed; 295, 3092, 4047, 6553, 9187 lufed; 777, 832, 1477, 2903, 13828 luffed; 773 lufed P yloued L; 2283, 2474, 5923, 7097, 9255 loue; 2305, 3871, 7366, 7522, 7659 loued; 3786L louede (P differs); 6929 lufed P louede L; **Ch2** 781, 2387, 2392, 7464, 7670 luf; 2834 loue; 3586, 5692, 6267, 7037 lufes; 162, 3804 luffed; 168 lufed P loued L; 820 lufed P liued L; 1196, 3528, 5459, 6797, 7045 lufed; 2610 loued; **HS** 1433, 1670, 7436 loue; 257, 1444 louede

louely, lufly adj./adv. [OE luflic] lovable, beautiful; willingly, graciously **Ch1** 2449, 3117 lufly; 7425 loueli; **Ch2** 657, 6666 lufly; **HS** 3065, 3907, 5155, 10101 louely; 10100 louelyest

louh, lough n. [Celtic; cp. OIr loch] arm of the sea, bay, lake **Ch1** 1413 lough P low L; 1414 louhes P loughes L; 1415 louh P lough L; 10037, 10039, 10131, 10134 louh; 10057 louhes

P loughes L

louh v. [see lauht, lauh, louh, v. (2)]

louh adj. [see lowe, adj./adv.]

louyngge, lufyng ger. [OE lufung] love; inordinate affection **Ch1** 2298 lufyng; **HS** 6223 louyngge

lounes n. [from ON lagr, adj.] humility, meekness **Ch1** 8650 lounes P lownesse L

lous, los adj. [ON lauss, louss] loose **HS** 4806, 5098 lous; 10586 lose; 10626 los

loute v. [OE lutan] bow, kneel; obey, submit **Ch1** 1353, 2664, 4469, 5759, 8976 loute; 3528 loute P aloute L; 9178 luke P lout L; **Ch2** 974, 2942, 6831, 7200, 7986 loute; 8146 lout; **HS** 5834, 9582 loute; 8250 louten; 12082 louteþ; 3574, 4042 loutede

low, logh v. [from ON lagr, adj.] to make lower **Ch1** 14902 low P lowe L; **HS** 11685 logheþ

lowe, louh, logh, lowly adj./adv. [ON, cp. OI lagr] low, wretched **Ch1** 2413, 3463, 4140, 4378 lowe; 6458 lowere; 10378 lawe; 11326, 13008 louh; **Ch2** 460, 2467, 6874, 7635 lowe; 7648, 7669 louh; 7639 lowere; **HS** 1143, 1395, 1615, 6562 logh; 358, 3073, 8384, 11339, 11786 lowe; 333 mercy *D* lowly

lowe n. [ON; cp OI logi] a fire, flame **Ch1** 8226, 14070 lowe; 8227 low P lowe L; **HS** 9665 lowe; 484 lowe GLOSS BH fere

lowed adj. [see lewed, adj.]

ludby n. [see loteby, n.]

luf n./v. [see loue, luf]

lufyng ger. [see louyngge, lufyng]

luke v. [see loke, v. (1), (2)]

lungeteyns adj. [OF lontains, lointain] distant, remote **Ch1** 4154 lungeteyns P long teymes L

lusk v. [cf. lusken, v.; MDu lusschen] to skulk, loaf **Ch2** 169 lusk

lussed ppl. [from lushen, v.; cp. OE leosan] tumbled, fell, crashed down **Ch1** 2949 lussed P lusched L; 12754 to lusshed P to lusched L

lust n. [OE] desire; sin **HS** 6546, 6626 lust

lusty, lustyly adj./adv. [from OE lust, n.] lecherous; voluptuously; eagerly **HS** 3184 lustyly; 7205 lustly; 7890 lusty

lustyn v. [from OE lust, n., and OE lystan] to wish for, desire **HS** 1734 be brennyng *C* more lustyn *D* be ardent

M

mace n. [OF] war club, weapon **Ch1** 12044, 12050, 12060, 12080 mace

mad adj. [see wode, adj.] [OE (ge)mædde] crazy, insane; infatuated; angry **Ch1** 604, 7494 mad; **HS** 273, 3117, 5642, 8524 mad

made v. [see make, v.]

mageste n. [AF maieste (MP)] majesty **HS** 11543 mageste

magnel, mangnel n. [OF mangonel] machine for hurling stones **Ch1** 1031, 5967, 6690 magnels P mangeneles L; **Ch2** 3070 mangnel; 4541 magneles P other gyles L

may, maiden n. [OE mæg, mægden] young woman; virgin; maid, girl **Ch1** 2009, 2937, 2967, 5486, 5492 may; 762 madan P maide L; 783, 1972, 2973, 3114, 6227 mayden; 2006 maydens P maydenes L; 2164, 2647, 6448 maydens; 2193 maydens P madenes L; 5269 maiden; 7487 maidin P mayden L; 7494, 7505 maidin; 14998 maiden P mayden L; **Ch2** 2326, 3785, 5716, 6111, 7503 may; 374, 655, 3781, 5069, 5995 maiden; 2302, 3418, 3901, 5224, 6109 mayden; 7967 maydens; **HS** 648, 1688 maydyn; 6005 mayden; 9728, 9729 mayde; 4541 ylka fyle GLOSS B eury mayde gerld GLOSS H maydgerle; 980 *D* may (B differs)

may, moun, mot, mowe, myght v. [OE mæg, magan, mot, moten, moste] can, may, must; in combination: cp. do and be **Ch1** 55, 2439, 5036, 6624, 9366 may; 8078 mouht; 7553 may P myght L; 174, 1287, 3116, 7926, 9047 mot; 547, 1236, 3287, 7861, 9138 myght; 4773 mote P mot L; 6644 myght P mighte L; 6756, 7375, 8194 might; 7232 mouh P mowe L; 7588 mot P myghter L; 9689 might P myghter L; 7248, 7772, 10574 mote; 5013 myht; 4352 myht P myght L; **Ch2** 3623 moun; 59, 1253, 4770, 6518, 8265 mot; 142, 4204, 5766, 6816, 8323 may; 55, 1302, 4193, 6114, 8272 myght; 7110, 7574 mowe; 7726, 8353 most; **HS** 41, 90, 1349, 6826, 10568 may; 484, 2660, 9904 mowe; 557 mow; 8019 mowen; 11597 moune; 320, 1400, 1824, 5889 myghte; 7740 myght; 7570 mought; 9587 maght; 202, 975, 4240, 5495, 11663 mote; 11367 most; 5668, 8681, 12410 moste; 134 seye & *D* seyn ȝe moun; 1689 may *C* mown; 1863 mowe *C* mown *D* moun; 1879, 2317 mowe *C* may *D* myȝt; 2284 may *C* myth *D* myȝtte; 4232 mowe *O* may; 35 mote *D* behouyth; 4073 byrde GLOSS BH moste

maille n. [OF] armor with rings **Ch1** 13264L, 13286L maille (om. P)

mayn n. [OE mægen] strength, vigor, power **Ch1** 5197 myght & mayne P myght & mayn L; **Ch2** 1350, 1724, 2411 myght & mayn; **HS** 10354 mayne; 5024 mayn GLOSS BH strenkþe

maynhed ppl. [OF mahaignier] maimed, wounded **Ch2** 7449 maynhed

maynpis v. [from OF mainprise, n.] release or arrange bail for a prisoner **Ch2** 3395 maynpis

maynten v. [OF maintenir] to uphold, support; preserve **Ch1** 20, 4095, 6672, 9010 mayntend; 885 mayntende; 3626 mayntend P mayntende L; 3478, 6667, 7134 maynten; 5375 maynten P vndertake L; 1466 mantend P meintened L;

7590 mantende P meyntende L; 6427 mayntend P meyntende L; 8967, 15497 mayntene; 7592, 7596 mantend; 15873 maynten P meintene L; **Ch2** 464, 2452, 5188, 6846, 8057 mayntend; 474, 1164, 2347, 6861, 8193 mayntene; 1479, 2157, 4173, 5781, 7647 maynten; 2454 maytenyng P mayntenyng L; **HS** 6560 maynteynest; 7654 maynteyne; 636 maynteyne *D* susteyne

mayntenour, mayntenure n. [OF mainteneour] supporter, helper; commander **Ch1** 3194 mayntenoure P mayntenour L; 12493 mayntenure P mayntende (v.) L; **Ch2** 3597, 7622 mayntenours; 4111 mayntenour; 6151 mayntenoure

maistre, mayster n./adj. [OE magester; OF maistre] master, leader, guide, teacher **Ch1** 57, 177, 189 mayster; 45 maysters; 5301, 5521, 5705, 7955 maister; 6055, 7186, 7852, 8106 maistres; 3472 maistres P mayster L; 8047 masters; 8006, 8042 maisters; 11793 maistres P mariners L; 12592LR maister (om. P); **Ch2** 3261 maistre; 3034 maistir; 2344 maistres; 2291, 4865, 5357, 7451, 8039 maister; 7240 maistere; **HS** 73, 1899, 2074, 7775, 11418 mayster; 1614, 1432 maystyr; 7910 maystred (ppl.)

maistrie, mastry n. [OF maistrie] superiority; power, authority; victory **Ch1** 309 mastry P maistrie L; 487, 508, 881, 5033 maystri; 496 maystrye P maistrie L; 1546, 3707, 5429, 7068, 11794 maistrie; 2235, 2699, 9103, 12196 maistri; 6405, 6559 maistry; 6143 mastrie; **Ch2** 578 maistri; 131, 1677, 2357, 5080, 8229 maistrie; **HS** 532, 2933, 4975, 8360, 12080 maystry; 3956, 4584, 7643 maystrye

make, made v. [OE macian] create; construct, build; produce; compose **Ch1** 8221, 8626, 9332 mak; 3774 make P made L; 4755 makis P made L; 4923 makes P makeþ L; 4978, 8571, 8892, 9283 make; 8762 makes; 11483 makis; 3663 mad P maden L; 3938, 4947, 5317, 8406, 9203 mad; 3721, 4055, 4663, 8211, 9017 made; 3056 maked P mad L; **Ch2** 4024, 4268, 4388, 6100, 8108 make; 5894, 6545, 7636, 8279 mak; 4005, 4562, 6875, 7596, 8318 mad; 6371 makand; 8256 mas; **HS** 110, 557, 1017, 3220, 11446 make; 51, 1591, 2296, 3220, 9558 made; 6891 makes; 10324 makþ

malencoly n. [OF] bad temper; irascibility **HS** 3712 malencoly

males n. [OF male, malle] bag, pouch **Ch2** 5988 males

malice n./adj. [OF] ill-will, hostility **Ch1** 5579 malice; 6115 malicius; **HS** 7588 malyce

malison n. [OF maleison, malison] curse, malediction; imprecation **Ch1** 2802 malisoun; **Ch2** 1023 malison; 4016, 7770 malisoun; **HS** 9630, 9651 malysoun; 1076, 12320 malysun; 1247 malysun *C* bannyng *D* maleys

man n. [OE] man; one, anyone **Ch1** 126, 1096, 4032, 6849, 13082 man; 208, 2403, 4505, 6509, 9354 men; **Ch2** 108, 1633, 4318, 6872, 7632 man; 1619, 2325, 4325, 5151, 5797 men; **HS** 378, 471 man; 8, 43, 57, 2050 men

manace n. [OF manace, menace] threat **Ch1** 2989, 4849, 6265, 7177, 9208 manace; **Ch2** 1580, 3077, 4490, 5269, 6175 manace; 3855 manace P manas L; **HS** 5772 manas

manace v. [OF manacer, manasser] threaten, warn **Ch1** 1046 manace; 4874, 9206 manaced; 4896 manaces; 8734 manaced P manased L; **Ch2** 5028 manaced; **HS** 3683 manase; 10301 manaceþ

manage, menage n. [OF] household retainers; troops, army **Ch2** 1924 manage P meynage L; 3788 menage

◆ **manauntie** n. [OF] residence **Ch2** 7948 manauntie

mandement, maundement n. [OF] command; a pope's decree **Ch2** 7475 maundement; 7487 mandement

maner n. (1) [AF manere] kind, sort; nature, character; custom **Ch1** 822 maner P manere L; 664, 2774, 3976, 7812, 9288 maner; 56, 1083, 5437, 7155, 15150 manere; 1341, 1350, 2192 maneres; 3865, 3923, 6073, 7052 maners; **Ch2** 806, 1913, 4527, 5508, 7663 maner; 1658, 3058, 4422, 5189, 7734 manere; 2121, 4680, 5692, 6657, 8061 maners; **HS** 130, 1737, 7329, 10566, 12591 maner; 45, 3521, 6978, 9643, 12427 manere; 461 maneyr; 70, 387, 2416, 5690, 5848 maners; 12417 maneres; 2759 maners *CO* wyse *D* wyses

maner n. (2) [AF] manorial estate; stronghold, mansion **Ch1** 7325, 7395 maners; **Ch2** 1367 maner; 2095, 3299, 3562, 6978 maners; 1353 manere P lordschupe L; **HS** 8675 maners

manhede, manhode n. [from OE man, mann + hædu] masculinity; virtue, dignity **Ch1** 4136 manhode; 10342 manhede; **HS** 655, 683, 5058, 11349, 11819 manhede

manyon n. phr. [from OE manig + on] many a one, person **Ch1** 120, 8774, 8951 manyon; **Ch2** 308, 318, 7176 manyon; **HS** 361, 414, 4010, 7224 manyon; 1283, 4509 manyoun; 2287, 2780, 11275 manyone

maniores, mangers n. [OF mangeoire] feeding trough for animals **Ch1** 10964 maniores P mangers L

mankynd n. [from OE mann + cynd] human race; people **Ch1** 5270 mankynd; 7862, 14281 mankynde; 7961 mans kynde; **Ch2** 3525 mankynde; **HS** 728, 6428 mankynde; 4150 mankynd

manly adv. [OE manlice] bravely **Ch1** 12248

manly P vaillaunte L; **Ch2** 4446, 5726 manly
manne v. [OE mannian] to take charge **Ch1** 6336L manne (P differs); **Ch2** 5498 manned
manqualm n. [OE man-cwealm] death from plague or pestilence **Ch1** 15677 man qualme P man qualm L; 15706 qualme P manqualme L; 15760 manqualme P moryne L; **HS** 1370 pestlensse *C* weniawns *D* man qualm
mansbond n. [ON; cp. OI manns-barn] slaves, rabble **Ch2** 2803 mansbond
manslauȝter n. [see slauhter, n./adj.] [OE mannslæht, man-slieht] murder; killing in battle **HS** 1334 slaghtyr *C* deth *D* manslauȝtter; 1710 slaghter *C* man slawth *D* manslauter
mantel n. [AF mantel (MP)] overgarment; robe **Ch1** 10971 mantles P manteles L; 11175 mantels; **HS** 11377, 12479 mantel
marreþ v. [OE merran] to spurn **HS** 8184 marreþ
marble n. [OF marbre] marble tomb **Ch2** 5644, 8351 marble
marchand n. [see merchaunt, n.]
marchaundie n. [see merchaundie, n.]
marche n. [OF] boundary; border district **Ch2** 300, 2034, 5779, 6587, 7732 marche
marchen v. [see merched, v.]
marchis n. [OF marchis, marquis] title of an English nobleman between the ranks of duke and earl **Ch2** 4390, 4394, 4400, 4401, 4738 marchis
mareis n. [OF] swamp, quagmire **Ch2** 7940 mareis
mariage n. [OF] marriage vow; wedding ceremony **Ch1** 2322, 6248, 6437 mariage; **Ch2** 2585, 3347, 3774, 5718, 8275 mariage; 7361 mariages
marie v. [OF marier] to give or take in marriage; formally wed **Ch1** 2332, 2407, 6251, 6449, 8981 maried; **Ch2** 3863 marie; 5223 maried
marinere n. [AF] seaman; boatman **Ch1** 5813, 5832 mariners; 11788 maryners; **Ch2** 3042 maryner; 3945, 6285 maryners; 2575 marinere; 4195 marinere P messenger L
mariole n. [OF] image of the Virgin Mary **Ch2** 2277 mariole
marite n. [OF; L marite] spouse, husband **Ch2** 5160 marite
mark, merk n. (1) [see marche, n.] [OE marc] boundary mark, gravestone; target; sign **Ch1** 9886 merk P merke L; 1432 markes P merkes L; **Ch2** 3001, 6564 merk; 3162, 3183, 7807 merke; 1895 merkes; 8194 merkis; **HS** 7860 mark; 2331 mark *D* tokene
mark, marc n. (2) [OE, OF marc] monetary unit: 160 pennies **Ch2** 377, 3308, 3321, 3325, 7937 marke; 2363, 3852, 4328, 5116, 5713 mark; 3310 marce; **HS** 6324 mark
mark, merk v. [OE mearcian, ON merkja] mark with a sign **HS** 7850 merked; 7855 marked
market, merket n. [OF; L mercatus] place for buying or selling **Ch1** 2759 merket P market L; **Ch2** 7189 markettis; 8015 markette
marschalcie n. [OF mareschaucie] position of the chief officer in a kingdom **Ch1** 7000 marchaucie P marchalsye L; **Ch2** 7093, 7099 marschalcie
marschalle n. [OF mareschal] steward; high officer of the royal court; military commander **Ch1** 10961 marschalles P mareschals L; **Ch2** 2968, 3595, 4501, 7081, 7613 marschalle
martir, martere n. [OE, L] one who suffers torture or death for Christian faith **Ch2** 780 martere; 2141, 3468, 3653, 5653 martir; 3654, 5679 martire; **HS** 8274 martyr
martirdam, martirdom n. [OE martyrdom] torture and execution of a martyr; suffering, torment **Ch1** 6492 martirdam; 10847 martirdom; 14726 martire; **Ch2** 3643 martirdam; 8268, 9024 martyrdom
masers n. [OF masre, mazre] drinking vessels made of wood **Ch1** 11176 maȝers P masers L
mason n. [OF] stone mason **Ch1** 6601, 8596, 8620 masons
mast n. [OE mæst] mast of a ship, a spar **Ch1** 682, 1302, 4292, 5527, 6477 mast; 4582 mastes; 2949, 4649 maste; **Ch2** 1727, 3648, 4606 mast
mastif n. [OF mastin, mestif] large hunting dog **Ch2** 4696 mastif
mastlyoun n. [OF mesteillon] mixture of grains **HS** 10132 mastlyoun *O* mastillion *SV* foule desires
matal n. [see metal]
mate v. [OF mater] checkmating; to render powerless **Ch1** 8440 mate
mate griffoun n. portable seige tower used by Richard I **Ch2** 3878 mate griffoun
matere n. [OF] affair; subject of discussion **Ch1** 342 matere; 15780 mater; **Ch2** 7838, 8354 matere; **HS** 11204 matere
matyng ger. [from OF mater] checkmating; defeat **Ch1** 11157 matyng
matyns n. [OF matin] the first canonical hour **Ch1** 14494 matyns; **HS** 823, 827 matyns; 9060 matynes
matrymony n. [AF matrimoine (MP)] marriage **HS** 1659, 1837, 1868 matrymony; 11163 matrymonye
mattok n. [OE mattuc] a pick, pickaxe **HS** 939, 941 mattok
maufesours n. [OF malfesour; AF meffesours] criminals, enemies **Ch2** 5174 maufesours
maugre n. [OF] blame, reproach, ill-will, resentment, wrath **Ch1** 957, 12530, 12534 maugre;

Ch2 3845, 7096 maugre; **HS** 6909, 7779 maugre

maugre adv./prep. [OF] in spite of; notwithstanding **Ch1** 5916, 6170, 10102, 11662, 11988 maugre; **Ch2** 1403, 4557, 5728, 6414, 7256 maugre; 4736 magre (?error) P maugre L; **HS** 4478, 6220 maugre

maumet n. [OF mahomet] idol; fig.: object of worship; false god **Ch1** 813 maumet P mawmet L; 1338 maumet; **HS** 190, 192 maumette *C* mawment; 221 maumet *C* mawmet; 227 maumet *D* þat deuyl; 256 maumet *C* fynde

maumetrie n. [from maumet, n.] worship of idols, images; Mohammedanism; vices, especially avarice **Ch1** 1329 maumetrie P maumetry L; 5672 maumetrie P maumetries L; **Ch2** 7819 maumetrie; **HS** 6158 maumetry; 4976 maumettry; 6159, 8257, 10218, 10247 maumetrye; 186 maumetrye *C* mawmentis

mede n. (1) [OE med] royal or noble endowment; reward, wealth **Ch1** 129, 2038, 7386, 10353, 11131 mede; **Ch2** 611, 6425, 8037 mede; **HS** 102, 2444, 6550, 8329, 11716 mede

mede, medue, medow n. (2) [OE mæd, med] a meadow, moor **Ch1** 1890 medew P mede L; 10841 medes; **Ch2** 1656, 7433, 7576, 7853 mede; 42 medew; 1869 medow; 4831 medue; 7573 medis; **HS** 1393 medue

medicine n. [OF medecin; L medicina] medicine; fig.: a remedy, solution **Ch1** 4433, 8703, 8897 medicyne; 13342 medicyne P medisine L; 4448 medecine; 8892 medicyn; **HS** 9236, 11574 medycyne

medle n. [see mele, v.] [OF medlee, mellee] battle; dispute **Ch2** 7594 medle

medle, medele v. [OF medler, meller] mingle; become confused; fight, dispute **Ch1** 13002 medled; 13902L medlande (om. P); **Ch2** 336 medeled; 2035 mykelle P medlyng L; 2635 deles P medleþ L; **HS** 10130 medled; 10134 medle *O* melle *SV* ȝiue to; 238 dele wyþ *C* medele

megge v. [see menge, v.]

meyne, meigne n. [AF meine] household retainers, servants; retinue **Ch1** 2382 meigne P meygne L; 2390 meygne P meyne L; 2393, 2396 meygne; 5657 meigne P men L; 5946 meigne P mene L; 9150 meigne P meyne L; 9030 meigne; 3987 meingne P meyne L; 8313, 11154, 11206 meyne; 5387 nauie P meynye L; 13564 meyne P meynee L; **Ch2** 260, 1583, 3004, 5470, 6910 meyne; 2371 mayne P meyne L; **HS** 3419, 3520, 5060, 7690, 10645 meyne

meke, mekely adj./adv. [ON; cp. OI mjukr] gentle, quiet; benevolent, kind **Ch1** 1471, 3724, 6651, 14958, 15642 meke; 3111 meke P plesaunt L; 8561 mekely; 8536 myldely P mekely L; **Ch2** 2241, 4132, 4786, 6851 meke; 4005 douhteli P mekely L; **HS** 259, 5837, 8645, 10101, 11476 meke; 12262 myke *H* meke *O* myke; 5834 mekely; 1998 meke *CD* mylde; 2869 myldely *C* mekely *O* mydelly; 4044 meke *O* mylde

meke v. [from ON meke, adj.] subdue, chastise; to be humble, become soft **Ch1** 5159 mekes P mekeþ L; 7718 meke; **Ch2** 1092 mekes; 7117, 7310 meke; **HS** 783 mekyþ; 11266, 11478, 12117 mekest; 3908, 5827 mekede; 6575 meken; 1618 meke *C* make *D* makyn

mekenes n. [from ON meke, adj.] humility **Ch1** 3288 mekenes; **Ch2** 4626 mekenesse; **HS** 5938, 10103, 11458, 11461 mekenes; 11422 mekenes *O* myldnese

mekyl n./adj./adv. [see mykelle]

mele n. [OE melu] a meal, food; ground grain **Ch1** 9806, 10273 mele; **HS** 1330 a melys mete; 7234 mele

mele v. [see medle] [OE mælan, ON] speak, engage **Ch1** 9937 mele

melk n. [OE milc] milk **HS** 514, 4845 melk

melodie n. [OF] tunefulness, harmony; performance of music **Ch1** 4006, 11036 melodie; **HS** 4711 melody

melte v. [OE meltan] to melt, dissolve **HS** 5054 melte

membre n. [OF] limbs; sexual organ; component part **Ch1** 1755 membris; **Ch2** 3185 membre; 5427 membres; **HS** 683 membre; 8910 membres

memorye n. [AF memorie (MP)] commemoration **HS** 7959, 10317 memorye

menage n. [see manage, n.]

mencyun n. [OF mencion] account; a reference **HS** 10502 mencyun

mende n. [see amende] [from OF amender, v.] recompense **Ch2** 7370 mende

mende v. [OF amender] alleviate, cure; repent, reform **Ch1** 692 amend P mende L; 2428 amend P mended L; 6451 mend P mende L; 6903 mendid; 7113, 9095 mende; 13902L mended (om. P); **Ch2** 1700, 3337, 4354, 6654, 6711 mend; 1912, 3737, 4822, 5891, 7643 mende; 5517, 8008 mendid; **HS** 8633 mende; 10410 amende *V* mende

mene n. [OF moiien, meen] the tenor voice **Ch1** 11031 mene

mene adj. [OE gemæne] people inferior in rank **Ch1** 5436, 13965 mene folk; 6554 mene; 10976 mener; **Ch2** 4153 mene folk P men & folk L

mene, mone, ment v. (1) [OE mænan] intend, mean, signify; mention, remember **Ch1** 81, 173, 2460 mente; 940, 2338, 8939, 10822, 15854 ment; 214, 327, 2770, 3961, 14205 mones; 7817, 8097, 8982 mene; 802, 1348, 4764, 5497 mone; 14745 neuen P mene L; 8127 menis; 8971 menes; **Ch2** 203, 1150, 4874,

6118, 8082 ment; 3690, 5659, 7968, 8061, 8183 mene; 2879 mone; 3831 menes; 3135, 5374 mones; 1748 mynt P ment L; **HS** 1541, 2178, 8863, 10507, 12281 mene; 8600 menyng; 10889 menes; 6676 menest; 10226 ment; 9402 mente; 7068 mynte; 7231, 10850 meneþ; 10133 meneþ *O* meenes *SV* bimeneþ

mene, ment v. (2) [OE mænan] complain, moan; lament, pity, sympathize **Ch1** 1834, 3465, 8337, 8911 mene; 3825, 8345, 11937, 15027 ment; 8946 mone; 8603 ment P mente L; **Ch2** 3690, 8183 mene; 6747 mone; 5074, 5857, 6165 ment

menge v. [see mong, n.] [OE mengan, mængan] to mix, blend, mingle **Ch1** 2843 nempe P mynge L; 5794 mengyng P megge L; 7864 menged; 7962 menge it P mengyt L; 10154 meng; 10158 mengyng; **Ch2** 7254 menge; **HS** 5358 mengest; 11634 mynged

mengyng ger. [from OE mengan, v.] mingling **Ch1** 7999 mengyng P mengynge L

menyng ger. [from OE mænan, v.] intention; interpretation; remembrance **Ch1** 719, 15641 menyng P menynge L; 5589 menyng; 15925 menyng P meninge L; **Ch2** 526 menyng; **HS** 611, 4358, 11281 menyng; 5210 mennyng; 10503 mencyun *O* menynge

menyuere n. [AF] squirrel fur **Ch1** 10972 menyuere P meneuer L

mensk n. [ON; cp. OI mennska] honored state, respect **Ch2** 2559 mensk

mensk v. [from ON mennska, n.] to adorn **Ch1** 12140 mensk P menske L

merchand, merchaunt n. [AF merchaunt] businessman, pedler **Ch1** 614 merchand; 14263 merchanȝ P marchauntȝ L; **Ch2** 3309 marchandȝ; 4156, 6315 merchant; 4956 merchandes; 6301 marchant; 5476 merchaunt; 6973 merchantȝ; **HS** 5547 marchaunt; 5947 marchaundes; 6315 marchound

merchandise, marchaundie n. [OF] trade, commerce; goods **Ch1** 626 merchandyse; 672 merchandise; 14250L marchaundie (om. P); **Ch2** 6800 merchandise; 6863 merchandie; 8017 merchaundie; **HS** 5794, 5978, 9478 marchauandye; 6354 marchaundyse

merchaunt n. [see merchand, n.]

merched v. [OF marchier] to border on, adjoin **Ch1** 7815 merched P marchen L

mercy n. [OF] pardon, forgiveness, clemency; a fine **Ch1** 551, 3819, 5168, 8578, 9127 mercy; 8441, 8537, 8583 merci; 8529 merci P mercy L; 10352 mercy P meyne (?error) L; **Ch2** 1459, 4154, 5678, 6582, 7986 mercy; 593, 2414, 5211, 6774, 7941 mercie; 6773, 7134, 7598, 7750, 8066 merci; **HS** 162, 2691, 6670, 10004, 11798 mercy; 9177 mercy *O* grase

mercy v. [AF mercier, AL merciare] to forgive; levy a fine **Ch2** 2719 mercied P merced L; 6930 merci; **HS** 5492 mercye

mercyable adj. [OF] forgiving **HS** 3795, 5322 mercyable

mercyment n. [shortened form of OF amerciment] penalty, punishment **HS** 5496, 5498 mercyment

mery adj./adv. [see myry, adj.]

merk n. [see mark, n.]

meruaile, merueile n. [OF] event causing astonishment, surprise; account of a marvel **Ch1** 2249 meruaile P meruaille L; 2803, 4223, 4952, 8044 meruaile; 9252 meruailes; 8044 meruaile P merueille L; **Ch2** 4423, 8163 mervaile; 3221 meruailes; **HS** 2482, 10530 merueyle; 2242, 4072, 6026 meruayle; 133 merueylys; 1823 wndur *C* merueyle *D* ferly; 7876 wunder *O* mervell; 11981 wnder *O* mervale

meruail, meruelle v. [OF merveillier] to be amazed, surprised, astonished **Ch1** 961 meruelle P merueille L; 972 merueyled P merueillede L; 8937 meruailed; 12465 marvailed; 11221 meruails P merueilles L; 11222 meruailand P merueillyng L; **Ch2** 1594 me meruailes P men meruailleþ L; **HS** 517, 1426 merueylde; 11047 merueylede

meruaillus, merueilous adj. [OF merveillos] wonderful, astonishing **Ch1** 3709L merueillous (om. P); 4528 meruailous; 5571 meruaillus P merueillous L; **Ch2** 4324 meruailouse; 5602 merveilous; **HS** 1420, 4074 merueylus; 1752 merueylouse; 5259, 9239, 11038 merueylous; 10224 perylous *OSV* meruelouse

meruaillus, meruellosly, merueylusly adv. [from adj.] wonderfully, horribly, exceedingly **Ch1** 3709 ouer mesure P merueillous L; 7492 meruelik P merueillyke L; 1687 meruelly P merueyloslike L; 12334 mervaily; 13717 meruailous; **Ch2** 2265 meruellosly; **HS** 10298 merueylous; 12077 merueylusly

mes, mese n. (1) [OF, from L missus] dish, serving of food **Ch1** 9158 mes P mees L; **HS** 6619 mese; 6621 mese *O* almus; 6627 mes

mes n. (2) [OF] an affliction **Ch2** 3880L mes (om. P)

mes, messe n. (3) [OF messe] mass, the ceremony **Ch1** 11012, 11028, 14494 messe; 11043, 14235 messes; 7510 mes P messe L; **Ch2** 456, 2289, 4525, 6898, 8242 messe; 2496 cristes messe P cristemesse L; 6995 kandilmesse; **HS** 823, 2297, 6362, 9061, 10425 messe; 10389 messes; 8828 mas

meselle n./adj. [OF mesel, ML misellus] a leper; hospital for lepers **Ch2** 3419 meselle; 3328 meselle houses; **HS** 11466, 11474 mesel; 4129 mesels; 7450 meseles, 10245 meselles

meselrie n. [OF meselerie] leprosy **Ch2** 3423

meselrie; **HS** 10217 meselrye
message n. [OF] a communication; utterance; news; messenger, envoy, courier **Ch1** 1495, 5084, 6420 message; 2484 massage P message L; 3323 massages; **Ch2** 929, 5279, 6208 message; 1941 message P messenger L
messenger, messager n. [OF] courier; envoy **Ch1** 1285, 7872 messengeres P messegers L; 2492, 4760 messengere; 2497, 9000 messenger; 2983 messengeres; 4669, 5470, 5480, 6072, 7903 messengers; 8638 messager; 6527 messagers; **Ch2** 146, 1710, 3513, 6122, 7707 messengers; 651, 3670, 5524, 6657, 7585 messengere; 1048, 6278 messengeres; 2146, 3191, 4054 messenger; 6419 messengres; 7687 messengrs; 4195 marinere P messenger L; 1941 message P messenger L; **HS** 4813, 4818, 8139 messager; 5813 messagers; 12089 messagere
mesurable adj. [OF] moderate, discreet **Ch1** 3788, 3867 mesurable; **HS** 6528, 6536 mesurable
mesure n. [OF] moderation in food or drink; excessive or extreme **Ch1** 2661, 3709, 4032, 5849 mesure; 7493 messure; **Ch2** 3168 mesure; 2943L mesure (om. P); **HS** 390, 3324, 5951, 6530, 7250 mesure
mesure v. [OF mesurer] to make measurements **Ch1** 1848 mesured
mesurly adv. [from OF mesure, n.] moderately **HS** 5452 mesurly
metal, matal n. [OF metal, metail, matal] made of metal **Ch1** 4445 matal P metal L; **Ch2** 6591 metalle; **HS** 6160, 9363 metal
mete n. [OE] food, provisions; dinner, mealtime **Ch1** 5052, 7073, 9803, 10361, 15046 mete; **Ch2** 1326, 2476, 4336, 7980, 8157 mete; **HS** 407, 2363, 5386, 6966, 10362 mete; 4604 metes
mete adj. [OE gemæte] the right size **Ch2** 807 mete
mete, mette v. (1) [OE metan] to meet, encounter; assemble; welcome **Ch1** 3240 met; 3817, 4331, 15614 mett; 538, 2093, 3498, 4610, 9000 mette; 3354, 6209, 8303, 13021 mete; 1485 metis; 2916 mete P met L; 8735 mette P met L; **Ch2** 1445, 4716, 4847, 7694, 7724 mete; 329, 2281, 5499, 7340, 8243 mette; 2745 met; **HS** 180, 2849, 3452, 4496, 8349 mete; 366 mette
mete, mette v. (2) [see dreme, n./v.] [OE mætan] to dream **Ch1** 1394 mette P met L; **Ch2** 2281 mette; **HS** 384 mette; 387 mete; 391 dreme of *C* mete for *D* metyn of; 7580 dremyng *O* in mette
mette, moten v. (3) [OE metan] to take measurements **Ch1** 14346 mette; 9888L meten (P differs); **Ch2** 439 moten P about L
◆ **metegift** adj. [?for mete-ȝife: meat-giver] generous, hospitable **Ch1** 4044 metegift P lyberal L
metesel n. [from OE mete, n.] midday dinner **Ch2** 8154 metesel
metyng ger. [from OE metan, v.] a meeting, gathering **Ch1** 1009, 8736 metyng; **HS** 363 metyng
metir n. [OF metre] metrical verse pattern, poetry **Ch1** 196 metir
mette n. [OE gemet] in measurement **Ch1** 14346 mette P met L
mettis n. [see mette, v. (3)] [OE gemet] a measure **HS** 2906 ples *H* pleys *O* mettis or
meuede, moued v. [AF moveir] to shift, shake; wag the head **Ch1** 6430L meued (P differs); 13378 moued P meoued L; **Ch2** 5046 moued; **HS** 2291 meuede *C* wagged *DH* mevyd
meward pron. [OE] towards me **Ch2** 4200 meward P aȝenward L; 4702 meward
mydelle n. [OE] middle of the body **Ch1** 12089 mydelle P middel L
midsomer, midsomeretide n. [see somer] [OE midsumer] time period about the summer solstice **Ch2** 3368 midsomer; 5501 midsomeretide; 7551 midesomers tide
myght n. [OE miht] power; control, dominion; military might **Ch1** 1300 ryght P myght L; 1269, 3572, 6154, 7709, 9327 myght; 7346, 8540, 9327 might; 6524 myghtes; **Ch2** 21, 1350, 3255, 6411, 8301 myght; **HS** 276, 558, 2213, 7769, 12531 myght; 2 myȝtys
myght, myghty, myghtful adj. [OE miht] powerful, great, strong **Ch1** 5166 myghty; 5570 wilfulle P myghtful L; **HS** 8701 myght
myghtles adj. [OE mihtleas] powerless, helpless **Ch2** 6780 myghtles
mykelle, mekyl, moche n./adj./adv. [see more, most] [ON mikell, OE micel, muchel] great, to a great extent; much, more **Ch1** 53, 1530, 4661, 8366, 12910 mykelle; 1693, 2999 mykelle P mykel L; 3093 inouh P mykel L; 12037 mykille P mykel L; 2605, 2293, 3548, 8342, 9327 mykille; 10209 mikille; 3091, 4515, 5854, 9168, 15347 mikelle; 3945L muche (om. P); **Ch2** 660, 3715, 4750, 6709, 7921 mykelle; 1756, 2853 mikelle; 916L muche (om. P); 1127, 1756 mikelle P muche L; 786L mikel (P differs); 2559L, 3482L muche (P differs); 1933 mykelle P muchel L; **HS** 255 mochyl; 1384, 3892, 4013, 11386 moche; 1142 moche *H* meche; 2644 mykyl GLOSS B moche; 1142 moche *D* meche; 166 mochyl *D* gret; 258 mochyl *CD* gret; 255 mochyl *C* ful redy; 276, 374 mochyl *C* mekyl; 376 gret *C* mekyl; 1088, 2007, 1911, 2156 moche *C* mekyl *D* meche; 1530 moche *D* mechil; 3117, 3529, 4764, 5174, 11386 moche *O* mekyll; 10094 meke *O* mekyll *S* mochel *V* muchel; 2644, 5947, 8135, 8366, 8490 mykyl

mykillehed n. [from OE micel, muchel, adj.] size, magnitude **Ch1** 12822 mykillehed P mikelhed L

myht, myght, mote v. [see may, moun, mot, myght, v.]

mylde adj. [see meke, adj.] [OE, ON] merciful; forgiving **Ch1** 14419 mylde; **HS** 5825, 5840 mylde; 5826 mylder

mile n. [OE mil, from L] measure of distance; time spent in going a mile **Ch1** 655, 685 myle; 14568 miles; **Ch2** 439, 798, 5089, 7168, 8156 myle; 2991, 5350 mile; 4920 miles; **HS** 64 myle

♦ **millers, milleners** [OF milier] a military unit of a thousand men **Ch1** 3509 milleners P mylers L; 13005 millers P milers L

mylnes n. [OE mylen, myln] a military engine devised by Richard I **Ch2** 4303 mylnes P milnes L

mynde n. (1) [OE gemynd] memory, remembrance; reason, intention; thought **Ch1** 1358 mynde; **Ch2** 3526, 5152 mynde; **HS** 727, 1013, 8660, 11566 mynde; 7709 mynde *O* þe menchyone; 9917, 10864 mynde *O* menynge

mynde n. (2) [?from OE gemynd] multitude, crowd **Ch1** 1884, 2605 mynde; 15680 myndes

mynde adj. [OE gemynde] thoughtful, kind; mindful of **Ch1** 876 mynde; **HS** 727, 5116, 5313, 6502 mynde

myne n. [OF mine] tunnel, passage **HS** 10745 myne

myne v. [OF miner] undermine, dig a tunnel **Ch1** 6734 myand (?error) P mynynge L; **Ch2** 4441, 4443 myned

mynge v. [see mynt] [OE mynegian] mention **Ch1** 2843 nempe P mynge L

minystre n. [OF] ministers **Ch2** 6902 minystres; 7623 ministres

ministre v. [OF ministrer] provide religious services **Ch2** 2001 ministre

minour n. (1) [AF minere] miner for metals, coal; one who undermines fortifications **Ch1** 3403 minours P mynours L; 8039 grauers P mynours L; **Ch2** 4441 minoures; **HS** 10738, 10741 mynur; 10739 mynurs

minour n. (2) [OF menour] a Franciscan, minorite **Ch2** 8073 Minours; **HS** 9606 frere menor

mynsyng ger. [?OE mynsung] remembering **Ch1** 324 mynsyng; **Ch2** 4935 mynsyng P myndyng L

mynstere, mynstire n. [OE mynster] church, cathedral **Ch1** 14522 mynstire P mynstre L; **Ch2** 1588 mynstere P churche L; 1919L minstre (P differs); 7346 mitere (?error for minstere); **HS** 2588 mynstyr

mynstral n. [OF menestral] singer, musician; story-teller **Ch1** 4694 mynstrals; 11141 mynstrals P mynestrales L; **HS** 4691, 4704, 4711, 4717, 4732 mynstral

mynstralcie, mynstralsy n. [AF menestralsie] music, entertainment **Ch1** 3994, 3997 mynstralcie P mynstrecye L; 11035 mynstralcie P menestralcie L; **HS** 4720, 4754, 4778 mynstralsy

mynt v. [see may, mene, v.] [OE myntan] intend, plan; attempt **Ch1** 7121, 12059 mynt; **Ch2** 1748 mynt P ment L

miracle n. [OF; L miraculum] a marvel; extraordinary event; miracle plays **Ch1** 7654, 8542, 15417 miracle; 5640, 15346 miracles; 14487 myracle; **Ch2** 810, 814, 2038 miracle; **HS** 3888, 3896, 10526 myracle; 4642, 4643 myracles

myre n. [ON, cp. OI myrr] marsh, bog **Ch1** 3059 myres; **Ch2** 1737 myre; 7454, 7576 mire

myry, mery adj./adv. [OE myrige] cheerful, merry; happily **Ch1** 1439 mery P myry L; 1442 mery; 5619 miri; 7203 myri P myry L; 7762 meri P mury L; 11147 myry P merye L; **Ch2** 728 myri; 2038 myrie; 3194, 3483 mirie; 7505 miry; **HS** 4263 mery; 7484 myry; 1130 wiþ al merþe *C* mad hem mery *D* al mery; 2860 ioye (n.) *C* mery

myrk n./adj. [OE mirce, ON myrkr] darkness, night; dark in color **Ch1** 259 myrke P merk L; 6471 myrk P derk L; 6473 mirk; **Ch2** 1791L myrke (om. P); 4376 mirke; 5422 mirk; **HS** 2164 myrk GLOSS BH derk

mirknes n. [from OE mirce, adj.] darkness **Ch1** 9131L, 14282L merknesse (om. P); 9691 mirknes P derknesse L

myrrour n. [OF mirour] a mirror **HS** 6503 myrrour

mirth, merþe n. [OE myrgþ] happiness, delight; rejoicing; entertainment **Ch1** 4717 mirth; 5485 mirth P myrthe L; 11148 sounde of glew P gret murþe L; **HS** 1130 wiþ al merþe *C* mad hem mery *D* al mery he spak

mis n. (1) [see misse, v.] [OE, ON] offense, sin; guilt, wickedness, evil **Ch1** 1196, 4737 mys; **Ch2** 6567, 7223, 7372 mys; **HS** 634, 8600 mys

mys n. (2) [OE mus, mys] mice **HS** 5385, 5387 mys

mis adj./adv. [see amysse, adv., misse, v.] [from OE mys] wrong, wicked; sinfully, improperly **Ch2** 4061 a mysse; 6286 mis; 7223 mys; **HS** 152, 4552, 4844, 8686 mys

mysauentour, mysauenture n. [OF] mishap, bad fortune, accident **Ch1** 5105 misauentour P misauentur L; 9097 mysauntour P mysauentour L; **Ch2** 1664 misauentoure; 4114 misauentour; 6630 misauentours; **HS** 515, 3291, 3334, 5952 mysauenture; 2768 a mysauenture *C* euyl auenture *O* yll aventure; 6365 mysauentur *O* mysauentures

misbede v. [OE misbeodan] maltreat, injure **Ch1** 2082 misbede P misbed L; **Ch2** 2523, 3205, 5841 misbede

mysbeleue n. [from OE belefan] false religion, heresy **HS** 10035 mysbeleue

misbileued v. [see misleued] [from OE belefan] to hold a false religious belief; be heathen, pagan; faithless **Ch1** 14574 misleued P misbileued L; **HS** 9860 mysbeleue; 7736 mysbeleuyng/r **misberyng** ger. [see mysbore, v.] [from OE beren] illegal warfare **Ch2** 8206 misberyng

mysbetide v. [from OE bitidan] be defeated, fail **Ch1** 11567 mysbetide P misbytide L

mysbore, misborn v. [from OE beran] acted foolishly or wickedly **Ch2** 6385, 8132 misborn; **HS** 1208 mysbore

mysbreyd n. [from OE brægd] misdeed **HS** 94 mysbreyde; 3494 mysbreyd

mischance n. [OF meschance] misfortune, accident **Ch1** 431 myschaunce P meschaunce L; 4714, 13991 mischance; 7178 mischefe P meschaunce L; 7497 meschaunche P meschaunce L; **Ch2** 2521, 3807, 5633, 6403, 7908 mischance; 3907 mischuos (adj.) P myschance L; **HS** 3383, 4103, 4623, 5666 myschaunce; 2062 myschaunce *C* sorowe *D* myshap; 2218 myschaunce *C* comerawnns

◆ **myschaunsful** adj. [from OF meschance] unfortunate, unlucky **HS** 3926 myschaunsful *F* mischaunful *H* myschaunceful *O* mysschamful; 4626 myschefful *F* mischeful *O* mischansfull

mischefe n. [OF meschef] misfortune, affliction, trouble, plight **Ch1** 944 myschefe P meschef L; 2488, 9716, 13545 mischefe P meschef L; 7178, 13975 mischefe P meschaunce L; 8487 mischefe P sorewe L; 15538 mischeue; **Ch2** 2515 mischeue P myschance L; 1763L myschiffe (P differs); 2233, 6989 mischeue; **HS** 9167 myschef *O* sorowe

mischeue v. [OF meschever] suffer harm **Ch2** 4242 mischeue; 8040 mischeues

mischuos adj./adv. [from OF mischef] causing distress **Ch1** 13549L mescheuously (P differs); **Ch2** 3907 mischuos P myschance (n.) L

miscomforte n. [from OF comfort] distress **Ch1** 2964 miscomforte P mysconfort L

myscumforte v. [from OF comforter, cunforter, v.] to be distressed **HS** 8512, 8573 myscumforte

misdede n. [OE misdæd] sin, crime; damage **Ch1** 1240 mysdedis P skaþes L; 5100 misdede; 8490L mysdedes (P differs); **Ch2** 3576, 4935, 5775, 5911, 7077 misdede; **HS** 1016, 3495, 4395, 8600, 12106 mysdede

misdo, misdede v. [OE misdon] do wrong, to sin, do harm **Ch1** 3183 mysdos; 13618 misdone P hys misdede (n.) L; 14754 misdon; **Ch2** 3166 misdo; **HS** 1054, 1886, 3493, 6832, 7933 mysdo; 5838 mysdede; 781 mysdedyst; 1101, 4340, 7354 mysdoun

◆ **misdryuen** ppl. [from OE drifan] offending **Ch2** 2831 misdryuen

miseyse n. [AF meseise (MP)] discomfort, distress **Ch1** 2442L meseysey (error) (om. P); **Ch2** 796 miseyse; **HS** 1097, 6059 mysese

misfalle v. [from OE fallan] be grieved, defeated **Ch1** 1999 misfalle P mysfalle L; 13699 misfalle; 10563 misfelle P mysfel L; **HS** 10893 mysfalle

misfare, misferd v. [OE misfaran] come to grief, fail, be injured, die **Ch1** 4879 misferd; 5909 misferd P þus ferde L; 6811 misferd P mys spedde L; 7851 misfare P misferde L; 15602 misferd; **Ch2** 1513, 7032 misfare; 2877 misfore; 3440, 3908, 5494, 5808, 6709 misferd; **HS** 5270, 6062, 6630 mysfare; 5256 mysferde; 3650, 6568 mysgone; 3992 mysgoun; 12377 mysȝede

mysȝyue ppl. [from OE giefan] misgiven **HS** 10986 mysȝyue

mishap n. [from ON happ] misfortune, accident **Ch2** 2482, 2838 mishap; 4337 mishappes; **HS** 2062 myschaunce *C* sorowe *D* myshap

mishappes v. [from OE happen] to have bad luck **Ch1** 4910 if þou spede not P for þou myshappedest; 9892 mishapped; 12782 mishapned P myshapped L; **Ch2** 7016 mishapnes

mishappenyng, mishappyng ger. [from OE happen, v.] misfortune **Ch2** 1672 mishappyng P mys schapyng L; 1758 mishappyng; 7037 myshappenyng

myshope v. [from OE hopian] to despair **HS** 8443 myshope

misleued, misleuande v. [from OE leuen] to lack faith or belief; to be in doubt **Ch1** 1328 misleuande P myslyuande L; 14574 misleued P misbileued L; **Ch2** 199 misleued; **HS** 7736 mysbeleuyng *O* myslefande

mysleuyng ger. [from OE misleuen, v.] unbelief, paganism **Ch1** 1340 mysleuyng P mysleuynge L; **Ch2** 7819 mislyuyng

myslike n. [from OE like, n.] unhappiness **HS** 5167 myslyke

mislyke v. [OE mislician] to offend, disturb **Ch1** 2411 mislyke P myslyke L; 4458 mysliked; 2478 mislyked P myslyked L; **Ch2** 4300, 4314 mislikes

misnam v. [from OE nimen, v.] commit an offense **Ch2** 5190 misnam

mispaye v. [OF mespaier, mispaier] to displease, anger, irritate **Ch1** 7696L mispaye (om. P); **Ch2** 4241 mispaied; 7906 mispayed; **HS** 490 myspaye; 11836 myspayd

misproude n./adj. [from OE prud, prut] arrogant person; haughty **Ch1** 10764L mysproude (om. P); 13782 misproude P mysproud L; **HS** 3049 mysproud; 3497 mysproud *H* mysprout; 8624 ouerdo proud *O* ouer mysprowed

myssay v. [from OE secgan] speak ill of, insult, slander **Ch1** 3457 missaid P missayde L; 4871 myssay; **HS** 6886, 7110 myssey; 4853, 4909, 8718 mysseye; 3484 mysseydyst; 6431 mysseyd

missawe n. [from OE saue] insult, slander **HS** 3496, 6893 myssawe; 778 myssawe *C* gret awe *D* þat sawe

misse v. [OE missan] miss, lose the way; lack **Ch2** 5604 misse; **HS** 10487 mysse; 7872 myssed; 1294 mysse GLOSS BH fayle

myst n. [OE] weather condition **HS** 1423 myst

mistake v. [ON] make a mistake, transgress **Ch1** 5088L y mystok me (P differs); 5986L mystaken (om. P); **Ch2** 3382 mistake

mister, mester n. [OF mester] an office; occupation, profession or trade; need, necessity **Ch1** 582, 7078, 11334 mystere P mester L; **Ch2** 2291 mister; 3630L mestere (om. P); 4196 mistere P mester L; 4785 mystere; **HS** 1202 mystere; 4279 myster; 6862 myster GLOSS BH nede; 3949 craft *O* myster; 5087, 6342, 10884 nede *O* myster

mystrouyng v. [ON; cp. OI mistrua, v.] distrust **HS** 3609 mystrouyng *O* wand lysand

myswent v. [see misfare, v.] [OE miswendan] err; transgress **HS** 9521 myswent *O* myswente

mitere n. [OF mitre, L mitra] a bishop's cap **Ch2** 7346 mitere; **HS** 11114, 11116 myter

mythed v. [OE miþan] restrain oneself **Ch1** 13083 mythed P meþed L

mo adj./adv. [see more, most]

moble n. [OF moeble] movable possessions **Ch2** 3556 mobles P noblis L

moble adj. [OF mueble, adj.] movable, changing **Ch2** 7298 moble

moche n./adj./adv. [see mykelle]

mod n. [MDu modde] mud, mire; murky water **Ch2** 5830, 7454 mod

mode n. [OE mod] mind, character, temper; arrogance, anger **Ch1** 1280, 3222, 4482, 5115, 14419 mode P mod L; 3186L mod (P differs); **HS** 5840, 10193, 10238 mode

moder n. [OE modor] mother; the Virgin Mary; ancestress **Ch1** 846, 2639, 5573, 6134, 7929 moder; 840, 2076, 3188, 5784, 6247 modere; **Ch2** 842, 3776, 4663, 5664, 6515 moder; 5675 modere; 382, 825 stepmoder; **HS** 1058, 1066, 1093, 2585, 3857 modyr; 6596, 8078 moder

mody adj. [OE modig] arrogant, angry **Ch1** 3709 mody

♦ **mokerard** n. [?ON; cp. OI myki] a miser **HS** 6232 mokerard

mokerers n. [?ON; ME mokeren, v.] misers, hoarders **HS** 6067, 6070 mokerers

molde n. [OE] earth; the soil **Ch1** 442 erth molde; 9893, 11172, 15451 molde; 4230 molde P mold L; **HS** 7024, 10741, 11378 molde

mone, moyne n. (1) [OE mona] the moon **Ch1** 3364, 3369, 3372 mone; 7959 moyne P mone L; **HS** 2233 mone; 2240 mone *D* mone lyȝt

mone n. (2) [OF moneie] money; a bribe **Ch1** 8881 mone; **Ch2** 5736, 6185, 6993, 7008, 7526 mone; **HS** 7002 mone

mone n. (3) [?OE *manan, v.] moaning, lamentation; weeping, sorrow, anxiety, regret **Ch1** 930, 2434, 3825, 5980, 9091 mone; 5369 mone P mon L; 7780 mon; 15144L mone (om. P); **Ch2** 2273, 3710, 4314, 4818, 4956 mone; 3959 vow P mone L; **HS** 698, 3176, 4025, 7455, 10847 mone

mone v. (1) [see mene, mone, v. (1)] [ON, cp. OI muna] admonish; reflect, remember; suppose, imagine **Ch1** 802, 4764, 8975 mone; 356 mon P mone L; 214, 327, 14205 mones; **Ch2** 2135, 2879 mone; 5374 mones; **HS** 1141, 7988, 12527 mone; 4766, 5008 mones; 11896 monne; 1119 mone GLOSS BH warne

mone v. (2) [prob. from OE *manan] lament, grieve, utter moans **Ch1** 7804, 8946 mone; 8133, 8655 mons; **Ch2** 6747 mone; **HS** 7675 mones

monenday n. [OE monan-dæg] Monday **Ch2** 3605 monenday

monessed v. [OF monester] admonish **Ch1** 9927 monessed P bad L

moneth n. [OE monaþ] a month's time; months in a year **Ch1** 6080 moneth; 298 monyth; 10599 moneth P monþe L; **Ch2** 213, 2715, 3569, 6631, 8331 moneth; 545, 3478, 5035, 7977, 8347 monethes; 735 monethis; 1623, 2617 moneþes; **HS** 6405 moneþ; 2874, 2885 moneþes; 3815 twel monþe; 7778 twelue monþe; 9087, 9089, 9095 twelf month; 9179 twelfmonþe; 10759 twelue moneþ

mong n. [see menge, v.] [OE gemang] a mixture; confusion; association **Ch1** 5794 mong P monge L; 6435, 7278 monge

monk, munk n. [OE munuc, from L.] monk; friar, canon **Ch1** 6947, 6957, 7143, 8891, 14709 monk; 6895, 6943, 6951, 6974 monke; 6985 mokes (error) P monkes L; 8887, 14642, 14787 monkes; 14626 monkes P monke L; **Ch2** 2010, 3012, 4248, 6183, 7966 monke; 4238, 4257, 5755, 6451, 8295 monk; 1985, 2784, 3324, 5111, 5186 monkes; **HS** 171, 317 munk; 11087 monkes; 11111 monk

monkhed, munkhede n. [from monk, n.] monastic life, monasticism **Ch1** 6972 monkhed P monkhod L; **HS** 201 munkhede *C* munkis wede

more, mo, mest n. [OE mare] subject larger in size or amount **Ch1** 1269, 4786, 5854, 6639,

7109 more; 7556, 8093, 13572 mo; **Ch2** 852, 1917, 3208, 5020, 7528 more; 480, 1420, 7803 mo; 6609 meste; **HS** 135, 679, 1006, 9365, 11434 more; 517, 2883, 7725, 10481, 12584 mo

more, mare, most, mest adj./adv. [OE mara, mæst] more, greater, higher; the biggest **Ch1** 295, 2327, 6103, 7090, 9119 more; 7243, 7261, 7565 mo; 300 mest P most L; 510 mast P principale L; 18, 1778, 1966, 2834, 3015 mast; 2325 maste P mest L; 3547, 11128 maste; 2560 mest; 1276L moste (om. P); 725, 2392, 4041, 6967, 8434 most; 4862, 9379, 12481 moste; 4967, 7056, 12481 moste P most L; 2064, 5989, 13443 mare; **Ch2** 735, 1126, 3088, 5747, 8092 mo; 781 mare; 969, 1235, 2491, 3770, 5669 more; 609, 3173, 4683, 5394, 7726 most; 2183, 2258 meste; 2623, 3149, 4067, 4402, 4650 maste; 3067, 5598 moste; **HS** 1052, 3055, 6026, 8335, 12614 more; 2636, 6280, 8061, 11530, 12568 most; 4472 moste; 6767 mest

more n. [OE mor] wasteland, moor, heath **Ch2** 5821, 5830, 7853, 8212 more; 7573, 7848, 7940 mores

mored ppl. [from OE mor, n.] rooted; moored **Ch1** 15805 mored P ymored L

moreyne, moryne n. [OF morine] plague, death **Ch1** 15689 moreyne P moryne L; 15760 manqualme P moryne L; **HS** 1369 moryne

morn, morowe, morwe, morue, mornyng n. [OE morgen] morning, dawn; the next day **Ch1** 818, 1180, 5544, 5548, 8987 morn; 1181, 9348, 11842 mornyng; 1681, 3391, 5542 morn tide; 9334 morne tide; 8142, 9116 to morn; 2434 morowe P morwe L; 8964 to morne P to morewen L; **Ch2** 1179 morn P morwe L; 319, 1660, 3977, 7420, 7595 mornyng; 906 morow; 2279, 3969, 4710, 7513, 8337 morn; 3838 morne P morwen L; 4371 morne; 6673, 7649 to morn; 7587 mornes; 2267L morwe (P differs); **HS** 9129, 10489, 11115 morn; 9450, 9741, 9393 morne; 1577 morow; 236, 373 morue; 375 þe day *C* at morowen; 245 to morue *C* tomorwun; 3102 morun *F* moru *H* morwe; 10418 morne *SV* morwen; 10610 morn *SV* morwe; 363 morue *C* morwyn

morne v. [OE murnan] to grieve for; worry, be sad **Ch1** 9386 morne; 2442L (add, l. 6) mournes; **Ch2** 383 murne; 3429 morne; 2297 mournand; **HS** 5677, 8536 mornyng; 6133 morenand; 11970 mornyng *O* murnande

morselle, musseles n. [OF] a bite, a mouthful; a delicacy **Ch1** 12364L musseles (P differs); **Ch2** 1337 morselle; **HS** 10066 morselles *V* mosseles; 10067 morsel *V* mossel

morter n. [OF mortier, L mortarium] cement, plaster **Ch1** 7845, 7864, 7865 morter

mosard, musard [OF musarde, musart] fool, wretch, villain **Ch2** 5618 mosard; 6422 musard

◆ **moshon** n. [?AF musket: sparrow-hawk; OF muissuns (Wace)] a sparrow **Ch1** 14084 moshon P mischeroun L

mostred, mustird v. [OF mostrer] show, demonstrate **Ch1** 6524 mustird P schewed L; **Ch2** 5119 mostred

mot, mote v. [see may, moun, mot, v.]

mote n. [OF] walled embankment **Ch2** 4079 kastelle mote

mote v. [OE motian] argue, complain; plead a cause **Ch2** 1418, 6524 mote; **HS** 2701 pletede *C* motyn *D* motedyn; 9810 mote GLOSS BH plete

moten v. [see may, moun, v., and mette, v. (3)]

motoun n. [OF mouton] mutton **Ch2** 4330 motoun

moued v. [see meued]

mountayn, mouns, mountes n. [OF montaigne, AF mount] mountain or hill, a mountain range **Ch1** 9081 montayn; 1885, 3320, 3326, 6874 mountayns; 2737 mountanes; 13378 mountayn P montayn L; 3256 mountayne; 3262, 7841 mount; 3331 mounte; 11511 mouns P mountȝ L; 13378 mountayn P montayn L; 13467 mountayns P mountes L; **Ch2** 1950, 7579, 7848 mountayns; 3954, 4750, 5821 mountayn; 4712, 4762, 4831, 5013 mount; **HS** 2268, 10766 mounteyne

mountouns n. [OF montance] the amount of **HS** 5770 mountouns

mouth n. [OE muþ, muþa] mouth **Ch1** 74, 2028, 8972, 13474, 15856 mouth; 8078 mouht; 8658, 8926, 12723 mouthe; **Ch2** 678, 1337, 4584, 6828, 7283 mouth; **HS** 98, 111, 218, 2859 mouþe; 2639 mouþ; 6214 mouth

mowe n. [OF moe, moue] grimace; derisive expression **HS** 3958 mowe

◆ **mucche** n. [see muccheþ, v.] ?a place for hiding valuables **HS** 6229 mucche

◆ **muccheþ** v. [?OF muchier] to hoard something **HS** 6233 muccheþ

muk n. [ON; cp. OI myki] excrement, dung, waste **HS** 2300 muk hepe *D* muk hyl; 2301 muk *D* muk hil; 6546 [MS *O*, l. 92] muke hyll

mul n. [cf. OE myl, MDu mul] rubbish **HS** 6200 mul

mule n. [OE, OF mul] a mule **Ch2** 4336 mules

multiplie v. [OF multeploier] increase, grow; produce offspring **Ch1** 1881 multiplied P multeplyed L; 7245 multiplie; 6386 puplise P multeplie L

munk n. [see monk]

munkhed n. [see monkhede]

musik n. [OF musique, L musica] music **Ch1** 3998 musik

musyng ger. [from OF muser] investigation;

pondering **Ch1** 7859 lotes kestyng P musyng L

N

nacouns n. [OF nacion] a nation, race, people **Ch1** 4152 nacouns P nacions L; 14252 nacoun P nacion L

nages n. [OF nage, nache] buttocks **Ch2** 6713 nages

nayle n. [OE nægl] a nail; fingernail **Ch2** 1734 nayle P chanel L; 643 nayles; 4912 iren nayles; **HS** 9156 nayles

naked adj. [OE nacod] unclothed, nude **Ch1** 3164, 9786, 11933 naked; 6517 nakyd P naked L; 7371 nakid P naked L; **Ch2** 7065, 8207 naked; **HS** 5699, 7519, 11767 naked

nakned v. [from OE nacod] to make bare, naked **Ch2** 6713 nakned

nam v. [see nym, nam, nomen, v.]

namcouht, namecouth adj. [OE namcuþ] well-known, renowned **Ch1** 13457 namcouht P name couþ L; **Ch2** 3426 namecouth; **HS** 3619 namecouth

name n. [OE nama, pl. namen] name; personified virtue or vice; reputation **Ch1** 136, 2245, 4412, 6320, 8623 name; 121, 1925, 4078, 5912, 7253 names; **Ch2** 6, 1666, 3036, 5789, 8241 name; 570, 3135, 3515, 6830, 7761 names; **HS** 59, 1051, 3604, 6844, 12224 name; 9031 names

name v. [OE namian, genamian] give a name to; praise **Ch1** 333, 1927 named; 9021 named P alosed L; **HS** 31, 8308 name; 2039 named; 11641 namest

namely, namly adv. [OE nameliche] especially, in particular, chiefly **Ch1** 13942 namly; 15254 nameli P nameliche L; **Ch2** 3565, 6997 namely; 4521 namly; **HS** 1023, 7888, 11323 namly; 2725 namlych; 4151 namely; 847 namlyche *C* sertaynly *D* namely; 10393 namly *SV* nomeliche; 1242 specyaly *C* namely

nape n. [?OF hanap, goblet] nape of the neck **Ch2** 5174 nape

narow adv. [see nerewe, v.] [OE nearu] closely, strictly **Ch1** 9074 narow; **Ch2** 278 narow P straite holdes L

♦ **nasee** adj. [see nese] [AF; cp. ML nasatus] having a mutilated nose **Ch2** 4150, 4167, 4175 nasee

naselle n. [OF nasel] noseguard of a helmet **Ch1** 9894 naselle P nasel L; 8438 naselle P vyser L

nat adv. [see noght, nouht, adv.]

nature n. [OF; L natura] characteristics **Ch1** 7967 nature

nauie, nauy n. [AF navei] fleet of warships **Ch1** 2982, 4939, 5823, 13868 nauie; 5387 nauie P meynye L; 2146, 4562 nauye; 6502 flete P nauye L; 3146, 5753, 15200 nauy; **Ch2** 3614 nauy; 3621, 3936, 4191, 5079 nauie

nece, nyftes n. [OF; OE nift] niece **Ch1** 832, 11854, 11961, 12166 nece; 10805 nyftes; **Ch2** 538L (add, l. 39) nece

neddre n. [OE nædre] adder **HS** 4174, 4175 neddre; 5275 addres

nede n. [OE ned] necessity, compulsion; what is required **Ch1** 587, 2037, 4349, 6582, 9069 nede; 3120, 5804, 8904 nedes; 6159, 7330, 9615 nedis; 12235 nedis P nedes L; **Ch2** 406, 4230, 5596, 6859, 7845 nede; 2782, 6747 nedes; 772, 2448, 6268, 7574 nedis; **HS** 155, 2250, 6306, 9602, 12369 nede; 10938, 11528 nedes; 2919 neyde

nede v. [OE nedan, neodian] to force; to be obliged to **Ch1** 4773, 4783, 5002, 8363 nede; 9965, 12235 nedis; 7110 nedes P nede L; **Ch2** 3294, 5958 nedes; 6508 neid; 7726, 8353 nede; **HS** 1229 nedyþ; 2891 nedyd; 7839 neded; 8898, 11203 nedeþ; 11514 nedeþ *O* aghte

nede, nedely adv. [from OE ned, n.] necessarily **Ch1** 1071, 13605, 14010 nedly; 4282 nedeli P nede L; 7926 nedeli P nedlike L; 14896 nedely; **Ch2** 250 nedly; 3294 nedes burd P nedes byhowed L; **HS** 202, 3468, 6118, 7858, 11698 nede; 5668, 9941 nedes; 10084, 11367, 12398, 12410, 12593 nedely; 6466 nedly *O* nedlynge

negh, neigh v. [OE] to approach, move close to **Ch1** 3012 nehed P neyghed L; 3266 neghed P neighed L; 3345 negh P neighe L; 4982 neihed P neighed L; 5354, 13019 neghed P neyghed L; 9711, 13019 neghed; 12916 neghes P neigheþ L; 12375 neihed P neghed L; **Ch2** 936 negh P neyhe L; 8154 neghed; 6695 neghand nehi; **HS** 9913 neyghed nye

negh, nehi, ny, nygh adj./adv. [see nere]

neihburs n. [OE nehebur] neighbors; fellow citizens **Ch1** 5846 neihburs P neygheburs L; **HS** 1352 neghbur; 1346, 2904, 2924, 3930 neghburs

neihand adv. [see nerhand]

nek, nekke n. [OE hnecca] the neck **Ch1** 3823, 8439, 11158 nek; 3161 hals P nekke L; 8535, 12561 nek P nekke L; 12113 hede P nekke L; 1815, 3005, 3008 nekkes; **Ch2** 6821 nek; **HS** 2122, 11559 nekke; 2688 hals GLOSS B necke GLOSS H nek

nemne, nempe v. [see neuen, v.] [OE] to name, specify, speak of; ppl. nemned: renouned **Ch1** 2843 nempe P mynge L; 7251, 10902, 11146 neuen P nemne L; **Ch2** 385 neuen P nemne L; 738 neuen P nemene L; 7535 nemnid; **HS** 2287 nemnede *C* nemelyd; 1910 neuene *C* nemen *D* neuene; 2309 nemnede *C* nemelyd *D* nempned *F* namede; 6785 nemne *O* neuene; 8247 nemne *F* whenne (?error) *O* neven; 10506 neuene *SV* nempne

nere, negh, nehi, next, ny adj./adv./prep. near by, close; nearly, almost **Ch1** 104, 2792, 6343, 9268, 10599 nere; 1650, 8275 nehi P ney L;

2792 nere P nerre L; 5016, 8334, 8431, 9922, 12195 nehi; 8779 neih; 9711 neghi; 10166 nehie; 5354 ner; 5846 nere P ney L; 2669, 3793, 4935, 7768, 11914 next; 3508 neste P next L; 7755 next P nest L; 10432 heire P nerrer L; 13019 nehi P ney L; **Ch2** 804, 2295, 4985, 6695, 8041 nehi; 936, 2740, 3931 nerre; 2365 nerre P nyr L; 45, 3902, 4989, 5346, 8154 nere; 591, 2228, 3894, 5663, 7841 next; 5405 aldernext; **HS** 971, 4041, 5895, 9247, 12056 nere; 7373 ner; 2500, 7486 ny; 2703, 8478, 8954 nygh; 10908 nye; 4408, 9207, 9646, 10352 nest; 1352, 4749, 8879, 11381, 12216 next; 9130, 11065 nexte; 2522 almost *CD* ny *O* nere; 4462, 4728 nygh *O* nere; 7504, 7506 nygh *O* nerehande; 9913 neyghed nye *O* ne hye *SV* hym neih; 860 nygh *C* nerhand

nerewes v. [from OE nearu, adj.] to make narrow, constrict **Ch1** 4533 nerewes P nareweþ L

nerhand, neihand adv. [OE] close to; nearby **Ch1** 10566 nerhand P nerhande L; **Ch2** 1591 nerhand P þe nyr L; 3983 neihand; 4104 nerhand P neyhand L; **HS** 5425 nyrhonde; 6093 nerhond; 860 nygh *C* nerhand; 10544 almost *SV* nerhonde; 7504, 7506 nygh *O* nerehande

nesch, nessh n. [OE hnesce] soft, easy, comfortable; phr.: all times, all circumstances **Ch2** 4166 nesshe & hard; 5609, 6283 nessh or hard; 5822, 7313, 7355 nesch & hard

nese, nose n. [see nasee, naselle] [OE nasu] the nose **Ch1** 1817 nese P nose L; **Ch2** 4114 nese P nose plat L; **HS** 704 nose

neste n. [OE] bird's nest **Ch1** 10044 neste; 10137 nestes

nete n. [OE neat] cattle **Ch2** 2867 nete; **HS** 5120 nete

nette n. [OE] net for catching fish or game **Ch1** 14059L nettes (om. P); **Ch2** 1297 nettes; 1298 nette

nettille, netle n. [OE netele] a nettle; fig.: sin, vice; an enemy **Ch2** 6779, 6780 nettille; **HS** 7516, 7521, 7523 netles

neuen v. [see nemne, v.] [ON; cp. OI nefna] to name, speak of **Ch1** 138, 2285, 7898 neuen; 7251 neuen P nemne L; 14745 neuen P mene L; **Ch2** 7011, 8329 neuen; 385 neuen P nemne L; 738 neuen P nemene L; **HS** 6380, 12283 neuene; 7682 neuende; 1910 neuene *C* nemen; 2918 neuene *O* newyn; 6785 nemne *O* neuene; 8247 nemne *F* whenne (?error) *O* neven; 8272 nemned *O* nevende; 10162, 10506 neuene *SV* nempne

neuer adv. [OE næfre] never **Ch1** 80, 2551, 5104, 7135, 9174 neuer; **Ch2** 1720, 3025, 4625, 6603, 8308 neuer; **HS** 119, 230 neuere; 538, 1348, 1855, 2719, 10678 neuer; 2250, 5480, 9063, 10275, 10361 neure

neuerþeles adv. [see noþeles, adv.]

neueu, neuow, niouh n. [OF nevou, neveu] nephew **Ch1** 4305, 4605 neuoȝ P neuews L; 4393, 4852, 4872 neuow; 4707 nouowe; 5199 neueue P neuewe L; 10431 neuow; 10805 neuous P neueus L; 10429, 10467 niouh P neuew L; 12399 nevowe P neuew L; **Ch2** 2842 neueu; 1668, 1704, 2540, 5345 neuow; 1697 neuow P nevew L; 2464 nevow

new, neuly adj./adv. [OE neowe, niwe] fresh; made recently; renewed **Ch1** 770, 1894, 4045 new; 1240, 3468, 6722, 8573, 9042 newe; **Ch2** 1992, 2267, 4275, 5956, 7950 new; 2877, 3814, 6048, 7217, 8024 newe; 1653 neuly P newely L; **HS** 1980, 2708, 6429, 10066, 12270 newe

newe v. [OE neowian, niwian] to renew, resume **Ch2** 3998 newed; **HS** 12261 newe; 9323 neweþ

newyng ger. [from OE niwian] produce **HS** 898 þyngys *C* tythyng *D* newyng

nyce adj./n. [OF] foolish, wanton, wicked; stupid **Ch1** 5628, 13828, 15456, 15457 nyce; **Ch2** 5689, 5880 nyce; 6711 nisse

nycely adv. [from nyce, adj.] wickedly **Ch2** 7223 nycely

nycete n. [OF] foolishness **Ch2** 3005 nycete; **HS** 4723 nycete

nyftes n. [see nece]

nyght n. [OE niht] nighttime; darkness **Ch1** 670, 2431, 4415, 7988, 9325 nyght; 6611, 7436, 7511 night; 5080 nyghtes; **Ch2** 692, 1840, 3967, 6308, 8335 nyght; 4243, 5599 night; **HS** 297, 464, 7739, 11270, 11976 nyght; 384 nyþt *C* nyth *D* nyȝt *H* nyght *F* niȝt

nyghtede v. [from OE niht] to spend the night **HS** 7731 nyghtede

nygon, nygun n./adj. [ON *hnigg; cp. nigard] miser, niggard **Ch1** 5628 nygon; **HS** 6057 nygones; 5578 nygun; 5340 nygun *O* negun

nygromanci n. [AF nigremancie (MP)] witchcraft **Ch1** 2236 nigromanci P nygromaunci L; **HS** 340 nygromaunsye

nygromancyen n. [AF nigromancien (MP)] magician, socerer **HS** 8156 nygromancyene *O* negrymencyan; 8176 nygromancyen *O* negrymencyane

nikers n. [OE nicor] water monsters; sirens **Ch1** 1439 nikers; 1447 nykeres

nym, nam, nomen v. [OE niman] take, pick up, seize, carry off; travel, go, come, depart **Ch1** 7023 take P nyme L; 8582 nimes P nymes L; 702, 2731, 5014, 7196, 13160 nomen; 219 cam P nam L; 1609, 3150, 6708, 8725, 10332 nam; 36 namen; 4296 nomen P ynomen L; 3560 nam P nom L; 3612, 4327, 7308, 8545, 8989 nom; 4589, 7316 nome; 5916 nam P wan L; 10626 nomen P nome L; 7753, 7765 takis P nymeþ L; **Ch2** 7046 nym; 6060 nymme; 76, 4716, 5280, 6970, 8244 nam; 956, 4386, 4506, 7848 nom; 270, 2107, 3438, 5506, 8316 nomen; 1946 nomen P take L; 8074 nome; **HS** 5084 nymes; 5899, 6653, 6956, 8191, 10338 nam; 3835 namme; 9692 name; 4498, 4938, 10044 nome; 6869, 8166 nam GLOSS BH ȝede; 6960 nome GLOSS B take; 8191 nam GLOSS H toke; 9950 nomes GLOSS B takeþ; *O* mones *S* names *V* nemes; 1306 ȝeme *C* neme *D* queme; 9751 name *O* came

nine, nien, ninetie, nientend, nynþe numeral [OE nigon, nigontig, nigende, nigoþa, nigonteoþa] nine, nineteen, nineteenth, ninety **Ch1** 1368, 2232, 4117, 5617, 5779 nyen; 1365, 1369, 5779, 6760 nien; 7564L nyne (om. P); 15890 nyne; 14206 nien P nynetene L; 14207 niented P nynetene L; 14208 nienten; 14211 nientend P nynetenþe L; **Ch2** 410 nene P nyne L; 585, 761 nien P nyne L; 813, 1770, 2082, 3640, 5035 nien; 2183 nyen; 3661, 3703 nine; 3481 nyne; 5033 nyent; 3685 ninetie; 4231, 5039 nienti; 3248 nientend; **HS** 12123 nyne; 12123 nynty; 2903 nynþe; 11705 nyghenþe

niouh n. [see neueu, n.]

♦ **nypped, nymped** v. [?blend of OE niman and ME nippen] nipped, gnawed **HS** 10215, 10243 gnapped *O* nypped *SV* nymped

nyth, niht n. [OE niþ] malice, envy, spite **Ch1** 3925 niht P ire L; **Ch2** 231, 5724 nyth; 6011 nythe

nythyng n. [ON niðingr; OE niþing] niggard **HS** 6725 nythyng

no, non, noun adj./n./pron. [OE nan] no one, none, not any **Ch1** 761, 3251, 6990, 9335, 10383 non; 1754, 3716, 3828, 7772, 8673 none; 1864 non P any on L; **Ch2** 69, 1290, 5977, 7644, 8345 non; 482, 3025, 4845, 7447, 8146 none; 1455L noun (P differs); **HS** 56, 379, 466, 1223, 1361 no; 2275, 4908, 8575, 10126, 12586 noun; 2827 noon; 3649, 10539 none

noble, nobille, nobilly, noblie adj./adv. [OF noble, adj.] valorous, strong; splendidly, boldly **Ch1** 269, 942, 6117, 8293, 15642 noble; 8800 noble P nobleste L; 448 nobly; 7166 noblie P nobly L; 3988, 5140, 7545, 9512 nobille; 5503 nobilly P noblely L; 10648, 13817 nobilly; 1279, 4310, 6111 noblest; 9626 nobilly P nobliche L; **Ch2** 389, 3420, 4669, 6255, 8120 noble; 574 douhty P noble L; 1712 nobly; 4073, 5575 nobilly; 8348 noblie; **HS** 6018, 8751, 9373, 11463 noble

nobley, noblay n. [OF noblei] nobility, dignity; splendor, magnificence; fame **Ch1** 105 nobleye; 11632, 15653 nobley; **Ch2** 2163 noblay; 1018, 2542, 7480, 8111 nobley; **HS** 8744 nobleye; 10957 nobley

noen n. [see noun, noen, n.]

noght, nouht, nouȝt, nat adv./n. [OE naht, noht] not, none, nothing **Ch1** 75, 1216, 3801, 7499, 8659 noght; 1025, 4203, 5453, 7107, 9248 nouht; 3010 nouhted (?error) P nought L; **Ch2** 211 nouht P nought L; 1652, 2415, 4828, 5577, 8119 nouht; 1811, 4722 nouht P noȝt L; 7428 nouhut (?error); **HS** 30, 31, 37, 210 nouȝt; 370, 2280, 6777, 9901, 11290 noght; 7939, 11695 naght; 539, 3074, 5885, 7901, 12562 nat

noyance n. [from OF anoiaunce] trouble, difficulty **Ch1** 3416, 3606 noyance P noyaunce L

noye n. [shortened from OF anoi] misfortune, affliction; injury **Ch1** 6504 noie P noye L; **Ch2** 4556, 6752 noye; **HS** 375 noye; 10512 noye *O* ony *SV* nuy

noye v. [see anoy, onoy, v.] [from OF anoier, v.] to harm, assail, defame **Ch1** 15556 noye; 785, 3643 noyed; 4840 noied P noyed L; 6766 noies P noyes L; 7567 noied P onoyed L; 2050 dispite P onoy L; 15399 anoies P onoyes L; **Ch2** 1030 noye; 4565, 7275 noyed; 5489 noied; 5576 noie; **HS** 1855 noye; 5981 noyeþ

noyse n. [OF] noise, din; quarrel, disturbance **Ch1** 5940, 5996 noys; 1148, 3366, 11702 noyse; 3357 noyse P noise L; 13392 noise; **Ch2** 3521, 4307, 4309 noyse; **HS** 1388, 4712, 4720, 9067 noyse

noke n. [?ON; cp. Norw. dial. nok] particle; the least bit **Ch2** 597 ferþing noke; **HS** 5812 a ferþyng noke GLOSS B a corner

nombre, numbir n./v. [see numbre, n./v.]

non, none adv. [see no, non, noun, adv.]

none, noen, noon n. [see noun, noen, none, n.]

nones, nons n. phr. [from OE phr.] meaningless tag: for the time, occasion; nonce **Ch1** 1258, 2720, 6462, 11500 nons P nones L; **Ch2** 812 nones; 2628 nons P nones L; **HS** 2263, 7477, 8693 nones

nonne n. [see nunne, n.]

nonnerye n. [see nunrie, n.]

norise, noryst v. [see norture] [OF stem of norriss-, norrir] to nourish, nurture, rear **Ch1** 5200 norissed P noriced L; 5254 norissed P (L differs); 5622 norist P norysed L; 5839 norissed P norysched L; 6894 norish P norice L; 10243 to norise; 10248 norised; 11959 norisshed; 11323, 11327 norisches; 11963 norisch; **Ch2** 219, 5854 norised; 476 norised P norisched L; 5602, 6795 norise; **HS** 2156 (add line) *C* norchyn; 2876 noryst ben *CO* were norchyd *D* norysched

norman, normanȝ n. [OF] the people of Normandy; the French **Ch1** 4069 normandȝ P normaunȝ L; **Ch2** 1858, 2850, 4302, 6084, 6452 normans; 2457, 6310, 6440 normanȝ; 6148 normand; 6370 normant

norreis, northren, norwais adj./n. [AF noreis;

ON norroenn] Norwegians; northern inhabitants of Scotland and England **Ch1** 2790, 2791, 2793 northren P norþerne L; 3207 north P norn men L; **Ch2** 860 norwais P norweye men L; 542, 742, 1867 northeren; 712, 3240 northren; 202 noreis P norreys L; 557, 716, 1873, 2766, 8284 norreis; 751 norreis P noreys L

north n./adj./adv. [OE norþ] north; northern direction **Ch1** 37, 2378, 4438, 7549, 9135 north; 2776 north P northward L; 2789 northward; 6506 northe; 1954, 2548 northwest; **Ch2** 231, 5777, 7246, 8124 north; 130 north P northerne L; 2926, 5086, 5996, 7408, 7855 northward; **HS** 10531 norþ

northend n. [cp. OE norþ] the north part of the country **Ch1** 6604 north end; **Ch2** 263, 714, 1237, 2788 northende

norture, nurture n. [see norise, v.] [OF nourture] upbringing, education; breeding **Ch1** 4259L nurture (P differs); **Ch2** 4669, 5217 norture

nose n. [see nese]

notarye n. [AF notaire (MP)] scribe who authenticates legal documents; a secretary **HS** 5750 notarye

note n. [OE note, notu] benefit, profit; task, usefulness; a note in music **Ch1** 3996, 11788 note; 9700 notes; **HS** 4752 notes; 963, 2615 note; 2073 note GLOSS BH seruyse

note v. [OE notian] to use; become useful **Ch1** 2397 notes; **Ch2** 4186 note; **HS** 146 proffyte *D* note; 2601 note GLOSS B okepye

noþeles, neuerþeles adv. [OE na-þe-læs] nevertheless, in spite of **Ch1** 2467, 7147, 8531 neuerþeles; 5287 neuerþeles P neyþer L; 4386, 6592 neuerþeles P naþeles L; 9716 neuerþeles P netheles L; 12083 noþeles; **Ch2** 105, 2319, 3747, 5066, 7486 noþeles; 277, 1502 neuerþeles; 1596, 1629 neuerles P naþeles L; 2362 neuerlesse P naþelese L; **HS** 35, 1559, 3403, 5891, 8125 noþeles; 2803, 10585 noþeles *O* neuer þe lesse

noþer, noiþer, nagher adv./conj./pron. [OE nahwæþer, nawþer] neither; none of them **Ch1** 1149, 5052, 5243 noþer; 6009 nouþer P neyþer L; 1275, 7182 noþer P non oþer L; 4821, 5545, 6757, 7345, 14979 nouþer; 1559, 8848, 10258 noiþer; 2340 noþere; 2156, 3067, 6251, 7655, 9290 a noþer; 6009 nouþer P neyþer L; **Ch2** 163, 1025, 1917, 2441, 3007 noiþer; 166, 437, 712 noþer; 2567, 4570, 5635, 6548, 8219 a noþer; 548, 3666, 5270, 6204, 7457 nouþer; 2337L neyþer (P differs); **HS** 1360, 4694, 5338, 8091, 11487 noþer; 1899 nagher; 3818 nagher *O* nowere; 1094 noþer *CD* neyther

nottes n. [OE hnutu] kernel of a nut **Ch1** 14061 nottes P notes L

nouht adv./n. [see noght]

noun, noen, none n. [OE non, L nona] noon; the canonical hour of nones **Ch2** 339 noen P noon L; 4187, 7447, 8146 none; 6574 non; **HS** 846, 891, 970, 1023, 7210 noun; 4064, 4311 none

nouelrye n. [AF nouelerie (MP)] strangeness; innovation **HS** 3344, 3355 nouelrye

noure, nower adv. [OE na-hwær] at no place, nowhere **Ch1** 5026 noure P nower L; 9844 noure P no whar L; 10154 noure; **Ch2** 283 noure P nowhere L; 8211 noure; **HS** 3818 nagher O nowere

nouowe n. [see neueu]

numbre, nombre n. [AF numbre (MP)] a number, amount; the number of a collection or group **Ch1** 2565 noumbire; 3557, 11698 noumbre; 13674 nomber P noumber L; **Ch2** 666 numbere; 7761 numbir; 4698, 5341, 5591, 8176 numbre; **HS** 7788, 12521 numbre

numbre v. [OF numbrer] to count; calculate **Ch1** 8260 nombere; 10569 noumbre; **Ch2** 2654 pundred P a numbred L; 3482 pundred P numbred L

nunne, nonne n. [OE nunne; L nonn] a female religious; an anchoress **Ch1** 7915 nonne; 7730 nunnis (?error) P merueille L; 10848, 11011 nonnes; **Ch2** 5854, 5864 nunne; 776, 7946 nunnes; **HS** 1547, 1551, 1571 nunne

nunrie n. [from OE nunne] a nunnery **Ch1** 13657 nunrie P nonnerye L

nurture n. [see norture]

O

obaist, obessed v. [see abaist] [from OF obeir] to be governed by or subject to; obeyed **Ch1** 3125 obessed P obeysed L; 5005 obaist P abaischt L; 5371 obaist P abayscht L; 7774 obeist P abayscht L

obak adv. [OE on bæc] backward, to the rear **Ch1** 12349 obak

oblaunchre n. [OF blaunchet] cosmetic powder for whitening the skin **HS** 3221 oblaunchre *O* blaunchette

oble n. [see vbble]

obligacioun n. [OF] a binding pledge **Ch2** 3284, 4012 obligacioun; 6216 obligacion

oblige v. [OF obligier] impose an obligation, bind by oath **Ch1** 15246 obligid P obliged L; **Ch2** 1269 bond P obleschud L; 2172, 3378, 3381 obliged; 4055 oblige

obowen prep. [see abouen] [OE onbufan] above, about **Ch2** 963 obowen P about L

obrode adv. [OE on brode] at large, wide open **Ch2** 2927 obrode

o chance adv. [cp. OF chance] by chance **Ch1** 1593, 2479, 4542 o chance; 12052 o chaunce; **Ch2** 2968, 3921, 5080, 6624, 8008 o chance

od adv. [ON odde; cp. OI oddi, odd number] singly; by odd numbers **Ch1** 4570 ilk an od P ilkon od L

o drehi, a drey adv. [see drie, drehi, adj./adv.]

ofright v./ppl. [OE fyrhtan] to be afraid, terrified **Ch1** 12822 ofright P aflight L; 13952 ofright P afright L; **Ch2** 1738 ofright P offriȝt L; 3901 ofright P of fraȝt L

offrande, offrynge n./ger. [OE offrung; from offrian, v.] sacrifice, gift **Ch1** 4684 offryng; 7700 offrynges; **Ch2** 6071 offryng; **HS** 897 offryngys; 4938, 7966, 10754, 10802 offryng; 10424, 10729 offrynge; 10798 offrande *O* offerande

offre v. [OE offrian] to make an offer or gift **Ch1** 4686L offred (P differs); 8711 offred; **Ch2** 4450, 6072 offred; **HS** 10372, 10721 offre; 7953 offreþ; 10505, 10755 offred

ofspryng, ospryng n. [OE] lineal descendants, progeny **HS** 4148 ospryng *F* ospring *H* ofspryng *O* of sprynge

oft, often adv./adj. [see eft] [OE oft, oft-siþ; ON oftsiþas] many times, repeatedly **Ch1** 897, 6298 oft P often L; 1199, 4810, 5094, 7074, 9166 oft; 7945, 7946 ofte; 4075, 5732, 5891, 6590, 6625 often; 5034 often P ofte L; 10856 oft tymes P often L; **Ch2** 4423, 4607, 5173, 6121, 7401 oft; 2478, 3546, 5480, 8133 often; 208 often P ofte L; 3166, 7016 often tide; 4575 oft tide; **HS** 126, 1517, 10341, 11493 ofte; 8123, 8677 often; 11433 ofter (comp.); 129 ofte syþys; 9322 ofte syþe; 3085 often stoundes; 5981 often tyde; 8291 ofte tyme; 12435 often tyme

ogast v. [see agast] [OE] aghast, terrified **Ch1** 14910 ogast P agast L; **Ch2** 3042 ogast

ogate adv. [from OE gata] astray **HS** 10896 ogate

oght, ouht, ouȝt, aght n. [OE awiht, owiht] anything, something **Ch1** 668 ought; 5110, 5277, 6644, 8194, 9172 ouht; 7099, 7101, 7930 ouht P ought L; **Ch2** 249, 536, 4408, 5477, 7350 ouht; **HS** 152 ouȝt; 340, 3388, 5055, 8616, 11929 oght; 4480 oghte; 2149 oght *D* owht; 2547 oght *C* owt; 4873 aght

oghte, ouht v. [see auht, owe, v.]

♦ **oglift, aglyfte** adj. [see glift] [ON glepja; prob. phr.: on glifte] afraid, terrified **Ch1** 3374, 15394 oglift P aglift L; 12047 oglifte P o glyft L; 12589 oglifte P a glyft L o glift R; **Ch2** 1737 oglyft P o glift L; 1781 oglift P aferd L; 2510 oglift P a glift L; **HS** 3589 aglyfte GLOSS BH feryd

♦ **ogrant** v./ppl. [see agraunte] [modeled after OF acreant] in agreement **Ch1** 1793 wele o grante P wel of . . . graunt L; 5189, 7937 o graunt P of graunt L; **Ch2** 1218 wele ogrant P grant (n.) L

ogrefe adv. [OF phr. en grief] angrily, with resentment **Ch2** 3831 ogrefe P on greff L

ogrisen, agros v. [see agrisen, grew]

oynement n. [AF oignement (MP)] unction, unguent **HS** 11240 oynement

okepye v. [OF ocuper, L occupare] take possession, use **HS** 2601 note GLOSS B okepye

oker n. [ON okr; cf OE wocor] money loaned at interest; unjust profit **HS** 2394 oker *CD* gowle; 2395, 2457 oker *C* gowle *D* goul; 2417 vsery *CD* gowle

okerer n. [from ON okr] a userer, money-lender **HS** 2415 okerers *C* goddis leris *D* gouleris; 2419 okerere *C* gowlyery *D* gowlere; 2562 okerer *CD* gowler; 2591 okerers *C* gowlers *D* gouleris; 2596 okerer *CD* gowler; 2604 vserere *D* gowlere; 2611 vserer *CD* gowlere; 2632 vsurers *C* gowler *D* gouleris *O* okeres; 2634, 2472 okerers *C* gowleris *D* gouleris *O* okerrkes; 5555, 5940 okerers

okeryn v. [from ON okr, n.] to lend money at interest **HS** 2456 okeryn; 2620 okered *D* goulyd *O* okyrryde; 2622 gadered *O* gouleyde

okeryng ger. [ON from verb] the practice of usery **HS** 2465 okeryng *C* gowle *D* goulyng; 5944 okeryng

oknowe v. [see know, v.] [OE on-cnawan] acknowledge, reveal, confess **Ch1** 8549 oknowe P aknowe L; **Ch2** 1718 oknowen P aknowyn L

oliche, olyke adv. [OE onlice; from ON olike] in the same manner, equal, similarly **Ch1** 41, 10212 oliche; 3425 only P olyke L; 6370 onlyche P oliche L; 7035L onlyk (om. P); 6425 olike P oliche L; 8223 olike P lyk L; 8921 onlik; **Ch2** 7335 oliche; **HS** 2644 ylyche *C* in lyke *D* onlyche *O* elyke

olife, alyue adj./adv. [OE on life] alive, living **Ch1** 2047 olyue P on lyue L; 2437, 7670 olyue P alyue L; 2625, 3189, 7670, 9132 olyue; 3777 on liue P alyue L; 2424, 6884 of lyue; 7194 of lyue P alyue L; **Ch2** 348, 1880, 2230, 4745, 5652 olyue; 5216 o lif; 5232 olife; **HS** 1138, 8005, 11291, 12591 alyue

olypraunce n. [AF] ostentation; vanity **HS** 4582, 4696 olypraunce

olyue n. [OF olive] olive tree branches **Ch1** 11204 olyue

oloft adv. [ON phr. on loft] on top; high above **Ch2** 4190, 6633 oloft; 5917 olofte

oloude, aloud adv. [OE phr. on hlud] loudly; audibly **Ch1** 14956 oloude; **HS** 3484 aloud

omang adv. [see among]

ond, hand n. (1) [ON; cp. OI andi] breath **HS** 1175 hand *C* honde *D* ond

onde n. (2) [see nyth] [OE anda] hatred, spite **Ch2** 5724, 6011 onde

only, onely, onelyk adj./adv. [see oliche] [OE

anlic] only, alone; solely **Ch1** 1570, 3980, 4538, 5174 only; 1576 only P onelyk L; 2364 only P onlike L; 3425 only P olyke L; 6370 onlyche P oliche L; **Ch2** 5610, 6394 only; **HS** 6772 only; 4386, 5772, 9151 onely; 5764 onelyche

onoy n. [see noye, n.] [OF anoi] harm **Ch1** 2050 dispite P onoy L

onoy, anoy v. [see noye, v.] [OF anoier] to disturb, offend **Ch1** 3643 noyed P onoyed L; 7567 noied P onoyed L; **Ch2** 859 anoyed

onor n. [see honour]

open v. [OE openian] to open, unfasten **Ch1** 8647 opyn; 3771 opind P gaped L; **Ch2** 3220 open; 1968 opned; **HS** 121 opone; 8775 opunde

openly adv. [OE openliche] openly, freely **Ch2** 7322, 8035 openly; **HS** 29, 34 oponly; 2608, 10852, 12166 opunly; 633 soþly *C* opily

opon, vpon adj./adv. [see vpon, vppon]

or, ore adv./conj. [see ere, oþer] [OE ærest, oþer] before; first, then; either . . . or **Ch1** 796, 1612, 1700, 2754, 3871 ore; 5430, 5809, 7378, 7756, 8492 or; 5431 or P er L; 5986 ne P or L; 2741 ore P or L; 9991 ore P raþer L; **Ch2** 1843, 4823, 4852 or; 203, 2391, 4418, 5717, 7846 ore; **HS** 50, 1315, 2961, 7500, 10153 or; 653 ar *D* or

ordeyn v. [AF ordeiner] appoint, establish; put in order **Ch1** 541, 1268, 2372, 4658, 14537 ordeynd; 1792 ordaynd P ordeyned L; 1792 ordaynd; 1796 set P ordeyned L; 2403 ordayned; 3067 ordand; 3835 ordaind; 5660 ordeyned P ordeigned L; 9877 ordeyne; 5675 ordeynd P ordeyned L; 5681 ordeynd P ordened L; 6140 left P ordeined L; 10942 ordeynd P ordeigned L; 12207 sent P ordeynd L; **Ch2** 7704 ordeyn; 1599, 3450, 6332, 7507, 8257 ordeynd; 427 atired P ordeined L; 553 purueied P ordeyned L; 2538 mad P ordeyned L; 4045 loke P ordeyn L; 7498 ordand; **HS** 4983, 5370, 6402, 9140, 12134 ordeyned; 2588 ordeynde; 854 ordeynyd *C* sett in *D* ordeyned to; 1605 stablede *D* ordeynd; 1981 ordeynyd *C* mad; 2211 ordeynyd *C* ordeyn *D* ordeyned; 7409 ordred *O* ordayned; 8642 ordred *O* ordenyde

ordeynours n. [OF ordener] trustees **HS** 6310 ordeynours

ordenance n. [OF] order, arrangement, plan; approval; military equipment **Ch1** 3333 ordenance P ordynaunce L; 3402 ordenance P ordeyned (v.) L; 9330, 14739 ordenance; **Ch2** 2077, 3454, 7365 ordenance; 2483, 4431, 5297, 7551, 7723 ordinance; 4477 acordance P ordynance L; **HS** 1325, 1461, 6257, 8377, 12374 ordynaunce

ordre v. [see ordeyn]

ordynaryys n. [OF ordinaire, L ordinarius] lesson, course of study **HS** 10917 ordynaryys *O* ordynars

◆ **ordine, ordryd, ordineȝ** n. [OF ordine] the ordained; the clergy **Ch2** 3157 ordine; 5169 ordineȝ; **HS** 1541 ordryd

ordine adj. [OF ordene] orderly; well-regulated **Ch2** 5516 ordine

ordire n. [OF ordre] orderly arrangement; rank **Ch1** 4964 ordire; **HS** 3574 ordyr; 4635 order

ore n. [OE ar] rudder, oar **Ch1** 613, 1303, 2935 ore; 11767 ores

orely adv. [see orly]

orfreis n. [OF] a decorated cap **Ch2** 2857, 2858 orfreis

organes n. [OE, OF] musical instruments, esp. pipe organs **Ch1** 11034 organes P orgnes L; **HS** 4775 organes

orison n. [OF] prayer; praying **Ch1** 7510 orison P orysoun L; **Ch2** 2498 orisoun; **HS** 1793, 8513, 10461 orysun; 310 orysouns; 4035 orysown

orkyn v. [see irke, yrken]

orly, orely adv. [see arely] [OE arlice from ær; ON ar, adv.] early **Ch1** 8987 arely; **Ch2** 693 orly P erlich L; 4515 orely P erliche L

orryble adj. [OF] monstrous, huge **HS** 4473 orryble *O* horribill

ospryng n. [see ofspryng]

oskere adj. [see skere]

ostage n. [OF] person held as security for an agreement or treaty; being a hostage **Ch1** 3036, 3301, 3619, 8570 ostage; 3044 ostage P hostage L; 5210 ostages P hostages L; 5238, 8588 ostages; 13478 hostage; **Ch2** 629, 4864, 5162, 6468, 7310 ostage; 1923 ostages

ostagers n. [OF] collective term for hostages **Ch1** 3421, 3546, 4926, 5350 ostagers P hostagers L; **Ch2** 3406 ostagers; 6656 ostegers

oste, host n. [OF] army; herd; encampment **Ch1** 982, 4827, 6182, 9378, 14054 oste; 1667, 2088 oste P ost L; 1990 oste P host L; 3735, 6186, 6501, 7134, 8165 ost; 1541, 3155, 3240, 4314, 4982 ostes; 3611L, 5756L host (P differs); 2518 hoste P host L; **Ch2** 73, 198, 7566 ost; 276, 2867, 4649, 6659, 7958 oste; 885, 982, 1510 ostes; 538L [interpolation, l. 76] host; 574 oste P host L; 1706L hostes (P differs); **HS** 9360 oste

osteyl, ostele n. [OF ostel] lodging **HS** 1938 osteyl GLOSS B herborue; 12478 ostele *H* hostele

ostiled v. [OF osteler, hosteler] to provide lodging for **Ch1** 5466 ostiled P hosteld L

ostray adj./adv. [OF estraie] wandering, astray **Ch1** 4337, 8393 ostray; 12499 ostrey P astray L

ostrut adv. [cp. strut, n. from OE strutian]

strutting, standing defiantly **Ch1** 8769 ostrut

osundere, asonder adv. [see sondre, sunder, v.] [OE phr. on sundran] apart, distant; separated **Ch1** 480 asondere P asonder L; 989, 8759 osondere P asonder L; 3346 osondere P asondres L; 3389 osundere P osunder L; 3469 osundere P asondres L; 5546 osundere P asonder L; 4217 osundire P osunder L; **Ch2** 4320 osonder; 6841 osundere; **HS** 9216 asundyr *F* asunder *O* in sondere; 1672 asundre; 8955 asondre; 9095, 10616 asunder

otes n. [OE ate, aten] oats, grain **HS** 10018 otes *O* hauer

oth n. [OE aþ] an oath **Ch1** 3426 oth; 3044, 3851, 15566 othe; 11293 othes; **Ch2** 1715, 2739, 3736, 5260, 8094 oth; 1709, 1866, 3180, 6413 othe; **HS** 933, 2712, 4381, 8361 oth; 666, 712 oþys

oþer, ouþer, toþer adj./conj. [see or, ore, adv./conj.] [OE oþer, awþer] different than; except; either . . . or **Ch1** 190, 2421, 5678, 6673, 9335 oþer; 6499 oþir; 89 outhere; 736 outher; 2131 ouþer; 3923 other; 279, 2934, 4039, 6953, 9159 toþer; 3327, 14189 oiþer P eyþer L; 14811 oiþer P oþer L; 8086 toþer P oþer L; **Ch2** 69, 2125, 4348, 5683, 8276 oþer; 117, 1202, 5450, 7004, 8336 toþer; 2931 toþere; **HS** 566, 1026, 1042, 4585, 5365 oþer

otuyn, otwynne adv. [see tuynne, v.] [ON phr. on twinne] separated in two **Ch1** 2055 otuynne P otwynne L; 8061 otuynne P atwynne L; **Ch2** 2477 otwynne; 3049 otuyn; 4552 otuynne P atwynne L; **HS** 1817 otwynne; 1848, 9181, 11419 atwynne; 85 otwynne *D* atwynne

oughtes adj. [OE ahtes, sg. gen. of awiht, aht n.] brave, courageous **Ch1** 9284 without P oughtes (?error) L

ouht n. [see oght, n.]

ouht v. [see owe, v.]

out, oute adv. [OE ut] of direction, location; in combinations **Ch1** 52, 1434, 2565, 5359, 9375 out; 3438, 4847, 7493, 9065 oute; 4843 out of score; **Ch2** 125, 1035, 3709, 4420, 5624 out; 1086, 2541, 5363, 7218, 8153 oute; 5835 out cam; 6719 out camen; 5943 out gon; **HS** 218, 1567, 2076, 8800 out; 2157 oute

outen adj. [OE utan, adv.] alien, strange **Ch1** 1928 outen folk P straunge folk L; 14985 outen pathes P sties & paþes L

outheys n. [OE blend of hæs, hæst] clamor **Ch2** 8291 outheys

outlandes, outlandiche n./adj. [OE utland, utlenda] a foreign land; alien or foreign; foreigners **Ch1** 1318, 1417, 5818, 6687, 13504 outlandes; 6501 outlandis; 5718 outlandes P outlandeis L; 5825 outland P outlandeys L; 5850, 6568 outlandes P outlandeys L; 5815 outlandes P outlandesmen L; 10913 outlandes P outlandische L; 3184 vnkouth londes P outlandes L; **Ch2** 882 outlandes P outlandiche L

outlawed v. [OE utlagian] to banish or exile, declare an outlaw **Ch2** 729, 732, 1548 outlawed

outrage n. [OF] excess of food, drink, lust; evil deeds, treachery; presumption, insolence, pride **Ch1** 941, 2576, 3100, 4521, 5518 outrage; 3292 outrage P vtrage L; 4737 outerage; 2394, 4767 outerage P outrage L; 11356 rage P outrage L; **Ch2** 1272, 2685, 3509, 5148, 8276 outrage; **HS** 22, 1663, 3223, 8608, 10281 outrage; 9908 wrong *O* outerage

outrage adj./adv. [OF from noun] presumptuous, wicked; exceedingly **Ch2** 6344 outrage; **HS** 3033, 10242 outrage

outrage v. [OF from noun; cp. oultrager] go astray **HS** 10899 outrage

outraious, outraiusly adv. [AF outraious (MP)] excessively, immoderately **HS** 5492 outraious; 2196 outraiusly *C* with wronge *D* outtrageusly

outrely adv. [OE utera, uttere] utterly **Ch1** 11278 þat þou ert P outrely L

outsaid v. [from OE secgan] accused, informed on **Ch2** 5739 outsaid

outschoke v. [from OE sceacan] shake out **Ch1** 14062 outschoke

outwyn v. [from OE winnan] get out, escape **Ch1** 8390 out wynne; **Ch2** 3681 outwyn

ouer adj./adv./prep. [OE ofer] above; higher; more, in excess; from one side to the other; beyond the sea **Ch1** 879, 2548, 3567, 6657, 7032 ouer; 322, 3157, 6382, 7174, 9140 ouer alle; 98, 3808, 6519, 6524 oueral; 2480, 2515, 8717 ouer þe se; 8314, 8680, 8726 ouer þe see; 5119 ouer cruele; 4376 ouer fer; 4384 ouer fere; 1694 ouer feire P ouer fer L; 15740 ouerhand P heyer hand L; 3759 ouer hardi; 159, 2437 ouer long; 3709 ouer mesure; 779 ouer myght; 3956 ouer mykelle; 3770 ouer nere; 13309 ouerpriked; 4140 ouer proude; 5296 ouer stoute; **Ch2** 3359, 5361, 6843, 7212, 8224 ouere; 458, 2227, 4539, 5794, 7466 ouer; 350, 1715, 4192, 5508, 8258 ouer alle; 2370, 3223, 5337, 7030, 8273 ouer þe se; 502 ouer þe see; 6780 ouer fer; 8068 ouer hie; 806 ouer litelle; 6133 ouer lyue; 5029 ouer nere; 2943 ouer stoute; 7636 ouer strange; **HS** 390, 3001, 5827, 9934, 10833 ouer; 123, 915, 1750, 4399, 12182 oueral; 12013 ouerall; 5166 ouerdrede; 4290 ouerlate; 6520 ouermoche; 6614 ouertymely

ouercast v. [OE ofer + ON kasta] place across, throw over; fig.: change color **Ch2** 1733 ouer kast; **HS** 5472 ouercaste

ouercharge v. [OE ofer + OF charger] overburden, overload **Ch1** 7234, 8072 ouercharged; **HS** 6849 ouercharge

ouercome v. [OE ofercuman] to conquer, defeat **Ch1** 2539, 4859, 5545, 7600, 8544 ouercomen; 8683 ouercomes; 11422 ouercome; **Ch2** 85 ouercome; 269, 1708 ouercomen; 75 ouerkam; 543 ouercam; 5477 ouercomyng; **HS** 4974, 6959, 7503, 12037 ouercome; 12079 ouercomest

ouerdo adj./adv. [OE oferdon] excessive **HS** 3072, 8624 ouerdo

ouergete v. [see ouertok] [from ON; cp. OI geta] overtake, catch **Ch1** 12362 ouergete; 13353 ouertoke P ouergat L

ouergo, ouergon v. [see ouerwend] [OE ofergan] overtake, pass over, cross; go beyond, overrun; disregard, fulfill **Ch1** 3739, 5115 ouergo; 2608, 7406 ouer ȝede; **Ch2** 1358 ouer ȝede; 1618 ouergone; 5377 ouergo; **HS** 8576 ouergon

ouerhaf n. [OE ofer + healf] more than half **Ch2** 7210 ouerhaf

ouerhaf v. [OE oferhebban] ignore; overcome **Ch1** 13218, 14114 ouerhaf; **Ch2** 5912 ouerhaf; **HS** 6913 ouerhaf

ouerhipped v. [OE ofer + *hyppan] skip over; cheat, pass by **Ch1** 64 ouerhippis; **Ch2** 6778, 7210 ouerhipped; 4652 ouer hoppe

ouerhope n. [from OE hopa] presumption, overconfidence **Ch1** 6190 ouerhope P ouerwenyng L

ouerlepe v. [OE oferhleapan] omit, skip over **HS** 2913 ouerlepe *O* ouer skype

ouernome adj. [OE oferniman] overpowered **HS** 12038 ouernome

ouerpriked v. [see prike, v.]

ouerproude adj. [see proud, adj./adv.]

ouerreche, ouerrauht v. [OE ofer + recan, rohte] to overtake **Ch1** 4946 ouer reches; 1560 ouertok P ouer raught L; **Ch2** 4218 ouer rauht

ouerride v. [OE oferridan] to ride over; trample, overthrow **Ch1** 3264 ouer rode; 3328 ouer ride; **Ch2** 340 ouer riden

ouerronnen, ouerran v. [OE oferyrnan] run over; overpower, ravage **Ch1** 2580, 5796 ouerran; 4664L ouer ronnen (om. P); 15552 ouer runnen P ouer ronne L; 12919 ouer runnen; **Ch2** 340 ouer riden & ronnen; 3001L ouer ran (P differs); 3041 ouer ronnen; 2127, 3989, 7270 ouer ran; 4474 ouer ron

ouerschaken, ouerschoke v. [OE ofer + scacan] plundered, dispersed **Ch1** 10565 ouerschaken; 12603 ouerschoke; **Ch2** 5494 ouerschaken

ouersette v. [OE ofersettan] ravage, overthrow **Ch1** 6571 ouersette

ouersyttes v. [OE ofersittan] omit, delay **HS** 10291 ouersyttes

◆ **ouerstad** v. [from OE stad, ppl. of steden; cp. ON stadde] overwhelmed **Ch1** 12416 ouerstad

ouerstreit adj. [from OE streccan] too perilous **Ch1** 12772 ouerstreit

ouertake, ouertoke v. [OE ofer + ON taka] overtake, encounter **Ch1** 1236 ouer take; 1094, 3757, 4406 ouertoke; 1560 ouertok P ouer raught L; 8997 ouertaken; 13353 ouertoke P ouergat L; **Ch2** 196 ouertake; 5701 ouertoke; 3269 ouertok (?error) P oure men tok L; **HS** 12234 ouertoke

ouerþynke, ouerþoughte v. [from OE thinkan] to grieve, have regrets; repent **Ch1** 2344, 2702 forþouht P ouerþoughte L; 7111 forþenkes P ouerþynkes L; 12348L ouerþynkeþ (om. P)

ouerthuert adj./adv. [from OE þweorh, ON þwert] crosswise, perverse; against **Ch1** 856 ouerthuerte P ouerthwert L; 2312 ouerthuert P ouerþwerte L; 3072, 5736, 5741, 6602, 9175 ouerthuert; 8651 ouerthourt P ouerthwert L; **Ch2** 5795 ouerthuert; **HS** 8138 ouerthuert *O* outwerde

ouerturned v. [OE ofer + turnian] overthrown; tipped over **Ch1** 4583 ouerturned P ouerterned L; **HS** 5422 ouerturned *O* ouer topnyde

ouerwarpen v. [OE oferweorpan] overthrow, destroy **Ch1** 8083 ouerwarpen P ouerwepen L

ouerwend, ouerwent v. [OE oferwendan] go across, pass over; cross the sea **Ch1** 7686 ouerwent; **Ch2** 1710 ouerwent P beþ went L; 6459 ouerwend

ouerwene v. [OE oferwenan] be presumptuous **HS** 5166 ouerwene

ouerwenyng ger. [OE from verb] arrogance, presumption **Ch1** 4114, 9498 ouerwenyng; 6190 ouerhope P ouerwenyng L; **Ch2** 2369 ouerwenyng

ouerwhelm v. [OE ofer + *hwelman] overturn, throw down **Ch2** 4720 ouerwhelm P ouer heluyn L

oure, houre n. [AF houre, oure (MP)] hour; ecclesiastical hour **Ch2** 462 houre; 470, 473 houres; **HS** 95, 4781 oure; 4066, 9180, 11390 our; 6131 oures

owe, awe, ogh, oghte, ouht v. [see auht, oght] [OE agan] possess, rule; to be obliged; as modal: expressing obligation **Ch1** 271 aught P augste (error) L; 960 owe; 4254 wrouhtis P oughtes L; 1251, 7113 ouht; 5149 owe P oughte L; 5145 awe P aughte L; 6831 auh; 11468 ouh P schold L; **Ch2** 1541 ouht; 3858 auht; 3184, 7647, 7670 ouh; **HS** 836, 954 owyþ; 2401 owyst; 5499 owest; 11359 oweþ; 10105 ogh; 1178 owyn; 1024 owyþ *C* xulde *D* schulde; 9600 oweþ *O* he awe; 5154 ogh *H* hogh; 8645, 9953, 11526 oghte; 806 oghte *C* owest *D* owe; 1542 oghte *C* xuld ben *D* owyn *H* owtȝ; 9953 oghte *H* ogh *O* awe; 9955 oghte *O* awe *SV* schuld; 10019 oghte *SV* schulde; 1539 owte *CD* owyn *H* owtȝe; 11141 oghtest; 11557 oghtest *O* burde; 1089 oghtyst; 1593 awys GLOSS BH feryþ *C* owes; 1641 oghtyst *C* owe *D* owist

owne, owen adj./pronoun [OE agen] their, his, its own **Ch1** 1183, 2880, 4388, 5092, 6439 owen; 5462 ow P owen L; 1272, 2374, 5362, 7634, 9046 awen; 7521 owne; **Ch2** 942, 2469, 4209, 5525, 8036 owen; 1757 awen P owyn L; 1757, 3671, 4533 awen; **HS** 4444, 6495, 8792, 12358 owne; 811 oune *D* owyn

oxe n. [OE oxa] oxe **HS** 4324 oxe

P

pace n. [see pas, n.]

page n. [OF] servant, groom; messenger **Ch1** 5085, 6739 page; 12271 pages; **Ch2** 7965 page; 4044, 6714, 7226 pages; **HS** 5893 page

pay n. [OF pai] satisfaction, pleasure; money **Ch1** 593, 2010, 5561, 6985, 7576 pay; 2335 paie; **Ch2** 3786, 5797, 6323 pay; **HS** 298, 1689, 4784, 9736, 11790 pay

pay v. [OF paiier] to please, satisfy; recompense **Ch1** 4489, 5125 pay; 1949, 3128, 12784 paied P payed L; 3119, 4167, 4419, 15946 paied; 2383 payed; 8548, 15197 paid; 14583 paies; **Ch2** 114 paye; 134, 4042, 7624 pay; 1133 paied P apaied L; 1219 payd P gladed L; 1825 paied P liked it L; 2419 paied P yformed L; 1436, 1999, 5132, 7492, 8247 paied; 4567, 6043, 6304, 7287 payed; **HS** 1056 pay; 7719 paye; 195 payde *C* payd *D* a payȝed; 3224, 3359, 3926, 10736, 11841 payd; 6993 payed; 12545 payeþ; 2447 *C* pay (om. B); 1171 payd *D* plesyd; 2292 payd *C* plesyd *D* plecyd; 1479 plesyd *C* payd; 2657 plese *D* a peyre *O* pay; 10473 payde *SV* apayd; 11841 payd *O* pasede

paien, paen, paynym n./adj. [OF] pagan, heathen; Moslem **Ch1** 7259, 15084 paen; 8217 paens; 7660, 8516, 13665, 13922 paien; 7508, 8134, 9134, 13412, 14042 paiens; 15292 peaen; 8950, 9066, 13670 paiens P payens L; 7276, 7388, 7390 paen P payen L; 13001 paien P payen L; **Ch2** 276 paiens P paynymes L; 302, 517, 2013, 4683, 4725 paien; 294, 306, 334, 390, 416 paiens; 3079 payens; 3528 paen; **HS** 9359 paynym; 10576 paynyms

payenie, paemie n. [OF] heathen lands, pagandom **Ch1** 12930 payenie P paynye L; 13126 paemie; 13355 paemie P payenye L; **Ch2** 2501, 3504 paemy; 3622, 3686, 4812, 5595, 5655 paemie; 4843 paiemie; **HS** 5243 paynye

payn, peyn n. [see pine, n./v.] [OF paine, peine] punishment, torment; execution; vengeance **Ch1** 996, 11874, 11970 payn; 431, 451, 670, 707, 1457 peyne; 2958, 3016, 4386, 4721 peyn; 4903 payne; 5073 peynes; **Ch2** 3216, 3230, 3277 payn; 7788, 7984, 8278 payne; 2647 paynes; 1125, 7005 peyn; 8341 peyns; **HS** 1514 payne; 102, 2114, 6673, 8055, 11194 peyne; 1080 penaunce *C* peyne *D* pyne

paired v. [see apeyre, v.]

pais n. [see peis, n.]

pais v. [see pese, v. (1)]

palace, palaised v. [OF palisser] enclose in a fence **Ch1** 1051 palace P pale L; 9800 palased P palysed L; **Ch2** 2669 palaised P paleysed L

pale adj. [OF] pallid **Ch1** 8943 pale

paleise n. [AF paleis (MP)] palace; court of a king **Ch1** 5738 palis P pale L; **Ch2** 3720 paleise; **HS** 6846, 7021, 7042, 7068, 7075 paleys

palfrey n. [OF palefrei] a fine riding horse **Ch1** 10966 palfrey P palfray L; 11178 palfreis; 12019 palefreis P palfreys L; 13419 palfreis P palfrays L; **Ch2** 1683 palfray

palis, pale n. [OF pal, pel] palisade **Ch1** 5738 palis P pale L

palle n. [OE pæl, OF paile] robe of fine cloth **Ch1** 11007 palle P pal L

pallesye n. [AF paralesi (MP)] palsy; paralysis **HS** 11928 pallesye

pallion n. [OF pallion, L pallium] archbishop's vestment **Ch2** 3489 pallion; 3648 pallioun

palmer n. [AF] a pilgrim **Ch1** 15128 palmers P palmeres L; **Ch2** 693 palmere; **HS** 2343 palmers

pan n. [OE] the skull, head **Ch1** 10699 pan; 12114 panne

pances n. [OF pancier] armor covering the paunch **Ch1** 9880L paunȝ (om. P); 13030 pances P paunces L

pane, paene n. [OF pan] a cloak or mantle; fur lining or trimming of a coat **Ch1** 12132, 12143, 12151, 12155 pane; 12139 paene P pane L

pantelere n. [AF paneter] officer of the pantry **Ch2** 733 pantelere P trethour L; 736 pantelere P panter L

panterie n. [AF panetrie] pantry **Ch2** 731 panterie

pap n. [L papilla] the breast; nipple **Ch1** 11958 pap; 3173 pappes; **HS** 6024 pappe

pape, pope n. [OE papa] a pope **Ch1** 250 pope; 5644, 14305, 14315, 15828 pape; **Ch2** 6894 pope; 79, 2998, 5445, 6889, 8336 pape; **HS** 809, 1074, 6261, 4133, 11058 pope; 10954 popes

paradis n. [OF] the Christian heaven; the garden of Eden **Ch1** 5691 paradis; **Ch2** 8352 paradis; **HS** 1604, 4147, 5212, 7947 paradys; 11167 paradyse

parage, perage n. [OF] lineage; heritage; rank **Ch1** 2816, 3110, 3846 parage; **Ch2** 3784 parage P perage L; 6099 parage

parceyue v. [see perceiue]

parcelles n. [OF parcel] portions; particulars, details **Ch2** 3306, 4542 parcelles; **HS** 11831, 11885 parcelles *O* perceuels

par charite phr. [see charite]

parche adj./?n. [cf. perishen, v. from OF perir] burned, laid waste; desert **Ch2** 5824, 7516 parche

parchemen n. [OF parchemin] parchment **HS** 9285, 9295 parchemen

par fay exclamation [AF par fai] by my faith **Ch2** 4803 par fay

parfite adj. [OF parfit] flawless; completed **Ch1** 8886 parfite P parfit L; **Ch2** 3379, 6138 perfite; **HS** 1957, 12172 parfyte; 3863 parfyt

parfytely adv. [from OF parfit, adj.] perfectly **HS** 12100 parfytely

paringalle, parvigalle n. [OF parigal, paringal] persons of equal rank; on an even basis **Ch2** 2995 paringalle P parvigalle L

parisches, parshe, parysshenes n. [OF parroche, paroisse] parishioners; as adj.: the parish priest; the parish **Ch1** 5681 parisches P paroschens L; **HS** 8664, 10171, 10890, 10904, 10914 parysshenes; 9193, 11613 parysshe; 10167 paryssh; 3883 parshe *O* paschyn

parke n. [OF parc] the royal forest **Ch2** 2669 parke P parkes L

parlement n. [OF] discourse, communication; formal conference; assembly **Ch1** 1723, 2124, 3466, 5927, 8816 parlement; **Ch2** 2192, 2516, 3096, 4877, 5715 parlement

parloure n. [OF parleor] chamber; conference room **Ch1** 6963 parloure

parson, persone n. [AF persone (MP)] a religious; clergyman; rector of a parish; a person of high rank; fig.: analogous to the persons of the Trinity **Ch1** 5682 parsons; **Ch2** 1805, 6313 person; 4955 persons; **HS** 3598, 7557, 9447, 9457 persones; 4821, 4849, 9456, 11615 persone; 6176 persoune; 8796 persoun

part n. [see party] [AF part (MP)] share, portion **Ch1** 242, 1787, 3445, 6281, 15120 parte; 250 parte P partie L; 1949, 7724 partis; 4991 partes; **Ch2** 1237, 1436 parte; **HS** 1166, 5099, 7636, 10435, 11725 part

partable adj. [see partineres, n.]

parte v. [OF partir] separate, divide, share; depart from **Ch1** 223, 1145, 1948, 2773 parted; 230 departid P parted L; 2336, 5202 parte; 1420 partid P passede L; 1684 partid; 4744 departed P parted L; **Ch2** 4018, 7849 parte; 1158, 4477, 7205 parted; 1236 portiond P partid L; **HS** 6106, 6344, 9095, 10057 parte; 1848 partyd; 5940, 7952 parteþ; 6360 parted *O* delt

party, partise n. [see part, n.] [OF partie] part, portion; faction; a part of; somewhat, a little; a group, class **Ch1** 411 partie P parti L; 454, 1869, 4363, 6275, 8402 partie; 8432 parti; 1006, 2700, 4342, 6716, 8738 parties; 228, 232, 3889 partye; 3336, 7540, 7596 party; 223, 226, 1112, 5457, 5551 partys; 1869, 2633, 5515, 11501 partie P party L; 11340 party; 10289 parties P partis L; **Ch2** 292, 3349, 4207, 5692, 8082 partie; 3948 partie P partye L; 6738 parti; 5538, 5539 partis; 2549, 3602, 7592, 8346 party; 1158, 1456, 2932, 7666, 8277 parties; 6212 partys; 7676 partise; **HS** 1832, 2342, 10170, 10539, 11272 partys; 1820, 3981, 10745, 12272 partye; 112, 5643, 7808, 11035, 12487 party

partineres, parceners n. [OF parcener] partners; fellow-sinners **Ch1** 5143 partineres P parceners L; 5149 partinere P parceners L; **HS** 2980 partable (adj.) *C* partener *O* partenell; 4634 partyners *O* parcenere

pas, pace n. [OF] passage in a story; a pace, step; way, path; event, a course of action, affair **Ch1** 192, 1018, 5973, 6689, 15288 pas; 3487 pas P paas L; 3325 pace P pas L; **Ch2** 1266 pase; 1398, 3870, 4346, 6502, 7593 pas; **HS** 337, 2510, 6538, 10428, 12210 pas

pas, passe v. [OF passer] pass by; cross, go beyond; escape, proceed, travel **Ch1** 843, 1054, 3292, 4203, 12183 passe; 856, 1412, 4158, 6572, 9376 passed; 3269, 12186 passand; 13020 passand P passing L; 1002 pas; 4972 renge P passe L; 5027 passe P issue L; 6507, 15786 passid; **Ch2** 4649, 7054, 7162 pas; 285, 2370, 4428, 5742, 8295 passed; 2066, 6223 passid; 3168, 4665, 5799, 6699, 7845 passe; 5479, 6628 passand; **HS** 1429, 1437, 3055, 6466 passe; 721 passyd; 4066 passede; 1440 passyng (ger.); 10391 passyng; 10500 passeþ; 10760 passed

pask, pasch n. [OF] Easter; passover **Ch1** 9144, 10775 pasch P pasches L; 15350 paske; 15351 pask; **Ch2** 677, 2704, 6379, 6565, 7957 pask; 62, 5721 paske; 1375 pask P ester L; 2704 pask P estertid L; **HS** 2023 estyr *C* paske *D* pasch; 9731 estyr tyme *O* þe paske; 9735 ester *O* paske; 10175 esterne *SV* asterne

passage n. [OF] journey, expedition; road, route; ford, crossing **Ch1** 2806, 5825, 6811, 11900, 13454 passage; **Ch2** 660, 2580, 4650, 6122, 7846 passage; 4658 passage P passing (ger.) L

passagers n. [OF passageor] travellers **Ch1** 15809 passagers

passyng ger. [from OF passer] a passing, crossing **Ch1** 3331 passyng; **HS** 1440 passyng

passion n. [OF passion, L passio] suffering; the passion of Christ **Ch1** 14406 passion; **Ch2** 305, 409, 3218, 3625 passion; 342, 4009, 4357 passioun; **HS** 856, 8555 passyun; 3870 passyown; 2743, 8244, 8249, 9913 passyoun

past, paste n. [OF] dough for pastry or communion bread **HS** 10105 past; 10129 paste

pastour, pasture n. [AF pastour, pasture] pastureland, a field **Ch1** 468 pastoure P pastour L; 7244 pasture; **Ch2** 1869 pastur; 7572 pastours; **HS** 506, 516, 10908, 10911 pasture

pateyn n. [OF patene] plate for sacramental bread **HS** 10065 pateyn *F* patain *O* patayne *SV* patin

pathe n. [OE pæþ] path, lane, by-way **Ch1** 14985 outen pathes P sties & paþes L; 8318 pathe; **HS** 10329 paþ; 10905 paþe; 11039 path

patriark n. [AF patriarch (MP)] an Old Testament father; chief priest **Ch2** 3965 patriarke; 5636 patriark; **HS** 4928, 6920 patryark; 6841 patryarke

pauillon n. [OF paveillun, pavillon] tent, pavillion **Ch1** 1153 pauilloun P pauyloun L; 1178 pauillon; 4600 pauillons; 4601 pauilons; 10960 pauillons P pauilons L; 12269 pauilloun; 12335, 14003 pauillons; **Ch2** 3763, 4049, 4993 pauillon; 3265, 4363, 6381, 6617, 7065 pauilloun; 291 pauillons

pauiment, paument n. [OF pavement] paved street; floor of a building **Ch2** 6526 pauiment; **HS** 1576 pament; 9186 paument

pautenere n./adj. [OF pautonier] rascal, scoundrel; traitorous **Ch2** 7811, 8140 pautenere

pecche n. [OF] impurity; sin **HS** 82, 84 pecchees; 6526 pecches

pece n. [OF] fragment, bit, portion **Ch1** 156, 11962, 15061 pece; 2649, 6561, 8506 peces; 13180 pecis; **Ch2** 646, 4442 pece; **HS** 3580 pecys

pechere, picher n. [OF pichier, AF picher (MP)] a pitcher **HS** 10756 pechere *SV* picher

pedaile n. [see poraile] [AF pedaile] common people; group of soldiers; group of criminals **Ch1** 6388, 14255 pedale P pedaille L; 4671, 13493 pedaile P pytaille L; 891 pedale P pytaille L; 6510 pedail P pedaille L; 6554 poueraile P pedaile L; 15178 pedaile; **Ch2** 3034, 4744, 7466 pedaile

peiht, peyt n./adj. [OE peoht, peht, piht] Picts **Ch1** 5578, 5585, 5594 peiht P peyt L; 5602, 6910, 6917, 6923, 7079 peiht; 5614 peight P peiht L; 5604, 5733, 5870, 6487, 7176 peihtes; 5716 peihtes P peytes L; 7079 peiht P peight L; 5723, 6609 peihtlond P peytes landes L; **Ch2** 118 peihtes

peyne n. [see payn, n.]

peyne v. [see pyne, v.] [OF peinir, var. of pener] take pains to do; to suffer pain **Ch1** 4355, 5552 5554, 8357 peyned; **Ch2** 1615 pyne P peyne L; **HS** 5367 peyne; 677 he shedde *C* was peynyd

peyntyd ppl. [see depeynt] [OF peintier, peint] represented in painting; decorated **HS** 1412, 1414 peyntyd

peire, paired v. [see apeyr, v.] [from OF apeirer] to impair, hinder, ravage **Ch1** 8601 paired P peyred L; 12974L peyre (om. P); 8200 peire; **Ch2** 5247 paires; 5514 peyres; 7190 peires; 7648 peired

peyrment n. [see apeyre] [from OF apeirer, v.] diminution, degradation; sexual bondage **Ch1** 2389 apayrment P peirement L; **Ch2** 1401 peyrment

peis, pais n. [AF peis] weight; in balance; value **Ch1** 8677 pais P peys L; 11047 pris P peys L; **Ch2** 4910 peis; 5626 pais; 8067 pays; **HS** 5670, 5951, 9471 peys

pele, peyl, pyle n. [AF pel; OE pil, L pilum] a pointed missile; pole, stake; stockade or fortress **Ch1** 4567 peeles P pyles L; 4578 peles P pyles L; 4588 pelis P pyles L; 4593 pele P peel L; 15192 pele P pel L; **Ch2** 3871 pele; 3878, 3882 pele P pile L; **HS** 2166 peyl; 2120 peyl GLOSS BH perche *D* pel

pele, pile v. [OE pilian, OF piller, peler] rob, steal; defraud **Ch1** 6183L pylede (P differs); 6572, 9443 robbed P pylede L; 7306 robbid P pylede L; **Ch2** 969 piled; **HS** 2357 pele; 5452 pyll; 6803, 6797 pyle; 6792 pelyn *O* pylles

pelore, pelure n. [OF] skin; fur trimming **Ch1** 10972L, 11076L pelure (om. P); 11068, 11187 pelore P pelure L

penance n. [OF] penance; reconciliation; penalty for sin **Ch1** 9541L penaunce (om. P); 15722, 15734, 15829, 15880 penance; **Ch2** 8, 80, 1470, 2750, 7384 penance; **HS** 112, 1089, 6715, 10885, 12634 penaunce

pencel n. [OF penoncel; AF pencel] pennon attached to a lance; streamer identifying a knight; a banner **Ch1** 12189 pencels P penceles L; **Ch2** 3938, 5836 pencels; 4191 pencelle

peny, pens n. [OE penig] penny, silver coin; money **Ch2** 134, 1565, 2423, 5741, 7295 peny; 5965, 6959, 7538, 7682 penie; 3499, 3575, 4334 penyes; 4968, 5942 penies; **HS** 6988, 6471 peny; 6136, 9467 penys; 9459 penys *H* pens; 2620, 5579, 6091, 6326 pens

penyblely, peynyble adv. [OF penible, AF peinible] concerned, painstaking **HS** 5802 peynyble; 10346 penyblely *H* peynybly *O* benyngly *SV* ful apertely

penne n. [OF; L penna] a pen **Ch1** 11613 penne; **HS** 9285 penne

peple, people n. [see popille]

perage n. [see parage, n.]

perauenture adv. [OF] perhaps, perchance; possibly **Ch1** 2863 perauentour; **HS** 1775 perauentur; 4293, 5356, 6881, 9885 perauenture; 8349 perauentoure *O* thrughte aventure

perbrake v. [OF par-braken, var. of breken] break through, penetrate **Ch1** 7836 perbrake P perebrake L

perce v. [OF percer, AF perser] pierce, penetrate **Ch1** 2922, 3414, 3518 perced P persed L; 4998, 13093 perce; 2928, 4344, 6175, 12485, 13395 perced; 3404 to hole P to perce L; **Ch2** 2769 pres P perce L; 7431 perce; 5415 perced; **HS** 10770 perced; 3358 perced *O* party

perceiue, parseyue v. [AF parceivre; cp. aparceivre] notice, see, observe **Ch1** 2862 perceiue P aparseyue L; 1139, 4641, 6916, 9186, 13293 perceyued; 5367, 7235 perceyue; 1125, 15515 perceyued P perseiued L; 2459 perceyued P parceyued L; 9591 perceyued P aperceyued L; 12018 perceyued P perceiued L; **Ch2** 333, 4370, 5255, 7149, 8153 perceyued; 4427, 5615 perceyue; **HS** 2433, 6504 parseyue; 3811, 3884 parseyuede; 6143 parseyued; 11727, 12054 parceyued; 508 parseyuyd *C* aspyed

perchance adv. [AF parcheanse] possibly, perhaps, maybe **Ch1** 15569 perchance; **Ch2** 8022 perchance; **HS** 386 chaunce *C* perchawnes; 996 chaunce *C* perchawns

◆ **perd** n. [see pert, n.]

perde exclamation [OF par deu, parde] by God; in truth **Ch2** 5371 perde

pere n. (1) [OE peru, pere] a pear; something of little value, worthless **Ch2** 2033 pere (?error) P paynge L; 4334 pere; **HS** 769 pere

pere n. (2) [see fere, n.] [OF per, AF peir] a person who is equal; a companion; nobleman **Ch1** 550 pere P per L; 1689 pere; 1349, 4239, 5142 peres; 3422, 4927 pers; 4257 peris; **Ch2** 92, 2995, 4673, 7088, 8101 pere; 2557, 3595 pere P fere L; 2247L peris (P differs); 2250 peres P peris L; 1875, 2111, 3277, 6219, 7694 pers; **HS** 1043, 4376, 12090 pere; 3100, 6078, 12418 peres; 1924 pere *C* fere

pere adj. [OF per] equal in rank or worth **HS** 3080 pere

perfite adj. [see parfite, adj.]

perile, perel n. [OF] danger, jeopardy; fright **Ch1** 740L perille (om. P); 1451, 10618 perile; 2947, 2952, 4789, 4919, 5000 perille; 10121 perille P peryl L; 12566 a pile P perile L peril R; **Ch2** 2869, 6081 perile; 6483, 7107, 7660, 7783 perille; **HS** 1008, 3742, 7419, 8110, 9719 perel; 4404 peryle; 5686, 7435 peryl

perilouse adj. [OF perillos] dangerous, at risk **Ch1** 13296 perillous; **Ch2** 5153 perilouse; **HS** 4693, 6601, 8641 perylous; 9661, 10744 perylus; 10224 perylous *OSV* meruelouse

perist, perysshe v. [OF periss- from perir] to perish, die **Ch2** 8184 perist; **HS** 4838 perysshe

perre n. [AF perre] jewel, precious stone **Ch1** 9894L perre (om. P)

persone n. [see parson]

pert n. [see apert, adj.] [OF perde, var. of perte] something lost; a loss **Ch1** 2002 a pert; 3811 pert P perd L

pes, pays n. [OF pes, pais] a pact of peace or friendship; law and order; reconciliation **Ch1** 1932, 4769, 7196, 9369, 11304 pes; 3878, 7554 pese; 15790 pes P pees L; **Ch2** 250, 2173, 4026, 5717, 8279 pes; 8067 pays; **HS** 1039 pees; 1981, 2197, 3858, 6805 pes; 2605 pes GLOSS B pax

pesabille, peysibly adj./adv. [OF paisible, peisible] peaceable; gently; harmoniously **Ch1** 3052 pesabille P pesyble L; 4009 pesabille P pesable L; 7196 in pes P peysibly L

pese v. (1) [OF paisier, AF apeser (MP)] to pacify, reconcile; satisfy, alleviate; atone **Ch1** 4526, 11307 pesed; **Ch2** 7330 pese; 3293, 4277, 5191, 5541 pesed; 2708 praised P ypesed L; 2364 pesed P peised L; 3244 peysed; 4871 pesed P paised L; 6026 pesid; **HS** 5570 pese; 10310 pes; 12066 peseþ *O* pleses; 10860 pleseþ *O* peses

pese v. (2) [OF peser] to weigh, put into balance **HS** 5570 pese

pestlensse n. [OF pestilenes] pestilence, plague **HS** 1370 pestlensse

peticioun n. [OF] supplication; entreaty **Ch2** 7280 peticioun; 7656 peticions

pharysu n. [OE phariseus; AF phariseu (MP)] a Pharisee; member of a Jewish sect **HS** 11653, 11659, 11661, 11682 pharysu

picher n. [see pechere]

pygace n. [OF] to be equal to **HS** 3690 þy pygace GLOSS BH so gret as þou

pyk, pycch n. [OE pic] pitch, tar **HS** 6580 pycch; 11548 pyk; 12596 pykke

pike n. [OE, OF pic] pick, pickaxe, spike **Ch1** 9799 pikke; 15130 pike P pyk L; 15162 pike; **HS** 941 pykeys; 942 pyke

pike v. [OE *pican; ON, cp. OI pikka] dig with a pick; embellish, pick out; rob, despoil; drive a stake; pitch a tent **Ch1** 4600 piked P pyght L; 4601 piked P picched L; 9799 pikke; 10969 pike; 12190 pikke P wyk L; 14596 fitched P pighte L; **Ch2** 6598, 6715 pike; 6599 pikit; 6600 pikes; **HS** 6738 pyke

piked adj. [from OE pic, n.] pointed **Ch2** 8014 piked

pikyng ger. [from ON pikka, v.] digging with a pick **Ch2** 6601 pikyng

pile v. [see pele, v.]

piler n. [OF] pillar; a pedestal **Ch1** 1436 piler

pilgrime n. [OF peligrin, var. of pelerin] a pilgrim; a traveller to holy places **Ch1** 14430 pilgrimes P pylegryms L; 15132 pilgryme; **Ch2** 3315 pilgrimes; 3692 fulle grim P pilgrym (?error) L; 3911 pilgrime; 4693 pilgryn P pilgrym L; **HS** 6845, 6864 pylgryme

pylgrymage [OF peligrinage, AF pelerignage (MP)] pilgrimage; a foreign journey **Ch2** 77 pilgremage; 3792, 7384, 7403 pilgrimage; **HS** 5875, 6860, 7302 pylgrymage

pylours n. [OF pilleor] robbers, pillagers **Ch1** 6583 robbours P pylours L

pylt v. [see spilte] [OE *pyltan] strike; cast down **HS** 1296 pylt (?error) GLOSS B cast *C* spylte *D* spylt *F* pilt

pine, pyn n. [see payn] [prob. OE; cp. pinian, pinere] torment, disease; sin, punishment; affliction **Ch1** 1988 pyne P pyn L; 4118, 5443, 8385, 9276, 15409 pyne; 3584 pyn; **Ch2** 265, 1263, 4911, 5785, 8066 pyne; 4359, 4709, 4750, 7994 pyn; 2481 pynes; 5040 pine; **HS** 1588, 5290, 7312, 8164, 10390 pyne

pyne v. [see peyne, v.] [from OE pyne, n.] to torment, punish, afflict, grieve **Ch1** 4404 pyne; **Ch2** 1258, 3440, 5930 pyne; 1615 pyne P peyne L; **HS** 680 pyne; 721 pynyde; 3242, 6807 pyned; 4484 pynede; 10859 pyneþ; 9920 pynyng

pynyng ger. [from OE pynian, v.] woeful torment **HS** 2521 pynyng

pinched v. [OF pincier, AF pinchier] cavil, blame **Ch2** 7666 pinched

pipe n. [OE] wind instrument **Ch1** 11143 pipes; 13018L pipes (P differs)

pypyng n. [OE pipian] playing pipes **Ch1** 1771L pypyng (om. P); **HS** 8996 pypynge

pystel n. [OE pistol] an epistle, message **HS** 7124, 7172 pystel

pyt, putte n. [OE pyt] ditch, cave; hole, grave **Ch1** 15686L pyt (om. P); **Ch2** 2038 pitte; **HS** 3004, 5170, 6243, 9135 pyt; 5260 putte *H* pytte; 5273 pytte

pytaille n. [see pedale]

pytaunce n. [OF pitance] donation to a religious house; fig.: scanty rations **HS** 10454 pytaunce

pite n. [OF] compassion; generosity, charity **Ch1** 321 pite P pitee L; 3806, 3862, 5153, 8446, 9126 pite; **Ch2** 2579, 5175, 6355, 7589, 8293 pite; **HS** 163, 4879, 6939, 8074, 12322 pyte

pitous, pitously, pytysfully adj./adv. [from OF pite, n.] merciful; mournful; sad, sorrowfully **Ch1** 3864 pitous; **Ch2** 879, 1448 pitously; **HS** 1495 pytysfully *C* petowsly *D* pytously *H* pytyffully

place n. [AF place (MP)] space, location; house; situation **Ch1** 558, 1802, 5883, 7781, 11135 place; 4749 space P place L; **Ch2** 283, 2130, 3291, 6712, 7694 place; **HS** 1809, 3252, 6054, 8664, 12174 place

play n. [OE plega] mirth; sport, games; dramatic play **Ch1** 2164 play; 11134 pleih; **Ch2** 5368 play; **HS** 985, 1017, 2961 play; 4662 pleyys

play, pleye v. [OE plagian] to play, dramatize **Ch1** 1792, 3815, 4870, 6915, 7880 play; 2073 played; 4701, 11150 plaied; 11570L pleye (om. P); **Ch2** 5026, 5367, 5834 play; **HS** 1044, 4646, 7897 pleye; 2989 sey *C* playe

playeng ger. [from OE plagian, v.] merrymaking; recreation, pleasure **Ch1** 11129 playeng; **Ch2** 1195 playeng P pleyng L; **HS** 4539, 7816, 7898 pleyyng; 3090 pleyynges

playn, plener adj. [OF] of justice, restitution, obligation, pardon, victory; complete, perfect **Ch1** 1719, 1768, 8104, 8606, 14189 playn; 8284 playn P pleyn L; 2522 plenere P ful L; 3731 plein P pleyn L; 4457, 5727, 6738, 7290, 10421 pleyn; 13467, 14189 playn P pleyn L; 10953 plenere P plener L; **Ch2** 1475, 3270, 6108, 7358, 7770 pleyn; 1584, 3946, 4043, 6249, 7721 plenere; 2973 plener; 229, 2997 pleynere

playn, plenerly adv. [from OF playn, adj.] completely, entirely **Ch1** 5215 plenere P plener L; 12124 pleynere P plener L; 13467 playn P pleyn L; **Ch2** 2973 plener; 229 pleynere; 7438 plenere; 2088, 3063, 3113, 3752, 6757 plenerly; 2020, 3757 pleynerly; 228 pleynerlie P prively L; 3880L plenerliche (om. P); **HS** 5811, 12244, 12475 plenerly; 11720 plenerlye *O* priualy

playne, pleyne n. [OF plain] a level open space; flat land, field **Ch1** 1886, 6875 playnes; 5619, 7761, 8338, 9080, 12808 playn; 7729, 7736 plain; 7739 plein; 11928 pleyn; 10633 playne P pleyne L; **Ch2** 1950, 5426, 7853 playn; 8283 pleyn; 7579 playnes

playtour n. [from pleten, v., OF plaideon, n.] a lawyer, advocate **HS** 8748, 8749 playtour

planke n. [OF] gangplank, board **Ch1** 11774 plankes; **Ch2** 1733 plankes; **HS** 5261 planke

plat v. [OE plættan] chop off someone's head **Ch1** 13357 plat

plate n. [OF] plate armor **Ch1** 8361 schelde P plate L; 11182 plates

pleyne v. [OF plaindre] complain, lament, bewail, appeal **Ch1** 2089, 13556, 15410 pleyned; 2936 pleyned P playned L; 3824 pleined; 4733, 4893 pleyne; 7569 praied P pleyned L; 4871L pleyneþ (om. P); 15708 pleynt P pleynyng L; **Ch2** 7628 pleyn; 3173, 5432, 7618, 8003 pleyned; **HS** 1146 pleyned; 4103, 4105, 4721, 4940 pleynede; 10542 pleyneþ; 10751 pleynede *SV* bimenede

pleynt n. [OF; cp. plaindre, v.] lamentation, mourning; petition **Ch1** 2489, 3196 pleynt; 5106 pleynte P pleint L; **Ch2** 2998, 5173, 5919, 7625, 8256 pleynt; 5923 pleyntes

plente n./adj. [OF] abundance, wealth; plentiful **Ch1** 956, 1294, 4313, 5871, 10861 plente; **Ch2** 1970, 3221, 5951, 6084, 6591 plente; **HS** 850 plente

◆ **plentyue** adj. [OF plentif] fertile **Ch1** 750, 6345, 7225 plentyue

plentyuous adj. [OF plentivos] rich, abundant **Ch1** 1382 plenteuous P plentiuous L; 6339 pleytiuous P plentyuous L; **Ch2** 2802 plentyuous

ples n. [OF plai, plait] strife, legal conflict **HS** 2906 ples *H* pleys *O* mettis

plese v. [OF plaire; AF pleisir (MP)] to please, satisfy; gratify, flatter **Ch1** 7334, 7338 plese; **Ch2** 1681 plesed P plese L; **HS** 1479, 2004 plesyd; 2657 plese; 10860 pleseþ

pletede v. [OF plaitier, var. of plaidouer] litigate; plead **HS** 2701 pletede aboute *C* motyn & botyn *D* & motedyn aboute; 9801 mote GLOSS BH plete

plight n. [OE pliht, AF plait] danger, harm; guilt, blame; pledge **Ch1** 11183 plyght; **Ch2** 3204, 5569, 6475 plight; **HS** 626, 7823, 9818, 10656, 12159 plyght; 1512 perel *C* plyt; 2676 plyght *C* trespas *O* plyghte; 4856 plyght *O* perlyȝth; 1434 sauely *D* safly a plyȝt

plyght v. [OE plihtan] promise, pledge; vow **Ch1** 6979, 8836 plight; **Ch2** 1500, 3787, 4626, 5389, 6475 plight; **HS** 1643, 8797 plyght; 1721, 5774, 8355, 8396, 10689 plyghte; 1494 plyght (n.) *D* plyȝt (v.)

plouhes, plowes n. [ON; OE plog, ploh] tool for tilling the soil **Ch1** 2757 plouhes P plowes L

podels n. [OE pud] a puddle; dirty water **Ch2** 1295, 5491 podels

poere n. [see pouer, n.]

poined v. [from OF poindre] troubled, harassed, annoyed **Ch1** 13309 poined P poyned L; 15474 poyned

poynt n. [OF] a small amount; critical moment; example, instance; point of a weapon **Ch1** 3152, 5738, 6731, 10671 poynt; 7966, 13292 poyntes; **Ch2** 267, 2674, 4979, 6176, 8199 poynt; 2680, 5286, 7432, 7620, 8277 poyntes; 7482 poyntis; **HS** 1376, 3062, 5270, 7417, 9928 poynt; 11631 poynte; 17 poyntys; 9600 poyntes

poynt v. [OF pointer] having a point **Ch1** 5738 poynt P y poynt L

poyson n. [OF; AF puson] poison **Ch1** 8901 poysoun; **Ch2** 210, 5205 poyson

poyson v. [OF poisoner] to poison someone **Ch1** 7659 poisond; 7658 poson P poyson L; 8915 poysond

pol n. [?MDu pol] head of a person **Ch1** 4011 pol; **Ch2** 6775 pol

poleyns n. [OF polaine] kneecap of plate armor fastened to the thigh piece **Ch1** 9880L poleyns (om. P)

polk n. [from OE pol, n.] a puddle, pool **Ch2** 6713 polk

pomelle n. [OF] knob of a sword-hilt **Ch1** 9887 pomelle P pomel L

pompe n. [AF pompe (MP)] ostentatious display; shows of the devil **HS** 4665, 4669 pompes; 8782 pompe

ponde, pounde, punde n. [OE pund, from L] English monetary unit based on a pound of silver **Ch1** 5214 punde; 8881 pound; 11174 pondȝ; **Ch2** 902 ponde; 1938, 3576, 4415, 6474 pounde; 2173 pound; 3770 pundes

ponder n. [see pundred, v.] [from L pondus, ponderis, pondere] weight; what something weighs **HS** 9471 weyghte *O* ponder

ponysshed v. [OF punir, puniss-] to be punished **HS** 4832 ponysshed

pope n. [see pape]

popyll v. [from pople, n., a bubble; cp. MDu popelen, v.] to bubble up **HS** 10214 burble *O* popyll *SV* welleden

popille, people n. [AF peple, people] persons, common people **Ch1** 3584 popille P people L; 3999, 7242 pupille P people L; **Ch2** 1303 comonalte P peple L; 2673 folk P peple L; 3127 popille; **HS** 6792, 6948 peple

poraile, poueraile n. [AF poverail] poor people; the wretched; poverty **Ch1** 13965 poraile P poraille L; 15137 poraile; 6554 poueraile P pedaile L; 6565 poueraile P poraille L; 7632 apparaile P porayl L; **Ch2** 3081, 3082 poraile

porche n. [OF] roofed sructure, porch **HS** 9069 porche

porcion n. [OF] inheritance; part of a kingdom **Ch1** 14225 porcion

pore adj. [see pouer, adj./n.]

port n. [OE; OF port] a harbor, haven; gate, entrance **Ch1** 2963 porte; 7202 ports; **Ch2** 678 portis P hauenes L; 2336, 2338, 2344 portes

porter n. [AF porter (MP)] gate-keeper, doorkeeper **Ch2** 4540 porters; 7965 portere; **HS** 4708, 5900, 5906, 5911 porter

portiond v. [OF porcioner] to divide **Ch2** 1236 portiond P partid L

poson v. [see poyson, v.]

pot n. [OF] vessel; container **HS** 4999, 5001 pot; 5828 pottes

pouce n. [OF pous, pulse] the pulse **Ch1** 8896 pouce P pous L

poudre n. [OF] powder; pulverized preparation **Ch2** 6703 poudre

pouer, pore, poure, pure adj./n. [see poraile] [AF poure (MP)] poor; the poor people **Ch1** 3190, 6388, 10779 pure P pore L; 4505, 6550, 15471 pouere; 5806 pure P pouere L; 7112 pore P pouere L; 15155, 15348 pouer; 15358 pouer P pouere L; **Ch2** 116, 2940, 5745, 7582, 8346 pouere; 476 pouer P pore L; 2255 pouer P poure L; 5211, 6277 pouer; **HS** 772, 1326, 2220, 7106, 7107 pore; 5622, 6848 pore *O*

pure; 2185 poure *CD* pure *H* powre
pouer, powere, poere n. [see pouste] [OF poer, AF pueir] power, force, authority; ability to do **Ch1** 549 poere P power L; 581, 584 powere P poer L; 7758 poer; 1367, 7172, 10661 powere P power L; 607, 4150, 7030, 9098, 15473 powere; **Ch2** 451, 2465, 5229, 7087, 8304 powere; 2405, 4787, 5776, 6799, 7669 power; **HS** 656, 1216, 3684, 6447, 8002 power; 8207, 10391, 10500, 10639 powere
pouerte n. [AF] destitution; want, need **Ch1** 2445, 3822, 3824 pouert; 3812 poueret P pouert L; 6881 pouerte P fere L; 11423 pouerte; **Ch2** 6868 pouert; 3311, 7026 pouerte; **HS** 3336, 5756, 6682, 9484 pouert; 1094 pouerte; 11718 pouertee
pound n. [see ponde, n.]
pouste n. [see pouer] [AF pouste (MP)] power, strength, authority; control, dominion **Ch1** 1167, 1238 pouste; **Ch2** 6206, 6593 pouste; **HS** 4202, 6032, 9819, 11482, 11845 pouste
power n. [see pouer, n.]
pray n. [OF praie, preie] booty, plunder; a human victim **Ch1** 2881 praie; 4473 pray P praye L; 9231 pray; **Ch2** 4981, 6504, 6614, 6722, 7398 pray; **HS** 2169, 3362 pray; 7720, 12164 praye
pray, preye v. [AF preier (MP)] ask, beg, entreat; plead with **Ch1** 133 prayes; 171, 8909 prayed; 530, 630, 965, 9096 pray; 543 preye; 555 preyed P preied L; 1631 pray P ypreye L; 5089 pray P prey L; 5981 said P preyed L; 6268, 7626 praie; 13441 praies; 2985 praied P preynge L; 3098, 5751, 6751, 7853, 8939 praied; 2056 prayd; 6130 bisouht P preied L; 8644 praid; 7435 praid P preyenge L; **Ch2** 3437, 4136, 5675, 6908, 7484 pray; 1336, 2431, 4032, 6307, 7078 praye; 695, 1791, 3911, 7547 praie; 3524 praies; 94, 3553, 4674, 6969, 7926 praied; 8146 preid; **HS** 728, 748, 2273, 2552, 7709 preye; 6423 preyþ; 299, 1793 preyd; 3378, 10199, 10422 preyde
prayere, praiere n. [from OF preier, v.] a request, entreaty; prayer **Ch1** 130 prayere; 1365 prayere P preyere L; 3221, 5179, 5183, 9203 praiere; 4769 praiere P preyere L; 5117 praiere P preiere L; 5201 praiere P biddyng L; **Ch2** 1809, 2362, 3711, 7035, 7598 praiere; 471 preyere; 4516, 7674 prayere; 1497, 2033, 2593, 4922, 5108 praier; 2503 praieres; **HS** 5719, 10510 preyere; 1039 preyer; 272, 2751, 11399 preyers; 1007 preyerys
praying ger. [from pray, v.] praying, entreaty, petition **Ch1** 2993 prayng P praieres L; **Ch2** 7482 praying; **HS** 476, 10458 preyyng
praise n. [from AF preiser, v.] praise **Ch1** 9166 praise
praise v. [AF preiser (MP)] offer praise, esteem **Ch1** 83, 322, 503 praysed; 3091, 4150, 5805, 7089, 7443 praised; 3598 praised P preyse L; 4554, 4555, 6934 praise; 11561 preise; 4805, 5967 praises; 7075 praised P preised L; **Ch2** 1926 praise; 2008 preise; 1969, 2708 praised; 5745 prayses; **HS** 2666, 3963, 6720, 11899 preyse; 3024, 3141 preysed; 2005 preysede
praisyng ger. [from OF preiser, v.] commendation, worship; being worthy of veneration **Ch1** 12897 praisyng P preysynge L; **Ch2** 7600 praysing; 8318 praisyng; **HS** 3147, 3324, 7155 preysyng
preche v. [OF preechier, AF precher (MP)] to preach, teach, talk **Ch1** 2220, 2590, 5511 preched; 5507, 5652, 14431, 14483, 15343 preche; 5278 preche P prechen L; **Ch2** 2795, 4575, 5555 preche; 4846 preches; 7695 preched; **HS** 745, 4301, 4555, 7937, 11713 preche; 8101 precheþ
prechement n. [OF preechement] exhortation **Ch2** 5446 prechement
prechyng ger. [from AF precher, v.] preaching a sermon **Ch1** 5509, 14415, 14484 prechyng; **Ch2** 3554, 5179 prechyng; **HS** 1276, 3898, 5241, 10976 prechyng
prechoure, prechur n. [OF preecheor] preacher; Dominican friar **Ch2** 7966 prechoure; **HS** 4354, 4356 prechur
precyus adj. [OF] valuable; of great worth **HS** 1412 precyus
predycacyoun n. [AF predicaciun (MP)] exhortation **HS** 11499 predycacyoun
preise v. [see prayse, v.]
prelate n. [OF prelat] ecclesiastic of high rank **Ch2** 6230 prelate; 1604 prelates
pres, presse n. [OF presse] crowd, assembly; an army; turmoil, rush of events **Ch1** 367, 4835, 6949, 7716, 13309 pres; 716 prees; 11025 presse; **Ch2** 336, 4557, 4746, 5415, 7583 pres; 1764 presse; **HS** 1764 wasteyn *C* prees
pres, prest v. [OF presser] hasten, crowd, press forward; press clothes **Ch1** 4970 prese; 8400, 15376 pres; 10969 presse; 13079, 13267 presed; **Ch2** 3007, 4367 pres; 2769 pres P perce L; 4550 presse P prece L
present n./adj. (1) [OF] presence; the present time **Ch2** 3754, 4396, 5102, 6227, 8192 present; **HS** 6992, 4223, 9558, 10048 present
present n. (2) [OF] gift, present; proposal **Ch1** 2968, 7140 present; 9177, 9185 presentȝ; **Ch2** 638, 2508, 5194, 7598 present; **HS** 4612, 5526, 9115, 10729, 11446 present
present v. [OF presenter] introduce; exhibit; offer a present **Ch1** 3191, 3298, 8448 present; 3304 present P presented L; **Ch2** 328, 5427 present; 1552 presentid; 7099 presented; **HS** 10782 present
presentement n. [see presthod] [OF] nomina-

tion, presenting for a benefice **HS** 10952, 10993 presentement
preson n. [see prison, n.]
prest adj./adv. [OF] ready, armed for battle; eager, hasty **Ch1** 648, 818 prest; 1108, 13261 preste; 11667, 12902 preste P prest L; **Ch2** 1754, 4544, 6552, 6644, 6999 prest; 2348, 2883, 3889, 4513 preste; 3273L prest (om. P); 6714 prester; **HS** 416 fraystys *D* prest
prest n. [OE preost, from L] cleric, priest **Ch1** 1351, 5675 preste; 14723 preste P prest L; 7509 prest; **Ch2** 1523, 2961, 5745, 7807 preste; 1604, 1892 prestes; **HS** 185, 1437, 1679, 3016, 11292 prest; 2287, 6075, 7938, 7982, 8030 prestes; 843 prestys
prest v. [see pres, prest, v.]
presthod n. [see presentement] [OE preosthade] holy orders; priesthood **HS** 10950 [caption: not in text] presthod
preuayle v. [OF prevaloir; L praevalere] to win, overcome **HS** 1872 *D* preuayle (B differs)
preue v. [see proue]
pride n. [OE] unreasonable self-esteem; the sin of pride **Ch1** 105, 1578, 4141, 6188, 11568 pride; 8652 pryde; 1139 tide P pryde L; **Ch2** 1093, 2776, 5784, 6380, 7634 pride; **HS** 1004, 2128, 3119, 6021, 11782 pryde
prike, prykke v. [OE prician] to vex; pierce, stab **Ch1** 5361 priked; 13309 ouerpriked P pryked L; 9074 prikke P prykke L; **HS** 5185, 10117, 11929 prykke; 7523 prykked; 4582 prekyng
prikelle, prykyl n. [OE pricel] a point; pointed object, goad **Ch1** 15474 prikille P prykel L; **HS** 8489, 8578, 10119 prykyl
◆ **prikelle** v. [from OE pricel, n.] bristle, protrude **Ch2** 7428 prikelle
◆ **primalte, primaute** n. [OF] preeminent office in an ecclesiastical province **Ch2** 3381 primalte; 6866 primaute
primate n. [OF primat, L primas, adj.] chief church official **Ch1** 14654, 14659 primate P prymat L; **Ch2** 1802 primate; 8091 primatis
prime n. [OE prim] first division of a day; hour of sunrise; number of a given year used in calculating Easter **Ch1** 11844 prime P pryme L; **Ch2** 5860, 7447, 8358 prime; **HS** 4281, 7210 pryme
prince n. [OF] sovereign; governor, leader; king's son **Ch1** 3808, 7235 princes; **Ch2** 1701, 3361, 5215, 7663, 8123 prince; 1600, 1892 princes
principale n./adj. [AF principal (MP)] foremost; chief part **Ch1** 510 mast P principale L; **HS** 9507 pryncypalle; 10758 pryncypall; 10876 pryncypal
pryores n. [OF prioresse] a prioress **HS** 7810 pryores
priorie n. [OF priore] a religious house **Ch2** 4957, 5318 priorie; **HS** 65 pryore
priour n. [OE, OF prior] head of a religious house **Ch1** 6962 prioure; **Ch2** 1804, 5098 prioure; 3012, 5105, 5107 priour; 8132 priours; **HS** 10447, 10455 pryour
pris, prise n. [OF] value; payment; distinction, fame, worth; praise **Ch1** 195, 3088, 6746, 9160, 14150 pris; 3719, 3782, 7320, 8643 prise; 13422 pris P pride L; **Ch2** 342, 1661, 4952, 5670, 7968 pris; 2926, 5926, 7558 prise; **HS** 1603, 3042, 5216, 6534, 11109 prys; 11168 pryse
prison, prisoun, preson n. [OF] imprisonment; a captive, prisoner; prison **Ch1** 1073, 2541, 3884, 7811, 9133 prison; 1013 preson P prisons L; 1090, 1192 prisoun; 3022L prisoners (P differs); 8533 prisons P prisoners L; 12708, 12760, 12767 prisons; **Ch2** 1667, 4266, 5335, 6392, 7744 prisoun; 1256, 1494, 1668, 1956 preson; 1675 presoun; 1706 presons; 2033, 4267, 5344, 6482, 8192 prison; 3926, 5017, 6466, 8029 prisons; 3678 prisoune; 5440 prisouns; **HS** 1313, 3849 presun; 2063 prysone; 6058 prysones; 10517 prysoun; 12226, 12250 prysun
prison v. [OF prisoner] to confine, imprison **Ch1** 5194 prison P prisone L; 8474 in prison (n.) P enprisone L; 12440 prisonde P prisoned L; **Ch2** 2475 prisoned
priue n. [OF] a secret; privacy; private parts; confidant, adviser **Ch1** 5368 priuies P priues L; 9176 priueȝ P priues L; 10794, 13621 priueȝ; **Ch2** 942 priue; 7100 priues
priue adj. [OF] secret, concealed, confidential **Ch1** 3382, 5975, 6556, 9240, 13979 priue; **Ch2** 450, 2857, 3696, 5959, 6915 priue; 3502 priue P priuey L; **HS** 467, 4421, 5919, 9719, 12567 pryue
priue adv. [from OF priue, adj.] secretly, confidentially **Ch1** 3365 priue P pryue L; 5870 priue
priued v. [OF priver, L privare] to deprive, deny **Ch2** 1806 priued
priuely adv. [from OF priue, adj.] secretly, covertly **Ch1** 1147, 4940, 6926, 8859, 15115 priuely; 6558 priuely P sodeynly L; 3881 pryuely; 4800, 9110, 9121 priueli; 5914L pryuely (P differs); **Ch2** 895, 1547, 4129, 5619, 7139 priuely; 4904 priueli; 228 pleynerlie P priuely L; 334, 5462, 5814, 7100 priuelie; **HS** 437, 1625, 2428, 3182, 6233 pryuyly; 5899 preuyly *F* preueliche; 2432 stylleche *C* preuely *D* stillyche
priuete n. [OF privete] privacy, secrecy; concealment; intimacy **Ch1** 540, 2068, 3828, 7442, 8660 priuete; **Ch2** 5532, 5614 priuete; **HS** 30 pryuytees; 9, 3661, 8123, 10653, 12031 pry-

uyte; 2038, 2486, 5751, 5850 preuyte; 7582, 8411 pryuytes; 2039 preuytes *C* priuy synnes

processe n. [OF] a sequence, procedure **Ch2** 5281 processe

procession n. [OF] parade; religious procession **Ch1** 11025, 11027 procession; **Ch2** 414 procession

procure v. [OF procurer] to cause; connive, conspire **Ch1** 3432, 7356 procure; **Ch2** 2907 procore; 6212, 6747 procure; 4865 procurand

procurement n. [OF] contrivance; inducement, improper influence **HS** 2909, 6391 procurement; 5955 procurment

profe n. [OF] striving, effort **Ch2** 8348 profe

profere, profred v. [AF profrer] to offer a gift, battle, love **Ch1** 5459 bed P profred L; **Ch2** 4794 profers; 7969 profred; 8013 profere; **HS** 3907 profrede; 7828 profred *O* bed

professioun n. [OF; L professio] vow upon entering a religious order **Ch2** 4258 professioun; **HS** 7385 professyun

profit n. [OF] benefit, interest **Ch1** 1217 profite; **Ch2** 3923 profit

profyte v. [from OF profit, n.] to benefit **HS** 146 proffyte *D* note; 8445, 11076 profyte

prophecie n. [OF profecie] prediction of events; prophesying **Ch1** 2220, 2590, 11527, 15831 prophecie; 8105, 15853, 15857 prophecies; **Ch2** 6843 prophecie; **HS** 7133, 10969 prophecye; 12276 prophesye; 7167 prophecyes

prophecie v. [OF prophecier] foretelling the future **Ch1** 2229 prophecied P prophesied L

prophete n. [OF profete] a prophet, seer **Ch1** 2106, 2219, 2591, 5272, 8509 prophete; 13979 profete; **HS** 455, 5157, 7635, 11515, 12108 prophete; 5216 prophetes

prophetised v. [OF profetisier] to prophesy, foretell **Ch1** 15822 prophetised P prophetysed L

propire, propre n./adj. [OF propre, L proprium] private property, privately owned **Ch1** 2374, 13979 propir P propre L; **Ch2** 7933 propire; **HS** 11621 propre

propirte, properte n. [OF proprete] ownership; attribute, characteristic quality; particulars of a story **Ch2** 5022 propirte; **HS** 3975, 10149, 12263 properte; 10089 propertes; 12294 propretes; 10147 propertes *SV* parties

proud, proudly adj./adv. [OE prut; OF prod, prut] arrogant, obstinate; gratified; bold, valiant; splendid **Ch1** 4488, 6115, 8481, 13747, 14955 proude; 11026 proudere P proudly L; 4140 ouer proude; **Ch2** 153, 2842, 7017 proude; **HS** 1414, 3203 proudly; 3019, 10098 proude; 3045, 3483, 5159, 8784 proud

proue, preue v. [OF prover] to test, try, attempt, assay **Ch1** 2473, 3313, 4244, 6415, 8005 proue; 1825, 2704, 3733, 8294 proued; 12300 proue P prof L; 2306 reproued P proued L; **Ch2** 1747, 3815, 4849 proue; 1491, 3838, 5187, 5189 proued; **HS** 167 preuyd; 3643 preued; 5125, 6881, 12107, 12291 proue; 2251, 2841, 5557, 8437 preue; 6885 proueþ

prouend, prouender n. (1) [OF provende] fodder for animals; an ecclesiastical allowance **Ch1** 10533 prouend P prouende L; **Ch2** 5171 prouendes; 5213 prouendis

prouendere n. (2) [AF prouendir, provendre, var. of provende] prebendary; canon of a cathedral **Ch2** 2003, 6313 prouendere

prouerbe n. [AF prouerbe (MP)] maxim; proverb from the Old Testament or Book of Proverbs **HS** 7673 prouerbe *O* a bysen; 8085 prouerbe *O* forbysyn; 7240 forbysyn *H* prouerbe *O* forbysen *F* forbisin

prouest, prouoste, preuest n. [OF prevost, provost] chief magistrate; manager, steward, overseer **Ch2** 6467, 6473, 6493, 7137 prouest; 6492 prouoste; 7147 preuest

prow, prouh, pru, prew n. [OF prou, pru, pro] benefit, profit, advantage; honor, victory; for the common good **Ch1** 1474, 4820, 7109, 7377 prowe P prow L; 3216, 3255, 4394, 5161 prow; 1878, 2298 prouh P prow L; 6976 prue P prow L; 7652 prue; 12400 prowe P prew L; 8705, 15550 pru; **Ch2** 3542 prouh; 6298, 6745, 7630, 7759 prow; 1959, 2060, 2360, 4571, 7607 prowe; **HS** 1302, 4306, 6056, 9532, 10401 prow; 2380 prowe; 2304, 2854, 11944, 12609 pru; 2598 prew GLOSS B profyte *C* knowe *D* on trew *O* wyll prowe

prowes, pruesse n. [OF prouesce, proece] valor, skill; moral or spiritual courage **Ch1** 3314 prowes; 3598, 5588, 8157, 11326, 11591 pruesse; 3091, 6672, 6747 pruesse P prowesse L; 5805 prowesse; **Ch2** 1753, 4846, 4508, 8183 pruesse; 2887 pruesse P prowesse L; 7246 prowes

prut, tprut, trut interjection [AL ptrut, phrut, OF trut] exclamation of contempt or disapproval **Ch2** 7760 trut; **HS** 3016 prut *F* tprut *O* ptrute

psalme n. [L salmus] song **Ch1** 15703, 15705 psalme P salme L

publykan n. [AF publican (MP)] Roman tax collector; the Biblical publican **HS** 11656, 11681 publykan; 11675 publykan *H* pupblycan

pul v. [OE pullian] to pull **Ch1** 1819 pulled; **HS** 9289 pul; 8763 pulde

pulle, pul n. [from OE pullian, v.] a bad turn; a wrestling hold **Ch1** 1805, 3929 pulle P pul L

pulpite n. [OF pulpite, L pulpitum] church pulpit **Ch2** 7347 pulpite

pundred v. [see ponder] [OF ponderer, L ponderare] it was reckoned, calculated **Ch2** 2654

pundred P a numbred L; 3482 pundred P was numbered L; 5659, 5694, 5861 pundred
pupille n. [see popille, poraile, people]
puplise v. [OF puplier, publier] to announce; to populate a country **Ch1** 6386 puplise P multeplie L; **Ch2** 2191 puplised P puppliced L
♦ **purale** n. [AF, AL purale] official perambulation to determine boundaries of manors or forests **Ch2** 7483, 7491, 7519, 7604, 7683 purale
purchace n. [AF purchace] acquisition; booty **Ch2** 2131, 2139 purchace; 2133L purchas (P differs); 2137 purchace P purchas L; **HS** 6053, 6065, 9482 purchace
purchace, purchase v. [AF purchaser] acquire, gain; cause **Ch1** 962, 2200, 5053, 7240 purchace; 7356 puriace P purchace L; 8822 purchesed P purchaced L; 13867 purchaced P purchased L; **Ch2** 2135 purchased; 5456 purches; 5270, 6479 purchace; **HS** 4380 purchase; 5347 purchased; 12064 purchaceþ; 12084, 12091 purchasest; 1458 trespace *CD* purchase
purchasour n. [AF] a purchaser, buyer **HS** 9463 purchasour; 6051, 9461 purchasours; 1105 purchasours *C* purchesowris *D* purchasourys
purgatorye n. [AF purgatorie (MP)] place of punishment after death **HS** 4784, 6252, 7960, 10318, 11073 purgatorye
purified v. [OF purifier] to purify after childbirth **Ch2** 7565 purified
purpos n. [AF] intention, plan **Ch2** 2527L purpos (P differs)
purpure n. [OE, AF purpre] purple clothing; rich fabrics **Ch1** 11022 purpure; 612, 4697 purpure P pourpre L; **HS** 6638 purpure
purse n. [OE purs] pouch; money bag **Ch2** 6715 purses; **HS** 6120, 6136, 6144 purs
purse v. [from OE purs, n.] to put money in a purse **HS** 6150 purse
pursent adj. [AF purceint] surrounding a precinct **HS** 8918 pursent
purtenance, purtynaunce n. [see apurtenance] [AF portenance] a benefice, belongings; appendages **Ch1** 7364 purtenaunce P strengþe L; **Ch2** 2159, 6053 purtenance; **HS** 10956 purtynaunce
purtreit, purtraid v. [AF purtraire] drawn, engraved; to depict **Ch1** 14452 purtreite P purtraied L; **Ch2** 1214, 4425 purtreit; 2295 purtraid; 8351 purtreied
purueiance n. [AF] foreknowledge; preparation; provisions; military force **Ch1** 1028, 7060, 10592 purueiance P purueaunce L; 15113 purueiance; 9224 purueance; **Ch2** 3075, 4063, 5448, 6558, 7503 purueiance; 3849 purueiance P appurtenance L; 4968L purueance (P differs); **HS** 5148 purueyaunce; 12432 purueyaunces
purueie v. [AF purveier] arrange, prepare, procure; foresee **Ch1** 611 puruoie P puruey L; 7746 puruey; 982, 9226 purueyd; 7760 puruaid; 1110 purueied P knew L; 1020, 3146 purueied; 7433, 13517, 15110 purueid; 15817 purueied P ordeyned L; **Ch2** 52 purueie P layen L; 3449, 4576, 6937, 7410, 8273 purueie; 3587, 3601 purueis; 3889 purueies; 204, 1837, 3495, 4605, 7783 purueied; 210, 2332, 2914, 3275, 7783 purueid; 552 purueied P assingned L; 553 purueied P ordeyned L; 574 purueied P assembled L; **HS** 3166 purueyd; 1562, 3564 purueyde; 12433 purueyst
put, putte v. [OE; cp. pytan, potian] push, thrust, put; strike a blow; overcome; endanger; blame **Ch1** 146, 4919 putt; 2413, 2445, 6551, 8772, 13683 put; 2442L [add, l. 12] puttest; 4255 sette P put L; 4261 putte; 6213 put P breken L; 8772 put; 8763 putte P potte L; **Ch2** 1257, 5319, 6869, 7639, 7806 put; 1337 putte; 2725 putt; 776 did P putte L; **HS** 488, 818, 3850, 12358 putte; 3350, 4269, 7796, 8702, 8758 put; 2793, 4519 puttyþ; 6475, 12350 puttest
puttyng ger. [from OE pytan, v.] striking, pushing **Ch1** 8774 puttyng P pottyng L; 10957 puttyng P puttynge L

Q

quaynt, queynt, quante adj. [OF queinte] wise, clever, prudent; proud; skilfull; ingenious, intricate, deceptive **Ch1** 109, 6930, 7050 quante; 535 quante P quynte L; 2240 quante P queynte L; 1904 quant; 4485, 8276, 13990 quaynte; 7548 quynte; 7548 quynte P queynte L; **Ch2** 1310 quaynte; 5920, 7258 quaynt; **HS** 2378, 11773 queynt; 3043, 3063 queynte
quaynted v. [cp. OF cointier, from aqueinten, v.] to become acquainted **Ch2** 5516 quaynted
quayntise, quantise, queyntyse n. [OF quentise] wisdom, intelligence, skill; guile, cunning, deceit, trickery **Ch1** 18, 1070 quantyse; 8894, 9281, 9307 quayntise; 1071, 2831, 5626, 6725, 7331 quantise; 4697 quantise P desgysede L; 615, 661, 2713, 7044 quantise P queyntyse L; 8683 quayntise P queyntise L; 10386 þing P queyntise L; 15504 quayntes P queyntise L; **Ch2** 124, 2653, 3171, 6408, 7071 quantise; 567L queyntyse (P differs); 4535, 4585, 4981, 5811 quayntise; **HS** 519, 4915, 5519, 8187, 11775 queyntyse
quayntly, queyntly, quantly adj./adv. [OF from queinte, adj.] wisely, cleverly, discreetly, cunningly **Ch1** 1122 quantly P queyntely L; 7147 quantly; 8695, 15135 quayntly; **Ch2** 1874 quantly; 2798 quitely P queyntely L; 2951 quantly P queyntely L; 5830 quayntly; **HS**

3358 queyntly
quake, quoke v. [see quik, adj.] [OE cwacian, cwacode] tremble with fear, shudder; shake with anger; quicken, awake **Ch1** 10637, 11920 quake; 10529, 10955 quoke; 8073, 10529 quoke P quok L; 14907 quoke; **Ch2** 7090 quoke; **HS** 7756, 7840, 8038 quake; 1382 quakede *C* quekyd ageyn *D* awok; 2528 to shoke *D* sore quook; 8046 quoke *O* schoke
qualm n. [see manqualm]
quante adj. [see quaynt, adj.]
quarelle, querel, quirel n. [OF quarel] bolt for a crossbow, an arbalest or seige engine **Ch1** 1034 quirels P quarels L; 6724 querels; 3407, 6718 querels P quareles L; 8200L quarel (P differs); **Ch2** 5030, 6579 quarelle; 5032 querelle
quarre adj. [OF quarre from carrer] having a square shape **Ch1** 10146 quarre
quarter n. (1) [OF] dry measure of approximately eight bushels **Ch2** 4328 a quarter whete
quarter n. (2) [OF] a fourth part; a quarter of a body or corpse **Ch2** 5536 quarter; 5882, 5883, 8060, 8063 quarters
quassed v. [OF quasser] to nullify, veto, reject **Ch2** 5120, 5125, 5307 quassed
quath, queþe, quod v. [OE cweþan] exclaim, pronounce; bequeath, grant **Ch1** 1218 quede P queþe L; 15433 quod P quaþ L; **Ch2** 3317 quathe; 3318, 3765 quath; **HS** 2319 *C* quod (B differs); 6292 queþe; 6294 queþe *O* wytte
qued n. [OE cwead, cwed] wicked person, devil; harm, mischief **Ch1** 5530 qued; 8480 quede P qued L; **HS** 5605, 8028 quede; 6281 qued GLOSS BH a shrewe
quede v. [see quath, v.]
quelle v. [OE cwellan] kill, strangle **Ch1** 13906 quelle; **HS** 1753 quelle; 2194 deye *C* qwelle
queme n. [from OE gecweme, adj.] pleasure, satisfaction **Ch1** 7284 queme; **HS** 11321 queme
queme v. [OE cweman] to please, gratify **Ch1** 574 quemes; 2012, 6057, 7024, 14844, 15738 queme; 7492 quemid P quemed L; **Ch2** 2670 queme P comyne L; 6954 queme; 7494 quemed; **HS** 146, 1305, 6515, 9909, 12638 queme; 1903 quemyþ; 11216 quemeþ; 1302 queme *C* plesyth *D* plese
quenche v. [OE acwencan] destroy, eliminate **Ch1** 15605L quenche (P differs); **HS** 7082 quencheþ; 8426 quenched; 12004 quenche
quene n. [OE cwen] a noble woman; wife of a king or emperor **Ch1** 432, 2097, 5567, 6090, 11755 quene; 784 quene P quen L; **Ch2** 66, 3199, 4897, 5991, 7867 quene; 2557 quene P queyne L; 3139 quen; **HS** 7267 quene
quert n. [ON; cp. OI kvirt, adj.] health; comfort, safety **Ch1** 9844 quert; **Ch2** 3024 querte; **HS** 6982 quert *O* vnqwerte
quest, questis n. [OF queste] inquest, judicial inquiry; court **Ch2** 4251, 4287, 8029 quest; 5737 questis; **HS** 5508, 5509 quest; 8917 queste
questword, quethword n. [see witeword]
queþe v. [see quath, v.]
quik, quyk adj. [OE cwic, cwicu] living; alive, vigorous **Ch1** 12541 quikke P quik L; 3500 quike; 4350 quyk; 15618 quike P quyke L; 12372L quyk (om. P); 15540 quik; **Ch2** 704, 6576, 7252, 8054 quik; **HS** 2574, 9566, 10054 quyk; 10724, 10725, 10727 quyke
quik, quicly adv. [from OE cwic, adj.] swiftly, at once; vigorously **Ch1** 3517, 15618 quike; 6623 quicly P quykly L; 5832, 8517 quicly; 7668 quikly P quykly L; 13768 quikely P quitly L; **Ch2** 1953, 3237, 3583, 5543, 6637 quik; **HS** 5573 quyk
quiked, quakede v. [OE cwician] come to life, rise from death **Ch1** 12750L quiked (om. P); **HS** 1382 quakede *C* quekyd ageyn *D* awok
quit, quite adj. [OF] excused, exempt, free and clear; acquitted **Ch1** 1218, 3804 quite P quit L; 2318, 2324, 3033, 7822 quyte; **Ch2** 2067, 2420, 4262, 5417, 7836 quite; 1200, 6450 quyte; 1935 quik P quyt L; **HS** 3146, 4402, 7524, 9835, 11075 quyte; 7973 quyt
quitance n. [OF] compensation; document in evidence; forgiveness **Ch1** 1203 a quitance; **Ch2** 3864 a quitance; **HS** 10820 aquytaunce
quyt cleyme v. [AF quiteclamer] renounce **HS** 199 quyt cleyme
quite, quitely adv. [from OF quit, adj.] completely, altogether, entirely **Ch1** 497, 3427 quite; 1002 quite; 1194 quitely P quytly L; 12323 alle quite; 13768 quikely P quitly L; **Ch2** 1355, 2798, 6415 quitely; 1068, 4595, 5161, 7803 quite; **HS** 11952 quyt
quite, quyt v. [OF quiter] to pay for, recompense; avenge **Ch1** 9934 quyte; 11580L quyte (om. P); **Ch2** 3389 quite; **HS** 6244, 7973 quyt; 9589, 10348, 11778, 12503 quyte; 11432 quyteþ; 1338 quyte *C* late go
◆ **quiteclamance** n. [AF] renunciation of a claim **Ch2** 4624 quiteclamance P couenant L
quysseaux n. [OF quisseuz] leg armor **Ch1** 9880L quysseaux (om. P)
quod v. [see quath, v.]
qware adv. [see þer, adv.]
qwat adv./pronoun [see what]
qwen adv. [see when]
qwere adv. [see where]

R

rad v. [see rede, v.]
radde adj. [OE hræd; cp. OF rade] rash, hasty **Ch1** 12801 radde
raf n. [AF rif et raf] rabble, riffraff; everybody

Ch2 876 riffe & raf; 2679 rif no raf; 3323 suilk raf; 3728, 6692, 6704 rif & raf

raft v. [see reue, v.]

rage n. [OF rage, raige] madness; a rash act; combat **Ch1** 907 rage; 11356 rage P outrage L; 15434L rage (om. P); **Ch2** 2777 rage; **HS** 7672, 8907 rage

rage v. [OF rager, ragier] to play; behave wantonly **HS** 7897, 8926, 9721 rage; 4541 rage *O* rache

ragyng ger. [from OF rager, v.] wild behavior **HS** 9722 ragyng *F* iaping

rayne, reyne n. [OE regn, ren] rain **Ch1** 6473 rayne P reyn L; 6726 reyn; **Ch2** 7578 rayne; **HS** 9154 reyne

rayne, reyne v. [OE regnian] to rain **Ch1** 2603 rayned P reyned L; 2943 reyned; 6471L reyned (P differs); **Ch2** 855 rayned

raise, reise v. [see rise, v.] [ON; cp. OI reisa] to raise; hold or lift up **Ch1** 2800 raised P to reyse L; 3536 raised P reisede L; 3562, 3569, 4482, 4544, 8758 raised; 3419 reised; 5966, 7637 raise; 12326L reyse (om. P); 11227, 11230 reise; 7090 vp araised; **Ch2** 795 raise; 477, 3311, 5157, 7681, 8081 reise; 1334, 3556, 5917, 6304, 8130 reised; 1968 vp raised; 1927, 2009 vpreise; 4766 heised P raised L; 5725 raised; 5773 rais; **HS** 344, 6719, 9722 reyse; 2008 reysyn; 7403 reyseþ; 2369 reysyddyst; 10014 reysed; 10886 reysen

ram n. [OE ramm] a male sheep **Ch1** 441 rame; 445 ram

ran, renne, runnen v. [ON renna, OE rinnan] go, hasten; spread or descend from; attack, ravage **Ch1** 418, 3264, 5701, 6041, 8423 ran; 1486, 4225, 5233, 8190 rennes; 1889 rynnen; 3095, 11572 runnen; 3540, 10056 rynnes; 2580, 5796 ouer ran; 4946 ran P ronne L; 4951, 5007, 10174 renne; 6805 ronen; 8143 ren; 6836 ran P ronnen L; 10661 ronnen; 8035 rynnand P rennyng L; 14628 ronne; 12582 rounn L gate R (om. P); **Ch2** 15, 2268, 5727, 7249, 8165 ran; 340, 2801, 3540, 6358, 6833 ronnen; 403, 930, 2769, 7394, 7752 renne; 2743, 5166, 5789 rennes; 2127, 3989, 7270 ouerran; 3041 ouer ronnen; 4474 ouerron; 3001 ran P ouerran L; **HS** 2529, 6144, 7502, 8540, 9147 ran; 4296 renþ; 1388 rennyngge; 2524 rennyng; 3173 rennyng O rynnande; 5021 rennyng O rennand

rank adj. [OE ranc] strong; swollen with infection; gross, indecent **Ch1** 9585, 13263 rank; **HS** 5095, 12537 rank

rank v. [from OE ranc, adj.] fester, swell **Ch2** 5032 rank

rape n. [from ON hrapa, v.] haste; incitement **Ch1** 7330 rape; **HS** 2143 rape; 7045 rape GLOSS BH haste

rape v. (1) [ON hrapa] hasten, rush, charge **Ch1** 7634 rapid P raped L; 8458, 8995, 12360 raped; 8352 abated P raped L; 12916 rapes; **Ch2** 4203, 6890, 7143, 7469 rape; 2191 raped

rape v. (2) [AF raper] abduct, ravish **Ch2** 7542 rape

rascaile, rascale n. [OF rascaille] foot soldiers; common people, rabble **Ch1** 1534 rascaile P raskayl L; 6685 rascale P rascaille L; **Ch2** 749, 1750, 2803, 2874, 7258 rascaile; 7217 rascail

raske v. [ON raska, OE racsan] to stretch oneself **HS** 4283 raske

rathe, raþer, raþely adv. [OE hraþe, hraþer] quickly, soon, readily; earlier **Ch1** 5540 sonere P raþer L; 9862, 11399 rathe P raþe L; **Ch2** 159, 2146 rathe; 2743 raþely; **HS** 1255, 9761 raþe; 3669, 5131, 6172 raþer; 3052 raþe GLOSS BH sone

rauht v. [see reche, v.]

raumpand v. [OF ramper] rearing, as beasts on a heraldic banner **Ch2** 5820 raumpand as leouns; 7437 raumpand þre lebards

rauyssh, rauyst v. [from OF ravir, raviss-] seize, steal away; rape a woman **Ch1** 434 rauyst P rauisched L; **HS** 7394, 7404, 7423 rauys; 2177, 2185 rauysshe; 5011 rauysshed; 1377 take *C* rauasched; 2174 rauyssh *C* rauasche *D* rauaschyn

raundon n. [OF randon] with speed or violence **Ch1** 13694 raundon

raunson n. [AF ransun (MP)] payment to release a prisoner or buy off a hostile army; a fine; hostages; redemption **Ch1** 2543, 3304, 7812, 8360, 15240 raunson; 8296 raunsoun; **Ch2** 3966 ransoun; 1957, 4917, 5552, 7946, 8033 raunson; 4908, 6988 raunsoun; **HS** 5296, 10669, 10701 raunsoun; 5765 raunsun; 5809 raunsoune

reame, reme, reume, reome n. [OF reaume, realme] kingdom, country, realm **Ch1** 1950 remes P royames L; 2626 reume P royalme L; 4907 reme P reame L; 5791 reume P reome L; 6290 rengne P reome L; 6336 reume; 6805 remes P lande L; 13636L reme (P differs); 13739 regne P roialme L; 13743L roiame L (om. P); 14147 reame P roialme L; 14158 remes P reomes L; 14224 reames; 14812, 15339 reame; **Ch2** 61 reame P roiwme L; 166, 2093, 4171, 6782, 7961 reame; 3540, 4862, 6172, 7204 reames; 3268 reme (?error) P toun of Roone L

rebelle adj. [OF] rebellious **Ch2** 5454 rebelle

rebours n. [see robours, reburs, n.]

rebuk v. [AF rebuker] to reprove, reprimand; repulse **Ch1** 6261 rebuke P rebuk L; **Ch2** 5916, 5926 rebuk; 4466, 4820, 6256 rebuke

recchesse n. [see riches, n.]

receyue v. [see raise, reise] [OF recevoir] take

possession, accept; succeed to the throne; take the sacrament; be granted, raised **Ch1** 50 receyued; 1483 receyues; 2246, 6973, 7670 resceyue; 6360, 8134, 9322 resceyued; 2507 resceyued P receyues L; 13579 reseue; **Ch2** 483, 1989, 3325, 7475, 7804 resceyued; 6033 resceyue; **HS** 236 reseyue; 2592, 4845, 8830, 10966, 10300 receyue; 10201 receyuede; 2369 reysyddyst *C* take *D* receydist *F* reiseddest

recet n./v. [see rescet, n./v.]

reche v. (1) [OE reccan] explain, teach **Ch1** 14548 reche P teche L

reche, rouht v. (2) [ON, OE recan, rohte] care about, take notice of **Ch1** 7086 rouht P roughte L; 13097 rouh (?error) P roughte L; **Ch2** 1607L recched (P differs); 8258 rouht; **HS** 5411, 5763, 10836 recche; 6238, 7726 rekke; 8549 roghte; 4331 reyghte *H* roght; 210 rouȝte *C* charged; 1221 recche *C* reckyn

reche, rauht v. (3) [OE ræcan] attain, strive for; reach out, stretch, come to **Ch1** 1312, 10344, 13339, 14548 reche; 3070L reches (P differs); 4946 reches; 9996 rauht P raughte L; 12115 rauht; 15344 reche P wreche L; **Ch2** 4218, 5626, 5794, 7236 rauht; 4845 reches; 4144 rouht; **HS** 1930, 5486 reche

rechelesshepe n. [from OE recan, v.] ?negligence, heedlessness, rashness **HS** 2558 rechelesshepe *C* ȝetylede *D* ientylnesse *F* rechelessnesse *O* for gytelsheppe

recorde v. [OF recorder] repeat, remember; ponder **Ch2** 143 testimons P recordeþ L; 4271 recorded; **HS** 4195, 10845 recorde; 8706 recorded

recouere n. [OF recovir] recovery from poverty; release from prison; succor **Ch1** 15472 recouerere P recouere L; **Ch2** 5362, 6844 recouere; **HS** 7108 recouere

recouere v. [see couer, v.] [OF recovre; AF recouerer] to recover, be restored **Ch1** 1833 recouerde; 13402 recouer P relye L; **Ch2** 538 [L interpolation, l. 68] recouere

recreant adj. [OF] cowardly; surrendering **Ch1** 5107 recreant P recreaunt; 11832 recreaunt; **Ch2** 178, 4855 recreant

♦**recreie** v. [OF recroire, recreire] to yield in battle; to tire out a horse **Ch1** 13319 recreie P recreye L; **Ch2** 5351 recreied

recure v. [L recurare] to recover **HS** 2186 socoure *CD* recure

rede, reade n. [OE] advice, counsel; teaching **Ch1** 860 rede P to red L; 4808, 5603, 7665, 8913, 9275 rede; **Ch2** 1251, 2045, 5343, 6691, 8086 rede; 1128 reade P red L; **HS** 950, 1216, 4410, 9594 red; 2244, 4018, 9993, 10749, 12362 rede

rede adj. [OE read] of red color **Ch1** 8064, 8065, 8088, 8922, 8968 rede; **Ch2** 2148, 2310, 4305, 6579, 8328 rede; **HS** 3505 rede

rede, red, redde v. [OE rædan, redan] advise, counsel, teach; read, describe **Ch1** 65 redes; 194, 10404 redis; 1193, 8473 red P redden L; 2401, 4126, 7023, 9389, 14465 rede; 8530, 9372 red; 4780 what is to spede P rede L; 13530 red P redde L; 15174 redde; 15488 rad P radde L; **Ch2** 320, 2192, 5375, 6860, 8209 rede; 2303, 3125, 4061, 6717, 8232 red; 1598 redis; 5022 redes; **HS** 5532 red; 420, 1015, 4443, 8202, 12303 rede; 456, 4446, 7031, 7038, 9282 redde; 118 redys; 5174, 6706, 10805 redes; 10082 reden; 10724 redeþ; 2365 rede *C* counsell; 1560 *BH* as men er hedys (?error) *CF* as men redis *D* as men redys

redy v. [from OE ræde, adj.] prepare **Ch1** 2995 redied P al redy L; **Ch2** 7714 redy

redy adj./adv. [OE ræde] prepared; armed for combat **Ch1** 638, 4289, 6714, 8858, 12498 redy; 4988 redye; 8328, 8348 redi; 13608 redie P redy L; 13626 redie; **Ch2** 287, 2599, 6547, 7715, 8164 redy; 2294, 4850, 6950, 6998 redi; 1723, 2415, 3937, 7094, 7400 redie; 61 redie P redy L; **HS** 164, 1260, 2870, 5145, 12544 redy

redely, redilie adv. [from OE ræde, adj.] fully, entirely; in order; easily, quickly, clearly **Ch1** 6075 redely; **Ch2** 2561 redilie P al redy L; **HS** 234, 2139, 2332, 12099 redyly

redyng ger. [from OE redan, v.] reading **HS** 126, 127, 9270 redyng

refous n. [OF] rejected, worthless rabble **Ch2** 2803 refous

reft v. [see reue, v.]

refus v. [OF refuser] to reject **Ch2** 2508 refused; 8076, 8140 refus

refusyng ger. [from OF refuser, v.] rejection **Ch2** 5299 refusyng

refute n. [OF] refuge, sanctuary **Ch1** 8145 refute P recet L

regalle n. [OF] kingship, sovereignty **Ch2** 1770, 2249 regalle

regaunte, regaute, regalte n. [AF regalte, regaute] sovereignty **Ch1** 3861 regaunte P regalte L; 3913 regaute P regalte L; **Ch2** 1377, 3248, 6018, 6020 regalte; 253 regaute P regalte L; 1204 regaute

reght n./adv. [see right]

region n. [AF regioun] kingdom, country; dominion, a nation **Ch1** 2128, 3921, 3940 region; 6682 regions; **Ch2** 3457, 6838 regions; 3387 regioun; 4874L region (P differs)

regne n. [see reame] [OF] sovereignty, dominion **Ch1** 3716, 3809, 6393, 7013, 13739 regne; 6290 rengne P reome L; 9164 regne P reome L; 11662 renge P regne L; **Ch2** 228, 1593, 2732, 3064, 4140 regne

regne, regnand, reyned v. [AF regner (MP)] exercise royal power; reign **Ch1** 6291, 7539,

8152 regne; 4073 remouyng P regnynge L; 789, 3529, 4033, 8722, 13795 regned; 14471 regned P rengned L; **Ch2** 1177, 3303, 4388, 8333 regne; 159, 1372, 3477, 5642, 8348 regned; 3677 regnes; 816, 2056 regnand; 1724 regnand P regnyng L; **HS** 2683 greuyþ *C* reynnyth *D* regnyth; 4149 reyned *O* regnys; 9369 reynede *F* regnede *O* regnede

reyme v. [OF raiembre, reimbre] to redeem; plunder, ravage **Ch2** 627 reymed; 1011 reymed P destrued L; 4594 reyme P ref L; 6360 reyme

reyne n. [see rayne]

reioyse, reioshe v. [from OF rejoir; cp. AF reioysse] to possess, occupy; enjoy **Ch1** 3894 ioyed P reioysed L; 5261L reioisede (om. P); **HS** 2032 reioshe *C* reioye *D* ioyȝe in

reise v. [see raise]

◆ **reyued** v. [ON, cp. OI reifa] revealed, disclosed **Ch2** 7150 reyued

rekene, rakend, rekne v. [OE recnan, recenian] to mention; count up; number **Ch1** 157 reknes; 10910 rekne; **Ch2** 3688 rakend P rekened L; 5661 rekened; **HS** 2036 rekene; 5585 rekenede

relefe, releue n. [OF relief, AF relif] an heir's feudal payment to take possession of his estate; recompense **Ch2** 4965 releue P releff L; 5249, 5253 relefe

relene v. [see lend, v. (2)]

reles n. [OF] remission, forgiveness **Ch2** 4596 reles

relie v. [OF relier] assemble, reassemble, rally in battle **Ch1** 999, 12515 relied P relyed L; 5335 alied P relied L; 13120 relied P relie L; 12707 relied; 8392L relye (P differs); 13294 alied P relyed L; **Ch2** 5484, 7550, 7757 relie

religion n. [OF] religious order; religious life; monastic vow **Ch1** 6945 religion; 7915 relig-ioun; **Ch2** 5759, 6612 religioun; 1804, 3326, 8053 religion; 4957 religions; **HS** 173, 213, 1195, 1971, 7386 relygyun; 7558 relygyones; 10007 relygyoun

religious n./adj. [OF religios] members of a religious order; monks, nuns, friars; pertaining to religious life **Ch1** 14631 religious; 14633 religious P religiouses L; **Ch2** 1997, 2003, 3354 religiouse; 3332 religiouses; **HS** 7384, 8642, 8643, 10591 relygyous; 7389 relygyus

relikes n. [OF relique, relike] part of the body of a saint **Ch1** 10078, 10126 relikes; 13945 relikes P reliqes L; **HS** 5000, 5013 relykes

reme n. [see reame, n.]

reme v. [OE hreman] to cry out, shout, roar **HS** 7859 reme

remembre v. [AF remembrer, remembrir] reflect; consider, meditate **Ch2** 3570, 7994 remembre; **HS** 100 *D* remembre (om. B)

remenant n. [AF remenaunt] remaining part; a small part **Ch1** 3650 remenante; 3310 re-manans P remenauntȝ L; **Ch2** 270 remenant P remenaunt L; 2796 remenant

◆ **rempede** v. [see rimethed] [OE rempan] to do or to go at once, hasten **Ch1** 3464 rimethed P rempede L; **Ch2** 337 rimthed P remede L

remue, remoue v. [OF remuer, remouier] take away, dismiss; raise a seige **Ch1** 164, 9315, 9873, 12804 remue; 3307 remoued P remued L; 4073 remouyng P regnynge L; 5767 remoue P remue L; 8679 remoue; 8691 remoue P remewe L; 8761 remued; 9058 remue P re-mewe L; **Ch2** 2463, 4694, 6654, 7629 remue

rene, renne v. [see ran, v.]

◆ **rengaile** n. [see renge, n.] [OF ringaille, ren-gaille] formation, rank **Ch2** 2814 rengaile

renge n. [OF] line, rank, row; military forma-tion **Ch1** 1530, 1549, 4969, 9336 renge; 4964 ordire P renges L; **Ch2** 7442 renge

renge v. [OF rengier] array in ranks or battle positions; ring around, surround **Ch1** 3417, 6556, 8143, 8832, 9336 renge; 4964 renge P arraied L; 4972 renge P passe forþ L; 2892, 4637 rengid P rengede L; 4300 rengid P renged L; 3468, 3482, 8328, 8752 renged; 4332, 12874 rengid; 4987 renged P enbatailled L; 11586 rounge P ryng L; **Ch2** 930 renge; 3937 renged

◆ **renome** adj. [from OF renomer, v.; AF re-numee] renowned, famous **Ch2** 5013 renome

renoun n. [AF renun, renume] fame, reputation; report, rumor; excellence, value **Ch1** 1915, 6805 renoune; 1964, 2162, 4061, 11348 re-noun; 4946 renoun ran P tydynges ronne L; 13234 ronons P renouns L; 14139 ronoun P renoun L; **Ch2** 1806, 3206, 5472, 6625, 7760 renoun; 5100 ronoun; **HS** 1917, 3244, 8724, 9240, 10008 renoun; 3231 renouns GLOSS BH name

rent n. [OF] revenue from property; income **Ch1** 2405, 3137 rente; 8593 rentes; 5809 rent P rentes L; 2340, 5676, 7106, 7504, 7816 rent; 6968 rent P rente L; **Ch2** 1466, 4462, 5239, 6759, 7710 rent; 753, 1122, 2257, 3557, 4948 rentes; 3063 rentis; **HS** 5365, 6075 rente

rent v. [OE rendan] destroy; tear up, rip **Ch1** 2139 rente P rent L; 3163, 8084 rent; **Ch2** 3639 rent; **HS** 1474 rente

reome n. [see reame, n.]

repeire n. [OF] go home, return **Ch1** 7964 repeire P repeir L

repent v. [OF repentir] feel regret, sorrow **Ch1** 4836, 5121 repent P repente L; **Ch2** 4052, 4938, 6173 repent; 1921 repentis; **HS** 4333, 4501 repent; 3709, 4236, 5129 repente; 251 repentyd; 11057 repented; 12127, 12586 re-pentest

repentailles n. [OF] regrets **Ch1** 11570L repentailles (om. P)

repentance n. [OF] penitence, contrition **Ch1** 15404L repentaunce (om. P); **Ch2** 1339 repentance; **HS** 588, 4338, 8012, 10857, 12619 repentaunce

repentaunt adj. [OF repentant] penitent, contrite **HS** 4426, 12122, 12612 repentaunt

reprefs n. [from AF reprove] slander, an insult **Ch1** 7882 vpbreide P reprefs L

repreue v. [OF reprover, AF repruver] to rebuke, censure **Ch1** 2306 reproued P proued L; 11421 vpbraide P repreue L; **HS** 3724 repreuedest O reprouyd

request n. [OF requeste] request, petition **Ch2** 6439 request

requiem n. [from L requies] a requiem mass; eternal rest **HS** 2615, 2625 requiem

rerbras n. [AF] armor for the upper arm **Ch1** 9881L rerbras L (om. P)

◆ **rere** n. (1) [from rereward, n.] the rear guard **Ch2** 4997 rere

◆ **rere** n. (2) [cp. MDu reren, to roar] noise, clamor **Ch1** 10049 rere

rere v. [see arere] [AF] force to retreat **Ch2** 1750 rere

rere soper n./adj. [AF rere supers (MP)] last meal of the day; a late supper **HS** 7261, 7269, 7293 rere sopers

rereward n. [AF] rear guard of an army **Ch2** 4732 rereward P warde L

res n. [OE ræs] violent motion, rush; attack; anger, rage **Ch1** 1232, 15591 res; 3443L res (P differs); 4768 res P rees L; 5124 rees P res L; 12692 with res P þe pres L þe res R; **Ch2** 1521, 3684, 5711, 7876, 8206 res

resceyue v. [see receyue, v.]

resceyuour n. [AF receivour] receiver of stolen goods; a government official, treasurer **Ch2** 6152 resceyuour; 6966 resceyuoure

rescet, recet n. [AF reset] place of refuge, shelter; protection **Ch1** 916, 4323, 4426, 7374 rescet P recet L; 1611 rescette P rescet L; 6693L recettes (om. P); 1337, 7392 rescet; 12200 resette P recet L; 8145 refute P recet L; 13578 reste P recet L; **Ch2** 5960, 7064 rescette

rescet v. [OF receter] to take refuge **Ch2** 1860 rescet

rescous, rescus, rescours n. [from OF rescorre, v.] rescue, escape; help, deliverance **Ch1** 2911 rescous P rescours L; 5317 rescus; 12626 waiting PR rescours L; 12643 rescous PR rescours L; 12735 rescowes P rescours L; **Ch2** 8212 rescus

rescue, rescowe, rescouh v. [from OF rescorre; AF rescure] deliver from captivity, fire, death; aid in battle; relieve **Ch1** 4909 rescowe; 5198 rescue P rescuwe L; 9059 rescue; 8384 rescued P rescowed L; 8760 rescued; 12512L rescowed (om. P); 12568 rescouh P rescouse LR; **Ch2** 6653 rescue

reson n. [AF] intellectual faculty; course of action; argument, claim **Ch1** 1961, 4254, 6827, 9241, 10123 reson; 1215 resons; 3600 resone; 7389 resoun; **Ch2** 1680, 2074, 4050, 6016, 7282 reson; 1686, 2688, 4014, 5055, 7697 resoun; 7539 roson; 3453, 6022, 6543, 7618, 8270 resons; **HS** 817, 2112, 5650, 8630, 12473 resun; 2202 resoune; 11799, 11825, 12281 resoun

reson v. [OF raisoner, resoner] question; call to account **Ch1** 6941 reson

resonabille adj. [OF] capable of reasoning; intelligent **Ch1** 11391 resonabille; **HS** 10964 resonable

respite n. [OF respit] extension of time for action; delay; decision **Ch1** 4729 respite; **Ch2** 4596, 6652, 6895, 7094, 7789 respite; **HS** 4401, 11383 respyte

respone v. [OF respondre] make reply **Ch1** 4202 respone P respoune L

respons n. [OF] reply, answer **Ch1** 11652 respons P respouns L; **Ch2** 2397, 3925, 4196, 6293, 7493 respons; 3186 respouns

rest n. [OE] peace; death; repose **Ch1** 817 rest; 7197 reste P rest L; 13578 reste P recet L; **Ch2** 60, 1755, 3530, 4051, 7866 rest; 2632, 3890, 4514, 5632 reste; **HS** 359, 5937, 6092, 6147 reste; 2619, 7053, 7734 rest

rest v. [OE restan] sleep, relax; leave off **Ch1** 705, 3646, 4657, 8986 reste; 4147, 8273 reste P rest L; 1107, 1774, 6576, 7588, 8467 rest; 2551 restis; 3464 rest P reste L; 5814 duelle P reste L; 1610 restid P rested L; 8747 rested; **Ch2** 2266, 8178 reste; 2531, 5878, 6672, 7827, 8138 rest; 3967, 5245, 8079 rested; 1897, 2023 restid; 283 restyng; 7130 restis; **HS** 830, 11158 rest; 1939, 10141, 11877, 12481 reste; 831 restede

resteie v. [OF rester, arester] arrest, capture **Ch2** 7102 resteie

restyng ger. [from OE restan, v.] place of rest; dwelling **Ch1** 3465 restyng; **HS** 6656 restyng

restore v. [OF restorer] repay; return; recover **Ch1** 3617, 3811, 7635, 8267, 8595 restore; 4510 restored; **Ch2** 2431, 2433, 6250 restore; **HS** 2082, 5796, 10686 restore

resurreccioun n. [OF] resurrection of Christ; dramatization of the resurrection **Ch2** 4010 resurreccioun; **HS** 4646 resurreccyun

retenanȝ, retenance n. [AF] retainers, band of followers **Ch1** 15265 retenance P retenauntȝ L; **Ch2** 2456 retenanȝ P retenance L

retoure n./v. [OF retor, retour] return, retreat, flight **Ch1** 5393, 5409 retoure P retour L; 1711 com ageyn P retorned L (v.)

retted v. [AF retter] accused, charged **Ch2** 1573

retted

reue n. [OE refa] warden, reeve **HS** 8796 reue

reue, reft, raft v. [OE reafian, reafod] deprive, seize; plunder **Ch1** 3193, 5749, 7368, 8657, 15598 reue; 911, 2005, 5075, 8265, 12806 reft; 3100 held P reftym L; 6945 take P reue L; 4767 reues P reuest L; 5851, 8503 refte; 7146 reued; **Ch2** 403, 3731, 5475, 6200, 8084 reue; 2203 reued; 1564, 3008, 4742, 6075, 7805 reft; 4636 reues; 6816 raft; **HS** 2905, 3317 reue; 1522 reuyst; 2368 reft; 1320, 1321, 4893, 8060, 12168 refte; 12057 rafte; 2264 refte *CD* stalle; 9301 to drofe *O* rafe; 9535 leue *O* refe

revel n. [OF] carousing; game **HS** 992 *D* revel (om. B)

reuelacyun n. [AF reuelaciun (MP)] disclosure of future events **HS** 441 reuelacyun

reueld v. [OE; cp. rifelede, p.ppl.] to be tangled **Ch1** 4585 reueld P ryuereled L

reuerence n. [OF] respect; veneration **HS** 4991 reuerence

reuery n. [from OE reafere, n.] robbery, plundering **Ch1** 5734 robberie P reuery L

reuers adj. [OF] opposite, contrary **HS** 11120 reuers

reuested, reustat v. [OF revestir] dressed in ceremonial vestments **Ch2** 811 reustat at (?error) P reuested atte L; **HS** 9062 hym reueste

reuful adj. [from OE hreow, n.] doleful, piteous; compassionate **HS** 5695, 6940, 7150 reuful

◆ **reufulhed** n. [from reuful, adj.] compassion **Ch2** 6355 reufulhed

reuile v. [OF reuiler] to insult, rebuke, taunt; degrade **Ch1** 6262 stouted P reuiled L; 11433 reuyle P reuille L; **Ch2** 3203, 3985, 7634, 7891 reuile; **HS** 11554 reuylest

reuly, rufully, rulych adj./adv. [OE hreowlice] pitifully, miserably **Ch1** 10084 reuly; **HS** 8757 ruly; 2512 ruly *CO* rewly; 730 rulych; 3854 rufully

reume n. [see reame]

reuth, rewþe, rouþe n. [see rew, v.] [from ON; cp. OI hrygð] pity, sympathy; sorrow, grief **Ch2** 1756 reuth P ruthe L; **HS** 2775 rewþe; 8382 reuþe; 12346 rouþe

rew v. [OE hreowan] to pity, regret, be ashamed; be grieved **Ch1** 10127 rewed; 11515, 11940 rewe; **Ch2** 7706 rew; 3684 rewe; 5711, 8227 rewes; **HS** 9324 reweþ; 10935 reueþ *O* rewes

reward n. [AF] prize, fee; value **Ch2** 3856, 4030, 4812 reward

reward v. [AF rewarder] to give a reward; consider, watch **Ch1** 11192 rewarded; 13098 tentid P rewarded L; **Ch2** 3534, 7152 reward

◆ **rewardons, rewardoun** n. [prob. AF; cp. OF reguerredon] reward, gift; payment, recompense **Ch2** 2353 rewardons; 3497 rewardoun P guerdons L

rewe n. [OE hreow] in a row; successively **HS** 2575 al be dene GLOSS B rewe (?error)

ribaudie, rebaudye n. [OF ribaudie] debauchery, dissipation; jesting; lechery **Ch1** 906 rebaudye P rybaudie L; **Ch2** 5401, 5689 ribaudie; **HS** 1292, 2657, 3766 rybaudy; 3678 rybaudy *O* rebaldry

ribbes n. [OE ribb] side of the body; ribs **Ch1** 1829 ribbes

riche, rike n. [OE rice, ON riki] sovereignty, authority; kingdom; the rich **Ch1** 6553 ryche; **Ch2** 812, 2940 riche; 6715 rike

riche adj. [from OE rice, n.] rich; wealthy **Ch1** 754, 4678, 6682, 9147, 10779 riche; 632, 666, 771, 1882 ryche; 5489 rych; 2663, 3303 richest; 11067 riche P god L; **Ch2** 867, 2255, 5194, 6313, 7880 riche; 4799 riche P richer L; 3141 richest; 3537 richer; **HS** 689, 2700, 4214, 6637, 11668 ryche; 4213 rycher

richely adv. [OE riclice] splendidly, magnificently, sumptuously **Ch1** 11022 richeli P richely L; 5891, 6291, 6453, 11023, 11081 richely; **Ch2** 774, 1699, 2595, 3452, 5643 richely; 3359, 3761 richeli; 5212 richelie; **HS** 6755, 9376 rychely

riches, richesse, richenesse n. [OF richese] wealth, opulence **Ch1** 681 ryches; 2441, 4111, 4515, 12447 richesse; 7042 richesse P richesses L; 755, 2435 rychesse; 2190 rycheise P richeyse L; 3524 riches; 12447 richesse P prowesse L; **Ch2** 660 richesse; 4279, 6594 ricchesse; 2800 rechesse; 3834 richenesse; 4224, 4450 riches; **HS** 3053, 4203 rychesse; 4388, 6684 ryches

rycolage n. [OF rigolage] revelry **HS** 7275, 12568 rycolage

ride v. [OE ridan] ride a horse; ride to battle; travel; to sail **Ch1** 8248, 8860 ride; 8301, 9136 rode; 2484 rode P rod L; 4562, 14202 ride P ryde L; 9006, 12260, 12365 ridand; 9995 houe P ryde L; 12338 riden P prykede L; 14628 riden; **Ch2** 308, 1103, 1533, 3661, 7234 ride; 7178, 7846 rode; 340 riden; 7248 ridyng; **HS** 1934, 3293 ryde; 9054 rode; 3432 rydyng

rif n. [see raf, n.]

rife, ryf adj. [OE hrife, rife] widespread, abundant; commonly known **Ch1** 3789 rife P ryf L; 6147 rife; 9163 ryfe P ryf L; **Ch2** 532, 1484 rife; **HS** 3244, 8725, 10961 ryff

rife, ryf adv. [from OE hrife, adj.] abundantly, widely, commonly **Ch1** 5640, 6147, 10766 rife P ryf L; 7655 ryfe P ryf L; **Ch2** 1673 rif P riȝt L; **HS** 3159 ryf; 6500 ryff

righ n. [OE reohhe] the ray fish **Ch1** 14550 righ P righe L

right n. [OE riht] justice, rights; territory **Ch1**

514, 2447, 7512, 11415, 14324 right; 19, 964, 1300 ryght; 4095 right P ryght L; 6656 rightes P right L; 12237 rightes; 11572 reght; **Ch2** 189, 2660, 3676, 6956, 8215 right; 33 righ (error) P right L; 3403, 4525, 4744, 5910 rightes; **HS** 741, 2204, 4757, 9470, 11269 ryght; 6320 ryghte

right v. [OE rihtan] restore; set in order **Ch1** 11763 right P righte L; **Ch2** 1700 right

right adj. [OE riht] true; proper, correct, complete **Ch1** 33 ryght; 2656, 3654, 5659, 6857, 9338 right; **Ch2** 94, 2179, 4397, 6776, 8302 right; 2239 righter; **HS** 1523, 1713, 3310, 10169, 11416 ryght; 383 ryþt *C* ryth *DF* ryȝt *H* ryght; 2035 ryght *D* trewe; 9530 clere *O* ryghte

right, reght adv. [OE rihte] precisely, exactly, justly; exceedingly **Ch1** 333, 3437, 6552, 7689, 8541 right; 61, 68, 216 ryght; 1355, 1481, 3926 reght; 882 fulle P right L; 1405, 7307 reght P right L; 5510 late P right L; 15036 right P ryught L; **Ch2** 158, 1684, 3702, 5371, 8245 right; **HS** 682, 2878, 9467, 10212, 12547 ryght; 145 ryþ *FH* ryȝt; 244 ryþtnow *C* ryth *D* ryȝt now *F* riȝt now *H* ryghtnow; 875 ryþt now *DH* ryȝt now *F* riȝt now; 3294 ful moche *H* ryȝt moche

rightfulle adj. [OE rihtful] appropriate; fair, just **Ch1** 323 ryghtfulle P rightful L; **Ch2** 3598 rightfulle P riȝtfully L; 5911 rightfulle

ryghtfulnes n. [from OE rihtful, adj.] fairness, justice, equity **Ch1** 321 rygfulnes (error) P rightfulnesse L; **HS** 600, 601 ryghtfulnes *D* ryȝtwysnesse

rightly adv. [OE rihtlice] righteously, correctly; justly **Ch1** 1231, 4182, 9336, 15944 rightly; **HS** 1433, 1956, 9334, 10170, 11308 ryghtly; 793 ryghtly *C* rytȝly *D* a ryȝt *H* ryȝt *F* riȝth; 9334 ryghtly *F* trewli; 9986 ryghtly *SV* verrey; 11914 ryghtwus *O* ryghtly

rightwis, ryghtwslye adj./adv. [OE rihtwislice] righteous; virtuously, fairly **Ch2** 8037 rightwis; **HS** 11164 ryghtwslye; 11414 ryghtwys; 11914 ryghtwus *O* ryghtly; 7156 ryghtwys *O* ryghtful; 7163 ryghtwys *O* ryghte; 600, 601 ryghtfulnes *D* ryȝtwysnesse

rike n. [see riche, n.]

ryme n. [OF] rimed verse; measure, meter, rhythm; a poem, story **Ch1** 28, 85, 118, 200, 5477 ryme; **Ch2** 533, 6371, 7602, 8234, 8357 ryme; 2227L ryme (P differs); **HS** 46 rymys; 51, 74, 2138, 8629 ryme; 9004 rymes

ryme v. (1) [OE ryman] to retreat, depart; die **Ch1** 9729, 13318 ryme; **Ch2** 1750 ryme

ryme v. (2) [OF rimer] to make verses or rimes; recite poems **Ch1** 63 rymes; 180, 190 rymed; 3574, 4694 ryme; **Ch2** 5020, 8122 ryme; 6712 rymed; **HS** 10946 ryme

rimethed v. [OE rymþ] to make room, clear a way **Ch1** 3464 rimethed P rempede L; **Ch2** 337 rimthed P remede L

rynce v. [OF rincier] to clear land of crops **Ch2** 7853 rynce

rynde n. [see rote, n.]

ryng n. [OE hring] symbol of kingship; wrestling ring; battlefield **Ch1** 4612 ryng; 11586 rounge P ryng L; **Ch2** 2087, 3129, 5742, 8091 ryng; 7172 rynges; 7442 renge; **HS** 991 ryng

ryng v. [OE hringan] ring a bell, jingle; echo, resound **Ch1** 1129 ryng P rynge L; 3493, 12066 rong P ronge L; 12482 rong; 14236 rongen; **HS** 891, 909 ryngge; 4259 rynge; 923, 928 rong; 970, 7284 runge; 4775 ryngyng

rynne v. [see ran, v.]

ryot n. [OF; AF rioute] loud revelry **HS** 994 bobaunce *C* thyngis *D* ryot

◆ **rioterie** n. [OF] riotous behavior **Ch1** 2400 riotry P ryotrye L; 11334 rioterie mystere P lechours mester L; **Ch2** 5400, 8281 rioterie

rise v. [see aryse, raise, reise] [OE risan, arisan] rise to battle, take up arms, rebel; increase, grow; come, appear; become powerful, become stormy **Ch1** 973 risen; 1251 rise P ryse L; 1823, 2786, 4710, 6379, 7332 rise; 770, 2945, 4115, 6426, 8916 ros; 4953 rose; 4533 risand P rysande L; 4616L ruysed (P differs); 10175 risand P rysyng L; 14927 rises P so ryst L; 6476 risand P arysen L; 8895 vp ryse; **Ch2** 74, 3254, 5452, 6787, 8022 rise; 1328, 3363, 5874, 6378, 8154 ros; 1065 rises; 1330 be risen P þe risyng L; 3698, 3811, 5709, 6341, 6606 risen; **HS** 109, 3568, 4780, 9812, 12268 ryse; 2481 rys; 522, 867, 2719, 4647 ros; 708 resyn

rysyng ger. [from OE risan] rising, standing up; resurrection; moving upward **Ch1** 1181 rysyng; 9116 risyng; 13801 tisyng (error) P; rysyge L; **Ch2** 1330 be risen P þe risyng L; **HS** 4293 rysyng

ryþt, ryth, ryȝt [see right, adj./adv.]

ryuage n. [OF] coast, shore **Ch1** 1459, 3636 ryuage; 7562 ryuages

riuale n. [OF rivaille, rival] sea coast; shore; landing place **Ch1** 1288 ryuale P ryuaille L; **Ch2** 3777 riuale P ryvaile L

riue, rofe, riuen v. (1) [ON; cp. OI rifa] tear up, demolish, break up **Ch1** 1842 to ryuen; 4584 riuen P ryuen L; 10052 ryue; 11872 to rofe P to rof L; 13330 ryuen; **Ch2** 3638 ryuen; 4212 to rof; **HS** 9113 ryue; 9292 rofe; 6796 to ryues; 12252 to ryue

riue v. (2) [see ariue, v.] [OF river] come to shore; go, travel **Ch1** 6182, 6870 ryued P aryued L; 2869, 6286 ryue; 4654 vp ryue P aryue L; 5914 ryuand; 15215 aryued P ryued L; **Ch2** 189, 677, 2596, 5932 ryued; 2404 ryued P aryved L; 2349, 4206 ryue; 3662 riue;

7130 riues; 13, 2526, 4746 vpryue; 3945 vpriue; 7712 vp rif
riuelyng n. [OE rifeling] a rawhide shoe; fig.: derogatory epithet **Ch2** 6824 riuelyng
riuer n. [AF rivere] river; a river bank where hawking is done **Ch1** 3107, 8044, 10837, 13957 ryuere; 15670 ryuer; 3815, 14598 riuere; 6005 broke P riueres L; 6343 riuers; **Ch2** 2286, 3606 riuer; 4998 riuere
ryues n. [see ryuage, n.] [OF; cp. AL rivus] ?river bank; ?stones for grinding **Ch2** 4307 ryues P ryves L
riuyng ger. [from OF river, v. (2)] arrival, landing **Ch2** 1731 riuyng P aryvyng L
ro, roo n. [OE ra, raha] the roe deer **Ch1** 15056 roo P ro L; **Ch2** 2850 ro
robbe v. [OF rober, robber] to plunder, spoil **Ch1** 4472, 4757, 5580, 7288, 7552 robbe; 3185 robbe P robben L; 1428, 2752, 5582, 6740, 8485 robbed; 3727, 7306 robbid; **Ch2** 896, 5475, 6280, 6754, 8012 robbe; 859, 2229, 5773, 6614, 7872 robbed; 1104 robbes; 2185, 7870 robband; **HS** 2170, 2202 robbe; 6732 robbed; 9361 robbud
robbery n. [AF robberie] stealing, plundering **Ch1** 5734 robberie P reuerie L; 8835 robbery; 8854 robberie; **Ch2** 878, 1942, 3009, 7940, 8040 robberie; 8052 robbrie; **HS** 1312 robbrye; 2210, 2219, 2449, 11636 robborye; 3363 robbory
robbour n. [AF robbere] thief **Ch1** 1978 robbour; 1417, 5821, 5835 robbours; 6583 robbours P pylours L; 12984L robbours (om. P); **Ch2** 1602, 7913 robbours; 4263 robboure; **HS** 4935 robbours; 6129 robbour
robe n. [OF] robe, gown **Ch2** 6715 robis; **HS** 3350 robe
robours, reburs n. [OF rebors, rebours] antagonism; with perversity **Ch1** 5108 at robours P at reburs L; 12316 at rebours
roche n. [OF] boulder; cliff, crag **Ch1** 1839, 10136 roche; 1173, 1450, 11043, 11871 roches
rochere n. [OF rocher] a stony cliff **Ch1** 10041 rochere P rocher L
rode n. [OE rod, rode] the cross; a crucifix, rood **Ch2** 1906, 2275, 6770 rode; **HS** 724, 1787, 3845, 5286, 8247 rode
roialme n. [see reame, reme, n.]
roillant adj. [OF roillier, v.] rampaging; rough play **Ch2** 2919 valiaunt P roillant L
roke n. [OF roc, rok] the rook in chess, a castle **Ch1** 11155 roke
rolle n. [see huche] [OF] scroll of documents **HS** 9263, 9288, 9292 rolle; 9807 rolle O huche
rollyng ger. [from OF roller, rouler] enrollment; recording a document in a scroll **HS** 9809, 9811 rollyng
romance n. [AF] narrative, poem, chivalric tale; book or document written in French **Ch1** 178, 4453, 15917 romance; 15921 Frankis stile P romaunce L; **Ch2** 2878, 4909, 5024, 5625, 8323 romance; 4688 romans P romance L
rombed v. [prob. OE *ramian] roll or toss about **Ch1** 8084 rombed P rubbed L
ronnen, runnen v. [see ran, v.]
ronoun, ronons n. [see renoun, n.]
rope n. [OE rap] rope, cord **Ch1** 1040, 2948, 4585, 8768, 11763 ropes; 9864L rop (om. P); **Ch2** 4404 runcys P ropys L; **HS** 8057 rope
rore v. [OE rarian] shout, bellow; thunder **Ch1** 2942 rored; 6470 rorand; **Ch2** 2873 roryng
roste v. [OF rostir] to roast meat, cook **Ch1** 12038 roste P rostyng L; 12039 rosted; 15062 roste P rostoid L; **Ch2** 4336 roste
rote n. [ON rot] root of a tree or plant; fig.: the source; fig.: rote & rynde: utterly, completely destroyed **Ch1** 1971 rote; 15671 rotes; 4250 rute P rote L; 5919, 12925, 15744 rote & rynde; **Ch2** 8126 rote & rynde; **HS** 7620 rote; 9809 croppe & rote
rote v. [OE rotian] to rot, wither **Ch1** 15367 rote; **HS** 4130 rotede; 6757 rote
rotefast adj. [from ON, OE rot, n. + fæst] established; fixed **Ch1** 2102 rotefast P roted fast L
roten adj. [ON rotinn] decayed; rotten **Ch1** 15679 roten; **HS** 6766 roten
roþer n. [OE roðer] rudder, oar **Ch1** 6477 roþer; 11768 roþers P roþeres L; **Ch2** 4606, 7030 roþer; **HS** 4628 roþer
rotour n. [OF roteor] one who plays the rote, a stringed instrument **HS** 1042 rotour
roun, rom n./v. [OE rum, rumian] clear a battlefield of hostile troops; give way **Ch1** 12582 rounn L gate R (om. P); **Ch2** 4448 redy roun P redy & rom L
roun n. [OE run, rune] language; a rune **Ch1** 13221 roun; 15013 roune P roun L
round, rounde aboute adj./adv. [AF rounde, rund] round; in a circle, surrounded; all around **Ch1** 5018 round; 8668 rounde about; **Ch2** 3575, 5741 rounde; 7432 rounde aboute
roune v. [OE runian] to whisper, take counsel; speak in confidence **HS** 6932 rounede; 12516 roune; 1344 *D* rowne [other MSS differ]
rounge n. [see ryng, n.]
roungers n. [from OF roungier, v.] one who clips coins **Ch2** 5737 roungers
rous n. [ON; cp. OI hrosan] a boast; pride, vainglory **HS** 2385 rous GLOSS BH proude wrdys; 5160, 7426 rous GLOSS BH bost
rouht, route n. [OF rote, route; AF rute] troop, band; company **Ch1** 1697, 6177, 8832, 11079, 12484 route; 6175 þorghoute P rout L; **Ch2** 1750 rouht; 3629, 4660, 6689, 7752, 8154 route
rouht v. [OE hrutan] cry out, shout **Ch1** 7086

rouht P roughte L
rouht v. [see reche, v.]
route n. [see gate] [AF rute] way, road, path **Ch1** 1135, 3367, 3380, 4637, 6177 route; 10808 gashadles P grete routes
route v. [OF aroter] assemble **Ch2** 2353 loute P route L
rouþe, ruthe n. [see reuth, n.]
rowe n. (1) [OE raw] line, row **Ch1** 1679 rowe; **Ch2** 8169 rowe
rowe n. (2) [from OE ruh, rug, ruwe] being rough, shaggy **Ch2** 5274 rowe
rowe adj. [OE ruh, ruwe] rough, rude, angry **HS** 3017 rowe
rowe v. (1) [OE rowan] to row a boat **Ch1** 10174 rowe; 11864 rowes; **Ch2** 5699 rowe
rowe v. (2) [OF roer, ruer] to flow, flood **Ch1** 10174 rowe; 11864 rowes
rubbed v. [cp. LG, Fris. rubben, Norw. rubba] scratched, clawed **Ch1** 8084 rombed P rubbed L
ruly, rulych adv./adj. [see reuly]
runcy n. [OF roncin, AF runcin] charger; riding horse; work horse **Ch1** 11180 runces P rounsyes L; **Ch2** 1187 runcies P hurdels L; 4404 runcys P ropys L

S

sabatons n. [from ML sabatum] steel foot-armor **Ch1** 9880L sabatons (om. P)
sacrament n. [AF sacrement (MP); L sacramentum] sacrament of the Church **HS** 1619, 1837, 1980, 10808, 11993 sacrament; 23 sacramentys; 11267 sacramentes
sacre, sakare n. [OF sacree] part of the mass; ceremonial, anointing **HS** 7299 sakare; 7951, 8831, 8849, 10014 sacre
sacred, sacrid v. [OF sacrer] to consecrate; celebrate the eucharist **Ch2** 3155 sacred; 5114 sacrid; **HS** 9957 sacred; 10083 sacreþ
sacrifise n. [OF sacrifice] making a sacrifice; a victim of sacrifice; a spiritual offering **Ch1** 2069, 4667, 4693, 4866, 5936 sacrifise; **HS** 341, 2851, 7737 sacryfyse
sacryfyed v. [AF sacrifier (MP)] perform sacrificial rites **HS** 10059 sacryfyed; 9957 sacred *O* sakryde *SV* sacrefyed
sacrilage n. [OF sacrilege] stealing church property; outrage against sacred things or persons; irreverent behavior **HS** 21 sacrilage; 4682, 8599, 8612, 8637, 8797 sacrylege; 8994, 9009, 9258, 9496, 11140 sacrylage
sad, sadly adj./adv. [OE sæd] sated; weary, hard, steadily, strongly; completely **Ch1** 4382 sad; 4972 sadly P sadlyk L; 13020 sadly; 13292 sidelynges P sadly L; **Ch2** 4912, 7432 sad; 7433 sadly; **HS** 1117 sad
sadelle, sadille n. [OE] saddle for a horse or donkey **Ch1** 4337, 12382 sadille; 10667, 13045 sadelle; 12398L sadel (om. P); 12570LR sadels (om. P); 13078L sadeles (om. P); **Ch2** 7248 sadelle
saf adj. [see saufe]
saffrund v. [AF safroneȝ (MP)] of saffon color **HS** 3447 saffrund
sage n. [OF] an ancient authority **Ch1** 11528 sage
say, seie, sais, said v. [OE secgan] to tell, speak; agree on, claim **Ch1** 70, 3723, 5598, 8251, 10651 say; 7333 sai; 234, 1216, 3268, 7662, 8119 seie; 539 seye; 2292 sey; 1727 saie; 61, 374, 1731, 2199, 5635 says; 1978, 3732, 6493, 8045, 15626 sais; 157 sayes; 560 seys; 3751, 6487 seis; 11352 seise; 1309 seies; 1077, 2865, 5086 saye; 7975 sayn; 712, 14163 sais P seys L; 1626, 2395, 5981, 8004, 15580 said; 71, 284, 485, 1790, 2029 sayd; 2289 saied; 1121, 1473, 6632, 7465, 8048 seid; 1133 seied; 2974 sayden; 2362 teld P seyde L; 2473 said P seyde L; 6537 sais P seyþ L; **Ch2** 98, 1321, 4573, 6161, 7877 sais; 8192 seis; 7346 says; 205, 2594, 5047, 6714, 8323 say; 494, 840, 1407, 6263 seye; 584, 1639, 3479, 5973, 8274 seie; 804, 1686, 4011, 6080, 8349 said; 1678, 1720 seid; 2305 saiden; 2513 sayd; 7358 saied; 945 said P seide L; **HS** 521, 1515, 2779, 6833, 11776 sey; 551, 595, 676, 4371, 11307 seye; 632, 3493 seyd; 2735 say; 664, 4166, 4859 seyþ; 624, 6526 seyse; 589, 942, 2639 seys; 11386 seyt; 381, 737 seyyn; 4168, 4956 seyen; 240, 2543, 9431, 10470, 10693 seyde; 1136 seyyng; 634 seyst; 3489 seydyst; 5887 seyden; 1977 spak GLOSS B seyd
saies n. [see asay] [AF assay; short form of assai, n.] a feat, trial **Ch1** 3997 þe saies P þer assayes L; 9701 þe saies P þasayes L
saile n. [OE segl] sail of a ship **Ch1** 682, 2949 saile P sayl L; 613, 1302, 3612, 4559, 7631 saile; 1405, 5527 sailes; **Ch2** 1443, 1727, 3867, 4606, 7374 saile; 4229, 4304, 4306 sailes; **HS** 8887 sayl
saile v. (1) [see assaile] [from OF assaillir, v.] attack, make assault **Ch1** 4326 saile P assaile L; 4354 saile P saille L; **Ch2** 2818 saile
saile, sailand v. (2) [OE seglan, seglian] sail on a ship **Ch1** 1287, 1307, 2152, 3624 saile; 1311, 2939, 4590, 5528, 6467 sailed; 5858 farde P sayled L; 8139 sailand P saylynge L; 13877 sailand; **Ch2** 4193, 5699 saile; 4632 sailes; 3627, 3686, 4232, 4633, 5583 sailand; 1730 sailyng
sayled v. [OF salir] to dance, leap **HS** 2820 tumblede *C* salyed *D* sayled
sayng ger. [from OE secgan, v.] talking, speaking **Ch1** 96, 103 sayng; 198 saiynge; 8116 saing; **Ch2** 3770, 6226, 6228 sayng; **HS** 542,

734 seyyng

saynt n./adj. [OE sanct; OF saint, seinte] holy person; divinely inspired; canonized saints; a title **Ch1** 52, 5226, 5507, 6024, 7642 saynt; 3069, 7916 seynt; **Ch2** 90, 1626, 3032, 6047, 8189 saynt; 3336, 3654, 6853 seynt; **HS** 640 seyntys; 1290, 2787, 7173, 7645, 11515 seynt; 2475 seynt *D* seyn

sak n. [OE sacc; AF sac (MP)] bag; sackcloth garment **HS** 1152, 1156, 1158, 1165 sak

sake n. [OE sacu] for the benefit of; regard, consideration **Ch1** 1894, 2766, 4051, 5553, 6306 sake; 2238 sak P sake L; **Ch2** 1462, 3317, 6969, 7084, 8107 sake; **HS** 1230, 2902, 6487, 7454, 8885 sake

sakles adj. [OE sacleas] blameless, guiltless **Ch2** 4522 sakles P gultelis L

salyne n. [OF saline] a salt pit **Ch1** 1413 salyne P salynes L

salle, suld, schal, schulde v. [OE sceal] to have to; must; be about to (modal aux.) **Ch1** 21, 1156, 2470, 6665, 8157 salle; 2306 salle P schal L; 542 schalle; 5196 salle P schol L; 2912, 6972 salle P schalt L; 4243 suld P schalt L; 2568, 5375 salle P schal L; 1085 salt P schalt L; 2031 salt; 8983 salle P schullen L; 90, 1288, 4563, 6189, 8120 suld; 1507, 3814, 4415 suld P scholde L; 5194L schost (om. P); **Ch2** 907, 2042, 4823, 7619, 8299 suld; 67, 1038, 4042, 7639, 8329 salle; 61 suld P schulde L; 696 suld P schalt L; **HS** 36, 226, 2150, 2187, 12558 shal; 10075 shall; 122, 1514, 2188 shalt; 3, 10093 shul; 6416, 6613 shull; 32, 9061 shuld; 97, 1544, 2484, 4438, 9061 shulde; 2381, 5132, 11756 shust

saluacoun, saluacyoun n. [OF salvacion, L salvatio] salvation from sin; being secure; protection **Ch1** 14548 saluacoun P sauacion L; **HS** 4427, 5310, 5352 saluacyoun; 9930 saluacoun

salue n. [OE sealf] medicinal ointment; remedy **Ch1** 8890 salue

same pron./adj./adv. [ON samr] equal, similar; the same thing **Ch1** 62, 1333, 5353, 6372, 8188 same; **Ch2** 97, 1905, 4418, 7854, 8249 same; **HS** 288, 3280, 7294, 9441, 11107 same

samen, samned v. [OE samnian] to gather, assemble **Ch1** 2915, 4868 samen; 1928 samed P ysamed L; 2514, 3614, 5471, 6555 samned; 13141 samend P samned L; **Ch2** 49, 1508, 2529, 5310, 7752 samned; 1532, 6855 samen

samen adv. [OE samen] together, in company **Ch1** 10, 4003 samen; 12694LR samen (om. P); **Ch2** 443 samen ȝede P togydere ȝede L; 2167, 2867, 4026, 4504, 6720 samen

samenyng ger. [from OE samnian, v.] meeting, gathering; union; battle **Ch1** 2696L samnyg (om. P); 3436 samenyng P samnyng L; 6619 samenyng P sampninge L; 11029 samenyng P samninge L; 14695 samnyng P somonynge L; **Ch2** 3506, 4076, 5430, 5771, 7153 samenyng; 7554, 7617 samnyng

sample n. [see ensample] [AF saumple, OF essemple] example **HS** 5237, 7475, 11426 sample

sand, sond n. [see sond]

sangesters n. [OE sangestere] singers **Ch1** 4001 sangesters; 11147 sangsters P gestours singers L

sanȝ faille phrase [OF saun(s), prep. + faille, n.] certainly, without doubt; assuredly **Ch1** 4458, 6239 sanȝ faile; **Ch2** 639, 5906, 6577, 7508 sanȝ faile; **HS** 6025 sauntȝ fayle

saracen, saraȝin n./adj. [AF saraȝin (MP)] a saracen, pagan **Ch1** 6484, 6488 saracens; 6494 sareȝins P sarsyns L; 13107 saraȝins; 15271 sareȝin; 15290 sareȝyn; **Ch2** 1226, 3430, 3891, 4752, 5617 saraȝin; 4570 saraȝyn; 2480, 3422, 4308, 5556, 6628 saraȝins; 2492, 4370 saraȝines; **HS** 5242, 5343 sarasyn; 185, 193, 221 sarasyne; 5556 sarasyns; 6161 sarasynes

sare adj./adv. [see sor, sare, sory] [OF sere, sarre, ppl. of serrer] holding closely together; in close order **Ch1** 12698 sarer P sykerer L sarrer R; 13014 sarrely; **Ch2** 7423 sare

sargeancie n. [see sergeancie]

sargeanȝ n. [see sergeant]

satled v. [OE setlan] become lower in estate; to settle, sink **Ch1** 8072 satled P schok L; **Ch2** 5514 satled

saue v. [see vouchsaue, v.] [OF sauver, salver, saver] to save, deliver, rescue **Ch1** 735, 2352, 5102, 7047, 8547 saue; 261, 7649 saued; 15690L saue (om. P); **Ch2** 233, 2501, 5011, 7144, 8253 saue; 3806 saues; 325, 1152, 3235, 4222, 5152 saued; **HS** 627, 3846, 6102, 9598, 10320 saue; 900 sauyþ; 10313 saued; 9823 saue *O* defende

saue, safly, sauely prep./adv. [from OF sauf, adj.] safely, without danger; except **Ch1** 904 saue; 986, 7379, 7866 sauely; 3037 sauely P safly L; 6523 sauely P sauelike L; 7830 sauely P safliest L; **Ch2** 1993, 3642, 4746, 5434, 7741 sauely; **HS** 1434 sauely *D* safly; 9119 saue; 10261 *S* saf *V* saue (om. B)

saueoure n. [OF] savior **Ch1** 5267, 14304 saueoure; **HS** 10816 sauueour

sauf, saf adj. [OF sauf, saf] unscathed, unhurt **Ch1** 6469 sauf; 12679 saufe P siker L sauf R; **Ch2** 1992 saf

saufte, suate n. [OF sauvete, AF saute] safety; custody **Ch1** 1055 suate P suwaute L (errors); **Ch2** 5706 saufte

sauht v./adj. [see saut, n.] [OE sehtan] make peace; be reconciled **Ch1** 2470 sauht; 13787 seldom sauht P sonder sauht L; 15502 was brouht P were al saught L; **HS** 4140 vnsaght

O saught

sauhtillyng, sauhtlyng ger. [OE sauhtiling] reconciliation, agreement **Ch1** 3228 sauhtlyng P saughtlyng L; **Ch2** 1154 sauhtillyng P in his departyng L; 3277, 3288, 6963 sauhtillyng

sauer, sauour n. [OF savor, savour] taste, smell **Ch1** 14260 sauour; **HS** 9996 sauer; 1398, 9985, 11575 sauour

sauer v. [OF savorer] to have a taste, smell, flavor **HS** 9994 sauerþ; 1396 sauerede *C* smellyd; 9996 haþ sauer *SV* hit sauereþ

saut n. [see assaut] [short form of OF assaut] attack, battle **Ch1** 5054 sauht P saut L; 5057 saute P saut L; 9221, 14026 sautes; **Ch2** 3072 saut; 4366, 4367, 7791 sautes

sauter n. [AF sauter (MP)] psalter, Book of Psalms **HS** 4772, 5158 sauter; 11625 sautere; 9974 sautere *SV* psauter

sautre, sautreours n. [OF sauterie] psaltery, a musical instrument **Ch1** 11144 sautreours; **HS** 4774 sautre

sauuage adj. [OF sauvage, AF sawage] wild, uncultivated; fierce **Ch1** 5607 sauuage P sauage L; **Ch2** 2773 sauuage P sauage L

saw n. [see say, se, see, v.] [OE sagu] saying, discourse; tale; decree, proverb **Ch1** 21, 951, 2788, 6265, 9957 sawe; 8657 saw; 7120 falsnes P sawes L; 2554 sawes; 7353 sau P sawe L; **Ch2** 381, 2090, 3505, 6682, 8075 sawe; 532, 5095, 6037 saw; **HS** 13, 4905, 5455, 7744, 11657 sawe; 6720 sawes; 550 sawe *D* sawhe; 625 sawe *C* tale; 1382 sowe *D* seyȝen

saxon, sesson n./adj. [OE seaxan; L saxo; AF sessoun] Saxon; the Saxon language: English; the country of Saxon origin **Ch1** 1917 sessons; 1921 sesson; 7462 sessoun P saxoun L; 15532 saxone P saxoyn L; 15764 saxons; 15769 sessons . . . sessoyne; 15795 sessoyne P saxoyne L; 15789 sessons P saxons L

scabbed adj. [from ON scabbe, n.] dirty, wretched **Ch2** 6821 scabbed

scape v. [see skape]

scarlet adj. [AF escharlet (MP)] color scarlet **HS** 11377 scarlet

scathe n. [see skathe]

scatred v. [prob. OE; cp. MDu scateren, MLG schateren] dispersed **Ch2** 6603 scatred

SCH- and SH-

schad, sched, shedde v. [OE sceadan, scadan] to divide, separate; to split, shed, scatter **Ch1** 989 schad P schadden L; 6177 schad P to schadde L; 7995 schad; **Ch2** 2853, 2913 schad; 3940 schede; 4320 sched; 7443 shad; 1791 gette P sched L; **HS** 677, 8248 shedde

schaft n. (1) [OE sceaft] shape, appearance; creation **Ch1** 9261 schaftes; **HS** 8286 shaft; 480 deuyls craft *C* deuyll chafte *D* deuelys awȝt

schaft n. (2) [OE sceaft, scaft] staff, pole; shaft of a spear; darts; axe handle **Ch1** 4335, 6717, 13285 schaftes; **Ch2** 4425, 4430 schaft

schake, schok v. [OE sceacan] hurry; flow; shake, agitate; beat, attack **Ch1** 1819, 6980, 8074 schoke P schok L; 8072 satled P schok L; 5425, 7638, 12371 schake; 13562 schaken; 8074, 10956, 11630, 12514, 14062 schoke; 11934 schaked; **Ch2** 894, 2867, 3067, 7896, 8124 schoke; 5292 schok; 2181 schaken; 195, 2972, 5328 schake; **HS** 2528, 7001 shoke; 3191 cheke *F* scheke *O* schake; 8046 quoke *O* schoke

schal, scholde v. [see salle]

schame, skam n. [OE sceamu, scamu] feeling of humiliation; harm, evil; injury **Ch1** 941, 3896, 6018, 10096, 13648 schame; 4815L schame (om. P); 14768L scham (om. P); **Ch2** 508, 3090, 4009, 6820, 8200 schame; 3870 skam P schame L; 7248 skam; 4296, 7904 scham; **HS** 674, 1446, 6894, 11434, 12579 shame; 4686, 8992 shames

schame v. [OE sceamian, scamian] to feel shame; to put to shame; to injure **Ch1** 7893, 7973 schame; 3082, 14561 schamed; 2343 aschamed P schamed L; **HS** 11856 shamede; 12037 shameþ

schamfulle, shamely adj./adv. [see aschamed, oschamed] [OE scamful, scamlic] shameful; disgracefully **Ch1** 1001 schamly P schamely L; 5087, 6574, 6793, 11983 schamly; 3424 schames dede; **Ch2** 4113 schamfulle P schamful L; 5974 schames dede; **HS** 7, 6518 shameful; 2053, 12053 shamely

schank n. [OE sceanca, scanca] a leg **Ch1** 4346 schankes; **Ch2** 1328, 1334, 4700, 5031 schank; 807, 808 schankes

schap, shape n. [OE gesceap] form; physique, design **Ch1** 156 schappe; 7194, 7208 schap; 7936 schap P wyght L; **Ch2** 2483 schap P schape L

◆ **shapandys** n. [cf. OE scieppend, scippend] the Fates as shapers of a child's destiny **HS** 572 shapandys *C* schappande *D* schepandys

schape, schop v. [OE scippan, sceapan] to make, devise; ordain **Ch1** 11945 schaped P schape L; 3211L schapest (P differs); 4326L schept (P differs); 4521 compassid P schopen L; 5222L schope (P differs); 7329 skape P schape L; 7744L schop (P differs); 7793 schapid P scaped L; 11758 dight P schop L; 12915 schapes; **Ch2** 6108, 7324, 7690, 7721 schape; 574 dight P schop L; 4923 schaped; **HS** 574 shapyn; 3755 shope; 9669 shape *O* schappynge

shaper n. [from OE sceapan, v.] shaper of destiny; the Fates; God as creator; **HS** 579, 581 shaper; 585 shapers; 9663, 9665 shapperes

schare, shorne v. [OE sceran] to cut, inflict a wound **Ch1** 2648, 10672, 12724 schare P schar L; 15061 schare; 13170 schaar P schar L; **Ch2** 5427 schare; **HS** 1158 shorne *CD* schorn; 10060 share; 11660 shore

scharp adj. [OE scearp] sharp of edge or point; keen-witted **Ch1** 3003, 4334, 15129 scharp; 1005, 1008 scharpe; **Ch2** 641 scharp; **HS** 4748, 7520 sharpe; 8522 sharp

scharply adv. [from OE scearplice] sharply; openly **Ch1** 11815 scharpli P scharply L; **Ch2** 5420, 5876 scharply

schaue v. [OE sceafan, scafan] shave the face or hair; to be tonsured **Ch1** 8888, 9704 schaue; 15920L schauen (om. P); **HS** 3478, 3479 shaue

sched v. [see schad]

shedyng ger. [from OE sceadan, v.] dividing sins in confession **HS** 12426 shedyng

schelde n. [OE scild, scield] shield with a heraldic device; symbol of authority; government **Ch1** 914, 3217, 5433, 10291, 14190 schelde; 4372, 4383, 7514 scheld; 472 schelde P scheld L; 2709, 3003, 3373 scheldes; **Ch2** 417, 1713, 2058, 3888, 3961 schelde; 417 schelde P elde L; 467, 1627, 3604, 5725, 8206 scheld

schelde v. [see schilde, v.]

scheltron, cheltroun n. [AF chiltron; OE scild-truma] battle formation; a compact body of troops; phalanx **Ch1** 3484, 3542 cheltroun P scheltroun L; 4615 þer hardynes P þe scheltrom L; **Ch2** 7443 scheltron

schende, schonde v. [see schond, n.] [OE scendan] to injure; destroy, disgrace **Ch1** 82 schente; 700, 3640, 7602, 8264, 11426 schent; 15571 schende; **Ch2** 903, 2166, 7821 schende; 2042, 3035, 5736, 6629, 8261 schent; 5556 schond; **HS** 2065, 2755, 4942, 11227, 12061 shende; 349, 1002, 2609, 11225, 12048 shent; 494 shende *C* blende; 664 lore *C* schent

schene adj./adv. [OE scine] beautiful, shining **Ch1** 11022L schene (om. P); **Ch2** 6120 schene

shenshepe, shenshype n. [from OE sceand, scond, n.] ruin, destruction **HS** 8252 shenshype; 12036 shenshepe

schepe n. [OE sceap] domestic sheep; a parishioner; meek, long-suffering person **Ch1** 4689, 11250, 13344, 14724 schepe; **Ch2** 1616 schepe; **HS** 4051, 4100, 4822, 5120, 10892 shepe

scheperd n. [OE sceaphirde] shepherd; a spiritual leader **Ch2** 1616 scheperdes; **HS** 4825, 10891, 10895, 10906 shepherd

shere adv. [see schire, adj./adv.]

scherefe n. [see schirue, scherefe, shereue]

schete, schot v. (1) [OE sceotan] hasten, attack; shoot an arrow or missile; to kill; fig.: drunk **Ch1** 854 schote P schete L; 1034 schote P schotten L; 1134 schette P schet L; 1520 schotte; 2927, 3001, 3407 schote; 2054 schet P schoten L; 3766 scet P schet L; 3768, 4335, 6717 schoten; 11398 schoten P yschoten L; 4990, 11395 schot; 6692 schote P scheote L; 7450 cop schotin P cuppe schoten L; 11398 schoten P yschoten L; 8304, 13022, 15684 schete; **Ch2** 437 schotte; 2275, 4219, 4424, 5486, 6536 schete; 2294 schoten; 2850 schet; 4424, 6579 schot; **HS** 1372, 3583, 8517 shete; 3579 shette

schete v. (2) [OE scyttan] close, complete; shut **Ch2** 6536 schete; **HS** 4456 shette; 4486 shet

scheuerd v. [?OE; cp. MDu scheveren] to shatter, splinter **Ch1** 13285 scheuerd P schiuered L

schewe v. [OE sceawian] to see, perceive; announce; demonstrate; explain, confess, reveal **Ch1** 1341 schewed P scheweid L; 132, 700, 4210, 5831, 8056 schewed; 23, 1359, 11892, 12124, 12163 schewe; 627, 3179, 5101, 5588, 11887 schew; 9631L schewes (om. P); **Ch2** 1742, 3813 schewes; 5406 scheawes; 4575, 7367 schew; 1299, 3178, 5614, 6871, 7642 schewe; 131, 2104, 4423, 5645, 7987 schewed; **HS** 4, 400, 7351, 11007, 11189 shewe; 432 shewyd; 498 shewyþ; 12169 yshewed; 5 shewe *D* eschewe

schewyng ger. [from OE sceawian, v.] revelation; confession **Ch2** 4434 schewyng; **HS** 3200, 11435 shewyng

schilde, shelde v. [OE scildan, sceldan] protect, keep safe **Ch1** 7250L schildes (om. P); 9097L schulde (P differs); **Ch2** 416, 7420, 8218 schilde; **HS** 1686 shyld; 2899, 3703, 5187 shelde; 12344 shylde; 1599 shelde *C* chylde

schine, shyne, schone v. [OE scinan] to shine, to be bright **Ch1** 3364 schane P schon L; 3372 schyne; 8929, 11812 schone; 8932 schynand; **Ch2** 3649 schone; **HS** 2300 shynes; 2302 shynyngge; 7028 shynyng; 2233 shoun *H* shone

shynyng ger. [from OE scinan, v.] radiance from a source of light **HS** 2236 shynyng

schip n. [OE scip] sea-going vessel; cargo ship **Ch1** 2931, 3017, 4646, 6461, 7423 schip; 613, 1294, 1322, 3048, 4290 schippe; 2006 schyppe; 4550, 8165 schipes; 738, 1404, 3014, 6179, 15111 schippes; 7420 schippis; 11776 schippis P schipes L; 1456, 6480 scippes P schipes L; **Ch2** 13, 1443, 3645, 5698, 7399 schip; 700 schippe; 46, 894, 2346, 3703, 6454 schippes; 3908, 6568 schippis; **HS** 4628 shyppe; 12520 shyppes

schipman n. [OE scipmann] sailor, seaman; master of a ship **Ch1** 1448, 1452, 14246 schipmen; **Ch2** 3046 schipman; 3638, 3656, 4216 schipmen

schipped v. [OE scipian] to embark; travel by ship **Ch1** 3241, 6463 schipped; **Ch2** 1427,

5572 schipped

schipwright n. [OE scipwyrhta] ship builder **Ch2** 951 schipwright

schire n. [OE scir] county, shire **Ch1** 2093, 7869, 13761 schire; 3685 schires; **Ch2** 82, 2890, 5137, 6942, 7575 schire; 2753 schires

schire adj./adv. [OE scire] bright, shining; glittering **Ch1** 8922, 11904 schire P schir L; **HS** 2496 shere; 12445 shyre

schirue, scherefe, shereue n. [OE scirgerefa] administrator of a shire; a sheriff **Ch1** 6156 scherefes P schirreues L; **Ch2** 1988 schirue P shyreve L; 6796 shireues; **HS** 6795 shereues

schold v. [see salle]

schod v. [OE scodden, ppl.] iron attached to the feet as torture **Ch1** 4569, 4593 iren schod; **Ch2** 4912 iren . . . schod

schoke v. [see schake, to schoke]

schond n. [OE sceand, scond] shame, disgrace; destruction **Ch1** 13642L schonde (om. P); **Ch2** 6312 schond

shone n. [OE sco, sceo, shone] shoes **HS** 3831, 10335 shone

schonne, schone v. [OE scunian] refuse to do, refrain from; shun **Ch1** 13566 schonne P schone L; **Ch2** 2626, 2687, 7244 schonne; **HS** 4 shewe *D* schone

schop v. [see schape]

schorne v. [see schare]

schort adj./adv. [OE scort, scortlice] of short length, less than adequate; a brief time, soon; rapid speech **Ch1** 151, 1905, 12017, 15127 schorte; 3554 schorte P schortly L; 3581 schort; 388 schortly; 7411 schorter; 7351 scort P schort L; **Ch2** 5441 schorte; 7673 schortely; 6349 schortly; 1659 smertly P schortly L; **HS** 11284 short; 3167, 5267, 6009, 9266, 11331 shortly

schorte, schorten v. [OE scortian; cp. OI skorta] to shorten; decrease **Ch1** 3555 schortid; 9924 schorten P schorte L; **Ch2** 4353 schorten; 6814 schorte; 1170 scorted P schorted L; **HS** 1029 shortyþ

schote n. [OE scot, sceat] a missile, dart, arrow; a swift movement, a rush **Ch1** 857, 1734, 2095, 15018 schote; 2922 schotes P schutes L

schotyng ger. [from OE sceotan, v.] shooting of a weapon **Ch1** 11400 schotyng P schetyng L; 13029 schotyng

schoure n. [see stour] [OE scur, scurra] shower of blows or darts; an assault or attack; trouble, misfortune **Ch1** 6717L schour (P differs); 11422 schours P stours L; **Ch2** 4113 schoure; 8131 schoures

schouue, schoue v. [OE scufan, sceufan] push, shove; thrust with a weapon **Ch1** 8769 schoued P schouued L; 12484, 13292 schouen; **Ch2** 6715 schouue

schrew, schreward n. [?OE screawa] rascal, rogue; scoundrel **Ch1** 3929 yuel men P schrewes L; 6009 schrew P schrewe L; 12134 schrewe; **Ch2** 169 schrew; 5739 schrewe; 6341 schreward; **HS** 1896, 2936, 7352, 11008 shrewe; 3062 shrew; 4907 shrewes

shrewed adj. [see schrowe, v.] [?from OE screawa, n.] wicked, depraved **HS** 4906 shrewed

shryfte n. [OE scryft] confession; sacrament of penance **HS** 25, 3416, 9310, 10830, 11909 shryfte; 7306 shrifte; 12348 shryft; 588 shreue; 3658 shryfte *W* schrifte; 3661, 3668 shryfte *W* shrifte; 3664 shryfte *W* shrift; 956 shryfte *C* howsyl & thryfte

shryftefader n. [from OE scryft + fader] a confessor **HS** 11592 shryftefadyr; 11601 shryftefader

schrille, shryl adj./adv. [?ON; cp. LG schrell] of a piercing sound **Ch2** 649 schille (?error) P schrille L; **HS** 8757 shryl

schrine n. [OE scrin, L scrinium] reliquary; decorated tomb **Ch1** 15370 schryne; **Ch2** 445, 1968 schryne; 3219 schrine; **HS** 4994 shrynes

schriue, schryuen v. [OE scrifan] to absolve, hear confession; impose penance **Ch1** 15884 schroue P schrof L; **Ch2** 1609 scryuen P yschryven L; 2808 schryuen; 6813 schriue; 3384, 5844 schryue; **HS** 264, 11375 shrof; 1081, 4162, 8416, 10853, 12209 shryue; 16, 35 shreuyn; 750, 3443 shreue; 8569 shrofe; 12206 shroue; 12324 shroff; 12253 shryuen; 2388 shryue *C* telle *D* amende; 11840 vnshryue *O* noghte schreuene

shryuyng ger. [from OE scrifan, v.] confession; absolution **HS** 11493, 12636 shryuyng

schrowe, schrewe v. [from OE screawa?, n.] to curse **Ch2** 3930 schrowe P schrewe L; 5692 schrowe

shrubbyþ v. [cp. MLG, MDu schrubben, schrobben] scratch or rub oneself **HS** 4285 shrubbyþ

schuldres n. [OE sculder, sculdra] shoulders **Ch1** 13357 schuldres

scirt, skirt n. [ON; cp OI skyrta] lower part of gown or robe **Ch1** 7770 scirt P skirt L

sclaunder, skandere n./adj. [OF esclandre] false accusation, lie; shameful distress, misfortune; notoriety, disgrace **Ch1** 54 sclaundire; **Ch2** 8228 skandere; 1273 skandre P sklandres L; **HS** 7936 sclaunder; 1292 ernyst *D* sclaunder; 1532 vyle *D* sclaundrous; 1535 slaghtyr *D* sclaunder; 6546 [MS *O* interpolation, l. 95] sclaunder

scole n. [OE scol; AF escole (MP)] school; institution for training **Ch2** 5606 scoles; 6776 scole; **HS** 7998, 8166, 8167 scole; 8169 scole hous

score, skore n. [OE scoru, from ON; cp. OI skor] limit, boundary; track, way; notch, tally; twenty **Ch1** 3349, 4873, 4971, 5779 score; 2597, 4284, 6033 foure score; 13162 skore P score L; **Ch2** 1311, 3481, 5747, 6067, 6561 four score; 5929 forscore; 6724 fiue score; **HS** 1545, 3100, 3681, 6874, 11233 skore

scorne, scarne n./v. [see skorne, skurne]

scoupe n. [from OF escope; cp. MDu scoppe] water bucket **Ch1** 8054 scoupes P scopes L

scoupe v. [from scoupe, n.] bail out water **Ch1** 8050, 8052 scoupe

scourge n. [AF escorge] whip, lash **HS** 10926, 10928 scourge

scrite, scris n. [see skrite, skryt]

scrowe n. [AF escrowe] parchement document **HS** 11117 scrowe

sculk v. [see skulke]

scumfyghte v. [see discomfite]

se, see n. (1) [OE sæ] ocean; a large body of water **Ch1** 656, 2480, 4168, 6318, 7675 se; 686, 1427, 2148, 4165, 8139 see; 5737, 5755 sees; 2892 seis; **Ch2** 1977, 2401, 4929, 6804, 8273 se; 502, 1727, 2007 see; 947 sees; **HS** 1741, 3799, 5445, 10737, 12519 se; 877, 5700, 7785 see

se, see n. (2) [see sege, n.] [OF sie, se] throne of a bishop; seat; a bishop's territory **Ch1** 7646 see P sege L; 5660, 11548 archbisshop see; 5671 bisshop sees; 6770 bisshop se; 14640 se; **Ch2** 1820, 2313, 3982, 6909 se; 6001 bisshop se; 7840, 7906 papes se; **HS** 11481 se

se, saw, sauh, seen, sene v. [OE seon] notice; to be seen; observe; to witness **Ch1** 672, 1669, 5382, 8038, 14266 se; 93, 668, 3901, 7438, 7531 see; 7062 sees; 4056, 6338 ses; 1043, 4328, 5359, 6344, 7443 saw; 148, 1269, 3142, 7145, 14271 sawe; 7623, 7899, 8031, 11983 sauh; 493 saugh; 7912 sowe P sawe L; 4628, 9587 sowe; 7173 sauh P sey L; 13748 sauh P seye L; 11960 seste; 624, 2508, 4116, 5094, 7343 sene; **Ch2** 142, 1433, 3220, 5922, 7959 se; 1967 see; 1190, 5615, 6269 sees; 1696, 5342 ses; 3649 sihi P sey L; 6364 seen; 814, 2764, 5198, 6688, 8151 sene; 765 seene; 276, 675, 3302, 5003, 8234 sauh; 257 sauh P seye L; **HS** 40, 281, 1384, 1791, 10076 se; 324, 1109, 1249 see; 7581 ses; 81, 10148 sees; 4584, 7507 seeþ; 6358 seþ; 218, 1421, 1795, 3884, 4192 sagh; 1372, 1819, 9213, 9593 sawe; 1571, 2716, 3886, 8039, 10056 saye; 1382 sowe; 29 seen; 5532, 6283, 10040 sen; 317, 523, 1667 seyn; 1440, 4454, 9120, 11546 sene; 134, 1580, 5281, 5312, 7500 seye

seale n. [see seel, n. (2)]

seculere n. [OF seculer, adj., L secularis] clergy not living under a rule; a religious not cloistered **Ch1** 14626 seculere; **Ch2** 5854 seculere

secunde, secound n./adj. [AF secund (MP)] the second number; next in order after the first **Ch1** 12867 secound; **Ch2** 3123 secunde; 4685 secund; **HS** 9795, 11381 secunde

sede n. [from L sedes] seat; a capital **Ch1** 15460 sede

sedgeyng ger. [see sayng, seyying] [from OE secgan] a written account **Ch1** 93 sedgeyng

seel, sele n. (1) [OE sæl, sel] happiness; time, occasion **Ch1** 6902 seele P sel L; **Ch2** 1995 non seel P no while L; **HS** 5879 sele; 4067 cele GLOSS BH godely; 5781 sele GLOSS H man; 6970 sele GLOSS B tyme GLOSS H þat tyme; 536 al weyl *C* þat sel; 786 *C* an sale (B differs)

seel, seal, sel n. (2) [OF seal] figure affixed to seal a document or letter **Ch1** 2748 seal P sel L; 4217 seel P seal L; 5828 seale P sel L; **Ch2** 622, 1695, 3609, 4163, 6256 seale; 826, 2552 seele; 6994 seales

seere adj. (1) [OE sear] dry, shriveled **Ch2** 347 seere

seere, sere adj. (2) [ON; cp. OI ser, pron.] various, diverse; distinct, individual; much; in all, all told **Ch1** 435 seere P ser L; 3011, 3469, 5320, 5627 sere; 709 sere P seer L; 5028, 7871 seres; 1286 seres P sers L; 7255 sere P seeres L; 7326, 13006 sers P seers L; 7970 sere P here L; 8106 sere P ser L; **Ch2** 353, 3945 seere; 1889, 2011, 4158, 7849, 8192 sere; 5458, 6286, 8059 sers; 2617 sere P more L; **HS** 2029, 2603, 8072 sere

sege n. [OF siege (MP)] seat, chair; besieging a city, castle; the episcopal see **Ch1** 1027, 1057, 5025, 5960 sege; 7646 see P sege L; **Ch2** 2463, 4090, 5524, 6620, 7977 sege; **HS** 10045 sege

sege v. [see besege] [from OF siege, sege, n.] besiege a city or castle **Ch1** 3296 seged P byseget L; 5422, 5537 seged; **Ch2** 2459, 6570 seged

seggers n. [from OE secgan, v.] reciters, minstrels **Ch1** 76 seggers

seignory, seynurye n. [AF seignurie] lordship, dominion, authority; land, domain; control **Ch1** 2626L seignurie (om. P); 2822 sengnori P seygnury L; 5187, 5190 seignorie P seignurye L; 3890, 5699, 6974, 14155 seignorie; 11455 senyorie P seynurye L; 11464 seingurie P seignurye L; 5683 seignories; **Ch2** 490, 764, 5546 seignory; 1157 seignories; 798, 3615, 4462, 5252, 7544 seignorie; **HS** 8665 seynurye; 10533 seynurrye; 2209 seynorye GLOSS H lordshyp *C* maystry *D* seyngnorye

seyyng ger. [see sayng, ger.]

seine adv. [OF sene, AF segne] discreetly, in an orderly manner **Ch1** 11205 seine

seynt n./adj. [see saynt]

seise v. [OF seisir, saisir] confiscate, capture; establish; endow **Ch1** 6289 sese; 6338 ses; 2098, 2566, 4101, 7040 seise; 2681 seised P seysed L; 2726, 3247, 6217, 6542 seised; 1869, 11308 sesed; 3005 seised P sesede L; 1522, 6153, 8183 sesid; **Ch2** 1045, 1487, 2248, 4765, 6635 seised; 2095 seised P sesed L; 2208 seise; 2377 sayse; 2519, 6141 seysed; 3234, 3400, 4278, 4927, 5192 sesed; 4313, 4754, 5402, 7746 sesid; 4947 seises

seisine n. [OF saisine, seisin] possession or right to land or property **Ch1** 2522 seisen P seysyne L; 3132 seisyn P seysyn L; 7511 seisine P sesyn L; **Ch2** 229 seyseyn; 1799 seysyne P ysesed (v.) L; 2020 seisen P seised (v.) L; 2088, 6249 seisyn; 3066 seysen; 3113 seysine; **HS** 6014 sesyne

seke, seche, souht v. [see besouht, biseke] [OE secan, sohte] look for, try to find; request, beseech; search **Ch1** 1208, 2462, 4492, 7717, 13427 seke; 2881 sekis P sekes L; 5152 sekes; 3641, 12988, 13134, 13368 souht P sought L; 3144, 4818 souht P soughte L; 1594 souht P seke L; 1494, 2213, 3628, 7904, 14026 souht; 1358 souht P bysoughte L; 6429, 6784 sought; 5209 bisouht P sought L; 12472 sek P sekeþ L; 1717L soughten (P differs); **Ch2** 951, 3978, 4785, 5479, 8027 seke; 1091, 1953 sekes; 432, 2935, 4919, 6070, 7406 souht; **HS** 176, 260, 5615, 8646, 11475 seke; 5896 seche; 3923 sekþ; 6576 seken; 2345, 8550, 8855, 11567 soghte; 8773 soght

seke, syke adj. [OE seoc, sioc] injured; in ill health **Ch1** 3831 seke; **Ch2** 347 seke P siknesse (n.) L; 2495 seke P sik L; 4766 seke P syk L; 1107, 3115, 3690, 4332, 5314 seke; **HS** 696, 1375 syke

sekenes, syknes n. [OE seocness] illness; physical disorder **Ch1** 6094, 15527 sekenesse; **Ch2** 1089, 1591, 4608, 8128 sekenes; 2497 seknes; 3471, 3698 sekenesse; **HS** 2225, 3165, 3254, 4405 syknes; 6957, 6979, 6998, 11295, 11472 sekenes

sekesteyn n. [AF segerstein, OF secrestaine] sexton of a church or religious house **HS** 11101, 11105, 11108 sekesteyn *F* sexstein *O* seggerstane

sekke v. [from OE sec, sæc, n.] to pack in a sack; hoard **HS** 6237 sekke GLOSS H fyl þe bag

sekutour n. [see executour]

selcouth, selkouth adj./n. [OE selcuþ, seldcuþ] strange, unusual; a marvel; a wonder; peculiar or amazing **Ch1** 121, 14057, 15855 selcouth; 8077 selcouht; 4535 selcouth P selcouþe L; 5264, 7188, 7860, 8757 selcouth P selcouþ L; 8635 selcouthes P wondres L; 13356 selcouth P wonder strok L; **Ch2** 631 selcouth P wonder L; 738 selcouthest P wonderest L; 2984, 6827 selcouth; 4306 selly P selcouþ L; **HS** 444, 448 selkowþ; 3889 selkouth; 4865 wndyr *O* selcuth

selcouthly adv. [from OE selcuþ, adj.] wondrously, strangely **Ch1** 7229 selcouthly P selcouþloker L; **Ch2** 2263, 8047 selcouthly

seldom, selde adv. [OE seldan] infrequently; rarely **Ch1** 13787 seldom P sonder L; **HS** 3058, 7681 selde

sele v. [AF seieler, OF seeler] put a seal on a document **Ch1** 4799 sele; **Ch2** 622, 7930 seled; 1052 sealed; 2154 selid; 7304 sele; **HS** 7011 sele

self, selue, seluen adj./n./pronoun [OE self] intensifying a previous or following noun or pronoun; the very same **Ch1** 314, 923, 1518, 1604 hymself; 2570, 3760, 5004, 7135, 8008 himself; 2030, 2043, 7061, 8146 þiself; 7721 þemself; 2279, 5943, 6672 þamself; 2544 hirself; 3289 our self; 3020 him selue; 5343 him P hymseluen L; 6843, 7396 myself; 4848, 6845 miself; 6663, 6666, 6676 ȝourself; 4272 ourseluen; 4459 þamseluen; 7713 himseluen; 10740L selue (om. P); **Ch2** 434, 1322, 4545, 6045, 7517 himself; 5652 himselue; 3897 his self; 1159, 1260, 1732 him seluen; 3754, 3755 hir seluen; 1069, 5613, 7297 þam self; 827 þam seluen; 4847 our seluen; 4796, 6178 myself; 4333 it selue; 1490, 2079, 6304 self; **HS** 2297 seluen

selyng ger. [from OF seeler, v.] confirming, certifying **Ch2** 7305, 7682 selyng

selle v. [OE sellan; ON selja] sell; give **Ch1** 665, 14265 selle; 652 sellis; 14264 seld; **Ch2** 3557, 4224, 5763, 6800, 6973 selle; 3588, 4155 sellis; 4329, 4926, 7664 sold; 7022 solde; **HS** 1193, 5514, 5754, 6010, 10580 selle; 2618 solde; 4194 sold; 5529 selles; 9460 selleþ; 9486 selþ

sellers n. [from OE sellan, v.] merchants **HS** 2460 sellers *D* soweris *F* silleris

selli, cely adj. [OE selig, sellic] lucky; blessed, holy; surprising **Ch1** 14525 selly; **Ch2** 4306 selly P selcouþ L; 5630 selli; **HS** 1410 cely *D* sely

selue pronoun [see self]

semblande, semblant n. [AF semblant (MP)] appearance, form; a pretense; countenance **Ch1** 6335 semblande P semblaunt L; 2448, 7148 semlant P semblaunt L; 7490, 11982 semblaunt; **HS** 4057, 10649 semblant; 8469 semlant; 3509 semlaunt *O* semlande; 4175, 4178 semblant *O* semlande

semble n. [short form of assemble; cp. AF semblee] assembly, meeting **Ch1** 14764 semble; **Ch2** 1823 semble

seme v. [see bisemed] [ON; cp. OI soema] to appear to be, to feign; to be appropriate, suitable **Ch1** 7283 seme; 96, 531, 600, 8970 semes; 11640 semes P semeþ L; 3110, 7130, 8066, 12264 semed; 7491 semid; 8068 semand;

4534 seme P semeþ L; **Ch2** 3832 semes; 3830 semed; 1230, 7486 semand; **HS** 12419 seme; 1357 semede; 10662 semed; 2623, 3347 semyþ; 5152, 8538, 11770, 11772 semeþ; 4656 semys; 9949 comes *SV* semes

semely adj./adv. [ON; cp. OI soemiligr] beautiful; gently, courteously; attractively **Ch1** 8301, 12259, 15460 semely; 14271 semly; 7426L semly (P differs); **HS** 8174 semely

semes n. [OE seam] ditch, gutter **Ch1** 13418 semes

semlant, semblant n. [see semblande]

sen, syn adv./conj. [see sithen]

senatour n. [OF] senator of ancient Rome **Ch1** 3280 senatoures; 3297 senatours

send, sent v. [see bisent] [OE sendan] send a message or messenger; cause to be sent **Ch1** 951, 2889, 5924, 7055, 8666 send; 4808 send P sendeþ L; 3130, 4890, 5081, 7049, 7114 sende; 205, 1533, 4800, 7984, 11569 sent; 2482 sente; **Ch2** 1348, 2145, 6537, 6653 send; 3738, 4964, 6199, 7644, 8272 sende; 653, 2906, 3886, 4940, 5098 sendes; 6220 sendis; 19, 692, 3191, 6727, 8185 sent; **HS** 1782, 9043, 11312 sende; 1200, 4314, 4612 sendyþ; 1796, 6746, 12564 sent; 5515 sente

sendal n. [OF cendal] costly fabric used in winding sheets **HS** 11091 sendal *O* sedall

sene n. [OF] Senate **Ch1** 3283, 6118, 6127 sene; 4192 seene P see L

sengle, sengli adj./adv. [OF] single or unmarried person; individually, separately **Ch1** 9403 singelle; 9825 sengli; 11107 syngle; 5988L senglely (P differs); 7732 simpli P senglely L; **HS** 7355, 7365, 7932 sengle

sentence n. [OF] judgment **Ch2** 7351, 7917 sentence

sepulcre n. [OF] a tomb **HS** 2345 sepulcre

serch v. [OF sercher, cerchier] search, explore; ransack; devise means **Ch1** 1500, 7056, 11910 serche; 5841, 13147 serched; **Ch2** 1840 serch; 6487, 6489 serchis; 3615 serches; 3213, 6491 serched; 8172 serchid

sergeancie, sargeancie n. [AF serjancie] a body of soldiers, knights' attendants **Ch1** 11697 sargeancie P seriauntye L; 12887 sargeancie P seriauntȝ; **Ch2** 2059 sergeancie

sergeant, sargeanȝ, seriaunt n. [see seruant] [AF sergant, seriant (MP)] officer in a lord's retinue; attendant **Ch1** 891 sergeantes P seriauntȝ L; 6446 sergeanȝ; 7108 sergeanȝ P squiers L; 14583 seruant P seriaunt L; 11732 sargeanȝ P seriauntȝ L; 15266 sergeance; **Ch2** 1094, 1441, 2723, 3493 serganȝ; 7245, 7795 sergeantȝ; 4543, 4953, 4979, 7638 sergeanȝ; 4158 sergant; 8241 sergeant; **HS** 12017 seruaunt *O* sargante

serke n. [OE serc, ON serkr] undergarment **Ch2** 3987 serke; 8168 serkis & surplis

sermoun n. [OF sermun] talk, discourse; a sermon **Ch2** 2691 sermon; 3650 sermoun; **HS** 9629, 9894 sermoun

sermonyng ger. [from OF sermoner, v.] a speech, counsel **Ch1** 8709 sermonyng P sermonynge L

sermun v. [OF sermoner, AF sarmuner] to speak, preach **HS** 6937 sermun GLOSS BH speke

seruage n. [OF] bondage; feudal obligation **Ch1** 864, 1202, 4268, 6581, 12923 seruage; **Ch2** 140, 1244, 2737, 4160, 6316 seruage; **HS** 5756, 5795, 5894, 9562, 10580 seruage

seruant n. [see sergeant] [OF] servant **Ch1** 11082 seruauntȝ P seriauntȝ L; 11263 seruant P baron L; **Ch2** 6501 seruant; **HS** 5503 seriaunt *O* seruande; 12017 seruant; 2361, 4425, 5503, 5959, 6853 seriaunt; 5873 seriauntes

serue v. (1) [OF servir, AF serveier] be employed; work **Ch1** 2810, 7105, 7576, 11083 serue; 7123 serues; 2632, 3118, 4672, 6910, 7341 serued; 3111 meke to serue P seruisable L (adj.); 6865 seruand; **Ch2** 731, 3121, 5670, 7810, 8306 serued; 3646, 3764, 4587, 5944, 7671 serue; **HS** 1132, 1989, 5314, 9376, 10279 serue; 835, 2073 seruyþ; 8843, 9364, 9423 serued

serue v. (2) [OF deseruir] to deserve **Ch1** 4268 serue; 4851 serued; **HS** 9573 serued

seruise n. [OF] religious ritual; feudal duty; wages **Ch1** 2779, 2824, 3647, 4268 seruyse; 4266, 4867, 5904, 7296, 11564 seruise; 7639 seruys; 13004 seruis; **Ch2** 2241, 3578, 6042, 7056, 8344 seruise; **HS** 803, 3256, 5954, 9347, 12180 seruyse; 5152 seruise; 2073 note GLOSS BH seruyse

seruitour n. [OF servitor] a servant, attendant **Ch1** 11060 seruitours P seruiturs L; **Ch2** 1326 seruitour; 4099 seruitoure

ses n. [OF ces, cesse] stop, conclusion **Ch1** 182 ses; 15175 ses P sesse L

sesyne n. [see seisine]

seson n. [OF sesoun] a period of time, occasion **Ch1** 1324 seson

sesse v. [OF cesser, cessier] to stop, cease **Ch1** 15375 ses; 2608 sesed P sesede L; 13080, 13268, 15767 sesed; 12555 sesse P ses L sese R; **Ch2** 4549 sesse P sece L; 7730 ses

sesson n./adj. [see saxon, sesson]

set, sete n. [OE, ON sæte] habitation, home **Ch1** 11308 setes; **Ch2** 6825 sete; **HS** 2600 set

set v. [see biset, besette] [OE settan] make, sit; place, dispose; strike a blow; appoint, build; begin a battle; establish **Ch1** 537, 713, 1805, 4045, 14265 sette P set L; 6349 sete P byset L; 7750 sett P set L; 1430, 2080, 4966, 9946, 12286 set; 1542, 2094, 12697, 14003 sette; 814, 3856, 7455, 8594, 15613 sett; 4558, 6349, 13518 sete; 11063 sate; 473, 6920, 7335, 8425 sat; 13277 set P sett L; **Ch2** 577, 1343, 5926, 7003, 8274 sette; 374 sett; 6235 settes; 594, 2973, 4090, 6504, 7960 set; 1553, 4099, 4287, 7695 sat; 1171 satte; 4522 sate; **HS** 189, 1205, 4440, 7776, 12515 sette; 4441, 9083 sett; 2589, 3208, 6356, 7484 set; 2775 settyst; 804, 3015 settyþ; 9583 settest; 6434, 10909 setteþ

seth, sothen v. [OE seoþan, soden] to boil, seethe **Ch1** 12039 sothen P sode L; 15671 seth P seþ L

setnesse n. [OE setnes] law; established custom **Ch2** 6409 setnesse

sette n. [OE set] an attack, onslaught **Ch1** 14982 sette P set L

settyng ger. [from OE settan, v.] sitting down for meals **HS** 7210 settyng

seuen, seuenten, seuenty numeral/n./adj. [OE seofon, seofunda] the number seven; seuen, seventeen, seventy, seventh **Ch1** 889, 2064, 3891, 5541, 8979 seuen; 2598, 5777 seuenten; 6411 seuenty; 7790 seuenti; **Ch2** 446, 4573, 5862, 7041, 8330 seuen; 702, 1213 seuentene; 1623, 2259 seuenten; 3687, 5859, 6863 seuent; 8331 seuend; 2556 seuentend; **HS** 19, 2917, 7341, 7357 seuene; 7351, 7793 seuen; 7429, 11239, 11583, 12157 seuenþe; 830, 2047 seuenþe *C* seuened

seuenyght n. [OE seofon niht] a week; seven days **Ch1** 5537 seuen nyght; 9230 seuenyght P wyke L; **Ch2** 6224 seuenyght; **HS** 275 seuenyght; 10029, 10042 seuen nyght

sewe, sue v. (1) [OF seure, siure] pursue, chase **Ch1** 8383 sued P sywed L; **Ch2** 1914 alowed P sowed L; 8041 sewed

sewe, sowe v. (2) [OE sawan] scatter seeds; perform sinful deeds; beget **Ch1** 1850 sowe; 7934 sewe P sew L; **HS** 3983 sowe

sex, sexti, sexten, syxe numeral/n./adj. [OE] six, sixty, sixteen **Ch1** 349, 1696, 3558, 4550, 6033 sex; 7564L six (om. P); 7274 sext; 7420 xiii P sexten L; 2165, 5224 sexty; 3558, 6460, 6481, 7778, 10135 sexti; **Ch2** 2, 179, 1623, 4743, 8103 sex; 6301 sext; 8251 sexte; 480, 5492 sexty; 386, 831, 1625, 3576, 5693 sexti; 702, 831, 3401, 5207, 7794 sextene; 6561 sexten; 3092 sextend; **HS** 64, 387, 401 syxe; 1601, 11163 syxte; 6517 sext

sexe n. [OE seaxe, sexe] a knife or dagger **Ch1** 7760 sexe P sex L; 7753, 7765, 7818, 7820 sexis P sexes L; 8176 sexis

sexstein n. [see sekesteyn]

sib, sibbe n./adj. [from OE sib, adj. used as n.] kin, family, clan **Ch1** 4092, 6385 sibbe; 2440L sibbe (P differs); 6891, 12312 sibbe P syb L; 7360 sib kind; **Ch2** 4282 sib P sub L; **HS** 1198, 7373 syb; 7656 sybber; 7446 syb kynd

sibred n. [from OE sib + rede] consanguinity; relationship by marriage; kinship **Ch1** 6832 sibred P sybrede L; **Ch2** 6102 sibred

side n./adj./adv. [OE sid, side] one of two parts; long, something hanging down; to a great length **Ch1** 7397 side P syd L; 1036, 2722, 6247, 8170, 9344 side; 1808 syde; 3401, 5003, 5323, 7746 sides; 15140 o side; **Ch2** 412, 2190, 4069, 6007, 8212 side; 1395, 1768, 5793 sides; **HS** 705 sydys; 1575, 2563, 4440, 7832 syde; 3226, 3442 syde GLOSS BH long

sidelynges adj./adv. [cp. OE sidling-weg] sideways, obliquely **Ch1** 10184, 10669 sidelynges; 13292 sidelynges P sadly L

sidenen, sidenhand adv. [from OE side + honde] sideways, at an angle **Ch1** 4962 sidenen P sidenhand L

◆ **sideslepis** adv. [from OE side + lepis] sideways, sidelong **Ch1** 12670 sideslepis P aside L o side R

◆ **sygaldryd** v. [from OE sige + gealdor, n.] bewitch; speak an incantation **HS** 503 sygaldryd *C* wyched . . . with gyn *F* sigaldrid

sigh, syke v. [OE sican] to sigh **Ch1** 2477 sighed P syked L; 3167 sighed P sykede L; **HS** 5677 syghyng

sight n. [see site, v.] [OE siht] spectacle, view; opinion, judgment; observation **Ch1** 620, 2014, 3744, 8067, 14271 sight; 215 syght; 9185 sightes P delites L; 9318 sightes; 3744 be sight; 9022 in sight; **Ch2** 1969, 2611, 4274, 6171, 7956 sight; 2987 syght; 5368 be sight; 7486 bi sight; 1312, 2505, 7360 with sight; 3132, 6024, 7642, 7668 þorgh sight; **HS** 283, 1356, 7597, 8410, 12160 syght; 1410, 1722 syghte

signe, seyne n. [OE segn, seign] indication, evidence; token; portent, omen; pennant **Ch1** 1341 signe P syngne L; 5379 seyne P seigne L; 9878 seyne; 10006 syne P seyne L; **Ch2** 3065, 3302, 8090 signe; **HS** 3904, 5717, 6535 sygne; 1583 sygne GLOSS B a tokene; 8225 sygne *O* taken

signe v. [see assigne]

signifiance n. [OF signifiance] enigmatic sign; symbolic meaning **Ch1** 8096 signifiance; 8129 signefiance

signifie v. [AF signifier (MP)] to stand for, be an emblem or symbol **Ch1** 8125 signifise; 8919 signifye; 11830 signified; **HS** 10139 sygnyfye

syke adj. [see seke, adj.]

syknes n. [see sekenes]

siker v. [from OE sicor, adj.] promise to do; to assure, confirm **Ch1** 14102 sikerd P sykerede L; **Ch2** 1695 sikere; 1268 sikerd; 758, 3609 sikered; 4163 sikred P sikered L; **HS** 8216 sykere; 10667 sykerd

siker, sekyr adj./adv. [OE sicor] safely, certainly, surely **Ch1** 1237, 7374, 7375, 12595 siker; 12679 saufe P siker L; sauf R; 7530, 7533 sikir;

3035, 5487 sikere; 4571 sikerly; 4575 sikerli; 6432, 7365 sikerer; 12698 sarer P sykerer L sarrer R; 13676 sikerer P sykerere L; **Ch2** 946, 1962 siker; 6007, 6191 sikere; 6204, 6472 sikerer; 4176 better P sikerer L; 1270 sikerly; **HS** 2370, 3903, 7916 sekyr; 9806, 9833, 12033 syker; 8563 sykerer; 5071 sykyrlyche; 7231, 11251 sykyrly

sikernes n. [from OE sicor, adj.] security, agreement, assurance **Ch1** 1104 sikernes; 8571 sikernes P sykernesse L; 12680 sikernes PR sykernesse L; **Ch2** 2338, 3607, 8010 sikernes; 3394, 7736, 7915 sikernesse; **HS** 5766, 9798 sykernes; 6691 sekernes; 9816 sekernesse

sikes n. [OE sic; ON, cp. OI sik] ditch, trench **Ch1** 8051 sikes P sykes L

silk n. [OE seolc; ON] silk **Ch1** 9882 silk; **Ch2** 5623 silke

siluer n./adj. [OE seolfor, silfor] silver; money **Ch1** 3290, 4229, 10354, 15355, 15452 siluer; 4513, 11541 siluere; **Ch2** 595, 1957, 3541, 5951, 6591 siluer; 1943, 4143, 7383, 7399 siluere; **HS** 5393, 5798, 6160, 10742, 11721 syluer; 1338 seluyr

symonie n. [OF; L simonia] buying or selling an ecclesiastic office or possession **Ch2** 7818 symonie; **HS** 5511, 5540, 1105 symonye

simple, simpli adj./adv. [OF] innocent, guileless; common; sincerely, honestly; humbly **Ch1** 73, 77, 1366 symple; 7716 sempely P simplely L; 7732 simpli P senglely L; **Ch2** 7021 simple; **HS** 7299 symply

symphan, synfan n. [OF symphoine] a stringed musical instrument **Ch1** 11145 synfan P symfan L; **HS** 4773 symphan

syn adv. [see sithen]

syn, synne n. [OE synn] transgression; moral failure **Ch1** 6955, 13650, 15701, 15884 synne; 2133, 6959 syn; 202 syne; 15104 synnes; **Ch2** 1882, 7019, 7818 synne; 8, 2133, 2807 synnes; 2722 syn; **HS** 4, 5, 7, 18, 12579 synne

syn, synne v. [from OE synn, n., synnian] commit a sin **Ch1** 15731 synned; **Ch2** 8305 synne; **HS** 12554 synne; 161 synnyd; 1324 synnyst; 1640 synnedyst; 3741 synnyþ; 9349 synnest; 2644 synnyn; 4689 synnen

synful, synfully adj./adv. [OE synfull] of sinful behavior; immoral; corruptly **Ch1** 15717, 15724 synnfulle; 13497 synfully P synfullyke L; **HS** 5232, 8029, 12090, 12210, 12285 synful; 9742 synfully

syng v. [OE singan] chant; sing the mass; lament **Ch1** 1442 synge; 7427 singe; 11030 syng; 7093, 11033 songe; 1439, 11147 song; 7510, 7639 songen; 15710 song P songen L; 14395 sang; 14449 singand; 14453, 15703 sunge; **Ch2** 240, 866, 5214 syng; 4273 songen; 5952 song; **HS** 823, 2289 syngge; 6363, 10496 synge; 10312 syng; 12287 syngeþ; 2340, 4545, 10382 song; 9267 songe; 2615 sungge; 7126 soung; 4196, 9049, 9160, 10432, 10679 sunge; 10474 sungen; 7484 syngyng

synger n. [see sangster] [from OE singan] singer **Ch1** 3993 syngere; **HS** 3059 synger; 3061 syngere

synke, sank, sonken v. [OE sincan] to be submerged, drown; sink into the ground; ruin, be destroyed **Ch1** 4580 sinke; 10016 synk; 7990 sinkes; 4379, 13264 sank; 11990 sonken; **Ch2** 3050, 5804, 7020 sank; 4228 sanke; 6400 sonken; **HS** 1108, 8456, 10835 synke; 8315 sank

sire n. [OF] ruler; as title **Ch1** 13762 sire; **HS** 2583 syre

sysours n. [from OF assisour] persons deputed to hold assizes **HS** 1336, 2636, 8919 sysours

sister, suster n. [OE suster; ON systir] a sister **Ch1** 10805, 13475 sistir; 2301, 2322, 2531 sistres; 2319 sestres P sistren L; **Ch2** 223, 2627, 3671, 5069, 7471 sister; 654, 1701, 4901 sistere; 2699, 3863 sistir; 3790L sustere (om. P); 3899L suster (om. P); **HS** 7704, 9104, 9118 syster; 572 sustrun; 1689 sustren

site n. [ON syt, syti] grief, lamentation **Ch1** 1015 sorow & site P sorw in sight L; 8024 with site P wyþ syt L; 10158 with site P wyþ sitte L; 15025 site; **Ch2** 69 sorow & site; 2513 site; **HS** 4981 syghte; 8470 sorowe & syte

site v. [from OF site, cite] to sit in judgment upon; be becoming, suitable **Ch1** 658 sitte P syte L; 14888 site; **Ch2** 8028 site

siþe n. [OE siþ, syþ] time, occasion; many times **Ch1** 1369 siþes P syþe L; 6590 siþe P syþe L; 13822 siþe; 7487 sithes; **Ch2** 122, 2408 siþes; **HS** 5197, 8884, 11738 syþe; 6680 sythe *O* oft syth

sithen, syþe, sen, syn adv./conj./prep. [OE siþ, siþþan] since, afterwards; also; consequently **Ch1** 24, 1862 sen; 3874 syn; 290, 4938, 5097 siþen P syn L; 1621 sen P sithen L; 177, 2819, 5419, 6761, 7948 siþen; 7303 sethen; 13401 sþen P syn L; 15028L sith (om. P); **Ch2** 26, 3469, 4641, 6071, 8307 siþen; 91, 605, 2428, 6179, 8319 sen; 703 siþen P syn L; 3976 siþen P siþþe L; **HS** 19 syþyn; 259, 461, 1277 seþyn; 263 seþþyn; 2343, 3855, 6148, 6720, 11179 syn; 1383, 9274, 7866 seþþe; 3667 seþþen; 1637 seþen; 8793, 12254 syþen; 1637 seþen *C* sythen *D* siþþin; 1638 aftyr *C* sythen; 1960 syn *D* siþþe *H* syþ; 2133 syn *D* siþþin; 2489 seþþe *C* sythen *D* siþþe; 3882 aftyr *A* sethe *O* sythen; 10644 afterward *SV* siþen

sitte v. [OE sittan] be seated; kneel; remain, dwell **Ch1** 10 sitt; 7755 sittis; 10373 siten; 11932 sittand P sittande L; **HS** 1418, 1899, 4616, 7275, 8372 sytte; 318 setyn; 952 syttyþ;

1228 syt; 4470, 5467, 6181 sate; 6021, 6408, 7488, 12518 sat; 7490 syttand; 5729 syttyng; 11481 sytteþ

six, syxte numeral [see sex, sexti, sexten]

skandere n. [see sclaunder]

skape, askape, escape v. [AF aschaper, eschaper (MP)] to get away safely, free oneself **Ch1** 994, 1141, 4572, 9109 scape; 5331 ascape; 1050 ascape P skape L; 1122, 2958, 5979, 8342, 9049 scaped; 7633, 7781 scapid; 3016 escapid P skaped L; 6029 ascapid; 7793 schapid P scaped L; 13756 skaped; 370, 1997, 5949, 6221 ascaped; 5071 escape; 7329 skape P schape L; 217, 740, 1171, 3390 escaped; 12608 scap P ascape LR; 15428 skape P scape L; **Ch2** 3392 skape; 3966 scape; 2472 skapes; 2951, 4245 skaped; 3971, 5337, 5363 scaped; 5474 scapid; 6482 skapid; 3002 escape; 3905 askeped P skaped L; 7144 ascape; 463, 3986 askaped; 2190, 7179 ascaped; 4924 escaped; 7416 escapid; **HS** 2144, 4398, 4890, 8361 skape; 6716 askape; 8044 ascaped; 10675 eschape *SV* skapynge

skathe, scaþe n. [ON skaði, skaþa] harm, injury; loss, misfortune; danger; sin **Ch1** 1240 mysdedis P skaþes L; 3901 schathes P skaþes L; 5122 skath; 10892 scathe; 1834 scathe P skaþe L; 5847 scaþe P skaþe L; 6613, 11400 scathe P scaþe L; 7628 scaþe P slaughter L; 7965, 10187 scaþe; 6721 skaþe; 13802 skathe; **Ch2** 1531, 3932, 5927 skaþe; 2147 skathe; 4471, 7323 scathe; 4480, 5812, 6172, 6906, 7111 scaþe; **HS** 3051, 5989, 10656 scaþe; 4917, 9760, 10906 skaþe; 3422 harm *O* skathe; 3654 synne *O* skath

skellis n. [OE scill, scell] nut shells **Ch1** 14063 skellis

skere adj. [ON] aslant, awry **Ch1** 4383 oskere P osker L; 7822 quyte & clere P quit & sker (?error) L

sky n. [ON, cp. OI sky] heavens; clouds **Ch1** 2944 skye; 6471, 6473, 6474 skie; **HS** 5477 sky

skilfulle adj. [from ON skil] prudent, clever **Ch2** 7599 skilfulle

skille n./adj./adv. [ON skil] reason, discretion; intelligence; prudent; appropriate **Ch1** 505, 4198, 5120, 6076, 7535 skille; 969, 6430 skille P skyle L; 6387 skil; 1211 skilles; 8568 skille P skil L; 10224L skyle (om. P); 7394L skylfulle (P differs); **Ch2** 156, 2393, 4581, 5922, 8012 skille; 7599 skilfulle; **HS** 87, 2951, 6291, 7295, 11387 skyle; 2358, 2368 skele; 4759 skeyl; 7667, 8119, 8493, 11589, 11685 skyl; 5457, 6437, 7200 skyll; 8641 skyles

skyn n. [OE scinn; ON, cp. OI skinn] skin **Ch1** 1374 skyn; 12078 skynne

skip v. [ON skopa] jump, leap; hasten, flee, escape; attack **Ch1** 4699 skipped P lepen L; 11123 skipped P skipte L; **Ch2** 4491, 5004, 6144, 6919, 7400 skip; 4528 kip P skippe L

skirme v. [AF eskirmir, eskermer] fight with a weapon; wrestle **Ch1** 4698 skirmed P skirmede L; 4704 skirme P skyrmen L; 4708 skirme P skyrme L; 11124 wrestild P skirmed L; 11126 skirmed P wrastled L

skirmyng ger. [from AF eskirmir, v.] fighting with swords **Ch1** 4870 skirmyng

skirt n. [see scirt]

skitte n. [ON] dung, trash **Ch1** 15930 skitte P skyt L

sklandre n. [see sclaunder]

skof n. [ODan skuf, skof] a jibe, banter **Ch1** 7476 skof

skoler n. [OE scolere; AF escoler (MP)] student, reader **HS** 3079, 8071 skolere; 8001 skoler

skore n. [see score]

skorne, scorn n. [OF escarn; AF escharn (MP)] feeling of contempt **Ch1** 2392 scorne; 5302 skorne P scorn L; 11247 skorne; **Ch2** 6599 scorne; **HS** 3132 scorne; 3482 skorn; 12503 skorne; 2964 skorne *C* schorne *O* scorne; 2042 teyl GLOSS BH scorn

skorne, scorne, skurne v. [OF escharnir; AF escarnir] to be contemptuous, despise; ridicule; be frightened; fall back **Ch1** 120, 7681, 13365 skurne; 1810 scurn P spurn L; 7681 skurne P scurne L; 6724, 8428 scurne; 12985, 13042 skurned; 12494L scurne (om. P); **Ch2** 4724 skurne P skorn L; 4842 skornes; 6371 scornand; 2177L scornes (P differs); 6598, 6734 scorned; **HS** 416, 4910, 5132 scorne; 3131 scornedyst; 3486 skorn; 3488, 12489 skorne; 3196 scarne GLOSS B scorne *O* tharne

skorner, scorner n. [from OF escharnir, v.] one who scorns, despises **HS** 3137 scorners; 4936 skorners

skornyng, scornyng ger. [from OF escharnir, v.] feeling of contempt, disdain **HS** 3134 scornyng; 12492 skornyng

skrape, shrape v. [ON skrapa, OE scrapian] to scrape, shave **HS** 7046 skrape; 7048 shraped

skrite, scrite, scris n. [OF escrit; AF scrit] written document, letter; writings **Ch1** 7957 skrites P scrytes L; **Ch2** 1269 skrite P scrit L; 1395, 2421, 3098, 3542, 4163 skrite; 5489 scris; 2116, 5714, 6251, 7804, 8354 scrite; **HS** 7004 skryt; 7005, 7011 scryt

skryueyn n. [AF escriuein (MP)] a writer **HS** 8094 skryueyn

skulke, sculk v. [ON] move furtively, slink; hide **Ch1** 6873 sculked P skulked L; 8173 sculk P skulke L; 15169 skulked P sculked L; **Ch2** 5826 skulkand; 5867 skulkes; 7872 skulked; 2949 stokked P schulked L

skulkyng ger. [from ON, v.] sneak attack, ambush **Ch2** 52 skulkyng P enbuschement L

slayn, slawen v. [see slo, slouh]

slake, slek v. [ON; OE slacian] stop; abate, overcome; quench, extinguish **Ch1** 3195 slake; 4786 slek P fle L; 9344 slaken; **HS** 5995 slaken

slauhter, slaghter n. [ON *slahtr; cp. OI slatr] murder, assassination; massacre; disaster, strife **Ch1** 708, 709 slauhtere P slaughter L; 729, 3016, 5443, 5972 slauhter; 2127 slauhtere; 7628 scaþe P slaughter L; **Ch2** 843, 2234, 3177, 5078, 5927 slauhter; 846 slauhter care P treson & care L; **HS** 5400, 10919, 12526 slaghter; 1535 slaghtyr; 1334 slaghtyr *C* deth *D* manslauȝtter; 1710 slaghtyr *C* manslawth *D* manslauter

sle v. [see slo, v.]

sledyr adj. [OE slidor] slippery, treacherous **HS** 5262 sledyr

slehi, slye, sligh adj./adv. [ON sloegr] cunning; wise, ingenious **Ch1** 2252, 11793 slie P sleye L; 3403, 7843, 10522 slie; 7695 slily P sleightly L; 9441 douhty P sley L; 9710 slehi P sley L; 8276 slehi; **HS** 4916 slygh; 6100 slye

sleiht, sleght, sleghþe n. [ON; cp. OI sloegð] trickery, deception, guile; cunning **Ch1** 5023 sleght P sleight L; 5587 sleht P sleight L; 5887 sleihtes P sleightes L; 6911 sleiht P deseit L; 7049 sleghtes P sleytes L; 8685, 8686 sleght P sleyght L; 8741 sleiht P sleight L; 4566L sleigþe (P differs); **Ch2** 3171 sleiht; 228L sleiþe (om. P); **HS** 10096 sleghþe

slenge n. [?MLG slinge, slenge] sling for throwing stones **Ch1** 3002, 6719 slenges P slynges L; **Ch2** 4541 slenges

slepe n. [OE slep] asleep; death; dream **Ch1** 1166, 11804, 11821 slepe; **Ch2** 472, 2268 slepe; **HS** 432, 1567, 4263, 7020, 9317 slepe

slepe v. [OE slepan] sleep, rest; to be dead **Ch1** 7379, 14896 slepe; 290 slepte; 11337 slept; 1376 sleped; 1159 slepand; **Ch2** 692, 1746, 6183, 7827 slepe; **HS** 1258, 4355, 7753, 9235, 12551 slepe; 426 slepys; 7839 slept; 9151 slepte

slide v. [OE slidan] to slip; fall asleep **Ch1** 8036 slide oslepe P slyden oslep L; **HS** 1468 slyde

slyked ppl. [OE *slician] specious, deceptive **HS** 11771 slyked

slyppe v. [cp. OE slipig, slipor] to slip **HS** 3411 slyppe

slo, slouh, sle, slayn v. [OE slean, slagen; cp. ON sla, slo] strike, cut off heads; kill **Ch1** 840 slo P sloo L; 1158 slo P sles L; 1163, 1590 slouh P slow L; 1322, 2837, 5585, 8218, 13792 slouh; 6565, 13215 slow; 3731, 3734 sleu; 4715 sleuh; 6539, 7789, 8131 slou; 7768 sloh; 7176 slouh P slough L; 8501 slawen; 2544, 5330, 6201, 7757, 12520 slo; 1528, 3412, 12714 slowe; 13336 slos P sleþ L; 338, 2095, 5196, 8175, 15300 slayn; 782 slayne; 1592 slaen P slayn L; 6513 slain; 1142 slone P flayd L; **Ch2** 116, 1572, 3089, 5036, 8012 slo; 130 slouh P slowe L; 698, 1332 slouh P slow L; 136, 1176, 3027, 6444, 8311 slouh; 2531, 7760, 8176, 8328 slowe; 4882, 5464, 6615, 7239, 8148 slayn; 5976, 8052, 8200 slawen; **HS** 1308, 1499, 1505 slo; 1310, 1349 sle; 1521 slos; 1026 sleþ; 1526 sles; 1749, 3751, 4732 slogh; 3804 slow; 5010 slough; 996, 1499, 3288 slayn; 1513 slayne; 10066 sleyn; 1527 slekþ *CD* sleth; 1534 slawe *F* islawe; 1752 slough *C* slowe *D* slow; 4355 slogh *O* so slaw; 5153 slogh *O* slawe

slogh, slowe adj. [OE slaw] slothful, indolent **HS** 4249, 4554, 4849, 5053, 5177 slogh; 4257 slowe

◆ **sloghnes** n. [from OE slaw, adj.] slothfulness **HS** 4241, 10116 sloghnes; 4251 slownesse; 4278 slownes; 4591 sloghnesse; 4632 sloghnes *H* sloghtnesse *O* sclawnes; 5326 sloghnes *O* sleuth

slouþe n. [OE slæwþ] sloth, indolence **HS** 12534 slouþe

◆ **sloghþehede** n. [from OE slaw, adj.] slothfulness **HS** 4523 sloghþehede *O* slewthheued; 5073 sloghþehede *O* sleuth; 5075 sloghþehede *O* sleuthhede

slomer, slomber n. [?from MDu slumeren, v.] sleep; a doze **Ch1** 11804 slomer P slomber L

◆ **slop** n. [?ON sloppr] a magic bag **HS** 514 a melk slop *C* a storop *D* a meche sop; 522, 526, 537 sloppe *C* storpe *D* bagge

smale adj. [OE smæl] small **Ch1** 4287, 6457, 6953 smale; **Ch2** 555 smale; **HS** 8, 2366, 12444 smale; 6304, 6489, 7144, 7610 smal

smert n. [cp. OE smeart, adj., *smeortan, n.] annoyance **HS** 3966, 10825 smert

smert adj./adv. [OE smeart] sharp, stinging; painful; alert, prompt; severe **Ch1** 1639, 4333, 7311, 15216 smert; 4343, 6821, 6925, 8355, 15232 smerte; **Ch2** 154, 1304, 3522, 5796, 7090 smerte; 7633 smert; **HS** 112, 3785, 7561 smerte; 4818 smart; 4862, 5706, 8543, 10264, 11526 smert

smerte v. [OE *smeortan; cp. OE smeart, adj.] to cause pain **Ch1** 4793 smerte P smert L

◆ **smerthed, smartnes** n. [from OE smeart, adj.] severity, harshness **Ch2** 7468 smerthed; **HS** 4968 smartnes *O* smerthede

smertly adv. [from OE smeart, adj.] vigorously, promptly **Ch1** 2094, 2728, 5585, 6279, 6563 smertly; 7587, 15239 smertli; 8354 smertli P scharply L; 15226 smertlier P smertloker L; **Ch2** 919, 4977, 6643, 7796, 8244 smertly; 1659 smertly P schortly L; **HS** 6999 smartly; 841 smartly *C* wurthely

smyle v. [?ON; cp MHG smielen] to display scorn, deception, disbelief **Ch1** 6933 smyle; 7478 smiland; **Ch2** 4603 smyle; **HS** 3509 smylyng semlaunt

smyte, smot v. [OE smitan] strike, beat **Ch1** 756, 1651, 4333, 8081, 8286 smyten; 1782, 7311 smite; 1150, 3152, 4578, 7756, 12122 smyte; 3006 smyte P smyten L; 4384 smot; 8514, 11914 smote P smot L; 15617 smote P smette L; 782 smyte P faught L; 3003, 4375, 6924, 8355, 12064 smote; 8426 smat; 11915 smote P stod L; **Ch2** 293, 2856, 5744, 7105, 8299 smyten; 328, 1643, 4748, 6578, 8077 smote; 920, 4990, 5741, 6684 smyte; 5616 smite; **HS** 1373, 2180, 11928 smete; 939, 2494, 4493, 7815, 9775 smote; 8636, 8644 smyte

smoke n. [OE smoca] smoke **Ch1** 12011 smoke

snacches v. [?OE *snæccan] to snatch, seize **Ch1** 13335 snacches

snelle adj. [OE snel] swift, prompt **Ch2** 3227 snelle

snewe v. [from OE snaw, n.] to snow **Ch1** 13027 snewe

♦ **snore** n. [from OE fnora, sneezing] snorting of the nose **Ch1** 1817 snore

snoute n. [?OE; cp. MDu, MLG snute] the nose, used derisively **Ch1** 11662 maugre his snoute

snowe, snogh n. [OE snaw] snow **Ch1** 13027 snowe; **Ch2** 2975, 2987 snowe; **HS** 5054, 9154 snogh

sobbyng ger. [?from MDu or MLG sabben] weeping **Ch1** 14907 sobbyng

soberte n. [AF sobrete (MP)] sobriety **HS** 5974, 7272 soberte

sobre adj. [OF] moderate, serious **Ch2** 7595 sobre

socour n. [AF] aid, comfort; relief, rescue **Ch1** 917, 3098, 4899, 5109, 13960 socoure; 3806, 5009, 6196, 6521 socour; 5043 socour P socur L; 6579, 6751 socours; 5109 socours P socurs L; 9435 socoure P socuring L; **Ch2** 234, 1448, 3468, 6472, 7979 socour; 909, 1020, 2831, 6645, 7283 socoure; 7387 socoure; **HS** 1223, 4206 sokour; 6253, 10316, 10448 socour; 2186 socoure *CD* recure

socour v. [AF socurer] help, attend; relieve **Ch1** 6802, 12424 socoure; 7363 socour; 6531 socourd; 7078 socoured; 12452 socoured P to sokere L; **Ch2** 296, 461, 4854 socour; 4524, 7031, 7285 socoure; 3874 couere P socore L; **HS** 1096 susteyne *C* socorne

sodanly, sodenly adv. [from AF sudein, adj.] all at once; unexpectedly, immediately **Ch1** 6558 priuely P sodeynly L; 7774 sodenly; 13826 sodanly P sodeynly L; **Ch2** 1411 sodanly; 1374 sodenly; 7791 sodeynly; **HS** 7495 sodeynlye

sodom n. [L sodoma] unnatural sin **Ch1** 2133 syn of sodom P synne of sodome L; 13824L synne of sodome (om. P)

♦ **sodomike** adj. [from L sodoma, n.] pertaining to sodomy **Ch1** 13824 synne sodomyke; **Ch2** 7818 synne sodomike

soft, softeli adj./adv. [OE softe] tender, pliant; gentle; easily, slowly **Ch1** 1366, 3839 soft; 3487L softe (om. P); 13020 softeli; **Ch2** 4189, 4360 soft; **HS** 5837, 10342 softe

sogettys n. [see sugette, adj.] [OF suget, soget] a subject **HS** 1177 sogettys *C* sudiecte *D* soget

soioure, soiorne n. [see iorne] [AF] temporary stay or residence; delay **Ch1** 3097, 7190, 7825 soioure P soiour L; 3532, 6706, 8466 soiorne; 13587 soiorne P soiour L; **Ch2** 3795, 5894, 6646, 7991, 7996 soioure; 5942 soiour; 3795 soiore; 1776, 4353, 5358 soiorne

soioure, soiourne v. [AF; OF sejorner] delay, remain temporarily; stay **Ch1** 4147 soioure P soiourne L; 4655 soiornde; 6167 soiorned; 6706, 10717 soiorne P soiourne L; 13367 soiorned P taried L; **Ch2** 60, 993, 1473, 5400, 7565 soiorned; 1975, 3996, 4498, 5357 soiorne; 4181 soiourne; 2177 soiornes P scornes L; **HS** 4062, 5182 soiurne; 6546 [MS *O* interpolation, l. 8] soȝerne

soiornyng ger. [from AF sojour, v.] staying in a place; a resting place **Ch1** 9757 soiornyng P soiournynge L; **Ch2** 1990 soiornyng

soke v. [see sugke, v.]

sokour n. [see socour, n.]

solace n. [OF solas, solace] pleasure, happiness; entertainment, recreation **Ch1** 9, 134, 144 solace; **Ch2** 6075 solace; **HS** 1909 solas; 4048, 4108, 4122, 4752, 6685 solace

solace v. [OF solacier] please, cheer up **Ch2** 64 to solace

solemnyte, sollempnyte n. [OF solemnite] religious celebration, ceremony; feast day **Ch1** 5503, 5938, 6205 solempnite; 10980 sollempnyte P solempnete L; **Ch2** 1587, 3126, 5052, 7510 solempnite; 3999 sollempnite; **HS** 916 solemnyte; 9640 solempte

solempne, sollemly, solempnelie adj./adv. [OF solemne] ceremonious; reverent; sacred **Ch1** 2525, 5774 solempnely; 9004 solemply P louely L; 14743 sollemly P solempnely L; **Ch2** 10 solemplie; 1812, 2327 solemply; 3414 solemplie; 5209 solempnely; 6879 solempne; 8318, 8344 solempnelie; **HS** 8734 solemply *H* solempny *F* solempni

solied, solowed v. [from OE solgian; cp. OE solian] to defile, soil; to become dark or dirty **Ch1** 12041 to solied P to soilled L; 10966L to soille (om. P); **HS** 9157 solowed *O* tholyde; 9229 solowed *O* changed

some adj./adv./pronoun [see sum]

somer, somerstide n./adj. [OE sumer, sumor] summer; descriptive of the season **Ch1** 13465 somer; 5235, 5557 somerstide; 5481 somorestide; **Ch2** 259, 5582, 5784 somer; 345, 2160, 7841 somerestide; 3368 midsomer; 5501 midsomeretide; 7551 midesomerstide; **HS** 903 somurtyde; 10208 dayes lyght *SV* somer liht; 4685 somur; 8991 somour

somons n. [AF somunse] order or command; an official writ **Ch1** 975, 2226, 4303, 8060 somons; 7741, 11512 somouns; **Ch2** 273, 2151, 3375, 6398, 7534 somons; 5896 somouns

somoun, somon v. [OF sumuner] invite; order to appear; call upon **Ch1** 3237, 4860, 6324 somon; 3900, 4201, 5930 somoune; 6986 somoun; 11665 somone; 10266, 10556, 10830 somond; **Ch2** 2759 somon; 2206, 4249 somoune; 2716 somoun; 589, 5072 somond; **HS** 510 somoune; 1800 sumne

sond, sand n. (1) [OE] sandy beach, shore; river bank **Ch1** 2148 sond; 10064 sandȝ P sandes L; 11774, 13878 sand; **Ch2** 1733 sond P lond L; 2576 sond; 57, 1899, 6804 sand; 726 sande P land L

sond, sonde n. (2) [OE sond] message, ordinance, command; report; envoy, messenger; summons **Ch1** 5083, 5962, 6440, 7625, 9202 sonde; 8639 sond; 4918, 6216, 7446, 8627, 9473 sond P sonde L; 7557, 7867 sondes P sonde L; 10755 sonde P sond L; **Ch2** 964, 1101, 1342, 2760, 5723 sonde; 2052, 2316, 3534, 5277, 7049 sond; 2023 sonde P tydyng L; **HS** 1990 sondys

sonder, sondre, sundre v. [see osondere, adv.] [OE *sundrian] divide or separate; scatter; leave **Ch1** 4416, 8372 sondred; 8169 sundird P asondred L; 8286 sundred P sondred L; 12662 sonder PLR; **Ch2** 586, 4222, 5040, 5452, 5652 sundred; 3940 sondre; 4552 sondred

sonderlypes, sunderleps adj./adv. [see osonder] [OE sunder lipes] separately, severally, individually **Ch1** 3849 sunderleps P sonderlypes L; **HS** 9226 sundre lepes *H* sundyrlepys

sone, sonnes n. [OE sunu, suna] male child, descendant **Ch1** 262, 3124, 4038, 5633, 6244 son; 801, 2616, 4765, 6419, 7927 sone; 3599, 3702, 13891 sonne; 1945, 2168, 3776, 4749, 7525 sons; 2116, 2769, 3960, 4037 sones; 213, 427, 2120, 2175 sonnes; **Ch2** 70, 973, 3472, 6076, 8321 sonne; 5050 sons; 320, 1191, 2614, 3460, 5426 sonnes; **HS** 1, 1123, 1231, 9898 sone; 4906 sones

sone, soun adj./adv. [OE sona] soon; immediately; hastily **Ch1** 853, 2685, 4331, 5538, 6184 son; 989, 1803, 3367, 5251, 8124 sone; 5540 sonere; 7021, 8352 soner; **Ch2** 3266 sonne; 2913, 4827, 5157, 6510, 8008 son; 259, 2146, 4126, 6755, 8286 sone; 1622, 4828, 7910 soner; **HS** 1381, 1561, 6317, 9122, 12111 sone; 6906 soun; 386, 789 soner; 2254, 8034, 10395 sunner; 3056 sunnere; 3252 sunnest

sonenday n. [OE sunnan-dæg] Sunday; first day of the week **Ch2** 834, 3485, 5025, 5663 sonenday

song n. [see sing, v.] [OE sang, song] a song, poem; lyric **Ch1** 93, 1446, 1453, 3994, 4004 song; 11036, 11040, 11042 songe; **Ch2** 4271, 6598 song; **HS** 3057, 9058, 9160, 12120, 12288 song

sonne, sunne n. [OE sunne] the sun as a heavenly body **Ch1** 1181, 9116 son; 11842, 11843 sonne; **HS** 57, 2126, 2299, 10208, 12601 sunne

sop n. [OE sopp; OF sope] a light meal **Ch1** 7437 sop

soper, soupere n. [AF soper (MP)] supper; a meal **Ch2** 1033 soupere; **HS** 7261, 7269, 7293 rere sopers

sore n. [OE sar] pain **Ch1** 1242 sore; **HS** 2329 sor

sore, sare adj./adv. [OE sar, sare] grieved, in pain; bitter, hard; intensely, exceedingly **Ch1** 1270, 4836, 7111, 8958, 9890 sore; 8946 sore P sorewe L; 12090, 13556 sare P sore L; **Ch2** 200, 1513, 5358, 6165, 8227 sore; **HS** 680, 1375, 3589, 7516, 11991 sore; 707 sor

sory adj. [OE sarig] woeful, sorrowful; sorry **Ch1** 7096, 7148 sory; 696 sary P sory L; 5980 vnglad P sory L; **Ch2** 2562 sory; 4554 sorie; 5629 sori; **HS** 267, 706, 887, 5247, 5732 sory; 162 sory *C* sorowfull

sorow n. [OE sorh, sorg] grief, pain; affliction **Ch1** 451, 3584, 5070, 7655, 15025 sorow; 3178 sorowe; 2433 sorewe; 5615 ire P sorewe L; 15746 grete P sorewe L; **Ch2** 117, 905, 2098, 5070, 6932 sorow; 69 sorow P sorewe L; 1629, 1886 sorowe; 102, 103, 109 sorowes; 4896 soioure P sorwe L; **HS** 374 sorue; 1578, 1776, 1830 sorow; 2468, 10710 sorowe; 6101 sorous; 9167 myschef *O* sorowe

sorowe v. [OE sorgian] to be in pain; to lament, bewail **HS** 11541, 11936 sorowe; 12208 sorowede

sorowful, sorowfully adj./adv. [OE sorhfull] regretful; grievously **HS** 706 soruful; 3922, 5867 sorouful; 8051 sorowful; 5288 sorowfully; 162 sory *C* sorowfull; 2515 sorowfully *CD* dolfully *O* dulefully

sot, sottis n. [OF sot] fool, madman; wretch, rascal **Ch1** 6009 sotte P sot L; 6039 sot; 9856 sottis P sottes L; **Ch2** 6735 sottis

soþ, sothe n./adj. [see forsoth] [OE soþ] truth, true; indeed, truly; accurate, authentic; facts **Ch1** 1133, 2453, 5275, 10651 soth; 3800 sothe P soþes L; 5275 soth P soþ L; 9382, 10399, 13553 sothe P soþe L; 11954, 12363, 12987, 13999 soþe; 10102 soth P forsoþe L; **Ch2** 584, 708, 2625, 6540, 7678 soth; 1980, 3298, 6329, 8274 sothe; **HS** 485 soþ; 128, 2113, 10625, 11743, 12470 soþe; 7674, 9014, 11755 soth

sothfast adj. [OE soþfæst] authentic; just, righteous **Ch1** 14360 sothfast; **HS** 7160 sothfast

sothen v. [see seth, sothen]
sothfastnes n. [OE soþfæstness] certainty **HS** 2733 sothfastnes
soþly adv. [OE soþlice] in truth; really, assuredly **Ch2** 7262 sothly; **HS** 633 soþly; 9901, 10379 soþely
soþnes n. [from OE soþ, n.] truth, reality **HS** 10037 soþnesse; 614 soþnes *C* trowth *D* soþnesse
soth sawe n. [OE soþ sagu] true statement **Ch1** 2292 soth sawe P soþe sawe L
souche v. [see sugke, v.]
souched v. [OF souchier] become suspicious **Ch2** 6258 souched
soudan n. [OF] the sultan; a Moslem ruler or knight **Ch2** 648, 3435, 4602, 4767, 5607 soudan; 5614 soudone
souder, soudioure n. [OF soudier] servant; common soldier **Ch1** 3144, 7051, 9220, 13664 souders; 13805, 15533 soudeours P souders L; **Ch2** 6783 soudioure; 2643, 6976 souders
souereyn n. [OF souerain, souerein] a superior; lord, master **Ch1** 14115 souereyns; **HS** 3018 souereyn
souht v. [see seke, v.]
souke n. [OE soc] sucking milk from the breast **Ch1** 11958 souke
soule, saule n. [OE sawol, sawel] spiritual or rational element in man; spirit of a dead person **Ch1** 5691, 15891 soule; 4009 soule P saul L; 13116, 15624 saule; 15430, 15433 saules; **Ch2** 184, 2632, 3317, 4614, 8352 soule; 1042 saule; 1615, 3111 soules; 5414 saules; **HS** 840, 6312, 10112, 10511, 11970 soule; 2066 saule; 2512 saules; 12596 soules
soun, sounde n. [OE son] a sound, noise **Ch1** 1154, 3555, 11032 soun; 11142 souns; 11148 sounde; **HS** 7131 sown
soun adv. [see sone, adv.]
sound adj. [OE gesund] safe, unharmed **Ch1** 8020 sounde; **HS** 7010 sound
souper n. [see soper, n.]
sour adj./adv. [OE sur] bitter; severely, harshly **Ch2** 1621, 3469 soure; **HS** 96, 4094, 4782, 8492, 10106 soure; 10107, 10109 sour
sowe v. [see sewe, v. (2)]
space n. [AF; OF espace] land, territory; an interval of time; proper time; a place **Ch1** 2135, 2511, 5250, 7782, 15722 space; 4749 space P place L; **Ch2** 2133, 3551, 5227, 6711, 8178 space; **HS** 2260, 4506, 7327, 11300, 11779 space; 7030 spas
spake v. [see speke, v.]
◆ **spake** adj. [ON spakr] gentle, tame **HS** 319 spake; 7488 spake GLOSS H tame
spare v. [OE sparian] leave unhurt; forgive, take pity on; cease **Ch1** 2691, 3450, 3714 spare; 1158 spares; 1163, 3440, 3985, 5851 spared; **Ch2** 1352, 2761, 5476, 6205, 8345 spare; 1523, 1873, 1907, 6197 spared; **HS** 806, 2402, 5388, 6277, 11001 spare; 1693 wonde GLOSS BH spare
sparkeld v. [OE spearcian] sparkle, glitter **Ch1** 8923 sparkeld P sparkled L; 13188L sparklyng (om. P)
sparkes, sperkes n. [OE spearca] fiery particles **Ch1** 8082 sperkes; 8430, 10694 sparkes P sparkles L
sparowes n. [OE spearwa] small birds **Ch1** 14060, 14065, 14083, 14086 sparowes
sparpled v. [AF esparplier] scatter, disperse **Ch1** 8374 sparpled P sparplyed L
spas n. [see space, n.]
spece, spyce n. [AF espece (MP)] way, manner; type or kind; the human species; portion, part; characteristic, attribute **Ch1** 900 spece; **HS** 2413, 7280, 8323 spece; 2919 spyces; 3529 spyce; 6521 speces; 28 spyce *D* speche; 115 speche *D* spycys; 7587 vyce *H* spyce *O* spyse
speche n. [OE spec, spæc] speaking; language **Ch1** 73, 1905, 5571, 7411, 10343 speche; 1918, 2159, 3105, 4074, 7273 spech; 4947 spechis; 15926 spech P speche L; 15930 spech P spekynge (ger.) L; **Ch2** 657 spech; 6257 speche; **HS** 4302, 6374, 8291, 10651, 12438 speche; 28 spyce *D* speche; 115 speche *D* spycys
special, specyaly adj./adv. [OF especial] exceptional; in extraordinary circumstances **Ch2** 453, 1517, 2417 specially; **HS** 8323 specyal; 59, 278, 2246, 7554, 10437 specyaly
specialty n. [OF especialite] a special favor **Ch1** 530 specialty; 5236 specialte; **HS** 9733 specyalte
sped, spede n. [OE sped] fortune, success; haste **Ch1** 588 spede; 13666L sped (om. P); **HS** 10446 spede
sped, spede v. [OE spedan] prosper, succeed; travel swiftly; depart in haste **Ch1** 1536, 4465, 7874, 9756, 11836 spede; 2497, 3208, 6202, 9231, 15623 sped; 9251 spede P sped L; 6332, 7846, 9564 sped P spedde L; 8790 spedis P spedeþ L; 7497 led P spedde L; **Ch2** 495, 2598, 5086, 6502, 8286 sped; 2099, 2493, 4185, 5776, 8210 spede; 7939 spedis; 2963 sped P fledde L; **HS** 365, 7800 sped; 1768, 5019, 6856, 9446, 11404 spede; 4817 spedyþ
speire, speyr n. [AF espeir] hope, expectation **Ch1** 2354 speyre P speyr L; 3123 speire; 5697, 10430, 13739, 13850 speire P speyr L; 6237 speire P espeir L; **Ch2** 1267, 2516, 2622, 3442, 6077 speyre; 1779 speyr; 4046 speyre P no dispeir L; **HS** 6478 speyr *O* espayr
speke, spak v. [OE specan] speak; tell **Ch1** 2348, 3839, 6834, 7199, 13907 speke; 5640 spek; 5565 spekes; 12525 spekis; 6921 speken; 7336 spekin; 6628 spekand; 389, 1502, 4152, 7188,

15846 spak; 330, 2799, 3027, 8159, 10132 spake; 947, 1867, 2017, 3229, 4484 spoken; **Ch2** 29, 1430, 4293, 6822, 8273 speke; 7473, 7621 spake; 372, 2304, 3612, 6763, 7801 spak; 2464, 4584, 5840, 6139, 8277 spoken; 1081 oft speke P of wel spekon L; 3998L spekeþ (P differs); **HS** 30, 798, 1536, 2635, 8363 speke; 315, 1552, 4904, 9217 spak; 5589, 9192 spake; 4083 spakk; 1537, 6025, 8609 spoke; 1034 spokun; 5897 spekyng; 1977 spak GLOSS B seyde; 2129 seyde *CD* spake; 6937 sermun GLOSS BH speke

speker n. [from OE specan, v.] speaker **HS** 8295 speker

spekyng ger. [from OE specan, v.] conference, assembly; talk, a language **Ch1** 15930 spech P spekynge L; **Ch2** 7325, 7570, 8074, 8267 spekyng; 7775 spekynges; **HS** 8289, 9504 spekyng

spel, spell n. [OE] story, tale; sermon **Ch1** 4004 spelle; **HS** 4703 spell; 9725 spel; 10915 spelles

spele v. (1) [OE spelian] save, hoard, spare; neglect, set aside **Ch1** 12110, 13692, 13874 spele; **Ch2** 2331, 5438, 6186, 6458 spele

spele v. (2) [OE spellian] speak, tell, recount **Ch1** 10419 spelle; 58, 15346 spelles; **Ch2** 528 spellis; **HS** 402, 1180 spellyþ; 688, 3898, 4345, 10128, 11853 spelle; 7034 spelles; 12337 spelleþ *O* telles; 12338 telleþ *O* spelles

spellyng ger. [OE spellung] discourse, speech **HS** 10983 spellyng

spence, spense n. [OF espense, spence] money; payment, reward **Ch2** 2768 spence P spences L; 3329 spense P despens L; **HS** 6859 spenses

spend v. [see dispende] [OE spendan; OF despendre] spend money, wealth; use, employ **Ch1** 7102 spende; 6639 dispendid P spended L; 10605 spended P despended L; 13258 spendid; **Ch2** 3150, 5116 spend; 470 spended; 2767, 5518, 7526 spendid; 3321 spende P despende L; 2833, 5878 spendes; **HS** 6508 spende

spendyng ger. [OE spendung] money, wealth; expense, **Ch2** 3082, 4968, 6784 spendyng

spenser n. [AF despenser] dispenser of money or provisions; steward, an almoner **HS** 6072, 6448, 6840 spenser

spere n. [OE] javelin, dart **Ch1** 1765, 1788 spere; 1007 lance P spere L; 1542, 3766 launce P spere L; 4987 helme P spere L; 2927 speres; 3496 lances P speres L; **Ch2** 2858, 7419 spere; 7423 speres

sperre, sperd v. [see spire, v.] [ON; OE gesparrian] lock a gate, door; shut up; imprison **Ch1** 11560 sperre; 9371L sperre (om. P); 8386, 11380, 13659 sperd; 5952, 12674 sperd P sperde L; 1392, 9218 sperde P sperd L; **Ch2** 5782 sperre; 2271, 2471, 3876, 4294, 7317 sperd; 2225 sperd P stret L; **HS** 6136 sperde; 6140 sperd; 3658 sperd *F* sprede *O* speryde *W* sperid; 4456 shette *O* speryd; 4486 shet *O* speryd; 6200 sperd *F* spred

sperkes n. [see sparkes, n.]

spycerye n. [AF especerie (MP)] aromatic spices **HS** 1396 spycerye

spie n. [OF espie] scout; lookout, guard **Ch1** 3347 spie; 6704, 7870 spies; **Ch2** 124, 2380, 4567, 5813, 6996 spie; 1098, 8144 spies

spie v. [see aspie] [OF espiier] seek information stealthily; scout **Ch1** 3324, 14032 spie; 6207, 7593, 14038 spied; 1532, 14001 spied P aspied L; 2717 spiand; 13146 spies P aspieþ L; **Ch2** 918, 2215, 4810, 6470, 8239 spie; 4648, 5521, 5828, 5832 spied; 8236 spiand; 8284 spiyng

spikke n. [OE spic] animal fat, lard **Ch1** 12041 spikke P spyk L

spille, spilte v. [OE spillan] to kill, destroy; punish; mutilate; to flow from a container **Ch1** 4759, 4855, 8547, 10628, 15570 spille; 9231 spilte; 13092 spilt P spild L; **Ch2** 2761, 4399, 6754 spille; 3179 spilte; **HS** 736, 6646 spylle; 552, 1332, 6948 spylt; 3847 spylte; 5294 spyll; 8440, 8928, 9328, 12046, 12452 spyl; 1296 pylt GLOSS B cast *CD* spylt

spillyng ger. [from OE spillan] shedding blood **Ch2** 4578 spillyng

spire, sperre, spird v. [OE spirian] ask, question, search out **Ch1** 7870, 7874 spire; 7905, 15134 spired P spirde L; 9379, 15349 spired P spyrde L; 10809 spir P spirde L; 13983 spirde P spyrede L; 14249 spired P spyred L; **Ch2** 3301 sperre; 2715 spire; 2752 spires; 8001 spired; **HS** 1936 askede *C* speryd *D* aspyed

spirit n. [AF espirit (MP)] the soul; demon, ghost; holy spirit; divine power **Ch1** 7958, 7973 spirites; **Ch2** 8340 spirit; 2811 spiritu sancti; 4426 spiritus sancti; **HS** 288, 316, 12205 spyryte; 1377, 4725 spyryt

spiritualle, spyrytuele adj. [AF spirituel (MP)] of the spirit; divine **Ch2** 6868 spiritualle; **HS** 3014 spyrytual; 12178 spyrytuele

spirred v. [see sporede, v.]

splaied v. [see display, v.] [from AF despleier] to display or unfurl a banner **Ch1** 9778 splaied

spoiled v. [OF espoillier, AF espuiller] to strip off armor, despoil, pillage **Ch1** 5341 spoiled P dispoilled L; 12606, 13400 spoiled

spors n. [OE spora, spura] spur for a horse **Ch1** 12371 sporse P sporede (v.) L; 12681 spors P haste L sporis R; **Ch2** 2846 spors

sporede, spirred v. [from OE spora, n.] spur a horse **Ch1** 12371 sporse (n.) P sporede L; 5392 spirred

sposage n. [OF esposage] marriage; wedding rite **Ch2** 3787 sposage

spourge v. [OF espurgier] to purge **HS** 10925 spourge

spousayle n. [AF spousaille, esposaille (MP)] marriage, wedding **Ch2** 7507 spousale; **HS** 1673, 1718, 4207, 7368 spousayle; 2035 spousale; 1622 spousayle *C* spousehede

spouse v. [OF esposer, AF espuser] give a daughter in marriage; betroth **Ch2** 188 wedded P spoused L; 661 spoused; 5154 spouse

spousebreche n. [from OF spous + breche] adultery; marital infidelity **HS** 7364 spousebreche; 7366 spoubreche

spouted v. [?OE; cp. MDu spouten] a dragon: spitting fire **Ch1** 8082 spouted

spred, sprad v. [OE *sprædan] stretch or draw out; extend out; scatter **Ch1** 618 spredde; 934, 1490, 4297, 8166, 15407 spred; 7372, 7398 sprede; 3083 spred P yspred L; 8374, 8979 spred P spredde L; **Ch2** 324, 2852 sprad; 5589, 8063 spred; 854, 1665, 7849 sprede; 6780 spredis; 1933 spred P spredde L; **HS** 5583 spredde; 6205, 9454 spred

spring v. [OE springan] sprout, grow; be born; arise; breaking of dawn **Ch1** 2239 springes; 11841 spring; 4993 springe; 3494, 10694, 12481, 13407, 14597 sprong; 3386 sprong P sprang L; **Ch2** 914 spronge; 7174 sprong; **HS** 882 spryngge; 2881 sprynge; 5447 sprong

spurne n. [from OE spornan, spurnan, v.] a rush **Ch1** 12405 spurne

square adj. [see quarre, adj.] [OF esquarre] weapon ground to a cutting edge **Ch1** 15129 square

squier n. [OF esquier, AF esqier] esquire; soldier rank below a knight; servant **Ch1** 5471, 6865, 10967, 12020, 15266 squiers; 4603 suaynes P squiers L; 7108 sergeanȝ P squiers L; 1492, 3143, 4670, 4696, 5029 squyers; 2984 squyeres; 5085 squiere; 11884 squyere; **Ch2** 2855, 2865, 4044 squier; 2996, 3146, 6314, 7716, 8080 squiere; 4041 squieres; **HS** 3254, 3308 squyer; 4375 squyere; 4629, 5873, 7270 squyers

squierie n. [from OF esquierie] group of military squires, retainers **Ch1** 2399 squyery; **Ch2** 5809, 7013 squierie

squyler n. [AF scuiler] scullion **HS** 5913 squyler

stable v. [OF establir] establish; fix, ordain **Ch1** 2747, 7653 stabled; **Ch2** 3412, 3599, 7537 stabled; 5891 stabille; **HS** 11167, 11243 stabled; 1604 stablyd *CD* mad; 1605 stablede *D* ordeynd

stable, stabille adj./adv. [OF stable, estable] steadfast, firm, solid; stationary **Ch1** 3868, 9183, 10398, 15746 stable; 8026, 11392 stabille P stable L; **Ch2** 3399, 3589, 7370, 7930 stable; 3100 stabilly; **HS** 471, 1991, 3502, 6535, 7550 stable; 10759 stabely

stables n. [OF estable] stables for animals **Ch1** 10964 stables

staf n. [see staues] [OE stæf] rod, club, weapon **Ch1** 14190, 14594, 14596 staf; 15127, 15161 staffe

stage n. [OF estage] platform; a period of time; story of a building **Ch1** 11899, 13230 stage; 4535, 12272 stages; **Ch2** 4058, 6235, 7932 stage

◆ **stage** v. [from OF estage, n.] construct a bridge **Ch1** 3062 stage

stak n. [ON; cp. OI stakkr] corn heap **Ch1** 14068 stak P stakkes L

stake v. [from n.; cp. MDu, MLG staken] stake out a boundary; fix fortification stakes in a line **Ch1** 1848, 4568, 4588, 7407 stake; **Ch2** 7536 stake

stakerd v. [ON; cp. OI stakra] to stagger, sway **Ch1** 12067 stakerd

stal v. [see stele, v.]

stalle, stale n. [OF estal] place, position; armed men placed for ambush **Ch1** 5020, 6712, 9916, 11642, 13582 stalle P stal L; **Ch2** 3599, 3854, 6848, 7983 stalle; **HS** 11880 stale

stalworth adj./n. [OE stælwierðe] strong, courageous; valiant **Ch1** 466, 882, 5803, 7283, 13272 stalworth; 5058 stalworth P strong L; 3741 stalworth P stalwordest L; **Ch2** 550, 819, 2965, 7427, 8303 stalworth; **HS** 5865 stalwrþe; 9827, 9841 stalworth

stalworthly adv. [from OE stælwirþe, adj.] bravely, valiantly **Ch1** 490 stalworþely P stalworly L; 8325 stalworthest P starworþest L; 8990 stalworthly; **Ch2** 4095 stalworþely; 4217 stalworthly; **HS** 7183 stalwrþly; 7513 stalwrthly

◆ **stampe** n. [see stank, n.] [?from OF estanc] pool of water **Ch2** 7010 stampe

stanch v. [OF estanchier] stop the flow; to end strife **Ch2** 4880 stanch; 6102 stanche

stand, stond v. [OE standan, stondan] stay in place; rise up; stand and fight **Ch1** 1558, 4626, 6644, 7988, 8022 stand; 570, 1327, 2695, 3009, 4422 stande; 7931 standen; 374, 2600, 3539, 4184, 5619 standes; 8191 standis; 7788 stond; 7856, 8000 stonde; 501, 4570, 4617 stod; 1335, 2926, 5321, 6512, 8769 stode; 596 stode P stoden L; 1653 stoden; 4614 riden P stoden L; 579, 1033 stude; 6310 stande to P assayeþe L; 10643 stude P stode L; 1814 stode P stod vp L; 11899 standand P standynge L; **Ch2** 750, 1229, 3550, 5297, 7792 stand; 391 stand P stonde L; 4737, 6396 standen; 437, 1790, 4960, 6635, 7274 standes; 2007 standis; 2027, 6494 stond; 1415 take P stonde to L; 4391 stund P stonde L; 150, 2275, 3240, 7458, 8320 stode; 5352 standand; **HS** 812, 1571, 6569, 11289 stonde; 844 stond; 5715, 5835 stande; 12223 stanst; 5887, 7122 stant; 8998 standeþ; 7735 stondyng; 305, 1379, 3271, 8047, 11028 stode

standard n. [AF estandard] flag or banner on a pole **Ch1** 13294, 13305 standard; **Ch2** 2790

standard
stank n. [OF estanc] a pond or pool **Ch2** 1685 stank P strong L
stare v. [OE starian] gaze intently **HS** 8902 stare; 10212 staryng
starfe, sterue v. [OE steorfan] to die; die from hunger **Ch1** 7622 starfe P starf L; **Ch2** 4588 sterue
stark adj./adv. [OE stearc] strong, severe; hard, unyielding; rigid **Ch1** 8018, 10497, 13732 stark; **Ch2** 401 starke; 1065, 1850, 2394, 4327, 5714 stark; **HS** 4989 stark; 6842 starke
state n. [OF estat, AF astat] rank, social position; physical condition **Ch1** 12, 5808, 6783, 7671, 11064 state; 10976 mener state P mener stat L; **Ch2** 1803, 2075, 5247, 6229, 7057 state; 4100 stat; **HS** 213, 2211, 4146, 6182, 11802 state
stature n. [OF estature, L statura] height, posture **Ch1** 150, 7187 stature
statute n. [OF estatute] law, decree, proclamation; ordinance **Ch2** 5285, 5720, 6875, 7289 statute
staues n. [see staf] [OE stæf] a stick, pole, or club used as a weapon **Ch1** 4345 staues P wyfles L; **Ch2** 8014 staues
stede n. (1) [OE] place, position; town, locality; property, estate **Ch1** 1895, 3637, 5845, 7085, 11015 stede; 14740 sted; 7326 stedis; 1717, 4868, 5756, 7839, 15804 stedes; 5028 stedes P wardes L; 10962 stedes P innes L; **Ch2** 148, 2271, 5458, 7263, 8059 stede; 1889, 2742, 3945, 5969, 6286 stedes; 8192 stedis; 1885 wonyng stede; **HS** 1879, 2020, 5817, 7732, 9223 stede; 9250 stedes; 1404 wonyng places *D* stede; 1418 stedys *CD* place; 1808 stede *D* place; 1809 place *D* stede; 1858 stede *CD* place; 2016 place *C* stede; 2020 stede *C* place; 2485 stedys *D* a place; 9342 place *O* stede
stede n. (2) [OE steda] a horse, steed **Ch1** 1113, 5376, 10664, 11886, 13419 stede; 10962, 11171, 12019 stedes; 12236, 12488 stedis; **Ch2** 3018, 4548, 6572, 7436, 8173 stede; 6701 stedes
stedfast, stedfastly adj./adv. [OE stedefæst] firm, steady **Ch1** 8664 stedfast P stedefast L; 14892 stedfast P studefast L; **Ch2** 79, 7043 stedfast; 6038 stedfaste; **HS** 1908 stedfast; 2310, 7517, 9847, 10263, 11214 stedefast; 313 stedfastlyche; 864 stedefastlye; 3591 stedfastly
steem n. [cp. F estime] esteem, worth **Ch1** 98 steem
steih, stegh v. [see stie, v.]
steke v. [OE *stecan] be hindered; lock up; shut or fasten **Ch1** 1449 steke; 12102 stoken P loken L; 12570 steke L stoken R (om. P); **HS** 7746, 11232 steke; 11837 stoken *O* lokene; 11838 loken *O* stokene
stele n. [OE stel, stile] steel implement or weapon; fig.: hard, stiff, strong, faithful **Ch1** 1102, 4813, 9516, 10654, 13263 stele; **Ch2** 819, 1477, 1827, 7745 stele; **HS** 2338 steyl
stele, stal v. [OE stelan] to rob; escape; conceal **Ch1** 5745 stele; 6693L stele (om. P); 1089 stolne; 9670 stolne P stolen L; 290, 1116 stollen; **Ch2** 3510 stele; 1909, 1911 stal; **HS** 2048, 2111, 2149, 10584 stele; 1203 stelyþ; 2198 stelyst; 2434 stelst; 2190, 3693, 11868 stole; 2464, 6732 stall; 9375 stal; 2153 stale; 11832 steles; 3178 stolne
stelth n. [prob. OE *stælþ] a furtive act **Ch1** 2881 stelth
stem n. (1) [OE stemn] trunk; the source **Ch2** 7194 stem
stem, steme n. (2) [OE steam] vapor, hot breath **Ch1** 1814 stem; **HS** 2526 steme
sterynges ger. [from OE styrian, v.] incitement **HS** 8522 sterynges
sterisman n. [OE steores-mann] helmsman of a ship **Ch1** 12600 sterisman P steresman LR
sterne n. [ON stjarna] star **Ch1** 1678, 8916, 8968 sterne; 10855 sternes; **Ch2** 3977 sterne
stert v. [see stirt, v.]
sterue v. [see starfe, v.]
steuene n. [OE stefn] sound of the voice **HS** 10069 steuene
stie n. [OE stig] path, narrow way, road **Ch1** 5949, 10807 stie; 5031, 6705 sties; 2606 sties P styes L; 13625 stie P sty L; 14985 outen pathes P sties & paþes L; **Ch2** 4648, 4986, 7792 stie
stie, steih, stegh v. [OE stigan] ascend, rise up; climb **Ch1** 8227, 11133 stegh P stey L; 9962, 14409 steih P stey L; 11809 vp stegh P vp stey L; **HS** 321 steye *CD* stey
stiffe n./adj./adv. [see stith, adj.] [OE stif] rigid, inflexible **Ch1** 3009, 4614, 5042, 13362 stifly; 8283 stifly P styf L; 10497 stiffe P styf L; **Ch2** 87 stiffe; 312 stifely P stifly L; 6447, 7254 stifly; 2889 stouter in strife P stinter & stiff L; 4799 stith P stiff L; **HS** 272, 1774 weyl to *C* styfly
stik, stykkes n. [OE sticca] a stick; fig.: every stick, total destruction **Ch2** 2749 ilk a stik; **HS** 12444 stykkes
stike, stykke v. [OE stician] to pierce, thrust with weapons **Ch1** 3499 stike P styke L; 5360 stiked; 7756 smyte P stykeþ L; **HS** 5186 stykke; 5168 styke *O* stryke
stile n. [OF] characteristic mode; language **Ch1** 10772, 15921 stile
stille, stilly adj./adv. [OE stille, stillice] yet, still; in addition; motionless; quietly **Ch1** 1180, 3646, 4514, 7771, 8047 stille; 2069, 3356 stilly; 15144 stilly P stille L; **Ch2** 54, 1330, 3880, 6586, 7313 stille; 3983 stilly; **HS** 308, 526, 2125, 4470 styll; 1189, 3271, 5960, 6413, 9188 stylle; 9257, 10252 styl; 2432 stylleche

stynk, stank v. [OE stincan] to stink **Ch2** 7019 stank; 4392 stinkand; **HS** 6520 stynk; 6757, 6759 stynke; 8316, 11682 stank; 1420 stynkyng; 1387 stynkyngge *C* styngande *D* stynkende; 2301 stynkyngge

stint v. [OE styntan] stop, cut short; stay **Ch1** 7318 stint P stynt L; 10664, 10689, 11896, 12067, 13574 stynt; 10702 stynt P stinte L; 12555 stynt P stynte L stint R; **Ch2** 193, 5384 stynt; 2331 stound P stynte L; 4555 stint; **HS** 524 *D* stente (B differs)

stynte n. [from OE styntan, v.] cessation, a stop **Ch1** 6712 stynte P stynt L

styntyng ger. [from OE styntan] stopping, ceasing **Ch2** 15 styntyng

stirop n. [OE sti-rap, stig-rap] stirrup **Ch1** 12398L stirop (om. P)

stirre, stere v. [OE styrian] move, stir; prompt, incite; steer a ship **Ch1** 3530 stir; 8775, 10955 stired; 1445, 11798, 13541 stere; **Ch2** 6184 stirre; **HS** 8039 stere; 12284 styreþ; 5188 steryþ *O* wayttes

stirt, sterte v. [see vpstirt] [OE styrtan] leap, jump, caper, spring **Ch1** 6627, 6949 stirt P stirte L; 7769, 12998 stirt; 11288 stirte P sterte L; 12047 stirte vp; 4970, 5184, 7138, 12088, 13547 stirte; **Ch2** 3941, 4115, 7812 stirte; **HS** 1569, 5603 sterte; 6218, 7848 styrte

stith adj. [OE stið] strong; unyielding **Ch2** 4799 stith P stiff L

stiward, steward n. [OE stiweard] domestic official, steward **Ch1** 4301, 13074 stiward P styward L; 10783 steward P stywarde L; 11065 stiward; **Ch2** 191, 4148, 4964, 6755, 7642 stiward; **HS** 5423 stywardes; 5425, 5495 styward; 4419 steward *H* stuwarde

stodye v. [see studie, v.]

stodyyng ger. [from OF estudier, v.] studying **HS** 443 stodyyng

stok n. [OE stoc] trunk of a tree; instrument of punishment; block of wood **Ch1** 9800L stok (om. P); **Ch2** 1772 stoure P stokes L; **HS** 940, 12446 stok; 9113 stok *O* tre

stokked v. [from OE stoc, n.] punish in stocks; imprison **Ch2** 2949 stokked P schulked L

stole v. [see stele, v.]

stond v. [see stand]

stone n. [OE stan] jewels; grave stone, monument; missiles for slings **Ch1** 449, 5590, 5600 ston; 1782, 1842, 6600, 7864, 14020 stone; 1031, 3002, 4699, 6719, 8063 stones; 7782 stonis; **Ch2** 1041, 1370, 6437, 7425, 8351 stone; 4307, 5007, 7446, 7972 stones; **HS** 1810, 2269, 8740, 9778, 11923 stone; 1412, 8784 stones

stoned, stonyed v. [OF estoner] to daze or astound; be amazed, stunned **Ch1** 10677 stonyed P dunede L; 12067 stonyed P stoneyd L; 15844L stoneyed (om. P); **Ch2** 5352 stoned

stop v. [ON stoppa; OE *stoppian] obstruct, block; plug up **Ch1** 2574, 5031 stop; 6575 stop P stoppe L; 9593 stopped; 12988L stopped (om. P); **Ch2** 4022, 4492 stop; 4651 stoppe; 4454, 4650 stopped; **HS** 10549 stopped

store n. [OF estor] store, hoard; provisions **Ch2** 7980 store; **HS** 5393, 6083, 6246, 6351, 10896 store

store v. [from OF estorer] supply with stores, provisions **Ch1** 1323, 1422, 15806 stored; 10588 store P warnische L; 2888 stroyed (?error) P storede L; **Ch2** 3973 store; 4085 stored P astorred L

store, stour adj. [see stour, n.] [ON storr, OE stor] violent, fierce; stubborn **Ch2** 1789 stoure; 7660 store; **HS** 11479 stour

story n. [from AF estorie; OF estoire] narrative, history **Ch1** 3, 327, 1614, 2532, 3961 story; 712 storyes; 5565 stories; **Ch2** 520, 1216, 2696, 5406, 5865 story; 4680, 4684 stori; 2560, 5674, 7039 storie; 1, 535 stories; 94 gestes P stories L; **HS** 6251 storye; 7034, 11460 story

stork n. [OE storc] the white stork **Ch1** 13956 stork

storme n. [OE] violent weather **Ch1** 2941 storme; 13028 stormes

storpe, storop n. [see slop]

stound n. [OE stund] short while; moment, space of time; often; season **Ch1** 1376, 3946, 5322, 8149, 12015 stounde; 12868 stound; 11090 stond (v.) P stounde L; **Ch2** 104, 5630 stoundes; 3819, 5222, 6570, 6592, 7684 stounde; 901, 1339 stound; 2331 stound P stynt L; 4391 stund P stonde L; **HS** 7243 stound; 5934, 10910, 11751 stounde; 3085, 10569 stoundes; 4470 stounde *O* thraw; 6933 stound GLOSS H tyme; 12235 stounde *O* thorowe

stounded, stonde v. [from OE stund, n.] remain, stay; to rest **Ch1** 10702 stounded; **HS** 8808 stonde

stoupe v. [OE stupian] bow; look down **Ch2** 1741 stoupe; **HS** 5615 stoupede

stour n. [OF estour, AF estur] armed combat, fight **Ch1** 1186, 2735, 5144, 6030, 11581 stoure; 6635, 7547 stours; 726, 843 stoure P stour L; 5895 stoures P stours L; 11422 schours P stours L; **Ch2** 87, 298, 2826, 5221, 8320 stoure; 1772 stoure P stokes L; 3434, 3984 stour; 4578, 6639 stours

stour adj. [see store, stour, adj.]

stoute v. [from OF estout, adj.] to behave haughtily or defiantly **Ch1** 6262 stouted P reuiled L; **HS** 2948, 3405, 8457, 10930 stoute; 1077 stoute *C* stande *D* stant *F* stout *H* stonde

stoute, stoutly adj./adv. [OF estout] proud, fierce, brave, resolute; furious **Ch1** 912, 2107,

5116, 6174, 7689 stoute; 1686, 2704, 3726, 4392 stout; 5296 ouer stoute; **Ch2** 1130, 1850, 2790, 5831, 7199 stoute; 4214, 4460, 6546, 6700 stout; 2889 stouter; 2742, 5421 stoutly; 2744 stoutely; 2943 ouer stoute; **HS** 4038, 4989, 6016, 10213 stout; 4959 stoute; 3523, 4287, 4903, 10916 stoutly

straied v. [see ostray] [OF estraier] escape from confinement; wander away **Ch1** 3284 straid P strayed L; 12514 straied P astraied L; **Ch2** 5360 straied

strait, streit, streight adj./adv. [OF estreit] tight, narrow, close; tense, strict, rigorous; difficult **Ch1** 3326, 9280 straite; 4534 streght P streight L; 1801 streit; 4913 straitly P streitly L; 4997, 5978, 8453, 15561 streite P streit L; 9074 strayte P streit L; 9797 strait P streit L; 10595 straite P streit L; 15650 streitly; **Ch2** 2070, 2082, 3399, 5825, 7150 streite; 1953, 5256 streit; 2898 straite; 278 narow P straite L; 6320 streiter; 6786, 8245 streitly; **HS** 3816, 5330, 6057, 11818 streyt; 5340 strayte; 3813 streytly *O* strangly

strange adj. [OF estrange] foreign; unfamiliar; cold, unfriendly **Ch1** 78, 116, 4063, 4531 strange; 1928 outen P straunge L; 11198 vnkouth P straunge L; **Ch2** 821, 1198, 4815, 5257, 7943 strange; 2136 strange P estrange L; **HS** 7547, 8111 straunge

strangle v. [AF estrangler (MP)] to kill; choke to death **Ch1** 15576 strangle; **Ch2** 1336 strangle; 733, 1322, 1338 strangled; **HS** 972 stranglyd; 3191 strangle; 6408 strangled

stranlyng v. [see strinkled, v.]

streit, streight adj./adv. [see strait]

streke, strekid v. [OE streccan] stretched out, extended **Ch1** 12357 strekid P streked L; **HS** 944 streke *F* steke

stremes n. [OE stream] river, stream **Ch1** 2946, 13417 stremes

streng n. [OE streng] thread, rope, cord **Ch1** 8534 streeng P streng L; 14550 streng

strength, strenkþe n. [OE strengðu] violence, outrage; a stronghold, fortified place; power; an abortifacient **Ch1** 1690, 1824, 1833, 5969 strength; 4492 force P strengthe L; 7040 forcelettes P strengþes; 7364 purtenance P strengþe L; **Ch2** 300, 933 strength; **HS** 3049, 8341 strenkþe; 3719 strenþe; 5227 strenþe *H* strenkþe; 7199 strengþe

stresse n. [see destres, n.] [OF estrece, destresse] hardship; force, affliction; compulsion, violence, oppression **Ch1** 6095, 15528, 15555 stresse; 3320, 3444 stresse P destresse L; **Ch2** 3395, 6810, 7860 stresse; 627 stresse P destresse L; **HS** 8234, 8348 stres; 5502, 8816 stresse; 2798 stresse *D* distresse; 3941 stresse *O* dystresse; 4406, 5006 stres *O* distresse; 7316 destresse *O* stresse

stresse v. [short form of OF estrecier; cp. OF estrece, n.] to restrain, compel; dissuade **Ch1** 6095 stresse; **HS** 3728 stres

strete n. [OE stret, L strata] path, road **Ch1** 3057, 3353, 5949, 6208, 10807 strete; 2606, 3076, 6705 stretes; **Ch2** 2871, 4648 strete; 8150 stete (error); **HS** 179, 1371, 2101, 2850, 8461 strete; 2610, 3451 stret

strewed v. [OE strewian] scattered, dispersed **Ch1** 4347 strewed

strife n. [OF estrif] enmity, dispute; antagonism **Ch1** 770 stryf; 516, 788, 5446, 7881, 15555 strife; 2986, 7590 stryfe; 3931 striue; **Ch2** 464, 1124, 2889, 5057, 7641 strife; 2109, 2368, 5046, 5290 strif; 4471 scathe P striff L; **HS** 1192, 1517, 5140, 7403, 7447 stryff

strike n. [from OE strican, v.; cp. AF estriche] a distance **Ch1** 1048 stryke P stryk L; 1412 strike P stryke L; 5737 strike; 11686 strike P stryk L; 13848 strik P stryk L

strike v. [OE strican] go, pass, proceed; deal a blow; stab, cut **Ch1** 1730, 4345, 13029 striken; 3659 striken P stryken L; 490, 9953, 10970 strike

strinkled ppl. [?altered from sprinkle, v.] a sprinkled surface **Ch1** 10972 strinkled P stranlyng L

striue v. [OF estriver] to be hostile; fight, quarrel **Ch1** 2328, 2626, 6274, 7894 stryue; 2122 stryuen; 1210 striues; **Ch2** 908, 6134 stryue; 7128 striued; 7129 striues; **HS** 1984, 6493, 7781, 7950 stryue; 11238 stryues

stroye v. [see destroy] [AF destruire (MP)] to demolish; ravage a country or crops; conquer **Ch1** 706 destroye P struye L; 2888 stroyed (?error) P storede L; 446, 720, 5919 stroyed; 6505 stroie; 6015, 6018 stroied; 4757L struye (om. P); **Ch2** 966, 7350, 8059 stroied; 4555 stroye; 8327 stroie; **HS** 8079 stroye

stroke n. [OE *strac; cp. OE stracian, v.] a blow; a thrust with a weapon **Ch1** 1585, 4372, 4409, 9951, 12079 stroke; 1564, 1686, 2697, 3495, 9938 strokes; **Ch2** 2295, 4718, 5031 stroke; **HS** 4496 strokes *O* strakes; 8648 strokes *O* stakes

stronde n. [OE strand] shore, coast **Ch1** 13491 stronde

strong, strange adj. [OE strang, strong] vigorous; severe, difficult; deadly, fierce **Ch1** 484, 1060, 6675, 8127, 13175 strong; 3293, 7239 stronge; 15464 strange P stronge L; 1290 strangest P strengeste L; 14231 strangest; 15729 strangere P straunger L; **Ch2** 484, 1217, 4475, 5783, 5951 strong; 1791 stranger P strenger L; **HS** 1339, 1441, 2478, 2506 strong; 2034, 8620, 12415 stronge

stroupe n. [ON strupe] throat, neck **Ch2** 4719

stroupe

strut n. [see ostrut, adv.] [OE strutian] manner of walking: to strut **HS** 3349 strut *O* sturte; 3745 strut *O* stryt

studie n. [OF estudie] perplexity; reflection, reverie; a study room **Ch1** 11319 study P studie L; **Ch2** 1410, 4836, 5599 studie; **HS** 399, 4749, 6121 stodye

studie v. [see stodyyng, ger.] [OF estudier] learn by study; meditate; observe; to be in doubt, perplexity **Ch1** 3679, 8522 studied; **Ch2** 473, 1293, 6866 studied; **HS** 7748 þoghte so *O* stodyde; 11605 stodye

stumble v. [prob. ON; cp. MDu stommelen] trip; stagger, fall **Ch1** 12116L stombled (om. P); 12570 stumbled L stomblid R (om. P); **HS** 6523 stumble

stund n. [see stound, n.]

sturble v. [see desturble] [OF desturble, destrobler] to bother someone; prevent, hinder **Ch1** 4717 turbled P sturbled L; **Ch2** 2841 sturbled; **HS** 1713 desturble *C* strobyll; 1725 desturble *C* distrobyll *D* stourblyst; 1876 dysturble *C* strobyll *D* distourble; 4717 sturbled *O* dystrubyd; 5405 sturbled *O* dystrube; 11142 sturble *O* destrube

stut adj. [see stout, adj.] [?ON stuttr] short-spoken, imperious **HS** 8701 stut *F* stout *O* stutte

suage v. [see asuage] [AF suager, swagier] appease, mitigate **Ch1** 888 asuage P a suwage L; 4526 suaged P swaged L; 9541 suaged P yswaged L

suayn n. [see sueyn, n.]

sualhid, swalud v. [OE swelgan, ON svelga] to swallow, devour **Ch1** 3756 swaloud P swelwed L; 3771 sualhid P swelwed L; 3773 swalud

suate n. [see saufte, sauely]

suatte, swete v. [OE swæten] to perspire, sweat **Ch1** 15044 suatte P swatte L; **HS** 4262 swete

subdekene, suddekene n. [see dekene] [AF; cp. OE deacon, diacon] the lowest clerical order **HS** 1051 subdekene; 1681 suddekene

successoure n. [AF, L] heir; a descendant **Ch2** 1798 successoure

sue v. [see sewe, v. (1)] [AF suer] follow, pursue **Ch1** 8383 sued P sywed L

sueyn, suayn n. [OE swan; ON sveinn] attendant; soldier, follower **Ch1** 1144, 2638, 6329 suayn; 5785 suayne; 6447 sueyns; 7302 swain; 7421 swaines; 1579, 13970 sueyn P swayn L; 4603 suaynes P squiers L; 8396, 9120 suayn P swayn L; **Ch2** 1817, 5380, 5801, 6670 sueyn; 4540 sueynes

suelhu n. [OE swelh] water, a whirlpool **Ch1** 1449 suelhu P swelw L

suerd, swerd n. [OE sweord] sword **Ch1** 2923, 3498, 4454, 12073 suerd; 4360, 4875, 4975, 12076 suerde; 1555 swerde; 3769 swerd; 1007, 3004, 4334 suerdes; 12570LR swerdes (om. P); **Ch2** 178, 908, 3942, 6684, 8312 suerd; 1037, 1225 suerd P swerd L; 5983 suerde; **HS** 351 swerde; 991 swerd; 1572 swerdys

suere, swere v. [see forsuore] [OE swerian] make an oath, vow, promise; curse, blaspheme **Ch1** 3849 swere; 3844 swere P sweren L; 1529, 2430, 5457, 7810, 12941 suore; 3044, 3851, 5852 suorn; 12941 suorne; **Ch2** 1542, 2674, 5259, 6802, 7863 suere; 604, 1868, 3372, 5297, 7659 suore; 2407, 4152, 5261, 6175, 7657 suorn; 3837 suorne; **HS** 608, 770, 2899, 4571, 5629 swere; 2682 sweren; 692 sweryn; 2760 sweryþ; 2772 swerþ; 637 swerys; 961, 2717, 2819, 5625, 6343 swore; 11731 swor

suete, swete adj./adv. [OE swete] fresh, attractive; sweet-smelling **Ch1** 7490 swete; 14417, 15066 suete; 11032, 14260 suete P swete L; **Ch2** 3651, 5069, 5224, 6667, 7473 suete; 2307 sute (error) P swete L; **HS** 1396, 2102, 4183 swete; 3314 suet; 11516 suete; 4215 swetter

suetnes n. [OE swetnes] being sweet or pleasant **HS** 10108, 10111 suetnes; 12119 swetnes

sueuen, sweuenyng n./ger. [OE swefen, ON svefn] a dream, vision **Ch2** 2268 sueuen P sweuene L; **HS** 5726 sweuenyng

suffer, suffir, suffre v. [AF suffrer] endure or undergo pain, loss, injury; submit, permit, tolerate **Ch1** 3646, 4845, 6659, 15571 suffre; 3840, 4755, 10508 suffir; 4790, 5087 suffire; 3189 suffire P suffre L; 4773 suffre P suffren L; 2373, 5044, 6040, 6633 suffred; 9790 þoled P suffred L; **Ch2** 265, 1047, 1939, 2647, 7781 suffre; 83, 1943, 3160, 4009, 7219 suffred; 3643 suffred P þoled L; **HS** 1460 suffryþ; 1477, 2114, 2262, 4124, 11070 suffre; 11076 suffreþ; 675, 723 sufferyd; 1446, 3845 suffrede; 2072 suffryd; 1450 þole GLOSS B suffre; 3299 drygh GLOSS BH suffre; 3545 drye GLOSS BH suffre; 8099 drye GLOSS H suffre

sufferable adj. [OF suffrable] patient, merciful **Ch1** 15745 sufferable P suffrable L; **HS** 8645 suffrable

sufferance n. [AF; OF sofrance] endurance; allowance; forbearance **Ch2** 6461, 7584, 7780 sufferance; **HS** 2690, 4979, 9768, 11959, 12373 suffraunce

suffise v. [AF suffiser] to be adequate, enough **Ch1** 1284 suffise

sugette adj. [see sogettys, n.] [OF suget] obligated; obedient **Ch1** 14222, 14671 sugette P suget L

sugke, souche, soke v. [OE sucan, sugan] to suck, imbibe; entice **Ch1** 3173 soke; **HS** 1624, 7698 souche; 6024 soke; 504 soke *C* sokyd *D* sok; 516 sugke *C* sowkyn *D* soukyn; 546

sokun *D* soukke

suyft adj. [OE swift] fast, moving quickly **Ch2** 5353 suyft; 5355 suyftest

suyke, suoke v. [see bisuike] [OE swican] deceive, cheat **Ch1** 2412 suyke P swyke L; 11156 suoke P byswok L

suilk, swych, sweche adj./pron. [OE swelc, swilc] such, such as, such a **Ch1** 106, 2822, 3130, 3977 suylk; 4260, 4592, 6958, 8113 suilk; 469 suilk P swylk L; 1511 suylk P sylk (error) L; 4225 suilk P silk L; 1336 suilk P swich L; 7296 swilk; 1252 suylk P swylk L; 6512 swik P swyche L; **Ch2** 276 suylk; 606, 3174, 4819, 6422, 8256 suilk; **HS** 45, 194, 469, 481, 1737 swyche; 577, 2687, 3046, 7983, 8730 swych; 243 sweche; 4543 swylk; 216 so moche *CD* swych; 990 swylk *H* swyche; 1363 swyche *C* such *D* suych; 2399 *D* sueche (B differs); 2451 sweche *D* swech; 3335, 3341, 7198, 7569 swych *O* swylke

suyme, suown, swown n./v. [OE swima, geswogen] dizziness; to swoon **Ch1** 8286 suyme P swyme L; 1837 suoune P swowene L; **HS** 6222 suown; 9187 swon *F* sowoun *H* swone *O* swone; 10544 swown; 11294 swyme

suimme v. [OE swimman, swam] to swim **Ch1** 3753 suimmes; **Ch2** 7170 suam

suyne n. [OE swyn] pigs **Ch1** 12038 suynes flesch P a swyn L

suynhird n. [OE swin-hyrde] keeper of swine **Ch2** 170, 216 suynhird

suypte v. [ON; cp. OI svipa; OE *swipian] rush away **Ch1** 11817 suypte P swypte L

suyth, swyþe adj./adv. [see asswyþe, adv.] [OE swiðe] strong; swift, quick; wise; very much, extremely, strongly **Ch1** 762 suyth P swythe L; 847 suythe P swiþe L; 975, 1633, 5307, 7139, 9362 suyth; 2497, 11947, 11995 suythe; 12336 suythe P hasted L; 2094 smertly P swyþe L; 7310, 8168 swiþe; 3487 suythere P swyþer L; **Ch2** 23, 1059, 2265 suythe; 275 suyth; 1059 suythe P swyþe L; 1291, 1962, 4301, 4876, 7175 suiþe; **HS** 7845 swyþe; 183 swyþe C anon; 1453 asswyþe *C* anon *D* also swyþe; 3859 swyþe *A* sone

sum, som adj./adv./pronoun [OE sum] someone, one; an indefinite number; somewhat, sometimes **Ch1** 90, 2402, 4078, 6655, 8107 som; 6541 som P somme L; 6120 some; 3746, 7532 sum; 6934, 7016 somdele; 7540 sum delle; 2064, 4027, 7961 somwhat; 7333 some þing; 5731 sumtyme; 5730, 6301, 6636, 6804 somtyme; 11053 somtyme P whilom L; **Ch2** 645, 2051, 3055, 6914, 8288 som; 1381 summ; 438 somwhat; **HS** 942, 1424, 1788, 2678, 9525 sum; 133, 589, 1623, 2655 some; 1121, 2238, 6637, 7736 sum tyme; 4363 sum whyle; 9754 sum whore

summe n. [OF some, somme, summe] amount, total **Ch2** 3305, 4223 summe; **HS** 6996 summe

sumne v. [see somoun, v.]

sundre v. [see sonder, v.]

sunne n. [see sonne, sunne, n.]

suoune v. [see suyme, suown, n./v.]

suowe n. [?rel. to OE *sweg(h), swoȝen, v.] impetus, a forcible movement **Ch2** 4212 suowe P swow L

suppose v. [OF supposer] to believe; to think, expect **HS** 2791 suppose *D* hopyn *O* hope; 6972 soposede *O* hopyde; 9695 suppose *O* hoppede; 10633 supposeþ *O* hopes *SV* leeueþ; 10646 supposede *O* hoppede *SV* leeuede

suppriour n. [OF] monastic official below the rank of prior **Ch2** 5105, 5107 suppriour

surfeyte, surfeture n. [OF surfait, surfeiture; AF surfet (MP)] excess, overindulgence **Ch2** 7588 surfeyte; **HS** 389 surfeture *C* fetowur

surplis n. [AF] loose vestment of white linen **Ch2** 8168 surplis

◆ **sursaute** adv. [AF sursaut] unexpectedly **Ch2** 8243 sursaute

suspecion n. [AF suspicioun] mistrust; conjecture of guilt **Ch1** 2877 suspecion; 4904 suspicion; **HS** 3973 susspecyun

suspend v. [OF suspendre] to place under interdict, debar **Ch2** 1803, 5126 suspended

susteyn v. [AF sustenir] support, maintain; provide help **Ch2** 378, 3171, 5781 susteyn; 476 sustened; 3597 sustene; 7936 susteynd; **HS** 3495, 7643 susteyne; 5392, 7164 susteyneþ; 1096 susteyne *C* socorne

sustenance n. [AF sustenance (MP)] livelihood; food, provisions **Ch1** 5679, 10276 sustenance; 14446 sustenance P sustinaunce L; **Ch2** 7871 sustenance; **HS** 1111, 1326, 7215 sustynaunce

suster, sustren n. [see sister]

sute adj. [see suete, adj.]

◆ **swagge** n. [prob. Scand. origin; ?cognate with sway] ?swaying bundle; a bulging bag **HS** 502 swagge

swalud, swaloud v. [see sualhid]

swan n. [OE] a swan **HS** 4324 swan

swerd n. [see suerd, n.]

swere v. [see suere, v.]

sweryng ger. [from OE swerian, v.] making an oath or vow **HS** 615, 635, 2724 sweryng; 2737 swerynges

swete adj. [see suete, adj.]

swete v. [see suatte, v.]

swetnes n. [see suetnes, n.]

sweuenyng ger. [see sueuen, n./ger.]

swych, swech adj./pron. [see suilk]

swyer n. [OE swira] the neck **HS** 5030 swyer GLOSS BH nekke

swyke, suoke v. [see suyke, v.]

swykel adj. [see suyke, v.] [OE swicol] deceitful,

false **Ch1** 3798 fikille P swykel L

swyle v. [OE swillan] wash, rinse out **HS** 5828 swyle *HF* swele

swyme n. [see suyme]

swyn n. [see suyne, n.]

swynk n. [OE swincan] labor, toil **HS** 7221 swynk

swynke v. [OE swincan] work, labor **HS** 6546 [MS *O* interpolation, l. 34] swynke

swyþe adv. [see suyth]

swolle, swal v. [OE swellan, swæl] swell, distend, dilate **HS** 8871 swal; 10213, 10241 swolle

T

taar v. [see teryst]

tabard n. [OF tabart] sleeveless garment **Ch2** 6778 tabard

table rounde, tabille n. [AF tabler] a table; Arthur's round table **Ch1** 10943 table rounde; 10359, 10909, 13702 rounde table; 12841 rounde tabille; **HS** 4997 table

tables, tabler n. [AF tabler (MP)] backgammon board; game of tables or backgammon **Ch1** 11150, 11332 tables; 11153 tablere P tabler L; **HS** 1044 tablere *C* tabelyrye; 4310 tabler

tabour n. [OF tabour] a small drum **Ch1** 2696L taber (om. P); 11143 taboures; **HS** 4773 tabour; 8996 tabure

tache, tak v. [?OF tache, n.] tie up, attach; set ropes for sailing **Ch1** 11764 tache; **Ch2** 7718 tak; 644 tached

tay, teye v. [OE tiȝan; cp. ON teygja] tie up; secure tackle on a ship **Ch1** 10966L teye (om. P); 11764 tay P teye L

taile n. (1) [OE tægl] the buttocks; tails on fish or other creatures **Ch1** 14550 tailes P tailles L; 14554, 14560, 14564 tailes; **Ch2** 1735, 1751, 6692 taile; **HS** 3187, 4176, 4179, 5418, 8888 tayl

taile, tale n. (2) [OF taille] tally, count; a reckoning, a number **Ch1** 6456 tale; 892, 1308 tale P taille L; 4690 tale P noumbre L; 14709 taile P tale L; **Ch2** 5241 taille; 7804, 7806 taile; 4726, 5401 tale

taile, tale v. [OF taillier] to count up, tally; trim, make ready; impose a tax **Ch1** 2376 taile P taylle L; 11789, 15774 taile P taille L; 13574 tale P taille L; **Ch2** 2813 taile

tayled ppl. [from OE tægl, n.] having a tail **Ch1** 14558 tailed; **Ch2** 3920 tayled P tailled L

take, toke v. [ON taka] take, seize **Ch1** 543, 1671, 4850, 6955, 7961 tak; 809, 2439, 5533, 8130, 10959 take; 10187 latche P take L; 7665 takes; 7753, 7765 takis P nymeþ L; 5216 tan; 3899 takyn; 1010, 2034, 3080, 5310, 7863 taken; 228, 6596, 6761 tok; 202, 1306, 5448, 7163, 10516 toke; **Ch2** 8, 2832, 4159, 7306, 7718 tak; 611, 1535, 2287, 4866, 7904 take; 2223, 2636, 4875, 5737 takes; 2014 takes P takeþ L; 6828 takis; 429, 1813, 2717, 5708, 8283 taken; 335, 2595, 5044, 6614, 7693 tok; 113, 2937, 4414, 6801, 8252 toke; **HS** 224, 1151, 1377, 2702, 11790 take; 6892 takes; 770 takyþ; 7361, 9259 takþ; 2082 tan; 5996 taken; 261, 1938, 4018, 7672, 10749 toke

takille n. [cp. MLG takel] ship's rigging **Ch1** 11789 takille

takyng ger. [from ON taka] seizure, capture; taking possession **Ch2** 5453 takyng; **HS** 407, 12342 takyng

tald v. [see tell, told]

tale n. [OE talu] story, narrative; discourse **Ch1** 93, 454, 4288, 6952, 7483 tale; 1935, 5491, 7876, 8185 tales; **Ch2** 1181, 1323, 1838, 2877, 6516 tale; 1683, 2201, 5674, 6839 tales; **HS** 46 talys; 1739, 2473, 3241, 4387, 12443 tale; 11083 tales

taliage n. [OF taillage] arbitrary tax, levy, toll **Ch2** 971, 1026, 1621, 3558, 6943 taliage; 1024 taliage P tallage L; **HS** 9259 taylage

talk v. [from OE tellan] speak, converse **Ch1** 10420 talk

tame adj. [OE tam, ON tamr] of animals: submissive **Ch1** 4692 tame; **HS** 4050, 4070, 4079 tame

tapise v. [OF tapissir] to lurk, creep; skulk, lie hidden **Ch1** 3382 tapise P huyden L; 11287 tapise P tapice L; **Ch2** 51 tapised

targe n. [OF, OE] a shield or buckler **Ch2** 4543, 4546, 4547 targe

taske n. [OF tasque] job, task **HS** 4284 taske

tast n. [from OF taster, v.] test, attempt **Ch1** 5311 tast

tasted v. [OF taster] to attempt; examine, explore by touch **Ch1** 8896, 13288, 15222 tasted; **Ch2** 208 tasted

tateles n. [cp. LG tateln (v.), to gabble, cackle] idle talk, chatter **Ch2** 5855 tateles

tauerne, tauernere n. [AF tauerne (MP)] tavern, inn; frequenter of a tavern **HS** 1018, 1022, 1025, 1043, 7226 tauerne; 6546 [MS *O* interpolation] (l. 7) tauerne; (l. 24) tauernere; (ll. 68, 119, 125) taverne

tauht v. [see tech, v.]

tauuarsyns n. [see kauersyns]

taxe n. [OF] compulsory tax to support government **Ch2** 5968 taxe

taxed v. [OF taxer] assess a levy or fine; impose a tax **Ch1** 5213 taxed; **Ch2** 5970, 6904 taxed

team n. [OE] offspring, family; race **Ch1** 4092 team; 4747 teame P teem L; **Ch2** 388 team; 3418 teme

tecchis n. [OF teche] fault, vice **Ch1** 3869 tecchis P tecches L

teche, tauht v. [see bitauht, betauht] [OE tæcan] teach, show, direct **Ch1** 3654 tech; 5506, 5653,

6935 teche; 3869 tecchis; 2469, 3348, 7683 tauht; 14548 reche P teche L; **Ch2** 2794 tech; 4858, 6661, 7235 tauht; **HS** 24 techyn; 422, 4516 techyþ; 1797, 9714 teche; 8102 techeþ; 9588 taght; 1167 techyst *C* leryst *D* lernyst; 1937 taghte *CD* tawtyn; 2787 techyþ *C* seyth *O* kennys; 2990 shewe *O* teche; 3172, 5036 lere GLOSS B teche; 4863 techeþ *O* lere; 7539 techeþ *O* kennes; 9584, 11896 teche *O* lere; 9623 teche *O* ken

techyng ger. [from OE tæcan, v.] teaching, learning **HS** 2093, 10915 techyng

teye v. [see tay]

teyl n. [OE tæl] detraction; blame, scorn **HS** 2042 teyl GLOSS BH scorn; 8625 teyl

teynt ppl. [see ateynt, v.] [OF; aphetic form of attaint] troubled; condemned; convicted **Ch1** 5107, 10703, 11882 teynt

teised, teisand v. [OF teser] aim an arrow, poise a weapon in taking aim **Ch1** 10706 teisand P teysande L; 12060, 13167 teised P teysed L

telde n. [OE] tent, pavillion, dwelling **Ch1** 645, 3664, 12268 telde

telde v. [OE teldian, from n.; ON tjalda] pitch a tent, encamp **Ch1** 12258 teldid P telded L; **Ch2** 5830 teld

tell, teld, tald, told v. [OE tellan] recount, enumerate, reckon; explain **Ch1** 62, 1488, 3501, 8043, 10420 telle; 28, 56, 152 telles; 66, 192, 5593, 7222, 7790 tellis; 7428 tellit; 248, 2394, 7954, 12277, 14691 teld; 4288, 7179 telde; 8057 said P telde L; 1339, 2485 telled; 849 teelde P teld L; 2067, 5261, 7860, 12853 tald; 1525, 11504 talde; 5818 talde P tolde L; 33, 2761, 4173, 7262, 10383 told; 128, 2776, 4468, 8006, 12758 tolde; **Ch2** 460, 2264, 5302, 6452, 7968 telle; 110, 802 telles; 527, 1570, 2654, 4340, 5674 tellis; 6827 tels; 21, 2031, 3509, 5112, 8338 teld; 1683, 3390, 6125 tald; 901, 1630, 2429, 5896, 8098 told; 2325, 3502, 4170, 6985, 7628 tolde; **HS** 4165 tell; 345, 1485, 5267, 11875, 12589 telle; 1931, 3162, 8419, 11721, 12632 tolde; 41, 5073, 5541, 11005 told; 11011, 11012, 11013 telþ; 1547 tellys; 6731 telleþ; 7033 telles

tellyng ger. [from OE tellan, v.] account, description **HS** 2903, 8322 tellyng

teme v. [see team, n.] [OE tieman] to turn or draw to **Ch1** 10959 teme; **HS** 9553 teme

tempest n. [AF tempeste (MP)] violent storm of wind; calamity, misfortune **Ch1** 1408, 2956, 2962, 6470, 15765 tempest; **Ch2** 3041, 3638, 3660, 3896, 3903 tempest; **HS** 852, 900, 913, 7789, 9169 tempest

temple n. [OF; OE templ] edifice for divine worship **Ch1** 1335, 1344, 1399 tempille; 1327, 2244, 2749, 4437, 5937 temple; 5662, 5672 temples; **Ch2** 2499, 4865, 4896 temple; 4887 temple P templers L; **HS** 4937, 5016, 7735, 9361, 9364 temple

Templer n. [AF] member of the Knights Templars **Ch2** 3318 temples P templers L; 7450 templer; 7451 templere; 4679, 4728, 4736 templers

temptacyun n. [AF temptaciun (MP)] enticement, attraction **Ch1** 11324 temptacoun P temptacion L; **HS** 174, 393, 411, 7591, 8572 temptacyun; 8521 temptacyons

tempte v. [AF tempter (MP)] to test, try; attract, entice **HS** 175 temptyd; 3093, 7526, 8560 tempted; 11699, 12049 tempte

temptyng ger. [from AF tempter] temptation, attraction **HS** 7496, 7508, 8510, 8567, 12058 temptyng; 8548 temptynges

ten, tende, tenþe adj./numeral [OE ten; cp. ON tiundi] the number ten; tenth in a series; the tenth part **Ch1** 2109, 3693, 5630, 6904, 7790 ten; 14471 tende P tenþe L; 13557 tendele P tenþe del L; **Ch2** 122, 2991, 4329, 5565, 7445 ten; 571, 605, 6320 tend; 784, 3559, 5986, 6877, 7290 tende; **HS** 15, 69, 2985, 7722, 12541 ten; 2922 tende; 2923 tenþe *C* tende; 2981, 11765 tenþe

tenante n. [OF tenant] possessor of lands by a title; one owing fealty to a lord granting land **Ch2** 4157 tenant; 4056 tenante; 360 tenantȝ P barons L; 5888 tenauntȝ

tende v. [see tent, v.]

tendre, tendirly adj./adv. [OF tendre] soft, delicate; weak **Ch1** 7230 tendre; 2011 tendirly; **Ch2** 6077 tendre; **HS** 1135 tendrere

tene n. [OE teona] harm, trouble; grief; injury, damage; wrath **Ch1** 1244, 2046, 4622, 5615, 8098 tene; 11838 tenes; **Ch2** 1067, 5694, 6562, 7191, 8018 tene; **HS** 2462, 4086, 6401, 9527, 12048 tene

tene v. [OE teonian; ON tyna] to vex, anger, annoy **Ch1** 5732, 14000 tene; 5312 tende P tened L; **Ch2** 1581 tened; **HS** 7474 tene

tenement n. [AF] tenure; possession of land; a dwelling **Ch2** 768, 2517, 4799, 6156, 7412 tenement; **HS** 2910 tenement

tent n. (1) [see entent] [OF atente] attention, care; intent, purpose **Ch1** 2723, 5997, 6922, 7105, 13540 tent; 683, 852, 2459, 5358 tente; 8033 tent P entent L; **Ch2** 5375 tent; 3559 þe tende P þe entent L; **HS** 6185, 6761, 11631, 12201 tent; 1631, 5253, 5956 atent; 477 tent *D* entent; 5917 tent *F* entent

tent n. (2) [OF tente] a portable shelter supported by poles **Ch1** 4600 tent; 12262, 14003 tentes; **Ch2** 3265, 4049, 4510, 4993 tent; 3981 tente; 3985 tentes; 1657, 3967 tentis

tent, tende v. [OF atendre] pay attention to; care for **Ch1** 1672, 11328, 11331 tent; 651 tente P tende L; 12687 tentid P tente L tent

R; 13098 tentid P rewarded L; 13542 tent P tenden L; **Ch2** 2218 tent; **HS** 10570 tende

tentefully adv. [from OF atente, n.] carefully, attentively **HS** 10731 bysyly *O* entently *SV* tentefully

teres n. [OE tear] tears, teardrops **Ch1** 14905 teres; **Ch2** 6836 teres; **HS** 7979, 11570, 11577 teres

teryst, taar, torn v. [OE teran] to tear, pull apart **Ch1** 13169 taar; **Ch2** 5882 torn; **HS** 725 teryst

Termagaunt n. [OF Tervagan] an imaginary Mohammedan deity **HS** 4322, 4674 termagaunt; 197 teruagaunt *D* termagaunt *H* termagaunt

terme n. (1) [AF terme (MP)] appointed time; duration of time **Ch1** 3239, 5287, 13808, 15826 terme; 7351 time P terme L; 5215, 10545 termes; **Ch2** 4058, 6401, 7520, 7737, 7932 terme; 4044 termes; **HS** 2410, 2411, 3307 terme

◆ **termes** n. (2) [?AF therme; termes (MP)] public bathing establishment **HS** 11041 termes *O* teryns

testament n. [AF, L testament] a will, testament **Ch2** 377, 3305, 3315, 3739, 5639 testament; **HS** 1214, 6396 testement; 1979, 2470 testament

testimons v. [OF testimoiner] to bear witness, testify **Ch1** 5592 testemons P wytnesseþ L; **Ch2** 143 testimons P recordeþ L; **HS** 7646 wytnesseþ *O* testymonys

teth n. [OE toþ, teþ] the teeth **Ch1** 1817 teth; **HS** 9290 teþ

tewe v. [synon. with OE taw] to dress leather **Ch1** 12133 tewe

þak n. [OE þæc] thatch; roofing **Ch1** 14067 þak P þakkes L

þan, þen, þo adv. [see þien] [OE þanne, þenne] then, at that time **Ch1** 187 than; 34, 1005, 1552, 4063, 8099 þan; 1669, 1911, 5970 þen; 4198 þan P þenne L; 2015, 4632 þo; **Ch2** 17, 2931, 4302, 6652, 8154 þan; 3224, 5231, 7998 þen; 1855 þo; **HS** 13, 5664 þan; 365 þanne; 871 þen; 4764 than; 3377, 3813 þo

þan, þen conj. [OE þonne, þanne, þænne] than **Ch1** 296, 2188, 5008, 6977, 7892 þan; 1270, 1995, 4813 þen; **Ch2** 548, 2493, 4375, 6322, 7639 þan; **HS** 34, 936, 2466, 4214 þan

þank n. [OE þanc] thanks; gratitude **Ch1** 2035 þank; 7092 þanke; **Ch2** 3051, 3535 þank; **HS** 6835, 7182, 9378, 10319, 12538 þank

þank v. [OE þancian] to thank for, express gratitude **Ch1** 3170, 7486 þank; 9353 tanke P þank L; 1395, 1742, 5649, 13425 þanked; 1603 thanked; 7700 þankid; 15893 blisse P þanke L; **Ch2** 4351, 4752, 5572 þank; 1052 þanke; 415, 2881, 3547, 4923, 6586 þanked; **HS** 323 þankyd; 5096 þank; 1861, 3887 þankede; 11299 þanke; 11663 þanked

þankyng ger. [from OE þancian] expression of thanks **Ch2** 4433 þankyng; **HS** 3894, 12129 þankyng

thar, thort, dar v. [see dar, durst] [OE *þarfan, þearf] it needs; it is necessary; to be obliged **Ch1** 6786 þar; 6937 þar P nedeþ L; 7133 þar P þarf L; 4113 thorte P þurt L; 4826 thurte P þertestow L; 4829 thurte P þart L; 7901 may P þart L; **Ch2** 3630L þurfte (om. P); **HS** 8285, 8962, 9124, 9563 þar; 7392 thar; 119 darst *D* þar; 2249 darst *C* thar *D* þar; 1229 nedyþ *C* þare *D* thore; 5826 þurt *F* durst; 4290 dar

þar, þare, þer pronoun [ON þeir, þar; OE heora] their, theirs **Ch1** 4320, 5865, 6405, 6704 þar; 21, 161, 1272, 1534, 8156 þare; 9427 þaire; 1235, 4091, 5519, 7324, 8078 þer; 7807 þers; 12455 þars P þeires L; **Ch2** 1444, 2047, 2413, 4952, 6617 þar; 1462, 1613, 1750, 2090 þare; 717, 7320 þers; 4016, 5689, 6603, 7522, 8314 þer; 1070 þairs; 3016 þeir; **HS** 5590 þayr; 874 her *H* þeyr; 914 here *H* þeyr; 1783 here *H* þere; 3343 here *H* þer; 26, 52, 488, 4634 here; 6273 heren

þar, þare, þer, þore adv. [see qware, qwere] [OE þær, þer] there; at that place; where **Ch1** 4442, 4801, 5077 þar; 318, 4629, 7624, 13555, 15516 þare; 1289, 3791, 4715, 5983, 7825 þer; 1372, 3790, 4828, 5780, 7675 þere; 3021 þor; 1019, 2902, 4837, 8160, 10144 þore; 5379 was þer P waster L; 7469 qware P þer L; **Ch2** 1855, 2017 þar; 7632, 7644 thar; 3913, 5297, 6337, 7866, 8115 þare; 590, 5178, 6163, 7263, 8335 þer; 343, 4222, 5010 þere; 437 þer where; 676 þer þere; 201, 1823, 5431, 7126, 8244 þore; 3125 þair; **HS** 69, 851 þer; 1400 þore; 2478 þyr; 6652 þare; 558, 1436, 1731, 10905 þere

þarmys n. [OE, ON þarmr] entrails, viscera **HS** 702 þarmys GLOSS BH guttys *C* harmes *D* armys

tharne n. [ON þerna] a maiden **HS** 7355 tharne GLOSS BH a wenche

the n. [OE þeoh] the thigh **Ch1** 7748 the P kne L; 15061 thee P þe L; **Ch2** 4748 the; **HS** 1474, 1484 thes; 4638 the; 2327 þe *C* they *D* skyn

þe v. [see þriue] [OE þeon] to thrive; in imprecations: ill-wishes **HS** 4240 þe

thede n. [OE þeod] a people, nation, country **Ch1** 10389 thede P stede L; **Ch2** 349, 366 thede P þede L; **HS** 10571 thedes

þedyr adv. [see thider, adv.]

thefe, theues n. [OE þeof] a thief **Ch1** 2138 deueles P þeues L; 6532 þeues; 11579 theues; **Ch2** 6527, 8255 thef; 1902, 3030, 3390, 5739, 5976 thefe; 729 thefe P þef L; 4269 cheitefe P þeff L; 1602 þefes; 5740, 7870, 8039, 8194 theues; 4053 theues P þeffes L; **HS** 1338, 1339, 2418 þef; 2070, 5205 þefe; 2080, 2115, 2416 þeuys

þeft, thyfte n. [OE þeofð, þeoft] theft **Ch2** 1908, 3013, 3177, 8289 theft; **HS** 2110, 2131, 2449, 8920 þefte; 2367, 2394 þeft; 2068, 2069, 2073, 2084, 2094 þyfte; 2077 thyfte

þeke adj./pronoun [see þylke]

þenk v. [see þink, v.]

þenne adv. [see þien, adv.]

þer adv./pronoun [see þar, þore]

þeþen adv. [see þien, adv.]

thew n. [OE þeaw] custom, usage, habits, qualities; manners, virtues **Ch1** 9612, 12901 thewes P þewes L; 9631L þewes (om. P); **Ch2** 2873 thewe (error: ?threwe); **HS** 3061 thew; 3110, 4863 þewes; 6532 vertues *O* thewes; 8726 hew *O* thewes

thider adv. [OE þider] to or towards that place, thither **Ch1** 674, 3669, 4802, 6131, 10835 þider; 7310 þidir P þydeward L; 7442, 8169, 9559, 10830 þidir; 4590, 8323 þidire; 931, 4933, 5539, 6617, 7401 þidere; 12105 þidere P tyder L; **Ch2** 27L þyder (om. P); 89, 1291, 3374, 6665, 8263 þider; 506, 3309, 4485, 6145, 7893 þidere; **HS** 602, 1475, 1798, 9226 þedyr; 6927, 7730, 10349 þyder; 7044 þydyr

þiderward adv. [OE þiderweard] in that direction, towards that place **Ch1** 10035 þiderward P þideward L; 5412, 11588 þiderward; **Ch2** 1409, 3680, 3926, 5638, 6339 þiderward; **HS** 8505 þyderward; 2497 þedyrward *C* þeþer *D* to hymward

þien, þeþen, þenne adv. [ON þeðan] from there, hence, thence **Ch1** 1045, 3232, 4163, 14832 þien P þeþen L; 6312 þien P þenne L; 7216 þien P fro þennes L; 7294 þine P þennes; 13237 þiþen; **Ch2** 7, 4728, 6770, 7405 þien; 1652 þien P for þan L; 3988 þien P þen; **HS** 2537 þeþen; 9145 þenne; 10550 þenne *F* þanne *SV* þennes

þik, þykly adj./adv. [OE þicce] thick; densely, closely crowded **Ch1** 4532, 5739, 6726, 10900 þik; 4343, 9075, 9800, 12189 þikke; 2927 þik P þykke L; 13042L þyk (om. P); 13370L þykke (om. P); 6718, 6728 þikli; 3518 þike; **Ch2** 5158 þik; 6989, 7423 þikke; **HS** 4481 þykly; 12596 þykke

þylke, þeke adj./pron. [OE þylc] that same; that, this, those **Ch1** 379 þat ilk P þylke L; 7237 þat ere P þulke L; **Ch2** 4394 þat ilk P þilke L; **HS** 182, 6153 þeke

thing n. [OE þing] object, matter; affair, cause **Ch1** 304, 1382, 4634, 5459, 7956 thyng; 2457, 3655, 5885, 6846, 8019 þing; 8011 þyng; 15, 4512, 7175 thynges; 5761, 8099 þinges; **Ch2** 3383 thyng; 802, 1601, 4090, 6800, 8006 þing; 738 cas P þyng L; 5568 þyng; 2095, 3293, 6073, 7626 þinges; **HS** 20, 2107, 6314, 7691, 11732 þyng; 910 þyngge; 7648 þynges

þink, þenk, þouht v. [see forþenke, beþenke, v.] [OE þyncan] think, intend; ponder **Ch1** 1229 thenk; 2316, 3178, 7358, 7469 þink; 6681 thynk; 7438 þinke; 5100, 6254, 6930 þenk; 3215, 6694, 10186 þinkes; 11649 þenkes; 980, 1377, 2392, 2629, 7929 thouht; 1136 thouth P þoughte L; 579 thoght; 1394, 2351, 4594, 7136, 13009 þouht; **Ch2** 6695, 6849 þink; 2461, 4937, 6647, 6769 þenk; 6556 þenkes; 8097 þinkis; 2121 thnke (error) P beþenke L; 6775 þouhtis; 825, 2179, 4504, 5349, 7138 þouht; 5158, 6990 þouh; **HS** 1287 þenkyþ; 1978, 4427, 6297, 12556 þenke; 4169, 4569, 5676, 8455, 10836 þynke; 5440, 7714 þenche; 427 þenkys; 1348, 5662, 7682, 10053 þoght; 251, 368, 458, 11858 þoghte; 9279 þught; 448 þoghttyst

þinkyng ger. [from OE þyncan] thought, cogitation **Ch1** 11927 þinkyng; **Ch2** 6083 þinkeng

þynne adj. [OE] thin **HS** 10137 þynne

þis, þise, þase, þes, þo pronoun [OE þis, þas] this, these, those **Ch1** 1211, 2599, 5621, 7247, 8147 þis; 1944, 3174, 6110, 7547, 8104 þise; 2008 þase; 220 þes; 1937, 1939 þese; 212, 1143, 4676, 7161, 8185 þo; **Ch2** 488, 1080, 2098, 2602, 3730 þis; 527 þise; 601 þese; **HS** 44, 77, 350, 2003, 10221 þys; 13, 15, 7330, 12540 þyse; 223 þose; 9448, 10356, 10953 þese; 270, 415, 4435, 6128, 12599 þo

þof, þogh conj./adv. [ON þo, *þoh] though, although **Ch1** 958 þat P þaw L; 1518, 4828 þof P þey L; 4827 þof P þaw L; 15326L þowh (om. P); **Ch2** 845, 1333 þof; **HS** 235, 1585, 7876, 10214, 11259 þogh; 1087 þogh *C* thow *D* alþowh; 1101 þogh *C* þwow; 970 þogh *D* þowh *H* þoght; 1357 þogh *C* thow; 1815 þogh *D* þowh; 2213 þogh *C* þow

þole v. [OE þolian] to suffer, be afflicted with evil **Ch1** 9790 þoled P suffred L; 14407 þoled P tholede L; 15256 tholed P þoled L; **Ch2** 3643 suffred P þoled L; 4357 þoled P þolede L; **HS** 1450 þole GLOSS B suffre; 9024 suffred *O* tholede; 9157 solowed *O* tholyde

þolemode adj. [OE þolemod] meek, submissive **HS** 10932 þolemode

þolmodnesse n. [OE from adj.] humility **HS** 5831 þolmodnesse

þore adv. [see þar, þer, þore]

þorh, þorgh, þurgh adv./prep. [OE ðurh, þurh] through, throughout; on account of; by, by means of; completely **Ch1** 3041, 4902, 5637, 7727, 11321 þorh; 11231, 11335 þorh P þorow L; 306, 434, 1190, 11578 thorgh; 340 thurgh P þorow L; 5587, 9021 þourh P þorow L; 722, 3004, 5658, 8017, 13303 þorgh; 6538, 7756 þrou; 3814, 7741 þoru; 1518, 4827 þof; 5090 þof P þaw L; 1418, 4198 þorgh P þorow L; 8652 þrow; 1685, 10611 þorhout; 3053, 3064, 4861 þorghout; 6175 þorghoute; 6618 þorghout P þorwout L; 7690 þorghoute P þorowout L; **Ch2** 22 þorh P þurgh L; 844, 2010, 5189, 6395 þorh; 111, 1424, 4244, 6810, 8326 þorgh; 2222 þorgh P thurghe L; 917 þorgh P thurw L; 1170 thorgh P thurw L; 4550 þorgh P þurw L; 4107L, 4797L þurw (om. P); 14, 331, 4844, 5889, 6733 þorghout; 7431 þorghoute; 4219, 4461, 6004, 6164, 8043 þorght; 845, 1333 þof; 567L þurght (P differs); **HS** 457, 5519, 12135 þurgh; 295 þurgh *D* þorw; 996 þurgh *C* þer; 1316 þurgh *C* þer thorw *D* þerþorwh; 2447 þurgh *D* þorw; 11514, 9400 þurghout

þornes n. [OE þorn] thorns **Ch1** 9075 hesils P þornes L; **HS** 7515, 7520 þornes

thort, þurt v. [see thar, thort, dar, v.]

þouht n. [OE þoht] mind; thinking; remembrance; idea **Ch1** 564, 568 thoght; 2803, 4913 thouht; 2628, 5208, 8032, 8162 þouht; **Ch2** 1596, 2096, 3822, 6258 þouht; **HS** 209 þouȝt; 1134, 1627, 2558, 9743, 10179 þoght

thousand n./adj. [OE þusend, þusendu] a thousand; ten times one hundred; a large number **Ch1** 186, 985, 1645, 3021, 6497 thousand; 3558, 4686, 5317, 6850, 7701 þousand; 2696 þousande; 3013, 3470 thousandȝ; **Ch2** 114, 1373, 4231, 6561, 8330 þousand; 5039, 5592, 7042 thousand; **HS** 76, 8097, 12520, 12541 þousynd; 7790 þousand

þraldom n. [OE, ON] bondage, captivity **Ch1** 956 thraldom P þraldam L; **Ch2** 6317 þraldam

þralle n. [OE, ON þræl] a servant, slave, serf **Ch1** 2813, 10779 þralle P þral L; 6448 thralles P þralles L; **Ch2** 141, 1220, 2063 thralle; **HS** 9561 þral

þre, þred, þrid n./adj./numeral [OE þrie, þreo, þridda] three; third **Ch1** 501, 2008, 5068, 7184, 13200 þre; 511, 5082, 6139, 13823, 14515 þrid; 12881 thrid; 14137 thrd (error) P þrydde L; **Ch2** 114, 1623, 3226, 6019, 8330 þre; 916, 2496, 4249, 6924, 7944 þrid; 4678, 7545 þridde; **HS** 76, 1780, 8026, 12520 þre; 792, 801, 2747, 6105 þredde; 6870 þred; 5099 þryd

þrepe v. [OE þreapian] argue; rebuke **HS** 4356, 6067 þrepe

þrete v. [OE þreatian] to threaten **Ch1** 5114 þrette; 11505 þrette P þret L; 12319 þrete; **Ch2** 1028 thrette P þretnede L; 2222 þretis; **HS** 6399 þrete

þretty, þritty adj./n. [OE þritig] thirty **Ch1** 2422, 3671 thritty; 1410 thritty P þrittyþe L; 2167, 2696, 3622, 6480, 12948 þritty; 4687 þritty P þre L; **Ch2** 71, 1441, 4743, 5010, 6503 þritty; 3777, 7204 þritti; 7380 þretty; **HS** 6324, 6951, 6991, 7009 þretty; 6934 þrytty

þryft n. [see vnþrifte, n.] [ON þrift] prosperity, health, strength **HS** 3116, 11646 þryfte; 5054, 8304, 5625 þryft

thrilled v. [OE þyrlian] pierced **Ch2** 641 thrilled P þyrlede L

þring, þrong v. [OE þringan] press, thrust **Ch2** 1260 þring P put out L; **HS** 2514 þrong *C* donge *O* thrange

thrinne, þris adv. [ON þrinnr, OE þrinna, þries] thrice, in three parts **Ch1** 383 thrinne P þrynne L; 11098 þris P þrys L; 11099 þris P þries L; **Ch2** 2506, 2507, 3045 þris; 4316 þrin P twynne L; **HS** 8199, 8209 þrys

þris adv. [see thrinne]

þrist, þirst n. [OE þurst] thirst **Ch1** 3640 þriste P þurst L; 10020 thrist P þirst L

thrist v. [ON þrysta] to thrust, force; press on, rush out **Ch1** 8769 þrist P þriste L; 8772 þrist P þryst L; 11819 þriste; **Ch2** 5310 thrist; 6704 þrist

þristyng ger. [from ON þrysta] thrusting **Ch1** 10957 þristyng

þrittene, þirtende n./adj. [OE þreotene, ON þrettande] thirteen, the thirteenth; the last of thirteen **Ch1** 14473 þrittene P þrytty L; **Ch2** 813, 6444 þrittene; 86 þirtende P þrettenþe L

þriue v. [ON þrifa-sk] thrive, grow; prosper **Ch1** 1881 throfe P þrof L; 6445 þriuen P þryuen L; 7226 þriue; 9908 þro; 7226 þrod P kynde (n.) L; **Ch2** 5768 thro; **HS** 1298, 4618, 11333 þryue

thro n. [see throw, þrawe, n.] [ON þra] struggle, trouble; strife; a contest **Ch1** 54 thro; 10046, 10957 þro; 13370L þro (om. P); **Ch2** 2854, 7685 þro; **HS** 10577 thro

þrod adj. [see þriue, v.]

throfe, thro v. [see þriue]

þrong n. [OE geþrang] crowd, tumult, throng **Ch1** 13176 þrong; 13380 throng P þrong L; **Ch2** 4476, 5008 þrong; **HS** 947, 3439 þrong

þrong v. [see þring, v.]

throstel n. [OE þrostle] a song-thrush **HS** 7482 throstel; 7493 þrostel *O* vnsell

throte n. [OE þrote] the throat **Ch1** 2648, 3007 throte; 12356, 12724 þrote; **HS** 964, 2074, 6758 þrote

throw, þrawe n. [ON þraȝ, þrah] time, occasion **Ch1** 141, 871, 6576, 9586 throwe; 4627 þrowe; 3890 throw P þrowe L; 3306 while P þrowe L; 685, 2414, 3464 throwe P þrowe L; 12173 no while P no þrowe L; 12204L þrawe (P differs); 13018 þrewe P þrowe L; 13150 thrawe P þrawe L; 13283 þrow P þrowe L; **Ch2** 459, 3660 throwe; 8236 throw; 2755, 4471, 4836 þrawe; 4841 þrowe; **HS** 1381, 7277 þrowe; 3101, 3273, 4258, 4275 throwe; 3571 a trowe; 4437 þrowe GLOSS B whyle; 4470 stounde *O* thraw; 12235 stownde *O* thorowe

þrow adv. [see þorh, þorgh, adv.]
throwe, threwe v. [OE þrawan, þreow] to throw; to twist, turn **Ch1** 1038 throwe; 4346, 5856, 13179 threwe; 3384 trewe (?error) P þrew L; 14022 þrewe; **Ch2** 4306 þrewe; 8314 threwe; 2873 thewe (error: ?threwe); **HS** 10924, 10926 þrowe; 10927 þrawe; 3004 threw
thrum n. [see þrong] [OE þrymm] host, multitude **Ch1** 12953 thrum P þrom L
þumbe n. [see tomb, n.]
þundur n. [OE þunor] thunder **HS** 9158 þundur
thurft v. [see thar, thort]
thurte, thorte, þurt v. [see dar, dur, durst, v.] [ON þurfa, þarf] to be obliged to do; it is necessary **Ch1** 4113 thorte P þurt L; 4826 thurte P þertestow L; 4829 thurte P þart L
tyce, tysyn v. [OF enticier, atiser] entice, lure **HS** 7717, 8128 tyce; 3060 tycyþ; 92 tysyn *D* techith; 2152 tyce *C* tysen *D* teche; 2970 to tyll *C* to tysen; 1504 entycedyst any *C* cowncellyn hym
tycement n. [OF] inciting, tempting to do evil **HS** 3924, 12024 tycement; 367 tycement *C* tysement *D* tysyng (ger.); 2146 entycement *C* tysment
tide n. [OE tid, ON tið] time; an age, season; tide of the sea **Ch1** 1139, 2920, 4561, 6207, 7014 tide; 1643, 1830 tide P tyde L; 1313, 5533 euen tyde; 3391 morn tide; 5235, 5557 somerstide; **Ch2** 2567, 4070, 5590, 6446, 7457 tide; 3487 tyde; 4310 euentide; 345, 2160, 7841 somerestide; 5501 midsomeretide; 3701 heruest tide; **HS** 505, 903, 2127, 2381, 3819 tyde
tide v. [see bitid, betyde, v.] [OE tidan] happen, befall **Ch1** 5406 ben tid P bytid L; 11515 tide P bytide; 11517 tides P bytydes; **Ch2** 1248, 2201 tid P bytidde L; 7678, 7873 tide; **HS** 5043 tyde *O* betyde
tide adv. [see tite, adv.]
tiding, tiþand, tiþing ger./n. [OE tidung] news, reports **Ch1** 629, 2498, 5908, 7191, 12254 tiþing; 6282 tiþinges; 4455 tiþeng; 4946 renoun P tydynges L; 3268 tiþng P tydynges L; 2875, 2895, 2972 tiþing P tydyng L; 4948 tiþand P tydant L; 6184 tiþand P tydand L; 12252 tiþng P tyding L; 13519 tiþng P tydyng L; 6792 tiþnges; 15216 tiþand P tydande L; **Ch2** 924, 3222, 5584, 6935, 8322 tiþing; 573 tyþng P tydynge L; 401, 1834, 3743, 6632, 7271 tiþinges; 1481 bode P tydyng L; 1850 tyþynges; 3088, 3933, 4824 tiþand; 1864, 2331, 3416, 6512 tiþng; **HS** 5018, 5022, 6389 tydyng
◆ **tyffe** v. [see atiffement] [OF tifer] to attire, dress **HS** 3208, 3312 tyffe; 3203 tyffyst; 3225, 11771 tyffed; 3245 tyffyng (ger.)
tyffure n. [OF tifeure] ornament, adornment **HS** 3292 tyffure
tight v. (1) [OE tyhtan] to draw to, proceed **Ch2** 4984, 6349 tight
tight v. (2) [?OE stihtan, dihtan] appoint; devise, get ready; arrange **Ch1** 3281, 5767 tight; 5399 tight P tyght L; **Ch2** 2267 tight P tiȝt L; 3825 tight P ment L; 7844 tighte
tihtes n. [OE tyht] behavior **Ch1** 9184 tihtes P tyhtes L
tikelle v. [?cp. OE tinclian] pleasantly excited **Ch2** 2757 tikelle
tikelle adj. [from v.; etymology obscure] ?tickled **Ch1** 12909 tikelle P tykel L
tille v. [OE tilian] labor, work for, strive, cultivate; entice **Ch1** 8262, 8569, 10842, 15682 tille; 6431 tille P tyle L; 5606, 6340, 6391, 15762, 15802 tile; 1850, 3666, 6509, 8587 tilled; 15793 tiled; **Ch2** 5386, 5766 tille; **HS** 2970, 7616 tyll; 5674, 7093 tylle; 9042 tyl; 2446 ere *C* tyl *D* eryn; 9045 tolled
tille, tyl adv./prep./conj. [see vntille] [OE] to, as far as, so as to reach; onward, to that time **Ch1** 27, 1151, 1536, 6017, 7121 tille; 3719 til; 2047 tille P whil L; 2484 tille P whyle L; 4272, 5197 tille P while L; **Ch2** 58, 2133, 5336, 6834, 7933 tille; 348 tille P while L; **HS** 7436, 9433, 11367, 11686 tyl; 5458 tyll; 314 til; 2646, 4677 tyl GLOSS B to
timbere, timbir n. [OE timber] wood, timber **Ch1** 1041 tymbere; 14020 timbir; **HS** 9344 tymber
timbred v. [OE timbran] to build, construct; fig.: to frame, cause **Ch1** 3664 timbred telde P tymber teld L; **Ch2** 1067 timbred
time n. [see bityme, betymes, adv.] [OE tima] time, occasion **Ch1** 22, 1316, 2589, 6936, 9728 tyme; 3726, 3900, 6518 time; 12406 tome P leyser L; 288, 435, 1365 tymes; 4154 lungeteyns (?error) P longe teymes L; **Ch2** 74, 881, 3417, 4860, 8356 tyme; 157, 2505, 3636, 6850, 7594 tymes; **HS** 52, 825, 2010, 7237, 9756 tyme; 4068 tymes; 3307 terme *O* tyme; 12570 whyle GLOSS BH tyme
tympan n. [see chyme, n.] [L tympanum] a drum; ?a timbrel or tambourine **HS** 7130 tympan *O* chyne (?possibly chyme)
tyne, tynt v. [ON tyna] lose; destroy **Ch1** 1008, 7122, 15624 tynt; 2736 tynt P lost L; 4474, 5442, 5447, 12194, 12978 tyne; **Ch2** 267, 6886, 6905, 8066 tyne; 998 tynt P lost L; 1795, 4038, 4722, 6364, 6777 tynt; 6685 tint; 4088 tynd P sey hym L; 5878 tynes; **HS** 11933 tyne; 7067 tynte; 2083, 3321 tyne GLOSS BH lese; 2299 tynes GLOSS B lesyþ; 9456 tynes GLOSS B lest
tinselle n. [ON *tynsla, from tyna, v.] loss, destruction **Ch1** 2346 tynselle; 5334, 9697, 10579 tinselle P los L; 13546 tynselle P lost L; 5334 tinselle; **Ch2** 7111 tinselle
tippet n. [?OE tæpped, tæppet] loose sleeve **Ch2**

6778 tippet

tirant n. [OF tyrant] absolute ruler; usurper **Ch1** 6549 tiraunte; **Ch2** 1226 tirant; **HS** 10238 yrous *SV* tyrauns

tire n. [see atire, n.] [from OF atirier, v.] attire, dress **Ch1** 11045 tire P atir L

tirede v. [see atire, v.]

tirpeil, tirpelle n. [from OF trepeil] uproar, trouble, tumult, battle **Ch1** 1661 tirpelle P turpel L; 6259 tirpeile P tyrpeyl L; 6765, 9257 tirpeile P turpeyl L; 14762 tirpeil P tyrpayl L; **Ch2** 2387, 2837, 3253, 5284, 7059 tirpeile; 6165 tirpeil

tysen, tysyn v. [see tyce, tysyn, v.]

tite adv. [see tide, n., astyt, adv.] [ON titt, tiðr] soon, as quickly as possible **Ch1** 704, 2930 tyte P tyt L; 4455 tite; 4728 tyte; 8063 tite P tyt L; 12324 tide P tyt L; 12739 tide P tit L; **Ch2** 3543, 5724, 6142, 7084, 8238 also tite; 1294 also tite P as tid L; 1945 also suiþe P als tid L; 151, 1836, 2510, 2883, 3924 fulle tite; 4992, 5329, 6583, 6651, 7790 tite; **HS** 1765 tyte; 7235, 12556 fultyte; 2660 fultyt GLOSS B sone; 3153 astyt *O* tytte; 6557 astyt *O* full tyte; 6784 astyt *O* all so tytte

tiþand, tiþing ger./n. [see tiding]

tiþe n. [OE teoþa, adj.] tenth; payment to support priests or religious establishments **Ch2** 367 tiþe; **HS** 911 tyþys; 9321 tyþe; 11668 tyþes

tiþe v. [OE tiȝþian] to pay tithes **HS** 898 tyþyth *C* tythyng (ger.); 9324, 9340 tyþe *O* tende; 9334 tyþeþ *O* tendes

title, tytyl n. [AF title (MP), L titulus] inscription; subject matter; a title-deed **Ch2** 143 title; 6000 titles; **HS** 7050, 7051 tytyl

to prep. [OE] expressing a prepositional relationship in which an infinitive stands to a preceding verb, adjective, or noun. [OED] (See the following individual examples.)

to blast v. [OE toblawan, blæst] ruined, blasted **Ch1** 9170 to brast P to blast L; **HS** 7509 to blast; 8870 to blaste

to brast, to barst v. [OE toberstan] shattered, burst asunder **Ch1** 2258 to brast P to barst L; 5945 to brast; 11819 to braste P to barst L; **HS** 9292 to brast; 10612 to breste; 10680 to braste

tocome n. [OE tocyme] arrival, coming; advent **Ch1** 5485 tocome; 10804 tocome P þer come L; **Ch2** 5921 tocome

today n. [OE to dæg] this day; present time **Ch1** 9102 today

to draw, to drouh v. [OE to + dragan] drawn asunder; torn apart **Ch1** 13400 to drouh P to drow L; **HS** 702 to drawe; 1474 to drowe

to dryuen, to drofe v. [OE todrifan] scattered, dispersed; dashed to pieces **Ch2** 278 to dryuen; **HS** 9301 to drofe

to fade v. [OE to + OF fader] spoiled **HS** 9299 to fade

to fraped v. [?OF frapper] struck, beaten **Ch1** 10012 to fraped; 12442L to fraped (om. P)

to frete v. [OE to + fretan] gnawed to pieces **HS** 3628 to frete

to frusched v. [OE to + OF frusch, v.] smashed, broken to pieces **Ch1** 1174 to frusshed; 2950 frussed P to frusched L

togge v. [ON toga] to pull, tug **HS** 9291 togge

togider adv. [OE togædere] together; against each other; accompanying **Ch1** 482, 782, 1003 togydere; 1541, 2698, 5384, 10562, 14843 togider; 1542, 2686, 4295, 5439, 6302 togidere; 4295 togidire; 4333 togidre; 1994, 6920, 7001, 11202, 14821 togidir; **Ch2** 118, 1683, 4486, 6203, 7656 togider; 494, 3610, 5793, 6146, 8010 togidere; 4528, 6829 togidir; **HS** 86, 1666, 9227 togedyr; 1966, 1984, 2008 togedere; 11175 togyder

to gnawe v. [OE to + gnaȝen] gnawed to pieces **HS** 704 tognawyn; 3676 to gnawe

to hewe v. [see hew, v.] [OE toheawan] cut up, cut to pieces **Ch1** 2649, 6560, 8505 to hewe; 13180 tille hewe P to hew L; 13181 to hewen; **Ch2** 331, 7252 to hewe

toye n. [obscure] amorous sport **HS** 7893 þe toye *O* þe toys

token n. [OE tacn, tacen] a sign, symbol; sign of the cross **Ch1** 1348 token; 14093 tokne; 8649 tokyn P tokene L; **Ch2** 444, 4813 token P tokne L; 2351 token; **HS** 630, 2323, 3877, 6376, 8240 tokene; 444 tokene *CD* takyn; 1583 sygne GLOSS B a tokene; 8225 sygne *O* taken

tokenede v. [OE tacnian, getacnian] to signify **Ch1** 8098, 11826 tokned; 8969 betoknes; **HS** 11576 tokeneþ; 3391 tokenede *O* lyknyde

tokenyng ger. [OE tacnung] signification, meaning, sign **Ch1** 1360, 15816, 15848 tokenyng; **Ch2** 692 tokenyng; **HS** 2352, 7016, 10109, 10182, 11339 tokenyng; 3309 tokenyng *O* taken

tollere n. [OE] a toll-collector **HS** 5572, 5816, 5888 tollere

to lusshed v. [see lussed] [prob. imitative] crashing down **Ch1** 12754 to lusshed P to lusched L

tomb, toumbe n. [AF tumbe; OF tombe] place of burial; a monument for a burial **Ch1** 7677, 11975, 12170 toumbe; 11930, 11935, 11939, 11960 towmbe; **Ch2** 800 tombe P toumbe L; 1214 toumbe P tombe L; 214, 546, 811, 2299, 8350 toumbe; **HS** 1810, 1817 towmbe; 9235 toumbe; 8740, 8787, 11096 tumbe; 353 þumbe (?error) *C* thowmbe *D* tombe

tombled, tumbled v. [OE tumbian] dance; fall

from a stumble, tumble **Ch2** 1735 tombled P tumbled L; 6604 tombled; **HS** 2820 tumblede
tome adj. [OE tom, ON tomr] empty, vacant, void **Ch1** 4337 tome; 3381 tome (error: time) PL; **Ch2** 4765 tome P toom L; 6778 tome; **HS** 7854 ler vessel *O* tome wessell; 7855 empty *O* tome; 7865 ler *O* tome
to morn, to morue adv. [see morn, morue] [OE to + morgenne] tomorrow **Ch2** 6673, 7649 to morn; **HS** 236 to morue; 245 to morue *C* to morwun; 3102 to morun *F* to moru *H* te morwe; 9393 to morne
toname n. [OE to-nama] surname, nickname **Ch1** 800, 6897, 7819, 9034 toname; 5783L toname (om. P); **Ch2** 4150 toname; **HS** 4745 toname
tonge, tung n. [OE tunge] tongue; language **Ch1** 198, 4680 tonge; 4152, 6941, 11608, 13943 tong; 14454 tunge; 15704 tunge P tonge L; **Ch2** 570 tonge; 6697 tunge; **HS** 44 tonge; 1591, 2616 tungge; 3579 tung; 7125 toung; 7942 tong; 3675 tung *W* tunge
to pyle v. [see pele, v.] [OE to + *pylian] robbed, plundered **HS** 6797 to pyle
to pulle v. [OE to + pullen] pulled to pieces **Ch1** 10052 to pulle
to rathe adv. [OE hraðe] too quickly, too soon **Ch2** 159 to rathe
to rente v. [OE torendan] torn to pieces **Ch1** 2139 to rente P to rent L; **Ch2** 3639 to rent; **HS** 712 to rent
to ryue, to rofe v. [OE to + ON rifa] burst asunder, split, torn apart **Ch1** 1842 to ryuen; 11872 to rofe P to rof L; **Ch2** 4206 to ryue; 4212 to rof; **HS** 6796 to ryues; 12252 to ryue
torn v. [see teryst, taar, torn, v.]
torment n./v. [see tourmente, turment]
to schad v. [OE to + sceddan] scattered, divided **Ch1** 6177 alto schad P to schadde L; 15620 to schad
to schaked, to shoke v. [OE tosceacan] shaken apart **Ch1** 11934 schaked P to schaked L; **HS** 2528 to shoke *D* sore quook
to solied, to soilled v. [OE to + OF soillier] defiled, soiled **Ch1** 12041 to solied P to soilled L
to spred v. [OE tosprædan] scattered, dispersed **Ch1** 2953 to spred; **Ch2** 324 to sprad
to sprunge v. [OE tospringan] sprung apart **HS** 10680 to sprunge
to sualle, to suelle v. [OE toswellan] swollen, puffed up **Ch1** 10676 to sualle P to swal L; 12726 to suelle P to swel L
touch v. [AF toucher (MP)] touch; mention, refer to **Ch2** 4720, 6257 touched; **HS** 799, 1623, 7697, 7849, 12295 touche; 2327, 2984 touchede; 139 touchyþ; 2563, 6538, 8589, 11139, 11156 touched; 4925, 10398 toucheþ
touchyng ger. [from AF toucher] caressing **HS** 7698 touchyng
toumbe n. [see tomb]
toumbed v. [from AF tumbe, n.] to entomb **Ch2** 1145, 5643 toumbed
toun, towne n. [OE tun] a town, village **Ch1** 820, 3303, 5310, 6378, 14150 toun; 791, 1914, 1916, 5931 toune; 6523 touns; 1847, 4079, 5856, 7042 7067 tounes; **Ch2** 160, 1794, 4232, 6593, 8294 toun; 740, 4250 toune; 1859, 2935, 6724 touns; 508, 2095, 4158, 6758, 8205 tounes; **HS** 509, 1343, 2076 toune; 997 towne; 6794 touns; 10167 toun
tour n. [OF tour, OE tur] tower; tall building; stronghold **Ch1** 3595 tour; 1627, 3567, 5954, 13959, 14035 toure; 5992 toures; **Ch2** 1794, 5941 tour; 1184, 3070, 5886, 7274, 8180 toure; 2378 tours; **HS** 7653 tour
tourment, torment n. [AF turment (MP)] anguish; suffering, pain **Ch1** 5068 tourment; **Ch2** 3634 torment; 5640 tourment; **HS** 3280 turment; 4622 tourment; 12524 turmente
tourmente, turmente v. [OF turmenter] to torture; cause pain **HS** 763 turmente; 4621 tourmente
tourmentours, turmentours n. [OF turmentour] a torturer, tormenter **HS** 762 turmentours; 4620 tourmentours
tournament n. [AF turneiment (MP)] joust; military game **HS** 4611 tournament; 4575, 4590, 4610 tournamentes
tourne v. [see turne, v.]
tourneours n. [AF turneiurs (MP)] jousters **HS** 4619 tourneours
toward adv./prep. [OE toweard] towards; in the direction of **Ch1** 256, 2690, 4148, 5268, 6614 toward; **Ch2** 451, 1305, 3622, 6700, 8332 toward; **HS** 2490, 2529 toward
to whille, to whils conjunctive adv. [see while, whilom, adv.] [OE to + hwil] during, while **Ch1** 3722, 6522, 6644, 7137 to while; 2625 to whils P þe while L; 681, 4276, 4646 to whils; 4109 to whille P to whyle L; 6525 to whyle P þe whyles L; **Ch2** 5398, 5402, 7395 to whils; 1752, 4097, 5681, 6944, 8213 to while; 5327 to whille; 4311 to while P þe whiles L
tray, treie, trey n. [see bitray, betraised] [OE trega, ON tregi] deceit; trouble, grief **Ch1** 1244 treie & tene; **Ch2** 5672 treie & tene; 7402 tene & tray; **HS** 2462 losse or tene *D* trey & tene
trayle v. [OF trailler] to drag, trail **HS** 3442 traylyng; 3446 traylyþ
trailebastoun n. [AF traille-baston] gang of outlaws in time of Edward I; the laws against them **Ch2** 8024 trailebastoun; 8028 trailebastons
trayn n. [OF traine] delay, tarrying **Ch2** 7182

trayn; 6365, 6393, 7787, 7983, 8213 trayne

traist, traised v. (1) [ON treysta] to make safe; to trust **Ch1** 7539 traist P trist L; **HS** 415 traystys GLOSS BH beleuyn

traist, traised, tresond v. (2) [from OF traiss-, stem of trahir] to betray **Ch1** 5370 traist P trayscht L; 5897, 5900 traised P traysched L; 12746 traiste P trayst L; **Ch2** 1175 bitraist P trayed L; 1484 traised; 3810 be bitraied P ben traised L; 2539 tresond

traist, treist, triste adj./adv. [ON traystr] faithful; trustworthy; firm, safe **Ch1** 3536 triste & trewe; 8278 triste P traist L; 12746 traiste; **Ch2** 4355 treist; 7043 traist

traitour n. [OF traitre] betrayer, traitor **Ch1** 6905 traitour; 7177 traitoure; 5894 traitoures; 7026 traitours P traysons L; **Ch2** 943, 2843, 5884, 7137, 8065 traytour; 1965, 4260 traitour; 600, 4102, 4394, 5837 traitoure; 465, 1491, 6498, 7935, 8181 traytoure; 1187, 2383, 2524, 6514, 8141 traytours; 5738 traitoures; 1186 traytoure P traitour L; **HS** 1344, 2530, 3644 treytours; 3837, 4195, 4199, 4210 treytur; 12607 treytour

traitourie, treytory n. [OF traitre] treachery, betrayal **Ch1** 9563 traitorie P trayterye L; **Ch2** 1483 traitourie; 3830, 4403, 6774, 7381 traytorie; **HS** 6250 treytory

translate v. [L translatus] move, transport **Ch2** 5096 translate

trauaile n. [OF] labor, toil; hardship, suffering, harm **Ch1** 694, 2538, 3942, 5138, 6840 trauaile P trauaille L; 104, 112, 114 trauayle; 747 trauayle P trauaille L; 3810 trauaille; 1044, 2848 trauaile P trauaylle L; **Ch2** 288, 2768, 4638, 6679, 7994 trauaile; 3802 trauaile P availle L; **HS** 840, 886, 7219, 10322 trauayle; 4344, 5072, 6103 traueyle

trauaile v. [OF trauaillier] to labor; torment; to weary **Ch1** 134 trauayled; 6755 trauailed P trauailled L; 7672 trauaile P trauailleþ L; 13158 trauersid P trauailled L; **Ch2** 6208 trauail; 1137, 4916, 7193, 7979 trauailed; 1139 trauailes; 6463 trauaild; 55, 1383, 1755, 2817, 5358 trauaile; **HS** 3167 traueyld; 4384, 4469, 6037 traueyled; 2412 traueylyst; 5065 traueyleþ; 9480 trauayleþ; 1952 traueylyd; 5050, 5067, 10416 traueyle

trauers n. [OF travers] sideways, crossways **Ch1** 12890 trauers

trauersid v. [OF trauerser] to cross over, run across or through **Ch1** 1551, 2720, 5001, 12403, 12852 trauersed; 3349 trauers; 8407 trauersede; 13158 trauersid P trauailled L

tre n. [OE treo] a tree; trees in a forest **Ch1** 286, 5020, 15441 tre; 1035, 1779, 1782, 5030, 8768 trees; **Ch2** 438, 3872, 5007 tre; 914 þre P tre L; **HS** 3845, 4762, 5207, 8239, 12359 tre

trechery, trichery n. [AF trecherie (MP)] guile, deceit **Ch1** 3882 trichery P tricherie L; 6929 tricherie P trycherye L; 15748L tricherye (om. P); **Ch2** 1095, 1495, 4813 tricherie; 1940 trecherie; 5690 treccherie; **HS** 3066 trechery

◆**trechet, trecther** v. [from OF trichier, trechier] to cheat, deceive **Ch2** 7662 trechet; 4062 trecther P trechere L; 4060 trechettyng (ger.) P trechiryng L

trechour, trethour n. [OF] deceiver, traitor **Ch2** 733 pantelere P trethour L; **HS** 5976 trechour

treget, trypet n. [OF] trickery, deceitful plot **Ch1** 2883 treget P trypet L; **Ch2** 4657 tregette P treget L

treie, trey n. [see tray, n.]

treist v. [see trist, v.]

treytorie n. [see traitorie]

treytour n. [see traitour]

◆**treyturhede** n. [from OF traitre, n.] treason **HS** 4208 treyturhede

tremble, tremle v. [AF trembler (MP)] to tremble, shake **Ch1** 10637 tremble; 3167 trimbled; 3155 trembland; **HS** 9398 tremle *F* tremble *O* trymbyll

tremlyng ger. [from AF trembler] trembling, shaking **HS** 4914 tremlyng *O* twynkand

trenchand, trenchaunt adj. [OF trenchant] having a sharp edge **Ch1** 4376 trenchand P trenchaunt L

trencheour n. [AF trenchour] a knife **Ch2** 4112 trencheour

treson n. [AF tresun, traisun (MP)] treachery **Ch1** 702, 2125, 4930, 6918, 13795 treson; 6538 tresoun; 6655 tresons; 13778 þorgh treson P treterously (adv.) L; **Ch2** 614, 3383, 6404, 7319, 8200 treson; 2051, 4260, 5762, 6378, 7743 tresoun; 2237, 3444 tresoune; 7067 tresons; **HS** 394, 4197, 10266 tresun; 8335 tresoun; 12525 tresoune; 3644 tresun *O* felon

tresond v. [see traist, v.]

tresore n. [OF tresor] wealth; riches; money **Ch1** 737, 2151, 4537, 7037, 11592 tresore; 1185, 3588, 4540 tresoure; 3721, 3799, 6309, 11566 tresour; 11539 tresure; 3298 tresours; **Ch2** 1972, 3459, 5226, 7224, 8345 tresore; 4412 tresoure; 5963 tresour; 2385 tresours; **HS** 5391, 6083, 6922, 9362, 9430 tresour; 6095 tresore; 6205 tresur

tresorere n. [OF tresorier] court official who keeps the treasure **Ch2** 6793, 6911, 7325, 7625, 7797 tresorere; **HS** 6071 tresorer

tresory n. [OF tresorie] place to keep valuables; the funds of a king or the state **Ch1** 3104 tresory; 4546, 7067 tresorie; **Ch2** 5488 tresory; 1938, 3327, 5494, 6864, 7653 tresorie; **HS** 6079, 6099 tresourye

trespas n. [OF trespas] transgression; sin, fault;

felony **Ch1** 209, 2751, 6653 trispas; **Ch2** 1184 trispas; 1286, 2043, 4032, 5471, 8288 trespas; **HS** 268, 338, 12242 trespas; 1430 trespasse; 1458 trespace

trest n./adj. [see triste, n. (1), triste, adj.]

trest v. [see triste, v.]

trestel, trestille n. [OF trestel] a support, beam, bar; frame **Ch2** 3760 tretels P tresteles L; 3767 trestels; 5626 trestille; 5627 treste

tretable adj. [OF traitable] docile, affable **HS** 1992 tretable

trethour n. [see trechour, n.]

treuage, trewage, trouage n. [OF treuage] tribute; an acknowledgement of fealty **Ch1** 5169, 5170, 5212 treuwage; 3040, 3291, 3300, 3545, 11575 trewage; 3608, 4544, 5286, 6636, 13438 treuage; 869 treuwage P truage L; 3034 trewage P truwage L; 5516 treuage P true L; 11414 treuage P trewe L; 11471 treuage P trewage L; 13442 treuage P truwage L; **Ch2** 113, 594, 1027, 1343, 7383 treuage; 1301 treuwage; 3722 trouage

◆ **treuwagers** n. [from OF treuage] subject to tribute; a tributary **Ch1** 4240 treuageres; 5351 treuagers; **Ch2** 1047 treuwageres P truwagers L

treuth, trouth, trew n. [OE treow] a vow; truce; tribute **Ch1** 2123 treus P trewes L; 14979 treus P trewe L; 3036 treuh P bond L; 3572 trewth P trowþ L; 4556 trew P trewe L; 5997 tru P trew L; 6979, 13490 trouth; 7724 treus P trewes L; 7727 treus P trues L; 11472 trew; 2034, 6907 treuth; 11472 trew P trewe L; 11401, 11647 trewe; **Ch2** 1500, 3787, 4626 trouth; 79, 1757, 4355, 6232, 8134 treuth; 4852, 7777 trew; 4781, 6668, 7395 trewe; 4830, 4841, 6671, 7586, 7733 treus; 4832 treue; 4839 treu; **HS** 356, 394 trowþe; 2776 trewþe; 5774, 8375, 12345 trouþe; 8381 treuþe; 1721 trowþe *C* trowthes *D* truþis

trewe, treuely adj./adv. [OE treowe, triewe] steadfast; faithfully, truly **Ch1** 3352, 3783, 10398 trew; 3801, 4878, 5625, 6642, 15638 trewe; 3536 triste & trewe; 6415 lele P trewe L; 520 certanly P truely L; 7036 trewly; **Ch2** 949, 1827, 2390, 5017, 7218 trewe; 4349, 5545, 7952 trew; 2637, 2907, 5017 trowe; 7864 treuly; **HS** 1912 trew; 2320, 2707, 3310, 6430, 12282 trewe; 2712 trewly; 4114, 10690, 12286 trewely; 11999 truly

trewman, trwman n. [from OE treow] a true, faithful man **HS** 1337 trwman *CDF* trewe man *H* trewman

tribille n. [OF treble] the high voice in a musical arrangement **Ch1** 11031 tribille

tribulacioun n. [OF tribulacion] oppression; distress **Ch2** 5057 tribulaccoun; 6377, 6528 tribulacioun

tricherous adj. [from AF trecherie, n.] deceitful, perfidious **Ch1** 15748L tricherous (om. P)

trie v. [see atrie] [OF trier, L triare] to judge; separate, set apart **Ch1** 12762 souht P tryde L; **Ch2** 6540, 7649, 7656 trie

tryfele v. [OF truffler] to deceive, cheat **HS** 2412 traueylyst hyt *C* tryfele hym

tryfle n. [OF trufle] false or idle talk or tale **HS** 5033 tryfle

trinite n. [OF] God in three persons **Ch1** 14360, 14500 trinite

triours n. [AF *triour; cf. F trieur] judges **Ch2** 6037 triours

trip n. (1) [prob. from OF treper, triper, v.] a trick; ?a mistake **Ch1** 1821 trip; **Ch2** 3848 trip

trip n. (2) [etymology obscure] ?troop, host **Ch2** 4992 trip

trispas n. [see trespas, n.]

triste n. (1) [OE *trust, ON traust] confidence, faith, trust **Ch1** 3514 trist; 5888, 5890 triste; **Ch2** 2491 triste; **HS** 7230 tryst; 378 beleue *C* no trost *D* not trewe

triste n. (2) [OF] a hunting station; rendezvous, appointed place **Ch1** 854 triste; **Ch2** 2292 trist; 3891 trist P tryyst L; 4447 triste

triste adj. [from triste, n. (1)] trustworthy **Ch1** 1102 treste P tryst L; 3352 treste P trist L; 3536 triste P trist L; 4813 tristeliere P tristiloker; 5021 trostere P tristi L; **Ch2** 1477 trost; 4355 treist

triste, treist, trost v. [ON treysta, OE *trystan] to believe in, rely on; to hope **Ch1** 1693 trost P triste L; 6969 triste; 2868 triste P tristed L; 3429 tristed; 11891 trasted P tristed L; 13502 trosted P tryste L; **Ch2** 1054 troste; 6697, 6999 trost; 8048 trest; 7315 trosted; 4439 treistid; 2909 treistes P tristes L; 5680 trestes; **HS** 1228, 4114 truste; 2315 trust; 2690 trusten; 370 beleue *C* to trostyn til; *D* to truste til; 379 beleue *C* trost *D* trowe; 10800 truste *V* trustneþ

trod v. [see trow, v.]

trompe n. [OF] trumpet **Ch1** 2696L trompe (om. P); 1771L trompes (om. P); 3493 trompes P trompe L; 13471 trompes P trumpes L; **Ch2** 2466, 3669 trompes; 7160, 7165 trumpes; 649 trumpes P trompe (v.) L; **HS** 4774 trumpes

trompors n. [from trompe, n.] trumpeters **Ch2** 2847 trompors

troteuale n. [entymology obscure] idle talk, tale-telling **HS** 48 trotouale; 5972 troteuale; 8082 troteuale *O* trotyuayle; 9249 troteuale *O* troteuayle; 6546 [MS *O* interpolation, l. 26] troteuale

trouhes n. [var. of OE trog] boats **Ch1** 10058 trouhes P trowes L

trouht, trowþyd v. [see betrowþe] [from OE treowe, n.] to promise; to betroth **Ch2** 6475 trouht; **HS** 1705 betrowþe *C* trewth ply3th *D* truþe; 1724 trowþyd *C* trewth plyth *D* truþid

trouþe n. [see treuth, n.]

trow, trod v. [OE truwian, treowian] to believe; suppose, hope; verify **Ch1** 887 trowe P trowed L; 1521, 2827, 4243, 9613, 11837 trowe; 3423, 6375 trow; 7252 trod P trowd L; 1133, 5277, 7120, 7153, 7254 trowed; 7998 be trod P be bytrowd L; 10664 trow P trowe L; **Ch2** 674, 1374, 4425, 6519, 7727 trowe; 1655, 4787, 5194 trow; 2526 trowed; 2902 trod P trowed L; 4352, 4911, 8298 trod; **HS** 483, 1483, 3894, 9013, 11118 trowe; 497 trowst; 9246 trowed; 474, 478 trowe *C* leue; 479 beleue *C* trost *D* trowe; 1141 trowe *D* þou3tte; 2647 beleueþ *C* trowe *D* telle *O* trowys; 3105 vndyrstode *O* trowyde ore vndyrstode; 3108 troud *O* trode; 11255 trowest *O* hoppes

trowyng ger. [from OE treowian, v.] belief **HS** 498 trowyng

truely adv. [see trewe]

trulle n. [?ON trull] ?a prostitute; wench, girl **Ch2** 6817 trulle

trumpes n. [see trompe, n.]

trumped v. [from OF trompe, n.] to blow a trumpet **Ch1** 13018 trumped P trumpes (n.) L; **Ch2** 649 trumpes (n.) P trompe L

trut, tprut interjection [see prut]

tueie, tweye, tuo, toon, two n./adj./numeral [OE twege] two **Ch1** 540 tweye P beye L; 2358 tuey P tweye L; 5781 tuo P tweye L; 436, 3071, 5652, 6850, 7175 tuo; 5614 tu P two L; 6494, 6530 two; 277, 280, 365 tua; 13745 to; **Ch2** 493, 1406, 3366, 4572, 6817 tueye; 1202 tueie; 47, 1073, 4806, 5767, 8156 tuo; **HS** 85, 794, 1695, 1820, 7095 twey; 795 toon; 1156, 5283, 6691, 9284, 12542 two

tueyn, tweyen n./adj. [OE twegen] two **Ch1** 482 tueyn; **Ch2** 1819 tweyn; 2583 tuayn; 2892, 3466 tueyn; **HS** 1869 tweyyn; 10173 tweyen

tuelf, tuelue, tuelft n./adj./numeral [OE twelf, twelfta] twelve, twelfth **Ch1** 241, 1349, 1603, 1826, 3018 tuelf; 2205, 3019 tuelue; 248 tuelft; **Ch2** 3478 tuelf; 2262, 4334, 5651 tuelue; 1100, 3064, 3605, 5485, 6862 tuelft; 1492 tuelft P twelfthe L; **HS** 25, 6880, 11619, 11891 twelue; 11825 twelfeþe

tuelmoth, twelfmonth n. [OE twelfmonþ] a year, twelve months' time **Ch1** 3129 tuelmoth; **HS** 3815 twel monþe; 7778 tuelue monþe; 9087 twelfmonth; 9179 twelfmonþe; 10759 twelue moneþ

tuenty, tuentende, tuende n./adj./numeral [OE twentig, twentigoða] twenty, twentieth **Ch1** 436, 2135, 3703, 5663, 11444 tuenty; 1933 tuenti; **Ch2** 2082, 3478, 6551, 7052, 8347 tuenty; 1623, 4438, 5016, 6846, 7965 tuenti; 3559, 6877 tuende; 7538 tuentende; **HS** 1965, 7790, 12584 twenty

tuynne v. [see otuyn, otwynne] [from OE twinn, adj.] to divide in two **Ch2** 2131 tuynnes; 3287 tuynne

tuys adv. [OE twi3es] twice; two times **Ch1** 4662, 5035 tuys P twys L; 4823, 5040, 6643, 12914 tuys; **Ch2** 152, 4697, 5715, 5839, 5840 tuys; **HS** 3182 twyys; 4060, 4974, 4982, 9686, 11667 twys

tumblede v. [see tombled, v.]

tunder n. [OE tynder] tinder to light a fire **Ch1** 14063 tunder; 14069 tundir P tonder L; **HS** 7926 tunder

turbe n. [?OF; cp. L turbella, a little crowd] a crowd, troop **Ch2** 4685 turbe P warde L

turbled v. [see sturble, desturble, v.]

turcus n. [cp. F turquin] pumpkins **HS** 2105 gourdus *C* growndis *D* turcus

tureile n. [see tour, n.] [OF tourelle, torele] tower, turret **Ch2** 4429 tureile P tourel L

turmente n./v. [see tourment]

turne n. [OF torne, from tourner, v.] occasion; turn **Ch1** 1809 turne P turn L; 12111 turne; **Ch2** 2533, 3803, 4723 turne; 2968 turne P iourne L

turne, torne v. [OE tyrnan, turnian; AF turner (MP)] change; leave; move, retreat; become **Ch1** 118, 1449, 3337, 6707, 12406 turne; 8651 turn; 8050 turne P turn L; 8372 gaf back P turd þe bak L; 4473, 5049, 6680, 9261 turnes; 179, 1859, 4389, 7117, 15673 turned; 8395 turned P turde L; 1480 turnede; 9297 tourne; 9387 torne; **Ch2** 7923 turn; 198, 2835, 4089, 5828, 7838 turne; 877, 1962, 3880, 6947, 8174 turned; 2751 tourned; 516, 2950, 3614, 5393, 6494 turnes; **HS** 77 tournede; 124, 1153, 5181, 8716 turne; 5131 torne; 2963 tourne; 6586 turnest; 4627, 12606 turned; 810 turne *C* chawnge *D* tourne

turnyng ger. [from turne, v.] reversal, retreat; change in direction **Ch1** 12496 turnynges; **Ch2** 5803 tournyng; **HS** 8844, 8879 turnyng

twynkelyng ppl. [from OE twinclian] winking; fig.: in an instant **HS** 9184 twynkelyng

♦ **twyxten** prep. [aphetic form of atwixt, betwixt] between **Ch1** 2276 bituex P twyxten L

two numeral [see tueie, tuo]

UV

vbble, oble n. [OF oblee, obleie] sacramental wafer **HS** 10013 vbble *HV* oble; 10091 vbble *V* oble; 10105 vbble *H* vble *V* oble

vmbeleid, vmbilaid v. [OE ymbe + belecgan] beseiged, surrounded, covered **Ch1** 8164 be layd P vmbyleyd L; 8347 vmbileid P vmbyleyden L; 13600 vmbileid P vmbyleide L; **Ch2** 4660 vmbeleid; 7232 vmbilaid

vmbilapped v. [OE ymbe + læppa, n.] surrounded **Ch1** 1140 vmbilapped P bylapped L

vmbreide n. [see vpbraid]

vmwhile adv. [OE ymb hwile] sometimes, formerly **Ch1** 1407, 1822, 5712, 7564, 14040 vmwhile; **Ch2** 5480, 5812, 8213 vmwhile; **HS** 2780 vmwhyle GLOSS B sum tyme *C* many qwyle *D* sum qwyle; 3065 oþerwhyl *O* vmqwyle; 3069 oþerwhyl *O* sum qwyle; 4363 sumwhyle *O* vmqwylle; 5335 oþerwhyle *O* vmqwyle

vnbynde v. [OE unbindan] loosen; release from bonds **HS** 1014, 4528, 5654, 6463, 11593 vnbynde; 9220, 10630 vnbounde

vnbiweued v. [OE bewæfan] uncovered **Ch2** 2858 vnbiweued

vnbore adj. [OE unboren] unborn **HS** 4857 vnbore

◆ **vnbryche** adj. [OE unbryce] useless, unserviceable **HS** 6788 vnbryche *O* vnbryghte

vnbuxyme n. [from vnbuxom, adj.] disobedience (prob. error) **HS** 10178 vnbuxyme *F* vnbuxynne *O* vnbuxsome thynge *VS* corsyng inne

vnbuxom, vnbuxum adj. [from OE *buhsum] disobedient **Ch1** 14722L vnbuxom (om. P); **HS** 3013, 6559 vnbuxum

vnbuxumnes n. [from adj.] disobedience **HS** 3012 vnbuxumnesse; 6568, 11343 vnbuxumnes

vnce n. [OF] an ounce; unit of weight **Ch2** 1314 vnce; 3769 vnces

vncerteyn adj. [from OF certein] doubtful; indeterminate **Ch2** 7916, 8176 vncerteyn; **HS** 5997 vncerteyn; 6690 vncerteyne

vncharged adj. [from OF charger] unburdened **HS** 11950 vncharged

vnconyng n. [see con, conne, v.] [OE onconning] ignorance, stupidity **Ch2** 6178, 6179 vnconyng; **HS** 8632 vnkunnyng; 9598 vncunnyng

vncouth, vnkouth adj. [OE uncuþ] strange, unknown **Ch1** 2909 vnkoth P vncouþ L; 3184 vnkouth londes P outlandes L; 10440 vncouþe P vncouþ L; 11198 vnkouth P straunge L; **HS** 3067, 4300 vncouth; 9880 vncouþ

vncurteise, vncurteisly adj./adv. [see curtays, adj.] [from OF curteis] discourteous, inconsiderate **Ch1** 11562 vncurteise; **Ch2** 3511 vncurteisly P envyesly L; **HS** 6800 vncurteys

vnder adj./adv./prep. [OE] beneath, lower than; subordinate **Ch1** 645, 2062, 5661 vndere; 5360 vndire; **Ch2** 42, 1644, 3425, 4998, 7527 vnder; 1650, 4548 vndir; 4441, 6994 vndere; **HS** 1194, 2270, 2818, 3446, 12227 vndyr; 10741 vndur

vnderfong v. [OE underfon] receive, undertake, accept **Ch1** 242 vnderfang P gan fonge L; 3893 vndirfong P vnderfonge L; **Ch2** 1388, 3170 vnderfong; **HS** 9506 vndyrfongeþ

vndermye v. [see myne, v.] [from OF miner] undermine a wall **Ch1** 3404 vndermye

vndersette v. [cf. MDu ondersetten] held up, supported **Ch1** 284 vndersette P vnder feet L

vnderstand v. [OE understondan] comprehend; reckon, suppose **Ch1** 308 vnderstande; 1738 vndirstand; 4803, 6608 vnderstond; 921, 2457, 3221, 4134, 7006 vnderstode; 940 vndrestode P vnderstonde L; 11557 vndirstode; **Ch2** 1414 vnderstand; 1290, 2053, 6041 vnderstond; 6029 vnderstandes; 7698 vnderstondes; 5135 vnderstod; 1207, 2896, 4601, 6035, 8203 vnderstode; **HS** 84, 1481, 6351, 11586 vndyrstonde; 614, 2727 vndyrstande; 9870 vnderstondeþ; 2471, 3105 vnderstode; 586, 1629, 10171, 10440 vndyrstode; 571 vndyrstandys; 5086 vndyrstondes

vnderstandyng n. [OE understonding] comprehension; agreement **Ch2** 611, 772 vnderstandyng; **HS** 11588 vndyrstondyng

vndertake v. [OE under + ON taka] accept, receive willingly **Ch1** 880, 893, 5810 vndertake; 4752 vndertoke; 12620 vndertoke PL vndirtoke R; **Ch2** 1463, 3608 vndertake; 4146 vndirtoke; 5785 vndertoke; **HS** 43, 9992, 11336 vndyrtoke

vndron, vndurne n. [OE undern, ON undorn] third hour of the day; nine a.m.; middle of the morning **Ch2** 339 vnderon P vndern L; 5860 vndron; **HS** 4061 vndurne

vnfayn adj. [OE unfæȝen] unhappy; sorry, reluctant **Ch1** 10013 vnfayn; **Ch2** 2461, 4749, 7318 vnfayn

vnfest v. [from OE fæstan] unfasten, untie **Ch1** 647 vnfest

vnfolden adj. [OE unfealdan] open up **Ch2** 6883 vnfolden

vngyuen ppl. [ON ugefinn; MDu ongegeven] not given in marriage **Ch1** 6444 vngyuen

vnglad adj. [OE unglæd] unhappy, sorry **Ch1** 5980 vnglad P sory L

vngracious, vngraciously adj./adv. [from OF gracious; cf. MDu engracioos] without grace; discourteous **Ch2** 2507 vngracious; 5460 vngraciously; 7038 vngraciouse

vnhalowed v. [see halewe, v.] [OE unhalgod] profaned; not consecrated **HS** 8613 vnhalewed; 8799 vnlawe (n.) *O* vnhalowe

vnhap n. [ON uhapp] misfortune, mishap **Ch1** 4591 vnhap; **Ch2** 6616 vnhap

vnhende adj./adv. [OE ungehend] discourteous; faithlessly, rudely **Ch1** 14434, 15300 vnhende; **Ch2** 6244 vnhende; **HS** 4941 vnhende

vnkynd adj./adv. [OE uncynde] unnatural, unfaithful **Ch1** 2129 vnkynde; 2134, 2643 vnkyndly P vnkyndely L; 15765 vnkynd P vnkynde L; **Ch2** 1527, 4931 vnkynd; **HS** 766, 2950, 6790, 8623, 11552 vnkynde; 5126, 6268 vnkyndely; 1167 vnkyndly *C* vnskylfully *D* vnkynd; 1172 nat kynde *C* vnkende *D* vnkynde

vnkyndhede n. [from OE uncynde] unnatural conduct; baseness **HS** 5095 vnkyndehede; 3648, 4837, 6510 vnkyndhede

vnkyndnes n. [from OE uncynde] unnatural conduct **Ch1** 2644 vnkynes P vnkyndenesse L; **HS** 5123 vnkyndenes

vnknawen n. [OE ungecnawen] strange, unfamiliar persons **Ch1** 2729 vnknawen P vnknowen L

vnkonand n. [from OE cunnan, v.] ignorant persons **Ch2** 5892 vnkonand

vnkunnyng n. [see vnconnyng]

vnlace v. [from OE lacier, lachier] unfasten laces **Ch1** 3223 vnlace

vnlawe n. [OE unlagu] illegality **HS** 8799 vnlawe *O* vnhalowe

vnliþe adj. [see liþt, adj., and vnride, adj.]

♦ **vnmayn** n. [OE unmæȝness] weakness **Ch2** 1333 vnmayn

vnmyght n. [OE unmiht] weakness, feebleness **Ch1** 14894 vnmyght P vnmight L; **HS** 7912 vnmyght

vnneþe, vnneþis adv. [OE uneaþe] with difficulty; scarcely, hardly **Ch1** 1170, 1593, 6730, 8343, 13025 vnneþis P vneþes L; 5331 vnneþis P vnneþe L; 3017 vneþis; **Ch2** 1871, 1880, 5372, 7179, 7190 vnneþis; 2230 vnneþis P vnnyþe L; 6536 vnnethis; **HS** 1071 vnneþys; 3649, 5076, 7043, 9477, 9481 vnneþe; 6092 vnneþes; 2598 *C* oneth (B differs)

vnride adj. [OE ungeryde] rough, violent, severe; enormous, numerous **Ch1** 1035, 3407 vnride P vnryde L; 11016 vnrid P vnryde L; **Ch2** 4309 vnride P vnliþe L; **HS** 904 vnryde *C* wunt abyde *D* gan vphyde

vnright n./adj. [OE unriht] wrong, injustice, evil; crime **Ch1** 11271 vnright; **Ch2** 4408 vnright P vnriȝt L; **HS** 6404, 9739, 11178, 11915 vnryght; 2265 wyþ oute ryght *C* wyþ vnrytȝ *D* wyþ out ryȝt; 6512 vnryght *O* deyde na ryghte; 7912 vnmyght *F* vnriȝt

vnsauht, vnsaght adj. [OE unsæht] unreconciled; hostile **Ch1** 8420 vnsauht P vnsaughte L; **HS** 482 vnsaght; 4140 vnsaght GLOSS B at debate *O* saught

vnsele n./adj. [OE unsæl] misery; unlucky **Ch2** 6736 vnsele; **HS** 8802 vnskyl *O* vselle

vnsemly adj. [cf. ON usæsmiliger] indecent, unfitting **Ch2** 4240 vnsemly

vnshent ppl. [see schende, v.] [OE unscended; MDu ongescent] unpunished **HS** 2730 vnshent

vnshryue ppl. [see schriue, v.] [from OE scrifan] unconfessed **HS** 11840, 12151 vnshryue

vnsyb adj. [OE ungesib] not related, not of kin **HS** 1198 vnsyb

vnskyl n. [cf. ON uskil, oskil] folly, wrongdoing **Ch1** 12309 vnskille P vnskyle L; **Ch2** 7634 vnskille; **HS** 8802 vnskyl *O* vselle

vnskilfully adv. [from vnskyl, n.] unreasonably **Ch2** 3750 vnskilfully; **HS** 1167 vnkyndly *C* vnskylfully *D* vnkynd

vnslayn adj. [ON; cp. OI usleginn] not killed **Ch1** 13756 vnslayn

vnthank n. [OE unþanc] unwillingness; displeasure; a curse **Ch1** 6000 vnþank P vnthank L; 13610 vnþankes; **Ch2** 5803 vnthank

vnthende adj. [from OE þeon, v.] unlucky **HS** 2888 *C* vnthende (B differs)

vnþewes n. [OE unþeaw] bad habit or custom **HS** 4852 vnþewes *O* vnchastynge

vnþrifte n. [cf. ON uþrifnaðr, sluggishness] a shiftless or dissolute person **Ch1** 7127 vnþrifte P vnþrift L; **HS** 12347 vnþryft *F* vpþrift *O* anoþer vnthryfte

vntille prep./conj. [see vnto] [cp. ON til] in, into; for; at, to **Ch1** 862, 2067 vntille; 2848 vntille P þe while L; 4973 vntille P til L; 4783, 5010, 6135, 6195 vnto P vntil L; **Ch2** 182, 1358, 2477, 6756, 7894 vntille; **HS** 5996, 6068, 6184, 8386 vntyl

vntime n./adj. [OE untime, untima] an evil moment; untimely **Ch2** 5584 vntime; **HS** 2962 vntyme

vnto prep./conj./adv. [see vntille] [?OE *unto] to, until; for, at **Ch1** 25, 1018, 3280, 5389, 6882 vnto; **Ch2** 7, 1251, 4034, 7327, 8246 vnto; **HS** 187, 1624, 4452, 9060, 11788 vnto

vntrewe, vntrewly adj./adv. [OE untreowe, untreowlice] faithless, false **HS** 10303 vntrewe; 1834 vntrewly

vnwar adj. [OE unwær] unwary, imprudent **Ch2** 6735 vnwar

vnwarned adj./adv. [OE unwarnod] not warned or forewarned **Ch1** 12437 vnwarned; **Ch2** 212 vnwarned

vnwedded ppl. [from OE weddian] unmarried **HS** 7354 vnwedded

vnwetyng ppl. [see wete, v.] [OE unwitende] without knowing **HS** 11261 vnwetyng

vnwylland adj. [OE unwillende] unintentional **Ch1** 858 willand not P al vnwylland L

vnwis adj. [OE] indiscreet, imprudent, foolish **Ch2** 156 vnwis; 5373, 5925 vnwise; **HS** 9685 vnwys

vnwysdom n. [OE] folly, stupidity **HS** 5048 vnwysdom

vnwrshyply adv. [OE unweorþscipeliche] irreverently **HS** 981 vnwrshyply *C* vnwurthely *D* vnworþily

vnwrþy, vnwrþyly adj./adv. [from OE unweaorþe; cp. ON uvirðiliga, scornfully] unfit;

unmerited **HS** 11002 vnwrþy; 11006 vnwrþye; 10255, 10960 vnwrþyly; 981 vnwrshyply *C* vnwurthely *D* vnworþily; 3039 vnwrþyly *O* wykkydly

vparyued, vpryue v. [OE up + OF river] to arrive on shore, land **Ch1** 2486 vparyued; 4294 vpryue; 4654 vp ryue P gon þey aryue L; 5577 vpryued P aryued L; 5914 com vpryuand P come pryuely L; 6483 vp ariuen; **Ch2** 13, 4746 vpryue; 3945 vpriue; 5574 vp ariue; 7712 vp rif; 7822 vp ryf; 858, 3262 vp aryued

vpbraid, vmbreide n. [from OE up + brægd] a reproach, reproof **Ch1** 3457 vpbraid P vmbreides L; 7882 vpbreide P reprefs L; 7885 vpbreid P vmbreyd L; 11423 vpbraide P vmbreyd L; 14564 vpbraid P vmbreyde L; **Ch2** 5370 vpbraid; **HS** 673, 1986, 2632, 6432 vpbreyd; 5843, 6675 vpbreyde

vpbraide, vpbreid, vmbreyde v. [OE upbregdan] censure, find fault with, reprove **Ch1** 7890 vpbreid P vmbreyde L; 11421 vpbraide P repreue L; **HS** 672, 1530, 3880, 5739, 8756 vpbreyde; 4844 vpbreydyng; 724 vpbreydyst *C* breydyst *D* vpbroydyst

vpbraidyng ger. [from OE upbregdan, v.] reproach or reproof **Ch2** 7767 vpbraidyng; **HS** 766 vpbreydyng

vpdrouh v. [see drawe, drouh, v.] [from OE dragan; cf. MDu opdragen] pull up **Ch1** 1779 vpdrouh

vphelde v. [from OE uppheald, n.; MLG upholden, v.] to support **Ch1** 4336 vphelde

vplaid v. [see leih, lay, v. (1)] [from OE lecgan] put in place **Ch2** 4838 vplaid

vpland n. [OE uppe land] rural districts; areas outside towns or cities **Ch1** 10288, 15668 vpland; **HS** 1315 vpland

vplift v. [see lift, v.] [cf. ON lypta upp] elevate in rank or honor; support, assist **Ch1** 3373 vplift; **Ch2** 1319, 1780 vplift; 1736 vp him lyft; **HS** 11410 vp lyfte; 7088 vp lyft; 11922 vplyfte

vpnam v. [see nym, nam, v.] [from OE niman; cf. OFris. opnima] to take up **Ch1** 4372 vp nam

vpon, opon, oppon, apon adv./prep. [OE uppe on; ON upp a] on; during; about, near, above; on condition of **Ch1** 682, 1458, 4462, 7865, 8813 vpon; 4548, 4552 vppon; 855, 2255 apon; 572, 8368 oppon; 905, 2115, 4350, 7505, 9148 opon; **Ch2** 189, 541, 2576, 3078, 3273 vpon; 122, 329, 422 vppon; 465, 1463, 4068, 6721, 7996 opon; **HS** 1447, 1919, 2533, 6506 vppon; 8834 vppoun; 384, 952 opon

vpreise, vpraise v. [OE up + ON reisa] to erect, raise up **Ch1** 12842 vpraised P vp reysed L; 7090 vp araised; **Ch2** 1927, 2009 vpreise; 1968 vp raised; **HS** 11900 vpreyse

vpride v. [from OE ridan, v.] ride up on the shore **Ch2** 2161 vpride

vpright adj./adv. [OE uppriht] erect; in a vertical position **Ch1** 1730, 8670 vpright; 1302 on hyght P vpright L; **Ch2** 8130 vpright

vprise v. [OE up arisan] to rise up **Ch1** 1823 vprise; **Ch2** 4138 vp rise; 6184 rise vp; 7082 ros vp; **HS** 5319, 8188 vpryse

vpryue v. [see vparyued, v.]

vpset v. [OE up + settan] to erect, set up, raise up **Ch1** 13358 vpsat; **Ch2** 1727, 2340, 3882 vpsette

vpspede v. [OE up + spedan] to build quickly **Ch2** 1895 vpspede

vpstirt v. [see stirte] [OE vp + styrtan, *stertan] spring up, rise up quickly **Ch1** 1213 vpstert P vp styrte L; 1799 vpstirt P vp he stirt L; 11298 vpstirte P vp stirt L; 5184, 12047 stirte vp; 6627, 6949 stirt vp; **HS** 1569 sterte vp; 5603 vp sterte

vpward adv./prep./adj. [OE upweard] to or toward a higher position **HS** 5274, 6666, 11677 vpward

vpwright v. [OE up + wyrhte, n.] build, erect **Ch2** 2178 vp wright

vryne n. [OF] urine **Ch1** 8896 vryne P vryn L

vsage n. [OF] habit, custom **Ch1** 3554, 15800 vsage; 15794 vsages; **Ch2** 7631, 8221 vsage; 7627 vsages; **HS** 7671 vsage; 10572 vsages

use v. [AF user (MP)] to act, conduct oneself; to be accustomed; employ **Ch1** 122 vsed; 5629 had P vsed L; **Ch2** 3474, 7620 vse; 5145, 5738 vsed; **HS** 1299, 1536, 2391, 2398, 2636 vse; 8789 vsedest; 7450 vsen; 2170 to robbe *D* vsyd to robbe

vsure, vsery n. [OF usure] usury **Ch2** 5490, 7818 vsure; **HS** 2417 vsery

vsurer n. [OF vsurer; AF vserer (MP)] userer **HS** 2604 vsurere; 2611 vsurer; 2453, 2632, 8737 vsurers

U as V

vaile n. [AF veile] headdress of a nun **Ch1** 13658 vaile

vaile v. [see auaile] [from OF valoir] to be of value, of use or service; to benefit **Ch1** 1043, 2636, 6686, 6841, 8271 vaile P vaille L; 5055 vaile P availle L; 5928 vale P vaille L; 12250L vaille (om. P); **Ch2** 202, 4611 vaile; **HS** 9479, 10979 vayleþ; 10683 vayled

vale, valeie n. [AF valeys; OF val, valee] tract of land between ranges of hills; a dale or valley **Ch1** 3059 valeiȝ P vales L; 5488 vale; 12811 vale P veleye L; 1110, 3359, 4962, 14567 valeie; 4985 valaye; 14569 valeys; **HS** 7136 valeye

valiant adj. [AF vaylant] brave, bold, courageous

Ch1 6849 valiant P valliaunt L; 12248 manly dede P vaillaunte dede L; **Ch2** 158, 177, 2827, 3676, 4389 valiant; 2919 valiaunt P roillant L; 3538 valianter; 7246 valiantȝ; **HS** 4374 vaylaunt *O* waylande

valiantise n. [OF from vaillant] valor, bravery, courage **Ch1** 11893 valiantise P vaillauntise L; **Ch2** 4152 valiantise

valow, value n. [OF value] worth; rank; valor **Ch1** 4862 valow; **Ch2** 2061 valowe; 2462 value; 4037, 4851 valow; **HS** 5968 value

vamward, vaumward n. [OF var. of vauntward] vanguard of a host or army **Ch2** 4675, 4682, 4997 vamward; 8163 vaumward

vanatours n. [see auoutours]

vanysshed v. [from OF evanir] become invisible **HS** 8197 vanysshed

vanyte n. [AF vanite (MP)] frivolity **HS** 381, 3348, 3433, 3691, 4295 vanyte; 9862 vanytes

vassalage n. [OF] vassal's deeds; courageous acts; body of vassals **Ch1** 5295, 13229 vassalage; 2829 vassallage P vasselage L; 12029 vassalage P vasselage L; **Ch2** 2126 vassalage; 4670 vassalage P vyage L; **HS** 4614 vasselage

vaumbras n. [OF] armor for the arm **Ch1** 9881L vaumbras (om. P)

vaunsed, vaunsement v./n. [see auaunce, auauncement]

vauasoure n. [OF vavasour, vavaseur] feudal tenant ranking below a baron **Ch1** 10792 vauasours; **Ch2** 297, 4104, 5468 vauasoure; 6640 vauasours

veyn adj. [OF vein, vain] useless, futile, in vain **Ch1** 5183 in veyn; 11927 veyn P vayn L; **Ch2** 7674 in veyn; **HS** 391, 2001, 5352, 9170, 10260 veyn; 465, 8736 veyne

veire n. [OF vair, veir] squirrel fur for trimming garments **Ch1** 611 veire P veir L; 10972L veyr (P differs); 11175 veire P veyr L

venery, venrie n. [OF venerie] hunting beasts or game; the chase **Ch1** 852 venery P venerye L; 3976 venrie P venurye L

venyson n. [AF veneson, venyson] flesh of game, deer **Ch1** 1323, 1526, 15045, 15059 venyson; 10839 venison; **Ch2** 1561 venysons; 2717 venysoun

venge v. [OF vengier] to punish wrongdoing **Ch1** 1529, 3418, 6400, 6828, 7181 venge; 1630 venged P venget L; 2053, 5150, 6557, 8144, 12120 venged; 3428 venged P wroken L; **Ch2** 197, 1576, 3892, 5564, 8325 venge; 247, 1603, 2384, 3207 venged; **HS** 3808 venge

vengeance, veniaunce n. [AF veniaunce, vengance] punishment; retribution **Ch1** 1172, 4454, 15683, 15727 vengeance; 2652, 4719, 8837 vengeance P vengaunce L; 3711 veniance; 3928 veniaunce; 4795 vengence; 15089 vengeance P veniaunce L; **Ch2** 610, 1599, 2485, 7414, 8300 vengeance; **HS** 778, 789 vengaunce; 1370, 1462, 1850, 2731 veniaunce; 9786 warnyng *O* venganse

vengement n. [OF] vengeance; retribution **Ch2** 4883, 7411 vengement

venyal adj. [OF venial] light or forgivable sin **HS** 11250 venyal

venom n. [AF venim, venin] poison **Ch1** 2552 venom; 8890 venom P venyn L; **Ch2** 4203, 4225 venom; **HS** 4176, 4179 venym

venomouse adj. [see envenomed] [AF venimus] poisonous **Ch1** 15810 venomouse P venimouse L

venquis v. [OF] overcome in battle; vanquish **Ch1** 5131 venquised; 7290 venquis P vencuse L; **Ch2** 6309 venquised

verrey, verray adj./adv. [AF verrey, verrai] true; in truth, in reality **Ch2** 2061 verrey; 4037, 4693, 7509 verray; **HS** 1659, 9973 verrey; 12268 verry

verreylyk, veryly adv. [from AF verrey] in truth, in reality **Ch2** 4517 verrayly; **HS** 10053 verreylyk; 10076 veryly

verrement adv. [OF vraiement, verreiment] truly; assuredly **HS** 651 verement; 10877, 11172 verrement

verse n. [OF, ON] a metrical composition; lines of poetry **Ch1** 15707 verse; **HS** 11117, 11119 vers

verseild v. [from L versiculus] to sing verses from the Psalms **Ch1** 15704 verseild P versled L

vertue, vertew n. [AF vertu] power, strength, courage; peculiar property; miracle **Ch1** 3717 vertues; 6977, 7651 vertue; **Ch2** 342 vertew; 4574 vertewe; 4668 vertu; 8183 vertuȝ; **HS** 2303, 2853, 5854, 11459, 12610 vertu; 6532 vertues *O* thewes

veselle n. [AF vessel (MP); L vessel] utensil, plate, receptacle; a ship **Ch1** 11085 vesselle; **Ch2** 3761 veselle P vessel L; 3777, 3903 busses P vessels L; **HS** 5180, 6325, 7854, 7861, 9210 vessel; 6203 vesseles; 9423 vesselles

vesellement n. [AF vesselement (MP)] church vessels or plate **HS** 9346 vessellement; 9488 vesselment

vestement n. [AF vestement (MP)] garment; vesture worn by clergy **HS** 4679, 9345, 11092 vestement

viage n. [AF veiage, veage] journey, expedition **Ch1** 3620, 6625, 8725 viage; **Ch2** 2199, 3510, 6352, 7291, 7714 viage; **HS** 3748 vyage

viandoure n. [AF] a liberal host, hospitable man **Ch1** 4044 viandoure P vyaundour L

vicarie n. [AF vicare (MP); L vicarius] office of a vicar; a benefice **Ch1** 5682 vicaries; **Ch2** 6873 vicarie; **HS** 11615, 11797 vycary

vice n. [OF] depravity; wicked conduct or

habits; fault **Ch1** 6977 vice; 5629 vyce; 3872 vices; **Ch2** 1807, 2586 vice; **HS** 4377, 5329, 6276, 7587, 10136 vyce; 5969 vys

vilany, vilenie n. [AF vilanie, vilenie] shameful deed, disgrace; evil, insult **Ch1** 3454, 4260, 11937, 14042 vilany; 13648, 14556 vilanie; 3038 vilany P vileny L; 6489 vilani P vileny L; **Ch2** 4168, 4628, 5302, 7825 vilanie; 4289, 5510, 8018, 8187 vilenie; 1286, 4134 vilany; 6420 vileynie; **HS** 1536, 1549 vyleyny; 3771, 6833, 8289, 8414, 11630 vyleynye; 6518 vylaynye; 49 velanye; 3528 velany; 4940 vyleny; 12536 vyleyne; 7596 vilonye *H* felonye; 5986 felonye *F* vilenie; 8718 fouly *O* vylany; 10900 felonye *O* velany

vile adj./adv. [AF vil, vile] cheap, common, base; shameful **Ch1** 2814, 10617 vile P vyl L; 6744 vile; **Ch2** 7019 vile; **HS** 1532, 3135, 4403 vyle; 1819 vyly; 1586 vyle *C* fowle; 2597 vyler *CD* werse *O* foulere; 2609 vyly *C* fowl *D* opynly; 3040 yl *O* vylle; 6762 vyle *O* evyll; 6767 vyle *O* evyle; 7671 vyle *H* foule *O* wyke; 11124 wykkedly *O* vylyly

vileyn n./adj. [AF vilein, vilain] a scoundrel, base-born person; opprobrium **Ch2** 1273 vileyn; **HS** 11565 vyleyn

vilens, vilensly, vilaynly adj./adv. [OF vileins] foul, shameful; vilely **Ch1** 12314 vilensly P vyleynlike L; **Ch2** 5491 vilaynly; **HS** 1555, 1847 vylens

vilte, vilete n. [OF vilte] vileness; crime **Ch1** 5426 vilte P vylte L; 9199 vilte P vilenye L; 11261 vilete P vilte L; **HS** 5208 vylte

vineis, vynys n. [OF vine, vigne; L vinea] vine plant; grape vine **Ch1** 10740 vineis P vynes L; **HS** 882, 900, 905, 917 vynys

vyolence n. [OF violence] a violent act **HS** 11150 vyolence

virgine n. [AF virgine (MP)] an unmarried or chaste woman; the Virgin Mary **Ch1** 5778 virgine; **HS** 580 virgyne; 863 virgine; 8274, 9077, 9232, 9237 vyrgyne

virgynyte n. [AF virginite (MP)] chastity **HS** 2875 virgynyte

vis n. [OF vis] face; honor **Ch1** 9161, 10733, 12437, 14048 vis P vys L; 3718 vise P vis L; 5483 vys P vis L; 5034 vys P auys L; **Ch2** 2533, 2989, 3808, 7521 vis; 3880 vys P wyle L

visage n. [OF] the countenance; face **Ch1** 3109 visage; **Ch2** 7523 visage; **HS** 5889 vysege; 8487, 10241 vysage; 10209 vyseges; 10213 vysege *O* vegase *SV* visage

vyser n. [from OF vis, face] front of a helmet **Ch1** 8438 naselle P vyser L

vision n. [AF visiun, visioun] an apparition; revelation **Ch1** 14753 vision; **Ch2** 1617, 1891 vision; 1598 vision P avision L

visite v. [AF visiter (MP)] to comfort or benefit someone; pay a friendly call **Ch1** 3836 viset; 6768 visite; **Ch2** 64 visitte; 2022, 5086 visite; **HS** 4392 vysyte

vitaile n. [AF] food, provisions **Ch1** 737, 1064, 4558, 5315 vitaille; 1220, 1421, 1535, 2151, 3623 vitaile; **Ch2** 3778, 3972, 4086, 6993, 7131 vitaile; **HS** 10563 vytayle

vitailled v. [from AF vitaile, n.] to provide a food supply **Ch1** 449 vouted (?error) P vitailled L

voice n. [AF voice, OF vois] opinion, reputation; the words said; the one who speaks; singing in unison **Ch1** 14394, 15396 voyce P voys L; 14454 voice; 15814 voyce; 15847 voyce P vois L; **Ch2** 303, 3526, 4358, 5122, 5756 voice; **HS** 1925, 8224, 11024 voys; 7492 voyce

voide n./adj. [see tome, adj.] [AF] vacant; an empty vessel **Ch2** 4761, 7447 voide; **HS** 5180 auoyde vessel *O* a vayle; 7861 a voyde vessel *O* & voydyde; 7863 voyde *O* voydyde; 7868 a vessel voyde

voide v. [AF voider] to empty, rid, make void; depart, remove from; expel **Ch1** 5299 void P voyde L; 13930 voide; **Ch2** 233, 5962 voide; 962, 5241 voided; 8095 woyde

voydes n. [AF voider] a piece of armour **Ch1** 9880L voydes (om. P)

voket n. [AF aduocat (MP)] an advocate, lawyer **HS** 5404 voket

vouch, vouchsaue v. [from OF voucher] to warrant, grant, permit; to swear or allege; assert **Ch1** 694, 6346 vouch it saue P vouche hit saue L; 1266 vouched on þam saue; 488 vouchsaue P vouche hit saue L; 2359 vouched saue; 5461 vouch hir saue P vouche hure saue L; 5611 vouched non saue P vouched nought saue L; 9271 vouch it saue P vouche saue L; **Ch2** 6289 vouches it saue; 6484, 6864 vouched saue; **HS** 6347 vouchede hit saufe

vouted v. [see vitailled, v.]

vow n. [see auowe, n.] [AF vu, vou] solemn promise, vow **Ch1** 4668 vowe; **Ch2** 3959, 4259 vow; 4615, 7069, 7265, 8327 vowe; **HS** 2795, 2812, 2848, 2888, 2901 vow

vowe v. [see auowe, v.] [AF vouer (MP)] admit, claim; acknowledge; to promise, swear **Ch2** 4470, 4529 vowe; **HS** 2804, 2807, 3424 vowe; 2825 vowede

vrle v. [OF ourler, from ourle, urle] to provide with a border or trim **Ch1** 12143, 12152 vrle

W

wage n. [AF] a pledge, security; payment for services **Ch1** 7561, 13805 wages; **Ch2** 4043, 7225, 7803 wages; 3400, 7805 wage; **HS** 2396 auauntage *C* wage

wage v. [OF wagier] to employ for wages **Ch1**

3144 hired P waged L

waggyd v. [OE wagian] moved the head **HS** 2291 meuede *C* waggyd *DH* mevyd

way, weye n. [OE weg] road, path; method of proceeding **Ch1** 2024, 3563, 5472, 6946 way; 6737 way P wey L; 4984 waye; 1170, 2706, 3318 wey; 983 weye; 6701 away P weye L; 1728, 3654 waie; 1100, 1254, 2574, 4963, 6395 weie; 62, 190, 2200, 2865 ways; 6673 ways P weis L; 7082, 11916 wais; 3733 wais P weys L; 1364, 5193 oþerweis; 4882 oþerwais; **Ch2** 337, 3816, 5876, 7513, 8244 way; 2775, 8286 wey; 3367, 6626, 6857 weye; 1119, 4022, 5821, 6382, 7409 weie; 5005 ways; 3014 wayes; 3872, 4348, 4611 wais; 6302, 7870 weis; 6749, 7255, 7923, 8293 weys; 1150 oþer waies; **HS** 1797, 5582, 5698 way; 522, 1212, 2489, 2893, 12009 wey; 8460, 11308, 11324 weye; 4655 weyys; 7124, 12400 weys; 2640, 9472 ouþer weys

wayers n. [AF wayour] a horse pond **Ch1** 10966L wayers (om. P)

wayfarand, weyferyng ppl./adj. [OE wegferende] pertaining to a journey **Ch1** 3631 wayfarand; **HS** 10518 weyferyng

◆ **waile** n. [see weld, wold, n.] [from OE weald, n.] being in someone's power or control **Ch1** 5247 waile

wayn n. (1) [OE wæȝn] a wagon; large open cart **Ch1** 6739 wayn

wayn n. (2) [OF wain] profit, advantage; booty, possessions gained by conquest **Ch1** 1479, 1853, 2205, 5858 wayne; 13940 wanes; **Ch2** 3085, 6200, 6840, 7240 wayn; 130 wanes

waise [OE wase] ooze; mire, slime **Ch2** 1735 waise P wose L

wait, wate, weyte v. (1) [OF waitier] lie in wait; keep watch **Ch1** 1072, 1232 wate P wait L; 2718 wate (?error) P what L; 1493 witt P waite L; 3325, 8136, 8318 waite; 5029 waite P wachem L; 8460 waited P wayted L; 2971 waited; 6705 waitand; **Ch2** 2292, 3936, 4068 waite; 2936 waited; **HS** 825, 2159, 5100, 5986, 6612 weyte; 3802, 6012 weytede; 12439 weytyng

waite v. (2) [ON veita] be cruel to, plot against; ensnare **Ch1** 1230 wate; 6655 waite; 7020 waite P wayte L; **HS** 4190 weytede; 5989 weyte

wake, woke, wakned v. (1) [OE wacnan] awaken; rouse, incite **Ch1** 4324 waken P awake L; 14908 woke P awoke L; 1159 wakand; 11338 wakand P wakynge L; 11340 wakned; **Ch2** 1747 wakand P wakant L; 2959 waken; 2936, 7405, 7793 woke; **HS** 5830, 7755, 12551 wake; 1567 wakyd; 8045, 8062 woke; 427, 2230, 7840 wakyng

wake v. (2) [OE wacian, wæcnan, wok] to remain awake, be kept awake; keep watch; to be imprisoned; to cause woe **Ch1** 8460, 9077, 9774, 15237 waken; 14030 wake; 8180 wakin P wake L; 14006 woke; 7175, 8444 wakned; **Ch2** 2849, 3462, 4456, 5016, 6620 waken; 3964 wake; 4243 woke; 6567 wakend; **HS** 8036, 8037 wake; 4347 wakyng

wakest adj. [OE wac, ON veikr] weak; without strength **Ch1** 1810 waikest P waykest L; 14231 wakest P febleste L

wakres n. [see watches]

wald v. [see weld, v.]

wale n. [OE walu] the gunwale of a ship **Ch1** 11770 wale

walk v./ger. [OE walcan] to walk; walking **Ch1** 4688 walkand; **Ch2** 8150 walk; 8151 walkand; **HS** 2994 walkyd

walle, wogh, wowe, wawe n. [OE wall, wag, wah] rampart for defense; wall of a city or castle **Ch1** 3414, 4615, 5968, 6603, 6713 walle; 3536, 3562, 5415, 5953 walles; **Ch2** 1973, 3873, 4441, 7975 walle; 997, 1861, 1927, 2378 walles; 7972 wallis; 5158 groundwalle; **HS** 4731, 9293, 12181 wal; 8678 walles; 1144, 9386 wogh; 4276, 9410 wowe; 6546 [MS *O* interpolation, ll. 48, 57] wawe

walled v. [OE *weallian, from OE wall, n.] surround with a wall **Ch2** 7425 walled

wan adj. [OE wann] gloomy, sad **Ch1** 2962 wan

◆ **wanbodyes** n. [OE wanbodig] infidels **HS** 6161 wanbodyes

◆ **wandelard** [AF] a criminal, traitor **Ch2** 2791 wandelard P wanlard L

wane n. [see wone, n.] [ON van] property; dwelling **Ch1** 13940 wanes P wans L; **Ch2** 130 wanes

wane adj. [OE wana] lacking, absent **Ch1** 8215, 12140 wane

wane v. [OE wanian] decrease, dwindle **Ch1** 1249 wane P wanye L

wanhope n. [OE wanhope; cf. MLG, MDu wanhope] despair **HS** 4522, 5168, 8425, 10124, 12311 wanhope

wanisid v. [see warnisch, v.]

wanlace n. [AF wanelace] a trick, deceptive movements **Ch1** 12496 wanlaces; **HS** 4379, 12016 wanlace

want, wantyng n. [ON vant] something missing **Ch1** 1910 want; **HS** 1902 noght *D* wantyng

wapen n. [OE wæpen] weapon **Ch1** 5933 wapen; 1781 wapen P wepen L; 5060 wapyn; 13034 wapens P axes & daggares L; 14847 wapen P wepne L; **Ch2** 4661 wapen

wapentake n. [ON vapnatak, OE wæpengetæc] subdivision of some English shires **Ch2** 3560 wapentake P wapintake L

war n./v./adj. [see ware, n./v./adj., were, v. (1)]

warant n. [OF] a protector, defender; safeguard, defense **Ch1** 1468, 1503 warant; **Ch2** 1536L

warrant (om. P); 4546 warant
warant v. [OF warantir] to defend **Ch1** 5824 warant P warante L
warantie n. [AF] covenant requiring the giver to yield lands of equal value if the grantee is evicted from the original land **Ch2** 6361 warantie
warantyng ger. [from OF warantir, v.] security **HS** 12412 warantyng
warde n. (1) [OE weard] guarding; charge, care; a prison; prison guards; being in custody **Ch1** 4954 warde; 5028 stedes P wardes L; **Ch2** 3229, 7963 warde; 3492, 4756, 4893, 5017, 5253 ward; 1772 ware (?error) P warde L; 5249, 6447, 6725 wardes
warde n. (2) [OE weard] an army division **Ch2** 4685 turbe P warde L
wardeyn n. [OF wardein] guardian; governor of a prison **Ch1** 6140, 6150, 6156, 6611 wardeyns; 12620 wardeyns PL wardeins R; **Ch2** 1862, 6445, 6581, 7466, 7527 wardeyn; 1794, 4640, 5891, 7732, 7989 wardeyns; 3589 wardans; **HS** 8756 wardeynes; 1566, 1577 wardeyns *C* keperis
ware n. [OE waru] goods, merchandise **Ch1** 631, 652, 1303 ware; **Ch2** 3975 ware P whete L; **HS** 2940 chaffare *C* ware
ware, were v. [OE werian] [see were, v. (1), wary, v.]
ware, warn, were v. [OF warnir] to fortify, defend; protect **Ch1** 7182 were P war L; 7921, 8721 werne; 13349 ware; **Ch2** 886, 6480 warned
ware, ywar adj. [OE wær] aware; cautious, on guard **Ch1** 4149, 4804, 5162, 8122, 11256 war; 5103, 5397, 6063 ware; **Ch2** 153, 2222 war; 5612 ware; **HS** 2061, 8976, 9892 war; 2978, 5534, 6751, 8086 ware; 4201 ywar
wary, wery v. [OE wiergan, gewiergan] to curse; afflict with evils or calamities **Ch1** 203 waryed; 11956 waried P waryed L; **Ch2** 7787 wery; **HS** 1289 warye; 1244 kurse *C* banne *D* waryen; 1268 kursynge *D* waryed; 1290 waryyþ *C* a cursed *D* warye; 1288 waryyþ *C* bannyth *D* waryyth; 3763 curse *O* ware; 4872 cursed *O* weryd; 4874, 4895 cursede *O* werid; 5384 weryed; 5540 cursed be *O* weryd worth; 7972 kurse *O* wery
waryerys n. [from OE wiergan, v.] one who curses **HS** 1297 kurserys *H* cursers *D* waryerys
waryyng ger. [from OE wiergan, v.] cursing **HS** 1286 waryyng GLOSS B cursyng *F* cursing; 1293 waryyng; 1300 kursyng *D* waryyng; 1304 kursyngge *C* bannyng *D* waryyng
warison, warnisoun n. [OF] possessions; protection; giving possession; give a woman in marriage **Ch1** 1276L warisoun (om. P); 2196 warison P warisone L; 2339 warisoun; 2342 warison; 6451 warison P waryson L; **Ch2** 400 warisoune; 478, 1717, 4897, 7937 warisoun; 3495 warnisoun P warisoun L; **HS** 2190, 8376 warysun
warly adv. [OE wærlice] cautiously, prudently **Ch1** 8460 warly
warme adj. [OE wearm] warm **Ch1** 8902 warme; **Ch2** 808 warme; **HS** 5584, 9111 warme
warne, werne v. [OE warnian, warenian] forbid; refuse, prevent **Ch1** 2496, 6960 warne P werne L; 44 werne; 926 warned; 2440 warned P warnyng L; 14447 warned P wernde L; **Ch2** 1611 warne; 6508, 6514 warn; 886, 1172, 3953, 5814, 7161 warned; **HS** 228, 1021, 3195, 6069, 8978 warne
warnyng ger. [from OE warnian, v.] admonishment **Ch1** 8649 warnyng; **HS** 9786 warnyng
warnisch, warissed, warisched, warnised v. [AF warniss-, wariss-, stem of warnir, warir] save, protect, fortify; furnish with supplies and equipment **Ch1** 1023 warnised P warnysched L; 7797 warnyst P warnyscht L; 7938 warnissed; 8186, 8194 wanisid P warnyschet L; 9211 warnisced P warnisched L; 9540 warisced P warysched L; 10026 warissed P warisched L; 15187 warnysch P warnische L; **Ch2** 5997 wanissed; 7132 warnised
warnisoun n. [see warison, n.]
warnisours n. [see warnistour, n.]
warnissed, warnyst v. [see warnisch, v.]
warnistour, warnisour n. [AF warnisoun, warnesture] provisions, stores; a garrison **Ch1** 7025 warnisours P garnysons L; **Ch2** 3495 warnisoun P warisoun L; 4482 warnistour P socour L
warp v. [OE weorpan] cast, throw, fling **Ch1** 15161 warp; **HS** 7519 wrappe
wars, wers, worse n./adj. [OE wyrsa] more reprehensible; more harmful or grievous; more difficult **Ch1** 2472, 6653 wers; 2426 wers P wors L; 8581 wers P wirse L; 5853 wers P worse L; 10109, 15619 wars P worse L; **Ch2** 412 wers; **HS** 2298, 2832, 8397, 11009 werse; 1140, 6812, 6814 wers; 1220, 5169 werst; 7369, 7449 werste
was, were, ware v. [OE wæs, wæron, wære] forms of the verb: to be; was, had been, were; would be, should be, might be **Ch1** 26, 1539, 2385, 3593 was; 12184 wasse; 288 are P wore L; 693 was P were L; 17, 1205, 2006, 3283 were; 330, 2820, 5423, 6460, 11588 ware; 10810 waren; **Ch2** 5800, 7846 wasse; 3904 waren; 643, 2309, 7188 war; 110, 1772, 5324, 7571, 8237 ware; 7043, 7276, 7432 wer; **HS** 69 was; 314, 1406 were; 537 wore; 6138 ware
wassail n./v. [ON ves heill, OE wes hal] saluta-

tion in response to a toast: drink to your health **Ch1** 7457, 7471 wassaille P wassayl L; 7470 wosseille P wassail L; 7473 wosseille; 7481, 7483, 7484, 7486 wassaille P wassail L; 7488 wassailed; **HS** 6546 [MS *O* interpolation] (l. 33) vessayle, (l. 77) wessaylle

wasshe v. [OE wæscan, wascan] to wash; fig.: baptism **Ch1** 8699 wesch; **HS** 9516, 9552, 10332, 11044 wasshe; 9554 baptysed *O* weschyn; 10352 wysshe *F* wesschede *O* weschede *SV* wusch; 11578 wyssh

wasshele n. [from OE wæscan, v.] a bath; a vessel for washing **HS** 11041 wasshele *O* wessell

wasshyng ger. [from OE wæscan, v.] washing **Ch1** 8701 wasshynges; **HS** 10330, 11040 wasshyng

waste n. [OF wast, waste] barren country; sin; useless talk **Ch1** 8261 waste P ways L; 3661 wildernes P wast L; 11112 waste P wast L; **Ch2** 5496 waste; **HS** 1884, 7263, 7462, 12398 waste; 9617 wast

waste adj. [from OF waste, n.] wild, uncultivated; vain, idle words **Ch1** 1316, 5607, 6879 wast; 1326, 8499, 9236 waste P wast L; 6879 wast P wasted L; 11877 waste; **Ch2** 1525, 7991 wast; 1949, 5496, 5766 waste; **HS** 1552, 1586, 1743, 3028, 11388 waste; 9668 wast

waste v. [AF waster] devastate; to ravage, ruin **Ch1** 2988, 3728, 4846, 7022 waste; 1318, 2693, 5725, 5844, 6506 wasted; 2839, 7808 wastid P wasted L; **Ch2** 119, 2011, 7842 waste; 207, 1829, 2763, 7623, 7858 wasted; 1104 wastis; 1110, 7820, 7859 wastid; **HS** 1031 wastyþ; 10896 wasteþ

wasteyn, wasten n. [AF wastine (MP)] desert, wilderness; barren country **Ch1** 14091 wasten; **Ch2** 1869 wasteyn; **HS** 1764, 6114, 7731 wasteyn; 1807 wasteyn *C* wast place

watches, wakres n. [OE wæcce] company of watchmen, guards **Ch2** 4513 watches; 4640 wacres P wakres L

wate v. [see wite, v. (1)]

water, watres n. [OE wæter] river, pool **Ch1** 751, 1287, 3055, 5233, 6478 water; 1175, 3062, 6341 wateres; 1889 waters; 10054 watres; **Ch2** 291, 2975, 4650, 6436, 7170 water; 5360 watere; 6829 watres; **HS** 826, 1256, 1386 watyr; 9900 watres; 11053 water

waþe n. [ON veiðr] the right to hunt game, booty **Ch1** 10188 waþe; **Ch2** 7112 waþe

wawe n. [see walle, wogh, wowe, n.]

wawes n. [OE wæȝ, ON vagr] waves **Ch1** 2945, 6475, 10175, 10179 wawes

wax, wex v. [OE weaxan, wexan] grow, become; increase in number; ppl.: grown up, adult **Ch1** 1249 waxe; 881, 2536, 2676 waxen; 7224 waxand P waxynge L; 7231 waxen P wexen L; 7233 waxen P woxen L; 833, 1882, 3557, 6032, 13381 wex; 3665, 5795 wex P wax L; 6680, 6693 waxes; 12903 waxes P wexeþ L; **Ch2** 347, 2652, 3202, 6073, 8104 wex; 2443 wex P waxed L; 5769, 6819 wax; 1613 waxen P wexen L; 2274, 6078 waxen; **HS** 707, 1743, 2256, 9229 wax; 3942 wexe; 4129 waxe; 4518, 4852 wexyþ; 7997, 8048 woxe; 1117 wexyn *C* yrken *D* orkyn; 2493 waxe *D* wexyn

waxdam n. [cp. OE weaxan, v.] maturity **Ch1** 6445 waxdam P þryuen L

wed, wedde n. [OE wedd] pledge, security for payment **Ch1** 8290 wed; **Ch2** 5950 wed; 1549 awed (?v.) P wed L; **HS** 2389 wedde

wed, wedde v. [OE weddian] engage, pledge, wager to do; marry **Ch1** 766, 2018 wed; 2333, 2354, 5486, 6089 wedde; 11540 wed sette; 783, 2058, 2132, 5500 wedded; 372, 1974, 4016 weddid; **Ch2** 1717, 2599, 3996, 7499 wed; 1721, 5697, 6103 wedde; 180, 1084, 2699, 5047, 8116 wedded; 382, 531, 2073, 3427, 5203 weddid; **HS** 1703 wed; 438 weddyde; 1129, 7360, 11178 wedded; 1658 weddede; 2175, 2973 weddyd; 11174 wedden; 11217 weddeþ; 1664, 1683, 8391 wedde; 1695 wede

weddyng ger./n. [from OE weddian, v.] wedding **Ch1** 1296 weddynge; 2900 weddyng; **Ch2** 2135, 2548, 2593, 4000, 7490 weddyng; 3995 fest P weddyng L; **HS** 1629, 1713, 7767, 11220 weddyng

wede n. [OE wæd] clothing, apparel **Ch1** 15645 wede; **HS** 2343, 6855, 6871 wede

wede adj. [see wode, adj.]

weder n. [OE weder] weather **Ch1** 11799 wedir; 10262 wedir P weder L; **Ch2** 4189 weder

wedlaike, wedlok n. [OE wedlac] wedlock; the marriage vow **Ch2** 6132 wedlaike; **HS** 1627 wedlok; 1635, 1833, 1978, 8986, 11209 wedlak

wehere n. [see were, weyr, werre, n.]

wey, weie n. [see way, n.]

weyghte n. [OE (ge)wiht] measurement by weighing **HS** 9471 weyghte

weyue v. (1) [AF weyver] abandon, forsake; deprive, outlaw; relinquish **Ch1** 1726, 2464, 6972, 10029, 13580 weyue; **Ch2** 6500 weyued; **HS** 235 weyue *D* forsake; 2591, 2649 weyue GLOSS B fle; 6599 weyue GLOSS BH forsake; 8328 weyue GLOSS H forsake; 10086 weyue *S* leve *V* weyue

weyue v. (2) [ON veifa] wave; stray, wander, waver **Ch2** 3938, 5836 weyued; **HS** 4846, 10299, 10841 weyue

weke, wouke n. [see woke, n.]

wel, weyl adj./adv. [OE wel] good, happy, plain; much, very; fully; quite correctly; bravely **Ch1** 196, 1243, 3377, 6088, 7185 wele; 4655, 6045 wel; 1376 welle; 1793, 8831, 11640 wele P wel L; **Ch2** 494, 2959, 5838, 6167, 8350 wele; 1993, 2902, 2955, 3235, 3804 welle; 7018 wel; 4742 welnere; **HS** 40, 1140, 9311, 10633, 12021 weyl; 7646 weel; 9414 well; 7233, 12177 wele; 10910 wel; 456 weyl *C* wyll; 2000 ryght *C* wol *D* ful

welcom, wolkomyng n. [OE wilcuma] assurance of welcome; greeting **Ch1** 689, 3160 welcom; **Ch2** 4770, 5450 welcom; **HS** 2858 wolkomyng

welcomed v. [OE wilcumian] to greet a visitor **Ch1** 15071 welcomed

weld, wold n. [OE weald, geweald] command, control, possession **Ch1** 3187, 5070 wolde P wold L; **Ch2** 3143 wold; 3972 weld

weld, welte v. [OE wealdan, wieldan] to rule, govern, command; control, possess **Ch1** 646, 3116, 4100, 7238, 15368 welde; 3741 weld; 6347 weld P welde L; 6359 weld P weldit L; 7942, 15702 welte P welt L; 11778 weldes; **Ch2** 467 weldid; 844, 848, 4661 weld; 182, 908, 1832, 4610 welde; **HS** 1094, 1164, 6440 welde; 6460 wald; 9899 weldes; 9427 weldande

wele n. [OE wela] wealth, well-being **Ch1** 673, 1409, 3485, 5047, 6584 wele; **Ch2** 6926, 7069, 8149 wele; **HS** 2056, 3265, 5088, 6442 wele

◆ **wele** v. [ON velja] to choose, pick out, cull **Ch1** 7236 wele; 2703 weled P colede L

weleawey, weylaway interjection [cognate with OE wa la wa] woe, "alas" **HS** 2374 weylaway; 11222, 11230 weleawey

wele fare, weyl fare n. [OE wel + faru; cf. ON velferð] well-being, welfare **Ch2** 5150 wele fare; **HS** 1715, 3920 weyl fare

welle n. [OE wella] a well; source **Ch1** 8636, 14602 welle; **HS** 2262, 11313 welle

welle v. [OE wellan, wiellan] to boil, seethe, bubble **HS** 6580 wellyng; 11125 welleþ; 10214 burble *O* popyll; *SV* welleden

welth n. [OE wel, welaþ] wealth, riches; ?bliss **Ch1** 2443 welth; 3139 weth (error) P welþe L; **Ch2** 182 welth; **HS** 1410, 6440 welþe

wem n. [OE wamm, wam] injury; blemish; stain of sin **Ch2** 1884 wem; **HS** 3113, 7449, 10772 wem

wemles adj. [from OE wamm, n.] spotless **Ch1** 7792 wemles

wenche n. [see tharne, n.]

wend, went v. [see ȝede] [OE wendan] turn, change; overcome; depart, go **Ch1** 660, 1724, 4423, 6131, 8238 wende; 1473, 3046, 4155, 5505, 6614 wend; 6311, 9820 wend P wende L; 312, 3853, 5344, 7693, 8083 went; 851, 2140 wente; 4846 wendes; 1525 ȝede P wenten L; 1767 wonde; **Ch2** 181, 2007, 3294, 4608, 7785 wende; 1238 wende P leynde L; 63, 2144, 3632, 4828, 5560 wend; 3600 wendis; 2212, 3112, 4632, 4809, 4939 wendes; 145, 3029, 4800, 6814, 8155 went; 7292 wendand; **HS** 124, 3047, 9086, 12062, 12621 wende; 220, 1103, 4334, 8193, 12273 went; 1783, 6772, 7013, 12523, 12625 wente; 4611 wendyþ *O* comys

wendyng ger. [from OE wendan, v.] a change or turn; journey **Ch1** 4596, 11610 wendyng; **Ch2** 3038, 5075, 5703, 6291, 7469 wendyng

wene, wend, went v. [OE wenan] suppose, expect; think, believe; intend, hope, wish **Ch1** 1243, 3681, 5524, 6786 wene; 13238 wene P were (error) L; 1019, 2428, 4575, 4954, 5310 wend; 986, 4891, 6469, 9343 wende; 6918 wend P wende L; 7226 wend P byþought L; 5261L wend (P differs); 8145 wote P wenst L; **Ch2** 126, 1145, 5037, 6453, 8117 wene; 1520, 2765, 4714, 5833, 8042 wend; 971, 1071, 5708, 7426, 7743 wende; 1138 wend P wente L; 4062, 5868 wenes; **HS** 625, 4349, 9405, 9528 wene; 1380, 2535, 10748, 10604 wende; 2144 wenyþ; 11821 wenest; 12305 weneþ; 651 wene *C* leue; 9750 wyl wene *O* sall thynk

wening ger. [from OE wenan, v.] thinking **Ch1** 7317 wening

went n. [from OE wendan, v.] course of action, contrivance **Ch2** 1535, 1939 went; **HS** 529 went; 567 went (v.) *C* went

wepe n. [OE wop] weeping **HS** 5723 wepe

wepe v. [OE wepan, weop] to weep, cry out **Ch1** 2900 wepe P wepede L; 6699 wepe P wep L; 11952 wepes; 14904 wepte; **Ch2** 691 wepe P wep L; 3439 wept; 1969 wepte; 2359 lept P wepte L; 4360 wepand; **HS** 1568, 1771, 2281 wepe; 5732 wepest; 9166 wepte; 10970, 11573 wepyng

wepyng ger. [from OE wepan, v.] weeping **HS** 2882 wepynge; 2521 wepyng *O* grett

werche, wrouht v. [see wirk, v.]

werd n. [see werld]

were, wehere, weyr n. [OE werre; OF guere, were, weire] danger, peril; confusion, turmoil; war **Ch1** 824 were P wer L; 437, 4542, 6295, 9255, 10642 were; 2888, 6511, 11838, 13791, 15376 werre; 435, 2790, 5446, 7054, 10335 were P werre L; 2120 wehere P wer L; **Ch2** 72 wehere P wer L; 433 were P wher L; 6861 were; 467, 2364, 3445, 5781, 8218 werre; 2028, 4786, 5597, 7461, 7798 wehere; **HS** 462 weyr; 5678, 9529, 10775 were; 2197, 10578 werre; 4988 were GLOSS B bateyle; 8098 were GLOSS H dysese; 8526 a wer *O* twyrathe

were, ware v. (1) [OE werian] defend, guard, protect; spend, employ **Ch1** 1766, 4272, 9189, 10292 were; **Ch2** 1057, 2093, 3456, 5260, 6866 were; 1087 ware; **HS** 9159, 11966 were; 5798, 7679 ware; 11982 wereþ; 1317, 4080, 4217 were GLOSS BH kepe; 3672 were GLOSS BHW saue; 11437 weres GLOSS BH kepeþ; 9821 defendeþ *O* weres

were, werre v. (2) [from OE werre, n.] to make war, to fight **Ch1** 4739 were; 3309 were P werren L; 6302, 9855, 10336 wered; 6038, 5703 wered P werreyed L; 5708 werid P werreyed L; 11559 werre; **Ch2** 2741, 5783, 6332, 6807, 7217 werre; 469, 513, 5724, 6353, 7187 werred; 6743 werand; 7184 werrand; **HS** 3111, 4972 werre; 5644 bewreyyng *O* wereand

were v. (3) [OE werian] to wear **Ch1** 15125 were; **HS** 2405, 5720 were; 6638 werede

wery v. [see wary, v.]

wery adj. [OE werig] weary, tired of **Ch1** 3737, 4496 weri P wery L; 4421, 5547, 9083 wery; 4496, 15224 weri; 13416 werie P wery L; 14571, 15133 werie; **Ch2** 5352, 7787 wery

werydnes n. [from OE wiergan, v.] cursedness **HS** 7228 kursednes *O* werydnes

werynes n. [OE werignes] fatigue, weariness **HS** 9148 werynes

werke n. [OE weorc] deed, work; business; a building **Ch1** 203 werke; 5674, 15935 werk; 7991 werke P werk L; **Ch2** 475, 1893, 2258 werkes; 2000 werke; 5225 werk; **HS** 831 werkys; 2379, 4012, 6312, 8635, 10768 werk

werk, werche v. [see wirk, v.]

werkmen n. [OE weorcmann, ON verkmaðr] workers **Ch1** 6510 werkmen

werld, world, werd, wold n./adj. [OE weorold, worold] of the world; the world **Ch1** 1390 werlde; 5276 werld; 222, 3270, 4132 werld P werd L; 4235 wordes; 4156 werldis; 719, 2296, 5041, 11232, 11236 world; 7224 werld P werde L; 11096 werldes P wordles L; 15331 world P werd L; 5222L werld (om. P); 11093L werd (om. P); **Ch2** 2479, 4258, 6267, 6524 werld; 4261 worldes; 569, 3532, 6415, 8301, 8313 world; 4717 world P wordle L; **HS** 1351 wrld; 2764, 8270 werld; 9757 werldes; 3116, 4139, 10975 wrldly; 450 wrlde *C* warde *D* word *FH* world; 599, 654 wrld *D* word; 650 wrld *C* warde *D* world; 829 wrld *C* warde *DH* word *F* world; 1100 wrldys *C* wardis *D* worldys; 1510 wrldys pay *C* wardis prey *D* wordes pray; 2386 wrld *C* werde *D* word; 2387 wrld *C* ward *D* word *FH* world; 3412 wrdys of wrshyppe *O* þe werldys wyrschype; 4196 werld *O* welde; 6069 wrd *F* world *H* wurde; 7390 þe wrld *O* welde; 10248 wrly *F* worldli *HV* worldly *O* werlde

werre n. [see were, n.]

werre v. [see were, v. (2)]

werre adj. [ON verri] phrase: much worse **HS** 474 weyl werre *C* is warre *D* þe werre

werreour n. [OF werreieor, werrieur] a soldier **Ch1** 2701, 6013, 6849 werreour; 2798 werreoures; 3880 wereours; **Ch2** 599, 4105, 4318 werreoure; 4105, 4374, 5769 werreour

werryng ger. [from OE werre, v. (2)] warfare **Ch2** 393, 2932, 6390, 6458, 7814 werryng

wers adj./n. [see wars, worse]

west adj./adv./n. [OE west, adv.] westerly direction; to the west of; western region or country **Ch1** 37, 1379, 3888, 5741, 6598 west; 4148, 4155 weste; **Ch2** 364, 1046, 4076, 7718, 7850 west; **HS** 829, 10740 west

westreis n. [from OE westerne] men from the west **Ch2** 297 westreis

wete adj. [OE wæt] damp, liquid **Ch1** 9808, 14906 wete

wete v. [see wite, wate, v.]

wete v. [OE wætan] to moisten; to flood with water **Ch1** 10176 wete; 10179 wetes; **HS** 6671 wete

wettenes n. [from OE wæt, adj.] moisture; being damp **Ch1** 10188 wettenes P wetynge L

wethere n. [OE weðer] a castrated ram **Ch1** 11248 wethere

wex v. [see wax, v.]

what, qwat interrog. adj./adv./pron. [OE hwæt] what, whatever; how, why, when **Ch1** 7336, 7376 qwat; 837, 1573, 3733, 7054, 9324 what; 2718 wate (error) P what L; **Ch2** 165, 2094, 3417, 6456, 8356 what; **HS** 20, 206, 4886, 7846, 10527 what; 442 wat

whele n. [OE hweol] wheel **Ch1** 5046 whele; **HS** 3275, 3277 wheyl

whelp n. [OE hwelp] whelp, pup; fig.: son of the devil **Ch2** 6815 whelp; **HS** 7242 whelpe *O* hounde

when, whan, qwen adv. [OE hwanne, hwænne] what time; whenever **Ch1** 1377, 2698, 3673, 5908 when; 637 when P whan L; 369, 2443, 4712, 5930, 7180 whan; 2971 whenne; 3851 qwen; **Ch2** 3256, 3984, 5973, 7743, 8329 whan; 1151, 1431 whan P when L; **HS** 118, 289 wan; 364 whan; 458, 3514 whanne; 1206 when

where, whar adv. [OE hwær, hwar] what place; combinations **Ch1** 5115 wher; 970, 2510, 3937, 6674, 6756 where; 7910, 11522, 12164 whare; 7332 qwere P wher L; 12546 whore P whar L; 14435 whore; 11534 wharto; 48 where of; 2821 wherfor; 2948, 5608 aywhere; 3265 ay whore; 3006 ai whore; 1206 elleswhere; 5298 where so euer; **Ch2** 437 þer wher; 705, 3863, 5183, 8011, 8315 where; 1937, 4664 wherefor; 4829, 4949, 6258 wherfore; 1414, 2240, 4846, 5382, 5995 wherfor; 1155 wharfor; 3919, 4787 wherto; 433 were P wher L; 1930 aywhare; **HS** 119 whar; 1383, 9408 where; 5784 wher; 7494, 8067 whore; 1825, 1872, 2474, 10581 wharfore; 3008 wharyn; 463 wharof; 9466 wharwyþ; 4998 wharon; 8153 whereso; 4501 wharto *O* qwarto; 2766 wherþurgh *C* þere of *D* þer þorw

whete n. [OE hwæte] wheat, grain **Ch2** 3800, 4328 whete; 3975 ware P whete L; **HS** 10099, 10115, 10117, 10131 whete

wheþen adv. [ON hvaðan] whence **Ch1** 11239 whiþen P wheþen L; 15179 wheþen; **Ch2** 5701 wheþen; **HS** 10344 whenne *O* qwyne *SV* wheþen

wheþer, wheþir, whedir pron./adv./conj. [OE hwæþer] whether, if; which is which **Ch1** 1193, 5085 wheþer; 1494, 1791 wheþir; 2287 wheþire; 4016, 5450, 4883, 4915 whedire; 696, 11826 whedire P wheþer L; 7982, 8098, 11369, 11824, 12720 whedir; 8473, 13554, 15182 whedir P wheþer L; **Ch2** 3300, 7678 whedir; 2131 whedir P wheþer L; 7092 whedere; 3449 wheþer ys wheþer; **HS** 1486, 2483, 3022, 6413, 10022 wheþer; 226 wheþyr; 7257 wheyþer; 617 wheþer *C* qweyther *D* qweche; 3449 wheþer ys wheþer *O* wheþer es qweþer; 12202 whyder *O* qweþer

whette v. [OE hwettan, ON hvetja] fig.: to incite, urge on **Ch1** 2800L whette (P differs)

why interrogative adv. [OE hwi] reason why, cause **Ch1** 2604, 3542, 6787 why; 2821, 3628, 4248, 5232, 11951 whi; **Ch2** 7133, 7201, 7529 whi; **HS** 543, 1825, 4760, 7308, 10774 why

which interrog. pron./adj. [see whilk] [OE hwilc, hwelc] which; which time **Ch1** 715 þat P which L; 722 þer P whiche L; 4965, 13374 whilk P whiche L; **HS** 1000, 10172, 10202, 12184 whyche; 5203, 8418, 9756 whych; 1674, 2767, 3977, 4094 wheche

whider, whiderward adv. [OE hwider] to what place, whither **Ch1** 2876, 5393, 15180 whider; 9360 whider; 2462, 6917, 12546 whidere; 3624, 9329 whidire; 12514 whidire P whiderward L; 14078 widirward P whiderward L; **Ch2** 5182 whider; 6204, 7122, 8009 whidere; 4064 whiderward; **HS** 5818, 5820, 5918, 6143, 6186 whyderward; 12202 whyder *O* qweþer

while n. [see to while] [OE hwil] time; a portion of time **Ch1** 2632, 2879, 3966, 6907 while; 3306 while P þrowe L; **Ch2** 168 while P whilom L; 60, 4495, 5534, 6270, 7244 while; 1995 non seel P no while L; **HS** 1745, 4542, 7101, 11284, 12493 whyle; 12570 whyle GLOSS BH tyme

while, whiles conj./adv. [OE hwile] sometimes, formerly; meanwhile; once; whilst **Ch1** 4272, 5197 tille P while L; 2047 tille P whil L; 290, 4050 whils; 11228 whils P þe whiles L; 10040 whiles P whyles L; 13544 to whils P while L; **Ch2** 1020 tille P whiles L; 3824 a wiles P sone L; 3669, 5482, 6743, 7459, 8146 while; **HS** 6239 whyle; 4237, 5315, 7242, 8808, 8998 whyl; 3388, 6237, 6296, 10883 whyles; 1175, 1706, 1708 whylys

whilk pron./adj. [OE hwilc] which, who **Ch1** 17, 1212, 2278, 4326, 6939 whilk; **Ch2** 525, 1246, 4366, 5757, 8273 whilk

whilom adv. [see vmwhile] [OE hwilum] once, at times; at that time; formerly **Ch1** 1342, 3543, 4809, 6808, 14631 whilom; **Ch2** 96, 1287, 2460, 6254, 8221 whilom; 6589 wholom; **HS** 6637, 7736 sumtyme *O* whylome; 12171 ones *O* qwylome

white adj. [OE hwit] white **Ch1** 151 whyte; 1357, 2075 white; **Ch2** 8169 white; **HS** 3505, 7285, 10143 whyte; 3222 whytter; 284 flyght *D* qwhyȝt

wicche n. [see wik, n.] [OE wicce] a witch **Ch1** 499 wicches; **HS** 499, 521, 525, 1711 wycche; 2649, 8152 wycches

wychecrafte n. [OE wiccecræft] magic arts, supernatural power **Ch1** 14387 wychecrafte P wichecraft L; 14388L wychecraft (om. P); **HS** 479, 515, 8145, 8279, 10630 wycchecraft; 342 wycchecraftys *C* wychecaste; 1712 wycchecraft *C* wycchecaste

wyched v. [OE wiccian] bewitched **HS** 503 sygaldryd *C* wyched

wide adj./adv. [OE] spacious; far and wide **Ch1** 1617 wyde; 3771L wyde (P differs); 3083 wyde spred; 4584 wide; **Ch2** 2191, 4535, 5589 wide; **HS** 2994, 3430 wyde

widouhed n. [OE widewanhod] being a widow **Ch1** 2529 widouhed P wydewehod L

widow n. [OE widewe] a bereaved wife **Ch1** 8500 widow

wife, wyff, wyue n. [OE wif] a married woman **Ch1** 787, 2115, 2936, 3676 wyfe; 2864, 3205, 5243, 6890, 11878 wife; 368, 778, 2897, 3960, 4675 wyf; 208, 214, 6433 wyfes; 2048, 2870, 3121, 6232, 6287 wyue; 1209, 2166 wyues; **Ch2** 63, 1698, 4083, 5646, 7773 wife; 1775, 3040, 5146, 7343, 8112 wif; 563, 1192 wifes; **HS** 1128, 1135, 1662, 1728, 1731 wyff; 7361 wyf; 9886 wyue; 1287, 1740 wyuys; 7424 wyffes

wiffin adj. [?OE wefan, v.] ?pertaining to a devious person or plotter **Ch2** 6716 wiffin

wyfles n. [OE wifel, ON vifr] spears **Ch1** 4345 staues P wyfles L

wight n. [OE wiht] creature; a person; thing; a moment **Ch1** 7737 wiht P wyght L; 7931 wight P wyght L; **HS** 3353, 8669, 12217 wyght; 2221 wyght *D* whyȝt

wight adj./adv. [ON vigt] strong, brave; swift **Ch1** 3475, 10476, 10649, 11762 wight P wyght L; 5913, 13235, 15284 wight; 4037, 5836, 10350 wyght; **Ch2** 322 wyght; 4722, 4953 wight; **HS** 4606, 4918 wyght

wightly adv. [from ON vigt, adj.] swiftly **Ch1** 9975 wightli P wightly L; **Ch2** 2863 wightly

wik n. [?OE wicce] evil, wikkedness **Ch1** 838 ille P wykke L; 12190 pikke P wyk L; **Ch2**

6588, 6705 wik; **HS** 2553 maystry *C* wyk; 2649 wycches *C* wythnes *D* wikke

wyk v. [OE wician] encamp; pitch a tent **Ch1** 12190 pikke P wyk L

wik adj./adv. [?OE wicce, wicca] wicked, evil **Ch1** 2426 wik P wycke L; 838 ille P wykke L; 3455 wikke P yuel L; 9858 wik P wyk L; **Ch2** 6990 wikke; 7137 wik; **HS** 4242, 5574, 6445, 11547 wyk; 7671 vyle *H* foule *O* wyke; 6546 [MS *O* interpolation, l. 69] wike

wikked adj. [?from OE wicce] wikked, evil **Ch1** 1230, 1232 wikked P wykked L; 3869, 6931, 15679 wikked; **Ch2** 826, 1920, 4808, 6902, 7829 wikked; **HS HS** 575, 714 wykkyd; 3611 wykkede; 9668, 12585 wykked; 1896 wykkyd *D* euyl; 2073 wykkyd *C* euyl; 3198 wykked *H* foule *O* fals; 12278 wydded (error) *H* wykked *O* wykkyde

wikked hals, wikhals n. [?from OE wicce] rogue, evil fellow **Ch2** 6464, 6529 wikhals; 7385 wikked hals; **HS** 6546 [MS *O* interpolation, l. 103] wykkyde hals

wikly, wykkedly adv. [?from OE wicce] perfidiously; with evil intent **Ch1** 2799 wikly P ful euele L; 6657 wikly P yuel L; 2554 wikkedly; 3795 wykkidli; **Ch2** 3040 wikly; 4414 wikkedly; 6244 wikkidly; **HS** 776, 6414 wykkedly; 1717, 2808, 3612 wykkydly; 1203 wykkedlyche *D* wikkydly; 3039 vnwrþyly *O* wykkydly; 11124 wykkedly *O* vylyly

wiknes, wikkednes, wykkydhede n. [?from OE wicce] iniquity, evil **Ch1** 6678 wikkednes; 14749 wikkidnes; 15605 wikkednesse; **Ch2** 607 wiknes P yuel L; 1613 wiknes P wikkednesse L; 612, 1916, 5141, 5196, 6506 wikkednes; 3159 wikkednsse; **HS** 612, 3727 wykkydnes; 773 wykkydhede; 6731 wykednes; 11350 wykkednes; 720 wykkydnesse *D* wikkyd hede

wilde adj./adv. [OE wilde] crazy; unruly, reckless, sinful **Ch1** 1039, 4481, 6883, 13252, 15955 wilde; 834, 2674 wylde; 11186 wyld; **Ch2** 1949, 3041, 4215, 6169, 8208 wilde; **HS** 714, 3806, 4176, 4852 wyld; 4848, 8337, 9871 wylde

wyldernes n. [OE wildeornes] wilderness, waste land **Ch1** 954, 3661 wildernes; **HS** 5005 wyldernes; 172 wyldyrnesse *C* waste place

wile n. [ON vel] trick, deceit; a plot **Ch1** 535 gyle P wyle L; 536 wyle P gyle L; 12565 wile P wyle L wil R; **Ch2** 2868, 4808, 5349 wile; 8064 wiles; **HS** 361 wylys

wylyeste adj. [from ON vel, n., OE wig] most tricky **HS** 3562 wylyeste

willand ger. [from OE willan, v.] consent; desire, wish **Ch1** 858, 8831 willand; **Ch2** 1451, 1937, 2725, 5588, 6167 willand; **HS** 4813, 6220 wylland

wille n. [OE willa] desire, pleasure; mind, disposition; intention **Ch1** 580, 2282, 4319, 6077, 7137 wille; 14914 wille P wyl L; **Ch2** 991, 3623, 5732, 5922, 6720 wille; **HS** 111, 7150, 10251, 11360, 12127 wyl; 248, 2126, 11366 wyll; 735 wylle

wille, wild, wold v. [OE willan, wolde; ON vilja, vilda] wish, intend; will to do **Ch1** 107, 2839, 4759, 7162, 9154 wild; 3714, 5337 wild P wold L; 2053, 3378, 3633, 5869, 6057 wild P wolde L; 4241 wild P wilt L; 11867 wold P wylde L; 820, 4195, 6169 wilde; 7038 wilt; 13091 wilt P wyld L; 2562, 3198, 15583 wilte; 201, 2415, 4187, 5982, 7021 wille; 5091 wille P schal L; 160, 2277, 4147, 4961, 5610 wald; 44 walde; 3032, 5175, 5516, 6641 wolde; 4551 wille P wyly L; 4809L wylned (P differs); 10574 wild P wold L; 11241 wildes P wyldes L; 11990 wild P wilde L; 12526 wille P wol L; 13219 wild . . . wold P wold . . . wolde L; 15850 ȝerned P wilned L; **Ch2** 153, 1032, 4371, 7439, 8355 wild; 18, 515, 2419 wild P wolde L; 6370 wild . . . wolden; 1550 wille P wolde L; 1040, 2832, 4012, 5578, 6785 wille; 164 wald P wolde L; 1514, 2195, 3297, 4172, 7242 wald; 6370 wolden; 5212, 5438, 5798 wild; 5526, 6651, 7927 wilde; 1794, 2230, 5764, 8279 wold; 1405 wild P wolde L; **HS** 11, 46, 11881 wyle; 3764 wylle; 4208 wyll; 121, 551, 3730, 3732 wylt; 16 welyn; 4787 welen; 206, 396, 545 wolde; 934, 2483, 4891 wlde; 6952 wold; 4840, 6397, 6935 wylde; 8034 wyld; 3025 wldest; 3421, 3938, 5292 wst; 7147 wyltow; 8440 wyltou; 2557 wyllyng *C* wyllandly

wille adj./adv. [ON villr] perplexed, uncertain **Ch1** 2951 wille; 11906 wille P wyl L

wymple n. [AF wimple (MP)] woman's headdress; a veil **HS** 3450 wymple; 3447 wymples

wynd n. [OE] stormy air; wind for sailing ships **Ch1** 1305, 3147, 4653, 6472, 11798 wynd; 2942, 4293, 4560 wynde; 15679 wyndes; **Ch2** 2348, 3631, 4233, 5573, 7400 wynde; 3661 wynd; **HS** 12523 wynd; 9900 wyndes

wyndas n. [AF windas] ship's windlass **Ch1** 11795 wyndas

wyndowe, wyndous n. [ON vindauga] window **Ch1** 4536 wyndous; **HS** 2235 wyndowe

wyne n. [OE win] wine **Ch1** 1356, 11076 wyne; **Ch2** 3968, 4155, 4687, 7902 wyne; 5700, 7132 wynes; **HS** 7227 wyn; 9979 wyne

wynke n. [from OE wincian, v.] a wink **HS** 9151 wynke

wynly adj. [OE wynlic] splendid, beautiful **HS** 1411 wynly wones GLOSS B sekyr dwellyngys *D* wurþi *F* worþi

wynne n. (1) [OE gewinn] profit **HS** 5552 wynne

wynne n. (2) [OE wynn, gewinn] joy, pleasure **Ch1** 6359, 14278 wyn P wynne L; 9482 wyn (v.) P wyn L; 15702, 15883 wynne; **Ch2** 5601,

5854 wynne

wynne, wan, wonne v. [OE winnan] conquer, capture; seize; make one's way, reach **Ch1** 13, 441, 3248, 4622, 6796 wan; 1186, 2933, 4662, 6064, 6660 won; 3096 wunnen; 4075, 6333, 6804, 10662, 12910 wonnen; 4444 won P wonnen L; 3658, 4145 wonen; 8343 cam P wan L; 443, 2036, 4839, 6197, 9056 wyn; 4154 wyne; 4156, 4472, 5148, 8222 wynne; 5057 wynes; 5059, 5067 wynnes; **Ch2** 485 wanne; 872, 3424, 4500, 7204, 8309 wan; 3496 won; 4166, 4763, 5593, 6363 wonne; 3539, 4126, 4737, 6309, 6833 wonnen; 994, 3742, 4299, 5326, 6297 wyn; 22, 3446, 4818, 6181, 7522 wynne; 1417, 2130, 2823, 4322 wynnes; 268 wyne P wynne L; **HS** 1107, 5051, 8288, 11004, 12080 wynne; 20 wynnys; 4244, 7350 wynnes; 2422, 5213, 10566 wan; 7720 wonne; 2937, 5944 wune; 7834, 9443, 9467 wunne; 6608 wynne *O* brynge

wynnyng ger. [from OE winnan, v.] booty; conquered land; benefit, profit **Ch1** 1873, 6365 winnyng; 1606 wynnyng; 6847 wynning; **Ch2** 4620, 6360, 6486, 7205, 7591 wynnyng; **HS** 2652, 5548, 6103, 9341 wynnyng

winter n. [OE] the winter; years **Ch1** 2110, 2658, 3550, 5234, 15109 wynter; 15274 wynter P ȝer L; 2165, 5556 wyntere; **Ch2** 396, 1015, 2759, 5784, 7865 wynter; 115 ȝere P wynter L; 259, 5581 wyntere; 2974, 5089, 5783 wynter tide; **HS** 72, 7821 wyntyr; 7793 wynter

wipped, wyppyng v. [?ON vippe] strike **Ch1** 8083 wipped P wyppyng L

wiri n. [?OE were = wergeld] ?money value of ransom [prob. invented for rime] **Ch2** 6988 wiri

wirk, werche, wrouht v. [OE wyrcan, worhte] build, create; make **Ch1** 3186 wirke; 5650, 14487 wirk; 4944 wirk P wyrke L; 1234, 2570, 4426, 6589, 15923 wrouht; 116, 746 wroght; 2072, 14216 wrouht P wrought L; 4254 wrouhtis; **Ch2** 656 wrouht P ywrought L; 1588, 2000, 3843, 6872, 8074 wirke; 827, 1597, 3562, 5140, 8350 wrouht; 6776 wrouhtis; **HS** 556, 9210, 11131, 12566 werche; 1884 werchyst; 4343 wyrk; 100, 496, 1347, 9160, 9174 wroght; 5450, 9170 wroghte; 29 wrouȝt

wirschip, worschip n. [OE weorðscipe, worðscipe] dignity, importance, rank; reverence, honor **Ch1** 2828, 3591, 4815, 5492 wirschip; 6997 wirschip P worschipe L; 7256L wyrschip (P differs); **Ch2** 4452 worschip; 6060 worship; 305, 2009, 4258 wirschip; 3543L worschupe (P differs); 4368 forgetilschip P envye of worschupe L; **HS** 3, 434, 908, 2942, 3470 wrshepe; 3412 wrshyppe; 10300 wrshype; 3178, 8695 wrshepe *O* honour

wirschip, worschip v. [from OE worðscipe, n.] honor, confer dignity on, show respect to **Ch1** 1400, 2510, 6997 wirschip; 757 worchipped; 1329, 1333 worschipped; 1390 wirsciped; 7260 wirschip P worschipe L; 7263 wirschip P wyrschipe L; 7269 worschip P worschipen L; 7274 worschip P worschipe L; **Ch2** 4048 wirschipid P worschuped L; 4050, 4921 wirschipped; 773 wirschiped; 4434, 8064 wirschip; **HS** 6, 4246 wrshepe; 1010, 10232 wrshype; 854 wrshepe *D* honoure; 1301 wrshepyþ *C* honowur *D* honouriþ; 8270 wrshyped *O* honerde; 9076 wrshepeþ *O* honors; 10015 wrshepe dede *O* honouryde *SV* honourede

wirschiply, worschipfully adv. [from OE worðscipe] respectfully, in an honorable manner **Ch1** 4102 wirschiply P worschipfoly L; 12142 curteisy P worschipfuly L; **Ch1** 2004 worschiply; **HS** 9905 wrshypfully

wisdom n. [OE] wise teaching; being wise **Ch1** 11, 557, 2469, 4486, 4787 wisdom; 514 wysdom; 585, 3905 wisdam; **Ch2** 4672 wisdom; 5189, 5810 wisdam; **HS** 1179, 4202, 9987 wysdom; 6529 wysdoms

wise n. [OE wise] way, manner, fashion; mode, custom, habit **Ch1** 4607, 5647, 6160, 7043, 10941 wise; 625, 1898, 2811, 4267, 5627 wyse; 5937 wise P gyse L; 6200 wise P wyse L; **Ch2** 1112 wyse; 1391, 2423, 4830, 6559, 7932 wise; **HS** 249, 4535, 6506, 9439, 11807 wyse; 8483 wyse *O* gatte

wise, wisse adj. [OE wis] having sound judgment; certain, sure **Ch1** 2350, 3678 wis; 470, 3087, 4135, 5162, 6134 wys; 2224 noble P wys L; 3783, 5913, 6105 wise; 17, 721, 1069 wyse; 586 wisere P wyser L; 5440 wisest; **Ch2** 177, 550, 2116, 2785 wis; 771, 3879, 5288, 6307, 7106 wys; 2652, 4153, 7699, 7775, 8316 wise; 4262 wisse; 6031, 7655 wisest; **HS** 418 wyse; 3041, 6005, 6533, 7196, 9892 wys; 4211 wyser; 8095 wysere

wise v. [OE wissian, wisian] guide, direct **Ch1** 10756 wise P wyse L; 11916 wised; 13166 wysed; **Ch2** 2525 wisse P wyse L; **HS** 1015, 4834, 6456 wysse; 9396 wys

wisely, wysly adv. [OE wislice] carefully, skillfully; certainly **Ch1** 1931, 10530 wisly; 3050, 3117, 5332 wisely; 3571 wysly; **Ch2** 3562 wisly; 5363 wisely; **HS** 457, 9681 wysly

wiseman, wysman n. [OE wis + man] wise man, sage **Ch1** 5255, 6628 wiseman; 6249 wisemen (error) P wysman L; **Ch2** 7366 wysemen; 7590 wisemen; **HS** 3716 wysman

wyt, witte n. [OE witt] knowledge; mind, memory; skill; meaning **Ch1** 113, 2442, 5207, 9268, 15929 witte; 10855 wittes; 972 witte P wyt L; **Ch2** 5615, 6775 witte; **HS** 1227, 2727, 4748, 8900, 11587 wyt

wyte n. [OE wite] sin **HS** 12394 wyte

wite, wate, wost, wote, wete v. (1) [OE witan] know, learn; discover, see **Ch1** 80, 110 wate; 146, 2604, 4792, 6674, 7015 wote; 429 wyten P witen L; 1613 witten; 6668 wittes; 11710 wit; 92, 664, 4204, 5450, 7058 witte; 5591, 7151, 15146 wite; 1470 wist P wyste L; 81, 2301, 4138, 7072, 10019 wist; 5011, 7908 wist P wystey L; 5094 wist P wyst L; 7064 wote P wost L; 1493 witt P waite L; 2047 wote P wost L; 3786 witand P louede L; 8288 wate P wot L; 12981 wate P wyte L; 14166 witen P wyten L; **Ch2** 3210 wit; 108 wote P wot L; 211, 4431 wiste; 1331, 2835, 6387, 7133, 8078 wote; 8270 wot; 288 wate; 240, 2366, 3353, 6915, 8117 witen; 5848 wyten; 148, 1453, 3256, 5155, 8144 wist; 1069, 3298, 4943, 7122, 8264 wite; 2061, 3295, 4656 witte; 4262 wost; **HS** 39, 134 wetyn; 463, 512, 1451, 9028, 12627 wete; 377, 6573, 7000, 7052 wyte; 1417, 1645 wytte; 88, 2802, 6579 wote; 403, 466 woot; 157, 2165, 4579, 11803 wost; 10292 wytes; 6358 weteþ; 3168, 3886, 10607, 12603 wyste; 445, 7818 wyst; 5961 wystest; 613 wetande; 1067 wetand; 2740 wetynge; 9349 wytyng; 10271 wytand; 39 wote *D* knowe; 1874 wote *C* knowyst *D* wost; 2953 wystyst *C* wyst *O* wyste

wite v. (2) [OE æt witan] blame, accuse, reproach **Ch1** 5146 wite; **Ch2** 2929 wited; **HS** 1900, 5988, 8643 wyte

witeword n. [OE witword] will, testament **Ch2** 3759 witeword P questword L; 3768 witworde P quethword L

withalle, wiþal adv. [OE mid alle] moreover; altogether **Ch1** 4446 with al; 6374 with alle; 2266 withalle; **Ch2** 1219, 2159, 2708, 3475, 3874 withalle; **HS** 2463 wyþ all; 4032, 9112, 9364, 9376 wyþ al; 10757 wyþ alle; 11097 wyþalle

wyþdrawe, widrouh v. [OE wiþ + dragan] retreat, flee a battle; refuse; recant, withhold **Ch1** 1659 withdrouh; 6049 drouh P wyþdrow L; 3218 widraw P wyþdraw L; 12014 widrouh P wyþdrow L; 12396 fleand P wyþdrawande L; **Ch2** 1898 withdrouh; 3500 widrouh P withdrow L; 4586, 6681 withdrawe; **HS** 1501, 2379 wyþdrowe; 2811 wyþdrow; 2437 wyþdraghst; 5336, 10880 wyþdraghþ; 777, 1533, 3601, 12105, 12498 wyþdrawe; 2431 wyþdraghst *C* wythholde; 2435 wyþholdyst *D* withdrawe

withhold v. [OE wiþ + haldan] hold back, keep **Ch1** 6656 with hold; **Ch2** 1253 withhald; **HS** 2435 wyþholdyst; 5349, 8603, 11722, 11827, 12631 wyþholde

within prep./adv. [OE wiþinnan] inside; in limits of **Ch1** 685, 1057, 2879, 4577, 7053 within; 656 within P wyþynne L; **Ch2** 459, 2380, 4488, 5630, 7967 within; 4551 withinne; **HS** 7049 wyþ yn; 326, 1818, 3198, 5941, 12611 wyþynne

withoute adv./conj./prep. [OE wiþutan] outside of, beyond; besides; lacking; except **Ch1** 324, 1202, 4224, 7156, 9303 withouten; 619, 1038, 3022, 6734 without; 642, 1354, 5537, 5956, 6715 withoute; 788, 1179 withoutten; 7271 withouten P wyþouten L; 13234 withouten P wiþoute L; **Ch2** 1315, 2656, 4369, 6752, 8066 withouten; 3710, 4536, 6880, 7057, 7965 without; 5089, 6602, 7483, 7971 withoute; **HS** 9 wythoutyn; 190 wyþoutyn; 1436, 1751, 3198, 12198, 12289 wyþoute; 7563, 12622 wyþouten

withsay, withsaid v. [OE wiðsæcga] renounce, contradict, deny; refuse, oppose **Ch1** 9181 withsaid P ne seyde L; 15782 withsay P wyþseye L; **Ch2** 149 withsaid P wyþseyde L; 236, 4458, 5988, 6555, 6560 withsaid; **HS** 9808 wyþseyd; 12304 wyþseyþ

withsette v. [OE wiþsettan] resist, oppose; beset, prevent **Ch1** 2893, 13524 withset P wyþsette L; 12983 withsette P wyþset L; 15212 withset P wyþset L; **Ch2** 4658, 8244 withsette

withsitte v. [OE wiþ + sittan] resist, contradict; hinder **Ch1** 8024 with site P wyþsyt L; 10158 with site P wyþsitte L; **Ch2** 7206 withsitte

wyþsperd v. [see sperre, sperd, v.] [from OE gesparrian] prevented **Ch1** 14982L wyþsperd (om. P)

withstand v. [OE wiþstondan] oppose, stand aside; stop **Ch1** 3338 withstand; 3284 withstode; 12426 stode P wyþstode L; 12677 withstand P wyþstande L withstande R; 4853L wyþstodit (P differs); 12984L wyþsted (om. P); **Ch2** 7434 withstand; 15 styntyng P wiþstandyng L; **HS** 8562 wyþstode; 12024, 12051 wyþstonde; 12057 wyþstondyng (ger.); 470 knowe *C* wythstande

wyþþe n. [OE] withe; willow twigs for a halter **HS** 11559 wiþþe

wytyng ger. [from OE witan, v.] knowledge, awareness **Ch2** 3510 wytyng; 5283, 6880 wittyng; **HS** 8605 wytyng

witnes n. [OE] testimony, evidence; oath **Ch1** 4850 witnes; 11987 witnesse; **Ch2** 3754, 3862, 5531, 6138, 6828 witnes; 5256 wittnes; **HS** 136 wytnesse; 616, 2356, 2705, 4657 wytnes

witnes v. [from OE witnes, n.] testify, bear witness **Ch1** 461 wittnes; 712 witnes; 1363, 15418 witnes P witnesseþ L; **Ch2** 2039 witnes; **HS** 2651 wytnessyn; 7646 wytnesseþ

wlate v. [OE wlatian] to feel disgust or loathing **HS** 3540 wlatys GLOSS BH loþeþ *O* lathes; 4234 wlates GLOSS H ys wrothe *O* slatys; 9940 wlates GLOSS H steynyst *S* bateþ *V* bates; 9990 wlate *SV* wyþstonde; 6520 abomynable *O* vlatefull (adj.)

wlf, wlues n. [see woulf]

wlle n. [see woule]

wo, wa, wouh, wogh, wow n. [OE wa, woh] worry, sorrow, anguish; wrong, evil, injury **Ch1** 53, 1042, 3023, 5047, 6829 wo; 4712, 7175 wouh P wough L; 13247 wouh P wow L; 13791 wouh; 15420 wa; **Ch2** 827, 2922, 3026, 3462, 6567 wouh; 2849, 6974, 7069, 7267, 8149 wo; **HS** 2117, 3801, 5771, 6442, 9160 wo; 2518 wone; 1459, 4091 wogh; 574 euyl *C* woo

wode n. [OE wudu] woods, forest **Ch1** 851, 1123, 2136, 5389, 12256 wod; 3814, 3816 wode; 1887, 2737, 3055, 6341, 10297 wodes; 6874 woddes P wodes L; 10018 woddes; 952, 4688 wod P wode L; 1966 wodelond; **Ch2** 2285, 2715, 5440, 7453, 8212 wod; 2669 wodes; **HS** 9054 wode; 9900 wodes

wode adj. [OE wod] insane **Ch1** 4481, 4637, 12056, 13152, 13253 wode; 1547, 6472 wode P wod L; 12086 woder; **Ch2** 2274, 4714, 5136, 6011, 8207 wode; **HS** 1274, 1698, 5839, 11034, 12485 wode; 3588 wede GLOSS BH mad

wodehede n. [OE wod + *hædu] madness, folly **HS** 9021 wodehede

wofare n. [OE wa + faru] trouble, woe **HS** 6483, 10705 wofare

wogh, wowe, wawe n. [see walle, n.]

woyde v. [see void, v.]

woke, weke, wouke n. [OE wucu] week **Ch2** 833 wouke; 3625 woke; 6573 weke; **HS** 270 woukys; 293, 300, 4255 wouke; 9757, 10381, 11667 woke

wold n. [see weld, n.]

wolde n. [see werld, n.] [OE wald, weald] forest, country; fig.: on the earth **Ch1** 3187 wolde P wold L; 5070 wolde; **Ch2** 3143 wold

wolkomyng n. [see welcom, n.]

woman, women n. [OE wifmann, wimman] woman, women **Ch1** 608, 635, 1317, 4014, 6059 woman; 929, 1442, 4013, 5610, 6457 women; **Ch2** 180 womans; 988, 1104, 2135, 2390, 3783 woman; 869, 1870, 3350 women; 3346 women P wommen L; **HS** 180, 290, 7363, 8847 womman; 999, 7430 wommen; 1927, 1953, 2000, 4609, 7440 wymmen; 7692 wymmens

wombe n. [OE womb] belly, womb **Ch1** 3175 wombe; **HS** 7229 wombes

wonde n. [OE wunde] wound, injury **Ch1** 4880 wond; 1242, 4360, 4434 wounde; 4402, 12109 wondes; 1786, 14407 wondes P woundes L; **Ch2** 444 wonde; 3177, 5624, 8078 wounde; 4757 wondes; 103, 5629, 5640 woundes; **HS** 673 wndys; 6650, 10570 woundes; 11849 wndes

wonde v. (1) [OE wundian] wound, injure **Ch1** 13291 wounde; 4339, 4656, 12765 wonded; 4446 wonded P wounded L; 3767 woundyd; 5135 wounded; **Ch2** 154, 734, 6851, 7009, 8080 wonded; **HS** 1374 wndede; 3746 wndedyst

wonde, wounden v. (2) [OE windan] wind, twist, writhe; bind **Ch1** 13948L wounden (om. P); 5527, 15135 wond; **Ch2** 1297, 2857 wond; 4910 wonden; **HS** 8057 wonde; 9181 woned *O* wane

wonde v. (3) [see wend, went, v.] [OE wandian] shrink, hesitate, refuse **HS** 1693 wonde GLOSS BH spare; 1846 wonde *C* withstande

wonder n. [OE wundor] a marvel, prodigy; cause of astonishment **Ch1** 479, 990 wondere; 4218 wondire; 3390 wondere P wonder L; **Ch2** 4319 wonder; 6829, 6842 wondere; **HS** 1385, 5264 wndur; 7925 wunder; 8195 wundyr; 8958, 9217, 12313 wndyr; 10219 wndres; 1823 wndur *C* merueyle *D* ferly; 7485 ferly GLOSS H wundyr; 10614 wunder *O* ferly; 11981 wnder *O* mervale

wondere, wondirful adj./adv. [from OE wundor, n.] strange, marvellous **Ch1** 6475 wondere P wonder L; 3747 wondirful; **Ch2** 7368 wondere; 631 selcouth P wonder L; 738 selcouthest P wonderest L; **HS** 1570 wndur; 12246 wndyrly; 2495 wndurful; 3639 wnder; 3707 wndyr; 3483, 4107 wndyrly *O* ferly; 11975, 12232 wnder *O* ferly; 4865 wndyr *O* selcuth

wondre v. [see forwondred, v.] [OE wundrian] be surprised, wonder **Ch1** 4259L wondreþ (P differs); **Ch2** 5748, 5768, 5930, 5980, 6562 wondred; 4460 asked P wondred L; **HS** 1671 wndre; 1282 wundrede; 8956 wondre

wondring ger. [OE wundrung] amazement; ?wandering **Ch2** 4311 wondryng; **HS** 6287 wndryng *H* wundryng *F* wondring

wone n. (1) [see wone, wont, v.] [OE wone, wune] habit, usage, custom; manner, fashion **Ch1** 11124 wone P won L; **Ch2** 3578 wone; 2065, 2905, 3582 wonne; 2553, 2729 wonne P wone L; **HS** 6848, 8739 wone; 845, 1742, 3559 wnt *F* wont; 1465 wnt *F* woned; 9728 wonte; 10564, 10698 wont

wone n. (2) [see wane] [ON van] dwelling; domain, territory **Ch1** 8834 wones; **Ch2** 1878 wone; 1562 wones; 1919 wones P minstre L; **HS** 1411 wynly wones GLOSS B sekyr dwellyngys

wone, wont v. [OE wunian, gewunod] dwell, remain; become accustomed to; prevail, persist **Ch1** 7, 866, 958, 1347, 2204 wone; 2036 wons P wones L; 13565, 13892, 14296 wonne; 51, 3754, 5596 woned; 4060, 4476 wonned; 1361, 1740 won; 5048 wont P wond L; 7314 won P wond L; 15051 wonte; 14600 wonand P wonyng L; 13902L wonede, wone (om. P); **Ch2** 2137, 3578, 7787 wone; 873 wonned; 6604 woned; 296, 1080, 3582, 7710, 8036 wonne; 1043, 2564, 3459 wonnes; 1919 wont; **HS** 72, 1879, 9709, 9897, 11020 wone; 3535 wunne; 4765, 4905, 5042, 7675 wones; 1747 wonede; 4768 woneþ; 1760 wonande *D* duellende; 1762 wonede *C* dwellyd *D* duellede; 9717 dwelle *O* wone; 845 wnt *CF* wont; 1742 wnt wonyng *C* wone in *F* wont

wonyng ger. [OE wonung] dwelling, place of residence **Ch1** 1381, 1772, 6810, 14435 wonyng; 1441 wonynge; 1888, 14481, 15820 wonnyng; 1208 wonyng P wonynge L; **Ch2** 1985, 4397, 5969 wonyng; 1885 wonyng stede; 3726 wonnyng; **HS** 2997 wonyngys; 1813, 4200, 7053, 8949 wonyng; 1466 wonyng *C* dwellyng *D* duellynge; 1742 wonyng *D* duellyng; 1404 wonyng placys *D* wonyng stede

word n. [see bodword, witeword] [OE] word, speech **Ch1** 2285, 2457, 3556, 4871, 6698 word; 1360, 3868, 4925, 5272 worde; 1366, 4486, 4710, 5881, 6860 wordes; **Ch2** 1041, 2283, 4526, 5377, 8298 word; 993, 1262 bode P word L; 1337, 4417 worde; 839, 1346, 4816, 6660, 7494 wordes; **HS** 90 wrde; 782, 1914, 2001, 6896 wrd; 1898 wrdus; 12125 worde

world, wold n. [see werld]

worm, wrmes n. [OE wyrm] maggots **HS** 6758 wrmes *FO* wormes *H* wurmes

wors, worse n./adj. [see wars, wers, worse]

worschip, wirschiply n./v./adv. [see wirschip]

worth, worþi adj./adv. [OE weorþe, wyrþe] deserving, honorable; having rank; excellent **Ch1** 215, 2309, 3094, 6336, 15927 worþi; 1870, 2454 worthy; 2416, 2835 worth; 11840 worþe; 9624 worþi P worthly L; 11174 worth P wyþ L; **Ch2** 38, 5124, 5213 worþie; 2500, 3591, 4849, 6951, 7821 worþi; 4490, 5005, 7036 worþe; 4276, 5884, 7036 worth; 3988L worþ (om. P); **HS** 769 wrþ; 7563, 8554 wrth; 349, 820, 4816, 8551, 11315 worþy; 10201 worþyly; 841 smartly *C* wurthely; 1584 dygne GLOSS B wrþ; 3960 wrþ *O* worthy; 6943 wrth *O* wroth; 9904 wrþy *SV* digne

worþe, wroþe v. [see wryþys, wroþe, v.]

wost, wote v. [see wite, v. (1)]

wouke n. [see woke, weke, n.]

woule, wlle n. [OE wull; ON ull] wool **Ch2** 4155 woule; **HS** 4845 wlle *F* wolle *H* wulle *O* woule

woulf, wolues, wlf n. [OE wulf; ON ulfra] wolf, wolves **Ch1** 2137 wolues; 11248, 13252, 13344 woulf; 14724 woulf P wolf L; **Ch2** 440 woulfe; 442 woulf; 874 woulfes; 1806 woulfes; **HS** 5522, 5523 wlf *F* wolf; 4848 wlues *F* wolues; 10892 wlfe *F* wolf

wouwe v. [OE wogian] to court a woman, woo **Ch2** 912 wouwe P wowe L

wowe n. [see walle, n.]

wrake n. [OE wracu] vengeance, punishment **HS** 3391 wrake

wrappe v. [see warp, v.]

wrask adj. [OE wræst, wrast] skillful **Ch2** 4216 wrask P wrast L

wrast v. [OE wræstan] to turn or twist something **Ch1** 3166 wraste P wrast L; 12570 wrast LR (om. P); 13045 kast P wrast L; 13046 wrast P cast L; **Ch2** 4216 wrask P wrast L; **HS** 6197 wraste

wrastle, wristille v. [see skirme, v.] [OE wræstlian] to wrestle **Ch1** 1794 wristille P wrastle L; 4699 wristled P wrastlede L; 11126 skirmed P wrastled L; 11124 wrestild P skirmed L

wrastlyng, wristelyng ger. [from OE wræstlian] a wrestling match **Ch1** 1796, 1798 wristelyng P wrastlyng L; **HS** 992, 3689 wrastlyng; 8991 wrastlynges

wrath, wrathhede, wroth n. [OE wræþþu] anger, indignation, resentment **Ch1** 2337, 5095 wrath; 2345 wraþe; 604 wrath P wrayth L; 2028, 3229, 3231 wreth; **Ch2** 83, 1358, 4768, 5918, 7136 wrath; 1320 wraþe; 3165 wreth; 2436, 5382, 6402 wroth; **HS** 1266 wraþ; 3915, 9422 wraþþe; 12468 wrathhede; 780 wraþþe *D* hate; 3720 wraþþe *O* wreth; 3723 wraþþe *O* ire; 3730, 3740, 3754, 3902, 3913 wraþþe *O* wyrth; 3801, 3910 wraþþe *A* wreth *O* werth; 3794, 3911 wraþþe *O* werth

wrath v. [OE wræþan] to become angry; to annoy, anger **Ch1** 10122 wrethis P wraþest L; 11235 wreth; **Ch2** 3679 wrathes; 151, 2682, 3164 wrathed; **HS** 3770, 8588 wraþþe; 3711 wraþþyþ; 3773 wraþþe *O* werth; 6784 wrathede *O* wyrthyde

wrecched adj. [from OE wrecca] wretched, miserable **Ch2** 2617 feble P wrecchede L; **HS** 5497 wrecched *O* wyrchede

wrecche n. (1) [OE wrecca, wræcca] an unfortunate person; niggardly, parsimonious person **Ch1** 13036L wrecche (om. P); **Ch2** 6735 wrecchis; **HS** 6205 wrecche

wreche, wreke n. (2) [OE wræc] vengeance **Ch1** 202 wreke P wreche L; 10576 wreche; **Ch2** 5556, 7074 wreche; **HS** 4556, 5485, 8285, 8292, 10310 wreche

wreche, reche v. [see reche, rauht, v. (3)] [from OE wræc, n.] to rescue or deliver **Ch1** 15344 reche P wreche L

wreie, wrey v. [see bewray] [OE wregan] to accuse; reveal **Ch1** 1099 wreie P wrye L; **HS** 345 wrey; 8921 wreyest; 11489, 11674 wreye; 3533 bewreyþ *O* wryes; 3608 bewreye *O* wray

wreke, wroken v. [OE wrecan] to avenge; punish **Ch1** 7348, 9699, 13908, 15032 wreke; 3428 venged P wroken L; 8240 wroken; **Ch2**

1082 wreke P wrekon L; 4294 wreke; 1095 slo P awreke L; 1916, 2839 wroken; **HS** 2918 *C* wrecchest (B differs)

wrenk, wrenche n. [OE wrenc] trickery, deception **Ch2** 1419 wrenke; 5938 wrenk; **HS** 7713 wrenche

wrye v. [OE wrion] to cover up **HS** 1148 wrye *C* hylle *D* hyl

wrightes n. [OE wryhta, wyrhta] craftsman, builder; carpenter **Ch1** 8596 wrightes P whrightes L; **Ch2** 1559, 1563 wrightes; 951 schip wright; **HS** 9168 wryghtes GLOSS H carponters

wrihte, wright, wrouht v. [from OE wryhta, n.] build, construct **Ch1** 4426, 4530, 4620 wrouht; 8599, 8692, 9779 wrouht P wrought L; 4254 wrouhtis; **Ch2** 7843 wrihte; 2178 vp wright; 1998, 3054, 4934, 5578, 6506 wrouht; 6776 wrouhtis

wryng, wreng v. [OE wringan] wring the hands **Ch1** 10639 wreng P wrynge L; **HS** 5028 wryng

writ n. [OE] letter, order; a writing, book **Ch1** 971 writte; 4222 writte P lettere L; **Ch2** 2039, 3370, 3829 writte; 3814 writ; 6163 write; **HS** 1365, 2728, 4847, 7646, 11588 wryt

write, wrote v. [OE writan] to write, draw **Ch1** 937, 4209, 5590, 5958, 10410 write; 143 wryte; 140, 723, 3683, 4414, 15923 wrote; 4, 12, 71 wryten; 1614, 4028, 5506, 6759, 6830 writen; 10406, 10413 wrote P wrot L; **Ch2** 92, 5065, 6117, 8353, 8357 write; 102, 523, 8256 writes; 2154 wreten; 96, 2114, 4840, 6495, 8251 wrote; 395, 2561, 4430, 6916, 8355 writen; **HS** 527, 7051, 8974, 9386, 11777 wryte; 785, 4998, 9286, 12008 wrote; 2088 wroot; 3749 wrot; 2179 wrete; 40, 133, 169, 410, 419 wretyn; 7029 wryten

wryþys, worþe, wroþe v. [OE wriþan, wrað] turn, twist; bend **Ch1** 12099 wroþe P wroþ L; **Ch2** 3018 lepe P worþeþ L; **HS** 130 wryþys; 5473 wroth

writhyng ger. [from OE wriþan, v.] twisting **Ch1** 1822 writhyng

wrytyng ger. [from OE writan] something written; the act of writing **Ch1** 722, 5591 writyng; **Ch2** 110 writing; 1594 boke P writyng L; **HS** 4675, 7031, 9299 wrytyng

wroken v. [see wreke, v.]

wrong, wrang n. [OE wrang, ON *wrangr] something unjust, illegal, unfair; improper **Ch1** 19, 3200, 3787, 6643 wrong; 6648 wronges; **Ch2** 824, 2329, 5910, 6978, 8206 wrong; 1982, 7024 wronges; **HS** 1442, 2420, 4385, 6432, 9908 wrong; 12416 wronge; 9590 wrang; 11162 no wrons *H* wronges *F* no wrong *O* na wrange

wrong, wrongfulle, wrongfully adj./adv. [OE wrang, ON *wrangr] unjust; with evil intent; illegally **Ch1** 1444, 15036 wrong; **Ch2** 6245, 8031 wrong; 5188 wrongfulle; **HS** 1356, 2026, 2729, 5448, 12188 wrong; 11077 wrongly; 776 wykkedly *C* wrongfully

wrong, wrang v. [from OE wrang, adj.] to do wrong, to harm **Ch1** 11596L wranges (P differs); **Ch2** 6414 wrong

wroth, wrothfulle adj./adv. [OE wraþ] irate, fierce; angrily **Ch1** 1521, 3425, 4621, 6292 wroth; 2121, 2458, 5467, 6043, 13829 wroþe; 4518, 5120, 11570 wrothe; 2027 wrothfully P angrily L; **Ch2** 1305, 3202, 4405, 5134, 6948 wroth; 497, 1040, 2117, 2930, 7360 wroþe; 2435 wrothe; 839 wrothfulle; 7089 wraþefully; **HS** 967, 1967, 3397, 6873 wroth; 2617 wroþe; 8101 wroþ; 12301, 12339 wroþer; 7153 irus GLOSS H wraþful; 3740 wroþe *O* wrath

wroþe v. [see wryþys]

wroþerhaile, wroþerheile ?adv. [OE wraþre + hæle] with bad luck or ill fortune; unfortunately, disastrously **Ch1** 2570, 3456 wroþerheile P wroþerhayl L; **Ch2** 2527 wroþerheile; 4913 wroþerheile P with ille heil L; 5424, 6392 wroþerhaile; **HS** 3674 wroþer heyl *F* wroþerheil *H* wroþer in helle *O* wrothire hayle *W* wroþerhele

wrouht, wrought v. [see wirk, werche, wrouht, wrihte, v.]

wrshepyng ger. [see wirschip, v.] [from OE worðscipe, v.] worshipping **HS** 9380 wrshepyng

wrþ v. [OE weorþan] to come about, happen **HS** 10472 wrþ GLOSS H most þou *F* worþ *O* worthe

Robert Mannyng of Brunne: The Chronicle edited by Idelle Sullens completes the edition of the works of Robert Mannyng of Brunne, 1303–1338, which was begun by Sullens' *Robert Mannyng of Brunne: Handlyng Synne* (MRTS, vol. 14, 1983). Mannyng's purpose in *The Chronicle* was to compile a history in English verse of the British people from the "beginnings"; Part I is a translation of the French *Roman de Brut* of Wace (1155) and Part II is nearly all from the Anglo-French chronicle by Peter of Langtoft. The two parts form a coherent whole.

Sullens has undertaken the evaluation and collation of the many manuscripts of this work in order to present an edition as free as possible of the errors which beset earlier editions. A full introduction provides Mannyng's biography and discusses the extant manuscripts, the scribes, the earlier studies, and Mannyng's style, use of sources, and his influence. Part I and II each has its own introduction. Lines are numbered; there are side notes to the text describing the differences in the manuscripts, extensive endnotes, a select bibliography, a complete glossary, and four plates.